THE PRAGUE SPRING 1968

A NATIONAL SECURITY ARCHIVE DOCUMENTS READER

Compiled and edited by

JAROMÍR NAVRÁTIL
chief editor

**ANTONÍN BENČÍK, VÁCLAV KURAL,
MARIE MICHÁLKOVÁ, JITKA VONDROVÁ**

Members and Associates of the former Czechoslovak Government
Commission for Analysis of the Events of 1967–1970

Translation by
MARK KRAMER, JOY MOSS, RUTH TOSEK

Headnotes and additional documents provided by
MARK KRAMER

Editorial coordination by
MALCOLM BYRNE, PETER KORNBLUH

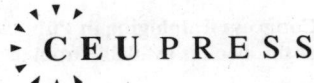

CEU PRESS

CENTRAL EUROPEAN UNIVERSITY PRESS

Central European University Press
Október 6 utca 12
H-1051 Budapest
Hungary

Distributed by
Plymbridge Distributors Ltd., Estover Road, Plymouth PL6 7PZ, United Kingdom
Distributed in the United States by
Cornell University Press Services, 750 Cascadilla Street, Ithaca, New York 14851-0250, USA

ISBN 963–9116–15–7

Library of Congress Cataloging in Publication Data
A CIP catalog record for this book is available from the Library of Congress

Printed in Hungary by Akadémiai Nyomda Kft.

CONTENTS

PART THREE

REVISION, REFORM, REVOLUTION?

PART SIX

THE AFTERMATH

PART SEVEN
DOCUMENTARY EPILOGUE

Jsem rád, že ze spolupráce National Security Archive ve Washingtonu a české nadace Pražské jaro 1968 vzešel tento obsáhlý sborník dokumentů, který, doufám, přiblíží americkému čtenáři dramatické události, které před třemi desítkami let tehdejší Československo prožívalo.*

Václav Havel

---

* I am happy that the cooperation between the National Security Archive in Washington and the Czech foundation, Prague Spring 1968, has resulted in this voluminous collection of documents, which, I hope, will lead American readers to a closer understanding of the dramatic events that the then Czechoslovakia lived through three decades ago.

PREFACE[1]

Václav Havel

The fundamental break with communism decided upon by our society which has been recently set in law, has resulted, quite understandably, in attention to the events of 1968 in Czechoslovakia. These events are today mainly restricted to a slackening of criticism of the half-hearted and self-contradictory program and policies of the reform communist leadership of the time. For that reason, it will not hurt us to be reminded of some of the additional elements and dimensions of those events.

Above all, it must be remembered that the personal and conceptual changes which occurred early in 1968 in the leadership of the communist party and the country were not simply a coup of top party people, nor were they just the result of ever-increasing pressure by reform communists working at the time within the structures of power. This course of events was, in its most profound sense, the result of a deepening chasm between the true opinion and will of society on the one hand, and official political ideology and practice on the other, of a social crisis which was becoming increasingly pronounced and of a distinct public yearning for change. It is no wonder, then, that our society began to take advantage of the growing freedoms created by the policies of the so-called post-January leadership. This the society did rapidly and often with an energy and a consistency that took the state leadership by surprise and often was not particularly welcomed. Newspapers began to print the truth, people gathered in independent organizations and clubs, and the free exercise of citizenship and free political thinking began to awaken and develop.

Thanks to the efforts of citizens of the most divergent political orientations, Czechoslovakia became an island of freedom and a relatively dignified state living in the gloomy gray ocean of the Brezhnev Soviet bloc, earning itself great respect around the world. The Prague Spring became for many people of both East and West a great—and sometimes, given the true state of affairs, disproportionate—source of hope and inspiration. For the West it signified that not only hopelessly manipulated slaves lived under communist overlordship, but that there was a great, if repressed, creative potential here requiring little in order to arise and begin to transform itself into democratic institutions and a democratic public consciousness. In the East, it became a call of inspiration for all forces of opposition and defiance.

A clear conception of our country's history is one of the basic conditions for building genuinely democratic self-awareness in our society. And for this reason it makes sense to point out the extent of those events which some of us—immersed in the current atmosphere—would rather forget or relegate to obscurity.

When foreign troops invaded our country on the night of the 20th to the 21st of August, 1968, and abducted its political representatives, something took place a parallel for which would be difficult to find in modern history. Within several hours our society began to unite quite unexpectedly in a peaceful and dignified demonstration in defense of the independence of the state and the civic freedoms that had been achieved. An entire civilian population stood against an enormous army armed to the teeth essentially; a population which had developed thousands

---

[1] This Preface is based on remarks President Havel originally gave on Czechoslovak radio and television on August 20, 1993, on the occasion of the 25th anniversary of the Warsaw Pact invasion.

of methods for confronting power non-violently, for thwarting its intentions and rendering it for all practical purposes ineffective. "Spirit will prevail over brute force!" read one of the countless banners which sprouted almost overnight on the streets of our cities. The mass media, by the most varied and sometimes almost unbelievable methods, outwitted the occupiers and moved and mobilized the entire society against the powerful will of the aggressors and some of their helpers at the time. The country simply refused to pay attention to the occupation.

This situation, which undoubtedly belongs to the critical life of an entire generation, did not endure, nor in the given state of affairs could it endure. Nevertheless, the great, admirable, and genuinely brave uprising of our society at the time remains living proof of the beneficent powers that lie dormant within it. If only a part of those beneficent powers, which are in each of us, could turn itself to the service of the common cause. The demanding tasks which the far-reaching transformation of our society and the creation of a democratic state place before us need the cultivation of precisely those good qualities which we have proven ourselves able to uncover and so magnificently unleash even in such limiting circumstances as August 1968 or November 1989. The better we cultivate these good qualities, the more easily we will make ourselves equal to the great tasks of our time.

FOREWORD

As the great events of 1968 recede into history, it becomes more important than ever to recapture them in their full reality and significance. The year 1968 was a time of greatness of spirit which remained embedded in the consciousness of the two nations, but it was, too, a time of ignominy and humiliation which also persisted as an indelible element of Czech and Slovak historical memory. However, Czechs and Slovaks, and the outside world, have begun to forget what really happened in that tragic yet fascinating period of Czechoslovak and world history. Such forgetfulness exacts a serious toll. Without a historical memory a nation is lacking one of the salient features of its own identity and is incapable of understanding its place in world history. Moreover it may fail to see the relevance of these events to the more recent past—the Velvet Revolution of 1989–1990 and the collapse of communism—and may not realize some of the continuing implications for the post-communist present and future in the countries of Eastern Europe.

It is the task of historians to search out the background and meaning of such events and make their findings available to the Czech and Slovak people, as well as to the interested world public. Thanks to the fall of communism and the end of the cold war we are now unexpectedly in possession of voluminous new materials which shed important light on 1968. This is the result of the opening of the archives of the Eastern bloc and the publication of memoirs and interviews given by important figures of this period. This new evidence was discussed at a conference in Prague in 1994 which brought together, in a splendid act of intellectual cooperation, scholars of different political persuasions and from many countries, including all the former communist countries of Eastern Europe and the United States and Canada. This was a sequel of a long process of research by an unusual commission of Czech and Slovak historians established by the Czechoslovak government for the analysis of the events of the years 1967–1970. At the same time scholars in other former communist countries were able to explore the newly opened archives of their own countries.

The conference was co-sponsored by the National Security Archive and has now culminated in this extraordinary collection of documents compiled and edited by the Czech historians associated with the governmental commission. This is but part of the Archive's even broader program of multinational cooperation whereby documents from various national archives, hitherto sealed from scholarly research, are being made available on historic events in Eastern Europe, such as the Prague Spring and the Hungarian Revolution of 1956.

The volume constitutes an unparalleled resource of primary documentation on the events of 1968, which is of inestimable value for future researchers, and equally valuable for classroom use and for a broader attentive public. The documents give one the impression of sitting in on meetings of the Soviet Politburo or conferences of the bloc states, looking over the shoulder of Brezhnev as he wrote letters to Dubček, reading the top secret dispatches of Soviet ambassadors and generals, and listening in on telephone conversations between Brezhnev and Dubček at the height of the crisis in August.

The main virtue of the volume lies in its documentation of the discussions and decisions at the topmost leadership levels in Eastern Europe and the Soviet Union. In many cases these documents confirm earlier portrayals of the course of development and tentative conclusions reached in previous studies, including my own book, *Czechoslovakia's Interrupted Revolution*. They provide, however, fascinating new evidence about crucial events and the positions of the major participants, hitherto cloaked in secrecy.

These documents attest to the overwhelming fear of the Soviet and other bloc governments about what was happening during the Prague Spring and their deep concern about the spread of this infection to their own states and testify also to their fear of the breakdown of the military and political unity of the bloc. They also demonstrate the continuing intervention of Moscow in the internal affairs of Czechoslovakia and the unremitting pressure on Dubček to change course. They also show that, although some of the Soviet bloc states, such as Poland and East Germany, were more rabid and Hungary slightly more reticent, they were at one in their fears and concerns about the danger in Prague and their resolve to put a stop to it. They indicate the readiness of the Soviet Union, as early as May, to consider the use of military force and their beginning of preparations, from July on, for an invasion, but also their reluctance to implement these plans without serious efforts to achieve this goal by non-violent means. They show the important role of the KGB and the military in preparing the ground for the invasion.

Revelations concerning the U.S. attitude are more meager, but reveal clearly their unwillingness to give any support to Prague or to take any action against the actual military intervention which they recognized as likely as early as June. There is absolutely no evidence that either the State Department or the CIA took any measures to use the Prague Spring as a means of destabilizing or subverting the Soviet bloc, in spite of constant Soviet propaganda about the sinister efforts of Western imperialism to do so.

New light is thrown on certain crucial episodes, for instance, the visit of Brezhnev to Prague in December 1967 and his notorious dictum—"eto vashe delo." During his forty-eight hour sojourn he had individual talks with each of the top Czechoslovak leaders. Although he had no confidence in Novotný's leadership capacity, he sought, in vain, to unite the presidium behind him. He seems to have had no role in the ultimate selection of Dubček to succeed Novotný.

Successive conferences at Dresden, Moscow, Warsaw, etc. revealed Brezhnev's determination to curtail the reform movement, by forceful intervention if necessary, the vigorous support of his position by East Germany, Poland and Bulgaria, and the ready acquiescence of Hungary in this policy, as well as, of course, the opposition of excluded states, Romania and Yugoslavia, to Soviet intervention. There is no evidence of serious divisions within the Soviet leadership, and Brezhnev clearly exercised decisive influence. The final decision to invade was made by the Soviet Politburo on August 17, and transmitted to the other bloc leaders in Moscow on August 18.

The documents also show the resistance by Alexander Dubček to Soviet pressure and at the same time his desperate efforts to persuade the Soviet comrades of the errors of their ways. They reveal the conviction of certain Czechoslovak leaders, such as Vasil Biľak, "the healthy forces," as Brezhnev called them, to support the Soviet Union in its efforts to curtail or reverse the Prague reforms. This culminated in their infamous letter soliciting military action, the existence of which was vigorously denied after the occupation. In fact the letter of invitation was delivered by Biľak to Shelest in a lavatory during the Bratislava conference and transmitted at once to Brezhnev. The text of this letter, given here, was ultimately turned over to Prague by the Gorbachev government and was published in 1992.

Although the main provisions of the actual reform program were undoubtedly feared and condemned by the Soviet and other communist regimes, as well as by the conservatives in the Czechoslovak leadership, the main concerns expressed during the months of crisis was what they described as the "counterrevolutionary" tendencies in Czechoslovakia and the unwillingness and inability of the Czechoslovak leadership to curb them or to control the situation. Over and over again Soviet and bloc leaders complained of the freedom of expression in the press, the emergence of "anti-socialist forces" such as the Social Democratic Party, KAN and K-231, the "anti-socialist" activities of the intelligentsia and the students, and the openly counterrevolutionary position taken by certain leaders such as Čestmír Císař, František Kriegel and others. All of these threatened, they argued, to undermine socialism (as they conceived it!) and had to be curbed by the Prague leaders.

This culminated at the conference in Čierna nad Tisou in early August when these accusations were repeated and the Prague leadership was called upon to take the necessary action. Unfortunately documentation of the conference is meager, and there is no report at all of the *conversation à deux* between Brezhnev and Dubček. There is no hard evidence as to whether Dubček did in fact make any promises or that any agreement was reached about putting a stop to these tendencies. Brezhnev, in his later telephone conversations with Dubček, repeatedly stated that there were such agreements and pressed Dubček to carry them out. Dubček later denied that there were any such promises or agreements, but during the phone conversation he was evasive in his responses and kept insisting that it would take time to deal with these matters. Yet it seems clear that it was the alleged failure of the Czechoslovak party to take such steps which finally tipped the scales in favor of military intervention.

Interesting, too, that in these final phone conversations Dubček's sturdy defense of the Czechoslovak party's course becomes clear. However, he gave no signs of a will to resist a Soviet military invasion or even to warn of such resistance. His only response was to express his willingness to step down from the leadership post and to challenge Brezhnev to take whatever measures he wished. Brezhnev for his part asserted the obligation of the socialist camp to act collectively against the Prague regime, but did not openly threaten with military intervention. Within several days, in an act of unparalleled perfidy, he launched the already planned invasion.

The documentation of the Moscow confrontation is also somewhat limited. Brezhnev justified the invasion by "the failure (of Dubček) to fulfill your commitments", and warned of civil war and a military dictatorship if the Czechoslovak leaders did not agree to the Moscow Protocol. Dubček put up a strong defense of the Prague Spring and described the invasion as "the greatest political mistake" which would have "tragic consequences." Ironically, twenty years later the Soviet leaders, in an official apology to Czechoslovakia, in effect confirmed his judgment and his prediction. In the end Dubček reluctantly decided to sign—an act later branded as a surrender by many of his former supporters.

This volume concentrates its attention on the elite level of communist politics and was not intended to be a full study of this climactic year in Czechoslovak history. It does not throw new light on another crucial aspect of the Prague Spring, the rise of an embryonic civil society or the spontaneous wave of resistance after the occupation. Although these have been documented in previous studies, there has been a tendency in some circles to play down what may be called the "non-capitulationist tradition" within Czechoslovak society in favor of the so-called "capitulationist tradition" of the top leadership. The surrender of Dubček and the entire leadership except for Kriegel was one of the main reasons for the dampening down of these societal movements of protest and for the apathy and passivity of Czech and Slovak society in the following two decades. On the other hand the continued resistance for one year after the occupation and the later emergence of the dissident movement played a role in the outburst of long-suppressed anger and resentment which culminated in the revolution of November 1989 and provided the context for the transition to democratic governance.

The volume raises questions in the mind of the reader about the nature of the Prague Spring. Did it constitute a mere reform of the existing system or was it a genuine revolution, fundamentally transforming the existing system? This invites one to reflect on the differences between 1968 and 1989 in this respect and to seek out the causes of these differences, especially in the nature of the regimes in power and of the beliefs and actions of the people. In 1968 the conservative regime of Brezhnev, unlike Khrushchev in 1956, denied the need for any reform of Soviet communism but like his predecessor, was determined to prevent basic change in the other communist countries. In Czechoslovakia the leaders were strongly in favor of reform, but were divided within their ranks. Dubček and the reformers lacked the will to stand their ground and resist Soviet and domestic pressures.

It is difficult to know what would have happened had Dubček rejected the demands of Moscow, appealed to the world communist movement and the international community and threatened forceful resistance. The documents suggest that this would have led to Soviet military intervention at an earlier date, the imprisonment of Dubček and his colleagues and the establishment of military rule or the installation of a highly reactionary regime even worse than that of Husák's in 1969. The ultimate effect on world communism cannot be predicted. It might have accelerated the decline and fall of communism in Russia, but alas, there were at that time no forces in Soviet Russia capable of bringing about serious changes in the regime, still less its replacement.

In 1989 the situation was in a way reversed. This time the Gorbachev regime recognized the need for reform at home and the right of Czechoslovakia and the other East European states to work out their own fates independently. In contrast the Czechoslovak regime was obscurantist in the extreme but in a state of decline and was confronted with independent and progressive reform tendencies capable of offering a decisive change. Similar situations existed in other East European countries. The way was thus opened for drastic revolutionary transformations in Eastern Europe and ultimately the collapse of communism in the USSR itself. No doubt the experience of 1968 contributed to this long delayed result but the changes in 1989 went far beyond the more limited aims of 1968.

In my own book I somewhat grandiloquently stated that the revolution would perhaps be resumed, but under changed conditions and in new forms that cannot now be known. It turned out that I was right in anticipating a new revolution, which in fact occurred some twenty years later, but I did not anticipate it in the near future nor did I foresee the form it would take. Nor was I aware of the degree to which the 1989 revolution would eclipse the interrupted revolution in 1968 in its scope and intensity. It would indeed by contrast demonstrate how limited and incomplete the actions of the ruling elite had been in 1968 and how the mood for radical change on the part of the people had been frustrated by the lack of will of that elite to carry through the change to completion and to defend it against outside pressure.

In retrospect the documentation of the Prague Spring reminds us of the terrible costs of the Soviet action and Czechoslovak capitulation. It began the process of the dismantling, under Dubček's leadership, of the Prague Spring and the introduction of retrogressive "normalization" by Gustáv Husák. This meant the postponement of all attempts to reform the system for two decades, the maintenance by force of an outdated and oppressive social and political order and the suppression of alternative social and political forces. It slowed down the course of urgently needed economic reform, ruined the careers of tens of thousands of persons and wiped out the intellectual achievements of the sixties. Moreover the communist party and the idea of socialism generally had been totally discredited by the post-1968 years of normalization under Husák. This had a boomerang effect. All reformist elements within the party had been liquidated so that there was no alternative leadership to replace them and to embark on another round of reform in the spirit of Gorbachev.

It also set back the cause of reform in the Soviet Union itself. In Poland it led to repeated conflicts and the military takeover in 1981. In Hungary it was a setback to the gradual and partial steps towards reform. It irrevocably divided the communist world, weakened the strength of Eurocommunism in Western Europe and of radical and socialist struggles in Asia, Africa and Latin America, and strengthened Chinese communism. On a broader international front it led to an intensifying polarization of world affairs and the escalation of the arms race and culminated in the "second cold war" during the Reagan and Gorbachev era.

It was only some twenty years later that progress toward reform was renewed, and this time at the cost of the total collapse of communism in the Soviet Union and Eastern Europe. Even then, however, the legacy of communism and the survival of communist forces and tendencies blocked the full implementation of reform in Russia and hindered the development of civic and democratic social solidarity and the attainment of full democracy elsewhere in East Europe. This suggested that the full achievement of reform in 1968 in Czechoslovakia would not have been easy and might even have been impossible, even if there had been no outside intervention. The meaning of 1968 will continue to be the subject of controversy as post-communist Europe struggles to determine the course of its transformation to democracy and a free market system in a changing global order.

H. Gordon Skilling
North York, Ontario

ACKNOWLEDGEMENTS

As the product of a remarkable multinational cooperation, this book benefited from the contributions of scores of individuals and institutions in the Czech Republic, Slovakia, the U.S., Russia, Poland, Germany, Hungary, France and Italy. The authors' team and the National Security Archive would particularly like to thank the following:

• The members and staff of the former Governmental Commission of the Czechoslovak Federal Republic for the Analysis of the Events of 1967–1970. In addition to the authors' team, these included Prof. Vojtěch Mencl, Dr. Miloš Bárta, Dr. František Janáček, Dr. Eduard Kubů, Dr. Ondřej Felcman, Dr. Josef Belda, Dr. Karel Krátky, Ivana Ryzcová, Anna Marková, and Alexandra Janácková. On the parallel Slovak Committee were Dr. Jozef Žatkuliak and Dr. Josef Jablonicky. (From the authors' team, Marie Michálková also contributed the chronology of events.)

• The President of the Czech Republic, Václav Havel, for contributing the Preface to this volume, receiving the multinational participants in this project at the Prague Castle, and helping make available key documents from Russian archives.

• Prof. H. Gordon Skilling, an early supporter of this project and eminent participant in the jointly organized international conference in Prague in 1994, as well as contributor of the Foreword to this volume.

• The members of the President's Office (Prague) who provided essential support for the efforts leading to this book, namely Luboš Dobrovský, Ivan Medek, and Pavel Seifter.

• Prof. Radomír Luźa, for his significant role from the very beginning in making possible the collaboration between the authors' team and the National Security Archive, especially during the preparations for the 1994 international conference in Prague and for the publication of this reader.

• Drahomira Vohryzková, for her vital role as intermediator between Prague and Washington in the final stages of book preparation.

• Dr. Vilém Prečan, the director of the Institute for Contemporary History, Academy of Sciences of the Czech Republic, where the documentary collections gathered by the Commission are preserved, and which sponsors the ongoing publication in Czech of the documentary record of the Prague Spring. The Institute has granted permission for those materials from its collections to be reproduced in this volume, while accepting no responsibility for the accuracy of the English translations.

• Prof. Jiří Valenta, former director of the Institute of International Relations in Prague, for encouraging this project at the beginning and making arrangements to support this work in the Institute.

• The many international scholars and archivists who contributed documents and analyses incorporated in this book, especially the Russian archivist Dr. Rudolf G. Pikhoya; the German historians Prof. Manfred Wilke, Prof. Lutz Priess, Prof. Rudiger Wenzke; the Polish historians Florian Siwicki and Lech Kowalski; and the Hungarian historian Iván Pataki.

• Dr. Mark Kramer of the Harvard Project on Cold War Studies, who contributed significantly to this book through his translations, annotations, glossary work and selections of additional documents, and who has done some of the most important recent work analyzing these materials and the wider universe of new evidence on the events of 1968 in Czechoslovakia.

• Ruth Tosek and Joy Moss, who prepared the initial translations of the documents and essays for this book; Malcolm Byrne and Peter Kornbluh of the National Security Archive staff, who performed the final rewrites and copy-editing of the complete text; and Catherine Nielsen and Greg Domber, also of the Archive staff for their assistance in proof-reading the galleys.

• Deborah Harding, whose funding support for this project, first at the German Marshall Fund of the United States and now at the Open Society Institute, made possible the initial travel and the ultimate partnership that produced this book.

• George Soros, Aryeh Neier, Dr. Alfred Stepan, Anthony Richter, and Robert Kushen of the Open Society Institute, New York, whose long-term support for the National Security Archive's partnerships with East and Central Europeans has underwritten this book and many more to come.

• Dr. Adelle Simmons, Dr. Kennette Benedict, and Dr. Kimberly Stanton of the John D. and Catherine T. MacArthur Foundation, Chicago, whose long-standing support for the National Security Archive was vital to the 1994 Prague conference and this book.

• Dr. Marin Strmecki and Dr. Samantha Ravich of the Smith Richardson Foundation, Westport (Connecticut), whose support for the National Security Archive and the Cold War International History Project helped make this book possible.

• P. J. Simmons, whose excellent reconnaissance work on behalf of the Cold War International History Project introduced the National Security Archive to the Commission.

• Dr. Jim Hershberg, Director Emeritus of the Cold War International History Project, who not only dispatched P.J. to Prague, but joined in with enthusiasm and ingenuity in all the resulting projects.

• Our thanks to the ambassador of the Czech Republic in Moscow, Rudolf Slánský, for his help and support in organizing conditions for Czech historians studying the newly available documents in the Russian archives.

• The Hon. William Luers, former U.S. Ambassador to Czechoslovakia, and Wendy Luers, President of the Foundation for Civil Society, for their encouragement and wise advice.

• All those who attended, contributed documents, and presented papers at the International Conference on the Prague Spring, 18–20 April 1994, organized by the Prague Spring 1968 Foundation, the Institute of Contemporary History of the Czech Academy of Sciences, the National Security Archive of George Washington University, and the Cold War International History Project of the Woodrow Wilson International Center for Scholars. We especially thank the then-Ambassadors to the Czech Republic, the Hon. Adrian Basora of the United States, and the Hon. Alexander Lebedev of the Russian Federation, for their support for and participation in the Prague conference.

• Dr. Frances Pinter, Executive Director of the Center for Publishing Development of the Open Society Institute, and Walda Metcalf and Klára Takácsi-Nagy, former and present directors of the Central European University Press, Budapest, with whom it is a delight to work.

We dedicate this book to the memory of our friend and colleague, Dr. František Janáček, who contributed so significantly to this project, to the work of the Commission, to his country, and to international understanding.

ACRONYMS AND ABBREVIATIONS

BCP — Bulgarian Communist Party
BTA — Bulgarian News Agency
CC — Central Committee
Cde. — Comrade
CMEA — Council for Mutual Economic Assistance
ČNR — Czech National Council
CPCz — Communist Party of Czechoslovakia
CPS — Communist Party of Slovakia
CPSU — Communist Party of the Soviet Union
ČSSR — Czechoslovak Socialist Republic
CzPA — Czechoslovak People's Army
ČTK — Czechoslovak Press Agency
FRG — Federal Republic of Germany
GDR — German Democratic Republic
HSWP — Hungarian Socialist Workers' Party
ICP — Italian Communist Party
KAN — Club of Committed Non-Party Members
KGB — Committee for State Security
KSČ — Communist Party of Czechoslovakia
LM — People's Militia
NATO — North Atlantic Treaty Organization
NF — National Front
NS — National Assembly
PCC — Political Consultative Committee (of the Warsaw Pact)
PUWP — Polish United Workers' Party
ROH — Revolutionary Trade Union Movement
SED — Socialist Unity Party of Germany (East Germany)
SNR — Slovak National Council
SPD — Social Democratic Party (West Germany)
StB — State Security
USSR — Union of Soviet Socialist Republics
WTO — Warsaw Treaty Organization (Warsaw Pact)
YLC — Yugoslav League of Communists

Abbreviations Used in Document Source Citations

AAN = Modern Records Archive (Warsaw)
A.j. = *Archivní jednotka* (Archival Number)
APRF = Presidential Archive of the Russian Federation
AVPRF = Foreign Policy Archive of the Russian Federation

AÚV KSČ	=	Archive of the CPCz CC
D.	=	*Delo* (File)
Dok.	=	*Dokument* (Document)
F.	=	*Fond* (Collection)
GS/OS	=	Operational Directorate of the General Staff (CzPA)
KC PZPR	=	PUWP CC
KV	=	Komise vlády ČSFR pro analýzu událostí let 1967–1970
Ll.	=	*Listy* (Pages)
MfS	=	Ministry for State Security (former GDR)
MHKI	=	Archives of the Hungarian Defense Ministry
MV	=	Ministry of the Interior (Prague)
MZV	=	Ministry of Foreign Affairs (Prague)
MNO	=	Ministry of National Defense (Prague)
NS	=	National Assembly (after 1969, Federal Assembly)
Op.	=	*Opis'* (Inventory)
P.	=	*Paczka* (Record Group)
PTTI	=	Hungarian National Archives
SAPMDB	=	Foundation for the Archive of Parties and Mass Organizations of the GDR under the Federal Archival Service (Berlin)
Sb.	=	*Sbírka* (Collection)
Sv.	=	*Svazek* (Record Group)
T.	=	*Tom* (Volume)
TsKhSD	=	Center for Storage of Contemporary Documentation (Moscow)
ÚSD	=	Institute for Contemporary History (Prague)
VHA	=	Military History Archive (Prague)
Vondrová & Navrátil	=	Vondrová, Jitka and Jaromír Navrátil, eds. *Mezinárodní Souvislosti Československé Krize 1967–1970*, vols. 1 & 2 (Brno: ÚSD, 1995 & 1996)
Z/M	=	Materials provided to the Czechoslovak Commission by the Hungarian Government
ZPA	=	Central Party Archive of the SED (Berlin)
Z/S	=	Materials provided to the Czechoslovak Commission by Boris Yeltsin (4/92, 7/92)
Z/S-MID	=	Materials provided to the Czechoslovak Commission by the Soviet Foreign Ministry (12/91)

Letters Following "KV"

D	=	CPCz Central Committee Archive
K	=	Foreign Ministry Archive
B	=	Interior Ministry Archive
A	=	Gifts from Citizens to the Commission
V	=	Archive of copies of interrogations at the Prosecutor General's Office and the Federal Interior Ministry

CHRONOLOGY OF EVENTS
CZECHOSLOVAKIA 1967–1969

1967

June 27–29, 1967: The 4th Congress of the Czechoslovak Writers' Union in Prague criticizes the cultural policy of the Communist Party of Czechoslovakia, especially restrictions on the creative freedom of writers.

September 26–27, 1967: The Plenum of the Central Committee of the Communist Party of Czechoslovakia (CPCz CC) decides that the Ministry of Culture and Information will edit the weekly magazine of the Union of Czechoslovak Writers, *Literární noviny*. Klíma, Liehm, and Vaculík are expelled from the CPCz.

October 30–31, 1967: At a CPCz CC plenum, Alexander Dubček criticizes the first secretary of CPCz and president of Czechoslovakia, Novotný.

October 31, 1967: Police violently suppress a demonstration by Prague university students protesting poor dormitory conditions.

December 8–9, 1967: Brezhnev arrives in Prague at the personal request of Novotný for a brief, unofficial visit. He carries out separate talks with several members of the Presidium of CPCz CC.

December 11, 1967: An extraordinary session of CPCz CC Presidium discusses dividing the posts of the first secretary and the president of the republic. Five members vote for separation, five against. At the meeting, the CPCz CC Presidium also discusses Novotný's position on Slovakia.

December 19–21, 1967: During a CPCz CC meeting, Novotný is criticized and asked to resign as first secretary. The meeting is adjourned until January 3, 1968.

1968

January 3–5, 1968: The so-called January meeting of CPCz CC takes place. The posts of first secretary and president of the republic are separated. Dubček is elected first secretary. Novotný remains president.

January 20, 1968: Upon Dubček's request, János Kádár meets him in Topolčianky, Slovakia.

January 22–23, 1968: At a plenary session of the Central Committee of the Communist Party of Slovakia, Vasil Biľak is elected first secretary.

January 24, 1968: The Czechoslovak Writers Union elects Eduard Goldstücker chairman. The Union decides to publish *Literární listy* as its own new weekly magazine.

January 29–30, 1968: Dubček meets Brezhnev and Podgorny in Moscow.

February 4, 1968: Dubček meets Kádár in Komárno. Zoltán Komócsin and Károly Erdélyi also represent the Hungarian side.

February 6, 1968: The CPCz CC Presidium decides that reports from the sessions of the CPCz CC Presidium and Secretariat will be published in the media.

February 7, 1968: Dubček meets Władysław Gomułka in Ostrava (Northern Moravia).

February 22, 1968: At Prague Castle, Dubček delivers the main address at a ceremonial session of CPCz CC, the Central Committee of the National Front of the ČSSR, and the government, on the occasion of the 20th anniversary of February 1948. Also speaking are Brezhnev, Gomułka, Ulbricht, Kádár, Ceauşescu, Zhivkov, and Vlahovič.

March 4, 1968: The CPCz CC Presidium begins the process of abolishing censorship.

March 8, 1968: For the first time, the Czechoslovak press prints a demand for Novotný's resignation from his post as president.

March 13–20, 1968: Two meetings take place in Prague between young people and political and cultural officials (as many as 20,000 participants), at which discussions of formerly forbidden topics take place. Participants in the second meeting send a letter addressed to Novotný demanding his resignation.

March 14, 1968: The CPCz CC Presidium decides to accelerate the rehabilitation of citizens who were unjustly persecuted during the 1950s.

March 14–15, 1968: The Slovak National Council presents its demand that Czech–Slovak relations be organized in accordance with the principles of the federation.

March 18, 1968: East German journalists are prohibited from visiting the Czechoslovak Embassy and the House of Czechoslovak Culture. They are forbidden from reporting information about Czechoslovakia, and all private and official business trips to Czechoslovakia are prohibited.

March 19, 1968: The information office of the previously prohibited Scout organization "JUNÁK" opens in Prague.

March 22, 1968: Novotný resigns as president.

March 22, 1968: The "Action Group for the Restoration of the Social Democratic Party" formally comes into being.

March 22–23, 1968: The fourth session of the CPCz CC Control and Auditing Commission takes place. Chairman Pavel Hron and the leading members of the commission resign. The commission votes for the total rehabilitation of former General Secretary Rudolf Slánský and other prominent communist party members persecuted in the 1950s (Otta Šling, Marie Švermová, Josef Smrkovský, Hanuš Lomský, Vilém Nový, Koloman Mokovic, Vítězslav Fuchs, Růžena Dubová and Bedřich Geminder). The commission further declares void the expulsions of writers Klíma, Liehm and Vaculík from CPCz and cancels disciplinary proceedings against Milan Kundera and Pavel Kohout.

March 23, 1968: Top officials of the communist parties and governments of Bulgaria, Czechoslovakia, Hungary, East Germany, Poland, and the Soviet Union meet in Dresden. The only topic on the agenda is the "Czechoslovak question."

March 24, 1968: A commentary on possible Soviet intervention in Czechoslovakia is published for the first time in the western press (*Sunday Express,* London).

March 26, 1968: A senior secretary of the East German Socialist Unity Party (SED), Kurt Hager, delivers a sharp attack against the policies of the CPCz and Smrkovský.

March 27, 1968: In Prague, K-231 establishes a preparatory committee representing Czechoslovak citizens who were victims of persecution in the 1950s.

March 28, 1968: At a CPCz CC plenary session, Svoboda is recommended for the post of president with 105 of 197 votes. Novotný's resignation is accepted unanimously.

March 28, 1968: Bulgarian authorities block tourist travel to Czechoslovakia due to the political situation there.

March 30, 1968: The National Assembly elects Svoboda president by a vote of 282 to 6.

April 1–5, 1968: A CPCz CC plenary session adopts the CPCz Action Program, completes the formal rehabilitation of all persons unjustly persecuted in the 1950s, and elects a new Central Committee Board consisting of Barbírek, Biľak, Černík, Dubček, Kriegel, Piller, Rigo, Smrkovský, Špaček, Švestka.

April 3, 1968: The Minister of National Defense, Army General Bohumír Lomský asks to be relieved of his position.

April 3, 1968: A new investigation begins into the circumstances of Jan Masaryk's death.

April 6, 1968: The ČSSR government resigns. Oldřich Černík is asked to set up a new government, which is appointed two days later.

April 8, 1968: František Kriegel is elected chairman of the Central Committee of the National Front of the ČSSR.

April 9–10, 1968: At a hastily summoned session, members of the CPSU Central Committee consider the situation in Czechoslovakia, promulgating the resolution: "We will not give up Czechoslovakia."

April 14, 1968: Soviet Ambassador to Czechoslovakia Chervonenko hands Dubček a letter from Brezhnev, dated April 11, which expresses dissatisfaction with developments in Czechoslovakia. In a telephone conversation on the same day, Brezhnev proposes to Dubček that both sides meet for talks.

April 18, 1968: At the 22nd meeting of the National Assembly, Smrkovský is elected chairman of Parliament.

April 19–20, 1968: Warsaw Pact Commander-in-Chief Yakubovskii negotiates with Polish military and government officials in Warsaw. He holds further negotiations on April 21–22 in Berlin, on April 23 in Sofia, and on April 27 in Budapest.

April 23, 1968: The T.G. Masaryk Association is founded in Prague.

April 23–25, 1968: During an official visit to Czechoslovakia, Marshal Yakubovskii requests that training for the Šumava military exercises be held from June 20 to 30, not in September as originally planned.

May 2, 1968: Literární listy publishes an appeal to the National Assembly to abolish the People's Militia.

May 3, 1968: About 4,000 Prague citizens take part in an open discussion in the Old Town Square voicing demands for the establishment of an opposition party and expressing support for Polish students.

May 3, 1968: Radio Prague announces that East German authorities have begun jamming its German broadcasts.

May 4–5, 1968: The Moscow meeting of top party and state officials from Czechoslovakia and the Soviet Union takes place. The Soviets characterize the situation in Czechoslovakia as a counterrevolution and declare that they are ready to take even the "most far-reaching steps".

May 5–7, 1968: The First Secretary of the Italian Communist Party Luigi Longo visits Prague.

May 7, 1968: The Minister of the Interior Josef Pavel announces that the jamming of western radio stations has been stopped.

May 8, 1968: At a secret meeting in Moscow, top party and state officials from Bulgaria, Hungary, East Germany, Poland, and the Soviet Union ("the Five") discuss the situation in Czechoslovakia.

May 8–14, 1968: Without an official invitation, a Soviet army delegation led by Marshals Koniev and Moskalenko visits Czechoslovakia.

May 10, 1968: In a letter to Černík, Soviet Premier Kosygin points out that "the completely abnormal and dangerous situation" which is occurring on Czechoslovakia's borders with West Germany and Austria [comes] as a result of the lenient policies of Czechoslovak authorities toward western tourists.

May 10, 1968: At the NATO defense ministers' session in Brussels, General Secretary Manlio Brosio declares that the organization considers direct Soviet intervention in Czechoslovakia improbable.

May 10–23, 1968: Military maneuvers take place in southern Poland. One Soviet and one Polish tank army participate, with a total force of more than 80,000 troops and 2,800 tanks.

May 13, 1968: KAN issues its policy manifesto.

May 15, 1968: Dubček writes to Soviet Ambassador Chervonenko asking that he inform Brezhnev about Czechoslovak concerns over not being included in the meeting of "the Five" held in Moscow on May 8.

May 15, 1968: According to a report from the Czechoslovak ambassador to East Germany, the situation in Czechoslovakia is on the agenda of the Politburo of the SED. According to the report, "A struggle is going on between the forces of capitalism and socialism. If the balance of powers changes to the detriment of socialism, the GDR will regard it as its duty to intervene in the ČSSR, because this affects the defense of socialism."

May 17–22, 1968: Kosygin is in Czechoslovakia "for a short-term visit and treatment." During his stay, negotiations take place in Prague and Karlovy Vary with Svoboda, Dubček, Černík, Císař, and other Czechoslovak officials.

May 26, 1968: Brezhnev sends a letter to Dubček providing information about the meeting of "the Five" in Moscow on May 8.

May 28, 1968: U.S. Ambassador Jacob Beam informs Czechoslovak Foreign Minister Hájek that "the U.S. government and the president were watching the developments in Czechoslovakia with great attention and a constructive interest." For the time being, he states, they are avoiding active steps which could put the Czechoslovak government in an unpleasant situation.

May 29, 1968: The Bishop of Prague František Tomášek says in the Italian newspaper, *Il Messagero*, that the position of Catholics has significantly improved in the last two months.

May 30, 1968: 16,000 Soviet soldiers arrive in Czechoslovakia for the Šumava exercises.

June 1, 1968: The Governmental Expert Commission is established to solve economic problems associated with the new constitutional arrangement of the republic. Ota Šik is named chairman of the Commission.

June 4–15, 1968: A National Assembly delegation led by Smrkovský visits the Soviet Union. Brezhnev and Podgorny receive the delegation on June 14.

June 6, 1968: The Czechoslovak government agrees to abolish censorship.

June 6, 1968: In a report to the Hungarian party's Politburo, Zoltán Komócsin denies that there is a counterrevolution underway in Czechoslovakia and requests support for Dubček.

June 12, 1968: Soviet Ambassador Chervonenko hands Dubček a personal letter from Brezhnev which includes an invitation to a bilateral, confidential, and unofficial meeting on June 15–16, "somewhere along the Soviet–Czechoslovak border." Dubček declines due to his work load and asks instead whether the meeting could be held after the regional party conferences, i.e. after July 14, at the earliest.

June 13–15, 1968: During an official visit to Budapest, Czechoslovak leaders sign the Treaty on Friendship, Cooperation, and Mutual Assistance between Hungary and Czechoslovakia.

June 17–18, 1968: The ČSSR and GDR foreign ministers hold talks in Berlin on the development of mutual relations. Ulbricht unofficially receives Hájek.

June 19, 1968: Dubček addresses 10,000 participants at a nationwide rally of the People's Militia.

June 19–30, 1968: The Šumava command and staff exercises take place on Czechoslovak territory. About 27,000 Soviet troops, along with small units of the Polish, Hungarian, East German, and Czechoslovak armies participate under the supervision of Marshal Yakubovskii.

June 20, 1968: At a CPS CC plenary session in Bratislava, members decide to convene an extraordinary congress of the CPS in October 1968.

June 21, 1968: The State Statistical Bureau reports that 21,117 people applied for permission to open private businesses.

June 21, 1968: Pravda publishes a letter to the Soviet people from participants of the June 19 nationwide rally of the People's Militia. (*Rudé právo* publishes the letter only on July 13.) Over the next 14 days, *Pravda* publishes letters and resolutions from Soviet workers informing their Czechoslovak counterparts that they are ready to provide help in the common defense of socialism.

June 24–28, 1968: The National Assembly adopts a law on preparing the federative arrangement of the republic. (As part of the law, the Czech National Council is established as the country's representative political body.) The assembly also adopts a law on judicial rehabilitation, and incorporates the abolition of censorship into an amendment to the law on the press.

June 27, 1968: The "Two Thousand Words" Manifesto, authored by Ludvík Vaculík, is published in *Literární listy*, *Práce*, *Zemědělské noviny* and *Mladá fronta*. On the same day, the CPCz CC Presidium releases its negative reaction to the document, followed on June 28 by similar statements from other official bodies.

June 27–July 4, 1968: A Hungarian delegation consisting of Kádár, Fock, and Aczél meets Brezhnev and Kosygin in Moscow. Their assessments of the situation in Czechoslovakia are coming closer together.

June 28–30, 1968: A series of extraordinary CPCz district and regional conferences are held. About one-third of them support the "Two Thousand Words" proclamation, one-third consider the reaction to the proclamation inappropriate, and one-third agree with the CPCz leadership's negative assessment of the document.

July 1, 1968: As of this date, the CPCz has 1,677,565 members. Within 6 months in 1968, 18,282 new members join the party and 6,956 members are expelled.

July 2, 1968: The magazine *Lidová armáda* publishes a memorandum from researchers at the Klement Gottwald Military-Political Academy recommending changes in Czechoslovak military doctrine.

July 4, 1968: The CPSU CC Politburo sends a letter to the CPCz CC Presidium. During the next two days, the GDR, Bulgaria, Hungary, and Poland send similar letters.

July 5, 1968: In a telephone conversation, Brezhnev tells Dubček that it is urgent that the communist parties of six socialist countries meet. Dubček writes to Brezhnev inquiring about the subject of the meeting.

July 6, 1968: Brezhnev sends Dubček a letter including an invitation to a meeting of six communist parties in Warsaw, scheduled for July 10 or 11, to discuss the situation in Czechoslovakia.

July 8, 1968: The 83rd session of the CPCz CC Presidium discusses the letters sent recently by the communist parties of Bulgaria, Hungary, East Germany, Poland, and the Soviet Union.

July 10, 1968: The National Assembly elects the 150-member Czech National Council (85 members for the CPCz, 22 members for the Czechoslovak People's Party, 22 members for the Czechoslovak Socialist Party, and 21 nonpartisan members). Čestmír Císař is elected chairman.

July 11, 1968: The Šumava exercises conclude. In the next two days, the first foreign units leave the country.

July 12, 1968: The CPCz CC Presidium declines the invitation to meet "the Five" communist countries in Warsaw, proposing instead to hold bilateral talks with each party's representatives.

July 13, 1968: At Dubček's request, he and Černík meet Kádár and Fock in Komárno, on the Hungarian–Czechoslovak border, just after 5:00 P.M. Kádár says that "the refusal of the CPCz to go to Warsaw was the biggest mistake that the CPCz leadership had made since January."

July 13, 1968: The Czechoslovak army command hands a letter to the military attachés of the Warsaw Pact countries and Yugoslavia expressing the army's unconditional support of Dubček's leadership of the CPCz.

July 14–15, 1968: The Warsaw meeting of "the Five" takes place. The CPCz CC Presidium sends a letter (signed by Dubček and Černík) to the Czechoslovak ambassador in Warsaw requesting that it be handed to Brezhnev and to the delegations of the other communist parties taking part in the meeting.

July 15, 1968: Gen. Prchlík, the head of the State Administrative Department of the CPCz CC, makes remarks at a press conference that are critical of the military and security policies of Czechoslovakia and the Warsaw Pact.

July 15, 1968: In a visit to Moscow, an Italian Communist Party delegation (Galuzzi and Pajetta) express their support for the "Czechoslovak experiment."

July 16, 1968: The 87th session of the CPCz CC Presidium discusses the joint letter of "the Five" from the Warsaw talks, and adopts a resolution to propose to the leadership of the CPSU to hold bilateral talks on July 20–21.

July 16–18, 1968: A French Communist Party delegation, led by Waldeck Rochet, meets Brezhnev in Moscow.

July 17, 1968: The Politburo of the French Communist Party proposes to call a meeting of all European communist parties as soon as possible to deal with the situation in Czechoslovakia. The proposal receives the support of the Italian, Austrian, and Belgian parties.

July 17–18, 1968: The CPSU CC Politburo discusses the situation in Czechoslovakia.

July 18, 1968: A special edition of *Rudé právo* publishes the letter from "the Five" and the CPCz CC Presidium's response. At the same time, the letter is debated by the National Assembly and the ČSSR government, the Presidium of the Central Committee of the National Front, the CPS CC, and the Central Council of the Trade Unions. All express approval of the presidium statement.

July 18, 1968: Marshal Yakubovskii sends Dubček a letter in which he accuses General Prchlík of unjustly criticizing the activity of the Political Consultative Committee of the Warsaw Pact at the July 15 press conference, and of disclosing strictly confidential information about the structure and circumstances of the Warsaw Pact joint command.

July 18, 1968: U.S. Secretary of State Rusk denies rumors that the United States has warned the USSR against using military force against Czechoslovakia.

July 19, 1968: The CPCz CC plenary session unanimously approves the presidium's response to the letter from "the Five."

July 19, 1968: The CPSU CC Politburo proposes that the CPCz CC attend a bilateral meeting in the Soviet Union. The CPCz CC Presidium rejects the Soviet proposal two days later. On the 21st, TASS announces that the talks will be held in Czechoslovakia.

July 19–20, 1968: In Prague, leaders of the French Communist Party (Rochet and Kanapa) discuss developments in Czechoslovakia over the last six months with Dubček, Černík, Lenárt, Císař, and others.

July 20, 1968: The Czechoslovak government receives a Soviet note expressing concerns over the discovery on July 12 of weapons in the Sokolov region. Czechoslovak authorities had found five backpacks containing 20 Thompson submachine guns, 1,600 cartridges, and 30 Walther pistols with 11 reserve cartridges.

July 23, 1968: The Presidium of the Union of Czechoslovak Film and Television Artists sends a letter to related organizations in Bulgaria, Hungary, GDR, Poland, and the Soviet Union including an invitation to visit Czechoslovakia in order to learn about what is really happening in the country. The Czechoslovak Writers Union, the Union of Czechoslovak Composers, and the Czechoslovak Academy of Sciences send similar letters.

July 23–August 10, 1968: The "Nemen" logistical training exercises take place in western Russia and the republics of Belorussia, Ukraine, and Latvia. It is reported to be the largest training event for rear-guard troops in the history of the Soviet Armed Forces.

July 24, 1968: The French Party Politburo adopts a resolution to publicly denounce the Soviet Union if it takes any military action against Czechoslovakia.

July 24, 1968: The CPCz CC Presidium declares in a letter to the French Party Politburo that it considers a call for a meeting of European communist parties inappropriate.

July 25, 1968: The 90th session of the CPCz CC Presidium deals with preparations for the 14th Extraordinary Party Congress. The presidium decides to abolish the State Administrative Department of the CPCz CC and to transfer General Prchlík to a different position. On the same day, the Military Council of the Ministry of National Defense backs up Yakubovskii's criticism of Prchlík.

July 25, 1968: Literární listy publishes a "Message from the Citizens to the Presidium" expressing confidence in the leadership in their negotiations with the Soviet Union.

July 25–31, 1968: Soviet Air Defense forces under the command of Marshal Baticky take part in the "Sky Shield" exercises. More Soviet air power is transferred to the GDR in the course of the operations.

July 29, 1968: The Czechoslovak embassy in Moscow is handed a letter from five Soviet communists expressing agreement with the CPCz's new direction, and denouncing Soviet pressure on Czechoslovakia.

July 29–August 1, 1968: The Čierna nad Tisou talks take place between the CPCz CC Presidium and the CPSU CC Politburo. Among other things, the joint communiqué notes that both sides have agreed to hold multilateral talks on August 3 in Bratislava.

July 30, 1968: The Czechoslovak embassy in Warsaw reports high concentrations of Soviet tanks in Poland moving toward the Czechoslovak border. The Czechoslovak embassy in Berlin is informed about the presence of heavy tank and missile units at the Czechoslovak border, and that three years of reserve soldiers have been called for training. On August 1, the Czechoslovak embassy in Budapest reports that Hungarian and Soviet troops have been moving toward the Czechoslovak border for two days.

August 3, 1968: The Bratislava meeting of "the Six" takes place. Among other things, the joint proclamation emphasizes that the protection and strengthening of socialist achievements in individual socialist countries are "the common international obligation of all socialist countries." During the talks, Radko Kaska, an aide to Drahomír Kolder, hands Shelest a draft "letter of invitation" appealing for assistance in the face of "counterrevolution."

August 5, 1968: General Sergei Shtemenko, an expert on offensive operations, replaces Mikhail Kazakov as chief of staff of the Warsaw Pact armed forces.

August 7, 1968: Soviet Ambassador Chervonenko meets Dubček and Černík.

August 7, 1968: At a meeting of the CC of the Hungarian Socialist Workers' Party, Kádár reports on the talks at Čierna and Bratislava: "If this is not achieved by political means, the use of other means is not excluded."

August 9, 1968: In a telephone conversation, Dubček and Brezhnev discuss the fulfillment of agreements from Čierna and Bratislava.

August 9, 1968: A petition is begun in Prague calling for the dissolution of the People's Militia. Investigators later discover that more than 50 undercover state police agents have infiltrated the activist groups.

August 9–11, 1968: Tito leads a party delegation to Czechoslovakia.

August 11, 1968: TASS announces that "liaison units and staffs of the Soviet army, the National People's Army of GDR, and the Polish People's Army [have begun] joint training on the western borders of Ukraine and in southern parts of Poland and the GDR."

August 12, 1968: SED leaders, including Ulbricht and Honecker, meet Dubček, Smrkovský, Černík, Kolder, Lenárt, and Kolář in Karlovy Vary.

August 12–15, 1968: At Yalta, Kádár debates Brezhnev, Kosygin, and Podgorny on developments in Czechoslovakia. Kádár is asked to talk once more with Dubček.

August 13, 1968: In a telephone conversation with Dubček, Brezhnev expresses his dissatisfaction with the lack of fulfillment of the agreements reached at Čierna and Bratislava.

August 13, 1968: Soviet Minister of Defense Grechko and Chief of the Main Political Administration of the Soviet Army General Yepishev arrive in Dresden.

August 14, 1968: The CPCz CC publishes an opinion poll among delegates to the CPCz district conferences (held at the end of June): 88% welcomed the extraordinary congress, 90% considered the personnel changes made at the May CPCz CC plenary session to be insufficient; 52% believed the CPCz was capable of carrying out the changes it had undertaken; 75% were convinced that the party's direct management of state and economic entities was detrimental.

August 14, 1968: Soviet Ambassador Chervonenko hands Dubček a CPSU CC declaration expressing dissatisfaction with the failure to fulfill agreements from Čierna and Bratislava.

August 15–17, 1968: An extended session of the CC CPSU Politburo ends with the decision to intervene militarily in Czechoslovakia.

August 16, 1968: Soviet Deputy Minister of Defense Pavlovskii is appointed commander of the intervention troops.

August 17, 1968 (evening): As proposed by the Soviet leadership, Kádár meets Dubček at Komárno.

August 18, 1968: In Moscow, Polish, East German, Hungarian, and Bulgarian leaders unanimously approve the Soviet stance on intervention in Czechoslovakia.

August 19, 1968: A large group of KGB officers, disguised as "tourists" arrive in Czechoslovakia. They go to the Soviet embassy as well as to Czechoslovak army headquarters.

August 19, 1968 (10:10 P.M.): At Prague Castle Chervonenko hands over the final letter of warning from the CC CPSU Politburo to President Svoboda in the presence of Dubček and Černík.

August 19, 1968 (night): Warsaw Pact forces move into position to begin the intervention.

August 20, 1968 (2:00 P.M.): The 93rd meeting of the CPCz CC Presidium takes place.

August 20, 1968: At his request, Soviet Ambassador Dobrynin meets President Johnson. Dobrynin informs him about the decision to send troops to Czechoslovakia. According to Dobrynin, the Czechoslovak party and the government's highest representatives have requested the intervention.

August 20, 1968 (11:00 P.M.): Černík, attending a session of the CPCz CC Presidium, is informed by telephone that troops of the "Warsaw Five" have crossed over state borders. He requests verification.

August 20, 1968 (11:10 P.M.): Western information services lose radar contact with Prague and its environs, and long-range signals begin to be jammed.

August 20, 1968 (11:30 P.M.): Chervonenko arrives at Prague Castle and informs president Svoboda that "allied troops [have] entered Czechoslovakia." During the Soviet ambassador's mission, the president receives a telephone call from Smrkovský asking him to attend a session of the CPCz CC Presidium.

August 20, 1968 (11:40 P.M.): Černík informs the members of the presidium about a report received from Minister of National Defense Dzúr concerning the invasion of Czechoslovakia by "allied troops."

August 20, 1968 (after 11:00 P.M.): The CC CPS Presidium meets in Bratislava. The text of "the letter of invitation" is presented along with the comment that the document was accepted by virtually all members of the CPCz CC Presidium in Prague, including Dubček. Only Smrkovský and Kriegel were opposed. Six out of 10 members of the CC CPS vote to accept it, while four vote against (Falt'an, Daubner, Turček, and Ťažký).

August 21, 1968: General Dzúr issues an order that all Czechoslovak army troops are to remain in their barracks to avoid armed resistance to the intervention. On the contrary, Czechoslovak units are to provide intervening troops with "maximum all-around assistance."

August 21, 1968 (00:45 A.M.): General Dzúr orders Air Force commanders to ban take-offs by Czechoslovak aircraft. Safe landing is to be provided for Soviet aircraft at the Prague and Brno airports.

August 21, 1968 (approx. 1:00 A.M.): President Svoboda leaves the CPCz CC Presidium session and returns to Prague Castle.

August 21, 1968 (approx. 1:30 A.M.): The CPCz CC Presidium adopts by a 7 to 4 vote the text of a proclamation "To all the People of the Czechoslovak Socialist Republic." (Barbírek, Černík, Dubček, Kriegel, Piller, Smrkovský, and Špaček are in favor; Biľak, Kolder, Švestka, and Rigo against.) This statement condemns the intervention as an act that "not only contravenes all principles governing relations between socialist states, but also violates the fundamental provisions of international law."

August 21, 1968 (1:30 A.M.–2:00 A.M.): The CC CPS Presidium, after receiving the authentic text of the CPCz CC proclamation, revokes its earlier resolution and accepts a new proclamation supporting the CPCz CC position.

August 21, 1968 (1:30 A.M.–2:00 A.M.): Two Soviet military aircraft land at Prague's Ruzyně airport. Several dozen Soviet soldiers on board occupy the main airport building and disarm airport personnel.

August 21, 1968 (1:50–2:00 A.M.): Czechoslovak radio repeatedly broadcasts the text of the CPCz CC Presidium proclamation.

August 21, 1968 (shortly after 2:00 A.M.): The airborne operation begins. At intervals of less than one minute, a total of 120 AN–12 aircraft land at Prague-Ruzyně airport. The operation is covered from the air by 200 MIG 19s and 21s. By morning, one airborne division has landed. Acting under instructions from General Dzúr, the supreme commander of the Czechoslovak Air Force ensures that the runways are well lighted and that the Soviet commanders have been contacted.

August 21, 1968 (approx. 2:15 A.M.): The CPCz CC Presidium session comes to an end. Černík returns to the presidium offices, Švestka leaves for the *Rudé právo* office, and Biľak and Indra leave for the Soviet embassy in Prague. The other presidium members remain in Dubček's office.

August 21, 1968 (approx. 3:00 A.M.): Černík is arrested by Soviet airborne troops at the presidium offices.

August 21, 1968 (approx. 3:00 A.M.): Soviet Marshal Grechko orders General Pavlovskii, the commander-in-chief of the intervention operation, to move his staff from Legnice, Poland, to Prague.

August 21, 1968 (approx. 3:00 A.M.): In an altercation between the occupying forces and the local citizenry of Liberec (in northern Bohemia), several Czechs are seriously wounded. They become the first casualties of the invasion.

August 21, 1968 (4:30 A.M.): TASS publishes an official statement to the effect that Warsaw Pact forces have entered Czechoslovak territory upon the request of the Czechoslovak party and various state officials whose names are not mentioned.

August 21, 1968 (approx. 4:30 A.M.): The first Soviet armored cars, led by a Prague Soviet embassy limousine, arrive at the CPCz CC building and begin occupying it.

August 21, 1968 (approx. 5:00 A.M.): A special Soviet plane carrying Kirill Mazurov, a member of the CPSU CC Politburo, lands in Prague. Mazurov, alias General Trofimov, has been assigned to oversee the political direction of the intervention.

August 21, 1968 (approx. 5:50 A.M.): Dubček, Smrkovský, Kriegel, Špaček, and Šimon remain in Dubček's office.

August 21, 1968 (approx. 8:30 A.M.): The initial battle for control of the Czechoslovak Radio building erupts between Soviet occupiers and Czechs. 17 people are shot; 52 of the most seriously wounded are transported to hospitals.

August 21, 1968 (8:30 A.M.): Czechoslovak Radio broadcasts President Svoboda's first address to the nation, in which he calls on the people to stay calm. He neither condones nor condemns the invasion.

August 21, 1968 (approx. 9:00 A.M.): Two Soviet officers and three members of ČSSR State Security arrive at Dubček's office and lead him away, along with Smrkovský, Kriegel, and Špaček, informing them that they are under arrest pursuant to orders from the revolutionary tribunal headed by Indra.

August 21, 1968 (10:00 A.M.): An emergency session of the Presidium of the National Assembly is convened. In an appeal addressed to leaders of the Warsaw Pact countries, the presidium protests the invasion and requests that all foreign troops be withdrawn immediately.

August 21, 1968 (12:00 noon): A general strike is called in Prague.

August 21, 1968 (2:35 P.M.): An extraordinary plenary session of the National Assembly condemns the occupation, and demands that all arrested constitutional representatives be released and that all occupying forces be withdrawn.

August 21, 1968 (7:00 P.M.): The Czechoslovak government publishes its declaration, "To all the People of the Czechoslovak Socialist Republic," condemning the invasion.

August 22, 1968 (11:00 A.M.): President Svoboda meets Soviet Ambassador Chervonenko and the commander of the intervention forces, General Pavlovskii; he requests a meeting with the Soviet leaders in Moscow.

August 22, 1968 (11:00 A.M.): The 14th Extraordinary Congress of the CPCz is convened at ČKD, the largest heavy industry factory in Prague. 1,192 of the 1,543 regularly elected delegates take part.

August 22, 1968 (12:00 noon): The general strike in Prague begins.

August 22, 1968: Petitions circulate throughout Prague demanding the withdrawal of occupying troops, the release of arrested Czechoslovak leaders, and support for legal state authorities.

August 22, 1968: The conservative faction of the CPCz spends the entire day in meetings at the Soviet embassy. At about 5:00 P.M. an agreement is reached on the personnel structure of a "provisional revolutionary government" headed by Indra. A delegation led by Piller arrives at 9:15 P.M. at the Castle, where they present this arrangement to President Svoboda, who rejects it for tactical reasons and insists on visiting Moscow.

August 22, 1968 (approx. 9:30 P.M.): The Extraordinary 14th Congress of the CPCz ends. A new central committee of the CPCz and a new presidium are elected; the latter unanimously elects Dubček to the post of first secretary. In his absence, Šilhán is appointed as leader of the CPCz CC.

August 22, 1968 (approx. 11:00 P.M.): Svoboda meets Chervonenko again to discuss his demand that he be allowed to hold talks with Soviet leaders in Moscow.

August 23, 1968 (8:45 A.M.): Czechoslovak Radio broadcasts Svoboda's speech in which he informs the public of his departure for Moscow.

August 23, 1968 (afternoon): From a prison in Ukraine, Dubček is taken to Moscow, where he meets Brezhnev, Kosygin, and Podgorny. Černík is also present at the meeting.

August 23, 1968: The UN Security Council votes on a draft resolution condemning the intervention: 10 votes for, 2 against (USSR and Hungary), and 3 abstentions (Algeria, India, and Pakistan). On the same day, delegates from Brazil, Denmark, France, Canada, Paraguay, Senegal, the United States, and Great Britain submit a draft resolution asking the UN general secretary to send an emissary to Prague to insist upon the release of arrested Czechoslovak officials and guarantees for their personal safety.

August 23–26, 1968: Czechoslovak and Soviet officials meet in Moscow. The Czechoslovaks include: Svoboda, Dubček, Smrkovský, Černík, Biľak, Barbírek, Piller, Rigo, Špaček, Švestka, Jakeš, Lenárt, Šimon, Husák, Indra, Mlynář, Dzúr, Kučera, and Koucký. The Soviet side consists of: Brezhnev, Kosygin, Podgorny, Voronov, Kirilenko, Polyanskii, Shelest, Katushev, Ponomarev, Grechko, and Gromyko. On August 26, the Moscow Protocol and a joint communiqué are signed. Kriegel, a member of the CPCz CC Presidium, refuses to sign the documents.

August 24, 1968: At a session of the UN Security Council, Hájek, the Czechoslovak minister of foreign affairs, states that neither the Czechoslovak government nor any of its constitutional officials had requested military assistance from the states of the Warsaw Pact, and that the government considers the occupation of the country an act of violence.

August 24–25, 1968: In Bratislava, a plenary session of the CC CPS demands the immediate withdrawal of the intervention forces and decides to convene an extraordinary congress of the CPS.

August 26, 1968 (9:00 – 9:15 A.M.): A nationwide work stoppage takes place.

August 26–29, 1968: The 14th Extraordinary Congress of the CPS is held in Bratislava. A new CC of 107 members is elected. Husák, who had reported to the delegates on the negotiations in Moscow, is elected first secretary, replacing Biľak.

August 27, 1968: Early in the morning, the Czechoslovak delegation returns to Prague from Moscow. In a radio broadcast, Dubček and Svoboda report on the meetings in Moscow. The information they provide is general, leaving the public unsatisfied.

August 27, 1968: Soviet units begin withdrawing from the center of Prague and from the area around Prague Castle.

August 28, 1968: A plenary session of the National Assembly issues a proclamation classifying the occupation as an illegal act in contravention of the UN Charter as well as of the statutory norms of the Warsaw Pact.

August 29, 1968: The Czechoslovak government initiates talks with Soviet commanders on the withdrawal of all military units from Prague and from all press, radio, and television buildings.

August 30, 1968: Deputies to the National Assembly unanimously declare that they did not invite, either in writing or orally, the governments of the Warsaw Pact countries to intervene militarily in the ČSSR.

August 30, 1968: Soviet occupation units begin distributing *Zprávy* ("News"), a journal edited by the "Editorial council for Soviet troops" and printed in Dresden (GDR).

August 31, 1968: A CPCz CC plenary session is held in Prague at which CC members are informed of the wording of the Moscow Protocol, and a new Presidium of the CPCz CC is elected. Dubček, Smrkovský, Černík, Biľak, Piller, Špaček are all reelected. Newly elected members include Svoboda, Erban, Husák, Šimon, and Mlynář. During the session, a very well informed Brezhnev telephones Dubček to criticize "the undemocratic methods by which the CC was elected," i.e., the inclusion of some of the delegates to the extraordinary congress in the new CC.

August 31, 1968: Josef Pavel, minister of the interior, is recalled from his post. Josef Pelnář is named as his replacement.

August 31, 1968: In Washington, NATO ambassadors meet representatives from the State Department. Their communiqué notes that invasion represents "the largest presence of Soviet military forces since W.W. II.", and that the situation "poses a menace to the security of the U.S. and its allies."

September 1, 1968: A comprehensive report on the occupation of Prague states that 25 people were killed and 431 seriously wounded. Additionally, many buildings were heavily damaged by gunfire.

September 2, 1968: Ota Šik is removed from his post as deputy prime minister and reassigned as economic adviser to the Czechoslovak embassy in Belgrade.

September 5, 1968: The Ministry of Foreign Affairs refuses to approve the statutes of KAN and of K-231.

September 6, 1968: Kriegel resigns his post as chairman of the CC of the National Front of the ČSSR.

September 6, 1968: In the presence of Dubček and Černík, President Svoboda receives Foreign Minister Hájek and informs him it will be impossible for him to remain in his position. On September 14, Hájek will resign as foreign minister.

September 6, 1968: Soviet First Deputy Foreign Minister Kuznetsov arrives in Prague as plenipotentiary of the Soviet government. He remains until early December, becoming a key figure in asserting Soviet control over the "normalization" process in the ČSSR.

September 10, 1968: Svoboda, Dubček, Smrkovský, Černík, and Husák publish a proclamation to the Czechoslovak people, in which they express their determination to continue with the policy of reforms that was begun in January 1968.

September 10, 1968: Černík leads a delegation meeting with Brezhnev, Kosygin, and Podgorny in Moscow to discuss economic cooperation between the ČSSR and the USSR. Issues such as the presence of Soviet troops in Czechoslovak territory and the problems surrounding normalization are discussed.

September 16–17, 1968: In Mukaczevo (USSR), Ministers of Defense Dzúr and Grechko meet to discuss problems connected with the number of Soviet troops temporarily remaining in Czechoslovak territory.

September 17, 1968: The presidium removes Pelikán from the position of director of Czechoslovak Television and Suk from the post of director of the Czechoslovak Press Office.

September 27, 1968: The leaders of "the Five", Brezhnev, Zhivkov, Gomułka, Kádár, and Ulbricht, meet in Moscow to discuss the Czechoslovak situation. On the same day, Svoboda receives Warsaw Pact Chief Marshal Yakubovskii in Prague.

September 28, 1968: Defense Minister Dzúr expands the number of military areas accessible to Soviet troops.

October 3–4, 1968: Czechoslovak–Soviet talks convene in Moscow. The delegations of Dubček, Černík and Husák from the Czechoslovak side and Brezhnev, Kosygin, Podgorny from the Soviet side discuss questions of "normalization" and the billeting of intervention troops on ČSSR territory.

October 14–15, 1968: Negotiations commence between the ČSSR and the Soviet Union delegations on the conditions of the residence of Soviet troops on Czechoslovak territory.

October 16, 1968: Following two more days of negotiations in Prague, Kosygin and Černík sign a treaty on the "Temporary Presence of Soviet Troops in the ČSSR."

October 18, 1968: The National Assembly approves the above-mentioned treaty, by a vote of 228 to 4 with 10 abstentions. More than 50 deputies are not present. Svoboda ratifies the treaty the same day.

October 30, 1968: In Bratislava Castle, Svoboda signs the constitutional law on the federative arrangement of Czechoslovakia.

November 7, 1968: Massive anti-Soviet demonstrations take place in the streets of Prague, Bratislava, Brno, and České Budějovice. 176 persons are arrested in Prague.

November 14–17, 1968: At a CPCz CC plenary session, a new executive committee of the presidium is elected. Members include Dubček, Černík, Erban, Husák, Sádovský, Smrkovský, Svoboda, and Štrougal. Mlynář is relieved of all posts at his own request.

November 17, 1968: Following rejection of a request to hold a parade, Prague University students begin a 3-day strike to support their demands; students in other cities immediately join in.

December 7–8, 1968: Talks among the top officials of the CPCz and CPSU take place in Kiev.

December 12–13, 1968: At a plenary session, the CPCz CC decides on nominations for senior governmental positions in connection with the new federative arrangement of the ČSSR.

December 27, 1968: The Soviet government protests the publication of the so-called Czech Black Book (*Sedm pražských dnů*, August 21–27, 1968), compiled by the Historical Institute of the Czechoslovak Academy of Sciences.

1969

January 1, 1969: Svoboda is appointed president of the first federal government of the ČSSR. Černík is appointed prime minister.

January 2, 1969: The Presidium of the Slovak National Council is appointed, with Sádovský as chairman of the first government of the Slovak Socialist Republic.

January 9, 1969: Dubček receives Konstantin Katushev, the CPSU CC official responsible for intra-bloc relations, who is in Czechoslovakia as the head of a Soviet delegation from December 27 to January 10.

January 16–17, 1969: At a CPCz plenary session, Peter Colotka is appointed chairman of the Federal Assembly and Smrkovský is appointed vice-president.

January 16, 1969: In front of the National Museum on Wenceslas Square in Prague, Jan Palach, a student at the Faculty of Philosophy at Charles University, attempts suicide by self-immolation. He calls his act a protest against the restoration of censorship. He dies three days later.

February 21–March 2, 1969: Defense Minister Dzúr heads a 10-member military delegation to the USSR, where he is received by Brezhnev on February 27.

February 27–March 12, 1969: A delegation of the CPSU Central Auditing Commission, headed by Arvid Peľshe, visits Czechoslovakia as part of the process of overseeing "normalization".

March 21 & 28, 1969: Victories by the Czechoslovak ice hockey team over the Soviets at the World Championships in Stockholm spark spontaneous anti-Soviet demonstrations throughout the ČSSR.

March 31, 1969: Following an extraordinary session of the CC CPSU Politburo the previous day, Marshal Grechko and Vice-Foreign Minister Semenov arrive in the ČSSR without notice. They meet Czechoslovak officials to discuss the demonstrations of March 28–29. Semenov and Dubček hold numerous meetings over the next 10 days. On April 10, Grechko orders the transfer of nearly 8,000 Soviet soldiers from the GDR to Czechoslovakia.

April 17, 1969: At a CPCz CC plenary session Dubček is relieved of his post as first secretary and replaced by Husák. A new Presidium of the CPCz CC is elected with 11 members instead of the former 22: Husák, Biľak, Colotka, Černík, Dubček, Erban, Piller, Poláček, Sádovský, Svoboda, Štrougal.

August 19–21, 1969: Demonstrations take place in 31 towns on the first anniversary of the invasion; Prague and Brno are the sites of the largest protests. After 35,000 members of the National Militia and Czechoslovak People's Army are called in to suppress the demonstrators, clashes ensue, leaving five persons dead, 33 seriously wounded, and 287 arrested.

September 25–26, 1969: A plenary session of the CPCz CC disavows the August 21, 1968 resolution of the CPCz CC Presidium condemning the invasion of Czechoslovakia, and starts the "purge" process in the CPCz and Czechoslovak society.

PART ONE

'A SUN SUDDENLY RISEN'
A PRELUDE TO THE PRAGUE SPRING OF 1968

INTRODUCTION

The reader of this anthology may wonder why it is being published at this time—why, years after the collapse of communism in Eastern Europe, the history of the failed Czechoslovak attempt in 1968 to transform "real socialism" into "socialism with a human face" would be of interest in today's world. Yet, as Eastern Europe struggles to emerge from the shadows of its communist past, the Prague Spring, as the reform effort in Czechoslovakia was called at the time, remains relevant and compelling. In a speech to the Czechoslovak Federal Assembly in 1990, then-British Prime Minister Margaret Thatcher recalled the aborted era of Czechoslovak reform as a "sun suddenly risen from long darkness." Representatives of other European states and the United States have shown renewed appreciation for that effort at socialist reform that was mown down by Soviet tanks. The idea of the Prague Spring was one of the foundations of our own dissident movement for the 1989 Velvet Revolution in Czechoslovakia. During the overthrow of the old regime, a key demand of our CIVIC FORUM (the organization for coordinating civic activities and also for negotiating with the government) and PUBLIC AGAINST VIOLENCE (performing the same function in Slovakia) was that the Soviet Union, and the CPCz leadership who aided and abetted the repression of reform, officially apologize for their role in 1968. For those reasons, the meaning of the Prague Spring and its main protagonist, Alexander Dubček, has experienced a comeback rarely seen in politics.

Today, euphoria over the collapse of communism is replaced by a sober analysis of our nation's history. And this analysis highlights the question of the means and objectives of this attempt at reform—as well as the consequences of its defeat. The first part of the answer, at least in the opinion of the editors, lies in the history of Central and Southeastern Europe, the sub-continent upon which two world wars were fought. During the second and most destructive war in the history of mankind, this sub-continent was the target of Hitler's attempt at European hegemony and, became, directly and indirectly, a component of his Great German Reich. The drive of fascism wrought human and material devastation, horrific social upheaval, and the unparalleled terror of Nazi brutality, depriving entire nations of their ethnic origins and culminating with the Holocaust.

The abject evil of nazism provided the Soviet system with a beneficent image it would not otherwise have garnered. Josef Stalin exploited Eastern European sympathy for the performance of his victorious armies on the battlefield as well as their position on the river Elbe by transforming Central and Eastern Europe into the "borderland" of the Soviet Empire. In our nation, as well as the others in this region, Moscow asserted its hegemony not only through political influence but through the presence of Soviet troops. Throughout what would become the "Eastern Bloc" Stalin implanted a Soviet-model socioeconomic and political system based on what Lenin called the "dictatorship of the proletariat"—in reality a dictatorship of the communist parties, or rather the top party leaders who swore allegiance to the Kremlin. The communist party apparatus was based on a system of mass organizations degraded to the role of mere "transmission belts" in a stilted bureaucratic order. Under this order, the peoples of Eastern Europe had no voice to assert their needs and desires, let alone dictate the demands of a nation. Indeed, the Soviet-sponsored systems brought severe suppression of elementary democratic liberties and human rights including the outright repression of non-communists and opponents in the ranks of the communist parties.

In Romania, Poland, Hungary, East Germany, and perhaps with some exception in Bulgaria, the Soviets presented this system as the sole historically justified and logical model of socialism. (In fact, Moscow's brand of communism stemmed as much from the historically restricted individuality of pre- and post-revolutionary Russia as it did from the ideological writings of Marx, Engels and especially Lenin.) An outside force, the Kremlin imposed this system against the will of the populations of Eastern Europe, the majority of whom were not inclined towards socialism.

The Czechoslovak Road

Czechoslovakia represents a unique historical case: in the Czech lands, socialist ideas had become very attractive during the war and during the German occupation. In the first post-war elections, held freely in 1946, socialist parties won a substantial majority in the Czech Lands (and in Slovakia established themselves as an influential minority). The "Czechoslovak Road to Socialism," as it was called at the time, was an accepted part of the national political landscape.

Nevertheless, general acceptance of socialism by Czechoslovak society in no way meant copying and implanting the Soviet system. In the spirit of the anti-fascist resistance struggle of the Second World War, the Czechoslovak people were drawn to democratic socialism—a concept based on T.G. Masaryk's visions of a synthesis of political and economic democracy, complemented by Eduard Beneš' idea of a future convergence of capitalism and socialism. To be sure, the Soviets' liberating role in the Second World War—the part they played in the defeat of Hitler and in saving the Czechoslovak people from national liquidation at the hands of the Nazis—led to respect and sympathy for the USSR, augmented by a feeling of Slavonic mutuality. But under no circumstances did that translate into a longing to live under a Soviet system and have it transposed onto our nation.

The "Czechoslovak Road" might have advanced if the anti-Hitler coalition had been kept alive after the war. But the demise of that coalition, the advent of the Cold War, and the threat of a "hot war" between the East and West undermined any chance that Prague could continue on an independent path toward socialism. In February 1948, the Czech Communist Party forced a major political confrontation over the resignation of twelve democratic ministers in the Gottwald government. The CPCz managed to use the collapse of the government to impose the dictatorship of one party—its own—on the Czechoslovak political system.

Under the regimen of the CPCz, the first half of the 1950s brought a radical transformation of Czechoslovak society. The economy experienced rapid growth, fueled in part by the rearmament of the military for an expected war with the West. At the same time, the capitalist classes and the petty bourgeoisie were decimated, along with the intelligentsia. This devastation of the country's social structure was accomplished through severe repression—imprisonment, police surveillance, labor camps, even the execution of some 200 "enemies." In the countryside, repression was used to impose a Marxist system of collective agriculture on a resistant peasantry; in the cities repression was used to squash the national leadership that had grown out of the years of anti-Hitler resistance, among them members of the movement led by Beneš. Czechoslovakia's writers, scholars, and leading political thinkers were now forcefully excluded from playing an active role in politics as well as in the economy, science and culture of our nation. The newly emerging intelligentsia (among them some of the editors of this book) were essentially conformist. Only much later would this group "sow their intellectual oats" and take a leadership role in a major movement toward reform.

By the end of the 1950s, the Soviet-style system of communist rule was fully imposed upon Czechoslovakia, as well as on its neighboring countries. All aspects of the Czechoslovak Road to socialism had been eliminated; whatever traces remained would be wiped out "with an iron broom," as the CPCz leader Klement Gottwald put it in 1952.

After the exposure of Stalin's brutality at the 20th CPSU Congress in 1956, a certain thaw in state repression occurred in Russia, which trickled down to Czechoslovakia. The state continued to exercise firm control, however; the CPCz did not even take advantage of Khrushchev's policies for redressing the worst of Stalin's repressive techniques, for example, the possibility to rehabilitate innocent victims of the trials. Nevertheless, gradually a national consciousness developed on the unsuitability of the current system of Czechoslovak communism and the necessity for fundamental changes. Change was mandated both by the interests and requirements of the new social structure, by the need for economic growth, now stifled by a centralized planning system and by the growing hostility among the Czechoslovak people against the repressive apparatus of the CPCz. A move for reform was also spurred on by a national awareness, and a historical memory, of Czechoslovakia's democratic past and of the original vision of a just social system that Czechoslovaks had been yearning for in the years following the Second World War.

These conditions, along with the continuing thaw in international relations and changes in neighboring nations, contributed to a national crisis of power that steadily spread through Czechoslovak society during the mid-1960s. It was essentially a crisis of Soviet-sponsored socialism. Increasingly, the Czechoslovak people, led by the intelligentsia and the student movement, began to voice criticisms of the foreign, repressive, and economically regressive components of the Soviet-imposed model. A political and moral crisis within the governing elite fed growing social pressure to liberate Czechoslovakia from the strait-jacket of the totalitarian bureaucratic system.

The Beginning of Reform

In the political climate of the Khrushchev reforms, the CPCz leadership, headed by Antonín Novotný, agreed to a slow and hesitant retreat from the existing rigid methods of ruling society. Of most significance was Novotný's decision to re-appraise the political trials of the early 1950s and rehabilitate the victims of these injustices. In 1963 the Ministry of Justice acknowledged publicly that more than 400 former communist officials had been "unjustly persecuted" and would have their sentences revoked—in some cases posthumously. Symptomatic of the regime's superficial commitment to this reform, however, a report by a special party commission whose task was to investigate the political trials was never published; and the prosecutions and imprisonments of tens of thousands of innocent non-communists for political crimes were not reviewed.

Novotný's decisions to prepare and implement an economic reform program were similarly limited. A blueprint for reform had been prepared by a team of mostly non-conformist economic scholars headed by Professor Ota Šik; it wanted to combine a new conception of strategic planning with elements of a market economy. In its final form, the proposed economic program reflected a compromise imposed by the party leadership. Nevertheless it gave business enterprises a certain latitude to formulate their own production programs and introduce a degree of market incentives in their planning. Though limited in concept, the economic reform still marked a blow to Czechoslovakia's centralized and command-based economic system.

Around the world, the 1960s were marked by a "scientific and technological revolution" which penetrated the Iron Curtain. In Czechoslovakia, this revolution manifested itself in the development of science and an increase in the role of intellectuals in society. Economists, historians, sociologists and lawyers took up the cause for economic and political modernization. Political scholars and philosophers also began to lay out ideas and visions for a new society. Remarkably, military strategists, long silenced by the binding dogma of communism and by Soviet military doctrine, began to find their own voice on the issues of Czechoslovak national security. Culturally, Czechoslovak arts, literature, film and especially theater also emerged from the confines of the totalitarian regime, with creative achievements that were appreciated not only throughout Europe but also in America. Indeed, the 1960s represented a golden age of artistic creativity in Czechoslovakia.

These groups filled the ranks of the "frontline fighters" against the totalitarian regime. In the extraordinary era of the 1960s, they garnered the experience of challenging the regime, and achieving the first small, but significant, changes in the system. They drew their strength from the growing social consensus on the need for reform, as well as from the formation of social and political organizations determined to achieve these changes. In the forefront of this movement were the intellectuals—scientists journalists and artists—as well as students, both communist and non-communist. So dynamic was their growth that First Secretary Novotný waivered between accepting the opposition and suppressing it.

The initial manifestations of a Czechoslovak reform movement triggered the concern of the Kremlin. In 1964, Khrushchev had been replaced as first secretary of the CPSU by Leonid Brezhnev—a move that boded ill for Moscow's future support for Novotný. Similarly, outright criticism was voiced in the German Democratic Republic (GDR) where party leader Walter Ulbricht feared any deviation from orthodoxy that could endanger the stability of his regime.

The Eastern Bloc camp of ossified "real socialists" also feared a weakening of the Warsaw Pact if reforms in Prague led to an independent Czechoslovak foreign policy. Czechoslovakia, which together with Poland and the GDR, formed the so-called northern flank of the Warsaw Pact, was geographically situated on the main route of anticipated war operations against the NATO military powers on the European battlefield. It was also the only country with no Soviet troops on its territory, despite multiple Soviet attempts to base forces there to bridge the gap in its northern flank. At the end of 1945, Soviet and U.S. liberation armies left Czechoslovak territory simultaneously. During the civil strife in February 1948, Stalin had demanded that Czechoslovak communists request Soviet military aid in the struggle against "reaction." The CPCz resisted this pressure, fearing the political backlash from a nationalistic populace. In 1955, in connection with the Austrian state treaty, Soviet, U.S., British and French occupation troops withdrew from the newly sovereign state of Austria. At the same time this boded a change in the military-strategic situation of the Central European region, increasing the geostrategic significance of the Czechoslovak area in Soviet military considerations. Soviet political and military authorities sought at that time to redeploy some of the Soviet troops withdrawn from Austria in neighboring Czechoslovakia. The CPCz leadership was prepared to accommodate these demands as a gesture of self-preservation. In the end, however, Khrushchev decided not to go ahead with the transfer. After his removal by Brezhnev's neo-Stalinist group, the Kremlin revived its efforts to establish a military presence on Czechoslovak soil.

During Khrushchev's tenure, Soviet military doctrine had been based on the premise that the outbreak of war would be preceded by a period of increased tension in international relations. Under Brezhnev, the Soviet military put forward the thesis that the imperialists were continuing preparations for an unexpected nuclear strike. According to new Soviet operational planning, in the event of war frontline Czechoslovak units would be immediately placed in a state of full combat alert, ready to fight within a period of between thirty minutes and three hours. According to original plans from the early 1960s, Czechoslovak missile troops would receive warheads located on Soviet territory after 18 to 22 hours at the earliest. Whereas the adversary already had nuclear weapons at the regimental level, the Czechoslovak army would have to fight, initially, only with the support of strategic weapons located at a relative distance from Czechoslovakia's borders. To rectify this problem, the Soviet representatives, headed by the commander-in-chief of the Warsaw Pact Joint Armed Forces, concluded that the deployment of warheads on Czechoslovak territory be considered, contingent on the presence of Soviet forces to handle and safeguard this forward-based nuclear arsenal. The Soviets determined that Prague should request this deployment; the Kremlin would then give its consent.

The deployment actually advanced to the stage where, in 1966 and 1967, three silos were built to store special tactical warheads. At the time of the Prague Spring, some 500 Soviet soldiers were scheduled to arrive to handle the stored nuclear material—the beginning of a process that was to end with the official deployment of Soviet troops on Czechoslovak territory. The deployment plan underscored the strategic significance of the Czechoslovak region to Soviet authorities, and was a major factor in their concern for Prague's complete subordination to Moscow's dictates.

1967

The year 1967 brought both hopes and dangerous risks for the course of the Czechoslovak reform movement. During that twelve-month period, developments in Czechoslovak political and economic life raised the curtain on the drama to which history has given the name "Prague Spring."

Ironically, a key catalyst occurred far beyond Czechoslovakia's borders. In June 1967, tension in the Middle East erupted into the Arab–Israeli conflict. The world was shocked not only by the outbreak of war but by its progress and by its unequivocal and meteoric outcome. "The world of socialism" was doubly shocked; in the period preceding the Six-Day War, Eastern Europe had provided considerable military assistance—weapons, trainers, intelligence—to the Arab countries. The defeat of the Arab countries was thus a defeat for the Soviet bloc and its international prestige.

In the aftermath of the war, the totalitarian regime reasserted its most militaristic character, giving the Czechoslovak generals a greater social predominance then they had previously held. At the same time the Czechoslovak intelligentsia, led by members of the Writers' Union who opposed Prague's role in the Arab–Israeli conflict, used the occasion of the 4th Czechoslovak Writers' Congress to openly condemn, for the very first time, the CPCz's aggressive stance against Israel. The Writers' Congress became the first forum for unprecedented criticism of Novotný's international and domestic policies, as well as the first forum for open debate about Czechoslovakia's future.

The 4th Congress met in Prague on June 27–29, 1967. As on many occasions in modern Czechoslovak history—recall 1917, 1938, 1956—Czechoslovak writers again asserted themselves as the interpreters of the fundamental needs and aspirations of society. In a demonstration of the transformation of virtually the entire cultural and scientific community into opponents of the communist party leadership, members of the congress articulated a principled judgement of the past and present, and of the need to prepare for a new concept of the country's future at considerable risk to themselves and their professional careers. "I [am] truly fascinated by the courageous openness of some of the speakers, the reasoned arguments heard from the rostrum, the enthusiasm and frankness that marked attempts to discern various fundamental certitudes and fundamental doubts that today accompany our work," the prominent young playwright—and future president—Václav Havel noted in his address (Document No. 1).

For years, Czechoslovak writers had been calling for a "European context"—a return to the civilized cultural sphere corresponding to the history and traditions of the Czechoslovak people. At the Congress, they expressed their sovereign and independent attitudes—on issues ranging from Prague's role in the Middle East to amending the law of the press to allow freedom of speech—as well as their determination to back their convictions on what the writer Milan Kundera called their "responsibility for the very existence of their nation." As Havel pointed out, "instead of uttering a thousand bold words of which a hundred are later gradually retracted, it is always better to utter only a hundred but to stand behind them to the very end." The writers who spoke out were condemned by the CPCz secretary, Jiří Hendrych (after Novotný the most powerful man in the Politburo), "for the presentation of views that run directly contrary to the state, socialism, and even [the] national interests of our people." Several were expelled from the communist party; others were reprimanded and subjected to disciplinary action.

The Writers' Congress tested the ground for open non-conformity; the flawless functioning of the so-called leading role of the party was suddenly cast in doubt. Administrative repression against the writers—in addition the Central Committee banned their journal *Literární noviny* and replaced it with a new weekly under the control of the Ministry of Culture and Information—only fueled the spread of political ferment and public criticism of Novotný's leadership.

In response to the outbreak of open opposition, the CPCz leadership attempted to revise its ideological agenda—to abandon the idea of an all-people's state and return to one of the state as the dictatorship of the proletariat and the priority of class principles in political practice. At a graduation of military colleges on September 1, 1967, First Secretary Novotný announced a special directive committing the army to the ideological struggle against "liberalism" and moving the military as an institution onto the front line of the political struggle against reform. The first secretary and his supporters made it abundantly clear that the armed forces were firmly behind him. The speech, which had not been cleared by the Presidium, was widely considered Novotný's ill-conceived attempt to consolidate his political position and personal power.

Novotný's crude abuses, his refusal to entertain necessary economic reforms, and his rejection of grievances voiced by Slovak representatives over the unequal conditions facing the Slovaks in the Czechoslovak state, caused the social crisis, in October 1967, to penetrate the highest echelons of the communist party. The fragmentation of the treasured cohesion of the party manifested itself at a CPCz Central Committee Plenum on October 30–31, 1967 (Document No. 2). The anti-Novotný forces used the agenda, which included extremely vague language "on the position and role of the party in the present phase of the development of our socialist society," to criticize the highest party officials—the first time any Central Committee member had dared to do so since the communist party seized all power in 1948. They understood that democratization within the party itself was a prerequisite for advancing democracy throughout the country.

The criticism raised at the Plenum was directed above all against Novotný, and against his concentration of power as first secretary, president of the republic, supreme commander of the armed forces and supreme commander of a kind of private army of the CPCz, the People's Militia. Alexander Dubček, the first secretary of the Slovak Communist Party, angered Novotný by stating during the Plenum that government and party "tasks must be carefully separated, especially in central leadership and management. "The party and its Central Committee are not the government. The government must govern, this is something I have in mind, and it applies chiefly to the communists in the government, especially in its leadership, who should show sufficient initiative in improving the work of the government. This is precisely what the government leadership is lacking and there is nothing to justify this."

Dubček also called on the CPCz to "deepen intra-party democracy," and readdress the top-down control that the centralized Central Committee leadership exercised over almost every aspect of Czechoslovak life. "To lead the party consistently in a Leninist spirit toward the strengthening of its leading role," he noted, "means less ordering about and more practical work with communists whom the party has entrusted with jobs in any sector of its activity." Here, Dubček articulated the hostile feelings of many Czechs that the CPCz had usurped the power of all state, economic and social institutions by interfering at will in their functions and authority.

Novotný was also criticized during the Plenum for his handling of ethnic grievances and nationalism, most notably the Slovak issue. Slovakia's evolution into a modern nation generated strong and often emotional national feelings. At the same time, the Soviet model emphasized minimizing nationalism and nationalist identity to the greater good of the central communist state. Under Novotný's regime, Slovaks chafed at the restrictions on many of their national institutions and the abject control of the Czechoslovak party bureaucracy over their daily lives. Novotný's arrogance in the face of escalating calls for change in the Central Committee's policies toward Slovakia prompted Dubček and his followers to make "mutual relations" a major issue at the Plenum. Perhaps more than any other issue, this enhanced Dubček's image among the anti-Novotný forces. The Slovak question thus became the catalyst of the entire subsequent development towards the "Prague Spring."

Dubček's speech at the Plenum—by American standards surely very mild, but unprecedented in the CPCz—signaled the existence of serious conflicts even within the CPCz Presidium. Novotný responded with indignation—only confirmed his intransigent, arrogant, and increasingly isolated position. The CPCz first secretary accused his main detractor of advocating "bourgeois nationalism," and of falling "under the influence of incorrect local interests." His remarks only inflamed and emboldened the anti-Novotný forces at the October Plenum. For the first time, a severe division within top party ranks was openly manifested, reflecting the growing unrest in Czechoslovak society.

By early December, Novotný had lost power within the CPCz. At the beginning of the Presidium meeting, half of the members—Drahomír Kolder, Jiří Hendrych, Oldřich Černík together with the last leader of the Gottwald generation, Jaromír Dolanský, and, last but not least, Alexander Dubček—joined to challenge the regime's leadership. In Novotný's camp stood Prime Minister Jozef Lenárt; Bohuslav Laštovička, chairman of the National Assembly; Michal Chudík; chairman of the Slovak National Council (the only organ of Slovak autonomy); and Otakar Šimůnek, deputy prime minister of the Czechoslovak government and its permanent representative to CMEA.

To break this stalemate, and undermine his opponents, Novotný desperately sought the support of Soviet leader Brezhnev. Without informing any of his party colleagues, Novotný invited Brezhnev for a brief, unofficial visit to Prague in early December. Clearly, Novotný hoped that Brezhnev's visit, and presumed endorsement, would help him reconsolidate power. But that proved not to be the case. Brezhnev acted diplomatically. Over a period of 18 straight hours, he spoke to almost all the members of the Presidium individually—learning that Novotný was widely unpopular—and then attended a Presidium meeting on December 9, 1967, where he made a brief and carefully worded speech (Document No. 3). "I did not come to take part in the solution of your problems . . . you will surely manage to solve them on your own," Brezhnev told top party officials.

"*Eto vashe delo*—This is your affair," Brezhnev is reported to have privately told CPCz officials. In fact, he subtly tried to help Novotný by urging the party leadership to come to a consensus in the Presidium on issues over CPCz leadership, rather than allow the 150-member Central Committee—where Novotný had even less support—decide them. "Under the circumstances," Brezhnev admitted in a phone call to Hungarian leader János Kádár following the visit to Prague, "I could not create the impression that I was interfering in their internal affairs, while at the same time something had to be done to restore the unity of the Presidium and the Central Committee and to support Cde. Novotný" (Document No. 4).

When the Central Committee opened its Plenum session on December 19, the future of Czechoslovakia was at a crossroads. Novotný's failure to secure Brezhnev's open support further eroded his backing in the CPCz. At the very least, his posts as first secretary and president, and commander-in-chief would now be separated. The profound implications of this seemingly bureaucratic reorganization soon became apparent in the early days of 1968.

DOCUMENT No. 1: Proceedings of the 4th Czechoslovak Writers' Congress, June 27–29, 1967, and a Follow-up Resolution by the CPCz CC Plenum, September 1967 (Excerpts)

Sources: (1) *IV. Sjezd Svazu československých spisovatelů (Protokol), Praha, 27.–29. června 1967* (Prague: SCSS, 1968), pp. 131–162; (2) VHA, MNO-HPS, RS 18–1/1968; and (3) Sb. KV, D IV – ÚSD, AÚV KSČ, F. 01

The 4th Czechoslovak Writers' Congress in June 1967 symbolized, more than any other event, the growing political and intellectual ferment in Czechoslovakia during Premier Antonín Novotný's last year in power. The congress became a forum for unprecedented public criticism of the CPCz, and of Novotný personally. These excerpts, from speeches by Milan Kundera, Václav Havel, Ludvík Vaculík, and Pavel Kohout, convey both the spirited nature of the debate and the main demands put forth by the writers—for greater freedom of expression and an end to censorship. The response of the top communist party official responsible for cultural affairs and ideology, Jiří Hendrych, reflects the communist party leadership's hard-line position against such "hostile views."

Kundera, Havel, Vaculík, and Kohout were among Czechoslovakia's best known writers. Kundera gained prominence for his satirical and existential writings, a style he continued and perfected while living in exile after 1968. Havel, only 31 years old in 1967, had already earned a reputation as a gifted and courageous playwright. Vaculík was regarded as one of the finest writers in Czechoslovakia and had recently published his acclaimed novel Sekyra *(The Axe). He subsequently authored the famous "Two Thousand Words" Manifesto (see Document No. 44). Kohout was a celebrated playwright and in mid-1968 became widely known for his "Message from the Citizens," which was published in* Literární listy *and signed by hundreds of thousands of Czechs and Slovaks on the eve of the Čierna nad Tisou negotiations (see Document No. 63). The willingness of these four writers and their colleagues to speak out so boldly posed a danger to their careers, their livelihood, and even their personal safety.*

Hendrych's speech represents the CPCz leadership's extreme dissatisfaction with the Writers' Congress. In his remarks, he condemns the regime's critics for espousing views "fundamentally at odds with the policy of our republic and the policy of the communist party." He promises to exact retribution against the "hostile" speakers—a pledge fulfilled three months later, in September 1967, when the CPCz Central Committee adopted a disciplinary resolution against several of the writers.

Excerpts from Milan Kundera's Speech

Large European nations with a so-called classical history look upon the European continent as something natural. But Czech history is interspersed with periods of awakening and periods of slumber, and missed certain major stages in the progress of the European spirit so they were forced to interpret the European context simply for themselves, to master it, and to re-create it. For the Czechs nothing was ever a matter to be taken for granted, neither their language nor their "Europeanism." . . .

In his letter to Helvetius, Voltaire wrote that beautiful phrase: "I disapprove of what you say, but I will defend to the death your right to say it." This formulates a fundamental ethical principle of modern culture. Anyone who goes back in history to the period before this principle takes a step backward from modern times into the Middle Ages. Any suppression of views, even when the views that are being forcibly suppressed are erroneous, must lead, in the final analysis away from the truth, for truth can be attained only through the interaction of views that are equal and free. Any interference with freedom of thought and words, no matter how discreet the technique or name given to such censorship, is a scandal in the twentieth century and a shackle on our emerging literature.

Czech writers have borne responsibility for the very existence of their nation, and this is true even today because the standard of Czech writing, its greatness or smallness, courage or cowardice, provincialism or all-embracing humaneness will to a large extent determine the answer to the nation's vital question: Is the existence of the nation even worthwhile? Is the existence of its language worthwhile? These most basic questions, embedded in the foundations of the modern existence of this nation, are still awaiting final answer. That is why everyone who—through bigotry, vandalism, uncivilized behavior, or closed-mindedness—undermines cultural progress is, at the same time, undermining the very existence of this nation.

Excerpts from Václav Havel's Speech

This is the first writers' congress I have attended. And after yesterday's proceedings, especially the morning session, I must say that I was truly fascinated by the courageous openness of some of the speakers, the civilized arguments given from the rostrum, the enthusiasm and frankness that marked attempts to discern various fundamental certainties and fundamental doubts that accompany our work today. . . .

But once I recovered somewhat from this initial astonishment and fascination and when some of the speeches in the afternoon permitted me to immerse myself for a while in my own thoughts, the first doubts gradually began to enter my mind. I asked myself: Is all this peculiar to this specific congress, or has it always been like this? All that has been said here surely has some weight irrespective of all contexts, and yet I said to myself that it would be worthwhile finding out whether such an atmosphere is not something entirely normal and typical at congresses; whether this whole suggestive theater is not in reality some kind of ritual—in the good sense of the word—which must take place over and over again, and always a little bit differently . . . It occurred to me that when all is said and done, this is more or less the way things must have appeared at the Third Congress, not to mention the second and even, to some extent, probably the first. At that point I was a little puzzled: Some kind of a tradition would in itself certainly be nice, to display openness and passionate commitment once every four years while airing problems and coming forward with bold demands that could not be uttered anywhere else; this in itself would be a noble mission—or, a ritual, if you like—of writers' congresses. The only thing that made me nervous was the thought that even though such a gathering always has a direct social impact, this impact soon fades—and is all this still binding in the end? Is there any guarantee that tomorrow's reality will not simply once again, as so many times before, spit at today's beautiful words? It is sufficient to recall how many such beautiful and courageous declarations made from congress rostrums had to be retracted sooner or later; it is sufficient to recall how many of these fine resolutions were soon negated by the reality that followed. How many times, after various congress speeches were made, after tempers cooled and those who made them returned from the realm of mass psychosis to the realm of everyday life, did they apologize for or clarify or criticize their speeches, often by emphasizing precisely this mass psychosis? Congresses are in no way simply an example of mass psychosis or suggestion, but if this feature of them can regularly be used as a pretext for subsequent efforts to touch up and justify one's remarks, then such a psychosis is a luxury we writers simply cannot afford. And I thought about all these things until I gradually became convinced that instead of uttering a thousand bold words of which a hundred are later gradually retracted, it is always better to utter only a hundred but to stand behind them to the bitter end.

I am not really familiar with the diplomatic rules of writers' organizations, but I would like to believe that, as an internal matter of this congress, reading Solzhenitsyn's letter is all to the good.[1] However, now that the letter has been read out I see no reason why I should not be able

---

[1] Havel is referring here to Aleksandr Solzhenitsyn's Letter to the 4th Congress of the Soviet Writers' Union. In the letter Solzhenitsyn condemned censorship and bitterly criticized the leaders of the Soviet Writers' Union, who promptly forbade any mention or dissemination of the letter. Copies of the document were distributed in Czechoslovakia, and most of the delegates at the Czechoslovak Writers' Congress had seen it. When one of the participants, Alexander Kliment,

to comment on it, again as an internal matter. It struck me as a splendid example of a true ethical stance, that is, a stance commensurate with one's given possibilities and one's awareness of them: Although I have no way to verify the matter, I fervently believe that in the letter the author said only what he himself is totally capable of guaranteeing with his entire life right to the very end. Such unusual openness is based on a precise awareness of the limits of what can be guaranteed . . . In this light I believe it was most useful, leaving aside all diplomatic considerations, that the letter was read out here; its moral strength, which is derived not from grand words but from its great cogency and which therefore inevitably wins the respect of even his most ardent opponents, can serve as a perfect lesson for all of us of the supreme, self-reliant poise of a writer. . .

Excerpts from Pavel Kohout's Speech

I believe it is the duty of our congress, the congress of a union to which the great majority of writers and commentators belong, to demand an amendment to the press law so that each author should have the right to defend the freedom of their speech within the framework—I stress, within the framework—of the constitution. In the past and even today each author has a threefold responsibility for their views and work: a moral responsibility if they are exposed to public criticism, a material responsibility if their work is censored and thus not paid for, and a legal responsibility as demonstrated by the court proceedings against the cartoonist Lidak. In return for this threefold responsibility, authors are entitled to one inalienable right: namely, to defend themselves under the terms of the same law that is used against them to the extent that they have violated it. I propose that this demand be incorporated in the congress resolution as a separate point.

Excerpts from Ludvík Vaculík's Speech

. . . when casting around for an explanation of why we have lost so much moral and material strength and why we have fallen behind economically, the ruling circles claim that this was a necessity. I believe that this was not a necessity at least not for all of us; it was perhaps necessary for the intellectual advance of the institutions of power that have essentially forced all advocates of socialism to accompany them along this road. It must be acknowledged that over the past twenty years not a single human problem—including basic requirements such as housing, schools, and a prospering economy, as well as more subtle requirements of a kind that un-democratic systems through the world are incapable of solving, such as a sense of fulfillment in society, the subordination of political decisions to ethical criteria, faith in the worth of even the most menial jobs, and the need for trust among people and a better education for the masses—has yet been solved. What is more, I am afraid that we have not advanced on the world scene and that our republic has lost its good name. We have not contributed any original thoughts or good ideas to humanity, and that, for example, we have not come up with any solutions of our own about how to produce and not drown in goods. . . .

I am not saying that we have lived in vain and that all this is meaningless; there *is* a meaning here, but the question is whether the price of this meaning is a warning. Human knowledge would advance in any case, but instrument should not have been a country whose culture was aware of this danger.

---

explicitly mentioned and supported Solzhenitsyn's letter, he was warmly applauded. Kohout then got up and read aloud a Czech translation of the document. This was the specific action that prompted Hendrych to storm out of the hall.

Excerpts from Jiří Hendrych's Response

. . . All that has taken place, especially at certain stages of the congress, cannot leave any genuine communist indifferent. The direction in which certain individuals are steering the congress proceedings was bound to cause serious concern. It is evident that this was a group of people who had agreed on such a course of action, most of them party members who had expressed views fundamentally at odds with the policy of our republic and the policy of the communist party . . .

On Tuesday, the Presidium of the Party's Central Committee discussed the congress's first day. We condemned attempts to ignore the actual problems of the Writers' Congress and misuse its forum for the presentation of views that run directly contrary to the state, socialist, and even national interests of our people. . . .

It is difficult at this point to analyze the various speeches in the discussion and to define where they turned into outright attacks and slanders against the socialist system, against the domestic and foreign policies of our republic, and against the communist party. Similarly, there is no time to spell out where and on which points aggressive polemics were put forward . . . Therefore, I will simply make a few brief remarks on views that every honest communist must repudiate.

First of all, we vigorously condemn efforts to disparage the revolutionary achievements of our people and the communist party, as well as efforts to negate and vilify 20 years of our socialist achievements and place them virtually on a par with the period of darkness and the Nazi occupation. We will always oppose attempts to imbue general slogans of freedom, humanism, and democracy with the demand for the right to have hostile views and to obstruct the fruits of the labor of our people. . . .

We cannot help noticing that despite the discussion at a meeting of the party branch of the congress and despite the decision reached there, Cde. Kohout found it necessary to express to the congress an erroneous view on the question of the Middle East.[2] We can understand a certain lack of clarity, but we can neither understand nor tolerate a communist who publicly expresses criticism of the government's policy, attacking his communist government at a time when fronts worldwide have precariously split apart and when shots are being fired. Likewise, we must severely criticize Cde. Kohout for having publicized a Soviet document that was not addressed to the congress and that had not been published as a document of the fraternal writers' union.[3] This act must be qualified as an irresponsible move, which has seriously damaged our fraternal ties. . . .

I say sincerely, comrades, that in view of the rhetoric of symbols, allegories, and insinuations that were frequently heard at the congress, one cannot help but wonder what objectives certain writers are pursuing. . . .

One cannot help but wonder what Vaculík and others like him are seeking and what Havel and his ilk are after. Maybe some of you have seen the last issue of Tigrid's *Svědectví*. Prior to the congress an attempt was made to smuggle in several hundred copies of this issue containing instructions for the writers' congress—instructions which in their details, persons, and names are identical to what we have witnessed at the congress. There is no need to discuss who Tigrid is; we know this only too well and shall demonstrate that he is an agent employed by the American intelligence service, which also finances his magazine.[4]

---

[2] Hendrych is referring to the meeting of the party branch of the Writers' Union that was held the day before the 4th Congress opened. He convened that meeting to ensure that the CPCz's line would prevail at the congress.

[3] Hendrych is referring here to Solzhenitsyn's letter.

[4] Pavel Tigrid is a well-known Czech journalist who lived in exile in Western Europe after the communist takeover in Czechoslovakia in 1948. He was, however, able to maintain close ties with reformist elements in his homeland. In addition to editing the emigré quarterly *Svědectví* in Paris, Tigrid wrote two illuminating books about the 1968 crisis: *Le printemps de Prague* (Paris: Seuil, 1968) and *La chute irresistible d'Alexander Dubček* (Paris: Calmann-Levy, 1969).

Recent historical experience teaches us that things that start off with the same irresponsibility end in sharp conflicts. . . . It is our duty to put a stop to such irresponsibility and attacks. We will not permit irresponsible people to hold on to inflammatory materials. Patience has its limits, and so has tolerance. We will not allow anyone to subvert this republic. Those who act in this way, putting forward a variety of anarchic views and attacks as Vaculík does, are breaking ranks with the party. We will inform the party and, if necessary, will transfer this conflict to the forum of the entire party . . .

The proceedings of the congress and two meetings of the party branch of the congress have demonstrated that there are dangerous tendencies within the Writers' Union which . . . in the ideological sphere are undermining and forsaking Marxist–Leninist positions. . . .

The supporters of these tendencies and of organized activities to promote them, as well as of political ambitions, are confined to a relatively small group of writers, especially journalists gathered mainly around the periodical *Literární noviny*, and previously around the magazines *Květen* and *Tvář*, which have ceased publication. . . .[5]

Resolution of the September 1967 CPCz CC Plenum

After considering the report of the Presidium of the CPCz Central Committee regarding the party discussion of the proceedings and results of the 4th Congress of the Czechoslovak Writers' Union as presented by Cde. J. Hendrych, the Central Committee of the Communist Party of Czechoslovakia:

a) endorses the organizational and political conclusions set out in the report;

b) releases Cde. Jan Procházka from the post of candidate member of the CPCz Central Committee, based on the proposal of the Presidium of the CPCz Central Committee and based on the statement of Cde. Jan Procházka himself, since by his misguided and irresponsible action in the preparation of the 4th Congress of the Czechoslovak Writers' Union and during its proceedings and in his writings, he has demonstrated that his political and ideological standards do not correspond to the requirements arising from this office;

c) expels Comrades Ivan Klíma, Antonín J. Liehm, and Ludvík Vaculík from the Communist Party of Czechoslovakia;

d) delivers a reprimand with a warning to Cde. Pavel Kohout; and

e) agrees that the Central Control and Auditing Commission should start disciplinary proceedings against Milan Kundera.

---

[5] For further details about these literary outlets, see A. French, *Czech Writers and Politics 1945–1969*, East European Monographs No. 94 (Boulder, Col.: East European Quarterly, 1982). See also Dusan Hamšík, *Writers Against Rulers*, trans. by D. Orpington (New York: Random House, 1971) and other references cited in Vladimír V. Kusin, *Political Grouping in the Czechoslovak Reform Movement* (New York: Columbia University Press, 1972), pp. 66–67. Hamšík was head of the editorial board of *Literární noviny* and, later, of *Literární listy*.

DOCUMENT No. 2: Speeches by Alexander Dubček and Antonín Novotný at the CPCz CC Plenum, October 30–31, 1967

Source: Sb. KV, D IV—ÚSD, AÚV KSČ, F. 01

The presentations at the CPCz CC plenum in late October 1967 record the power struggle between the supporters of Antonín Novotný and those in the Central Committee who wanted to remove him as CPCz leader. Alexander Dubček, the first secretary of the Slovak Communist Party, used his speech to argue that the CPCz first secretary had pursued "inappropriate methods of political leadership" and that "a great deal must be improved and changed in practice," with "far greater care given to political and professional maturity." Dubček also came out decisively in support of separating top party and state posts, which in the context of contemporary debates within the party could only be construed as another anti-Novotný position. In a vigorous rebuttal, Novotný accused Dubček of duplicity and of succumbing to "narrow national interests." Novotný also charged Dubček and other Slovak officials with promoting "erroneous tendencies" and "playing into the hands of various petty bourgeois elements."

The plenum was unprecedented in its open criticisms of the CPCz leadership; only the most superficial details about the proceedings were released to the public.

Excerpts from Alexander Dubček's Speech

. . . Our main energy should not be concentrated on a defensive struggle *against* something, but on efforts to understand the causes of the problems, find a solution to them and to work *for* further progress—and I deliberately emphasize the word "for." On many occasions, and recently with increasing frequency, I have encountered the idea of giving people of all ethnic origins and social classes in our republic more concrete objectives, to show them ways and methods as well as the power of ideas, and to help them find their place in the worldwide struggle in a more vivid and active sense.

It is for this idea that we must make a substantial contribution to consolidate the unity of our people and of Czechoslovak statehood in view of relations between the nationalities. The past economic, political, and cultural development of Slovakia triumphantly confirms the success of the policy of our Communist Party of Czechoslovakia. The policy of leveling out discrepancies and of creating equal conditions for the work and life of people in all parts of our Czechoslovak Republic, as laid down by the party, remains the primary way to strengthen this unity.[6] We must make better use of positive tendencies in the struggle and life of the Czech and Slovak peoples for their national and social freedom and for their coexistence in a united Czechoslovak state. Where Slovakia is concerned, this requires—more so than in the recent past—the rectification of the party's perception of our revolutionary national past. National interests naturally must not be placed above international interests, but all that unites us in the Leninist understanding of mutual relations—which have always had a beneficial influence on the coexistence of Czechs and Slovaks and the life and work of our peoples and nationalities—and all that is progressive must today, as in the distant past, be put to the service of consolidating relations between Czechs and Slovaks as well as other ethnic groups in order to strengthen Czechoslovak patriotism, Czechoslovak statehood, and our Czechoslovak socialist republic. We know that no policy can be pursued automatically and that it is necessary to fight for it, eliminate all reasons for the failure to implement it, and translate it into reality which is precisely what we, as communists, are striving for and must continue to do.

---

[6] Dubček is referring to Slovakia's long-standing goal of "parity" with the Czech Lands. Many Slovaks perceived themselves to be living in a country in which "majority domination" *(majorizacia)* was destined to prevail.

But even this major social issue requires a better programmed and conceptual approach; this consolidation is only possible to a full extent as part of the process of the dynamic movement of society as a whole in which even Slovakia will play a more active role. I believe that in the broad initial stage on the road toward the scientific-technical revolution, the question of the progress of Slovakia will emerge in a different light, as a factor of great resources and possibilities, capable of making an adequate contribution to and playing a more active part in the development of society with the help of its material and, above all, its subjective factors. In turn, the current problems of Slovakia cannot be properly solved without the progress of the entire Czechoslovak society since they are an inseparable part of it. I believe that such an active role, together with the development—and I would emphasize the word "development"—of a general national life will allow for a sound national awareness to become an active component of the struggle in preparing for a communist society and to give national development its principles of internationalism and Czechoslovak patriotism. We must combine all these factors correctly into a united procedure and activity. But this also requires an integral, comprehensive program in the party's nationality policy, linked with development. . . .

The third question I want to address and which I wish to emphasize is the fact that the new phase and new tasks basically require new, more precise, and more appropriate methods of political leadership and management methods, as well as more precise relations between them. In this respect the most important issue is, and must be, a fundamental shift of methods and substantial changes in the work of the party. We must literally change over from replacing, as the theses state, to providing political leadership of the construction and development of socialism. Ever more profound consideration of the tasks and methods of political leadership impels us to stress the principle that the party is not directing but leading society, as was pointed out at the May plenary session of the Communist Party of Slovakia's Central Committee. The party is leading society—as correctly specified in the theses when listing the primary methods of implementing the party's leading role—by a profound and truthful understanding of the paths of development and by guiding development toward objective tendencies by winning over and mobilizing people for conscientious activity as outlined in the program. The party is doing this by setting out the content and determining the crucial path to take and ensuring the implementation of the program as well as providing the personnel. We realize that this is a complicated problem that has not yet been worked out in detail, and that these issues are of pressing social importance and must be tackled by science. Nevertheless, to make myself understood, I will put forth several clear thoughts.

The difference between leading society and managing individual sectors of its activity is not only a question of theory but one that is pertinent and practical. There are evidently different categories of content and form which have their dialectical relationship and their unity, but also their contradictions. The contradiction is given by the fact that society must have a government, discipline, and a legal system—in brief, a certain stability yet at the same time changes and revolutionary transformations are necessary. That very same society must be permeated by socialist revolutionary ideas, and this must be done at an optimum pace. The leadership has its tasks and methods, which include direct leadership by one section alone, while governance, state power, the management of economic processes, and other duties also have their practical tasks and methods. These relationships must be clarified and I am inclined to support those comrades who discussed this with me earlier on.

The party directs the activity of its bodies, organizations, and members, through whom it carries out its leading role in the whole of society. This intra-party leadership inevitably includes democratic centralism and the constant growth thereof; it also includes greater democracy in shaping the policy of the party without which the party would not discern the truth about development. We must deepen intra-party democracy, as we have pointed out in the statement of the Presidium of the Central Committee, but we must also consolidate unified discipline of action by implementing this democracy. To lead the party consistently in a Leninist spirit toward the strengthening of its leading role means less ordering about and more practical work with communists whom the party has entrusted with jobs in any sector of its activity. The leading role of the party must be reinforced also by having communists take a far more active part in formulating and implementing the policy of the party to which they belong, as well as in non-party organs because the party does not consist merely of party organs and its apparatus. It is on this question of a Leninist understanding of intra-party democracy that a great deal must be improved and changed in practice so that communists in all sectors should feel they are communists with equal rights, fully entitled to express their opinions and ultimately responsible for the formulation and implementation of the policy ensuring that the party is not divided into layers. Let us not have any illusions that this will happen all on its own. The Central Committee, too, will have to consider this in its entirety and take measures, for without them we shall never succeed in channeling the party into unity of action.

This is inseparable from the cadre policy, which requires far greater care to be given to political and professional maturity, as pointed out in the theses, but also to moral and personal qualities that are essential for an individual who wants to and is supposed to fight for progress. These qualities include such things as honesty, individual courage, and above all devotion to the party and not to one's working arrangements or personal ambition. These personal qualities often determine whether or not an individual succeeds in applying professional and political knowledge, which is why greater attention must be given to such qualities in our work with cadres.

The party has all the conditions and instruments by which it is able to ensure that the state bodies should govern and administer affairs in keeping with the program and other political decisions of party bodies. These tasks must be carefully separated, especially in central leadership and management.[7] The party and its Central Committee are not the government. The government must govern, this is something I have in mind, and it applies chiefly to communists in the government, especially in its leadership, who should show sufficient initiative in improving the work of the government. This is precisely what the government leadership is lacking and there is nothing to justify this. If these bodies are not governing sufficiently well and are not leading as required, as pointed out in the theses, the party cannot replace or take over their work and responsibilities. Instead, the party must once again insist that these bodies do their jobs. And if it really has to do so, then it should be done only as a necessary evil and only as a form of self-criticism of the mistakes of the party leadership, from which conclusions must be drawn for the improvement of the leadership itself. If we do not want anarchy—which we must also fear, just as we must fear lack of a programmed approach—it is unthinkable that pertinent bodies and individuals work without proper responsibility. The government and economic bodies should have, must have scope for practical leadership—and if they are lacking it they must create it—because to lead means to take decisions. And taking decisions means having a choice between alternatives and bearing responsibility for the alternatives and solutions that are chosen. . . .

Excerpts from Antonín Novotný's Speech

. . . The members of the Presidium of the Central Committee, whether Czech or Slovak comrades, bear responsibility for solving matters for the state as a whole. And it is on this point, I believe, that there is no total agreement. Take a look at today's session, comrades, compare the different approach in the speeches of the Slovak comrades, and look at the last session where Cde. Dubček spoke. After the last session of the party's Central Committee in September I told Cde. Dubček that I did not agree with his speech and that this speech would be discussed at a Presidium session. I told him that, after all, you approved the nationwide plan, and this means that you, too, take responsibility for it—yet you speak out and raise new problems. You know

---

[7] Here Dubček is addressing the question of the "separation of posts" (dekumulace funkci).

15

the economic problems with which we are grappling at the Presidium, and you, too, have a say in these matters, yet you speak out at the Central Committee plenum against the decision.

That would be bad enough, but there is still more. I listen to the radio and watch television and I read most Slovak papers. What is the response of the public to such a speech? I want to say quite openly that things are then depicted as a conflict between Prague and Bratislava and they become a national issue. We have already once before dealt with such opinions, feelings, and contradictions at the Presidium of the Central Committee. At a joint session to which the Presidium of the Central Committee of the Slovak Communist Party was invited, the Presidium of the Central Committee of our party was obliged to criticize the Presidium of the Central Committee of the Slovak Communist Party for certain deviations and for inconsistent implementation of resolutions adopted by the party Presidium.[8] I must stress that in my private conversations with Cde. Dubček I warned him that he was not pursuing a correct and responsible policy as first secretary of the CPS CC, an office whose chief responsibility is to oversee the policy of the CPCz in Slovakia. I also warned him that he had fallen under the influence of incorrect parochial interests, that he did not confront erroneous views on a consistent basis, and that he was even in the grip of certain narrow national interests. . . .

In this connection I would like to say quite openly that I opposed certain demands raised by some Slovak comrades, especially Cde. Dubček. Why? Comrades, I want to stress once more that our main task today is not to allocate new investments, our main problem is to modernize existing production facilities and to give them new production life and a new productive content. That is what we really need. I am not referring to further necessary investments in Slovakia; these are only natural. We have an industrial base, we have skilled engineers and qualified workers. We are introducing a new system of economic management, but if this new system is not backed by new technology we shall continue to have to subsidize it from the top and production will be costly and of inferior quality. What will the consequences be if we continue to pay subsidies so as not to reduce living standards? And so, what is needed is a new system of management, as well as new technology and new technical equipment for existing industry. It is within the framework of these economic measures that Slovakia must naturally be developed so that it should be on a par with the Czech Lands.

I think here it must be said frankly that the policy pursued by the communist party has had extremely positive, I would even say, excellent results. But what do we need, comrades? We need the Slovak comrades to implement whatever is fundamental and to mention these problems in their speeches as well. They must point out that national interests—not only local interests, but national interests—are what are most important and what will help us raise Slovakia to the standard of the Czech Lands. That is the only way we can achieve a uniformly high standard of the entire Czechoslovak economy. And that is where there are certain contradictions. That is why I cannot agree with the statements made, for example, by Cde. Dubček in September. After all, this would again be a one-sided solution and that would not help the progress of the national economy as a whole.

The question of dualism is connected with this. The question of dualism is understandably linked with national and international problems. Are we to set up certain parallel bodies in the government and in Slovakia and in the Slovak National Council, or are we to set up a fundamental central body based on statewide interests and in the interest of a unified economy?[9] It is logical of adjustments, requirements, and the demands of national interests that we are to establish a Slovak national body; that goes without saying, but not where this is not expedient. On the contrary, let the Slovak comrades work within the central organs and let them gather their forces into one area.

---

[8] Novotný is referring to a Presidium meeting held in early September 1967.

[9] Until 1968 the Czech Lands, unlike Slovakia, had no government bodies of their own; this discrepancy rankled many Slovaks because it implied that the central government functioned on behalf of the Czechs.

That is why we want the Presidium of the Central Committee of the Slovak Communist Party, including all its members and its Central Committee, to adopt an open stance on certain erroneous views regarding economic matters. With the help of radio and television, these views are being spread within the party and the whole state by certain economists employed by the Slovak Academy of Sciences or at universities. I am referring, for example, to Comrades Pavlenda, Kočtúch, and several others. Figures are deliberately being distorted in articles to demonstrate a wrong approach in the economic sphere in Slovakia, and that is how anti-Prague sentiments are being fuelled. But this is not the truth, comrades. A logical analysis of the economy and a logical analysis of the state's revenue show that we are constantly obliged to shift a portion of state revenue produced in the Czech Lands to the development of Slovakia. I stress that we must do this. We really want to raise the standards in Slovakia, but this can be done only on the basis of statewide economic results and on the basis of statewide results of state revenue. That is why we must shift a portion of the state's revenue, produced in the Czech regions, to Slovakia; otherwise this process of balancing standards would take perhaps fifty years since the entire economy is constantly growing. That is why investments in Slovakia must be greater, there is a bigger population there, a greater number of workers, and so forth.[10]

However, if these erroneous tendencies continue to be spread in Slovakia and nothing is done to counter them, I said that I would come to the Central Committee and demand the establishment of a Czech National Council. If there is a Slovak National Council then, given the current atmosphere, there must also be a Czech National Council. Such voices are already emerging. I warned the comrades. I said, comrades, I do not really want to come forward with such a proposal. It is now up to you whether you will oppose such incorrect tendencies. For if a Czech National Council were to be set up, it would be the body to decide what to do with the state revenue produced in the Czech Lands. And this is something that would play into the hands of various petty bourgeois elements in the Czech Lands. We can all surely imagine this kind of development, all the haggling.

Forgive me for coming back to this. Cde. Sedláková has raised certain problems connected with the last session of the Central Committee; I am surprised she raised them.[11] I think we must realize that the enemy is extremely active. We are again back to what I already said. A NATO meeting in Munich in 1961 decided how to fight in this context against the socialist countries, including our country. That is precisely what they are doing. I cannot go into details, it cannot be done. But I again affirm that the enemy is working exceptionally hard.

---

[10] What Novotný means here is "a higher population growth rate and a greater potential workforce," *not* a larger population. Slovakia's population was only about half that of the Czech Lands.

[11] He is referring here to Mária Sedláková, who at the time was one of the editors of the Slovak daily *Pravda* and was also one of the earliest critics of Novotný's leadership. In 1968 she was appointed a secretary of the Slovak Communist Party.

DOCUMENT No. 3: Remarks by Leonid Brezhnev at a Meeting of Top CPCz Officials, in Prague, December 9, 1967 (Excerpts)

Source: Sb. KV, D VII—ÚSD, AÚV KSČ, File for A. Novotný; Vondrová & Navrátil, vol. 1, pp. 30–31.

Leonid Brezhnev's carefully worded speech conveys his caution against overtly siding with the unpopular First Secretary Novotný. Although invited to Prague by Novotný as a way to bolster his flagging rule, Brezhnev tried to avoid taking a decisive position in the CPCz leadership dispute—"I did not come to take part in the solution of your problems"—and instead focused his remarks on restoring unity in the fractious party. Some of Brezhnev's comments during his meeting with top CPCz officials on December 9, especially about the proper role of the Presidium vis-à-vis the Central Committee, were openly supportive of Novotný against his opponents. But the Soviet leader's backing was far less enthusiastic than Novotný had either hoped for or needed.

[Brezhnev first spoke about the good results achieved by the Soviet Union and then discussed the defense capability of the Warsaw Pact.]

The Soviet Union is forced to allocate vast resources to defense. Although the budget officially refers to 22 percent, much more than that actually must be spent. Several institutes working for the defense industry are referred to as being civilian. That is why two recent plenary sessions of the CPSU Central Committee discussed international issues; the Soviet comrades are aware that concern for the defense of the USSR and the entire socialist camp must at all times have pride of place. The only thing ordinary people want is that there should not be another war, since the distress caused by the last war has not yet been fully alleviated. That is why we are continuously working to consolidate the Warsaw Treaty Organization and to ensure that unity on this question will prevail among all its members. No one can offer guarantees regarding the future course of events. Experience from the time of the civil war and the world war teaches us that we must have a powerful army. The reasons that the imperialists do not dare attack Czechoslovakia, Poland, or the other socialist countries, is that they are aware of the immense military strength of the Soviet Union. The Americans leave in peace those countries with whom the Soviet Union has concluded a treaty because they know only too well that we are superior. They constantly talk about a balance of forces, but they are fully aware of the actual disposition of forces. They do not even dare touch North Korea. The U.S. Air Force is bombing all kinds of targets in the Vietnamese Democratic Republic except for ports where Soviet ships are anchored, even though they know only too well that those ships are transporting arms to Vietnam. That is why unity on all military matters is essential so that we need not abandon our achievements.

[After dealing with the international situation, Brezhnev explained the circumstances of his present visit.]

This time I am here under circumstances in which the situation has escalated, if that is how we are to characterize it. I have been briefed by Cde. Novotný, and I had talks with other comrades as well. What am I to say? I did not come to take part in the solution of your problems. We do not do this, and you will surely manage to solve them on your own. I consider what Cde. Novotný said was quite correct, namely, not to submit matters of principle to the Central Committee at least until such time as they have been adopted unanimously by the Presidium.[12] That is the way

---

[12] By endorsing this view, Brezhnev came down squarely on Novotný's side on a particularly contentious issue. The anti-Novotný forces had been demanding a preeminent role for the Central Committee as opposed to the Presidium.

we do things. The Politburo deals with all fundamental issues. The question of party unity is a supreme principle that begins at the nucleus of the party: the Presidium. Unity within the Presidium is the guarantee of unity within the Central Committee, and this in turn is the guarantee of unity within the entire party. Unity of the Presidium and the Central Committee not only guarantees the unity of our party but also of the successful accomplishment of their tasks. As far as I know, the decisions of the 13th Congress [June 1956 — ed.] are being carried out successfully and, if I am correct, even your economy is not doing badly. Cde. Novotný pointed out that the situation has really improved. I shall not deal with the problems that have arisen in your country. I agree with Cde. Novotný that the problems should first of all be discussed by the Presidium. I know your party and the road it has traveled along, and that is why I am confident that this time, too, it will adopt the kinds of decisions that are in a Leninist spirit.

Brezhnev's insistence that the Presidium should remain the dominant organ partly qualifies the remark often attributed to him, "*Eto vashe delo*" ("This is your own affair"), when he was asked to intervene in the CPCz leadership dispute. Even if Brezhnev's chief motivation in favoring the Presidium over the Central Committee was simply to avoid a precedent that could later affect other communist parties (including the CPSU), his position was identical to Novotný's and thus could be construed, whether rightly or wrongly, as a broader gesture of support. For evidence that his whole visit was interpreted this way, see "Informatsiya k voprosu o polozhenii v rukovodstve KPCh," Cable No. 110 (SECRET) from I. Kuznetsov, Soviet consul-general in Bratislava, to A. A. Gromyko and K. V. Rusakov, 28 December 1967, in TsKhSD, F. 5, Op. 60, D. 299, Ll. 9–14.

DOCUMENT No. 4: János Kádár's Report to the HSWP Politburo of a Telephone Conversation with Leonid Brezhnev, December 13, 1967

Source: Sb. KV, Z/M; Vondrová & Navrátil, vol. 1, pp. 32–34.

This transcript of a December 13, 1967, phone call from Leonid Brezhnev to Hungarian communist party leader János Kádár records the Soviet premier's reaction to his visit to Prague and his negative impression of Novotný's political situation. Brezhnev tells Kádár that Novotný "hasn't the slightest idea about the true state of affairs" and "is himself to blame for all these problems because he does not know what collective leadership is and how to handle people." Despite Brezhnev's deep misgivings about Novotný's abilities, the Soviet leader indicates, as he did during his meetings in Prague, that he agreed with Novotný about the need to proceed slowly in separating the top party and state posts in Czechoslovakia, preferably leaving the matter to a "later stage." At the end of the conversation, Kádár informs Brezhnev that Novotný has cancelled the Hungarian leader's scheduled trip to Prague.

TOP SECRET

Information for Members of the Politburo

Cde. Brezhnev phoned me this morning (13.12.1967) and conveyed to me the following information:

"I consider it my duty to inform Cde. Kádár about my trip to Prague. The trip was quite unexpected; it was arranged at the personal request of Cde. Novotný.[13]

Even before the request there were signs that certain events had taken place in Prague, that a large number of people at the October plenary session had spoken out directly against Cde. Novotný. There were proposals to introduce a secret ballot in party elections, and the Slovak issue was raised in very tense terms. All this demanded our close attention, and that is why we decided I should go to Prague. Although I am very much pressed for time—we are preparing a session of the Politburo—I nevertheless left on an unofficial friendly visit.[14]

My first conversation was with Cde. Novotný. He informed me about the October plenary session, but it was evident that he was not aware of the scale these problems had assumed and the way things had evolved before the session of the Central Committee. Later on, the plenary session was interrupted, and certain urgent problems that had arisen were left unresolved because the comrades were about to leave for a ceremony marking the 50th anniversary of the October Revolution.

At the conclusion of the Central Committee session it was announced that another session would meet in December to deal with the plan and the budget, and that the discussion could continue there. Cde. Novotný fell sick after his return from Moscow and was unable to get up until the last day (his back was hurting).[15]

I spoke with the members of the Politburo one by one. In my talks I discovered that each of them was preoccupied with his own concerns; no one really cared about the plenary session, but merely about carrying on the discussion. Even at the previous session the discussion had been spontaneous and, as a result, various groupings formed. Cde. Novotný hasn't the slightest idea

---

[13] The following passage has been deleted here: "who even insisted twice on this matter."

[14] The manuscript originally said "under the pretext of an unofficial friendly visit," but the words "under the pretext" were subsequently crossed out.

[15] Novotný's trip to Moscow in early November was a routine visit to take part in the celebration of the 50th anniversary of the October Revolution of 1917, but, unbeknownst to the other members of the CPCz CC Presidium, he also used the occasion to invite Brezhnev to come to Prague in December.

about the true state of affairs. There are two dominant problems. Novotný himself is to blame for the legally ambiguous status of Slovakia; no one knows whether it is a federal republic and it has no capital city. In short, for years he has been sweeping the entire issue under the carpet. What is more, at the plenary session he accused Dubček of nationalism. Dubček is a totally honest person, but the situation angered him, and the other Slovak participants were infuriated as well, and all this produced an undesirable atmosphere.

The way I understood it, the crucial issue of the discussion was the separation of the two top posts. Had this problem been handled spontaneously, in an unanticipated manner, and without any preparation, the impression would have been left that the first secretary had been unseated, and this would be dangerous. Once I realized this, my mission became extremely delicate. None of the comrades with whom I spoke said that the party line was erroneous, or that it did not rest on Marxist–Leninist positions, or that there were no successes, or that there was no friendship with the fraternal parties. In this respect, everything was in order.

It appears, however, that the main cause of these difficulties is the fact that Cde. Novotný is incapable of cooperating with the comrades; he takes too many things upon himself and is unable to participate in a collective leadership.

Under the circumstances I could not create the impression that I was interfering in their internal affairs, while at the same time something had to be done to restore the unity of the Presidium and the Central Committee and to support Cde. Novotný.[16]

During the 48 hours I spent there I had three hours for my personal hygiene and food, while the remaining 45 hours were devoted to work. I spoke to each of them separately: to Lenárt, Hendrych, Dolanský, and Dubček. Afterwards we gathered at a planned dinner. We agreed that Cde. Novotný would report briefly about my visit without, however, connecting it with internal matters, and that I would speak about friendship and unity without raising their internal matters, but in such a way that they would all understand the issue.

I tried to have them postpone the plenary session because the Presidium was not following a united policy. It will be good if the Presidium debates these issues, adopts constructive decisions, and submits them to the Central Committee with a recommendation to adhere to the status quo for the moment, while leaving the Slovak question and other pressing issues to be considered at a later date. As a result of my successful talks, they themselves decided to put off the plenary session, and the joint dinner then proceeded.

Their Presidium has been meeting since the day before yesterday (yesterday until 2.00 A.M.). Cde. Novotný is due to speak this morning. He will make a critical analysis of the attitude adopted toward the Slovak question, and he may possibly succeed in creating a good atmosphere.

Lenárt has a good and firm position, he supports unity and stability. I had a four-and-a-half hour discussion with Dubček. At first he was very upset, but in the end he gave me his word to strive for unity. Comrades Chudík and Laštovička also hold correct positions.[17]

Today's speech by Cde. Novotný will determine whether or not correct decisions will be adopted (I tried to explain to Cde. Novotný that in situations such as this one there is no place for considerations about pride, vanity, or prestige). In my opinion, there is no unity in the Presidium, the forces are divided roughly five to five.[18]

During our talk, Cde. Novotný discreetly pointed out that my visit coincided with certain internal problems, but that they would make every attempt to show sufficient wisdom to solve them.

[16] As Brezhnev explicitly acknowledges here, he did use his visit to offer support for Novotný, despite serious misgivings. But he did so in such a half-hearted way that it ended up having the opposite effect.

[17] Michal Chudík, the chairman of the Slovak National Council, and Bohuslav Laštovička, the chairman of the National Assembly (parliament), were both full members of the CPCz CC Presidium and both were supporters of Novotný.

[18] This in fact was precisely the division; Those on the CPCz Presidium supporting Novotný were Laštovička; Chudík; Jozef Lenárt, the Czechoslovak prime minister; and Otakar Šimůnek, a deputy prime minister. Those opposing Novotný included Dubček, Drahomír Kolder, Jiří Hendrych, Oldřich Černík, and Jaromír Dolanský.

I can tell Cde. Kádár in all confidence that Cde. Novotný is himself to blame for all these problems because he does not know what collective leadership is and how to handle people. I would like to add that Cde. Hendrych's position is bad; I must conclude that we were unaware of the true nature of this person.

The problem is that the Czechoslovak comrades are dealing with these issues so impulsively that they fail to consider the wider repercussions of such difficulties with regard to the country, the party, and the international workers' movement. I think I managed to get them to think about all those matters, although I touched on them only indirectly when I spoke about the importance of our friendship, COMECON, the Warsaw Pact, and so forth.

I do not think the issue of separating the posts needs to be dramatized, and it should be done gradually and preferably at a later stage, rather than in a headlong manner, so that people will learn about it from the newspapers.[19]

Yesterday I informed Cde. Ulbricht very briefly about these matters prior to his departure, without going into details. He, too, is aware of the problems."

Cde. Brezhnev pointed out that the Czechoslovak comrades were awaiting the arrival of Cde. Kádár, and Cde. Kádár believed that his trip would be most useful and necessary. Cde. Brezhnev was invited to come during the same period, but this could not be arranged as a result of a visit by a Romanian delegation to Moscow. I informed Cde. Brezhnev that I had today received a message from Cde. Novotný in which he was cancelling the visit.

[19] Here again Brezhnev sided with Novotný, though his comments preceding this statement indicate that his support for the CPCz leader was far from enthusiastic.

DOCUMENT No. 5: Andrei Aleksandrov-Agentov's Memoir of the Pre-Crisis Period (Excerpt)

Source: A. M. Aleksandrov-Agentov, *Ot Kollontai do Gorbacheva:Vospominaniya diplomata, sovetnika A. A. Gromyko, pomoshchnika L.I. Brezhneva, Yu. V. Andropova, K. U. Chernenko i M. S. Gorbachev* (Moscow: Mezhdunarodnye otnosheniya, 1994), pp. 144–147.

This excerpt from the posthumously published 1994 memoir by Andrei Aleksandrov-Agentov provides an insider's account of Leonid Brezhnev's visit to Prague in December 1967. As the Soviet general secretary's long-time foreign policy adviser, Aleksandrov-Agentov attended the one-on-one meetings between Brezhnev and top CPCz officials that took place for eighteen consecutive hours. The memoir confirms that Brezhnev's original intention was to "save" Novotný, but that this goal had to be set aside when almost all the Czechoslovak officials, even erstwhile supporters of Novotný, "insisted that Novotný was no longer capable of effectively leading the party and the country and had lost all his authority." Aleksandrov-Agentov acknowledges that Brezhnev's decision to return early to Moscow, after having told the Czechoslovak leaders to sort out their own affairs, was enough to "determine Novotný's fate."

The memoir also explains why Czechoslovakia was of special importance to Brezhnev, and addresses his relations with key CPCz officials—especially Jozef Lenárt, Vasil Biľak, Miloš Jakeš, Václav David, and Alexander Dubček himself.

Brezhnev always believed that our relations with [Czechoslovakia] were one of the central elements both of our European policy and of a reliable balance of forces between East and West. He regarded Czechoslovakia, along with Poland and the GDR, as the core of the Warsaw Treaty Organization, and also the most reliable and trustworthy component of this core (both politically and economically).

Leonid Ilyich knew and loved Czechoslovakia. The main reasons for this were: the memories he still had of the joint military operations in which he took part with a Czechoslovak brigade in the Carpathian region toward the end of the war; his personal friendship with the brigade commander, Ludvík Svoboda; and his close friendship with the circles who had led the anti-fascist national uprising in Slovakia in 1944 (Šverma, Husák, etc.). It is undoubtedly not by accident that one of the first official trips in Europe by Brezhnev when he was the young chairman of the USSR Presidium of the Supreme Soviet was his visit in May 1961 to Czechoslovakia. (It was precisely during that visit that my job with Brezhnev began.) Prague, Bratislava, Plzeň, Ústí nad Labem—Brezhnev toured all these cities and several other settlements during his visit to the ČSSR. He spoke frequently at meetings both inside halls and outside the Prague Kremlin, on the squares of Bratislava and Ústí, and at large factories. In addition he held many meetings and negotiations with Czechoslovak leaders.

Over the years Leonid Ilyich's wife, Viktoriya Petrovna, often visited the spas at Karlovy Vary.

During discussions about *economic* ties with the CMEA members, Brezhnev invariably gave Czechoslovakia one of the top-priority places.

Relations with the ČSSR leadership were always regarded in Moscow as good overall. No serious political disagreements had arisen, and any problems that did emerge (mainly about economic issues) were resolved peacefully in some way or other and in conformity with normal procedures. As far as *personal contacts* with the leaders in Prague are concerned, the picture was more complicated. In general Brezhnev and his colleagues got along well with the president of the republic and leader of the CPCz, Antonín Novotný, and they regarded him as a loyal ally. Nevertheless, it was evident, and Leonid Ilyich mentioned this in private numerous times, that Novotný was not an especially strong leader: He had a poor grasp of economics and lacked great political authority; he basically had to work cabinet-style. ("He's not a Gottwald or a Zápotocký," said Brezhnev.) There were times when Brezhnev, during his conversations with Novotný, would explicitly criticize certain aspects of Novotný's policies, for example his tactlessness in dealing with the Slovaks and the tendency toward wage-leveling. ("What good is it when a qualified engineer and a simple worker receive the same salary? This is too hasty a transition to communism!") Novotný would accept these remarks calmly and without taking offense, but it seemed that in practical terms he never derived any special conclusions from them.

The members of the Czechoslovak leadership to whom Brezhnev was closest included the following: the Premier Jozef Lenárt; the Second Secretary of the CC Presidium Vasil Biľak; the Chairman of the Central Auditing Commission Miloš Jakeš; and the Minister of Foreign Affairs Václav David. Brezhnev was more guarded in his relations with such officials as O. Černík and L. Štrougal, believing that they were too "technocratic" and therefore might be too inclined to "lean toward the West." Brezhnev had a very low opinion of the CC Secretary J. Hendrych, regarding him as merely an ambitious apparatchik-careerist. Relations with Dubček, when he was CC first secretary in Bratislava, were fine.

As for the segment of the Czechoslovak "nomenklatura" that became the backbone of the future "Prague Spring," and reflected the aspirations chiefly of the pro-Western intelligentsia (for example, Kriegel, Císař, Pelikán, Šik, Smrkovský, etc.), Brezhnev and his colleagues, in my view, simply knew nothing about them and did not even take them into account (unless, of course, definite information came in from our embassy).

In short, by the end of 1967, when the situation within the Czechoslovak leadership sharply deteriorated and dark clouds began to hang over Novotný, it was not wholly unexpected for Brezhnev and other members of the Soviet leadership. But they had not foreseen and did not expect the negative sentiments among the masses, as manifested in the events of the "Prague Spring."

It was clear, however, that Novotný's position was under threat and that the replacement of him might have unforeseen political consequences. The officials who were closest to us (Lenárt, Biľak, etc.) warned us about this via the Soviet ambassador.[20]

And that is when Brezhnev decided on a step unusual for him, but characteristic of his belief in the possibility of "personal diplomacy." Toward the end of December 1967[21] he unexpectedly flew to Prague where, without losing any time, he entered into direct personal discussions, one after another, with all the most prominent and influential members of the Czechoslovak leadership in order to prevent a crisis, mollify the disputing sides, and "save" Novotný. All the negotiations were one-on-one (the only others present were the Soviet ambassador and the author of this memoir), and they continued for 18 hours without a break—by day, by night, and into the next morning.

This was an attempt to persuade the leading officials of the CC Presidium at that time to avoid threatening the stability of the party and the country, and to avoid endangering the normal course of development of Soviet–Czechoslovak cooperation. Most of the officials who took part insisted that Novotný was no longer capable of effectively leading the party and the country and had lost his authority. These accusations typically focused exclusively on personal matters, and none of the officials, as far as I remember, said even a word about changing course internally, much less in foreign policy. They complained about Novotný's arbitrariness and obstinacy, which in their view would create social and ethnic tension in the country. Dubček even had tears in his eyes when he complained that he, as CC first secretary of the Slovak Communist Party who had lived for many years in the USSR, had been passed over by Novotný for the delegation celebrating the 60th anniversary of October in Moscow.[22] And when Brezhnev directly asked the CPCz CC Secretary Hendrych who, in his view, had sufficient skill and authority to replace Novotný in

---

[20] The Soviet ambassador at the time was Stepan Chervonenko.
[21] Actually, the trip was on 8–9 December, not toward the end of the month.
[22] The anniversary in fact was the 50th not the 60th.

his posts (the secretarial and presidential), Hendrych immediately replied, without batting an eyelid: "I do." When Hendrych left the room, Brezhnev only shook his head in dismay and spat.[23]

In short, the 18-hour negotiating marathon essentially produced no results. He had not succeeded in persuading the Czechoslovak officials to join ranks. The whole affair ended when Brezhnev, having finally given up, said "Do as you wish" and then flew back to Moscow. That determined Novotný's fate and also the further course of events.

All evidence suggests that neither Brezhnev nor the other members of the CPSU CC Politburo could begin to imagine the full scale of the process that had already begun to eat away at the CPCz and Czechoslovak society, or the depth of the protest against the administrative-bureaucratic regime that had been established in the country. Nor could they imagine the scope of organization and activity of anti-socialist forces in the country (above all a significant portion of the intelligentsia) and the strength of their ties with the West, especially with the social-democrats.

---

[23] See Dubček's equally jaundiced assessment of Hendrych in *Hope Dies Last: The Autobiography of Alexander Dubček*, trans. and ed. by Jiří Hochman (New York: Kodansha International, 1993), pp. 120–123.

PART TWO

FROM JANUARY TO DRESDEN

INTRODUCTION

On January 6, 1968, the Czechoslovak public learned that, the day before, Alexander Dubček had been named first secretary of the CPCz Central Committee. A brief notification in the official press provided the first hint of a shake-up in the communist party leadership. "January," as this session of the CPCz Central Committee came to be called, launched the Czechoslovak reform experiment.

This lengthy meeting, which followed the CPCz CC session in October, actually spanned the months of December and January. After addressing the officially set agenda—including an indispensable evaluation of economic and political developments—the Committee's discussion, according to the Plenum resolution, "assessed the present situation within the party and highlighted existing shortcomings in the methods and style of work, in internal party management, and in the practical application of the principles of democratic centralism and intra-party democracy" (Document No. 6).

The discussion focused primarily on the separation of the top communist party and state posts. Excessive power was concentrated in the hands of Antonín Novotný: he held the titles of president, supreme commander of the army, chairman of the Central Committee of the National Front of the ČSSR and, first and foremost, the omnipotent first secretary of the CPCz Central Committee. After a lengthy and confrontational debate, dominated by criticism from the Slovak representatives, the Central Committee concluded that decentralizing the authority of the CPCz leadership structure as a whole was fundamental to reviving the party apparatus. The top posts would now be divided; Novotný would retain only the title of president—at that time a more or less decorative function. After a series of behind-the-scenes talks, including consultation with the Kremlin, the choice for the key post of the first secretary of the CPCz Central Committee went to Dubček, the head of the Slovak Communist Party.

January Plenum—The Road to Change

"January" inspired the entire subsequent development of Czechoslovak reform. Its importance, however, must not be overrated. To be sure, strong criticism of the untenable state of affairs was spreading throughout society, and the January session offered an invaluable debate over the methods of addressing and resolving the crisis. In the political area, nevertheless, the outcome of the Central Committee meeting reflected both the combination, and conflict, of the two poles of power within the party. The progressive trend, represented by Dubček, intended to introduce an element of reform and democracy into its party base. Subsequent developments demonstrated those intentions.

The progressive forces within the party based their efforts on elaborating an Action Program pushed by Dubček at the plenary session. On January 5, the Central Committee Plenum adopted a resolution directed exclusively at elite party members; the document was kept from the public at large (Document No. 6). Although the resolution did not specify the conflict within the party, it did call for "far greater encouragement of an open exchange of views," and characterized the

27

new separation of official posts as "a logical part of the democratization process in the state and political spheres."

Thanks to several more radical party officials, especially Josef Smrkovský whose articles—"What is it about?" in *Práce*, January 21, and "What Lies Ahead?" in *Rudé právo*, February 9—provided the first information on the relevance of the CPCz CC plenary session and the initial explanations of the reform movement, Czechoslovak society gradually learned that the decisions at the January Plenum went beyond a replacement of personnel in the leadership. The rotation of leaders, according to Smrkovský, reflected

> the imperative to remove the obstacles that for some time have been obstructing the party's progressive efforts. . . . I am referring to a series of tasks that should have been performed a long time ago, as well as to topical and pressing matters in the economic and social system. It is also essential to eliminate everything that has been distorting socialism, hurting people's souls, causing pain, and depriving people of their faith and enthusiasm (Document No. 9).

This growing public awareness inspired greater activism for change, which, in turn, influenced the policy of the CPCz where attempts were slowly moving toward a reform of the political system on a bigger scale than the post-Novotný bloc had originally anticipated.

Eastern Bloc Opposition

Czechoslovakia's Eastern allies watched these initial moves with extreme vigilance. The CPSU which, in the post-Khrushchev era, had done its utmost to reinforce the leading role of the party, was particularly disturbed by the way the CPCz had divided its top posts and addressed the "democratization" of the party structures and society at large. Brezhnev's Kremlin feared any destabilization in the Eastern bloc that could endanger a *modus vivendi* with the United States on nuclear weapons (SALT I) and/or escalate the potential for struggle against socialism through the West's exploitation of nationalist and revisionist elements emerging in the Soviet bloc countries. The primary concern of the CPSU was preserving the status quo, with as little change as possible.

The GDR and Poland adopted the most critical attitude towards developments in Czechoslovakia. They believed the present situation in Europe was extremely tense, a result of the policy of the Federal Republic of Germany. Foreign Minister Willy Brandt's Ostpolitik was perceived not as a way of terminating and overcoming the Cold War, but simply a new type of revanchism. Therefore, it was essential to strengthen ideological unity and the unified defense of the European socialist countries, already threatened by Yugoslavia's and Romania's autonomous policies.

These rebel countries were now to be joined by Czechoslovakia. Apart from the fear that Czechoslovakia might change its foreign policy and move closer to West Germany, the Polish and East German authorities were concerned that Czechoslovak developments might well trigger similar reformist pressures against their own regimes. High-level reservations about the course of events in Czechoslovakia were shared during an unofficial visit by Brezhnev, Podgorny and Kosygin to Poland on January 12–14, and to the GDR on January 15–16.

As a result, Brezhnev asked First Secretary Dubček to visit Moscow without delay. Prior to the visit, Dubček solicited support from Hungarian leader János Kádár. (Since Hungary also was attempting a moderate social reform, Kádár's Hungarian Socialist Workers' Party would become the only communist bloc organization evaluating developments in Czechoslovakia more or less positively and objectively.) "[T]here was not another person in the world with whom [Dubček] would have been able to discuss the same subjects in the same manner, for obvious reasons," Kádár reported back to his Politburo after the "frank" discussions (Document No. 7).

During his visit to Moscow, Dubček mollified the fears of the Soviet leadership, telling Brezhnev and his colleagues that he would "do my utmost to assist the efforts by our party's Central Committee to seek the further consolidation of our fraternal friendship and stronger all-round cooperation" (Document No. 8). With such assurances, Dubček won some latitude from the Soviets for his decision to replace certain hard-line Czechoslovak party and government officials. Kádár confirmed the Kremlin's acceptance of these changes during another meeting with Dubček at Komarno on February 4.

Dubček's desire to explain the essence of the changes in Czechoslovakia to the Polish communist chief Władysław Gomułka prompted a meeting in Ostrava on February 7. According to Dubček in 1990, during an unofficial walk in the countryside he suggested to Gomułka that the communist parties of Hungary, Czechoslovakia, Poland, and Romania, with the support of Yugoslavia, establish a reform bloc within the Warsaw Pact.[1]

Although a one-time reformer himself, First Secretary Gomułka refused to accept this proposal. Ongoing tensions in Polish society had transformed Gomułka into one of the staunchest opponents of tinkering with the status quo of communist party power. Indeed, Dubček's ideas of reform confirmed Gomułka's suspicion that a careful eye would have to be kept on the new Czechoslovak leader.

The only parties in Eastern Europe to welcome the January session were the Yugoslav and Romanian communists. Both showed immediate interest in more active relations with the Czechoslovaks; they regarded Dubček's reform ideas as support for their positions, which would be presented at the international conference of communist and workers' parties, planned for the autumn in Moscow. Yugoslavia and Romania watched closely as these ideas began to appear in the Czechoslovak media. Radical articles by Smrkovský (Document No. 9) were followed by several other statements illuminating a Czechoslovak road to socialism, with reforms in the existing structures of power, enhanced civil liberties, a freer press, and the transformation of passive people into active citizens of the state.

The Prague Spring Advances

Indeed, following Dubček's appointment as first secretary, work on the party's Action Program proceeded rapidly. On February 19, the CPCz Presidium was able to discuss the first version of the Action Program, which emphasized the development of socialist democracy in society and changes in the political system to give back to socialism its humane function and human face. However, the Action Program did retain the leading role of the CPCz, albeit with the condition that the party would no longer have a monopoly on administering of society. Although the Action Program was limited in its call for reforms, it also paved the road for successive changes.

In the internal debate over this draft of the Action Program, the anti-Novotný bloc still acted as a united force; the leading role of the CPCz as such had not yet been questioned, and there was still no open pressure or disagreement with Czechoslovakia's Warsaw Pact allies. Critical fissures within the party apparatus remained, however.

And Soviet concerns were severe, if at this juncture not openly expressed. Drawing on contacts with hard-line Czechoslovak communists, the soviet ambassador in Prague, Stepan Chervonenko, reported back to Moscow that the Czechoslovak reforms constituted a right-wing threat as well as an anti-Soviet and anti-socialist drive. Still, as of February, the Soviet leadership had not yet resorted to open polemics against the Prague Spring. This also reflected contradictions within the CPSU and Brezhnev's as yet unconsolidated leadership. Soviet society itself, one Czechoslovak journalist reported, was divided between groups with an "extremely negative"

---

[1] Dubček oral history interview with the KV ČSSR, August 1990.

opinion, which viewed the reforms as "revisionist and dangerous," and those with a "highly positive" opinion who saw events in Prague as "healthy and democratic" and not a threat to the Soviet Union (Document No. 11).

The Warsaw Five's growing concern became evident during the 20th anniversary celebrations of the 1948 creation of a socialist Czechoslovakia, held in Prague on February 22–23, 1968. The Eastern European nations sent unusually large delegations headed, with the exception of Yugoslavia, by the first secretaries of their communist parties. Their harshly critical attitudes were reported by the Czechoslovak escort staff of the various delegations. The guide for the Soviet delegation, for example, observed that "certain developments in our public and political life . . . provoked their astonishment, fears, and concern," and that the Soviets "made adverse comments about articles by some of our leading comrades" (Document No. 12). Brezhnev personally forced Dubček to revise his keynote speech; the first draft, according to the Soviet leader, was too critical of Dubček's predecessors. Although he toned it down, Dubček still used the speech to state that "things must be thoroughly changed" in Czechoslovakia (Document No. 10).

The Warsaw allies', escalating concern over the breadth of reforms contrasted sharply with the rapid radicalization of Czechoslovak society. The mounting movement for significant reform was spurred by the mass media, which took full advantage of the relaxation of censorship and, at times, according to Dubček officials, even abused it. A new-found freedom of speech allowed the press to inform the public about the affair of General Šejna—a scandal which roused the silent majority and pushed civic activities in the direction of an organized civil movement.[2] For the first time, the public learned of cases of corruption involving top representatives. This was followed by politically sensitive subjects, until then taboo, such as Tomáš Garrigue Masaryk and his role in Czechoslovak history, the mysterious death of Jan Masaryk, the problem of opposition parties, and the Slovak issue. Through such reporting, the press, television, and radio became vehicles for the animation of the Prague Spring.

A freer press was accompanied by greater freedom of speech at public meetings with leading politicians in Prague on March 13 and 20. Demands were put forward for the guarantee of elementary democratic liberties, and an unadulterated economic reform. Czechoslovak citizens publicly called for the resignation of Novotný as president of the republic—a demand that would have been unthinkable under his previous, strict communist regime.

Certainly the leaders of the movement toward a more open Czechoslovak society were its writers and students of Charles University, long the leading critics of rigidity in the communist system. The Czechoslovak Writers' Union played a major role in the Prague Spring from the very beginning, demanding the full rehabilitation of all citizens who had been unlawfully imprisoned, persecuted or hurt professionally after February 1948. New youth groups—including the Czechoslovak Union of Youth—appeared to challenge the official communist organs. Non-communist parties (the Czechoslovak Socialist Party, the Czechoslovak People's Party in Bohemia, and two small parties in Slovakia) also utilized small windows of opportunity in order to expand their activities and foster an incipient opposition movement. For example, an action group for the restoration of the Social Democratic Party[3] was formed on March 22; a preparatory committee for Club-231[4] was set up on March 27, and its constituent assembly met on March 31.

In the meantime, party meetings continued to debate the unfolding regime. On March 9–10 and on March 16–17, the regular CPCz district conferences were held. The majority of party members accepted the conclusions of the January session of the CPCz Central Committee and

---

[2] Gen. Jan Šejna, a senior officer with responsibility for political affairs and a close friend of the son of Antonín Novotný, defected to the West on February 25, 1968. Because of his position and intimate knowledge of sensitive military secrets, his defection was considered a serious blow to communist authorities in Prague and Moscow.

[3] This party existed until 1948 when it was pressured to join the CPCz against the will of the majority of its members.

[4] This organization consisted of former political prisoners; it took its name from the law under which they had been incarcerated in the 1950s.

post-January developments. However, the first signs of divergence among the membership also appeared. Some who spoke up expressed their concern about the fate of socialism in Czechoslovakia; they criticized the mass media from dogmatic, pro-censorship positions; they disagreed with the one-sided criticisms of the past being expressed and with the allegedly excessive advance of democracy. Other members of the rank-and-file, however, feared a return to pre-January conditions and expressed an impatience with the pace of developments so far.

It was at the district conferences that the membership heard for the first time straightforward information about the circumstances surrounding Novotný's resignation as first secretary. Members demanded that Novotný and others who had committed serious mistakes in the past and had no intention of backing the democratization process leave their posts. (Under mounting pressure, Novotný would be forced to resign on March 22.)

Similar discord was manifested at a Presidium meeting on March 14, which was held to assess the first round of the party district conferences. Some CPCz representative speakers decried the radicalization of society, blaming the mass media for the growing social demands for liberalization. Yet Dubček's followers, who defended the revival process, prevailed in the end. At a subsequent meeting on March 21, the Presidium devoted great attention to certain new problems related to the attempt to restore social democracy in the country. After a heated debate, members rejected proposals for the formation and functioning of opposition parties in the process of so-called democratization; even the reformers in Dubček's camp were not prepared to share power. The Presidium also discussed the country's constitutional arrangement, a question which had already been widely discussed in the mass media as well as at district conferences. The majority favored a Czechoslovak federation. Finally, the Presidium addressed the many demands for the resignation of Novotný.

The Dresden Meeting

At this session, Dubček announced that a meeting of five communist parties and the CPCz had been scheduled in Dresden on March 23. (He had been informed, and summoned, by telephone the week before by Brezhnev, Kádár and Gomułka—see also Document No. 13.) Dresden would mark the first open clash between the Warsaw allies and Czechoslovakia about the Prague Spring.

The Czechoslovak leadership was already aware of the increasing opposition to the post-January developments among the allies in the East. At the March 6 meeting of the Warsaw Pact Political Consultation Committee in Sofia, Bulgaria (convened at the initiative of the Romanian party in connection with the nuclear non-proliferation treaty), Czechoslovak representatives heard substantive criticism of the position of the Romanian party as well as of developments in Czechoslovakia. Poland expressed a particularly negative attitude against the Czechoslovak reforms, as did the GDR. At the time, Poland was grappling with growing discontent among its own population, especially student revolts in early March, to which it reacted totally out of proportion, even accusing its adversaries of Zionism. The GDR was also tightening its policies, including introducing the first series of visa requirements directed against the Federal Republic and West Berlin. Polish and East German criticism went so far as to allege that counterrevolutionary tendencies were gaining the upper hand in Czechoslovakia.[5] Hungary's position was not as critical.

Only the Yugoslav League of Communists and the Romanian Communist Party offered any appreciation for Czechoslovak developments, though not without certain reservations. Yugosla-

---

[5] According to the CPCz delegation, these verbal attacks indicated a lack of understanding and familiarity with the situation in Czechoslovakia. As a result, the Presidium attempted to confront critical voices in these countries by providing more substantive information of what was really happening in Czechoslovakia.

via saw in the Prague Spring a confirmation of the correctness of its own model of self-administrative socialism, while Romania expressed a hope for a change in Czechoslovakia's foreign policy. Their positions, of course, were overshadowed by the Soviet Union.

At Sofia, the Soviet position remained as veiled as before. According to a March 7 political report by the Czechoslovak embassy, the Soviet leadership had adopted a wait-and-see attitude even though it was evident that its stance on several problems differed significantly from the position of the CPCz. On March 16, Dubček received a letter from Brezhnev inviting him to Moscow for talks "at the highest level" to "discuss with you, in a fraternal way, questions of interest to both sides." Although the letter was warm and friendly, it clearly reflected a Soviet effort to address the growing apprehension within the Warsaw Pact over developments in Prague.

Even before the Moscow meetings, Dresden would provide a multilateral forum to demand a suppression of the reform movement in Czechoslovakia. The conference of the six communist parties on March 23 was a significant watershed in the history of the Prague Spring—the first time the Soviet-led bloc applied outright pressure on Czechoslovakia in an attempt to halt so-called "counterrevolutionary" developments under Dubček. Dubček and his comrades were invited under the pretext of discussing economic cooperation in the Eastern bloc. They sat stunned when the GDR's Walter Ulbricht opened the meeting by stating that the Warsaw Pact leaders had gathered to learn "the plans of the Central Committee of the Communist Party of Czechoslovakia" (Document No. 14).

Both Ulbricht and Gomułka were particularly direct in their attacks, with the Polish leader demanding that Dubček "launch a vigorous counteroffensive against the counterrevolutionary forces and against the revisionist forces, who have now begun to operate on a large scale in Czechoslovakia." Kádár was more measured, although even he criticized the situation in Czechoslovakia as "strikingly reminiscent of the prologue to the Hungarian counterrevolution."

The position of the Soviet delegation at Dresden remains unclear; the available documents, including Documents Nos. 14 and 17 in this book provide only a partial account. Brezhnev called for "serious" but "friendly discussions" at Dresden; he requested an explanation for the phrase "liberalization of society" in Czechoslovakia. Rather than accusing the CPCz delegation outright of fostering a counterrevolution, the Soviets pressed the Czechoslovak delegation to keep the situation from becoming even more radical. According to intelligence gathered by the Italian Embassy in Moscow, at Dresden the Soviets proposed "maximum support" for a Dubček strategy "to control internal turmoil and elements opposing the regime" (Document No. 17). The Kremlin's insistence on a crackdown was reinforced by the ostentatious presence of several Soviet generals and colonels. Their symbolic participation was not lost on the Czechoslovak delegation.

In the aftermath of Dresden, the Warsaw Pact antagonists stepped up their attacks on the Czechoslovak reform process. On March 26, Kurt Hager addressed a philosophers' congress in Berlin with a withering critique of the CPCz policy and Smrkovský personally. Hungary's Zoltán Komócsin went on Hungarian television to state concerns about the fate of socialism in Czechoslovakia. According to one diplomatic cable to Prague, Komócsin reported to his own Politburo that he had told Dubček at Dresden that "the communist party in the ČSSR had lost control of events and that decisions about the way things in the ČSSR should proceed were now being made in the streets" (Document No. 18).

Upon his return to Prague, Dubček provided only oblique information about the serious nature of the allied attacks on the Prague Spring. In a report to the Presidium on March 25, he referred only to "the specific concerns and advice" the Czechoslovak delegation received. "There was some concern that certain activities should not be misused in our development," he told his colleagues (Document No. 15).

Ironically, "Dresden" acted as a spur for the revival process, prompting even stronger radicalism with an anti-Soviet flavor. The domestic pro-reform movement quickly moved to assert its own weight on the government. An open letter signed by 134 writers and cultural figures on March 25, for example, called on the CPCz to "stand up to [international] pressure motivated by doubts about the nature and objectives of our internal measures," and to move the nation toward "permanent democracy" (Document No. 16). On the other side of the political spectrum, external pressure from the Soviet bloc helped rally Czechoslovak conservatives around Novotný and triggered a division within the anti-Novotný forces over how far and how fast to proceed. The potential for internal and external conflict around the Prague Spring now became a reality.

"Dresden" marked the first manifestation of the internationalization of the Czechoslovak problem—at least within the socialist bloc. The Czechoslovak representatives found themselves unable to respond effectively to the Soviet-led pressure for two reasons: first, after the meeting of the seven Warsaw Pact member states in Sofia, Czechoslovak diplomats had obediently joined the Kremlin's game by agreeing to discuss issues regarding Romania without Romanian participation. With the assistance of the Czechoslovaks, the "Seven" turned into the "Six" (Document No. 15). Dubček had unwittingly contributed to setting a precedent that the Kremlin would now use against Prague: transforming the anti-Romanian "Six" into an anti-Czechoslovak "Five." Secondly, under massive pressure, the Czechoslovak representatives had agreed that their internal affairs could be discussed at a meeting of the remaining five nations; inevitably, Czechoslovakia was transformed into the accused, judged and condemned party.

These errors, and the threatening nature of the diplomatic attacks on Prague, dictated the need to keep the Czechoslovak public in the dark. Dubček did not want Czechoslovak society to become openly antagonistic toward the Soviets at a time when he was trying to convince the Kremlin that they had nothing to fear from the Prague Spring. Therefore, most members of the party leadership were given no more than general and oblique information about the Dresden meeting (Document No. 15). With the public and the party largely unaware of the mounting external pressure, the Czechoslovak representatives were thus caught in the tentacles of Soviet policy behind closed doors, without the national support an informed citizenry would have provided. This weakened Prague's position in all subsequent negotiations with the Warsaw Pact nations. And at every turn, Dubček and his aides found themselves constantly on the defense.

DOCUMENT No. 6: Resolution of the CPCz CC Plenum, January 5, 1968, Electing Alexander Dubček as First Secretary

Source: Sb. KV, D IV—AÚV KSČ, F. 01.

In this resolution, the Central Committee replaces Antonín Novotný with Alexander Dubček as the new first secretary of the party. The document also records the decision to separate this post from the state presidency—under Novotný both offices had been combined—"as a logical part of the democratization process in the state and political spheres."

The large majority of Czechs and Slovaks, unaware of the acute power struggle in the CPCz's leadership, learned about the changes from terse announcements and press reports in the newspapers the next day.

. . . The new stage of development places greater demands on the work of the party and on the assertion of its leading role. In this light the plenary session of the CPCz Central Committee discussed relations among party, state, and social organs and the working methods of the central party organs. The Central Committee carried out its work in a democratic and critical manner, with full responsibility for the concrete implementation within its own ranks of the conclusions drawn by its October session. The Central Committee again assessed the present situation within the party and highlighted existing shortcomings in the methods and style of work, in internal party management, and in the practical application of the principles of democratic centralism and intra-party democracy. . . .

. . .

The Central Committee will create better conditions for thorough and open discussion at its plenary session on all items on the agenda so that each of its members has every opportunity to state and defend their position. Different positions on how to seek a correct solution are natural and objectively necessary. Members and candidate members of the Central Committee must take part in the preparation of resolutions and their implementation through the intermediary channels of commissions and in other ways in order to judge the correctness of decisions and measure them against reality. Members and candidate members of the CPCz CC and its organs must serve as an example to the lower echelons of party leadership, showing them how to promote intra-party democracy, how to ensure democratic centralism, collective leadership, criticism, self-criticism, and cadre work, and above all how to fulfill their tasks. . . .

. . .

Along with this, the members should specify analyses and proposals regarding the party statutes and the role of the CC Presidium, which has to discuss fundamental issues pertaining to the elaboration, implementation, and preparation of Central Committee decisions. In its work the Presidium must concentrate more on dealing with conceptual and programmatic aspects of party policy. The Presidium is to inform the Central Committee regularly about all its activities and testify before the Central Committee plenum about the status of these activities. In the event of a dispute in dealing with certain matters, the Presidium is required to provide information about the views and positions of its members. It must ensure that the work of all officials is regularly and collectively assessed in their presence, especially on the basis of party discipline and performance while at work. Their activity must be assessed favorably and any mistakes that may occur must be criticized openly and in a timely manner. That is the only way to create comradely relations corresponding to communist ethics.

To that end, there must be far greater encouragement of an open exchange of views, and all officials must create the conditions for such an exchange. The qualities of a communist include a sincere, comradely attitude toward human beings and an awareness of and respect for the needs of fellow workers. Collective party leadership helps bond talent, knowledge, and popular experience, all to the benefit of the party's collective judgment.

Bearing in mind the great demands and complexity that the present stage of development is placing on the leading work of the party and its organs, and also bearing in mind the need for better application of Leninist standards of party work, the Central Committee has assessed the existing state of affairs and—in line with the decision of the October session of the CPCz CC that the "excessive cumulation of offices does not benefit the quality of work and that it is therefore necessary to eliminate that practice as soon as possible"—has decided to separate the post of president of the republic from that of first secretary of the CPCz CC and entrust these posts to two different persons. The growing complexity of socialist development in our country and the assertion of the leading role of the party are accompanied by rising demands on the leading activity of the central apparatus and of individual top officials. In the present complicated situation the combination of the highest party and state posts is beyond the capacity of a single official, no matter how qualified.

This decision is based on the overall concept of our policy of creating a profoundly democratic and advanced socialist society. The separation of the two highest posts is a logical part of the democratization process in the state and political spheres. It is motivated by the need for a division of labor and for new relations between the supreme party and state organs, while emphasizing the significance of the president's office as a symbol of workers' power and the socialist regime in this state.

For these reasons the plenary session of the CPCz CC approves Cde. Antonín Novotný's personal request as president of the ČSSR to be released from the post of first secretary of the CPCz CC.

The CPCz CC simultaneously appoints Cde. Alexander Dubček to the post of first secretary of the CPCz CC, in the conviction that he will safeguard continuity of party leadership and in appreciation of his long years of experience in party work.

The current first secretary of the CPCz CC, Cde. Antonín Novotný, has been at the head of the party for several years. His personality is linked with important successes that the party achieved during those years both within its ranks and in the international communist movement. It was a period in which Leninist standards were renewed and the repercussions of the personality cult were dissipated, in which socialism was constructed and conditions were established for the general progress of socialist society. The CPCz Central Committee highly values the worthy and dedicated work which Cde. Novotný has accomplished at the head of the CPCZ CC during this complicated and challenging period.

The Central Committee further decided that under present circumstances it is impermissible to accumulate leading posts in party, state, and social organs. This principle, however, must not be understood in the sense that leading representatives of state, economic, or social organs and organizations may not be elected as members of party organs. The Central Committee instructs the Presidium to prepare concrete principles on this matter.

The party's Central Committee further decided to increase the number of members of the Presidium of the Central Committee and elected Comrades Josef Borůvka, chairman of the Dolany United Agricultural Co-operative, Jan Piller, deputy minister for heavy engineering, Emil Rigo, chairman of the Slovak Communist Party factory branch in the East Slovak Iron Works at Košice, and Josef Špaček, a leading secretary of the South Moravian regional CPCz committee, as members of the Presidium. In addition, the future first secretary of the CPS CC, who will replace Cde. Dubček, will also be appointed as a member of the CPCz CC Presidium.

In keeping with the conclusions of the October session of the CPCz Central Committee and with Leninist principles, relations between party and non-party organs will have to be elaborated in greater detail and adjusted: Necessary scope for initiative is to be given to communists working in non-party organs and their responsibility to the party is to be increased.

Accordingly, the CPCz CC plenum instructs the Presidium to elaborate principles governing mutual relations, a division of labor, and other ties between central party and central state and economic organs and organizations of the National Front. The Presidium is to submit these principles to the plenary session.

The CPCz Central Committee has noted that the government and Presidium of the Slovak National Council will present concrete recommendations to the party Central Committee on how to improve their activity. In so doing, it will proceed from the conditions inherent in the new system of management and from the deliberations and proposals submitted by the December and January plenary sessions of the CPCz Central Committee.

The CPCz Central Committee further maintains that in the interest of preserving the unity of the Czech and Slovak nations during the further advance of the socialist society, and in the interest of pursuing a comprehensive expansion of ties between our fraternal nations and nationalities, all questions pertaining to nationality policies under the new conditions must conform to the spirit of a Leninist solution. Such an approach will be based on the preparatory work carried out by the CPCz CC Presidium, with pertinent analyses submitted to the plenary session of the CPCz CC.

To implement the conclusions of the October, December, and January meetings of the CPCz CC with purpose and consistency, the Central Committee will adopt an Action Program providing for the implementation of the stipulated tasks; it will do this with full responsibility and on the basis of a timetable for the implementation of these tasks.[6] It also will create conditions for drawing up a long-term party program.

[6] See Document No. 19 below.

DOCUMENT No. 7: János Kádár's Report to the HSWP Politburo on His Meetings with Alexander Dubček, January 20, 1968 (Excerpts)

Source: Sb. KV, Z/M 3; Vondrová & Navrátil, vol. 1, pp. 35–39.

This document records a secret meeting between the leader of the Hungarian Socialist Workers' Party, János Kádár, and Alexander Dubček two weeks after his election as first secretary of the CPCz. Kádár reports back to the Hungarian Politburo that "Cde. Dubček is a communist on every major issue without exception, and he maintains high principles." He nevertheless warned Dubček about the need to take account of the effect developments in Czechoslovakia could have on other Warsaw Pact countries, especially the Soviet Union.

Kádár's report also provides details on Dubček's election as first secretary, the apprehension he felt about being the first Slovak to head the CPCz, and Dubček's clashes with Novotný.

About six to eight days ago, a message arrived from Cde. Dubček. This was followed by a meeting that was actually held in two places. . . .[7]

The atmosphere was very pleasant, and our discussions were very frank. One of things that Cde. Dubček mentioned is that there was not another person in the world with whom he would have been able to discuss the same subjects in the same manner, for obvious reasons. . .

. . . It must be pointed out that Cde. Dubček, whom I know well by the way, made a very good impression on me insofar as he showed no sign of smugness or arrogance. On the contrary, one could say just the opposite: He is even a bit annoyed that they decided to elect him, of all people; he has misgivings, feels the burden of his responsibility, and is deeply concerned.

In my considered judgment, Cde. Dubček is a communist on every major issue without exception, and he maintains high principles. This is noticeable even in subjective matters, for example in his assessment of Cde. Novotný. There is no sign of hatred or anything of the kind.

On the basis of all this, even though our talk was almost exclusively a kind of interference in Czech affairs—after all, we spoke of nothing else—it must be said that our talk was correct and comradely. . . .

The first subject of our conversation, though other political issues were covered as well, centered for some two hours on my recent and current invitations.[8] From the discussion I learned that at the time—and this is connected with the attitude to the present meeting—Cde. Novotný had not mentioned a single word to the Presidium or the Secretariat about his invitation to Cde. Brezhnev and me. . . . This, in part, explains why Cde. Brezhnev's visit was received with such unease even by the leadership. In short, they found out that he was coming only after he had already arrived.

Besides, during our entire talks I had the distinct impression that Cde. Dubček felt he had to come up with an explanation. It appears that he is worried about how he is perceived internationally in the context of certain matters. He spoke about that at great length so that he could display his working methods on a trivial issue, but then he spoke a great deal about the political circumstances preceding the entire affair and explained at which point he first clashed with Cde. Novotný.

I told him that our Politburo took a positive view of their decision, its features and nature, and the communiqué, and that we believed, given the situation, it was the best that could have been done. I made it quite clear how pleased I was that the communiqué spoke in favorable terms about Cde. Novotný, since this was of great political importance. It was politically significant

---

[7] The first hunting lodge near Nové Zámky did not have adequate accommodations, so the meeting was moved to a lodge near Topolčianky.

[8] The "recent" invitation to which Kádár alludes here is the one Novotný extended to him and then canceled in December 1967. See Document No. 5 above.

in general because it revealed how the socialist countries were treating such matters. I told him that it was the same as the question we had discussed with the Soviet comrades when Khrushchev was removed. I said that we were pleased about Cde. Dubček's election and that we congratulated him and wished him good health and success in his work, but I recalled also what I had decided to do on my own, namely, to greet him straightaway by saying: our congratulations, but please also accept our condolences.

I further told him that he must try to understand Cde. Brezhnev and avoid any misunderstanding. I added that if he had spoken to me in the same circumstances, he should be aware that I would have had the same opinion that Cde. Brezhnev did when he told him: "Yes, the posts must be separated, but not now, under pressure; instead, it should be done at a suitable moment, on the basis of a united stance of the Politburo. Let Cde. Novotný himself make a proposal to that effect."[9] To this Dubček replied that he had been of a similar opinion when the question first arose—not today, but approximately a year ago. However, the situation had now reached the point where the matter could no longer be postponed. Had they continued dragging their feet, the waves of discontent might have submerged the whole party. That is why he changed his mind and came out in favor of separating the posts.

He also said that although he supported what had happened, he had not wanted to be elected himself. A nominating commission had drawn up a list with five names: Lenárt, Černík, Kolder, Štrougal, and his own. Members of the nominating commission had a preliminary talk with him. He asked not to be proposed as a candidate because he had on several occasions advocated the separation of the posts and he did not want to give the wrong impression. Finally, he agreed with the nominating commission to propose him as a candidate but only as fifth in order of preference. The election proceeded in such a way that a vote was initially taken on the first candidate on the list, then on the second, until the time came for his own nomination to be considered, and that was the one that the Central Committee passed unanimously. He immediately added that even now he realized the election had not been very good, especially considering that their party had existed since 1921 and a Slovak had never been first secretary before; this might create problems in his party.

He then stressed that the change in no way implied a modification of the party's line in either domestic or foreign policy; on this score there was absolute unity in the Central Committee.

He pointed out that although there had been several items on the agenda, including the problem of the Slovaks, this had not been a nationality-based issue. Of the Central Committee that elected him, some 85 percent were of Czech origin.

He then dealt at length and in detail—and this was really the main problem he had wanted to raise—with the causes and origin of the situation. He spoke in general about Cde. Novotný's erroneous working methods but emphasized that, of course, the party is a political institution, and even though problems existed with regard to working methods, the main issue always concerned policy. He added that he had several times clashed with Cde. Novotný, but always about matters of policy. He spoke about those issues in detail, and they are all fairly important.

He recalled four or five policy problems that were discussed mainly in Presidium circles. He had opposed Cde. Novotný's proposals and remarks, but he had always been isolated in the Presidium. He had been the one to raise various matters, but had always remained in a minority. In this context he mentioned an interesting thing: When the Central Committee reached its decision, Cde. Novotný also congratulated him and said that Cde. Dubček is the only one who stood up on various matters and who highlighted his [Cde. Novotný's—Eds.] mistakes.

What were the matters under discussion? The first clash between them occurred on the question of rehabilitation, about which there had been a long debate. Dubček was a secretary of the CPCz Central Committee at the time. The Presidium had set up three commissions to deal with rehabilitation matters and he was the head of one of these. The other two commissions

[9] See Document No. 5 above.

declared that the questions they were to discuss were closed, whereas his commission stated that the matter was not closed because measures had to be taken. The crux of the issue was that there was unanimity about the need for full state rehabilitation of all who had been unjustly convicted in trials that violated the law, and that this would be the end of the whole matter. Dubček and his supporters argued that these people must also be rehabilitated as members of the party and the movement, because otherwise the whole thing would be no more than a half-hearted gesture. This was an issue they had been discussing for some two years. Dubček then recalled how the matter had been under discussion in the Presidium, and Cde. Novotný had left for Košice where he made a speech declaring his own view that those who had been executed deserved civil rehabilitation but could not be rehabilitated along party lines because they had committed mistakes as party members.

After that the entire matter was raised in the Central Committee, which decided to give instructions for party rehabilitation. In the discussion Cde. Novotný was asked to adopt an official stance in the name of the Central Committee, but he declared this was something he would never do.

The second argument and confrontation came partly over the same matter. It was on the question of Bacílek. Someone pointed out that at the time of the trials Bacílek had been minister of the interior. Many people attacked Bacílek, and it became clear that he had to be dismissed as first secretary in Slovakia. Novotný firmly defended him. The Presidium even adopted a resolution demanding Bacílek's dismissal, but on the condition that he and someone else might be members of the Slovak Politburo. Cde. Dubček had argued a great deal at the time, but in the end the Presidium decided that this was how things should be. To explain this, Dubček added that material discovered from the time of the trials had made it clear that when Bacílek was interior minister he had praised Cde. Novotný in one of his speeches, saying Novotný was someone who had done a great deal to expose the enemy. At the time, Novotný was the Prague first secretary and secretary of the Central Committee. In the discussion about Bacílek, Novotný had said something to the effect that you are going to regret this because you, too, will discover that you might need Bacílek.

After that there was the Slovak Congress where the atmosphere was such that it was impossible to propose Bacílek, and in fact no one did. That is why he did not get onto the Politburo. The following day Dubček wanted to tell Novotný on the telephone why it had not been possible to carry out his proposal, but Cde. Novotný interrupted him by saying, "Very well, everything is clear," and he slammed down the receiver.

The third such major dispute concerned economic questions at a time when problems had arisen in connection with the decision to transform the Five-Year Plan into a Seven-Year Plan. This decision was preceded by stormy arguments. Cde. Dubček had been against the idea because he felt it would achieve nothing and the situation would not improve, which is precisely what happened later on.

The fourth such dispute concerned Slovakia. The perpetual debate about how to develop the backward regions of the country had turned into an argument between Slovaks and Czechs because there are two economically backward areas in the country, and one of these is in Slovakia. (The other is in the German border region.) There are numerous Congress decisions about the development of Slovakia, but a struggle has been going on for years within the party leadership between those who want to develop Slovakia and those who prefer concentrating on the Sudeten area, putting forward proposals for that area. For example, the latter group wanted factories that were under construction in Košice to be relocated to the Sudeten, even though there were no favorable conditions in these parts. There was no suitable manpower and that is why they wanted to move 50,000 families there from Slovakia. Cde. Dubček opposed such proposals, and as a result he was labeled a Slovak nationalist.

In the end the whole matter [concerning the separation of posts—Eds.] was placed on the agenda in accordance with the Presidium's decisions referring to the need for improvement in the party's working methods. But a conflict arose around this question. In the discussion on the party's working methods it was argued that party cells were not functioning properly. It was further argued that the party itself was not working properly and that this was the reason for the deficient work of party cells. It was also claimed that the government was not performing well, yet the government had no authority. During the discussion Cde. Dubček said it was the Central Committee and the Presidium that were performing badly and that this was the cause of the deficient work of party cells.

We also spoke with Cde. Dubček about their future program and about what they intended to do now. It is a fact that the entire working program of the Central Committee needs to be reformulated because it also includes the proposal to place the question of technical development on the agenda at the beginning of March. Although this is a serious matter, now is not the time to deal with it.

After that I "interfered in internal affairs" in a subtle manner. This happened to be possible at the time, and I warned them against certain things. I said that the unity of the people and the working class and the unity of the party are naturally very important, but he should bear in mind that this, too, has a mechanism of its own. The people cannot be united if the party that unites them is itself divided. The party cannot be united if the Central Committee is not united, and the Central Committee can hardly be united if there is no unity in the Presidium. This is what I recommended: Forget the arguments that have taken place. I said: There is, for example, your celebrated vote of 5:5. The whole world knows about it. In this connection I would suggest that you not use this to determine your allegiances, because you may well be in for a surprise. It is possible that there were honest people among the five who did not want the posts to be separated right away, and it is also possible that the other five included some who wanted the separation for goodness knows what reason. Here I recalled the example of Khrushchev at the exhibition of paintings.[10] Dubček, too, gave examples of various people who were genuinely tormented by the question of whether the posts should be separated or not. I said: There is only one good way for you to find out who holds what principles. Progressive proposals must be submitted and then see who votes in favor of them. I suggested that they act in a humane manner and stop worrying about who voted when for what, but that they should show no mercy because otherwise progress will be impossible.

Among the concrete issues I mentioned was the nationality question. They, too, had discussed the matter and agreed that a federation was a reactionary idea. I said I did not want to meddle in their affairs, but I asked whether there exists a Slovak nation. He said "no," because these people already talk in Czech but they have a different mentality. I replied that when viewing the whole situation in this light, one had the impression that one leg of the state was longer than the other. If there was a Slovak National Council why wasn't there a Czech one, or if there was a Slovak Central Committee, why wasn't there a Czech one, and a Czechoslovak entity above the two? One might wonder: If the name of the state is the Czechoslovak Socialist Republic, should the whole construction really be changed? And one would have to see whether the Slovak Central Committee really could be regarded as a governing body. The Slovak Central Committee has, in fact, been doing nothing.

Cde. Dubček then spoke of the position of writers in his country. That issue, too, had bolstered their fears that if they continued to drag their feet the party would no longer be in a position to retain control of matters. There had been the Writers' Congress. Imagine, comrades, that 75% of the Writers' Union are party members, and not just any kind of party members: Many are veteran members of the party and former partisans, and for eight months they have not managed to give the Writers' Union proper leadership. No one wants to take over the leadership.

---

[10] On December 1, 1962, the Soviet leader visited an art exhibition in Moscow which contained some abstract works whose presence infuriated him. The incident led to a dramatic, albeit temporary, curtailment in cultural freedoms in the Soviet Union.

I reminded Cde. Dubček of one other international matter. I said: You must show great patience. Our Politburo has adopted the position I mentioned regarding your decision, but on the international scene there are different opinions and I do not know whether you are aware of these. The election of Dubček was not received with wild enthusiasm. This must be accepted and accepted calmly, it would be wrong to take offense. The way you must view this is that those people are not aware of the circumstances and do not know your stance on various matters. Once they get to know this, they will assess matters accordingly.

Yesterday, when I consulted Cdes. Komócsin and Erdélyi,[11] it occurred to me that it would be necessary to contact Cde. Brezhnev. I called him and briefly told him the essence of the matter. He said he thought it was good that the meeting had taken place and thanked me for informing him.[12]

Cde. Zoltán Komócsin: We naturally do not wish to interfere in their affairs, but we are able to help by taking advantage of these favorable political and personal opportunities.

The political crisis, as well as the crisis in the leadership that has been fermenting for some time, have now come out into the open; but, as demonstrated also by reports, the actual burden of work is only just beginning. Cde. Dubček will not have it easy, and in fact the Czech comrades have not yet overcome the bulk of their difficulties. They have to grapple with a series of problems of a political nature, and here we are able to offer reasonable assistance.

---

[11] Károly Erdélyi was the Hungarian deputy foreign minister. Komócsin, in a speech to the Politburo, advised that "it appears that we can also offer help with regard to the international arena — again, it goes without saying, in a solid and unobtrusive manner, starting with the Soviet comrades. I believe Cde. Kádár's talk with Cde. Brezhnev has been useful. It is true that the Soviet comrades will accept Cde. Dubček, but it might be necessary to press the Soviet comrades a bit further, as far as we are able. Or, for example, with the Germans and in relations with the Poles it is essential that we use our influence if the necessity should arise."

[12] In his memoirs, Dubček expressed dismay that "immediately after meeting me, Kádár called Brezhnev and informed him in great detail about our discussion. It now seems probable that the initiative to meet me came from Brezhnev" (*Hope Dies Last,* p. 133). Dubček's irritation may be partly warranted, but it is clearly overstated in the broader context of Kádár's report. Moreover, it was Dubček, not Kádár or Brezhnev, who initiated the meeting. Dubček's remarks about this occasion would apply more accurately to Kádár's subsequent encounters with Dubček, especially those in July and August (see, for example, Document No. 85).

DOCUMENT No. 8: Report Submitted to the CPCz CC Presidium on Alexander Dubček's Visit to Moscow, January 29–30, 1968 (Excerpts)

Source: ÚSD, AÚV KSČ, F. 02/1; Vondrová & Navrátil, vol. 1, pp. 39–44.

This document provides a summary of the issues Dubček and Brezhnev covered during the Czechoslovak leader's visit to Moscow at the end of January. Their conversations focused on Soviet–Czechoslovak ties as well as on internal developments in the two countries. Dubček pledges to "strengthen fraternal friendship and all-round cooperation between our parties and countries," adding that "friendship and alliance with the Soviet Union are the cornerstone of all our activity." He also commits to uphold and strengthen the essential features of Czechoslovakia's socialist system, including the "leading role" of the CPCz and the practice of "democratic centralism" within the party. In response, according to the summary, Brezhnev indicates he is "pleased that your Central Committee, the leadership of your party, and Cde. Dubček personally intend to contribute to the expansion and deepening of our friendly ties." Brezhnev also expresses full confidence that the CPCz under Dubček's guidance would be able to solve Czechoslovakia's "acute and critical internal problems."

Brezhnev invited Dubček to Moscow after a top Soviet delegation, consisting of Brezhnev, Podgorny, and Kosygin, traveled unofficially to Poland and East Germany in mid-January and heard ample expressions of concern from Gomułka and Ulbricht.

During his stay in Moscow, Cde. Dubček had talks with Cde. Brezhnev and Cde. Podgorny. On the Soviet side, those present included Cdes. Gromyko, Goreglyad (first vice-chairman of the USSR Gosplan), Rusakov (first deputy head of a department at the CPSU Central Committee), Kolesnikov (head of the Czechoslovak–Polish section at the CPSU Central Committee), and Chervonenko.[13] On the Czechoslovak side were Cdes. Pavlovský and Synek.[14]

Cdes. Dubček and Brezhnev exchanged views about certain current international problems and the international communist movement, and informed each other about the domestic situation in their countries.

Cde. Dubček then went into detail about some of the conclusions contained in the resolution of the January plenum of our party.

Cde. Dubček added that the passages in the plenary resolution about our relations with the Soviet Union and the CPSU expressed the unequivocal and clear position of our Central Committee which we firmly endorse. This position expressed the will of our entire party and our people. Thus, it was nonsensical and foolish for anyone to believe that the personnel change in the leading post would cause a reversal on this score. "I would like to stress once again that fraternal friendship and firm alliance with the Soviet Union are not a question for individuals in our party. As far as I am concerned, I would like to give you my assurance—and I hope you never had any doubts about this—that in my new post I will act, as I always have up until now, to do my utmost to assist the efforts of our party's Central Committee to seek the further consolidation of our fraternal friendship and stronger all-round cooperation between our parties and countries. It goes without saying that problems may arise, but I am convinced that our Central Committee and our party will always solve them, bearing in mind that friendship and alliance with the Soviet Union are the cornerstone of all our activities.

---

[13] Andrei Gromyko was the Soviet foreign minister; Stepan Chervonenko was the Soviet ambassador in Prague.

[14] At the time, Oldřich Pavlovský was the Czechoslovak ambassador in Moscow. Later on he became minister of domestic trade in the Czechoslovak government and was one of the hard-line supporters of the Soviet invasion. Ivan Synek was a specialist on intra-bloc relations in the CPCz CC International Department. Unlike Pavlovský, he supported the Prague Spring and was a champion of "the inalienable right of every socialist country and every communist party to determine for itself the forms of socialist construction suitable for its own country."

Our party's leadership gives maximum attention to international issues. We are watching the growing aggressiveness of world imperialism and the situation in Vietnam and in the Near and Middle East with great concern. You will surely understand that for us, as direct neighbors of the Federal Republic of Germany, developments in that country are of exceptional importance. We are fully aware that there will be continued attempts by the FRG to 'penetrate' our country and influence public opinion. We realize that we will have to remain on guard, keep close watch over all trends in the FRG's policy, and wage an active struggle against the revival and growth of fascism. In the near future we intend to send a delegation to the German Democratic Republic, and during our talks with the German comrades (as well as in a communiqué afterwards) we intend to reiterate our unambiguous support of the GDR as well as our fundamental position on the situation in West Germany." . . .

Cde. Dubček then dealt with our domestic problems. He said that new conditions had arisen in our country that have placed qualitatively new tasks before the communist party. First of all, there is no longer class antagonism in our country. In dealing with new tasks we will continue to proceed from the principle of the leading role of the party and the leading role of the working class. Those who think we will surrender this leading role to anyone are badly mistaken. But we must also thoroughly analyze the new situation and pay close attention to critical views expressed by the party membership. This applies chiefly to the following tasks: to the expansion and promotion of intra-party democracy while maintaining the principle of democratic centralism, to the encouragement of activity by party members, and to the quest for forms and ways of improving the work of communists employed outside party organs and outside the party apparatus. We must create conditions for work by communists in the government, ministries, national committees, and public organizations—in short, wherever party decisions are being translated into reality. We must correct the party's relations with the intelligentsia, improve our work among young people, and so forth.

In our future activities we do not intend to be guided by the principle that everything in the past was bad and now all will be fine. This would not even be true. In the past we did some great work. There is no doubt about that. We must assess the past critically but with a positive approach, and now we have to turn our attention to new tasks. The March plenary session of our party will start implementing these new duties. First, we want to increase the role of the CC plenary session and create conditions that would give all members of the Central Committee every opportunity to play their part in confronting the crucial problems of this country. We will have to consider how to improve the activity of all sectors of our system of management and, above all, of the government. We also will have to come up with a more accurate definition of the relationship between the party (the CC) and the government and state bodies, and a more accurate definition of the relationship between the political and economic leadership under new conditions of management now that a new economic system is coming into being.

We realize that at a time when certain difficulties have arisen in the party, there is fertile ground for those who have an axe to grind, for those who want to restrict the leading role of the party, and for others of a similar bent. This is only natural. Various negative tendencies, petty bourgeois dispositions, and anarchist visions, which are unacceptable to the party, have been manifested for some time, and not simply in the context of the recent CC sessions. There is no doubt that we must watch these manifestations closely, but this is by no means enough. Neither is it sufficient merely to highlight these phenomena. We must, above all, consider why such manifestations are finding fertile ground and why they have not been firmly repudiated by party activists. This only demonstrates that there is something wrong with our work and that things are not totally clear within the party, which accounts for the apathy and indifference toward erroneous views. We must improve our work and give back to the party its certainty and faith, thus limiting the scope for those espousing such erroneous views. That is why under no circumstances will we announce at the March plenum any sort of 'grand celebratory' activities. Instead, we will build on the resolutions and conclusions of the January session in earnest. . . .

The work that awaits us, Cde. Dubček went on to say, will not be easy. The conditions in which we are going to deal with it are not exactly the best. It is, however, a good sign that there is not a single party branch that did not endorse the conclusions of the January session. I know only too well that it is not important who is first secretary. The party expects better work at all levels in the interest of the general progress of our socialist society. That is what matters now, and I am certain we shall succeed.

Cde. Brezhnev thanked Cde. Dubček for having accepted the invitation of the CPSU Central Committee to come to the Soviet Union and for having found a way to attend this meeting despite the complex situation and a heavy workload.

Our friendship, he further stated, is not a coincidence; it has deep roots. It is based on the principles of our parties and our common Marxist–Leninist teachings. Our relations with the Communist Party of Czechoslovakia have always been good and they remain good. We naturally want this to be so in the future as well. That is why we are pleased that your Central Committee, the leadership of your party, and Cde. Dubček personally intend to contribute to the expansion and deepening of our friendly ties. I would like to take this opportunity to stress that we, too, shall do everything in our power to move in this direction.

You certainly have a number of domestic and internal party problems today that you will have to solve step by step. Yours is a party with great traditions and a wealth of experience, and that is why we do not doubt that you will find the right solutions. I would also like to assure Cde. Dubček that he can always count on our total and absolute support for his work.

Our party does not have such acutely critical internal problems today. We are naturally striving to consolidate its ranks and are successful. . . .

On the question of European security, we are adamant that we cannot lose the GDR and that we cannot fritter away the results of World War II; we must insist on stable European borders. These principles cannot be abandoned in exchange for money.[15]

A revolutionary process is taking place in the world, albeit with great ups-and-downs and complications. Let us mention, for example, China or Indonesia.[16] In view of these complications, the coordination of our activities and of our course of action is of particular significance. You are aware of our position on the Budapest meeting.[17] We know that certain difficulties will crop up there as well, and this is something we must take into account. We believe, however, that we should not postpone a meeting of the world communist and workers' parties but insist that it be held this year.

---

[15] A reference to the attempts the ČSSR had been making to obtain a large hard-currency loan from the FRG even though the West German government was not yet formally willing to accept the permanence of the inner-German border and the Oder–Neisse line.

[16] Brezhnev's references here are to the Cultural Revolution in China (and of course the Sino–Soviet split) and the unsuccessful coup attempt in Indonesia in 1965, which led to mass reprisals against the Indonesian Communist Party.

[17] The meeting in Budapest at the very end of February 1968 set up a preparatory commission for the worldwide conference of communist parties that was due to be held in Moscow in November 1968. The participants at the Budapest meeting agreed to invite all communist parties to be represented on the preparatory commission and to attend the worldwide conference.

DOCUMENT No. 9: "What Lies Ahead," by Josef Smrkovský, February 9, 1968

Source: "Jak nyní dál: Nad závěry lednového pléna ÚV KSČ," *Rudé právo*, February 9, 1968, p. 2.

This article, published only a month after Dubček's election, became the most significant initial manifesto of the reform movement. In it, Josef Smrkovský emphasizes the desirability of forging links between intellectuals and workers, the need for greater scope of action and dissent in the party's lower and middle ranks, and the intention of the CPCz Central Committee "not to be a mere rubber-stamp body any longer."

In writing this reform manifesto Smrkovský hoped to demonstrate that the January plenum had in fact marked a break with the past and that the CPCz would henceforth be addressing issues that had been ignored or glossed over under Antonín Novotný. As a senior member of the CPCz Presidium (after the April Plenum) and a close aide to Dubček, Smrkovský became one of the leading architects of the Prague Spring. Both this article and another he had written earlier (on January 21) in the daily Prace *were intended to help generate popular support for the reforms Dubček proposed.*

WHAT LIES AHEAD

On the Conclusions of the January Plenum of the CPCz CC

The questions that the Central Committee of the party considered and resolved in December and January have set the entire party in motion, and the public at large has been paying great attention to them. This is so even though we failed to ensure the prompt and sufficient release of information. We must put this right, and that is precisely what we are doing, since there must be no discrepancy between our statements of Leninist principles and democratic traditions, on the one hand, and our future practical activities, on the other.

We can already say that in general the last Central Committee session has met with a favorable response in politically active sections of society. As more information has become available, discussions have been gaining momentum, and this in turn has generated greater enthusiasm for political activity. Yet even sincere persons who in the past have often been disappointed still show signs of skepticism. Old practices are still embedded in the activities of many of our organs and in the minds of people working in them. This creates doubts and insecurity. People are demanding guarantees.

It is at this point that I would like to say something about certain pressing issues, though I do not mean to impose my opinions regarding future decisions of the party on anyone.

A Common Republic

Of all the decisions of the January session of the party's Central Committee, the one that has attracted the most attention is the resolution to divide the highest party and state posts. This has given rise to many questions: Is this not merely a rotation of individuals? What is the actual meaning of the decision? Does this not simply amount to the replacement of the "Czech government" by a "Slovak government"? As a result of certain reports, the question is even being raised whether the separation will diminish the workers' component of the party, whether it is a concession to "all kinds" of intellectuals, and so forth.

The Slovak issue was widely discussed at the last session and it is indeed one of the fundamental problems we have to solve. However, it is certainly not the only problem or the paramount one.

We failed to notice that the Slovaks have every reason to insist on the resolution of certain matters of principle concerning relations between our two nations and especially the everyday reality of our coexistence. We have become accustomed to looking at Slovakia as though all problems had been settled there and as though the task of equalling economic standards with those in the Czech Lands had been totally resolved, thanks to certain sacrifices on the Czech side. But we did not notice that the gradual narrowing of the "Košice" arrangement of Czechoslovak relations, especially the last constitutional arrangement in 1960 together with the practical reinforcement of "Prague" centralism, created a serious political problem.

"Commercial arithmetic," as practised by some of our people, divides the population into thirds—two Czech and one Slovak—but this will no longer do. If we leave aside ethnic minorities (though we must give consideration to them as well, so that they genuinely feel at home in our republic), the republic is not made up of three thirds, but merely of two national entities, both equal and with equal rights. To respect this reality naturally does not mean to give priority to Slovak interests and ignore those of the Czechs. One cannot turn things upside down. There is no greater Czech national interest than the strength of this republic, which one cannot imagine without the Slovaks. The years 1938–1939 taught a lesson not only to the Slovaks but to us Czechs as well! Let us not forget that the first free voice of Czechoslovakia rang out on domestic soil at Baňská Bystrica in 1944! I meet a great many people and unfortunately I notice that a segment of the Czech public—and I am afraid it is not just a negligible segment—have still not grasped the Slovak question and are unaware that the problems of Slovakia need to be addressed. Our way of looking at Slovakia is still burdened by old prejudices that have again been fueled by allegations of so-called Slovak nationalism. True, "our" Czech patriots have their counterparts in Slovakia. National exaggerations are not the domain of one nation alone.

Still, the common interest in truly maintaining the republic's internal unity demands that we rely on proven traditions, stemming from the joint anti-fascist liberation struggle, and that we come to grips with the issue of our relations in the interest of a modern socialist community. Following some indications in the past, the CPCz CC has now realized all this, as is evident in the relevant sections of the resolution. For the first time in the history of the CPCz, a Slovak communist has been placed at the helm of the party. Cde. Dubček has become first secretary as an honest and experienced communist. At the CPCz CC session it was not at all a question of a "power seizure by the Slovaks" as we sometimes hear because of a lack of information in Czech circles.

Confidence in the Intelligentsia

By the same token, no one has threatened the working-class nature of the party. Those who spoke in the discussion could not be divided into intellectuals and workers, as is claimed erroneously in certain quarters. The open and passionate debate included intellectuals as well as workers and peasants, who were motivated by the same sincere concern for the cause of the republic, the interests of the people, and the improvement and consolidation of socialism. As a workers' official, which I consider myself to be, this is something I wish to emphasize. And I also want to say that a revolutionary workers' party has always been characterized by ties between the working class and scientific socialism. That, too, is part of the best traditions of our party. A significant number of the leading figures in Czech and Slovak science, literature, and art, as well as teachers, doctors, and others, have always fought in the party's ranks and even laid down their lives for it. The present era of the scientific-technical revolution—in which, unfortunately, we are badly lagging behind—demands more than ever that the creative forces of the working class, the peasantry, and the intelligentsia combine their efforts.

To put the matter simply: If in the last century a revolutionary workers' party could never have been founded and developed without Marx and without Lenin, in 1968 it is even more inconceivable that socialism could be built without science and without the intelligentsia! That is why efforts to stir up mistrust between workers and intellectuals are totally out of place and are damaging to the cause.

Even further from the truth is the suggestion that what happened at the recent sessions of the CPCz CC was no more than a personal quarrel and a rotation of individuals. Of course, no one finds it easy to set aside his personal biases, not even at sessions of the party's Central Committee. Nevertheless, the personnel changes were in fact motivated by considerations that are of far greater urgency and importance to the party: the imperative to remove the obstacles that for some time have been obstructing the party's progressive efforts, and the need to remove everything that has prevented the conclusions of the 13th Congress from being implemented and that inhibits the activation of all healthy forces in the party and among the people. I am referring to a series of tasks that should have been performed a long time ago, as well as to topical and pressing matters in the economic and social system. It is also essential to eliminate everything that has been distorting socialism, damaging people's spirits, causing pain, and depriving people of their faith and enthusiasm. This means we must do whatever is necessary to rehabilitate communists and other citizens who were unjustly sentenced in political trials so that we, as communists, can look ourselves in the face without shame. We must face the truth of history, as well as our historical legacy—especially the progressive traditions of the resistance struggle—and we must grant all our citizens whatever they are entitled to.

We should draw appropriate theoretical and practical conclusions from the fact that there are no more antagonistic classes in our country. It would be a setback for us if the current problems were to be resolved by the same methods and means that were used—albeit in a different form—during the years when a struggle was being waged to see "who would prevail over whom."[18]

The CC session attempted to find the cause of the passivity and indifference in our country, things which we can no longer conceal. There is a conviction growing that everything we have achieved in transforming the structure of the society will facilitate—indeed will absolutely necessitate—a basic change of course. Such a change must be aimed at the democratization of the party and the society as a whole, and must be brought about consistently and honestly; it also must be backed by realistic guarantees that are understood by the majority to ensure that it will not be undermined by hedging and reservations.

This is why the CC has decided to draw up an Action Program and start work on a project for the advancement of socialist society. The project will include all tested practices and progressive national traditions that were at the root of our victory. What, then, lies ahead? We shall find no ready-made solutions. It is up to us, both Czechs and Slovaks, to launch out courageously into unexplored territory and search for a Czechoslovak road to socialism. We can even regard this as our duty to the whole international socialist movement. It means strengthening our unity with the Soviet Union and with all socialist countries on the basis of tested equal rights principles.[19] It also enables us to establish the type of socialism that may even have something to offer to industrial countries in Europe and to their advanced revolutionary workers' movements.

---

[18] The phrase in Czech is *"Kdo s koho,"* a formulation first used by Lenin (in the Russian phrase *"Kto-kogo"*) to denote the Bolsheviks' approach to gaining power.

[19] The notion of a "Czechoslovak road to socialism" and of the need for "equal rights" in Soviet–Czechoslovak relations drew harsh comments from the Soviet ambassador in Czechoslovakia, Stepan Chervonenko, in a top-secret memorandum to Konstantin Rusakov and Andrei Gromyko on 16 February 1968 (Cable No. 169, in TsKhSD, F. 5, Op. 60, D. 299, Ll. 112–121.) Chervonenko claimed that Smrkovský was advocating a "more independent" foreign policy that would place relations with the Soviet Union on "an entirely new basis." This seems to go well beyond what Smrkovský was actually saying, but the allegations were typical of the slanted reports that Chervonenko was sending back to Moscow throughout the Prague Spring.

These are, in my view, the main problems that have left their mark on the most recent session of the CPCz CC. The members of the CPCz CC have tried hard and sincerely to find democratic solutions to all these problems.

The Example of the Central Committee

I would say that this quest was largely successful. True, there was no "volte-face," white did not change to black, nor vice versa. In a meeting of some 150 speakers and in the subsequent unity of the entire CC—the unity of which need not be absolute at all times—the CC plenum became what it should be: namely, the truly supreme organ of the party. It became an organ that contributed not only a democratic spirit, but also made fundamental and significant democratic steps that have not been made by the party for decades. It introduced and carried through a task that accords with the democratic sentiments of our people and with their awareness of everything our public life ought to be—straightforward, truthful, and decent—while retaining a principled and critical outlook in accordance with the sound rule of "the truth, come what may." Thus, the CC set an example to one and all, as well as to itself, of how to conduct both the practical work of the center and the everyday work of lower-echelon organs. This is an example to the present and to the future, an example that still must be thought through and taken to its logical conclusion.

The Central Committee has now demonstrated that it does not intend to be a mere rubber-stamp body any longer. It has become the real spokesman of the party and has finally given voice to issues that have long been troubling every communist who is sincere toward the movement and honest with himself. The CC has now started to confront the question of the party's authority in society and, above all, its internal problems which for so long have been side-stepped or addressed sporadically. This applies also to relations and duties toward non-party members and the society as a whole.

So, what are we to do after "January"? How are we to ensure that words will be turned into deeds and translated into reality, that the program and line of the 13th Congress—as fully endorsed by the CC session—will be implemented with consistency, that hopes which are finally beginning to emerge in the party will not be dashed, and that the activity accompanying these hopes will not be squandered?

The first task is to inform the party, the whole party, of the content of the discussion at the CC session. We must reveal the spirit and methods underlying the proceedings of the most recent session to the entire party and to all its sections. Scope must be given to a sincere and frank exchange of views from top to bottom, with priority to be given to the cogency of the arguments rather than to the power of the voice or the office. Priority also will be given to action instead of to indifference and passive submission. All truly progressive and responsible trends must be given a chance, and their chance must be given boldly and judiciously, sooner rather than later.

No mistake would be greater than to start carrying out these tasks on the basis of obsolete procedures, in the form of a one-off campaign that would, as usual, pay lip-service and then wither and die a few months later. We must not gamble frivolously with the confidence shown either by the party or in the party. This can only be solved on a systematic, long-term basis. Not everything has been solved. I would say that the first "test of statesmanship" for us will be to summon up the will and the courage to inform the party in detail about all that has happened and about the views expressed in connection with these events. We must inform the party concretely and honestly from top to bottom, and from bottom to top.

To that end, we must fully implement all provisions of the party statutes that are today on the agenda, and we must rid the party of formalism and command methods and replace them with genuine, straightforward, and ideologically sound arguments. This must be done not by the authority of rhetoric and office, but with the help of ideas, evidence, and acts. The whole process must imbue the party from top to bottom and vice versa. If the CC has now proclaimed everything that the party wanted to hear, it also has declared that the CC itself needs to know what the party and the people are saying.

The whole set of tasks and problems that are accumulating today before us can best be characterized as a steady process of democratization within both the party and the state. This process is the main precondition for a truly mature and thus voluntary form of discipline, without which the party would lose its capacity to act. Although we must cure and revive the whole party organism, we cannot do so through some "back-door" method. Nor can we compensate by relying on even the most hard-working apparatus. The entire party and each of its members must be convinced that the party as a whole is responsible not only for the implementation of tasks, but also for their conceptualization—that is, for the formulation of party policy, in which each communist must participate so that they can then regard it as their very own.

No doubt, we must "clear the table"—a phrase one often hears among comrades nowadays—but this must be done peacefully and in a businesslike manner so that we can prudently return to our former work and can reaffirm and develop whatever has been successful in the past, while rectifying shortcomings and mistakes in a just and sincere manner. Let us give to the past what it deserves—truth, purity, and justice. Let us do this without further delay and without scandals and recriminations, and let us do it consistently so we can then fully concentrate on what has always been the main interest of all communists: the future.

What Kind of Program Do We Need?

The decision of the January CPCz CC plenum to prepare a party Action Program will move us in precisely that direction. The Action Program must express the fundamental needs—and thus also the political interests—of individual groups within the population. The Central Committee intends to include principles that are clearly formulated and that will guide us when we approach various strata of society and their interests, as well as when we confront urgent economic, social, and ideological problems. The program will be a rallying point that can unite all progressive and patriotic forces and that can restore an atmosphere of trust between individual classes and groups of society as well as between the party and the people.

However, an atmosphere of trust can only be created after we succeed in overcoming certain areas of friction and tension that have emerged in the past. I have in mind especially the tension between the party leadership and the intelligentsia, and the tension between the party leadership and some of our young people, particularly students.

We also realize that we must adopt a new approach when we confront social problems that have emerged as a result of our protracted economic difficulties. Social problem number one is the need for improvement in the housing situation. An effective solution to this matter means we will have to adopt certain emergency measures to get things moving. In the Action Program the party's Central Committee should also state clearly and openly what steps it proposes to adopt regarding prices, wages, taxes, and social policy.

If a climate of mutual political confidence is to be restored, the people must be given sufficient factual information about everything that concerns their living standards. Prompt information is among the most important prerequisites of the democratization of public life; without it, political stability cannot be achieved.

All citizens are entitled to know how their lives are going to develop so that they can plan for the future realistically and responsibly. Frequent changes in living conditions do not promote stability. Although some changes are necessary, we can ensure that people do not feel insecure and that they do not have to live from one day to another always wondering what those "above" will think up next.

This last point is especially important. If the thesis about the party's leading role is to be more than a hollow phrase, the projected Action Program cannot be the affair of the party alone. The party's Action Program must be addressed to our entire public.[20] All segments and groups of the population must find in it a reflection of their aspirations, requirements, and demands. The program, which is being devised by the party's Central Committee at the instruction of the Presidium, must be a program for the whole of society, the whole of the state, and the whole population. The forthcoming 50th anniversary of our republic will be the most suitable occasion for the elaboration and full implementation of the Program.

The Position of the Party

What we must do now is clarify relations between party and state organs, between state organs and enterprises, between state administrative bodies and the economic sphere, and between the apparatus and elected bodies. Unless all these relationships are precisely demarcated and the jurisdiction and responsibility of individual organs are properly established, it will not be possible to improve the quality of management or to implement the demand that each of us must be accountable for our actions, work, and decisions. The public must know not only who decides at what level but also who takes full responsibility for that level.

The new Action Program must also clearly stipulate the tasks of individual social and professional organizations and the appropriate relationship between these entities and state and party organs. Because we know that progress in a socialist society takes place through the interaction of economic, social, and political interests, we must strive to establish a mechanism of political leadership that will provide for the routine settlement of all social conflicts and preclude any need for emergency administrative measures, which would give rise to new points of friction and political tensions. Naturally, the same applies to certain nationality problems.

Ultimately, the Action Program—and, above all, the way it is implemented—will determine whether the expectations that the January session of the CPCz Central Committee has generated within the party and among the people will be fulfilled, and whether this session will become a landmark in our development and the beginning of a new climate not only in the ranks of the party, but in the society as a whole. Let us not have any illusions. Nothing will happen on its own, without a struggle, or without some effort. Nothing will fall into our laps, and no one should expect charitable donations. There must be a sense of responsibility both "at the top" and "at the bottom."

People have emerged from various quarters who talk about a shake-up and turbulence; more such people will emerge, and the talk will continue. This eventful session, where people spoke frankly, openly, courageously, critically, and self-critically, may appear turbulent to some. But there are different types of turbulence. I think it will be a good thing if the December and January plenary sessions bring a real shake-up—a shake-up that is beneficial in releasing and reviving new and fresh forces that can move our society and our socialist republic forward into a new phase. All this is fully within the power of the party and within the power of our 1.5 million communists, who can count on the total help and support of broad masses of the population who want the same things that we do.[21]

---

[20] See Document No. 19 below.

[21] The article was applauded by supporters of reform, but rankled many hard-liners in both Czechoslovakia and the Soviet Union. A senior member of the CPCz CC Presidium, Drahomír Kolder, expressed misgivings about the article in an interview on Czechoslovak television in early March. Soviet Ambassador Chervonenko voiced even stronger reservations about the article in cables he sent back to top officials in Moscow.

DOCUMENT No. 10: Alexander Dubček's Speech Marking the 20th Anniversary of Czechoslovakia's "February Revolution," February 22, 1968 (Excerpts)

Source: *K otázkám obrodného procesu KSČ: Vybrané projevy 1. tajemníka ÚV KSČ A. Dubčeka* (Bratislava, 1968), pp. 31–58.

Dubček delivered this speech at the 20th anniversary celebration of the communist seizure of power in Czechoslovakia. In it, he offers a generally favorable evaluation of the two decades of communist rule in Czechoslovakia, suggesting that most of the "negative phenomena" and "excessive centralization" had come about only over the previous few years. Although Dubček alludes to the disgruntlement that was spreading in the party's ranks and pledged to take "decisive action" to remedy the country's ills, most of his prescriptions, especially his insistence on the need to "uphold democratic centralism" and "enforce the leading role of the party," appear cautious. He does admit, however, that "things must be thoroughly changed," and offers a "firm rejection of the directive-based methods of managing the economy."

An earlier draft of the speech was significantly stronger. Because party and state officials from all of Czechoslovakia's Warsaw Pact allies, including the Soviet Union, were due to attend the celebration, Dubček showed a draft of the speech to Brezhnev beforehand. The Soviet leader became upset and demanded revisions. The final version of the speech was less critical of Dubček's predecessors than the earlier draft; any innovative formulations about foreign affairs were removed; and it did not even signal any notable departures in the CPCz's domestic policies.

. . . I know that for some time serious rumblings have been heard from the ranks of our workers and peasants. They have been saying that it is no longer good enough to fix something here and there in the party and in society as a whole. They believe, instead, that things must be thoroughly changed in the spirit of the old and tested Leninist methods and traditions of the labor movement—not by words but by decisive action. This objective corresponds to the wishes of our working people.

We have several times attempted to bring about a change in many spheres: in industry, agriculture, culture, and science. We have achieved certain successes, but we sensed that these were not commensurate with our capabilities and the effort we expended. If we look back today at all these endeavors, we come up against the real key to the solution of everything, the focal point of all our burning problems. The area in which we must start is politics, the political sphere. This conviction is dictated by that very same political sphere, by life itself, and by our past experience. It is no coincidence that this is where negative phenomena have recently been spreading—phenomena that we know only too well—and where we are most alarmed by the growth of political apathy, passivity, and a certain type of resignation even among communists.

A series of unresolved questions have been accumulating in the political sphere. We cannot afford all this to become entangled in a web we would find hard, very hard, to disentangle. This is, therefore, the point where we must begin to tackle matters, where a turnaround is essential, and where a remedy is most needed. There are indications and signals warning us that this need has been and is being felt by the public and the whole party. The same applies to the party leadership, which also has launched a more intensive discussion about these matters since the October plenary session [in 1967—Eds.].

These discussions did not refer to the policy or resolutions of the 13th Party Congress [in June 1966 — Eds.]. After all, we know that the documents of the 13th CPCz Congress provide a sufficiently broad basis for the solution of pressing problems. The discussion centered mainly on working methods, on the course of our further progress, and on whether we could accomplish the tasks set by the 13th Congress with the old methods or whether those old habits would lead us not forward but into a blind alley.

These debates and disputes featured a confrontation of views, and their purpose was to facilitate a progressive advance.

What was the result or what were the first results—insofar as these are just initial steps?

I believe the correct and progressive position has triumphed, the view that we cannot preserve past values simply by defending them all the time, but by looking new problems boldly in the face, and that we shall tackle these in a new and creative manner, in a manner dictated by our present reality. I am probably not simplifying matters when I say that today more than ever the important thing is not to reduce our policy to a struggle "against" but, more importantly, to wage a struggle "for." That, in my view, is the crux of the matter. . . .

We have analyzed and firmly rejected directive-based methods of managing the economy, which no longer correspond to the existing level of the forces of production and which are remnants of a specific period when the economy could still be developed extensively. Similar problems exist in the political sphere as well.

In this situation we have futilely racked our brains about the alarming tendency toward passivity, and we have called in vain for responsible activity and greater discipline. Appropriate and favorable conditions must still be created for the kind of activity that is vital for socialism's existence. Political directives, too, will have to be worked out with the far greater participation of those at whom they are targeted, such as the trade unions or the Youth League. In some sectors of our life responsibility for one's work has diminished. Lack of discipline and a peculiar type of passing the buck have become rife.

Naturally it will be essential and effective to promote the kind of discipline we need—a mature and voluntary discipline. In applying the Leninist principle of party organization and party work, and in building the state, we must proceed from the principle of democratic centralism. We must take a closer look at its foundations and application in our work. There must not be excessive centralization, which only weakens the democratic factor. This was, incidentally, one of the crucial issues discussed by the Central Committee in October and December 1967 and again in January 1968.

It was not for nothing that it was stressed time and again that conclusions must be drawn from the fact that socialism has already triumphed in our country and that new relations have been created between classes. We must live up to this new social situation in practice, and not by words alone. That is where the key to the majority of our current political problems lies.

Therefore, the discussion must not focus on whether to enforce the leading role of the party in the advancement of society and in the implementation of policy with regard to the economy, culture, the trade unions, or the youth movement. The question, instead, is how to enforce the leading role of the party more effectively in the existing conditions of socialist construction. This flows directly from the Leninist principle that the party must constantly struggle to uphold its leading position in society.

Over the past few years the view of the party that was so prevalent in the past—regarding it as a force which, instead of exercising political leadership in society, would instead often make authoritarian decisions about even the most superfluous, marginal, and trivial matters—has again won the upper hand in this country.

We have to think seriously about the consequences and repercussions of this mode of thought, insofar as the shortcomings are directly linked with the problem of decision-making and power, as discussed at the recent sessions of the Central Committee. There will probably be no disagreements about the fact that it was this concept of the running of society and its actual practice that have done so much to deprive the work of many state, economic, and social institutions of the essence of their content and responsibility. This concept gave rise to a situation in which insufficient scope was given to them to apply beneficial social initiatives, and stamped many of our activities with a seal of formality.

I believe these circumstances recall the words of Klement Gottwald when, after February 1948, he warned us against administrative and command methods in relations between the party and society.

It will certainly not be easy to deal with this problem, as it contains a whole set of intricate theoretical and practical issues. Impatience and improvization will not help, although we cannot keep postponing a proper solution. The party must formulate political objectives that are understandable to the people, together with a corresponding concept of our policy. All new concepts must be expressed in new terms, without abandoning continuity with past developments, which have molded the present situation in our society and its thinking. We must forget wishful thinking and must respect what we have and transform it fundamentally and patiently. That was the crux of the matter at the last sessions of the Central Committee, and this point is best reflected in the demand for, first, an Action Program, and then, a few years later, a long-term political program that gives all our citizens—Czechs, Slovaks and other ethnic groups—new prospects and answers to their questions, to their needs, and to everything else they expect from the forthcoming period in which a socialist society is constructed and refined in Czechoslovakia.

Suggestions for the Action Program covering the immediate period up to the preparation of the 14th CPCz Congress, which we are going to review over the next few months, are among the main duties that will enable us to figure out how to implement the conclusions of the January Central Committee session in a practical and positive manner.

We want to rally all the citizens of our republic to implement the progressive objectives of socialist development and strengthen confidence in the party. The only way to do this is to rectify all mistakes and shortcomings and to promote intra-party democracy, providing a guarantee for the widest possible inclusion of the party's members and officials in the formulation and implementation of the party's policy.

In the Action Program we cannot specify the practical steps of each section of society, but we can and must open political space to allow individual groups and all social institutions and organizations to formulate their most urgent practical objectives and tasks. In this way, each citizen of our state should be able to pursue their interests directly and effectively, especially at work, as part of their social activity.

I believe the Action Program should also be a starting point for the formulation of key issues in a prospective long-term program running through the year 1970. Long-term objectives and concepts of the general progress of socialism should reflect the most innate sense of the socialist revolution, the transformation of the material and intellectual conditions in society, and the genuine liberation of people.

The solution of many problems in our party will be of great—I would even say, decisive—importance in this work, based on the decisions of the 13th Congress which we shall have to elaborate further during our preparations for the 14th CPCz Congress. The recent sessions of the Central Committee have already provided substantial and valuable new ideas.

I believe we have succeeded in confronting the problems that have been worrying all of us—our entire party and all its members—for a long time. To enforce the leading role of the party under present conditions, we must create the necessary prerequisites for the promotion of initiative, greater scope for opinions to be compared and exchanged, and greater efforts to inform all communists thoroughly and objectively about events at home and abroad in a timely manner, allowing them to form opinions about the policy of the party and, above all, to participate not only in the implementation but also in the formulation of the political line and procedure of the party, especially in their work sphere. In brief, this means that at the present stage we must place the strongest emphasis on the premise that while preserving the necessary degree of centralism, democratic forms must be developed more actively and, above all, more thoroughly; this must be done not in the highest party institutions but mainly "from below", in organizations and among the membership. In intra-party life we must eliminate excessive centralism in decision-making and place greater emphasis on the role of party branches and elected bodies.

Expert studies and science must play a major role in shaping the party's policy. The party today has a large number of scientists and experienced personnel, who are capable of devising well-considered and well-founded solutions.

Recent sessions of our Central Committee have offered convincing evidence that democratic forms in party life are the most suitable method for responsibly approaching the problems of practical tasks. We want to draw all necessary conclusions from this and to anchor the result of all these deliberations in a set of well-elaborated and scientifically justified measures. I already mentioned that several dozen scientific workers and experts in a variety of fields are working on the draft Action Program under the guidance of the Presidium of the CPCz CC. That is also how we are tackling other burning questions connected with party life.

The solution to these problems will surely inspire many suggestions relevant to other branches and organs of the party which, like the Central Committee, must start confronting them on their own, in keeping with the requirements of the day and the views of the majority of party members.

The work of local branches and of district and regional conferences will be decisive in determining whether we succeed in laying the foundations for activity and in fostering a creative, productive work atmosphere.

We must find ways of rapidly, objectively, and courageously solving the problems that have accumulated, but, most importantly, we must do so with circumspection. The only way to forestall the possible extremes that are naturally and logically emerging and that we must oppose is through positive action by the whole party. There is no other way of overcoming them.

* * *

Our entire effort and all our endeavors are directed toward a true invigoration and unity of all constructive and progressive forces in the republic. That is the necessary prerequisite for a new inception of socialism in our republic. The object of this development is to build an advanced socialist society based on sound economic foundations and to build a socialism that corresponds to the historical democratic traditions of Czechoslovakia, in accordance with the experience of other communist parties. . . .

DOCUMENT No. 11: Report by Czechoslovak Television Reporter on Soviet Reactions to the Events in the ČSSR, February 28, 1968

Source: ÚSD, AÚV KSČ, F. 07/15; Vondrová & Navrátil, vol. 1, pp. 52–54.

Czechoslovak television journalist, O. Výborný, compiled this report two months after Dubček's election. His survey indicates that officials and ordinary citizens in the Soviet Union divided their assessments of Czechoslovakia between two distinct perspectives. One important group viewed everything in a negative light, arguing that the new leaders in Prague were moving away from socialism, endangering relations with the Soviet Union, and giving in to bourgeois nationalist pressures. A second, and very different, group perceived the reforms in Czechoslovakia with great excitement and relief, hoping that the events would pave the way for similar changes in the Soviet Union. They were particularly intrigued by the latitude given for free expression in Czechoslovakia. Those holding this opinion acknowledged that a certain degree of caution was necessary to avoid giving the hard-line elements in Moscow a pretext for cracking down. But they also believed that Czechoslovakia's embrace of its "own road to socialism" need not attenuate relations with the Soviet Union.

Výborný also evaluates the problems of Czechoslovak journalists reporting from the Soviet Union, commenting that "a great deal of skill and tact is needed to tell our people about the problems encountered by the USSR while not offending the Soviet authorities." The Výborný report was delivered to Dubček on March 4 by CzTV Director Jiří Pelikán.

The response in the USSR can be divided into two categories:

1. highly negative
2. highly positive

In between the two is a large section (a third undifferentiated group) of those who, because of a total lack of information or covert reports by Western radio stations, are unable to find their bearings in the present situation and thus cannot characterize events in our country correctly. It can be said that their assessment of what is going on in our country depends on the extent of their knowledge.

1. Negative

Negative assessments are not confined to a specific group. One comes across them in the highest places as well as among ordinary people. Those who hold this view have been frightened by the developments in our country. They disagree with the results of our plenum and are worried about future developments. They compare our situation with the Yugoslav road, and regard it as revisionist and dangerous. They are afraid that just as in Yugoslavia, our party will become no more than a political education center and will not be the leading force in the state. They allege that Czechoslovak policy is becoming nationalist; they believe we are exaggerating our attempt to set out on our "own road to socialism." Instead, they point to the USSR, which consistently sticks to positions of internationalism.

They furthermore regard our new road as concealed criticism of the old road—the road pursued by the USSR—and fear that we will deviate from this path. They criticize us for our faltering struggle against petty bourgeois tendencies, and they maintain that the voices of the latter have been particularly conspicuous in recent events. Some point to the nationalist factor; they interpret the plenary sessions as attempts by the Slovaks to achieve a political and economic settlement. They are concerned lest these tendencies be taken up in the USSR as well. They emphasize their own problems with nationalist tendencies: for example, in the Transcaucasian and Baltic republics and in Ukraine.

These adverse assessments of our plenum account for the attitude of certain comrades toward their own economic reform. They do not want to hurry its implementation, and they point to the bad experience of the USSR. In addition to the political impact, they focus also on the economic impact. They believe that certain inflationary tendencies have arisen precisely because of the economic reform.

This group has curtailed and restricted all substantive information. The press has published only the TASS report about the plenary session, which was transmitted by ČTK, along with Dubček's biography and his speech on the February anniversary.[22] The powers that be are guided by the old Soviet dictum: If I provide information it means that I agree. If I do not give information, it means that I disagree.

All substantive *Rudé právo* articles are carried only in the white TASS. Although our embassy used to receive this version of TASS regularly, it is no longer made available to the embassy. Nor is it sent to the embassies of the other socialist countries.

TASS has issued two versions of Cde. Dubček's speech—one with omissions for the press, the other without omissions for the white TASS.

2. Positive

People in this category welcome events in our country and hope that they will have some influence on domestic developments in the USSR as well. They merely warn against criticism of the USSR and against any unfavorable assessment of past relations with the USSR. They realize that such criticism would immediately be exploited by conservative comrades. They believe we will be in an extremely isolated position: Apart from Hungary, where a transition is under way to highly unusual forms of management, the socialist countries (Poland, Bulgaria, etc.) are experiencing the opposite sort of trend. Certain people have their doubts whether Dubček will be able to cope with all the demands put by various groups; they are aware of the complex situation and understand that the January session has no more than publicized all the problems, and that now they will have to be solved.

They hail the speeches and the discussion that have appeared in our press, especially the fact that these have been published by members of the Central Committee and that they are airing their views so openly. They believe it is healthy and democratic that everyone should be able to express their opinion alongside the official party statement. They regard this as free discussion. They consider efforts by the ČSSR to move along its own road to socialism, based on its own traditions and experiences, to be correct. They do not think that this represents a turning away from the USSR.

The events in our country have done much to increase interest about us in the USSR; this interest must be kept up.

Problems Connected with the Work of Correspondents in the USSR

Correspondents in Moscow now find themselves at a disadvantage. Although in our country greater scope has been given to reporters, in the USSR it is actually being narrowed. The availability of information has become more restricted and there is no access to places that in the past were open. Rumor has it that screws will be tightened still further in the cultural sphere to put an end to free discussion and curtail excessive relaxation.

We, too, are encountering difficulties in reporting from the USSR. There are still no opinion polls in our country, and it is not clear to whom we are speaking or what exactly people want to hear from us. The younger generation no longer sees our relationship with the USSR as an emotional matter the way our generation used to. On what is the new generation's thinking based? In reality nothing is known about the current state of our friendship with the USSR. This problem

---

[22] This assertion tends to understate the lengthy biography of Dubček and the warm congratulatory message from Brezhnev to Dubček which appeared in Moscow newspapers, including *Pravda,* on 6 January 1968.

should be neither overlooked nor dealt with spontaneously, but should be approached on a genuine scientific basis.

Under the circumstances, Moscow correspondents will have to show a great deal of skill and tact in telling our people about the problems encountered by the USSR while not offending the Soviet authorities; they will have to reconcile their own remarks and commentaries with the atmosphere in our country.

DOCUMENT No. 12: Observations by Czechoslovak Escort-Guides on the Views of Foreign Delegations Attending the Celebrations of the "February Revolution," February 1968

Source: ÚSD, AÚV KSČ, F. 07/15; Vondrová & Navrátil, vol. 1, pp. 54–62.

This report contains brief observations by the staffers who were assigned as escorts to the high-level "fraternal" delegations that attended the February 1968 festivities in Prague. It was prepared by the International Department of the CPCz Central Committee. The guides convey the views held by East German and Polish leaders, who argued that developments in Czechoslovakia were "endangering socialism" and "providing grist for the mill of Bonn's global strategists." The document suggests that even at this early stage, Ulbricht had come to believe that it was "useless to try to do anything" with the CPCz authorities. Comments by some of the Soviet officials who were present also revealed deep anxiety about the Czechoslovak reforms.

The report also transmits the highly favorable assessments expressed by Yugoslav leaders, who argued that the processes under way in Czechoslovakia were in keeping with the ČSSR's reputation as "the most advanced socialist state" and its "deeply-rooted democratic traditions." The guide accompanying the Romanian delegation relates how disappointed Ceauşescu was that the new Czechoslovak leaders were not seeking a more independent foreign policy, and the guide escorting the Hungarian participants was able to detect, from a brief conversation with Kádár, that the Hungarian leader's position was far more moderate than the views of his East German and Polish counterparts. The guide escorting Polish leader Władysław Gomułka describes a lengthy and agitated conversation that Gomułka had with several of his Warsaw Pact counterparts, including Brezhnev, Ulbricht, and Kádár, about an unknown topic. Although Gomułka was "extremely upset" during much of the conversation, according to the report, he appeared satisfied by the end that he had "managed to convince" his Soviet interlocutors.

The Communist Party of the Soviet Union

During their visit to our country, members of the CPSU delegation—including members of the political entourage as well as officials from the Soviet Embassy—expressed their total confidence in our party's Central Committee and in Cde. Dubček. They did so both during their toasts and in discussions with us. They said they were convinced that things in our country would settle down, that relations between our parties and peoples would in no way be jeopardized, and that the CPCz, which enjoys great authority in the international communist movement, would continue to enjoy this authority provided it advances on an internationalist Marxist road. However, they also pointed to certain developments in our public and political life that provoked their astonishment, fears, and concern. Some of these were directly connected with the situation after the January plenum; others dated further back.

For example, they were astonished by the well-known appearance of Prof. Goldstücker on television and by the manner in which the publication of *Literární listy* was launched; they wondered why it was possible that the so-called preliminary issue of the magazine was circulated along with *Rudé právo*. In general, they argued that *Rudé právo* was too liberal, and that it gave space to a variety of views that were often directly contrary to the views of the party. They made adverse comments about articles by some of our leading comrades that dealt with the results of the January session, claiming that each of them interpreted the results in their own way, and so forth.

The delegation received Cde. Gomułka to its residence, and several of our leading comrades also had discussions with its members. Since none of the staff of the International Department was ever present at these talks, we are unable to report on them.

Socialist Unity Party

Comrades Dubček, J. Hendrych, O. Černík, J. Špaček, and L. Štrougal, as well as an official of the CPCz Central Committee International Department, had talks with the delegation on various occasions. The conversations were mainly critical toward us and covered all aspects of CPCz and ČSSR policy. . . .

In connection with Cde. Ulbricht's remark about the continuing discussion on the draft of a new GDR Constitution (in which, according to Cde. Mittag a whole series of critical proposals have been made that have not yet been published in the GDR) . . ., Cde. Ulbricht was astonished that we intend to modify certain articles of our socialist Constitution since, as he said, only a relatively short period of time has passed since it was adopted. In this context he mentioned an article by Cde. Slavík, featured in *Rudé právo*, in which the author demands a greater democratization of Czechoslovak public life and the restoration of civil rights.[23] He had felt consternation when reading the translation of the article by a member of the CPCz Central Committee. (Cde. Ulbricht said they were thoroughly informed about everything, even about the latest sessions of the CPCz Central Committee sessions.) According to Ulbricht, the article must be characterized as advocating the demand of the restitution of bourgeois rights, or at least as a demand to return to the situation that had been settled by the national democratic revolution in 1945. (Note: The question was raised whether it is really appropriate to use the term "national democratic revolution" when discussing our situation, since that phrase is usually applied nowadays to Third World countries.)

According to Cde. Ulbricht, Czechoslovak journalism, but, above all, articles by Czechoslovak writers were frequently a tool for Bonn's global strategy against the socialist countries. For example, an article by Pavel Kohout in the Hamburg *Die Zeit*, later published also in *Frankfurter Allgemeine Zeitung*, contained instructions for activities against the GDR *("Anleitung für die Handlung gegen die Regierung").*[24] Citizens of the GDR are being acquainted with such ideas by West German television. The SED does not react to such articles and does not place them in their right perspective. It acts on the principle that the CPCz is responsible for reacting to them. . . .

In a subsequent discussion Cde. Hendrych raised certain questions and spoke about the situation on the cultural front and about a certain crystallization of activity among writers. . . .

Cde. Ulbricht again stressed that Czechoslovak writers were essentially espousing an anti-socialist platform. They speak defensively about capitalist countries, attempting some kind of false objectivity. They admire the West, and that provides grist for the mill of Bonn's global strategists. He stated his doubts about the possibility of uniting our working class with those types of intellectuals. He even went so far as to claim it would be absolutely impossible. In this context he had harsh words to say about the Hungarian writer Lukács and the fact that he was readmitted to the HSWP—even though this was the affair of the HSWP, as he noted.[25] (Cde. Ulbricht's preferred tactic is to offer severe criticism of conditions, because in conclusion he can always add that the solution of this or that problem is of course the affair of the specific party in question.) He said Lukács had been a revisionist as far back as the days of the Weimar Republic.

Despite a host of critical remarks on a number of questions in various spheres of our life, the members of the SED delegation said that Ulbricht was very pleased by our country. It was evident

---

[23] Václav Slavík was a leading reformist on the CPCz Central Committee who was appointed to the CPCz CC Secretariat in April 1968. Earlier, he headed an Institute of Political Science under the CPCz CC.

[24] The German title of the article translates as "Instructions for Action against the Regime."

[25] The writer in question is György Lukács, the controversial Marxist theorist who, ironically enough, ended up supporting the military intervention in Czechoslovakia.

that the section in Cde. Dubček's report devoted to the GDR had achieved its aim. However, the situation changed considerably on the last evening of the delegation's stay in the ČSSR on returning from the Soviet reception where its members had a discussion with Cde. Černík.

At first we were unable to find out exactly whether the delegation's fury had been caused by the discussion with Černík (because we did not know its content), or whether there had been other causes. One could merely hear a few agitated phrases such as "it is clear that it's useless to try to do anything with them," etc. Later on, when Ulbricht had left, we tried to find out the reason for the agitated discussion.

It appears that the main cause had been two words—recognition of the GDR—additionally handwritten in Cde. Novotný's speech which he made at the Old Town Square demonstration. W. Krolikowski, a member of the delegation, told us in a discussion we had that it was "symptomatic of our position that the president of the republic himself did not even see fit to include in his speech such an important formulation as the demand for recognition of the GDR, and that it was added only when some official had drawn his attention to this." We tried in vain to convince Cde. Krolikowski that this had been no more than a technical hitch.

The episode demonstrates that the SED delegation, especially its leaders, adopted a highly critical attitude toward the situation in the ČSSR while they were here, and openly stated their concern about future developments in our country.

Yugoslav League of Communists

Against all expectations, the Yugoslav delegation did not ask obtrusive questions about the outcome of the most recent sessions of the CPCz Central Committee and about matters directly connected with it—at least not in the conversations where I was present, or in which I participated—but it was evident that they were well informed about our problems and that they were observing developments in the ČSSR very closely. Their comments were aimed at grasping the general context of events. Cde. Siljegovin had more to say about current problems. He evaluated present Czechoslovak developments most favorably and frequently stressed that they corresponded to the objective possibilities of our country as the generally most advanced socialist country with deeply-rooted democratic traditions. It was, therefore, logical that it was making the greatest progress in the democratization process, greater than Yugoslavia, where opposing traditions still go very deep.

Both comrades highly appreciated Cde. Dubček's speech at the festive session as well as his address on the Old Town Square. . . .

Polish United Workers' Party

The conversations among members of the delegation and their entourage (if they took place in my presence) do not allow me to draw a conclusion on their attitude to the outcome of the December and January CPCz Central Committee sessions other than that it is full of reservations. . . .

Immediately upon his arrival Cde. Gomułka asked to make a telephone call to Cde. Brezhnev and, after talking to him, left with Cde. Gierek for the Soviet delegation's residence, where he spent nearly two hours. Most of Cde. Gomułka's official meetings were with Cde. Brezhnev throughout his stay here: He talked to him for about 20 minutes before the festive session at the Castle on 22 February and then again at the reception following the session. Cde. Gomułka spent the whole time (more than an hour) in conversation with a group initially including Dubček, Brezhnev, Ulbricht, and Kádár. In the end, only Brezhnev, Gomułka, and Kádár were left at the table, and they were engaged in an agitated conversation (Gomułka especially seemed upset), which went on for about 40 minutes.[26] Upon leaving for his residence Cde. Gomułka told the other members of his delegation: "I have worked so hard, slaved away, and explained more than at any mass gathering. But I have managed to convince them." When I later tried to find out what the conversations had been about, one member of the entourage intimated that they had probably spoken about the proposals of the Soviet comrades that the Budapest meeting should be a preliminary gathering and should be followed soon afterwards by a further consultative meeting in Warsaw.[27] Cde. Gomułka was against these proposals, arguing that the Budapest meeting should be sufficient for consultations and that a world conference should follow after a longer period of time. . . .

At the celebrations I met the special ADN correspondent who had come to Prague with the SED delegation; in reply to my direct question what the GDR delegation thought about the latest developments in our country and the changes taking place, he replied that in a conversation about these matters Cde. Ulbricht had said: "This is going to happen to me, too. It will now be my turn."

. . .

Conversations with members of the entourage of the Soviet delegation (Cde. Kolesnikov and Cde. Brezhnev's secretary) focused solely on routine topics.[28] Even so, they confirmed the detailed information the Soviet comrades had of everything going on in our country, including minor and totally insignificant personnel transfers in the CPCz Central Committee apparatus.

The Romanian Communist Party

Cde. Ceaușescu did not comment about the proceedings of the 20th anniversary of the February victory celebrations nor about any of the speeches. Only when giving a general outline of the policy of the Romanian CP did he remark, with a touch of indignation, that "instead of fighting for the liquidation of military blocs they are speaking about strengthening the bloc, even here in Prague—this is incomprehensible!"

The Hungarian Socialist Workers' Party

When talking amongst themselves the Hungarian comrades on principle did not comment on current Czechoslovak problems. It is worth mentioning only an unspecified remark by Cde. Kádár that the departure of officials of long standing did, after all, make one feel sad.

Shortly before leaving Prague, in the car Cde. Kádár spoke to me for about 10 minutes about the problems connected with the forthcoming meeting of communist and workers' parties and about his participation in the February celebrations. He emphasized the complicated situation in

---

[26] A top-secret memorandum in the former CPSU archives that refers to this conversation indicates that it dealt with the situation in Czechoslovakia, contrary to what a member of the PUWP entourage claimed below. See *"Zapis' besed s zam. zav. mezhdunarodnom otdelom TsK KPCh tov. M. Millerom v fevrale 1968 goda,"* Cable No. 211 (TOP SECRET) from I. I. Udal'tsov, minister-counselor at the Soviet embassy in Czechoslovakia, to M. A. Suslov, K. V. Rusakov, and A. A. Gromyko, 5 March 1968, in TsKhSD, F. 5, Op. 60, D. 299, Ll. 111–114.

[27] The reference here is to the meeting of communist parties in Budapest at the very end of February, which was intended to prepare for the worldwide communist party conference scheduled for November 1968 in Moscow.

[28] Sergei Kolesnikov was the head of the sector on Czechoslovakia and Poland in the CPSU CC Department on Ties with Communist and Workers' Parties of Socialist Countries. He played an important role in 1968 in channeling information to top CPSU officials.

the international communist movement and said that under the present conditions one can hardly expect a united stance (even in the form of a declaration or appeal) on the issues under discussion. Nowadays it was essential to devise a new concept of these meetings as outlets for an exchange of opinions, rather than to insist on declaring formal unity at a time when it was evident there was no such unity. As an example he mentioned the Moscow meeting in 1960.[29]

[29] Kádár is alluding to the meeting of 81 communist parties in Moscow in November 1960. The meeting came just as the Sino–Soviet split was widening beyond repair, yet the party leaders tried to achieve a united stance, at least on the surface.

DOCUMENT No. 13: Letter from Leonid Brezhnev to Alexander Dubček Inviting a ČSSR Delegation to the USSR, March 16, 1968

Source: ÚSD, AÚV KSČ, F. 07/15, Zahr. kor. c. 787.

This is the first of six confidential letters that Leonid Brezhnev wrote to Alexander Dubček during the 1968 crisis. It is an invitation to the Czechoslovak authorities to send a delegation to Moscow for bilateral talks. Although Brezhnev and his colleagues were already having misgivings about the events in Czechoslovakia, Brezhnev's letter addresses Dubček in a warm and friendly tone.

(For Brezhnev's other letters see Documents Nos. 21, 35, 39, 49, 85.)

---

16 March 1968
To the First Secretary of the Central Committee
of the Communist Party of Czechoslovakia,
Cde. A. Dubček

Dear Cde. Dubček!

During your visit to Moscow at the end of January of this year, we spoke about the necessity of further developing contacts between the party and state leaders of our countries. During those talks the opinion was expressed that a ČSSR state and party delegation should visit the Soviet Union this year.

On the basis of this preliminary agreement, the CPSU CC, the Presidium of the Supreme Soviet, and the Soviet government invite a ČSSR state and party delegation to visit the Soviet Union for talks at the highest level at a time that is most convenient for the Czechoslovak comrades.

While your delegation is in the USSR, we can discuss with you, in a fraternal way, questions of interest to both sides. We are convinced that the visit of a ČSSR delegation to the USSR will play an important role in strengthening the fraternal friendship and all-round cooperation between our parties and peoples.

With communist regards

L. Brezhnev
General Secretary, CPSU CC

DOCUMENT No. 14: Stenographic Account of the Dresden Meeting, March 23, 1968 (Excerpts)

Source: SAPMOB, ZPA, IV 2/201/778; Vondrová & Navrátil, vol. 1, pp. 73–117.

This stenographic account of the Dresden meeting of the Warsaw "Five" leaders is the only comprehensive record of the concerns and pressure put on CPCz leaders at the time. It is particularly useful in highlighting the way they were deceived about the intent of the conference. The Czechoslovak delegation, consisting of Dubček, Černík, Jozef Lenárt, Drahomír Kolder, and Vasil Biľak, had come to Dresden expecting to discuss questions of economic cooperation among the East-bloc states. This expectation seemed to be confirmed by the invitations extended to the heads of central planning from all the participating countries, but the presence of those officials proved to be almost wholly cosmetic. Walter Ulbricht laid out the real agenda of the meeting in his opening remarks, explaining that the assembled leaders wanted to learn about the "plans of the Central Committee of the Communist Party of Czechoslovakia" and about the status of the CPCz's "Action Program." The transcript underscores how uncomfortable Dubček and his colleagues were when the underlying purpose of the meeting was described to them. The CPCz first secretary expressed a strong "reservation" from the outset about the sudden change of agenda, but he and the four other Czechoslovak officials did not refuse to take part. Their participation inadvertently legitimized the notion that Czechoslovakia's "internal affairs" were a valid topic for a multilateral conference.

The transcript is also valuable in showing how the "Five" Warsaw Pact countries came to adopt different approaches during the early stages of the crisis. Gomułka's pronounced hostility toward the Prague Spring clearly stemmed in part from the difficulties he had been encountering at home, which he suspected were being inspired, at least indirectly, by the events in Czechoslovakia. Dubček's inability to assuage the Polish leader's concerns became evident a few days after the Dresden meeting, when Gomułka told a secret conclave of PZPR regional first secretaries that the talks in Dresden had confirmed that "anti-socialist" youth and intellectuals in Poland were like "vessels in communication" with the reformist elements in Prague (AAN, KC PZPR, P. 1, T. 298). Ulbricht, for his part, was also wary of the domestic repercussions from the Prague Spring, but he was even more eager to ensure that the Dresden conference would reaffirm Czechoslovakia's stand against "our common mortal enemy, imperialism," and specifically against the "revanchist" brand of imperialism in the FRG. Brezhnev's approach was less extreme than Gomułka's—which was beneficial for the "Five" in many respects because it made the Soviet leader appear conciliatory by comparison—but all the CPSU delegates, especially Aleksei Kosygin, made no attempt to hide their growing dissatisfaction with recent developments. Of the leaders of the "Five," only Kádár had any hope that the "Czechoslovak comrades themselves know best" how to cope with their own problems. Even Kádár, however, sought to convince Dubček and the other CPCz officials that resolute measures must be taken soon to prevent the onset of a full-fledged "counterrevolution" in Czechoslovakia.

The positions of the various countries remained essentially along these lines until just after the Warsaw Meeting in mid-July (see Document No. 52), when a greater consensus emerged among the "Five" (and within Moscow) about the need for military intervention if prompt and decisive steps were not adopted by the CPCz leadership. In the meantime, the differing approaches of the "Five," as the Dresden conference well illustrated, proved useful for the Soviet leadership. The harsh views of Gomułka and Ulbricht helped put pressure on the Czechoslovak authorities, whereas Kádár's approach facilitated Soviet attempts to rely on "comradely persuasion" as well as coercion. The Dresden conference thus served as a microcosm of the way Brezhnev managed the whole crisis during the first seven months of 1968.

Only recently it came to light that a secret stenographic record—albeit a somewhat incomplete one—was kept by East German officials, thanks to a hidden recording system. The proceedings were apparently taped and transcribed without the knowledge of the other participants, including the Soviet delegates. This excerpt—characterized by the sometimes impenetrable language of the monologues—is based on that secret record.

. . . .

L. Brezhnev: Unfortunately, we do not have full information on the course of the December Plenum and the January Plenum. It is, of course, no secret——one can take a look at it in the archives—that we were informed more extensively, that we ourselves informed the Politburo better, more extensively. But this time we were simply told in general terms: We had a plenum on the democratization of society. One cannot, of course, draw any conclusion from such general information. We were reserved in this case, did not ask any questions so we could not be accused of dictating anything. We were tactful. It is difficult for us to say what took place, what was meant by democratization and liberalization. By the way, when Alexander Stepanovich was with us—we once shared a ride, Comrade Podgorny, he and I—I asked: well, we understand what is meant by the democratization of the party. No secret understanding exists. Perhaps something needs to be changed. But let us clarify what you mean by the liberalization of society. I still do not understand this thesis today. How should this term be understood? What does the Politburo mean by "liberalization of society"? For 25 years you have been building socialism. Have you not had democracy until now? Or how else could this be understood? Perhaps the phrasing is not quite exact in this regard. But what do we want? This is not the worst thing. We see a danger, and we want to talk about it. Against the background of these decisions, against the background of the search for a correction of various deficiencies in policy which had existed. We do not object to that. Each party has the right to find and correct its deficiencies and mistakes; this is the obligation of each party—not to be satisfied, but to search for mistakes and shortcomings. [Against this background] a wave of public and political activities of an entire group or of entire centers has come into existence which has brought the entire public life of Czechoslovakia to counterrevolution. I would like to prove this now by stating facts. I cannot give a full account here. If it is necessary, this can be done with documents. I just would like to emphasize the fact that these questions were dealt with by the Politburo based on factual information and on the information which the Politburo received from your party. What is the main point? What main processes developed after the CC Plenum? I do not criticize the Plenum nor the Action Program, which we do not even know. This is a matter for the Czechoslovak comrades—whether or not they think it necessary to inform us or show us this program. As I said, that is their concern. But what happened in the country after the Plenum? There were public attacks on the Central Committee. This turned into a denunciation of the actions of the entire party, of all of [its] achievements and of all of its work in the past 20 to 25 years. Just look at *Rudé právo*. I have it here on the table. You can make a thick program of denunciations against the party out of it. And this in the central organ of the party! This runs from phrases such as "decayed society" and "outdated order" right up to demands to create a new party which will bring something more alive than the current bureaucratized police and administrative apparatus. This is the result. This went out over the entire country and the entire world. It was stated at demonstrations. It was repeated on TV. And it is also in *Rudé právo*. It will be reprinted in West Germany, in America, in Austria, everywhere. We can easily compile these materials for you. It is really not difficult. The second thing is the attack on the leading cadres of the party, the government, the Ministry of Defense, the Foreign Ministry, the Interior Ministry or however it is called in your country, etc. Everything is denounced. But this is not only aimed at Novotný's activities. All of the activities of the government are defamed, thus Lomský was attacked as well. Of course, I do not agree with Šejna either. That is a really an embarrassing story. But this was only the immediate cause, a matter that was used to disrupt the army. I think the army is currently not combat-ready. But what kind of an army is it then that constantly holds meetings without unified command, where the ministers and military district commanders etc. do not know any longer whether they enjoy confidence or not. Radio, TV and the press have achieved this wonderfully. Or let's take the Foreign Ministry! There are personal attacks on [Foreign Minister Václav] David. But dirt is thrown on all political activities and the entire foreign policy of the republic. And then the doctrine of autonomy in foreign policy was postulated: independent of the Soviet Union, of the socialist camp, etc. We have characterized individual personalities. But please allow me to point out that David worked in the underground as well. He had been secretary of the illegal Prague Committee. A good, honest communist! For 20 years he had led the fight against imperialism in cooperation and agreement with us. He appeared before the U.N. In the political arena, he was not a representative of the working class in any way. But even he was smeared with dirt to create a basis for an "independent foreign policy". In the background of this wave, in this anti-socialist background, the tendencies for a "Czech socialism" came into being. Some said: we need a Masaryk socialism, not a Marxist socialism! And what happens after that, Comrade Dubček, Comrade Černík, Comrade Lenárt? Well, what happens next? For now it is still called Masaryk socialism. What are you going to come up against during the second phase? You say: there are huge economic difficulties in Czechoslovakia. And whose fault is that? The system of socialism was to blame. Friendship with the Soviet Union, economic cooperation with the Soviet Union and the other socialist countries was to blame. A way has to be found to the West. Credits and aid in general have to be received. You stated this as a cover-up. That the prosperity of the workers must be taken care of, that is a cover-up. The policy and the goal is to disrupt and tear apart the economic cooperation. We are, of course, not of the opinion that Czechoslovakia has managed to achieve everything. Even we have not yet achieved everything. All fraternal parties are making efforts to strengthen their economies. We are helping each other. We will probably need to work for a good many years in this area until we will have reached the right level. But we must state that no situation in Czechoslovakia justifies attacks on the party and government, because such difficulties would arise that demand the abandonment of cooperation with the socialist countries, and above all with the Soviet Union, which allegedly has been robbing Czechoslovakia. That's exactly the phrase used in your country. I do not know if you have enough time to read your own press. But we are obliged to read it, and we are very concerned. This is, so to speak, the general tone. Radio, TV and press are without leadership, without guidance. You do not need any special proof for that.

The comrades themselves know this. It is perhaps a bitter truth. But if you are communists, Leninists, then you have to get to the bottom of this truth. [. . .]

I cannot exhaustively deal with everything which has caught the attention of our Politburo. We have spent dozens of hours analyzing the events. We have put all our other work aside, have looked at the documents, have evaluated everything from the political point of view, and have perceived the dangerous trend of events. We would like to tell you as friends: we are still convinced that the situation can be changed, that the counterrevolution can still be dealt a blow. But one needs the desire, the willpower and also the courage in order to implement the necessary actions. We have the authorization of our Politburo to express to you who are present here our hope that you will be able, under the leadership of Dubček, to change the course of events and stop these very dangerous developments. We are ready to give you moral, political and democratic support. I would be glad and happy—and our party would be as well—if I could express at the same time the support of all other parties present. But even if this is not possible. If you disagree, we still cannot remain indifferent to the developments in Czechoslovakia. We are tied to each other by ties of friendship, by commitments of an internationalist nature, by the security of the socialist countries, by the security of our countries. We have a great number of obligations which were signed by our government, and our Central Committee, as well as your government and your Central Committee, obligations which express the popular and party will. For the time being I will finish my statement.

[. . .]

Władysław Gomułka: Our government and our people are concerned about the situation which has developed in fraternal Czechoslovakia since the January Plenum. We consider today's meeting vital. It is necessary for us all, for the representatives of all parties in order to be able to assess by means of an exchange of opinion the situation which has developed not only in Czechoslovakia, but in our camp; and it seems to me that it is particularly necessary for the Czechoslovak comrades to hold this meeting. Our delegation agrees with the assessment which we heard from Comrade Brezhnev who stated the point of view of the Soviet delegation, the

CPSU Politburo, and as we heard, this was a very thorough analysis of the situation. We are completely in agreement with this assessment. We see all the dangers, the real dangers, with which the Czechoslovak party, the Czechoslovak people are confronted, and we are of the opinion that it is still possible today to counter these dangers, I would say, in a peaceful manner, but only with an energetic counter-offensive which, in our opinion, the leadership of the Communist Party of Czechoslovakia would have to take against the counterrevolutionary forces, against the reactionary forces which have appeared and are quite active in Czechoslovakia. It seems to me that it is impossible to say how long this would take in the current situation. Measures will have to be taken immediately, and this has to happen very quickly. This depends, in the opinion of our delegation, particularly on an understanding of the situation, on an understanding by the leadership of the Communist Party of Czechoslovakia, but above all on an understanding of the comrades of the Communist Party of Czechoslovakia present [at this meeting]. We have the impression that, as the first secretary, Comrade Dubček, stated, the leadership of the communist party perhaps underestimated the dangers. Therefore we want to be clearly understood. We are under the same impression as the other delegations. We do not intend to interfere in domestic affairs but there are, of course, situations when so-called domestic affairs naturally become external affairs, thus affairs of the entire socialist camp. We have commonly concluded agreements, and these agreements oblige us, of course, as well, and the Czechoslovak comrades certainly will agree with this completely. But all of what happened in the ČSSR, and in a certain sense in Poland, affects in a certain way our agreements, our pacts, and requires consultations, requires that we take certain measures, frankly, in order to block the path to counterrevolution. The situation is, after all, if I understand correctly, that the Czechoslovak comrades still do not view the matter that way. This is a question, if I may say so, not just of knowing the facts, it is also a matter of experience, of one's own experience and that of others. And we have a little experience ourselves, and from of this experience conclusions must be drawn. Why shouldn't we draw conclusions from the experience which we aquired in 1956 in Poland? Why not draw conclusions from what happened in Hungary? That all began in a similar way, comrades. In our country and in Hungary everything began with the writers. It started with the Petőfi Circle in Hungary, and it is the same [in Poland]—the intellectuals have been acting this way since 1956—this time it was again the case with the writers. And in your country it also started with the intellectuals. Let us look at the reality of the situation correctly, as it happened. In your country it is also coming from there! And it did not start just today! Later it develops into something new. I don't want to remind you, comrades, of the student events in our country; because I have already talked about this subject very extensively before the Warsaw party activists, and there is an extensive evaluation of the situation. I have the impression that this evaluation fits your situation 90%, Czechoslovak comrades. The more you look at it and exchange some facts, the more it looks the same. It starts with the arts. Under the flag of the defense of culture and the defense of freedom, under this mask the enemy, the counterrevolution works, foreign intelligence services work. They want to stir people up and achieve their goals this way. [. . .]

I think what is necessary is the following: We cannot leave here without results. We have to come to certain decisions, to such decisions which are meaningful for internal and external enemies, for the counterrevolution, to decisions which unequivocally state that the counterrevolution will not succeed in Czechoslovakia, that the leadership of the Czechoslovak party and Czechoslovakia's working class will not permit that, that Czechoslovakia's allies, that is, those who are gathered here, will not permit it. This seems to me to be the most important conclusion which we must take from today's meeting.

János Kádár: [. . .] I want to say that the Central Committee of the Hungarian Workers' Party, the government of the Hungarian People's Republic, and our workers are preoccupied with their normal planned tasks. But I have to add that, starting with the Politburo and the Central

Committee of our party, our entire public has been intensively concerned with the situation in Czechoslovakia for two, three months. This is, after all, understandable. The people in our country are very much concerned with the situation which has developed there, and they are also concerned with the question of what will happen. I want to move on to the subject which has been mainly dealt with here. Above all I want to express, in the name of the comrades of our party assembled here, our gratitude for the information which Comrade Dubček gave, and for the deliberations which he laid out here and with which the Czechoslovak comrades are concerned. I also consider it necessary to underline that we are, like Comrade Brezhnev and Comrade Gomułka, of the opinion that the events concern the internal affairs of the Czechoslovak party and that the right to make decisions lies with the Czechoslovak comrades, and that we of course do not have the intention to interfere in domestic affairs, and could not do so. But I would like to add that we stand by the Czechoslovak fraternal party, and the Czechoslovak people and believe and wish that the great and difficult problems which are on the agenda will be resolved successfully, and in a manner by which the Czechoslovak fraternal party and the Czechoslovak Socialist Republic will come out of this situation strengthened. . . . [A]nd the situation today can be justifiably characterized as a critical one. [. . .] The second aspect is that the Czechoslovak comrades have to understand and accept that our parties and our countries are extremely interested in the shape and further development of the Czech situation, that they are also interested in solving the unresolved questions on the agenda in favor of socialism. It is quite understandable, quite clear, why this is so. Above all, because there is a direct connection between important events which happen in any socialist country, and the domestic situation in other socialist countries. This has been confirmed again in this situation. Secondly, as we state in celebratory speeches, not as empty phrases but as reality, that we have common successes as well as common worries. One does not need to clarify especially why this is so, because party membership and public opinion in the socialist countries ask our parties questions regardless of what is happening in other socialist countries, and they expect an answer from us to these questions. The Czechoslovak comrades have to understand this. If we sometimes passionately but with the same feelings and the same intentions raise certain questions, then we ask that it be understood literally that communists have gathered here, comrades, brothers-in-arms, and allies. We have come together and we talk about our common affairs in this capacity. It is extremely important for us to receive in such a situation appropriate information, and statements on all questions; and these are not demands based on non-existent rights but requests which result from the situation. It is necessary to understand the real situation in Czechoslovakia, in order for us to have some idea what the thoughts of the Czechoslovak party leadership are. This is a basic requirement since we have stated that we stand by them. This is the truth. We are honestly convinced of this, and we state that we have to come together, we have to help each other and work together. For this, we should, of course, have very detailed information as to where we need to, and must, help each other, since it is otherwise very difficult for our parties to make their respective decisions. We also need the statements and information from the Czechoslovak comrades because we have certain obligations toward our party members, toward public opinion in our countries, which we have to keep informed. Only if we receive declarations and information from the Czechoslovak comrades will we be able to report on the situation there. If we do not receive information, we nevertheless need to give some information to our comrades but we will give information based on our own conclusions, comrades, and we may perhaps have to diverge from your point of view, from the Czechoslovak point of view. I want to talk about some questions, for example general questions. Comrade Gomułka already touched upon the fact, and I agree with him, that there are certain historical experiences, for example direct ones, which relate above all to Hungary and Poland, where a few years ago similar events already took place. We are of the opinion that this is a shared experience which we all will need to take advantage of. Of course, we always add that even within our own ranks, in the most intimate circle, when we talk about it in the Politburo, there are great differences. But at the same time one should not deny that there are very many similar aspects. I have to state frankly, comrades, that we have to understand that the situation in the Czechoslovak Socialist Republic and within the Czechoslovak fraternal party is very complicated. We also know that not only what the Central Committee or Comrade Dubček and his comrades decide comes to pass and occurs, because other forces make decisions there, and that it is very important for us in our estimate of the situation to be able to separate one from the other. The word "counterrevolution in Czechoslovakia" was used here. We have also talked about it. I cannot officially express my opinion in the name of the Politburo and the Central Committee of our party since there have been no decisions with regard to the situation in the ČSSR; but there have been information and exchanges of opinion several times, and what we say here expresses the opinion of our Central Committee and the Politburo. The Czechoslovak comrades know best, I believe, what is happening in Czechoslovakia today. But the process which we observe, what we see and hear, and what we do not yet see—permit me to explain—this process is extremely similar to the prologue of the Hungarian counterrevolution at a time when it had not yet become a counter-revolution. This means that this is the process which took place in Hungary from February 1956 to the end of October. And we ask you to think about this. [. . .]

Ulbricht: [. . .] In a situation in which we all are interested in having the socialist camp and the Warsaw Pact countries appear unanimous, now that U.S. imperialism and its global strategy is in a difficult position, exactly in this situation you start letting down your own party, you give the enemy material for a campaign against the socialist countries. And West German imperialism, of course, exploits this and is running a massive campaign. Look, Comrade Dubček, I do not even blame the leadership as it has been elected now. I will tell you frankly that this development has been going on for six or seven years. Five years ago the capitalist world press had already written that Czechoslovakia was the most advantageous point from which to penetrate the socialist camp. Why? Because within your intelligentsia—I am speaking now of writers and artists—the Western oriented forces are the strongest. Perhaps some Soviet and other comrades will not quite understand this, because actually it should be [the GDR] where [that] ideology is the strongest since we are, after all, a divided country. But the odd fact of history is that Western influence is strongest in Czechoslovakia. And why? Because for 10 years no ideological battle has been fought there, no systematic ideological fight, not for 10 years! This is a fact. Now this all boils over, now we see it all in black and white. Previously it had been covered up. There was the discussion about Kafka, then about other issues. It was mashed as democracy, as humanism. Now the matter is clear, now it is all concentrated. But this is a development of five to eight years. Now, comrades, let us talk once very openly. Novotný bore a great responsibility as first secretary, but Novotný after all was not the only member of the Central Committee in this entire time! Other comrades were in the Central Committee and in the party leadership besides Novotný and a few others. [. . .]

Todorov: [. . .] The communists in Bulgaria are concerned about the fact that such a strong party as the Czechoslovak one is being attacked by unhealthy elements in such a negative fashion. The Bulgarian communists wonder why the leading party of the working class did not respond adequately and in a timely way to the questions raised. Instead opinions on the great principal questions were presented in such a spontaneous manner that some resulted in the distortion of Marxist–Leninist practice. Principles on the construction of socialism, even in the area of politics and on relations with the fraternal parties, are stated in new ways by which the role of the communist party in the construction of socialist society is decreased. Various people play games with young people, abuse them. Criticism of mistakes made becomes degradation, a negation of the 20 years of achievements of the Czechoslovak republic. Apparently some of the positions of some unhealthy elements in the ČSSR who have been misled, who have been deluded, coincide with the positions and intentions of the enemy of socialism, who have the objective of dividing the cadres and playing them off against each other, of weakening the party, who obviously, above all, wish to break the backbone of the party which has carried the major load, the heaviest burden in the antifascist struggle and in the construction of socialism. It does not seem normal to us that some representatives of Czechoslovakia, such as Smrkovský, present the political line and explain their political objectives on West German radio, not in the appropriate bodies of the party. We do not understand why the right of the party to lay out the main line in the media is permitted. Moreover and finally, it is completely incomprehensible to us how one can tolerate opinions which are in the interest of the bourgeoisie and constitute a mesh of bourgeois democracy and socialism.

Kosygin: [. . .] It can probably now be said without doubt that the entire world is currently looking at Czechoslovakia. The attention of the entire world, of all forces which fight along with us, is currently focused on the events in the ČSSR. This is completely natural because the ČSSR is at present the chain link where the forces of socialism, of progress and the forces of communism and imperialism evidently intersect. If we look at the international press altogether, we see that the entire international press is commenting on the Czechoslovak events two or three times a day. These are no singular instances, nor temporary events. These are events which the imperialists will not let rest until they have been severely rebuked. It is currently a fact that the organs which convey the thoughts of the leadership and our thoughts to each worker, farmer, student, and intellectual, are in the hands of the enemy. These are the TV, radio and even the newspapers. There is no need for me to explain and expose all of the massive material which is in our hands and to state all the occurrences in the Czechoslovak press. I would only like to discuss those issues which are currently of interest to the Czechoslovak press, that is the negative comments on the relations between the ČSSR and the USSR. You find such negative statements in the press of the ČSSR almost every day, statements which are directed against the international communist movement, statements against the Council on Mutual Economic Assistance. Then there are contrasting remarks on the role of the party, in particular with regard to [its] approach toward the development of a socialist position. This is a problem which concerns the entire socialist camp. These problems concern not only the entire socialist camp but our entire international communist movement. I have to say that the events in the ČSSR also appear in the entire communist press and communists worldwide worry about it. For this reason our collaboration today is of a very, very important nature. The leadership of the Czechoslovak Socialist Republic and of the government of the ČSSR have to find a resolution, a remedy to the situation in which the ČSSR finds itself now. I would like to say that besides these general political problems in the ČSSR, economic issues will now be dealt with in a very far-reaching manner, with the discussion proceeding in various ways. For quite a long time, for at least two months, I have not found a single article in the Czech press which supports socialist cooperation in the field of economics. If you check these articles, you only find critical remarks. You do not find a single article which actively states that the economic collaboration of the socialist countries is the only correct solution for the further development of the ČSSR economy.

[. . .]

Jozef Lenárt: I would like to make a few remarks. Above all I think that we were told much we can learn from by Comrade Brezhnev, by Comrades Gomułka, Kádár, Ulbricht and other comrades who appeared here. We cannot counter the facts which have been listed here, and we ourselves can add such facts. We could offer, as an example, how the reactionary Catholic clergy is becoming more active, something we view as an important element in the current situation. This is one facet.

On the other hand, I believe the following: The characterization of the situation in Czechoslovakia given here sounds as if a state of counterrevolution has already occurred. I do not know if this evaluation is correct. I think that, as far as I know the situation, we are not dealing with a counterrevolution at this point. This is the first point. The second question is whether a counterrevolution is at all possible.

I say: Yes, counterrevolution in Czechoslovakia is possible in a situation in which our party, our governmental order fall into passivity and leave the field to spontaneous developments of the situation, in which our party leadership and our state leadership do not at present proceed on grounds of principle and flexibility. As far as I know Comrade Dubček and the core of the comrades in the CC and in the districts and counties, the situation can be characterized as one in which the party is capable today of mastering the situation with principle and flexibility. [. . .]

Drahomír Kolder: For the first time I am able to participate in such an important consultation. Of course, we have to be concerned after the cold shower which we received here. Above all I think we need to make available to our comrades the minutes of the December and January plenums, on the basis of which it can be seen that these plenums undertook a deep political analysis of the situation in our countries, that it was not about a gathering of officials but about a principled discussion in which 152 members and candidates of the CC participated. Secondly, I think that we have to send our comrades in the central committees of the fraternal parties official information, estimates on how the situation in the party is developing without underestimating the danger which we see as well, with regard to the impact of the mass media. So much as an introduction.

Now, comrades, regarding the main question: Above all I understand that there is the question: How can one characterize the current situation in our country? After hearing the comrades' statements, there are two views: According to the first point of view, a counterrevolutionary situation exists in our country. According to the second view, today's situation is critical and measures have to be taken to master the situation. We came together for a meeting on economic questions—this was what we were told. We have not had the opportunity to consult here. But in the Presidium we assessed the situation the day before yesterday. In my opinion, the situation today is complicated, is critical, and we—as they say, the Komsomols of this leadership—have to undergo a great Leninist test if we are to master the situation. In assessing and evaluating the situation, questions about the causes have to be asked above all else, how this situation came about. The analysis of causes allows us to find the correct solution. [. . .]

Oldřich Černík: This is my first time at such an important meeting of the representatives of the fraternal party [sic]. I would like to say right away that we have had very harsh words directed at us, at the five of us who represent the communist party here. In the spirit of our internationalist relations we can assure you that we will give serious thought to what has been said, and not only that: What we in the Presidium and the CC consider correct, necessary and useful for our work, we will implement. Everybody was convinced that everything is in order in our party. We both certainly have an interest in a strong Czechoslovakia, in a strong communist party. Unfortunately the situation has developed so that, given the impression that the party was strong and our relations firm, we did not imagine that something unhealthy could develop. We have started a general discussion in our party about our party the only objective being that the party will emerge stronger out of the resulting discussion and facts. One gets the impression that we should feel guilty that we started to improve party work. I will pass to an assessment of today's discussion, from two viewpoints:

What is the situation in Czechoslovakia? Is it a counterrevolutionary situation, or is it of a mostly pro-socialist nature? Comrades, for this we need very profound analyses, factual analyses. A one-sided assessment of the situation does not help us or our party. We have to know the motives of the people, have to know how they act and what they do in order to be able to explain that such-and-such a situation exists. We in the party leadership—we will also convey this assessment to the CC—are of the opinion that the situation is serious, that the danger of an attack from left or right exists, and that progressive forces do exist. But we see today's state of affairs in Czechoslovakia as overwhelmingly progressive and pro-socialist in character. What do we base this on? Comrades, since February 1948 we have not had such waves of political interest within our party, such activity of the working class and intelligentsia, as we now witness.

Thousands of meetings are being held, in factories, villages and cities. The halls are overcrowded, and the party members are implementing and defending the policy of the party. Millions of people attend the party meetings and other gatherings. For years we have had a situation in which halls had been empty, passivity was evident and increasing. We stated that a certain degree of passivity among the masses and party membership existed. We said that we could not blame the masses but the leadership for this. We, comrades, can say that our party has a very healthy core. That which is happening within our party and within our society—believe us, comrades—is not creating an atmosphere of fear. There is an unusual interest in the political life of Czechoslovakia, in the fate of socialism.

DOCUMENT No. 15: Alexander Dubček's Presidium Report on the Dresden Meeting, March 25, 1968

Source: ÚSD, AÚV KSČ, F. 02/1; Vondrová & Navrátil, vol. 1, pp. 117–119.

First Secretary Dubček presented this report to the CPCz CC Presidium just after the Dresden conference of March 23. It begins, however, with brief comments about a meeting of the Warsaw Pact's chief political organ, the Political Consultative Committee (PCC), in Sofia on March 6.

On the Dresden talks, Dubček conveys only the barest outline of the multilateral discussions, downplaying the harsh criticisms and belligerent questioning from other leaders like Gomułka and Ulbricht, and the general displeasure of the Soviet authorities. Conceding that the internal situation in Czechoslovakia was discussed at Dresden, Dubček reports that "the specific concerns and advice we heard were prompted by the fact that the comrades are on our side and want things to work out."

Information on the Experience of the CPCz Central Committee Delegation at the Meeting of Six Communist Parties in Dresden, 23 March 1968 (Dubček orally)

On my return from the meeting of the Political Consultative Committee in Sofia I informed you that at the end of the meeting there was a consultation among six of the communist parties.[30] I told you that in this loose gathering new questions were raised in the discussion on the work of CMEA, the Political Consultative Committee, and the international communist movement. It was noted at the meeting that judging from experience, measures within CMEA, the economic division of labor, and other matters could not always be settled with the participation of every member state. It was further pointed out that the proposals for modifying the Joint Command had still not been settled, and that the question of whether to rotate the headquarters of the Warsaw Pact has also not been resolved yet.[31] As became evident at the meeting in Sofia, no common language could be found when discussing moves in the United Nations on the non-proliferation of nuclear weapons.[32]

In Sofia we noted that it would be desirable if these six communist parties were to meet from time to time to discuss the conclusions and measures on which a common language could be found. At the first meeting of the six, a joint procedure was agreed on action to take in the UN when the non-proliferation of nuclear weapons was discussed. This was soon achieved with the proviso that every country would have the right to state its own position. It was also said that it

---

[30] The Sofia meeting began with all seven members of the Warsaw Pact. When it became clear at the start of the PCC meeting that Romania disagreed with most of the Soviet Union's proposals on how to reorganize the alliance, the other six states decided to meet separately, leaving Romania on the sidelines. This decision may have seemed expedient and "desirable" (to use Dubček's phrase) at the time, but for Czechoslovakia the precedent of going along with the ostracism of a pact member turned out to be a crucial mistake. Subsequently, the group of "Six" that had excluded Romania became a group of "Five" arrayed against Czechoslovakia.

[31] Since the mid-1960s, the East European members of the Warsaw Pact, especially Romania, had been attempting to gain a greater say in the pact's decisions and activities. One proposed way to achieve this was through a restructuring of the Joint Command that would permit East European officers to serve in high-level posts, which had previously been reserved exclusively for Soviet marshals and generals. Another idea was to rotate the headquarters of the pact periodically from country to country, rather than always having it in Moscow.

[32] The Treaty on the Non-Proliferation of Nuclear Weapons (NPT) was signed in 1968 after many years of debate in the United Nations and other international bodies. A few of the East European countries, most notably Romania, had raised serious questions about the connection between the treaty and the procedures for nuclear weapons decision-making within the Warsaw Pact. Ceaușescu refused to sign the joint statement on the NPT that emanated from the Sofia meeting, much to the Soviet Union's dismay.

would be good to come back to some other issues. Cde. Kádár mentioned the experience of the Budapest meeting.[33]

The main conclusion of the Sofia meeting was that it would be good to meet more often in a group of this composition.

So we met in Dresden. I would like to say that we were reassured in our view on the procedure and need to strengthen the Warsaw Pact. This means that in the coming period the members of these communist parties and the representatives of these states will have to work faster in preparing a proposal about the Joint Command, the Military Council, and the Technical Committee.[34] We adopted the communiqué without discussion.

Cde. Kosygin spoke about certain questions pertaining to economic cooperation of the states within CMEA and updated certain political aspects. What problems were these? First, in his speech Cde. Kosygin said that the proposal of mutual cooperation within CMEA was very good and that positive results had been attained. He mentioned these results because he felt that they were being approached in a pessimistic manner, and that the community of socialist states was experiencing good results in economic cooperation. In this context he said it was necessary to take advantage of the positive results of our economic cooperation.

In our propaganda it will be necessary, so to speak, to avoid downplaying this factor and to highlight the positive results of economic cooperation. He pointed to further possibilities of deepening economic cooperation. He mentioned that in their country there are huge crude oil deposits (about 11 billion tons). Why did he mention this? He wanted to show that far from all possibilities of cooperation are being exploited within the CMEA and that they as a country with raw material reserves are able to go further. He said there would have to be a race against time, as in the case of the construction of the gas pipeline, etc.

He also spoke about the economic conditions in the United States. This section was amazing for many comrades. What was so surprising? His contention was that the United States is approaching a real shock. The problem concerns the value of the dollar. The United States is looking for a way of propping up the dollar. It resorted to and is still taking a number of internal measures. It has even turned to the Soviet Union. He said that as a result of this state of affairs the economic situation was not very good.

It was also said that the State Planning Commissions of countries working on Five-Year Plans should work more efficiently and aim to coordinate to a certain extent. Cde. Kosygin's remarks made it clear that things had to be worked out better and taken up more actively. Officials from individual states should get together and prepare materials for top-level negotiations in order to find further ways of economic collaboration.

There was also an exchange of views and information at the meeting about our communist parties. I would like to say that in my introduction I spoke about certain conclusions of the January CPCz CC plenum and about its consequences. I also spoke about the preparation for the March plenum of the CPCz CC and certain connections. Other comrades spoke after me. What was there in common? There was some concern that certain activities should not be misused in our development. Cde. Gomułka spoke about the Polish experience, or how certain elements were hangers-on of the new movement. The parties must always remember this.

I can say that the specific concerns and advice we heard were prompted by the fact that the comrades are on our side and want things to work out.[35]

---

[33] Kádár is referring to the meeting in Budapest in late February 1968, held in preparation for the worldwide communist party conference scheduled for November.

[34] Proposals to create the second and third of these bodies had been bandied about since the mid-1960s, but no action had been taken by the time of the invasion. Not until March 1969 was the pact restructured, and even then the modifications did not go as far as most of the East European states had hoped.

[35] Dubček's misrepresentation of the criticisms and pressure leveled at his government at Dresden reflected a tendency he displayed throughout the Prague Spring of withholding certain negative information both from his colleagues and from the public. Apparently, he feared that if he revealed the true extent of Soviet and East European "interference in

Cde. Gomułka recalled the situation in his country. There they have problems with anti-Soviet attitudes and religious fanaticism. Then there are the Zionist problems.[36] They have difficulties. And now we are pushing things. We ought to give the comrades the materials of the Central Committee session. Cde. Koucký should prepare them for the six parties and later we will have to consider how to inform our representatives in the socialist countries and in the capitalist ones as well.[37]

Cde. Kolder: Their views are mostly printed in our press. The comrades are concerned and worried whether the party will manage to deal with the situation.

Cde. Biľak: They were astonished that the resignation of the president of the republic took place before the Central Committee plenum. In addition, regional secretaries are resigning and they are asking whether this was because of their disagreement with the policy after the January plenum.

Cde. Lenárt: They clearly do not have sufficient information about the district conferences. There was talk about the question of criticism. How were developments progressing? Whether this would not reflect on living standards. They said: We are allies, we want to know things. The Slovak question, too, was explained there.

Czechoslovakia's internal affairs," it would heighten tensions and lend impetus to a public backlash against Czechoslovakia's Warsaw Pact allies, prompting them to engage in further attacks of their own. Although Dubček, as he later acknowledged, was often uneasy about putting a better gloss on events than was actually warranted, he believed that too candid a presentation would merely provoke a reaction that everybody would later regret. After the invasion, however, the fact that Dubček had at times withheld information from the Presidium and the Central Committee, as well as from the public, became one of the charges lodged against him by hard-line CPCz officials.

[36] Under pressure from hard-line nationalists and from one of his chief political rivals, Edward Gierek, Gomułka had promoted a widespread anti-Semitic campaign in Poland in the spring of 1968.

[37] At the time Vladimír Koucký was still a CPCz CC secretary, a post from which he was removed at the April 1968 plenum of the CPCz CC. Soon thereafter he was appointed Czechoslovak ambassador in Moscow, replacing Oldřich Pavlovský.

DOCUMENT No. 16: Open Letter from 134 Czechoslovak Writers and Cultural Figures to the CPCz Central Committee, March 25, 1968

Source: "Otevřený dopis 134 čs. spisovatelů a kulturních pracovníků ÚV KSČ,"
Literární listy (Prague), No. 5 (March 28, 1968), p. 1.

Published in the immediate aftermath of the Dresden meeting, this open letter dramatizes the extent of support that the reform process had generated among the intelligentsia and cultural elite in Czechoslovakia. Signed by many of the country's most celebrated artists and writers, including Jaroslav Seifert (later a Nobel Prize winner), the letter urges the CPCz Central Committee to preserve and build on the reforms that had begun with the January 1968 plenum. The signatories referred directly to the Dresden communiqué when they exhorted the CPCz leadership to continue "standing up to pressure motivated by doubts about the nature and objectives of our internal measures" and to bear in mind "that your responsibility for this country is above all for its own people."

The pressure that CPCz leaders encountered at Dresden was one of the major factors behind the letter's publication; another important consideration for the 134 signatories was the high-level personnel changes that had occurred in late February and March, especially the dismissal of Novotný from the presidency. Although most of the new appointees were of a distinctly reformist bent, the signatories of the letter wanted to "democratize" the selection process—through public input and discussion of nominees—so that popular support for reform would have a direct bearing on those responsible for governing the country.

---

25 March 1968

Esteemed Comrades!

We are appealing to you at a time when, we believe, political developments in Czechoslovakia are entering a new phase. The resignation of Antonín Novotný as president of the republic was a sign of important change at home, while the preceding phase was marked by growing political activity among our citizens. And the reputation of communists has also improved thanks to those who have been carrying out the proposals of the December and January sessions of the CPCz Central Committee soberly, judiciously, and with determination. The great majority of the citizens of our state are confident that things will turn out for the better—by this they understand unequivocally the socialist character of our society. What is most gratifying in this process is that the project for democratic socialism has been taken up by the younger generation, who consider it exciting and remarkable.

Nevertheless, comrades, we would like to draw your attention to several points whose solution will be viewed as a litmus test of the sincerity of all statements about democratic socialism. The first point concerns international relations. We know and understand that on various occasions delegations of the CPCz are obliged to explain the nature of the democratization process in our country to other communist parties. We realize what we owe the socialist countries and our allies. However, the Dresden communiqué, for example, has made it clear to us that the CPCz CC must stand up to pressure motivated by doubts about the nature and objectives of our internal measures. Thus, although we want to assure you that you have our full support in all your statements, we emphasize that the need to maintain international solidarity among socialist states should not cause you to forget that your responsibility for this country is above all to its own people.

We see the current democratization process as a road that will lead to permanent democracy, and not as a process in which certain people are to be replaced by others while their thinking and working methods remain unchanged. That is why we attach major importance to the question of who will be appointed to vacated high posts in the state, and to the way this is going to be done. We believe it would not be appropriate to the situation if decisions on this matter were made exclusively after internal discussions in certain organs—in other words, decisions made behind closed doors. In our view, decision-making will have taken on a truly democratic shape only if the public is informed about proposed changes and is given the chance to express its views on them in various quarters. We know that until the elections we must live with some kind of provisional arrangement based on "a word of honor." But even though we have no new deputies in Parliament we are now on the threshold of electing a new president. That is why it is especially important to know who the candidates for this office will be. We are convinced that the deputies will be able to cast their votes in accordance with the wishes of the people only if the candidates are able to live up to the public's expectation that the president should be a generally respected and well-known person with the kind of energy needed to cope with this post—a person, in other words, who is capable of independent and penetrating thought. In our view, it goes without saying that this must be someone involved in the democratization efforts so that their election will be ample evidence of the fact that democratization is really gaining the upper hand.

We therefore expect a president who is sufficiently firm but also judicious, educated, and astute, someone whose arrival in office can rectify the moral damage that the office of the president has suffered in past years. We would consider it ideal if someone is chosen who is linked with the workers but close to the intelligentsia or the other way around. We are therefore hoping for a sufficiently dynamic personality who would play a full part in the first stage of socialist democratization, but we also expect that in the subsequent phase this person will be properly limited in keeping with the future constitution. We believe that the same yardstick must be applied to the future prime minister. We also believe that maximum attention must be given to changes in the government. We agree with the demand often heard nowadays that major ministries such as the Ministry of Interior and the Ministry of National Defense must be entrusted to people known to the public for their favorable qualities and whose character alone would provide guarantees that they would not abuse their power. With regard to the minister of national defense, we would like this to be someone known at least in the army for his work on behalf of worthy objectives, someone whose progressive views and democratic thinking did not emerge only this past January. We state that this is not merely a question of filling a post but of cleaning the slate.

Recently, we have done our best to demonstrate that we were anxious to bring Czechoslovak socialism out of its tragic isolation. But our past commitment also pledges us to react to phenomena that may signal stagnation and, later on, even a reversal of our course. That, comrades, is how we want you to understand the motives behind these words. . . .

DOCUMENT No. 17: Soviet Reactions to Events in Czechoslovakia and the Dresden Meeting, as Assessed by the Italian Embassy in Moscow, April 1968

Source: ÚSD, AÚV KSČ, F. 07/15.

This report, prepared by the Italian embassy in Moscow shortly after the Dresden conference, contains both general observations about the situation in Czechoslovakia and specific comments on the meetings in Dresden. The report suggests that the liberalization in Czechoslovakia had raised widespread fears in Moscow about the risk of a political "spill-over" into other Warsaw Pact countries, including the Soviet Union itself. It also addresses the potential effect the reforms would have on Czechoslovakia's role in CMEA. The report predicts that Moscow would, if necessary, resort to strict economic sanctions to bring Czechoslovakia back into line, arguing that the "decline in power of the Soviet regime" ensured that Moscow would be "unable to impose its will on Czechoslovakia by armed force as it had done in Budapest in 1956."

TOP SECRET
INFORMATION

Obtained by the Italian Embassy in Moscow[38]

To a large extent, Czechoslovakia's drama and its recent attempts to establish socialist democracy in the country will be determined by the country's geographical position and economic situation, as well as by the political and economic relations that tie the country to the Soviet Union and the other CMEA countries. . . .

. . . Roughly one-third of Czechoslovak foreign trade is with the Soviet Union, and the total value of Czechoslovakia's trade with the socialist countries, including the USSR, amounts to nearly 70 percent of its total foreign trade. One must realize that virtually all raw material supplies such as energy resources and industrial raw materials (crude oil, gas, iron ore, fertilizer, cotton) come from the Soviet Union, while a large portion of Czechoslovak exports, including industrial equipment, machinery, and finished industrial goods, are absorbed by the Soviet market. Even if we leave aside political, military, and ideological factors, which also play a significant role, the economic ties that exist between Czechoslovakia, on the one hand, and the Soviet Union and the other CMEA countries, on the other, will be a formidable barrier to the efforts of Czechoslovakia's new political leadership.[39] These ties will hamper the leadership's attempts to go even some way toward meeting the urgent demands of the people for the liberalization and democratization of political, social, and economic life in the country. *It goes without saying that the leaders of the other CMEA countries—and, above all, the leaders of the Soviet Union—cannot permit Prague to choose its own national road of building socialism,* which in the case of Czechoslovakia would be even more dangerous than Togliatti's well-known dictum.[40] For if the

---

[38] The authors of the report are not identified. The Italian ambassador at the time was Federico Sensi, and the report presumably was issued in his name.

[39] Many of these same points were emphasized by Nikolai Baibakov, the head of the Soviet State Planning Commission, in a classified memorandum to a senior member of the CPSU Politburo, Andrei Kirilenko, on 26 July 1968 (TsKhSD, F. 5, Op. 60, D. 562, Ll. 3–12).

[40] The allusion here could be to any of several phrases coined by the long-time Italian Communist Party leader, Palmiro Togliatti. In the mid-1930s Togliatti proposed that the ICP aim for a "democracy of a new type" as an alternative to a "proletarian dictatorship." The phrase quickly caught on among other West European communists. Later on, in 1956, Togliatti devised the concepts of "unity in diversity" and "polycentrism" to promote greater independence among the

Czechoslovaks sought to democratize communism in earnest, *this would mean the destruction of communism for Soviet ideologues.*

It is clear that what Moscow really fears is not economic reform. After all, the other CMEA member countries, including the Soviet Union, have embarked on reform themselves. What really terrifies Moscow is the will of the Czechoslovak people to *rid itself once and for all of the heavy bonds of bureaucracy,* which have been patterned after the Soviet model. Over the past twenty years these bonds have ravaged Czechoslovakia's economy, which in the past was on a high level of industrialization and technology. Thanks to these bureaucratic methods Czechoslovakia has dropped to the level of the Soviet Union, which itself is only just emerging from the stage of an essentially agricultural economy.

The fact that Prague is determined to overcome its bureaucracy is demonstrated not only by the words and speeches of political and economic representatives and Czech intellectuals, but also by the administrative measures recently adopted in Czechoslovakia to carry out changes in the posts and organization of public institutions that have the task of running the country's economic life.

If Prague abandons directive-style centralized planning within the country and refuses to coordinate its economic development plans with those of the Soviet Union and the other countries of the socialist camp, and if it strives to enlarge its economic and trade relations with Western countries, including West Germany, what will the CMEA do and how will it end?

If Prague really succeeds in introducing its own political, economic, and social structures as part of its democratization process, what would the consequences be and what would the repercussions be in countries such as Poland, Hungary, Romania, and even the GDR where the population is desperate for more freedom and greater prosperity? Not even the Soviet Union could escape the turmoil and unrest, and the consequences for the entire socialist movement and the ideological and political position of the Soviet Union could be unpredictable.

These uncertainties have irritated, and still irritate and anger, Soviet officials, who at the Dresden meeting, with the assistance of the Bulgarians, Hungarians, Poles and East Germans, did their best to convince Czechoslovakia not to force the situation at such speed and to avoid excessive changes in the political, economic, and social structure of the country.

According to reports that have been leaked to us, *these are the arguments the Soviets used in Dresden*:

1. The right of each individual state of the socialist camp is confirmed to carry out the type of economic reform deemed inevitable and suitable to adapt to new requirements and new production technologies.

2. *The reforms must not transgress the fundamental principles of the socialist organization of the economy of the country concerned*; these fundamental principles are collective ownership of the means of production and *centralized economic planning.*

3. Under no circumstances must the reforms detract from the supreme interest of a socialist country in *forming a bloc together with the other friendly parties and governments of the socialist camp.*

4. It is too dangerous to give free rein to the liberalization efforts of the mass of the Czechoslovak population, especially students and intellectuals. The Soviets are said to have warned that the situation may easily get out of hand even for reformers who mean well. The methods used to restore a normal situation could be extremely painful and, in many cases downright bad.

---

world's communist parties and to deny that a "single directing party" (as the CPSU had long styled itself) could exist in the communist movement. Although Togliatti subsequently watered down his commitment to independence from the CPSU (he endorsed the invasion of Hungary, for example), he continued to espouse the desirability of a unique "Italian path (via italiana) to socialism."

The Soviets reportedly made *the following proposals* to their Czechoslovak comrades:

a) Maximum financial, economic, and technical assistance by the Soviet Union and the other socialist states to Czechoslovakia during this highly delicate phase of the latter's economic development.

b) Maximum support for the current political leaders of the ČSSR to be in a better position to control internal turmoil and elements opposing the regime as well as centrifugal tendencies vis-à-vis the CMEA of certain industrial and economic sectors in Czechoslovakia.

To ensure that resources are available to achieve the targets mentioned under a), the participants in the Dresden conference decided to call an economic summit to be attended by the chairmen of the parties and governments of the CMEA member countries.

In Dresden the Soviets scored a tactical success since they succeeded in putting a brake on and blocking attempts to jeopardize the cohesion and unity of the CMEA at least temporarily, as well as efforts to undermine the political and ideological power that the Kremlin has been usurping.

A tactical success is, however, not victory; it is more a way out for someone who feels they have neither the means nor the strength to bring about a decisive and definitive solution.

The Dresden conference is also very important because it revealed the decline in power of the Soviet regime, which is today no longer in a position to order an excommunication as in the case of Belgrade in 1948 and is unable to impose its will on Czechoslovakia by armed force as in Budapest in 1956. It can merely recommend moderation, promise help, and, in the worst of cases, threaten to use possible economic sanctions.

The only weapon Moscow possesses and is able to use against the rebels in Prague is *economic ransom.* Without the Soviet Union the Czechoslovak economy would collapse straightaway, since the country has no raw materials for its industry nor other markets where the Czechoslovaks could sell their products. The country certainly has no market that would be equal to the Soviet market. The conclusion it can draw is that two dramas—that is, the drama of Czechoslovakia, which would like to carry out a swift democratization of its political, economic, and social life, but is unable to; and the drama of the Soviet Union, which wants to stop the course of history, but cannot—are taking place, at times even pitifully, on the same stage.

In the coming days and months we will witness further acts of those two dramas, which will most likely proceed without ostentatious effects, since the two main propagandists (the main actors) are not keen to bring the situation to a head. Prague is certain to want to carry out its reforms in peace—not only in the economic but also in the political and social fields—and to avoid stirring up too many domestic and foreign conflicts, whereas Moscow wants everything to take place in a surreptitious manner so that the CMEA is not impaired or destroyed and, most important of all, so that the germ of democratization from Czechoslovakia and Poland should not spill over and spread even to the territory of Mother Russia.

It is probable that at the next economic summit to be attended by all CMEA countries, a large number of major concessions will be made to Czechoslovakia in the sphere of finance and the economy, while the screw is being tightened on possible excesses of liberalization by Soviet intellectuals. Brezhnev confirmed this in his speech at the 19th conference of party organizations in Moscow on 29 March and at the recent CPSU Central Committee session.

DOCUMENT No. 18: Dispatch from Budapest Outlining Hungarian Concerns about Events in Czechoslovakia after the Dresden Meeting, April 6, 1968

Source: Sb. KV, K—Archiv MZV, Dispatches Received 2950/1968; Vondrová & Navrátil, vol. 1, pp. 128–129.

This cable, from the Czechoslovak ambassador in Budapest, Jozef Púčik, transmits a summary of a meeting of the HSWP Politburo a few days after the Dresden conference. The views of Zoltán Komócsin, that the CPCz "had lost control of events and that decisions about the way things in the ČSSR should proceed were now being made in the streets," are highlighted. Although Komócsin publicly defended the Prague Spring, privately he predicts to the Politburo that Czechoslovakia is on its way to becoming a "bourgeois democracy."

The cable includes a final paragraph on a comment by an official from the Bulgarian embassy in Budapest, V. Pangelov. Pangelov asserts that Czechoslovakia is of greater security importance to the Warsaw Pact than even the GDR, and predicts that the socialist countries will resort to joint military intervention in Czechoslovakia if the Prague Spring creates a "breach in the socialist camp."

The plenary session of the HSWP Central Committee met on 27 March. The press contained only scanty reports about the proceedings. Komócsin reported on the meeting in Dresden, and at a later gathering of top party officials he made an assessment of the events in the ČSSR. He said there had been fundamental changes in the political life of the ČSSR, which were continuing. The HSWP was worried that as the situation unfolded, the Action Program would gradually take on a revisionist character. The HSWP had expected the situation to calm down after the January CPCz plenary session, but the very opposite happened. They were afraid that a situation analogous to that in Hungary in 1956 would arise. Komócsin said they had told this to Dubček, who rejected such an allegation, arguing that Prague would not become Budapest. Dubček went on to say that an internal revolution and a process of renewal were taking place in the ČSSR gradually, and that political leadership was firmly under the control of the CPCz. The HSWP did not share this assessment and did not agree.[41] The HSWP had its own information indicating that the communist party in the ČSSR had lost control of events and that decisions about the way things in the ČSSR should proceed were now being made in the streets rather than in the CC. The Czechoslovak press and radio openly approved efforts to introduce a new electoral law that would provide for a system of bourgeois democracy in the future. There are no signs that the party can regain control over events. Everything is being solved in the streets. Communists, including members of the CPCz Central Committee, have joined forces with elements in the streets and are backing them. They are acting on the basis of their own political platform, including some who want to rehabilitate themselves in the public's eyes and others who wish to do so for their own peace of mind. Some time ago Dubček invited journalists from the press, radio, and television to see him and asked them to stop putting down the results of 20 years of work, to avoid writing in anti-Soviet terms, and to abandon demands for neutrality. Such activities, Dubček said, were giving impetus to a pro-Western orientation, and that did not serve the interests of the CPCz. . . .

---

[41] In late May, the HSWP CC International Department prepared a memorandum combining both optimistic and pessimistic views of events in Prague for the HSWP Politburo. For a copy, see "Zapis' besedy s zam. ministra inostrannykh del VNR tov. Karoem Erdei, 29 maya 1968 goda," Cable No. 500 (SECRET) from N. N. Sikachev, minister-counselor at the Soviet embassy in Hungary, to K. V. Rusakov, 30 May 1968, in TsKhSD, F. 5, Op. 60, D. 339, Ll. 2–9.

Pangelov, a secretary at the embassy of the Bulgarian People's Republic, declared that diplomats of the socialist camp in the Hungarian People's Republic were of the same opinion that there must not be a return of capitalism in the ČSSR. It is possible for our camp to lose the GDR but never the ČSSR, which is neither Vietnam nor Korea. It is in the center of Europe. The fate of the world revolution will always be determined in Europe. If there were a breach in the socialist camp, the socialist countries would not hesitate to use military force against the ČSSR as a last resort.

PART THREE

REVISION, REFORM, REVOLUTION?

INTRODUCTION

In April, the Kremlin decided to escalate its interference in Czechoslovakia's internal affairs beyond mere diplomatic pressure. The KGB was directed to step up operations and intelligence gathering in Czechoslovakia. Not surprisingly, KGB agents began filing distorted reports on the advance of counterrevolution in Prague—drawing on similarly slanted information from hard-line anti-Dubček officials, and reflecting the Soviet secret police's own bias against the reform movement. In particular, the KGB focused on the ferment on the cultural and intellectual fronts, labeling writers, artists and poets as the main enemies of the socialist state. This was particularly true after 134 writers and cultural leaders sent an open letter on March 25 to the CPCz, calling for Dubček to "stand up to [external] pressure motivated by doubts about the nature and objectives of our internal measures" (Document No. 16). In April, Andrei Gromyko dispatched a KGB report to the leaders of the Warsaw Pact transmitting alleged intelligence on a "front of intellectuals" in Prague, dedicated to "shake the foundations of the socialist system, undermine the leading role of the CPCz, and compromise Soviet–Czechoslovak friendship" (Document No. 20).

The Action Program of the CPCz

Dubček tried to extricate the CPCz from growing foreign and domestic pressures by pushing through a blueprint for political and economic reform around which progressive forces both in the communist party and in Czechoslovak society could unite. His hope was that this "Action Program" would demonstrate to the rest of the Eastern Bloc that the reforms were quite popular, and not at all threatening to the socialist community. While the plan envisioned small steps toward "political pluralism" and "reform [of] the whole political system so that it will permit the dynamic development of social relations appropriate for socialism," its authors stressed the solidarity of Czechoslovak foreign policy with the Soviet bloc. "We stand resolutely on the side of progress, democracy, and socialism in the struggle by the socialist and democratic forces against the aggressive attempts of world imperialism. . . .The basic orientation of Czechoslovak foreign policy . . . revolves around alliance and cooperation with the Soviet Union and the other socialist states" (Document No. 19).

At the CPCz Central Committee meeting of April 1–5 (the so-called April session), Dubček's Action Program was formally adopted. Its most significant provisions focused on a new concept of "justifying" the party's "leading role in society." The communist party, representing "a monopolistic concentration of power," would be transformed and reorganized into a true political party with a mission "to inspire socialist initiative" rather than dictate it. The party would endeavor to secure its leading role in society through exemplary work and political activity. In addition, the Action Program demanded that the other political parties of the National Front be raised from their present humiliating role of "transmission belts" into "partners whose political work is based on the joint political program of the National Front." Through political reform and a "democratization program of the economy," which envisioned greater independent business activity, the Action Program sought to preserve the socialist order while introducing political and economic pluralism.

The plan did not abandon the principle of the leading role of the communist party nor did it establish the "bourgeois" concept of parliamentary democracy with parties in power and in opposition. It did, however, call for changing the bureaucratic administration of society and its repressive tendencies. The Action Program not only proclaimed but demanded immediate legal steps towards the securing and protection of full civil rights and liberties—freedom of speech, freedom of assembly, freedom to travel—for Czechoslovak citizens. No less significant was the demand for the full rehabilitation of all citizens—communists and non-communists—who had been victims of unlawful practices over the past 20 years. The Action Program also called for "a crucial change in the constitutional arrangement of the relations between Czechs and Slovaks, and to carry out the necessary constitutional modifications." A "socialist federal arrangement," according to the plan, would redress the Slovak problem and provide for "the legal coexistence of two equal nations in a common socialist state."

In addition to traditional ties with the socialist community and developing countries, the section on international relations contained the noteworthy demand for an "active European policy." To prevent Czechoslovakia's isolation, Dubček and his followers sought more active participation in international organizations, especially the UN and its bodies. Prague, according to the plan, "will formulate its own position toward the fundamental problems of world politics" (Document No. 19).

The Soviet Reaction

There was, however, another "April session"—not in Prague but in Moscow. From April 9–10, the CPSU Central Committee met and discussed the situation in Czechoslovakia. The deliberations and conclusions of the CPSU CC were kept secret at the time; its protocol is still not available to historians. However, Brezhnev's retrospective review, contained in his speech to the session of the CPSU Central Committee on July 17, 1968, partly lifted the veil: he confirmed that the Czechoslovak question had been a critical issue at the April session, and that the CPSU had decided on an approach to deal with the so-called Czechoslovak crisis. The essence of Soviet strategy was to provide assistance to the healthy forces, particularly within the CPCz, in order to prevent the loss of socialist achievements in Czechoslovakia and its withdrawal from the "socialist community." Brezhnev stated unequivocally that the Soviet Union would not permit changes in the Czechoslovak social system which might jeopardize Prague's filial role in the Soviet bloc.

Dubček's Action Program, in fact, called for such changes in areas which Moscow considered of fundamental importance and sensitivity. In what he called a "friendly letter" dated April 11, Brezhnev informed Dubček of the issues that "disturb me" and the Kremlin: any challenge to the party and its leading role, ideological impurity, lack of restraint on the mass media, and the question of "loyalty to the Warsaw Pact." Using a fraternal tone, Brezhnev warned Dubček "that events are still not unfolding in quite the way that the CPCz CC and all your friends in the fraternal parties would like. . . .we get the impression that the longer this situation lasts, the more likely it is that internal and external enemies will be tempted to exploit this situation . . . " (Document No. 21).

A similar message was transmitted by one of the foremost representatives of the Soviet Ministry of Foreign Affairs, Leonid F. Il'ichev, in a conversation with the Czechoslovak ambassador in Moscow, Oldřich Pavlovský. "He argued that there are internal forces not willing to respect the efforts and aims of the party and that their personal arsenal even included anti-Sovietism and aimed at disrupting our alliance," Pavlovský reported back to Prague on April 17 (Document No. 22).

The same day, the Soviet ambassador in Warsaw, Averki Aristov, reported after a conversation with Polish First Secretary Władysław Gomułka, that a consensus with the other members of the "Five", especially with Berlin and Warsaw on the approach of the Soviets towards Czechoslovakia, had been reached. According to Aristov's top-secret dispatch, Gomułka "expressed the need for us to intervene immediately, arguing that one cannot be an indifferent observer when counterrevolutionary plans are beginning to be implemented in Czechoslovakia." During their meeting, Gomułka phoned Brezhnev on the "Hot Line" to discuss the situation. "[I]t was obvious that Cde. Gomułka was very pleased with what he heard from Cde. Brezhnev," Aristov reported back to Moscow (Document No. 24).

Faced with escalating hostility, and anti-Czechoslovak activities by the "Warsaw Five," Czechoslovak diplomats sought to counter the inaccurate and distorted information about the reform movement by proposing a number of meetings between Czechoslovak and Eastern Bloc representatives to "facilitate the process of mutual understanding" (Document No. 25). A proposal from Foreign Minister Hájek, submitted on April 20 to Prime Minister Černík, observed that "with few exceptions the Soviet comrades do not understand the situation in our country. They are not familiar with Czech history, the composition of Czechoslovak society, the mentality of our people, or our democratic traditions. That is why the openness of the Czechoslovak press and radio has provoked such bewilderment, and why opinions have been expressed that this development is abetting the enemies of socialism" (Document No. 25).

Hájek made "vigorous efforts to influence the state of Czechoslovak–Soviet relations," by accepting Brezhnev's February invitation to talks in Moscow and preparing a Dubček-led delegation to address a series of key questions of concern to the Kremlin.

Despite such efforts, other initiatives of the Prague Spring continued to incite the wrath of neighboring socialist nations. In keeping with the call of the Action Program to promote a variety of international contacts, for example, considerable attempts were made to encourage more normal relations with the Federal Republic of Germany. To be sure, the Warsaw Pact treaty constrained Czechoslovakia's latitude in its foreign policy toward the West. Nevertheless, Prague sought at least initial steps toward the establishment of diplomatic relations between the USSR and West Germany. Given the sensitivity of the situation, an exploratory meeting was held on April 17–19—not at an official government level, but on a party level, e.g. between the authorized representatives of the CPCz and Egon Bahr, who served both as an envoy of the chairman of the Social Democratic Party and of the West German Ministry of Foreign Affairs (Document No. 26). Although these talks did not go beyond clarifying each country's position, they generated harsh criticism by the "Warsaw Five", especially the USSR and GDR who accused Czechoslovakia of violating its strategic commitments towards the Warsaw Pact.

The military factor in the Czechoslovak crisis was raised substantively in April. On April 24, the commander-in-chief of the joint armed forces of the Warsaw Pact, Marshal Ivan Yakubovskii, arrived in Prague for talks with Dubček, President Ludvík Svoboda, Prime Minister Oldřich Černík, and Minister of National Defense Martin Dzúr. Dzúr's report on his talks is the only available document on the visit (Document No. 27); it reveals that the purpose of Yakubovskii's trip was to obtain the consent of the Czechoslovak representatives to advance the Pact's Šumava military exercises, scheduled to take place on Czechoslovak territory from September, to May. Dzúr, according to his report, "explained why such a step would be untimely," and requested a postponement until 1969: "I gave as the reason our internal political situation as well as the duties now confronting the new army command." Marshal Yakubovskii reiterated his demand at the meeting with top-level Czechoslovak representatives. According to the testimony of direct participants, he did not receive consent there either, but the Czechoslovak side did not reject the demand outright. Dubček, Černík and Svoboda maintained, however, that May would be unrealistic. Their position raised further suspicions in the Soviet Union about the Czechoslovak commitment to the Warsaw Pact.

The Moscow Meetings

Immediately after Marshal Yakubovskii's departure from Czechoslovakia, Dubček received an invitation from Brezhnev to visit Moscow. Brezhnev had originally intended to meet only Dubček, but he soon changed his mind and invited a delegation of the CPCz Central Committee to Moscow. On the basis of his experience in Dresden, Brezhnev assumed that Dubček and Černík would be accompanied by Biľak and Kolder, both of whom the Kremlin viewed as "healthy forces" and on whose support Brezhnev therefore counted in the negotiations. Dubček decided to appoint Jozef Smrkovský as a member of the delegation instead of Kolder—a move subsequently accepted by Moscow.

The CPCz Central Committee delegation met with its CPSU Central Committee counterparts in Moscow on May 4–5 for bilateral talks (Document No. 28). There, Dubček and his colleagues encountered withering Soviet criticism of the Czechoslovak reform process, along with a forceful demonstration of the CPSU's determination to halt the progress of that reform. Soviet demands, according to a stenographic transcript of the meeting, took on the character of threats and ultimatums. "The situation, I repeat, is very serious," Brezhnev warned solemnly. "This is no longer an 'internal matter'." The Czechoslovak delegation, with the exception of Biľak, who identified with the Soviet position, defended the program of Czechoslovak reform, repeatedly reiterating the need for a political solution to social conflicts. Under pressure, Dubček did offer one good-will gesture—agreeing that the allied maneuvers demanded by the Soviets could take place on Czechoslovak territory before mid-1968.

Upon the delegation's return to Prague, the CPCz Presidium met on May 7–8 to discuss the situation. Dubček's colleagues appeared shaken by their experience in Moscow, convinced that they now faced a crisis at home and abroad. "If you permit me to say so," Smrkovský told the Presidium, "I as a communist official certainly do not want to live to see a counterrevolution in this country" (Document No. 30). A consensus emerged at this meeting on accepting Moscow's view of the advance of socialism's enemies; Dubček's main supporters in Presidium, Černík and Smrkovský especially—probably concerned about the possibility of Soviet intervention—became insistent on inevitable, energetic, and essentially administrative measures against the so-called anti-socialist forces.

Dubček, however, called on his comrades "to maintain that the first priority . . . is to pursue what is positive, the socialist factor that endorses the Action Program" (Document No. 30). Temporarily in a minority in the Presidium, the first secretary based his position on the results of the CPCz conferences in the districts and regions which had demonstrated a clear majority for progressive, pro-reform forces within the communist party. At four regional conferences—in Prague, Brno, Plzeň and České Budějovice—the demand had been made to convene an extraordinary CPCz congress immediately. The rank-and-file appeared to be pushing for the resignations of the large numbers of leftovers from the Novotný regime and for fundamental changes in direction of the CPCz leadership.

In the wake of the Presidium meeting, the Kremlin convened a secret meeting of the "Five" in Moscow on May 8; Czechoslovak representatives were neither invited nor informed. This was the first of several meetings of the five-member group of Warsaw Pact members—the USSR, Poland, Bulgaria, the GDR and Hungary—called to discuss and decide the fate of Czechoslovakia.

This initial meeting confirmed that a military counter-action against Czechoslovak reform was viewed as an acceptable solution for most of the "Five"—although Brezhnev stated that "for the moment we will not mount an attack on the new CPCz leadership as a whole," according to minutes of the meeting (Document No. 31). The Soviets, however, hoped that allied military maneuvers on Czechoslovak territory "might turn out to be one of the most decisive factors enabling us to turn events around." For Brezhnev, the maneuvers signified military assistance to the anti-reform forces within the CPCz and its leadership in their endeavor to halt the reforms and return developments in Czechoslovakia to the limits of the Soviet model.

Prague's International Position

At the Moscow meeting on May 8, Brezhnev postponed a final solution of the Czechoslovak question: "First it is necessary to see what [Dubček's officials] do, how they address the people, and how the people and army respond to this," he told Gomułka, Kádár, Ulbricht and Todor Zhivkov. Except for Hungary—Kádár called for moderation at the Moscow meeting—Czechoslovakia was in total isolation within the coalition; all that was left were possible closer contacts and informal consultative meetings with Kádár and his representatives. Although Prague had the ostensible moral support of Romania, it was not expressed at the Warsaw Pact summits for the simple reason that, during this critical period, Romania was not invited. On the European political scene it was Yugoslavia's President Tito who was the most outspoken pro-Czechoslovak personality; at his meeting with Brezhnev on May 9, Tito not only opposed the Soviet leader's assessment of the Czechoslovak situation—"Tito said he could not share [Brezhnev's] fears," according to a cable to Prague on the meeting—but told him that Dubček "enjoys great support among the party members" (Document No. 32).

The largest and most respected communist party in the West, the Italian CP, also provided key assistance to Czechoslovakia. In their considerations and actions in the world communist and workers' movement, the Soviets had to take account of the Italians' position. At a meeting between Dubček and the general secretary of the Italian Communist Party, Luigi Longo, in Prague on May 5–7, the Italian leader expressed his approval of the Czechoslovak reform process so forcefully that it triggered Brezhnev's spontaneous comment at the meeting of the "Five" on May 8. Brezhnev stated his regret that the Italians had praised and supported "liberalization" and "the new model" (Document No. 29).

The western democracies, above all the leading superpower, the United States, did nothing to support Czechoslovakia's fragile effort at reform. Even on small bilateral issues—the return of the gold deposited in the U.S. during WW II or gaining most-favored-nation status—Washington's foreign policy showed no favor toward the Prague Spring. The Johnson Administration consistently refused, diplomatically, economically or covertly, to lend assistance to Dubček's efforts. The U.S. ambassador in Czechoslovakia, Jacob Beam, who was received at his own request by Jiří Hájek on May 28, conveyed Washington's "hands-off" policy. The American administration was watching developments in Czechoslovakia with great attention and constructive interest, but for the moment they wished to avoid any steps which could place the Czechoslovak side in an embarrassing situation, given the reaction which was bound to follow from the USSR and the other allies. A special CIA intelligence assessment—"Czechoslovakia: The Dubček Pause"—was given to President Johnson in June. In it, the CIA noted that Dubček had made some concessions to the Kremlin but predicted: "there is a good chance that relations between Prague and Moscow will again become very tense. The Soviet leaders, or at least most of them, wish to avoid drastic and costly military action. Nevertheless, should Dubček's control threaten to collapse, or should the Czech regime's policies become, in Moscow's view, 'counterrevolutionary', the Soviets might once again use their troops to menace the Czech frontier" (Document No. 42).

For the Soviets, the invasion option was enhanced by indications from Washington that there would be no military counter-move by the West.

Power Struggles

Soviet policy toward the Prague Spring cannot be understood without understanding the ongoing struggle for political power within the Soviet political leadership in 1968. Brezhnev's position as general secretary of the CPSU was not yet fully consolidated. There were various signals concerning the nature of this struggle within the Soviet Politburo. In mid-May, Czech correspondent Jan Riško reported that a faction of the Politburo, led by Alexander Shelepin, sought "to take over the leadership from Brezhnev" (Document No. 33). The CIA's June intelligence assessment noted the possibility of "splits within the quadrumvirate itself," particularly between Kosygin and Brezhnev (Document No. 42).

Dubček faced similar problems in the Presidium. Soon after the Dresden meeting two of its participants, Bil'ak and Kolder, took up the Soviet position in Prague, creating a nucleus of Soviet agents in the Czechoslovak political leadership. Bil'ak, as noted above, excelled in siding with the Soviets at a meeting of two four-member delegations from the CPCz and the CPSU in Moscow on May 4. Smrkovský later described Bil'ak as the "fifth member of the Soviet delegation." Smrkovský and Černík wavered, but only temporarily, at the Presidium on May 6–7; thanks to the progressive nationwide movement, both soon came to terms with their Moscow trauma and fully backed Dubček's reform position.

Their stance was significant as the CPCz Central Committee prepared to meet at the end of May—a session that holds a special place in the course of the events of 1968. It was convened as a result of the Moscow talks of the CPCz and CPSU delegations earlier in May—a "Soviet plenum" designed to provide evidence, as demanded by the Soviets, of Dubček's determination to meet the allegedly dangerous threat from the "Right." (In Soviet terminology, the "Right" was synonymous with the so-called counterrevolutionary forces.) On the crucial issue of the threat of counterrevolution, the Czechoslovak political leadership was divided; discussion of this question at the CPCz Central Committee plenary session of May 29–June 1 produced a further split.

Dubček's position, offered in his speech to the Central Committee, reflected the Soviet pressure. The "situation has changed," he stated. "Anti-communist tendencies have grown stronger and certain elements are attempting to engage in more intensive forms of activity. The large majority of the party have come to realize this danger which is today the main threat to the democratization process" (Document No. 37).

The first secretary of the CPCz nevertheless consistently defended the progress of the reform process as being decisive for the advance of Czechoslovak society, and he rejected the arguments that right-wing forces were threatening socialism. Most significantly, Dubček argued, attacks by extremist forces from the Right and from the Left would be countered by "democratic means," by a policy of taking the offensive without using methods of repression.

Vasil Bil'ak's speech expressed a harshly opposing view. He articulated the Soviet belief that events were "not purely our own, Czechoslovak affair" because the "socialist commonwealth" was at stake. In contrast to Dubček, Bil'ak advocated repressive measures in the struggle against the Right. Not surprisingly, he fully endorsed Moscow's position that the enemy—even its "leading center"—could be found within the communist party itself (Document No. 37).

The Extraordinary CPCz Congress

The May session of the CPCz Central Committee failed to bring a decision on the party's future role; instead it confirmed the profound schism between the hard-line and pro-reform members of the CPCz. This session did, however, offer a potential solution to the conflict; the decision was made to convene an Extraordinary 14th CPCz Congress in early September 1968, two years earlier than scheduled. The date became a marker for Soviet intervention because of the likelihood that the congress would make the Prague Spring politically irreversible. Indeed, the progressive forces within the CPCz had sought the special session in order to achieve both radical changes in the composition of the central party bodies and take a decisive step toward transforming the communist party from a ruling institution into a political party.

The fact that at the May session even the conservative wing in the communist party leadership suddenly agreed to the congress—while back in Moscow Biľak declared on May 4 that the Slovak communists would not attend the extraordinary congress, even if this were to lead to a split—was due to certain new circumstances which appeared to give the conservatives new hope. Conservatives, led by Biľak, interpreted growing Soviet pressure as outright support for their political goals. The preparation of allied military maneuvers on Czechoslovak territory also gave them confidence. In May, a Soviet military delegation, headed by the USSR Minister of Defense Marshal Grechko, arrived in Prague. The delegation insisted on the earliest possible date for the exercises and finally forced the Czechoslovak side to give its consent to have them start on June 20. From May 10–23, the Soviets conducted massive military exercises in southern Poland, near the Czechoslovak border, involving one Soviet armored unit of 80,000 men and 2,800 tanks. The maneuvers coincided with a visit for "medical treatment" by Soviet Premier Kosygin in Karlovy Vary which, as Brezhnev later admitted, was a subterfuge by the Soviet Politburo to have a high official observe the situation in Czechoslovakia personally.

The idea of an early Extraordinary 14th CPCz Congress—a normal congress should have been held in 1970—was greeted with enormous interest and support by the Czechoslovak public. Indeed, the month of June was marked by increasing activity not only within the ranks of the communist party, where delegates for the extraordinary congress were being elected, but also among the public. In addition, Czechs witnessed a revival of the non-communist political parties in the National Front which up till then had been nothing more than window dressing, serving to bolster the regime's argument to the world that Czechoslovakia had a multiparty system. These parties continued to advocate cooperation with the communist party but they now argued that it should take place under conditions of a correct and generally respected partnership with guaranteed participation in formulating policy, and mutual public control.

The increased activity of the Club of Committed Non-Party Members (KAN), reflected the determination of the Czechoslovak people to advance towards political pluralism. On May 13, this group issued a political declaration signed by a number of eminent personalities from Czechoslovak scientific, cultural and sporting life, among them the future president of the republic, Václav Havel. The KAN manifesto called for a contemporary, "modern form" of the ideals which were present at the birth of the modern Czechoslovak state in 1918—"the idea of human and civil rights and civil equality," as well as "the humanist tradition of Czechoslovak culture." The manifesto also stated its support of the "current impressive idea of the Czecho-slovak experiment, which is to combine democratic socialism with the noble program of individual freedom" (Document No. 38).

Even though KAN had all the attributes of an emerging political party, its registration was authorized by the ČSSR Ministry of Interior. The social democrats who wanted to restore their activity, terminated in 1948 by their so-called joining (in fact an imposed merger) with the communist party, were denied permission to register, however. The consent to restore social democracy in Czechoslovakia was not a matter of free decision by the reformers in the CPCz. For doctrinal reasons, the Soviets forcefully opposed any step in the direction of social democ-racy. The Czechoslovak political leadership could not fail to note that the harsh, critical tone uttered by the highest representatives of their socialist allies was often accompanied by the revving of massive combat hardware engines in neighboring Warsaw Pact member countries. The Polish–Soviet maneuvers on May 10–17, which concentrated on exercises on the Czecho-slovak border, were immediately followed by similar maneuvers in southern regions of the GDR. The latter involved one Soviet armored car army and two German motorized divisions with a total strength of 60,000 men and 1,800 tanks. These maneuvers, as in Poland previously, brought massive Soviet fire power increasingly close to the Czechoslovak border. At the time, the intent of these maneuvers was not even suspected by Western intelligence analysts; in retrospect it is clear they were designed to create an armed aggressive bulwark along Czechoslovakia's northern border.

The Šumava Maneuvers

In the course of this feverish military activity the allied maneuvers code-named Šumava began on Czechoslovak territory on June 20. Brezhnev had originally hoped to use the maneuvers as a demonstration of military strength against the Czechoslovak reform and in support of its adversaries. But events overtook Brezhnev's original intention and Šumava became part of the preparation for military intervention in Czechoslovakia.

Even before the maneuvers began, a number of incidents raised the fears of Dubček and his colleagues in the leadership. According to a June 17 report by the Minister of National Defense General Dzúr for the Presidium of the CC of the CPCz the Soviets had redefined a "command-staff" exercise with a minimum number of combat units involved as "strategic operational command staff." Now, Dzúr advised, "between 30,000 and 40,000 personnel" were expected to be involved in the exercise—"unusually high for an exercise of this nature" (Document No. 40). Dzúr also reported to his superiors that the commander-in-chief of the Joint Armed Forces of the Warsaw Pact, Marshal Yakubovskii, would determine the final size of the forces involved, but only after his arrival in the ČSSR on June 18. As the subsequent course of events leading up to the August intervention in Czechoslovakia by the armies of the Warsaw Five demonstrated, the Šumava exercises had two objectives: conducting a dress rehearsal for the future military intervention; and providing Moscow with the opportunity to deploy Soviet troops on Czechoslovak territory whose presence would help pacify the situation and, with the aid of domestic anti-reform forces, gradually terminate the Czechoslovak experiment.

For this purpose the Soviets encouraged the activity of hard-line actors who could turn the course of events in Czechoslovakia. The Kremlin focused its attention mainly on the People's Militia—a kind of private communist party army within Czechoslovakia's armed forces. The activities of this unpopular paramilitary unit increased in May and June without any justification. The People's Militia demanded to be identified in the statute of the CPCz as "the armed corps of the communist party." In support of these demands, they announced plans to organize assemblies of their members in Prague and in other industrial centers and conduct street marches in full gear. This was to have been a repetition of what the militia did in the February crisis of 1948, which became one of the decisive factors in the success of the communist *coup d'état*.

Dubček succeeded in preventing the show of force of the People's Militia in the streets of Czech and Slovak towns by proposing to hold a nationwide assembly of People's Militia representatives. The meeting took place in the hangar of the Prague airport on June 19. Dubček seemed successful in controlling the proceedings and averting open confrontation. The resolution adopted by the assembly reflected a compromise between Dubček's line and the militant position taken by elements of the militia (Document No. 41).

Yet, at a plenary session of the CPSU Central Committee on July 17, Brezhnev stated that the political manifestation of the People's Militia had taken place "on the basis of our (Soviet) repeated recommendation and urgent advice." Indeed, the organizers of the assembly, headed by secretary of the CPCz Central Committee Alois Indra, made sure that a "Letter to the Soviet People" was adopted, the content of which had clearly been agreed upon with the Soviet side in advance (Document No. 41). The Soviet press published it as early as June 21; the authorities reacted with well-tested methods, organizing "the response of Soviet workers." Within a fortnight more than 16,000 resolutions arrived in Czechoslovakia from Soviet factories and other institutions with a chorus of assurances that "they are prepared to give Czechoslovak workers help in the common defense of socialism." Such language became the first "working" version of the subsequent slogan of "providing fraternal, internationalist assistance" used during the invasion. The letter from the Czech People's Militia assembly became an important tool for the Soviets to use in escalating their propaganda campaign against Czechoslovak reform, and preparing the Soviet citizenry psychologically for a possible military solution to the Prague Spring.

"Two Thousand Words"

The attack against reform, both at home and abroad, naturally aroused concern among the Czechoslovak public. The pro-reform forces, led by the intellectuals, decided to launch an active defense of the Prague Spring. The key initiative came from members of the Czechoslovak Academy of Sciences who asked writer and journalist Ludvík Vaculík to draw up a manifesto. In this document, scientific, cultural, sports and other personalities addressed the citizens of the republic, mobilizing them to a fresh upsurge of political activity in support of democratic social change.

The "Two Thousand Words" manifesto appeared on June 27. It was published in the weekly of the Czechoslovak Writers Union *Literární listy*, as well as in three Czech dailies: the trade union paper *Práce*, *Mladá fronta* and *Zemědělské noviny*. Along with the CPCz Action Program, it became the most important document of the 1968 Prague Spring. Vaculík eloquently drafted a vision of the fate of Czechoslovak society, especially after World War II, and the promise of a different future, if, and only if, the Czechoslovak people mobilized in support of reform:

At this moment of hope, albeit hope still under threat, we appeal to you. Several months went by before many of us believed it was safe to speak up; many of us still do not think it is safe. But speak up we did, exposing ourselves to the extent that we have no choice but to complete our plan to humanize the regime. If we do not, the old forces will exact cruel revenge. We appeal above all to those who have just been waiting to see what will happen. The time approaching will determine events for years to come (Document No. 44).

Vaculík, and the seventy other prominent members of the Czechoslovak cultural, intellectual and scientific community that signed the manifesto intended to support the Dubček wing in the CPCz. Their vision for the future of Czechoslovak society, however, went beyond the official policy offered by the CPCz Action Program. In its final section, "Two Thousand Words" attempted to outline a plan for progress, calling among other things for civil disobedience—strikes, demonstrations, picketing at the front doors of those "people who abused their power, damaged public property, and acted dishonorably or brutally." In the face of the threat of intervention from abroad, the manifesto concluded, "all we can do is stick to our own positions, behave decently, and initiate nothing ourselves. . . . The spring is over and will never return. By winter we will know all" (Document No. 44).

"Two Thousand Words" set in motion a series of events which its authors and supporters could not have anticipated. The Kremlin seized on the document as the "smoking gun" of the counterrevolution and used it to justify finalizing the Warsaw Five's preparations for transforming the Prague Spring into Czechoslovakia's "hot summer."

DOCUMENT No. 19: The CPCz CC Action Program, April 1968
(Excerpts)

Source: "Akční program Komunistické strany Československa," *Rudé právo* (Prague), April 10, 1968, pp. 1–6.

The Central Committee's adoption of an Action Program of economic and political reform marked the culmination of lengthy efforts to devise a blueprint that would preserve Czechoslovakia's socialist order yet introduce key elements of liberal democracy. The program had several significant features, among them: a new role for the communist party as a political organization competing for popular influence rather than holding a "monopolistic concentration of power"; allied political parties which would be genuine partners rather than subservient organs of the CPCz; the enforcement of civil rights and personal liberties routinely denied under the communist regime; equal status for the Czechs and Slovaks to create two equal nations in a federalized state; and bold economic reforms to provide much greater scope for private enterprise, a shift from heavy industry to consumer production, the liberalization of foreign trade, and a reduced and more clearly defined role for state planning. In a separate section on foreign policy, the Action Program pledged to uphold Czechoslovakia's traditional commitments in the "struggle against the forces of imperialist reaction." At the same time, the program affirmed the need for "a more active European policy" and urged that Czechoslovakia "formulate its own position vis-à-vis the problems of world politics."

The document was not as radical as some of its proponents portrayed it; it did not, for example, envisage any circumstances in which the communist party would be removed from power, and it rejected the "bourgeois" notion of a formal political opposition. Nevertheless, the reforms did represent the first tentative steps toward what the authors described as "political pluralism," and it was intended as the prelude to a longer-term program of sweeping reform that would be worked out by the government and the legislature.

. . . [Introductory sections deleted.]

The Leading Role of the Party: A Guarantee of Socialist Progress

At present it is most important that the party adopt a policy fully justifying its leading role in society. We believe this is a condition for the socialist development of the country. . . .

In the past, the leading role of the party was usually conceived of as a monopolistic concentration of power in the hands of party organs. This concept corresponded with the false thesis that the party is the instrument of the dictatorship of the proletariat. That harmful conception weakened the initiative and responsibility of state, economic, and social institutions, damaged the party's authority, and prevented it from carrying out its real functions. The party's goal is not to become a universal "caretaker" of society, bind all organizations, and watch every step taken in fulfillment of its directives. Its mission instead is primarily to inspire socialist initiative, to demonstrate communist perspectives, their modes, and to win over all workers by systematic persuasion and the personal examples of communists. This determines the conceptual side of party activity. Party organs should not deal with all problems; they should encourage others and suggest solutions to the most important difficulties. But at the same time the party cannot turn into an organization that influences society by its ideas and program alone. It must develop through its members and bodies the practical organizational methods of a political force in society. . . .

As a representative of the most progressive section of society—and therefore the representative of the prospective aims of society—the party cannot represent the full range of social interests. The National Front, the political face of the manifold interests of society, expresses the unity of social strata, interest groups, and of nations and nationalities in this society. The party does not want to and will not take the place of social organizations; on the contrary, it must ensure that their initiative and political responsibility for the unity of society are revived and can flourish. The role of the party is to find a way of satisfying the various interests without jeopardizing the interests of society as a whole, and promoting those interests and creating new progressive ones. The party's policy must not lead non-communists to feel that their rights and freedom are limited by the role of the party. . . .

For the Development of Socialist Democracy and a New System of the Political Management of Society

. . . We must reform the whole political system so that it will permit the dynamic development of social relations appropriate for socialism, combine broad democracy with scientific, highly qualified management, strengthen the social order, stabilize socialist relations, and maintain social discipline. The basic structure of the political system must, at the same time, provide firm guarantees against a return to the old methods of subjectivism and highhandedness. Party activity has not been directed systematically to that end and, in fact, obstacles have frequently been put in the way of such efforts. All these changes necessarily call for the commencement of work on a new Czechoslovak Constitution so that a draft may be thoroughly discussed by professionals and in public and submitted to the National Assembly shortly after the party congress. . . .

The entire National Front, the political parties that form it, and the social organizations will take part in the creation of state policy. The political parties of the National Front are partners whose political work is based on the joint political program of the National Front and is naturally bound by the Constitution of the Czechoslovak Socialist Republic. The National Front is based on the socialist character of social relations in our country. The Communist Party of Czechoslovakia considers the National Front to be a political platform that does not separate political parties into government and opposition factions. It does not create opposition to state policy—the policy of the entire National Front—or lead struggles for political power. Possible differences in the viewpoints of individual components of the National Front or divergent views regarding state policy are to be settled on the basis of the common socialist conception of National Front policy by way of political agreement and the unification of all components of the National Front. . . .

The implementation of the constitutional freedoms of assembly and association must be ensured this year so that the possibility of setting up voluntary organizations, special-interest associations, societies, and other such bodies is guaranteed by law, and so that the present interests and needs of various sections of our society are tended to without bureaucratic interference and free from a monopoly by any individual organization. Any restrictions in this respect can be imposed only by law, and only the law can stipulate what is anti-social, forbidden, or punishable. Freedoms guaranteed by law and in compliance with the constitution also apply fully to citizens of various creeds and religious denominations. . . .

Legal standards must also set forth a more explicit guarantee of the freedom of speech for minority interests and opinions (again within the framework of socialist laws and following the principle that decisions are taken in accordance with the will of the majority). The constitutional freedom of movement, particularly that of travel abroad for our citizens, must be explicitly guaranteed by law. In particular, this means that a citizen should have the legal right to long-term or permanent sojourn abroad and that people should not be groundlessly placed in the position of emigrants. At the same time it is necessary to protect by law the interests of the state, for example, with regard to a possible drain of some specialists, etc.

Our entire legal code must gradually come to grips with the problem of how to protect, in a better and more consistent way, the personal rights and property of citizens, and we must certainly remove statutes that effectively put individual citizens at a disadvantage with the state and other institutions. In the future we must prevent various institutions from disregarding personal rights and the interests of individual citizens as far as personal ownership of family houses, gardens, and other items is concerned. It will be necessary to adopt, as soon as possible, the long-drafted law on compensation for any damage caused to any individual or to an organization by an unlawful decision of a state organ.

It is troubling that up to now the rehabilitation of people, both communists and non-communists, who were the victims of legal transgressions in previous years, has not always been carried out in full, regarding political and civic consequences. . . .

In the interest of the development of our socialist society it is absolutely essential to strengthen the unity of the Czechoslovak people and their confidence in the policy of the Communist Party of Czechoslovakia, to effect a crucial change in the constitutional arrangement of the relations between Czechs and Slovaks, and to carry out the necessary constitutional modifications. It is equally essential to respect the advantage of a socialist federal arrangement as a recognized and well-tested form of the legal coexistence of two equal nations in a common socialist state.

Socialism Cannot Do without Enterprises

The democratization program of the economy places special emphasis on ensuring the independence of enterprises and enterprise groupings and their relative independence from state bodies; the full implementation of the right of consumers to determine their consumption patterns and lifestyles; the right to choose jobs freely; and the right and opportunity of various groups of working people and different social groups to formulate and defend their economic interests in shaping economic policy. . . .

Decision-making about the plan and the economic policy of the state must be both a process of mutual confrontation and harmonization of different interests, that is, the interests of enterprises, consumers, employers, different social groups of the population, nations, and so forth. It also must manifest a suitable combination of the long-term development of the economy and its immediate prosperity. Effective measures protecting the consumer against the abuse of monopolies and economic power of production and trading enterprises must be considered a necessary part of the economic activity of the state. . . .

The drafting of the national economic plan and the national economic policy must be subject to the democratic control of the National Assembly and specialized control of academic institutions. The supreme body implementing the economic policy of the state is the government. . . .

The Central Committee believes it is essential to raise the authority and responsibility of enterprises in the concrete implementation of international economic relations. Production and trade enterprises must have the right to choose their export and import organizations. At the same time it is necessary to lay down conditions that would entitle enterprises to act independently on foreign markets. . . .

The International Status and Foreign Policy of the Czechoslovak Socialist Republic

We will be implementing the Action Program at a time when the international situation is complicated. The development of that situation will influence the fulfillment of certain key aspects of the program. On the other hand, the process of socialist renewal in Czechoslovakia will make it possible for our republic to influence this international situation more actively. We stand resolutely on the side of progress, democracy, and socialism in the struggle by socialist and democratic forces against the aggressive attempts of world imperialism. It is from this viewpoint that we determine our attitude toward the most acute international problems of the present and our role in the worldwide struggle against the forces of imperialist reaction.

Taking, as a point of departure, the existing relationship of international forces and our awareness that Czechoslovakia is an active component of the revolutionary process in the world, the ČSSR will formulate its own position toward the fundamental problems of world politics.

The basic orientation of Czechoslovak foreign policy took root at the time of the struggle for national liberation and in the process of the social reconstruction of the country. It revolves around alliance and cooperation with the Soviet Union and the other socialist states. . . .

We will actively pursue a policy of peaceful coexistence vis-à-vis the advanced capitalist countries. Our geographical position, as well as the needs and capacities of an industrialized country, compel us to pursue a more active European policy aimed at the promotion of mutually advantageous relations with all states and with international organizations, and aimed at safeguarding the collective security of the European continent.

DOCUMENT No. 20: Cable from Andrei Gromyko for Todor Zhivkov, János Kádár, Walter Ulbricht, and Władysław Gomułka Regarding the Internal Security Situation in Czechoslovakia, April 1968

Source: ÚSD, Sb. KV, Z/S, MID 1.

In this top-secret cable, Soviet Foreign Minister Andrei Gromyko relays KGB intelligence on the alleged activities of "hostile" and "subversive" elements in Czechoslovakia to the communist party leaders of Bulgaria, Hungary, the GDR, and Poland. The cable asserts that an "illegal, anti-state" group has been formed under the leadership of a dissident writer, Jan Procházka, and a professor at the University of Prague, Václav Černý. This group, according to the KGB, is dedicated to "subvert[ing] the foundations of socialism in the ČSSR."

The cable reflects the KGB's efforts to put the most negative light on events in Czechoslovakia. During the Prague Spring, top KGB officials consistently advocated drastic action to halt the Czechoslovak reforms. Toward that end, they abandoned balanced intelligence gathering, and began preparing alarming reports for the Soviet Politburo on the basis of what was, in fact, relatively innocuous information. Gromyko's transmission is an example of how the KGB, with tacit approval from the CPSU leadership (or at least certain members of the leadership), manipulated the flow of intelligence during the crisis.

(See also Document No. 130.)

Visit Cde. Zhivkov (Kádár, Ulbricht, Gomułka) personally and pass on to him the following information, which has been sent by diplomatic pouch.

The Committee on State Security of the USSR Council of Ministers wishes to inform you about the activities of the illegal, anti-state group in Czechoslovakia headed by Professor Václav Černý of Prague University and by the deputy chairman of the Union of Czechoslovak Writers and a former candidate member of the CPCz Central Committee, Jan Procházka.[1] According to our information, the former chief of the General Staff of the Czechoslovak People's Army, Krejčí, the editor of the newspaper of the Czechoslovak Socialist Party, *Svobodné slovo*, I. Černý, authors Kohout, Vaculík, Beneš, Kundera, Havel, and Hamšík, an employee of the Czechoslovak Academy of Sciences, Konůpek, Professor Řehák, and others are also taking part in the activities of this anti-state group. The leaders of the illegal group have set out to discredit the CPCz in the eyes of the Czechoslovak people, to subvert the foundations of socialism in the ČSSR, and to gradually return the country to the path of bourgeois development.

Černý and Procházka maintain contact with Tigrid, the leader of the reactionary Czechoslovak emigré center in Paris and editor of the emigré journal *Svědectví*, who is linked to American and French intelligence.[2]

Černý has broad contacts among leading figures in culture and science in Czechoslovakia, recasts their work in a hostile spirit, and receives information from them about the situation in various spheres of general, cultural, economic and political life in the ČSSR.

Grouped around Procházka are literary people who are against the policy of the CPCz. At the 4th Czechoslovak Writers' Congress in June 1967, Procházka and his cohorts worked on the speeches of a large number of writers who criticized party policy and forced the congress to adopt an anti-party platform.

This illegal group has forged links with opposition-minded students and inspires them to hostile activities.

---

[1] Procházka was dismissed from the CPCz Central Committee in September 1967 for his role in the 4th Czechoslovak Writers' Congress. See Document No. 1 above.

[2] Pavel Tigrid was a well-known emigré journalist; for further details about him, see the annotations in Document No. 1 above.

At present, it is known that Černý and Procházka have gone about creating a "front of intellectuals" and in the future intend to form a "committee of the Czechoslovak intelligentsia," which will conduct political work among the people and have its own press organ. In Procházka's view, the intelligentsia, and above all the writers, must be an active political force capable of "keeping CPCz leaders on the defensive and instilling fear in them."

Following the January plenary session of the CPCz Central Committee a process of democratization began to develop in Czechoslovakia which, in the opinion of Černý and Procházka, created favorable conditions for the attainment of their own goals. Their gamble is that the activities of the new CPCz leadership under A. Dubček will objectively prepare the groundwork for the seizure of power by individuals who will "revive" the Czechoslovakia of Masaryk's time.

Using the situation that has developed in the ČSSR, the Černý–Procházka group has drawn up a plan of activities divided into two stages. In the first stage the group's task, in the view of its leaders, is to do everything possible to promote the democratization process and criticize the mistakes of the old CPCz leadership. This, they believe, is the "main work" needed to shake the foundations of the socialist system, undermine the leading role of the CPCz, and compromise Soviet–Czechoslovak friendship, which the communists, involuntarily, "will carry out themselves."

Černý and Procházka have declared it necessary to secure Dubček's final victory so that the communists "will launder the party's dirty linen" in front of the Czechoslovak public and thereby undermine the authority and strength of the CPCz in the country.

Then, in the second stage, when the CPCz, in the view of Černý and Procházka, loses its leading role in the country and is no longer able to control the further course of events, the group should declare itself an independent political party and take charge of all forces that oppose the current regime. This, the conspirators believe, will cause great difficulties for the CPCz leadership in implementing its "Action Program"; and it might then be used for a struggle against the CPCz.

On 16 March, while assessing the situation in the country, Procházka told Černý that it is developing rapidly and "that matters are going ahead." Procházka stressed that it looks as if the CPCz is beginning to "lose control of events." In his words, "the road will be clear" after the army, state security organs, and state apparatus break down. At a meeting with writers Beneš and Havel on 23 March, Černý spoke about the need to move up the date of the National Committee elections to the autumn so that supporters can strengthen their positions in them. He warned Beneš and Havel against taking any "reckless steps" and pointed out, at least that for the time being, they must avoid organizing "mass actions." Černý himself believes it necessary at this moment to remain in the background.

Judging from the data at hand, the Černý–Procházka group represents one of the illegal centers directing the activities of hostile elements in Czechoslovakia.

Tell Cde. Zhivkov (Kádár, Ulbricht, Gomułka) that this information is of an exceptionally confidential nature and that the Soviet side has no intention of publishing it in any form.

Send any reply by telegraph.

A. Gromyko

DOCUMENT No. 21: Letter from Leonid Brezhnev to Alexander Dubček Expressing Concern about Events in Czechoslovakia, April 11, 1968

Source: ÚSD, AÚV KSČ, F. 07/15, Zahr. kor.; Vondrová & Navrátil, vol. 1, pp. 132–135.

This is the second of Leonid Brezhnev's six letters to Alexander Dubček. Brezhnev wrote it just after the adjournment of a CPSU Central Committee plenum which had considered the situation in Czechoslovakia and about a week after the close of the CPCz CC's own April plenum. Like his initial letter in March, this correspondence is generally warm in tone; unlike his earlier one, this letter contains personal reflections and digressions. Although the letter reveals Brezhnev's concern about the developments in Czechoslovakia and the opportunities that were being opened up for "world imperialism," his language does not suggest that, at this date, the Soviet leader holds Dubček personally responsible for those dangers.

Brezhnev's letter was given to Dubček by the Soviet ambassador in Prague, Stepan Chervonenko, on April 14. That same day, Brezhnev telephoned Dubček to gauge his reaction to the letter and to request that the two sides hold negotiations. Two days later, Dubček informed the CPCz CC Presidium about the letter and about Brezhnev's phone call and proposal. It was on the basis of this proposal that Soviet and Czechoslovak party leaders held bilateral talks in Moscow on May 4th and 5th.

(See also Document No. 28.)

---

11 April 1968

Dear Alexander Stepanovich!

It's already late at night, but I'm not yet asleep. Obviously I won't be able to fall asleep for a long time yet. My mind is filled with impressions from the CPSU CC plenum that has just ended and from the conversations I had with secretaries of the republic-level CCs and regional party committees. The plenary session went well. In brief, we talked about the current intensification of the class struggle between the two world systems, and about the place and historical role in this struggle of the communist parties, the working class, the socialist camp, and the bulwarks of world communism.

And, as always, in such cases one thinks not only about one's own affairs, but also about one's friends and brothers who are fighting side by side in a single line along our common, wide, and complicated front.

I would like to have a conversation with you and ask your advice, but it's too late now even to call by phone. I want to put my thoughts down on paper, not bothering too much about how I express them.

I want to tell you frankly that in my speech as well as in the speeches of my comrades, we paid special attention, naturally, to the events in Czechoslovakia and expressed friendly concern in that regard. Alexander Stepanovich, you know very well what enormous respect our party and the Soviet people have for the Czechoslovak Communist Party and for your people. This is well known both to our friends and to our enemies.

The fraternal ties between our countries and peoples were consummated in the brutal clashes with the class enemy, and were sealed by the blood we jointly lost.

And we, you and I, Alexander Stepanovich, were not merely disinterested bystanders during those harsh and heroic days when the intense battles with the enemy solidified our countries' friendship, which will remain forever sacred.

In the twenty years of our friendship, there has been, as you well know, no cloud that has overshadowed our friendship, even though both you and we have encountered many difficulties and disappointments.

Our mutual confidence was always firm. It is still firm now, and I believe that in the end no one will be able to disrupt or cause irreparable damage to our nations' friendship.

I very well understand how great your responsibilities and concerns are now that your party has elevated you to such a high office.

The fate of your party and state are now directly connected with your actions and your personal responsibilities. I was glad to learn that even in the complicated situation that has now emerged in Czechoslovakia, you received expressions of full confidence and support.

I read your speech, the closing speech at the plenum and your other speeches very carefully. I admit that I haven't yet read the full text of the Action Program that you adopted at the plenum.[3] We don't yet have the full text.

As I see it, you and your comrades are now trying to find the most effective route for the further development of your socialist society and the development of socialist democracy. I understand very well that your work is aimed at overcoming certain difficulties, the most important of which is that amidst the healthy trends, revisionist and hostile forces are seeking to divert Czechoslovakia from the socialist path. However, this poses not only difficulties for you, but great dangers as well.

We couldn't help but notice that in your speeches, as well as in those of several of your comrades on the CPCz CC, you alluded to this danger.

Now, when I think back on and try to draw conclusions from the exchanges at our own plenum, I always come back to the prudent Leninist warning that as long as imperialism exists, it will fight with great tenacity for every position it holds and will try to attack the positions of socialism, looking for weak links in the chain.

Not long ago we jointly celebrated the 50th anniversary of the Great October Revolution. When we look back on the way our people have developed, we can see that along the entire way the main strength and support for new socialist relations came from the working class. Even now the working class still provides our main strength. The experiences of the revolution and subsequent years show that when the communists firmly relied on the working class, they emerged from these hard tests even stronger than before.

Dear Alexander Stepanovich!

I sincerely hope that you will understand and excuse my frankness, knowing that it stems from the best of feelings. As your comrade I wish to share with you some of the thoughts that disturb me. I realize that you're now busy in dealing with the problems that were mentioned in your recent plenum. When reading over your materials, I get the impression that in the current situation you're attempting to find immediate solutions to all the problems that have accumulated. This desire is understandable. But I can tell you quite frankly that life and experience show that overly hasty corrections of past mistakes and imperfections, and the desire to solve everything at once, can make for new and even greater mistakes and consequences. That's why I want to point out the danger that the current emphasis on immediately solving a broad array of complicated questions, which can evoke disagreements, could possibly undermine the very important process of consolidation that you've just started.

I and my comrades noticed that at your plenary session many spoke about the leading role of the party. It is very important that precisely this matter—the party's position in the country—be secured as soon as possible. It seems to me that this very issue is the key to solving your fundamental problems.

I'd like to divulge another matter to which the participants in our plenum devoted much attention. This concerns the ideological work of the party. Imperialism is now poised with its propaganda, attempting to launch an attack on the ideological front. The forms and methods of

---

[3] For the Action Program, see Document No. 19.

its actions are, as you well know, diverse and treacherous. After the plenum I studied the most recent information about what is happening in the ČSSR. I also read what is being written about this in the bourgeois press. I can't help but think that events are still not unfolding in quite the way that the CPCz CC and all your friends in the fraternal parties would like. What especially strikes me is that some people in your country, who clearly do not subscribe to socialist positions, are continuing to make statements that are contrary to the measures adopted by the Communist Party of Czechoslovakia to stabilize the situation in the country.

This cannot but be worrying.

The current moment for all of us is serious and demanding. I keep on thinking just how much we, as communists, now have to be vigilant and united!

Dear Alexander Stepanovich!

Judging from what your press, radio, and television are saying, and even from the speeches by some of your leading officials—in which, incidentally, some important and fundamental questions are interpreted differently—we get the impression that the longer this situation lasts, the more likely it is that internal and external enemies will be tempted to exploit this situation in fighting for their goals.

One thought keeps coming to the forefront at this time.

It seems that now, after the new leadership has been formed, the necessary conditions have been created to display unity of will and action and to forestall any opportunity for the revisionist and anti-socialist elements to influence the course of events. Alexander Stepanovich, when I sat down to write this friendly letter, as my heart was telling me to, I did not intend to touch on all problems. That would be hard to do in such a short letter.

I merely wanted to focus on the most important things—about the party, socialism, friendship, and the working class. The motive for this letter to you was precisely that feeling.

In closing this letter, I return in my thoughts to the many discussions I've had with you and your comrades in Prague, Sofia, and Dresden, in which we expressed complete confidence that neither the socialist gains of the Czechoslovak people nor friendship with socialist countries and between our peoples and parties can ever be shaken. The party will be in the forefront, relying on the working class as the leading force of your society. All this, as well as loyalty to the Warsaw Pact, is the guarantee of national independence and the security of the Czechoslovak Republic and the entire socialist community.

From the bottom of my heart I wish you and your comrades success in solving the problems you are facing.

In closing, I want to assure you from myself and, literally, from all our comrades that you can always count on our full support in the struggle to bolster the cause of socialism, the cohesion of the socialist countries, and the unity of the world communist movement.

I am sending you this letter unofficially. Feel free to do with it whatever you like and think is necessary.

In a friendly spirit I firmly shake your hand.

L. Brezhnev

DOCUMENT No. 22: Cable from Czechoslovak Ambassador Oldřich Pavlovský on a Conversation with Soviet Deputy Foreign Minister Iľichev, April 17, 1968 (Excerpts)

Source: ÚSD, Sb. KV, K—Archiv MZV, Dispatches Received, No. 3375/1968;
Vondrová & Navrátil, vol. 1, pp. 145–146.

The Czechoslovak ambassador in Moscow, Oldřich Pavlovský, transmitted this cable shortly before he was recalled to become the minister of domestic trade in the new Czechoslovak government. The cable recounts a conversation with the Soviet deputy foreign minister for East European and African affairs, Leonid F. Iľichev, during which he conveys alarm at developments in Czechoslovakia motivated by "anti-Sovietism" and "aimed at disrupting our alliance." Ambassador Pavlovský reports that he assured Iľichev that "our relations were not jeopardized;" but the cable recommends that the Czechoslovak government move as rapidly as possible to shore up Czechoslovakia's fraternal alliance with the Soviet Union.

Files in the former CPSU archives in Moscow indicate that Pavlovský, and his replacement, Vladimír Koucký, were hostile to the Prague Spring and often fed information to Soviet authorities that heightened their concerns about the reform movement.

. . . Iľichev got very upset when we spoke about developments in our country. He spoke with tears in his eyes. Since there are sincere and trustworthy relations between us he stated his open concern about future developments. To my assurances that our relations were not jeopardized and that we would never permit them to be undermined, pointing to speeches by Cde. Dubček and the other representatives as well as to the outcomes of district conferences and public meetings, etc., he said it would be good if these speeches and events were not disrupted by phenomena that seriously worried him about where everything was headed (attacks on communists, now even in villages, as well as the incomprehensible and inhuman treatment of party officials, leading secretaries, and secretaries of district committees who were not elected, etc.). He argued that there are internal forces not willing to respect the efforts and aims of the party, and that their political arsenal even included anti-Sovietism with the aim of disrupting our alliance. The concerns he expressed, he said quite openly, were not his view alone. All the comrades in the leadership were of the same opinion. I myself would like to add that this kind of concern is noticeable among all the people we meet. Speaking about the degree of information available to the Soviet public, he said (clearly as his own opinion in connection with my earlier conversation with Gromov) that they are often criticized by their own people for the paucity of available information. Finally, since providing information may be construed as approval of the course of events, they are compelled to provide information to the public precisely in this light.[4] I believe it would be useful to take well-considered, active steps, without waiting any further, in order to show our determination, for propaganda and practical purposes, not only to maintain but reinforce our concept of alliance with the Soviet Union, both for domestic and for international political reasons.

---

[4] The very same point is raised in Document No. 11 above, where a Czechoslovak television correspondent reports on Moscow's obsessive desire to control the dissemination of news.

DOCUMENT No. 23: Memoir of Andrei Aleksandrov-Agentov on Internal Soviet Deliberations about Czechoslovakia (Excerpts)

Source: A. M. Aleksandrov-Agentov, *Ot Kollontai do Gorbacheva: Vospominaniya diplomata, sovetnika A. A. Gromyko, pomoshchnika L. I. Brezhneva, Yu. V. Andropova, K. U. Chernenko i M. S. Gorbacheva.* (Moscow: Mezhdunarodnye otnosheniya, 1994, pp. 147–149.)

Aleksandrov-Agentov affirms that, despite numerous other pressing domestic and international issues—Vietnam, Sino–Soviet tensions, agricultural shortfalls among other problems—the Czechoslovak crisis dominated the CPSU Politburo's agenda after March 1968. Initially, according to Aleksandrov-Agentov's account, CPSU leaders were sharply divided in their views of what to do about Czechoslovakia. For a considerable time, Brezhnev "was undecided and was still thinking things over, and he wanted to hear what others thought." Not until later on, when Brezhnev finally decided to take the lead in forging a consensus, were the disagreements among Politburo members overcome. Aleksandrov-Agentov argues that although Brezhnev did not want "blood to be spilled," he believed the "loss of Czechoslovakia" would endanger other communist regimes in Eastern Europe (notably East Germany and Poland) and possibly his own position as CPSU general secretary.

(See also Document No. 5.)

. . . A long and arduous period of searching for a resolution to the "Czechoslovak problem" began for the Soviet leadership and its allies. The question of the situation in Czechoslovakia never left the agenda of Politburo sessions or of contacts with our allies. And of course it was always present during contacts with Prague.

The arguments were long and heated. Once I had to attend a session where a group of roughly 15 people (members and candidate members of the Politburo, CC secretaries, and one or two heads of CC Departments) collectively drafted the text of a letter, the purpose of which was to help the CPCz leadership "see the light." What a horrible spectacle that was! It took many hours to draft the text, particularly because everyone tried to add their two cents, often contradicting what others had said. There were "hawks," there were some who came close to being "doves," and there were some who were cautious and reserved. The only thing missing was a common, unified approach to the matter. And Brezhnev at that point was not yet ready to serve as a tuning fork. He himself was still undecided and still thinking things over, and he wanted to hear what others thought. This sort of thing happened on numerous occasions.

As the process of "liberalization" in Czechoslovakia gathered pace, calls were voiced with increasing urgency for the sending of troops into the ČSSR to halt what was regarded as a dangerous process. The most urgent calls of all came from Ulbricht and Gomułka, who were worried about the security of their own countries if Czechoslovakia broke away from the alliance. We, too, had our hotheads who demanded that we "intervene decisively." During one of these sessions (sometime in the spring of 1968), the Soviet ambassador to the ČSSR, Chervonenko, who was taking part, said bluntly: "If we resort to such a measure as the sending of troops without necessary political preparations, the Czechoslovaks will resist—and blood will be spilled." No one wanted this. For several months Brezhnev adhered to an extremely cautious position. Nevertheless, during one session he temporarily left his chairman's seat and, sitting down for a minute next to Chervonenko, said to him: "If we lose Czechoslovakia, I will step down from the post of general secretary!"

The "political preparations" to which the ambassador referred, or rather the search for some sort of mutually acceptable agreement with the Dubček leadership of the CPCz, continued for a long time—more than half a year—in different forms.

DOCUMENT No. 24: Cable to Moscow from Soviet Ambassador to Warsaw Averki Aristov Regarding Władysław Gomułka's Views on the Situation in Czechoslovakia, April 16, 1968

Source: ÚSD, Sb. KV, Z/S—MID No. 2.

In this cable Soviet ambassador Averki Aristov reports on how internal developments in Poland are affecting First Secretary Gomułka's assessment of events in Czechoslovakia. In the face of spreading civil unrest—during student demonstrations protesters held up signs reading "Polska czeka na swego Dub-czeka" ("Poland is awaiting its own Dubček")—and internal challenges to his power, the Polish leader's position is that "counterrevolutionary plans" were being hatched in Czechoslovakia and that the reform movement is having "an ever greater negative effect on Poland." Gomułka, according to the cable, favors "immediate intervention" by the other Warsaw Pact countries to halt and undo the Prague Spring reforms.

During his meeting with Gomułka, Aristov reports, the Polish leader placed a call to the Kremlin on the "Hot Line" and "was very pleased with what he heard from Cde. Brezhnev" about Czechoslovakia.

TOP SECRET

I visited Cde. Gomułka today and informed him about the CPSU Central Committee plenary session. Cde. Gomułka thanked me for the information. Cde. Gomułka was personally pleased with the assessment of events in Poland given by Cde. Brezhnev in his report to the plenary session.

I acquainted Cde. Gomułka with the full text of the part of the speech that dealt with events in Poland. Cde. Gomułka said he fully agrees with what Cde. Brezhnev stated in the report. It was clear that he is very pleased with this assessment.

During the conversation Cde. Gomułka returned to the events in Czechoslovakia. It was evident that he is very disturbed by what is going on in Czechoslovakia. In his view, the process whereby socialist Czechoslovakia will be transformed into a bourgeois republic has already begun. He pointed to several places in the resolution of the recently concluded CPCz plenum and to separate articles and remarks about the liquidation of democratic centralism, about the leeway for bourgeois expression, about trade unions without communists, about national committees without communists, and so forth. The many reports he used during this conversation were underlined in places and, on the opposite side of the page, there also were his notes and remarks. Cde. Gomułka once again expressed the need for us to intervene immediately, arguing that one cannot be an indifferent observer when counterrevolutionary plans are beginning to be implemented in Czechoslovakia. At that very moment Cde. Gomułka called Cde. Brezhnev on the "Hot Line." From what I could gather, their conversation focused on Czechoslovakia, too. It was obvious that Cde. Gomułka was very pleased with what he heard from Cde. Brezhnev.[5]

As for the internal situation in Poland, Cde. Gomułka noted that not everything has yet been done to cleanse the party of its Zionist elements. While speaking about this Cde. Gomułka said that there are many people in his country who want to repeat what is happening in Czechoslovakia and one cannot help seeing the events developing there as having an increasingly negative effect on Poland. This influence is also affecting the other people's democracies.

There have now appeared in our newspapers and journals, said Cde. Gomułka, several articles of a harmful nature; and we intend to take necessary measures against the editors of these papers

---

[5] What exactly Brezhnev said that met with Gomułka's approval is unclear, but it seems likely that the Soviet leader mentioned a key decision which the CPSU Central Committee had adopted at the April 9–10 plenum only a few days earlier. Newly released materials record that the plenum resolved to "lend assistance to the healthy forces [in Czechoslovakia] and above all to the Communist Party of Czechoslovakia and not to permit the loss of the ČSSR and its withdrawal from the socialist community."

and journals and against the authors of the articles. All this must be corrected in time. We will not allow a repetition, Cde. Gomułka noted, of what happened in Czechoslovakia where the press, radio, newspapers, journals, and even members of the Central Committee Politburo and the CPCz, are beginning to interpret party policy each in their own way. There must be only one policy of the party and its Central Committee. Just recently, said Cde. Gomułka, a party meeting in the Polish Embassy in London adopted a decision to release ambassador Morawski from his post. This, said Cde. Gomułka, is anarchy. Taking decisions about ambassadors is the work of the Central Committee and the government. And we do not intend to hand over these functions to any other organization. I already took measures to drop Morawski from the Politburo; we know what an active revisionist he was in the past. We, ourselves, will decide the question about him. That is our right. And anyone who carried out such an illegal directive will answer for it.

16 April 1968

A. Aristov

DOCUMENT No. 25: "Proposal for a Number of Major Political Measures to Facilitate the Process of Mutual Understanding in Relations with the USSR," by Czechoslovak Foreign Minister Jiří Hájek, April 17, 1968 (Excerpts)

Source: ÚSD, AÚV KSČ, F. 07/15.

Foreign Minister Jiří Hájek made this proposal to the Czechoslovak leadership two weeks before a delegation traveled to Moscow for bilateral talks. It reflects his awareness of the growing tensions in Soviet–Czechoslovak relations, and records his suggestions on easing the pressure from Moscow.

Hájek's proposal assumes that the main reason for the deterioration of Soviet–Czechoslovak ties is that "with few exceptions, the Soviet comrades do not understand the situation in our country." If Czechoslovak officials could do a better job of "convincing the leaders of the CPSU and the Soviet state of the overwhelmingly positive nature of the developments in our country," they would eventually succeed in winning Moscow over, according to this position. For this reason, Hájek recommends that Dubček accept the Soviet invitation to come to Moscow for bilateral consultations in order to address "the particular lack of clarity" in the Kremlin concerning the reform movement.

Proposal for a Number of Major Political Measures to Facilitate the Process of Mutual Understanding in Relations with the USSR

Relations between the ČSSR and the USSR have existed on a purely formal basis over recent years. This situation was undoubtedly caused by the position adopted by the CPCz CC regarding the dismissal of Cde. Khrushchev.[6]

Transformations in the Czechoslovak economy and certain traits in Czechoslovak culture have aroused doubts among several leading officials in the USSR, more often than not because of insufficient and inaccurate information.

Consequently, recent developments (from the plenum in October) have been followed with unusual attention.

In general one might say that, on the one hand, there are many people in the USSR who are keenly interested in the recent developments in Czechoslovakia, but on the other hand, the public at large is not properly informed. The result is a wide spectrum of views and responses, ranging from fears and fundamentally negative views to restraint and even great optimism. . . .

. . .

Response to the January Session of the CPCz Central Committee

The results of the January session of the CPCz CC, and the measures adopted there, have made a strong impression in the USSR. It is understandable that in such an agitated atmosphere a number of inaccurate or distorted views emerged. For example, concerns were expressed that Czechoslovakia had set out on the road of revisionism and was following the example of Yugoslavia or Romania. There were even suggestions that our policies were being driven by the difficult economic situation in our country or that our decisions were meant solely to alleviate nationality problems in the ČSSR. In these circumstances, it was a good thing that the Soviet

---

[6] This is a reference to Antonín Novotný's opposition to Khrushchev's ouster, a position that hardly endeared him to Khrushchev's successors.

press published the resolution of the January session of the CPCz CC along with Cde. Dubček's biography. That helped dispel the concerns mentioned above, though it by no means totally eliminated them. It is worth noting that after the January session of the CPCz CC, officials at the Czechoslovak embassy in Moscow and Czechoslovak delegations arriving in the USSR found that their Soviet counterparts had considerable misgivings and reservations when they talked about recent developments in Czechoslovakia. Soviet officials were extraordinarily unwilling to discuss or even listen to information from Czechoslovakia. This situation did not change even after Cde. Dubček's visit to Moscow. The visit received almost no publicity, except for a brief mention of it by Cde. Brezhnev in his speech in Leningrad (a speech that, incidentally, was not published in the central press). . . .

. . .

For a long time the Soviet press refrained from commenting about subsequent developments in Czechoslovakia. This led to a variety of interpretations in the USSR: for example, that the silence was intended to convey the Soviet leadership's disagreement, or that Soviet officials were maintaining a wait-and-see attitude and that this carried over to the Soviet press, or that Soviet officials wanted to avoid making hasty judgements, or some other explanation. For the Soviet public, and particularly among CPSU activists, any development in the socialist countries arouses immediate concern about the USSR's allies. The causes of the rifts with Albania, the People's Republic of China, and Romania are not fully understood even now, and frequently one can hear remarks addressed to the CPSU leadership stating that a more intelligent policy would have averted these breaks.

Based on information at our disposal, we can report that the efforts to democratize our party and Czechoslovak society as a whole have been received with little understanding in the USSR, especially among officials at medium levels and even, judging by recent information, at higher levels. A distinct segment of the Soviet intelligentsia, however, welcomes events in the ČSSR, stirring hopes that have created frictions in Soviet society.

It is evident that, with few exceptions, the Soviet comrades do not understand the situation in our country. They are not familiar with Czechoslovak history, the composition of Czechoslovak society, the mentality of our people, or our democratic traditions. That is why the openness of the Czechoslovak press and radio has evoked such bewilderment, and why opinions have even been expressed that this development is abetting the enemies of socialism. The situation in the ČSSR also has met with an unfavorable response in the upper levels of the Soviet army.

It can be said that even after Cde. Dubček's visit to Moscow and after the Dresden meeting, the leaders of the CPSU and of the Soviet state have still not been convinced of the overwhelmingly positive nature of the developments in our country.

It is essential that we make vigorous efforts to influence the state of Czechoslovak–Soviet relations, which affect the attitude of some other socialist countries toward the developments in our country. . . .

. . .

It is, therefore, proposed to comply as soon as possible (by the middle of May) with the invitation conveyed to Cde. Dubček in February for a Czechoslovak party and government delegation to visit the USSR. The situation in the ČSSR should once again be explained during the talks and the party's Action Program should be elucidated in detail.

There is a particular lack of clarity on the following issues:

1) The internal situation in the party in connection with the progress and results of conferences held so far, and the removal of officials.

2) The concept of the leading role of the party, the Czechoslovak road to socialism, and the growing activity of non-communist parties and of some internal reactionary forces.

3) Rehabilitations in cases where the Soviet organs and the activities of Soviet advisers were involved; the impact this may have on bilateral relations; the newly-established organization consisting of those who suffered, known as "K-231"; and the possible effect on the USSR.

4) The situation in the Czechoslovak economy and its possible influence on Czechoslovak foreign policy (foreign credits, licenses, a greater orientation toward the capitalist states, etc.).

5) Economic reform: the new system of management and the ease of control from the center.

6) Issues of conflict in Czechoslovak–Soviet economic cooperation.

7) Czechoslovak foreign policy (lack of clarity about the meaning of our own image, our independent policy, our desire to respect our own interests and Czechoslovakia's specific conditions, etc. Among concrete issues, the greatest attention is devoted to future policy toward the FRG).

8) A solution to the nationality problem in the ČSSR.

This state of affairs necessitates a meeting of Czechoslovak and Soviet representatives.

These visits may be of great help in overcoming a variety of doubts and ambiguities in the ČSSR's relations with both the USSR and the other socialist countries.

17 April 1968

DOCUMENT No. 26: Report on Secret Discussions between the CPCz CC International Department and Egon Bahr of the West German Social Democratic Party, April 17–19, 1968 (Excerpts)

Source: ÚSD, AÚV KSČ, F. 02/1.

This report, prepared by the CPCz CC International Department, summarizes the issues discussed by a high-ranking representative of the West German Social Democratic Party, Egon Bahr, during a secret and unofficial visit to Prague on April 17–19. The CPCz–SPD talks clarified the respective positions of the two sides on a number of issues, including nonproliferation and potential political and economic ties, but did not achieve any concrete decisions beyond an agreement that relations between the FRG and Prague "could be improved even without direct diplomatic relations."

The meeting was another step toward improved ties with West Germany that had begun under Novotný when an FRG trade mission was authorized in Prague. A section in the CPCz CC Action Program explicitly called for Czechoslovakia to "pursue a more active European policy" and to "promote mutually advantageous relations with all states." When word of the meeting leaked, however, it prompted fierce criticism from the other Warsaw Pact countries (with the exception of Romania which established diplomatic relations with West Germany in 1967). In particular, East German leader Walter Ulbricht accused the Czechoslovak authorities of having reneged on the commitments undertaken at the April 1967 Warsaw Pact conference at Karlovy Vary when the USSR, Poland, Czechoslovakia, Hungary, Bulgaria and East Germany agreed not to significantly improve relations with the FRG unless the West German government formally recognized the permanent existence of two German states and accepted the Oder–Neisse border and the border between the two Germanies as inviolable.

(See also Document No. 19.)

In accordance with a decree adopted by the CPCz CC Presidium in March 1968, meetings were held on an unofficial and confidential basis with an SPD spokesman at the request of the SPD chairman, Willy Brandt. The meetings took place in Prague on 17–19 April 1968. The talks were conducted by Cde. Josef Šedivý, the deputy head of the CPCz CC International Department, who was accompanied by two other ID officials, Cdes. Mikeštík and Janout. The German side was represented by Egon Bahr, a confidant of the SPD chairman and envoy of the Bonn Foreign Ministry, who was accompanied by Hans Bock, an official of the SPD Presidium and former head of the West German mission in Belgrade. Toward the end of the brief discussions with E. Bahr, Cde. O. Kaderka, the head of the CPCz CC International Department, joined the others. . . .

. . .

In further comments, Bahr explained the SPD's motives in suggesting that the next state with which there should be talks about the renunciation of the use of force in mutual relations is the ČSSR: Not only is the ČSSR a neighbor of both German states, but its contiguity with the FRG makes a possible treaty especially important. The same applies to the GDR. Because of a series of factors, including the current renewal process in our country, the SPD believes that the ČSSR has a real chance of pursuing a more active policy vis-à-vis its partners in the Warsaw Pact.

The SPD believes the significance of a treaty on the renunciation of the use of force in mutual relations, if it were part of a set of treaties that included the GDR, the ČSSR, Poland, and the USSR, would be mainly in the improvement it would bring in the general atmosphere in Europe and in the progress it would make toward the *de facto* normalization of relations. By concluding such treaties, the FRG would in fact take a positive and sufficiently convincing stand regarding the existing borders in Europe, including the Oder–Neisse border as well as the borders between the FRG and the GDR. A final settlement of the border issue, however, would be left until a future peace treaty.

Clarification of such a treaty with the ČSSR, the GDR, Poland, and the USSR would be of great importance in view of issues still outstanding between the FRG and these countries, especially considering that similar problems do not exist with the other socialist countries.

On the Question of Establishing Diplomatic Relations between the ČSSR and the FRG

Bahr spoke about this issue in very general and non-committal terms. He said that in the FRG there was full understanding of the priority given to the present domestic political tasks of the ČSSR. However, the FRG's offer to negotiate these problems still stands, and it is now up to the Czechoslovak side to decide when negotiations are to open. In this context, Bahr wanted to know whether we still insist on the conditions we had raised in connection with the establishment of diplomatic relations with the FRG. He broached the possibility of fulfilling the conditions linked with the establishment of diplomatic relations between the FRG and the socialist countries in the following manner:

— treaties on the renunciation of the use of force would provide a satisfactory solution to the question of European borders until a peace treaty was signed;

— it is a virtual certainty that the FRG would join the treaty on the nonproliferation of nuclear weapons, which would fulfill another of the socialist countries' demands. However, in subsequent talks, Bahr said that on this question there would be a bitter discussion in the FRG between the SPD, on the one hand, and the CDU and even more the CSU, on the other. He did not rule out the possibility that conflict on this issue could lead to the collapse of the coalition;

— the problem of Munich may be settled in bilateral FRG–ČSSR relations;

— relations with the GDR remain a problem; Federal Germany does not close its mind to any agreement, although it states that these could only be solutions which would exclude the interpretation of international legal recognition of the GDR by Federal Germany;

— Bahr did not adopt a position on the problem of West Berlin.

The Czechoslovak side stressed that the matter of diplomatic relations could not be seen as a formality if this act were to have any real significance and that the establishment of diplomatic relations would have no effect on mutual relations unless progress was achieved on controversial matters. Bahr agreed in principle with this argument but said it might be worth considering and acknowledging the purely political significance of such an act for improving the atmosphere and promoting relations in all spheres, including the possibility of dealing, for example, with compensation for damages caused by persecution. It was agreed in the discussion that in the present situation relations between the ČSSR and the FRG could be improved even without direct diplomatic relations.

The Munich Agreement Issue

The SPD regards the existence of the Munich agreement as a serious stumbling block to the normalization of relations between the ČSSR and the FRG. In this context, the representatives of the SPD made several concrete proposals which, in the opinion of the SPD, could lead to the elimination of this problem in a manner to satisfy the ČSSR. Following the well-known declarations by the Federal German government, Bahr feels that the conflict now focuses on whether the agreement was null and void from the very beginning or whether it is simply null and void now. The SPD believes the problem of the Munich agreement could be settled within the framework of a treaty on the renunciation of force or in a separate treaty, but in any case by a bilateral contractual act between the FRG and the ČSSR. According to the SPD, one of the following three formulations of the joint declaration could be used in the treaty: either (1) that there are no conflicts between the two sides on the question of Munich, (2) that there are no conflicts between them and that any areas of disagreement will be settled by peaceful means, or, (3) that they will shape their relations with a view to future peaceful developments—in other words, as though the question of Munich had never existed. . . .

Bahr and Bock agreed that the political aspects of the Munich agreement and their solution would have to be separated from subsequent legal and economic aspects. Bahr, furthermore, expressed concern that a hasty solution of these legal and economic consequences of Munich would lead, on both sides, to an accumulation of demands and the revival of support at home for their fulfilment, causing the entire Munich issue to acquire insurmountable proportions. The SPD, therefore, suggests that a political solution to Munich should now be explored and concrete negotiations about Munich should commence later. The SPD's vision is such that in addition to constitutional matters the negotiations should deal also with property issues, in other words, Czechoslovak property claims connected with Munich and property claims by the so-called Sudeten Germans from the time of their expatriation.[7] Bahr replied that for the SPD these demands and the actual negotiations have a purely domestic political function since this enables them to fend off allegations that they have abandoned these demands. Otherwise the negotiations could drag on for several years. The SPD would also be prepared to examine another way of exploring the demands, for example, by a joint commission of experts whose task would be to prepare a specialist report for the governments of the two countries.

We told Bahr that acceptance of property claims for the expatriation of Sudeten Germans was totally unacceptable. Besides, arguments about domestic political considerations do not withstand scrutiny if we remember that the expatriation had nothing to do with Munich but with the outcome of World War II, and the FRG government could transfer these demands to peace negotiations. In addition, one cannot overlook the fact that, under law, former Sudeten Germans have already received some compensation in Federal Germany and, as a result, cannot expect anything in this respect even from the West German government.

The multitude of proposals made it clear that the SPD spokesmen had a positive and keen interest in liquidating the Munich issue. Yet it was also evident that the proposals—notwithstanding their interesting nature—still remained only half baked. The West German side still resists an unequivocal declaration on the nullity of the Munich agreement from the very beginning, as requested by the ČSSR. . . .

Relations between the CPCz and the SPD

The SPD spokesmen said that they were maintaining unofficial contacts with certain communist parties in Europe and that, in their opinion, the leadership of the SPD and of the CPCz could maintain contacts and hold consultations on a variety of problems pertaining to relations between the ČSSR and the Federal Republic, and possibly between the CPCz and the SPD. However, they cannot agree to full normalization of relations. Contacts could be arranged in such a way that SPD officials would have talks with the CPCz at their own request but with the consent of the party leadership.

The Czechoslovak side stressed that we were in favor of normal contacts between communist and socialist parties, but that we understood that this could be achieved only step by step, especially since the resolution of the Socialist International still prevents socialist parties from cooperating with communist parties. . . .

---

[7] The Sudeten property claims arose from the mass expulsion of ethnic Germans from western Czechoslovakia just after World War II. Neither at the time nor since then has the Czechoslovak government (and now the Czech government) been willing to entertain such claims.

Promotion of Economic Relations between the ČSSR and the FRG

Bahr emphasized that the SPD as well as the Federal Republic were in favor of greater cooperation; he believed that the Federal Republic could assist the solution of urgent problems of the Czechoslovak economy in various forms. Credits possibly of as much as DM 200–300 million would not be a problem. . . .

At the end of the talks two joint records were adopted, stating the outline and subjects of the talks. At Bahr's request it was decided not to inform the public of the talks. However, a press release was drawn up in case a report of the meeting was leaked. . . .

DOCUMENT No. 27: Report by ČSSR National Defense Minister Martin Dzúr on a Meeting with Marshal Yakubovskii, Commander-in-Chief of the Warsaw Pact Joint Armed Forces, April 24–25, 1968

Source: ÚSD, AÚV KSČ, F. 02/1.

Marshal Ivan Yakubovskii's official visit to Prague on April 24–25, 1968, was part of a week-long series of visits to all the East European members of the Warsaw Pact (other than Romania). His trip was officially intended to cover "questions concerning a further increase in the combat readiness of the Warsaw Pact member states." When he was in Warsaw, East Berlin, Sofia, and Budapest, however, Yakubovskii also focused on the military implications of recent events in Czechoslovakia and obtained the consent of each government to begin joint preparations and contingency planning with the Soviet Union for possible military actions "in defense of socialism."

While in Prague, Yakubovskii met Dubček, Svoboda, Černík, and National Defense Minister Martin Dzúr. The Soviet marshal requested that military exercises known as the Šumava maneuvers be brought forward to June 20–30, 1968, rather than being left until September as originally planned. Dzúr, according to his own report, "explained why such a step would be untimely," because the volatile political situation in Czechoslovak society and in the Czechoslovak army would preclude holding joint exercises until sometime in 1969 at the earliest.

TOP SECRET

Marshal I. I. Yakubovskii, commander-in-chief of the Joint Armed Forces of the Warsaw Pact member states, paid an official visit to the ČSSR on 24–25 April 1968.

The visit was part of his tour of all the Warsaw Pact countries.[8]

The talks focused on three groups of subjects:

1. Official introduction to our party and state representatives in his post as commander-in-chief.

2. Consolidation of the military institutions of the Warsaw Pact.

3. Elaboration of the front maneuvers to be held in the ČSSR this year under a plan approved by the Joint Command.

The negotiations had the following results:

Re. 2. In the discussions about ways to strengthen the Warsaw Pact's military institutions, the officials who took part—which in our case was the minister of national defense, Lt. General Dzúr—considered proposals sent to us in advance. Since these proposals had been discussed on several occasions since 1965, he [Dzúr—Ed.] stated his agreement. His remarks focused on how to resolve three fundamental questions:

a) the nature of the relationship between the Warsaw Pact's military institutions and the supreme party and state bodies of the member states.

The Soviet proposal did not maintain the principle applied in all protocols as well as in the treaty itself, to wit, that the armed forces of the member states assigned to the Joint Armed Forces should remain directly subordinated to their national command structures, which are fully responsible for the quality of their combat capability. Certain proposed revisions in the

---

[8] Yakubovskii's trip started on April 19 with two days of meetings in Warsaw, then shifted to East Berlin on April 21–22, moved to Sofia on April 23, and then to Prague on the 24th and 25th. The trip concluded with a visit to Budapest on April 27.

jurisdiction of the pact commander-in-chief were in contradiction to this principle. We therefore proposed adjustments in the pertinent section of the statutes. The commander-in-chief accepted our proposals as totally correct and it was agreed that the commander-in-chief must base his activity not only on the decisions of the Political Consultative Committee, but also at all times on the consent of the governments or defense ministers of the member countries concerned;

b) the appointment of the chief deputies of the commander-in-chief.

The proposal stated that the chief of the main staff of the Joint Command, the commander of the Joint Air Defense Forces, and the commander of the Technical Committee may be chosen from among the armed forces of any member country. Since no representative of any army, with the exception of the Soviet army, has the possibility of holding these posts, we proposed that these officials be appointed from among the ranks of Soviet generals;

c) the authority of the Technical Committee.

We insisted on the demand that the proposed authority of the Technical Committee be enlarged to also cover the sphere of military research & development, since the existing state of affairs leads to redundant expenditures of resources by all the member states and to unnecessary waste. Cde. Yakubovskii agreed and promised that this will be taken into consideration in the final formulation of the documents.

All in all, it can be said that full agreement was reached in the discussion of this issue and all our views were taken into consideration. The commander-in-chief declared that our remarks were unequivocally aimed at clarifying and strengthening the content of the proposed basic documents of the treaty in the military sphere.

Our remarks will be incorporated in the more specific drafts of these documents, which will be evaluated once again at the ministerial level of all member states prior to being debated by the Political Consultative Committee.

Re. 3. In the discussions regarding the front operational maneuvers due to be held on our territory, the ČSSR minister of national defense explained why such a step would be untimely. He requested that exercises on this scale be held neither in June as requested by the commander-in-chief, nor at any other point this year. He cited his reasons: our internal political situation as well as the duties now confronting the new army command. He added that after making personnel changes, the command of the Czechoslovak People's Army felt it expedient to take certain internal measures to bring about a cohesion of the commands and staffs and planned to take part in allied front exercises no earlier than 1969.

In conclusion I would like to point out that the talks with the commander-in-chief of the Joint Armed Forces took place in a spirit of full understanding; he received our points of view with an open mind and the negotiations contributed to the clarification of our sincere efforts as well as to the strengthening of mutual relations.

DOCUMENT No. 28: Stenographic Account of the Soviet–Czechoslovak Summit Meeting in Moscow, May 4–5, 1968 (Excerpts)

Source: ÚSD, Sb. KV, Z/S 2; Vondrová & Navrátil, vol. 1, pp. 165–191.

This 74-page typed Russian transcript of the bilateral Soviet–Czechoslovak meeting in Moscow in early May 1968 details Moscow's efforts to manage and negotiate the crisis. Brezhnev called for the meeting just after Marshal Yakubovskii left Czechoslovakia in late April without Prague's consent to host joint military exercises in May.

The minutes of the meeting record sharp Soviet criticisms of the Czechoslovak reforms and pronounced disagreements between the Czechoslovak delegation, led by Dubček, and the Soviet authorities, led by Brezhnev. Soviet negotiators expressed multiple concerns about events in Czechoslovakia: the Czechoslovak army and security forces were being weakened and subverted; the CPCz was being deprived of its most loyal (i.e., pro-Soviet) cadres; West Germany and the United States were covertly undermining the Czechoslovak regime; Czechoslovak foreign policy was becoming (or would soon become) openly pro-Western; and the counterrevolutionary forces were, as Brezhnev put it, "raging in full force." Brezhnev and his aides hinted that the Soviets would act decisively to "defend socialism" in Czechoslovakia if Dubček did not meet their concerns.

Minutes of Talks with ČSSR Delegation, 4 May 1968[9]

Representing the Czechoslovak side in the talks: Cdes. A. Dubček, O. Černík, J. Smrkovský, V. Biľak.

Representing the Soviet side: Cdes. L. I. Brezhnev, A. N. Kosygin, N. V. Podgorny, K. F. Katushev, K. V. Rusakov.

[After Brezhnev welcomed the participants, Dubček explained the current situation in Czechoslovakia.]

. . .

A. Dubček: In brief, after the April plenum the people's trust in the communist party increased. This is the most important thing for us; we regard it as our real source of strength. The changes carried out were entirely necessary. It was impossible to confine ourselves to less. Now it is essential that Cde. Novotný leave the Central Committee. The regional party conferences objected to the fact that the January plenary decisions are not being fulfilled systematically. We are accelerating work to prepare the party congress. Its exact date has not yet been decided. This will be done at the CC plenum in May. According to the statutes, the congress should be held in 1970, but we'll have to hold it earlier.

A. N. Kosygin: Will it be an extraordinary congress?

A. Dubček: It will be an extraordinary, pre-term one, but the main thing is not the interval at which the congress takes place. The important thing is the content of its work and what problems will be discussed. We will have to consider, among other things, several questions of a constitutional nature (that of the federation), the question of the party statutes, and other issues concerning the future work of the party. At present we are busy putting together a plan on how to prepare for the congress. We'll try to finish this work by the end of the year or in the spring of 1969. There are many questions that simply cannot be resolved without calling a congress.

---

[9] In the aftermath of the collapse of the Soviet Union, the Russian government turned over this document to Czech authorities, making it available for public evaluation for the first time.

N. V. Podgorny: Some regional conferences have urged that the congress be held this year. What is the CC Presidium's response to that?

A. Dubček: We still don't know when we'll finish preparations and so we still haven't considered the date, but we want to hold the congress as soon as possible. The need to bring the congress forward to 1968 was approved by two conferences: one in Brno and the other in Prague.[10] As for the necessity of calling an extraordinary congress: any congress, if we convene it before 1970, will be an extraordinary, pre-term one. This is essential because we face large and complicated problems. And linked to this is the fact that we have to put off elections to the National Assembly, which had been planned for the autumn, to a later date.

N. V. Podgorny: But only one thing is important for those who want an extraordinary congress: to bring about changes in the present composition of the CC.

A. Dubček: We reject the demand to hold congresses only for such purposes. All the resolutions of the regional party conferences now speak not only about a new composition of the CC, but also about ways of solving certain problems, in particular problems connected with the situation in industry and agriculture.

And now, if you don't object, I'll briefly describe the situation in our industry and agriculture.

N. V. Podgorny: Excuse me, Cde. Dubček, but we wish to know what is happening with regard to radio, television, and the press. One gets the impression nowadays that anyone who wants to can be heard speaking about anything he pleases. Is it possible that the means of mass information and propaganda, including *Rudé právo*, have fully slipped out of your control?

A. Dubček: That was why we instructed the government to strengthen the leadership of these media. I am dealing with this myself; I had a talk with the staff of *Rudé právo*. I especially emphasized that this paper is the organ of the Central Committee. I asked them directly whether they wished to work independently of the CC. The talk was lively and good. We are drafting a special proposal to improve the work of *Rudé právo*. At the Presidium session on 14 May we will consider that proposal. Communists working in these organs should assume greater responsibility.

N. V. Podgorny: It is very important that the press, radio, and television remain under the control of the Central Committee, and that they carry out its wishes. Otherwise, any solution will be only so many words.

A. Dubček: We see this and are taking appropriate measures. The government is dealing with this, as I've already told you.

N. V. Podgorny: Does the government have the power to change the situation in this sector? After all, this is a question of ideology and personnel—that is, it's a matter that the Central Committee should have handled.

A. Dubček: It's necessary to issue special laws, which is a matter for the government to handle. But we in the CC Presidium are also dealing with this matter.

K. F. Katushev: And how are things as regards the CPCz's influence on the press organs of the other political parties, the organs of the Writers' Union, and so forth?

A. Dubček: That's a task that can't be completed in a single day, but we'll deal with it.

A. Kosygin: Do you intend to change the personnel working in the organs of the mass media?

---

[10] Two other regional conferences, in Plzeň and České Budějovice, also had called for an extraordinary congress to be held in 1968, as reported in *Rudé právo* on April 27, 1968.

A. Dubček: Yes, that's being planned. We'll also conduct our work also with the communists in the press organs of the Writers' Union and others, and especially those in the publishing houses. In Slovakia, the situation overall is better. Influential authors there are firmly upholding party positions and are resisting anti-party acts. The Writers' Union in Slovakia has a strong and authoritative party branch which is speaking out firmly against ideological subversion. We intend to place a newspaper at its disposal. In Prague, there are more petty bourgeois elements among the writers and not a strong enough party core. In the writers' organ published in Prague, *Literární listy*, there are two tendencies: a bid to set up a political opposition, and an effort to halt uncontrolled democracy. We will rely on the Slovak writers. In a word, on this issue I personally and the other comrades have much to do. We'll have to speak systematically with influential figures.

We intend to go over the matter of Mňačko.[11] If he returns, we'll criticize him. He was condemned not long ago by the Slovak Writers' Union.

Cde. Smrkovský will also deal directly with questions relating to writers.

A. N. Kosygin: Was any decision adopted about the responsibility of editors?

A. Dubček: You mean to imprison them, or what? The only real solution is to work with them as we did in Bratislava. That's the only way out of the situation, to win them over to our side. I'll have to work personally with these people and speak to them. In Prague, I don't have such a strong position in these circles, and past roots are stronger there than in Slovakia. On the whole, comrades, we regard the situation to be complicated and difficult.

Now, as concerns our industry and agriculture. How do matters stand at the end of the first quarter? The plan for industry in the first quarter was not only fulfilled but overfulfilled by 7—or perhaps—6 percent. The quality indices are also good. The relationship between the growth of productivity and wages continues to improve. In agriculture the plan is also being fulfilled. Spring planting went on successfully. But, as the saying goes, don't count your chickens before they're hatched.

For a long time in our country there was stagnation in the economy. Only in 1964 did a slight improvement begin, as you know.

It should be said that there is considerable interest in our economic affairs among different firms, including firms in influential circles in the FRG and other Western countries. They are determined to offer us aid, credits, and so on. There have also been personal contacts, in particular with West German social democrats. Matters have advanced so far that a representative of Brandt came to our Central Committee, to Cde. Lenárt, and asked that he be received for talks. We discussed this among ourselves and decided not to receive him.[12]

Such interest indicates, above all, that West Germany is looking for new markets and outlets for capital investment. Of course, they want to use economic levers for political ends as well. This accounts for their concern about our economy, a situation that they know very well.

A. N. Kosygin, N. V. Podgorny: This, of course, isn't real help but an effort to exploit their influence. They're less interested in new markets.

---

[11] Ladislav Mňačko was a Slovak writer whose novels, short stories, and essays were celebrated for their anti-Stalinist themes. Mňačko also gained prominence for his condemnation of the CPCz's periodic reliance on anti-Semitism. In the summer of 1967 he strongly criticized Czechoslovakia's opposition to Israel during the Six-Day Mideast War. In a further gesture of protest against Czechoslovak policy he traveled to Israel in August 1967. The CPCz authorities promptly denounced Mňačko as a traitor and stripped him of his citizenship, forcing him to live in exile. His case became one of the main pretexts for Hendrych and Novotný to shut down *Literární noviny.* Mňačko was not permitted to return to Czechoslovakia until mid-1968. Following the Soviet invasion he had to leave the country again, and at that point settled in West Germany.

[12] According to Document No. 26, Bahr was received unofficially by senior officials from the International Department. Although it is true that Bahr did not meet with Lenárt or other members of the CPCz CC Presidium, it is not entirely correct to say, as Dubček did, that the Czechoslovak authorities "decided not to receive him."

A. Dubček: I know, I know. This is help in quotation marks, that was how I used the word.

L. I. Brezhnev: Some of the socialist countries have already experienced such "help," and then they didn't know how to cope with the consequences.

N. V. Podgorny: There's no such thing as a free lunch.

A. Dubček: We should of course remember that even earlier there were certain economic contacts between us and some West German firms. This is more or less normal, provided that it is carried on within well-defined parameters. It even led to overtures by some of West Germany's competitors, especially the French. We have a somewhat different attitude to them, taking into account France's policy. On the whole, we support the expansion of economic ties, above all with the Soviet Union as well as with the other socialist countries. This is important economically, strategically, and in other ways. It is important for the future development of our economy. I wish to emphasize here, once again, that the CPCz and the government of Czechoslovakia will not retreat an inch from cooperation with the Soviet Union. And I must also say that we will not manage without an internal injection to support our economy. The enemies are counting on the fact that we will not succeed in improving our economic affairs and that this will leave us vulnerable.

We ask you, comrades, to consider and then to decide, perhaps during the visit of our party-state delegation, the question of providing Czechoslovakia with long-term credits in convertible currency. We have in mind a credit period of 8, 10, and 15 years. We also ask that you examine the question of increasing supplies to us this year of wheat, an increase of approximately 300,000 tons above what was already agreed upon by treaty.

. . .

L. I. Brezhnev: Nowadays one hears more frequent talk about some sort of "new model of socialism" that has not existed until now. It's as if there should no longer be the kind of socialism built by the CPCz in the course of many years, based on the working class. Is it not for these aims that Western credits are being offered to you?

Less than a week after the new CC Presidium was elected, there were louder and louder cries that some Presidium member was a conservative, another a traitor, and President Svoboda was even elevated to being "an enemy of the people"! These loudmouths don't even spare Cde. Smrkovský, who was just elected chairman of the National Assembly; and even Cde. Dubček is not to their liking. Someone must be methodically organizing this wild mayhem.

In such circumstances, comrades, it's especially important to maintain unity in the CC Presidium itself. Such unity is the basis for success. To our dismay we see signs that imply a lack of such unity. For example, Cde. Dubček gave a good speech at the regional party conference in Brno, but immediately after him, the central committee secretary Cde. Císař spoke and said just the opposite. This, of course, is an isolated instance, but it tells us something. The mistakes made in the past should be rectified. That is not the issue. If someone was unjustifiably humiliated, then matters should be rectified. But the problem is not this. By the way, I'd like to mention the following. Don't imagine that we here are acting in the role of some sort of defenders of Cde. Novotný. I officially inform you here in the name of our Politburo that we are not.

There were attempts to cast a suspicious cloud over my visit to Prague in December of last year.[13] This visit took place after an invitation was extended to me in the name of the CPCz CC Presidium, and I accepted it with the intention of taking a short rest and getting in a bit of hunting, as well as having a comradely exchange of views on general themes. But once I was in Prague I unexpectedly found myself in the very midst of events that were reaching a climax. When I learned that it was a matter of a proposal to separate the posts of CC first secretary and president

---

[13] See Document No. 3 above.

of the country, I immediately said that I saw no problems arising from it. As you know, the separation of leading party and state has been carried out in our country, and also by the Hungarians and the Poles.[14] And it never caused any particular problems. But I was already struck by the danger arising from the lack of unity in the leading party bodies. At the time I had talks with members of the Presidium and with CPCz CC secretaries, and for several hours I talked with Cde. Dubček. You probably remember, Cde. Dubček, what happened, don't you?

A. Dubček: I spoke about it at the CC plenum. I said there was no interference, and Cde. Smrkovský said the same thing at a mass meeting attended by 18,000 people.

L. I. Brezhnev: In a situation as complicated as the present one there is not so much danger from clergymen as from all those different "clubs" with their political demands. The government should restrict the activities of these clubs in some way.

Comrades, you know about the CPSU's principled position based on full respect for the independence of all fraternal parties and countries. But not every question is a purely internal matter. If, for example, 40,000 people from West Germany cross the border of Czechoslovakia every day without any control, and we have an agreement with you on friendship and mutual assistance and are obliged to defend one another, then this is no longer just an internal matter. If your army is being weakened, that, too, is not simply an internal matter. We rely on your strength just as you rely on the power of the Soviet Union. No one can guarantee that tomorrow a new war will not break out. This is not an internal matter for either side, it is our common affair as communists and Leninists. We, of course, can speak about committing errors and rectifying them, but in doing so we must not forget our main aims. And in your country, in Czechoslovakia, one already finds "officials" who proclaim to the whole world that Marxism–Leninism is an "outmoded dogma", that "Marx and Lenin understood nothing about agriculture," and so on and so on. And after all, your papers are also read by Soviet citizens, your radio is listened to in our country as well, which means that all such propaganda affects us, too.[15]

As regards the rehabilitation of those who were unjustly persecuted, that we understand. We experienced similar things. But to make this problem, today, the main one, means giving extra ammunition to the enemies of the CPCz. After all, unlawful acts were not carried out by the party as a whole, but now they are attempting to depict it in this way.

The situation, I repeat, is very serious. We welcomed the new composition of your leading organs, expecting that once you had corrected the mistakes you would move back along the path of socialist construction. But what is happening now requires an extremely serious reassessment.

For example, on 1 May at some demonstration or other in your country a resolution was adopted concerning Poland. At the demonstration it seems the people did not agree with what was happening in Poland and within the Polish leadership.[16] But this is already a provocation by anti-socialist elements who are also to be found in Poland. This is no longer an "internal matter." To carry out or not to carry out economic reform and in what form to carry it out—that, in the

[14] In the Soviet Union there was a separation of top party and state posts after Khrushchev's ouster, when a "triumvirate" was formed of Brezhnev, Kosygin, and Podgorny. This separation was feasible because the potential for abuse when too many posts were held by a single individual had been all too apparent under Stalin and Khrushchev. Gradually, however, as Brezhnev consolidated his power, he, too, began to accumulate functions, taking on the post of president (chairman of the Presidium of the Supreme Soviet) after Podgorny died. This same accumulation of posts was evident under Brezhnev's three successors, including Mikhail Gorbachev, who served simultaneously after 1989 as both CPSU general secretary and president of the USSR.

[15] This statement well illustrates the extent of Soviet concern about the political "spill-over" from the Prague Spring.

[16] Brezhnev is referring here to a large student demonstration held outside the Polish embassy in Prague on May 1 to express support for Polish students and to protest the forceful anti-Semitic campaign under way in Poland. An even larger student rally was organized near the embassy on May 3, the day before this meeting in Moscow. On May 6, the Polish government lodged a strong official complaint about these incidents.

end, is your affair. But there are questions about which communists in other countries cannot be silent. At the moment a vicious political struggle is going on. In these circumstances, communists should close their ranks; nothing should be able to break their unity.

When we began seeing stories that cast blame on the USSR as the instigator of Jan Masaryk's suicide, we particularly reexamined the whole issue to see how matters stood.[17] We searched the archives and made sure that all this was nothing but groundless rumors. . . .

A. Dubček: Our official information bureau ČTK published a statement by Masaryk's former private secretary, who was witness to the fact that for several days Masaryk was consciously preparing to commit suicide.

L. I. Brezhnev: But at first the shadow was cast on us. Such commotion was impinging on the Soviet Union, yet no one offered any resistance to it. This left us in the position of having to act alone, despite the shadow cast on us by the press, radio, and television.

When we express our concerns, we are not making up anything, we are not looking for artificial circumstances. The facts speak for themselves. In your country at a May Day demonstration the American flag was waving freely. What does that imply? Does it mean that the Czechoslovak people and the CPCz are now willing to stand by this flag? And I won't even bother to mention such things as the shameful telephone calls that are frequently being made to the USSR embassy, the threats that are made against us, the calls for us "to get out of Czechoslovakia," and so on. All this attests to the fact that counterrevolutionary forces exist in your country and are becoming more active.

. . .

V. Biľak: I understand and share your concerns, comrades. We are underestimating the anti-socialist forces. We have been somewhat blinded by what we regard as our achievements. The biggest mistake is that purely intra-party matters have become a subject of public discussion. The most secret party issues are now being discussed by students on the streets, demands are being raised for an extraordinary party congress, and so on. In our policy one feels a certain timidity. And one hears public statements to the effect that everyone in the leadership is in office only "temporarily."

I agree with what was said about the positive aspects of our policy, but that is weakened by acts that contradict it. The enemies are doing everything to prevent the consolidation of our forces; they want to impose methods on the party we do not regard as acceptable. The truth is that we have relinquished control over the press, radio, and television. Cde. Smrkovský may speak to an audience of 100,000, but the editors of newspapers write something else for an audience of 8 million readers. On 1 May in Ostrava, Cde. Černík was carried on the shoulders of marchers, but the editors of newspapers wrote that he "failed miserably."

A. Dubček: We've cleared up this question. It turned out that the editorial board of the newspaper included the spouse of a person who had been removed from his post earlier.

V. Biľak: As long as these people act this way we will not move forward. Their tactics are intended to lull us to sleep, to praise Dubček, and to discredit the others, exploiting the fact that there is no unity in the CC Presidium. And they are all too well aware of this. We intend to discuss the whole matter seriously.

The enemy intends to isolate Dubček so that the working class and the whole population no longer trust him; they want to discredit individual leaders and, through them, the whole party.

[17] On April 3, the Czechoslovak government announced that it was opening an investigation into the death of former Foreign Minister Jan Masaryk, whose purported suicide by defenestration occurred under suspicious circumstances in 1948. Numerous articles in the Czechoslovak press in the spring of 1968 alleged that Masaryk had in fact been murdered by Soviet agents.

Their first aim was to remove the "conservatives." Their next aim is to discredit the policy of the CPCz in the 1950s; the issue here is not only one of positions, but also such acts as the collectivization of agriculture. We all know that this was not easy work. We are proud of its results and its historical significance, but we know that when it was carried out, individual mistakes were made. Now the enemies are trying to cash in on this.

After that they intend to take up the events of 1948. One can already hear talk that a minority came to power, that it was allegedly an "undemocratic" act.

At first rumors were spread about the murder of Jan Masaryk, and now, unconfirmed by anyone, there is talk about "intellectual murder" by the communists. Next, attacks will begin against the resistance movement and an "analysis" will be made of the CPCz's policies in the period leading up to Munich. Communists will be blamed for daring to struggle against the "great Masaryk," because in our country today one increasingly hears the slogan "learn from Tomáš Masaryk."[18]

All this is being said in order to bolster a single conclusion: namely, that the Communist Party of Czechoslovakia, so to say, was never a party of the people, and that the state should be led by another, very different, party. Today in our country the communist party is being vilified daily. It can be said that in our country nowadays everyone is good, and only the communists are bad. Unfortunately, this is even being repeated by members of our own party. We know there are various people among them. One has only to remember that after 1948, 100,000 former members of the National Socialist Party entered the Communist Party of Czechoslovakia.

We are all thinking about how to strengthen the leading role of the communist party. Every day on radio and television people hear slander against the party. By our very actions, we ourselves are convincing the people that communists are "dirty people." What will young people think about the party?

The greatest danger is that the press, radio, and television are no longer in our hands.

. . .

[Recess in the talks.]

L. I. Brezhnev: Now, let's go back to what's happening in Czechoslovakia. It turned out that all recent events there were objectively aimed at discrediting the communist party, whether you wanted them to be or not. The party's enemies have succeeded in carrying out their evil intentions at this stage. First there was a great commotion, then the removal of cadres got under way. All of a sudden everyone turned out to be bad, including the minister of national defense, the minister of foreign affairs, and the minister of internal affairs, as well as other leading officials.[19] I don't know whether this was necessary, but removing these people undoubtedly cast a shadow over the whole party. Until that time no one had shown that your foreign policy was incorrect or that things were bad in the army. And these comrades were removed in such a way that it appeared they had done something terrible. Hence, it can be said that in this second stage the party's enemies succeeded in achieving their aims.

Under the guise of democratization the press, radio, and television, which have now eluded the party's control, are seeking to push malicious practice to the limit. I wish to emphasize, comrades, that this entire ideological machine is working in an organized way; all are aiming at a single target. They are attacking the party, attacking its cadres, attacking its theory, and impinging on inter-governmental relations with the socialist countries, including the Soviet Union. Insinuations are heard either about the economic difficulties of Czechoslovakia for which the Soviet Union is held responsible, or about the burden of spending on the army which is the

---

[18] Tomáš Masaryk was the charismatic founding president of the Czechoslovak Republic in 1918 and the father of Jan Masaryk.

[19] In order, these officials were Bohumír Lomský, Václav David, and Josef Kudrna, all of whom were ousted in March–April 1968, at around the same time that Novotný was removed.

"fault" of the Warsaw Pact, or about some other matter. All this bears the hallmark of being organized by a single center, and there is a great deal of evidence to prove it.

As a result, former political parties are increasing their demands, new "clubs" are appearing, hostile parties and student organizations have been activated, and many other things are going on about which you, comrades, may not even be aware. I think all this is in preparation for a new stage: in preparation for the overthrow of the CPCz Central Committee and its policy and the overthrow of the current leadership. Someone has already remarked that Dubček and Černík are "transitional figures," and that new people must come and take their place. And what kind of people are to replace them? No one says anything about that. Yet it is clear that the organizers of all these acts have their program, and they believe in what they do. They are supported by the USA and the FRG, but they are being warned: conduct yourselves cautiously, don't give cause for intervention from outside. They want the counterrevolution in Czechoslovakia to come about without a repetition of the Hungarian events.

Whether you want them to or not, comrades, matters are going on in this way; everything is becoming clearer, stage after stage. Cde. Biľak correctly analyzed the specific, serious circumstances of this trying period.

Your news agency ČTK transmits the Devil knows what, even defaming Lenin and Marx. I don't know whether you actually read such things, comrades. The truth is that drunken peasants at a country fair behave better than these journalists do.

In the end, you're entitled to your own assessment of the actions of the Polish leadership, but a struggle is a struggle. This leadership punched the enemies of the party in the nose and honestly said that they would not surrender workers' power to anyone. In Hungary the same thing began with the activities of the writers' clubs, and it ended when they started hanging communists.[20] And many hid behind slogans of friendship with the Soviet Union. And in your country the same kinds of threats are being heard in the villages. I don't want to be a prophet, but if you now let things drift along, it might end up with communists being hanged in your country. And not everyone will be saved then. And what then will Comrades Dubček, Černík, Smrkovský, and others say to the people? What can we say? If 1.7 million communists are done away with, then people will ask: And where was the CPSU, why did it not fulfill its internationalist duty?

You consider yourselves the "leading force," but secretaries from the CPCz district branches who've been released from their duties are not being hired by anyone else. They wander around starving, yet the young peacocks with their counterrevolutionary slogans freely gather on the squares.

Comrades, we have spoken about everything here very sharply but honestly, in a comradely way. I agree that in your country there are healthy forces, but you haven't turned to them. Everything happening in your country seems to be like a palace *coup d'état*. Something is about to erupt in Prague, yet you don't turn to the working class. The working class stands on the sidelines, it has not yet understood what is happening in your country, who is being changed for whom.

Take Procházka, is he a leading force in your society, a leader of your party? The party put its trust in him and Procházka does whatever he wants. And what a mild expression we use—"anti-socialist elements"! Are we communists or aren't we? Why are we afraid?

There are all sorts of things in your clubs.

That is why we express such concern and we think: What is going to happen next? We don't believe that you consciously wish to relinquish the leading role of the communist party and share power with, say, social democrats. We want to believe that you understand this is the most trying period in the history of your state and party, and in the history of socialist construction in Czechoslovakia. Some of the things that are going on in your country demand an official response

[20] An allusion to the formation of anti-Stalinist cultural and writers' groups such as the Petőfi Circle in Hungary in 1956.

from us. Let's say they're trying to vilify us by disseminating all sorts of fabrications about the death of Jan Masaryk. Our conscience on this matter is absolutely clear. We cannot put up with any reproaches. No one in your country is rebutting these attacks.

A. Dubček: True . . .

L. I. Brezhnev: And yet all this involves us, as a state. If we give our own theoreticians the right to reply to these "theoretical" explanations that Procházka and his ilk are currently spouting in your country, we'll see on whose side the truth lies.

The question has arisen of the unity of your state, of the unity of Czechs and Slovaks. It is not a simple question, not one to be solved at a moment's notice. In the past, it is true, some harm or other was done to the interests of the Slovaks for no valid reason. At one time we spoke very openly about this to Cde. Novotný. Why, for instance, were they afraid to call Bratislava the capital of Slovakia, what's so terrible about that?

N. V. Podgorny: I spoke to Novotný about that on the 50th anniversary of the October Revolution.

L. I. Brezhnev: As far as we are concerned, we never persecuted either the Slovaks or the Czechs. I know Czechoslovakia from long ago and from close up. In the war years I had to cross it, along with our fighters, from Čop to Prague, and I can say with full assurance: Both the Slovaks and the Czechs are dear to the Soviet people, like their own brothers.

I would like our talks about the situation that has emerged in Czechoslovakia to be more open in character. All along we've been hearing soothing pronouncements that things in general are all right, that in two or three weeks things will improve, and so on. Yet events continue to develop there and the situation is becoming ever more tense. The actions of hostile forces are acquiring an increasingly dynamic and organized character. Things have deteriorated so much that at demonstrations American flags are waved freely. This, comrades, is a serious fact when you think that it is happening in a socialist country. We're somewhat surprised, I would say, by the casual assessment of events that you've given us here. We believe that the events at present are being organized and directed by forces linked to the West. The thread that controls them clearly leads to France, to West Germany, in a word, you yourselves know where. Let us speak openly, comrades: Can one fail to emphasize the significance of facts such as the daily travel by 40,000 tourists from the West to your country? We know that in their time these "tourists" carried arms to Hungary in order to supply the counterrevolutionaries. If such matters don't upset you, they do upset the GDR, Poland, and the Soviet Union. After all, we're bound to you by a Treaty of Mutual Defense. We expect that the borders of Czechoslovakia will be protected, yet in reality it turns out that your border with the FRG is open. Don't misunderstand us, comrades. We are not against tourism as such. Tourism, when organized properly, is a natural thing, and it does not give rise to any questions. But when 40,000 people go, without any background check, to a country and travel around in their own cars to military units and wherever they want, this cannot but cause serious dismay. It might well be said beforehand that among these people a good half are Americans or West German spies. No money is being spared for such purposes.

We should very much like things to be as you say they are. We would be glad if Cde. Smrkovský's announcement is confirmed; if so, then within a few months matters will have been corrected.[21]

As for rehabilitations, it does no good to make such a ruckus about this issue. Instead, you should pursue political measures and an examination of specific cases, and avoid propaganda around the issue. The tragedy is that a purely intra-party matter in your country now has become

[21] Brezhnev is referring here to Smrkovský's pledge to introduce new border controls. In late March and early April the Czechoslovak border guards had dismantled a series of barbed-wire and electric fences along the border with the FRG. See "Les militaires enlèvent des barbeles à la frontière germano-tchèque," *Le Monde* (Paris), April 5, 1968, p. 5.

over a few days accessible to the man in the street. The life of the party, its plans, its errors, and its failures must and should be considered within the party. After the party decides, some of these things are then communicated to the public in a certain form. But to bring into the open the most delicate questions, especially considering the situation that exists in your country, hardly coincides with the party's interests. Yet issues like this have become accessible to all those "clubs" and immature young people. What is a first or second year student? A young person of 18 to 19. What do they understand about politics? There are special organizations for their political education; the Komsomol exists for that purpose, it is intended to educate such youth. And in your country these youngsters are insisting that they be allowed to run the country on the same level as the government. As you see, they want to set up an independent party and take part independently in elections to the National Assembly and to put forward their own program. Is it possible to tolerate such things in silence?

I'll tell you frankly, Cde. Smrkovský, I know that you are a strong-willed person, but in support of those general prognoses you laid out here for us, you said nothing about what can be done and will be done in concrete terms.

And I also want to say that I consider it incorrect to adopt all sorts of resolutions concerning Polish matters, the policies of the fraternal Polish party. That party has its own problems and its own difficulties, and it wants to solve them as it believes fit. Resolutions that you adopted in your country, naturally, will not help matters.

A. Dubček: That was a provocation.

L. I. Brezhnev: Of course, a provocation. But just look at how things turned out: the representatives of one or another of these circles sing praises of Dubček in one place, and in another place they demand that he be removed from the leadership. They act in a way that they consider advantageous to themselves. I'm sure that the working class of Czechoslovakia supports its communist party and will follow it. But the whole truth must be told, and it is necessary to remove those who do not support party policy.

I cannot understand: why are you able to remove the minister of foreign affairs and the minister of defense from their posts, yet are unable to decide to remove an editor of a newspaper who is following a line that is not in keeping with the party's policy?

I don't know what mistakes Cde. David made when he held the post of minister of foreign affairs. I only know that he always was a good communist and honorably upheld the cause of socialism. In the years of Nazi occupation he was a member of the underground party organization, and he fought against fascism. By the way, he probably fought with Cde. Smrkovský, and, as you see, in that period they were friends. Now for some reason he has been removed. And yet you do not have enough strength to insist that a high-handed editor toe the line. Look how many ministers you have recalled, comrades, and what kind of ministers! I don't know how all this can be explained to the working class, to the party.

It is necessary, comrades, to have a clear view of the purpose of events, to see where they are heading, and in which direction. And now attempts are getting under way to concentrate the attacks on Slovakia and its leaders. Such tendencies clearly exist insofar as people in Slovakia uphold correct positions and so the attacks are directed against them. You are surely well aware of this, even Cde. Biľak is described as one of the conservatives.

V. Biľak: They're already writing that.

L. I. Brezhnev: I don't know whether you're aware of it, but your television service has already put together special programs about prisons.[22] They're only waiting for the right moment to

---

[22] Here Brezhnev appears to know about this issue before Dubček and his top aides. The Soviet leader received a steady flow of information about "unhealthy" developments through the KGB, the Soviet Embassy in Prague, hardline Czech officials in the CPCz, and Czech state security and military forces.

broadcast them. You can well imagine what they'll feature on them. This obviously will be a new blow to the leadership.

Now you're saying that you'll be raising the question of the unjust acts of Cde. Gottwald and Cde. Zápotocký. I don't know what happened, possibly some sort of mistakes did occur, although in the end one cannot attribute all the unjust acts, let's say, to Gottwald personally. But to the counterrevolutionaries your accusations come as a gift. This will be still another blow to your party, comrades.

A. Dubček: The talk about Gottwald's role in these matters was begun by Cde. Novotný at the most recent plenum.

J. Smrkovský: We didn't want it.

N. V. Podgorny: Then you should have called Novotný to task.

L. I. Brezhnev: I can't imagine that the party was not in a position to restore order. Of course it has the capacity to do that. But at the given moment the counterrevolutionary forces, the successors of the bourgeoisie, are given freedom to act as they please, and they are raging in full force. This freedom of action was given to 1.5 million former members of the once-disbanded fascist and bourgeois parties. It is not the workers who are calling for the overthrow of the CC Presidium. They are not. The workers have never spoken out against Černík or against Dubček or against Smrkovský. Who, then, is speaking out? These actions are the work of forces which for the moment are underground, and they have in their hands radio, television, the press, and various "clubs." They are the ones who are organizing this work. We cannot have any illusions about the workers. For the moment the workers are only looking at what is going on. You yourselves say that the workers support the CPCz. Talking about the people as a whole does not make things entirely clear. More than half the people of your country, evidently, are workers, and a significant percentage are peasants. The intelligentsia is relatively small in numbers, although it pulls a certain weight.

If you were really to call upon the workers, the picture would be somewhat different. But on this matter, it seems, nothing is being done. I don't know: Perhaps, in the end, it is suddenly difficult to do, but we have the impression that all that could be done is not being done.

. . .

[Kosygin and Podgorny give further speeches reemphasizing the points made by Brezhnev.]
. . .

L. I. Brezhnev: The main thing is to decide in what manner the cause of socialism can best be defended in Czechoslovakia. This question concerns not only Czechoslovakia itself but your neighbors and allies, and the entire world communist movement. All of us are ready to offer assistance if it is needed. We ourselves are ready to do this, and because I know the views of Cdes. Gomułka, Ulbricht, Zhivkov, and the others I can say they are prepared for this as well. The world communist movement is looking at the CPCz. It seems to us that as a result of today's talks one could conclude that the moment has arrived when the CPCz CC Presidium should clearly state to one and all what kind of line it will pursue and point out the dangerous phenomena that have appeared in the country, and really explain which of these phenomena it does not support and will struggle against with all means available. This is the only way to defend your honor. You should honestly and directly tell the working class everything and name its enemies. It is incorrect to make concessions and to be reformists; one must truly serve the cause of the party of which you are members. You must be the real leaders of this party. This, if you will, is the only reliable path. To follow that path, you must have unity, courage, strong will, and the support of friends. You must find within yourselves the necessary unity, courage, and willpower. We are ready to offer our support. And if we all help you, that will be powerful support indeed.

If we all begin to speak in our press and on radio, openly citing facts and names, that, too, will be a great force. Now, while we're still discussing all these matters with you, we hear you and we believe you. But if it becomes necessary, we can begin to speak in such a way that everyone can hear, and then the working class will hear the voice of its friends. But it is better for you to do this now yourselves. That will be honest and just. If you uphold the positions that were mentioned here, then matters can be corrected.

. . .

DOCUMENT No. 29: Report on the Visit of Luigi Longo, Italian CP General Secretary, to Czechoslovakia, May 5–7, 1968 (Excerpts)

Source: ÚSD, AÚV KSČ, F. 02/1; Vondrová & Navrátil, vol. 1, pp. 227–231.

This internal memorandum of conversation records talks between Dubček and the general secretary of the Italian Communist Party, Luigi Longo, on May 6, 1968. Longo's two-day visit to Prague reflected the Italian communists' enthusiastic support of the Prague Spring. In his meeting with Dubček, Longo acknowledges that the ICP hoped to "take full advantage" of the excitement created by the reforms in Czechoslovakia to enhance its own electoral prospects and to legitimize its program of "open, democratic socialism" for Italy.

The ICP's endorsement of Czechoslovak reforms angered Soviet officials. Within a day of Longo's departure from Prague, Brezhnev complained that the Italian leader's positive remarks were being "exploited by the unhealthy forces in Czechoslovakia."

The reason for the visit of Luigi Longo, general secretary of the Italian Communist Party, to Prague was the desire of the Italian side to establish contacts with the new leadership of our party, to obtain more information about the current phase of our developments and their prospects, and to exchange opinions on current problems of the international communist and workers' movement.

The centerpiece of the visit was a discussion between Cde. Longo and the first secretary of our party, Cde. Dubček. This was followed by meetings and talks with Cdes. Smrkovský, Černík, Lenárt, Císař, Šik, Husák, Kaderka, and Pudlák. During his visit Cde. Longo granted a lengthy interview to *Rudé právo* and met Czechoslovak and foreign journalists at a final press conference.

* * *

The meeting and talks between Cdes. Dubček and Longo took place on Monday morning, 6 May 1968, at the headquarters of the CPCz Central Committee. Those present on our side included Cdes. Lenárt and Kaderka and two comrades from the international department, and on the Italian side Cde. Boffa from *L'Unità*.[23]

After a cordial welcome, Cde. Longo took the floor.

He pointed out that the Italian Communist Party welcomed our current internal political development because it confirmed the correctness of its own orientation toward "an open democratic socialism." The Italian CP was taking full advantage of this in its election campaign. However, political adversaries have been misusing our developments; they have exploited a variety of exposés about the negative aspects of our past, carried in the Czechoslovak media, in order to claim that there was no freedom in socialist Czechoslovakia and that human dignity had been trampled on.

In response, the Italian CP is highlighting the widespread suppression of civil rights and liberties in the capitalist world, especially in the USA. The party continues to criticize the "left of center" government and is focusing on the prospect of solving the problem of governing Italy. The party's objectives are to defeat the Christian Democratic government and to form a broader unity coalition of secular and Catholic forces.

Cde. Longo said he was convinced that the information he would obtain during his stay in Prague would be of value to their election campaign since, he stressed, the current policy of the CPCz represented a boost for the policy of the Italian CP.[24]

After that Cde. Dubček spoke.

---

[23] G. Boffa's coverage of the reforms in Czechoslovakia for the Italian communist newspaper *L'Unità* was highly favorable throughout 1968.

[24] After substantive gains at the polls during elections on May 19, Italian communist officials suggested that the ICP's showing was at least partly attributable to the boost gained from Longo's visit.

He explained the essence of the problems debated at the post-January session of the CPCz Central Committee and the position of the party leadership on a problem currently being widely discussed among the public: whether the future activity of the party can proceed via a confrontation of views within the National Front, or whether a political opposition is necessary.

When dealing with a variety of our problems we proceed from our specific needs and conditions, and we will always seek to capture our specific aspects as best as possible, always harmonizing them with all the general attributes of socialism. Under no circumstances do we wish to serve as a "model" for other socialist countries. In this respect far too many mistakes have been committed in the past. Nor will we engage in polemics with the others; this in itself would negate the existence of a variety of specific characteristics.

Nevertheless, the period we are now experiencing is complicated. A transition to something new is always accompanied by difficulties, extremes, and incorrect attitudes. On the one hand there is the tendency of some not to abandon practices that have become obsolete; on the other hand, there is the tendency of others to misuse current developments against socialism. We have staunch political adversaries whose ideas are still closely tied to the pre-Munich republic. These right-wing extremists may exploit our good intentions, oppose the direction we intend to pursue, and thus obstruct the democratization process.

Cde. Dubček then briefly explained our position vis-à-vis the church. He concluded by emphasizing our firm ties with the international communist movement, the Soviet Union, and the other socialist countries.

When Cde. Dubček finished, Cde. Longo again took the floor.

He expressed gratitude for the presentation, which will enable him to get a more accurate idea of our problems. He said that Italian communists valued our current efforts and were aware of the difficulties we had to overcome, as well as the many obstacles and threats that emerged whenever changes were taking place.[25] The situation is clearly even more complex because, in his view, these changes were taking place in our country somewhat belatedly. Yet it was necessary to pay the price for this delay because any further hesitation would in no way make a solution easier. On the contrary, the communist party could easily lose control over developments. It is therefore essential to adapt to existing conditions; certain demands were overstepping certain limits, but even this reflected the general situation.

The new conditions introduced by modern society in the economic, social, and political spheres compelled the Italian Communist Party to find a new solution for the relationship between political power and the masses and the fight for greater freedom. It was clear that eliminating the exploitation of man by man was a prerequisite for every type of freedom. In the socialist countries these liberties could already be applied in accordance with the current phase of development, and broadened in all spheres of social activity.

Under present conditions in Italy, and in the current international situation, the party favors plurality in the economy, the social sphere, and culture, along with a positive contribution to the progress of society from the forces that can be won over in the next higher stage of development (e.g., craftsmen). The strength and role of the intelligentsia must also be duly appreciated in the advanced society that now exists. The same is true of the political role of students, whose movement condemning the political institutions of the bourgeois state has acquired explosive proportions in Italy.[26] The Italian student movement, together with various political parties,

---

[25] In the face of ominous threats from Moscow in July and August, Italian communist leaders repeatedly called on neighboring states to refrain from "interfering in the internal affairs of Czechoslovakia." As military intervention began on August 21, ICP leaders condemned the "wholly unjustified" invasion and called for an immediate withdrawal of all Soviet and East European troops.

[26] The ICP came under serious challenge when the Italian student movement (*movimento studentesco*) erupted into violence during almost the whole academic year of 1967–1968. The party's own youth federation, the FGCI, was severely weakened by the rise of several leftist alternatives to the ICP, which succeeded in recruiting militant students who rejected the ICP's willingness to adhere to parliamentary norms.

frequently criticizes even the communist party. They are correct on some points; the party accepts this criticism and has entered into a dialogue with the movement, emphasizing that not all political parties are the same. What the party wants is that despite its sometimes naive, spontaneous, yet honest content, the movement should play an active role. The party is against underrating or even dismissing the student movement. Although the party has no intention of teaching the students a lesson, it wants to enter into a dialogue with them. The Italian CP adopts the same attitude to various left-wing intellectual groups: It holds discussions and argues with them.

The Italian CP respects the positions of the socialist countries and their communist parties, although it sometimes does not fully understand them, especially because there may be substantial differences between individual countries (depending on the kind of difficulties they are encountering). Nevertheless, the Italian CP does not wish to lecture to anyone. Its policy and position are determined by the realities in Italy, and that is why they are valid only for that party and cannot serve as a pattern to be imitated. The Italian CP welcomes our current efforts since they appear to be advancing in a direction that can be considered of a general nature and are able to communicate many things to many quarters. It is impossible to stick to obsolete visions, the idea of socialism must be continually developed and enriched, and modern and dynamic socialism needs to be reflected. Yet even though the idea remains basically the same, in various phases of the development of society it must take on different forms that allow it to achieve further progress and win greater confidence among the working people and the younger generation. In its work among Roman Catholics the party draws on certain positions adopted by the Ecumenical Council and contained in the latest papal encyclicals, since they offer fairly emphatic criticism of capitalist society. This creates conditions for a common struggle of communists, socialists and prominent Catholic forces against capitalism. The Italian CP collaborates with Roman Catholics on a fairly wide scale, some of their representatives have even agreed to stand in the elections on the list of candidates of the Italian CP. Under these conditions, higher church dignitaries are giving their unambiguous backing to the Christian Democratic Party. A close alliance has been established with Roman Catholic forces on the question of the struggle for peace and against US aggression in Vietnam.[27] People such as Cardinal Lercaro, who only ten years ago were in the frontline of the anti-communist struggle, are today prepared to cooperate. The circumstances and content of the recent meeting between Pope Paul VI and Johnson, who again rejected the Pope's request to stop the bombing of the Vietnamese Democratic Republic, strengthened such positions. . . .

[27] The ICP's vehement support of the North Vietnamese government and Vietcong in the war was manifested in such things as prayer vigils, demonstrations, public meetings, and press exchanges, often in conjunction with anti-war groups sponsored by the Church.

DOCUMENT No. 30: Minutes of the CPCz CC Presidium Meeting, May 7–8, 1968 (Excerpts)

Source: ÚSD, AÚV KSČ, F. 02/1.

This document provides a partial transcript of the CPCz CC Presidium meeting immediately following the bilateral Soviet–Czechoslovak negotiations in Moscow. The speeches by Dubček, Smrkovský, and Černík reflect the impact of the criticism they encountered, and the depth of Soviet hostility toward the reform movement. Smrkovský expresses dismay that "events [in Czechoslovakia] have been moving differently from the way we wanted them to," and Černík says he is now "convinced that counterrevolution is on the advance" in Czechoslovakia. Černík exhorts his colleagues to wage a vigorous struggle against the "international bourgeoisie," warning that the situation might otherwise develop as it had in Hungary in 1956. Even Dubček, who appeared somewhat less shaken than either Smrkovský or Černík, endorses his colleagues' remarks and urged the CPCz to do more to foster "socialist tendencies."

Cde. Smrkovský: Comrades, I firmly adhere to the principles we incorporated in the party's Action Program after the January session. When I accepted those principles, I was politically conscious of my action, and I have no intention of changing my mind now.

I say this by way of introduction to emphasize that I still support the direction in which we have set out. Even so, things are moving differently from the way we wanted them to. We want to democratize the life of society and the management of society, and we have won immense sympathy among the mass of the people. This is undeniable, it is a fact. We have regained tremendous support that the party did not enjoy last year.[28] It is a fact that the people once again have hope when they look to the new policy of the party. But while we are making speeches and want to democratize our life, certain others are not rallying around the Action Program or ways of implementing it (which is the other side of the coin of our efforts), but instead are preparing themselves to launch a frontal attack on our positions. On the basis of my convictions and of what I see and hear around me, I must declare my profound beliefs about this matter, rather than attempt to conceal them. I have not concealed them from the Presidium and I will not conceal them from the Central Committee or from our public. What I am going to say is not something I brought back from the Soviet Union because we spoke about these things when we flew out there, and we all said what we thought.

I want to point out that various forces are now rallying for a frontal attack on the position of the party; they want to use all possible means to drown the party—all possible means, they make no distinction. They do not see and do not want to hear about all the good that has been achieved. The mass media are from morning to night ferreting out all the bad things that have happened. Anti-communist forces and an anti-communist front are forming. . . .

If you permit me to say so, I as a communist official certainly do not want to live to see a counterrevolution in this country. . . .

Cde. Černík: I want to say that we regard this phase in the development of socialist democracy to be the advancement of democratic socialism in our country. It has a class character and is democracy for the majority, but is still very far from approaching the notion of democracy for all.

Now that we are facing new tasks of how to promote the development of democracy in this country, I want to say quite clearly that all of us, each one of us, above all each party organ, should be at the forefront of all that is sound and new, and all that is getting under way.

---

[28] A minor adjustment has been made in the translation to convey the proper meaning.

In my view, it is essential to work much harder in the party leadership on the tasks that would enable the party to be in a better position to take its place at the head of the renewal process and to earn the necessary support from all sound forces among our people. . . .

There are voices among the other partners in the National Front—in the other parties and in the columns of their press—saying that individual political parties should not be dependent on the policy of the National Front. They even claim that in the next elections these parties should put up their own candidates. In this situation, where the party does not have a clear position on the matter, events are literally being organized by the mass media in a way that encourages and activates the forces I mentioned earlier—forces that have not forgotten the way things were here in the past and, in some cases, still harbor hopes of revenge for February [1948].

The question is already being raised whether February in Czechoslovakia was historically correct and whether Czechoslovakia's socialist road should not have proceeded in a different direction. Čestmír, don't be angry with me, but I can't accept the notion that we have definitively rejected the Soviet model and without a historical context.[29] Let historians take up this matter; we will be able to analyze it. But if, under current circumstances, we base our policy on a negation of the period after 1948, I suspect we won't be able to generate a consensus within the party. Historians may try to prove this for us. But if, in a concrete situation when the party is blamed for everything and even we start talking in this vein, we're simply providing arguments to forces who today are skinning all of us alive, both from the left and from the right. They want to "prove" that in 20 years the party has not solved a single human problem in this country, that the party is incapable of leading the people during the next decade of social development, and that it is, therefore, necessary to constitute a party that has clean hands, a party that will advocate socialism, but that this will be a Czechoslovak socialism, a Masaryk and Beneš-style socialism. I don't want to fix the responsibility on anyone of us; I am simply telling you what the tactics of the enemy are: in brief, to discredit the party and undermine its leading role.

The assault on the state apparatus is crystal clear. I ask you not to underestimate this problem. Even this workers' regime, this socialist regime, must rely on a strong state apparatus. It is interesting to note against which quarters the attack is being launched: It is not being launched against the ministries in charge of the economy, even though the economy is a weak spot. The attacks, rather than being directed against the State Planning Commission, are being systematically directed against the army, the State Security organs, the police, the courts, the prosecutor's offices, the Ministry of Justice, and, last but not least, the party apparatus. In my opinion, there is an objective reason for this in the process we are encouraging. After all, we are not naive. Every time a campaign was being prepared against the institutions of power or certain components of power, it was always targeted at those places where power was exercised in a certain manner.

I don't want to panic, but I am personally convinced that counterrevolution is on the advance in this country. Counterrevolution does not mean that we have to start bashing each other over the head. It has its roots in certain tendencies, and the question is how one fights against them. Let us not forget that the international bourgeoisie has learned a lesson from Hungary and Poland, where it came out into the open. In Czechoslovakia the international bourgeoisie is in a different position. I don't think things will develop here as in the other countries. The situation here will be different if we do not show sufficient flexibility in standing up to the bourgeoisie properly.

[29] This statement was presumably addressed to Čestmír Císař, a CPCz secretary, who had given a speech earlier in the day to commemorate the 150th anniversary of the birth of Karl Marx. In the speech Císař declared that "every Marxist–Leninist party must have its own policy, which takes account of national conditions." He denied that any party (i.e., the CPSU) could have a "monopoly on the interpretation of Marxism in contemporary circumstances," and he chided those who wanted "a part of the communist movement to be subordinated to another part of the movement." The speech was swiftly condemned by Soviet officials.

Cde. Dubček: . . . As regards our next procedure and assessment of the political situation, I think that what is essential for our next steps forward are the socialist tendencies that, if not universal, are prevalent among an overwhelming majority. They are decisive in setting the tone and the conclusions of what our developments should be in the coming period. That is the decisive force. On the other hand, there are various countervailing pressure groups and efforts to form a political opposition, which were mentioned by Cde. Černík and certain other comrades. I am inclined to maintain that the first priority, which is also the decisive thing on which we must concentrate, is to pursue what is positive, the socialist factor that endorses the Action Program and the policy of the party's Central Committee.

DOCUMENT No. 31: Minutes of the Secret Meeting of the "Five" in Moscow, May 8, 1968 (Excerpts)

Source: ÚSD, Sb. KV, Z/S 3; Vondrová & Navrátil, vol. 1, pp. 193–216.

This transcript of the multilateral conference in Moscow on May 8, 1968 provides an internal account of how Soviet and East European leaders secretly assessed events in Czechoslovakia, weighed their options, and took a further step toward a consensus in favor of military intervention. Initially, Brezhnev informs the communist party leaders of Bulgaria, Poland, East Germany and Hungary of the earlier meeting with the Czechs in Moscow, and Dubček's lack of a "constructive" response. The meeting of the "Five," according to the transcript, then turns to an evaluation of events in Czechoslovakia. Both Ulbricht and Gomułka repeatedly insist that a full-blown "counterrevolution" was under way in Czechoslovakia and that the country was in danger of returning to a "bourgeois order;" Hungarian leader János Kádár, however, argues that counterrevolutionary forces will not gain the upper hand and that most of the negative developments in Czechoslovakia are attributable to Dubček's "fight against mistakes committed in the past" under Novotný. Although Kádár did not wholly discount some of the dangers that had emerged in Czechoslovakia, his clear preference is to work with, rather than against, Dubček and the other Czechoslovak reformers. In contrast, Gomułka, Ulbricht, Zhivkov, and most Soviet officials express the need for outside military intervention if the "healthy" forces within the CPCz are unable to reassert control and rebuff the "counterrevolutionary" forces.

---

8 May 1968

Participants in the talks:[30]
From the Soviet Union: Cdes. L. I. Brezhnev, N. V. Podgorny, A. N. Kosygin, and K. F. Katushev;

From Bulgaria: Cde. T. Zhivkov;

From Hungary: Cde. J. Kádár;

From the GDR: Cdes. W. Ulbricht and G. Axen; and

From Poland: Cde. W. Gomułka.

L. I. Brezhnev: Dear comrades, allow me in the name of the CPSU Central Committee to extend to you a warm welcome in the capital of our homeland, Moscow, and to thank you for responding promptly to our suggestion to meet and exchange opinions on such a pressing issue for all of us as the events in Czechoslovakia.

. . .

[Brezhnev next recounts developments in Czechoslovakia since the Dresden meeting and informed the others about the Soviet–Czechoslovak talks on May 4.]

L. I. Brezhnev: At the outset of our talks, Cde. Dubček informed us about the situation in the country. He spoke for two hours. After he was done, Cde. Černík spoke, followed by Cde. Smrkovský and Cde. Biľak.

I won't go into details about Cde. Dubček's remarks. They were quite similar to his speech in Dresden. He said nothing constructive; he limited himself to general assurances to the effect that they are coping with events. Not surprisingly, he said nothing about the May Day

---

[30] This transcript is one of a number of documents that the Russian government provided to the Czechoslovak commission in April 1992.

demonstration in Prague. He admitted that as yet they do not control the press, radio, and television, but was sure that they would cope with these, too. In other words, his remarks were, so to speak, of a reassuring character.

Cde. Smrkovský gives the impression of being a solid person, reserved, who doesn't speak very much. He spoke only briefly. He, too, had nothing constructive to say, but he answered several of our questions. He spoke about the need to conclude the rehabilitation process. On the whole he let it be known that the picture we described gives us much food for thought.

The most constructive, most appropriate, and most precise speaker was Cde. Biľak. He fully admitted that the communist party in Czechoslovakia today is being badgered by enemies who attack skillfully and in an organized manner. He expressed the view that a center must exist that is directing all this work, which is encountering no resistance at present except for the occasional delivery of speeches. Unfortunately, said Cde. Biľak, we do not control the press, radio, and television. The party is being attacked by all sorts of "clubs" that came into existence recently, by former social democrats, and by leaders of the socialist and national parties, who are now becoming active. One of the avenues of attack against the CPCz at present, in his view, is the demand for an extraordinary party congress. He is certain that the Slovak Communist Party is holding fast. There is demagoguery there, too, but the party leadership has the situation under control. The Slovak Communist Party does not support the proposal to hold an extraordinary congress of the CPCz. If a resolution is adopted to convene such a congress, Slovak communists will not attend.

For our part we said that we regard the current situation in Czechoslovakia to be exceptionally dangerous. We see that the CPCz Central Committee, because of its indecisiveness, is suffering losses and relinquishing one position after another, while counterrevolutionary, or as they call it, anti-socialist elements are gaining the upper hand. Things have deteriorated so far that these forces, who make no attempt to conceal their political demands, want a say in running the country.

The non-communist parties are insisting on "equality" and are demanding to be allowed to set up their own local and regional party branches, and to have the right to take part in elections on a par with the CPCz in the role of an opposition. The notorious "Club-231" has sprung into action; this club consists of former social democrats. A new "Club of Committed Non-Party Members" has emerged, which also has proclaimed itself a political organization and announced that it, if you please, has "clean hands" and is said to be supported by six million people outside the party.[31]

We emphasized once again that the CPCz CC does nothing to control the work of television, radio, the press, and especially its central organ, the newspaper *Rudé právo*.

We said all this in a sharp and disapproving tone. . . .

. . . In other words, the talks we had were serious, not less but if anything more detailed than in Dresden, insofar as the Dresden meeting was held when events that later took place in Czechoslovakia had not yet occurred. Events have since taken on an acute and open character. Therefore we had grounds to speak clearly about them. We had the feeling that the talks made a certain impression on the Czechoslovak comrades. True, Dubček has reacted to all this rather superficially. He said that the situation will be rectified and that the party will see to it that it takes the leadership of society into its hands, but he was unable to say in what way or how this will be done concretely.

We advised the Czechoslovak leaders in a comradely way: Put a member of the Presidium in the editorial office of *Rudé právo*, if only for a few months, and another Presidium member in the radio and television stations so that those people can take the work of these institutions under their control. We also suggested to the Czechoslovak comrades that they speak to their working

---

[31] See Document No. 38. The figure of six million was the approximate number of adults in Czechoslovakia who did not belong to the CPCz.

class openly, to tell it honestly and truthfully about the situation that has been created, and to call upon it to act.

What concrete steps have we taken recently? We sent a large military delegation, headed by Marshals of the Soviet Union I. S. Koniev and K. S. Moskalenko, to the celebrations of the 23rd anniversary of Czechoslovakia's liberation.[32] Delegations from twin cities, headed by regional committee secretaries, were also sent to Czechoslovakia for the celebrations.

Because the Soviet Union was in no way involved in the circumstances of Jan Masaryk's suicide, we believed it essential to publish a corresponding statement in TASS that would refute the provocative insinuations by reactionary circles in Czechoslovakia on this issue.[33]

Today in *Literaturnaya Gazeta* there is a major article entitled "Which Train did Procházka Miss?" This article uses pungent language to give Procházka a dressing-down for his attacks on Marxist–Leninist teachings and for his anti-socialist perorations.

Several more articles are being prepared, and if the course of events makes it necessary to publish them, we are ready to do so.[34]

We also intend to send a short letter to Cde. Černík in which we will set out, as we did during the talks in Moscow, our concerns regarding the ČSSR's borders with the West. These borders are, in fact, wide open, and we will stress the great danger this poses for the socialist camp, including the Soviet Union. The problem is that during the talks in Moscow we did not receive from the Czechoslovak comrades a concrete explanation of the measures they will take to seal off the borders to our enemies.

For certain reasons we'll explain to you later, we're deferring the delivery of this letter. We have the impression that by raising the question, we made the Czechoslovak friends pause and think. They saw that our concerns were not unjustified and that in light of these circumstances the CPSU and the Soviet Union will not remain mere bystanders or indifferent observers of what is going on.

It comes as little surprise that before leaving Moscow, the ČSSR leadership told us: "When we return to Prague, correspondents will meet us at the airport. What can we tell them about the talks in Moscow?" We replied: "Tell them honestly everything that happened. That's the way things are run in your country, you're supposed to tell the correspondents everything." They decided to consult with each other about this on their flight back to Prague.

Several conclusions can be drawn from our negotiations with the Czechoslovak comrades. Above all, these talks were clearly beneficial. Take Smrkovský, for instance. You remember that in my speech in Dresden I described him quite negatively, based on an interview he had given to West German television. Now, after the talks in Moscow, he said at the airport in Prague that "the talks were beneficial to socialism." You see, we still don't know Smrkovský well enough, we aren't fully aware of his political leanings.

The Czechoslovak comrades told us that on Monday a joint session of the CPCz CC Presidium and Secretariat would be held so that they can assess the results of the regional party conferences

[32] Marshal Ivan Koniev and Marshal Kirill Moskalenko were among the most distinguished Soviet military officers; in 1968 the former was inspector-general of the Soviet armed forces, and the latter was the chief inspector. They were heading a military delegation on an extended visit to fifteen Czechoslovak cities, ostensibly so that they could assess the combat preparations and readiness of Czechoslovak troops. But, as Brezhnev indicates in his speech, the main purpose of their mission was actually to exert political pressure on the CPCz leadership.

[33] The TASS statement, released the previous day (May 7), came in response to events following the ČSSR government's announcement about an investigation into the death of Jan Masaryk. Of particular concern from Moscow's perspective—what Brezhnev referred to as "provocative insinuations by reactionary circles"—were the frequent allegations in the Czechoslovak press that Masaryk was murdered by Soviet agents. The TASS statement insisted that these charges were being concocted by "enemies of socialist Czechoslovakia" who were seeking to "stir up anti-Soviet sentiments among politically unstable people."

[34] This effort was coordinated by V. Stepakov, the deputy head of the CPSU CC Propaganda Department. Detailed evidence of his work is contained in the once-secret files of the CPSU. See, in particular, the memoranda and reports in TsKhSD, F. 5, Op. 60, Dd. 24 and 25.

and evaluate the current political situation, and then determine the activities of the CPCz in the immediate future. In fact this meeting has begun and is continuing today for a second day.[35] From our preliminary information it is evident that after Cde. Dubček's report, a debate ensued. Six persons among those present offered a realistic and sober assessment of the way matters stand in Czechoslovakia and demanded that the struggle against counterrevolution be pursued. They are now considering having the government address the people and call for an offensive to be launched against the anti-socialist elements. Talks are under way about the best way for the Central Committee to regain control of the daily *Rudé právo* and of the radio and television.

On 11 May, as our friends have said, they intend to get together all the regional and district secretaries of the communist party in the ČSSR. Today we received a message that preparations for this gathering have been entrusted to Cde. Kolder. That's a good sign because recently Cde. Kolder, as we know, fully understood and agreed with the conclusions we drew in Dresden and with our assessment of the situation in Czechoslovakia. Now in the Central Committee he occupies a decisive position, the position of an active fighter against the advance of counterrevolution.

We also know that other comrades have taken a correct and principled position. This includes comrades Indra and Biľak. These comrades believe that perhaps Cde. Černík will join them. A correct position seems to have been taken by a member of the Secretariat—the Secretary of the Ostrava region of the party, the only one of the former regional secretaries who remained at his post—Cde. Voleník.[36]

Judging from this preliminary information, serious talks have begun in the party leadership. The session of the CPCz CC Presidium and Secretariat is continuing and discussion is going on pretty much along the same lines as yesterday. As yet we do not have any more concrete or more detailed information.

Unfortunately, there is no unity within the leadership among the Czechoslovak friends. Cde. Černík mentioned this during the talks in Moscow. We were informed—but just how precisely we still don't know—that at the CPCz CC Presidium and Secretariat session, Cde. Smrkovský used strong arguments. He spoke about the inception of counterrevolution and about the need to move from declarations and speeches to action. It will be good if he really upholds such a position.

We also have information about Cde. Smrkovský's speech at a meeting of activists in the Ministry of the Interior on 6 May, that is, just after he returned from Moscow. Cde. Smrkovský said it was necessary to struggle against counterrevolution and to appeal to the people for help and support. If the measures that the CPCz leadership and the government must take do not help, it will be necessary to act as in February 1948, that is, to have the working class come out into the streets with arms. If this information about Cde. Smrkovský's speech is accurate, then it's a good sign that the Czechoslovak leaders drew the proper conclusions from the Moscow talks.

We're not convinced that tomorrow everything will be fine in Czechoslovakia or that the situation will improve there overnight, but the very fact that urgent questions are now being considered at the level of the CPCz CC Presidium and Secretariat, combined with the tone of the discussion at the joint session, gives us hope that a more sober view is emerging and that our friends are beginning to look for concrete ways to fight counterrevolution.

I think we'll have to continue to exchange information about the way things develop in Czechoslovakia and to come up with joint measures to help our Czechoslovak friends defend the leading role of the party and uphold the cause of socialism in Czechoslovakia.

What is absolutely essential for us to do today? Above all we must make sure that in the press in our countries, in all our speeches, and in works put out by artistic unions and other

---

[35] See Document No. 30.
[36] Oldřich Voleník, a CPCz CC secretariat member, was widely regarded as one of the strongest opponents of the Prague Spring, yet he somehow retained his post.

organizations, nothing appears that might be construed as even slightly encouraging to the "new model of socialism" which the anti-socialist elements in the ČSSR claim to be creating.

Cde. Gomułka: No doubt, we'll have to speak out in general against the CPCz Action Program.

L. I. Brezhnev: I think the program can be a target later, in the next phase.

W. Ulbricht: We can't even publish this program in our country.

L. I. Brezhnev: It's not necessary to do that. We only let our people know about that program in abridged form.

Not everything Dubček says today is encouraging. It's hard to tell whether he lacks energy or is simply inexperienced. He and I have met many times and we've talked, and I personally sent him a letter, as directed by the CPSU CC Politburo. We explained our position to him and expected that he would understand it and agree with it to some extent and would draw the necessary conclusions. However, if after all this a person still comes to us with these general judgments and with empty hands, then it's hard to say whether this reflects mere inexperience or cunning.

At the present stage, obviously, we shouldn't embark on a struggle against the CPCz Action Program. This can be done during the next stage—the second stage—because, as is clear from the most recent news, the CPCz itself can launch a struggle against the counterrevolution.

If they succeed in breaking the counterrevolution and regaining control of the situation, some people, perhaps, cannot only be dismissed from their posts but removed altogether from any part in politics, and that will be an enormous step forward. We must do everything we can to help the CPCz take this step.

Moreover, we must try to get their consent to host joint military maneuvers on the territory of Czechoslovakia as soon as possible, and preferably this month, in May. This is an important measure about which we are all in agreement, and even the Czechoslovak comrades have agreed in principle to hold such maneuvers. So the maneuvers will facilitate the improvement of relations between fraternal parties and help the Czechoslovak friends to strengthen the army and stabilize the situation in the country. Cde. Yakubovskii, as the commander-in-chief, will go with his staff to the maneuvers in the ČSSR, and representatives of the other fraternal countries—Hungary, Poland, and Bulgaria—will also go, along with their staffs. We will send our troops there from Dresden and, perhaps, from Poland. As you know, the term for "designating the troops" means that army operations will be carried out using the symbols of military units (in place of an army there will be a division, in place of a division there will be a regiment, in place of a regiment there will be a battalion, etc.).

The presence of leading staff members and a large number of officers of all our armies will undoubtedly make an impression on our enemies, paralyze the counterrevolution, and be a substantial factor of support for our friends.

Therefore, it seems to us that we must reach agreement here so that full responsibility can be taken for preparations and the course of these maneuvers. In conversations with us Cdes. Dubček and Černík said that such maneuvers should be carried out. I gave Cde. Dubček the specific date of 10 to 12 May, but he said they would consider this matter back home within the leadership and would decide later about the right date. Cde. Černík, who talked with Cde. Kosygin about this question, agreed in principle to host the maneuvers. Cdes. Smrkovský and Biľak also supported the idea of holding the exercises.

Therefore we should take measures to ensure that nothing appears in our press or in the works of our propaganda and creative organizations that could be exploited by the counterrevolutionary forces in Czechoslovakia. Unfortunately, sometimes even statements by our good friends, for instance, Cde. Longo, are being exploited by the unhealthy forces in Czechoslovakia.[37] Without

---

[37] See Document No. 29.

question, offering praise for "liberalization" or "a new model" or some other thing does not bolster the healthy forces in the CPCz.

Now we'll see what the reaction is in Czechoslovakia to our article on Procházka. Cde. Kolder, for instance, told our comrades that publication of the TASS statement about Jan Masaryk was a big help.[38] We also believe that the article about Procházka will play a positive role. At the present time this article is being transmitted by our radio to Czechoslovakia.

We must constantly maintain contact on all these questions and consult among ourselves. We must monitor the way events unfold after the joint session of the CPCz CC Presidium and Secretariat that is now taking place, and we must wait and see what will appear in the appeal to the people that, as far as we know, they are now discussing there.

We must present a united front and follow a common line. In talks with Cde. Dubček through ambassadors we must emphasize our concern about the situation in Czechoslovakia and indicate that we are ready to make every effort to stabilize events in Czechoslovakia.

Well, that's everything we wanted to tell you. Perhaps some of our comrades want to add something?

. . .

[Speaking in succession, Ulbricht, Gomułka, and Zhivkov strongly endorsed Brezhnev's views—Ed.]

J. Kádár: Our Politburo has considered the situation in Czechoslovakia many times. Our conclusion is that there is no counterrevolution under way in Czechoslovakia. What is going on there is a process that began with a struggle against certain mistakes committed by the previous leadership. If we're going to criticize specific individuals, then I would criticize Cde. Novotný rather than Cde. Dubček. Of course it's not our prerogative to make judgments, but I want to remind you of a talk I had with Cde. Novotný, which took place in February in Prague.[39] Personally, I understand his situation and regard him to be an honest person. I spoke about that with Cde. Dubček, and he agreed with me. Subjectively, Cde. Novotný is an honest man. But when we spoke in Prague he told me the following in all seriousness: that everything went wrong because of the train. At the time of the celebrations of the 50th anniversary of the October Revolution, when he was returning from Moscow, he was forced to land at Košice. Because of bad weather he had to take a train that was organized in a hurry. Cde. Novotný caught a cold there, became ill, and after returning to Prague was unable to work for three weeks. During that time, preparations for the CC plenum were being made by other comrades. He believes it is precisely these circumstances that are the root of all his misfortunes.

W. Ulbricht: That's a good little story.

J. Kádár: No, you see, he said all this absolutely seriously. I spoke about it in a joking tone, but in fact it's a very sad story. If a person holding such a responsible post explains historical phenomena in this way . . .

A. N. Kosygin: If he said it that seriously, then obviously he's not a serious person.

J. Kádár: He said it absolutely seriously. In reality, the problem in Czechoslovakia is connected with phenomena that date back much earlier and undermined the position of the Czechoslovak party. Don't think me a cynic, but in 1956 I said it about Hungary and today I'll say it about Czechoslovakia: You have to do many things badly for many years for the situation to become so deplorable.

[38] This is a reference to former Foreign Minister Jan Masaryk whose alleged suicide in 1948 had become a subject of numerous news articles in Czechoslovakia alleging he had been killed by the KGB.

[39] This conversation took place when Kádár was in Prague for the 20th anniversary celebrations of the CPCz's "February Revolution" (see Document No. 10 above).

We should consider Cde. Dubček and those around him as communists who have begun a fight against mistakes committed in the past. But they are waging this struggle with great naiveté. It can be said that they are acting under the slogan: "Let the world perish, but justice shall triumph." Their CC plenum in January really amounted to a crossing of the Rubicon. The floodgates were opened. But the explosive forces had accumulated much earlier. What happened afterwards? Dubček and the others are continuing to fight against the earlier mistakes, to correct them, and Cde. Novotný was retired. They took power but in reality there was never any leadership in the party and still isn't. The CPCz CC and its Presidium differ. The key to the Czechoslovak situation lies precisely in this.

Does the CPCz at the present time have the majority on its side or not? We just don't know. One can speak only tentatively about that. But one thing is clear: The real leadership is not there. There is the CC, but 30 to 40 percent of its members are people who've already been removed from their posts. It reflects countless opinions, positions, and emotions. One thing is remarkable: how, under these circumstances, they were able to arrive at any sort of unified decision at the plenary sessions in January and March. Unfortunately, even when something is decided at a plenary session, the next day everyone just does as they wish once again. The current leadership of the CPCz is conducting a struggle simultaneously *against* the old mistakes and *for* the consolidation of the party's position. This cannot be denied. They are doing it voluntarily, even if only superficially.

A. N. Kosygin: What do you think, Cde. Kádár, of their Action Program?

J. Kádár: I'll come to that. In the very composition of the CC there are right-wing elements who have no place in the communist party. In a word, this is a very diverse group of people. That's why anarchy prevails there. The real leadership of the party, I repeat, does not exist. The main thing is the anarchy that is being used by the anti-socialist and counterrevolutionary elements in the country and in the West.

Unfortunately, agents and spies exist not only in detective stories but in real life as well, and it would be stupid if the imperialists did not exploit the circumstances that have arisen. They use Cde. Dubček, they use Cde. Smrkovský for what he is (I don't think that he's a representative of forces hostile to us). In short, the imperialists will exploit every opportunity. They have their own people in the Czechoslovak press, they are disorienting the party, and subverting the Interior Ministry and the army. It is said that the militia is unaffected by these processes, but we know that if there are 30 different views in the party, the militia cannot be united either.

As for the Action Program, it's a big zero, it is nothing.

W. Gomułka: What do you mean, a zero?

J. Kádár: I told Cde. Dubček in Sofia: You had the best authors write this document. They can write 8,000 pages for you and argue about words and specific formulations, but it won't mean anything. This is their program—a general socialist compromise. One can find absolutely everything in it. Its supporters can do whatever they want. They can either strengthen the party or dissolve it and in both cases they can refer to the Action Program to justify what they're doing.

Dubček said to me: We made a mistake when we did not inform the party about what was said at the January CC plenum. I replied: If you had done this it would have been the end of the party. Party members should know and carry out the decisions of the Central Committee. If they all read the minutes of the plenum and the debate that took place there, then it would be simpler just to broadcast everything to them directly over the radio and television. It is perfectly clear that in Czechoslovakia at the moment there is a weak leadership which does not have the party in its control, much less the society. Essentially, it is anarchy that prevails there, which is exploited by odd people of all stripes and even by the enemies of socialism. We believe that the situation is dangerous, but the forces of counterrevolution have still not gained the upper hand.

138

We approve of everything that was done by our Soviet comrades and what they said here. I believe that the way out of what is happening now will be decided *within* the CPCz and the Czechoslovak working class, and by the people of Czechoslovakia themselves.[40]

What should we do? We must do everything we can to help the CPCz extricate itself from this difficult situation. And, on the contrary, we must not do anything that could play into the hands of the enemy. But in order to give help there must be someone to give the help to. We believe that the measures being taken at this time are the right ones. The TASS statement was very timely and appropriate. It was good, in our opinion, but not complete, and I will speak about that later. The note of the Polish People's Republic was also correct. As for military maneuvers on Czechoslovak territory, we are for them and the longer they last the better.

But it is essential that in the Czechoslovak leadership there should be people who await our help, who count on it and accept it. If there aren't any, our steps can trigger the opposite response. All of us have a lot of experience. Cde. Brezhnev, Cde. Dubček, and Cde. Ulbricht were in our country, in Budapest, during our most trying period. In Czechoslovakia there must be forces who are awaiting our help, who have their plan of action. Then we can act together with them. Even if, perhaps, this seems difficult, we must support this very same Dubček and his aides in order to provide him with our help. Dubček, Kolder, and the other comrades find themselves in a situation in which they have never been before. They are being attacked by the enemy, and we, too, are attacking them, though for other reasons. But they have to carry out the leadership role. They are honest, albeit naive, people, and we must work with them. I hear and read their speeches. Dubček effectively reassures us and himself. They in fact have only one road ahead of them. They have to wage a struggle in two directions—against former mistakes (and there were such mistakes).

W. Gomułka: I don't understand, I don't understand, in what directions?

J. Kádár: In two directions: to fight against the enemies of socialism, the counterrevolutionary forces, and the agents of imperialism, and to fight against former mistakes.[41] The greater the right-wing danger and the danger of counterrevolution, the more attention this struggle attracts and the more strength it requires. The struggle against the former mistakes becomes less and less important. But if they do not fight on both fronts they will perish.

. . .

W. Gomułka: What does all this mean? It means equality for all existing ideologies; it means the legalization of bourgeois ideology. And that is not just to be found in some program. It exists in practice today in Czechoslovakia. That same Action Program says that this year guarantees of free assembly and opportunities to create voluntary social organizations conforming to the interests and needs of different strata of the population will be inscribed in the constitution.

L. I. Brezhnev: Those are the "clubs"!

N. V. Podgorny: This is going on in practice.

W. Gomułka: I could cite hundreds more such examples that show what their general line is.

The greatest difficulty in the current struggle is to find the healthy core in the communist party, the core that could come forward and redo the program. This, Cde. Kádár, is not a zero; it is the main document against which we will have to fight not only in Czechoslovakia but in other countries as well. This is the kind of document that the counterrevolution is using to pave the way for its struggle against socialism.

The most important thing for us now is to find the healthy core, to find the people in the leadership on whom we can rely, who can carry out the correct line. This will not be an easy

---

[40] Emphasis is in the original document.
[41] Kádár often used this same formulation to describe his own approach to reform in Hungary.

139

task since the counterrevolutionary forces will see to it that precisely such people are removed as quickly as possible. The name of Cde. Kolder was mentioned here. I remember that when we met in Dresden he didn't believe that counterrevolution was unfolding in Czechoslovakia.

In fact, right now in Czechoslovakia there must be only one struggle: the struggle against revisionism and counterrevolution. If we don't clarify this for ourselves, then, objectively speaking, we won't have a correct assessment of the situation, nor will our efforts achieve the desired results.

How do we look upon the situation now?

In Czechoslovakia today the only ones who are organized and determined are the opponents, the enemy. Whether they have one center, or two or three, is not of decisive significance. It's evident that they work along many lines simultaneously, but the direction of all their work is one and the same: namely, to compromise the communist party, to ruin it, and to remove it as the main enemy and thereby to open the way for the free development of counterrevolution. Neither from the leadership of the Communist Party of Czechoslovakia nor from the Central Committee is any effort being made to oppose all this. And that is no accident.

The essential feature of the current situation is that there is no active opposition to counter-revolution; this stems from the general line defined by the January CPCz CC plenum and its new Action Program. This program, comrades, is not a "big zero." If that were so, then the question would arise: why are we fighting? To tell the truth, everything happening in Czechoslovakia today is based on the text of this Action Program. . . .[42]

As for Cde. Dubček, of course it is not our task here to evaluate him. Perhaps it is not so important to determine whether his actions can be attributed to objective or subjective reasons. What matters is who he, as the CC first secretary, supports and to whom he is opening the way: to the healthy forces or to counterrevolution. Judging by everything that's gone on, his policy is opening the way to the forces of counterrevolution. This is not to say that he will not back the healthy core, if it is sufficiently strong. But it is clear that Cde. Dubček will not be the kind of leader the CPCz needs.

To say that everyone who is part of the present leadership of the CPCz is a communist is not enough. There are different kinds of communists. There are no immutable standards, including, in this case, even for communists. One person might have been a good communist in the party several years ago and now he is on the path to revisionism. Or the other way around: Life might teach a person a lesson, and he will veer onto the correct road and become a good communist. For instance, Kriegel fought in the Spanish Civil War, he fought against the fascists, and now he is laying the groundwork for counterrevolution. The minister of the interior, Pavel, also fought in Spain; and yet today, through his very actions, he is doing great harm to the communist party and to socialism. In effect he is liquidating the state security organs, dividing them into two parts: into counterintelligence organs, and into those dealing with public order, that is, the police. By the way, this step is mandated in the Action Program, where it says that security organs should fight only against foreign intelligence services and do not have the right to be concerned with the life and opinions of Czechoslovak citizens.

This means that today the leadership of the CPCz and the leadership of the ČSSR, as a socialist country, are rejecting the one thing that every state needs for its existence and are destroying the instruments of state power. And this is being done in conjunction with declarations that socialist democracy is "much more expansive than bourgeois democracy." Yet bourgeois countries maintain and strengthen their police forces and use them to fight against the communist movement. And I'm not even talking here about countries where communist parties are illegal

---

[42] At this point, Gomułka cites lengthy passages from the Action Program, which he claimed showed that the process of democratization was being abused. "Bourgeois ideology," he emphasizes, "can be opposed only by open ideological struggle that goes on in front of all the people."

and communists are physically liquidated. In those countries they believe it is right to use all means to fight against communists.

So, in Czechoslovakia the revisionists are "expanding" bourgeois democracy by destroying their own organs of state power. And this is called socialist democracy!

Comrades, if we do not make a correct assessment of what is going on and do not take the necessary remedial measures, then within a year or two we'll have to deal with a bourgeois Czechoslovakia and not a socialist one.

Look at what the paper *Rudé právo* of 6 May writes. It puts forth arguments in favor of a multi-party system in Czechoslovakia and asserts that there is nothing wrong about that.[43] What does this mean? It means that the paper is publicizing the emergence of new parties, which, incidentally, have in fact already begun to function, though they still hide under the name of "clubs." All this is set forth in the Action Program. Czechoslovakia is facing general elections with a new configuration of political forces. If we consider the attacks that have been directed against the communist party and the degree to which the party is paralyzed, we can't rule out that the reactionary forces will win the elections. Every democracy is a specific form of class dictatorship. The democracy that is now being discussed in Czechoslovakia already has the specific features of a class dictatorship of the bourgeoisie.

. . .

L. I. Brezhnev: From the first day we declared that we do not agree with the CPCz Action Program and published nothing about it.[44] We let the Czechoslovak leadership know that we did not agree with this program. It includes ideas of a bourgeois republic. Listen to what Císař said not long ago in a public address: "The communist party is dissociating itself from the sphere of state power and administration, from the sphere of industry and economics, and from the sphere of science and culture. This dissociation is a new type of relationship."[45] What will remain of the CPCz after this? Will it just step aside and return in the form of "Club-231"? But even "Club-231" intends to become a party tomorrow and insists on obtaining power.

N. V. Podgorny: The Action Program is also full of the ideas Císař expressed.

L. I. Brezhnev: There are elements in the CPCz leadership that are making one concession after another to counterrevolution. They have given us many assurances that, for instance, they will not allow the removal of one or another comrade, but in practice everything works out just the opposite.

What position must we take and how should we understand our tasks? The CPSU believes it is necessary to save scientific socialism in Czechoslovakia and to defend and maintain the communist party in power, the party that bases itself on the precepts of Marxism–Leninism. . . .

N. V. Podgorny: And that would be the leading force in the country.

L. I. Brezhnev: Yes, as it was until not long ago. These goals should determine our tactics at the present stage. As for criticism of the Action Program, that can come in the second stage. For now, it is essential to discover and consolidate the forces that can undertake the struggle against counterrevolution.

W. Gomułka: Irrespective of who this will be personally.

---

[43] This is another good example of the vast amount of raw information that Brezhnev had at his disposal during key negotiations—in this case, no doubt, courtesy of the Soviet embassy in Prague.

[44] Brezhnev's statement is incorrect. Although it is true that Soviet leaders made no attempt to conceal their disapprobation of the Action Program, excerpts from the Program were indeed published in *Pravda*, albeit belatedly, on April 17. Indeed, during this same session on May 8, in an exchange with Ulbricht and Gomułka (see above), Brezhnev himself noted that "we [in Moscow] have let our people know about the [Action] Program . . . in abridged form."

[45] This refers to the speech Čestmír Císař gave during the celebrations of the 150th anniversary of Karl Marx's birthday.

L. I. Brezhnev: Yes. It would obviously be desirable if the entire current leadership would adopt such a position. But if this is not to be, then it is necessary to support those who will embrace the party's positions and initiate the struggle against counterrevolution.[46]

N. V. Podgorny: We will support precisely these forces.

L. I. Brezhnev: That is our line. I think it can be said that all of us here are agreed on that. Although Cde. Kádár presented a somewhat different assessment, he, too, it seems to me, agrees with the measures proposed and with our general line.

Now, to a few particular matters. Actually, Bacílek came out with a statement that was mentioned here, but there are forces opposed to him. Cde. Biľak said here that after the interview with Bacílek was published they had to protect him against enraged workers. We have documents—correspondence between Stalin and Gottwald. From these documents it is evident that Stalin did not agree with the accusations against Slánský and stressed that as long as there was no proof of his guilt he was not to be arrested. And Gottwald agreed with this. Later, Stalin recalled our adviser on state security matters from Czechoslovakia and then, when Gottwald objected, Stalin wrote to him saying that another person could be sent, but that he was obliged to work under the leadership of the Czechoslovak Ministry of the Interior and under the control of the CPCz CC, and was not to act independently.

They are speaking about Mikoyan. True, he went to Prague and held talks on economic matters. We have the text of his notes to Stalin in which he reports on these talks and asks for instructions to reply to Gottwald on certain matters. As regards certain telephone conversations concerning the Slánský case, there are absolutely no documents from anyone confirming this. Mikoyan himself resolutely denied it. So the rumors being circulated in Czechoslovakia cannot be substantiated by anyone. On the contrary, Stalin warned Gottwald that to sow suspicion against workers is the enemy's method. He advised that if Slánský had shown he was not up to his job he should have been given a different one. Gottwald agreed to this. As for the interview with Bacílek, it is clear that it will be answered in due course.

How will we decide when the healthy forces reveal themselves in the CPCz leadership? Probably we'll receive some sort of answer to this question within the next few days. For two days now there has been a stormy session of the CC Presidium to decide what measures should be taken against the anti-socialist elements.

A. N. Kosygin: Černík told me when he was leaving that they will discuss fundamental questions at this session.

W. Gomułka: On 20 May there is to be a CPCz CC plenum.[47] Military exercises must be held before that. This will be extremely important for the healthy forces in the leadership.

T. Zhivkov: It is very important.

L. I. Brezhnev: We'll try, with your support, to do everything so that the exercises are carried out before that date.

We've just received a short item through the "Hot Line" from our Embassy in Prague that the session of the CPCz CC Presidium will be extended and that matters are going better.

W. Gomułka: But in *Rudé právo* things are not yet going better!

. . .

---

[46] Brezhnev's pivotal comment here marks a shift by the "Five" toward greater and more direct support for the "healthy" forces in the CPCz.

[47] Gomułka is in error here. The CPCz CC plenum began on May 29, as scheduled, not on the 20th.

[At this point Brezhnev read aloud an item about Smrkovský's address at a meeting of activists of the ČSSR Ministry of the Interior, held on May 6th.]

L. I. Brezhnev: This information clearly says that there are healthy forces in the Czechoslovak party although many of them, of course, are being repressed. They must be boldly supported so that they can sense this support. On the other hand, it is clear that there are counterrevolutionary forces in the country; otherwise we wouldn't be thinking about how to handle them.

Once again we thank you, comrades, for coming. Clearly we can agree, and I hope that Cdes. Ulbricht and Gomułka also agree, that at the given moment we will not mount an attack on the new CPCz leadership as a whole.[48] First it is necessary to see what they do, how they address the people, and how the people and army respond to this.

We will press ahead with military exercises. These may turn out to be one of the most decisive factors enabling us to turn events around. Clearly, we will have to meet after the exercises several times, since events might change. I would ask you to agree to respond just as promptly to a request for a meeting in the future. For our part we are ready to fly wherever it is suitable, day or night. Within two or three hours we can be in any city, no matter how busy we are. In defending Czechoslovakia, we are defending the cause of the socialist camp and the entire international communist movement. We must see where our strengths lie and be active.

[48] Brezhnev's conciliatory reference to Ulbricht and Gomułka reflects the pressure those two leaders were exerting for a more forceful and decisive response.

DOCUMENT No. 32: Cable from the Czechoslovak Ambassador to Yugoslavia, May 9, 1968, on Leonid Brezhnev's Recent Discussions with Josip Broz Tito

Source: ÚSD, Sb. KV, K—Archiv MZV, Dispatches Received, No. 4511/1968; Vondrová & Navrátil, vol. 1, pp. 216–217.

During Josip Broz Tito's visit to the Soviet Union on April 28–30, he and Brezhnev spent significant time discussing the Czechoslovak situation. This cable, from the Czechoslovak ambassador in Yugoslavia, Ladislav Simović, transmits the content of their conversations. Simović reports Brezhnev's view that the Yugoslav press, and by implication the Yugoslav authorities, underestimated the "danger" posed by internal developments in Czechoslovakia, which, according to the Soviet leader, were providing fruitful opportunities for "imperialist, ideological subversion" and "bourgeois elements." Tito, according to the cable, expressed his "faith" in Dubček's leadership and defended the Prague Spring. His position reflected Belgrade's support for the reforms undertaken by the CPCz as a vindication of Tito's own decision to pursue a separate "path to socialism."

. . . The situation in the CPCz and in the ČSSR took up a great deal of time in the talks between Tito and the Soviet leadership. Brezhnev stressed that the CPSU was concerned about the situation in our country which, in their opinion, is getting out of the party's control. Bourgeois parties that were previously banned are being revived in the ČSSR. There is a danger that a bourgeois state will be restored as a result of imperialist ideological subversion and increased espionage, concentrating chiefly in bourgeois elements and the intelligentsia. Because of the way the Yugoslav press is reporting the situation in the ČSSR, not enough attention is being given to this threat.

According to Popović, Tito said he could not share these fears.[49] Ever since his youngest days he has been keenly aware of the political maturity of the Czechoslovak working class, he knows the rich experiences and democratic traditions of the CPCz and the Czechoslovak people, and he knows that the Czechoslovak intelligentsia is always on the side of the CPCz. Tito said he has faith in the CPCz and in the ability of its leadership to inspire and muster the initiative and activity of the working class to ensure the prompt implementation of the Action Program. According to Tito, what the CPCz needs in the current situation is trust and support.[50] The Yugoslav League of Communists and the Yugoslav government are offering both of these to the Czechoslovak communists. Brezhnev expressed doubts about the reliability of the present CPCz leadership, which has been unstable in its declarations. Dubček reportedly assured him that there would be no personnel changes in some posts (David, Lomský), yet changes were made all the same.[51] Tito is said to have argued that there is only one CPCz leadership, that it enjoys great support among the party's members, and that there should be no apprehension about this matter. . . .

[49] Popović is a reference to Vladimir Popović, who accompanied Tito to Moscow. As a member of the Council of the Federation, a member of the YLC CC Presidium, and the general secretary of the Yugoslav Presidency, Popović was one of Tito's closest advisers. He also was a former ambassador to the Soviet Union (as well as to the United States, China, and Vietnam) and president of the Committee for Foreign Affairs and International Relations of the Federal Chamber of the Federal Assembly.

[50] In an effort to advance ties between Prague and Belgrade, Yugoslav officials tried, unsuccessfully, in the spring of 1968 to arrange a bilateral meeting between Tito and Dubček that would enable the two leaders to proclaim their joint commitment to diversity in the communist world. CPCz officials declined the Yugoslav offer mainly because they were concerned that such a meeting would stir undue anxiety in Moscow. Not until August did they finally consent to a visit by the Yugoslav leader.

[51] These are references to the post of ČSSR foreign minister and national defense minister.

DOCUMENT No. 33: Report by Czechoslovak Press Agency Correspondent Ján Riško from Moscow, May 12, 1968 (Excerpts)

Source: ÚSD, AÚV KSČ, F. 07/15; pp. 221–224.

In this survey, the correspondent of the Czechoslovak press agency (ČTK), Ján Riško, reports on Soviet public opinion about the Prague Spring as tensions escalated with Moscow. "The number of those expressing approval has dropped considerably," according to his assessment, and "more and more" Soviets are expressing "serious concern." By contrast, a report prepared two months earlier by the Czechoslovak television correspondent O. Výborný concluded that Soviet officials and citizens who were following events in Czechoslovakia were split almost evenly between those who supported the changes and those who were strongly opposed.

In addition to discussing the state of elite opinion in Moscow, Riško briefly describes the cool reception given to Czechoslovak Foreign Minister Jiří Hájek when he arrived in Moscow for a two-day visit on May 6.

(See Document No. 11.)

Change of Opinion toward the ČSSR

If, during the initial period after the CPCz CC plenum in January 1968 the response in the Soviet Union to developments in Czechoslovakia was rather differentiated—ranging from enthusiastic agreement to outright rejection—then four months later the situation has changed a good deal and the number of those expressing approval has dropped considerably, while there are more and more of those who express serious concern. The change of attitudes has clearly been brought about by certain items in our press that have had anti-Soviet undertones.

On questions of principle the current party and state leadership of the USSR is most concerned about positive developments for utilitarian reasons. According to many quarters, any shift by Czechoslovakia away from the Soviet Union and the CPSU would create great difficulties for the leadership at home. While it has been possible to explain the defection of Yugoslavia, China, Albania and Romania, it would no longer be possible to explain to the party and state apparatus or to the public a shift by Czechoslovakia.

In that case voices would emerge from the rank and file claiming that the Soviet leadership is not acting correctly in matters of the international communist movement. At the same time, the group in the CPSU leadership that would like to take over the leadership from Brezhnev and run all domestic and international affairs much more firmly could well attempt to achieve its goal. This group exists in the Politburo itself, but is in a tight spot at the moment; its main representative is Shelepin.[52] Events in Czechoslovakia are objectively reinforcing its positions, as has been confirmed by a well-informed source around the general secretary's associates. Foreign journalists widely believe that this group may try to achieve its objective against the general secretary before the end of the year but that is something the source I mentioned considers unlikely.

This may explain why at the April session of the CPSU Central Committee Brezhnev allegedly argued that the processes in Czechoslovakia are positive but that anti-socialist elements were trying to exploit and misuse those processes. Brezhnev's speech at the Central Committee session is said to have somewhat calmed the considerable fears in the Soviet Union about future developments in Czechoslovakia.

. . . [Section deleted on Moscow talks.]

---

[52] Other well-placed observers have offered similar speculation that Brezhnev's position vis-à-vis Czechoslovakia in 1968 was influenced by an internal challenge from Shelepin or others; see, in particular, Zdeněk Mlynář, *Nachtfrost: Erfahrungen auf dem Weg vom realen zum menschlichen Sozialismus* (Köln: Europäische Verlagsanstalt, 1978), pp. 167–169.

Minister Hájek's Talks in Moscow

Minister Hájek's first round of talks was twice postponed by an hour beyond what was originally stipulated because Gromyko was at the Central Committee, where he evidently consulted on how to conduct the talks and received instructions. Gromyko responded to Hájek's presentation of certain new aspects of our foreign policy (especially the geographic position and relations with Federal Germany) with an icy and dispassionate expression on his face. Some of his remarks appeared to be outright threats, especially that the USSR would do everything it could to prevent a change of the ČSSR's policy vis-à-vis Federal Germany. . . .

Referring to Hájek's statement that Czechoslovakia in its foreign policy would proceed from its geographic position in Europe, Gromyko said that geographic aspects never played any substantial role in the foreign policy of states, but only class factors. Hájek's talk with Gromyko appeared more like two monologues, whereby Gromyko simply did not react to Hájek's rejoinder, he made no notes, he was simply not interested. Someone present at the talk also saw among Gromyko's papers on the table materials coming from other socialist countries. . . .

DOCUMENT No. 34: Cable from the Soviet Ambassador in Warsaw to Soviet Prime Minister Aleksei Kosygin, May 22, 1968

Source: ÚSD, Sb. KV, Z/S—MID No. 5.

This cable from the Soviet ambassador in Warsaw, Averki Aristov, was sent at Brezhnev's request to Soviet Prime Minister Aleksei Kosygin during his "vacation" in Karlovy Vary. The cable recounts two points that Gomułka made in a recent conversation, which Brezhnev presumably wants Kosygin to raise with CPCz officials: that Yugoslavia and Romania are making a determined effort to forge closer ties with Czechoslovakia in the hope that the three countries would join ranks, at least informally, in a pro-Western bloc; and that Czechoslovakia is seeking to "reestablish diplomatic relations with West Germany," much as Novotný had done earlier. While accurate in certain respects, Gomułka's information is being transmitted to create alarming conclusions about the direction and nature of the Prague Spring.

[At the request of Cde. L. I. Brezhnev I am sending a telegram from our ambassador in Warsaw:]

In accordance with this message, I visited Cde. Gomułka today and informed him about the visits of Pham Van Dong and Broz Tito and about our reply to Romania.

In the talks that ensued, Cde. Gomułka's remarks on two questions are worthy of attention:

First, Cde. Gomułka knows that Ceauşescu has pressingly invited and is still inviting Cde. Dubček to visit Romania.[53] However, Cde. Dubček replied that at present he cannot accept this invitation. Ceauşescu then proposed that he visit Czechoslovakia, but it seems he has not yet received a reply from the Czechoslovaks.

Broz Tito is also pressing Cde. Dubček to visit Yugoslavia and would not be against visiting Cde. Dubček.[54]

In Cde. Gomułka's opinion these three countries are united by their attraction to the West. Their common wish is to leave the socialist camp and to set up something in the nature of an unofficial alliance that might be formed among them.[55]

It is known that when Novotný was still in power, Czechoslovakia wanted very much to reestablish diplomatic relations with West Germany. Last year, when a party and government delegation of the Polish People's Republic was in Prague in connection with the signing of a treaty on friendship and mutual assistance between Poland and Czechoslovakia, Cde. Gomułka had the feeling that Czechoslovakia was ready to send its representatives to Bonn. Thus, Dubček is merely continuing the line of rapprochement with West Germany that began earlier. And if the Czechoslovaks have not yet established diplomatic relations with West Germany, such relations, in fact, do exist. . . .

---

[53] This same matter is noted in secret reports and dispatches now contained in the former CPSU archives. See, for example, "TsK KPSS: O nekotorykh problemakh sovetsko-rumynskikh otnoshenii v svete pozitsii, zanyatoi rukovodstvom RKP v svyazi s sobytiyami v Chekhoslovakii," Report No. 686 (TOP SECRET) to the CPSU CC Politburo from A. V. Basov, Soviet ambassador in Romania, September 23, 1968, in TsKhSD, F. 5, Op. 60, D. 339, Ll. 106–121, esp. 107–109.

[54] On this point, see "Ob otnoshenii SFRYu k sobytiyam v ChSSR (Politicheskoe pis'mo)," Cable No. 495 (TOP SECRET) from I. A. Benediktov, Soviet ambassador in Yugoslavia, to A. A. Gromyko, K. V. Katushev, and K. V. Rusakov, October 20, 1968, in TsKhSD, F. 5, Op. 60, D. 278, Ll. 235–256, esp. 235–238. See also "Zapis' besedy s sovetnikom posol'stva ChSSR v NR Bolgarii tov. Krausom," Cable No. 519 (SECRET) from M. E. Pozolotin, minister-counselor at Soviet embassy in Bulgaria, July 22, 1968, in TsKhSD, F. 5, Op. 60, D. 278, Ll. 113–114.

[55] Gomułka's comments here stem directly from the meeting he and Dubček had in Ostrava, a city in northern Moravia, on February 7, 1968. During the meeting, the CPCz leader explained why sweeping reforms, including the rehabilitation of all those who had been unjustly arrested and punished, were essential. Dubček also hinted that Poland and Czechoslovakia might join informally together with Romania and Yugoslavia in presenting a reformist counterweight to the Soviet Union. Gomułka's response to this proposal was very cool, and afterwards Dubček suspected that the Polish leader had reported the exchange to Brezhnev as "evidence" of "negative" trends in Czechoslovakia. See Document No. 70 below, which goes slightly beyond the brief account in Dubček's memoirs. The minutes of the meeting compiled by the Polish side are available in AAN Warszawa, Arch. KC PZPR, P. 24, T. 193.

DOCUMENT No. 35: Letter from Leonid Brezhnev to Alexander Dubček Informing Him about the Results of the Moscow Meeting of the "Five", May 1968

Source: ÚSD, AÚV KSČ, F. 07/15, Zahr. kor. c. 797.

Leonid Brezhnev wrote this undated letter sometime around May 26. It is a response to a request that Dubček made on May 15 to the Soviet ambassador in Czechoslovakia, Stepan Chervonenko, for official information about the five-party meeting held in Moscow on May 8. Brezhnev's letter only nominally responds to Dubček's request for information and its tone is notably chillier than Brezhnev's two earlier letters. (He uses the formal second-person pronoun, "vy," when addressing Dubček rather than using the familiar "ty," as in earlier correspondence.) Moreover, the Soviet leader withholds information from Dubček. The letter does not mention that during the Moscow meeting Brezhnev raised, for the first time, the possibility of military intervention in Czechoslovakia; nor does Brezhnev provide any hint that large-scale Warsaw Pact military maneuvers are about to get under way on Czechoslovak territory.

[no date]

To the First Secretary of the CPCz CC
Comrade A. Dubček:

In connection with your letter asking me to inform you about the meeting of top officials from the Bulgarian Communist Party, the Hungarian Socialist Workers' Party, the Socialist Unity Party of Germany, the Polish United Workers' Party, and the Communist Party of the Soviet Union, which took place on 8 May of this year, I have been authorized by the CPSU CC Politburo to tell you the following:

At this meeting we exchanged views on a number of urgent international problems, especially those connected with the intrigues of the recently activated circles of imperialism and, above all, the revanchists and neo-Nazis in the FRG. We also touched on questions connected with the development of mutual cooperation among the fraternal parties and governments, especially in economic areas.

During the meeting the Polish comrades stated that they had prepared specific ideas for the further perfection of economic relations among the CMEA countries. The participants at the meeting agreed that the Polish comrades should send their materials to all the member states of CMEA.

At this meeting the same questions were discussed that were discussed at the previous meeting of Soviet and Czechoslovak officials. These are matters on which you and we, as we recently affirmed, have the same basic position. Obviously, at this meeting, as at other meetings of fraternal parties, we and the other participants would have preferred it if representatives also had been present from the Communist Party of Czechoslovakia, a party with which we have close fraternal ties and a relationship of complete trust, with no need to keep secrets from one another. But when we took into account that only a few days earlier a group of top officials from the CPCz and the Czechoslovak state, headed by you, had visited Moscow, we concluded that a request on our part for you to come again could be difficult for you in view of the large number of urgent matters in your country that demand your attention. This is all the more the case insofar as the general situation in Czechoslovakia at the time, as you yourself acknowledged, was still complicated. Irrespective of that, such a swift repetition of a visit by Czechoslovak officials to Moscow could have given rise to speculation and various reports about supposed difficulties emerging in relations between the CPSU and other fraternal parties, on the one hand, and the CPCz, on the other.

During the meeting of top-level representatives from the fraternal parties in Moscow, we informed the comrades about the talks that took place between the leading officials of the CPSU and CPCz during your recent visit to the Soviet Union. I must frankly tell you that we expressed the same concerns which we had already discussed with you during your visit to Moscow. We told the leading representatives of the fraternal parties, on the basis of what you yourself said, Cde. Dubček, and also on the basis of what other top officials from the Czechoslovak party and state—that is, Smrkovský, Černík, and Biľak—had said, that the CPCz and its CC will never permit the socialist order in Czechoslovakia to be undermined or the leading role of the communist party in society to be weakened. Nor will they permit any reduction in the traditional fraternal friendship between the peoples of Czechoslovakia and the Soviet Union and between Czechoslovakia and the other socialist countries. The representatives of the fraternal parties expressed their full solidarity with the CPCz and their determination to offer all necessary assistance and support to the new leadership of the CPCz CC, the Czechoslovak state, and the government of the Czechoslovak Socialist Republic in order to promote the consolidation and further development of the socialist order in your country.

With regard to the question you raised about your not having been informed in advance, not even the participants in the meeting themselves were able to come to any sort of timely agreement or exchange of information about this event.[56] Otherwise we obviously would have informed you that the meeting was being held. And today, to round out the information we provided you in our phone conversations and in your discussions with Cde. Kosygin, we realized it would be appropriate to send you this letter as well.

The CPSU CC Politburo has requested that I tell both you, Cde. Dubček, and all other comrades in the CPCz CC that the Czechoslovak communists and all workers in the Czechoslovak Socialist Republic can always in the future count on the Soviet Union and the Soviet people to be your true friends, fellow soldiers, and brothers-in-arms in the struggle for our common goals: for socialism, for peace on earth, and for the triumph of the great and invincible ideas of Marxism–Leninism.

With respect,

General Secretary, CPSU CC

L. Brezhnev[57]

---

[56] The original wording in Czech does not make sense as written, so it has been slightly smoothed out here to convey what Brezhnev meant.

[57] On May 28, Dubček informed the other members of the CPCz CC Presidium about the letter he had received from Brezhnev, and they briefly discussed it.

DOCUMENT No. 36: "On the Current Situation (Some Urgent Points Regarding the USSR's International Position)," The CPSU Politburo's Dissemination of Briefing Materials on the Crisis to CPSU Members, May 27, 1968

Source: "TsK KPSS," Memorandum No. 14194 (Top Secret), May 27, 1968, from V. Stepakov, K. Rusakov, and V. Zagladin, in TsKhSD, F. 5, Op. 60, D. 19, Ll. 109, 133–136.

This memorandum and the attached briefing materials were prepared by Vladimir Stepakov, the deputy head of the CPSU CC Propaganda Department, Konstantin Rusakov, the head of the CPSU CC Department for Ties with Communist and Workers' Parties of Socialist Countries, and Vadim Zagladin, the deputy head of the CPSU CC International Department. The documents were sent to the CPSU Politburo in late May 1968 pursuant to a May 16 directive instructing them to prepare briefing materials for party functionaries who were to conduct special meetings all over the Soviet Union to explain what was going on in Czechoslovakia and justify the Soviet response.

The propaganda package draws heavily on the speech that Brezhnev delivered at the April 1968 plenum of the CPSU Central Committee, "On Urgent Matters Regarding the International Situation and the CPSU's Struggle for Cohesion in the World Communist Movement," repeating entire passages verbatim. The materials illustrate how the CPSU Politburo conducted a top-down flow of information during the Czechoslovak crisis in order to ensure a uniformity of views throughout the party ranks, and forestall popular debate over the Soviet leaderships' chosen course of action.

TOP SECRET

In accordance with the instructions of the CPSU CC Politburo on 16 May 1968 (No. P81/XX), we are presenting draft material for speech-makers, propagandists, and agitators about the present state of affairs. The text of the material has been prepared on the basis of L. I. Brezhnev's report "On Urgent Matters Regarding the International Situation and the CPSU's Struggle for Cohesion in the World Communist Movement," which he presented at the April (1968) Plenum of the CPSU CC.

27. V. 68

V. Stepakov   K. Rusakov   V. Zagladin

On the Current Situation (Some Urgent Points Regarding the USSR's International Position), June 1968

In recent months Czechoslovakia has become one of the basic targets of political and ideological subversion carried out by imperialists.

In these circumstances the Soviet Union and the other fraternal countries have expressed their alarm at the events in Czechoslovakia. Their concerns have been met with understanding by the CPCz CC and the government of Czechoslovakia. Our internationalist duty is to help our Czechoslovak friends stabilize the situation and rectify the difficulties produced by the intrigues of forces hostile to socialism. Action on this matter, which is important for the entire socialist commonwealth, is being undertaken in close contact with the leadership of the fraternal countries.

At the meeting of the leaders of six European socialist countries in Dresden, a number of extremely important problems regarding their economic and political cooperation were considered, and the delegates from the ČSSR provided information about the situation in their country.[58]

---

[58] See Documents Nos. 14, 15, 17, 18.

A frank exchange of views then transpired. The Czechoslovak comrades stated that the CPCz will never permit events to develop in a way that would result in counterrevolution or that would turn Czechoslovakia away from the socialist path. Friendship with the Soviet Union and with other socialist countries, and the fulfillment of obligations to the Warsaw Pact, remain the cornerstone of its foreign policy.

As the March–April plenum of the CPCz CC showed, Czechoslovak communists are seriously troubled by the stepped-up activity of anti-socialist forces in the country. At the plenum there was an effort by the leadership of the party to gain control over events and to focus the attention of party organizations and all workers on the execution of constructive tasks of socialist construction in the ČSSR. Great attention was devoted to the necessity of further increasing the role of the party in the leadership of the country. Due note was taken of the significance of the activity of all links in the party and state apparatus, including those in the army and the state security organs.

As was reported in our press, on 12–13 May a conference of first secretaries of district, municipal, and oblast committees of the CPCz took place in Prague. It was convened in connection with preparations for a CC plenum, which has been recommended by the end of May. At the conference, Cde. Dubček gave an evaluation of the intra-party situation, having characterized both the positive and the negative sides of the process begun after the December and January plenum of the CPCz CC. The participants in the conference came to the unanimous conclusion that communists in Czechoslovakia under any circumstances will consistently defend, strengthen, and develop the achievements gained by the working class and by the whole nation under the leadership of the party. They expressed certainty that any attempt by anti-socialist forces to endanger the contemporary development of socialist society will receive a decisive rebuff.

The near future will show to what degree the decisions of the March–April plenum of the CPCz CC will be able to put things on an even keel. The CPSU sincerely wishes the Czechoslovak friends success in their endeavors to achieve complete stability in the party and the country.

The Communist Party of Czechoslovakia and the Czechoslovak working class possess extensive political experience; the communists of Czechoslovakia, as events have shown, are taking measures to control the situation and to avoid disrupting the ties of fraternal friendship between our parties and countries. However, it is not yet possible to rule out new complications. In all circumstances, no matter what happens, our principled position is clear: It is necessary to do everything possible to thwart the intrigues of the enemies of socialism.

Not long ago separate unsavory incidents occurred in the public life of fraternal Poland. A definite group of maliciously oriented figures from the revisionist school, including ideologically immature and unstable elements who were connected with bourgeois and Zionist circles in the intelligentsia, spoke out against the party's policy, and in essence against its leading role.[59] In their attempts to provoke mass anti-party and anti-state actions, they succeeded for some time in influencing a definte section of Polish students, above all in Warsaw. The roots and political nature of these events were deftly exposed in the speech of Cde. Gomułka, which was published in our press.[60] The leadership of the Polish United Workers' Party was able to mobilize within a short period of time against the attempts being made to subvert the party and was able to stabilize the situation in the country quickly. It is important to note that in the struggle against the attempts to spread anti-party and anti-socialist influence in Poland, the vanguard of the country's workers—the PZPR—acted decisively and militantly. To defend the party's policy, the cause of socialism in Poland, and Poland's friendship with the Soviet Union, party organizations displayed a broad front and kept their word to the working class.

[59] In effect, this passage is expressing approval of the vicious anti-Semitic campaign under way in Poland at the time.

[60] See "Vystuplenie tovarishcha V. Gomulki na vstreche s partiinym aktivom Varshavy," *Pravda* (Moscow), March 22, 1968, pp. 3–4. For secret CPSU reports on party members' reactions to Gomułka's speech, see "TsK KPSS," Memorandum No. 97983 (Secret), March 27, 1968, from V. Stepakov, deputy head of the CPSU CC Propaganda Department, in TsKhSD, F. 5, Op. 60, D. 19, Ll. 6–10.

DOCUMENT No. 37: Alexander Dubček's Speech to the CPCz CC Plenary Session, May 29 – June 1, 1968, with Discussion by Vasil Biľak (Excerpts)

Source: ÚSD, AÚV KSČ, F. 01.

In his speech and other remarks to the CPCz Plenum, Dubček makes clear that he favors a gradual approach to reform, an approach that would "transform" the existing system rather than "destroying" it all at once. In a gesture to more conservative elements, he declares that "anti-communist forces" had become active in Czechoslovakia, and he speaks harshly about the "excesses" and "irresponsible behavior" of the Czechoslovak press. Nevertheless, Dubček offers no concessions to defending the reform process per se, and he insists that "democratic means" rather than "administrative measures" (i.e., violent repression) are the only legitimate way to counter "extremist" elements of the right or the left.

The orthodox members of the CPCz Central Committee express harshly contrasting views, as demonstrated by the remarks of Vasil Biľak. The transcript records Biľak denouncing "right-wing," "counterrevolutionary," and "anti-Soviet" forces who had seized control of the party and warns, in an argument echoing the Soviet position, that these internal matters are "not purely our own, Czechoslovak, affair." A failure to uphold traditional Marxism–Leninism at home, he states, would amount to an attack on the country's "internationalist interests" and a blow against the whole "socialist commonwealth." Biľak openly endorses the use of mass repression, even of violent terror, to curb the activities of "anti-communist and anti-socialist forces."

This evident schism between the hard-line and pro-reform members of the Central Committee kept the plenum from significant decisions, with the exception of the removal of Novotný from the party and the vote to convene an Extraordinary 14th CPCz Congress on September 9, nearly two years ahead of schedule. In every respect, the congress held the potential to greatly expedite the process of liberalization; for that reason it became a marker for Soviet military action before September.

Cde. Alexander Dubček:

[In his opening remarks Dubček offers an evaluation of the current situation, a report on the activities of Central Committee bodies, the party's further tactical procedures, and preparation of the CPCz congress.]

. . . During the eight months since the April session the social process has further accelerated. While during the period immediately after January the trend was essentially one of unity, a gradual differentiation is now under way. A variety of specific interests are emerging, and individual political tendencies are coming to the fore with increasing evidence.

The differentiation of society is also reflected within the party in the different assessments of the current situation and of its causes as well of the party's future steps. There is growing concern, as demonstrated by resolutions adopted by party bodies and organizations, as to whether the party is not yielding some of its positions, whether it is not abandoning its leading role, and whether it is not paving the way for right-wing, anti-socialist forces. On the other hand, concern is also expressed that the party should not slow down the democratization process.

If we want to arrive at a truthful picture we cannot see only extremes and speak in absolute terms about marginal phenomena.

The fundamental nature of the current situation is determined by the positive social process begun in January. Following the April plenum, which correctly characterized the essence of the situation at the time, certain factors of political consolidation have been strengthened. . . .

The contradictions and conflicts that are quite natural in the current process and that are at times brought to a critical head perhaps even too dramatically, are neither the product nor the consequence of the policy on which we embarked in January. They are, rather, the fruit of a long social crisis that has been maturing over the years, a crisis in which a host of unsatisfied needs and unsolved problems had accumulated without redress from the previous regime. What is more, the previous regime by its actions even deepened these problems, even though many people had drawn attention to this fact since the 12th Party Congress, and even more so after the 13th Party Congress [in 1962 and 1966, respectively—Eds.]. In January we cleared the road to their solution. This naturally does not take place without conflicts and a certain degree of spontaneity. So, the fundamental source of the current difficulties lies in the burden of social conflicts, mistakes, and deformations that reached a critical state, especially over the past few years when personal power was so concentrated. . . .

But since then the situation has changed: Anti-communist tendencies have grown stronger and certain elements are attempting to engage in more intensive forms of activity. The large majority of the party has come to realize this danger, which is today the main threat to the further progress of the democratization process. Increasing sections of the progressive public are beginning to be aware of it as well.

The activation of right-wing forces has resulted in a certain inception of sectarian trends whereby attempts are being made to resolve the situation by largely incorrect methods that in turn might provoke undesirable tension and conflicts. . . .

In our view, the main way to struggle against right-wing, anti-communist forces is a positive approach by the party that will marshal all committed, pro-socialist forces in society to work constructively toward the progress of our society. We maintain that the fundamental path to follow is one that will have the full backing and recognition, above all, of the working masses, the working class, and cooperative farmers. The party leadership knows only too well that if anti-communist, right-wing forces emerge, the foundations of socialism cannot be safeguarded without the working class. That is what will guide the policy of the party.

Apart from fears of a right-wing danger, there are also now fears of the conservative forces in the party and of a return to the situation before January 1968. This danger stems from remnants of stereotyped thinking of the past and from the inertia of bureaucratic methods and activities.

Although the proponents of these views pay lip service to the new policy, they have not yet overcome old thinking, and instead assess social developments by fanning nervousness and mistrust in the policy of the party leadership and by readily giving the worst possible labels to each deviation from inertia or to even a slightly different socialist initiative. Some of these people are even pursuing deliberate actions against the policy of the party. I would like to mention examples, such as attempts to circulate slanderous leaflets within the party and among the public, the demagogic vilification of the party's policy, the attempts to bring about splits between the workers and the party, between party members and the leadership, and even within the party leadership itself.

It goes without saying that such views and attitudes undermine the party's capacity to act and could discredit the party in the eyes of the broad mass of the people, who are rightly coupling their hope in a new policy of the party with efforts to overcome old sectarian and dogmatic working methods. That is why firm action is necessary against this type of activity as well. All attempts to revive sectarianism, dogmatism, and pre-January conditions as such, albeit in the name of a struggle against anti-communism, would inflict great damage on the party and its policy and would, objectively, play into the hands precisely of such anti-communist tendencies. . . .

As is normal in politics, both extremes have the same objective impact in the final analysis and obstruct progressive development, which is and must be our main goal. We must and will not stop half way. That is why we are not so worried by tendencies that are obstructing the road in this direction. . . .

As demonstrated by the previous analysis, the reinforcement of the authority and influence of the party in society is the fundamental issue to be confronted. Without this, it would be naive to expect extremist tendencies not to exert pressure that might lead to attacks against the socialist system itself in our country. We have therefore concluded that without an extraordinary congress

the party will not unite at a sufficiently rapid pace and will be losing its authority. That is why the exceptional measure we are proposing—to prepare the congress during the three summer months—is a fundamental issue for the development of the entire internal political situation.
. . .

Vasil Biľak: Just as in the past many things were being simplified and idealized, the same is being done today. What was white is black, and what was black has suddenly become white. We would be deceiving ourselves if we were to speak about unity of action and unity of views within the party. After all, it is difficult to be at one with Comrade Novotný, but neither is it possible to be united with those who believe they will consolidate the party if they slander it as much as possible. Here, in the Central Committee, there is also no unity of views and of action, and we are more concerned with watching each other than with trusting each other. . .

Even if we pursue our Czechoslovak policy we must bear in mind that what we are doing is not purely our own, Czechoslovak, affair. The harmfulness of failing to respect national traditions and certain specific features that have been created by historical development in individual countries is well established. It is, however, no less harmful if Marxists do not see these national peculiarities in the context of internationalist interests since respect of the latter will multiply the strength of the socialist community, thus ensuring the progressive development of all the counties within it. . . .[61]

We cannot remain indifferent to many covert and open attacks against the socialist principles of our republic, against the Communist Party of Czechoslovakia, against Marxism–Leninism as our ideology, against the leading role of the working class, and against our alliance and friendship with the Soviet Union. Nor can we be indifferent to attempts to create an opposition party and so forth. It would be possible to give many examples of things that are like poison and contaminate people's thinking and that seek to provoke mistrust and even hatred of everything socialist. Anodyne voices urge us not to pay attention to this because these are no more than manifestations of individuals or only small groups. The Central Committee of the Slovak Communist Party has declared that we must not be lulled to sleep, but must give serious consideration to all negative phenomena. It is enough to take a look at the open program of Ivan Sviták and some others to understand whether they are speaking only for themselves or on behalf of anti-communist and anti-socialist forces that are already beginning to form.[62] They never imagined that after January such an opportune moment would arise for them to coalesce so quickly.

One may wonder where their roots are and where they have come from in our society. After all, in the past we declared that there were no longer any antagonistic classes in our society and that we were building an advanced socialist society. Twenty years, it appears, is not a long enough time for the disappearance in our society of all the forces against whom the working class, progressive peasants, and intellectuals had to fight under the leadership of the CPCz.[63] 1.7 million members of other political parties, including 320,000 members of Hlinka's Slovak People's Party and 230,000 members of the Democratic Party, of whom the great majority previously did not agree with the policy of the CPCz and were in active opposition to it, have also not disappeared into thin air from our society.[64] . . .

Members of the bourgeois classes whose property has been nationalized, starting with bankers and factory owners and ending with kulaks, will never become reconciled to the existence of

---

[61] This view is consonant with the argument made by Soviet officials both before and after the invasion.

[62] Ivan Sviták was an outspoken and controversial proponent of radical democratic reform who was closely associated with KAN.

[63] Biľak appears to be calling for a return to the terror of the late 1940s and early 1950s.

[64] Andrej Hlinka was an ultranationalist priest who founded the Slovak People's Party in the interwar period. His successor, Jozef Tiso, headed the party and state during Slovakia's brief period of "independence" (1939–1945) after Nazi Germany occupied the Sudetenland, Bohemia, and Moravia.

socialism, nor to the fact that their former property today serves the whole of society and its economic and cultural progress. And they are not alone. They are not the only ones who think in this way. It is more than likely that they brought up and still bring up their children and even their grandchildren to think this way.[65] . . .

All that happened last January was inevitable. But that is not the cause of the many complex problems and complications we now face in the party and in society. . . .

We are the ones who bear responsibility for the present, for all that is happening today, and we will not be able to twist and turn in the face of history. Was it the Soviet Union that forced its advisers on us? I am not defending the advisers: There were good ones, less good ones, and evil ones. The Soviet Union knew how to deal with them eventually. But I take the liberty of quoting from a letter from Stalin which he sent to the CPCz Central Committee on 25 June 1951, through the intermediary of Čepička.[66] It states, among other things: "If you really need an adviser in state security matters, you will have to decide this yourselves. In that case we will try to find a stronger and more experienced worker. Under all conditions and in any case we believe that our adviser must be supervised in his work and under the strict control of the CPCz Central Committee, and under no circumstances must he take the place of the minister for security." This is what Stalin wrote, and he was some authority!

. . . I am of the view that the congress should be held even though I see great danger in it unless we adopt certain inevitable measures.

In my view, these measures must ensure that the mass media do not create an anti-party atmosphere, that the choice and election of delegates at district and regional conferences does not turn into a public bidding game, and that this remains a strictly internal party affair. . . .

At a certain period of time it was possible to believe that some people who for years had been openly or covertly slandering, indeed attacking, our party for one reason or another, genuinely wanted the party to change its deformed working methods. They made a great show of their alleged struggle against Novotný. It is not difficult for me to remember that between the December and January plenary sessions some trembled like a leaf, wondering how it would all end. And they claimed that the main problem was the removal of Novotný. Novotný has now been removed,[67] many positive things have been done, and our democratization process continues and yet, they find it necessary to assail the party, to strike again and try to destroy it. However, the present makes it amply clear that they are not concerned about the communist party at all. There is a well-orchestrated drive under way to create an opposition to the communist party that will suit their way of thinking. . . .

[65] This statement forecast the notorious policy that was pursued by Gustáv Husák's regime in the post-invasion period of "normalization." Children often were denied access to education and other public goods simply because their parents were thought to have supported the Prague Spring.

[66] Alexej Čepička began his career as minister of trade in 1947. From 1948 to 1950, he held the post of minister of justice. In April 1950, he became minister of national defense and a member of the CPCz Politburo. He was one of the main architects of the political terror and show trials that took place in Czechoslovakia in the early 1950s, working closely with his father-in-law, Gottwald. In 1956, Čepička was stripped of all his official posts.

[67] Novotný as well as several other members of the Central Committee were removed at this plenum while an investigation was under way into their responsibility for the repressions of the 1950s.

DOCUMENT No. 38: KAN's Manifesto, May 1968

Source: "Manifest Klubu angažovaných nestraníků," *Svobodné slovo* (Prague), July 11, 1968, p. 1.

The Club of Committed Non-Party Members (Klub angažovaných nestraníků)—a group of 144 leading intellectuals and prominent social figures—released this manifesto on May 13, 1968 under the signature of the founding members as well as a few other well-known individuals. The document proclaims a commitment to "human and civil rights and civil equality," political pluralism, and the principles embodied in the UN Declaration on Human Rights. KAN's manifesto indicates that the club would seek to foster public debate about these principles and to enable members and supporters of KAN to take an active part in elections to the National Assembly.

KAN's main organizers were Jiřina Mlýnková and Ludvík Rybáček, who published several early statements of the group's aims in Literární listy. *At its height, KAN claimed a membership of nearly 15,000, though the actual number was probably closer to 3,000. (The number would have been much higher if not for restrictions imposed by the state, both formally and informally.) KAN was crushed by the Soviet invasion and was then formally proscribed in September 1968.*

The fiftieth anniversary of the Czechoslovak Republic inspires us to endorse the ideas that were present at the time our state and national independence was first achieved. We are convinced, as was the founder of this state, that states are kept alive by their loyalty to the ideals under which they were born. We declare our support for these ideals in their contemporary, modern form, stressing three fundamental principles as the ideological backbone of our CLUB.

We believe that the foundations of any modern European policy lie in the idea of human and civil rights and civil equality, anchored in the revolutionary declaration of human rights, which covers both the human being and the citizen, and which is today enshrined in the UN Declaration on Human Rights. We regard the defense of these rights against the dehumanizing forces of capitalism, fascism, and Stalinism to be the uninterrupted tradition of the democratic endeavors of the Czech and Slovak peoples, which we openly support as the reliable pillar of the Czechoslovak idea of statehood.

The second object of our political endeavor is the humanist tradition of Czechoslovak culture, which greatly inspired the advancement of our nations in the field of science, art, religion, ethics, and philosophy rather than on the battlefield or in attempts at world domination or simply in multiplying material well-being. In keeping with this international humanistic tradition of solidarity, peace, and cooperation, we do not believe the values of a nation, class, or race are decisive. Instead, we would emphasize the personality of the human being and their creation as the very meaning of human existence.

The third object is the current impressive idea of the Czechoslovak experiment, which is to combine democratic socialism with the noble program of individual freedom. The socialist system, the democratic exercise of power, and freedom of the individual are for us the points of departure in our political thinking as well as the objective for which we want to strive in the present transformation of political life.

The fact that in addition to the replacement of officials in leading posts there have been far more significant changes—a change of people's opinions and positions, a transformation of the atmosphere of fear into a climate of confidence and good will, and a change of the structure of people's political thinking—is a paradoxical yet logical outcome of the tempestuous political development in our country. We refer to hundreds of thousands of individual revolutions taking place within people who have understood that searching for a way to escape intact while hedging through the arbitrary totalitarian rule of a small group of people making undue claims to power is beneath the dignity of a human being. The internal transformations that are today taking place in every thinking citizen of this country—and that are, for the moment, the only guarantee that developments are irreversible and will not slide back into the past—motivate the need of individuals to come close to people, thinking and acting as they do. It is surprising and encouraging that this applies to thousands of non-members of the party who today claim their share of responsibility for the future progress of the political arrangement of the state. The call by non-members, which is growing stronger day by day, and therefore necessitates an organization capable of defending their interests, is the result of the abnormal situation of the past twenty years when a sharp divide was created between communists and non-communists. This discriminatory measure virtually prevented non-communists from holding any higher economic, political, and, hence, social position so that non-communists were manipulated as passive, scattered, and inferior elements in society. It is evident that this was a gross violation of fundamental human rights as set out in the UN Declaration, as well as a violation of our national traditions of humanism, democracy, and socialism.

The newly emerging structure of our political life, whose concrete shape and detailed forms we are for the moment incapable of anticipating, has certain common features, regardless of possible differences of views or political bearing, which unite non-members of the party and form the basis of the political activity of non-members of the party both within the CLUB and outside the CLUB. The political activity of our CLUB for the moment deliberately concentrates on this minimum program of common demands of non-members of the party because we expect that the further normalization of our social life will result in the establishment or transformation of political parties that are based on attributes, guided by a fundamental world outlook, and conceived with a long-term view. For the moment the CLUB has no aspirations toward such a role since it is still lacking the legal, organizational, and material prerequisites as well as the prerequisites of membership. We nevertheless see fit to draw the attention of the non-party public to key issues and to the need for adequate action to ensure that the fundamental rules of the democratic formation of political life and state power are observed and respected. All non-members of the party are today interested in such a program, irrespective of the questions that will be formulated at a later date in connection with elections, namely the content of the existing or future political parties' programs.

In accordance with fundamental human rights we consider equality of party members and non-members to be the minimum rule of the democratic game with which CLUB is launching its political activity. Without this principle it is impossible to substantially remedy the flaws in our public life. Nor can the crisis in the economy be overcome. Apart from the equality of the two sections of our political public, the crucial issues in the months to come are, in our view, democratic elections, which are conceivable solely as secret elections of separate lists of candidates from a number of political parties, and independent candidates as well. If the democratization process is not to be frozen at its inception the electoral law must fulfill these elementary demands with the citizen's free participation in forming the political bodies of the state, and it must offer genuine alternatives in political decision-making by the population. Finally, we wish to submit alternative political proposals not only on the question of elections, but on discussion of all major political issues. We want to be an independent political force of an entirely new type. We do not wish to shape our own political positions against the communist party but alongside it, working for a common objective—socialism, based on the foundations of humanism and democracy—an objective that has always been the longing of our two nations.[68]

[68] In September 1968, KAN was formally prohibited, and during the years of "normalization" under Husák and Jakeš, any sign of overt support for KAN was quickly squashed. Not until after communism collapsed in Czechoslovakia in late 1989 was KAN finally resurrected. The club never again approached the visibility it attained in 1968, but as of March 1993 it still claimed—perhaps in an overstatement—several thousand members in the Czech Republic. In the spring of 1995 KAN's leadership voted to merge with the Christian Democratic Party (KDS). The Slovak branch of the group was always very small both in 1968 and after 1989, and it ceased to exist altogether when the Czechoslovak state split apart.

DOCUMENT No. 39: Letter from Leonid Brezhnev to Alexander Dubček Proposing Another Bilateral Meeting, June 11, 1968

Source: ÚSD, AÚV KSČ, F. 07/15, Zahr. kor. c. 817; Vondrová & Navrátil, vol. 1, pp. 240–241.

This letter was given to Dubček by the Soviet ambassador in Prague, Stepan Chervonenko, on the morning of June 12, 1968—a day before Dubček left on a state visit to Hungary to sign a new bilateral treaty of friendship and cooperation. In it, Brezhnev expresses deep concern about the growth of "anti-socialist" and "counterrevolutionary" forces in Czechoslovakia, and proposes that the CPSU and CPCz convene another top-level bilateral meeting within a few days, preferably on June 15–16.

A handwritten note by Dubček on the letter indicates that after he conferred with Černík and Biľak, he "announced that at the present time I am too busy" to take part in such talks, and that "until the [regional and city] party conferences are over it will be impossible" to schedule a meeting. The conferences were selecting delegates for the upcoming CPCz congress from all over Czechoslovakia, and they were not due to be completed until the first half of July. This meant that sometime in mid-July was the earliest possible date for a Soviet–Czechoslovak meeting, a month later than Brezhnev had proposed. The note shows that Dubček "informed Cde. Chervonenko" of his decision and that Chervonenko "voiced his willingness" to transmit it back to Moscow.

With Dubček's rejection of the invitation Brezhnev became far more suspicious and mistrustful of the CPCz leader. Dubček's unwillingness to arrange a new bilateral meeting in June would later be cited by his domestic opponents and by Soviet officials after the invasion as evidence of his "irresponsible" behavior. They charged that he had violated the normal "comradely" procedures when he considered the invitation. Although Dubček consulted with Černík and Biľak, he did not present the letter to the full CPCz CC Presidium, and could not have done so until after he returned from Hungary.

[not dated]

To Esteemed Alexander Stepanovich!

Thank you for the information about the most recent plenum of the CPCz CC and about the situation in the state and the party, which we obtained via Cde. Chervonenko. We were satisfied upon receiving your news about the measures designed to activate the internal life of the party and to entrench the leading role of the party in socialist construction. At the same time we understand your worries and concerns about the attacks by anti-socialist forces against the party. As you know, we, too, are closely following the course of events in Czechoslovakia. We share your worries, and in a fraternal spirit we support you and your comrades in the fight you are waging for the defense and further development of socialist gains in Czechoslovakia and for the consolidation of the CPCz and its leading role. It has now become clear that your fight to achieve those goals is taking place against a backdrop of overt and growing pressure from anti-socialist forces.

Now, after the May plenum of the CPCz CC, you have entered an especially difficult period—a period in which preparations will be made for the extraordinary party congress. We well understand the great importance of the upcoming congress for the life of the party and the country. The preparations for the congress, as can now be seen, will be made at a time when your opponents have begun stepping up their attacks against the healthy forces in the communist party and its leadership, and have been perpetrating a campaign of intimidation, lies, and provocation; in this way, under the guise of waging a struggle against "conservatives," they will "shoot down" all the honest and loyal communists. The line faithful to Marxism–Leninism, to the cause of socialism, to internationalist duty, to the world communist movement, and to the Warsaw Pact, which, as was recently proclaimed, has been engaged in a sharp class struggle against bourgeois ideology, has encountered overt pressure from anti-socialist and counterrevolutionary forces. Unfortunately, we see that your mass media (the press, radio, and television) are still mainly espousing right-wing, bourgeois-liberal, and sometimes openly counterrevolutionary positions, irrespective of the results of the May plenum of the CPCz CC.

What especially worries us, as it does you and your comrades, is the existence of a "second center" in the CPCz, which obviously complicates the situation in the party and the country.[69]

We believe that in these circumstances you will find the appropriate solutions and will take the necessary measures to ensure the successful preparation for such an important congress.

Surely you understand that we are sincerely and fraternally standing by you in confronting the difficulties of your struggle, and that we, for our part, would like to lend you all possible assistance and support.

In that connection, it seems worthwhile, in our view, to arrange another unofficial, bilateral, and friendly meeting with you, Alexander Stepanovich, and your closest, like-minded comrades.[70] From our side, Cdes. Brezhnev, Podgorny, Kosygin, and Katushev could take part in the meeting.

This meeting could be held at any location that is suitable for you along the Soviet–Czechoslovak border, in the Tatras, or in Uzhgorod.[71]

We believe that in view of the current situation it would be best if the meeting were held confidentially, and that, for this reason, we suggest meeting on the morning of Saturday, the 15th, and Sunday, the 16th of June of this year after your return from Hungary. A friendly and confidential exchange of opinions would contribute to a better mutual understanding and coordination of our efforts in the struggle for the further consolidation and development of the cause of socialism and of Soviet–Czechoslovak friendship.

L. Brezhnev[72]

[69] Brezhnev's reference to a "second center" pertains to the group of pro-reform officials in the CPCz who were regarded by Soviet leaders as the nucleus of a "counterrevolutionary underground." It would have included such figures as František Kriegel, Čestmír Císař, Josef Špaček, Václav Slavík, Bohumil Šimon, Václav Prchlík, Jiří Pelikán, Ota Šik, and Jiří Hájek. On this point, see Document No. 130.

[70] According to the instructions transmitted by the CPSU CC Politburo to Chervonenko, the Soviet ambassador was supposed to explain to Dubček that the phrase "like-minded comrades" referred to Kolder, Biľak, Lenárt, and Švestka—in other words, the leaders of the orthodox, pro-Moscow faction.

[71] The Tatras are part of the central Carpathian Mountain range in southern Poland and northern Slovakia. Uzhgorod is the capital of Transcarpathia (in Ukraine), along the Ukrainian–Slovak border.

[72] Next to the signature is a note written by Dubček saying that the letter was "signed by Comrade Chervonenko" and that "the original was not delivered."

DOCUMENT No. 40: "Status of the Šumava Allied Exercise," Report to Alexander Dubček by ČSSR Defense Minister Martin Dzúr, June 17, 1968

Source: VHA, F. MNO, Gen. štáb, Sv. Šumava.

National Defense Minister Martin Dzúr's report on the Šumava exercises describes them as "strategic-operational command-staff exercises," a designation that implied a much larger role for combat forces than the original plan for the exercises in 1967.

The maneuvers were originally scheduled to begin in late 1968 or early 1969. In response to the Prague Spring, the Soviets decided to bring the date forward to mid-June, and expand the number of Warsaw Pact forces participating to 30–40,000 men. Dzúr informs Dubček that "the number of combat units taking part is unusually high for an exercise of this kind." Unbeknownst to Czechoslovak leaders, the Soviets designed the maneuvers as a "dress rehearsal" for the August intervention.

INFORMATION REPORT

TO: First Secretary of the CPCz Central Committee, Cde. Alexander Dubček

FROM: ČSSR Minister of National Defense

SUBJECT: Status of the Šumava allied exercise

Under the terms of an agreement between the ČSSR government and the commander-in-chief of the Joint Armed Forces, the Šumava allied strategic operational command staff exercises will be held on the territory of the ČSSR on 19–26 June 1968.

On the basis of information provided by the chief of staff of the Joint Armed Forces, General Kazakov, the following staffs and troops will participate in the exercise on ČSSR territory:

— two army staffs of the CzPA, each with one division staff, and each division with one regiment staff and one battalion of troops;

— one staff of the Soviet army from the Transcarpathian Military District, and two division staffs, each with one regiment staff and one motorized rifle battalion, with total personnel numbering 4,000, of which 1,000 are in combat units;

— one staff of the Soviet army from the Northern Group of Soviet Forces deployed on the territory of the Polish People's Republic, with two division staffs, each with one regiment staff and one motorized rifle battalion, with total personnel numbering 4,000, of which 1,000 are in combat units;

— one army staff and one division of the Hungarian People's Army with reduced numbers and total personnel of approximately 750;

— the air force of the Soviet army with 48–60 combat aircraft and ground-based logistical forces, with total personnel of about 1,900;

— the directorate of the exercise from the command staffs of the Joint Armed Forces and the General Staff of the Soviet army, with logistical and communications formations;

— a front staff from the Northern Group of Soviet Forces deployed on the territory of the Polish People's Republic.[73]

---

[73] In Soviet military parlance, a "front" was defined as "an operational-strategic formation of the armed forces . . . which is designated to carry out operational-strategic missions along a single strategic line or along several operational lines in a continental theater of military operations." See S. F. Akhromeev, ed., *Voennyi entsiklopedicheskii slovar'*, 2nd ed. (Moscow: Voenizdat, 1986), p. 787. The size of a front would vary considerably depending on its specific mission, but it could include as many as 200,000–300,000 troops.

In total, it can be expected that some 14,000 troops of the Soviet army will be on ČSSR territory during the exercise, including 2,000 in combat units, along with 48–60 combat aircraft and helicopters, and up to 750 personnel from the Hungarian People's Army, that is, a total of approximately 15,000 allied troops.

According to information available to us, additional troops from the border regions in the vicinity of the ČSSR, consisting of one Polish army and one army from the German Democratic Republic, will participate in the exercises on the territory of the Polish People's Republic and the German Democratic Republic.

The commander of the staff of the Joint Armed Forces anticipates between 30,000–40,000 personnel to be involved in the exercise.

The final number of personnel and their gradual entry onto our territory will be specified on 18.6.1968, by Marshal Yakubovskii after his arrival in the ČSSR.[74]

The following quantity of allied troops are already on ČSSR territory as of today:

— the directorate of the exercise: the Soviet section of 480 generals and officers;
— supply units for the exercise directorate and communications units amounting to 4,170 personnel and 1,327 vehicles;
— 747 personnel and 239 vehicles from the Hungarian People's Army;
— 1,297 personnel, 320 vehicles, and 21 aircraft from the Soviet Air Force;

Altogether, on 17 June 1968 there are 6,689 personnel, 1,886 vehicles, and 21 aircraft from allied forces deployed on ČSSR territory. These numbers will be increased both before and during the exercise up to the figures cited.

In addition to the participation of troops outlined above, the Soviet exercise directorate has insisted on the participation of a further staff from the 7th army of the National Air Defense Forces, along with two corps staffs from the National Air Defense Forces and, for a day or two, operational groups from the CzPA General Staff. These demands are increasing the originally agreed size of the numbers participating in the exercise, and that is why they have not yet been approved by the CzPA command.

The size of the exercise, especially the number of combat units taking part, is unusually high for an exercise of this nature.

I therefore request that agreement be given to hold the exercise in accordance with the proposal of the Joint Command, or to consider the following solution:

a) The exercise would be held in the size mentioned, but only up to division staff level, including the necessary communications and logistic units and without the participation of combat formations.

The troop maneuvers that the exercise directorate intends to carry out during the strategic-operational exercise can be held at any time during the year while not linking them to the nature of such an exercise. This is not only because similar exercises are not very effective for the training of troops but, above all, because at the present time of year it is difficult to avoid damage to crops and communications.

b) If the Joint Command so insists, the required combat units will be designated for individual missions of a tactical nature from the ranks of the CzPA.

The activities of the Joint Air Forces in ČSSR airspace will be limited, with essential tasks to be carried out by the CzPA 10th air force.

I recommend that Marshal of the USSR Yakubovskii be received within the next few days either by the CPCz CC first secretary or by the prime minister to provide overall information about the Šumava exercise.

---

[74] Since Yakubovskii was not due to arrive until the 18th, less than a day before the scheduled start of the exercises, the lack of knowledge of the final size of the exercises was of concern to Czech leaders.

The commander-in-chief of the Joint Armed Forces, Marshal of the USSR Yakubovskii, arrives in the ČSSR at Ruzyně airport on 18 June 1968; his reception is secured.

In the morning I will hold talks with Marshal of the USSR Yakubovskii on the following matters:

— the operational objective and organizational directives for the Šumava exercise;

— the number of troops participating in the exercise, and their quantity and specific location on ČSSR territory;

— the participation of the 7th Army and two corps of the National Air Defense Forces as well as operational groups of the CzPA General Staff;

— the date of the beginning and termination of the exercise, the duration of the assessment, and the deadline for the departure of allied troops from ČSSR territory;

— the method of carrying out the part of the exercise involving troops, and expected instances with which the original agreement did not reckon;

— an agreement that troops taking part in the exercise from the Polish People's Army and the German People's Army should perform their activity outside ČSSR territory;

— the official protocol connected with the exercise, especially the reception of top officials from the allied armies at an official luncheon at the Ministry of National Defense, their meetings with government officials, and a final luncheon arranged by the head of the exercise, Marshal of the USSR Yakubovskii.

I ask you to consider the measures proposed.

Col. General Martin Dzúr
Minister of National Defense

DOCUMENT No. 41: Resolution and Letter to the Soviet People from the National Conference of the People's Militia, June 19, 1968

Source: "Rezoluce celostátního srazu přislušníků Lidových milicí," *Rudé právo* (Prague), July 13, 1968, p. 1.

Approximately 10,000 to 12,000 members of the CPCz People's Militia—the paramilitary units who were traditionally among the most orthodox, pro-Soviet elements in the Czechoslovak Communist Party—approved this resolution and the accompanying message to the Soviet people at a national meeting in Prague. As adopted, the conference resolution echoed the general line of the CPCz, pledging that "the People's Militia will never be used against the interests of the people and of socialism." Although it did not directly criticize the reform movement of Dubček, the resolution did call for a "struggle against anti-communist tendencies," and it condemned those who were "exploiting freedom of expression and freedom of the press to assail the foundations of socialism and to engage in anti-communist and anti-Soviet attacks."

The "Letter to the Soviet people" also omits any positive allusions to the domestic reforms in Czechoslovakia, vowing "never to allow anyone to denigrate or threaten the principles of socialist construction and communism." The letter emphasizes that the People's Militia can provide the only reliable "guarantee—by virtue of our constructive political work, combat readiness, and loyalty to the ideals of Marxism–Leninism and the socialist camp"—that relations between the Soviet Union and Czechoslovakia would "remain firm and unshakable." Pravda published the letter with great fanfare in Moscow on June 21. Not until almost a month later, on July 13, did the letter appear in Rudé právo *in Prague.*

To the Central Committee of the Communist Party of Czechoslovakia in Prague
Esteemed Comrades:

The participants in the national conference of People's Militia units, gathered in Prague on 19 June 1968,[75] have heard a report by the CPCz CC first secretary and commander of the People's Militia in the ČSSR.[76] They have discussed the outcome of the May session of the CPCz Central Committee and the other tasks of the People's Militia, and have adopted the following resolution:

We fully and unconditionally endorse the resolution "On the Present Situation and on the Party's Future Activities," adopted by the CPCz Central Committee on 29 May–1 June 1968.

We reassure the CPCz Central Committee and the new party leadership that we will continue to offer complete support for the successful development of socialist democracy, which began with the January CPCz CC plenum. We will do everything we can to strengthen the unity of the party and its leading role and to ensure the consistent implementation of the party's Action Program.

We are satisfied with the decision to call an Extraordinary 14th Congress, and we express our belief that its proceedings and conclusions will give the party a solid base and a new central committee, and that it will lead to the consolidation of party unity as the prime condition for the party to be a leading political force in our society and to guide the future progress of our socialist society.

[75] The conference, which convened in the hangar of Ruzyně airport just outside Prague, took place on the same day that the joint Šumava maneuvers, involving tens of thousands of combat troops from the Soviet Union, Poland, East Germany, Hungary, and Czechoslovakia, began on Czechoslovak territory. Emboldened by this show of external support, many of the activists from the People's Militia expressed strong criticism of "right-wing forces" in Czechoslovakia, who, they alleged, were posing a "serious danger" to the country's socialist order.

[76] The conference grew out of mounting public debate over the role of the People's Militia. In response to criticism, militia leaders demanded that they be officially designated the "armed corps of the communist party," with a provision to that effect in the new party statutes. In support of this demand, units of the People's Militia intended to organize assemblies in Prague and other major cities and to stage marches along public streets in their uniforms and full combat gear—the very same tactic they used when buttressing the communist party's seizure of power in February 1948. Dubček was able to head off this idea by proposing that the People's Militia instead hold a nationwide conference.

We fully support the party's effort to introduce a new constitutional arrangement of the republic on the basis of a federation of Czechs and Slovaks as equal nations.

We support and endorse all steps taken by the Central Committee that are essential if the party is to rectify, to the maximum extent possible, all errors and unlawful practices in all instances where the law and the party statutes were violated.

However, we repudiate all tendencies and attempts whereby, hand in hand with the justified demand of rehabilitation, revolutionary measures are being attacked, measures that were unavoidable in seizing and consolidating the political and economic power of the working class.[77]

We deeply appreciate the attitude of the Central Committees of the CPCz and the Slovak Communist Party toward the People's Militia.

The People's Militia was formed as an instrument of the working class and other working people to defend the results and achievements of socialist revolution. The People's Militia has been fulfilling this task with honor and is prepared to continue fulfilling it.

It must be stressed that the People's Militia never had, and does not have, anything in common with the deformations and lawlessness of past years. The People's Militia never came out against the working people. On the contrary, its members joined the working people to build socialism and, moreover, in their free time trained and prepared to defend the socialist fatherland which is their paramount mission.

Immediately after January, members of the People's Militia unconditionally came out in support of the new party leadership, headed by Cde. Dubček. They have systematically demonstrated, and continue to demonstrate, high political activity and discipline during the democratization process.

We want to assure the Central Committee and the entire party as well as all working people that they can depend on the members of the People's Militia to support them reliably against any threat to the course on which we have embarked, no matter from which side it may come. We will do everything so that the conclusions of the May session of the CPCz Central Committee on reinforcing the political influence and authority of the party, as well as on the need for a struggle against possible anti-communist tendencies, should become the affair of communists at all places of work.

We fully agree with the Central Committee that there can be no return to the situation prior to January [1968] or prior to February 1948. The members of the People's Militia want to warn all who would like to gamble with the sincere endeavors of our party and exploit the democratization process for a revision of February 1948 or even a return to 1938, that the People's Militia units are guarding and will continue to guard the revolutionary legacy of February 1948 and our firm alliance with the Soviet Union and the other socialist countries.

The members of the People's Militia value the employees in the press, radio, and television who, by their objective information, are expediting the democratization process. They appeal to all journalists, both communists and non-communists, to continue giving their full support to the new party leadership and inspiring the confidence of citizens in the current development of socialist democracy. They call on these journalists not to permit the misuse of democracy against socialist principles and to help advocate and implement the Action Program of the communist party and the line of the National Front. We are convinced that all honest workers in the mass media, both communists and non-communists, will live up to the responsibility they hold because every day they freely address millions of people. We are confident they will help the working people find a positive solution to their problems and not permit individuals to exploit freedom of speech and freedom of the press to assail the foundations of socialism and to engage in anti-communist and anti-Soviet attacks.

---

[77] The reference to "revolutionary measures" pertains to the deployment of armed People's Militia units on the streets of Prague during the communist takeover in Czechoslovakia in February 1948.

As, despite the position of the CPCz Central Committee, the existence and activities of the People's Militia have lately become a target for polemics, we again stress that the People's Militia are performing tasks connected with the defense of the socialist state in conjunction with the other armed forces of the ČSSR.

The members of the People's Militia assure all citizens of our state that concern about the misuse of the People's Militia against the interests of the people and socialism is totally unfounded. The members of the People's Militia, being true to their traditions, will remain on the front line of the builders and defenders of our fatherland.

19 June 1968

Letter to the Soviet Embassy
from the National Conference of the People's Militia

Esteemed Comrades!

We, as members of the People's Militia who are assembled at a national conference in Prague, send you our fraternal and sincere greetings. We have heard a report by the CPCz CC first secretary, Cde. Dubček, on the current policy of our party and wholeheartedly welcomed his assurance that relations between our peoples are firm and unshakable as never before.

We, the members of the People's Militia—by virtue of our constructive political work, combat readiness, and loyalty to the ideals of Marxism–Leninism and the socialist camp—provide a guarantee that this is how things will remain. We will never allow anyone to vilify or attempt to threaten the principles of socialist construction and communism, as formulated by V.I. Lenin, for which the foundations were laid in our country in February 1948. We do not agree with and disassociate ourselves from the irresponsible activities of certain journalists who, by seizing on various fabricated reports from the Western press, want to jeopardize our friendship and alliance, which have been cemented throughout our socialist construction. We will never betray the ideals for which blood was shed in the Slovak National Uprising, on the Dukla Pass, and on the Prague barricades.[78] We will place all our forces at the disposal of our party's Action Program to help in the building of socialism and communism.

Long live the firm friendship between our nations and may it continue to grow stronger! Long live the Soviet people and their communist party!

19 June 1968

The Participants in the National Conference
of the People's Militia[79]

[78] These are references to the three largest battles in World War II involving Czech and Slovak units. The Slovak National Uprising, which began in late August 1944, was crushed after two months by the Germans after the Soviet army failed to lend assistance to the Slovak partisans, but the uprising became a revered occasion in Slovak history. The Battle for Dukla Pass witnessed the bloodiest fighting that Czech and Slovak units attached to the Red Army experienced, as more than 6,500 died. The battle proved successful, however, and the day the Red Army seized the Pass, October 18, later became a national holiday in Czechoslovakia. The Red Army's drive to liberate Prague, which also involved some Czechoslovak detachments, culminated in an uprising in Prague in May 1945, and the day of liberation also later became a national holiday in Czechoslovakia.

[79] After the letter was published in *Pravda,* Soviet newspapers featured a series of enthusiastic resolutions and letters (often of nearly identical composition) from Soviet "workers" who pledged their readiness to help "Czechoslovak workers" in the "joint defense of socialism." All told, more than 16,000 of these resolutions were sent from the USSR via the Soviet embassy in Prague to the People's Militia headquarters and the CPCz Central Committee. The "spontaneity" of both the message and the responses is belied, however, by documents in the former CPSU archives in Moscow, which reveal that the whole campaign was closely organized and coordinated by the Propaganda Department of the CPSU Central Committee. (See, for example, the documents in TsKhSD, F. 5, Op. 60, D. 1, Ll. 101–104 and TsKhSD, F. 5, Op. 60, D. 24, Ll. 104–126.)

DOCUMENT No. 42: "Czechoslovakia: The Dubček Pause," U.S. Intelligence Assessment of the Crisis, June 1968

Source: Czechoslovakia—Czech Crisis 8/68, Box 182, National Security File, Country File, Lyndon Baines Johnson Library.

The CIA issued this highly classified "Special Memorandum" in mid-June 1968. The Agency's Office of National Estimates prepared the report in coordination with another CIA division, the Office of Current Intelligence. The document provides an authoritative intelligence assessment of the crisis during the four-week period between the May plenum of the CPCz Central Committee and the start of the Šumava exercise on June 19, 1968.

The CIA analysts note the "temporary domestic equilibrium" in Czechoslovakia and the "uneasy truce with Moscow," but accurately predict that tranquility "is by no means assured indefinitely" and that "there is a good chance that relations between Prague and Moscow will again become very tense." The report observes that Soviet leaders are still hoping to resolve the crisis without having to invade Czechoslovakia, but acknowledges that the "threat of military intervention" was still "the principal instrument Moscow [can] employ against Prague."

The report describes three "concessions" by the CPCz leadership to Moscow: greater adherence to common bloc policy vis-à-vis West Germany, a reaffirmation of Czechoslovakia's military commitment to the Warsaw Pact (not least by hosting the Šumava maneuvers), and a reassertion of the CPCz's "leading role" in Czechoslovak society. CIA analysis also highlights, in sections 14 and 15, "three general theories concerning the impact of the Czechoslovak crisis on domestic Soviet politics." The first theory argues that the top four Soviet leaders—Brezhnev, Kosygin, Podgorny, and Suslov—are united in their assessments of the crisis and of the appropriate policies to respond. The second theory posits that the four leaders themselves and their Politburo colleagues are united, but that they have come under pressure from other influential quarters, perhaps from senior military commanders or members of the CPSU Central Committee. The third theory claims that the four leaders were not united in their assessments and policy recommendations. "There is no sure way to choose among these various hypotheses," the agency concludes, indicating the lack of CIA covert sources inside the senior policy-making community in Moscow.

According to handwritten annotations on the report's cover page, the CIA assessment was reviewed by National Security Adviser Walt Rostow, and President Lyndon Johnson.

Central Intelligence Agency Office of National Estimates

13 June 1968

SPECIAL MEMORANDUM [Excised][80]

SUBJECT: Czechoslovakia: The Dubček Pause[81]

1. The related crises in internal Czechoslovak politics and in Soviet–Czechoslovak relations seem to have eased—at home, into a delicate and perhaps temporary domestic equilibrium and, abroad, into an uneasy truce with Moscow. The regime of party leader Dubček and Premier Černík has, in effect, premised that it will control the pace of domestic reform; Moscow has gained the appearance of Czech compliance; but Prague seems at the same time to have been able to preserve the essential substance of its democratic experiment.

---

[80] The Lyndon Baines Johnson Library declassified this document in June 1991. Only brief passages of the report remain classified, and these have been noted in the text with brackets.

[81] This memorandum was produced solely by CIA. It was prepared by the Office of National Estimates and coordinated with the Office of Current Intelligence. [Footnote in original report.]

2. The compromise seems to have come about, sequentially, as a result of strong Soviet pressures, rising Czech concern, mildly concessionary Czech responses, and, finally, the Soviets' own anxiety to find some way to avoid direct military intervention. It is true, nonetheless, that if quiescence has been restored to the relationship, it is by no means assured indefinitely. [Several words excised] Soviets are currently engaged in a Warsaw Pact exercise on Czech soil; their presence serves, at a minimum, as an ominous reminder to the Dubček regime of Soviet power and of the USSR's continuing interest in Czech developments. The recently concluded plenum of the Czechoslovak Central Committee was reassuring to the Soviets in some respects but not at all in others. [Six lines excised]

Prague's Concessions, Domestic and Foreign

3. Prague yielded to the Soviets on two major foreign policy issues and on several domestic issues of great concern to the USSR. First, concerning policy toward Germany, the Czechs evidently discarded the possibility of an early move toward diplomatic recognition of West Germany. In addition, they reversed their recent public opposition to East Germany's claims on the Berlin access question and began to mute their bitter open quarrel with the Ulbricht regime.

4. Recent East German moves affecting West German access to West Berlin may cause the Czechs some considerable anxiety. A crisis over Berlin would perhaps give the Soviets a pretext for insisting that their troops in Czechoslovakia remain there at least for the duration. [Three lines excised] But, in the event of renewed trouble over Berlin—attended by strident Soviet propaganda against West German "fascists and revanchists"—Prague might find it difficult to demand the removal of Pact troops already present on Czech soil.

5. In any case, as a second concession to the Soviets, the Czechs had already reaffirmed their military commitment to the Warsaw Pact. They did so both in word and deed, the latter by permitting the Pact exercises now under way. This, of course, was of crucial importance to Moscow. The political significance of Pact membership is obvious. In Czechoslovakia's case, there is [two or three words excised] some considerable military significance as well. Geography aside, Czechoslovakia has contributed more manpower per capita to the forces of the Warsaw Pact than any other member state, including even the USSR, and by and large the Czechoslovak soldier is better equipped and better trained than all the others except his Soviet counterpart.[82] [One line excised] the Czechs might hold fewer training, exercises, decrease their participation in joint Pact exercises, shorten conscript terms, lower overall troop strength, and sharply reduce their military budget.

6. As a third concession to Moscow, the recent Central Committee plenum reasserted the leading role of the Czechoslovak Communist Party and implied that Czech political life would not be subjected to sudden and drastic change. (Even before the Plenum met, the Interior Ministry had indicated that no new political parties would be allowed to form at this time.) In a related move, the plenum—though disposing of Novotný—allowed most of the 40 or so relatively orthodox and pro-Soviet members of the Committee to retain their membership, at least for the time being. The plenum also went back on earlier party statements and, well aware of Soviet

---

[82] On a per capita basis, Bulgaria, in fact, contributed the most troops to the Warsaw Pact. Czechoslovakia was second. At the time, the Czechoslovak armed forces numbered 230,000 out of a population of around 14.5 million, or roughly 0.0158 troops per capita. The per capita figures for the rest of the Warsaw Pact were: USSR—0.0136; East Germany—0.0079; Poland—0.0084; Bulgaria—0.0182; Hungary—0.0094; and Romania—0.0096. All figures for military manpower and size of population are from International Institute for Strategic Studies, *The Military Balance 1968–69* (London: IISS, 1968), pp. 5, 12–14. The other qualities that the CIA ascribes here to the Czechoslovak armed forces reflect the situation before the invasion. After the invasion, as discussed in Part Six below, the morale of the CzPA was undermined, and the army lost much of its effectiveness.

sensitivities on this score, denied that the new Czechoslovak course was intended to be a model for other communist countries and parties.

7. Dubček personally dominated the plenum proceedings, and this must be comforting to Moscow. Whatever their suspicions of the man, the Soviets certainly prefer his leadership to some of the likely alternatives: a party without firm leadership and direction, threatening to collapse; or a party in the hands of ultra-liberals susceptible to non-communist and even anti-communist influences. In any case, the Soviets—though still apprehensive about the continued influence of these ultra-liberals in the present regime—now seem ready to accept that the Novotný forces probably cannot stage a comeback.

8. Finally, various Czech leaders promised to discourage anti-Soviet statements in the press. These had in recent weeks reached surprising proportions, suggesting that Soviet advisers were implicated in the death of Masaryk, the purge of Slánský, and the genesis of Czechoslovakia's present economic problems. Some articles had doubted whether the USSR had been willing to help defend Czechoslovakia in 1938—in other words, doubted whether alliance with the USSR had ever done the Czechs any good. But what the Czechs have not yet publicized, what some members of the regime still implicitly call for, is the chronicle of moves last winter by Soviet officials, especially the ambassador and Warsaw Pact representatives, as they intervened to try to save Novotný. That the Soviets are not yet satisfied with the degree of restraint the Czechs have shown and intend to keep the pressure on is indicated by Moscow's unusual resort a few days ago to a formal note protesting the anti-Soviet implications of an article on General Šejna in a Czech newspaper.

Prague's Gains

9. Clearly the principal instrument Moscow has employed against Prague during the past several weeks has been the threat of military intervention.[83] The Soviets are still in a good position to use military force, and it is likely that the Soviets would prefer to intervene under cover of an exercise. Yet most signs now indicate that Moscow has decided not to use force, at least for the time being. The decline of tensions during recent weeks and authoritative reports of a new "political understanding" [one line excised] are the best general signs of this. Other specific signs include the suddenly more cordial attitude toward Prague on the part of the previously hostile Polish regime and the decline of polemical innuendoes in the Soviet press.

10. The first and most direct "concession" the Dubček–Černík regime extracted from the Soviets appears to be that the Warsaw Pact exercise will be only an exercise. The second direct gain, related to the first, may have been that the Soviets agreed that there was no need to permanently station other Warsaw Pact forces in Czechoslovakia (an agreement which, in the Soviet view, might be subject to change in the event of a flare-up over Berlin).[84] An additional

---

[83] The extraordinary number and variety of visiting Soviet military figures have in themselves constituted ominous portents: first, Yakubovskii, the Warsaw Pact commander; then Marshals Moskalenko and Koniev attended by about *two dozen* Soviet generals; next the defense minister, Grechko, along with the chief of the Political Administration, Yepishev, and the commanders of the Soviet troops poised around Czech borders; then the chief of staff of the Warsaw Pact, Kazakov, along with more Soviet military equipment and personnel than the average Czechoslovak citizen expected or desired for a "staff" exercise; and probably Yakubovskii again, since he is scheduled to command the exercise. More than one of these Soviet officers apparently promised "good Czechoslovak communists" the aid of the Soviet army if they asked for it. [Footnote in original.]

[84] This assertion is highly problematic. There is no evidence to suggest that Soviet officials ever foreswore the option of permanently deploying troops on Czechoslovak territory. On the contrary, it was a demand that Soviet military commanders repeatedly made during their talks with CPCz leaders. Not until after the invasion, however, was the Soviet Union able to compel the Czechoslovak government to accept the "temporary presence of Soviet troops" on Czechoslovak soil via the status-of-forces treaty of October 1968 (see Document No. 133).

concession may be that Soviet Warsaw Pact representatives in Prague will be restricted in their activities and access to Czechoslovak officials.

11. Dubček has probably benefited indirectly from the USSR's handling of the crisis. Most Czechs and Slovaks are likely to hold the Soviets, rather than the leadership of the Czechoslovak Communist Party, responsible for the fact that concessions were made. Soviet pressure has been blatant, and the Soviets' press tirade against the elder Masaryk greatly aroused anti-Soviet sentiments among the people at large. Dubček and Černík are probably credited with forestalling Soviet intervention and staving off the worst of the Soviet demands. Thus the Czech party leaders still stand as symbols of national independence, an image cultivated to good effect by their counterparts in Romania. Finally, the USSR's military pressures presumably alarmed the ultra-liberals, along with everyone else, and this may have led them to ease their pressures on Dubček and Černík for further immediate moves of democratic reform.

12. The Czech regime may also have gathered additional sympathy in Eastern Europe for its independent position partly as a consequence of Soviet heavy-handedness. Early in May, there were plausible reports that János Kádár had cautioned the Soviets against exerting massive pressure on the Prague government. Foreign Minister Hájek's hurried trip to Budapest on 22–24 May evidently produced additional encouragement from Kádár; Hájek expressed gratitude for "Hungarian understanding for our foreign and domestic aims" and for "moral support."[85] It is clearly Prague's hope that Moscow's concern over such attitudes—both in Eastern Europe and within the communist parties of Western Europe—will help to deter any rash Soviet moves.

The Soviet Leaders

13. Prague (like Belgrade) seems to be convinced that the Soviet leaders are divided over how to proceed vis-à-vis Czechoslovakia—whether to be tolerant or rigid, whether to temporize, hoping for the best, or to move forcefully in order to forestall the worst. Even before tensions rose in May, some high Czechoslovak officials felt that the regime in Prague was counting on such a division to work in its favor. And in late May Pudlák[86] said publicly:

I have the impression that the official Soviet leaders. . . . support the (Czechoslovak) party leadership and the government. . . . But even (in the USSR) there exists a certain difference in opinions. . . . I think that our task is to truthfully explain the fundamentals of the political development and changes in Czechoslovakia and, at the same time, oppose unfounded criticisms and doubts.

If the Soviet leadership is in fact divided, Prague has some added room for maneuver. Dubček and Černík may believe (or hope) that concessionary gestures from Prague will help to strengthen the position of the moderates in Moscow.

14. [Two lines excised] There are, however, three general theories concerning the impact of the Czechoslovak crisis on domestic Soviet politics:

a. Soviet leaders reacted without major disagreements or strains on the collective system, banding together to present a solid front both to the Czechs and to their own party. (The evidence for this construction is largely negative, i.e. there is nothing on the public record to refute it.)

b. Though the four top Soviet leaders were united on the Czech issue, there was discontent elsewhere within the elite. Pressures were brought to bear on these leaders by those who feared

---

[85] Hungary's apparent moral support of Czechoslovakia was not an act of simple altruism. Hungary seeks closer relations with Western Europe and to free itself from what one Hungarian writer referred to as "Soviet Russian methods of economic policy making." Moreover, Kádár evidently wants to be a popular national figure in Hungary and something of a Danubian statesman. [Footnote in original.]

[86] Ján Pudlák was the ČSSR first deputy foreign minister.

the consequences of a "do-nothing" policy and who may, in addition, have seen in this issue an opportunity for personal political gain.[87] [Three lines excised]

c. There were splits within the quadrumvirate itself. Kosygin was opposed to rash action and hopeful of a satisfactory solution over time. Brezhnev, perhaps urged on by Suslov, came to favor forceful moves, partly because his earlier efforts to save the situation (e.g. his interference on behalf of Novotný) had obviously failed. Eventually, some sort of compromise was worked out; Brezhnev was permitted to make a forceful (troop) move, Kosygin was then allowed to go to Czechoslovakia to try to arrange a political solution. [Four lines excised]

15. There is no sure way to choose among these various hypotheses. Degrees and combinations of each are possible; indeed, we are inclined to think that there was pressure from below to do something tangible about Czechoslovakia—perhaps especially from a concerned military—and possibly differences within the top leadership as well. All the Soviet leaders were, of course, alarmed, but some foresaw the need for sudden and dramatic action; others did not, or were fearful that hasty moves might only accelerate Czech movement out of the camp and force the Soviets to intervene militarily. Something on the order of the compromise suggested above was then perhaps arrived at. And so far—with help from Dubček—the compromise seems to be working.

The September Congress and Beyond

16. Dubček has indicated that a main item on the agenda of the party congress scheduled for September will be the formal expulsion of his opposition from the Central Committee. With that done, Dubček, according to Soviet hopes and perhaps expectations, should begin to act as Gomułka did after 1956 by gradually reimposing firm party control over public activities. Among other things, the Soviets will look for signs that the party is reinstituting patterns of censorship which were in effect until January 1968, restoring the socialist and peoples' (Catholic) parties and the National Assembly to a state of political irrelevance, and emphasizing democratic centralism rather than intra-party democracy.

17. But Soviet hopes may be severely disappointed. Though his personality and his ideas remain in some respects unclear, Dubček does not appear to be a Gomułka, either in temperament or political disposition. He has already shown himself more tolerant of domestic criticism than Gomułka ever pretended to be, and many of his political preferences seem distincly [sic] unorthodox in communist terms. He believes that Marxist notions of class conflict have no relevance to his own country, and indeed this apparently was one of the major reasons he attacked Novotný last October. Dubček and other liberals in the party, as indicated at the recently concluded plenum, apparently wish to make the National Front a more meaningful organization, not merely windowdressing for the communist party.

18. Dubček's views presumably are to some extent a reflection of the company he keeps. Dubček was probably responsible for Zdeněk Mlynář's promotion at the plenum to full party secretary and head of the party's legal commission. In these posts Mlynář may continue to advocate some of his own, far-reaching ideas: e.g., in his words, the establishment of a "multi-chamber representative body" similar in function to the "House of Lords and House of Commons in Britain or the Congress of the United States."

19. In addition, Premier Černík is scheduled to present draft proposal for a new constitution at the September congress, and many of them will probably displease the Soviets. Černík has vigorously called for a "democratization of society" and seems to believe that the Czechoslovak

---

[87] Such pressures could have come, for example, from a stalwart on the Central Committee (someone like Yegorychev, the man who criticized the leadership's actions during the June War), or from a tough old hand in the high command (someone like Moskalenko, who in fact travelled to Prague and tried to intimidate the Czechs). [Footnote in original.]

government will function better if it is insured against "the system of personal power" and is made more responsive, through such means as regular press conferences and opinion polls, to the public at large. Moreover, Černík's economic proposals will probably be aimed at lessening Czechoslovakia's economic dependence on the USSR, and more important, will probably reduce Czechoslovakia's potential military contribution to the Warsaw Pact. He evidently concluded several years ago that Czechoslovakia's disproportionate emphasis on heavy industry, including defense industry, should be corrected. Černík and other economic reformers for some time waged an unsuccessful campaign against Novotný's inflated defense budget; now he will surely be able to set a lower figure. Also, Černík and the other ministers appear to be drafting serious proposals aimed at extensive, if not exhaustive, judicial rehabilitation of victims of the Stalinist period in Czechoslovakia. In any event, the Czechs, not the Soviets, are increasingly likely to make decisions of this nature.

20. At some stage in the game, as projected here, the Soviets will, of course, become aware that their earlier hopes for a return to anything like the *status quo ante* in Czechoslovakia were without foundation. It is the Czech hope that this realization will have come too late and that the Soviets' reactions will be minimal—limited to words alone. In part because of this hope, and in part to insure its own survival, the Czech regime will surely seek to control both the pace and scope of the process of democratization. Sudden alarm in Moscow could thus perhaps be forestalled, disagreements within the Soviet leadership could perhaps be encouraged, and a pretext for Soviet intervention—one good enough to overcome doubts and fears within the Kremlin, within the other socialist countries, and within other communist parties—could perhaps be avoided. Ultimately, if Dubček and Černík are thus able to continue to fend off both the Soviets and their potential critics at home, it is apparently their hope that a genuinely reformed and significantly freer Czechoslovakia will be able to achieve real independence within the Bloc and also restore its historic ties with the West.

21. This road, however, will certainly not be an easy one. So very much depends on the uncertain ability of the Dubček regime to hold both itself and the Czech people together. For the moment, the Czech party—having probably rid itself of the threat of a conservative, pro-Novotný revival—seems to be essentially united. But the party nevertheless includes the more or less cautious (and often vague) liberals of Dubček's stripe—who foresee a continued, though newly benevolent communist dominance of all political life—and the extreme liberals—who advocate a return to one form or another of genuine parliamentary democracy. A clash between these groups may eventually be inevitable. Moreover, given the extraordinary openess [sic] of the press and the growing feeling of political involvement among all sorts of non-communist elements, public participation in any such clash is a distinct (and complicating) possibility.

22. Thus there is a good chance that relations between Prague and Moscow will again become very tense. The Soviet leaders, or at least most of them, wish to avoid drastic and costly, military action. Nevertheless, should Dubček's control threaten to collapse, or should the Czech regime's policies become, in Moscow's view, "counterrevolutionary," the Soviets might once again use their troops to menace the Czech frontier.

FOR THE BOARD OF NATIONAL ESTIMATES:

Abbot Smith

Chairman

DOCUMENT No. 43: "On the Dissemination of the CPSU CC's Periodic Report on the Situation in Czechoslovakia and Certain Foreign Policy Steps of the Romanian Leadership": A Memorandum on Efforts to Provide CPSU Members with the Politburo's Latest Analysis of the Crisis, June 1968 (Excerpts)

Source: TsKhSD, F. 5, Op. 60, D. 1, Ll. 92–99.

Nikolai Petrovichev, deputy director of the CPSU CC Department for Party-Organizational Work, prepared this June 24, 1968 top-secret memorandum on dissemination of the latest Politburo report, "On the Situation in Czechoslovakia and on Certain Foreign Policy Steps of the Romanian Leadership." After the Politburo issued its report on June 18, the text was promptly distributed to lower-level CPSU organizations. Within three to four days, all senior party members had been apprised of the contents. Leaders of the different party organizations sent cables back to Moscow confirming that they had fulfilled the Politburo's instructions. Petrovichev, in turn, drew on these incoming cables when he wrote his memorandum informing the Politburo that the "party aktiv unanimously approves of the work carried out by the CPSU Central Committee in providing support to the healthy forces in the CPCz, which facilitates their effort to rebuff the anti-socialist elements. This process has been completed successfully."

Petrovichev's memorandum illuminates an obscure aspect of Soviet policy-making in 1968—the implementation of key decisions. The document reveals that Soviet leaders relied on elaborate monitoring and feedback mechanisms to ensure that their report would be handled exactly the way they wanted. All the secretaries of the republic, regional, oblast, and local party committees were obliged to report back to Moscow on the dissemination of the Politburo's analysis and the reaction they encountered. The report also demonstrates how officials in the CPSU CC Department for Party-Organizational Work monitored the performance of outlying party organizations and relayed this information to all the CPSU CC secretaries, including Leonid Brezhnev.

17254
TOP SECRET

CC CPSU

On the Dissemination of the CPSU CC's Periodic Report on the Situation in Czechoslovakia and Certain Foreign Policy Steps of the Romanian Leadership

The CPSU CC's report on the situation in Czechoslovakia and on certain foreign policy steps of the Romanian leadership was received in localities on 19–20 June of this year.[88] Within 3 to 4 days, all members of the CCs of the communist parties of the union republics, the regional party committees, the oblast party committees, the municipal party committees, and the district

---

[88] Beginning in mid-March, the Politburo transmitted periodic analyses of the crisis to lower-level party organizations. The issuance of these reports proved extremely useful for Brezhnev and his colleagues because it forced them to arrive at a broad consensus at various stages of the crisis, despite their continued disagreements. The reports also provided a convenient way for CPSU leaders to explain Soviet policy to other officials in the party hierarchy, especially those well outside Moscow. By setting forth the "official view" of events in Czechoslovakia at regular intervals, the Politburo took advantage of the CPSU's long-established practice of "democratic centralism," which strictly prohibited any dissent from policies made at higher levels. Soviet leaders thereby obtained ample leeway to define the party's stance during the 1968 crisis without unwanted interference from below.

party committees became acquainted with it. This report, as before, was greeted with keen interest and stimulated a lively reaction among the party *aktiv*.[89] It was noted that the report comprehensively discusses both the recent changes in Czechoslovakia and the position of the Romanian leadership, and provides a correct understanding of their political essence.

The party *aktiv* unanimously approves of the work carried out by the CPSU Central Committee in providing support to the healthy forces in the CPCz, which facilitates their effort to rebuff the anti-socialist elements. The letter from the participants in the nationwide party *aktiv* of the People's Militia, which was published on 21 June in our press, has been positively received.[90] Party members are encouraged by the resolve of the members of the Czechoslovak People's Militia, which, as the armed vanguard of the working class in Czechoslovakia, consistently protects the gains of socialism in the country and friendship with the Soviet Union.

Satisfaction was expressed with the measures undertaken by the CPSU CC Politburo to lend assistance to the CPCz in normalizing the situation in the country. In particular, the trip to Czechoslovakia by Cde. A. N. Kosygin was well received, as were the results of the recent negotiations between the government delegations from the USSR and ČSSR on matters pertaining to the further development of economic relations and cultural ties between the two countries. The positive significance of the Czechoslovak Cultural Festival, which was featured at the end of May and beginning of June in a number of oblasts and cities of the Russian Federation, was noted.[91] This was a clear demonstration of friendship between our peoples.

Intentions were also expressed to seek a further increase and deepening of contacts with representatives of the public and the workers in Czechoslovakia along all lines. In the Dagestan ASSR and the Stavropol area, a proposal was made to hold a meeting of veterans of the Great Patriotic War—participants in the liberation of the ČSSR with former soldiers of the Czecho-slovak army—which could adopt an appeal to the workers of the republic. In the Primorsk area, and in the Novgorod, Tula, Voronezh, and certain other oblast party organizations, the idea of sending communist activists to the ČSSR under the guise of delegations and tourist groups has been raised. These activists could propagandize the socialist way of life. It was also suggested that exchanges be increased for party delegations from oblasts and districts that support direct friendly ties with Czechoslovakia.

At the same time, the party *aktiv* are seriously worried because the CPCz still has not fully regained control of the situation in the country and because its leadership is wavering and is impermissibly lenient toward the enemies of socialism. "I, as a working man," said a member of the Minsk oblast party committee who is employed as a metal specialist at the Korolev auto factory, "completely fail to understand the position of the CPCz CC Presidium in the struggle against the intrigues of reaction. How can we put up with anti-socialist outbursts? In dealing with such matters one simply can't dilly-dally and give the initiative to the enemies. This could lead to the most unexpected results."

Members of the party committees of Ukraine, Belorussia, Kazakhstan, Turkmenia, and the Tatar ASSR, and the Volgograd, Kuibyshev, Kursk, Moscow, and other oblasts, express bewilderment at the CPCz's failure to take control of the press, radio, and television, which are not now under its influence, and at its willingness to permit the press to be used in stirring up anti-communist and anti-Soviet passions. "We are dismayed to see," said the secretary of the Balashikhinsk municipal CPSU committee in Moscow oblast, Cde. Rusanov, "that even such a newspaper as *Rudé právo*, whose editor at one time was a great friend of the Soviet Union, Julius

---

[89] Petrovichev's memorandum draws on cables sent back by regional and local party organizations. Among countless examples, see the top-secret cables to the CPSU Secretariat in TsKhSD, F. 5, Op. 60, D. 10, Ll. 15–19, 20–21, 22–23, and 24–26.

[90] See Document No. 41.

[91] Cultural exchanges were also being sponsored with Ukraine at this time. The festival in Moscow was opened on May 30 by the ČSSR minister of culture and information, Miroslav Galuška, who had been one of the chief proponents of a free press.

Fučík, a newspaper that during the bourgeois regime and the German fascist terror held fast to Marxist–Leninist positions, is now featuring simply unforgivable epithets directed against our country."

Noting the many instances of unfriendly attacks by the Czechoslovak press against the Soviet Union, party activists point out the necessity of displaying vigilance and of not giving further impetus to anti-Soviet propaganda. Speaking along these lines, the chairman of the State Committee on Radio Broadcasting and Television of the Council of Ministers of the Estonian SSR, Cde. Janimiagi, said: "Recently, Czechoslovak journalists and employees of radio and television have shown heightened interest in the national republics, including ours. Having arrived at the radio committee or at the editorial board of a newspaper, they often give ambiguous and, one might even say, provocative answers. Considering that the Czechoslovak press and other mass media continue to be outside the control of the party, we must be vigilant and not permit aspersions to be cast on Soviet reality."[92]

Party committee members are deeply interested in the position of the working class in Czechoslovakia as the situation unfolds. Typical in this regard is the statement by a worker at the Krasnodar oil equipment repair factory, Cde. Aleksenko, who said: "We are worried by the attempts of reactionaries in Czechoslovakia to sow discord in the working class and to oppose and bring about the ideological destruction of its communist party. It's time to put an end to the incitement of anti-party sentiments among Czechoslovak workers and the efforts of rightist elements who are trying to remove the trade unions from the influence of the CPCz."

Cde. Zuev—a member of the Essentusk CPSU municipal committee and a member of the party since 1918, said: "We old communists can fully understand the CPSU CC's anxiety about the events in Czechoslovakia. The slogans that are now bandied about—'Councils without communists'—and the creation of opposition parties and unions, are very familiar to us from the history of our party, when the slogan 'Councils without communists' were used by the most intractable reactionaries. For that reason, vigilance, vigilance, and still more vigilance must be shown toward these events."

Communist workers were startled and dismayed when they learned that in the ČSSR the right to strike was formally enshrined in law. Thus, a member of the CPSU Volga district committee of the Tatar ASSR who works at the "Radiopribor" factory, Cde. Pulataev, said: "We are very surprised that in a country in which power has been gained by the working class, the right to strike has been introduced. The working class of Czechoslovakia apparently does not understand that the very structure of the socialist order precludes such phenomena." A member of the Timiryazevsk district party committee in Moscow who is employed as a metalworking specialist toolmaker at the processing factory, Cde. Afanasyev, said: "It's upsetting that in Czechoslovakia the right to strike is legally enshrined. Workers don't need such a right, it just plays into the hands of the reactionaries." Very similar things were said in a number of other party organizations.

Exchanging opinions about this report, comrades who had traveled recently to the ČSSR or who had met with representatives of the country, made personal observations and cited facts that confirm the information of the CPSU CC about the situation in Czechoslovakia. To take one example, the deputy minister of trade in the Latvian SSR, Cde. Gorbachev, said: "I've just got back from Czechoslovakia, where I had the opportunity to meet many people. Even in discussions with leading comrades, one could sense the complacency in their evaluation of current events. They express certainty that the CPCz CC is rectifying the situation. However, it's not difficult to see that they are withstanding a force which is working against socialism. From discussions with faithful communists it is clear that no meetings of primary party organizations have been convened since January."

[92] The official in question here is E.-I. A. Janimiagi, who had been head of radio and television in Estonia since May 1962. He warned numerous times during the crisis about the political spill-over in the Baltic states.

After being briefed on the CC's report, the secretary of the party organization at the "Prikordonnik" collective farm in the Khust district of the Transcarpathian oblast, Cde. Kopanskii, offered his impressions of a recent visit to an area in Slovakia. He reported that the agricultural cooperative is interested in the work of the party organization. In his view, the role of party organizations there has greatly fallen, and the party assemblies do not take up vitally important questions. Most of the time, meetings and other activities are organized not by communists, but by different public organizations and clubs.

Speaking about the negative aspects of the events in Czechoslovakia, the comrades cited phenomena showing that the workers of this country are alarmed by the unfolding situation. An interesting example in this regard was cited by the secretary of the Moscow oblast Council of Trade Unions, Cde. Markeshin, who told of meetings and discussions he had had with delegations from the trade unions of the Eastern Czech oblast in the vicinity of Moscow. He declared that "members of a delegation gave completely disparate pictures of events in the country. For example, the chairman of the Council of Trade Unions, Cde. Kopecký, blatantly tried to downplay the significance and consequences of the student demonstration 'Majales' and to gloss over its manifestly anti-Soviet character."[93] He said that this was just the "curiosity" of youth. In contrast to this fuzzy statement, Cde. Stašek, a steelmaker, and Cde. Suchopárek, a railway worker, regarded this demonstration as an anti-socialist, hostile action. If workers had known about it beforehand, he declared, "they would have done whatever was necessary to suppress such hostile actions."

The first secretary of the Komsomol CC in Moldavia, Cde. Luchinskii, cited this point: "When I was recently in the GDR, we met a youth delegation from Czechoslovakia, who spoke with great alarm about the collapse of the Czechoslovak Youth League into a number of splinter groups.[94] The members of the delegation said that they will do everything necessary to ensure that the Youth League of Czechoslovakia retains a Marxist–Leninist position."

. . .

The materials sent out by the CPSU CC—"On the Current Situation" and "International Review"—are of great help to party organizations when carrying out explanatory work among laborers, in accordance with the decisions of the CPSU CC's April plenum.[95] Based on these materials, a broad campaign has been organized in all the republics, areas, and oblasts to read lectures and reports to the population. In Bryansk oblast, for example, more than 2,000 reports have already been presented, with more than 100,000 people having taken part. In Lvov oblast 846 workers' assemblies have been held on the theme of the current situation. Roughly 150,000 people took part, and 2,300 spoke.

Workers, collective farmers, and members of the intelligentsia listen to reports about the ongoing events with great interest and raise many questions. They are gravely alarmed by the

[93] "Majales" was the traditional student festival on May Day. The celebrations tended to be boisterous and irreverent, often to the displeasure of the communist authorities. During the brief and limited "thaw" in Czechoslovakia in 1956, students used the Majales in both Prague and Bratislava to call for major reforms, echoing demands made by Ladislav Mňačko and others at the 2nd Writers' Congress in April. Very soon thereafter the "thaw" came to an end, and Novotný banned the Majales until 1965. The revived celebrations, accompanied by flamboyant and off-color posters, again provoked official anger, especially when the American "beat" poet Allen Ginsberg, who was visiting Czechoslovakia, was elected "King of the Majales" in Prague. (Ginsberg was promptly expelled from the country.) In 1966, the festivities proved even more controversial, and over a dozen students were arrested. For an account of the Majales activities in 1968, see František Janáček and Jan Moravec, "Mezník i rozcestí reformního hnutí," in Václav Kural, ed., Československo roku 1968, Vol. 1: Obrodný proces (Prague: Parta, 1993), pp. 90–92.

[94] For an overview of the disintegration of the official Czechoslovak Youth League (ČSM) and the rise of alternative youth organizations during the Prague Spring, see Galia Golan, Reform Rule in Czechoslovakia: The Dubček Era, 1968–1969 (Cambridge: Cambridge University Press, 1973), pp. 69–78.

[95] See Document No. 19.

complex international situation, and they express firm resolve to exert all their energy to strengthen the might of our homeland and the unity of the world communist movement.

When the party activists were being familiarized with the CPSU CC's report, a number of questions arose. The most typical ones are attached.

24 June 1968

Deputy Head of the CPSU CC Department
for Party-Organizational Work

N. Petrovichev

LIST OF QUESTIONS

Raised by Party Activists During the Dissemination of the
CPSU CC's Standard Information

What were the objective and subjective reasons for the events in Czechoslovakia?

Why did the CPCz leadership not take take decisive measures against the anti-socialist elements?

Why did the CPCz CC not dismiss from their posts the editors of newspapers, radio, and television, and the employees who permitted the publication of anti-party items?

What prevented the CPCz CC from asserting control over the press, radio, and television that had openly taken positions against the measures taken by the CPCz CC?

What is the situation in the army of the ČSSR, and under whose control is it?

Can the command-staff exercises of the Warsaw Pact member states have a positive influence on the internal situation in Czechoslovakia?

How does the public in Czechoslovakia perceive these exercises?

Why don't Bulgaria and Romania take part in the command-staff exercises?

What measures might one expect from the Soviet Union vis-à-vis Czechoslovakia if the situation there becomes more complicated?

Should we provide economic assistance to countries that do not agree with the policy of the CPSU?

How do the leaders in Romania and Yugoslavia evaluate the situation in Czechoslovakia?

What is the internal situation now in Poland and Yugoslavia? Can't the CPSU CC provide more detailed information about this?

Why did the ČSSR government not take measures to close off the borders with the FRG?

Why did the government of Romania reject criticism for having established diplomatic relations with the FRG?

Who initiated the proposal to form a "Little Entente"?

What is the role of the National Front in Czechoslovakia?

Did Cde. Dubček take a correct Marxist–Leninist position on all questions?

Why were plenary sessions of the CPCz CC convened so frequently?

According to information previously supplied by the CPSU CC, Cde. Biľak declared that if an extraordinary CPCz congress is convened, communists from Slovakia would not take part in it. However, the CC plenum of the Slovak Communist Party decided to prepare for an extraordinary congress of its own. What was the reason for this fluctuation?

What is meant by "ceasing membership in the Communist Party of Czechoslovakia"?

What were the results of Cde. A. N. Kosygin's trip to the ČSSR?

DOCUMENT No. 44: The "Two Thousand Words" Manifesto, June 27, 1968

Source: "Dva tisíce slov," *Literární listy* (Prague), 27 June 1968, p. 1.

The "Two Thousand Words" Manifesto came to symbolize the Prague Spring more than any other document. The manifesto's author, writer Ludvík Vaculík, was joined by nearly 70 prominent individuals, including writers, cultural figures, distinguished scientists, and Olympic athletes, as well as a number of ordinary citizens who signed the "Two Thousand Words."

Although the "Two Thousand Words" strongly endorses the reforms that the CPCz had undertaken since January 1968, the signatories express serious misgivings about the durability of the reforms and warn of attempts by "retrograde" elements in the party who wanted to return to the "pre-January situation." The statement calls on ordinary Czechs and Slovaks to undertake direct action at the district and regional levels—through public criticism, demonstrations, strikes, and picketing—to compel anti-reformist officials to step down. Once these officials are out of office, the statement adds, a more vigorous grass-roots effort could be mounted to "improve our domestic situation," to "carry the renewal process forward," and to "take into our own hands our common cause and give it a form more appropriate to our once-good [national] reputation." The document concludes with a reference to "foreign forces" that might be preparing "to intervene in our affairs." The signatories pledge that they and other Czechs and Slovaks will "back our government, with weapons if necessary," against anyone who might interfere.

Three Czechoslovak daily newspapers (Práce, Mladá fronta, and Zemědělské noviny) as well as Literární listy simultaneously published the "Two Thousand Words" Manifesto on June 27; Dubček and his colleagues, who had not known of the document, were caught off-guard. They were especially dismayed by the exhortation to resort to independent initiative and action at the local level, which they regarded as a threat to their own measured approach. Czechoslovak leaders realized they could not allow the publication of the statement to pass without doing something to counter it and to mollify Soviet officials. Using a draft prepared by Čestmír Císař and Zdeněk Mlynář, the CPCz Presidium adopted a resolution condemning the "Two Thousand Words." From Moscow's perspective, however, these criticisms were far too moderate and no substitute for direct retribution against the author and signatories.

The Soviet embassy learned on June 26, from unnamed "friends," that a controversial document was about to be published. Not surprisingly, the "Two Thousand Words" infuriated Soviet leaders, who denounced it as an "anti-socialist call to counterrevolution." When Dubček refrained from taking harsh punitive action, the Soviet Union's impatience with the CPCz leader neared the breaking point. The episode became one of the catalysts for convening the Warsaw Meeting in mid-July, marking the point of no return for Soviet policy on rolling back the Prague Spring.

Two Thousand Words that Belong to Workers, Farmers, Officials, Scientists, Artists, and Everybody

The first threat to our national life was from the war. Then came other evil days and events that endangered the nation's spiritual well-being and character. Most of the nation welcomed the socialist program with high hopes. But it fell into the hands of the wrong people. It would not have mattered so much that they lacked adequate experience in affairs of state, factual knowledge, or philosophical education, if only they had had enough common prudence and decency to listen to the opinion of others and agree to being gradually replaced by more able people.

After enjoying great popular confidence immediately after the war, the communist party by degrees bartered this confidence away for office, until it had all the offices and nothing else. We feel we must say this, it is familiar to those of us who are communists and who are as disappointed as the rest at the way things turned out. The leaders' mistaken policies transformed a political party and an alliance based on ideas into an organization for exerting power, one that proved highly attractive to power-hungry individuals eager to wield authority, to cowards who took the safe and easy route, and to people with bad conscience. The influx of members such as these affected the character and behavior of the party, whose internal arrangements made it impossible, short of scandalous incidents, for honest members to gain influence and adapt it continuously to modern conditions. Many communists fought against this decline, but they did not manage to prevent what ensued.

Conditions inside the communist party served as both a pattern for and a cause of the identical conditions in the state. The party's association with the state deprived it of the asset of separation from executive power. No one criticized the activities of the state and of economic organs. Parliament forgot how to hold proper debates, the government forgot how to govern properly, and managers forgot how to manage properly. Elections lost their significance, and the law carried no weight. We could not trust our representatives on any committee or, if we could, there was no point in asking them for anything because they were powerless. Worse still, we could scarcely trust one another. Personal and collective honor decayed. Honesty was a useless virtue, assessment by merit unheard of. Most people accordingly lost interest in public affairs, worrying only about themselves and about money, a further blot on the system being the impossibility today of relying even on the value of money. Personal relations were ruined, there was no more joy in work, and the nation, in short, entered a period that endangered its spiritual well-being and its character.

* * *

We all bear responsibility for the present state of affairs. But those among us who are communists bear more than others, and those who acted as components or instruments of unchecked power bear the greatest responsibility of all. The power they wielded was that of a self-willed group spreading out through the party apparatus into every district and community. It was this apparatus that decided what might and might not be done: It ran the cooperative farms for the cooperative farmers, the factories for the workers, and the National Committees for the public. No organizations, not even communist ones, were really controlled by their own members. The chief sin and deception of these rulers was to have explained their own whims as the "will of the workers". Were we to accept this pretense, we would have to blame the workers today for the decline of our economy, for crimes committed against the innocent, and for the introduction of censorship to prevent anyone writing about these things. The workers would be to blame for misconceived investments, for losses suffered in foreign trade, and for the housing shortage. Obviously no sensible person will hold the working class responsible for such things. We all know, and every worker knows especially, that they had virtually no say in deciding anything. Working-class functionaries were given their voting instructions by somebody else. While many workers imagined that they were the rulers, it was a specially trained stratum of party and state officials who actually ruled in their name. In effect it was these people who stepped into the shoes of the deposed ruling class and themselves came to constitute the new authority. Let us say in fairness that some of them long ago realized the evil trick history had played. We can recognize such individuals today by the way they are redressing old wrongs, rectifying mistakes, handing back powers of decision-making to rank-and-file party members and members of the public, and establishing limits on the authority and size of the bureaucracy. They share our opposition to the retrograde views held by certain party members. But a large proportion of officials have been resistant to change and are still influential. They still wield the instruments of power, especially at district and community level, where they can employ them in secret and without fear of prosecution.

* * *

Since the beginning of this year we have been experiencing a regenerative process of democratization. It started inside the communist party, that much we must admit, even those communists among us who no longer had hopes that anything good could emerge from that quarter know this. It must also be added, of course, that the process could have started nowhere else. For after twenty years the communists were the only ones able to conduct some sort of political activity. It was only the opposition inside the communist party that had the privilege to voice antagonistic views. The effort and initiative now displayed by democratically-minded communists are only then a partial repayment of the debt owed by the entire party to the non-communists whom it had kept down in an inequal position. Accordingly, thanks are due to the communist party, though perhaps it should be granted that the party is making an honest effort at the eleventh hour to save its own honor and the nation's. The regenerative process has introduced nothing particularly new into our lives. It revives ideas and topics, many of which are older than the errors of our socialism, while others, having emerged from below the surface of visible history, should long ago have found expression but were instead repressed. Let us not foster the illusion that it is the power of truth which now makes such ideas victorious. Their victory has been due rather to the weakness of the old leaders, evidently already debilitated by twenty years of unchallenged rule. All the defects hidden in the foundations and ideology of the system have clearly reached their peak. So let us not overestimate the effects of the writers' and students' criticisms. The source of social change is the economy. A true word makes its mark only when it is spoken under conditions that have been properly prepared—conditions that, in our context, unfortunately include the impoverishment of our whole society and the complete collapse of the old system of government, which had enabled certain types of politicians to get rich, calmly and quietly, at our expense. Truth, then, is not prevailing. Truth is merely what remains when everything else has been frittered away. So there is no reason for national jubilation, simply for fresh hope.

In this moment of hope, albeit hope still threatened, we appeal to you. It took several months before many of us believed it was safe to speak up; many of us still do not think it is safe. But speak up we did exposing ourselves to the extent that we have no choice but to complete our plan to humanize the regime. If we did not, the old forces would exact cruel revenge. We appeal above all to those who so far have waited on the sidelines. The time now approaching will decide events for years to come.

The summer holidays are approaching, a time when we are inclined to let everything slip. But we can safely say that our dear adversaries will not give themselves a summer break; they will rally everyone who is under any obligation to them and are taking steps, even now, to secure themselves a quiet Christmas! Let us watch carefully how things develop, let us try to understand them and have our answers ready. Let us forget the impossible demand that someone from on high should always provide us with a single explanation and a single, simple moral imperative. Everyone will have to draw their own conclusions. Common, agreed conclusions can only be reached in discussion that requires freedom of speech—the only democratic achievement to our credit this year.

* * *

But in the days to come we must gird ourselves with our own initiative and make our own decisions.

To begin with we will oppose the view, sometimes voiced, that a democratic revival can be achieved without the communists, or even in opposition to them. This would be unjust, and foolish too. The communists already have their organizations in place, and in these we must support the progressive wing. They have their experienced officials, and they still have in their hands, after all, the crucial levers and buttons. On the other hand they have presented an Action Program to the public. This program will begin to even out the most glaring inequalities, and no one else has a program in such specific detail. We must demand that they produce local Action Programs in public in every district and community. Then the issue will suddenly revolve around very ordinary and long-awaited acts of justice. The Czechoslovak Communist Party is preparing for its congress, where it will elect its new Central Committee. Let us demand that it be a better committee than the present one. Today the communist party says it is going to rest its position of leadership on the confidence of the public, and not on force. Let us believe them, but only as long as we can believe in the people they are now sending as delegates to the party's district and regional conferences.

People have recently been worried that the democratization process has come to a halt. This feeling is partly a sign of fatigue after the excitement of events, but partly it reflects the truth. The season of astonishing revelations, of dismissals from high office, and of heady speeches couched in language of unaccustomed daring—all this is over. But the struggle between opposing forces has merely become somewhat less open, the fight continues over the content and formulation of the laws and over the scope of practical measures. Besides, we must give the new people time to work: the new ministers, prosecutors, chairmen and secretaries. They are entitled to time in which to prove themselves fit or unfit. This is all that can be expected at present of the central political bodies, though they have made a remarkably good showing so far in spite of themselves.

* * *

The everyday quality of our future democracy depends on what happens *in* the factories, and on what happens *to* the factories. Despite all our discussions, it is the economic managers who have us in their grasp. Good managers must be sought out and promoted. True, we are all badly paid in comparison with people in the developed countries, some of us worse than others. We can ask for more money, and more money can indeed be printed, but only if it is devalued in the process. Let us rather ask the directors and the chairmen of boards to tell us what they want to produce and at what cost, the customers they want to sell it to and at what price, the profit that will be made, and of that, how much will be reinvested in modernizing production and how much will be left over for distribution. Under dreary looking headlines, a hard battle is being covered in the press—the battle of democracy versus soft jobs. The workers, as entrepreneurs, can intervene in this battle by electing the right people to management and workers' councils. And as employees they can help themselves best by electing, as their trade union representatives, natural leaders and able, honorable individuals without regard to party affiliation.

* * *

Although at present one cannot expect more of the central political bodies, it is vital to achieve more at district and community level. Let us demand the departure of people who abused their power, damaged public property, and acted dishonorably or brutally. Ways must be found to compel them to resign. To mention a few: public criticism, resolutions, demonstrations, demonstrative work brigades, collections to buy presents for them on their retirement, strikes, and picketing at their front doors. But we should reject any illegal, indecent, or boorish methods, which they would exploit to bring influence to bear on Alexander Dubček. Our aversion to the writing of rude letters must be expressed so completely that the only explanation for any such missives in the future would be that their recipients had ordered them themselves. Let us revive the activity of the National Front. Let us demand public sessions of the national committees. For questions that no one else will look into, let us set up our own civic committees and commissions. There is nothing difficult about it; a few people gather together, elect a chairman, keep proper records, publish their findings, demand solutions, and refuse to be shouted down. Let us convert the district and local newspapers, which have mostly degenerated to the level of official mouthpieces, into a platform for all the forward-looking elements in politics; let us demand that editorial boards be formed of National Front representatives, or else let us start new papers. Let us form committees for the defense of free speech. At our meetings, let us have our own staffs for ensuring order. If we hear strange reports, let us seek confirmation, let us send delegations to the proper authorities and publicize their answers, perhaps putting them up on front gates. Let us give support to the police when they are prosecuting genuine wrongdoers, for it is not our aim to create anarchy or a state of general uncertainty. Let us eschew quarrels between neighbors, and let us avoid drunkenness on political occasions. Let us expose informers.

The summer traffic throughout the republic will enhance interest in the settlement of constitutional relations between Czechs and Slovaks. Let us consider federalization as a method of solving the question of nationalities, but let us regard it as only one of several important measures designed to democratize the system. In itself this particular measure will not necessarily give even the Slovaks a better life. The problem of government is not solved merely by having separate governments in the Czech Lands and in Slovakia. Rule by a state and party bureaucracy could still go on; indeed, in Slovakia it might even be strengthened by the claim that it had "won more freedom."

There has been great alarm recently over the possibility that foreign forces will intervene in our development. Whatever superior forces may face us, all we can do is stick to our own positions, behave decently, and initiate nothing ourselves. We can show our government that we will stand by it, with weapons if need be, if it will do what we give it a mandate to do. And we can assure our allies that we will observe our treaties of alliance, friendship, and trade. Irritable reproaches and ill-argued suspicions on our part can only make things harder for our government, and bring no benefit to ourselves. In any case, the only way we can achieve equality is to improve our domestic situation and carry the process of renewal far enough to some day elect statesmen with sufficient courage, honor, and political acumen to create such equality and keep it that way. But this is a problem that faces all governments of small countries everywhere.

* * *

This spring a great opportunity was given to us once again, as it was after the end of the war. Again we have the chance to take into our own hands our common cause, which for working purposes we call socialism, and give it a form more appropriate to our once-good reputation and to the fairly good opinion we used to have of ourselves. The spring is over and will never return. By winter we will know all.

So ends our statement addressed to workers, farmers, officials, artists, scholars, scientists, technicians, and everybody. It was written at the behest of scholars and scientists.

PART FOUR

THE JULY CRISIS

INTRODUCTION

The proceedings of the CPCz district conferences at the end of June caused great concern in Moscow, Berlin, Warsaw, Sofia and Budapest. The outcome of the conferences clearly indicated that the pro-Brezhnev conservatives would lose their posts at the forthcoming Extraordinary 14th CPCz Congress. In this context, the "Two Thousand Words" Manifesto became a welcome pretext for a new round of massive Soviet military, political and ideological pressures on the Czechoslovak reform movement and its leadership. For the Soviets, after all, the manifesto represented a platform for counterrevolution.

At that time, as part of Hungarian–Soviet friendship celebrations from June 27 to July 4, confidential talks were going on in Moscow between a Hungarian delegation led by János Kádár, and representatives of the CPSU Politburo led by Leonid Brezhnev and Aleksei Kosygin. Despite certain differing assessments of the Czechoslovak situation—the Hungarians judged the matter more moderately—their points of view grew closer together. Kádár, it is clear, endorsed a proposal to call another meeting of representatives of the five socialist countries (the "Five"), whether or not the Czechoslovak leadership was to be included. From the minutes of a meeting of the HSWP Politburo on July 7, 1968, it is evident that the situation in Czechoslovakia was to be discussed there.

Kádár also agreed with a critical letter from the CPSU Politburo to Prague (Document No. 48). Dated July 4, the letter began on a stark note, declaring that "[c]onditions in the ČSSR are becoming even more dangerous than before." After describing a litany of ominous developments inside the country, the authors arrive at "the crucial question . . . Will there or will there not be a socialist Czechoslovakia?"

Immediately afterwards, the CPCz Presidium received four letters from the leaders of the other members of the Five. While differing in the degree of criticism they leveled at the Czechoslovak situation, all were essentially based on the Soviet assessment. The note included a proposal for a meeting along the lines Brezhnev had expressed over the telephone to Dubček on July 5. The coordination of the letters by the Kremlin was obvious.

Meanwhile, the Czechoslovak leadership had to deal with serious complications which arose after the Šumava command-staff exercises. It turned out that Marshal Ivan Yakubovskii, commander of the Warsaw Pact Armed Forces, tried to prolong the exercise beyond the originally agreed-upon date (June 30), as well as delay the departure of Soviet troops from Czechoslovakia. It was only when Dubček and Oldřich Černík intervened personally that the exercises were reviewed (Document No. 45). The failure to provide for a joint assessment of the maneuvers was only one of the "irregularities" the Czechoslovak leaders discovered during a briefing they received from Yakubovskii on July 1. Dubček and Černík complained that "the continuation of the exercises is causing anxiety among our public and among the staffs and troops of the CzPA." Yet despite their demands to bring the maneuvers to an end, Yakubovskii never responded, and, notwithstanding various promises he and his staff had previously given, the withdrawal of troops dragged on until August 3. This naturally increased tensions in the country, a fact reflected in the critical reaction voiced by the Czechoslovak media.

The Political Pressure Campaign

The maneuvers and protracted troop withdrawal were clearly part of Moscow's campaign of political pressure aimed at supporting the "healthy, pro-Brezhnev forces" in Czechoslovakia; Šumava itself, in fact, represented a sort of dress rehearsal for military intervention. The Hungarian generals who participated in the maneuvers, István Oláh and Ferenc Szűcs, submitted a report to the Hungarian Party Presidium on July 5, which offers sufficient proof of this (Document No. 47). "With regard to domestic policy," they wrote, "the exercises were intended to influence the Czechoslovak events in the sense that a show of the strength and determination of the Warsaw Pact states would paralyze and frighten enemies at home; the exercises would also intimidate wavering elements (especially intellectuals) and bolster and safeguard true communists dedicated to the revolution and to socialism."

Noting further that the "Soviet comrades . . . proceeded from the conviction that there is a counterrevolutionary situation in Czechoslovakia or, to be more accurate, a situation on the verge of counterrevolution," the Hungarian generals added their assessment that the "Czechoslovak events were in general terms compared [by certain Soviets taking part in the exercises] to the Hungarian counterrevolution."

The letters from the Warsaw Five and their proposal for a joint meeting in Warsaw were on the agenda of two sessions of the CPCz Presidium, on July 8 and 12. It was clear that the Five had planned the meeting in advance; although its purpose was to deal with the situation in Czechoslovakia, its organizers did not see fit to consult with the Czechoslovak leaders themselves. Moreover, the content of the individual letters greatly distorted the situation inside Czechoslovakia, a function either of the ignorance or ill will of the authors. For these reasons, the CPCz Presidium declined to go to Warsaw as a defendant and refused to participate at all in the joint meeting. In their formal response to Moscow, they proposed instead to hold "bilateral negotiations . . . with representatives of the fraternal parties," including those of Romania and Yugoslavia, as soon as possible (Document No. 50). "In taking this position, the Presidium is upholding the generally recognized principles of socialist construction . . . while also respecting the specific features and sovereignty of every party on questions of its internal policy."

Brezhnev did not accept this proposal. Instead, the Warsaw Five sent another joint letter to Prague in which they reiterated the invitation, but the Presidium upheld its position. It is more than likely that Brezhnev et al. were actually somewhat relieved at this because it meant that they would be able to talk more freely without the Czechoslovak contingent in the room. On July 13, Dubček and Černík made one more attempt at least to try to influence the situation at a hastily convened meeting in Komárno with Kádár, Fock and Erdélyi. But during their flight, they learned from a ČTK report that the Soviet leadership was already arriving in Warsaw.

In a final attempt to sway the deliberations of the Five, Dubček and Černík wrote a letter to Brezhnev summing up their position and the current state of negotiations (Document No. 51). Remarking that the "assessments of the situation in the ČSSR by the Communist Party of Czechoslovakia, on the one hand, and the individual fraternal parties, on the other, are so divergent," they reiterated their view that "it would be useful to hold bilateral negotiations in the ČSSR prior to the joint conference." They also complained that they had not been informed in advance that a meeting was to be held to discuss the situation in their own country, saying, "We cannot understand why the view of our party is not being heard and why the party is facing a *fait accompli* brought about by a decision of several other parties." The Czechoslovak ambassador to Warsaw was asked to deliver the letter before the actual opening of the Warsaw meeting on July 14, but it did not reach Brezhnev until after the session had already concluded.

While a modern Constance[1] was taking place in Warsaw, in Czechoslovakia evidence of broad-based popular agreement with the party program was evident in the results of recent

---

[1] A council where the Czech medieval reformer, Jan Hus, was condemned as a heretic and burned at the stake in 1415.

regional and municipal CPCz conferences. As support for the reform leadership grew, the conservatives suffered a concomitant loss of standing in the eyes of the nation. At the same time, critical voices were being raised and resolutions passed around the country demanding the speedy departure of the Soviet troops. Dubček appealed to the mass media not to publish these resolutions in hopes of preventing a kindling of anti-Soviet feelings and the creation of more "causes" for criticism by the Five. Meanwhile, the countries of the Five unleashed a massive anti-reform campaign that was also intentionally provocative. Several caches of weapons in the Sokolov area, the location of which an anonymous German caller "disclosed" to Czechoslovak authorities even before they had been planted, was expanded in reports by the media of the Five into several caches, which they claimed were intended for use by Czechoslovak counterrevolutionaries. All of this happened before Czechoslovak authorities had even issued an official report about their discovery.

Meanwhile, the pressure campaign mounted steadily. *Moscow Pravda*, *Literaturnaya Gazeta*, and *Neues Deutschland* continued to attack the "Two Thousand Words" Manifesto as a counterrevolutionary platform. At the same time, military activities increased. On July 11, huge Soviet, Polish and GDR naval maneuvers under the name "Sever" (North) began, lasting until July 19. Moreover, Soviet Defense Minister Andrei Grechko was busy preparing another "exercise", in northern Hungary, for which he requested three divisions from the Hungarian minister of national defense. In response to these developments, signs of serious concern began to appear outside Czechoslovakia as well. In Italy, France, Yugoslavia, Romania, and several other European countries (and among their workers' and communist parties), the reform process raised considerable expectations.

The Warsaw Meeting and Letter

This was the atmosphere (described here in rough outline), in which the Warsaw meeting took place on July 14 and 15. It was hosted by Władysław Gomułka, but carefully stage-managed by Brezhnev (Document No. 52). In a lengthy speech, the Soviet leader reiterated his position about the "deteriorating situation" inside Czechoslovakia. He also pointed to the existence of an "attempt being made by the anti-socialist and counterrevolutionary forces to bring about the downfall of the Communist Party of Czechoslovakia." In laying out a number of actions that could be taken to prevent this outcome, he mentioned that "if the need should arise," the "fraternal parties" would have to "respond to the first call for help by the Czechoslovak comrades." Moreover, "[t]hey also must respond if . . . the Czechoslovak comrades for one reason or another find it difficult to appeal for help."

In spite of differences in the appraisals of the situation, the participants ultimately agreed on a common stance, formulated in what became known as the Warsaw Letter, which they addressed to the Central Committee of the CPCz (Document No. 53). The letter contained a rather obvious threat to use force if Prague should prove unwilling to respect the position of the Five: "we maintain that firm resistance to anti-communist forces and a decisive battle for the preservation of the socialist system in Czechoslovakia are not only your duty but ours as well." Intervention as such had not yet been fully decided upon, although military plans were being prepared in the meantime. The letter, along with the whole campaign of the Five, aroused further discontent, concern and fear, not only in Czechoslovakia, but in democratic countries abroad as well.

General Prchlík's Press Conference

Another event contributed to the escalation of the crisis: on July 15, at the initiative of the Union of Czechoslovak Journalists, General Václav Prchlík, the head of the CPCz CC State Administrative Department, held a press conference (Document No. 54). In his comments,

185

Prchlík spoke highly critically of a number of current aspects of military and security policy: the need to draw up a new Czechoslovak military doctrine; the position of Czechoslovakia and its army in the Warsaw Pact and in the Joint Command; the role of the Political-Consultative Committee; and, naturally, the protracted departure of the Soviet troops. As if predicting the contents of the letter of the Five, he was also critical of the unequal standing of the members of the Warsaw coalition, which failed to provide guarantees against factionalism within the coalition, and against violations of fundamental clauses of the treaty. More than anything else, these violations concerned matters of state sovereignty and the principle of non-interference in the internal affairs of the signatory states.

The response to Prchlík's conference in the Czechoslovak media triggered a sharp reaction on the Soviet side, from political and military leaders alike (Documents Nos. 57 & 60). Agreeing with the conclusions of Marshal Yakubovskii, a Soviet government diplomatic note chastised Prchlík on the grounds that he "deliberately distorted the real situation [regarding the Warsaw Pact] and went on to attack Soviet military commanders." The note called on Czechoslovak authorities to "exact the requisite measures against people who divulge secret information, with a view to the common interests of the security of the socialist countries."

Among the most ardent defenders of the Czechoslovak leadership were the heads of the communist parties of France, Italy and Spain. Delegations of the Italian and French communist parties held talks in Moscow during this period with this goal in mind (see, for example, Document No. 58). The Italian party passed a resolution supporting developments in Czechoslovakia. The leadership of the French Communist Party, after Waldeck Rochet's meetings in the Kremlin, and after consulting with his Italian counterparts, even proposed a meeting of communist and workers' parties to discuss the situation. The majority of these parties in Western Europe had turned down an appeal by the Kremlin to endorse the approach of the Warsaw Five and its letter. "To our immense regret," wrote the French party in a letter to Brezhnev, "it is impossible for us to comply with this request" (Document No. 59).

Responding to the Warsaw Letter

The Letter of the Five was conveyed to the CPCz Presidium on July 16. The Presidium decided to draw up a reply for discussion the following day, and to submit this "Statement" to the CPCz Central Committee for consideration on July 19. On July 18, in a special edition, *Rudé právo* carried the text of both the letter and the statement (Document No. 55). In a detailed way, the Statement alternately defended the actions of the Czechoslovak leadership and took exception to some of the arguments made by the Five. For example, the Presidium members were "astonished" by the allegation that West German policies and "revanchists" were "finding a sympathetic ear in leading circles of our country." The publication of both documents generated a tremendous wave of condemnation of the Warsaw meeting and backing for the statement. Public confidence in the reform leadership and its program was reaching a peak, as demonstrated by the thousands of resolutions and cables that appeared across the country in response. Even Vasil Biľak arrived in Prague at the head of a delegation from the Slovak Communist Party condemning the letter (although at a meeting of the Central Committee of the Slovak CP on August 18, he would later attempt to justify it).

On July 19, the day of the Central Committee meeting, to which a number of delegates to the forthcoming Extraordinary 14th CPCz Congress had been invited, the press again published the letter and the statement. Also appearing in print were a declaration of approval by the National Assembly Presidium, and statements by the ČSSR government, by the Presidium of the National Front Central Committee, and by the trade unions and youth organizations. That same day, French Communist Party leader Rochet arrived in the ČSSR for talks with Dubček, Černík, Císař and Hájek (Document No. 58). While sympathetic to their circumstances, Rochet warned of the "genuine danger" the French party saw in the event of a "split between you and the comrades in the socialist countries, above all with the Soviet Union."

The huge popular support that had arisen for the Dubček reform leadership in its quarrel with the Warsaw Five was clearly a surprise for Moscow and the other members of the Five. From that moment on, they no longer focused on winning over the entire leadership of the CPCz but on supporting and cooperating with its "healthy core." A series of events point to the increased urgency of the moment. On July 17, Brezhnev reported to the CPSU Central Committee about the negotiations in Warsaw, noting his uncertainty about how the CPCz would respond, and reasserting Moscow's "duty" to avert any attempts at counterrevolution. On July 18, Marshal Yakubovskii wrote to Dubček accusing General Prchlík of disclosing secrets about the Warsaw Pact, and categorically demanding that Dubček "take measures" as necessary (Document No. 57). Without waiting for a reply, Yakubovskii left for Moscow on July 19.

The same day, Marshal Grechko was suddenly recalled from an official state visit in Algeria. On July 20, the government in Prague received a note from the Soviet government (Document No. 60) again expressing concern over protection of the western frontiers and the discovery of arms caches in the Sokolov area, together with a sharp rebuke of General Prchlík's remarks. And most ominously, probably also on July 20, the Warsaw Five decided to place its armies on "combat alert." To put it more accurately, they began immediate preparations for "Operation Danube" *(Dunaj)*, the code name for the military intervention.

Military Preparations

At this stage, the Warsaw Pact's war machine went into top gear, and of all the participating members, Bulgaria and the GDR were the most zealous. On July 21, one Bulgarian battalion, to be followed by another, was dispatched to Ivanovo-Frankovsk. East German party leader Walter Ulbricht also acted swiftly: as Chairman of the GDR Defense Council, he issued orders on July 21 that the staff and first division of the Leipzig military region be put on combat alert. A few hours later, Warsaw Pact officials decided to raise the level of participation in Operation Danube to two divisions: the 7th Armored Car and the 11th Motorized. At the same time, they decided to include the full Second Polish Army of four divisions. On July 23–24, they included one reinforced Hungarian division. As the Hungarian chief of staff noted at the time, "The political objective of the maneuvers is to help the Czechoslovak people defeat the counterrevolution. We will explain this to the workers, peasants, and intellectuals and make it clear that afterwards we will withdraw. We will leave army units alone provided that they act loyally, but if they put up resistance they will have to be crushed" (Document No. 62).

Formations of the Soviet army, stationed in the GDR, Poland and Hungary, as well as in the Transcarpathian military region, would naturally be the decisive force in the operation being prepared. Marshal Yakubovskii's intervention staff made its headquarters in Legnica, Poland, where liaison officers from the GDR and Poland gradually assembled. The southern group of Soviet forces in Hungary had its staff in Mátyásföld where Hungarian liaison officers were heading. Detailed formations were supposed to be prepared to open Operation Danube on July 29.

Hand-in-hand with these preparations, further movements of huge armies started around Czechoslovakia. On July 23, vast rear exercises dubbed "Nemen" began in western Ukraine heading toward Poland's border with Czechoslovakia, and two days later, on July 25, "Nebesnyi Shchit" (Heavenly Shield) initiated air defense training in the Baltic–Moscow–Black Sea triangle. As expected, the ideological and political anti-reform drive continued unabated. For example, an article appeared in *Krasnaya zvezda* on July 23 under the title "Who does General Prchlík serve?"

While military units were swarming around Czechoslovakia and preparations for the operation continued at full speed, negotiations and bilateral meetings continued. The Dubček leadership, anxious to prevent a split, and following the spirit of the CPCz Central Committee decision of July 19, agreed to a Czechoslovak–Soviet meeting. However, they imposed two conditions: that the troops on maneuvers finally leave Czechoslovakia, and that the meeting be held solely on Czechoslovak soil. The venue chosen was the well-known railway trans-shipment station on the Soviet–Slovak border Čierna nad Tisou. At their July 22 session, the CPCz Presidium concluded that a meeting of communist and workers' parties, proposed by the leadership of the French Communist Party, was neither expedient nor relevant at that time.

Čierna nad Tisou

The CPCz Presidium spent the following days in intensive preparation for the Čierna meeting. Among other things, they agreed that all Czechoslovak participants at Čierna would take as their point of departure the July 19 Statement and a willingness to resolve the ongoing disputes. A report by Oldřich Černík, "On the Current Security Situation," which he presented to the CPCz Presidium on July 27, was part of these preparations (Document No. 64). The report made it amply clear that not only the United States but the West fully respected the current spheres of influence and Moscow's right to make decisions within its superpower domain; and that in the conflict between Czechoslovakia and the Warsaw Five, they were not prepared to lift so much as a finger on behalf of Czechoslovakia. "This restraint," Černík noted, "is motivated primarily by the need to maintain the current level of relations with the USSR." Consequently, regardless of the great sympathy and moral support Czechoslovaks enjoyed, the CPCz leadership could not rely on any effective help from the outside. Not only that, Czechoslovak radicals during this period were more than once the object of Western criticism because, according to critics, they unnecessarily irritated Moscow. Dozens of dispatches by Czechoslovak diplomats from all over the world fully bear this out.

The report of the planned meeting at Čierna nad Tisou was greeted positively at home and abroad and led, more than anything else, to a sense of relief that the imminent crisis had passed, and that fears of intervention had been exaggerated. But this relief was accompanied by popular concern inside Czechoslovakia over whether and how the country's representatives would be able to defend their interests in these negotiations. That prompted a new wave of support for—but also pressure on—the reform leadership. The most striking manifestation of this was a citizens' appeal addressed to the participants at Čierna, which adopted the slogan "Socialism, Alliance, Sovereignty, Freedom" (Document No. 63). "You are writing a critical page of Czechoslovakia's history on our behalf," the appeal read. "Write it with sound judgment, but above all with courage. To lose this unique chance would be our ruin and your dishonor. We trust you!" Within a matter of a few days after its publication on July 26 in a special issue of *Literární listy* (and on the following day by several other papers), about one million people had signed the document.

On July 29, the day the two delegations arrived at Čierna, some 20 divisions, armed to the teeth, were at the ready around Czechoslovakia and prepared to offer "internationalist assistance" in Operation Danube. Reports of the movement of these troops in the vicinity of the Czechoslovak borders came in a number of dispatches from Czechoslovak envoys in neighboring countries (Document No. 66). Reporting from East Berlin, for example, Ambassador Václav Kolář wrote: "At 10:00 A.M. an unknown major of the [East] German army reported the concentration of troops toward our borders. He expressed his sympathy with the ČSSR and immediately left." Yet, despite the exertion of such high pressure tactics, Ulbricht, Gomułka and Bulgarian leader Todor Zhivkov were not in the least enthusiastic about Brezhnev's consent to the meeting and objected to the decision. Gomułka regarded negotiations on Czechoslovak territory as an unacceptable concession to the Dubček leadership. And Ulbricht sent a dispatch to Brezhnev urging that "[i]t is necessary to consider when it would be politically more auspicious to announce the beginning of maneuvers by the armies of several Warsaw Pact member states" (Document No. 68).

A Deaf Monologue

On July 29, the trains bearing the two delegations arrived at the Čierna nad Tisou trans-shipment station. They met in the Railwaymens' House. On one side of the table sat virtually the entire Soviet Politburo (Kirilenko and Polyansky stayed in Moscow to manage affairs at home); on the other the CPCz Presidium, plus President Ludvík Svoboda. At the end of the first day of talks, a monologue of the deaf, it was evident that the monolithic Soviet delegation had not come to Čierna to listen to arguments by the Czechoslovak side, nor to discuss different approaches to building socialism since they regarded their own as the only possible and correct one. Brezhnev delivered a speech (Document No. 65), in which he repeated all of the accusations leveled against the reform process and its leadership at the meetings in Dresden and in May in Moscow, as well as in the Warsaw Letter and Brezhnev's speech in Warsaw. "Comrades," he intoned as he drew to a close, "If we objectively evaluate the essence of the political processes now under way in Czechoslovakia and the direction of their further development, we can arrive at only one conclusion, namely, that the threat of a counterrevolutionary coup in your country has become a reality. This is the main reason for the anxiety felt by the CPSU and the other fraternal parties."

The next to speak were Dubček and Černík, who forcefully defended the essentially positive developments of the reform process, and refuted each unfounded accusation, while also admitting the various negative consequences that accompanied the reform (Document No. 65). But the speech by Kosygin which followed made it more than clear that the Soviet side recognized only one truth—its own: "Your speech today did not convince us to any degree and provided no basis for saying that what is going on inside Czechoslovakia is the development of democratic roots within the framework of socialism, rather than counterrevolutionary activity. You did not convince us and I think that if you faced up to things honestly, you yourselves would not be so firmly convinced either."

The Soviet premier then advanced a new theory on common borders, whose alleged inadequate security, along with the developments inside Czechoslovakia, endangered the security of all the Warsaw Pact countries. At variance with the provisions of the Warsaw Pact, he deduced the right of the Joint Command to decide at will on the deployment and movement of Soviet troops. Kosygin's remarks were the subject of a special nighttime session of the CPCz Presidium, and the next day the Soviet side was informed that they had categorically rejected his demand. Around this time, Presidium candidate member Antonín Kapek, representing the so-called "healthy core" in the CPCz leadership, wrote the first letter requesting "internationalist assistance" (see Part Six).

Over the course of three-and-a-half days of talks, which gradually centered around four persons from each side and finally two—Dubček and Brezhnev—there were neither victors nor vanquished, despite the support given to the Soviet side by Biľak, and partly by fellow Presidium members Drahomír Kolder and Emil Rigo. Even during tense private discussions between the Soviet and Czechoslovak leaders in Brezhnev's personal train car, neither man was able to make any headway with the other (Document No. 67). By the end of the negotiations, the Soviets had not succeeded in opening a crack in the Czechoslovak ship of state large enough to sink it; on the contrary, the spirit of the Warsaw Letter seemed to have been shelved for the moment.

The essential outcome of the negotiations was an agreement to jointly convene a meeting of six communist parties, on Czechoslovak territory, which was to symbolize the two sides' "joint endeavor" to take positive steps. It was also agreed that the session would not refer to the Warsaw

Letter, to the Warsaw meetings, to the period following that meeting, nor to the situation in Czechoslovakia.

As Brezhnev boarded the train at Čierna, he said good-bye to the Czechoslovak delegation with the words: "You gave us a promise and we are confident that you are going to fight . . . we want to declare that we are prepared to give you unlimited help under the circumstances . . . if our plan is foiled, it will be very difficult to call a further meeting . . . That is when we shall come to your assistance."[2] According to Dubček, the Czechoslovak side gave no fundamental promises to Brezhnev at Čierna. In his view, this was Moscow's normal *modus operandi*: automatically to consider its own proposals and demands to be accepted and binding, then to impose their implementation with the argument that, after all, "it was agreed to, and accepted!"[3]

[2] Russian transcript from Čierna. ÚSD, Sb. KV ČSFR, Z/S 5.
[3] See Document No. 67.

DOCUMENT No. 45: Briefing on the Šumava Exercises for Alexander Dubček and Oldřich Černík by Commanders of the Czechoslovak People's Army, July 1, 1968, with Follow-up Talks between Dubček and Marshal Yakubovskii

Source: VHA, F. MNO, OS/GS, Sv. "Šumava."

These meeting "notes" are of a briefing on the Šumava military exercises given by three top Czechoslovak Defense Ministry officials to Dubček and Černík on July 1. The military officials report on "certain irregularities" during the maneuvers, informing Dubček that Soviet Marshal Yakubovskii "has sought to prolong the exercises" which were scheduled to end on June 30.

The stenographic account includes transcriptions of two phone conversations between Dubček and Marshal Yakubovskii, as Dubček attempts to ascertain why the exercises have been extended and when they will finish. Yakubovskii provides no satisfactory explanation, and flatly rejects Dubček's request that the maneuvers be ended on July 1. Only reluctantly does Yakubovskii agree to try to finish Šumava by the 2nd or 3rd of July—dates that he subsequently ignores. The transcript reflects the Soviets' dominant position over Czechoslovakia, where Dubček is forced to plead in much the same way that the leader of an occupied country would have to negotiate with military commanders of the occupying powers.

NOTES on Meetings between the Minister of National Defense Col. Gen. Dzúr, the Deputy Minister Lt. Gen. A. Mucha, and the Chief of the General Staff of the CzPA Lt. Gen. K. Rusov, with the CPCz CC First Secretary A. Dubček, and ČSSR Prime Minister O. Černík about the End of the Šumava Exercises.[4]

On 1 July 1968, between 10:00 A.M. and 12:00 P.M., the minister of national defense, the chief of the general staff, and the deputy minister of national defense briefed the CPCz CC first secretary and the prime minister on the Šumava exercises. They informed them:

1. that the exercises had taken place successfully on 20–30 June 1968;
2. that certain irregularities had arisen in connection with the exercises, including:

— the plan for directing the exercises was not worked out in detail and was not made available to the armies' adjudicative service;
— the exercises were arranged on an hour-by-hour basis, from one day to the next, on the basis of decisions by Marshal Yakubovskii;
— officials from the CzPA exercise directorate were not invited to consultations or to the start of the exercises and were not kept sufficiently informed about the intended procedures;

3. that when the Hungarian Minister of Defense Col. Gen. Czinege arrived, there was some irregularity in welcoming him on the part of Marshal Yakubovskii. The Hungarian minister of defense was welcomed only by the chief of staff of the Joint Armed Forces, Army General Kazakov. Marshal Yakubovskii's decision not to receive him and instead to designate Army General Kazakov drew comments in the staff of the Hungarian People's Army;

4. that there were irregularities in the agreement to carry out an analysis of the exercises. It turned out that for unknown reasons Marshal Yakubovskii has sought to prolong the exercises.

The state of the Šumava exercises as of 1 July 1968 was discussed and the main questions at issue were the reasons for (1) postponing the analysis of the exercises from the originally

---

[4] The Czech typescript contains some minor typographical errors, including the spelling of proper names, which have been corrected in the translation.

scheduled date of 1 July 1968 at 9 A.M. to a later date, and (2) the intention of the Soviet side to extend the maneuvers until 4–5 July 1968.

On the basis of recommendations by the Minister of National Defense Col. Gen. Dzúr, Cdes. Dubček and Černík decided:

1. The Ministry of National Defense is to prepare a letter to Cde. Brezhnev, the CPSU CC first secretary,[5] and convey it to Moscow today, requesting the Soviet side to terminate the exercises, carry out the final analysis, and withdraw all allied troops from ČSSR territory;

2. The Chief of the General Staff Lt. Gen. Rusov is to convey the following request from the CPCz CC first secretary and the ČSSR prime minister to Cde. Yakubovskii personally:

Cdes. Dubček and Černík were today informed by National Defense Minister Dzúr that the Šumava exercises, which, according to the original plan, were supposed to end on 30 June 1968, are still continuing. Because our public has been kept constantly informed about the progress of the exercises, and because the continuation of the exercises is causing anxiety among our public and among the staffs and troops of the CzPA that are taking part in the exercises, this does not help the consolidation of the political situation in our country.

Marshal Yakubovskii is requested to present a report by 12:00 P.M. on 1 July to the CPCz CC and the national government explaining:

1. why the Šumava exercises have not yet ended;
2. when they will end;
3. when the exercises will be analyzed.

It was requested that Marshal Yakubovskii should give these replies to Cde. Dubček personally and confirm this in writing by a courier.

After this report was transmitted, there was a telephone conversation between the CPCz CC first secretary and Marshal Yakubovskii on 1 July 1968 at 11:30 A.M.

Cde. Dubček asks Cde. Yakubovskii:

— Why, if the analysis was to have been carried out today, 1 July 1968, at 9:00 A.M., did neither I nor Cde. Černík know anything about a change of that date.

— I don't know why the analysis did not take place; this question should have been consulted with us. Neither the minister of national defense nor the chief of the General Staff was able to explain it to me because they had not been informed and did not know the reasons for the postponement.

— This puts me in an unpleasant situation because at a workers' assembly I announced the end of the exercises and wished the units and staffs taking part in the maneuvers a good return journey home.

Cde. Yakubovskii replies:

— Yesterday, the 30th of June, at 1:30 P.M., I finished listening to a report on the latest situation and issued instructions for the following additional activity:

1 July — sum up the results from the exercise needed for the final stage and compilation of the analysis;

2 July — carry out another analysis of the forces;

— the main analysis, as requested by Cde. Dubček, might also be carried out;

---

[5] Until 1965, Brezhnev's title was "First Secretary," but after that it was changed to "General Secretary," a title used by Stalin. Because the CPCz still used the title of "First Secretary," it was common to refer to the heads of other communist parties by that title as well.

— I possibly suggest the morning of 3 July depending on what is convenient for Cdes. Dubček and Černík.

Cde. Dubček again asks: But is this not possible on 1 July?

Cde. Yakubovskii: No, it cannot be done on 1 July.

Cde. Yakubovskii proposes that the analysis be made on 2 July and that he will adjust his plans. Following the analysis he wishes to host a festive luncheon.

Cde. Dubček says he will discuss it with Cde. Černík and will call Cde. Yakubovskii afterwards.

Cde. Dubček called Cde. Yakubovskii at 12 noon and told him that he and Cde. Černík agreed that the analysis should be held on 2 July 1968 at 9:00 A.M., with the proviso that those taking part will include the ČSSR president, the CPCz CC first secretary, Cde. Dubček, Cde. Černík, Cde. Smrkovský, Cde. Piller, and Cde. Prchlík, and members of the CzPA command on the basis of a decision by the Soviet side. In addition he asked Cde. Yakubovskii that the analysis, including lunch, be terminated by 1:00 P.M.

Cde. Yakubovskii said he would make arrangements in accordance with this request, but asked for greater participation by party and government officials in the analysis of the exercises.[6]

Cde. Dubček told him that because of a heavy work load at the CPCz Central Committee and preparations for CPCz district and regional conferences, other officials could not take part in the analysis. He then asked about Cde. Yakubovskii's general impression of the exercises.

Cde. Yakubovskii said he is satisfied with the progress of the exercises. The morale of the staffs and troops was good.

— He is satisfied with the work of the commanders and staffs that took part in the maneuvers, and offered high praise for the troops.

Cde. Dubček asked whether he could not manage to prepare the analysis on 1 July.

Cde. Yakubovskii replied that:

— he did not have the necessary background material from the exercise directorate and, even more important, he wanted to talk to the staffs of the maneuvering armies on those days,

— the actual exercises had ended officially on 30 June 1968,

— they will end completely once the analysis is over.

Cdes. Dubček and *Černík* gave instructions to the CzPA chief of the General Staff to respond in writing to the request of Army General Kazakov regarding the supply of additional special repair units to the ČSSR. The reply should state that all necessary repairs of the technical hardware of the Joint Forces can be carried out by repair units of the CzPA, and that a further transfer of units to the ČSSR could complicate the political situation and jeopardize consolidation.

Chief of the General Staff of
the Czechoslovak People's Army

Lt. General Karel Rusov

Deputy Minister of National Defense
Commander of Ground Forces

Lt. General Alexandr Mucha

---

[6] Yakubovskii's request here is a clear signal of the political motivations behind the decision to prolong the exercises.

DOCUMENT No. 46: Letter of the CPSU CC Politburo to the CPCz CC Presidium, July 4, 1968

Source: ÚSD, AÚV KSČ, F. 07/15; Vondrová & Navrátil, vol. 1, pp. 253–257.

This letter from the CPSU CC Politburo was the first of several concerned letters that the Czechoslovak authorities received between July 4 and July 6—part of a well-coordinated campaign by the "Warsaw Five" nations to step up their political pressure on Czechoslovakia. This communication harshly attacked the "ever more active anti-socialist forces," using the publication of the "Two Thousand Words"—an "open and cunning attempt" to "subvert socialism in Czechoslovakia"—as ammunition. "To ensure victory in this struggle," it advises, the USSR is "ready to provide all the necessary help."

The Politburo conveyed these views, as well as much of the phrasing of this letter, to the Soviet public a week later in a lengthy commentary by I. Aleksandrov (a pseudonym) in the CPSU daily Pravda, under the title "Attacks Against the Foundations of Socialism in Czechoslovakia." Subsequently, the July 4 letter became the basis for the drafting of the Warsaw communiqué approved during a meeting of the "Five" on July 14–15.

(See also Document No. 53.)

Conditions in the ČSSR are becoming even more dangerous than before. As a counterweight to the CPCz there is a growing political opposition, which rejects Marxism–Leninism, calls for a basic change in the current system of society and state management, and is seeking the restoration of a capitalist system in Czechoslovakia. In Prague, in other cities, and in outlying regions, countless legal and illegal groups have sprung up, and the tone of these groups has been set by non-proletarian elements and people from the exploitative classes.

Anti-socialist forces have become ever more active. They are dividing Czechoslovak society by pitting the party against the people, the trade unions against the party, the intelligentsia against the working class, and the younger generation against the older. They are persistently trying to achieve the destruction of the leading role of the communist party in the National Front, and to exclude communists from organs of power and management and from the leadership of social organizations. They are bringing together under one political roof everyone who can serve their anti-socialist aims, ranging from the muddle-headed and those who are disoriented by the complicated political situation to open class enemies of the socialist system, from right-wing social democrats to former Hitlerites, who are actively using the various "clubs" and other organizations for their subversive aims and are persistently working toward the establishment of a Social Democratic Party.

In their speeches, anti-socialist representatives have openly demanded the removal of the CPCz from the leadership of society. The mass media find themselves in the hands of anti-party elements who use them as a tribunal conducting incessant propaganda against the CPCz and socialism, and from which open counterrevolutionary and anti-Soviet appeals can be heard.

In fact, all activities and all the basic directions of CPCz policy have come under attack. We are firmly convinced that all attacks by anti-socialist elements are being led by a conspiratorial center of organization, which issues and changes slogans and indicates the direction of attacks at every turn in the situation.

What is particularly alarming is that these things are finding support among a certain section of CPCz members and even among individual members of the Central Committee. What is doubly and triply alarming is that all this is going on two months before the party's Extraordinary Congress begins its work.[7]

---

[7] The Extraordinary 14th Congress of the CPCz was due to start on September 9, 1968.

The right-wing forces are trying to use preparations for the Congress to deliver a decisive blow at the Congress itself against the healthy forces in the party, to put their people into key positions, and to force the CPCz to embrace a line that would necessitate the renunciation of tried and tested Marxist–Leninist principles and the transformation and disintegration of the socialist society.

The anti-socialist forces have already revealed their political platforms. The whole content of the "Two Thousand Words" platform is directed against the CPCz and is intended to weaken the position of socialism in Czechoslovakia.[8] It is an open and cunning attempt to denigrate the position of the entire communist party in the eyes of the Czechoslovak people and in front of world opinion.

The authors of the "Two Thousand Words" urge the promotion of subversive activities in every city, in every district, and in every factory. Their platform calls for the "creation of civic committees," the creation of their own press, and the establishment of their own police, which would be nothing less than a recipe for the disruption and undermining of the legal organs of government authority. Under the guise of false and hypocritical phrases about supporting "the progressive wing" of the CPCz, the platform demands the indiscriminate belittlement of party cadres and urges the use of pressure tactics such as strikes, demonstrations, and boycotts. A signal has been given to step up actions against the Communist Party of Czechoslovakia on all fronts. One cannot fail to note that this counterrevolutionary platform was published simultaneously by four central newspapers and that signatures for it were gathered in different cities of Czechoslovakia. This, too, is especially dangerous since behind it one discerns forces that have clearly been organized. The anti-socialist forces, in essence, are even posing the following threat: If you do not give up power "peacefully," we will use all means available, including the force of arms. Do you not understand that communists have a duty to expose the real face of such enemies before the party and that those who are honest and devoted to the cause of socialism will have to face the bores of rifles, unarmed? This would be death for the communist party, and it would mean the threat of tragic suffering for the Czechoslovak people as a whole.

Imperialist and emigré circles, who are carefully following events in Czechoslovakia, are inciting the activities of right-wing forces in all possible ways. Everyone knows that there are emigré organizations in Paris grouped around the magazine *Svědectví* that are collaborating with a number of imperialist intelligence agencies, from which they receive directives.[9] They have close ties to certain political figures in Czechoslovakia and are using them to influence the course of events. In turn, the reactionary forces inside the country itself, encouraged by counterrevolutionaries abroad, are becoming ever more insolent in trying to prevent the CPCz from normalizing the situation in the country.

Right-wing forces inside and outside the party are using this occasion to stir up hostile feelings toward the Soviet people and to shake the foundations of allied relations between the ČSSR and the Soviet Union and the other socialist governments. They are seeking ways of undermining the Warsaw Pact and discrediting the Council of Mutual Economic Assistance. They also are inciting hostile feelings toward the other socialist countries.

Our party, as well as the parties of the other fraternal countries, cannot regard with indifference these numerous statements in the press, on radio, and on television, as well as at assemblies and meetings, that attack the positions of the socialist countries on vital issues affecting the preservation of peace and security in Europe. The situation has deteriorated so much, as the CPCz leadership is well aware, that some Czechoslovak officials have made statements defending West Germany and its revanchist, militarist line. These statements confer *de facto* approval on the political course of a government that considers itself to be the true political heir to Hitlerite Germany.

[8] See Document No. 44 above.
[9] On the quarterly *Svědectví* and its editor, Pavel Tigrid, see the Editors' Note in Document No. 1.

At the same time, they urgently emphasize the notion that the place of Czechoslovakia in foreign policy should be based on its geographical location, that is, on its being "between the USSR and Germany." It is well known that such a "geopolitical" position did not save Czechoslovakia from the aggression committed by German fascism. In fact the question is not one of geographical location but of aggression, revanchism, and militarism, which are diametrically opposed to the unity of action of all peace-loving states and, above all, the unity of the socialist countries. We cannot help but be amazed that these irresponsible statements, which are directed against the maintenance of allied commitments and toward the reorientation of the ČSSR's foreign policy, are not receiving the necessary rebuff on the part of official state and party organs in Czechoslovakia. Our party, and the whole Soviet people, want to believe that the Czechoslovak comrades, the CPCz, and the Czechoslovak people will not passively accept such a situation. There have been too many victims borne by the peoples of our country, as well as by the peoples of Czechoslovakia, in the fight against Hitlerite Germany to make it possible to forget them. We cannot permit our enemies to succeed in weakening and crippling our ranks.

If we analyze the course of events, if we compare the basic facts with contemporary Czechoslovak reality, and if we study the more serious trends in the political life of the country, it becomes very clear that the crucial question at stake is: Will there or will there not be a socialist Czechoslovakia? We are compelled again and again to emphasize, comrades, that one cannot underestimate the extreme gravity of the situation or fail to notice how counterrevolution, released from its bonds, is seizing one position after another from the CPCz and acquiring a *place d'arms* for a decisive attack that might well bury the socialist system in Czechoslovakia. This is no dramatization of events but a sober appraisal, for which there is sufficient basis in fact.

There is no doubt that if the force of the working class and of other working people under the leadership of the communist party had been activated, anti-socialist platforms like the "Two Thousand Words" would never have seen the light of day.

Workers' collectives, party branches, nationwide corps of the People's Militia, and many members of the Central Committee are demanding that the anti-socialist forces be restrained and are urging the adoption of concrete and effective measures to bolster the positions of socialism. It would seem that the CPCz Central Committee, and above all the CC Presidium, should have supported these demands and committed itself to them in the fight to normalize the situation in the party and country. But in fact something very different is going on. The announcement by the CPCz CC's May plenum of its campaign against the right-wing and anti-socialist forces was not underpinned either ideologically or politically, and not even organizationally. In fact something different is happening. The forces hostile to socialism are exploiting this and becoming ever more insolent as they mount their subversive activities.

Comrades, it is clear to us that the forces of socialism in the ČSSR are, objectively speaking, far stronger than those who today are raising their fists against the socialist gains of the Czechoslovak people. The right-wing forces, despite the noise and attacks they have mounted, do not have the support of the broad mass of working people. But this does not mean that they cannot achieve success if they are not defeated. What is needed for this is a decisive, uncompromising, and consistent struggle against the right-wing forces.

But the problem is that not a single decisive blow has yet been delivered against the right-wingers or even against the counterrevolutionary forces who are now openly attacking the people's power. An insufferable situation has come about insofar as any demagogic statement by right-wing elements that is meant to discredit communists is converted immediately into the outright persecution of them, while the leading party organs refuse to give them any support.

The great historical experience of our party, as well as of the other fraternal parties, allows us to say that displaying irresolution and passivity, and a failure to mobilize the party and the people in a struggle against the attacks by anti-socialist forces at a time when they threaten the very existence of people's rule and the foundations of the socialist system, will drive the country to political catastrophe. Such, comrades, is the harsh truth, which we tell you as true friends, guided by our party conscience.

We want to tell you openly, comrades, that the resolution adopted by the CPCz CC Presidium on the "Two Thousand Words" statement was weak and, as a result, did not have the desired effect.[10] The situation is aggravated by the fact that individual, leading CPCz cadres went even further by offering support for the "Two Thousand Words," and those members of the Central Committee who took a principled party stance on this matter were subject to open attacks. In our opinion it is essential to reveal to all the people without delay the counterrevolutionary essence of the "Two Thousand Words" and who stands behind it.

There is not and cannot be any other way to strengthen socialist Czechoslovakia except by activating and opening up the political arena for the Czechoslovak working class—for the Czechoslovak workers who have sufficient means to halt the advance of hostile forces. Not a single day should be lost. The situation demands that concrete measures be immediately devised and adopted to put up effective resistance against the anti-socialist forces and defend the cause of socialism.

There is not and cannot be any other way to normalize the situation in the country except by rallying all communists and by strengthening the unity of the party on the foundations of Marxism–Leninism. Today it is not unity in general that is needed, but unity of the healthy forces in the party. All ties must be cut with those who by their actions aid the class enemies.

Today, as never before, it is imperative to carry out the Leninist principles of party action with consistency and to observe the principles of democratic centralism as strictly as possible. Experience has already shown that any compromise at the expense of this principle is fatal and will render the party incapable of acting. The communists who are in the leading party organs must be told to adhere firmly to the measures taken by these organs, regardless of the position they upheld until then. One cannot fail to see that the open attacks of right-wing elements within the party are aimed at revising Marxism–Leninism. Under the banner of defending the "right of the minority," they are violating basic organizational principles on which the party was built. Once factions and groups have been legalized, it is only a short step to the outright destruction of the party. That is the true nature of the line of the right-wing minority in the CPCz.

Success in the struggle against the anti-socialist forces and for the defense and development of socialist society in the ČSSR will be impossible unless you place the press, radio, and television—that is, all the mass media—at the service of these great aims. The party's immediate control of the mass media has a decisive significance at the present time.

Dear comrades, having openly told you our thoughts, we support the demand of the May plenum of the CPCz Central Committee "to secure the political administration of society by the communist party and effectively thwart all attempts to discredit the party as a whole, as well as attempts to foster mistrust in the party and oppose its moral and political right to lead society and be the decisive political force of socialist power."

Comrades! The events in your country are already being exploited by the enemies of socialism to mount a broad campaign of ideological subversion and to discredit the theory of scientific socialism and world socialist practices. All the greater therefore is the responsibility of the communist party, the working class of Czechoslovakia, and all the forces able to uphold the achievements of socialism and secure the further advance of Czechoslovakia toward the progress of socialist society and communism. Your victory over the anti-socialist forces will signify a victory not only for Czechoslovak communists and Czechoslovakia's working people, but a victory of our whole commonwealth and the communist movement.

In this difficult time of struggle against anti-socialist and counterrevolutionary forces you can be very certain, dear comrades, that the CPSU and the Soviet government are ready to provide

[10] For the Presidium's condemnation of the Manifesto, see "Předsednictvo Ústředního výboru KSČ k prohlášení Dva tisíce slov," *Rudé právo* (Prague), June 29, 1968, p. 1.

all necessary help to socialist Czechoslovakia to ensure victory in this struggle. The friendship between our peoples goes a long way back. The friendship grew immeasurably stronger after the Great October Revolution and especially after the liberation of Czechoslovakia from the fascist yoke by Soviet and Czechoslovak troops, as well as in the struggle for liberty and independence and for the ideals of communism. Soviet and Czechoslovak communists can state with a clear conscience that during the postwar years they have constantly felt close to one another, supported one another, and struggled together for the triumph of our great common cause. Soviet communists, and all the Soviet people, will always stand shoulder to shoulder with their Czechoslovak brothers.

Because of this, because of how much Soviet–Czechoslovak friendship meant and means to us, and particularly because the interests of socialism and the principles of proletarian internationalism are so dear to us—and knowing that close comradely relations exist between us—we think it possible and necessary to send you this letter expressing our concern and the views of Soviet communists and of all the Soviet people.

With communist greetings,

The Politburo of the Central Committee
of the Communist Party of the Soviet Union

4 July 1968
Moscow

DOCUMENT No. 47: Report on the Šumava Exercises by Generals I. Oláh and F. Szűcs of the Hungarian People's Army to the HSWP Politburo, July 5, 1968 (Excerpts)

Source: MHKI, 5/12/11.

This top-secret report offers a candid assessment of the Šumava military exercises by two senior Hungarian army officers who took part: Major-General István Oláh, a deputy minister of national defense; and Major-General Ferenc Szűcs, the deputy chief of the Hungarian General Staff. The two generals acknowledge that the exercises "were organized essentially for political reasons" and were designed as a "kind of camouflage" that would enable the Soviet Union to pursue its "political goals." They also note that the exercises were intended to have specific political effects in Czechoslovakia: namely, to "paralyze and frighten" the "anti-socialist forces," to "intimidate wavering elements," and to "bolster and safeguard true communists dedicated to the revolution and to socialism." On a more ominous note, the generals observed that the exercises allowed the Soviet Union and its Warsaw Pact allies to "gain greater experience in planning, organizing, supervising, and cooperating in large-scale military operations"—precisely the type of preparation necessary for an invasion in August 1968.

Their report is critical of the heavy-handed manner in which Soviet military officials conducted these operations. Marshal Yakubovskii, according to Oláh and Szűcs, "kept everyone in a state of maximum uncertainty" about the schedule for ending the exercises. Soviet commanders brushed aside the Czechoslovak complaints by drawing "comparisons between the events in Czechoslovakia and the Hungarian counterrevolution" of 1956, an analogy that the Hungarian generals curtly dismissed. Looking back on "the experience of the past 20 days," the generals concluded that the maneuvers had exposed "unacceptable shortcomings" in the Warsaw Pact, and they expressed particular irritation at the "unprofessional, crude, and insulting behavior of certain Soviet military commanders," whose conduct had been "objectively detrimental to the authority and reputation of the Soviet Union and the unity of the Warsaw Pact."

The commander-in-chief of the Warsaw Pact's Joint Armed Forces organized strategic-operational military command-staff exercises under the codename Šumava, which started on 18 June 1968.[11] Most of the exercises were held on the territory of the ČSSR, with some on the territory of the GDR, Poland, and the Soviet Union. Soviet, Czechoslovak, Polish, German, and Hungarian army and division staffs took part in the exercise: in total, these included the staff of one front, the staffs of seven combined-arms armies, one air force army staff, one air defense army staff, and the staffs of nine divisions, as well as subordinate intelligence and rear services units together with lower-level formations. Originally, the Germans were not included but in the last phase of preparations they joined on the basis of decisions of which we were totally unaware. The Hungarian People's Army was represented by the staffs of the 5th Army and the 11th Tank Division (altogether approximately 800 persons and 260 vehicles).

Romania and Bulgaria, under the command of their deputy chiefs of the General Staff, took part with three persons each, at the invitation of the commander-in-chief.

The exercise was organized essentially for political reasons and with political objectives, on the basis of an analysis of the situation worked out at the Dresden and Moscow conferences. The exercise and the preparation of the highest-ranking staffs were to serve as a kind of camouflage.

The objective of the exercise, its content and procedure, and above all the methods used in carrying it out revealed the extent and implications of the conflicting assessments involved. As a result, a tense, nervous, and antagonistic atmosphere arose in which views held by Czechoslovakia clashed with those of the exercise commanders, the Soviet comrades.

---

[11] Although most of the forces were in place on June 18, the exercises formally began on June 19.

On the basis of statements by the exercise commanders, the information they provided, and their activities, as well as on the basis of our own experience, the objectives of the exercise can be summed up as follows:

a) With regard to foreign policy, this was decidedly a demonstration of the strength and unity of the Warsaw Pact and a warning to the imperialists that speculation about the events in Czechoslovakia or about similar internal political developments elsewhere, as well as all provocative attempts, would be doomed from the very start.[12]

b) With regard to domestic policy, the exercises were intended to influence the Czechoslovak events in the sense that a show of the strength and determination of the Warsaw Pact states would paralyze and frighten enemies at home; the exercises would also intimidate wavering elements (especially intellectuals) and bolster and safeguard true communists dedicated to the revolution and to socialism.

c) Extensive meetings between senior military commanders and the staff participating in the exercise as well as members of units with the Czechoslovak people are to strengthen friendship and shore up the authority of the Soviet Union and the Warsaw Pact.

d) The exceptionally important strategic-operational exercises are designed to enable multinational army staffs to acquire greater experience in planning, organizing, supervising, and cooperating in military operations.

* * *

These planned objectives guided the exercise command in determining the scope of the exercises (the number of those involved), the timetable (making the exercises as long as possible), their content (deploying huge enemy and domestic forces against the ČSSR or for its defense), as well as the means to carry all this out.

The objectives of the exercise were determined by the position of the Soviet comrades in assessing internal political events in Czechoslovakia. They proceeded from the conviction that there is a counterrevolutionary situation in Czechoslovakia or, to be more accurate, a situation on the verge of counterrevolution. . . .

The assessment of the Czechoslovak comrades of their internal situation as well as their vision of the exercise and its requirements differed from everything that has been said above. They essentially agreed to the exercise after being convinced that all activities would take place on the basis of a mutual agreement, with Czechoslovakia's active participation and within the framework of specified military objectives.

But this did not happen, and that is why there was a tense atmosphere at the exercise from the very beginning. They were taken aback when they learned that although the exercise was not supposed to be held until the second half of June, some of the Soviet intelligence units and General Kazakov's preparatory staff had arrived on Czechoslovak territory as early as the end of May and beginning of June.

Moreover, during his stay of more than two weeks, Cde. Kazakov was unable or unwilling to inform the party, government, and military leadership of the objectives of the exercise, the dates of its commencement and termination, the forms it was to take, the planned progression and time schedule of the individual phases, and the size of the armies and staffs arriving on Czechoslovak territory. According to the Czechoslovak comrades, he merely informed them of requirements, especially with regard to intelligence activities. Referring to adequate information, he pointed out that this was the responsibility of the commander-in-chief, who was due to arrive on 10–11 June. This disconcerted the Czechoslovak political and military leadership, and they increasingly pressed for sufficient information, but to no avail. As a result, each demand of the Soviet comrades

---

[12] The Slovak typescript is slightly garbled here, so a few small adjustments have been made in the translation to convey the proper meaning.

to increase the number of units and formations triggered conflicts and heated discussions. This gradually increased the mistrust that was already present at the outset. . . .

The tension increased still further when the commander-in-chief delayed his arrival from the 10th or 11th to the 14th, and then finally arrived on the 18th, the day before the start of the exercises.

The arrival of the commander-in-chief further increased the tense atmosphere surrounding the exercises. The leadership of the Czechoslovak party again got no answers when it raised questions about the exercises. . . .

. . .

The date of the termination of the exercise was a constant problem not only for the Czechoslovak comrades, but for us as well. On this point the commander-in-chief kept everyone in a state of maximum uncertainty.

The repeated insistence by the Czechoslovak side that the exercise be terminated and that the armies be withdrawn made certain Soviet comrades ask the following question: If these commanders are truly friends of the Soviet Union, why do they object to a Soviet presence that, after all, is there for their benefit as well? Insinuations were made that the presence of Soviet units and military organs had been a problem in the past for Imre Nagy, though not for Cde. Kádár. (The Czechoslovak events were in general terms compared to the Hungarian counter-revolution.)

. . .

As we have pointed out, the Czechoslovak military leaders viewed their domestic situation as well as the objectives of the exercise and the need for it in a very different way from the Soviet comrades. That is why they tried their utmost to ensure that the exercise would not go in the direction it did.

In our opinion, there is no counterrevolutionary situation in the country.

. . .

The experience of the entire exercise unfortunately confirmed that there are unacceptable shortcomings, irregularities, and inadequate provisions in the Warsaw Pact. All this clearly demonstrates that sooner or later these deficiencies will erode the dignity of the Soviet Union and undermine the pact.

If such results are to be averted, the following steps are necessary:

— the text of the treaty must be made more specific on the basis of the Politburo resolution, as we had planned;

— in connection with the organization and conduct of the so-called joint exercises, matters of substantial and fundamental importance and their observance must be specified in advance.

On the basis of our experience during the past 20 days and prompted by a feeling of responsibility for the common cause, I take the liberty of proposing to use acceptable methods in explaining to the leaders of the Soviet party and government that the unprofessional, crude, and insulting behavior of certain Soviet military commanders is objectively detrimental to the authority and reputation of the Soviet Union and to the unity of the Warsaw Pact.

Budapest, 5 July 1968

Major-General István Oláh
Deputy Minister of National Defense

Major-General Ferenc Szűcs
Deputy Chief of the General Staff

DOCUMENT No. 48: General Semyon Zolotov's Retrospective Account of the Šumava Military Exercises

Source: "Shli na pomosch' druz'yam," *Voenno-istoricheskii zhurnal*, No. 4
(April 1994), pp. 15–18.

This memoir of the preparations and conduct of the Šumava exercises was written by Lt. General Semyon Mitrofanovich Zolotov, a top official in the Main Political Directorate of the Soviet armed forces. It details the logistical operations of the maneuvers and offers observations about the anxiety they produced inside Czechoslovakia. "We did not sense the fraternal warmth and friendliness that had previously distinguished the Czechoslovak friends," Zolotov writes; "instead, they seemed apprehensive."

Following the maneuvers, Zolotov became directly involved in preparations for the invasion as head of the Political Directorate and a member of the Military Council in the Transcarpathian Military District.

(See also Document No. 87.)

... In mid-May 1968 they informed us that in the very near future, joint military exercises involving troops from the member states of the Warsaw Pact would be held on the territory of Poland, the GDR, Czechoslovakia, and the Soviet Union. Issues concerning the organization and conduct of the exercises were examined during a visit to those countries by the commander-in-chief of the Joint Armed Forces, Marshal of the Soviet Union I. I. Yakubovskii. Originally, the exercises were intended to be live military maneuvers with significant military contingents taking part, but at the insistence of the Czechoslovak side, they were carried out simply as command-staff exercises. I learned about this, having been at the Main Political Directorate of the Soviet army and Navy.

After the May holidays I went with a group of comrades from the headquarters and the Political Department of the army to one of the garrisons, where I scrutinized the state of educational work and military discipline. Here we were given orders that the troops and command organs of the army would have to be brought up to combat readiness. It was up to me to return immediately to the headquarters and get in touch on a secure phone line with the leadership of the district's political directorate.

Within several hours, our plane touched down at Ivano-Frankovsk. The field command, the military communications units, and the support formations for the army staff were already prepared to march out. New formations had been added to the army's lineup, and these had been fleshed out with personnel called up from reserves. The situation was reminiscent of combat.

All the officers from the headquarters and political department of the army were in the military units. I met with political workers who had recently traveled around the units and formations. We reviewed a number of practical matters. We agreed, in particular, to keep each other informed about the exercises.

On 12 May our front-line units advanced to the region along the state border with the ČSSR. In Uzhgorod we held a meeting to consider matters of party-political work under field conditions and the organization of special propaganda for the upcoming exercises of the allied armies.

In the evening of that same day, the army commander, Lieut.-General A. M. Maiorov, got together with the commanders of the formations and units to consider matters connected with garrison service and the activity of military traffic control.[13] On 23 May we were at the Transcarpathian Oblast Party Committee, where we had a discussion with the party Secretaries,

---

[13] General Aleksandr Mikhailovich Maiorov, the commander of forces in the Transcarpathian, was appointed commander of the Central Group of Forces in the fall of 1968, at the same time that Zolotov was appointed head of the Central Group's Political Directorate.

Yu. V. Il'nitskii and B. I. Belousov. They briefed us on the situation in the Oblast and told us about the preparations for the upcoming Soviet–Czechoslovak friendship meeting in the region of Uzhgorod.

At the end of May, I was again summoned to Moscow to get instructions for the upcoming exercises on ČSSR territory. The instructions were given to me by the head of the Main Political Directorate, Army-General A. A. Epishev, and by other senior officers in the MPD. The discussion did not last very long. Aleksei Alekseevich issued a series of orders about the work to be performed, and he formulated guidelines for the behavior of Soviet soldiers on ČSSR territory, warning that any hint of insouciance or loss of vigilance would be impermissible.

Then we were received by A. A. Epishev's deputy, Col.-General N. A. Nachinkin, who had been given command of the party-political work during the preparations and conduct of the exercises in Czechoslovakia.

Early on the morning of 18 June 1968, the operational group of the army's field command crossed the state border of the ČSSR. The group was ordered to move expeditiously to the designated region to begin preparations for a regimental tactical exercise involving live fire. The group was commanded by the deputy head of the department for combat preparations, Colonel M. G. Popov; and the senior officer from the political department was Colonel K. A. Lebedev. At the border there was a low-key friendship meeting. The Slovak friends organized a warm reception for the Soviet soldiers.

Within three days, the main forces of the army that had been selected to take part in the exercises crossed the Soviet–Czechoslovak border. The weather did not cooperate: A torrential rain continued the whole night, and thunder bursts blinded the drivers. The narrow, winding mountain roads and the huge stream of military vehicles complicated matters even further. There was a danger of transport incidents on the road. The column rolled back for dozens of kilometers. Several vehicles stalled, and three swerved off into a ditch. However, all this transpired without loss of life or any other serious consequences.

From the very outset of the meetings on Czechoslovak soil it became clear that changes had occurred in the outlook and behavior of a significant proportion of Slovaks and Czechs. We did not sense the fraternal warmth and friendliness that had previously distinguished the Czechoslovak friends; instead, they seemed apprehensive.

On the night of 22–23 June our troops were concentrated at a training center in Libavá. It was located around 400 km from the state border with the USSR. The whole day had been spent on readying the facilities. The army commander summed up the results of the march along the roads of Slovakia and Moravia and specified future tasks. He demanded that the commanders, staffs, and political organs ensure a worthy military performance and the exemplary behavior of Soviet soldiers on the territory of friendly Czechoslovakia.

The commander-in-chief of the Joint Armed Forces of the Warsaw Pact member states, Marshal of the Soviet Union I. I. Yakubovskii, and his staff were based in Milovice. They ordered the army commander and me to come there, so that we could brief them on the march along the roads in Czechoslovakia and on the readiness of the staffs and troops for the exercises. The officers attending the briefing included the chief of staff of the Joint Armed Forces, Army-General M. I. Kazakov, and the deputy head of the Main Political Directorate, Col.-General N. A. Nachinkin.

The leadership, in particular, pointed out the inadequate study that had been done of the situation in places where troops were deployed, and recommended a more active effort to expand links with the Czechoslovak side. The army commander, Lieut.-General A. M. Maiorov, was assigned a task for the command-staff exercises, which had been given the codename Šumava We learned that staffs and troops from the ČSSR, Poland, the GDR, and Hungary would be taking part alongside us.

During the exercises there were numerous meetings and conversations between Soviet soldiers and the Czechoslovak friends. These encounters were frank and often polemical. We were convinced of the complexity and contradictory nature of the situation in the ČSSR. Thus, on 28

July the army commander and I were ordered to meet with the administration and workforce of a metallurgical combine in Nová Hut'.[14] This meeting left a bitter aftertaste. "How could the Czechoslovak people have become unrecognizable in such a short time?" I wrote in my diary. "They're no longer comfortable with the idea of friendship with the Soviet people . . ."

When the exercises were nearly done, a meeting of the political workers of the friendly armies took place in Milovice. All the leaders of the political organs of the Joint Armed Forces attended. In their speeches, many of them noted the signs of unfriendliness and even hostility on the part of some Czechoslovak citizens toward the allied soldiers. Slanderous attacks against the allies appeared in the press and on television. Especially fierce attacks appeared in such major newspapers and magazines of the ČSSR as *Mladá fronta, Literární listy, Student, Smena,* and *Svobodné slovo.* In June, one of the issues of the provincial newspaper in central Slovakia, *Smer,* featured a long article about the supposedly disgraceful behavior of Soviet servicemen during the Šumava exercises, having depicted them as drunks, marauders, and rapists. Underneath the article in small print a brief message was published saying that a check over the article had established that the facts were not corroborated. This underhanded approach—first to commit slander and smear with dirt, and then, as if by chance, to mention in passing that nothing of the sort ever occurred—was widely employed at that time in the Czechoslovak mass media.

On 1 July 1968 the command-staff exercises concluded. On the following day an assessment took place. Those taking part included the commanders of the Joint Armed Forces of the Warsaw Pact member states, the party and state leaders of Czechoslovakia—L. Svoboda, A. Dubček, O. Černík, J. Smrkovský, and the Minister of National Defense Col.-General M. Dzúr—and the military attachés of the socialist countries. The assessment of the exercises was conducted by Marshal of the Soviet Union I. I. Yakubovskii.

The Soviet and foreign press widely covered the exercises. In addition to the objective coverage of the exercises, attempts were made in the foreign press to depict these measures, which were carried out within the framework of treaty obligations, as some sort of "instrument" with which the USSR was trying to "impose its own strategic concepts on its allies." For the sake of objectivity, one must acknowledge that during the exercises a number of matters connected with the introduction of allied troops onto the territory of Czechoslovakia were settled.

On 12 July the newspaper *Krasnaya zvezda* published a lead article entitled "Invincible Combat Commonwealth," which summed up the results of the command-staff exercises of the armies of the socialist countries. It noted, in particular, that the command-staff exercises aimed "to work out matters of mutual assistance between the allied troops and their command-and-control while conducting modern operations, to raise still higher the combat readiness of the troops and staffs, and to further strengthen the friendship of the fraternal peoples and armies." True, the article did not mention certain things.

Although the tasks set for the exercises were in fact achieved, the allied troops still had not received orders from the command of the Joint Armed Forces to leave Czechoslovakia and return to their permanent bases. The reason for this was that negotiations were due to take place at Čierna nad Tisou in the very near future between the leaders of the CPSU and the CPCz.[15] The timeframe for the withdrawal of the troops of the Warsaw Pact member states depended on the outcome of these negotiations. It was not by chance that during the assessment of the exercises, Marshal of the Soviet Union I. I. Yakubovskii emphasized that although the exercises formally were over, the participants in the maneuvers would not be leaving the territory of the ČSSR. One cannot exclude the possibility, he said, that our military presence will continue here for quite a long time.

Events, however, developed in a way contrary to the scenario devised "at the top." A correspondent from one of the central Soviet newspapers who was covering the exercises in the ČSSR

[14] The text reads "28 July," but the context suggests that it should be "28 June."

[15] The reference to the upcoming Čierna negotiations is not consistent with the rest of the paragraph; the announcement that talks would be held at Čierna did not come until July 22.

prematurely relayed a feature about the conclusion of the exercises. This information prompted the Czechoslovak side to lodge a protest about the continued presence of the allied troops in their country and to demand the withdrawal of the units and formations as quickly as possible.

On 22 July a group of the highest-ranking officers of the CzPA, headed by the chief of the Main Directorate of the Ground Forces, Lieut.-General E. Blahut, came to the headquarters of our army. In the name of the ČSSR minister of national defense, they approached us with questions: Why, despite the promise made by Marshal I. I. Yakubovskii to pull out all Soviet troops by 21 July, were they still deployed in the area of the exercises? Why were we delaying, and what were our future plans? Having expressed their readiness to offer any sort of help to expedite the withdrawal of army troops, and even offering to create a special operative group for this purpose, the Czechoslovak comrades demanded, in the form of an ultimatum, immediate responses to the questions they raised. In a private conversation with me, Lieut.-General E. Blahut expressed bewilderment at our "prolonged and pointless presence" on their territory and said that "this situation does not serve the cause of our friendship and the strengthening of mutual relations."

We were left in a very difficult situation. This was precisely the time when the army commander, Lieut.-General A. M. Maiorov, was in Moscow, having flown there to see the defense minister of the USSR to get instructions on how to handle the pressure being exerted by the Czechoslovak government.

On 24 July the army commander returned, and I learned that we had permission to begin the withdrawal of troops. We promptly informed representatives of the CzPA about this. At the same time, in accordance with the instructions we received, we let the Czechoslovak comrades know that a large number of our vehicles were in poor technical shape after having traveled so many kilometers, and this could not help but take its toll on the rate of our movement back home.

On the way back to the motherland, our servicemen took part in meetings with Czechoslovak workers and soldiers from the CzPA.

Our personnel had already spent more than two months in field conditions. Physical and psychological fatigue was palpable. Those who were especially impatient to return home were the ordinary residents of the Transcarpathian region who had been called up from reserves for the exercises. Their hard work was needed at home for the harvest which was already in full swing.[16]

On 1 August we finally learned on our way back that the meeting of the leaders of the communist parties of the USSR and the ČSSR at Čierna nad Tisou had ended. The participants had suggested holding a conference in Bratislava as soon as possible among officials from all the socialist countries. This provided a basis for a certain degree of optimism.

Soon after we laid flowers and a wreath on the graves of soldiers who had perished during the Great Patriotic War and were buried in the Dargov cemetery near the city of Košice, we crossed the state border into the Uzhgorod region and within several hours were back at our garrisons.

[16] The point raised here illustrates the domestic costs that the Soviet Union experienced from such a large-scale mobilization in 1968. Civilians and regular soldiers who ordinarily would have been helping out with the harvest were instead diverted to combat duty, with predictable adverse consequences for Soviet agriculture.

DOCUMENT No. 49: Letter from Leonid Brezhnev to Alexander Dubček Inviting a CPCz Delegation to the Warsaw Meeting, July 6, 1968

Source: ÚSD, Archiv UV KSČ, F. 01, Sv. 210, A.j. 131.

This letter is one of several Brezhnev sent Dubček on July 5, 6, and 7 inviting him to come to Warsaw for the meeting of communist party leaders. During a phone conversation on July 5, Dubček had asked his Soviet counterpart to confirm in writing what the venue and purpose of the meeting would be; this brief letter constitutes Brezhnev's response.

At a session of the CPCz CC Presidium on July 8, a substantial majority voted in support of Dubček's view that the CPCz should refrain from sending a delegation to the Warsaw Meeting and should instead continue to seek bilateral negotiations with each of the "fraternal" countries, including Romania and Yugoslavia as well as the "Five."

(See Document No. 50.)

---

6 July 1968

To the First Secretary of the CPCz CC
Comrade A. Dubček:

At the behest and urging of the Central Committees of the Bulgarian Communist Party, the Hungarian Socialist Workers' Party, the Socialist Unity Party of Germany, and the Polish United Workers' Party, we appeal to you with a proposal to attend a comradely meeting at the very highest level to discuss the situation that has emerged in the ČSSR.

As things look now, this meeting will be held either on Wednesday the 10th or on Thursday the 11th of July in Warsaw.

At the head of the delegations from the fraternal parties will be the highest-ranking officials. The precise composition of each delegation will be left to the respective CC to decide.

We hope that you will show full understanding for our proposal and that a delegation representing the CPCz will come to the conference of fraternal parties in Warsaw.

With communist regards

L. Brezhnev
General Secretary, CPSU CC

DOCUMENT No. 50: Top-Secret Telegram from Ambassador Stepan Chervonenko to Moscow Regarding the CPCz CC Presidium's Decision Not to Attend the Warsaw Meeting, July 9, 1968

Source: AVPRF, F. 059, Op. 58, P. 124, D. 571, Ll. 145–149.

Soviet Ambassador Stepan Chervonenko transmitted this highly classified cable to Moscow on July 9, a few days before the Warsaw Meeting was due to start. Chervonenko reports that the CPCz CC Presidium has declined invitations from the Soviet Union and other Warsaw Pact countries to attend a joint meeting in Warsaw, preferring instead to hold a series of bilateral consultations as a prelude to a full multilateral conference. The cable advises that the Presidium wants bilateral talks to be held with Romania and Yugoslavia as well as with the "Five," and that the series of bilateral meetings could be arranged, for the sake of convenience, during the upcoming Extraordinary 14th CPCz Congress, when other communist party leaders would be in Prague. Chervonenko's cable also describes, at some length, the strong concerns he had conveyed to Dubček on behalf of the Soviet and East European authorities.

MINISTRY OF FOREIGN AFFAIRS OF THE USSR

TOP SECRET
Copy No. 1

CIPHERED TELEGRAM

From Prague
10 July 68

EYES ONLY
SPECIAL CLASSIFICATION

Today, 9 July 68, I was invited to the CPCz CC where, at Cde. Dubček's instruction, Cde. Lenárt gave me a formal response to the proposal to convene a meeting in Warsaw of representatives from the fraternal parties.

The response is as follows:

"Based on a review of letters we have received from the fraternal countries proposing that a meeting be held to consider the situation in the ČSSR and the CPCz, the CPCz CC Presidium states:

In principle we agree to and would welcome holding meetings and negotiations with separate communist parties at the level of the Presidium or in some other acceptable format, because at present we are not ready for a joint meeting of the six communist parties that may occur on Thursday, 11 July 1968.

The CPCz CC Presidium recommends that a meeting of the six communist parties not be held at this time to consider the current situation in Czechoslovakia and the CPCz, and proposes instead that bilateral negotiations be held with representatives of the fraternal parties, so that we can mutually inform one another about the situation in our countries and parties.

In taking this position, the Presidium is upholding the generally recognized principles of socialist construction, which hold that the close alliance and cooperation of our parties is a precondition for the successful development of individual countries, while also respecting the specific features and sovereignty of every party on questions of its internal policy. For our part, we will present complete information about the situation in our country and the CPCz and about the measures we are taking. To this end, the Presidium believes it would be appropriate and beneficial if the same sort of bilateral negotiations were held with representatives of the Communist Party of Romania and the League of Communists of Yugoslavia.

The Presidium further recommends that additional joint consultations with delegations from these parties might occur during the upcoming session of the CPCz's 14th Extraordinary Congress.

The CPCz CC Presidium has adopted a decision that a response to the letters from the presidiums of the central committees of the fraternal parties should be sent to them in written form."

For my part, having listened to this response, I expressed regret that the CPCz CC Presidium—and Cde. Dubček personally—had not gone along with the attempt of the CPSU and other fraternal parties to provide assistance to the CPCz leadership during this complex phase of its struggle.

The refusal of the CPCz leadership to meet representatives of the fraternal parties in order to exchange opinions on problems that have emerged will not be understood by Soviet communists or, obviously, other parties.

I added that from their response it was not apparent that they even had a sincere desire to meet the CPSU or any other party, because if they *were* sincere they would have proposed a specific time and venue for such meetings.

I said that with this step the CPCz leadership, and above all Cde. Dubček, are bringing their relations with the CPSU into a new phase. I stressed to my interpreter that he must convey to Cde. Dubček how alarmed the leaders of the CPSU and the other parties now are so that he will fully comprehend this, and I said that the problem was not only the internal situation in Czechoslovakia, but also whether the CPCz under his leadership would remain an internationalist component of the socialist camp and the world communist movement, or whether nationalist tendencies were becoming dominant under the guise of "specific features," "unique circumstances," etc.

The Soviet leadership has often said to the Czechoslovak comrades that Czechoslovakia's deviation from the agreed course of the countries of the socialist commonwealth will spur on the forces of counterrevolution, and that this will result in the destruction of the existing disposition of forces in Europe and could heighten international tension. At present, the working class and people of Czechoslovakia are being deluded; they are being swayed by grand promises and by the blessings they will supposedly receive from the new model of "Czechoslovak democratic socialism." But what will ordinary people say if Šik's theory is implemented and once again hundreds of thousands of simple people are left unemployed, as has been the unfortunate byproduct of Yugoslavia's path to socialism?[17] The people, regrettably, will only later grasp the full extent of the mistakes being committed by the comrades from the CPCz leadership, who are deflecting the good intentions of the CPSU and the other parties.

From the conversation one could see that Cde. Lenárt, undoubtedly, does not support either the decision of the CPCz CC Presidium or the response that was just made to Cde. Brezhnev's letter.[18] He said that stormy discussions within the Presidium are continuing, and that some of the speeches were so extreme that Cde. Dubček had to respond that he, as first secretary, would not permit such unfounded accusations to be made about the fraternal CPSU and the other parties, and that the proposal for a meeting, and also the letters from the CPSU and the other parties regarding continuing events in the ČSSR, stemmed from the best of motivations, reflecting

---

[17] The reference here is to Deputy Prime Minister Ota Šik. As the director of the Institute of Economics in Prague, Šik was one of the leading reform-minded economists during the Prague Spring. Early in his career he had been an orthodox Marxist economist, but he gradually evolved into one of the most ardent proponents of both economic and political liberalization. His ideas about economic reform prefigured the sorts of changes that Mikhail Gorbachev tried to carry out in the Soviet Union 20 years later.

[18] Here Ambassador Chervonenko appears to be highlighting Lenárt as one of the hardline Presidium officials who could contribute to the restoration of an orthodox communist regime once the reformers were ousted.

anxiety and fraternal concern about the CPCz, Czechoslovakia, etc. Even if one or more of these letters is formulated more sharply than is warranted, that's not the point. We must explain to the comrades how we view the situation and we must persuade our opponents if we can find sufficient arguments for this purpose, and so forth. . . .

9. VII. 68

Del.10.DII.

S. Chervonenko

DOCUMENT No. 51: Message from Alexander Dubček and Oldřich Černík to Leonid Brezhnev, July 14, 1968

Source: ÚSD, Sb. KV, K—Archiv MZV, Dispatches Sent, No. 2667/1968.

This message to Brezhnev expresses the consternation of CPCz officials on learning that the Soviet Union, Poland, Hungary, Bulgaria, and East Germany have sent delegations to Warsaw for a joint meeting without informing the authorities in Prague. The decision to go ahead with the multilateral conference, Dubček and Černík argue in their letter, would provoke "a new protest wave" of unrest and spur on the very forces that had given rise to such alarm in Moscow. Their communiqué was received by Brezhnev after the multilateral meeting had ended with the drafting of the "Warsaw Letter."

Hand to Brezhnev immediately.

The CPCz CC Presidium has received letters from the fraternal parties referring to efforts by the fraternal parties to state their position on the situation in the CPCz and the ČSSR. The CPCz CC Presidium was asked to take part in a conference of six parties to assess the situation in the ČSSR. The CPCz CC Presidium discussed the content of the letters at two meetings and unanimously decided that because the assessments of the situation in the ČSSR by the Communist Party of Czechoslovakia, on the one hand, and the individual fraternal parties, on the other, are so divergent, it would be useful to hold bilateral negotiations in the ČSSR prior to the joint conference. The CPCz CC first secretary, Cde. Dubček, having been entrusted by the CPCz CC Presidium, asked you, Cde. Brezhnev, for a meeting between the CPSU and the CPCz at the earliest possible time. He suggested two dates—Sunday, 14 July, and Wednesday, 17 July—or any other day convenient for you. We fail to understand why it has not been possible for you to comply with our request. On Thursday, 11 July, the CPCz CC Presidium received another letter signed by the five parties which again summons the CPCz CC Presidium to a joint meeting. The CPCz CC Presidium met on Friday and again had a long discussion about the content of the letter. After a very long debate and in light of the complicated situation in the CPCz and the ČSSR, the Presidium unanimously decided to send a letter to the fraternal parties in which we will again ask them to understand that at the present time we feel it would be useful to hold bilateral meetings prior to a joint conference. The CPCz CC Presidium was motivated by the desire to have a better opportunity to explain to each side the CPCz's position based on the resolution of the CPCz CC plenum in May, and also to agree on the procedure, content, and venue of a joint meeting. The letter was dispatched to the fraternal parties on Saturday, 13 July.

We regret to say that the deliberations of the CPCz CC Presidium on Friday, 12 July, were pointless. On Saturday, 13 July, we were informed by a ČTK report that the delegations of the fraternal parties were already assembling for a joint meeting. Referring to earlier letters, we can expect that the meeting will assess the situation in the CPCz and in the ČSSR without the participation of representatives of our party. We cannot understand why the view of our party is not being heard and why the party is facing a *fait accompli* through a decision by several other parties. Our party was never informed of the date of the meeting. We cannot understand why a summit meeting has been convened for Sunday in such haste. We fear the serious consequences of such a procedure. The CPCz CC Presidium and our entire party are working in an extremely complicated situation. Now, before the 14th CPCz Congress, we have to weigh every step most carefully. We expected a sensitive approach from the fraternal parties. It is to be expected that we will have to face a new protest wave that will strengthen both right-wing and sectarian forces in our country. In the interest of the future advance of socialism in our country and in the interest of international relations, we call on you, comrades, to refrain from steps that could worsen the situation in the ČSSR and relations between our fraternal parties. We would ask you to inform the other delegations at the meeting about the content of this letter.

Dubček, Černík

DOCUMENT No. 52: Transcript of the Warsaw Meeting, July 14–15, 1968 (Excerpts)

Source: "Protokol ze spotkania przywodcow partii i rzadow krajow socjalistycznych: Bulgarii, NRD, Polski, Wegier, i ZSRR," Archiwum Akt Nowych, Arch. KC PZPR, P. 193, T. 24, Dok. 4; Vondrová & Navrátil, vol. 1, pp. 269–297.

The Warsaw Meeting convened in a large hall in the Polish Council of Ministers building on the morning of July 14, 1968, and adjourned mid-afternoon the following day. The conference consisted of six formal sessions, many informal discussions, and an effort by a drafting committee to complete a joint communiqué and joint letter from the "Five" to the CPCz Central Committee. The six formal sessions were chaired on a rotating basis by one of the five delegation leaders. Brezhnev spoke last, allowing him to sort out any disagreements and establish the meeting's conclusions.

Of the speeches by the communist bloc leaders, János Kádár's reflects the most dramatic change in perspective on the Czechoslovak crisis. Unlike earlier meetings in Dresden and Moscow, the Hungarian leader made no attempt to defend Dubček and other reformist CPCz officials. Although Kádár stated at Warsaw that he did not believe the whole Prague Spring "can be uniformly regarded as counterrevolutionary," he conceded that "the situation in Czechoslovakia is steadily deteriorating" and "is now much more dangerous than in the past." Echoing what later became known as the Brezhnev Doctrine, Kádár emphasized that it was "both the right and the duty of the socialist countries to decide collectively" what to do about Czechoslovakia. Kádár also announced that Hungary was "prepared to take part in all joint actions" to resolve the crisis, a reference to military intervention.

Brezhnev used his keynote speech, which set forth conclusions for the whole meeting, to underscore the Soviet Politburo's growing dismay at the situation in Czechoslovakia. His remarks reflect no hopes of finding a solution with the existing CPCz leadership; instead he urged that the Five "continue the search for healthy forces in the party and to look for ways of appealing to the forces in the party that might take the lead in initiating a struggle to restore the leading role of the CPCz and normalize the situation in the country."

(See Document No. 53.)

SECRET
Copy No. 5

Protocol[19]

of the Meeting of the Heads of Parties and Governments of the Socialist Countries: Bulgaria, the GDR, Poland, Hungary, and the USSR

Warsaw, 14–15 July 1968

---

[19] Until very recently, all transcripts of the Warsaw Meeting were sealed from public access. A 91-page Soviet transcript is stored in the Russian Presidential Archive in Moscow but that version has still not been released, despite numerous requests. This 52-page Polish transcript was recently discovered in the Archiwum Akt Nowych (Modern Records Archive) in Warsaw, and is now freely available to researchers. Only six copies of the Polish document were produced, of which this is No. 5. For other accounts of the meeting see Brezhnev's speech to the Central Committee (Document No. 56) and János Kádár's recollections (Document No. 105). See also Kádár's detailed briefing on the Warsaw Meeting to the July 15, 1968 session of the HSWP CC Politburo, entitled "The Warsaw Meeting of 15 July 1968," which has become available at the Hungarian National Archive in Budapest (PTTI, 288, F. 5/462 oe); and Erwin Weit, *Eyewitness: The Autobiography of Gomułka's Interpreter*, trans. by Mary Schofield (London: André Deutsch, 1973).

Participants as listed in the communiqué.[20]
The meeting was held in the Council of Ministers building.

First Session—14.VII. 10:30 A.M.–11:30 A.M.

Cde. W. Gomułka presiding.

Cde. Gomułka: I extend heartfelt greetings to all the fraternal party leaders and heads of government of the socialist countries gathered here. We are meeting to exchange views and reach a common position on matters of the utmost importance for each of our countries and for the whole socialist commonwealth. We will consider the situation in Czechoslovakia and draw appropriate conclusions. The Czechoslovak leadership did not accept our invitations and has refused to attend the meeting.

I suggest we arrange the order of our proceedings. There are two items I would recommend placing on the agenda:

1) an assessment of the situation in Czechoslovakia;
2) conclusions and decisions.

It would be advisable to establish a uniform procedure for our deliberations. I recommend that our sessions last up to two hours. After each there will be a break of 20 minutes. Each session will be led by one of the delegations. I would recommend going in alphabetical order, using the Latin alphabet. Does anyone have any other suggestions?

Cde. Brezhnev: I think the agenda should only have one debate: "On the situation in Czechoslovakia." This debate would link the key questions, both the assessment and the conclusions and decisions.

Cde. Gomułka: That suggestion seems acceptable to me. I recommended two debates because I reckoned the delegations would first speak about the situation, and then others would have their turn and formulate the conclusions. I think, however, that we can all go along with Comrade Brezhnev's suggestion.

Cde. Brezhnev: It'll be better if each delegation formulates its conclusions and sets forth its propositions in its main presentation. Naturally this doesn't mean we can't proceed differently if there are other suggestions.

Cde. Gomułka: Are there any other suggestions? Apparently not. That means we'll go with the one debate, "On the situation in Czechoslovakia."

There has been no specific duration set for the meeting. It will depend on what we need. Perhaps the meeting can be finished today. If necessary it can continue until tomorrow. There's no need to decide now.

Comrades, let me, in the name of the Polish delegation, offer our point of view.

This is the third time we have met to consider the questions of interest to us today. The first time was at the meeting in Dresden, along with the Czech comrades.[21] The second time was at

---

[20] The Soviet Union was represented by Brezhnev, Podgorny, Kosygin, Shelest, and Konstantin Katushev, the CPSU CC secretary responsible for intra-bloc relations. The Polish delegation included Gomułka; the state president, Marian Spychalski; the prime minister, Jozef Cyrankiewicz; and a PUWP CC secretary and top aide to Gomułka, Zenon Kliszko. The Hungarian delegation consisted only of Kádár and Prime Minister Jenő Fock. The East German participants included Ulbricht; the GDR prime minister, Willi Stoph; and a senior SED Politburo member, Hermann Axen. (Another senior SED Politburo member, Erich Honecker, also was supposed to have taken part, but did not end up attending.) Participants from Bulgaria included Todor Zhivkov and three other senior members of the BCP Politburo: Boris Velchev, Stanko Todorov, and Pencho Kubadinski.
[21] See Document No. 14.

the discussions over the problem in Moscow, without the comrades from Czechoslovakia.[22] And finally we are gathered here for the third time, having invited the Czech comrades to take part only to find that they rejected the invitation and said in response that they would recommend bilateral meetings. At Dresden our assessment of events in Czechoslovakia was one and the same. Together we stated then that the events in that country are of an anti-socialist and even counterrevolutionary nature. Not all the Czech comrades accepted that position, although they acknowledged that certain things had been occurring over which they had no control. . . . There were no major differences of view, although the Czech comrades rejected the notion that the underlying process was counterrevolutionary. They wanted to disavow this assessment. At the meeting in Moscow there were divergent viewpoints, and our position was not so unified.

. . . What is the current situation in Czechoslovakia? What is the nature of events there? We believe that the country is being peacefully transformed from a socialist state into a bourgeois republic. At the current stage the process is still in its initial phase. Our second basic point might be put as follows: In Czechoslovakia a process is under way whereby the CPCz is abandoning the precepts of Marxism–Leninism and is being transformed into a social democratic party. This process is already far advanced, and its main stage will occur with the Extraordinary CPCz Congress scheduled for September. Fundamental changes in the nature and complexion of the party will be a prerequiste for the transformation of the country into a bourgeois republic. Without such changes, the transformation of the country would be impossible.

Our conclusion is that novel events are under way, with no parallel in the whole history of the socialist countries. No parallel at any rate in terms of scale. A new process has begun—a process of peaceful transition from socialism to neocapitalism. Until recently this problem hadn't even been conceived. As a result there had repeatedly been superficial approaches to the very concept of the process of counterrevolution. The whole essence of our understanding of the danger of counterrevolution was inappropriate. Today we are not talking about a return to capitalism in the classical sense, that is, in the way we understood it during the interwar period. To look at the problem in this way only would lead us down the wrong track. . . .

. . . It would be difficult to maintain that in Czechoslovakia today the same methods could be used as were used in Hungary in 1956. The Hungarian events in the fall of 1956 were of the classical counterrevolutionary type—armed counterrevolution. When speaking about the process of counterrevolution, many people operate on the basis of old assumptions; they think that the process will develop in the same way as in the past. Those who still rely on these old assumptions will not grasp our assertion that today the process is different. The means used now are different, and so are the methods of using them. The methods are aimed at the longer term. The sort of counterrevolutions we had in the past won't occur today; they will transpire differently. This is a process that might last many years. . . .

In the socialist countries class antagonisms have been suppressed. That applies to Czechoslovakia, too. There are no social classes right now capable of restoring the old order. However, reactionary forces are present. There is a social basis for counterrevolution. This is particularly true among the intellectuals and the whole mentality of broad social circles. . . .

. . . I think that a dominant majority of the leadership of the Czech party have become captives to revisionism. And it is always the case that when a government is taken over by revisionists, they first of all do away with all their ideological enemies. . . .

. . . We must frankly say that what is going on in Czechoslovakia could have grave consequences. The whole system of socialism is in danger of being weakened. Today if you take account of matters not from the standpoint of one country, but from the standpoint of the whole world, a single fundamental question still looms: Who will win out over whom?[23] We are living

[22] See Document No. 31.

[23] In Polish (and Russian) this is *"kto kogo,"* the phrase coined by Vladimir Lenin in the early days of the bolshevik party. The phrase amounts to a stark zero-sum conception of politics.

through very difficult times, when the international workers' movement has been beset by various negative and centrifugal tendencies: revisionism, nationalism, and even strands of anarchism. We can be a real force in the world only if there is unity among us. We must remember that those of us gathered here bear a special responsibility. Our countries are the fist of the socialist system. We provide an example of socialism to the world. It is we who provide that example—and not China, Korea, Cuba, or Vietnam. We are the showpiece of socialism, and the working masses of the entire world look up to us. The greater our strength, the greater our unity. ... We Poles are well aware that our borders can be safeguarded effectively only if the countries of the socialist commonwealth maintain a united stance. And this by no means applies just to our own borders; every attack on these borders is an attack on the whole of international socialism.

We therefore attentively and vigilantly watch for every possible attempt by the enemies of socialism to disrupt our unity. Such efforts are concentrated now in Prague, where we witness a variety of contacts and talks with representatives of the FRG—official, unofficial, and semi-official. . . .

All of the CPCz leadership's corrections and contradictions, and all these assertions, are not carried out in reality. We cannot take them seriously. We, after all, know what must be done. Recently we had the instructive example of the Yugoslavs. When we had a bit of trouble in March with student rioting, the Yugoslav press wrote incredible stories about it. We therefore called to the attention of their diplomatic representatives that the press was spreading false information about the events in our country. They replied to us that there is freedom of speech in their country, and that the press can write what it wants. However, when in Yugoslavia itself student groups took to the streets, the authorities immediately managed to deal with the press, which turned out to want to do what it was told.

It was not my intention to portray the situation in Czechoslovakia solely in a grave light. But I think we ought to look at the situation objectively and see things the way they really are. I say this because our conclusions will be appropriate only if our analysis is accurate. It is on this basis that we have sincerely and frankly presented our point of view.

* * *

Second Session—14.VII. 12:00 P.M.–2:30 P.M.

Cde. Kádár presiding.

Cde. Kádár: First of all I would like to express my satisfaction that our meeting has been convened. The problem on the agenda of our meeting affects the interests of all our countries, and therefore it is good that we are able to consider it jointly again.

To begin with some brief information. On Friday we held a Political Bureau session, at which the members were informed about the current situation in Czechoslovakia and about the proposal to convene our meeting. Among other things, we informed the Politburo that on that very same day another invitation had been extended to the Czechoslovak comrades to come to the meeting, and that the meeting would take place irrespective of whether the Czechoslovak comrades ultimately refused to attend. The session of the Political Bureau was prolonged, and the central question considered by the members was whether to hold a meeting with the Czechoslovak comrades.

After the meeting of the Political Bureau, at around 10:00 P.M., we received information from Prague that Dubček and Černík were requesting a confidential meeting with me on Hungarian territory. I was informed that they had simultaneously made a request for a meeting with Cde. Brezhnev.

We assumed that the Czechoslovak comrades wanted to communicate something to us about the proposed conference. That's why we agreed to hold the meeting with them. However, because it was late, we decided to wait until morning. We wanted to consult with the Soviet comrades. Because we didn't know who would be coming to Poland, we spoke to Cde. Suslov. Then we gave a further response to the Czechoslovaks. Cde. Fock and I met them at 5:00 P.M. on Hungarian territory. Our meeting lasted from 5:00 P.M. until 9:00 P.M.[24] I would like briefly to convey to our comrades the essence of our discussions. The first to speak was Dubček. He informed us about the situation in Czechoslovakia and about the latest developments. He spoke in great detail about the "Two Thousand Words" statement and about their response to the statement. Dubček said they wanted first to give a political response to that statement, but by its phrasing the statement does not have such visible results. The next topic of our discussion was the question of the meeting of our parties. Dubček spoke in detail about the motivations behind their response to our invitation. He explained why they proposed bilateral meetings. He said they were particularly eager to meet the CPSU. He also explained that the purpose of these meetings would be to discuss separately with each party the letters they'd received. We had the impression that the Czechoslovak comrades did not agree with the main themes of our letters. As Dubček listened I told him that the decision of the CPCz CC Presidium to refuse to participate in our session is a grave mistake. I said that this decision has created an entirely new situation. I reminded him that when a meeting of the five parties in Moscow took place, he had complained about being excluded from a meeting that discussed the situation in Czechoslovakia. I reminded them of Dubček's statement back then that he would have been ready to take part at any time, even at night, if only he had received an invitation. Well, now they had an invitation, I said, and yet the CPCz CC Presidium had responded by refusing to take part and had proposed holding only bilateral negotiations.

Cde. Dubček said that on the way to Hungary they had heard on a radio broadcast that Cde. Brezhnev had arrived in Warsaw. He said they hadn't realized the meeting would be convened so quickly. On Friday they discussed the joint letter from the five parties and prepared a response. Dubček had brought the response with him, and he handed it to me. Dubček said they had expressed their agreement to hold a collective meeting. The letter had explained, however, that they had turned down a joint meeting. We said that to him. I told him that the refusal to take part in our meeting was the greatest mistake they had made since the January plenum.

Our party, I stated, is troubled by the development of the situation in Czechoslovakia, and it is our duty and right to have a joint discussion with them about that situation. But they had avoided taking part in this discussion. I also told him that during the previous talks and discussions about the situation in Czechoslovakia there were certain differences of opinion. However, none of our parties disagreed in their assessment of the situation. In such circumstances it is the duty of communists to meet and discuss the situation jointly.

Toward the end of the conversation, when dealing with the international aspect of the question, I asked them a question: Where and with whom do they want to proceed?

My own impression is that neither Dubček nor Černík understands the full gravity of the situation. Perhaps they are in a stupor. Not until our joint conversation did they gradually begin to ask themselves about the gravity of the situation and take account of it. This is particularly true of Dubček, who was simply unable even to speak. Both of them cried. They began to ask what might be done now.

Cde. Brezhnev: They cry all the time.

Cde. Kádár: Dubček asked: what is to be done now that all the doors are being shut in our faces? They realized that we had not waited for their response and had decided to meet without them.

---

[24] Jenő Fock was the Hungarian prime minister at the time. Károly Erdélyi, a deputy foreign minister, was also present at the talks. For further details, see Kádár's report to the HSWP Politburo, entitled "Comrade Kádár's and Comrade Fock's Meeting with Comrade Dubček and Comrade Černík," July 15, 1968 (Top Secret), in PTTI, 288, F. 5/462 oe.

That was the essence of our conversation. We told them that their response to our letter was inappropriate, and that the situation in Czechoslovakia has caused us deep alarm. And with that we parted.

Cde. Erdélyi accompanied them to the Czechoslovak border. They said that when they returned to Prague they would convene the CC Presidium and discuss the situation that had arisen. That was about 9:00 P.M.

The Czechoslovak comrades explained that they would like to meet each of our parties bilaterally in the near term and then meet with all of them at once. We discussed this matter with them at some length. We said that the proposal to hold bilateral meetings amounted to a refusal to take part in a collective meeting. As for their proposal to hold a bilateral meeting, we didn't reply. We said that on Tuesday we would discuss this matter in the Political Bureau and then give them a response. That was, in a nutshell, the essence of our meeting.

If you have any additional questions on this matter, I will answer them. One fundamental point emerges from all this. They received our invitation but turned it down. . . .

Now I would like to touch upon the matter of the situation in Czechoslovakia. Our Political Bureau has discussed this question many times. During the meeting with Dubček I told him that holding discussions about the situation in Czechoslovakia is our right and our duty, and it is one of the most complicated problems we face. We have analyzed the problem many times, and have considered the matter jointly with the other parties and come to appropriate conclusions.

Comrade Gomułka recalled that during the session in Moscow there were certain differences of viewpoint. That was indeed the case. During our conversations about this with the Polish comrades in Budapest, we tried to state our different views precisely. We are troubled by the same issue. Namely, how to provide assistance so that events will develop not in a negative direction, but in a positive direction. We presented our position on this during the conferences in Dresden and Moscow.

We believe that in Czechoslovakia we are dealing with a very complicated process, a process in which anti-socialist and counterrevolutionary forces are present. We see this danger in the same way that Cde. Gomułka depicted it. Only our views of this matter differ somewhat.

If you consider the matter from the standpoint of the existing situation, the basic question is whether you would call what is going on there a counterrevolution or whether it should be called something else. The crux of the matter is whether the entire process can be uniformly regarded as counterrevolutionary. . . . In my view the whole process has dangerous tendencies within it. I would not say, however, that the party there is being transformed into a social-democratic party. I would say that in Czechoslovakia forces that might be regarded as revisionist forces have a vast amount of influence. In our view events are now developing in such a way that the political system is beginning to resemble the Yugoslav, and that at the next stage of development events mean the restoration of the bourgeois order. No doubt, the further development of the situation will be connected with the way the CPCz's Extraordinary Congress proceeds. There are no guarantees that the Congress will be conducted in the way it ought to be, that is, on the basis of a Marxist–Leninist solution to the problem. Most important of all is the situation in the CPCz Presidium . . . Our assessment is in line with your assessment that these events will be decisive for the future development of the situation. . . .

The situation in Czechoslovakia in our view is deteriorating. The danger is greater than in the past. It is unfolding in stages. The first stage is a transition to a Yugoslav-type system, which in those circumstances poses the danger of counterrevolution. The question for us to decide is how to help the communists of Czechoslovakia. We must determine who it is we should be helping, and how we should do that. Whom should we support and how?

. . . The Czechoslovak comrades have often told us that if the situation were in fact to become dangerous, they would then be able to resort to the use of appropriate forces—the Workers' Militia and the party organizations. Dubček has said that they have the ability to mobilize forces that could restore order within 24 hours. The situation is dangerous, even very dangerous, and yet we don't see that the CPCz has mobilized its forces. . . .

In reaching a decision we must remember the Hungarian events of 1956. We must recall the experiences of that period. The problem we are discussing, the struggle over the changing situation in Czechoslovakia, is of an international character, since that struggle has also come under scrutiny at the international level. During the struggle over Hungary in 1956 all the fraternal communist parties took part in lending us support. The question is to find what support we can provide now.

The situation in Czechoslovakia is steadily deteriorating. It is much more alarming than it was during our meetings in Dresden and in Moscow. Back then we expressed the wish that in Czechoslovakia itself forces would emerge that would be able to turn the situation around. Now this task is more urgent than ever. It is urgent to find Marxist–Leninist forces in Czechoslovakia, to whom we ought to provide full support.

Cde. Ulbricht: Our Political Bureau supported the idea of calling today's meeting. We had assumed that the CPCz CC Presidium would send its own representatives. We had hoped so because we observe that the situation in Czechoslovakia has given rise to new, negative elements. It therefore was appropriate and justifiable for us to want an exchange of views with them. However, the CPCz CC Presidium refused to take part in our meeting today and proposed bilateral meetings. . . . With the publication of the reactionary "Two Thousand Words" Manifesto, the leadership of the Czechoslovak party is not in a position to find a solution on its own. The only way is to find a solution jointly.

Cde. Kádár recounted his discussions with Dubček, which he called different things. They want to wait for a general disruption. Dubček does not grasp the situation. I am amazed by the analysis that Cde. Kádár gave. Do you not see, Cde. Kádár, that the question is not only about Czechoslovakia. Cde. Kádár said that we are dealing with revisionist forces there. I can't agree with that. The question is about counterrevolutionary forces. The "Two Thousand Words" Manifesto expresses their goal: to destroy the party's power. If the "Two Thousand Words" Manifesto is not counterrevolutionary, then certainly there is not a counterrevolution. The reality of the situation in Czechoslovakia indicates that there is a counterrevolutionary underground.[25] There is a gradual shift toward bringing this underground counterrevolution to the surface. . . .

The Czechs' plans for counterrevolution are obvious. There can be no further doubt about this matter. The counterrevolutionaries want to prepare the party congress in such a way that they can crush and eliminate the Marxist–Leninists. The "Two Thousand Words" is unambiguously counterrevolutionary. Their next move will be multi-party elections and they will try to get rid of the party, and then want to change the constitution.

I don't know, Comrade Kádár, why you can't grasp all this. Don't you realize that the next blow from imperialism will take place in Hungary? We can already detect that imperialist centers are concentrating their work now on the Hungarian intelligentsia.

In my view, Cde. Gomułka gave a principled and accurate assessment of the situation in Czechoslovakia. The interference by imperialism in Czechoslovakia is being carried out within the framework of a long-term global strategy, a strategy spanning at least ten years. . . .

The "Two Thousand Words" Manifesto was published within ten days of a report by the well-known American sovietologist Brzezinski, who was in Prague and delivered a public lecture.[26] Many people attended, and there was a discussion. No one there contested Brzezinski's

[25] This was the theme of KGB reports during the crisis; see, for example, Documents Nos. 20 and 130.

[26] Ulbricht's references to Zbigniew Brzezinski, both here and elsewhere in his remarks, were intended, in part, to please Gomułka, who detested Brzezinski and was always trying to depict him in a sinister light. Ulbricht's chronology is slightly askew. Brzezinski delivered his lecture on June 14, some 13 days before the appearance of the "Two Thousand Words." The lecture, which supported the CPCz's notion of "improving socialism," sparked angry commentaries in the Soviet, East German, and Polish media.

thesis. Not a single person there expressed opposition. Nor did Dubček express opposition. On the contrary, only one person had just a few doubts. Nynert was also in Prague, and he, too, delivered a lecture. And the response was the same.

I have a question for Cde. Kádár. What is going on here? Is it not a counterrevolution if an American anti-communist can speak publicly in Prague and purvey slanders about People's Poland before the members of the party, saying that this is a fascist country? And it was not only People's Poland that he attacked; he also attacked the Soviet Union. . . . We are dealing with organized activities by Bonn and Washington; that is what we must all understand. Can we see all this as merely a trivial matter? Is it a trivial matter if they are negotiating with West German associations of compatriots in Prague? Is it a trivial matter if the negotiations on this subject involve the return of 100,000 Sudeten Germans? For us this is not an insignificant matter, since we know that those lands were once settled by Henlein.[27] Today Henlein is dead, but they are discussing that same matter with his successors. . . .

. . . An idea has been floated to create a trilateral alliance among Czechoslovakia, Romania, and Yugoslavia. This is an old idea, which was first conceived during the time of Masaryk, who wanted to set up the so-called Little Entente consisting of those three countries. Back then this concept was aimed at establishing the "special authority" of Czechoslovakia in the framework of this alliance. Today the concept is intended to separate socialist Czechoslovakia from the Soviet Union and the whole commonwealth of socialist countries. Ceauşescu and Tito support it and have even given their official backing.[28]

. . . The fundamental question that must be answered is as follows: What are the deeper reasons for and sources of the events unfolding? The answer to this question is connected with the full array of complicated and difficult problems inherent in the stages of transition from capitalism to socialism. Each country is burdened by circumstances inherited from capitalism. The same applies to traditions; marked irregularities crop up during the economic development of individual countries. Similarly, the ideological level in the socialist countries is not uniform. . . .

I come to practical conclusions. I believe we ought to send a joint open letter to the CPCz CC, to the parliament, and to the Czech working class and intelligentsia. This letter should draw a connection between the internal developments in Czechoslovakia and the general developments in the international arena. It also should provide an assessment of the activities of counterrevolutionary groups and show how they are being controlled from outside. We must also show the way out of the existing situation. This would be the first step. The next step would be jointly to travel and present both our assessment and our conclusions. We will see whether they have the courage to eliminate the counterrevolutionary and reactionary elements. This absolutely must include the elimination of hostile elements from the mass media. That is the absolute minimum of what must be done. We also should consider how to deal with Slovakia, if there is a demand to hold maneuvers there. The need for any appropriate steps, the proper system of control, and so forth. These are our suggestions.

Cde. Zhivkov: The representatives of our Central Committee and Political Bureau of our party share the view of the situation in Czechoslovakia presented by Cde. Gomułka and Cde. Ulbricht. Unfortunately we cannot agree with the view offered by Cde. Kádár, nor with his conclusions. We want to depict things accurately by calling a spade a spade. That is how we see the question.

---

[27] Ulbricht's reference is to Konrad Henlein, the founder of the *Sudetendeutsche Heimatfront* (renamed the *Sudetendeutsche Partei* in 1935), a vehemently pro-Nazi grouping of ethnic Germans in the Sudetenland. Henlein's party received financial support from Nazi Germany and became the main champion of German irredentism in Czechoslovakia. For background on the origins and activities of the group, see J. W. Brügel, *Tschechen und Deutsche, 1918–1938* (Munich: Nymphenburg Verlag, 1974).

[28] Kádár brought up this issue during the meeting with Dubček and Černík on July 13; see his report (cited above) in PTTI, 288, F. 5/462 oe.

The current situation in Czechoslovakia is conducive to the stepped-up activity of foreign and internal counterrevolutionary centers and also to the activity of revisionists. Progressive forces are being terrorized. In Czechoslovakia one can observe a broad capitulation by all the healthy forces. The party is not a guiding force. The most active forces in the party are revisionists and counterrevolutionaries. The counterrevolutionary forces in Czechoslovakia are gaining strength day by day. All the counterrevolutionary centers controlled by the American and West German imperialists have been mobilized into action. We can't cite even a single fact that would suggest the healthy forces in the party have been mobilized for a struggle against the counterrevolution.

The question arises of what to do and how to counteract it.

Our parties are faced with a historic task and historic responsibility. The whole fate of socialism in Czechoslovakia is at stake. There is a very fierce conflict involving our whole commonwealth with the entire imperialist system. The imperialists have chosen to focus their efforts on Czechoslovakia, and it has become the main link in the struggle between the two systems.

We've already run out of all the possible actions that Cde. Kádár was speaking about. We've looked for different possible ways out of the situation that has arisen in Czechoslovakia. We've tried to rely on Dubček, but we haven't detected any progress. Right now neither Dubček nor Černík is deciding the situation in Czechoslovakia. Others are deciding it. . . .

There is only one appropriate way out—through resolute assistance to Czechoslovakia from our parties and the countries of the Warsaw Pact. We cannot currently rely on the internal forces in Czechoslovakia. There are no forces there that could carry out the types of tasks we wrote about in our letter. Only by relying on the armed forces of the Warsaw Pact can we change the situation.

In Czechoslovakia we must restore the dictatorship of the proletariat, which has been trampled underfoot. All the state and party organizations have been taken over by revisionists and counterrevolutionaries. The party Congress must be derailed. It is essential that we reestablish the party and restore the Marxist–Leninist content of its activity. We must prevent the social-democratization of the party. A decree must be prepared to dissolve the various counterrevolutionary and bourgeois organizations. There is no other way out.

We have not yet approached the schematic issue and been aware of the sort of activity that could also have highly negative results. A great uproar has emerged against us, and in particular against the Soviet Union. Perhaps certain adventurist forces wanted to benefit from this, even to the point of wanting violence to break out. No doubt, great difficulties may arise for the workers' movement in the capitalist countries. However, the positive results will be more valuable and more lasting if we preserve socialism in Czechoslovakia and preserve the unity of the Warsaw Pact. Besides, this will be one further lesson for the imperialists. They will see that they can't count on success. This might also have influence on the opportunists in the world communist movement. The opportunists have come out on all sides and are seriously weighing down the ranks of our movement.

Here I would like to mention the discussion I had with the member of the Political Bureau of the French Communist Party Central Committee, Cde. Garaudy, who said that the parties of the socialist countries should not undertake joint action on the question of Czechoslovakia.[29] Any intervention would cause, in his opinion, a loss of the party's influence among the French intelligentsia. It is essential to recall, however, that joint action on this matter would have great significance for the situation in our socialist countries. The majority of our parties are for such a solution. It would be a blow to the different forces—the revisionist, counterrevolutionary, and

[29] The reference here is to Roger Garaudy, a celebrated Marxist theorist whose concept of the "hegemony" of intellectuals was widely influential in CPCz circles. He strongly supported the Prague Spring and was officially reprimanded in October 1968 for his criticism of the revival of Stalinism in the Soviet Union. From then on, Garaudy was a dissident member of the French Communist Party who tried, unsuccessfully, to steer the party in a more liberal direction. He lost most of his positions at a party congress in 1970 and was later expelled from the French CP.

anti-socialist forces—that have emerged in our countries and our parties. Naturally these forces in our countries are isolated, but they still exist. They are engaged in preliminary activities in our countries.

* * *

Third Session—4:00 P.M.–5:30 P.M.

Cde. Brezhnev presiding.

Cde. Brezhnev:

Dear comrades!

In the name of the Central Committee of the Communist Party of the Soviet Union let me express my thanks for your common support of the proposal to hold this comradely meeting. Recently a large number of questions have cropped up that demand collective judgment at the highest level. The most important of these questions, which is the main reason for today's meeting, is the situation in Czechoslovakia.

Like all the other delegations present here, we understandably regret that the Czechoslovak comrades, whom we invited, are not taking part. No matter how their absence is explained by the CPCz CC Presidium, one cannot help thinking, comrades, that this is typical of the current situation whereby the Presidium does not wish to heed the advice and suggestions of its friends. It openly rejects the possibility of collectively assessing matters that not only concern Czechoslovakia itself, but also affect our common interests.

Despite refusing to take part in our meeting, the CPCz CC Presidium also does not want its new position to be examined here, at this collective forum, and given its proper evaluation. Judging from what was said by Cdes. Dubček and Černík to Cde. Kádár at bilateral talks held yesterday,[30] the task that Czechoslovak leaders have set themselves in proposing bilateral talks with all of us seems to be an attempt once again to convince each of us that there is nothing new or dangerous in the current situation. They don't want us to call a spade a spade, or to say clearly and unequivocally that counterrevolution is on the offensive, or to consider the measures that need to be taken as a direct result of this situation.

However, we are obliged to do precisely this—whether in their presence or as now, unfortunately, without them. No matter how any of us might characterize the potential consequences of the continuing offensive by the anti-socialist forces, one thing is clear: Czechoslovakia is at a dangerous phase on the path leading out of the socialist camp. And we must take all measures and use all means to prevent that.

The delegation of the CPSU Central Committee fully endorses the assessment of the situation in Czechoslovakia presented by Cde. Gomułka at our conference. We agree that the events taking place there are dangerous not only because they are openly directed against the socialist gains of the Czechoslovak people, but also because they undermine the positions of socialism in Europe and are playing into the hands of imperialism throughout the world. This is the essence of what Cdes. Ulbricht and Zhivkov said as well.

What is happening in the ČSSR passed long ago beyond a purely national framework and is now impinging on the fundamental problems of the vitality of the entire socialist system. One might say that Czechoslovakia has become one of the focal points of the bitter ideological and political struggle between imperialism and socialism. The attempt being made by the anti-so-

[30] When Brezhnev re-read the speech to the CPSU Central Committee, he interjected the following clarification at this point: "We met [in Warsaw] on Sunday, and it was on Saturday afternoon that Kádár and Fock had met Dubček and Černík unofficially in Hungary." This comment obviously was not included in his original presentation at Warsaw and is therefore not in the Polish transcript.

cialist and counterrevolutionary forces to bring about the downfall of the Communist Party of Czechoslovakia and remove it from power is essentially an attempt to strike a blow against our common ideological platform, the great Marxist–Leninist teachings, and thus to compromise the very principles of socialism.

One cannot help seeing the other side of the question as well. By jointly exploiting the events for their own purposes, the internal counterrevolutionary forces and the imperialist reactionary forces are counting on being able to turn Czechoslovakia back to the capitalist path, to weaken the strength of the Warsaw Pact, and to annihilate the unity of the socialist system and of the entire world communist and national liberation movement. It goes without saying that if the international reactionary forces succeed in carrying out their plans, there will be a direct threat to the security of our countries. That's why we agree it is essential to do everything possible to prevent such a development from arising.

In his speech Cde. Gomułka offered a quite detailed explanation of the possible future paths for the so-called "peaceful" evolution of the process in Czechoslovakia. In our opinion these are correct scenarios. In the final analysis, taking account of the enormous interest that imperialist circles have in Czechoslovakia as a state located in the center of Europe and in the very heart of the socialist camp, the possibility cannot be excluded that under the right conditions they might even resort to non-peaceful means to convert and reshape that country into a capitalist or perhaps neo-capitalist country. They will invest whatever means and resources are needed to achieve that end. This prospect, far from reducing the intensity of the question before us of the counterrevolutionary offensive in Czechoslovakia, greatly magnifies its significance.

We also understand that the development of events in Czechoslovakia has been a carefully disguised, counterrevolutionary process aimed at drastically transforming the country's social order without changing, insofar as possible, its external attributes and without even changing the form of political and state leadership of society. The particular danger that this poses is that the working people of Czechoslovakia, and even the working class, initially will be unable to comprehend where such developments might in the end lead. This is also precisely how an erroneous understanding of the situation can emerge even among communists outside Czechoslovakia. We already see signs of this in the case of the communist parties of France, Italy, and England.[31]

The question we have gathered here to discuss has been the subject of our collective and unflagging attention for a period of several months now. We have constantly returned to it during the many meetings and talks we have had with Cde. Dubček and the other members of the CPCz CC Presidium. We should repeat—or, better yet, we should recall—that at the end of March, in Dresden, we had a comprehensive exchange of views among the leaders of the six parties, which produced a collective assessment of the situation in the ČSSR and led to agreement on several crucial measures.

Based on a sober analysis of the facts, and taking account of the experience of our own and other fraternal parties, we seriously warned the Czechoslovak comrades about the menacing course of political developments in the ČSSR and about the existence there of a certain social milieu that is conducive to the activities of anti-socialist and counterrevolutionary forces. We urged them to be aware of the danger of taking a conciliatory approach on attacks made against the party and the socialist gains of the Czechoslovak people.

Not only did we express our concerns; we gave them comradely advice about a number of measures that could be taken to improve the situation. We recommended steps that might prevent

---

[31] Brezhnev's reference here to the very small British Communist Party is puzzling, especially when he could have mentioned a much larger party like the Spanish communists. The British Communist Party said little about the crisis in Czechoslovakia until August 21, 1968, when the party denounced the Soviet invasion.

things from developing in an undesirable way. The Czechoslovak comrades agreed with these suggestions, and they spoke about their own plans and about how the CPCz leadership is determined to put an end to the activities of counterrevolutionary elements and to assert control over the course of events.

Unfortunately, these proposals and plans were not carried out. The situation in the country has deteriorated as far as it can.

If we think in terms of the tendency or orientation manifested by the events in Czechoslovakia, we find that activities by anti-socialist elements are constantly increasing and that the leading role of the communist party is being undermined. The threat to the socialist achievements of the working class and the working people of the ČSSR is growing. It is appropriate here to recapitulate the course of these events in order to derive the proper lessons from them and to take the necessary measures.

We recall, comrades, that the CPCz CC's January plenum set for itself the relatively modest task of separating the top party and state posts. This was followed by mounting criticism of A. Novotný, which rather quickly evolved into criticism of the party's entire "pre-January" course. A number of issues arose that were already of political significance: the problem of rehabilitation, the allocation of responsibility for past repression, and the demand for complete information and freedom of the press.

At a particular moment everything was concentrated on the demand for Novotný to relinquish the post of president. But then a number of other personnel changes began occurring in the CC Presidium and in the government of the ČSSR; there was a wholesale change in the composition of the top layer of leading party officials. By that time, however, it was already clear that the question at hand was not just a rotation of individuals. Demands were being heard for changes in the entire political structure of the regime under the pretext that the existing structure had retarded the development of "real socialism."

These demands found support in the Action Program, which declared the need for changes in the political system. The leading role of the party was explained as something else; the Program reinforced *de facto* changes in the relationship among the partners in the National Front; the principle of "political pluralism" was included; the possibility of centralized leadership over the society was enervated; etc.

This was followed by a campaign to replace personnel from below based on the principle of "new politics—new people." Plenary meetings of regional and district party committees were held that led to substantial changes in the middle ranks of party leaders. Simultaneously, a purge occurred on all levels of the state apparatus.

The number of political problems snowballed; earlier ways of resolving these problems were said to be unsatisfactory. When the question arose about who was to blame for the mistakes of the past, they began to respond that it was not individuals but the party as a whole, and the entire political and social system, that should be held accountable.

From there it was only a small step before they arrived at an open repudiation of Marxism and of socialism in general. Unfortunately, it must be said that this step is being taken by some and in some ways it has already been carried out.

As events unfolded over these six months, they were inevitably accompanied by increased attacks on the socialist countries: on the GDR, Poland, Bulgaria, and the Soviet Union. At first these attacks only took the form of indirect assertions, which were concealed by demands for the rejection of a single model and for the elaboration of Czechoslovakia's own "national model" of socialism. Then the attacks became more direct and soon reached the point where demands were made for an end to joint activities with the socialist countries, for a reorientation of foreign economic ties, and for a radical reassessment of foreign policy.

Everything was used that could be used—from references to the role of advisers in political trials to claims about unequal trade relations and the "vice of economic dependence," from open insults about the unjust treatment of Czechoslovak legionnaires to offensive remarks about the Soviet troops that had liberated Czechoslovakia.[32]

The party's relinquishment of control over the mass media has led to a situation in which proclaimed freedom of speech has acquired a one-sided character. It is "freedom" to conduct a struggle against so-called conservatives, which is how the non-communist press considers all communists. At the same time, communists who find themselves assailed by public criticism and abuse are given no chance to defend their views. Newspapers don't publish their remarks. This is no longer freedom of information: It is freedom to carry out a political massacre against people who have absolutely no means of defending themselves against attacks organized by the press.

The danger of the current situation is aggravated many times over as a result of the emergence of factional activity within the party. Everyone who studies the history of the communist movement and who is familiar with the theoretical legacy of V. I. Lenin knows only too well that a party can act only if all its organizations and members fully and constantly uphold the principle of democratic centralism. Ignoring either aspect of this principle, either the democratic or the centralism, will inevitably weaken the party and its leading role, and lead to the transformation of the party into a bureaucratic organization or a mere discussion club.

V. I. Lenin, as is known, was an advocate of broad democracy in the party. He supported the full-fledged development of criticism, but he was categorically opposed to the kind of discussion and criticism that vitiates or hampers unity of action in party matters. And yet now, in the CPCz there is endless discussion, accompanied by hostile criticism. Is this not evidence of a violation of the principles of democratic centralism? Is there also not evidence of how much the authority of the Central Committee of the Communist Party of Czechoslovakia has declined when, for example, the various district party conferences, instead of carrying out the CC's orders and directives, choose an entirely different course and adopt decisions that are deliberately contrary to the line of the party leadership? This is precisely what happened with the CPCz CC Presidium's critique of the "Two Thousand Words" appeal. The Czechoslovak comrades themselves have said that one-third of the district conferences in Czechoslovakia did not support this appeal, one-third said nothing on the matter, and one-third (please note, not individuals but one-third of all district party conferences!) came out in support of this anti-socialist manifesto, that is, in opposition to the line of the CC Presidium. This was facilitated to a large extent by the fact that even some members of the CPCz CC Presidium were themselves willing to treat the "Two Thousand Words" in a manner that contradicted the decision endorsed by the CC Presidium. This is an appropriate place for a digression on something I wish to draw to our attention. The decision of the CC Presidium about the "Two Thousand Words" was not signed by the CC first secretary. It was not even signed by a member of the CPCz CC Presidium in the name of the Presidium.

Right-wing forces are quite openly trying to undermine the Communist Party of Czechoslovakia in order to transform it from a monolithic combat unit into an amorphous organization that includes a mass of fellow travelers who do not subscribe to Marxist–Leninist views. It is no coincidence that they are encouraged by Cde. Císař, who claims there is no need to worry if the Communist Party of Czechoslovakia now admits 200,000 or 300,000 young people into its ranks to give an aging party a healthy injection. Leaving aside the fact that this insulting type of comment is, in itself, aimed at undermining the authority of the CPCz, a legitimate question arises about the further intentions of Cde. Císař and those who share his views. What sort of

[32] Brezhnev alludes here to several controversial issues that were appearing in the Czechoslovak press at the time. His reference to the "role of advisers in political trials" pertains to the extent of Soviet complicity in, and guidance of, the political trials in Czechoslovakia in the early 1950s. The Czechoslovak government was getting ready to publish a lengthy report on the trials that would have documented the involvement of Soviet "advisers" (though as it turned out, the report was not published before the invasion, and was suppressed after August 1968). Brezhnev's reference to the "Czechoslovak legionnaires" pertains to the small detachment of Czechoslovak troops that had fought with the Allies against the bolsheviks in 1918.

"injection" do they have in mind, what are these 200,000 to 300,000 young people like who are to be admitted to the CPCz, and why admit young people and not true representatives of the working class? Is there not behind all this an attempt to bring into the party those who proclaim anti-socialist and anti-Soviet slogans at the "May Day" demonstrations and who march and shout slogans at mass meetings on the Old Town Square?[33] If so, such an injection is not intended to rejuvenate but to bury the party and give it an entirely different content, leaving only the name of the earlier organization.

Can one assume that the new leadership of the party is completely unaffected by these dangerous processes, or that it thinks they arose spontaneously? Of course, the answer to this question is not straightforward. There were unexpected elements that no one could have foreseen and that no political process could have avoided.

All the same, there is no doubt, in our view, that the recent line they have pursued has led to a deterioration of the situation. Erroneous acts were committed and dangerous passivity was allowed which disarmed the party. The replacement of leading party officials at the initiative of the CPCz leadership, the change in the emerging principles for governing society, the continuing shift to the Right of its political line—all this gives one cause to ask whether there is not a conscious, gradual re-orientation of the CPCz away from its role as a political party of the working class and of all the Czechoslovak working people, and as one of the stalwarts of the world communist movement?

Unfortunately, there are serious grounds for framing the question in this way. Recently there have been more and more references to the existence of a "second center" in the CPCz.

All the same, there is no doubt, in our view, that the line they have recently followed has facilitated the deterioration of ideological and cultural policy.

Let me be frank: We are extremely worried by facts such as these. They make us think: Are not the activities of the so-called "second center" linked with some members of the CPCz CC Presidium itself? And why is the Presidium so complacent about all the warning signals regarding the existence of a "second center," the signals that Cde. Dubček and other members of the Presidium admitted to us are justified?

As events unfold, one can truly see the organized activity of some sort of center, a center that exists in parallel with and perhaps even inside the CPCz CC. This center is conducting its activities in a well thought-out way. Clearly, the center did not come to fruition overnight; it was created gradually, but its leaders had thought out in advance what they are now doing.

At present, as some Czechoslovak communists are saying, the "second center" has worked out a new tactic, the meaning of which can be expressed in the slogan: "With Dubček without the Dubčekites." There is an intensified process under way to compromise Dubček's former co-workers, the people who are dedicated to the ideas of socialism and internationalism. According to reliable sources, the right-wing, anti-socialist forces have disseminated among counterrevolutionary "clubs" and organizations the names of party people whom they intend to vilify and compromise. The "Club of Committed Non-Party Members," evidently, received an order to compromise Cdes. Kolder, Biľak, Indra, and others as "refined conservatives" before the 14th Party Congress, and all this has been proceeding successfully.[34]

Some time ago Cde. Dubček said that everything would be settled within a month. Then this period was extended to two months. Then they began to say that everything would be solved in the course of the district conferences. And now Cde. Dubček vests all his hopes in the CPCz

---

[33] The May Day celebrations in Czechoslovakia in 1968 were one of the highlights of the Prague Spring. In contrast to the regimented and well-orchestrated activities on May 1 in previous years, the May Day celebrations in 1968 featured vast and exuberant crowds who turned out spontaneously to support Dubček and the reform program. Brezhnev is referring to several student rallies on May Day, including one held outside the Polish embassy to protest the Polish authorities' suppression of student unrest and their promotion of an anti-Semitic campaign.

[34] Next to this passage in the Polish transcript is a large exclamation point written by the official whose copy (No. 5) it was.

14th Congress. But comrades, one must think carefully about the full *gravity of the situation.* In the emerging circumstances the results of the congress might be such that afterwards not a single current member of the CPCz CC Presidium will be left on that body or, in the best instance, only a few will be left and their position will be such that they are unable to have any serious influence on the development of events in the party and the country and will be forced to retreat under pressure from the right.

If we think about recent months and weeks, *beginning with the Dresden meeting* and ending with the past few days, we can clearly see that *the situation is deteriorating* and that the CPCz leadership is relinquishing control of the situation in the country.

April — Performance by university student and artistic organizations on the Old Town Square with *anti-socialist and anti-Soviet slogans.*[35]

— Mass campaign to remove so-called conservatives from leading posts in party branches.

May — Open attacks and engagement in subversive activities by such organizations as the *"Club of Committed Non-Party Members"* and *"Club-231."*

— Student May Day march directed against the socialist system in the ČSSR and against Soviet–Czechoslovak friendship, and for the right of opposition groups and parties to operate legally.

— Creation of the *first branches of the socialist and people's parties in companies.*

— Reorganization of the activities of the Interior Ministry and the *security organs,* as well as personnel changes *in the army.*

June — Disruption of party unity and the actual *creation of factions* advocating different positions.

— Contempt for the principles of democratic centralism in the party and in its leadership.

— Appearance of *preparatory committees* working for the revival of the Social Democratic Party.

— Statement by the National Front that socialist state power *cannot be monopolized* by a single party.

— Publication of the "Two Thousand Words" appeal as a political platform for anti-socialist and counterrevolutionary forces.

— In Brno and other cities the circulation of *leaflets,* the display of *posters calling for the destruction of the CPCz* and local government bodies, and for a break in relations between the ČSSR and the Soviet Union and the other socialist countries.

The *danger of open attacks* by counterrevolutionary forces can be seen clearly. Imperialist agents and emigré organizations that were mentioned here are working actively toward this end.

Three months ago, during the meeting in Dresden, one might still have held out the hope—to some degree or another—that the CPCz, combining severity and firm principles with flexible tactics, would be able to effect a gradual change for the better in the situation in Czechoslovakia without having to resort to decisive measures.[36] Today there is no doubt that this did not happen. It is necessary to act now, before it is too late.

---

[35] It has since come to light that provocateurs employed by the KGB and the Czechoslovak State Security (StB) were chiefly responsible for the "excesses" at this event.

[36] The phrase "decisive measures" presumably refers to the imposition of martial law, as in Poland in December 1981. That phrase was used constantly by Soviet officials in 1980–1981 to denote what they wanted the Polish authorities to do. See Mark Kramer, "Poland 1980–81: Soviet Policy During the Polish Crisis," Cold War International History Project *Bulletin*, No. 5 (Spring 1995), pp. 1, 116–126.

The half-measures to which the Czechoslovak comrades resorted earlier can only encourage the anti-socialist forces to stage a counterrevolutionary coup. A failure to be decisive is incompatible with the gravity of the situation. The question now is: either the CPCz leadership finds enough courage within itself to change its views, inspire the party and the working class, and take decisive measures to defeat the reactionary forces and ensure the security of socialist positions, or the progressive forces of the party will be destroyed by our common enemies. In that case the fate of Czechoslovakia will be decided by completely different means and forces.

The open onset of counterrevolution may exact a high price from the Czechoslovak communists. The experience of the Hungarian events has shown that whoever capitulates to reactionary forces, whoever compromises with them, renders the party vulnerable to the cruel blow of counterrevolution.

We have repeatedly urged Czechoslovak leaders to make a realistic appraisal of the full extent of the danger and to draw appropriate conclusions from the fact that unrestrained reactionary forces are currently entering the political arena in Czechoslovakia. In such circumstances it is necessary to act, and to act swiftly and decisively. If they do not believe they have sufficient strength to do this, then the socialist countries have the right and even the duty to offer them their help, the help of sincere friends and allies for whom the cause of socialism in Czechoslovakia is so dear.

What concrete measures, in our view, should be adopted now to improve things?

In the first place, we must inform the Czechoslovak comrades about our collective assessment of the situation in Czechoslovakia and recommend, in a friendly way, that urgent action be taken in defense of the socialist system against counterrevolution. This could be done in a letter to the Central Committee of the CPCz in the name of our parties. If agreement in principle is reached on this matter, we are prepared to submit the first draft of such a letter for consideration by the others who are present here. This, if you will, is the first thing we believe should be done.

Perhaps it would be beneficial if representatives from, say, two or three parties met with the leadership of the CPCz and, in the name of all of us, expanded on the letter by explaining the measures that should be taken to turn things around and thereby strengthen the leading role of the communist party in the ČSSR. Presumably, we will have to consult about such measures here.

If we see that the CPCz leadership does not wish to heed our recommendations, then it will be necessary, obviously, to continue the search for healthy forces in the party and to look for ways of appealing to the forces in the party that might take the lead in initiating a struggle to restore the leading role of the CPCz and normalize the situation in the country. In that case it would be essential to organize a meeting of representatives designated by us with the members of this "initiating" group who would act on behalf of the healthy core of the CPCz CC Presidium. We would have to convey our views to them about the sort of political platform that would enable them to consolidate the party and deal a rebuff to the anti-socialist elements, and we would have to make clear our readiness to provide the necessary aid and support.

The fraternal countries will be obliged to follow the progress of events and, if the need should arise, they must respond to the first call for help by the Czechoslovak comrades. They must also respond if it becomes clear that such action is required and that the Czechoslovak comrades for one reason or another find it difficult to appeal for help.

The publishing outlets in socialist countries must develop their publications in a way that helps the Czechoslovak people understand the true essence of what is happening and the full extent of the danger looming over the socialist gains that the ČSSR has achieved in 20 years of its development.

It is necessary, in my view, to give special consideration to still another question.

Nowadays, on television and radio in Czechoslovakia, certain prominent figures refer to our recent meeting as some sort of interference in the internal affairs of the ČSSR. This issue, comrades, must be made more precise. When the plenum of the CPCz Central Committee recognized the necessity of removing Cde. Novotný from the post of first secretary and then of dismissing him from the post of president, we said nothing in regard to these changes. That was the internal affair of a fraternal party and country. When there was a change of secretaries of the Central Committee and of members of the Central Committee's Presidium, and also a change of ministers, we again, as you recall, said nothing about it (I mean we said nothing openly in the press).[37] We believe that this is the internal affair of a fraternal party, its Central Committee, and its National Assembly.

However, comrades, when the situation has developed into an open political massacre of all party cadres, when exhortations are made to change virtually the whole party leadership from top to bottom, when one hears ever louder voices calling for a reorientation of the CPCz, and when the fate of the whole party and of the socialist achievements of the Czechoslovak people is under challenge, then this is a different matter. If the threat that the political content of the CPCz will be transformed into some sort of new organization is real—in the best instance into a social democratic one or perhaps even into a petty bourgeois one—then this, I repeat, affects the interests not only of communists in Czechoslovakia and not only the people of Czechoslovakia, but the interests of the entire socialist system and of the whole world communist movement. We would be correct to regard such a turn of events as a direct threat to the world position of socialism and a direct threat to all our countries.

Any attempt to thwart such a process cannot be considered interference in internal affairs. This is an expression of our international duty to the whole communist movement and our international duty to the communists and working people of Czechoslovakia.[38] Confronted by the growing danger that socialism will be dislodged in one of the countries of the socialist commonwealth, we cannot shut ourselves off, comrades, in our own national apartments. That would be a betrayal of the interests of communism.

Communism develops and exists only as an international movement. All its victories and all its achievements are related to this. Anyone who departs from internationalism cannot consider himself a communist. Our countries are linked to the ČSSR by treaties and agreements. These are not agreements between individual persons but mutual commitments between friends and states. They are founded on the general desire to defend socialism in our countries and to safeguard it against all and any hazards.

No one has the right to dissociate themselves from their international commitments or their allied obligations. It must be stressed that the demagoguery we hear about this nowadays is out of place.

We respect the right of every party and the right of every nation. We recognize the idea of specific national forms of socialist development in different countries. But we also believe in a common historical fate. The cause of defending socialism—that is our common undertaking. Our parties were united in their understanding of this at the meeting in Moscow at the beginning of May.[39] We are certain that such unity characterizes our meeting this time as well.

There has never been a case in which socialism triumphed and was firmly entrenched, only to have a capitalist order restored.[40] This has never happened and we are certain it never will.[41] The guarantee of this is our common readiness to do whatever is necessary to help a fraternal party and people defeat the plans of counterrevolution and thwart imperialist plans in relation to Czechoslovakia.

---

[37] Brezhnev's aside here is an acknowledgment that he and other CPSU officials did comment behind-the-scenes about the personnel changes in the CPCz and the Czechoslovak government.

[38] The CPSU Central Committee plenum greeted this passage with applause when Brezhnev re-read it on July 17.

[39] See Document No. 31.

[40] Brezhnev's qualification here — in referring to socialist regimes that are "firmly entrenched" — is meant to exclude such cases as Béla Kun's communist government in Hungary in 1919, which was quickly overthrown.

[41] The CPSU Central Committee plenum greeted this passage with applause when Brezhnev re-read it on July 17.

Our delegation declares that the Communist Party of the Soviet Union, our government, and our people are fully ready to offer Czechoslovakia all necessary assistance.[42]

* * *

Fourth Session—14.VII. 68, 6:15 P.M.–6:30 P.M.

Cde. Brezhnev: We resume our meeting. All the delegations have already spoken. Which of the comrades would like to take the floor?

Cde. Kádár: I would like to say a few words about my earlier statement. Most of the comrades criticized my remarks, arguing that my convictions were not in line with our general stance. I would like to emphasize that the HSWP CC and the Hungarian government, which we represent both during our duties and during meetings with representatives from the other fraternal parties who are taking part in today's meeting, have been busy considering the situation in Czechoslovakia. Our assessment of the situation there is the same as the views of the other parties. I would like to offer two illustrations. Our party and government have maintained a resolute position on the "Two Thousand Words" statement. In our press outlets, we described this statement precisely as a platform for counterrevolution.

I also would like to draw attention to the statement by the Political Bureau of our party that the CPCz CC Presidium's rejection of our suggestion to hold a joint meeting has immensely complicated the situation and given rise to vast new problems. All of this has already been stated by our party.

I listened with great interest to the speech by Cde. Brezhnev, which contained a profound and accurate assessment of the processes under way in Czechoslovakia and which emphasized the dangerous elements in these processes. In this regard I believe it is worth saying that as far as the assessment and conclusions of the Soviet comrades are concerned, we completely agree with them and are prepared to take part in all joint actions.

Cde. Brezhnev: Which of the other comrades would like to speak? No one.

I believe further discussion of the problem on the agenda of our meeting—an assessment of the situation in Czechoslovakia—can be closed. The precise position can be worked out. I believe it is essential that we turn on behalf of all of us to the letter to be sent to the CPCz CC. The substance of the letter was discussed in the earlier sessions.

I suggest we establish a working group, which will set to work on the letter. To this end, each delegation should appoint a representative. The committee must work quickly, so that we can hold a plenary session tomorrow morning.

Cde. Gomułka: We can begin the session at 9:00 A.M.

Cde. Brezhnev: Everyone wants to prepare a good letter, which must be appropriately formulated. Drafting such a letter will take a good deal of political savvy. Let's agree, then, to meet here at 9:00 tomorrow morning. At that time each delegation will receive a draft for perusal. We'll take 30–40 minutes to go over it, and will then convene a plenary session. Do all the comrades agree with this proposal?

Cde. Gomułka: Who will chair the drafting committee?

Cde. Brezhnev: I suggest that the Polish comrades be asked to chair the effort.

Cde. Gomułka: Our delegation nominates Cde. Kliszko for this function.

---

[42] The CPSU Central Committee plenum also greeted this final passage with applause when Brezhnev re-read it on July 17.

Cde. Brezhnev: We support the candidacy of Cde. Kliszko. [All express approval.] We adjourn until tomorrow at 9:00 A.M.

* * *

Fifth Session—15.VII. 68, 9:00 A.M.–9:50 A.M.

Cde. Zhivkov presiding.

Cde. Zhivkov: The drafting committee needs roughly 30 minutes more to work out the remaining text of the letter. I suggest that in the meantime we discuss the press communiqué. Preparation of a draft was entrusted to the Polish comrades.

Cde. Brezhnev: Our delegation did not receive a draft of the communiqué. I suggest that the drafting committee also coordinate the draft of the communiqué.

Cde. Gomułka: I suggest we read out the draft of the communiqué and if there are any points to be taken up, we can refer them to the drafting committee to work out the remaining text.

[The draft of the communiqué was read out.]

Cde. Brezhnev: The question arises of whether we should repeat in the communiqué passages that are already in the letter. It's best to keep things brief in a communiqué, without fully developing them. That's why it would be better to shorten the communiqué. We don't need to include references to the Warsaw Pact; we can simply mention allied obligations without mentioning the pact. After all, Romania isn't represented here. It would appear that we were excluding Romania from the pact.

Cde. Gomułka: You're right, I've also made these changes.

Cde. Kádár: The communiqué should say that we also examined other matters: European security, Vietnam, etc.

Cde. Zhivkov: We will refer the draft of the communiqué to the commission to take care of the necessary changes.[43]

Cde. Gomułka: Which letter will we sign?

Cde. Zhivkov: We'll sign the original and send a copy at the behest of the Central Committees—

Cde. Brezhnev: When we publish a communiqué saying that we have sent a letter, an uproar will ensue. The text of the letter must be more polished, and it should be translated into Czech. We won't finish all that work until this evening. It would be advisable to send a special courier to Prague and instruct the ambassador to request a meeting with Dubček and deliver the letter to him. This will take some time, and therefore the letter will not be published immediately. We'll see what kind of response we get, and then after a few days go ahead and publish it.

Cde. Gomułka: I agree with this idea. The letter must also be translated into the languages of all the participants in this meeting. This, I imagine, will take around two days. The exact timeframe is still to be determined. By Tuesday or Wednesday everything should be set. How should we transmit the letter to the Czechs? We could give them the Russian text, in which case only the USSR's ambassador in Czechoslovakia should deliver it. Or each of our parties could deliver a version of the letter in its own national language, in which case the Czechs would

[43] For the final version of the communiqué, see "Vstrecha rukovoditelei partii i pravitel'stv sotsialisticheskikh stran," *Pravda* (Moscow), July 16, 1968, p. 1.

receive five copies of the text in different languages. They themselves could translate it into Czech. Dubček—I assume we're sending the letter to him—might receive the ambassadors individually, not all at the same time. The ambassadors should indicate on Tuesday that they want jointly to deliver the letter, and if he doesn't meet with them all at once, but only individually, they can hand over the text in their own national languages. We'll give the Czechs a couple of days to familiarize the CC with the contents of the letter, which means we can publish it on Saturday. In so doing we will display good will, by not appearing to want to inform the public before the CC. We should inform Dubček that we intend to publish the letter on Saturday. Whether they themselves will publish it is for them to decide.

Cde. Ulbricht: I believe that over the next few days the counterrevolutionary forces inside and outside Czechoslovakia will be launching an offensive. Our communiqué indicating that we have sent a letter might become the impetus for this campaign. Therefore the letter must be translated by this evening, and tomorrow morning the ambassadors will deliver it in their national languages. Otherwise, the anti-socialist centers that have stepped into action—together with the centers active in the CPCz CC—will begin engaging in indiscretions and leaks, and the West will learn the contents of the letter before the CPCz members do. I recommend we publish the letter on Thursday, and this is what we should tell the Czechs. It is not any great secret that they have their "Two Thousand Words," and we have a letter in which we lay out our position.

To be sure, Dubček said that the congress would reply to the "Two Thousand Words." We are helping the progressive forces to devise a counterplatform. It is best if the Soviet comrades provide such help, but we all ought to avail ourselves of these opportunities. The counterplatform might be put forward by different centers—for example, in Bratislava and in Brno. The only thing needed is to ensure that the efforts are coordinated. I recommend that the members of the drafting committee consult right now about these matters. We can't wait passively until the next meeting in August. It might be good if we were to take up the Czechs' invitation to hold bilateral negotiations, and thereby exert additional pressure on Prague. The motivation for this is in accord with our discussion. We can urge the CPCz leadership to take part in a joint conference in August. If the Czechs don't agree to a joint meeting in August, we can still meet, saying that the enemy is active and has achieved superiority in Czechoslovakia. This week we will publish materials about the intervention of hostile external forces in Czechoslovakia and will show who it is that is intervening. We want the CC secretaries to consult as soon as possible.

Cde. Zhivkov: We need to settle this matter. We have to decide how to deliver the letter and when to publish it. It would be good to deliver it tomorrow via a special courier. Perhaps one of us could perform this function? The letter must first be delivered in Russian, and then the texts in the other national languages can be sent. The text will be published Thursday morning.

Cde. Gomułka: I'll go along with this if it's what the majority wants.

Cde. Zhivkov: I therefore recommend we deliver the text in Russian with our signatures.

Cde. Gomułka: If the letter is to be signed, there's no need to send translations in the national languages.

Cde. Zhivkov: Let's settle, then, on how to deliver the letter. Perhaps via one of us? I propose that Cde. Gomułka deliver the letter.

Cde. Gomułka: I don't agree with this. If the text is in Russian, the USSR ambassador in Prague ought to deliver it.

Cde. Zhivkov: I propose, then, that the text in Russian be delivered tomorrow by Cde. Chervonenko, the USSR ambassador in Prague. Our ambassadors will work together with Cde. Chervonenko. The letter will be published this coming Thursday, and that's what we'll tell Dubček.

Cde. Ulbricht: Will the ambassadors go over there all at once tomorrow?

Cde. Gomułka: Will the letter be signed only by the First Secretaries?[44]

Cde. Brezhnev: It would be better if everyone signed it—all the members of the delegations. The Central Committees authorized the entire delegations to do so. If the document is to be signed, translations into the other languages are not particularly essential. We could therefore deliver the letter tomorrow and inform Dubček that we are going to publish it on Thursday.

Cde. Gomułka: In that case there's no need to deliver the text in the other languages to the Czechs.

Cde. Ulbricht: I think we absolutely should still deliver the texts in the languages of all the participants in the meeting.

Cde. Zhivkov: We, the whole delegations, will sign the text in Russian. Tomorrow the ambassadors will deliver the letter to Dubček, and on Thursday we'll publish it. With regard to what Cde. Ulbricht proposed, should we for the time being abstain from bilateral contacts? Should we wait and see what kind of reaction there is to our letter?

Cde. Brezhnev: We won't make a decision about this matter now. We'll think it over and consult. The most important matter now is the letter. It will be an indication that we have already given Dubček a response, that we went to a multilateral meeting, and that therefore we were not able to come to Prague.

Cde. Ulbricht: Please take into account that we've already corresponded about this matter with the Czechs and have agreed on a visit. They've invited the Hungarians to come there on the 20th of July and us on the 25th. I think we ought to go. We support having bilateral negotiations in July.

Cde. Kádár: On Saturday we were negotiating with Dubček and Černík. We discussed this matter. We received an invitation, but haven't yet decided whether to go. We're considering it. Our party can go along with the principle of having a series of bilateral meetings without having to set a specific date for the meeting. We can say the dates proposed by the Czechs are unrealistic, and we can't take them up on it. In our letter there is a proposal for a multilateral meeting. This does not mean we have to reject proposals for bilateral meetings in general, but simply can refrain from going to Prague on the dates proposed by the Czechs. Alternatively, we could insist that it would be better if they first held a Soviet–Czechoslovak meeting.

Cde. Gomułka: I'd bear in mind what the real intentions of the Czechs are. Their invitation to hold bilateral negotiations is merely a subterfuge connected with their refusal to take part in our conference. So let's not set a visit; let's consult and coordinate matters.

Only the letters need to be given to Dubček—evidence that he asked—and not the meetings themselves. These sorts of bilateral meetings in the current situation might be construed somehow—in principle—as an endorsement of their line. After all, at such a meeting Cde. Ulbricht would just say the same things that are in our letter. Rather than doing anything else right now, we should wait for a reaction to our letter. A positive reaction might induce the CPCz leadership to seek a collective meeting to discuss the matters raised in the letter. Dubček has placed everyone in a queue! Practically speaking, we'd do well to see what the reaction is to the letter, but what if it's very hostile? We'll come back to this question in August. At the same time, the position of the USSR is a special case. If Dubček would like to come to the USSR, that would be a different matter; the Soviet leadership could set a reasonable date. The Czech leader would then have to give a response either orally or in a letter, and we'll come back to this question later.

---

[44] The original transcript omitted the word "First" here, but a proofreader inserted the word in handwriting.

Hájek was due to come to our country. However, to avoid creating a false situation, we said that we weren't ready and wanted to change the date. It wouldn't be wise to hold bilateral meetings now.

Cde. Ulbricht: Cde. Gomułka spoke about the Czechs' initiatives. If he's referring to us, let me say we were the ones who proposed the meeting and Dubček the one who accepted our proposal.

Cde. Zhivkov: I propose we adjourn.

* * *

Sixth Session—15.VII. 68, 3:00 P.M.–3:20 P.M.

Cde. Ulbricht presiding.

Cde. Ulbricht: The drafting committee has finished its work. We thank them for carrying out their task. We now come to a decision about the communiqué. Since no one has asked to take the floor, I believe that all concur with the text of the communiqué. I would suggest it be published at 6:00 P.M. Warsaw time.

We now come to the letter. A text has been drafted by the committee.[45] Is there any comment about the contents? No. I believe the letter is unanimously approved. I would like to thank the PZPR CC and especially Cde. Gomułka. The conference was well organized. We achieved full agreement and adopted an extremely important document. The conference facilitates further cooperation in the struggle against the influence of reaction and counterrevolution, against the so-called "new Eastern policy" of the FRG, and against American aggression. The document serves the interests of the consolidation of peace and cooperation among our countries. I thank all the participants, and particularly the PZPR delegation and Cde. Gomułka. It's now time to sign the letter.

[Break while the letter is signed.]

Cde. Ulbricht: We're approaching the end of our meeting. The letter has been signed. In conclusion we can only hope that the Czech people and party will act in accordance with the spirit of the letter and be guided by the principles laid out there.

[45] For a first-hand account of the drafting of the Warsaw Letter, see Weit, *Eyewitness*, pp. 201–202, 215–217.

DOCUMENT No. 53: The Warsaw Letter, July 14–15, 1968

Source: "Tsentral'nomu Komitetu Kommunisticheskoi Partii Chekhoslovakii," *Pravda* (Moscow), July 18, 1968, p. 1; Vondrová & Navrátil, vol. 1, pp. 297–300.

The "Warsaw Letter" was approved at the meeting of the "Five" in Warsaw on July 14–15 for transmission to Prague. The final language derived from a draft letter that Soviet leaders brought to the meeting and was similar, both substantively and stylistically, to the letters that had been sent to the CPCz CC Presidium in the first week of July.

In their communiqué, the Five charge that the CPCz has lost control of events in Czechoslovakia and has "retreated more and more under the pressure of anti-communist forces." They express amazement at the CPCz leadership's failure to recognize that counterrevolutionary forces have taken advantage of the resulting vacuum to "seize one position after another from the CPCz" and to begin subverting the whole socialist order in Czechoslovakia. The letter claims that some members of the CPCz CC Presidium are "actively assisting hostile forces;" it warns that the situation could be rectified only if the "healthy forces" on the Presidium were able to repulse the "anti-socialist" and "reactionary" offensive. The CPCz leadership is urged to move immediately to reimpose censorship, restore "democratic centralism" within the party, dismiss reform-minded officials, and prohibit all non-communist political clubs and organizations. The signatories of the letter also pledge "solidarity and comprehensive assistance" to the "healthy forces" in Czechoslovakia to ensure that the outcome of the struggle will "block the path of reactionary forces" and promote the "common vital interests of all socialist countries." Toward that end, the communiqué asserts both a "right" and a "duty" for the Soviet Union and its allies to intervene in "defense of socialist gains."

The Warsaw Letter amounted to a clear ultimatum. CPCz leaders tried to have the Five retract the letter over the next month. On July 17, Dubček called Brezhnev to inform him that the Presidium had drafted a response and to urge that the exchange of letters be kept out of the public domain. The next day the Warsaw Letter was published with great fanfare in the Soviet Union and in the other countries that took part in the Warsaw Meeting. On July 19, CPCz leaders had no choice but to publish the letter from the Five along with the Presidium's point-by-point response.

(See Documents Nos. 52 and 56.)

TO THE CENTRAL COMMITTEE OF THE COMMUNIST PARTY OF CZECHOSLOVAKIA

Dear Comrades,

On behalf of the Central Committees of the communist and workers' parties of Bulgaria, Hungary, the GDR, Poland, and the Soviet Union, we are sending you this letter, which is motivated by sincere friendship based on the principles of Marxism–Leninism and proletarian internationalism, and by concern for our common aim of strengthening the positions of socialism and the security of the commonwealth of socialist states.

The course of events in your country arouses great apprehension. We are firmly convinced that the stance adopted by reactionaries against your party and the foundations of the social system in the ČSSR, a stance backed by imperialism, is threatening to divert your country from the road of socialism and, consequently, is endangering the interests of the whole socialist commonwealth.

We aired this apprehension at the meeting in Dresden and at many bilateral meetings, as well as in the letters that our parties recently addressed to the CPCz CC Presidium.

Recently we suggested that the CPCz CC Presidium hold another joint meeting on 14 July in order to exchange information and views on the situation in our countries, including the events in Czechoslovakia.

Unfortunately, the CPCz CC Presidium did not attend that meeting and thus did not take advantage of the possibility of the joint, collective, and comradely appraisal of the situation that has arisen. We therefore deemed it necessary to tell you sincerely and frankly our common point of view in this letter.

We want you to understand us well and evaluate our intentions correctly.

It was not and is not our intention to interfere in matters that are purely the internal affair of your party and state, or to violate the principles of respect for independence and equality in relations between communist parties and socialist countries.

We are not speaking to you as representatives of an old order that would seek to prevent you from remedying mistakes and shortcomings as well as the violations of socialist legality that have occurred.

We are not interfering in the methods of planning and running Czechoslovakia's socialist economy, nor are we interfering in the measures you have adopted to improve the structure of your economy and promote socialist democracy.

We welcome the basing of relations between Czechs and Slovaks on sound foundations of fraternal cooperation within the Czechoslovak Socialist Republic.

But at the same time we cannot agree that hostile forces should push your country off the socialist path and threaten to detach Czechoslovakia from the socialist community. This is no longer your affair alone. It is the common cause of all communist and workers' parties and states, which are bound by alliance, cooperation, and friendship. It is the common cause of our countries, which have united in the Warsaw Pact to safeguard their independence, to preserve peace, to maintain security in Europe, and to erect an impregnable barrier to the intrigues of aggressive and vengeful imperialist forces.

The peoples of our countries won a victory over Hitlerite fascism at the price of immense sacrifices. They have won freedom and independence and the opportunity to advance on the road of progress and socialism. The borders of the socialist world have been transferred to the center of Europe, to the Elbe and the Šumava mountains. We can never agree that these historic gains of socialism and the independence and security of all our peoples should be threatened. We can never agree that imperialism should break through the socialist system by peaceful or violent means, from within or from without, and change the balance of power in Europe to its advantage.

The strength and solidity of our ties depend on the internal strength of the socialist system of each of our fraternal countries, as well on the Marxist–Leninist policy of our parties, which are playing a leading role in the political and social life of their peoples and states. Policies that undermine the leading role of the communist party will lead to the destruction of socialist democracy and of the socialist system. Thus, the foundations of our ties and the security of the community of our countries will be placed in danger.

You know that the fraternal parties reacted to the decisions of the CPCz CC's January plenum with understanding, believing that your party, with a firm grip on all levers of power, would direct the entire process to serve the interest of socialism and would not permit anti-communist reaction to exploit the process for its own objectives. We were convinced that you would defend the Leninist principle of democratic centralism as the thing closest to your hearts. Ignoring either aspect of this principle, whether democracy or centralism, inevitably weakens the party and its leading role, and changes it into either a bureaucratic organization or a debating club. We spoke of these matters more than once at our meetings and always received your assurances that you were aware of all these dangers and were determined to deal with them.

Unfortunately, events have moved in a different direction.

By exploiting the party's weakened leadership in the country and by demagogically using the slogan of "democratization," reactionary forces have unleashed a campaign against the CPCz and against its honest and dedicated cadres, with the evident intention of destroying the leading role of the party, undermining the socialist system, and setting Czechoslovakia against the other socialist countries.

The political organizations and clubs that have recently emerged outside the National Front have essentially become staffs for the reactionary forces. The social democrats are arduously seeking to ensure that their party is formally established. They are organizing illegal committees and trying to split the labor movement in Czechoslovakia and force their way into the running of the state with the aim of restoring a bourgeois system. Anti-socialist and revisionist forces have seized the press, radio, and television and turned them into a tribune for attacks against the communist party in order to disorient the working class and all working people. They engage in unrestrained, anti-socialist demagoguery aimed at undermining Czechoslovakia's friendly relations with the USSR and other socialist countries. Some in the mass media are genuinely intent on perpetrating systematic moral terror against people who oppose the forces of reaction or who are voicing concern at the course of events.

Despite the resolution of the CPCz CC's May plenum, which cited the threat posed by right-wing and anti-communist forces as the main danger, reactionary attacks have escalated without encountering any resistance. For this very reason, the reactionary forces were given the opportunity, in public, to publish their political platform under the title "Two Thousand Words," which contains an open call for a struggle against the communist party and against the constitutional system, as well as a call for strikes and chaos. This appeal is a serious threat to the party, the National Front, and the socialist state. It is an attempt to foment anarchy. The declaration is, in its essence, the organizational-political platform of counterrevolution. No one ought to be misled by its authors, who claim they do not intend to overthrow the socialist system, that they do not wish to act without the communists, and that they do not want to undermine ties with the socialist countries. These are merely empty phrases, aimed at legalizing the platform of counterrevolution and overcoming the vigilance of the party, the working class, and all working people.

This platform, which has been widely circulated in the demanding period leading up to the Extraordinary CPCz Congress, was not only denounced, but found wholehearted supporters in the ranks of the party and its leadership, who are backing anti-socialist appeals.[46]

Anti-socialist and revisionist forces are denigrating all the activities of the communist party, conducting a campaign of slander against its cadres, and discrediting honest communists who are dedicated to the party.

This has brought about a situation totally unacceptable for the socialist countries.

In this atmosphere, attacks also are being launched against the ČSSR's foreign policy, and abusive comments are being made about the ČSSR's alliance and friendship with the socialist countries. Voices are heard demanding a revision of our common and coordinated policy vis-à-vis Federal Germany, even though the West German government has been pursuing a grim course hostile to the security interests of our countries. The enticing appeals by the FRG authorities and revenge-seekers are meeting with a positive response from leading circles in your country.

The entire course of events in your country during recent months demonstrates that the forces of counterrevolution, backed by imperialist centers, have launched a comprehensive assault on the socialist system and have not been rebuffed or opposed by the party and the people's regime. There is no doubt that centers of international imperialist reaction have become involved in the events in Czechoslovakia, doing everything possible to aggravate and complicate the situation and to incite anti-socialist forces. Under the guise of praising "democratization" and "liberalization" in the ČSSR, the bourgeois press is conducting a subversive campaign against fraternal socialist countries. The ruling circles of the FRG are particularly active and are trying to exploit events in Czechoslovakia, to provoke friction between the socialist countries, to isolate the GDR, and to carry out their revanchist objectives.

Comrades, can you not see this danger? Is it possible to remain passive under the circumstances and to confine yourselves to declarations and assurances of loyalty to the cause of socialism and

---

[46] In fact, the CPCz CC Presidium did promptly condemn the statement; see "Předsednictvo Ústředního výboru KSČ k prohlášení Dva tisíce slov," *Rudé právo* (Prague), June 29, 1968, p. 1.

commitments of alliance? Can you not see that counterrevolution is seizing one position after another from you? And that the party is losing control over the course of events and is retreating further and further under pressure from the anti-communist forces?

Is not the campaign by the press, radio, and television against the staff exercises of the Warsaw Pact armed forces aimed at sowing mistrust and hostility toward the Soviet Union and the other socialist countries?[47] Things have deteriorated so far that the staff exercises by our troops with the participation of a few additional units of the Soviet army, a perfectly normal part of any military cooperation, are being cited in unsubstantiated allegations about supposed violations of the ČSSR's sovereignty. And this is happening in Czechoslovakia, whose people honor the memory of Soviet soldiers who perished for the freedom and sovereignty of that country. Maneuvers by the military forces of the aggressive NATO bloc are taking place in the vicinity of your western borders, yet not a word is being said about this.[48]

The inspirers of this hostile campaign, as is self-evident, wish to poison the minds of the Czechoslovak people, disorient them, and deflect attention from the fact that Czechoslovakia is able to preserve its independence and sovereignty only as a socialist country and as a member of the socialist community.[49] Only the enemies of socialism can today put forward the slogan on "the defense of the sovereignty" of the ČSSR against the socialist countries—that is, against the very countries whose alliance and fraternal cooperation create the most reliable foundations of the independence and free progress of each of our nations.

We are convinced that a situation has arisen in which the threat to the foundations of socialism in Czechoslovakia also threatens the common vital interests of the other socialist states. The peoples of our countries would never forgive us if we remained indifferent and passive in the face of such a threat.

We live at a time when peace, security, and the freedom of peoples require the unity of all socialist forces more than ever. International tension is not lessening. American imperialism has not abandoned its policy of strength and open intervention against peoples fighting for freedom. It continues the criminal war in Vietnam, backs the Israeli aggressors in the Near East, and obstructs a peaceful settlement of the conflict. The feverish arms race has in no way been halted. The Federal Republic of Germany, where neo-fascist forces are on the rise, is attacking the *status quo* and demanding a revision of borders. It has no intention of abandoning its objective of devouring the GDR and obtaining access to nuclear weapons, and is thus opposed to disarmament proposals. In Europe, where huge quantities of weapons of mass destruction have been amassed, peace and security are maintained primarily as a result of the strength, cohesion, and peaceloving policy of the socialist states. We all are responsible for the strength and unity of the socialist countries and for the destiny of peace.

Our countries are linked by treaties and agreements. These major commitments of states and peoples are based on a common effort to defend socialism and guarantee collective security of the socialist states. Our parties and peoples have historic responsibility not to permit the revolutionary gains we have achieved to be shattered.

Each of our parties is responsible not only to its working class and its people but to the international working class and the world communist movement, and we cannot escape the

---

[47] The Soviet Politburo and Secretariat were receiving alarming reports in this regard from senior military officers stationed in Prague; see, for example, "Obzor pressy, peredach radio i televideniya v otnoshenii s komandno-shtabnom ucheniem i prebyvaniem sovetskikh voisk na territorii Chekhoslovakii," report (TOP SECRET) from Lieut.-General N. Trusov for K. F. Katushev, K. V. Rusakov, and A. A. Gromyko, July 18, 1968, in TsKhSD, F. 5, Op. 60, D. 311, Ll. 3–9.

[48] A reference to the preparations under way for NATO's "Black Lion" exercises, which were due to begin in September 1968. The NATO countries, particularly the United States, were worried that the exercises might appear "provocative" in light of the crisis in Czechoslovakia; hence, on July 24 the projected site of the maneuvers was shifted nearly 200 kilometers to the southwest, well away from the Czechoslovak border.

[49] The notion that Czechoslovakia's "independence" and "sovereignty" depended on its place in the socialist commonwealth later became a cardinal element of the Brezhnev Doctrine (see Document No. 128).

commitments this entails. That is why we must show solidarity and be united in defending the achievements of socialism, our security, and the international positions of the socialist commonwealth.

That is precisely why we maintain that firm resistance to anti-communist forces and a decisive battle for the preservation of the socialist system in Czechoslovakia are not only your duty but ours as well.

The defense of the power of the working class, of all working people, and of socialist achievements in Czechoslovakia demands:

— a decisive and bold stand against right-wing and anti-socialist forces, and the mobilization of all means of defense created by the socialist state;

— an end to the activities of all political organizations acting against socialism;

— a reassertion of control by the party over the mass media—the press, radio, and television—so that they will be used in the interests of the working class, of all working people, and of socialism;

— a closing of the ranks of the party on the foundations of the principles of Marxism–Leninism, unflinching adherence to the principles of democratic centralism, and a struggle against those whose activity aids hostile forces.

We know that in Czechoslovakia there are forces capable of defending the socialist system and defeating anti-socialist elements. The working class, working peasants, the progressive intelligentsia, and the overwhelming majority of the working people of the republic are prepared to do all that is inevitable for the future advancement of socialist society. The task of the day is to give these healthy forces a clear perspective, lift them to action, and mobilize their energies in the struggle against the forces of counterrevolution in order to save and consolidate socialism in Czechoslovakia.

Confronted by the threat of counterrevolution, the voice of the working class must resound with full strength in response to a call by the communist party. The working class together with the working peasantry has expended maximum efforts for the victory of the socialist revolution. The preservation of the socialist achievements is something they cherish most.

We are convinced that the Communist Party of Czechoslovakia, aware of its responsibility, will take urgent measures to block the road to reaction. In this struggle you can count on the solidarity and comprehensive assistance of the fraternal socialist parties.

. . .

238

DOCUMENT No. 54: Press Conference with Lt. General Václav Prchlík, July 15, 1968

Source: ÚSD, AÚV KSČ, F. 07/15.

This transcript of Lt. General Václav Prchlík's July 15 news conference reflects the growing tension between Prague and Moscow as well as the influence of the Prague Spring on the Czechoslovak People's Army. As the chief of the CPCz CC department for state organs, General Prchlík opened his press conference by outlining a number of changes in the security organs, including loosening centralized communist party control over the military, that his department planned to recommend for approval at the upcoming Extraordinary 14th Congress of the CPCz.

The key question asked by reporters dealt with the continuing presence of Soviet military troops on Czechoslovak soil, despite repeated promises by Marshal Yakubovskii to withdraw them and an-nouncements by Czechoslovak officials that they would soon be gone. Prchlík responded that he had carefully checked all the documents pertaining to the Warsaw Pact to determine whether any provisions in those documents entitled "certain partners to station their units arbitrarily on the territory of other member states." He declared that he had found no such provisions and that, on the contrary, all the relevant documents stipulated that troop deployments were permitted "only after agreement has been reached among the member states of the pact. I emphasize here: only after their agreement!"

Prchlík also used the news conference to voice complaints about other aspects of the Warsaw Pact. It was "deplorable," he stated, that the Soviet Union, East Germany, Poland, Hungary, and Bulgaria had chosen to "disregard our [the CPCz's] views" by going ahead with the meeting in Warsaw. Prchlík contended that the alliance had not yet provided for "genuine equality" or "genuinely equal rights" of its members. Echoing proposals voiced by Romanian leaders since the mid-1960s, Prchlík called for reforms in the Joint Command so that it could "perform its functions much better," and urged that every member state of the pact be permitted to "assert its own role." On this point, he advocated the "formulation of Czechoslovakia's own military doctrine," which would be distinct from the standardized doctrine of the Warsaw Pact. Both publicly and privately, the General's comments provoked swift denunciations from Soviet leaders.

(See Documents Nos. 68, 69, 84.)

In the past, the party always insisted on maintaining direct control over the army and security forces. Moreover, given the concept of the past model of the party, this principle of direct control was narrowed down even further. As a result, military and security policy was, in essence, determined by a small group of the party bureaucracy in the center. Indeed, serious matters often were decided by only a single person. In recent years it has become increasingly evident that this concept of direct control of the army and security forces, and the concept of political control over these institutions, did not provide for a complete and lasting solution of matters in their proper context. Rigid bureaucratic centralism in the running of things did not allow us to improve the quality of the process of deliberation and decision-making. On the contrary, it was a fertile breeding ground for amateurism and subjectivism. Not only was the entire command-and-control system in these institutions of power characterized by all the afflictions which we speak about nowadays in our critical analysis of the political system, but it was in precisely these institutions, as a result of the specific principles governing their development, that such ailments were most acute. The same applies to the party-political system. Increasingly serious conflicts and disputes emerged in these institutions in the past—that is, in the army and security forces—which were insoluble under the previous system. The mounting criticism of such phenomena by employees of these institutions, by party and political bodies, and by party organizations ran up against an insurmountable wall of bureaucratic incompetence and the inability of the previous political leadership to deal with these matters. . . .

The first analyses we are making in the sphere of military and security policy show that in the security sphere, for example, the state security forces had a number of very progressive-minded workers who had already come forward with criticism, suggestions, and new ideas in the past that went unheeded in the system which existed at the time. In regard to safeguarding the external and internal security of the state, we believe the party must abandon the principle of direct control over the armed forces and the security corps, and that it must prepare a new concept of political leadership and transfer control of these power institutions to state bodies. . . .

A proposal has been put forward to set up a State Defense Council. The functional relationship of the Council with the government, the concept of the Council's work, and the structure of its secretariat are still being assessed. We believe the State Defense Council should be a government body. This means that it should not be placed above the government and should not perform governmental functions, but that, on the contrary, it should be attached to the government as its organ of expertise in this area. The first task of the State Defense Council will be to assess the need for, possibility of, and essential conditions for a Czechoslovakian military doctrine. We expect the 14th Congress to say something about these problems as well. This is linked to the question of how to make further improvements in the quality of our military coalition, the Warsaw Pact itself. We maintain that necessary qualitative changes should also be carried out in the Warsaw Pact's concept of its function and in the establishment of relations within the Warsaw Pact. In our opinion, the first task should be to reinforce the role of the Political Consultative Committee, which should become a body that functions regularly, systematically, and purposefully, without having to rely on how it will be convened.[50] At the moment it is working rather sporadically and does not fulfill its function. If it were to operate as we propose, objective conditions would be created to ensure that military aspects would not be given precedence over political ones even in the pact's Joint Command system.[51] On the question of relations within the coalition, we believe they must be improved. Above all, we need to emphasize the genuine equality of all members of the coalition and ensure that they have genuinely equal rights, and we must enable each member state of the coalition, so to speak, to assert its own role and take a more active part and initiative in the conceptual work of the entire coalition. Moreover, we believe that unequivocal guarantees must be established making it impossible for individual members to form groupings within the coalition, so that to prevent factional activities, if we can call them that, within the coalition. No matter what the intentions or interests of their organizers, such factional activities in the final analysis always result in violations of the fundamental clauses of the Warsaw Treaty concerning state sovereignty and the principle of non-interference in the internal affairs of member states. Of course, in the materials for the congress we are raising several other problems as well, such as the overall structure—in other words, the function and structure—of the party's various institutions in the army and security forces, their command system, and a whole series of other matters.[52] . . .

Excerpts from the Question-and-Answer Session

In my view, it is deplorable that this meeting is taking place, especially since our allies were aware of the positions of our CC Presidium and government.[53] The Presidium and the government, as we know, rejected the meeting; they refused to take part in it and expressed disapproval

[50] The Political Consultative Committee (PCC) was the main political organ of the Warsaw Pact. Although the original Warsaw Treaty of May 1955 required the PCC to meet at least twice a year, the body convened a total of only seven times between 1955 and 1966, with no meetings at all in several years. Proposals to reinvigorate, replace, or supplement the PCC had been put forth since the early to mid-1960s.

[51] The Joint Command of the Warsaw Pact Armed Forces was another body set up under the original Warsaw Treaty. As its name implies, it was supposed to exercise command over all troops designated for the Joint Armed Forces. All the top officers in the Joint Command, without exception, were Soviet marshals or generals.

[52] See Document No. 61.

[53] Prchlík is responding here to a question about the Warsaw Meeting, which had begun the previous day and ended shortly before the news conference.

of efforts to hold a multilateral conference. They were more than willing, however, to engage in bilateral talks immediately with officials from each of the member states.

It is deplorable that a meeting is being held among allied states that have disregarded our views. I myself wanted to know whether in the Warsaw Pact there are some provisions that would give certain partners the right to deploy or station their units arbitrarily on the territory of other member states.[54] I went through all the available materials and did not locate such a clause in any of them. On the contrary, the Treaty on Friendship, Cooperation, and Mutual Assistance[55] provides for the further consolidation and promotion of cooperation and mutual assistance, and both the preamble and Article 8 emphasize the need to respect the sovereignty of states as well as the principle of non-interference in their internal affairs.[56] A document was drawn up in 1956 on the basis of Article 6 of the treaty which was called "Protocol on the Establishment of a Joint Command of the Armed Forces of the Warsaw Pact Countries." This protocol, too, respects the fundamental clauses of the Warsaw Treaty and stresses that all fundamental measures, especially those concerning the deployment of forces, will at all times be taken exclusively in keeping with the requirements of our common defense against the threat of an external enemy, and only after agreement has been reached among member states of the Pact. I emphasize here: only *after* their agreement![57] Similar provisions are also contained in the statutes of the Joint Command of the Armed Forces. When I went over to the General Staff, I asked the appropriate personnel there whether there are any secret clauses attached to the three documents I've just mentioned. They responded, with full responsibility, that they knew nothing about any such clauses, even though they had taken part in all the talks.

With regard to questions concerning the Joint Command of the Warsaw Pact itself, the situation at the moment is such that this command consists solely of marshals, generals, and other senior officers of the Soviet army, while the armies of the other member states have had to make do with mere "representatives" at the Joint Command who until now have had no duties and no share in decision-making. All they do is act as liaisons. That is also why our side has on several occasions come forward with proposals to establish the necessary conditions for the Joint Command to perform its functions much better. One of these conditions is the requirement that the Joint Command consist of appropriate experts from individual armies who would be able to participate in the formulation and implementation of policies during the whole process of decision-making and to take part in deliberations in the command system at all stages. Until now proposals to this effect have gone nowhere. In light of the future work of the Joint Command, we maintain that the position of the ministers of the individual countries also will have to be clarified; at the moment they serve, directly or indirectly, as mere deputy commanders of the

---

[54] Prchlík is responding here to widespread rumors in Czechoslovakia that the Warsaw Treaty contained secret provisions entitling the Soviet Union to deploy forces on the territory of the other member states. It is unclear whether Prchlík was aware of the numerous top-secret agreements that did in fact exist, including one signed in 1965 by the Soviet and Czechoslovak defense ministers providing for the storage of Soviet tactical nuclear warheads on Czechoslovak territory as well as the stationing of elite Soviet troops to protect those warheads. For details on this agreement and its significance, see Mark Kramer, "The Prague Spring and the Soviet Invasion of Czechoslovakia: New Interpretations," Cold War International History *Bulletin*, No. 3 (Fall 1993), pp. 8–10.

[55] This is the title of the original treaty of alliance signed on May 14, 1955.

[56] The Soviet intrusion on Czech sovereignty was, by this time, a major embarrassment for senior officials in Prague. In early July, General Prchlík had twice announced a "deadline" for the withdrawal of Soviet troops at the Šumava exercises, only to find those troops firmly in place on the announced day of departure. On July 13, a small number of Soviet forces were pulled out, but the withdrawal came to an abrupt halt the following day amidst rumors that new Soviet troops were flying in, and new equipment was being deployed at Soviet camps in Czechoslovakia. That same day, Marshal Yakubovskii informed CPCz leaders that Soviet troops would remain until at least July 21 without providing any reason for the delay.

[57] Emphasis is in the original Czech transcript.

Joint Command.[58] I believe that this relationship does not correspond fully to their position of equality. . . .

In my view, and it is now dawning on the government and Presidium as well, we have only one viable option, which is to insist that we will never allow our state's sovereignty to be violated and will never permit anyone to interfere in our internal affairs, and we will show ourselves capable of solving our problems on our own. What guarantees do we have? The guarantees, in my view, are that we will consistently adhere to the principles I just mentioned and will be uncompromising in our demands that all provisions of our treaties be observed.

. . . We have further guarantees arising from the fact that views within the Warsaw Pact itself are now divergent. As I see it, we must do what we can to exploit this divergency, and we must also take advantage of the different views expressed by fraternal parties outside the Warsaw Pact. . . .

Of course we are interested most of all in ensuring that common sense prevails and that contradictions do not multiply during this period of great tension. For our part, we will do nothing that would exacerbate the situation. But in taking this stance, we do not intend to make concessions or compromises which would be unacceptable to us. On the contrary, we will uphold this stance by insisting on the full and scrupulous implementation of principles embodied in a long series of documents adopted both within the Warsaw Pact and by the international communist movement.

---

[58] Prchlík alludes here to one of the more blatant manifestations of inequality in the Warsaw Pact structures at the time. The Joint Command overall was headed by the commander-in-chief, a Soviet marshal, who also served as a Soviet first deputy minister of defense. The defense ministers from the other Warsaw Pact states served as deputies on the Joint Command to the Soviet C-in-C. In other words, East European defense ministers were subordinated to a Soviet officer whom they nominally outranked. This problem was at least partly redressed in 1969, when a Council of Defense Ministers was established within the Pact, and the positions for deputies on the Joint Command were allocated to East European deputy defense ministers.

DOCUMENT No. 55: Response by the CPCz CC Presidium to the Warsaw Letter, July 16–17, 1968

Source: ÚSD, AÚV KSČ, F. 02/1; published also in *Rudé právo*, July 19, 1968, p. 1; Vondrová & Navrátil, vol. 1, pp. 310–316.

The CPCz CC Presidium adopted this point-by-point response to the Warsaw Letter at a session called by Dubček on July 16–17. The statement methodically rebuts the charges leveled in the Warsaw Letter and defends the specific policies as well as the broad nature of the Prague Spring. It invokes the Soviet Union's own rhetoric about the "sacred" principles of relations among socialist countries, especially the principle of non-interference in internal affairs, and it calls for bilateral talks between the CPCz and CPSU to help overcome the most serious of their disagreements.

A Soviet rejoinder to the Czechoslovak Presidium's response to the Warsaw Letter appeared in Moscow Pravda *on July 22. (Similar rejoinders appeared in East German, Polish, and Bulgarian newspapers.) The hostile and caustic tone of the Soviet reaction indicates that the CPCz Presidium's statement simply reinforced the Soviet Politburo's suspicion that the Czechoslovak leadership had no intention of complying with Moscow's demands.*

The Presidium of the Central Committee of the Communist Party of Czechoslovakia has thoroughly examined the letter sent to the Central Committee of our party from the meeting of representatives of five socialist countries, held in Warsaw.

The letter emphasizes that it is motivated by concern for our common cause and for the consolidation of socialism. Guided by this same end and by the same endeavor, we would like to be equally frank in setting forth our own position on the matters discussed in the letter.

In so doing, we are fully aware that the complex problems which are the subject of our attention cannot be fully explained in an exchange of letters; that is not the objective of our statement. Instead, it proposes direct talks between the parties.

Some of the concerns expressed in the letter were spelled out in the resolution adopted by the May plenum of the CPCz Central Committee. However, in our opinion, the causes of the contradictory political situation are the accumulation of these conflicts during the period prior to the January session of the CPCz Central Committee; these contradictions cannot be solved properly in a short period of time. It is therefore inevitable that in implementing the policy set out in the Action Program of our party the vast current of sound socialist activity is being accompanied by extremist tendencies, and that lingering anti-socialist forces in our society are attempting to take advantage of the situation, while dogmatic and sectarian forces linked with the erroneous policy pursued prior to the January session of the CPCz Central Committee are also becoming increasingly active. In this complicated situation not even the party is able to escape the internal contradictions that accompany the process of consolidation around the policy of the Action Program. The negative aspects of this process include the violation of the principles of democratic centralism in the activities of certain communists, which is the price we have to pay for the bureaucratic centralism imposed by the former leadership for many years and the suppression of internal party democracy. All this is making it impossible for us to achieve the results we desire in our political work.

We have no intention of concealing these facts, nor do we conceal them from the party and the people. That is why the May plenum of the CC clearly stated that all forces have to be mustered to avert a conflict situation in the country and a threat to the socialist system. Our party made it abundantly clear that if such a threat were to arise, we would resort to all means to protect the socialist system. In other words, we were fully aware of this threat. We understand that the fraternal parties in the socialist countries cannot remain indifferent. However, we see no objective reason to justify either the assertion that our current situation is counterrevolutionary or the allegation of an imminent threat to the foundations of the socialist system. Nor do we see any basis for the claim that a change in our socialist foreign policy is being drafted in Czechoslovakia or that there is a threat that our country will break away from the socialist commonwealth.

Our alliance and friendship with the USSR and the other socialist countries are deeply entrenched in the social system, in historical traditions, and in the experience of our peoples, their interests, and their outlooks on life. Liberation from Nazi occupation and the ushering in of a new life are permanently associated in the minds of our people with the historic victory of the USSR in World War II. They pay homage to the heroes who sacrificed their lives in this struggle.

The Action Program of our party is based on this. These traditions are our starting point.

The overriding orientation of Czechoslovakia's foreign policy was born and endorsed in the course of the national liberation struggle and during the socialist transformation of our country. It is alliance and cooperation with the Soviet Union and the other socialist states. We will do our utmost to ensure that friendly ties with our allies—the countries of the world socialist community—continue to evolve on the basis of mutual regard, sovereignty, equality, respect, and international solidarity. In this sense we will be more active and contribute to the common efforts of the Council for Mutual Economic Assistance and the Warsaw Pact on a well thought-out basis.

The letter mentions attacks that have been made against our socialist foreign policy, an offensive against our alliance and friendship with the socialist countries, and demands for the revision of our common and coordinated policy toward the FRG. It even claims that FRG and revanchist policies are finding a sympathetic ear in leading circles of our country. We are astonished by such allegations, for it is well known that the ČSSR is pursuing a consistent, socialist foreign policy. The principles of our foreign policy have been defined in the CPCz Action Program as well as in the government's policy statements. These documents and statements by senior Czechoslovak officials, as well as other acts taken by us, are consistently guided by the principles of socialist internationalism, alliance, and the promotion of friendly relations with the Soviet Union and the other socialist states.

We believe these facts are decisive and not irresponsible utterances by individuals in our country.

In view of the bitter experience of our peoples with German imperialism and militarism, it is unthinkable that any Czechoslovak government would ignore these experiences and recklessly gamble with the destiny of our country. It is even less likely that this would be done by a socialist government and we must reject all such suspicions. With regard to our relations with the FRG, it is generally known that the ČSSR, though a direct neighbor of that country, was the last to take certain steps toward a partial arrangement of bilateral relations, especially in the economic sphere. By contrast, other socialist countries settled their relations with the FRG in this or that way a long time ago without triggering any fears.

At the same time we consistently respect and defend the interests of the GDR, our socialist ally, and we are making every attempt to consolidate its international standing and authority. This is clearly demonstrated by all statements made by leading officials of our party and state throughout the period since January 1968.

The treaties and accords uniting the socialist countries are a significant factor for cooperation, peace, and collective security. The ČSSR honors all its contractual obligations and treaties, and systematically promotes a network of treaties with the socialist countries. Evidence of this comes from the new treaties of alliance we have recently concluded with the Bulgarian People's Republic and the Hungarian People's Republic as well as the planned treaty on friendship and cooperation with the Romanian Socialist Republic.[59]

---

[59] The treaty with Bulgaria was signed during a visit by Zhivkov to Czechoslovakia in April; the treaty with Hungary during a visit by Dubček and Černík to Hungary in June; and the treaty with Romania during Ceauşescu's visit in mid-August, a few days before the invasion.

In the same spirit as the authors of the letter, we affirm that we will never permit the historic achievements of socialism and the security of the peoples of our country to be placed in jeopardy or allow imperialism to breach the socialist system, either peacefully or by force, and change the balance of power in Europe in its favor. The paramount aim of our post-January development is precisely to increase the internal strength and stability of the socialist system and, as a consequence, our ties of alliance.

The maneuvers of the Warsaw Treaty armed forces on the territory of the ČSSR are a practical demonstration of our loyalty to these bonds of alliance. We have taken the necessary steps to ensure the success of the exercises. Our people and members of our armed forces have given a friendly welcome to the Soviet and other allied troops on the territory of the ČSSR. By their attendance, top party and state officials have demonstrated the significance and interest we attach to these maneuvers. The Czech public was not overwhelmed by skepticism and apprehension until the date of the departure of the allied armies from ČSSR territory and the date of the completion of the exercises were changed time and time again.

The letter from the five parties also deals with certain contemporary domestic political problems. We accept the assurance that the object of this concern is not interference in "the methods of planning and directing the socialist economy of Czechoslovakia" or in our "measures aimed at improving the structure of the economy and advancing socialist democracy," and that "the basing of relations between Czechs and Slovaks on sound foundations of fraternal cooperation within the Czechoslovak Socialist Republic" is welcomed.

We agree that the strength and solidity of our ties—unquestionably the common vital interest of all of us—depend on the internal strength of the socialist system in each of the fraternal countries. There is no doubt that undermining the leading role of the communist party would create a threat to the socialist system. That is precisely why it is imperative to understand correctly the factors on which the strength of the socialist system in Czechoslovakia depends today, and that these factors will reinforce the leading role of the communist party.

Based on past experience, we stated in the party's Action Program: "Today it is essential for the party to pursue the kind of policy that would justify its leading role in our society. We are convinced that in the present situation this is a prerequisite for the socialist development of the country. . . .

The communist party relies on the voluntary support of the people; it does not apply its leading role by ruling society but by dedicated service to free, progressive and socialist development. The party cannot enforce its authority; it must constantly gain it by its actions. It cannot impose its policy by decrees, but by the work of its members and by the integrity of its ideals."

We do not conceal the fact—and we said so frankly at the May plenum of the Central Committee—that there are attempts being made now in our country to discredit the party and to deny it the moral and political right to lead society. But if we ask ourselves whether it is correct to assess such phenomena as a threat to the socialist system and as the demise of the leading role of the CPCz under pressure from reactionary and counterrevolutionary forces, we conclude that this is not the case.

The leading role of our party has suffered badly in the past by deformations in the 1950s and by the irresolute policies of the leadership, headed by Antonín Novotný. It was his fault that many social disputes increased: between Czechs and Slovaks, between the intelligentsia and the workers, and between the younger and older generations. Inconsistent measures dealing with economic problems created a state of affairs in which we are not able to solve many of the justified economic demands of the working people and the efficiency of the entire economy is in serious jeopardy. Under this leadership the confidence of the masses in the party began to decline, and criticism and opposition were being voiced, but this was "solved" by the use of force against justified discontent, criticism, and attempts to solve social problems justly in the interest of the party and its leading position.

Instead of correcting mistakes in a gradual and well-considered manner, the leadership committed further errors and contradictions as a result of subjectivism in the decision-making process. In the years when objective conditions already existed for the gradual implementation of socialist democracy and when scientific management could have been introduced, subjective shortcomings were bringing social disputes and difficulties to a head. To the outside world it appeared that everything was in order in the ČSSR; the appearance was given of a conflict-free environment. The actual decline of confidence in the party was shrouded by external forms of directive party control. Although this regime was being presented as a solid guarantee of the interests of the entire socialist camp, problems were mounting within it, and their proper solution was being suppressed by the use of force against advocates of new and creative ideas.

The slightest intimation that there could be a return to these methods would trigger opposition among the overwhelming majority of party members and resistance among working people, cooperative farmers, and members of the intelligentsia. By taking such a step, the party would politically endanger its leading role and provoke a situation in which a true confrontation would arise. This would create a genuine threat to the socialist gains of the people and, consequently, to our common interests in the anti-imperialist front of the socialist commonwealth.

We agree that one of the primary tasks of the party is to thwart the plans of right-wing and anti-socialist forces. For this purpose our party outlined its tactical political procedure at the May session of the Central Committee and is dealing with these problems accordingly. This procedure consists of a set of measures that can produce results only if we have the conditions necessary to carry them out gradually, over a period of several months.

We maintain that one of the conditions for success is that the implementation of the Action Program and the preparation of the party congress should not be endangered by an inept step that would provoke a political and power conflict in our country. In its resolution at the May session the Central Committee stated this quite clearly:

"In the present situation the party considers as its paramount task the defusion of all threats to the socialist nature of the regime and to the socialist system, no matter from which quarter, whether by right-wing, anti-communist tendencies or by conservative forces that would welcome a return to conditions prior to January 1968 and that have been incapable of advancing socialism."

Our party is setting out the following major targets and stages in its political work:

1. To dissociate the entire party from deformations of the past for which specific people in the former leadership bear the blame. These specific people are rightly called to account.

2. To prepare the Extraordinary 14th Party Congress to appraise developments and the political situation following the January plenum and, in accordance with the principles of democratic centralism in the party, to lay down a policy binding for the entire party, adopt a political standpoint on the federal arrangement of the ČSSR, approve the new party statutes, and elect a new Central Committee that will have the full authority and confidence of the party and of society as a whole.

3. After the 14th Congress, take firm steps to solve all key internal political problems: the creation of a political system based on the socialist platform of the National Front and social self-administration, the settlement of the federal constitutional legal system, elections to state representative bodies (federal, national and local), and the preparation of a new Constitution.

We are now at a point where we must wage a political battle for the policy laid down by the CPCz CC's May plenum. It is a genuine battle; that is why there are not only victories but also setbacks. Yet the results of individual battles are not sufficient to permit a correct assessment of the outcome of the struggle as a whole. We nevertheless believe that since the May plenum we have succeeded in consolidating the political situation.

The special district and regional conferences held during the past few days have clearly demonstrated that the party is uniting on the basis of the course set forth in the Action Program. Delegates to the Congress have been elected who will guarantee that the party's future policy will not be decided by extremist forces, but by the democratically selected, sound, and progressive core of our party. The representatives of the new CPCz leadership, supporting the Action Program and the CC's May plenum, are all candidates for the new Central Committee to be chosen by the party's regional conferences. A definite and gradual stabilization is taking place within the party, and the first successful steps to prepare the Congress have been taken.

Communists are taking the initiative to form a politically binding platform of the National Front in accordance with the resolution of the CPCz CC's May plenum. On 15 June 1968, all political groupings of the National Front adopted a policy statement that unequivocally acknowledges the historically attained leading position of the CPCz and sets forth the principles underlying the socialist system as well as its socialist domestic and foreign policies. The National Front at the moment is debating its draft statutes, which ensure the socialist orientation of all political parties and organizations.

The law on legal rehabilitation essentially deals with the painful problem of the unlawful repression of innocent persons, which occurred in the past.[60] This has enabled the public and the mass media to avoid having to focus attention on these matters any longer.

In September, immediately after the Congress, several major new laws will be discussed: the constitutional law on the National Front, which is to endorse the permanent existence of the political party system within the framework of the National Front; and a law on the right of assembly and organization, which is to provide legal criteria for the establishment and activities of different voluntary organizations, groups, clubs, etc. This will make it possible to foil attempts by anti-communist forces to acquire organizational foundations for their public activity.

In keeping with the resolution of the CPCz CC's May plenum, communists are dealing actively with major problems connected with the work of the trade unions and workers' councils. For the most part, the party has been successful in withstanding political demagogues, who have attempted to use the justified demands of the workers to disrupt our system and unleash a spontaneous movement in the name of "workers' demands" in order to aggravate the economic and political situation in the country. Conditions permitting, we are simultaneously dealing with certain crucial social and political issues, such as raising low pensions and making urgent wage adjustments. The government is dealing step by step with the country's economic problems to give fresh impetus to production and to provide further improvement in living standards.

We have taken the measures necessary to guarantee the security of our borders. The party fully supports the consolidation of the army, the security services, the judiciary, and the courts. The party has adopted a clear stand on the question of the People's Militia, whose nationwide assembly has given the new CPCz leadership and the Action Program its full support. It is known that the significance of this move was hailed by the working people not only in our country but in the USSR as well.

We think that all this is the sound result of the execution of the policy laid down by the CPCz CC's May plenum, as well as a significant demonstration that the political situation is consolidating and that the influence of the party—no longer merely declared but now genuine—is growing stronger.

In spite of this, we are aware, and do not intend to conceal, that we are not carrying out all the conclusions of the CPCz CC's May plenum satisfactorily. At public gatherings and in the mass media there occasionally appear voices and tendencies alien to the positive endeavors of the party, state institutions, and the National Front. We regard the solution of this problem to be

---

[60] For a useful overview of this issue in 1968, see H. Gordon Skilling, *Czechoslovakia's Interrupted Revolution* (Princeton, NJ: Princeton University Press, 1976), pp. 373–411. For detailed background and statistics on the use of political repression in Czechoslovakia between 1948 and 1967, see František Gebauer et al., *Soudní perzekuce politické povahy v Československu 1948–1989: Statistický přehled*, Study No. 12 (Prague: Ustav pro soudobe dejiny AV ČR, 1993).

a long-term task, and are guided by the resolution of the CC's May plenum, which states that "political leadership cannot be exercised by old administrative methods and the use of force." The CPCz CC Presidium, the government, and the National Front distinctly repudiated the appeals contained in the "Two Thousand Words," which advocated anarchy and violation of the constitutional nature of our political reform. It is worth noting that following our repudiation of the statement, no further documents of that kind have appeared here, and that the "Two Thousand Words" appeal in no way endangered the party, the National Front, or the socialist state.

Various campaigns and groundless diatribes against individual officials and public figures, including members of the new CPCz leadership—diatribes that come from extreme right-wing and left-wing quarters—remain a harmful feature of our society. The CPCz CC Secretariat and other senior comrades have spoken out vigorously against these practices in specific instances.

We know that this has been made possible by the abolition of censorship and the passing of a law on freedom of speech and the press. All that used to be "told for one's ears only" can now be stated publicly.

However, if we ask ourselves whether it is right to regard such episodes as a collapse of the CPCz's leading political role under the weight of reactionary and counterrevolutionary forces, we must conclude that this is not so. After all, this is no more than one facet of our present situation. There is another, and in our opinion more decisive, element at work here: the growing authority of the party's new democratic policy in the eyes of the broadest section of the working people, as well as the escalating activity by the great majority of the population. The overwhelming majority of the population of all classes and segments of society backs the abolition of censorship and freedom of speech. The CPCz is trying to demonstrate that it is capable of leading society politically by means other than condemned bureaucratic political methods and above all by the force of its Marxist–Leninist ideas, its program, and its correct policy, which is supported by all the people.

Our party can win its difficult political struggle only if it is permitted to implement the tactical course of the May plenum and solve all fundamental political questions at the Extraordinary 14th Congress in the spirit of the Action Program. We therefore consider all pressure intended to compel the party to adopt a different procedure—that is, to deal with our political problems at a different time and other than at the 14th Congress—as a major threat to the successful consolidation of the party's leading role in the ČSSR. Such pressure is being applied by internal extremist right-wing forces as well as by those acting from conservative, dogmatic, and sectarian positions who are striving for a return to the situation prior to January 1968.

The appraisal of the situation contained in the letter from the five parties, and the undeniably sincere advice for our future procedure, fail to take account of the full complexity of society's dynamic motion, as analyzed by the CPCz CC's May plenum, and of the extensive conclusions adopted by that session. If our policy is to remain a Marxist–Leninist party, it cannot be based on superficial turns of events that do not always accurately reflect the profound causes of the development of society. Instead, our policy must grasp the essential features of this development and be guided by them.

The fraternal parties can today best serve the interests of socialism in our country by showing confidence in the leadership of the CPCz and giving their full support to its policy. That is why we proposed bilateral meetings with officials from our parties as the basis of the success of joint negotiations, and that joint negotiations be based on more thorough mutual consultations and objective information.

We sincerely regret that our proposals have not been accepted. It is not our fault that the meeting in Warsaw was held without us. On two occasions, at sessions of the CPCz CC Presidium on 8 and 12 July, we discussed the proposals of the five parties to convene this meeting, and immediately gave our opinion on what we considered the most appropriate way to prepare for such a meeting. Unfortunately, our deliberations on 12 July were already pointless, since the meeting had already been convened for 14 July regardless of the outcome of our discussions.

This became clear on 13 July in a dispatch of the Czechoslovak News Agency, from which we learned that officials from the five parties were already arriving in Warsaw.[61]

In none of the statements we sent to the five parties did we refuse in principle to attend a joint meeting. We merely stated our opinion on the desirability of holding such a meeting at this point and on the procedure to adopt in preparing it so that it will be truly objective and employ more thorough information about our complicated problems. The letters from the five parties, which were sent to us between 4 and 6 July 1968, lead us to believe that such information was absolutely essential if we are to avoid negotiations endangered *a priori* by the majority of participants' one-sided and insufficient information on the existing situation in Czechoslovakia.

This was our objective when we proposed holding preliminary bilateral negotiations. We were guided, not by attempts to detach ourselves from the community of our parties and countries, but, on the contrary, by a desire to contribute to the consolidation and development of the community.

We maintain that the common cause of socialism will not be served by arranging meetings at which the policy and activities of a fraternal party are judged without the participation of representatives from that party. We consider the principle, enshrined in the Declaration of the Government of the USSR of 30 October 1956, as still valid: "The countries of the great commonwealth of socialist nations, united by the common ideals of building a socialist society and the principles of proletarian internationalism, can shape their relations solely on the basis of full equality, of respect for territorial integrity and state independence and sovereignty, and of non-interference in their internal affairs." As you know, this principle was endorsed by the meeting of representatives of communist parties in Moscow in November 1957 and has been widely accepted. In our activities we intend to continue to strengthen and promote the deep international traditions that, we believe, must include an understanding of the common interests and aims of progressive forces throughout the world, while taking account of specific national requirements.

We do not want our relations to deteriorate further and are prepared to help stabilize the situation for the benefit of socialism and the unity of the socialist countries. We will do nothing that would conflict with this objective. However, we expect that the other side will assist our endeavors and show understanding for our situation.

We believe it is crucial to be able to arrange the bilateral negotiations we are proposing.[62] These negotiations would consider, among other things, the possibility of a joint meeting of the socialist countries, enabling us to set the agenda, composition, venue, and date. The decisive matter, in our opinion, is to agree within the shortest possible time on positive steps that would guarantee our continued friendly cooperation and provide convincing evidence of our common determination to promote and reinforce friendly relations. This is in the interest of our common struggle against imperialism, our struggle for the peace and security of our peoples, and our struggle for democracy and socialism.

---

[61] Dubček and Černík received this dispatch while they were still *en route* to their meeting at Komárno with János Kádár.

[62] Brezhnev accepted the proposal for a bilateral meeting when he spoke by phone to Dubček on July 19, and the two sides agreed a few days later to hold the talks at Čierna nad Tisou starting on the 29th. Brezhnev's willingness to accommodate the CPCz's request did not represent a major change of course, however.

DOCUMENT No. 56: Speech by Leonid Brezhnev to the CPSU Central Committee on the Proceedings and Results of the Warsaw Meeting, July 17, 1968

Source: ÚSD, Sb. KV, Z/S 4; Vondrová & Navrátil, vol. 1, pp. 316–321.

Leonid Brezhnev gave this lengthy presentation to a hastily-convened meeting of the CPSU Central Committee on July 17. He structured his debriefing of the Warsaw Meeting around three distinct areas: introductory comments to the CPSU Central Committee outlining the background to the Warsaw Meeting; the speech Brezhnev delivered at the Warsaw Meeting, which he read again in full to the members of the Central Committee; and his assessment of the Warsaw Meeting and actions to be taken in its aftermath.

The transcript records Brezhnev's uncompromising tone. Brezhnev emphasized that the Soviet Politburo had done its utmost to convince CPCz leaders that they should reassert control themselves. If the Czechoslovak authorities refrained much longer from adopting the requisite measures, he made clear, the Soviet Union would have to undertake coercive steps of its own, including military as well as political pressure. The Soviet first secretary insisted that Moscow had both a right and a duty to use any means necessary to thwart the impending "counterrevolutionary coup" in Czechoslovakia—a task that could be accomplished only by crushing the "second center" in the CPCz, which was behind the "reactionary onslaught." Although Brezhnev promised that the Soviet Union would "continue to expend all efforts" to find a political solution before resorting to "extreme measures," he conveyed the impression throughout his speech that the search for meaningful political steps was likely to be futile.

Brezhnev's lengthy speech won the "complete approval" and "unanimous endorsement" of the CPSU Central Committee plenum.

Results of the Meeting in Warsaw of Delegations from the Communist and Workers' Parties of Socialist Countries[63]

Comrades,

The CPSU CC Politburo believes it is necessary to convene this plenum in order to present the results of the meeting that took place in Warsaw on 14–15 July among the party and government leaders of Bulgaria, Hungary, the GDR, Poland, and the Soviet Union.

At the center of attention—that is, the basic question considered at this meeting—was the dangerous course of events in Czechoslovakia. Before presenting materials from the conference, let me explain that after the CPSU Central Committee plenum in April, which dealt with the Czechoslovak events, the CPSU CC Politburo believed at the time, as expressed at the April plenum, that it should help the healthy forces and above all the Communist Party of Czechoslovakia to prevent the loss of socialist achievements in Czechoslovakia and a rupture in the socialist community. In the meantime, the Politburo informed our party about the dangerous twists and turns in the political processes and political life of Czechoslovakia that had taken place recently.

There is no doubt that the situation in Czechoslovakia since the April plenum has become more and more complicated. We carefully followed the course of events and adopted a number of measures aimed at helping the leadership of the CPCz, in a comradely way, to correct the situation and thwart the danger looming over the socialist gains of a fraternal people. All the members of the Politburo and the CPSU CC Secretariat are taking part in this work.

---

[63] Russian President Boris Yeltsin turned this valuable historical document over to the Czechoslovak commission in 1992.

After the meeting in Dresden, which we reviewed at the last plenum, we invited the CPCz CC leadership to Moscow. Attending that meeting were Cdes. Dubček, Černík, Smrkovský, and Biľak.[64] At the meeting we stated our assessment of events in a tactical but sufficiently firm manner together with our views on how to cope with the anti-socialist and counterrevolutionary forces in Czechoslovakia. At that meeting, as in Dresden, the comrades assured us that they were taking all measures and would take additional measures to stabilize the situation in the party and country and then to control the mass media which, as is known, have slipped out of the party's hands. They told us that at the May plenum of the CPCz CC, the party would adopt the necessary measures to wage a decisive struggle against the danger from the rightists and against the anti-socialist elements.

In Moscow we talked to the Czech comrades about holding military exercises on the territory of Czechoslovakia, thinking that this would also help and support the healthy forces and have a certain political impact on the situation in Czechoslovakia.

It must be said in connection with the events in Czechoslovakia that all actions of our party's CC Politburo were and are fully consistent with the measures taken by the Central Committees of the communist and workers' parties of the other fraternal socialist countries—Poland, the GDR, Hungary, and Bulgaria.

On 8 May, as you know, there was a meeting of the leaders of the communist parties of these five countries in Moscow, which featured a wide exchange of opinions on the situation in Czechoslovakia. At this meeting, as well as later, there was full agreement regarding the danger to Czechoslovakia.[65]

Considering the development of events in Czechoslovakia, we felt it necessary to continue to adopt other measures to show support for the healthy forces both in the party and among the people.

At an important juncture, from our point of view, we gave Cde. Kosygin permission to take leave for treatment in Karlovy Vary (comrades, Karlovy Vary was a pretext), making it possible for him to meet Cdes. Dubček, Černík, and Svoboda, as well as several other members of the Czechoslovak leadership.[66] For this same purpose, we used members of the Central Committee and secretaries of regional party committees of twin cities and factories to exploit contacts already established in our country with twin cities in the ČSSR. During these months Cdes. Shelest, Shcherbitskii, Konotop, Shibaev, Kulichenko, Iľnitskii, Yazykovich, Borisenko, Yunak, Afanas'ev, Butoma, Bubnovskii, Kandryonkov, Kornets, and Ilyashenko, plus other party and government figures, visited Czechoslovakia.[67] The editor-in-chief of *Pravda*, Cde. Zimyanin, also went there for talks.

A great deal of work was accomplished by our comrades during the Decade of Ukrainian Art held in Czechoslovakia and the Decade of Czechoslovak Culture in the RSFSR.

In May, to mark celebrations of Czechoslovakia's liberation from fascism, we sent a group of outstanding Soviet military officers—led by Marshal Koniev and Marshal Moskalenko—and along with them a large group of generals and officers from our army who took a direct role in the battles for the liberation of Czechoslovakia. They used their stay to meet the president of Czechoslovakia, General Svoboda, and many communist war veterans of the liberation struggle.

---

[64] See Document No. 28.

[65] See Document No. 31. Brezhnev's statement here is not entirely accurate. Kádár's relatively calm assessment of the situation in Czechoslovakia at the time was vastly different from the assessments of Ulbricht and Gomułka, who insisted that a full-fledged counterrevolution was already underway.

[66] Brezhnev acknowledges here, in his aside, that the "medical treatment" Kosygin was supposedly undergoing at Karlovy Vary was merely a pretext to pursue additional contacts with CPCz leaders.

[67] Except for Shelest and V. V. Shcherbitskii, who at the time was the chairman of the Ukrainian Council of Ministers and a candidate member of the CPSU CC Politburo, all those listed here were local CPSU officials, including several who spoke at the July 17 plenum: A. I. Shibaev was the first secretary of the Saratov Obkom; V. I. Konotop was the first secretary of the Moscow Obkom; L. S. Kulichenko was the first secretary of the Volgograd Obkom; and Yu. V. Iľnitskii was the first secretary of the Transcarpathian Obkom.

They also spoke with the leadership of Czechoslovakia's armed forces and with workers.[68] At the same time, Marshal Grechko was sent to Czechoslovakia on a comradely visit along military lines.

From Moscow we maintained systematic contact with Cde. Dubček directly by phone or through the Soviet ambassador in Prague, Cde. Chervonenko, calling the attention of Czech comrades each time to a number of developments and trends, especially with regard to the mass media, and also to individual anti-socialist actions.

As you can understand, comrades, all this was intended not merely as an exchange of pleasantries or as a formal demonstration of our interest in the Czechoslovak comrades. We set out to use all means of political influence vis-à-vis people entrusted with great authority who are able to sway the course of events. At the same time we tried to have as many Czechoslovak officials as possible visit our country. We had a delegation from the National Assembly headed by a member of the CPCz CC Presidium, Smrkovský, and a delegation of workers led by a member of the CPCz CC Presidium, Cde. Barbírek. The minister of foreign affairs, Hájek, visited our country, as did the minister of culture and information, Galuška, the minister of technology, Hruškovič, the minister of transportation, Řehák, the chairman of the Central Council of Trade Unions, Poláček, the chairman of the CC of the Czechoslovak Youth Union, Zdeněk Vokrouhlický, and a number of others. In turn, our corresponding organizations in Moscow and Leningrad, and our central bodies that have relations with these persons, also carried out the necessary work. Regional and municipal committees of the CPSU welcomed delegations of CPCz regional and municipal committees.

All the work we carried out was aimed at strengthening our Czechoslovak friends' confidence in their own forces and their awareness that the communists of Czechoslovakia can count on the solidarity and support of Soviet communists and our people.

As you know, comrades, from information we circulated within our party, in May there was a CPCz CC plenum whose resolution correctly noted that the main danger for the party and the country came from actions from the Right. The resolution also noted that the Central Committee and party must wage a decisive struggle against the Right and defend socialist gains. The resolution contained very eloquent references to Czechoslovakia's friendship with the Soviet Union and the other socialist countries, and to Czechoslovakia's loyalty and commitments to the Warsaw Pact.

Unfortunately, we must state that these serious decisions adopted at the plenum were not backed up by any organizational measures by the CPCz CC Presidium. From being used to help in the struggle, the mass media went onto the attack. That is why, in fact, they had no favorable influence on the development of events.

Our comrades who were in Czechoslovakia, including those who are present here, spoke at our plenary session about the difficult circumstances in which the healthy forces in the CPCz—those who have correctly evaluated the course of events and are ready to defend socialism—are waging their struggle. They themselves observed how the reactionary forces are circulating more and more stories and fabrications in an attempt to paralyze the masses and confuse them with their demagoguery.

The development of events increasingly confirms that the CPCz CC Presidium is not in control of the situation and is not taking decisive measures. The fundamental principle of democratic centralism in the party is being violated. As a result, a situation has arisen in which individual district or municipal party branches instead of carrying out Central Committee decisions, adopt measures deliberately opposed to the party line, and in individual instances speak out openly against Central Committee directives.[69] The main role in this is played by the anti-socialist elements.

---

[68] Koniev's and Moskalenko's conversations with CzPA commanders and with Czechoslovak workers were intended to gauge the extent of support among these two groups for the reform movement.

[69] A reference, in particular, to the municipal party committees in Prague, Brno, and Ostrava, which had consistently been at the forefront of the reformist movement.

You must remember, comrades, that the mass replacement of cadres and the vile defamation of honest and devoted communists has created an atmosphere of mistrust throughout the party, as well as confusion and lack of faith within the party's ranks. This is especially true among the leading party workers against whom the rightists are concentrating their particular attacks, thereby creating an atmosphere of moral terror, labeling these comrades with such terms as "conservatives" and so on.

At our plenum, comrades, we must emphasize that this atmosphere of attacks on the party, this atmosphere of lies and calumny against honest communists, and these attempts in the media to depict the situation in the country as though everything is in order and a favorable process of democratization is under way—all this is being supported, unfortunately, in veiled and some-times open form by certain sections of the CPCz CC Presidium and Secretariat, so that what you see is the absence of unity in these leading bodies. The whole chain of events convinces us that all this hysteria, especially on the part of the mass media, is encouraged and guided very cleverly and is organized by a kind of second center whose representatives are, obviously, in the Central Committee itself.

At the same time, one thing is especially clear: This second, right-wing center is attracting mainly those who belonged to the former Social Democratic Party, a small circle of so-called intellectuals, many of whom support close links with the West, as well as various civil servants from offices and institutions. They are given the right to express their views in the press, on radio, and on television, whereas the voice of the working class is never heard in any of these media.

Taking this into account, we mentioned more than once to Cde. Dubček and advised him to turn to the working class, to rely on it, and to launch a decisive attack and struggle against the right-wing, anti-socialist, and counterrevolutionary elements. There have been and still are many signs that the working class of Czechoslovakia is seeking to take the initiative in the struggle against this looming danger, but in all cases these actions must be organized. After many of our recommendations and urgent advice, a nationwide meeting was held of representatives of the People's Militia of all the cities of Czechoslovakia.[70] As we were told, more than 12,000 people were present at the meeting. Comrade Dubček spoke to them. We do not have the full speech, only excerpts, from which it is evident that, fundamentally, Cde. Dubček spoke quite well to the workers. The workers warmly supported him and many asked for permission to send armed People's Militia units out into the street, to hold demonstrations and mass meetings in support of the May plenum decisions of the CPCz Central Committee, and to hold a mass meeting in support of socialist achievements. As you know, the gathering of the People's Militia adopted an appeal to the Soviet people.[71] This appeal was brought by the representatives of the gathering to the Soviet embassy, where they requested that it be forwarded to Moscow. The appeal was published in our press and received wide support from the working class and all the working people of our country, who then sent about 20,000 letters and telegrams to the ČSSR. But even such an important meeting of workers, addressed by the first secretary of the CPCz Central Committee, was not given a favorable interpretation in the mass media of Czechoslovakia, with the exception of a small item that appeared in Rudé právo. The appeal of the workers' meeting to the Soviet Union went almost unnoticed.[72] Moreover, the meeting itself and the response it evoked among the working people of the Soviet Union were depicted as further support for the process of so-called liberalization in Czechoslovakia. The CPCz Central Committee did not even react to this.

Comrades, a recitation of all the facts and actions of the radio, press, and television in the ČSSR that are anti-socialist and anti-Soviet in character would take a long time. We have informed you about many of them. It only remains to be said that articles and speeches have

[70] The meeting that Brezhnev cites is covered in Document No. 41.
[71] See Document No. 41 above.
[72] The appeal was not published in Rudé právo until June 13, nearly a month after it was published in Moscow.

appeared criticizing Marx, Lenin, and Leninism. The authors of these articles, both big and small, include not only former social democrats, but also none other than a Secretary of the CPCz Central Committee, Císař. You know that we replied to this in *Pravda*.[73] And we wrote articles in *Literaturnaya Gazeta* in reply to the anti-socialist attacks by the author Procházka and those like him. The absence of a decisive struggle by the CPCz CC Presidium has undoubtedly encouraged the Right. Day after day, they are expanding their front of attack against the party, taking up wider and wider questions not only on domestic matters, but also on foreign policy, including questions related to the Soviet Union and the socialist countries and, in general, to the whole political orientation of the ČSSR. This propaganda also includes attacks against the Warsaw Pact and against economic cooperation with the Soviet Union and the socialist countries, as well as an orientation toward an expansion of links with the West.

Because the right wing is not meeting bold and decisive resistance, it is becoming more and more insolent, and the situation has deteriorated so much that the openly counterrevolutionary platform, the so-called "Two Thousand Words," signed by a group of persons including well-known and unknown names, appeared simultaneously on the pages of four central newspapers of Czechoslovakia.[74] I might mention in passing, though this is only a detail, that we now have proof that some of the signatures to this letter are fabricated or phony.

This document is directed precisely against the CPCz, and amounts to an open call to struggle against constitutional power. Now it is being widely used to unite the anti-socialist forces and to serve as a platform for their action.

Speaking by phone to Cde. Dubček immediately after the appearance of this hostile platform, I urgently advised him to launch an immediate struggle against the anti-socialist, counterrevolutionary forces in the name of the CC Politburo. We pointed out to him that the "Two Thousand Words" provided the basis for decisive action against them, while relying on the support of the healthy forces in the party and the working class, and on the armed units of the People's Militia. Comrade Dubček replied that the CPCz CC Presidium was meeting at that very moment, and that he would pass on our recommendations and was certain that the "Two Thousand Words" would be condemned, and that very strong countermeasures would be adopted. Unfortunately, this did not happen. Although the CC Presidium adopted a resolution on this question, it keeps only a formal distance from the document. And the beginning of the Presidium resolution itself was similar to a bow or apology to the authors of this appeal.

Let me quote the way they began: "Independent of the aims pursued by the authors of this pronouncement," says the resolution, "and those who affixed their signatures to it, there is no reason in our country to doubt their good intentions."

[Commotion in the hall.]

Permit me to call your attention to still another circumstance: This resolution was sent to the regional party committees unsigned by the first secretary of the Central Committee but with the signature of Cde. Indra, who is a CC Secretary but not a member of the CC Presidium. We call attention to this fact because the next day the anti-socialist elements immediately began to attack Indra, and some Presidium members who were speaking at regional conferences, and who feared attacks against themselves, began to point their finger at Indra, too. Then a campaign got under way to badger CC Secretary Indra, who, in our opinion, espouses correct positions.

After this, CC Presidium members addressed various audiences in different cities. Here one should call attention to the fact that each of them spoke from his own point of view, independent

---

[73] The references here are to two items by Čestmír Císař and an article by Fyodor Konstantinov. The first of the items by Císař was a speech marking the 150th anniversary of Karl Marx's birth, which appeared in "Marxův myšlenkový odkaz je záštitou, oporou a inspirací: Večer k 150. výročí narození Karla Marxe," *Rudé právo* (Prague), May 7, 1968, pp. 1, 3. Konstantinov's article, which bitterly attacked Císař's speech, appeared in *Moscow Pravda* on June 14, 1968; and Císař promptly responded to Konstantinov in a lengthy article, "V čem je síla živého marxismu-leninismu: Odpověd' akademiku F. Konstantinovovi," *Rudé právo* (Prague), June 22, 1968, p. 3.

[74] See Document No. 44 above.

of the CC Presidium resolution, and interpreted it in a variety of ways. A Presidium member, like Kriegel, speaking on television, actually supported the authors of "Two Thousand Words," stating at the time that there are only 40 words of which he does not approve, and as for the rest, everything is fine.

In such conditions and in the absence of necessary resistance on the part of the CPCz leadership, anti-socialist actions and attacks against the CPCz are increasing. The CC Politburo of our party felt it necessary to evaluate these events and on 3 July sent a letter on this matter to the CPCz CC Presidium.[75] The contents of this letter are known to you since we reported it to party activists. We also sent the letter to the fraternal parties who fully supported the evaluation and conclusions reached by our Politburo, and who in turn sent letters to the CPCz Central Committee.

In the view of several members of the CPCz CC Presidium, who uphold correct positions, our letter and the letters of the fraternal parties made an impression and supported the position of the healthy forces in Czechoslovakia.

Since the response of the CPCz leadership to this letter was unsatisfactory, to say the least, we thought it was expedient to take the initiative and convene a meeting of the fraternal parties of Bulgaria, Hungary, the GDR, Poland, and the Soviet Union and to invite the leadership of the Communist Party of Czechoslovakia. The correctness and timeliness of our party's initiative in arranging this meeting can be seen from the rapid response and support we received from all the other fraternal parties. As a result, a joint letter from all the Central Committees of the parties was sent to the CPCz Central Committee regarding the desirability of convening such a meeting in Warsaw.

In view of the position of the Romanians, which would not be helpful at this conference, and considering the practices of previous conferences, there was a consensus among all the fraternal parties not to invite the Romanian comrades to this conference.[76]

We received an answer from the Czechoslovak comrades. They suggested changing the six-party conference to bilateral meetings and, in particular, a meeting between the CPSU and the CPCz, to be held in Prague.[77] Similar replies were sent to the other fraternal parties. These replies contained a schedule of meetings almost up to the time of the CPCz congress and stated that a fraternal, collective meeting might be held during the congress when our delegations will be there. At the same time, they stated the opinion that Romania and Yugoslavia might also take part. That kind of a position, comrades, obviously needs no comment. Its purposes are clear: to prevent a meeting of the fraternal parties, to space out the bilateral meetings until the Congress is held, and thereby to place before us a *fait accompli* of the further reinforcement of right-wing forces depriving the healthy forces in the CPCz of their ability to rely on the collective opinion of the fraternal parties.

In these conditions, the CC Politburo felt it necessary to consult with the fraternal parties and call a collective meeting. The fraternal parties fully supported the position of the CPSU CC Politburo without hesitation and, as you know, on 14 and 15 July a meeting of the five fraternal parties took place in Warsaw. At the same time it must be said that our party once again extended an invitation to the CPCz leadership to attend this conference. In no way, however, did we reject the significance of bilateral meetings. On the contrary, we indicated our support and our readiness to undertake such bilateral meetings after the collective one is held. . . .

. . .

---

[75] The actual date of the letter was July 4, but Brezhnev may be referring to the day on which it was drafted.

[76] The decision to exclude Romania was in line with the pattern that began at the Sofia meeting in early March and particularly at the Dresden conference in late March.

[77] See Dubček's brief, acerbic account in *Hope Dies Last: The Autobiography of Alexander Dubček*, ed. and trans. by Jiří Hochman (New York: Kodansha International, 1993), p. 162. See also Document No. 51 above.

Permit me, comrades, not to dwell on the details of the presentations by all the speakers. I've explained only their general meaning to you. But to give you a clearer idea of the position of the CPSU delegation, let me read the full text of our presentation to the Warsaw conference.[78]

. . .

It was on this note, comrades, that we finished our presentation in Warsaw.

After our delegation had spoken, the delegations of all the fraternal parties expressed full agreement with the analysis we presented as well as with our conclusions.

Everyone arrived at the same view about the need to send a letter to the Central Committee of the Communist Party of Czechoslovakia from all the parties attending the Warsaw Meeting. A drafting commission was then established to draw up this letter. Our delegation proposed its version of such a letter, which had already been considered by our own Politburo, and we brought it to Warsaw.

It should be said that our document was the basis for the letter that was adopted and has been distributed to you with, of course, the corrections, additions, and editorial changes made by the other fraternal parties.[79]

Yesterday morning, the 16th of July, this letter was delivered in Prague to the CPCz CC first secretary, Cde. Dubček, by the ambassadors of all the socialist countries that took part in the Warsaw Meeting.

We all collectively expect that the CC Presidium and the whole CPCz Central Committee will correctly understand our fraternal concern about the way events have developed in Czechoslovakia and will use this letter to adopt the correct decisions and measures.

It must be said that the CPCz leadership, evidently, did not understand the positive significance of the meeting of the five fraternal parties. Even as we were convening, the CPCz leadership once again sent a letter to the fraternal parties with a request either not to hold this meeting or not to say that it dealt with the question of Czechoslovakia.[80]

What can be said when judging the results of the Warsaw meeting overall? We are convinced that it demonstrated firm unity and loyalty to principles of Marxism–Leninism and of proletarian internationalism, and that it will occupy a great place in the struggle by the fraternal parties of the socialist countries to defend and strengthen the position of socialism in the ČSSR, as well as to seek the further development and strengthening of the entire socialist system. We are convinced that the line worked out in Warsaw will be supported by all steadfast fighters for the great ideals of socialism and communism.

A correct reading of events in Czechoslovakia by all communist parties is of great importance. This applies, in particular, to the French and Italian Communist Parties. That was why in two long conversations we informed Cde. Waldeck Rochet about the situation in Czechoslovakia and our assessment of what is happening there, as well as about the Warsaw Meeting.[81] This is of even greater importance in view of the fact that Cde. Rochet is going to Prague within a few days to meet Cde. Dubček.

Comrade Rochet expressed serious misgivings about the situation in Czechoslovakia; and at the end of our talks he stated that he agreed fully with the letter sent in the name of the Warsaw Meeting to the CPCz leadership, and that during his talks with Dubček he will support the position of this letter and fully recommend that the CPCz CC Presidium should heed the advice of the

---

[78] At this point, Brezhnev read the entire speech he presented during the third session of the Warsaw Meeting; see Document No. 52.

[79] A comparison of the draft letter and the final product reveals that most of these "corrections, additions, and editorial changes" were relatively minor. That is, the Warsaw Letter was really a document that Soviet officials had drafted well beforehand. The Soviet draft was used instead of a draft prepared by the Polish authorities. See also Documents Nos. 52 and 53.

[80] See Document No. 51.

[81] See Document No. 58.

CPSU, guided exclusively by the interests of the Czechoslovak people, of the cause of socialism, and of the whole communist movement.[82]

Similar talks took place with the leadership of the Italian Communist Party in Rome, which our delegation, led by Cde. Kirilenko, held not long ago, and in Moscow yesterday and this morning. The Italian comrades are gravely concerned about events in Czechoslovakia. In essence they support our evaluation of these events. The leadership of the majority of parties to which we sent our letter about the situation in Czechoslovakia received the information with understanding and supported our position. It should be said quite openly that a number of parties are still wavering and have doubts. In the first place, many of them, deprived of truthful information, cannot conceive of the gravity of the situation. Many parties expressed their gratitude to the CPSU for its frank information on the matter, which is of principled importance for the entire communist movement, and they promised to think of measures they themselves could take.

In addition to this, some comrades have expressed concern that if matters reach the point where it is necessary to resort to direct measures in the name of saving socialist Czechoslovakia, this will have extremely adverse consequences for the activities of the communist parties in the capitalist countries.

We can give only one possible answer in these difficult circumstances: In devising and implementing our policy, we will try to take account of all these considerations.

We cannot but mention, comrades, the position taken in connection with the most recent events in Czechoslovakia by the leadership of the communist parties of Romania and Yugoslavia. The Romanian leadership hastened to dissociate itself from the collective actions of the fraternal parties as quickly as possible. The Romanian leadership is playing a dubious game, to put it mildly. Bucharest is expressing its sympathy with the CPCz leadership and applauding it for its pursuit of a so-called independent political course.

The leaders of the Romanian Communist Party are clearly attempting to act as critics of actions agreed upon by the fraternal parties in connection with the events in Czechoslovakia. It must be said frankly, comrades, that this position, which corresponds to the general political line of the Romanian leaders, is miles removed from proletarian internationalism.

The leaders of the Yugoslav League of Communists are even more actively opposed to the position approved by the fraternal parties and the joint actions they have taken to support the healthy forces in Czechoslovakia.

The Yugoslav press and the whole propaganda apparatus of Yugoslavia has for a long time, with obvious enthusiasm and extreme tendentiousness, applauded the policy of "liberalization" carried out by right-wing elements in Czechoslovakia. It can be said that the Yugoslav leadership encourages and incites these right-wing forces in Czechoslovakia to undertake additional active measures[83] while, at the same time, opposing all attempts to support the healthy forces in that country. Matters have gone so far by now that Tito even considered it possible, in a public statement to the correspondent of an Egyptian newspaper, to describe the actions of the fraternal parties as "pressure" on Czechoslovakia and "interference in its internal affairs."

Comrades, one must call attention to the tactics of the imperialist circles. Our class enemies are trying to convince the whole world that one should not even dare to think there is a threat to the socialist gains of Czechoslovakia. The bourgeois press quotes anti-socialist comments taken from the Czechoslovak press as the "creative treatment of Marxism," and it praises the right-wing elements as "progressive Marxists."

At the same time the centers of imperialist propaganda are not sparing in their advice to the right-wing forces about where they are to strike, against which members of the CPCz leadership they should concentrate their fire, and so on. In recent times counterrevolutionary elements in

---

[82] Brezhnev's assumption that Rochet would endorse the Warsaw Letter proved unfounded; see Document No. 59.

[83] The phrase "active measures" in the Soviet lexicon was roughly equivalent to a combination of "covert operations" and "disinformation campaigns."

the ČSSR have been urged from abroad to change their tactics by reducing the strident tone of anti-socialism in their remarks, by conducting their subversive work in a more subtle manner, and by disguising the intentions of the reactionary forces more carefully.

Evidently, this is intended to lull the vigilance of communists, to create a heated atmosphere for the weeds of counterrevolution in Czechoslovakia to sprout, to give them a chance to grow stronger and proliferate, and then to stifle the healthy forces of the country.

The tactics of imperialism, as you can see, are distinguished by their cunning and invidiousness, and we must vigilantly confront their devious schemes to undercut and expose them in good time. We cannot but see a direct link between the tactics of imperialist reactionary forces and the actions of the anti-socialist and counterrevolutionary forces in Czechoslovakia.

Comrades! We do not know how the CPCz CC Presidium will respond to the collective letter from the fraternal parties. As before, we will vigilantly follow the course of events, and we will act in the spirit of the decisions taken at our April plenum, where the members of the Central Committee expressed their full support for the CPSU CC Politburo's determination not to permit the loss of socialist gains in Czechoslovakia. Before adopting any extreme measures, we will expend all efforts so that by pursuing a political path the actions of the healthy forces in the Communist Party of Czechoslovakia will themselves offer the necessary resistance to the anti-socialist and counterrevolutionary elements, preserve the CPCz as the leading force in Czechoslovakia, and uphold the cause of socialism in Czechoslovakia. We count on you, comrades, for your full support, and we await your remarks here. (Applause.)

DOCUMENT No. 57: Letter from Marshal Yakubovskii to Alexander Dubček on Gen. Prchlík's News Conference, July 18, 1968

Source: ÚSD, AÚV KSČ, F. 07/15.

This top-secret letter from Marshal Yakubovskii to Dubček was the first in a long series of complaints that Soviet officials lodged, both openly and behind-the-scenes, about Prchlík's remarks. As the commander-in-chief (C-in-C) of the Warsaw Pact, Yakubovskii addresses Prchlík's comments about the Pact, claiming that the Czechoslovak general had "distorted the essence" of the alliance, "divulged top-secret information about the organization and its structures," and "defamed Soviet military commanders." Yakubovskii demands that the Czechoslovak authorities "draw the proper conclusions in this case" to ensure that there would be "no further disclosures of interstate secrets dealing with the content of the Warsaw Pact or any further denunciations of the Supreme Command of the Pact"—a not-so-subtle recommendation that Prchlík be removed.

Dubious though Yakubovskii's accusations were, they reflected the broader concerns that Soviet leaders had about the effects of the Prague Spring on Czechoslovakia's military alignment and the strength of the Warsaw Pact. The specific allegations and much of the language in Yakubovskii's letter were subsequently incorporated in a formal note of protest from the Soviet government to the Czechoslovak government and in a bitter article published in Krasnaya zvezda on July 23 under the title "Whose Interests Is V. Prchlík Serving?" On July 25, Dubček yielded to this pressure and solved the Prchlík problem by closing the CPCz CC State Administration Department the head of which was Prchlík.

Commander-in-Chief of the Joint Armed Forces of the Warsaw Pact Countries

TOP SECRET

To the First Secretary of the Central Committee
of the Communist Party of Czechoslovakia,
Comrade Alexander Dubček

Prague

Esteemed Comrade Dubček!

On 16 July of this year, the newspapers *Rudé právo, Práce, Mladá fronta*, and others carried reports about a press conference held on 15 July in the Journalists' Club in Prague under the auspices of the CPCz CC State-Administrative Department, with the head of the department, V. Prchlík, as the main speaker.

As is clear from the newspapers, V. Prchlík spoke at length about the structure of the Warsaw Pact, which he believes is now outdated. At the same time, and without any justification or authority, he denounced the activities of the Political Consultative Committee of the Warsaw Pact Member States, describing it as an organ that is not carrying out its intended functions.

In explaining to the journalists the structure of the Joint Command of the Armed Forces of the Warsaw Pact countries, the organizers of the press conference not only distorted the essence of this structure and its organization, but went so far as to divulge some top-secret information contained in the protocol "On the Creation of the Joint Command of the Armed Forces of States Participating in the Treaty on Friendship, Cooperation, and Mutual Assistance" of 14 May 1955, and also in the "Principles of the Joint Command of the Armed Forces of the Member States of the Warsaw Pact," as approved by the Political Consultative Committee on 11 January 1956.

Furthermore, in the process of creating a distorted picture of the true composition of the Joint Command, V. Prchlík went so far as to defame Soviet military commanders. He told the audience that the "Joint Command consists only of marshals, generals, and senior officers of the Soviet army. The other member states of the Pact . . . have had to make do with mere representatives who wield almost no real power and whose role is simply to maintain a certain liaison among officers." He thereby defamed the composition and function of the Joint Command and the Joint Staff of the Joint Armed Forces.[84]

V. Prchlík also disclosed top-secret information about the deployment of the Joint Armed Forces on the territory of member states of the Warsaw Pact,[85] as set down in Article 5 of the Statement on the Joint Command of the Armed Forces.

Thus, the remarks of CPCz CC employees, especially of V. Prchlík, at the press conference on 15 July in Prague revealed facts relating to top-secret data contained in interstate agreements.

I am forced to remind you of the impermissibility of such statements insofar as they detract from friendship among members of the Warsaw Pact and undermine their military organization.

My position as commander-in-chief of the Joint Armed Forces of the Member States of the Warsaw Pact compels me to request that you take measures to prevent any possibility of further disclosures of interstate secrets dealing with the content of the Warsaw Pact and any further denunciations of the Supreme Command of the Warsaw Pact. I also request that you draw the proper conclusions in this case to which I have drawn your attention in this letter.

Yours sincerely,

I. Yakubovskii

Marshal of the Soviet Union,
Commander-in-Chief, Joint Armed Forces
of the Member States of the Warsaw Pact

18 July 1968

---

[84] Prchlík had merely pointed out the reality—that the Soviet Union dominated the Warsaw Pact and its structures. All the top officers in the Pact, including the C-in-C, the first deputy C-in-Cs, and the chief of the main staff, were from the Soviet army, and the Pact's wartime command structure was no more than the Soviet Union's own command structure for "coalition warfare." The "representatives" from the East European armies were, as Prchlík said, largely powerless and bereft of any role in allied decision-making.

[85] The "top-secret information" that Yakubovskii accuses Prchlík of divulging is presumably his reference to the possible existence of "secret provisions [in the Warsaw Pact's documents] entitling certain partners to deploy or station units arbitrarily on the territory of other member states." Prchlík said he had found no trace of such provisions, so it is difficult to see how he could be charged with "disclosing top-secret information." The inappropriateness of the allegation is especially glaring in light of new evidence (unearthed since 1991) which shows that the Warsaw Pact countries *did* in fact conclude numerous secret agreements over the years regarding force deployments. Far from "divulging" the content of these secret agreements, Prchlík denied—incorrectly, it now turns out—that they even existed.

DOCUMENT No. 58: Transcript of Discussion between Alexander Dubček and Waldeck Rochet, July 19, 1968 (Excerpts)

Source: *Kremlin-PCF: Conversations secrètes* (Paris: Olivier Orban, 1984), pp. 75–96; Vondrová & Navrátil, vol. 1, pp. 324–330.

This memorandum of conversation records a meeting between French Communist Party General Secretary Waldeck Rochet and Dubček. The purpose of the meeting was for Rochet to present his proposal for "true cooperation" between Prague and Moscow through a conference of all the communist parties of Europe that would provide a peaceful solution to the crisis. Along with two senior officials from the Italian Communist Party, Rochet traveled first to Moscow to argue for such a meeting—Soviet officials did not endorse his proposal—and then on to Prague.

According to the meeting transcript, Dubček was equivocal on Rochet's idea and rejected a number of his arguments. When Rochet urges Dubček to take whatever steps necessary to improve relations with Moscow and prevent "a rupture of your alliance with the Soviet Union," Dubček responds that the deterioration of Soviet–Czechoslovak ties "is not our fault," contending that the CPCz has "gone on the offensive" against "rightist forces." Dubček also expresses puzzlement and irritation at Soviet charges that Czechoslovakia's "western borders had been left exposed" to probes by NATO. He insists that, on the contrary, the border forces were "stronger than before." Finally, Dubček tells Rochet that any genuine improvement in Soviet–Czechoslovak relations would be difficult to sustain so long as Soviet troops remained on Czechoslovak territory against the wishes of the Czechoslovak government and population.

Ultimately, Rochet was not able to advance the FCP initiative to prevent a violent outcome to the crisis.

. . .

W. Rochet expresses his concern about the current Czechoslovak events and the deterioration of Czechoslovak–Soviet relations. . . .

In summing up, our party wishes to have friendly and fraternal relations with you and with the Soviet comrades, based on solidarity and the principles of proletarian internationalism.

But at this point the crucial question is not that of relations between the French Communist Party and the Communist Party of Czechoslovakia.

The crucial question for the whole international communist movement is the improvement of relations between your party and the Comunist Party of the Soviet Union.

Without wishing in any way to interfere in the internal affairs of other parties, we note that a most serious, I would even say dangerous, situation has arisen. This is all the more so since the imperialists are watchful.

I am convinced that you are as aware of the gravity of the situation as we are.

Yet I would, nevertheless, like to emphasize this.

Communists in our country—and I believe those in all countries—are worried by the prospect that there could be a split between you and the comrades in the socialist countries, above all with the Soviet Union.

On the one hand, they maintain that if there has been a shift to the right in your country, a shift that would endanger socialism, this would be a defeat for the whole international communist movement.

On the other hand, if your relations with the Soviet comrades were to deteriorate to the point of a split, this could lead to something even worse.

It appears there is a genuine danger of that. . . .

In any case, a rupture of your alliance with the Soviet Union would expose your country to all types of maneuvers by Germany, by Bonn, and by the United States. This would upset the whole balance of power in Europe, and European security would be in danger. It is understandable that the Soviet Union and the socialist countries cannot allow such a situation to arise.

As a result, the only solution to be envisaged is for the serious difficulties that exist between you and the comrades in the Soviet Union and the other socialist countries to be overcome by seeking an agreement and true cooperation. . . ."

A. Dubček disagrees with this point of view and explains the Czechoslovak situation to W. Rochet. . . .

"Our party is an internationalist party. It stands for unity with the USSR and the other socialist countries. There is nothing to prove otherwise.

You have pointed out that since April or May our relations with the USSR and the others have gone from bad to worse. I cannot give you a date, but we believe it is during the past few weeks that something has changed abruptly, around 28 or 30 June. That was the turning point. Perhaps this was due to the 'Two Thousand Words' or to something else. In any case, there has been a turning point. Yet I would not like to put forth a hypothesis about the cause of that turning point.

If our relations with the other socialist countries have changed, this is not our fault. . . .

Our party is naturally responsible for all that is happening in our country.

There are people who express ideas contrary to those of the party, that is true. But we are certain that this tendency has been diminishing and will continue to diminish. . . .

True, there has been a wave of euphoria about freedom regained; but that will pass. The events you referred to date back to March and April. They occurred more or less in the period leading up to the May plenary session. And it was precisely because of them that the party adopted the position it did at the May session. It is very likely that we do not have everything in order, in fact that is certain. But the important thing is that we have gone over to the offensive. And that should have improved our relations with the other fraternal parties. . . .

Is there a threat from the Right? Well, we say as much in our reply to the 'Five.' We are intent on eliminating the right-wingers as a political force in the eyes of the public.

After all, we hold power! And we are not afraid of a few people holding conversations in the streets."

[Dubček then briefly turns to the military and security measures taken by the Czechoslovak government on the country's western borders.]

"The Soviets are saying: 'You have exposed your western borders.' Yet we have turned over to them our military plans to demonstrate that we have actually reinforced the borders.

Koniev and other generals came, and they saw the border area and told Brezhnev: 'Everything is in order.' We have stronger forces on the borders now than before! Why? Because we are aware of the situation. That was the first thing we did in January; we gave orders to reinforce them.

The maneuvers? Soviet troops at present are leaving the territory. Černík and I were the ones who took the initiative to have the maneuvers in the first place. Why? To demonstrate to the whole world that we are an integral part of the Warsaw Pact and to ensure that Bonn would see this and realize that we have the socialist camp behind us.

And yet, there have been misunderstandings. When the date had been agreed, the commander-in-chief of the Joint Armed Forces, Marshal Yakubovskii, suggested late June or early July. In March–April the Western press reported that Czechoslovakia was about to be occupied by the Soviets. That is why, in order to put an end to such talk, Yakubovskii announced in public that the maneuvers would be over by the end of June or beginning of July.

It so happens that on 30 June or 1 July, I told a workers' meeting: 'The maneuvers are ending, and from this meeting hall we will send them our fraternal greetings.'[86]

And then something happened. No, it turns out, they are staying put. One week, very well. But after that? Why do they not move? People began to be worried.

Who has deceived whom?

As a result, people began to say: 'You know, maybe the Americans were right in April. . .'

[86] See Document No. 45.

262

Among the public there are people who say: 'There you are. They're going to stay here right up to the 14th Congress in order to apply pressure.'

Things had to be explained: At the Council of Ministers it was decided to ask Yakubovskii what the public was to be told. We got no answer. We said to him: 'If we give no explanation, public opinion will turn against us and this will serve as an anti-Soviet platform.'

For us, as Czechoslovaks, such things are difficult. . . .

We will do everything to solve the situation in a positive manner. That is what our Central Committee has decided. . . ."[87]

[87] This transcript was kept secret until May 18, 1970, when the French version was published in full in the FCP daily *L'Humanité*. The decision to publish the transcript came after a dissident French communist, Roger Garaudy, alleged—incorrectly—that the document had been turned over to Gustáv Husák's regime in Prague in November 1969 to be used as "evidence" in a potential trial of Dubček. French communist leaders stenuously denied the allegation and then published the transcript to show that it was still in their possession.

DOCUMENT No. 59: Letter from the French CP to Leonid Brezhnev, July 23, 1968

Source: *Kremlin-PCF: Conversations secrètes* (Paris: Olivier Orban, 1984), pp. 97–104; Vondrová & Navrátil, vol. 1, pp. 337–339.

In response to a request from Moscow to endorse the "Warsaw Letter" on Czechoslovakia, the French Communist Party sent this letter to Brezhnev on July 23. The FCP communiqué states that the French party cannot endorse the Warsaw Letter because it "constitutes blatant public interference in the internal affairs of a fraternal party" and thus "calls into question the fundamental principles" that should govern relations between communist states. On a surprisingly strong note, the French communists insist that "direct outside intervention of any sort" in Czechoslovakia would have the "most dire consequences" and therefore "must be totally excluded."

The FCP's opposition was unexpected in the Kremlin. Waldek Rochet had not been overly supportive of the Prague Spring in the past; indeed, during Brezhnev's speech before the CPSU Central Committee plenum on July 17, he had claimed that FCP officials "fully agreed with the [Warsaw] Letter." After the invasion, the FCP issued a statement of disapproval of Soviet actions.

Dear Comrade Brezhnev,

Following the reports received from your ambassadors in Paris and Prague, our party's Politburo wishes to inform you of its position on the problems arising from the situation in Czechoslovakia. This position has already been conveyed to you by comrade Waldeck Rochet during his visit to Moscow.[88]

You ask us to endorse the letter sent to the Communist Party of Czechoslovakia by the Warsaw Meeting on behalf of the Central Committees of the communist and workers' parties of Bulgaria, Poland, the German Democratic Republic, Hungary, and the Soviet Union.

To our immense regret, it is impossible for us to comply with this request. In effect, this letter calls into question the principles that ought to be the main factor in relations between communist and workers' parties, and it starts a process that could have the most dire consequences for the cause of socialism and the international communist movement. . . .

Because we believe that the letter sent by the Warsaw Meeting to the Communist Party of Czechoslovakia calls into question the fundamental principles, and that it constitutes blatant public interference in the internal affairs of a fraternal party, we are unable to support it. . . .

We are, therefore, fully aware that it is absolutely indispensable for the leadership of the Communist Party of Czechoslovakia to wage an effective struggle against all forces seeking to exploit the situation in order to do away with socialism in the country. Where we differ is on the method to be used to achieve this objective.

In our opinion, direct outside intervention of any sort must be excluded and the leadership of the Communist Party of Czechoslovakia must be persuaded to take action on its own, relying on the working class and on all other forces that regard socialism, and friendship and cooperation with the socialist countries, to be in their own interest as well as in the interest of Czechoslovakia. . . .

---

[88] Rochet's visit took place during and just after the Warsaw Meeting, from July 14 to 16. Initially, on July 14, he met Andrei Kirilenko, a senior member of the CPSU Politburo, and later on had talks with Brezhnev after the latter's return from Warsaw.

DOCUMENT No. 60: Soviet Government Diplomatic Note to the Czechoslovak Government, July 20, 1968

Source: ÚSD, Sb. KV, K—Archiv MZV, F. Gs "[TK]"; Vondrová & Navrátil, vol. 1, pp. 321–323.

The Soviet government transmitted this harsh diplomatic demarche in response to Gen. Prchlík's July 15 news conference. In it, the Kremlin denounces Prchlík's remarks as further evidence that Czechoslovakia's "obligations to the Warsaw Pact" are being "undermined" by "anti-socialist and anti-Soviet forces." Using virtually identical language to Marshal Yakubovskii's letter on the general's misdeeds, the note explicitly demands that the Czechoslovak authorities "exact the requisite measures against people" like Prchlík.

The Soviet authorities also allege that the situation around Czechoslovakia's western border had become "absolutely abnormal and dangerous" and was being "exploited by the intelligence organs of imperialist states." This was "not a purely, internal Czechoslovak matter," because it affected the "common safety of the socialist countries," and the USSR could "not be remain indifferent."

The Soviet government's note was drafted on the same day that top Soviet political and military officials met and decided to proceed with the final planning and preparations for an invasion. The Soviet ambassador in Prague, Stepan Chervonenko, passed it to Czechoslovak leaders two days later.

The Soviet government believes it is obliged to draw the attention of the ČSSR government once again to several serious matters affecting the vital interests and security of the Soviet Union and the other socialist countries in the Warsaw Pact.

1. Earlier on, the Soviet government drew the attention of the Czechoslovak side to the fact that actions are being taken in the ČSSR aimed at undermining the Warsaw Pact. It must be said that such actions are not a one-time occurrence, and far from decreasing, they have recently been stepped up in pursuit of a fully defined objective: namely, to undermine the obligations assumed by Czechoslovakia along with the other socialist states in the Warsaw Pact. All these actions cannot be regarded as matters relating solely to the internal affairs of a country; for they directly affect the security interests of the Soviet Union and all the other socialist countries.[89]

In this regard, one cannot help noticing that leading officials in the ČSSR, while stressing their loyalty to Czechoslovakia's alliance treaties and obligations, are doing nothing to rebuff all sorts of developments that are eroding the structure and principles of the Warsaw Pact. This inaction does great harm to the common interests of the socialist countries.

As is known, on 15 July of this year a press conference was held in the Journalists' Club in Prague under the auspices of the CPCz CC State-Administrative Department, with the head of the department, V. Prchlík, as the main speaker. At this conference, according to the Czechoslovak press, V. Prchlík argued, without offering any evidence, that the structure of the Warsaw Pact nowadays is obsolete.

In an unacceptable manner, he defamed the activities of the Political Consultative Committee of the Warsaw Pact Member States, declaring that this body does not fulfill its functions. Speaking about the structure of the Warsaw Pact Joint Armed Forces Command, the press conference organizers not only distorted the essence of this structure and its organization, but went even further and divulged some top-secret data contained in the protocol "On the Creation of the Joint Armed Forces Command of Member States of the Treaty on Friendship, Cooperation and Mutual Assistance" of 14 May 1955, and also clauses about the Joint Armed Forces

---

[89] Here and elsewhere the letter emphasizes the central theme of the Brezhnev Doctrine, namely, that the internal situation in Czechoslovakia was of vital concern not only for Czechoslovakia itself, but for all socialist countries.

Command of the Warsaw Pact Member States, as endorsed by the Political Consultative Committee on 11 January 1956.

V. Prchlík deliberately distorted the real situation and went on to attack Soviet military commanders.

At the press conference top-secret information was divulged regarding the deployment of the Joint Armed Forces on the territory of Warsaw Pact member states, as set out in Article 5 on the Joint Armed Forces Command. Top-secret information contained in interstate treaties was also revealed. Such actions damage the interests of the Warsaw Pact member states, undermine their military coordination, and impair their friendship. One is only amazed that the government of Czechoslovakia has not given due consideration to these facts until now.

Czechoslovak leaders and officials have more than once proclaimed their loyalty to the Warsaw Pact and called for the strengthening of this organization. Nevertheless, the events and actions that one finds nowadays in the ČSSR run contrary to all these statements and are, in fact, aimed at undermining this organization. It cannot be forgotten that membership in the Warsaw Pact obliges the participating states of this organization to move in unison and to operate together in a united front in the struggle for security and for the prevention of any attempts by the imperialists to weaken or threaten the unity of the socialist countries, or to drive a wedge in between them.

Because the government of the USSR attaches great importance to the security of the Warsaw Pact countries and wants to ensure that these countries fulfill their allied obligations, it draws the attention of the ČSSR government to the fact that at the present time anti-Soviet and anti-socialist forces in Czechoslovakia are openly striving to undermine the Warsaw Pact, and that in pursuit of these aims they have even been willing to divulge interstate secrets concerning the security of the socialist countries.

The Soviet government expects that the ČSSR government will take the necessary steps to prevent a repetition of matters of this kind and will exact the requisite measures against people who divulge secret information, with a view to the common interests of security of the Warsaw Pact member states.

2. As is known, on 10 May 1968 the chairman of the USSR Council of Ministers, Cde. A. N. Kosygin, in a letter to the premier of the ČSSR government, Cde. O. Černík, drew the latter's attention to the absolutely abnormal and dangerous situation on the borders of Czechoslovakia with the FRG and Austria. Thanks to the laxity of those responsible for Czechoslovakia, its western borders are virtually open. This was immediately exploited by the intelligence organs of the imperialist states, especially those of the FRG and the USA, which began sending their own spies and subversive elements into the ČSSR under the guise of tourists, so that they could carry out subversive work not only against Czechoslovakia but against the other socialist countries as well.

Cde. A. N. Kosygin's letter reflects deep concern and fear about this situation. This is understandable and perfectly natural because the defense of the ČSSR's western borders is not a purely internal, Czechoslovak matter. The question is how to ensure the safety of all the Warsaw Pact member states.

By penetrating the territory of the ČSSR, imperialist intelligence agents have secured access to a region of the socialist countries of Europe where, as is known, large defense forces of the Warsaw Pact governments are deployed. It is difficult to understand why the government of the ČSSR did not display the concern needed to secure the common safety of the socialist countries, as required by the ČSSR's commitments to the Warsaw Pact and by its bilateral agreements. Naturally, the Soviet government could not remain indifferent in the face of these developments.

The Soviet side asked to be told what measures the Czechoslovak government intends to take in order to close the borders of the ČSSR with the FRG and Austria and to establish the necessary strict controls on the borders, which would correspond to the security needs of the Warsaw Pact member states. Unfortunately, it must be said that the Czechoslovak government has not directly replied to this question.

In the reply from the ČSSR government, Prime Minister Comrade O. Černík disputes the notion that the ČSSR's borders with the FRG and Austria are open, and claims that the borders are being protected in a way that ensures the inviolability and sovereignty of the ČSSR. He goes on to declare that the borders will be protected in the interests of security of the Warsaw Pact member states.

Nevertheless, the facts show not only that conditions on the western borders of the ČSSR have failed to improve since we received a letter of reply from the Czechoslovak side, but that the border situation has deteriorated even further.

According to information received from Prague, the security organs recently discovered a secret cache of American-made arms in the vicinity of the well-known spa Karlovy Vary, near the border with the FRG. The arms were intended for Sudeten revanchists and reactionary forces that are currently attempting to tear the ČSSR from the socialist path and to carry out subversive action against the socialist countries.

Considering that the situation on the borders of the ČSSR with the FRG and Austria remains as unsatisfactory as ever, that the borders in fact remain open, and that this is being widely exploited by forces hostile to socialism in order to carry out subversive activities, the Soviet government believes it necessary once again to draw the attention of the ČSSR government to the danger of such a situation. Bearing in mind that Czechoslovakia has a responsibility to the Warsaw Pact, the Soviet government expects that effective measures will be taken to establish the necessary border control system on the frontiers with the FRG and Austria.

Moscow
20 July 1968

DOCUMENT No. 61: "Problems with the Policy of Safeguarding the Internal and External Security of the State, Their Status at Present, the Basic Ways to Resolve Them," Czechoslovakia's Plans for Future Changes in Military and National Security Policies, July 1968 (Excerpts)

Source: TsKhSD, F. 5, O. 60, D. 310, Ll. 121–153.

The State-Administrative Department of the CPCz Central Committee, headed by General Václav Prchlík, drafted this report in early July 1968. In its final form, the report would have provided the basis for changes in military and security policies scheduled to be discussed at the 14th CPCz Congress in September 1968.

Although the report states that Czechoslovakia "will take as a starting point its allied obligations before the Soviet Union and the Warsaw Pact," the Prchlík plan sought to redefine the whole nature of the alliance as well as Czechoslovakia's place within it. Internally, the report called for changing the "erroneous and obsolete premises" of Czechoslovak military doctrine, ending direct party control of the armed forces, and revamping the "illegal and inhumane" internal security apparatus. Externally, restrictions imposed by the Warsaw Pact, according to the authors, were contributing to the "deformations" and "recurrent crises" in civil–military relations in Czechoslovakia. These restrictions prevented the Czechoslovak leadership from developing "any conception of our own military doctrine," which would take full account of the country's "circumstances and capabilities" and would reject the "unrealistic and dangerous scenarios" that had long been the inspiration for the Pact's military doctrine.

Among those "scenarios" was nuclear war in Europe which, according to the report, would be "purely senseless" and would "bring about the total physical destruction of the ČSSR." At the time, the Soviet army had several secret agreements with Czechoslovakia entitling them to deploy nuclear weapons on Czechoslovak territory during an emergency and authorizing the Soviet Union to store nuclear warheads at three sites in western Czechoslovakia which were under construction at the time of the Prague Spring. The report's language implied that a military doctrine appropriate for Czechoslovakia would eschew nuclear weapons and nuclear warfare—a challenge to the most sensitive aspect of the Czech–Soviet military relationship.

Shortly before the invasion, a copy of this document was leaked to S. I. Prasolov, a counselor at the Soviet embassy, on a "highly confidential" basis by "Czechoslovak friends"—presumably from the Czechoslovak People's Army or State Security. The materials were then transmitted by the Soviet ambassador, S. V. Chervonenko, to a number of top Soviet officials, including Foreign Minister Andrei Gromyko, Defense Minister Andrei Grechko, and the two most senior CPSU CC officials who were directly handling the crisis, Konstantin Katushev and Konstantin Rusakov. In his cover memorandum, marked "TOP SECRET," Chervonenko noted that the main author of the report was the "infamous General Prchlík."

(See also Documents Nos. 68, 69, and 70.)

SECRET

PROBLEMS WITH THE POLICY OF SAFEGUARDING THE INTERNAL AND EXTERNAL SECURITY OF THE STATE, THEIR STATUS AT PRESENT, AND THE BASIC WAYS OF RESOLVING THEM

State-Administrative Department[90] of the Central Committee of the Czechoslovak Communist Party

1. Direction and Goals

I.1. In this report we examine the contemporary situation and current problems of the party's policy on defense and the protection of security. We seek to define the basic directions and main

---

[90] This was an alternative name for the Eighth Department, which Prchlík headed.

paths along which the further resolution of these problems must proceed. After refinement on the basis of further consultations or recommendations from party organs, the work will be the starting point for formulating decisions of the Extraordinary 14th Party Congress. Simultaneously it must permit a more precise elaboration of points of view regarding the content, methods of work, and organizational and personnel structure of party organs and other organizations in the military and security sphere.

. . .

The report has been compiled on the basis of materials prepared by the Ministries of National Defense and Internal Affairs, with especial attention to the materials for their action programs.[91] Assessments and documents of party committees, organs, and departments were used. When examining specific problems, we turned for help to certain comrade-activists. A significant contribution to the theoretical formulation of the problems examined here was made by the academic staff of the State-Administrative Department and others. This was particularly true when considering the results of the scientific-technical revolution and the revolution in the army, as well as their respective achievements, which have not been used in practice until now.

. . .

2. The Existing Approach to and Principles for the Policy of the State's Internal and External Security

II.1. At the basis of the party's existing policy to the state's internal and external security are principles and activities that took shape at the beginning of the 1950s. In essence the problem here is the same as the problems in the whole Czechoslovak political system, which have been critically scrutinized from a methodological point of view at recent sessions of the CPCz CC.

The foundation for Czechoslovakia's existing defense system was laid down during the tensest period of the Cold War when there was a possibility of a military clash between the superpowers. Consequently, a strategy was adopted to defend socialism against imperialist aggression, a strategy that simultaneously must allow for a strategic offensive and a complete victory by the socialist revolutionary movement in Europe under the leadership of the Soviet Union. An especially relevant position, from this point of view is the one formulated by J. V. Stalin in January 1949 at a Moscow conference on international relation problems and the military tasks arising from them.[92] One gets the impression that there has been no reevaluation of the coalition strategy worked out then, even though the conditions for its implementation have changed drastically.

For almost twenty years, Czechoslovak military strategy has been based on the notion of maximum expenditure of human and material reserves, often at very high rates and to the detriment of other important social demands. This has been the case even when international tension has significantly diminished and a policy of peaceful coexistence has gradually taken shape. One might say that this new state of affairs is only discernible in words, since in the economic and military spheres, despite some changes, the old approach still prevails. The ties of the coalition continued to be strengthened, particularly against an acute threat of aggression from German imperialism. But in fact this supposed threat was always a superfluous external factor, which served as a basis, on the one hand, for strengthening the unity of the socialist camp and, on the other, for justifying the extraordinary human and material resources that were demanded by the armed forces. The military factor in many respects compensated for the inadequate development of economic cooperation and other ties among the socialist countries.

---

[91] This document is largely a compilation of the draft Action Programs of the National Defense Ministry and the Interior Ministry, which Prchlík's department supervised.

[92] This is a reference to Stalin's speech proclaiming an irreconcilable struggle between the two "camps."

Such an approach became the source of political and ideological positions that embrace differences in historical development, differences in social-economic interests, and different levels of economic development in the individual countries. It reached the point where our participation in the events of 1956 and 1961 caused us to be dragged into a risky global policy, even though we were given insufficient opportunity to take part in the decisions on these very actions.[93]

The party's military policy was not based on an analysis of our national and state needs and interests. For this reason, the CPCz CC Commission on Defense, despite all its efforts, was not successful in taking on board national and international interests. The commission was unable to expose the roots of the continual state of crisis between the defense system and other systems of society, even crises within the defense system itself. The attempt to gloss over these profound contradictions by direct control basically accounted for the preservation of the extraordinary forms and methods of leadership in the armed forces in the first half of the 1950s. It was also telling that the concept of building socialism, of international relations, and of proletarian internationalism, was still carried out along the mistaken and obsolete ideological-political bases of the Stalinist era. Hence, the leadership was limited to a certain degree by individual measures that were deficient both in their logic and resolution. For the above-mentioned reasons, the Commission on the Defense System of Czechoslovakia did not propose any changes when it announced its decision on 14 February 1967. This decision absolutely failed to correspond to the genuine national and state interests and in many respects was simply bizarre. The widespread disaffection in this regard within the ČLA at present is proof of how bad the decision was.

One of the key reasons for the lack of success of the Czechoslovak defense system was that it was not based on formulations of Czechoslovak military doctrine and basic decisions of Czechoslovak political and military strategy. When it was devised, it was based on operational tasks set forth by the Warsaw Pact command, without taking into account whether the state had the human and material capacity to execute them. This was possible because the implementation of the individual articles of the Warsaw Treaty was drastically different from what was set down on paper, to the point where it did not even correspond to the spirit of the treaty. This fact, which has no legal basis, was reflected above all in the lack of any conception of our own military doctrine. Every government should be responsible for this most important sphere of state authority on both the national and the international levels. This led to a violation of the equilibrium in our society and a deformation in the organization of our armed forces and their removal from politics. There arose a basic crisis in the military organism, as it was torn from the social structure of its own society. In the process, the military lost its national sense and the feeling of being needed by the society. This was even more pronounced in the higher command structure, from which all the other representative and executive organs were excluded. This could not help but produce a rupture of ties among the political, economic, and military aims of the state. This also led to difficulties in creating good relations, between especially young people and the defense of the state, military service, and the command staff. Finally, the direct leadership of the armed forces by the party (*de facto* by a narrow party-state organ or individual persons) could not help but have negative consequences for the party itself and its internal procedures.

II.2.2. These and other factors had a negative effect on the party's ability to devise a policy for safeguarding security. At the same time that a definite, albeit unsatisfactory, model of a defense system was worked out for the ČLA, there was no general formulation of a sense and purpose for security policy. In its present state the National Security Corps is living with the serious mistakes made in the organization of the armed forces after 1945 and 1948, especially concerning its leadership and training. Thousands of new workers in the Corps still study the

---

[93] The authors are referring to the November 1956 invasion of Hungary and the August 1961 Berlin crisis, in which the Warsaw Pact had at least a peripheral role (more of a role in the latter than in the former).

methods of investigation and other things by following old secret police methods, some of which were borrowed from German prisons (the intelligence department COV II).[94] This obviously has had a negative effect. The problem was exacerbated by the fact that during the struggle for political power, when the legal system was being formed and its activity was directed against occupiers, collaborators, and traitors, a hard-line position, especially at the beginning, was widely accepted. In those first postwar years some impermissible habits, norms, and approaches used by certain workers or groups of the Corps took shape and carried over into subsequent years.

The necessity to purge the organs of national security and recruit anew during the complex internal and international situation post February 1948, and especially after 1951, in addition to the majority of tasks that confronted them—meant that it was impossible to carry out any professional training of the Corps staff.[95] All the units of the Corps were ordered to help carry out decisive political directives from the central regime. The main criterion at that time was absolute devotion to the party, almost to the point of absurdity, and a sacrifice of one's own interests, and so forth. To this end, many crude mistakes were made while performing service duties and it failed to live up to its principled instructions. Under qualified and armored agents meant that many of them used unacceptable pressure tactics and force during their investigations. Essentially these same factors accounted for the inefficacy of the Corps. Results were evaluated in a mechanical way. Individual agents, as well as entire groups, wanted to achieve results at any price. One of the main reasons for using secret police methods was once again the lack of qualified specialists in the field, so they were unable to penetrate hostile intelligence service centers.

The basic reason for all this is that the party did not have a comprehensive policy for safeguarding security. The measures adopted after 1945–48 did not take sufficient account of the changes that take place in the course of development of a socialist society. They were subordinated to ideology, particularly to the unilateral pronouncement on the relentless intensification of the class struggle and the necessity of searching for evil within one's own ranks.[96]

The specific consequences of this crude approach became especially apparent as they involved the essence of power. A one-sided evaluation of the political situation and the sociopolitical changes in society led to a consolidation of ruling habits which primarily relied on the instruments of power. The abuse of these organs during the internal political struggle rather than the use of political forms of leadership, prevented meaningful criticism and the correction of existing mistakes.

. . .

. . . The leading role of the party in this sphere went completely unchallenged. Among other things this resulted in a tendentious evaluation of the political situation, the adoption of political evaluations instead of genuine state security interests, and the manipulation of statistics. . . .

. . .

An entire series of reorganizational measures in the national security organs inhibited their further development and successful performance. The first measures were adopted in 1954 in accordance with the organizational model of the Soviet police and included the elimination of the anti-crime squad, which fundamentally reduced the effectiveness of the struggle against traditional criminal activity. . . . Every reorganization in the Ministry of Internal Affairs always led to the strengthening of state security organs' positions to the detriment of the administrative

[94] COV II was the Second Department of the State Security apparatus, whose nominal responsibilities included counterintelligence against foreigners on Czechoslovak territory.

[95] This passage refers to the period in which the political repression and show trials in Czechoslovakia reached their height (1949–1954).

[96] Stalin's dictum held that the class struggle intensifies (and hence the need for the suppression of "class enemies" increases) as socialism evolves into communism.

bodies and other functions in the ministry.[97] This was one of the decisive reasons that, despite criticism and periodic changes, there was no qualitative change in the understanding of the functions, methods, and style of work; and for the same reason nobody who bore responsibility for illegal and inhumane activities was sacked.

. . .

When the whole regime was controlled by an individual who had his own subjective whims, it was impossible to speak of a comprehensive, systematic framework in the intelligence service. The old ties between the intelligence service and state and economic organs, as well as with public organizations and individual citizens, were reflected in the centralized and bureaucratic model of the state.

In the course of the last twenty years leadership and control over party organizations in the intelligence service by the highest party organs meant administrative interference in the security organs. In essence, there was really no leadership to speak of. The intelligence service was formally subordinated to the first secretary and president of the republic, who never voiced any concerns at sessions either of the CPCz CC or of the government. However, he himself did not actually supervise the work. For this reason, the intelligence service was forced to find its own way, to satisfy the demands of different departments, and to recommend the duties it would carry out. In this way, a permanent situation of ambiguity arose concerning the way its work was directed and its methodology and organization. There was also no control over it by elected party organs. For this reason, the intelligence service was not able to operate as a true information bureau. The security organs were extremely secretive when it came to the party, state, and legislative organs and repeatedly served as the main arm of the repressive apparatus.

The socialist state did not evaluate at any stage of its development the existence of its own intelligence services and did not include them organizationally in the system of the Czechoslovak foreign service in a way that meant that they could fully serve the public interests of the state.

. . .

3. The Current Status of the Czechoslovak People's Army and the National Security Corps

3.1 We are only able to provide a preliminary assessment of the general situation in the Czechoslovak People's Army after the December–January plenum of the CPCz CC. . . .

. . .

In recent years the situation in the army was characterized by huge delays when it came to the solution of any basic theoretical and operational problems. The issue of the correlation between the country's defense demands and its actual capabilities was not clarified. Over a prolonged period, shortcomings in the organizational and leadership systems accumulated. The basic tension was caused by the fundamental disproportions between the demands, based on the obligations stipulated by the Warsaw Pact, and the conditions of their fulfillment. And also by the failure of its technical wing, combat equipment, and its support equipment to take account of the human factor. Serious problems accrued regarding the technical equipment of the whole system of organization and leadership. Frequent changes in the general concept of the organization of the army created a situation of permanent reorganization, which inevitably led to ill thought-out changes in the organization of branches of the forces. The technical level achieved and the structure of the armed forces were not commensurate with the norms demanded. And above all the quality and technological parameters of certain types of equipment and combat

---

[97] State Security (*Státní bezpečnost*, or StB) forces were headed by a deputy minister, who reported to and acted on behalf of the CPCz CC first secretary.

technology did not meet the standards of modern warfare (the air defense forces, anti-tank defenses, military aviation units, classical artillery, communications equipment, etc.). The problems just mentioned are connected, among other things, with the failure to work out ways of developing the Czechoslovak defense industry and its ties with other treaty member states.

The modernization of the army and the huge expenditures involved took place, to a large degree, at the expense of the living standards of the soldiers. For this reason this must be solved as soon as possible. The above-mentioned shortcomings weaken the preconditions for the successful operations of the forces in case of the sudden outbreak of war.

In the course of the army's organization, a whole series of major financial problems will arise. The basic problem is that expenditure on equipment is rapidly growing in light of the relentless increase in prices. The preservation of the army at its present size and its current financial state is extremely difficult to maintain.[98]

. . .

An important task is the search for a positive solution to the system of political supervision and political leadership in the army. The existing system is a mechanistic and ill-conceived conglomeration of very different and mutually incompatible types of activity within the party-political organs. This system does not accord either with the demands to strengthen the leading role of the party on the basis of new principles or with demands for leadership of the army under modern conditions.

The party-political organs have gradually overcome the depression of the first months and have more actively begun to organize political work with people. They inform servicemen in a quicker and more comprehensive way and spur on their activity in the spirit of the CPCz Action Program. The first steps toward the democratization of the leadership of party work were carried out. At the party conferences, in the spirit of the CPCz CC Presidium's decision, preparatory committees were set up and have begun their work. . . .

. . . .

Another characteristic tendency of the current political situation in the army is the gradual formation of a unity of views and a unified position in connection with the most important social and state issues.

This refers above all to the full support that the process of democratization in the society and in party life, the federal arrangement of the Czechoslovak Socialist Republic, and the fair solution to the nationality question enjoy. Categorical demands are being expressed for a split in the party in order to get rid of those who were responsible for deformations in the past, especially those members of the CPCz CC who compromised themselves by their activities. The necessity of the unity and mutual cooperation between the ČSSR and the Soviet Union and other socialist states is fully understood.

Although the majority of servicemen subscribe to a united point of view on the above-mentioned questions, there are still discrepancies and even contradictions that emerge, especially concerning the way to resolve them. Some express views that border on anarchism and are devoid of good sense. Others express a wait-and-see position. These include servicemen who have a negative view of their own situation and reject the process of democratization.

An important factor that markedly affected the political situation in the army was the development of public opinion vis-à-vis the army.

Strong pressure and a mass of published material evoked feelings of hostility in part of the command staff and channeled public sentiment both against individuals and against the army as a whole. Some commanders encountered physical violence. The command staff, which was

[98] Starting in the spring of 1968, the military press in Czechoslovakia had been featuring a lively debate about defense spending and economic tradeoffs.

blamed for all internal shortcomings, directed sharp criticism at the political apparatus. Gradually these hostilities faded. At present the public's relationship to the army is more level-headed and only occasionally becomes excessive.

3.2. The situation in the National Security Corps is complicated. The State Security service (counterintelligence) at present is in a state of crisis, both politically and in its work. This can be explained above all by the serious mistakes committed in the past, for which the former leaders of the Ministry of Internal Affairs and State Security organs bear responsibility. This includes direct ties with the previous political system of personal power and the negative consequences of direct party control over this sphere.

The State Security service, from its outset, was arranged on the basis of the old view that its work constitutes one of the pillars of the socialist system.[99] This false thesis corresponded with the spirit of the administrative-centralized system, which was condemned by the January plenum of the CPCz CC. The service had a highly privileged place as a specific organ of the party not only in relation to other parts of the executive apparatus of the National Security Corps, but also in relation to organs of the procuracy and judiciary. As a result of this, these organs were not genuinely controlled by the party leadership or socialist society, and they committed violations of the law with impunity, even after 1953. State Security organs did not often take into account the basic principles of professionalism, science, law and legality, socialist ethics and morality, and did not take account of the political consequences of the results of its work.

. . .

In accordance with the party's Action Program, it is necessary to begin with an objective and scientifically-based analysis of the intentions of the foreign enemy and the necessary risk in connection with preserving the country's security. Precise criteria must be defined, as must the methodology and approach to this sort of problem.

Exposing these intentions to public scrutiny and analysis demands coordinated work between the security organs and other organizations. One must have knowledge of corresponding military situations, and one also needs an apparatus for observations, analyzing hostile propaganda in the framework of psychological warfare, etc. These tasks go beyond the framework of the functions of the security organs and demand coordinated leadership within the framework of the entire state apparatus.

. . .

4. Basic Problems and Directions When Formulating the Party's Policy in Promoting the Internal and External Security of the State

A serious analysis of the contemporary situation clarifies the directions one should go in studying the problems of how to preserve the internal and external security of the state.

With regard to the country's defense:

4.1.1. In accord with the clarification of the general political doctrine of our socialist society, the elaboration of a Czechoslovak military doctrine as a brief formula of the country's military missions and needs is both a theoretical and an ideological precondition for a military-political strategy and the kind of Czechoslovak defense system that arises from it. The formulation of a military doctrine would be based on a comprehensive balance of the capabilities and demands of our state and on its dynamic development and the interests of the development of European socialism. Above all, one must realize the necessity for fundamental political, economic, and

---

[99] The authors are alluding to the Stalinist concept that evolved out of the bolsheviks' view that the security organs were the "sword and shield" of the revolution and the socialist state.

other changes in our society. Conclusions based on the study of the consequences of the scientific-technological revolution in separate spheres of public life must be employed as much as possible.

In this sense the military doctrine will be defined by a compromise between demands and real capabilities, between the hoped-for growth in scientific achievements, including the military sphere, and the actual development of technology and the necessity of continually deploying the most effective defense system. Further, it is worth adding that the demands placed on the Czechoslovak defense system are based primarily on an earlier operational plan of the Czecho- slovak army. An army which gave short shrift to both the human and material capabilities of the state, led to an irresovable contradiction between the demands of the armed forces and the capabilities of fulfilling those demands. This had serious negative consequences for the further development of our society.

In the future the doctrine will also take as its starting point the alliance obligations to the Soviet Union and the other Warsaw Pact partners. Simultaneously, it will recommend that the circum- stances and capabilities of individual countries be acknowledged in the decisions taken by the alliance. Such considerations are not strategic concepts, but yet we must not simply passively accept them.

In essence, Czechoslovak defense policy strives to be a policy of European security, a policy that helps ease international tensions, and a policy of friendly cooperation with all who have a direct interest in this. It strives to be a policy of close cooperation with all progressive forces. It must remain a valuable instrument of the whole Czechoslovak policy.[100] It must neither understate nor overstate the danger posed by the adversary, which in the end facilitates the development of conservative tendencies in both socialism and capitalism. It also does not underestimate the danger posed by different military confrontations, especially between oppos- ing sociopolitical systems.

. . .

It is necessary when formulating the state interests and needs of the ČSSR in the military sphere to encompass different versions of situations and to get rid of unrealistic scenarios and dangers of the past.

From the point of view of constituting Czechoslovak military doctrine as the most secure and most salutary unified approach, this is a method of simple logic. The notion of a general war in Europe that involves the massive use of nuclear weapons is, from Czechoslovakia's point of view, purely senseless. This form of war would bring about the total physical destruction of the ČSSR, irrespective of the scale of losses to its armed forces and also, ultimately, irrespective of the final results of the war.[101]

For this reason the aim should be to achieve a pragmatic stability of the state's defense system and the army's structure, a stability that flows from political demands and a dual goal: to prevent excessive danger on the part of the potential adversary, and to preserve the existence and sovereignty of the Czechoslovak Socialist Republic and in that way realize the necessary contribution of the ČSSR to the coalition, in the sense of fulfilling its internationalist tasks.

. . .

[100] The formulations in this paragraph not only were at variance with the Warsaw Pact's general approach, but were particularly galling to East German officials, who had long suspected that Czechoslovak leaders were seeking to establish "friendly cooperation" with the FRG.

[101] In 1965, the Soviet Union and Czechoslovakia secretly concluded two agreements on deploying Soviet nuclear weapons on Czech territory during an emergency, and a broader agreement authorized the Soviets to store warheads at three future sites in the western sectors of the country. Construction of the sites and deployment of the warheads were due to be completed by 1967, but last-minute delays meant that the facilities had not yet entered service when the Prague Spring began. This passage of the report, therefore, cast that agreement in doubt, as well as challenged the position of the Warsaw Pact at the time.

Guidance of the development of the army is only on the basis of simple logic, empirical analysis, and historical analogies, and if one speaks only of the interests of the coalition without taking account of one's own interests, that ultimately will contradict the interests of the coalition as well.

. . .

4.1.2. In connection with the prospective concept of the development of the country's defense and security, one must accurately define the relationship between the armed forces and the security corps.

We start with the assumption that the party, through its activities and policy, is struggling for a leading role in society. In the political system that currently exists, there are conditions for relatively independent operations and activity by each of its consituent parts and individual citizens. If one speaks about the sphere of the internal and external security of the state, the party rejects direct leadership over the armed forces. The use of the principle of direct leadership in peaceful circumstances is one of the signs of the command-administrative method of leadership. In the process, of course, one would not have to go so far as to slacken one's attention to such questions. The party, on the contrary, will seek to bolster its political influence over the armed forces and security corps. The interests of society demand that leadership of separate parts of the armed forces be unified and clear, and that it be carried out in the same way that political leadership is exercised.

. . .

DOCUMENT No. 62: Meeting Notes Taken by Chief of the Hungarian People's Army General Staff Károly Csémi on Talks with Soviet Generals in Budapest to Discuss Preparations for "Operation Danube," July 24, 1968

Source: MHKI, 5/12/11, Doc. 13.

This memorandum of a conversation between Hungarian and Soviet military officials reveals the state of the final military planning for the invasion—code-named "Operation Danube"—as of July 24. General Károly Csémi's notes from the meeting with Col. General Konstantin Provalov, the commander of the USSR's Southern Group of Forces; Lt .General Fyodor Marushchak, the chief of staff of the Southern Group of Forces and General Tutarinov, confirm that despite János Kádár's moderating influence earlier in the crisis, Hungary has participated fully in preparations for what Soviet officials describe here as "exercises" on Czechoslovak territory. Hungary's role was to provide one division to help "crush" any opposition from Czechoslovak army units and "defeat the counterrevolution."

(See also Document No. 66.)

On 24 July 1968 at 11:00 A.M. Cdes. Provalov, Tutarinov, and Marushchak came to see me.[102] Cde. Provalov informed me that he was planning maneuvers on Czechoslovak territory. He thanked us on behalf of Cde. Grechko for taking part in the exercises.[103]

He asked us to designate a division that would take part as well as the commanders. We were asked to decide whether the division should be involved in the first or second stage. They felt it would be more expedient to take part in the first stage.

I replied that I had merely been authorized yesterday to announce our participation in the maneuvers, and that I would have to report all other matters. We agreed that Major-Generals Szűcs and Reményi would leave for Mátyásföld on 25 July at 2 P.M. to prepare the plans and that they would report to me on the 26th.[104] It would be useful to include Major-General Kalázi in the preparations along with the commanders of the division and battalions and their chiefs of staff and political officers.[105] We will appoint a military operational liaison group to be attached to Cde. Provalov's staff for the duration of the maneuvers.

They also declared that although we will prepare for the exercises and be ready to carry them out, it would be good if we did not actually have to go ahead with them.

The political objective of the maneuvers is to help the Czechoslovak people defeat the counterrevolution. We will explain this to the workers, peasants, and intellectuals and make it clear that we will withdraw afterwards. We will leave army units alone provided that they act loyally, but if they put up resistance they will have to be crushed.

---

[102] All three of these Soviet generals played key roles during the invasion.

[103] Soviet "persuasion" over the preceding two weeks forced the Hungarian leadership to reluctantly agree to contribute Hungarian troops to the "exercises." On July 23, Kádár consulted with a few top aides and then explicitly confirmed Hungary's willingness to take part, a decision that prompted effusive expressions of gratitude from Brezhnev and Grechko. (See the top-secret *aide memoire* from the chief of the Hungarian General Staff, Col.-General Károly Csémi, July 23, 1968, in MHKI, 5/12/11, Doc. 12.)

[104] At the time, Mátyásföld (an outer district of Budapest) was the headquarters of the USSR's Southern Group of Forces. Following the general mobilization on July 27, the headquarters was shifted to Csákvár; and it was temporarily relocated once again, to Bratislava, on the day the invasion began.

[105] The three Hungarian officers mentioned here were, *seriatim*: Major-General Ferenc Szűcs, a deputy chief of the Hungarian General Staff; Major-General Gyula Reményi, another deputy chief of the Hungarian General Staff; and Major-General Lajos Kalázi, the commander of Hungary's 5th Army.

Three Soviet divisions will enter west of the Danube across the three bridges.[106] In the event that the bridges are blown up, the river will have to be crossed by the use of force. They would like to deploy our division in the first phase east of the Danube, if possible on a larger scale than has been already outlined.[107] The division is to be involved in administrative affairs on its territory.

We will be informed of the start of the maneuvers 5–7 hours in advance. At that point live ammunition is to be handed out, the formations are to receive concrete instructions, and the political purpose of the exercise is to be explained to the men.

Conclusions:

1. The exercises—if they take place—will cover a major portion of the territory and population of the country. It is therefore necessary to make arrangements to prepare public opinion in our country, prepare the troops of the People's Army, and take the necessary security measures.

2. If the exercises get under way, we can expect events to take place at any moment, at short notice, from the 26th or 27th on.

3. Regardless of the activities of the CzPA and the armed forces, armed clashes may occur.[108]

A decision must be taken:

— to determine whom we are to include in the preparation of the exercise,

— to make possible corrections in the choice of the location of the division (the first or second phase) and its composition on the basis of the definition of its tasks.

Budapest
24 July 1968

In the absence of Cde. Czinege (out of town)

Károly Csémi

---

[106] These three bridges were at Bratislava, Medvedov, and Komárno.

[107] The Hungarian troops were supposed to occupy portions of southern Slovakia (where the inhabitants were mainly ethnic Hungarians) after crossing the river Ipel', to the north of the Danube.

[108] Presumably, this means that the invading forces were prepared to subdue armed resistance from any quarter, whether organized resistance on the part of the CzPA or uncoordinated resistance by civilians.

DOCUMENT No. 63: "Message from the Citizens to the CPCz CC Presidium," July 26, 1968

Source: "Poselství československého lidu Předsednictvu ÚV KSČ," *Literární listy*, special edition, July 26, 1968, p. 1.

This "Message from the Citizens" to the Presidium, captures the degree of popular support for resisting Soviet pressure on the reform movement. The document was drafted by the well-known writer, Pavel Kohout; it was intended to bolster the morale of top Czechoslovak officials on their way to the meetings at Čierna nad Tisou with the "historic task" of "convincing the leaders of the CPSU that the renewal process in our country must be carried through successfully to the end."

The message calls on the Presidium to show "unity" and "courage" in "defending the path on which we have set out, a path we will not abandon as long as we live." The statement closes by reminding the CPCz negotiators that they were "writing a critical page of Czechoslovakia's history on our behalf," and that "we will anxiously follow your deliberations . . . We are thinking of you. Think of us!"

Such catchphrases and slogans devised by Kohout, along with the compelling sentiments expressed in the statement, ensured that the "Message" became an effective vehicle for ordinary Czechs and Slovaks—even those who normally had little interest in politics—to lend their support to the reform movement. After it was published in a special issue of the weekly Literární listy *on July 26, 1968, and featured the next day in many newspapers all over Czechoslovakia, including* Rudé právo, *over a million people signed it and countless others pledged their support in letters and telegrams.*

Message from the Citizens to the Presidium

Comrades,

We are writing to you on the eve of your meeting with the Presidium of the Central Committee of the Communist Party of the Soviet Union where you are going to discuss the fate of us all. As on many occasions in history, only a few men are going to decide the fate of millions of people. This is a difficult task and we would like to make it easier for you by giving you our support.

Over the past centuries the history of our country has been a history of bondage. With two brief intervals, we were condemned to shape our national existence illegally, and several times we were on the brink of annihilation. That is why our people so passionately hailed the democracy brought to them by liberation in 1918. It was a flawed democracy since it failed to provide its citizens with social security. And yet it was the working class that during Munich most firmly revealed its determination to defend this democracy against obliteration. This was another reason why our people so enthusiastically welcomed socialism, which our liberation in 1945 brought us. It was a flawed socialism because it failed to give creative freedom to its working population. But we tenaciously went in pursuit of it and began to find it after last January. . . .

The time has come when after centuries our country has once again become the cradle of hope, not only our own hope. The time has come when we are capable of demonstrating to the world that socialism is not some emergency solution for underdeveloped countries but the only true alternative for civilization.

We expected that this would be greeted with sympathy, above all by the entire socialist camp. Instead we are being accused of treason. We receive ultimata from comrades whose pronouncements increasingly reveal their ignorance of our developments and our situation. We are being accused of crimes we never committed. Designs are being attributed to us which we never had and do not have.

Comrades, we are threatened with unjust punishment which, whatever form it may take, would strike like a boomerang even on those who judge us, shattering our endeavors and, above all, tragically tarnishing the idea of socialism throughout the world for many years.

It is your historical duty to forestall such a danger! It is your responsibility to convince the leading representatives of the CPSU that the revival process in our country must be brought to a successful conclusion in accordance with the interests of our common fatherland as well as with the interests of progressive forces on all continents.

Everything we are striving for can be summed up in the words: Socialism—Alliance—Sovereignty—Freedom.[109]

Socialism and alliance give the fraternal countries and parties our guarantee that we will never tolerate developments that could endanger the true interests of peoples with whom we have been fighting a sincere battle for the common cause for more than twenty years. Sovereignty, on the other hand, provides our country with a guarantee against a repetition of the critical mistakes that only recently threatened to lead to a crisis.

Explain to your partners that extremist voices which can now and then be heard in our domestic debates are the product of the very bureaucratic police system that has been stifling creative thinking for so long, driving many people into internal opposition. Convince them by submitting countless examples that the authority of the party and the standing of socialism are today incomparably stronger in our country than at any time in the past.

Tell them that we need freedom, peace, and time in order to be more unflinching and better allies than at any time in the past.

In brief, speak in the name of the people, who at this point have ceased to be a poetic image but have once more become a force shaping history.

Comrades Barbírek, Biľak, Černík, Dubček, Kolder, Kriegel, Piller, Rigo, Smrkovský, Špaček, and Švestka, and Comrades Kapek, Lenárt, and Šimon, not all of you may hold identical views. Some of you, although you helped fight for January, are today the object of sharp criticism for the mistakes you committed prior to January. That is the fate of politicians, and the seven months since January have demonstrated that no one intends to transform this criticism into a vendetta. It would be tragic if the personal feelings of any of you were to prevail over the responsibility you hold at this moment for the fate of 14,361,000 people of whom you, too, are an inseparable part.

Go to the meetings and explain things, but do so in unity; and defend the road on which we have all set out, a road we will not abandon as long as we live.

Over the next few days we will anxiously follow your deliberations in our thoughts, hour by hour. We are impatiently awaiting your news. We are thinking of you. Think of us![110] You are writing a critical page of Czechoslovakia's history on our behalf. Write it with sound judgment, but above all with courage.

To lose this unique chance would be our ruin and your dishonor. We trust you!

At the same time we call on all our fellow citizens who agree with us to endorse this message!

---

[109] In Czech and Slovak, these four words all start with the letter "s" (*socialismus, spojenectví, suverenita, svoboda*), which makes for a more euphonious slogan than in English. After the appearance of this "Message" this quickly became a catchphrase of the Prague Spring.

[110] Even though this exhortation "We are thinking of you. Think of us!" (which in Czech is the rhyming phrase "Myslíme na Vás. Myslete na nás!") appears in Kohout's manifest, in popular memory the phrase became "Jsme s Vámi, buď'te s námi" ("We are with you, be with us!").

DOCUMENT No. 64: "On the Current Security Situation," Report by Oldřich Černík for the CPCz CC Presidium, July 27, 1968 (Excerpts)

Source: ÚSD, Sb. KV, B—Archiv MV, F. IM.

This top-secret report provides Prime Minister Černík's assessment of likely attitudes in the West toward an open Soviet–Czechoslovak conflict. His analysis addresses first the "hands-off" approach that the major Western governments had adopted, and second, Western governments' views of the way the crisis might be resolved, including the possibility of Soviet military intervention.

Černík confirms that Czechoslovakia could not count on outside assistance against a Soviet invasion. The major "Western countries, especially the United States, regard the ČSSR to be in the Soviet 'sphere of influence'," and the report observes that "respect for this sphere of influence is so entrenched that the United States . . . has refused any concrete commitment even in the event of Soviet military intervention in the ČSSR." The report notes, with some irony, that the strongest opposition to a possible Soviet invasion of Czechoslovakia had come not from Western governments, but from several West European communist parties.

Since July 20, however, the U.S. State Department, along with the French Foreign Ministry, had concluded that a Soviet invasion was "most unlikely and virtually out of the question." Černík himself takes no firm position on the likelihood of an invasion, but he suggests that with or without military action, Soviet "pressure on the ČSSR, especially in the political and economic spheres," would continue. Černík also notes that even if the Soviet and Czechoslovak governments eventually reached a compromise, such an arrangement, according to the U.S. State Department, would likely provide for Soviet troops to be permanently deployed on Czechoslovak territory, contrary to Prague's wishes.

On the Current Security Situation
. . .

1) *The Position of the Capitalist Governments vis-à-vis the Situation in Czechoslovakia*

In deciding what to do about a move against the ČSSR, there has been greater general restraint on the part of Western governments and political circles as a result of the latest developments, especially in connection with the letter from Warsaw from the five communist parties.

This restraint is so pronounced that, for example, the Austrian Socialist Party has refrained from issuing even a purely formal statement of intent, as had been proposed by the party leadership.

The U.S. State Department has explicitly instructed its diplomats abroad not to adopt any position on developments in Czechoslovakia, not even at the request of official quarters in the host countries. This restraint is motivated primarily by the need to maintain the current level of relations with the USSR.[111] Radio Free Europe has strict orders from the U.S. not to attack the USSR.

The French Foreign Ministry also refuses to express an official position because it, too, does not want to offend the Soviet Union.[112]

The Italian Christian Democratic Party, likewise, has a principle of not issuing public statements.

---

[111] This passage, though somewhat overstated, is generally borne out by newly declassified documents. See, for example, "Zapis' besedy s sovetnikom posoľstva SShA v NRB R. Dzhonsonom," July 17, 1968 (SECRET), from A. V. Sokolov, counselor at the Soviet embassy, in TsKhSD, F. 5, Op. 60, D. 278, Ll. 48–50. See also Memorandum No. 2588-Ts (TOP SECRET) from S. Tsvigun, deputy chairman of the KGB, to the CPSU Secretariat, November 15, 1968, in TsKhSD, F. 5, Op. 60, D. 311, Ll. 178–181.

[112] See "Zapis' besedy s sovetnikom posoľstva Frantsii v NR Bolgarii Gi Marten de la Bastidom," May 22, 1968 (SECRET), from A. V. Sokolov, counselor at the Soviet embassy, in TsKhSD, F. 5, Op. 60, D. 278, Ll. 51–54.

A partial exception was an internal statement by the French Government to the Polish representative that the success of Gomułka's planned visit to France would be helped if no "delicate problems" existed in Poland's neighborhood, which could be interpreted as a political move in support of the ČSSR.

West German Foreign Minister Brandt, in talks with representatives of the Austrian SPD, also spoke of the need to refrain from criticizing relations between the ČSSR and the USSR and from any "impulsive" statement in connection with the ČSSR.

There are, however, unofficial indications of moves in support of the ČSSR in the economic sphere. For example, the United States intimated on several occasions that Western economic aid was possible. The condition laid down by Federal Germany, France, and Italy is that the initiative must come from the ČSSR. There appears to be some tactical flexibility on this matter. The United States, for example, anticipates the possibility of loans along private lines but, from its point of view, only in an extreme situation. Apart from that, the U.S. is encouraging its Western allies, especially Federal Germany, not to be the first to take such steps.

The evidence suggests that in the present situation the capitalist countries do not wish for a radical turn in the situation in the ČSSR. Such a development might well have adverse international repercussions. They consider their own moves to be confined to a cautiously neutral official position. They are prepared to take economic steps to help the ČSSR, but not at their own initiative.

These countries, especially the United States, regard the ČSSR to be in the Soviet "sphere of influence," which, they believe, must be respected at present. This respect is so entrenched that the U.S., as it made amply clear and as is evident also in the assessment by the French Foreign Ministry, refuses any concrete commitment, even in the event of Soviet intervention in the ČSSR.

The French Left has played a certain peculiar role in the present situation. The French Communist Party, under some pressure by the Socialist Party SFIO, sent Cde. Rochet to Moscow.[113] In the opinion of the French CP, the visit forestalled an open crisis between the ČSSR and the five communist parties. While the French CP is fairly divided in its attitude toward the problem, the SFIO has stated unambiguously that open intervention by the USSR in the ČSSR under present circumstances would have an extremely negative influence on the Left in the West in general and would even result in an end to cooperation between the SFIO and the French CP.

2) Assessments of the ČSSR's Internal Situation

Following a certain lull, there has again been a surge of interest in the situation in the ČSSR. The original cause of this interest was the continued presence of Soviet troops on Czechoslovak territory. The meeting of the five communist parties in Warsaw further dramatized the situation. Until then the situation in the ČSSR was regarded as settled. Toward the end of June the American CIA noted that power in the country remained firmly in the hands of the CPCz and that the non-communist parties had won no significant positions. It was merely pointed out that developments confirmed the theory about specific roads toward socialism in individual countries.

However, in mid-July the French Foreign Ministry assessed the situation in the ČSSR as extremely tense. The cause of this, it felt, was the real danger of Soviet intervention motivated by fear that capitalism would be restored in the ČSSR and that Czechoslovak developments were having an adverse effect on the internal situation in the GDR.

West German Foreign Minister Brandt regarded the situation to be less dramatic. In talks with representatives of the Austrian Social Democratic Party, he welcomed developments in the ČSSR and merely expressed his view that things should not be accelerated in any way.

However, assessments by the U.S. State Department between 8 and 19 July concluded that in the ČSSR there was a noticeable rise in the influence of right-wing forces as well as mounting

---

[113] See Document No. 58.

conflicts within the CPCz about the future political and economic line to be taken. In their opinion, there is also disunity in the army and in the security services. In addition, they note that the United States enjoys growing prestige among the Czechoslovak population. Representatives of the Austrian SPD were surprised by the show of unity in the ČSSR in support of the CPCz in connection with the letter from the five communist parties. Yet they also spoke of the need for moderation in internal developments in the ČSSR. According to the SPD, every attempt should be made to prevent radical progressives from publishing articles in the press that could serve as a pretext for intervention by the USSR.

In its more recent assessment (after 20 July) the French Foreign Ministry also referred to the consolidation of the CPCz's position. But it added that lasting success depended on the solution of the CPCz's economic program.

All in all, it can be said that government and political quarters in the West basically agree that internal developments in the ČSSR are of an essentially orderly and tranquil nature. They do, however, point to the danger of extremist elements, which they do not regard to be desirable. This view is clearly motivated by fears of adverse international repercussions and the possible deterioration of the domestic situation in the ČSSR.

U.S. government circles have, moreover, expressed concern that a weakening of the prestige of the USSR as a result of Czechoslovak developments might result in attempts by the USSR (which would be unfavorable for the U.S.) to seek some kind of settlement of its conflicts with the Chinese People's Republic.

Considerations about concrete steps by the USSR have given rise to the question of whether Soviet military intervention in the ČSSR is likely. This scenario, according to the U.S. State Department and the French Foreign Ministry, is most unlikely and virtually out of the question. The reason is that, first of all, it would have a highly negative impact on the prestige of the USSR in the international communist movement and throughout the world and, second, that the position of the present CPCz leadership has been substantially consolidated.

It is considered likely, however, that pressure on the ČSSR will continue, especially in the political and economic spheres. The U.S. State Department believes that under a compromise arrangement the USSR will succeed in stationing its troops on Czechoslovak territory in some form since the CPCz leadership will not be able to put up effective opposition to such a demand.

The leadership of the Italian Christian Democratic Party believes that there will be a gradual easing of Czechoslovak–Soviet relations on the basis of a broader compromise. . . .

. . .

DOCUMENT No. 65: Speeches by Leonid Brezhnev, Alexander Dubček, and Aleksei Kosygin at the Čierna nad Tisou Negotiations, July 29, 1968 (Excerpts)

Source: ÚSD, Sb. KV, Z/S—5, 6; Vondrová & Navrátil, vol. 2, pp. 43–82.

The Čierna nad Tisou negotiations, named after the small railroad crossing town in Slovakia on the border with Ukraine where they were held, spanned three-and-a-half days of meetings and generated a transcript of several hundred pages from which Brezhnev's, Dubček's and Kosygin's speeches are drawn. The meeting represented the last bilateral opportunity to forestall a Soviet invasion.

The lead-off speech by Brezhnev, several hours in duration, set the tone for most of the negotiations. The Soviet leader issued a litany of charges and accusations, recounting how CPCz leaders had "retreated" and "failed to take any realistic measures" when the "anti-socialist and counterrevolutionary forces" both inside and outside the party "launched their attacks against the communist party, the foundations of socialism, and the friendship of the Czechoslovak and Soviet peoples." Drawing on a thick pile of press clippings he had brought with him to the meeting as "evidence" of the growing strength of the counterrevolutionary elements in Czechoslovakia, Brezhnev went into even greater depth about the CPCz leadership's alleged transgressions than he had in the past—bolstering his speech with a level of detail that made an effective defense against his accusations almost impossible.

The transcript of Dubček's speech records his attempts to respond to the concerns raised by the Soviet leader. His defense of the CPCz's actions throughout the Prague Spring addressed issues that were sore points in Soviet–Czechoslovak relations: the prolonged Soviet troop deployments, the press polemics, the threats of military intervention emanating from East Germany and Poland, the use of the Warsaw Pact as a means of generating pressure on the CPCz Presidium, and the reluctance of the Czechoslovak leadership to reverse key reforms. "The basic credo of our external political orientation is unchanged," he assured his Soviet counterparts.

To Dubček's strong defense of the Prague Spring, Soviet Prime Minister Aleksei Kosygin responded with a stinging denunciation of the CPCz and many of the Czechoslovak officials who were present, especially František Kriegel.

The negotiations produced few concrete results, even when Brezhnev and Dubček talked in private. Nevertheless, when the meeting ended the two sides agreed to convene a multilateral follow-up conference in Bratislava.

(See also Documents Nos. 76, 81, 82, 85, and 86.)

Brezhnev's speech:[114]

. . .

I tell you frankly, comrades, that we left Dresden with mixed feelings. On the one hand, we had the impression that the collective exchange of views had induced Czechoslovak officials to think again about the gravity of the situation and about their own responsibility, and to consider what must be done to rebuff the counterrevolution. On the other hand, we did not sense that the Czechoslovak comrades had any concrete plans or any concrete idea about what to do, in practical terms, to prevent the situation from heading in an ever more dangerous direction.

And again I regret to say that the course of events has borne out the conclusions of the fraternal parties rather than the unjustified optimism of the CPCz leaders. The March–April plenum of the CPCz CC was unable to stabilize conditions. What is more, the CPCz Action Program which was adopted at that plenum began to be used, in a number of instances, by the right wing as some

---

[114] The nearly 2,000 pages of Czechoslovak notes and negotiating transcripts, which had been placed in a special safe by Gustáv Husák at Soviet behest, became available soon after the "velvet revolution" of November 1989. Portions from the Soviet notes and Russian transcript were turned over to the Czechoslovak commission in 1992.

sort of legal basis for further attacks against the communist party, the foundations of socialism, and the friendship of the Czechoslovak and Soviet peoples. The right-wing forces went on the offensive, and the CPCz CC continued gradually to retreat.

Our worries increased when a broad campaign got under way aimed at discrediting all the earlier activities of the CPCz. These concerns increased still further when the large-scale replacement of party and government cadres began, and when a wave of anti-Soviet propaganda was vented in the press, on radio, and on television. Moreover, like mushrooms after a rain, all types of organizations began to sprout, placing themselves at odds with the communist party. In such a situation the CPSU CC deemed it necessary once again to take new steps to stress our fears. We expected the CPCz CC Presidium to move from words and assurances to deeds and practical resistance to the hostile forces. At the same time, it is self-evident that we understood the objective complexity of the situation and the difficult situation of the CPCz leadership itself. That is why the CPSU CC continued to refrain from any public evaluation and statements, proposing once again to hold confidential, bilateral talks.

At that meeting, held in Moscow on 4 May by mutual consent, Cdes. Dubček, Černík, Smrkovský, and Biľak spoke about the seriousness of the situation. Furthermore you declared that the negative aspects of internal political developments in Czechoslovakia "are going beyond our purely internal affairs and affect the fraternal countries, for instance, the Soviet Union and Poland." No one could disagree with this.

You also said you were ready to undertake the necessary measures to control the situation. Back then you said, and I quote: "The enemy is active, hoping to seize upon events in the interests of counterrevolution. To thwart this, what is needed is not cultural-educational work but a firming up of the army's stability. It is essential to whip the State Security organs into good shape from top to bottom. These organs are needed by the party as an apparatus of force. Perhaps it will be necessary to approve a special law on the People's Militia. . . ."

You admitted that the enemy is trying above all to discredit the communist party and weaken its influence on the masses. You also admitted that demands are growing to legalize political opposition to the CPCz, and that "if firm steps are not taken this might develop into a counter-revolutionary situation." You said that you know the specific people, and that you believe there is evidence of their links with imperialist circles. You also said you would put an end to this.

Your evaluations of this period coincided with those of the CPSU CC.

Our fears that the process of "democratization" which you have undertaken would turn into something exactly the opposite—by that I mean counterrevolution—were also expressed by A. N. Kosygin during his trip to Karlovy Vary. We spoke about these problems again in Moscow when a delegation of the National Assembly headed by Cde. Smrkovský and a delegation of workers headed by Cde. Barbírek visited us.[115]

At the CPCz CC's May plenum you admitted that the main danger to the cause of socialism in Czechoslovakia comes from the right. It seemed that this gave reason to hope you would move from words to deeds. You proclaimed your readiness to act decisively in defending socialist gains at conferences of the secretaries of party committees, at nationwide assemblies of the People's Militia, and at countless gatherings of party branches in factories and plants.

Unfortunately, the hopes of the healthy forces in the party and the country, as well as the hopes of all your friends, were unjustified. The decisions of the May plenum remained unfulfilled. The anti-socialist forces unleashed an attack against the line taken by the CPCz CC's May plenum. Attacks by anti-Soviet elements became even fiercer. The wave of attacks launched by anti-socialist forces became even bolder by the end of June, when the "Two Thousand Words"

---

[115] Smrkovský's lengthy visit, in his capacity as chairman of the National Assembly, took place in the first half of June. The visit aroused controversy back in Czechoslovakia because Smrkovský several times criticized "anti-socialist" phenomena in the Czechoslovak media. Upon his return to Prague, his popularity had declined, and he felt compelled to apologize for his remarks.

appeal was published. It amounted to an open summons to struggle against the CPCz and against the constitutional regime.

You remember, Cde. Dubček, in speaking to you on the phone that day we drew your attention to the danger of this document as a platform for counterrevolutionary activities. You replied that the CC Presidium would consider this question, and you would propose that the document be harshly criticized and that the most decisive measures would be adopted. But except for a weak resolution, no realistic measures were ever taken to carry out these words in practice.

All this compelled us and the other fraternal parties to consider the necessity of holding one more meeting with you. It was with this proposal that the CPSU and the other fraternal parties appealed to the CPCz CC, but, unfortunately, you refused to attend the meeting in Warsaw.

And so, comrades, for the last seven months Soviet and Czechoslovak leaders and the leaders of the other fraternal parties have been in close contact of the most diverse ways, ranging from telephone conversations to personal meetings and negotiations. If we were to assess the substance of this contact, one cannot but conclude that the CPSU CC has unwaveringly adhered to a consistent and clear position.

What, in brief, is the essence of our position?

In the first place, from the very beginning we fully appreciated the decisions of the CPCz CC that were aimed at rectifying mistakes and shortcomings, at improving party leadership in all spheres of public life, and at developing socialist democracy. We considered, and we still consider, these decisions to be an exclusively internal affair of Czechoslovak communists and of all the working people of your country.

Second of all, we continually emphasized that the only guarantee of the successful implementation of the measures adopted could come through the leading role of the party, ensuring that full control over the course of events is in the party's hands. In this regard we drew your attention more than once to the fact that a weakening of party leadership inevitably leads to the activation of the rightist forces, and even overtly counterrevolutionary forces, which seek to discredit the Communist Party of Czechoslovakia, remove it from power, tear your country out of the socialist commonwealth, and ultimately change the social system in Czechoslovakia.

Third, we supported, and still support, the notion that the fate of the socialist gains of the Czechoslovak people and the fate of Czechoslovakia as a socialist state bound by allied obligations with our country and the other fraternal countries is not purely an internal affair of the CPCz.[116] This is the common affair of the whole commonwealth of socialist countries and of the entire communist movement. That is why the CPSU CC believes it has an international duty to see to it that all measures lead to the strengthening of the CPCz, to the protection and strengthening of socialism in the ČSSR, and to the defense of Czechoslovakia from imperialist conspiracies. This, I repeat, is our international duty, it is the international duty of all fraternal parties, and we would cease to be communists if we refused to discharge it.

This, comrades, is the principled position of the Communist Party of the Soviet Union—a position based on the principles of Marxism–Leninism and on proletarian internationalism. Guided by these principles, we always considered it our duty not to hide our opinion from you and to speak the truth to you no matter how bitter and cruel our opinion might be. And that is what we intend to do today.

Let me dwell in greater detail on several aspects of the current situation in Czechoslovakia.

The first one, which is the one that causes us the greatest fear and concern, is the *situation in which the Communist Party of Czechoslovakia now finds itself*. We speak about this first of all because without strengthening the communist party and without securing its leading role in all spheres of social life, all references to the "improvement" of socialism are simply a deception.

---

[116] This paragraph presents the core of the "Brezhnev Doctrine," claiming both a right and a "solemn duty" for the Soviet Union to "protect and strengthen socialism in the ČSSR" and to "defend Czechoslovakia against imperialist conspiracies."

In recent months in Czechoslovakia the process of discrediting the communist party has been gathering steam and a real threat has arisen to the party's leading position in society. Of course, such a situation did not come about spontaneously. It is the result of the activation of anti-communist forces and, at the same time, the inevitable consequence of an incorrect position taken by some members of the CPCz leadership and of their deviation from Marxist–Leninist principles on a number of questions.

In particular, frequent calls by certain leading figures in the CPCz to "put an end to the monopoly of power by the communists," to "separate the party from the state," and to establish "equality" between the CPCz and other political parties, as well as calls to relinquish party leadership in the state, the economy, culture, and other spheres, served as the initial impulse and the basis for the development of an unbridled campaign against the Communist Party of Czechoslovakia, and also for the activation of forces attempting to destroy the CPCz and to deny it its leading role in society.

Attacks on the party began, as is known, under the guise of discussions about the necessity of putting an end to "obsolete" working methods and adapting them to present-day demands. Naturally, we understand that the party is a living organism which develops along with the whole of society, and that the forms and methods of party work and of party leadership can and must change in accordance with changes in society. But in this case that is not what has been occurring. What has been occurring is that some leaders of the CPCz have effectively ended up undermining the basic principles of the very political organization—the party—which they are responsible for leading and strengthening.

Only in this way can one explain the fact that although self-criticism is essential in every party, critical assessments in Czechoslovakia of various methods quickly led to the unrestrained and dangerous discrediting of the entire party. Exploiting the indecisive and wavering position of the CPCz CC Presidium, revisionists and right-wing forces have vilified all CPCz activities over the last 20 years, rejecting the party's right to lead society and the state.

Just look, comrades, at how far things have gone.

An article by a certain Liehm, printed on 13 June of this year in the weekly *Literární listy*, states: "The CPCz bears responsibility for all the mistakes of the 20 years since February 1948 and for all the illnesses and crimes in society . . ."[117] And he goes on to say: "The CPCz maintains its leading role even though it has neither a moral nor a political right to do so."

And on 9 June in the paper *Mladá fronta* one of the active spokesmen of the anti-party forces, Hanzelka, wrote that 1.5 million members of the CPCz have become fanatics of a sort who are used by certain party "despots" to further their own personal gains.[118]

At the meeting of the "Youth Club" in Semily someone called Temicek screamed hysterically: "The Communist Party of Czechoslovakia must be seen as the criminal organization it truly is, and should be expelled from public life." And these ravings were immediately published in *Literární listy*.

And the journal *Host do domu* (No. 5, 1968) published the following insolent statement by a member of its editorial board, V. Blažek, and I quote: "The CPCz, which was once the party of the intellectual and cultural elite and the party of the most mature section of the working class, has been transformed . . . into a party of the ragtail and riffraff and become subordinate to this rabble."[119]

---

[117] The author of this article, entitled "Tak vážně: Co konkrétné?" was the well-known writer and critic Antonín J. Liehm.

[118] Jiří Hanzelka, a prominent Czech writer-engineer and intellectual, was one of the signatories of the "Two Thousand Words" Manifesto. He took an active part in political groups supporting much more sweeping reform in Czechoslovak society.

[119] *Host do domu* was one of the main writers' monthly journals; Vladimír Blažek was a frequent contributor to it and to *Literární listy*, where he strongly supported reformist efforts.

One could cite analogous material in tens or even hundreds of other instances. And this whole stream, which is openly hostile to the communist party and to socialist ideas, pours forth daily on the heads of the working people. It is being suggested to them that the party of communists is something in the nature of an organization of bankrupt persons and should be banned from power.

Unfortunately, comrades, you did not reach the necessary conclusions that the party is being swallowed up by a vicious anti-communist campaign. Instead of resolutely rebuffing attempts that are being made to destroy the party, you are continuing to transform the CPCz into an amorphous organization unable to act, into something in the nature of a discussion club.

Today, in the CPCz, the main Leninist principles of party organization—the principles of democratic centralism and ideological-organizational unity of the party—are being violated.

The danger in this is mainly that the party itself is on the brink of legalizing factional groups and is breaking up into "autonomous units" with weak bonds between its branches.

Everyone who has studied the history of the communist movement and anyone acquainted with the theoretical legacy of V. I. Lenin, knows full well that only a Marxist party, all branches and members of which are consistently guided by the principle of democratic centralism, is able to act. Ignoring either aspect of this principle—either democracy or centralism—inevitably leads to the weakening of the party and of its leading role, and to the transformation of the party into a bureaucratic organization or into some sort of educational association.

Reactionary elements are seeking in all ways to pulverize and weaken the communist party while, at the same time, taking all measures to close their own ranks and bolster their organization. The weakening of democratic centralism in the CPCz serves their aims very well.

From information in the press it is clear that the revisionist elements in the party are planning to impose on the CPCz some sort of statutes transforming it into an organization devoid of Leninist party standards and devoid of party discipline and responsibility, that is, into a pulverized and amorphous party. All this is evident from your press.

The central press organ of your party, *Rudé právo*, came up with a suggestion on 23 July 1968 to adopt some autonomous principles for party bodies and organizations, in other words, to strengthen, through the new party statutes, their right to espouse their own positions with regard to decisions of higher authorities. Furthermore, the same newspaper proposes that the separately constituted sections of the party should not be bound by party discipline; it is suggested that they be voluntarily obliged "by associational ties" to "take shape from below . . . by cooperatively uniting branches." What does this mean, comrades? It means, in effect, that the CPCz Central Committee is making an assiduous effort to transform the party from a fighting, monolithic organization into some sort of "association" whose members act freely as they wish. By the way, this is not the first time *Rudé právo* has advocated this thesis, a thesis that cannot be described as anything other than a call to destroy the party.

It should be said that when the editor of *Rudé právo*, a member of the CPCz CC Presidium, Cde. Švestka, attempted to safeguard the party's imprint on this newspaper as the organ of the CPCz CC, he was subjected to the fiercest attacks on the pages of the Czechoslovak press and has not received the proper support from the leading party organs. Matters have reached the point where he was not even invited as a guest to the extraordinary nationwide congress of the Czechoslovak Journalists' Union that was recently held in Prague.

Attacks on the unity of the party's ranks are being waged on other fronts as well. Representatives of right-wing forces are working hard to include the "right of minority and group opinions," in the new party statutes, in other words, the right to act against party decisions after they have been adopted.[120]

---

[120] This proposed change in the CPCz statutes, which was included in the draft published on August 10, would have run directly contrary to the basic principle of "democratic centralism," namely, that open disagreement with decisions made at higher levels was prohibited.

In the view of the CPSU CC Politburo, all these considerations are contrary to Leninist principles of party organization. Just remember, comrades, Lenin's attitude to the question of party unity. The resolution that Lenin submitted to the 10th Congress of the Russian Communist Party, which was endorsed by the Congress, states: "It is necessary that all responsible workers clearly recognize the danger of factions, no matter what type. Despite all efforts by officials from different groups to defend party unity, the formation of factions will inevitably lead to the weakening of comradely work and to intensified, repeated attempts by the party's enemies, who have penetrated the party, to deepen the party's division and to use it in furthering the aims of counterrevolution." Unfortunately, even among members of the CPCz CC Presidium there are certain comrades who speak out openly against Leninist principles in party organization. In particular, the speech Cde. Špaček gave on these matters.[121]

As we well know world reactionary forces are not halting their attempt to take advantage of any weakening of party unity to step up attacks on communists and on socialism. In the world today, a bitter class struggle has emerged. In such conditions, actions that undermine party unity are tantamount to helping our class enemies.

The existence in your country of a *mass campaign to destroy the party's loyal personnel* is helping to undermine the CPCz's leading role. Criticism of individual leaders and the acknowledgment of certain mistakes have expanded into general demands for the sweeping removal of leading party workers. In the center and below (in local branches) many experienced, devoted party members and working class people who courageously fought against fascism in the years of Hitlerite occupation, and who have taken an active part in building socialism in Czechoslovakia, have been removed. An atmosphere has been created of a genuine pogrom, "a moral execution" of cadres.

A definite political line is emerging in the form of efforts to remove from active political life all those communists most versed in ideological-political attitudes and those who are decisively speaking out against the right-wing danger. This is the point of Cde. Císař's statement who asks that the CPCz admit 200,000 to 300,000 young people in order to provide an "injection" for what he calls the "older" party, while ignoring the class aspect of this grave matter.[122]

The line of mass destruction of leading cadres has affected not only the party apparatus. You have extended it to major bodies of the state apparatus, to the trade unions, and to the youth union. You replaced most members of the government. At the same time, comrades, among those removed are such workers whom you yourself, in talks with us after the January plenum, almost always characterized favorably as reliable and staunch communists. . . .

. . .

Comrades!

If we objectively evaluate the essence of the political processes now under way in Czechoslovakia and the direction of their further development we can arrive at only one conclusion, namely, that *the threat of a counterrevolutionary coup in your country has become a reality*. This is the main reason for the anxiety felt by the CPSU and the other fraternal parties.

[121] The text of the resolution has been quoted from V. I. Lenin, *Collected Works*, 4th edition, vol. 32, p. 217. The reference is made to Špaček's presentation at the April plenum of the CPCz CC (carried in *Rudé právo* on April 11, 1968), in which he advocated, *inter alia*, the formation of a political-theoretical journal that "would not be obligated to express the official views of the CPCz Central Committee."

[122] A reference to Císař's proposal, first made at a joint meeting of the CPCz CC Presidium and CPCZ CC Secretariat on May 21, to set up a separate youth wing within the party. The idea came at a propitious moment, for the Piller Commission had set forth a number of recommendations the previous month that would have eased many of the "older" communists out of the party.

On a number of occasions after our May meeting in Moscow, we proposed to hold another bilateral meeting with the CPCz leadership to consider the situation that had arisen.[123] However, every time we suggested that idea, you objected to it, giving a number of reasons.

Being faithful to the principles of internationalism, and guided by feelings of solidarity with fraternal Czechoslovakia and a sense of responsibility for the fate of socialism on our continent, the leaders of the fraternal parties of the Warsaw Pact decided to meet you to consider, in a comradely manner, the situation that has been created and to look for a way out of it and offer help to CPCz leaders.

Unfortunately, you refused this fraternal offer and were unwilling to meet us in Warsaw. Your reasons for rejecting this proposal are unconvincing. The excuse that you didn't know the precise date of the meeting does not conform with reality. As for the exact date of the Warsaw meeting, the Soviet ambassador in Prague informed you of it in accordance with our instructions.[124] The Hungarians also spoke to you about it. They even proposed delaying the meeting for a certain amount of time so that once again you could weigh up the situation and come to Warsaw. But you failed to do this.

Dubček's speech:

I would like to speak in Slovak and the comrades will interpret as they were unable to translate it into Russian in time.

Dear Comrade Brezhnev, esteemed friends, comrades!

First of all, I would like to thank you for coming to Czechoslovakia and to express satisfaction that this bilateral meeting of the leadership of our parties is taking place. We greatly appreciate your agreement in organizing a meeting on our territory. We will start with the fact that the traditional friendship and the many years of cooperation between the Communist Party of Czechoslovakia and the Communist Party of the Soviet Union, as well as the mutual trust that has always bound us together, all make it possible to clear up any misunderstanding and problems in our relations peacefully, without undue anxiety and without unnecessary dramatization, on the basis of mutual esteem and comradely frankness.

In the name of the entire Presidium I would like to assure you that we have come to today's meeting with a good will to try to eliminate the tension that has sprung up in recent times and to guarantee conditions for the further development of our cooperation.

All the members and candidate members of our Presidium who are taking part here, as well as the entire Central Committee of our party and our people, regard friendship, alliance, and cooperation with the Soviet Union as the natural and decisive component of the socialist development of our country, viewing it as the fundamental guarantee not only of the sovereignty and independence of our country, but also of the success of the general worldwide struggle by progressive forces against reactionary forces.

This attitude toward the Soviet Union in our country is due not only to sovereign, political, military, and economic aspects, but also to deep historical traditions.

We believe that this basic point of view must be taken into account in evaluating events in our country and our methods of solving internal matters related to the development of socialist society in Czechoslovakia.

Therefore it seems to us that it will be useful to approach matters in such a way so that our people do not feel that Czechoslovakia's alliance with the Soviet Union limits the opportunities to solve our internal matters, and in such a way that this alliance will correspond as much as possible to the country's needs and traditions. It is precisely this alliance that creates and preserves such possibilities. The knowledge that the Soviet Union fully respects the sovereign

[123] See, for example, Document No. 39.
[124] See Document No. 50.

rights of our people provides a reliable basis for the further development of our friendly relations and affords us the opportunity of acting against those who would wish to violate these relations.

We have taken into account that in the course of the post-January events various attacks have appeared in our press that affected the Soviet Union to one degree or another and contravened the opinion and line of the CPCz CC and the government of the republic. Along with these incorrect views, often inspired by hostile sources, one observes a second group of opinions that do not represent any anti-Soviet campaign. These opinions amount to criticism of phenomena linked to the personality cult and to deformations in relations between the socialist countries, which were decisively denounced by the Soviet Union itself.[125] One of the serious mistakes committed by the previous leadership was its failure to resolve or even consider these questions. One cannot help noting the increasing resonance of certain anti-Soviet and anti-socialist voices nowadays. It is these voices that are facing resistance from our people. I mean here acts by students in March and April of this year, which soon died out. Events in our country are not moving in a direction that would result in the destruction of the gains of the revolution, much less does one observe even the slightest departure from the socialist camp or from the foundations of socialism, as the letter of the five fraternal parties claims. Therefore one cannot compare our development with what occurred in certain countries in 1956.[126] I'll return to these questions in greater detail in another part of my address.

The situation I am speaking of seriously affects relations between our peoples and countries, and has important international implications. That is why we attach so much importance to our meeting today, a meeting that we sought and that was rendered even more necessary as a result of the Warsaw Meeting.

Believe us, comrades, when we say it is hard for us to understand and accept why our request was not taken into consideration. It would have been appropriate for you to wait until officials from the CPCz CC Presidium had met you before you held the Warsaw Meeting. Why was it so necessary to hurry, why was it not possible for the CPCz CC Presidium's letter, which we sent you the day after the conversation on Friday, to be considered at the CC Presidium sessions of the individual fraternal parties?[127] Practically speaking, there was no time to consider the CPCz's letter because on Friday we deliberated on your second letter, and on Saturday we sent the answer, and the meeting was already in session in Warsaw by Sunday. In effect, this means that from the outset the meeting was expecting no answer from us.

The Communist Party of Czechoslovakia, as you all know, never opposed and never will oppose general conferences of communist and workers' parties, collective consultations, or exchanges of views. On the contrary, the CPCz has always actively supported them. I would like to say that even at present we support holding multilateral conferences. But one cannot agree that parties which enjoy normal, comradely relations should get together to consider the situation in one of the individual parties against that party's will and without preliminary, serious consideration of the existing circumstances, without a series of mutual consultations, and so forth. The holding of such conferences, as in Warsaw, does not correspond to the principles of normal relations between fraternal communist parties. After the resolution issued by the Informburo there was no multilateral conference of any sort that might have judged the situation in the individual party or country and adopted a corresponding decision. Nor was a conference of this sort held even during the period known as the October events in Poland in 1956. How is one to regard the holding of such a conference and the assessment of the situation in a single party, and how is one to understand the fact that one party is told by the others how to solve its

---

[125] Dubček is referring here to the declaration that the Soviet Union released on October 30, 1956, shortly before the invasion of Hungary. The declaration acknowledged the "deformations" and "inequality" of Soviet relations with Eastern Europe under Stalin.

[126] Dubček is responding here to the comparisons that were being drawn, with increasing frequency, in the East European and Soviet press between the Prague Spring and the events in Hungary in October–November 1956.

[127] See Document No. 51.

internal problems? Can one avoid the impression that such measures were endorsed in violation of the principles governing relations between communist parties, and as an attempt to influence developments in this country, bypassing the existing leadership of the party and government? Who then will bear responsibility for the consequences of such measures? Only the participants in these conferences. If these conclusions turn out to have a negative effect on the situation in the Communist Party of Czechoslovakia and in the international communist movement, I think this would be an erroneous step in relation to the CPCz and to the international communist movement.

We tried to convince you and the other fraternal parties that it was undesirable to convene the Warsaw meeting before—and I repeat, before—holding bilateral talks because this would have adverse consequences.

In the letter we sent you prior to the Warsaw Meeting, we explained our conclusions and proposed that the meeting of the fraternal socialist countries should be preceded by bilateral talks. We did this in the belief that the fraternal parties, when assessing the situation in our party and country in the letters they addressed to the CPCz CC, did not take into consideration all the objective conditions and demands of our development. We therefore deemed it essential to explain, during bilateral talks, the situation that actually exists, as well as to consider questions connected with the organization of a multilateral meeting.

We also had to consider that Czechoslovak communists and working people would find it difficult to understand why their leaders always had to travel abroad to explain events taking place in our country. Up to now, all meetings between the CPCz and the CPSU—including three collective meetings and one bilateral—have been held outside our territory. Our wish to begin with bilateral meetings before another multilateral conference did not have the desired results because the Warsaw Meeting was agreed upon, apparently, without even taking account of our viewpoint. This is clear from the fact that our last letter of 12 July of this year was not dealt with by the CC Presidiums of the individual fraternal communist parties.

I must tell you frankly that we find it difficult to understand why this happened with such haste and why it was not possible to consider the letter and take it into consideration before the conference was held or at least during its proceedings.

Nor was our request that the Warsaw Meeting should make no assessment of the situation in Czechoslovakia heeded, or that the letter from the participants of that meeting should not be published in the press. What is more, the media in these countries have unleashed a campaign against our party, not against specific shortcomings that do not concern official policy, but in the form of a full-scale polemic against our entire party and its Central Committee. At the same time, the viewpoint of the CPCz CC Presidium in relation to the letter of the five fraternal parties has not yet been printed in these countries—neither in the party press nor in any other.[128] Consequently, the public in all the socialist countries has not yet had a chance to learn about the viewpoint of the Presidium. In the People's Republic of Poland the day before yesterday (I don't remember the precise date), our reply was published in the internal party journal *Život strany*.[129]

In our opinion the convocation of the Warsaw Meeting and the publication of the letter of its participants, as well as the press campaign, were not the best way to promote the development of relations among socialist countries. They also do not contribute to the resolution of the problems we are now discussing here with Cde. Brezhnev. Nor do they help consolidate the unity and trust among our peoples or add to the prestige of the socialist camp throughout the world. They merely serve as a basis for affirming that communists treat the national peculiarities of individual countries with a lack of sensitivity. Although the communists proclaim peaceful coexistence throughout the world, they are unable to solve problems in their own camp.

[128] See Document No. 55.
[129] Excerpts of the statement also had appeared in Hungary.

By way of information we must tell you that the Warsaw Meeting and its letter to the Central Committee of our party were perceived by us, the communists, and by our whole society as a means of generating external pressure on our party.

Worse still, it played into the hands of the right-wing and extreme sectarian forces. Such a step had a negative influence on the activities of the CPCz and on our internal situation, which in the wake of the CPCz CC's May plenum and the regional and district party conferences had considerably stabilized. Precisely because of this the CPCz Central Committee Presidium's viewpoint met with great support from our people.

It must also be said that the CPCz CC plenum unanimously reacted to those negative, right-wing, and other tendencies that are unacceptable to the party, the tendencies that cropped up especially in March and April of this year. The resolution of the May CPCz CC plenum was also directed against the very same tendencies.

All of this had a negative influence on a broader scale, on the situation in the international communist movement. As we prepare for the forthcoming Moscow conference, where we hope to settle controversial questions, the Warsaw Meeting did not go unnoticed by the communist and workers' parties.[130] Many of them even spoke out in support of our activities, while underlining their significance for their own policies.

An expression of the dissatisfaction of these parties was the proposal by the French Communist Party to convene a meeting of all European communist parties.[131] We asked the French comrades not to insist on such a meeting, particularly because many fraternal parties said their participation depended on the position adopted by our party. We did not, and do not, want to intensify the difficulties in the communist movement, which might then have a negative influence on the course of the approaching Conference of Communist and Workers' Parties in Moscow and on the activities of the fraternal communist parties. It also would not correspond to the interests of the socialist countries. We were particularly dismayed that a situation has arisen between the ČSSR and the Soviet Union that never existed before. If this policy continues, it may lead to a situation whose consequences one can scarcely foresee.

Despite the situation that has arisen, our party is fully determined and wishes to prove in practice that it wants to develop further cooperation with the socialist countries in a spirit of proletarian internationalism. We are seeking to find answers, based on cooperation, to the crucial questions of contemporary international development.

We are well aware that the complexity of the situation in Europe demands the coordination of efforts and unity of action from all socialist countries on fundamental questions.

Our policy in all these areas is based on straightforward principles and guided by clear objectives. We explain these objectives fully in our party's Action Program and will not deviate from them. We clearly stated that the basic credo of our external political orientation is unchanged and that it remains a consistent basis for all our foreign political activities. I am referring here to the strengthening of ties between the socialist countries, to our friendship and cooperation with the Soviet Union, and to our loyalty to the Warsaw Pact and commitments that stem from our treaties and relations with the socialist countries.

Especially dear to us is the question of preserving and bolstering fraternal and friendly relations with the Soviet Union and the Communist Party of the Soviet Union.

We are hurt by the fact that many accusations have been leveled against us, accusations that go far beyond the bounds of ordinary polemics conducted between parties and socialist countries.

The first unilateral steps to restrict our relations are also being adopted. We are sincerely interested in developing cooperation. At today's meeting we are ready to consider all aspects of our relations. We have shown an interest in the words of Cde. Kosygin, who said that even in

---

[130] Dubček is referring to the conference planned for November 1968 among the world's communist parties.
[131] See Documents Nos. 58 and 59.

the future the Soviet government will wish to continue developing mutual economic cooperation between our countries. We assure you that our party is also sincerely committed to this.

It is in the interest of both our parties to preserve and strengthen peace in Europe. We realize that the best guarantee of this is the existence of the Soviet Union, and that the Warsaw Pact is our common alliance. The ČSSR remains a firm link in the Warsaw Pact. It will loyally fulfill its obligations, although the situation of our government as a frontline state makes certain exceptional demands on us. This concerns the question of protecting our southwestern border. We find it hard to comprehend statements to the effect that the southwestern flank of the Warsaw Pact has been militarily weakened because these borders are said to be "open."[132] Such views are unfounded. We expect the USSR and our other allies to treat the ČSSR as a reliable, full-fledged member of the Warsaw Pact, the necessity of which is based on the commonality of our interests in ensuring peace and security in Europe. The aim of the Warsaw Pact concerns defense preparations and foreign policy activity.[133] The Pact would betray its aims and be seriously weakened if it were actually being used to try to influence internal developments in our state.

Comrades, in proposing to hold talks on a bilateral basis, we wanted to explain several differences that exist in the individual letters sent to us by the parties. I speak of this not from notes, but I remember that the letter from the fraternal Bulgarian Communist Party said that in Czechoslovakia counterrevolution is already rampant. The letter from the German comrades proposes to assist us via the Warsaw Pact—in other words by military action, for it is hard to imagine what else they could have in mind.

These and other questions deserve to be clarified on a mutual basis during a multilateral meeting. It would be useful to return to problems that were raised two months ago at our initiative when speaking to Cde. Yakubovskii in regard to the activation and improvement of the activities of the Warsaw Pact, especially its Political Consultative Committee.[134] This would seem to be the most suitable platform for judging all serious problems of common interest. There is no difference in opinion between us and the leadership of the CPSU on this matter.

In the Warsaw letter you speak about a "campaign" in connection with the military exercises in the ČSSR. In our reply we clearly explained why such concerns had arisen in our country. They arose not in connection with the maneuvers *per se*, but because of the frequent postponement of the withdrawal of allied troops from the ČSSR. Even now, almost a month since the last maneuvers ended on our territory, there are still two regiments left belonging to the other countries that took part in the maneuvers.

This is not such a crucial matter in itself, but if one bears in mind the tense situation in the ČSSR that was created by the letter from the five parties, it evokes conjecture and speculations that are not easy to refute.

Comrades, I sincerely wish to state that we, the communists and the majority of our working people, are not disturbed by the continued presence of Soviet troops on our territory after the maneuvers ended. But what is it that triggered certain feelings in this regard among the broader public? Before the maneuvers began, in conformity with the full agreement between you and us and the Joint Command—and Cde. Yakubovskii—it was decided that the maneuvers would end on 30 June. Many bourgeois news agencies have circulated reports that Czechoslovakia is now under threat of being occupied by Soviet troops, and so on. These stories have found their way into Czechoslovakia.

In seeking to undermine reactionary forces in Czechoslovakia on this issue, and being aware that the military maneuvers were due to end on 30 June or 1 July, we wanted to avoid the effect

---

[132] See, for example, Document No. 60.

[133] The sentence in Slovak does not make sense in the typescript, so it has been slightly modified here to suit the context.

[134] See Documents Nos. 27 and 45.

such news would have on the public. I took part along with the minister of national defense and Cde. Černík in a mass meeting of working people at which Cde. Chervonenko, the ambassador from your country, was present. This mass meeting was dedicated to strengthening the unity of our peoples. In my speech, not knowing that the pullout of troops would be delayed, I announced that the military maneuvers had ended those very days and that our friendly Soviet army was leaving Czechoslovakia. I said that we should send it off with our fraternal, comradely greetings. This was met by stormy applause, as Cde. Chervonenko can confirm. But later it became clear that things differed from what was written in the press. One or two days passed, and then a whole week, and so on—and people are still constantly raising questions about this. I tell you very frankly and sincerely that for us, too, these were questions to which we could not give an answer because neither the prime minister nor the president of the republic, nor even the CC first secretary of the party could explain it. It stands to reason that the whole matter has had unpleasant consequences. Again, comrades, you can believe us when we say we are not opposed to military maneuvers. On the contrary, as you well know, on the basis of mutual agreement we were prepared to hold these maneuvers and took all necessary measures for their successful conclusion. There has been, and is, no reason to doubt that the ČSSR has always displayed and shown an interest in broad economic cooperation with the other socialist states—the members of the Council for Mutual Economic Assistance. Within the framework of this organization we always have striven, and are continuing to strive, to improve the socialist division of labor and the adoption of progressive forms and methods of their activities. Our attitude to the CMEA derives both from an internationalist understanding of the role of this organization and from the actual needs of our economy. The Action Program of our party obliges the government to devise suitable proposals in this field. . . .

Kosygin's speech:

You, Cde. Dubček and Cde. Černík, have given us your appraisal. Comrade Černík speaks in a particularly soothing tone when he analyzes the events in Czechoslovakia, saying he has not found any counterrevolutionary forces and thinks that what is going on is merely the development of the socialist system and its further improvement and democratization. For our part, we have taken a very different view on all this and, ultimately, cannot agree with you about the processes under way in Czechoslovakia, which are being supported by all the imperialist forces and, above all by the U.S. imperialists, against whom we had to struggle throughout the 1950s in an acute conflict that sometimes verged on a direct military clash. We cannot agree that these processes in your country are democratic and not counterrevolutionary.

Your speech today did not convince us to any degree and provided no basis for saying that what is going on inside Czechoslovakia is the development of democratic roots within the framework of socialism, rather than counterrevolutionary activity. You did not convince us and I think that if you faced up to things honestly, you yourselves would not be so firmly convinced either. When you speak about this you present very unconvincing facts, and your judgments are of a general nature and are neither specific nor based on evidence. You are being carried away by chaotic events whose final result you have no way of predicting.

I want to return to the discussions we held in May during those seven days I was in Czechoslovakia at the instruction of the Politburo.

If you remember those talks, I do not believe there was anything new in what you had to say today, Cdes. Dubček and Černík, compared to what you said then. Then, too, you said it was time to take the press, radio, and television back into your hands. Cdes. Dubček, Smrkovský, and Císař all said at the time: Give us a little while—a month, say, or a month-and-a-half—and you will no longer recognize the press, radio, and television. At the time, the duties were divided up among you: Cde. Smrkovský was responsible for television, Cde. Dubček for *Rudé právo*, and Cde. Lenárt for radio. In other words, everything was assigned. All were responsible for carrying out this activity. When Cde. Smrkovský came to us he said: "If you wish, I'll turn on the television set and you'll see that everything has changed." But in fact, the most blatant anti-Sovietism has continued. We've told you that more than once.

By the same token, everything that Cde. Kriegel told us then about these matters did not correspond to reality or to his activities in the most recent period. Therefore, it is not by accident that L. I. Brezhnev presented a correct and harsh assessment of several issues about which he spoke again today. Kriegel occupies a position that impresses all those who would like to drive a wedge between our communist party and the CPCz. I would say that most of the questions we have considered with you have not been resolved.

Take such a crucial question as the division of the State Security organs. I was in your country more than two months ago. You said at the time that you wanted to strengthen the situation in the Interior Ministry. Truly honest employees should find protection and not be left exposed to insults. You told me about a decision that, incidentally, soon became known to all—in your country the press gains access to such decisions very quickly. At the same time, one knows from the Western press that the CC Presidium and the government of the ČSSR adopted a decision to split up the security forces and that Minister Pavel does not intend to let this happen. This decision is still being discussed and it continues to threaten the organs responsible for defending Czechoslovakia against its enemies.

And the last question I would like to touch upon concerns our interstate relations.

With full responsibility you, of course, have approached the agreements we have concluded. We also approach them with full responsibility. We regard the Warsaw Treaty as a treaty that binds our parties and our peoples together in the face of imperialism. And now maneuvers are beginning. What are we to think: where is your border and where is our border, and is there a difference between your and our borders? I think that you, Cde. Dubček and Cde. Černík, cannot deny that we together have only one border—the one that abuts the West and separates us from the capitalist countries.

Dubček: That was so even up to the Second World War.

Kosygin: This is a border we will never surrender to anyone. We say this quite directly, and this was envisaged in our state treaties. Does this please the imperialists in the West? Of course it doesn't. But they are not the ones to decide this question. They know only too well that we are the ones who decide it. And you, Cde. Černík, know that very well, but instead of determining how to fortify this important border, you are beginning to count how many tourists crossed it. This is a minor question—a hundred or a thousand tourists, give or take a few. But the border—that is a matter of principle for us and for the entire socialist camp. We will not permit, and indeed do not have the right to permit, anyone to violate it. That border is our common border, and if we must defend it together against the enemy, then how could a dispute arise on this question with the High Command of the Warsaw Pact Armed Forces, which ordered troops to be in a certain region for two to three weeks. It is obvious that this is necessary. And just imagine, Cde. Černík, that hostilities break out. After all, maneuvers are a way of checking on preparations for something close to a real combat situation. Should the High Command have to take a vote on the question? Do you guarantee that the NATO countries will not bring their troops up to the border tomorrow? We know how many American, British, West German, and French divisions are deployed there, and that these armies are very well armed. Why at this moment are all the forces in your country not focused on criticizing the rearmament of West German militarism? Why don't you tell your people that Soviet troops came here, and that when we liberated the Sudetenland we did not intend to surrender. Why don't you tell your people about that instead of making a fuss about the deployment of two or three of our regiments in Czechoslovakia? Why don't you tell them that instead of screeching about the deployment of troops and claiming that we are seeking to influence events in your country, when you know very well that these are just ordinary maneuvers? The whole world heeded your screeching. Why

296

don't you draw your public's attention to the fact that West Germany produced 2,500 tanks, thousands of planes, an enormous amount of ammunition, missiles, artillery, and so on. You, Cde. Černík, were reponsible for the military industry in the State Plan and you know what that means, that it is not done for fun and games. Why, at this moment, when maneuvers are going on, when all efforts are focused on a test of our military forces, why do you not mobilize mass propaganda, and why do you not show the people where the danger lies?

Why didn't you, as the head of government, speak out against this? If anyone of us in the Soviet Union had dared to speak against the Czechoslovak armed forces, he would have been given a reply worthy of our friendship. But instead you are still preoccupied with minor, crude provocations that serve the interests of Western countries and not our own countries. You say you cannot explain to the West why the two regiments remain in your country. But you should tell them that this is a question solely between you and us; it's none of their business. We know how many NATO armed forces are on the territory bordering your country. You should ask why they have 20 divisions there armed to the teeth, including nuclear weapons, and you should say that our forces are staying here to oppose them and that you are convinced of this. You know how warmly the Czechoslovak people welcomed our troops and not only were ours greeted that way; so too were the Poles, the Hungarians, and those from the GDR. But after that a campaign got under way by the right-wing forces, who are doing everything they can to complicate our relations. What is so special about holding maneuvers? That's just a natural part of the Warsaw Pact. Or are we seizing Czechoslovakia by force? Everything has taken place normally.

Brezhnev: Last year they held exercises and are holding exercises now, too.

Kosygin: Can we really believe you, Cde. Černík? Have you become such a naive politician that when this sort of question is put to you, you seize upon it and blow it up all out of proportion, as though it's a world-shaking matter? Didn't you understand that this was just bait which you so readily snapped up? Although you have sufficient strength to offer a proper rebuff to these forces, you didn't do that.

DOCUMENT No. 66: Dispatches from Czechoslovak Ambassadors in Berlin, Warsaw, and Budapest on the Deployment of Forces along ČSSR Borders, July 29–August 1, 1968

Source: ÚSD, Sb. KV, K. Archiv MZV, Received Dispatches, Nos. 7103, 7187, 7259, 7269/1968; Vondrová & Navrátil, vol. 2, pp. 35–36.

These four dispatches from Czechoslovak ambassadors in the East European countries surrounding Czechoslovakia (Václav Kolár in the GDR, Antonín Gregor in Poland, and Jozef Púčik in Hungary) report on the steady military build-up under way in the Eastern bloc. The Soviet army's "Nemen" logistic exercises in the Transcarpathian, Baltic, and Belorussian Military Districts—the largest such exercises ever conducted by the USSR—involved simulated nuclear strikes and large-scale offensive operations by armored and motorized infantry units. Begun on July 23, these maneuvers soon extended to the territory of Poland and East Germany, where Soviet and allied troops congregated along the Czechoslovak border. Also in late July, the Soviet Union and its allies embarked on a series of large-scale "Sky Shield" air defense exercises, just miles from Czechoslovak territory. By the time the Čierna nad Tisou negotiations opened on July 29, some 20 combat-ready Warsaw Pact divisions were already poised on Czechoslovakia's borders, waiting for orders to move ahead with "Operation Danube."

East Berlin:

At 11:00 A.M. today, 29 July, West Berlin radio confirmed our report (No. 249) concerning the southward movement of GDR motorized infantry units. In addition to GDR units, units of the USSR are heading toward the south in the Thuringian Forest area. A Czechoslovak citizen called on the telephone at 9 o'clock this morning and informed us of the movement of troops toward the Czechoslovak border in the Freiberg area. At 10:00 A.M. an unknown major in the East German army reported the concentration of troops toward our borders.[135] He expressed his sympathy with the ČSSR and immediately left.

Kolár 250

Warsaw:

It has been confirmed from other sources, including Poles who were present, that party meetings were held where the letter from the PUWP Central Committee was read aloud. The letter contains a highly critical description of events in the ČSSR, along with the Polish position on these events, and it criticizes Prchlík's statement and intimates that Brandt secretly visited the ČSSR.[136] The letter concludes that events in the ČSSR directly threaten the Polish People's Republic and that the Poles will defend their western borders with all possible means. The letter states that Soviet units are crossing Poland, but because our source was reporting to us on Monday, it is possible that at the time of the meetings units had already crossed the Czechoslovak border.[137] The source stated his opinion that in the event of disturbances in Warsaw, Soviet units deployed in the vicinity of Warsaw were to intervene.

Gregor 211

---

[135] In keeping with the standard Warsaw Pact lexicon, the cable referred to the East German army as simply the "German" army. The qualifier "East" has been added here for clarity's sake.

[136] Reports were rife at the time that the Czechoslovak government was holding secret negotiations with Willy Brandt and other top West German officials. In addition to the allegations of a trip by Brandt to Czechoslovakia, other sources contended that Czechoslovak Foreign Minister Jiří Hájek met Brandt secretly in Vienna.

[137] The "Monday" in question was the 29th of July, and the meetings were held on the following day.

East Berlin:

The Embassy was informed on 31 July by a female citizen of the GDR about the presence of powerful tank and missile units along the border with Czechoslovakia. A field airport was set up near Niederoderwitz, where Soviet transport aircraft loaded with military equipment have been landing.[138] Three reserve age-groups—1936, 1937, and 1938, and also part of 1939—have reportedly been called up for exercises.

Kolár 255

Budapest:

Over the last two days, Hungarian and Soviet troops have been detected moving north toward our border. This has been reported by embassy staff, by automobile drivers, by tourists, and by other sources. The Soviet airbase in Budapest is on full combat alert. No exercises have been announced. I am trying to verify these reports.

Púčik 143

---

[138] For clarity's sake, the phrase "four-engine aircraft" used in the cable has been rendered here as "transport aircraft."

DOCUMENT No. 67: Alexander Dubček's Recollections of the Crisis: Events Surrounding the Čierna nad Tisou Negotiations

Source: "Alexander Dubček vzpomíná: Původní rozhovor pro *Občanský deník* o pozadí srpnových událostí roku 1968," *Občanský deník* (Prague), Part 1, August 3, 1990, p. 3 and Part 2, August 10, 1990, p. 3.

The four-part interview with Alexander Dubček that appeared in Občanský deník *in August 1990 provides his most elaborate recollections of the 1968 crisis. These first two sections cover the period from the Warsaw Meeting to the Bratislava conference. Dubček's personal memory offers a behind-the-scenes account of the Čierna talks and his own role, thoughts, and decisions.*

In the interview, Dubček recounts his private meeting with Brezhnev, in the Soviet's leaders' private railroad car at Čierna nad Tisou, when no other officials were present. Describing what that meeting was like, he discusses the way the whole episode fit into the Soviet leader's broader negotiating strategy. Dubček also gives a detailed presentation of the demands that Brezhnev and other Soviet officials were seeking to extract from him, and he deals at some length with the question of whether "concessions" on his part—such as the reimposition of censorship, the dismissal of prominent reformers, and the dissolution of political groups—might have altered the Soviet decision. Dubček expresses skepticism that anything short of the wholesale repudiation of the Prague Spring and a reversion to "neo-Stalinism" would have been enough to mollify the Soviet Politburo. "Should I have used an iron hand?," he asks, and answers: "If I had I would have betrayed myself, the people, the nation, and everything we stood for."

PART 1

Memories of Dresden and Warsaw and of meetings at Čierna nad Tisou and Bratislava in the spring and summer of 1968 are still swathed in mystery, and many questions remain. This is even more the case with regard to the invasion of Czechoslovakia by the armies of five countries, as well as the Moscow talks between our delegation and representatives of the Kremlin. We asked the person who knows most about those events—Alexander Dubček—for a testimony and some personal memories.

Občanský deník: The threat to the renewal process from the Warsaw Pact actually began with the meeting in March 1968—the meeting at Dresden. But a more urgent threat arose at the meeting of the five communist parties in Warsaw in July 1968, when they drafted a letter. How would you characterize the situation at that time?

Dubček: As I see it, the Warsaw Letter was a turning point. A watershed. Until then, in my view, no decision was made on intervention. Brezhnev and the others were still working to find a "fifth column" in our country, including some elements from the State Security as well as some in the army and the CPCz. They wanted to do everything they could to stir up internal unrest in our country. But intervention had not yet been decided on. In my view, this was the logical progression of events.

And in this situation they prepared the Warsaw Letter, which was supposed to be the signal that a "fifth column" had been found. At that time they said we were refusing to negotiate with them. That's nonsense, we didn't refuse. We said we wanted the joint meeting to be preceded by bilateral meetings. We received threatening letters from individual parties. In particular, what Ulbricht wrote me was awful. So we said that first we wanted to meet these parties individually, and then these bilateral meetings would culminate in a joint meeting.

But they insisted on holding these meetings in such rapid sequence that it took us aback.

They did not accept our proposal, and decided to meet without us, without the bilateral meetings, and without having the Romanians and Yugoslavs present, contrary to what we had proposed. There is, in my view, another point to be made here, namely, that they attempted to destroy our national unity by threatening a dangerous confrontation and also by activating their supporters. They expected that in this kind of situation we would invite them ourselves.

We of course would never have done that; it was simply their way of thinking. And if Brezhnev claimed otherwise at the time, he was incorrect. I view it this way: If we had gone to the Warsaw meeting (about which we heard for the first time on the plane from Prague to Bratislava), they would, in our presence, have been able to do everything they had decided to do, and that would have been even worse.

They would have demonstrated to their fifth column in Czechoslovakia that we were giving up, or that we were in front of a tribunal similar to the new Constance Court.

Moreover, the "Warsaw" participants, in my view, had another key trick up their sleeve to try to disrupt the situation in our country. But none of their plans came to pass. . . . This was because they did not have as strong a position in our country as they thought they had. Events showed that our new ideas were already deeply rooted in the people, and we were able to unite the nation, as well as the army and a majority of the security forces, and even the militia (as you remember, it was they who later protected the Vysočany congress). Therefore, there was no chance they would have been taken over by a fifth column.

When I received the letter from Warsaw I immediately called Brezhnev. I told him: "I have the letter. But don't publish it. Let's hold a bilateral meeting, and then a joint one, together with Yugoslavia and Romania." But they refused to go along. They published it. And therefore I was presented with a *fait accompli.*

I thought to myself: I will go about my work and see what happens. But suddenly it was as if the "11th" hour had arrived. What could be done?

It's easy to say, "do it this way or that way," but when you stand at the captain's helm, your brain ticks over very fast. I walked over to the secretariat, got a few people together, and said: "What should we do? Let's convene the Central Committee." And all of them, though they were my supporters, said: "Are you so naive that you can't see that this is exactly what 'they' want—to provoke a confrontation there?" Imagine if I had retreated then, and not convened the Central Committee. Afterwards, of course, the CC, either because it had gained experience or because it was threatened by a domestic wave of discontent, agreed with our reply. There were a few people who disagreed and spoke strongly against it, like Kolder. But when the vote on the Warsaw Letter came, "their" position was rejected. That was another of "their" losses. "They" prepared their armed forces as early as the Šumava military exercises and got ready, as they are accustomed to do, for the worst-case scenario. I do not underestimate this scenario; the possibility had existed since Dresden. Nevertheless, they still were counting on some action from within, that is, an internal solution.

But the people in our country were more and more united behind the renewal process, and even the old CC took a stand against "them." Also, the leftist movement in Europe was more and more with us. All this tied "their" hands. But "they," in accord with their old stereotypes, believed that with constant goading and pressure on us, they would finally put together something that they could use as a pretext for intervention and for setting up a fifth column. But in practice of course that did not happen.

Občanský deník: What led Brezhnev to agree to the meeting in Čierna?

Dubček: If I remember correctly, one of the responses of the CPCz CC to the Warsaw Letter was that we would do everything we could to prevent a confrontation. And as I already mentioned, we wanted bilateral talks, not a "tribunal." I was obsessed with the idea of either eliminating Warsaw or somehow circumventing it. "They," on the contrary, wanted a meeting that would reaffirm Warsaw.

And from these different motives Čierna happened. To judge the meeting, one must see it in very close relation to what preceded it. Only then is it possible to understand it, to see what it was and why. At the meeting—as you can see from the speeches by Rigo, Biľak, and others, which were diametrically opposed to my position—"they" again tried to create a split within our ranks. That is why they kept yelling: "*A pochemu?*" "*Kto opportunist?*" "*Kotorye pravye?*"[139] They always needed to force the pace to the point where they had everything all sewn up and which they finally also realized. At Čierna they attempted to "smuggle" something into the documents, and they were masters at that—a normal person reads only what is written, but they would read what is not written, and whatever would bind us to Warsaw.

In my speeches I adhered to a line that conformed with what the CC Plenum and the Presidium had already agreed on. But that was not the usual approach. That's why afterwards Vasil Biľak repeatedly said that I did not have my speeches approved. I said: "Why should I have had them approved? I stuck by the already-agreed line." Biľak or others later on also accused me of not preparing for Čierna properly. They meant the railway station, etc.

I said before to the Soviets: "Why can't the meeting be held in Košice or somewhere else?" It was the Soviets' idea to hold the meeting in Čierna. They had everything prepared there. I didn't even know what the club in Čierna looked like, but they went there in all confidence. The fact that the meeting was on the border was itself a sign.

They might have thought that it would be easier to cause divisions and fragmentations among us on the border, and that they had us "in their pocket." From the speeches of Brezhnev and others it was clear they wanted to pressure us into accepting Warsaw. I told Brezhnev that I disagreed. I said that a new document had to be adopted affirming that we would be able to resolve everything in our own way, and that we really would have leeway to act in accordance with our Action Program. "A new document," I said, "would be worked out at a multilateral meeting." And that meeting took place later in Bratislava.

When the Soviets realized that I was supported by the majority (Kriegel, Smrkovský, Černík, Špaček, and others), they concluded that they had to change their tactics.

This change of direction roughly corresponds with the moment when Brezhnev announced that he was ill. He was jogging around there in his pajamas, but I saw that he was not ill. They needed time—they had their phones and transmitters—to be able, if their original plan didn't work out, to consult on new measures with others from Warsaw and find a solution. After consultations, they apparently reached an agreement, and so we came to the only conclusion that was also acceptable for us.

Občanský deník: Could you perhaps reconstruct for us the private discussion you had with Brezhnev in between the four rounds of talks in the train? Did it include some of Brezhnev's demands regarding the internal affairs of Czechoslovakia?

Dubček: The atmosphere in the car at that time was very tense, which was true of all the other discussions as well. I noticed that Brezhnev and the others were already extremely nervous during the joint meetings and during their speeches. It was apparent from their tone of voice, the expression of their eyes, and their whole demeanor. Personally I don't need much sleep, so I walked around the station and talked to the railway workers until the morning when the news came that Brezhnev was sick and could not attend the meetings. I sensed that something was not quite right, that something was going on.

In this context, I was informed that Brezhnev wanted to talk to me privately. And because he was sick it had to be in his train car. I went there, looked at him, and said to myself: "You really *are* sick."

That may have been in the afternoon, I don't remember it that well. Brezhnev was in his pajamas and tried to evoke sympathy. Maybe he was trying to wring concessions or something out of me that way. He had definitely made up his mind that the meeting would be in Bratislava on 3 August, and that it would not be postponed any longer.

---

[139] Dubček cites these phrases in Russian, which, seriatim, mean: "And why?" "Who is an opportunist?" and "Who are the rightists?"

Because the date of the meeting was near and it would be difficult to organize and prepare everything, I did not raise the question of having others participate again. I was led to believe that an "un-Warsaw" document would be adopted. I said that this time we agreed with what we had been talking about before and that we were ready to come to the meeting.

It was also decided that I would inform the members of our Presidium, and if there were no objections, the meeting would be held despite the time pressures (there were only 2–3 days to the scheduled start).

And then another matter arose. Brezhnev obviously returned to the things he always liked to get involved with: "*A chto takoe s etimi kadrami? Pochemu takoi Kriegel?*"[140] He was interested in how this issue would be resolved. I don't know whether there were other names mentioned, but I have the feeling that he did also mention Císař. And Pelikán, who had come under attack as early as the Dresden meeting. I told Brezhnev that these people had proven their abilities through their work. (I obviously later informed our own people about everything that was said in the train car.) We left the precise status of those people totally unresolved. As always, I declined to promise anything. I am not that naive. I had to leave myself as many open doors and as much room to maneuver as possible.

Soon after, Brezhnev brought up these personnel questions again, which showed that despite the new tactic they still had not given up the idea that we would speed up our own work and move ahead at full steam with certain personnel changes.

I strongly objected to making any such changes, and I actually did not make any until after the invasion, when we had to agree to make these concessions in order to minimize the consequences. For Brezhnev it was obviously a test of how far he could go on this issue, and he returned to it in Bratislava.

Therefore, I made no promises to him of any sort. But whenever "they" say something, they read it according to their old habits as "it was said." And whenever "it was said," it was, according to their leaders, also binding. It went automatically like this: "It was adopted, it was agreed upon, and there will be no changes." That was their approach.

In that sense, Čierna was like an intermediate step, which I regard, from the standpoint of what we said in the CC plenum and the Presidium, to have been a success. It was a success insofar as it moved us forward to the Bratislava meeting and what happened afterwards. You cannot treat them separately. I couldn't change the fact that what "they" described there was imperialism, etc. What was important was that the Bratislava document stated we should solve our internal problems according to what we thought was right (this was explicitly noted in the document), and it affirmed that this should be done on the basis of sovereignty, the inviolability of borders, and so forth. Even today I remember how vehemently the Germans, in particular, and perhaps others objected to this. But I insisted it was precisely these conditions—that we be permitted to solve our internal problems ourselves, that our borders were inviolable, and that our actions be based on our sovereignty—that must be included in the declaration. Otherwise I would never have signed any such document. That was clear. I acted in accordance with this principle, and that's why in a televised speech on 4 August I said we had succeeded because we had achieved what we promised at home. I also stressed that no other documents except the declaration had been adopted, that no split had resulted, and that we had maintained our sovereignty, and so forth.

Obviously, today anyone can reproach me and say I was naive when I believed all that. But the declaration was an international document that was valid before the whole international community, so why shouldn't I have relied on it? The rest of the world sympathized with us, but they left it up to us to solve our problems.

---

[140] Again, Dubček cites these questions in Russian; the translation in English is "What's the story with these cadres? Why tolerate someone like Kriegel?"

PART 2

Občanský deník: Let's get back to the train car. What did Brezhnev say initially?

Dubček: I may not remember it exactly. He resorted to arguments against the people I already mentioned (Kriegel, Pelikán, Císař) and so forth. He let me know they expected that the leadership of the party—meaning me—would take certain steps against these people. Their intention, as I indicated, was to create a schism within the progressive leadership. Any action would not have been limited to just these three people, though other names were not explicitly mentioned. I could sense—and Brezhnev also made this clear—that it would be necessary to get rid of all people who were "right-wing opportunists," "anti-socialist elements," and so forth. They always linked Kriegel with some sort of espionage on behalf of certain sinister powers as a result of his visit to Chiang Kaishek.[141] They tried to sow disunity among the progressive leaders with these same kinds of arguments. They tried to use all manner of influence against us so that they would provoke mistrust not only against me, but against others as well. That way they could foster a climate in which people would say "You might trust Dubček, but he's betraying us!" They needed somehow to compromise my integrity as well as that of Smrkovský, and others. They had to ensure that all of us would be rendered powerless in front of our people.

Let's not deceive ourselves. I grew up in this professional apparatus. I was active for years in the anti-fascist movement. I lived for years in the Soviet Union. I lived through all the changes there, from collectivization to the trials. When I lived through this and then again in Czechoslovakia for a second time, I had already developed a defensive layer. It had deformed me by the time Khrushchev came to power. Even so, they—the Soviets—are good enough psychologists to know they could discredit me because most people assume that anyone who grew up in that apparatus and in the Soviet Union must be untrustworthy and is "their" man. I am thinking out loud here because I want to make sure everyone understands what they were trying to do. They were trying somehow to isolate me somewhere, manipulate me in some way, and make me take a step that would alienate me from the people and thus cause people to think: "What were we saying? He's just 'their' man!" This was not specified formally, but it was very serious. I sensed this was also being done in the train car, and we got into a long and repetitive debate that cannot be described in any systematic way because it was not systematic.

Občanský deník: Did Brezhnev have some principal demands for changes in our internal policy and in connection with the mass media?

Dubček: These demands were all presented at every meeting beginning with Dresden. The same thing was done at Čierna nad Tisou. They said: "You have to do something!" Even to this day many historians have said that if we had made some concessions, we could have continued our reforms and everything would have been different. Kádár, too, said that if we had taken these warnings into consideration, the situation would have been better. But what exactly could I have done? Reimpose censorship? Get rid of those people? These were precisely the things they were seeking and demanding. I simply could not embrace the line they were trying to force on me. This was so during the whole crisis because they were trying to manipulate me into this position.

I just can't accept the hypothesis that if I had gone about making concessions, everything would have been fine. After all, we were not starting after a complete defeat, the way Kádár himself did! We were on the rise, we were moving upward. And if I had accepted a form of "Kádárization," which emerged in 1958 from the Hungarian defeat two years earlier, it would have been incompatible with our movement. It would have been nonsense in that time before

---

[141] This is an allusion to František Kriegel's service as a medical doctor for the "progressive forces" in both China and Spain during the civil wars in those countries, an experience that, in one of the typical ironies of the Stalinist era, became grounds for suspicion during the purges of the early 1950s. Another factor that was at least as important in accounting for Moscow's hostility toward Kriegel was his Jewish background.

"August," and I would have ended up the same way Gomułka did. And I didn't want something like that to happen, I couldn't let it happen. And all of this was in the air during the meeting at Čierna nad Tisou in the train car. To have done what they wanted us to do, to have made concessions, and to have reached for their hand and maybe have shaken it—all this was what they wanted to achieve. But these very things would have caused disunity among us and a split between the leadership and the people, and the armies might have arrived here even sooner than 21 August. We tried to get an agreement, an agreement that would provide reasonable self-limitations for radicalism and radicals; we tried to have them understand how far they could go and we could go in light of the external circumstances. They did not always understand, though in the end they did. But should I have used an iron hand to make them understand? If I had, I would have betrayed myself, the people, the nation, and everything we stood for. I could not have done that, it was not in my character. They were bound to be disappointed in that light.

Občanský deník: Besides insisting that those people be dismissed, did Brezhnev in the train car—or the Soviet leaders in general—demand the dissolution of KAN, the social democrats, K-231, etc.?

Dubček: In the train car he didn't raise that again. That came up in the earlier statements, when they claimed that those groups were anti-socialist elements, right-wing organizations, and so forth. But we viewed them as organizations that supported the new political course. These were people whom we had rehabilitated and had reintroduced into social life. Soviet leaders were always citing a few marginal things, one or two things against them. But if KAN had been evaluated objectively, it would not have been deemed an anti-state, anti-social, and anti-socialist organization; instead, it would have been seen as a group of people who had simply found their own way to fit into the new course. And we indeed saw this as a feature of pluralism, the expression of different views, which was in accordance with our policy. But "they" set themselves against these groups and on every occasion expressed serious warnings about them. At Čierna nad Tisou we did not assume any obligations on this matter.

Občanský deník: Did the members of the Soviet Politburo display a united front, or were they internally divided? Did some of them want some sort of concession from you to use as an argument against the "hawks" to show that military intervention was unnecessary? And where specifically did Brezhnev fit in? Did you sense a division?

Dubček: You would have to know them. You could see it only in their eyes, what they were like. I had thought initially that maybe the chairman of the trade unions, Grishin, might be a little more conciliatory.[142] I saw how they reacted to certain things. For example, about three of them reacted heatedly when Shelest jumped into the conversation and claimed that in our country there were movements to incorporate the Transcarpathian region of the Ukraine back into the ČSSR. At the time I said that if the meetings were to continue in this way, I would break them up and not be willing to negotiate any more. They then saw that I meant it seriously, and some of them were afraid they had gone too far. But to be frank, they were brought up in such a way that even if they had had inner doubts about what they were doing, they would never reveal those doubts or talk about them. I do not believe there were people among them saying: "Let the new socialists do what they want to do; we'll see what comes of it." No. I think that if they were linked by anything, it was by the power they were so accustomed to having.

---

[142] Dubček's reference here is in error. Viktor Grishin was a candidate member of the CPSU CC Politburo in 1968, but he was not chairman of the Soviet Trade Unions; instead, he was head of the CPSU's Moscow branch. The chairman of the Trade Unions was Aleksandr Shelepin, who was also a full member of the CPSU CC Politburo. This mistake does not detract at all, however, from Dubček's basic point. Neither Grishin nor Shelepin displayed any hint of a "conciliatory" approach during the crisis. Indeed, Grishin was the first member of the Soviet Politburo who explicitly offered "military assistance" to combat "counterrevolution" in Czechoslovakia, a formulation he used in April 1968 in a speech celebrating Lenin's birthday.

Občanský deník: Was there any occasion in 1968 when Brezhnev hinted that he was acting differently from the way he thought, so that he could mollify the "hawks"? Did he mention anything along these lines? Or did Kosygin? Did no one say so? Not even as an aside, as Brezhnev later did to Šimon?

Dubček: All of this was dissimulation. I knew them very well, their psyches, their way of thinking. They were very treacherous. An actor could not have done as well as they did. I did not see anything of the sort. No hint that they wanted to do one thing, but could not do so [because of pressure]. And what Brezhnev told Šimon in November 1968 was said only to create a better image. Nothing else. I don't believe in those things. I know that there were powerful militaristic circles in the Soviet Union, but I don't know what Brezhnev himself thought about them. You see, my own view is that they were all filmmakers whose aim was to destroy everything that was emerging in our country. I arrived at this opinion on the basis of the following consideration: Brezhnev, you'll recall, took part with the others in the conspiracy and coup against Khrushchev. And was Khrushchev's course at that time a reformist course? It certainly was. His course was against Stalinism in the economy, in politics, and everywhere else. Whatever else it may have been, it was reformist. And Brezhnev was in the forefront of the conspiracy not only against Khrushchev, but against the reformist course as well. So why should he grant leeway for reforms to the Czechs and Slovaks? Would he, Brezhnev, grant leeway to the Czechs and Slovaks to come up with something new and to disseminate a new way of thinking to the whole world? I don't believe it for an instant. If it's true that the era from 1953, beginning with the rise of Khrushchev, to 1964 was an era of attempts to combat Stalinism and to struggle for reform, then it is equally true that the Brezhnev conspiracy was a step that put an end to this process in the Soviet Union. I would use that date to mark the start of the period of neo-Stalinism. And that's why I don't accept the notion that Brezhnev might have been having some conciliatory thoughts. What I just recounted to you are facts that show just the reverse. The advent of Brezhnev's regime heralded the advent of neo-Stalinism, and the measures taken against Czechoslovakia in 1968 were the final consolidation of the neo-Stalinist forces in the Soviet Union, Poland, Hungary, and other countries.

Občanský deník: What was the role of Kádár?

Dubček: It is often said that Kádár was in a difficult position because he, after all, had to protect something of what he had accomplished in Hungary. But I would ask: How was he "protecting" it? Did he send his army? Yes, he did. Did he consent to the armed intervention? Yes, he did. The fact that he gave his consent in a more conciliatory tone hardly matters. As early as the spring there was a possible course of action which I explained to Gomułka when he and I were strolling near a playing field in Ostrava around the beginning of 1968. If he and Kádár—along with Ceauşescu, who at the time believed that every country should have the right to act on its own—had come to our defense, and if we had been part of a "Warsaw Four," I don't know what such a grouping would have looked like. I said to Gomułka that time in Ostrava: "Why don't you support us? Look at what we did to revise the political process. Here, too, we must correct things. Why shouldn't we do this together?" In response, he said that what I was talking about was a somewhat different thing—the correction of shortcomings. In Czechoslovakia this process was already going too far. I asked him: "How far?" Is the problem that we are enacting reforms and the people fully support the new course? I asked the same question of Kádár, Brezhnev, and the others. Whether some of them were or were not conciliatory, I don't know. Maybe instinctively they were. But all of them acted identically. None of their speeches even hinted that one of them was trying to get out of the circle and express a principled position at least in this sense: "Let's hold off and not interfere there, and we'll see how things work out."

Občanský deník: Did Brezhnev say anything in the train car to the effect that he was pursuing some sort of international political goal that would be endangered by a serious conflict in Czechoslovakia? Perhaps a treaty with the U.S.? Did he use that sort of argument?

Dubček: No, not at all. He just said that imperialism was growing in strength and that a threat to security was expected from this trend, and so forth. This of course was totally false. It is known that when they presented the U.S. leadership with a note justifying the invasion, American armies retreated some 200 kilometers from their original positions along the western border. This also reinforces the points I discussed in the first part about whether we should have resisted militarily or not. I talked about that with people who came here—for example, with Kissinger—and also when I was in the United States I discussed it with members of Congress. I asked them: "What would you have done?" And they responded: "You helped us out as well by not having fought. Fortunately, you kept a cool head. Any other course would have posed a danger, and a danger not only for you, but one that could have meant a catastrophe for all of Europe and ultimately, perhaps, for the whole world." Each and every one of them said this to me.

Občanský deník: In the train car did Brezhnev threaten you with military intervention?

Dubček: No, not at all.

Občanský deník: What effect did the speeches of our other delegates have? I'm thinking here of Biľak, Rigo, and so forth.

PART FIVE

AUGUST—THE MONTH OF INTERVENTION

INTRODUCTION

On August 3, the day the last Soviet units from the Šumava exercise finally left Czechoslovakia, communist party representatives from the USSR, Poland, Hungary, Bulgaria, the GDR and Czechoslovakia met in Bratislava on the basis of the agreement reached at Čierna. On August 2, the Warsaw Five had held separate talks where Brezhnev reported about the Čierna meeting. The views of the various participants differed: while Kádár welcomed the Čierna session because it had averted the acute threat of intervention, Gomułka and Zhivkov showed considerable skepticism, as did Ulbricht. The Polish leader was mildest, expressing only "[a] certain irritation . . . that the Soviet comrades had agreed to a bilateral meeting . . . at Čierna" (Document No. 70). Zhivkov stated bluntly to the Soviet ambassador afterwards: "It's impossible to trust Dubček, Černík, and Smrkovský . . . We must rely on other forces," while the East German Politburo on August 1 declared the need "[t]o deal a collective blow, using all available means, against the reactionary and counterrevolutionary forces in Czechoslovakia" (Documents Nos. 68, 69).

The Soviets convened the Bratislava meeting of the "Six" to ratify a Kremlin-drafted document on socialist unity and party development aimed at bringing Prague in line. After accepting several Czechoslovak remarks, the joint declaration was adopted. (As promised at Čierna, there was no further discussion of the Warsaw meeting.) On the one hand, Dubček succeeded in insisting on the right of each party to determine its own road to socialism in accordance with the specific conditions in its own country. On the other hand, the document retained the usual clichés about unity, a common anti-imperialist struggle, loyalty to Marxism–Leninism, and so forth. However, there was an additional formulation on joint responsibility for the defense of socialism which was soon to be invoked to justify the right of the Five to intervene. It later became the point of departure for the Brezhnev Doctrine.

The 'Solicitors' Emerge

At this point, an event of fundamental significance took place: five top Czechoslovak party officials handed over a "letter of invitation" to the Soviets for help against the threat of alleged counterrevolutionary forces within Czechoslovakia (Document No. 72). Acknowledging "a number of mistakes" by "our collective—the party leadership," the letter claimed that "[t]he very existence of socialism in our country is under threat." "In such trying circumstances we are appealing to you, Soviet communists . . . with a request for you to lend support and assistance with all the means at your disposal" (Document No. 72). Vasil Biľak handed the letter personally to Soviet Politburo member Pyotr Shelest. (According to Shelest, the delivery took place in a lavatory in the conference hall.) The document played an important part in justifying the approaching invasion.

After Bratislava

Shortly after the Bratislava meeting, the situation in and around Czechoslovakia calmed down to some extent. Fears of a military intervention were once again somewhat assuaged, and there were hopes of a solution through political negotiations. The CPCz Presidium, for example, published a statement describing the outcome of the Čierna and Bratislava meetings as "a fresh impetus for the promotion of mutually beneficial relations" among the socialist countries (Document No. 74). Hungarian leader János Kádár told his party's CC Plenum: "Our Politburo believes that . . . [the] main significance of the meetings [at Čierna and Bratislava] is that the conflict which arose among our six parties after 8 July has ceased to exist and unity has been restored among our parties" (Document No. 75). Czechs and Slovaks consequently toned down their polemics in the press, and generally began to enjoy the holiday season.

The Dubček leadership tried to take advantage of the respite to prepare the Extraordinary 14th CPCz Congress. The congress was to be the decisive watershed in the process of reform—it was already clear that the "conserves" (as the conservatives were called), would not get their way at the congress and that documents would be adopted endorsing a democratic, possibly even pluralistic, model of socialism. The congress was due to open on September 9 and was to be preceded by a congress of the Slovak Communist Party on August 26–29.

Initially, the Bratislava accord appeared to appease the Kremlin. Articles published in Moscow were moderate in tone. Also, the champions of a political settlement of the Czechoslovak issue appeared to have been given the opportunity, for example, to continue negotiations of the SALT I agreement and prepare for the world-wide conference of communist and workers' parties. On August 6, the Soviet Politburo endorsed Brezhnev's decisions at Čierna and Bratislava.

There were, however, indications of continuing concern within the Kremlin. After a meeting with Dubček, Soviet Ambassador Stepan Chervonenko reported to Moscow that the CPCz leader remained "internally torn" over how to deal with the situation in Czechoslovakia. "[A]t least for now he is not yet ready to embark on a consistent and decisive struggle against the rightist forces both within and outside the CPCz" (Document No. 76). Moreover, under pressure from hard-liners, the Politburo endorsed Čierna and Bratislava on the condition that Dubček demonstrate through his actions that he had interpreted the accords the same way as the Kremlin. Otherwise, the option of intervention, even prior to the Slovak CP congress, would be invoked.

Preparations Continue

The majority of the Politburo members then left on holiday, but military preparations continued. General Sergei Shtemenko, an expert in assault operations, was appointed chief of staff of the Warsaw Pact Joint Command. After the end of the "Nemen" exercise, rear units moved to join the assault formations in Poland, while on August 11 the "Horizon" exercises began in the southern part of the GDR, southern Poland and western Ukraine, with Hungarian units joining on August 15.

Covert operations continued as well. Beneath an ostensible calm, Czech and Slovak conservatives directly collaborated with Soviet diplomatic and intelligence officials to bring about what the group of "solicitors" had requested in their letter to Brezhnev—"assistance with all the means at your disposal" (Document No. 72). The activities of the Czechoslovak collaborators became one of the major factors between August 6 and 16 that tilted the scales in the Kremlin in favor of armed intervention.

The solicitors' objective was a last minute manipulation of the balance of power in the CPCz Presidium in order to prevent the 14th CPCz Congress from taking place—even if that meant a military invasion. To this end, they exerted massive pressure and coordinated action with the "healthy forces" within the CPCz leadership as well as within the Warsaw Five. On August 10,

Brezhnev asked GDR leader Walter Ulbricht to explore whether Dubček and his associates were serious about the commitments from Čierna and Bratislava (Document No. 79). The result was a report by Ulbricht following a meeting with a Czechoslovak delegation at Karlovy Vary on August 12. Ulbricht reported that Dubček's officials had no intention of halting the "creeping counterrevolution"; that secret talks were in progress between Bonn and Prague; and that Czechoslovakia and Romania were considering withdrawing from the Warsaw Pact (an assertion that was totally untrue, especially in the case of Czechoslovakia).

Three days of Soviet–Hungarian talks then began at Yalta on August 12. Kádár's record indicates that Brezhnev had not yet entirely decided that intervention was the only remaining option, but that he nonetheless tried to win Hungarian consent to exercise that option. As Kádár reported to his colleagues in Budapest: the "Soviet comrades have concluded that if the situation does not change. . . nothing more can be expected from the current CPCz CC Presidium" (Document No. 83). Brezhnev nevertheless asked Kádár to have "one more talk" with Dubček without telling him that the intervention was going to take place.

Brezhnev–Dubček Telephone Conversations

At the same time as these international moves were taking place, Brezhnev applied pressure directly on Dubček over the telephone and by letter. On August 9, the Soviet leader called Dubček to press him on his apparent failure to implement a number of the points discussed at Čierna and Bratislava (Document No. 77). Although he adopted an accommodating tone during the conversation, Brezhnev repeatedly pushed for specifics on the CPCz leader's willingness to cooperate with the "healthy forces" within the party Presidium, and on his timetable for effecting personnel and other changes the Soviets had been demanding.[1] Brezhnev closed the conversation by saying "we wish you all the best, Sasha," but he also reminded Dubček of the gravity of the situation: "In my opinion, this is very serious now."

By August 13, Brezhnev had hardened his position. The CPSU Politburo prepared a bluntly worded message for delivery that day to Dubček about "a series of grave facts demonstrating that the Czechoslovak side is clearly violating the agreement concluded at Čierna nad Tisou" (Document No. 80). Later in the afternoon, in another remarkable telephone conversation between the two first secretaries, Brezhnev repeatedly and sharply accused Dubček of "deceiving us" about his intentions to comply with his commitments. He warned that Dubček's actions were creating "a completely new situation which we, too, hadn't reckoned with, and that this obviously will compel us to reevaluate the whole situation and resort to new, unavoidable measures" (Document No. 81). Displaying moments of weariness and open aggravation toward the Soviet leader, Dubček tried to assure him: "I promise you, Cde. Brezhnev, that I'll do everything necessary to fulfill our agreement." Brezhnev and the Politburo followed up with instructions to Ambassador Stepan Chervonenko to restate the detailed litany of complaints the Soviet leader had already laid out to Dubček and Černík, and to meet President Ludvík Svoboda to express the Kremlin's hope that he would take the steps Moscow expected of Prague (Document No. 82).

Pressure by the Solicitors

One element of the coordinated—domestic and international—pressure tactics was the August 13 attempt by Drahomír Kolder and Alois Indra to force the CPCz Presidium to table their "Statement" on the current situation for discussion. It was a clear effort to prompt a reshuffling

---

[1] A number of documents, of course, remain closed in state archives in Moscow and elsewhere. One that no doubt would be of special interest here is the record of a long conversation Brezhnev had with Vasil Biľak on August 10.

of the membership of this key body. But thanks to the resistance of the Dubčekites, the plan misfired.

In the wake of this failure, the conservatives only increased their pressure campaign. At a weekend gathering at the government holiday center at Orlík, south of Prague, they worked out a coordinated political action plan for military intervention, and called for its immediate implementation. As part of the scheme, they promised that they would trigger a crisis at a meeting of the CPCz Presidium on August 20, the end result of which would be a call by the majority for "international assistance"; that the same would be arranged in the CPCz Central Committee, in the National Assembly and in the government; and that the conservatives would follow these steps by taking over the main organs of the media. It was an attempt to legalize the intervention both at home and abroad.

Indra handed this plan to the Soviet embassy in Prague, which passed it on to Brezhnev. It reached the general secretary's desk by August 17, or the morning of August 18 at the latest. In Bratislava, Biľak was kept informed.

On the basis of coordinated moves between the Kremlin and Czechoslovak conservatives, the Politburo gave the final green light to invade during a three-day meeting from August 15–17. The formal resolution, promulgated on August 17, begins: "After comprehensively analyzing the situation and events in Czechoslovakia in recent days, and after reviewing the request from members of the CPCz CC Presidium and the ČSSR government for . . . military assistance in the struggle against counterrevolutionary forces, . . . the CPSU CC Politburo unanimously believes that in recent days the course of events in Czechoslovakia has become as dangerous as possible."

Declaring that "all political means of assistance from the CPSU and the other fraternal parties have already been exhausted," the resolution continues, "the CPSU CC Politburo believes the time has come to resort to active measures in defense of socialism in the ČSSR, and has unanimously decided to provide help and support to the Communist Party and people of Czechoslovakia through military force" (Document No. 88).

At a meeting of the Five, convened at great speed on August 18, Brezhnev explained the Soviet Politburo's rationale for arriving at the decision, and for setting the timing of the invasion (Document No. 92). Filling his remarks with references to "hooligans" and "anti-socialist swine," who were allegedly responsible for a variety of attacks against the Soviet Union and other fraternal socialist countries at the instigation of "the Right," Brezhnev detailed the CPCz leadership's repeated failure to measure up to its alleged commitments from Čierna and Bratislava. He mentioned Dubček by name, charging that he "has gone over completely to the side of the Right," and noted that the CPSU Politburo agreed unanimously with the "healthy forces" in Czechoslovakia that the situation could only get worse. In describing the process the Kremlin had followed, Brezhnev implicitly acknowledged that the Politburo had taken the decision on its own, without the participation of Soviet constitutional bodies. Moreover, the summit of the Five was faced with an accomplished fact and merely had to endorse the decision—also clearly without the involvement of their respective constitutional bodies.

In addition to the Czechoslovak collaborators, top levels of the Soviet military unquestionably influenced the Soviet decision. The military actually proceeded with preparations for an invasion anticipating that the Kremlin, faced with unfolding developments, would be compelled to give its consent. For his part, in the week leading up to the invasion, Marshal Andrei Grechko traveled around the region meeting different elements of the joint Warsaw Pact forces (Document No. 84). Although he went under the pretext of a routine inspection tour, Brezhnev acknowledged his defense minister's real purpose in reply to a question by Ulbricht at the meeting of the Five on August 18: "Grechko has been everywhere and issued information on the preparations." Around August 15, Western intelligence discovered that parts of southern GDR and Poland had been declared closed areas, that the troops assembled there were being issued iron food rations, and that white stripes were being painted on military hardware for better orientation during black-outs.

On August 17, General Ivan Pavlovskii was appointed commander-in-chief of the joint invasion forces, and the Soviets resumed their anti-reform, anti-Czechoslovak campaign in the state-controlled media. The escalating attacks created concern and consternation within the Czechoslovak reform leadership. Visits by Yugoslav President Josip Broz Tito from August 9–11, and by Romanian leader Nicolae Ceauşescu from August 15–17, as well as meetings with other Warsaw Pact leaders and officials, failed to help the Czechoslovak situation. Instead, they only added fuel to the fire. At a press conference at the Hrzan Palace in Prague on August 17, Josef Smrkovský, František Kriegel, Oldřich Černík and Čestmír Císař told representatives of the press, radio and television that the situation was serious; as Kriegel put it, the sword of Damocles was hanging over the country by a thread.

On August 20, the group of "solicitors" attempted to carry out the scenario agreed upon with the Kremlin—to provoke a crisis at the meeting of the CPCz Presidium and muster a pro-intervention majority. But thanks to Dubček's insistence on following the planned agenda, Indra and Kolder's proposal to deal with the internal political situation, and force a change in the leadership, was not discussed until 8:00 P.M. As a result, the long and stormy arguments that ensued were never resolved.

The debate finally ended only when reports arrived that the invading armies had crossed the borders (Document No. 103). The Presidium then voted not on Kolder's and Indra's propositions but on the official posture they would adopt toward the Soviet incursion. And here the vote differed from what the "solicitors" had expected. The majority of the Presidium voted in favor of the anti-intervention statement: "The CPCz CC Presidium believes the border crossing not only contravenes all principles governing relations between socialist states, but also violates the fundamental provisions of international law" (Document No. 100).

Only Biľak, Kolder, Rigo and Švestka opposed the resolution, failing to muster the majority they had promised the Kremlin. (Indra was only a secretary and not a member of the Presidium, so he could not vote.) Barbírek and Piller, who had originally promised to vote for Kolder's statement, changed their minds and refused to endorse the invasion.

The promised pro-Kremlin majority never surfaced in the Presidium. A similar situation emerged in Bratislava at a meeting of the Presidium of the Slovak CP. This was the first in a series of political failures that accompanied the Soviet invasion. During the night, Josef Smrkovský's advisers managed to convene the Presidium of the National Assembly which also issued a declaration on the morning of August 21 condemning the occupation. The government press, scientific institutes and mass organizations reacted likewise, as did most of the population, which demonstrated its opposition in the streets of Prague, Bratislava and every other city and town. More than anything else, it was the courageous response of the citizens which delivered the final blow to the political scenario envisioned by the perpetrators of the occupation.

At this time, the radio played a role unique in history. Broadcasters prevented a prominent member of the "solicitors'" group, Karel Hoffmann, from delivering a pro-intervention declaration. Instead, they ensured that the censuring statement by the Dubčekite majority was broadcast. Later, when Soviet military units had seized the radio building, broadcasters continued to transmit via a network of studios and small regional and army transmitters. This made the radio a principal source of information for the population as well as an organizing force for the peoples' positions and activities.

The occupiers and those supporting them tried to take advantage of the rapid military success of the occupation; approximately 27 divisions, including 5,000 armored vehicles and 800 aircraft coming from the GDR, Poland and Hungary, swept through the country in a single day. When the "solicitors" failed in the first round to frame the move as coming at the request of Czechoslovakia's constitutional authorities, they concentrated on attempts to undermine Dubček and his supporters after the fact. The prerequisite for success was now the arrest, deportation—and possibly physical liquidation—of Dubček, Smrkovský, Černík, Kriegel, Špaček and Šimon, who were regarded as the rebellious core of the CPCz Presidium (Documents Nos. 101–103).

By eliminating the communist reform leaders, it would then be possible to remove the top representatives of the government, National Assembly, the National Front and the Prague CPCz organization, all of which the Soviets regarded as the so-called second ("counterrevolutionary") center. This would then make it possible to set up a purported revolutionary workers' and peasants' government (a typical tactic in cases of Soviet interference), which would replace the legally elected constitutional bodies and help save the discredited political scenario of the intervention.

The success of these plans relied on the "group of solicitors" and opportunists who participated in a CPCz Central Committee session at the Hotel Praha. It was labeled a plenary session, but in fact only one-third of the members were present. However, the main element of the plan in connection with the "revolutionary workers' and peasants' government" was intended to fall into place during discussions on August 22 at the Soviet embassy and at the office of ČSSR President Ludvík Svoboda (Document No. 115). Biľak, Kolder, Piller, Indra and nine others took part in the first session, which failed to yield a resolution to the question of who would assume the top leadership posts in the new regime. At the second meeting, attended by a smaller group including Ludvík Svoboda, the Czechoslovak president refused, after some initial hesitation, to sponsor the proposed government, thus dealing another blow to Soviet planners.

The second meeting took place in the Castle at 5:00 P.M. on the same day. President Svoboda received a small group led by Piller who suggested, at the recommendation of Chervonenko after he had checked with Moscow, forming a provisional revolutionary workers' and peasants' government with Svoboda at its head. Svoboda rejected the idea—not as a matter of principle, but because of its constitutional and tactical shortcomings. At the same time, he presented his own conception of how to reach the same goals by other means. He decided he would fly to Moscow and try to bring back the interned Czechoslovak leaders. He was sure that the Soviets would allow this, especially if he insisted that Dubček and Černík resign their posts and be judged by the responsible party and state organs immediately upon returning to Prague.

The Moscow Protocol

Meanwhile, members of the deported Czechoslovak leadership had been taken to the Kremlin, where they were interrogated separately by Soviet political "troikas" and "foursomes" (Document No. 116). To a person, and Dubček especially, they continued to reject Soviet aggression. In his first meeting with Brezhnev, Dubček declared: "I am certain that not only in Czechoslovakia and in Europe, but in all communist movements, this act will cause us to suffer the greatest defeat." The entire CPCz Presidium, including various secretaries (even Indra), was subsequently brought to Moscow, with the result that the pro-interventionists, or at least the opportunists, actually attained a numerical majority in the contrived Czechoslovak delegation (Document No. 117).

The reformers on the Czechoslovak side faced an extremely difficult situation. They were: isolated from information about developments at home (Zdeněk Mlynář,[2] sent by the 14th Congress, was one source of information); exposed to crude pressures by the Soviets; disavowed by Biľak who was systematically passing confidential information on to Brezhnev; and sharply attacked by President Svoboda. Given their dire situation, the reformers, headed by Černík, decided to negotiate. In explaining the view of the Czechoslovak delegation, Černík stated that: "Our country has fallen into a situation for which there is no parallel in the postwar period. We, the Czechoslovak communists, feel an immense responsibility to our people" (Document No. 117).

These talks resulted in the so-called Moscow Protocol (Document No. 119). Presented in the form of a Soviet ultimatum, the protocol stipulated, among other things, that the Czechoslovaks

---

[2] The role of Mlynář in the August events was very complicated and controversial in comparison with other leading Czechoslovak figures such as Svoboda, Černik, Husák and others. It is still the subject of ongoing research and analysis. In any case, in October 1968, Mlynář resigned his post in protest against the policy of normalization.

would face an occupation military government—and the prospect of bloodshed and civil war—of unlimited duration unless they accepted Soviet demands. The Czechoslovak delegation managed to secure only minor changes to the original Soviet draft, including eliminating the characterization of the Prague Spring as a counterrevolution; cutting a reference of approval of the intervention; and including a reference to the May plenary session which made it possible to endorse the Action Program. At the very end of the negotiations over the protocol, Dubček joined the meeting, gave a forceful speech which aroused Brezhnev's fury and even led the Soviet Politburo to walk out temporarily, and then signed the protocol. Kriegel remained firm and refused to sign.

A segment of the Czechoslovak public, as well as politicians, historians and political scientists, believed that signing the Moscow Protocol was an unpardonable, Munich-type capitulation, and that it brought an end to any possibility for reform in Czechoslovakia. Another group—some of the editors of this Reader among them—see the problem as more complex. There could not have been a united refusal to sign: the collaborationist part of the "pseudo-delegation" saw the protocol not as a defeat but as a victory, and would have signed the relevant section in any case. Furthermore, a refusal to sign would clearly have resulted in the imposition of an occupation regime, which would have relied on the collaborators and been accompanied by cruel acts such as arrests, deportations and bloodshed, even executions, along the pattern of repression that took place in Hungary after 1956.

Faced by the difficult decision of whether or not to sign, the reformers were clearly aware of these threats as well as of their historical responsibility (Documents Nos. 63 and 117). They understood that the protocol and its signature represented a defeat, but they also intended to take advantage of any loopholes in its interpretation. Moreover, they put their faith in the determination of Czechoslovak society to save at least a minimum of the reforms—possibly through a variant of "Kádárization" that became relatively successful in Hungary.

Against the reform group, however, stood an adversary who was not only powerful but perfidious. Under Brezhnev's stage-management, the antagonists were convinced that Dubček would have to submit to massive pressure by the "allies" and be forced to take unpopular measures himself that would eventually discredit and isolate him.

The return of the deported leaders to Prague was received everywhere not only with a feeling of relief and joy but also as a certain victory. However, the question soon arose as to what price had been paid for this victory, especially when, at Moscow's request, the protocol was not published in full. A crowd outside parliament, enthusiastically greeting Smrkovský, began to chant: "We want to hear the truth!" Suspicion spread when the first regressive decisions were taken—for example, writing off the "Vysočany" extraordinary congress. Dubček tried to offset abandoning the congress by coopting into the existing Central Committee 80 members who had been elected by the Vysočany congress. This compromise, ultimately more advantageous to the "old forces" at home and abroad, foreshadowed months of conflict with the Kremlin over how much of what was left of the reforms would be maintained during implementation of the so-called "normalization" policies.

DOCUMENT No. 68: Report by Soviet Ambassador to the GDR Pyotr Abrasimov on East Germany's Position vis-à-vis Czechoslovakia, July 28 and August 1, 1968

Source: AVPRF, F. 059, Op. 58, P. 124, D. 573, L. 79; Vondrová & Navrátil, vol. 2, pp. 33–34.

Soviet Ambassador to the GDR Pyotr Abrasimov recorded these two East German statements on Czechoslovakia: the first by Walter Ulbricht on July 28; the second from the Socialist Unity Party (SED) Politburo meeting on August 1. Both reflect the GDR's hostility toward the Prague Spring and the predisposition to "deal a collective blow" to Dubček's reform movement.

From a conversation with Ulbricht:

Cde. Ulbricht expressed the following desires:

(1) At the forthcoming meeting he is planning to discuss the draft of an appeal to the Czechoslovak population, an appeal that he assumes the Soviet side will introduce.

(2) He expects that at the meeting the political platform of the progressive forces of the ČSSR will be worked out and reviewed.

(3) He believes that, given the way circumstances have developed, coordination of the propaganda efforts of the five countries will be absolutely crucial.

(4) It is necessary to consider when it would be politically more auspicious to announce the beginning of maneuvers by the armies of several Warsaw Pact member states.

From the SED Politburo meeting:

The SED CC Politburo regards the following steps to be essential:

(a) To deal a collective blow, using all available means, against the reactionary and counter-revolutionary forces in Czechoslovakia.

(b) To expose the mistakes of both the past and the current leadership of the CPCz CC and the Czechoslovak government.

(c) To devise, through joint efforts, a program aimed at correcting the mistakes committed in Czechoslovakia and at remedying the situation in the country, with an eye to lending Czechoslovakia all necessary assistance in carrying out reforms in the economic, scientific, cultural, and other spheres.

At the SED CC Politburo it was noted that Dubček and his cohorts are "sly revisionists, and have turned out not to be such simple people as they seemed initially."

DOCUMENT No. 69: Report by Soviet Ambassador to Bulgaria A.M. Puzanov on Bulgaria's Position vis-à-vis Czechoslovakia, August 1, 1968

Source: AVPRF, F. 059, Op. 58, P. 124, D. 573, Ll. 95–96; Vondrová & Navrátil, vol. 2, pp. 150–151.

Soviet Ambassador to Bulgaria A. M. Puzanov recorded Bulgarian Communist Party leader Todor Zhivkov's hostile views on Czechoslovakia during two conversations on August 1. Justifying his opinions with anti-Semitic comments, Zhivkov directly advocates the use of force: "we will have to use all possible and necessary means, including the armed forces of the Warsaw Pact," Puzanov quotes him as stating, if "the situation in the ČSSR is to be changed."

Zhivkov's first remarks:

It's impossible to trust Dubček, Černík, and Smrkovský. They're not in a position to change the situation in their country, and even if they were, they consciously don't want to change it. We must rely on other forces. In our view, the situation in Czechoslovakia is extremely dangerous. Zionism is making active inroads in other countries as well. It is, one senses, applying enormous pressure on Cde. Kádár. Even here in Bulgaria we're experiencing some manifestations of it. . . . You know, that a secretary of the Bulgarian Communist Party CC, Cde. S. Todorov, has a Jewish wife . . . Her political leanings are unsound. S. Todorov is sufficiently mature and experienced as a political leader, but one sometimes notices the influence of his wife in his comments about certain matters.

Zhivkov's remarks later in the day:[3]

We [on the Bulgarian Politburo] believe it should be emphasized that regardless of the results from the bilateral negotiations at Čierna nad Tisou, the situation in Czechoslovakia and the whole history and course of events there give no reason to assume that the current leadership of the CPCz will be capable of changing the situation. The BCP CC Politburo reaffirms the opinion it expressed earlier: that if the situation in the ČSSR is to be changed and the communist party and socialist gains are to be preserved, we will have to use all possible and necessary means, including the armed forces of the Warsaw Pact if the situation so demands.

Dubček, Černík, and Smrkovský have offered no guarantees that they will turn events around. They are nationalists and revisionists, who have no love for the Soviet Union.

If we do not succeed in turning events around, this will be a catastrophe; it will be a blow against the Soviet Union, against our socialist countries, against the international communist movement, and against the development of our socialist countries.

What is going on? China broke away, and the same with Albania. The situation is only slightly better with Cuba, Romania, and Yugoslavia.

---

[3] Puzanov's memorandum begins with the following: "In the afternoon of 1 August I met Comrade Todor Zhivkov at his invitation. Comrades Stanko Todorov and Pencho Kubadinski, both members of the BCP Politburo, also were present. At first Comrade T. Zhivkov stated that the BCP CC Politburo had determined who would be in its delegation for the meeting in Bratislava on 3 August: T. Zhivkov (head of the delegation), Politburo members S. Todorov (BCP CC Secretary) and P. Kubadinski (deputy prime minister of Bulgaria), a counselor to the delegation, K. Tellalov (deputy head of the BCP CC Department on Foreign Policy and International Relations), and an interpreter. Then, Comrade T. Zhivkov, having emphasized that the Politburo and the BCP CC will always hang together with the CPSU CC Politburo, declared that he considered it essential to transmit the BCP CC Politburo's views on Czechoslovakia to Comrade L. I. Brezhnev and the CPSU CC Politburo."

We cannot and must not give any further ground!

We fully understand the difficulties that will be created within the international communist movement as a result of extreme measures we are being forced to take in Czechoslovakia. But what can we do?

We must clearly recognize how dangerously revisionism is developing in the international communist movement. Take the Italian Communist Party. It is no longer what it was ten years ago; social-democratic views have overwhelmed it. Just because the Italian Communist Party is a mass party does not means it is a truly Marxist–Leninist party.

Or take the French Communist Party, which has fallen strongly under the influence of Zionism.

We believe that the adverse consequences in the international communist movement and the hubbub being stirred up by international reactionary forces will pose only ephemeral difficulties.

If we restore Czechoslovakia to the path of socialism, we will strengthen the forces of the Warsaw Pact and the forces of socialism overall.

But if, on the contrary, Czechoslovakia leaves the Warsaw Pact or remains in it and behaves like Romania or some other revisionist state, the forces of the Warsaw Pact will be severely weakened and this will pose a great threat to the GDR, Hungary, and Poland. In the event of war, the Soviet army will end up having to fight not along the Czechoslovak–German border, but along the Soviet–Czechoslovak border.

If events in Czechoslovakia are not turned around quickly and decisively, that will amount to the rehabilitation of Tito. Khrushchev rehabilitated him once, and we did it a second time. And it will seem that Tito is the very best politician in the world.

A delegation from the BCP will be in Bratislava. We regard the forthcoming meeting of six parties to be a purely tactical move.

As concerns the course of events in the ČSSR, perhaps nothing will come of it. "But God help us if we are mistaken." The meeting will be fruitful only if we compel the CPCz leadership to sign a declaration or communiqué that is in the spirit of the Warsaw Letter both in its assessment of events in the ČSSR and in the measures it proposes to remedy the situation.

Our opinion is simple: Force them to capitulate. If they refuse, then we must resort to other, extreme measures.

DOCUMENT No. 70: Polish Views of the Situation in Czechoslovakia on the Eve of the Bratislava Conference, August 2, 1968

Source: ÚSD, Sb. KV, K—Archiv MZV, Received Dispatches No. 7289/1968.

This cable from the Czechoslovak Ambassador in Warsaw Antonín Gregor provides a brief summary of a conversation he had with Gomułka the day before the Bratislava conference. Gregor reports that the Polish leader expressed irritation that the Soviet authorities had agreed to hold the Čierna nad Tisou and Bratislava conferences, and remained skeptical that any political "solution" would prove viable under the existing leadership in Prague. Gomułka, as Ambassador Gregor notes, "feared a further impact of our developments on certain sections of Polish society," and "expects that the Bratislava meeting will not produce either a change of course or a solution."

2 August 1968

To the CPCz Central Committee

As the Polish delegation was leaving for Bratislava I had about a 20-minute talk with Gomułka. He voiced a certain discontent that the Soviet comrades had agreed to the Bratislava meeting and said, explicitly, that he could not agree with our Action Program because in it he saw the cause of all, in their opinion, negative events in our country. He does not believe an end to polemics is a real solution, even though he sees no guarantees that we will be able to live up to this pledge. It was abundantly evident that he was extremely worried by the continuing democratization process, which would be unacceptable under their conditions. This process has already caused them difficulties among various sections of the public, especially the clergy. Naturally he does not expect a change in the ownership of the means of production or the break-up of unified agricultural cooperatives in our country, especially in connection with the social security of cooperative farmers. He expects that the Bratislava meeting will not produce either a change of course or a solution. He explicitly said that this would have to be a long-term process, but from his hints it was obvious that he feared a further impact of our developments on various sections of Polish society. A certain irritation was evident on his part that the Soviet comrades had agreed to a bilateral meeting on our territory, at Čierna nad Tisou, and now a multilateral conference in Bratislava. He regards this as one-sided for prestige reasons and believes that it will also leave long-term shadows on inter-party relations. He further expressed annoyance at being labeled a "conservative" and "dogmatic." From the entire conversation I had the impression that once he states all his misgivings, he will not resist the conclusions adopted at Čierna nad Tisou, even though he said he was not informed of their content since he had only just returned from his holiday resort. . . .

DOCUMENT No. 71: Vasil Biľak's Recollections of the Bratislava Conference

Source: *Paměti Vasila Biľaka: Unikátni svědectví ze zákulisí KSČ*, 2 vols. (Praha: Agentura Cesty, 1991), vol. 2, pp. 85–89.

Vasil Biľak's two-volume memoir of his life as a hard-line anti-reformist leader of Czechoslovakia's Communist Party includes this discussion of the Bratislava multilateral meeting. Among the revelations in this unique historical account is Biľak's admission that he and other "reliable comrades" from the CPCz handed a "written request for fraternal assistance" to the Soviet authorities during the Bratislava meeting—a "letter of invitation" for an invasion if the situation deteriorated further. (When the letter was declassified from the Soviet archives in 1992, however, Biľak denied knowledge of its existence.) In his memoirs Biľak also takes the position that Dubček could have avoided an invasion if he had quickly implemented the "four steps"—including dismissing key reformers and cracking down on the media—demanded by the Soviets at the Čierna meeting.

(See also Document No. 72.)

We had only three days for the preparation of the Bratislava meeting, and the entire responsibility was left to the CPCz CC Presidium. The Bratislava meeting was set for 3 August 1968. The meeting in Čierna had ended on 31 July in the afternoon, and we left it full of good will.[4] It seemed that a critical point had somehow come and gone, and that things had taken a turn for the better. In the train there was a quite good, even festive, atmosphere. Černík sat next to me and whispered a proposal. He asked what my reaction would be to a deal whereby he would not reveal what position I had taken at Čierna nad Tisou, and I in return would help him remove Kriegel from the CPCz Presidium. Without thinking, I told him I had no objections to his revealing what my position had been at Čierna. What I said at Čierna was fully compatible with my conscience, and was truthful and candid. And in any event, if he revealed what I had said, that would be a breach of the agreement ensuring that nobody would be stigmatized for voting a particular way at Čierna. But even so, I repeated, I have no objections if you want to reveal what I said in Čierna. I will take what comes. And as for helping Černík to remove Kriegel from the Presidium, I said I would gladly help because Kriegel is a man who does not deserve to be on the Presidium. Kriegel does not work on behalf of the CPCz and the Czechoslovak people and the cause of socialism; he works instead against the party and against the people and against socialism. I gave this promise without knowing all the details that were agreed to at the meeting of the "four."[5]

When the counterrevolutionary elements in Prague learned about the results of Čierna nad Tisou, they were very disappointed. They instantly mobilized all the forces they could to negate the results of the Čierna negotiations and to reverse the situation at the meeting in Bratislava. They could not, however, prevent the meeting itself from taking place. To secure the meeting from curious onlookers and eavesdroppers, we had to find in Bratislava a suitable location. Nothing appropriate was available at that time, but fortunately the Recreation House of the ROH[6] had just been finished. It is on a pleasant site with a view of the Danube. We requested that the Slovak Trade Unions' Board let us use the site, and we began preparing it for an international meeting.

---

[4] Actually, the Čierna meeting ended on August 1, not July 31.

[5] The "four" to which Biľak refers are the four CPCz leaders—Dubček, Černík, Smrkovský, and Ludvík Svoboda—who ended up negotiating with four top CPSU officials in the last day-and-a-half of the Čierna talks.

[6] ROH was the acronym for the Revolutionary Trade Union Movement (i.e., the official trade unions).

The Soviet, Polish, Bulgarian, Hungarian, and GDR delegations came to Bratislava. All were led by their party first (or general) secretaries; other delegates consisted of prime ministers, the party secretaries responsible for international affairs, and other leading party members.

The Czechoslovak delegation consisted of A. Dubček, O. Černík, J. Smrkovský, V. Biľak, J. Lenárt, L. Svoboda, and Z. Mlynář. All the delegations stayed at the Recreation House, where the meeting itself also was supposed to take place. Foreign journalists streamed into Bratislava, including many from bourgeois countries. Any journalists who had been stationed in Vienna came to Bratislava. At that time travel was fairly free. Television crews, photographers, and reporters were allowed to attend the opening of the conference.

The meeting opened in the usual way. Dubček opened the session by welcoming all the fraternal parties and by laying out the schedule of the meeting. After the journalists and photographers departed, L. I. Brezhnev offered a proposal. Because there was very little time and the meeting was supposed to end that same day, and because the experts and staffs had not prepared any materials, he suggested that the meeting be broken up and that the general/first secretaries along with the prime ministers should move to the next room and prepare a draft of a document that would then be collectively reviewed and signed by the individual delegations.

This was the only meeting in my life—and I have participated in many international meetings—where literally every word of the document, from A to Z, was written by the first/general secretaries of the parties and by the prime ministers. I should add that they worked very hard, putting in a lot of effort and doing without lunch. The rest of us just walked around the building and its environs. We got word that nobody was supposed to leave the proximity of the building. Meanwhile, several Czechoslovak journalists were given access to the facility.

Smrkovský was unhappy not only because he was not present when the document was being prepared, but more so because he could not report back to Prague on what was going on and what sort of document would emerge. Out of sheer boredom, he gave three or four interviews. He was constantly screaming that he would never sign a document whose contents were unknown to him. Calls came in every minute from Prague wanting to know what was happening in Bratislava. The callers got no answer. No one could honestly say what was going on behind the closed doors. The document was scheduled to be completed by around three or four o'clock in the afternoon.

We thought about where such an important document should be signed. We concluded that the best place would be in the old Bratislava City Hall building. It was then decided that we should prepare the Mirror Auditorium, where other historic documents had been signed, including the peace treaty with Napoleon after the battle at Slavkov [Austerlitz].

At four o'clock all the television crews were summoned, but the document was not yet ready. Two more hours elapsed, but the document was still not ready. Not until about seven o'clock, or rather about half past seven, did we finally get word that it was possible to convene a plenary session of all members of the delegations of the fraternal parties, where the documents were to be submitted for consideration. And so, at half past eight the plenary session of the meeting opened in the above-mentioned Recreation House of ROH. After reading the document, each of the delegations indicated whether the document was suitable and whether the members would sign it. All the delegations said they would sign it, and thus all the members moved from the Recreation House to the old City Hall's Mirror Auditorium.

The occasion was very respectable and glorious. In the official rooms a small cocktail party was set up. At the same time, a public address system was installed on the balcony outside in case the heads of the delegations were willing to talk to the large crowds of people who had gathered on Primanacional Square. There were many people jammed as tightly as possible into the square. Unfortunately, a bad rainstorm set in, but even then people stayed in the square so that they could find out the results of the meeting. We knew that these people had not been organized by the CPCz CC or by the regional or city council of the party. A variety of people came to the square, including good honest people, as well as some unsavory types and provocateurs. Many Western journalists and tourists from Vienna were there as well. They simply wanted to see rather than to hear. They wanted to see the heads of the delegations. However, none of the delegations proved willing to speak from the balcony. Maybe that was because of the bad weather or because the meeting stretched into the late night hours and a celebratory dinner was scheduled to begin at ten o'clock in the building of the Board of Commissioners (today the Presidium of the Slovak government).

The reactionaries in Prague had already learned what sort of document we had worked out and signed. The result was that the colonel responsible for the security of the heads of the delegations called off his men, and an incredibly chaotic scene ensued in front of the City Hall.

It was decided that we would drive from the City Hall directly to the building of the Board of Commissioners, where the dinner was supposed to be held. It was extremely difficult to maneuver the cars parked in front of the City Hall through the crowds and in the direction of Klobučnická Street. L. I. Brezhnev, Dubček, and I were sitting in one of the cars. Dubček was constantly opening the window and shouting responses to people, whereas I kept my window closed the whole time to ensure that no one could come along in the darkness and rush and commit a provocation by throwing something into the car. I knew that I, as the main host, must not permit any sort of shadow to fall on Bratislava.

As we were leaving and trying to get over to Klobučnická Street, we could hear someone speaking into the public address system. Brezhnev asked who it was. Dubček said it was Smrkovský. That was in his nature. He went to the balcony and although no one had designated him to do so, he spoke to the crowd about what kind of document we had signed. He finished and then sang the national anthem. Brezhnev could not understand how such indiscipline could prevail in the party leadership. How, he asked, could a member of the presidium talk about such an important issue without the approval of the full body?

At the time Smrkovský was probably not even aware of what exactly he was praising or what he had signed, or that he had actually agreed on the need for "international assistance." In Bratislava we all collectively signed the statement that "the support, protection, and consolidation of these gains, which the nations achieved through their heroic efforts and through the devoted work of the people of each country, are the common international duty of all socialist countries. This is the unanimous opinion of all participants in the meeting, who have shown their unwavering determination to develop and protect the gains of socialism in their countries and to achieve new successes in building socialism."

Even before the official dinner started, Dubček had already been informed about the reaction to the meeting that had just finished. Counterrevolutionary forces were alarmed, he was told, and they were displaying their malevolence and anger. Even so, on that evening of 3 August, Kriegel saw fit to tell the representatives of the rightist forces who were gathered by Císař's office at the CPCz CC building that "it is being said that no losers or winners emerged. Clear-cut results are not possible in these sorts of meetings. But in any case, we have gained time. We must use it to keep the country agitated and prepare for a decisive confrontation."

Dubček grew frightened. At dinner he avoided conversations with the Soviet delegates, and he ignored them quite openly. Except for the GDR representatives, the delegations were scheduled to depart early the next morning. But when the Soviet delegates saw what kind of a situation had developed, they asked to leave on an overnight train, rather than to fly out the next morning. Only the GDR delegation stayed in Bratislava because Walter Ulbricht was interested in seeing Slovnaft.

Many good and reliable comrades reacted to the Bratislava Declaration with relief. They were convinced that the situation would finally turn around, as they had long hoped. I could name hundreds and thousands of those who were willing to take on any duty for the party so that they could contribute to the defeat and crushing of the counterrevolution.

Experience had taught us and led us to be cautious. We had lived through disappointments so many times in the past that we knew we could not rely on the promises of Dubček. But humans have a uniquely optimistic bent. Even in the most hopeless situations they still expect and believe things will change for the better. This where the saying 'hope dies last' comes from. We, too, believed and expected that Dubček might change for the better.

In Čierna nad Tisou we were clearly told that if the CPCz leadership should again resort to deception and fail to carry out its obligations as agreed on by all the fraternal parties, no more meetings would take place at this level. We knew that either there would be a true change, which was still possible at that time, or that a rapid deterioration would set in if the CPCz leadership were again evasive and deceitful.

As I already indicated, a written request for fraternal assistance had already been prepared in case the need should arise. During the Bratislava meeting a request, in the form of a letter, was given to the Soviet comrades, in which some members of the CPCz CC Presidium and the Czechoslovak government asked the Soviet leadership for assistance. The letter said that if the situation were to deteriorate further and the agreed-on responsibilities were not carried out, the comrades who signed the letter did not see any way to avoid the need for international assistance from their allies. We could not get out of this desperate situation through our own efforts alone, and we did not have time for a new meeting.

After the Bratislava meeting the pace of events accelerated. The reactionary forces embarked on a wild campaign against everything that had been agreed on in Čierna nad Tisou and against all the responsibilities flowing from the Bratislava Declaration. The reactionary forces knew very well that our "four" in Čierna nad Tisou—that is, Dubček, Černík, and Smrkovský, accompanied by the president of the republic, Ludvík Svoboda, to prove their integrity—had pledged that the CPCz CC Presidium would take the following four basic steps after returning to Prague:[7]

— František Kriegel would be removed from the CPCz CC Presidium.

— Čestmír Císař would be dismissed from his post on the CPCz CC Secretariat and would be appointed chairman of the Czech National Council.

— The functions of Interior Minister Pavel would be limited by removing the State Security organs from the ministry and placing them under the direction of another, more reliable comrade.

— Radical measures would be taken vis-à-vis the mass media. One measure would be the dismissal of Jiří Pelikán from his post as the head of Czechoslovak television, and another would be the reimposition of strict party and government control over all the main components of the mass media.

There was still enough opportunity to take these steps so that we could come to the Bratislava meeting with something positive. But Dubček did not use this opportunity. He claimed that the interval between the meeting in Čierna nad Tisou and the one in Bratislava was too short to carry out the four steps listed above. We let ourselves be convinced by him, expecting that after the Bratislava meeting these would be the first steps that would be taken.

---

[7] Judging from Dubček's speech at the CPCz CC Plenum in September 1969 (see ÚSD, AÚV KSČ, F. 01, Sv. 210, A.j. 131), Biľak may be justified in arguing that Dubček and the others made commitments of this sort at Čierna. See also Document No. 85 below.

DOCUMENT No. 72: The "Letter of Invitation" from the Anti-Reformist Faction of the CPCz Leadership, August 1968

Source: ÚSD, Sb. KV, Z/S 21.

This letter, drafted by a small group of pro-Moscow hard-liners in the CPCz, was given to Brezhnev at the Bratislava meeting on August 3. Written in Russian so as to be easy to read, the letter provided "an urgent request and plea for your intervention" to protect Czechoslovakia from the "imminent danger of counterrevolution." It was signed by Vasil Biľak and four of his colleagues: Drahomír Kolder, Alois Indra, Oldřich Švestka, and Antonín Kapek. Biľak quietly passed the letter to another member of the CPSU Politburo, Pyotr Shelest, in a meeting in the men's lavatory—the rendezvous was set up by the KGB station chief in Bratislava—during a break at the conference. Shelest went promptly to Brezhnev's suite and passed on the letter.

Brezhnev cited the "letter of invitation" when he met the leaders of East Germany, Poland, Hungary, and Bulgaria in Moscow on August 18 to inform them of the decision to invade. Brezhnev proposed to his East European colleagues that the letter be used as a formal justification for the impending military intervention. All the participants supported the idea, and the letter became a pretext for the invasion, though the "appeal" for "fraternal assistance" that was published in the Soviet press on August 22 was considerably longer and more detailed.

After the invasion, Soviet authorities stamped this key document top secret and locked it in the Kremlin archive with personal instructions from the head of the CPSU General Department, Konstantin Chernenko: "To be preserved in the Politburo Archive. Not to be opened without my express permission." For years, the letter, who signed it, and whether it even existed, remained a mystery. In July 1992, Russian President Boris Yeltsin provided the Czechoslovak government with a copy. Biľak, the only surviving signatory, was indicted by the Czechoslovak federal government in early 1992 on several counts, including charges of treason for trying to set up a "provisional revolutionary government of workers and peasants" after the invasion. Subsequently, those charges were broadened to include his part in the "letter of invitation." The breakup of the Czechoslovak federation at the end of 1992 prevented Biľak's trial.

Esteemed Leonid Il'ich,

We, conscious of the full responsibility for our decision, appeal to you with the following statement.

The basically correct post-January democratic process, the correction of mistakes and short-comings of the past, as well as the overall political management of society, have gradually eluded the control of the party's Central Committee. The press, radio, and television, which are effectively in the hands of right-wing forces, have influenced popular opinion to such an extent that elements hostile to the party have begun to take part in the political life of our country, without any opposition from the public. These elements are fomenting a wave of nationalism and chauvinism, and are provoking an anti-communist and anti-Soviet psychosis.

Our collective—the party leadership—has made a number of mistakes. We have not properly defended or put into effect the Marxist–Leninist norms of party work and above all the principles of democratic centralism. The party leadership is no longer able to defend itself successfully against attacks on socialism, and it is unable to organize either ideological or political resistance against the right-wing forces. The very existence of socialism in our country is under threat.

At present, all political instruments and the instruments of state power are paralyzed to a considerable degree. The right-wing forces have created conditions suitable for a counterrevo-lutionary coup.

In such trying circumstances we are appealing to you, Soviet communists, the leading representatives of the Communist Party of the Soviet Union, with a request for you to lend support and assistance with all the means at your disposal. Only with your assistance can the Czechoslovak Socialist Republic be extricated from the imminent danger of counterrevolution.

We realize that for both the Communist Party of the Soviet Union and the Soviet government, this ultimate step to preserve socialism in the Czechoslovak Socialist Republic will not be easy. Therefore, we will struggle with all our power and all our means. But if our strength and capabilities are depleted or fail to bring positive results, then our statement should be regarded as an urgent request and plea for your intervention and all-round assistance.

In connection with the complex and dangerous course of the situation in our country, we request that you treat our statement with the utmost secrecy, and for that reason we are writing directly to you, personally, in Russian.

Alois Indra   Drahomír Kolder   Antonín Kapek[8]   *Oldřich Švestka   Vasil Biľak*

---

[8] Kapek had previously written a letter of his own to Brezhnev in late July in which he deplored the "anti-socialist and anti-Soviet" trends in Czechoslovakia and requested "fraternal assistance" from the Soviet Union. Unlike this letter, Kapek's apparently had little or no impact.

DOCUMENT No. 73: The Bratislava Declaration, August 3, 1968

Source: "Zayavlenie kommunisticheskikh i rabochikh partii sotsialisticheskikh stran," *Pravda* (Moscow), 4 August 1968, p. 1; Vondrová & Navrátil, vol. 2, pp. 151–155.

The six communist party leaders from the USSR, Poland, Bulgaria, Hungary, East Germany and Czechoslovakia issued this joint declaration at the end of the Bratislava conference on August 3. The final document was based on a preliminary draft brought by the Soviet delegation. Czechoslovak officials were able to secure numerous small amendments to the text, but on the major points the Soviet delegates resisted pressure for modifications.

Some of the phraseology represented a genuine compromise between Czechoslovakia and the "Five." The declaration stipulated that "each fraternal party" must "take account of specific national features and conditions" when "deciding questions of socialist development." It also obliged the signatories to respect one another's "sovereignty, national independence, and territorial integrity."

Following the invasion, Soviet officials argued that those principles had to be understood within the context of the "laws of class struggle," and that Czechoslovakia could enjoy its "sovereignty," "national independence," and "territorial integrity" only by remaining a "socialist" state. Specific parts of the Bratislava declaration were cited as a justification for the armed intervention in Czechoslovakia. In particular, Soviet commentators emphasized that the declaration had enshrined "the common international duty of all the socialist countries" to undertake the "task of supporting, consolidating, and defending these gains" for the whole socialist commonwealth. Furthermore, Soviet officials argued that the declaration had bound the six governments to "increase their efforts to strengthen the defense capabilities of each socialist state" and to "bolster political and military cooperation within the Warsaw Pact." That, according to their post-August 21 justification, was one of the main objectives of the invasion.

"Statement by the Communist and Workers' Parties of Socialist Countries"

On 3 August 1968 a conference was held in Bratislava for representatives of the communist and workers' parties of the People's Republic of Bulgaria, the Hungarian People's Republic, the German Democratic Republic, the Polish People's Republic, the Union of Soviet Socialist Republics, and the Czechoslovak Socialist Republic. . . .

[Omitted passage lists the participants.]

Because the complicated international situation and the subversive acts of imperialism which are directed against the peace and the security of nations and against the cause of socialism, require the further cohesion of the countries of the socialist system, and also because the development of socialism involves new tasks the resolution of which is essential for the further unification of efforts by socialist states, officials from the communist and workers' parties of socialist countries believe it necessary to convene this meeting in Bratislava.

In deference to traditions, in conditions of absolute frankness, adherence to principles, and friendship of the fraternal parties, they considered topical questions concerning the struggle for socialism, the further strengthening of the socialist community, and the closing of ranks of the world communist movement. There was an exchange of opinions on problems connected with the current international situation and on the need to intensify the struggle against imperialism.

The officials from the communist and workers' parties considered ways of strengthening and developing fraternal cooperation among the socialist states.

In the years since the defeat of fascism and the accession to power of the working class, the peoples of European countries who set out on the path of socialism have achieved victories in all spheres of life. During these years the parties have overcome difficulties and gradually improved their work as they ensured in each socialist country the emergence of a powerful industrial base, as they transformed rural life, and as they achieved steady growth in national prosperity and the flowering of national culture. Millions of working people were mobilized for mature political life. The successes in building socialism and communism in the Soviet Union were especially great. The international influence of the socialist states and their role in solving significant questions of world politics have grown immeasurably.

The task of supporting, consolidating, and defending these gains, which were achieved through the heroic efforts and self-sacrificing labor of each nation, is the common international duty of all the socialist countries.[9] Such was the unanimous opinion of the participants in the conference, who displayed firm determination to develop and defend the socialist gains of their countries and to achieve new successes in the construction of socialism.

The fraternal parties are convinced, on the basis of their historical experience, that further progress along the path of socialism and communism is possible, but only through strict and consistent adherence to the laws of building a socialist society and above all through a consolidation of the leading role of the working class and its vanguard, the communist party. In this, each fraternal party decides all questions of further socialist development in a creative way, taking into account specific national features and conditions.[10]

Unwavering loyalty to Marxism–Leninism, efforts to educate the masses in the spirit of the ideas of socialism and proletarian internationalism, and a relentless struggle against bourgeois ideology and against all anti-socialist forces all guarantee success in strengthening the positions of socialism and thwarting imperialist conspiracies.

The fraternal parties uphold their unbreakable solidarity firmly and decisively, and maintain utmost vigilance against all attempts by imperialism and other anti-communist forces to weaken the leading role of the working class and the communist parties. They will never permit anyone to drive a wedge between the socialist states or to undermine the foundations of the socialist social order. In this regard, fraternal friendship and closed ranks are in keeping with the vital interests of our peoples and a reliable basis for solving the socioeconomic and political tasks on which the communist parties of our countries are working.

The fraternal parties believe it is their duty to demonstrate unyielding concern to increase the political activity of the working class, the peasants, the intelligentsia, and all working people to achieve comprehensive progress in the socialist social order and the further development of socialist democracy, as well as to improve the style and methods of party and state work based on the principles of democratic centralism.

The diverse tasks of building a socialist society in each of our countries are made considerably easier to solve through mutual aid and support. Fraternal ties expand and augment the opportunities of each socialist country. The participants in the conference expressed a firm desire to do everything they can to improve the all-round cooperation of their countries on the basis of the principles of equality, respect for sovereignty and national independence, territorial integrity, fraternal mutual assistance, and solidarity.[11]

The communist and workers' parties attach unusual significance to the effective use of the huge natural resources of our countries, applying the latest findings of science and technology and mastering the forms and methods of socialist farming. All this will ensure the further development of the economy and raise the material prosperity of the working people. An effective way of attaining these noble aims is to develop economic cooperation among the socialist countries on bilateral and multilateral bases. More significant than ever are improvements in the activities of the Council of Mutual Economic Assistance and the development of

---

[9] Czechoslovak officials did their best to get the Soviet leadership to modify this passage with a phrase that would pledge respect for specific national features, state sovereignty, territorial integrity, and the principle of non-interference in internal affairs. Soviet leaders were able to rebuff their attempted changes.

[10] This sentence was added at the insistence of the CPCz negotiators as a qualifier for the previous sentence.

[11] These principles do not include "non-interference in internal affairs," which in fact does not appear at all in the declaration.

cooperation and specialization carried out by the socialist countries, which will allow full use of the advantages of the international socialist division of labour.

In this connection, once again, the urgent need to hold economic consultations on the highest level, and in the shortest possible time, was confirmed.

The participants in the conference believe it is their duty to call people's attention to the fact that the aggressive policy of imperialism has caused the international situation to remain complicated and dangerous. In these conditions, the fraternal parties of the socialist countries, which are struggling to uphold universal peace and the security of nations and are organizing decisive resistance to the aggressive policy of imperialism while abiding by the principles of world cooperation among states with different social systems, once again confirm their readiness to harmonize and coordinate their actions on the international scene.

The working class, the peasants, the intelligentsia, and all working people desire peace and contentment for their countries and for all people on earth. The socialist countries have done, are doing, and will do all they can to ensure that these hopes come true. Our parties declare that in the future they, too, will cooperate in pursuing this noble task together with all communist and workers' parties and with all progressive forces in the world in the struggle for universal peace, freedom, independence, and social progress.

The communist and workers' parties of Bulgaria, Hungary, the German Democratic Republic, Poland, the Soviet Union, and Czechoslovakia once again solemnly proclaim their unyielding determination to continue supporting the heroic Vietnamese people in the future and to give them all necessary aid in their just struggle against the American aggressors.

We are also concerned about the situation in the Near East as a result of the aggressive policy of right-wing circles of Israel who are continuing to keep the region in a tense situation. Our parties will do all they can to liquidate the aftermath of Israeli aggression on the basis of the UN Security Council resolution of 22 November 1967, and to insist on the withdrawal of Israeli troops from occupied Arab territory.[12]

Examining the situation in Europe, the participants in the conference noted that the surge of revanchist, militarist, and neo-Nazi forces in West Germany directly affects the security of the socialist states and creates a threat to the cause of universal peace. In the future we will consistently pursue a coordinated policy on European matters, in keeping with the general interests of the socialist countries, and in the interest of European security. We will resist any attempts to revise the results of the Second World War and to change existing borders in Europe. We will continue to insist that the Munich agreement was invalid from its very conception; we will decisively support the German Democratic Republic, a socialist state of the German workers, which is defending the cause of peace. We will provide consistent aid to the Communist Party of Germany and all those forces fighting against militarism and revanchism, and for democratic progress.[13]

The communist parties of the socialist countries express their determination to achieve European security and to maintain the principles of the Bucharest Declaration and the Proclamation of the Conference of European Communist and Workers' Parties in Karlovy Vary. They are ready to do everything necessary to call a congress of the peoples of Europe in defense of peace on our continent. It is of decisive significance for the protection of peace throughout the world not to permit the breakdown of European peace. All our joint efforts will be directed toward the attainment of this aim, which affects the interests of all peoples.

Today, when the imperialist forces of the USA, the FRG, and other countries display their aggressiveness and are strenuously attempting to weaken the socialist community, officials of

---

[12] The UN Security Council resolution in question is Resolution No. 242.

[13] The Communist Party of Germany (KPD) was a small party in West Germany, not to be confused with the SED. The clause "all those forces fighting against militarism and revanchism and for democratic progress" was added at the insistence of the Czechoslovak delegates, and despite Ulbricht's objections.

the fraternal parties believe it is essential once again to emphasize the special significance of the Warsaw Pact. This pact, concluded by the socialist states in reply to the entry of revanchist West Germany into the aggressive, imperialist NATO bloc, was and remains a powerful factor for peace and security among the peoples of Europe. It serves as an invincible obstacle to all who want to revise the results of the Second World War. It reliably defends the gains of socialism and the sovereignty and independence of the fraternal states. It is aimed at strengthening European security and protecting world peace.

The current situation demands our increased efforts to improve the defense capabilities of each socialist state and of the entire socialist community. We must also strengthen political and military cooperation within the Warsaw Treaty Organization.

The participants in the conference believe it is their duty to reinforce as much as possible the cohesion of the international communist movement. They note that in recent times much work has been accomplished in preparing a new worldwide conference of communist and workers' parties. The fraternal parties hold this work in high regard and express the conviction that the forthcoming conference will be successful and will prove a serious contribution to the consolidation of all the revolutionary forces of today.

We believe more than ever that only a unified Marxist–Leninist world outlook, the role of the communist and workers' parties as the vanguard and leaders of society, and the socialist basis of the national economies of our states will serve as an effective means of guaranteeing the future cohesiveness of the socialist countries and of ensuring unity of action in the struggle for our common, great aims.

The parties attending the Bratislava conference present this Declaration, deeply convinced that it expresses positions and views in keeping with the interests of all fraternal countries and parties, and that it reflects the cause of inviolable friendship among the peoples of our countries and the interests of peace, democracy, national independence, and socialism.

DOCUMENT No. 74: Statement by the CPCz CC Presidium after the Talks at Čierna and Bratislava, August 6, 1968

Source: "Předsednictvo ÚV KSČ o výsledcích rozhovorů v Čierné a Bratislavě," *Rudé právo* (Prague), August 8, 1968, p. 1.

This brief statement, adopted by the CPCz CC Presidium at its regular meeting on August 6, conveys the optimism that most Czechoslovak officials and citizens felt in the immediate aftermath of the Čierna and Bratislava meetings. The presidium strongly endorsed the results of both sets of talks, and expressed gratitude to the citizenry of Czechoslovakia for displaying "political good sense" and "true socialist patriotism," and for maintaining "full confidence in the CPCz's policy." Although the statement includes a mild warning to the mass media in Czechoslovakia to refrain from provocative "reporting and commentary on events, especially in foreign policy," it offers no indication that the CPCz leadership intends to abide by Moscow's demand for the reimposition of censorship.

At its meeting on 6 August, the CPCz CC Presidium, in the presence of members of the CPCz CC Secretariat, discussed the outcome of the talks with the CPSU CC Politburo at Čierna nad Tisou. The presidium noted that in the four-day talks there had been a comprehensive and fruitful discussion that resulted in the adoption of significant conclusions for the benefit of future cooperation between the two fraternal parties. A significant decision emanating from the talks at Čierna was that a meeting would be convened among representatives of six communist and workers' parties in Bratislava. That meeting adopted a statement on the common position of the participants on major issues of socialist development and international relations.

The CPCz CC Presidium endorsed the procedure and work of the delegation of the CPCz CC Presidium at the Bratislava meeting. It noted that the proceedings and work of the delegation had contributed to the success of these talks.

The CPCz CC Presidium regards the outcome of the two meetings as the joint accomplishment of all participating delegations and a fresh impetus for the promotion of mutually beneficial relations among the fraternal parties and socialist countries on the basis of Marxism–Leninism and proletarian internationalism.

The CPCz CC Presidium expressed its appreciation to communists and all Czechoslovak citizens who in the past tempestuous days have shown full confidence in the policy of the CPCz and the Czechoslovak government and who, through their political good sense and increased work performance, have expressed their true socialist patriotism.

The CPCz CC Presidium expects workers in the press, radio, and television to continue working for the national and international interests of the Czechoslovak people and the state when reporting and commenting on events, especially in foreign policy, and to do so in the spirit of the policy of the CPCz and government.

The CPCz CC Presidium also reviewed preparations for the Extraordinary 14th Party Congress and, on the basis of remarks and proposals submitted by the CPCz CC political commission for the preparation of the congress, discussed the draft statutes of the Communist Party of Czechoslovakia. The draft will be published in *Rudé právo*, *Pravda*, and *Új Szó* on Saturday, 10 August, so that all members of the party will be informed and able to express their opinions. The draft statutes will be on the agenda of party bodies and organizations. Delegates to the congress must give special attention and consideration to the draft.

DOCUMENT No. 75: János Kádár's Speech at a Hungarian CC Plenum, August 7, 1968, Regarding Events since the Warsaw Meeting (Excerpts)

Source: PTTI, 288, F. 4/94 oe; Vondrová & Navrátil, vol. 2, pp. 161–164.

János Kádár delivered this two-hour speech, parts of which dealt with the Czechoslovak crisis, to an expanded session of the HSWP Central Committee a few days after he, Jenő Fock, and Zoltán Komócsin returned from the meeting in Bratislava. In contrast to the far more somber post-meeting assessments in Moscow and the other three bloc nations, Kádár tells the assembled delegates that the rift between Czechoslovakia and the other Warsaw Pact countries "has ceased to exist, and unity has been restored among our parties." The Hungarian leader expresses relief that "the contribution made by Čierna nad Tisou and Bratislava," with their emphasis on "political methods," had spared the "Five" Warsaw Pact allies the need to pursue "a much more difficult course." He concedes, however, that "internal developments in Czechoslovakia" were "not yet resolved" and might not be for a while, but he insists that the "conditions for the resolution of these problems are far more auspicious now" than before the Čierna and Bratislava meetings.

. . . Theoretically, it would have been entirely possible to avoid getting involved. We could have said we were not going to take part in the military preparations. But what would have come of that? We could see the anxiety of our Soviet comrades, of the Poles, and of the others, and naturally we had our own concerns, too, albeit less pronounced. What would it have meant if we had said we were not going to participate? In my view, it merely would have created greater anxiety. Nothing would have been achieved. On the contrary, it would have made for an even more complicated situation. Let me say quite frankly—since we all know the situation and the circumstances here—that these people would have pursued an even more unpredictable course of action.[14]

. . . The Bratislava meeting took place formally, so that we met on Friday—let me not get the days mixed up! First, and not in secret or *sub rosa*, the Soviet comrades informed our four parties about Čierna nad Tisou, and then, as was agreed, the Czechoslovak comrades joined us, and both sides informed us once more about Čierna nad Tisou. That was on Friday. The Soviets had prepared a draft communiqué and we agreed that we would take it as a starting point and that the plenary session the following day would not include opening speeches by the individual parties about such-and-such matters. Instead, by taking the draft as a starting point, we could set to work on a joint document that would express our positions. Any negotiation that was needed would be done when formulating the document. So on Friday night we agreed that we would not refer to the Warsaw Letter or to the standpoint of the CPCz Presidium because that would just take us back to where we were. There was no point in discussing this here any longer.

We took note of the information they presented about Čierna nad Tisou, and we agreed that all six parties together would declare to the whole world their unity and willingness to cooperate. Work on the second day actually concentrated on this. That's how the document was born; I make no claims about its stylistic merits, but its political content is good. It indirectly touches upon matters that have been the subject of discussion for 5–6 months: the leading role of the party, fundamental international laws of socialism, respect for national peculiarities, and so forth, as well as principles that demonstrate our unity and alliance from a different angle, that is, from the standpoint of the Warsaw Pact and other collective bodies. Without the slightest reservation, we can describe this as an exceptionally important document, a document that will have major implications.

---

[14] Kádár's phrase "these people" is a none-too-subtle reference to the Soviet Politburo.

The Czechs naturally announced that they will convene the presidium, since they had done nothing all week except negotiate with the Soviet comrades and then with us, that is how it went the whole week; so they will discuss what needs to be done, they will call party assemblies—I see that this has already been done—and they will carry on their work.

Finally, I would like to offer some conclusions without going into great detail.

Our Politburo believes that Čierna nad Tisou and Bratislava gave a fillip to the solution of the Czechoslovak question, or rather to its international conception. The main significance of the meeting—speaking just among ourselves—is that the conflict which arose between our six parties after 8 July has ceased to exist and unity has been restored to our parties. This is very important. I believe there is no need to stress the contribution made by Čierna nad Tisou and Bratislava or what this meant, and how many difficulties we have avoided. I think that even without any analysis, and without a great deal of imagination, everyone can envisage what sort of situation and what sort of problems could have arisen had the conflict between our five parties and the Czechoslovak party continued.

The second important point to be mentioned here is that political methods held sway among our fraternal parties in approaching the Czechoslovak situation—and now we are looking at it from an international point of view. This is very important.

The third conclusion I would also like to mention without dwelling on it is that the question of internal developments in Czechoslovakia still remains to be resolved, it is not yet settled. I could, perhaps, add that today domestic and international conditions for a solution of these problems are far more auspicious than at the time when our five parties were arrayed against the Czechoslovak side.

Another conclusion is that if it depends on us, or provided we could offer assistance in any form, the HSWP should continue to contribute in various forms and ways to a positive solution of the Czechoslovak situation.

Another question I wanted to mention, again without further analyzing it but so that we may reckon on it, is that the internal political situation in Czechoslovakia will become critical in the near future. I would say that this is an essential process and it can be regarded as a positive one. For if the situation there does not come to a head, if there is no unequivocal polarization, and if there is no healthy struggle, we will return to where we were. In that case the situation between us and the Czechoslovak side will once again become critical. We must be prepared for this, and I am not saying this as a clairvoyant but because this is absolutely evident and we must reckon on it in our future work. Besides, I would like to say that we had a variety of meetings with the Czechoslovak comrades over there, we talked to the members of the presidium as well as with others—in different psychological conditions—and they, too, reckon on this and are anticipating that the situation will now become critical and the political struggle that inevitably arises from a clash of different views will escalate. This is something to be expected.

DOCUMENT No. 76: Report by Soviet Ambassador Stepan Chervonenko to the Kremlin on His Meeting with Alexander Dubček, August 7, 1968

Source: AVPRF, F. 059, Op. 58, P. 124, D. 573, Ll. 183–185.

Soviet Ambassador to Czechoslovakia Stepan Chervonenko recorded his August 7, 1968, meeting with Alexander Dubček in this top-secret report to the Kremlin. Chervonenko requested the meeting on instructions from the Soviet Politburo, and conveyed a number of "concerns": about the unofficial clubs and political organizations, the "hostile" tone of the mass media, the delay in bifurcating the ČSSR Interior Ministry, the "vindictive" campaign against the 99 workers from the Auto-Praha factory, and Dubček's failure to replace certain key officials.

Chervonenko's conclusions that Dubček was oblivious to the "complexity of the situation," and "not yet ready to embark on a consistent and decisive struggle" against "rightist and counterrevolutionary forces," made a deep impression in Moscow. Soviet leaders promptly conveyed a copy of the report to the East German leader, Walter Ulbricht, so that he could cover many of the same points when he met a few days later top CPCz officials in Karlovy Vary. Some officials in Moscow welcomed the report as a vindication of their hard-line views and a further reason to proceed quickly with military action; others were disappointed that the CPCz leadership had refused to "close ranks with the healthy forces," whose strength and appeal Chervonenko greatly overstates at the end of his report.

. . . I asked Cde. Dubček to let me know what had already been done since the meetings in Čierna nad Tisou and Bratislava, and also what he personally, as CPCz CC first secretary, and the CPCz CC Presidium as a whole intended to do in the near future—that is, before the CPCz congress—to launch a struggle against the rightist and anti-socialist forces. I said I wanted to communicate all this to the CPSU CC Politburo, which had expressed confidence in him, Dubček, and in Cde. Černík and which hopes that the mutually agreed conditions needed to overcome the difficulties that have arisen between our parties will be firmly and consistently carried out by the Czechoslovak leadership. With regard to this I added that if the Czechoslovak comrades honestly and wholeheartedly wage a struggle against the rightist and anti-socialist forces, they can count on support and assistance from the CPSU and the Soviet Union.

I also emphasized that the fraternal parties that were represented at the Bratislava conference were avidly following and wanted to see what the CPCz leadership would do and what conclusions it had drawn from the Čierna negotiations and the Bratislava Declaration that it signed. They expected that the CPCz leadership would consistently abide by the provisions of the declaration, which specified the course to be followed in accordance with the internal interests of the country and the common goals of the socialist commonwealth. All those in the world communist movement and in the CPCz who realistically evaluated the situation were aware that the Čierna and Bratislava meetings had given the CPCz leadership ample leeway to act without losing face. Hence, they expected major, concrete steps and actions on the part of the CPCz leadership.

Dubček and Lenárt listened attentively and made notes of what was said. Then Dubček said that after the meeting in Čierna nad Tisou (he confirmed the profound and penetrating analysis of the situation in the ČSSR that had been offered by the Soviet leadership, particularly in the speeches of Brezhnev, Kosygin, Suslov, and other comrades) and the conference in Bratislava, the CPCz CC Presidium began to take certain measures. True, he, Dubček, had become somewhat ill and had to stay in Bratislava after the conference until Tuesday, and thus he had not yet had the chance to think through and discuss things with his comrades. Even so, at the first session of the CPCz CC Presidium, which was held on 6 August, several concrete matters were already raised, although the presidium meeting as a whole was devoted to a review of the state of preparations for the 14th CPCz Congress.

Dubček began to say that there was only a month left before the congress and the documents for the congress were still in the process of being worked out. So far, they had succeeded in publishing only the draft of the new CPCz statutes. A discussion about the congress documents lies ahead, and even now work is under way by delegates to the congress. . . .

He, Dubček, is going to be busy forming a new CPCz CC and other new party organs. The nature of the delegates and of the comrades who had been proposed for membership in the leading CPCz CC organs were the basis for hoping that the congress for the most part would avoid creating any stir with respect to the general line (the congress would reaffirm the post-January course and the Action Program) and with respect to the leading officials in the CPCz and the Czechoslovak government. He emphasized that the delegates this time had, in effect, been elected by local party organizations, and then the regional and provincial party conferences had confirmed their qualifications. The same procedure had been followed for those recommended for election to the leading CPCz CC organs. In other words, the majority of the delegates and of the officials proposed for election to the CC enjoyed the full confidence of the party rank-and-file. This would be highly advantageous for the new membership of the CC.

The preparations for the congress, Dubček continued, are being conducted in such a way that they will not permit any weakening of the leading role of the CPCz. This is the foundation of the new draft of the CPCz statutes. He, Dubček, sees difficulties ahead and believes there will be a fierce struggle over the congress and especially over the congress documents, including the adoption of the new party statutes. There will be harsh criticism at the congress, especially about the CPCz CC's activities in the pre-January period; and obviously there will be no shortage of hostile remarks aimed at the CPCz leadership that was chosen in January and after January 1968. Nevertheless, the prevailing atmosphere at the congress should be the same as the atmosphere at the regional and provincial party conferences that took place in July. . . .

Dubček then referred to the importance of the Čierna meeting and Bratislava conference, both of which he held in high regard. He said that the CPCz leadership would follow up on the conclusions and documents from those meetings, and that the spirit of the declaration and the guidelines it established would help the CPCz and would be incorporated into the basic framework of the 14th CPCz Congress.

Dubček noted that the mass media had changed their behavior after the meetings in Čierna nad Tisou and Bratislava, although serious work in this regard still lies ahead. Apparently it will not be possible to avoid controversy and clashes with journalists in the process. He wrote down a number of points that I cited from reports in the press and on radio and television on 4, 5, 6, and 7 August. My interpreter noted that the problems of the mass media will not be so severe at the congress, since measures will be adopted before the congress to establish an orderly arrangement for the media's activities. He said that the CC Presidium had ordered the comrades responsible for the mass media to put together proposals and a definite schedule for statements in the press and on radio and television by prominent party officials, statesmen, leading public figures, scholars, workers, and others. Lenárt had been instructed to devise a plan for specifying and publicly disseminating the main provisions of the Bratislava Declaration through the media. Along with this positive propaganda campaign, an effort will be made to thwart and repulse hostile, anti-communist attacks.

When asked to clarify this point, Dubček and Lenárt declared that practical steps will also be taken with respect to individual organs of the mass media, but they said nothing concrete about their intentions.

Dubček reported that on 7 August he, along with Černík and other comrades, had been busy considering measures that would have to be taken regarding the various clubs and newly-formed organizations with anti-communist leanings. A draft law about the National Front was considered, as was the draft of a law that would give government organs the right to ban the activity of various clubs and organizations and the right to break up demonstrations, spontaneous meetings, and other such things. The National Assembly would be approving these laws within the next two to three weeks. Even before that, steps and measures would be adopted to prevent clubs and organizations from acting outside the National Front.

In response to my question, Dubček was not able to say exactly when the question of the separation of the State Security organs from the Interior Ministry was to be settled. He acknowledged that if such a step were adopted, Pavel would resign immediately, and this would kill two birds with one stone. But Dubček did not indicate clearly enough how and when this would be done; he told me that an appropriate law must first be adopted, and so forth.

With respect to the campaign by rightist and anti-Soviet forces against the workers from the Auto-Praha factory, Dubček said that he had ordered a group of comrades to investigate the matter and report back to the Central Committee about what had transpired. He had not yet had time to read the group's report because he had received it only a short time before I arrived. He again said that the workers' letter to their "Soviet friends" was sound and proper, and he himself saw nothing wrong with their decision to send a letter to the Soviet Union. Letters of this sort, he noted, were sent almost every day in large numbers. He condemned Císař's behavior, although there had been reports that Císař was asked to come to the factory to mollify the workers after a threat of spontaneous action arose there. Dubček did not agree with this interpretation of the reason for Císař's appearance at the factory. He believed that Císař had played a deleterious role by addressing the Czech National Council and by identifying himself with the crackdown on the workers who signed the letter appearing in *Pravda*. Dubček said that the CC Presidium would take up the question of Císař's behavior.

Dubček did not mention anything concrete about personnel changes in the CC Presidium and other central organs. . . .

I did not insist that he answer the question because I suspected that he might be uncomfortable about speaking openly in Lenárt's presence.

In closing, Dubček said that the CC Presidium would meet again on 13 August for further scrutiny of the measures and steps required of the CPCz CC in light of the conclusions and provisions of the Čierna and Bratislava meetings.

This conversation bears out the general conclusion that Dubček does not see the complexity of the political situation, or at least that he approaches it in a way very different from the approach of the healthy forces in the CPCz leadership. There is also no reason to believe that on this occasion he was sincere and fully candid with the Soviet representative. The impression emerges that he is still internally torn and that at least for the time being he is not yet ready to embark on a consistent and decisive struggle against the rightist forces both within and outside the CPCz. In these circumstances, evidently, additional steps are needed both on the part of the CPSU and on the part of the other parties to apply pressure on him, Dubček, and on Černík.

At the same time, a propitious situation has emerged—and this is precisely the greatest benefit of the meetings in Čierna nad Tisou and Bratislava—for the establishment of a front to struggle against the rightist and anti-socialist forces, using conventional political and organizational forms and methods, at least for the time being. The healthy forces in the CPCz Presidium have taken heart and consolidated themselves, and they have closed ranks so that they are now a majority. If Dubček and Černík would join forces with them and rely on them, they would receive support in this struggle from an absolute majority of party and state officials in the center, in the provinces, in the regions, and in the locales. They would receive support from the CPCz and a majority of the people.

DOCUMENT No. 77: Summary Report and Transcript of Telephone Conversation between Leonid Brezhnev and Alexander Dubček, August 9, 1968

Source: Sb. KV, Z/S 8; Vondrová & Navrátil, vol. 2, pp. 164–167.

This transcript records one of several important telephone conversations that Brezhnev had with Dubček in the two weeks following the Bratislava conference. Brezhnev repeatedly expresses his concern that the CPCz leader has yet to implement personnel changes, reorganizations and social crackdowns that the Czechoslovak authorities had supposedly agreed to at the Čierna nad Tisou and Bratislava meetings. Although Brezhnev makes no explicit or even implicit threats of military intervention in this discussion, he does stress Dubček's need "to understand certain increasing concerns here" and how "in my opinion, this is very serious now."

(See also Document No. 81.)

---

9 August 1968

Cde. Brezhnev greets Cde. Dubček and inquires how things are going. A short conversation on general matters follows.

Then Cde. Brezhnev says that the Soviet party and people are concerned about a number of unpleasant matters appearing in the press and the remarks of Císař and others. One gains the impression that the proper conclusions have not been drawn from the meeting. Then Cde. Brezhnev goes on to say the following:

Brezhnev: . . . We understand perfectly well that it is the rightists who are doing such things, but communists and the people do not understand and have different attitudes toward the actions of the leadership as a whole. It is becoming difficult to hold back the wave of protests and replies to all this. Besides, we are gaining the impression that the commitments we approved with you in Čierna nad Tisou are not being fulfilled, as well as those approved at the bilateral talks in the presence of the entire CPCz CC Presidium, and also the personnel questions agreed upon at the multilateral conference.[15]

In such circumstances, Alexander Stepanovich, I wanted to ask in what way we can help. . . .

Dubček: I understand your concerns, Cde. Brezhnev. But at the moment I am not asking for any assistance.

Brezhnev: In analyzing what is happening in your country now and in view of all the information we have at our disposal, we have come to the conclusion that the rightists, and you know the people I'm referring to, once again are waging organized, subversive work against the decisions we adopted in Čierna nad Tisou.

Dubček: Yes, we also attribute everything negative in our activities to right-wing tendencies.

Brezhnev: In connection with this, Sasha, I would like to emphasize that we are now living through a very trying period. In many ways it will define our future links and relations. I always spoke the truth and was honest in keeping with circumstances and the situation. I have come to the conviction, the firm conviction, that you have the strength and people in the Presidium—the healthy forces—on whom you can rely and who will give you everything. The only serious

---

[15] In the last few years of his life, Dubček denied that he had made any specific commitments on personnel changes at Čierna, but the issue is by no means clear-cut, especially in light of the speech Dubček gave at the September 1969 plenum of the CPCz CC. For further discussion of this matter, see Document No. 85.

matter is your decision, whether to rely on these forces, to bring them close to you and to lead them in the struggle against the Right. I am telling you this because during the days we met I saw your concern, and along with it I noticed your doubts and vacillations. Therefore I want to tell you once more, Sasha, that without determined people, without determined assistance, without people dedicated to our cause, you will not be able to cope with the Right. Everything now depends on victory over the Right. Either we strengthen what is sacred to us—friendship between the CPCz and the CPSU—or we return to the difficult problems and decisions we were encountering until the meetings in Čierna nad Tisou and the conference in Bratislava.

Dubček: Černík and Lenárt are working on measures to carry out the agreements reached in Čierna nad Tisou.

Brezhnev: Well, to be matter-of-fact, Sasha, when do you expect to take up the question of personnel in accordance with the agreement we reached?

Dubček: That's a very complicated question and you know we cannot solve it without a plenary session. We are thinking of calling a Central Committee plenum in the near future and will probably take up these questions there.[16]

Brezhnev: But has a date been set for the beginning of your plenum's work?

Dubček: No. On Tuesday we'll consider this question and make a decision about the date of the Central Committee plenum.[17] But I think we'll convene the plenum in about ten days.[18]

Brezhnev: And then, at the plenum, you expect to take up the question of personnel?

Dubček: Yes, that's a question for the plenum. We can't decide it until the plenum meets.

Brezhnev: And the question of dividing the Ministry of the Interior. Evidently for that, it is not necessary to call a plenum. You remember then, at the meeting, that Cde. Černík, Cde. Smrkovský, and you said that this question can be resolved literally in a matter of several days, and your suggestion of candidates for the second post was a good one—Šalgovič.[19] All the same, how do you expect to solve this question, when do you expect to solve it?

Dubček: Our comrades are now considering this question but, of course, it also cannot be solved in a matter of two or three days.

Brezhnev: But Cde. Černík said very specifically at the meeting that in the course of five days he would be able to give Smrkovský a document. Smrkovský said that as soon as he received the document from Černík, the National Assembly would act favorably within five days on this question, and I think that the agreement was absolutely concrete and clear. I don't understand what new questions have arisen on this score.

Dubček: Purely organizational matters involving the structure of the ministry in connection with the division of Slovakia into a separate republic.[20]

---

[16] August 29, 1968, was eventually set for the plenum to which Dubček refers here, according to his speech at the September 1969 plenum of the CPCz CC (ÚSD, AÚV KSČ, F. 01, Sv. 210, A.j. 131). Presumably, that date was arranged by the Presidium at its meeting on August 13, as Dubček promised Brezhnev during this conversation.

[17] The CPCz Presidium normally met on Tuesdays. The Tuesday to which Dubček referred here was August 13.

[18] The date was actually set for somewhat later—on August 29. The difference between this later date and a date that would have been "in about ten days' time" (i.e., by August 19) was crucial because the Slovak party congress was due to start on August 26. Soviet leaders wanted the crisis to be resolved before that congress convened.

[19] The post in question was the head of the State Security (*Státní bezpečnost*, or StB) organs. Viliam Šalgovič was working for the Soviet KGB all through the crisis, and he supervised the StB's operations on behalf of the Soviet Union during and after the invasion.

[20] The proposed establishment of a federal Czechoslovak state in 1968, with separate Czech and Slovak republic-level governments alongside the federal organs, had created a good deal of uncertainty about the precise demarcation of functions and responsibilities.

Brezhnev: Alexander Stepanovich, I realize that you're very busy but I ask you personally to see how matters are going on these questions so that the comrades working on them don't drag out the decisions over a very long time.

Dubček: Yes, I'm busy with all this, I am personally following these matters.

Brezhnev: Sasha, I wanted to talk about another question. This concerns the witch-hunt against the workers of the Auto-Praha factory who signed the letter to *Pravda*.[21] If you remember, before this letter was published the Soviet ambassador showed it to you, and you said it was a very good letter. Yes, and it was good. That letter contains absolutely nothing contrary to, say, the spirit of our declaration in Bratislava. And I can't understand at all why such a situation is permitted where Císař organizes attacks on honest, good representatives of the working class, from one of the best enterprises in your country.

Dubček: That is the doing of the right-wing which expected different results from our talks. This is an attack by the Right. We spoke to Černík yesterday, and we will consider this and then take steps so that it doesn't spread to other factories and so that the press stops making a fuss about it.

Brezhnev: Well, and how are things as regards fulfillment of the other conditions agreed upon and approved by us, together, in Čierna nad Tisou?

Dubček: Černík and Lenárt are working on measures to implement the agreement, measures to prohibit spontaneous meetings.

Brezhnev: These meetings, as far as I know, are no longer spontaneous. They are being instigated by Císař and other anti-party elements.

Dubček: I was told that Císař took part in them. If that is so, then it is the work of right-wing-oriented forces. But I ordered an analysis of this question and an investigation of Císař's actions.

Brezhnev: Of course, that's good, if investigations of the activities of Císař are regular and objective. But all this depends on who does the investigating, Sasha. I think you should rely on the healthy forces in the CPCz CC Presidium, on the comrades who were always close to you—close to you in your work in Slovakia and in your work in the CPCz CC Presidium.[22] They'll fully support you in the fight against the Right if you, personally, accept their support. This is particularly serious now when the struggle with the Right has entered the most trying and decisive moment. In such conditions it is especially important to have united, collective action by the healthy forces and to be courageous. I think that you, yourself, understand this well.

Dubček: Yes, we take all decisions collectively and with the full approval of all members of the CC Presidium.

Brezhnev: In a word, Sasha, I wanted to remind you in this call about our agreements in Čierna nad Tisou and in Bratislava. I wanted you to understand certain increasing concerns here. These decisions are not being fulfilled and I wanted to request that you think about this and find the time and the means to carry out what was agreed upon. In my opinion, this is very serious now.

Dubček: We are working on these questions, Cde. Brezhnev.

Brezhnev: We wish you success, we wish you all the best, Sasha. Good-bye.

---

[21] This refers to the 99 workers at the Czechoslovak Auto-Praha factory in Prague, who supposedly co-authored and signed a petition that appeared in the Soviet press on July 30, 1968.

[22] This presumably is a reference to Biľak and perhaps to others who Brezhnev mistakenly thought were Slovaks.

DOCUMENT No. 78: Cables from the Czechoslovak Ambassadors in London and Washington on U.S. Reactions to the Situation in Czechoslovakia, August 10–12, 1968

Source: Sb. KV, K—Archiv MZV, Dispatches No. 7501, 7529/1968; Vondrová & Navrátil, vol. 2, pp. 167–169.

These two cables, the first from the Czechoslovak ambassador to London, Miloslav Růžek, and the second from Ambassador Karel Duda in Washington, reflect the tepid U.S. response to the continuing crisis. Ambassador Růžek reports on a meeting between Rusk and Dobrynin and on the U.S. and British reaction to the Čierna and Bratislava conferences. Ambassador Duda reports that the Johnson administration remains committed to a policy of "non-involvement in any form," and analysts have concluded that the Čierna and Bratislava meetings have produced favorable results for the Prague Spring, lessening any possibility of outright military intervention.

Dispatch from London:

According to reliable information from American quarters in London, after Rusk heard about the discovery of American weapons near Sokolovo, he summoned Dobrynin and told him categorically that the Americans had absolutely nothing to do with the entire affair.[23] He added that the anonymous insinuations as well as reports in the Soviet press had made it blatantly clear that this was a gross provocation. Rusk declared that if this or similar provocations were to lead to military intervention against the ČSSR, congress would refuse to approve the Nuclear Non-Proliferation Treaty. The Americans carefully assessed the outcome of the meetings in Čierna and Bratislava and have concluded that we achieved even more than had been expected. They did not understand what had caused the turnabout in the harsh position of the USSR, and they believe that we laid down the condition for the withdrawal of Soviet troops before the opening of negotiations. They believe that the results of Čierna are probably permanent, but that economic difficulties could be expected in our country which will cause discontent and could be exploited politically. They are now closely monitoring ČSSR–USSR economic relations to see whether there will be a curtailment and deterioration of Soviet deliveries. The British were surprised by the favorable outcome at Čierna; before the meeting they had thought we would retreat by restoring press censorship and consenting to at least the partial stationing of Soviet troops on our territory.

* * *

Dispatch from Washington:

All interested U.S. parties last week gave maximum attention to the outcome of negotiations at Čierna and Bratislava.

The only official reaction was a comment by the State Department spokesman, who reiterated the thesis about U.S. non-involvement in any form. He said the Bratislava formulation regarding U.S. subversive activities was regrettable and an unfounded accusation. Official circles look upon the results of the negotiations very favorably. They attach greatest significance to the victory of the moderate forces in the Soviet leadership, which might also help the further improvement of relations with the U.S.

Compared to last week, the press and other media have been paying less attention to Czechoslovak problems, but the major papers continue to devote front-page coverage to the

---

[23] Dean Rusk was the U.S. secretary of state; Anatolii Dobrynin was the Soviet ambassador in Washington.

situation in our country. Reports and commentaries show a lack of detailed knowledge about the negotiations and the concessions made by both sides. Commentaries are therefore mainly confined to speculation either about the reasons that a moderate line prevailed or about developments in the weeks to come, as well as the long-term repercussions. Their main source of information and conjectures is our press. The American press generally regards the present state of affairs to be temporary and soon to be followed by more negotiations. A further deterioration of relations in the near future is not ruled out, however.

The sympathy of the U.S. public and of Congress are unquestionably on the side of the ČSSR, albeit with different motivations. Expressions of sympathy for us in Congress and often in the press are accompanied by harsh attacks against the USSR.

DOCUMENT No. 79: Cables between Moscow and East Berlin Regarding the Approaching Czechoslovak–East German Meeting in Karlovy Vary, August 10–11, 1968

Source: ÚSD, Sb. KV, Z/S—MID Nos. 31, 32; Vondrová & Navrátil, vol. 2, p. 167.

This exchange of cables preceded a hastily arranged visit by East German leader Walter Ulbricht to Karlovy Vary, where he held a formal round of talks with Dubček, and his top aides. The first dispatch, from Brezhnev to Ulbricht, was transmitted via the Soviet ambassador in East Berlin, Pyotr Abrasimov, on August 10. In it, the Soviet leader briefly summarizes his phone conversation of the previous day with Dubček and passes on a copy of a cable he had just received from the Soviet ambassador in Prague, Stepan Chervonenko. The second cable, from Ambassador Abrasimov to Brezhnev on August 11, conveys Ulbricht's reply.

Ulbricht traveled to Karlovy Vary of his own accord (and at his own invitation, not the CPCz's). But he closely coordinated the whole trip with Brezhnev who sought to press for the "scrupulous fulfillment" of the Bratislava Declaration and the "full implementation of the agreements reached at Čierna nad Tisou." The East German leader, who firmly believed a military solution was necessary in Czechoslovakia, cabled back that he "had no illusions about the likely results of the forthcoming meeting." After his talks at Karlovy Vary, Ulbricht reported to Moscow that Czechoslovakia's "creeping counterrevolution" could no longer be halted.

Dispatch to Berlin:

Visit Cde. Ulbricht and tell him you have been empowered to inform him personally about the following communication from the Soviet ambassador in the ČSSR, Cde. Chervonenko, regarding a talk he had with Cde. Dubček at the suggestion of Cde. Brezhnev.

In addition, Cde. Brezhnev asked to tell you that on 9 August he talked by phone with Cde. Dubček and expressed interest in the way the results of the Čierna nad Tisou conference and the Declaration by the communist parties in Bratislava were being received within the party and by the people.[24]

The main emphasis of the phone conversation by Cde. Brezhnev was on the need to implement the agreements reached during the talks in Čierna nad Tisou, and particularly:

— the need for steps to control the mass media; and
— the need for steps to halt the activities of the Social Democratic Party and disband the clubs.

Cde. Brezhnev expressed concern about the incorrect explanation that the press was offering of the results of the conference and about the improper remarks by Cde. Císař.

During the phone conversation with Cde. Dubček, Cde. Brezhnev emphasized the need for the strict observance of the agreements reached between the leaders of the fraternal parties at the consultations in Čierna nad Tisou and in Bratislava.

Cde. Brezhnev hopes that during your bilateral meeting with the Czechoslovak comrades, you, too, Cde. Ulbricht, will give primary emphasis to the need for scrupulous fulfillment of the declaration of the fraternal parties, as well as to the need for the full implementation of the agreements reached at the meeting in Čierna nad Tisou, about which Cde. Brezhnev informed the fraternal parties in Bratislava in the presence of Cde. Dubček and Cde. Černík.

(The text of the communication from Soviet Ambassador Chervonenko is enclosed.)
Confirm by telegram.

* * *

---

[24] See Document No. 77.

Dispatch from Berlin:

After thanking me for the information, Cde. Ulbricht emphasized that during the forthcoming meeting in Karlovy Vary most of their attention will be devoted to the need for the comprehensive fulfillment of the declaration by the fraternal parties and for the full implementation of the accords agreed on in Čierna nad Tisou.

Cde. Ulbricht noted that he had no illusions about the likely results of the forthcoming meeting with the Czechoslovak leadership, since he views Dubček as an "adroit bourgeois diplomat who says one thing and thinks and does another." Clear evidence of this, in his view, can be seen in the publication just after the Bratislava conference of the draft of the new CPCz statutes, which permit factional activities within the party.[25] He also mentioned Dubček's latest conversation with the Soviet ambassador, in which Dubček did not give a concrete answer to a single one of the questions asked.

Cde. Ulbricht assumes that after the meeting in Karlovy Vary he will have a clearer idea of the line of the current CPCz leadership.

In conclusion, Cde. Ulbricht said that after his trip to Czechoslovakia he will fly directly to the Baltic Sea for a holiday. Cde. Honecker will stay behind as the acting head of the SED CC Politburo and will keep me informed about the results of the meeting in Karlovy Vary.

11 August 1968

P. Abrasimov

---

[25] The draft CPCz statutes were published as a 16-page supplement to *Rudé právo* and other newspapers on August 10.

DOCUMENT No. 80: CPSU CC Politburo Message to Alexander Dubček, August 13, 1968

Source: ÚSD, AÚV KSČ, F. 02/1; Vondrová & Navrátil, vol. 2, pp. 181–183.

The Soviet Politburo transmitted this brief message via the Soviet embassy in Prague on August 13; it was given to Dubček the next day. The communiqué addressed a spate of recent articles in the Czechoslovak press that were "unambiguously anti-socialist and anti-Soviet" in nature. The Politburo's intent was to persuade Dubček to launch an immediate crackdown on the Czechoslovak press, and disavow General Václav Prchlík who was the subject of a number of positive articles. The Politburo message demands to know whether the Prague daily Mladá fronta *is correct in asserting that "Prchlík still has the full confidence of the CPCz CC Presidium."*

Two days later, on August 15, the Czechoslovak Defense Ministry issued a statement of disapproval of the comments Prchlík had made at his news conference on July 15.

(On Gen. Prchlík, see also Documents Nos. 54 and 57.)

On 13 August 1968 Cde. Chervonenko handed Cde. Dubček the following message:

We have several times drawn the attention of the CPCz leadership to a series of grave facts demonstrating that the Czechoslovak side is clearly violating the agreement concluded at Čierna nad Tisou, which required that all the mass media—the press, radio, and television—be placed under the supervision of the CPCz Central Committee and the government, and that all anti-socialist and anti-Soviet publications be suspended.

Over the past few days several press outlets have carried fresh materials that are unambiguously anti-Soviet and anti-socialist. These materials distort the nature of the talks between our parties and the meeting in Bratislava; they are part of an attempt that is being made to impair relations between the USSR and the ČSSR and to arouse the mistrust and animosity of the Czechoslovak people toward the fraternal socialist countries.

These are not merely a few articles but an organized campaign. An especially inflammatory role is being played by *Literární listy*, *Mladá fronta*, *Reportér*, and *Práce*, which stubbornly continue to publish slanderous fabrications about the Soviet Union and the other fraternal countries. These periodicals are the mouthpiece of the right-wing, anti-socialist forces. Issue number 24 (8 August) of *Literární listy* carried an article entitled "From Warsaw to Bratislava," in which—incredible as it may seem—the policy of the fraternal socialist countries is compared to Hitler's policy and the press of the fraternal socialist countries is equated with the Goebbels propaganda machine. The paper brazenly states that "the professional mentality of the propaganda machine has not changed, insofar as it takes advantage of its monopoly and thereby skews all information, thus creating a deliberate and well-conceived lack of information."

The paper describes journalists in the other socialist countries as "publicist lackeys" and shamelessly speaks of "the rising cohorts of scribes who are capable of anything and who, on instruction from their ideological chiefs, have opened fire . . . on 'the Czechoslovak counter-revolution'."

The article "Friendship and Politics," featured in the same issue of *Literární listy*, is permeated by the same polemical, anti-Soviet spirit. Following the example of the bourgeois press, it propagates various slanders and filthy insinuations directed against the objectives and policy of the Soviet Union. The paper states: "Soviet leaders evidently did not trust the ability and desire of the whole people in Czechoslovakia to sustain and advance socialism voluntarily and democratically, and probably believed the only guarantee of the alliance could come from certain individuals."

Mladá fronta of 10 August carries an insulting assessment of the Bratislava Declaration and, with the most inflammatory of intentions, writes that "Bratislava is not the end but the beginning of discussion, possibly even of polemics. . . ."

In its most recent issue in August, the journal *Reportér* features an article entitled "The Luxury of Illusions." This article contains hate-filled diatribes against the Soviet Union and the other socialist countries and vilifies the socialist system. *Reportér* declares with impertinence that "we are threatening the bureaucracy, which slowly but surely was submerging socialism on a global scale. For this we can hardly expect to earn its fraternal solidarity or a spirit of mutual understanding or a full identity of views on questions under discussion. What is at issue is that we are moving toward the liquidation of the absolute power of a bureaucratic caste, which the Stalinist model of socialism has produced on an international scale."

An orchestrated, vociferous campaign has been unleashed and is spreading in defense of the statements by General Prchlík against the Warsaw Treaty Organization. We realize this is not a question of General Prchlík himself, but of using his name to launch more and more attacks against the Warsaw Pact. In this context we find it impossible to understand the statement in *Mladá fronta* (if we are to believe the paper) that Prchlík still has the full confidence of the CPCz CC Presidium.[26]

Hence, there is every reason to regard the emerging situation as a violation of the agreements reached at Čierna nad Tisou. This is the result not only of the activities of the right-wing forces, but also of the "non-interference" practiced by the CPCz and the government in these matters, which, in essence, is evolving into the *de facto* encouragement of anti-socialist elements. We state all this with full responsibility.

As you will surely understand, it would be only natural if we were to react to such statements openly, oppose these provocative affronts, and declare that it was your side that has violated the Čierna nad Tisou accord. However, we do not want to pursue such a course, and we hope that effective measures will be taken against periodicals such as *Literární listy*, *Mladá fronta*, *Reportér*, and *Práce*, whose activities are inspired by anti-Sovietism.

The unrestrained and hostile attacks in the Czechoslovak publications mentioned above are regarded in Moscow as extremely serious and critical.

[26] After a month of Soviet pressure against Prchlík's July 15th remarks about the Warsaw Pact, the Czechoslovak Defense Ministry issued a disavowal two days after transmission of this communication. The statement was published in all major Czechoslovak newspapers the following day. Although it is unclear whether there was a direct connection between the Soviet Politburo's message and the Czechoslovak Defense Ministry's belated disavowal of Prchlík's remarks, the evidence strongly suggests that the complaints voiced by Soviet leaders, both in this document and through other channels, were the main factor behind the ČSSR Defense Ministry's actions. (See, for example, the top-secret memorandum "Stanovisko Vojenské rady MNO: Případ V. Prchlíka," 13 August 1968, in VHA, F. Sekretariat MNO, 1968–1969, 129/AM.)

DOCUMENT No. 81: Transcript of Leonid Brezhnev's Telephone Conversation with Alexander Dubček, August 13, 1968

Source: APRF, Prot. No. 38; Vondrová & Navrátil, vol. 2, pp. 172–181.

On August 13, General Secretary Brezhnev called Dubček to admonish him for not taking immediate steps to reverse the Prague Spring reforms. A word-for-word transcription of this critical and dramatic conversation was apparently made possible by a KGB tape recording system which enabled Soviet leaders to keep track of important telephone calls.

In this conversation, Brezhnev adopts a far more aggressive and belligerent tone than in a call four days previously. The transcript records him repeatedly accusing Dubček of "outright deceit" and of "blatantly sabotaging the agreements reached at Čierna and Bratislava." The Soviet leader also issues oblique warnings about "the emergence of an entirely new situation . . . forcing [the Soviet Union] to consider new, independent measures that would defend both the CPCz and the cause of socialism in Czechoslovakia."

Midway through Brezhnev's attack, Dubček declares that he "would be content to go back to working at my old place," and step down as CPCz first secretary. With apparent exasperation, he tells Brezhnev that "if you [on the Soviet Politburo] believe we're deceiving you, you should take the measures you regard as appropriate." "Such measures," Brezhnev responds, "would be easier for us to adopt if you and your comrades would more openly say that these are the measures you're expecting of us."[27]

(See related Documents Nos. 77, 82, 85.)

Comrade L. I. Brezhnev's conversation with Comrade A. S. Dubček[28]

13 August 1968

Start of the conversation: 5:35 P.M.
End of the conversation: 6:55 P.M.

Brezhnev: Aleksandr Stepanovich, I felt the need to speak with you today. I called you early in the morning and then later in the day, but you were away the whole time in Karlovy Vary, and then you called me back, but at that point I had gone to have a talk with the comrades. Now that I've returned, they told me that you have a presidium meeting going on, and so I hope I'm not greatly disturbing you by having this conversation.

Dubček: No, not at all, the comrades already told me that you wanted to speak with me. I just now got back from Karlovy Vary. I had a meeting there with Cde. Ulbricht.

Brezhnev: How did the meeting go?

Dubček: I think it went well. Cde. Ulbricht and the comrades accompanying him returned today to the GDR, and I just finished seeing them off.

Brezhnev: We have little time, and so let me get straight to the point. I'm again turning to you with anxiety about the fact that the mass media in your country are not only incorrectly depicting our conferences in Čierna nad Tisou and Bratislava, but are also stepping up their attacks against

---

[27] Some Russian (and other) historians have looked at these remarks and concluded that Brezhnev may have construed them as a tacit green light for Soviet intervention. Others disagree, however, and it remains a matter of continuing debate.

[28] This transcript was declassified and released from the Russian Presidential Archive in April 1994 in connection with an international conference on the 1968 crisis held in Prague. It is one of nine documents presented at that time by the head of the Russian Archival Service, Rudolf Pikhoya, to Czech President Václav Havel. At times the transcriber of the tapes has editorially summarized Dubček's remarks rather than simply record them. Those places are marked with brackets.

the healthy forces and continuing to purvey anti-Sovietism and anti-socialist ideas. What I'm referring to here are not some isolated instances but an organized campaign; and judging by the content of the materials, these press organs have come to serve as a mouthpiece for the right-wing, anti-socialist forces. We in the Politburo exchanged views about this matter and unanimously concluded that there is every basis for regarding the unfolding situation as a violation of the agreement reached in Čierna nad Tisou. I have in mind the agreement you and I reached during our one-on-one discussions, as well as the agreement we thrashed out during the four-on-four meetings and the agreement that emerged between the Politburo of our party and the Presidium of the Central Committee of your party.

Dubček: I have already told you what sorts of measures we are taking to put an end to the anti-Soviet and anti-socialist manifestations in the mass media.[29] I have already told you what sorts of measures we are preparing and in what sequence we will carry them out. But I also told you at the time that it's impossible to do all this in a single day. We need time to take care of it. We're not able to restore order in the operations of the mass media in just two to three days.

Brezhnev: Sasha, that's true, and we warned you at the time that the rightist forces will not easily give up their positions and that it would of course be impossible to do everything in just two to three days. But a lot more time than two to three days has already passed, and the success of your work in this regard depends on your willingness to take decisive measures to restore order in the mass media. Of course if the CPCz leadership and the ČSSR government continue to pursue a policy of non-interference in this matter in the future, these processes will continue unabated. It's simply impossible to halt them through a policy of non-interference. You *must* resort to concrete measures. This is precisely the point on which we reached concrete agreement in connection with the role of Pelikán, and we said that it was essential to dismiss Pelikán. This would be the first step needed to restore order in the mass media.

Dubček: Leonid Ilyich, we studied these questions and are continuing to study them. I told Cde. Černík what sorts of measures we'd have to take, and I gave Cde. Lenárt the task of carrying out the necessary measures.[30] As far as I know, no sorts of attacks have been appearing recently against the CPSU or the Soviet Union or against the socialist order.

Brezhnev: How can you say such a thing when literally all the newspapers—*Literární listy, Mladá fronta, Reportér, Práce*—every day are publishing anti-Soviet and anti-party articles?

Dubček: That was going on *before* Bratislava. Since Bratislava that hasn't been happening.

Brezhnev: What do you mean it was only "before Bratislava"? On 8 August *Literární listy* featured an article entitled "From Warsaw to Bratislava," which was a full-blown, vicious attack against the CPSU and the USSR and against all the fraternal socialist countries.[31] The 8th of August, needless to say, was after Bratislava.

Dubček: That's an isolated case. I don't know of any others. All the rest appeared before Bratislava. We're opposed to this article and are now taking appropriate measures.

Brezhnev: Sasha, I can't agree with this. Over the past two to three days, the newspapers I mentioned have been doggedly continuing to occupy themselves with the publication of defamatory ravings about the Soviet Union and the other fraternal countries. My comrades on

---

[29] Dubček is referring here to the telephone conversation of August 9th. See Document No. 77.

[30] In regard to this, see Dubček's handwritten comments on the letter he received from Brezhnev on August 16th (Document No. 85).

[31] Brezhnev again demonstrates the extent of the information flowing into the Kremlin about the situation in Czechoslovakia from a variety of sources: the Soviet embassy in Prague, KGB agents, and the "healthy forces" on the CPCz, most notably Biľak, with whom Brezhnev spoke by telephone on August 10th.

the Politburo insist that we make an urgent request to you on this matter and that we send you a diplomatic note to this effect, and I'm not able to restrain the comrades from sending such a note.[32] But I only wanted to make sure that before a note is sent to you about this matter, I got a chance to speak with you personally.

Dubček: We had a meeting with members of the press. The session condemned the reporters at the newspapers you were speaking about for their incorrect actions; and a decision was reached there to put an end to all polemical expressions.

Brezhnev: Sasha, that's not the point—whether you had a meeting with members of the press or not. What we agreed about was not just to hold some meeting. We agreed that all the mass media—the press, the radio, and the television—would be brought under the control of the CPCz Central Committee and the government, and that you would put an end to anti-Soviet and anti-socialist publications after Bratislava. For our part, we in the Soviet Union are strictly abiding by this agreement and are not engaging in any sorts of polemics.[33] As far as the Czechoslovak organs of mass media are concerned, they're keeping up their relentless attacks against the CPSU and the Soviet Union and have even reached the point where they've been attacking the leaders of our party. They've already been branding us as "Stalinists" and other such things. And what, I might ask, do you say about this?

Dubček: [Falls silent.][34]

Brezhnev: I think I'm correct in telling you that so far we haven't witnessed any actions on the part of the CPCz CC Presidium that would fulfill the obligations taken on in this sphere. I must candidly say to you, Sasha, that by dragging your feet in the fulfillment of these obligations, you're committing outright deceit and are blatantly sabotaging the decisions we jointly reached. This posture toward the obligations you undertook is creating a new situation and is prompting us to reevaluate your statement. For this same reason we are considering new, independent decisions that would defend both the CPCz and the cause of socialism in Czechoslovakia.

Dubček: I only want to say to you, Cde. Brezhnev, that we are working in this direction. If you were able to be here with us, you'd see what great efforts we're expending in this direction. But this is a difficult matter and we're not able to resolve it in just two to three days, as I already told you. We need time for this.

Brezhnev: Aleksandr Stepanovich, I'm also obliged to say that we're not able to wait much longer and that you shouldn't force us to open new polemics with your mass media and to respond to all the articles and activities that are being permitted now in Czechoslovakia against our country, against our party, and against all the socialist parties.

During the negotiations we didn't force you to agree to anything. You yourselves took on the obligation to restore order in the mass media. And once you promised it, you should have been willing to carry it out. Well, fine, I perhaps can even agree with you that the restoration of order in this sphere requires time. But how are you coming along in carrying out the agreement on personnel questions? One must say that on this matter, too, we had a fully concrete agreement, and we also settled on a fully concrete timeframe for carrying it out.

Dubček: I would only like to say to you, Cde. Brezhnev, that these are very complex matters, which can't be resolved as easily as you might think.

---

[32] An initial "letter of warning" was sent to Dubček by the CPSU Politburo that same day; see Document No. 89.

[33] Brezhnev is only partly correct; by August 13, polemics had started to reappear in the Soviet press.

[34] This is one of several places in the transcript where the transcriber inserted a brief comment to sum up Dubček's response, rather than providing a verbatim record. In this case the third-person verb *molchit*, meaning "is silent," indicates a lack of response.

Brezhnev: I understand how complicated these matters are. I'm only asking you to resolve them along the lines we agreed on at Čierna nad Tisou. Was it not already clear to you and Černík and Smrkovský and Svoboda, when we met in our four-on-four sessions, how complex it would be to resolve these matters? Yet at the time you yourselves very easily and very independently, without any sort of coercion from us, raised these matters and promised to resolve them as soon as possible.

Dubček: I already told you, Cde. Brezhnev, that this is a complex question, the resolution of which requires that we convene a plenum. And in order to examine and resolve these questions, there must be due preparation. I must consult with the comrades about how best to resolve this question.

Brezhnev: But back in Čierna nad Tisou all your comrades were present, and I don't think you took on all these obligations then without having consulted among yourselves. We adopted the obligations, shook hands, and said that the question was decided and that you would take care of it as soon as possible.

Dubček: I didn't promise to resolve this matter in two to three days. We need ample preparation in order to resolve the question properly.

Brezhnev: But it's impossible to keep on resolving these questions *ad infinitum,* Sasha. When you were preparing for the last presidium meeting, you and I had a conversation. In particular, a conversation about personnel matters. I'm referring to my conversation with you on 9 August.[35] At that time you said to me that you weren't yet ready to handle things at that presidium meeting, but that you would definitely prepare these matters and resolve them at the next presidium meeting. And now you say that you have a presidium meeting under way. So, will you be considering these matters today at this presidium meeting, or will you not?

Dubček: These matters can be taken up only by a plenum of the Central Committee.

Brezhnev: Fine. You also told me that you were preparing to convene a plenum within the next ten days.

Dubček: Yes, we're thinking about holding a plenum by the end of the month. But it may be that it won't occur until the beginning of September.

Brezhnev: But will you be considering personnel questions at this plenum? Will you resolve them positively, as we agreed at Čierna nad Tisou?

Dubček: [Gives an evasive answer to this question, in the sense that what happens will be whatever the plenum decides.][36]

Brezhnev: This is where the problem lies. Both our problem and your problem. I'll tell you honestly that when you and I were speaking in Čierna nad Tisou, I thought that I was dealing with the leader of the chief party organ, the organ that has complete power. And everything that you promised us we accepted in good faith; and like friends, we believed you in all you said. Personally, Sasha, I can't understand at all why and to what end you've deferred the resolution of these matters until a new plenum, that is, an extraordinary plenum. We believe that today, at this presidium meeting, you could resolve personnel questions; and believe me, you could resolve them without any great loss. If you place these matters before the presidium today, it would still be possible—this would be the last chance—to salvage matters without great detriment or great loss. It will be worse if these losses are very large.

---

[35] See Document No. 77.

[36] This is another instance in which the transcriber inserted a third-person phrase to sum up Dubček's response.

Dubček: [Again insists that these matters can be resolved only by a plenum.][37]

Brezhnev: If I understand you correctly, you don't intend to consider these matters today. I want to ask you directly, Sasha, what you mean by this, and what I'm getting at here is that you're deceiving us! I'm not able to regard it as anything other than deceit.

Dubček: Leonid Ilyich, if you could see how these matters are being prepared now in the presidium, you wouldn't talk this way. We promised to resolve these matters, and we are taking all the measures needed to resolve them correctly.

Brezhnev: Sasha, I'm not just speaking here personally for myself. The entire Politburo has instructed me to speak with you[38] and to ask you concretely: Will you be resolving the personnel questions or not?

Dubček: [Evades a direct answer, explaining that it is impossible to resolve all the personnel questions at once, that these questions are very complex and imposing, and that, as he already said, these questions must be considered by a plenum.][39]

Brezhnev: My comrades are interested in finding out, and I would ask you to let me know so that I can transmit your answer to the members of our Politburo, what sorts of questions you are thinking of considering today at the CC Presidium meeting?

Dubček: [Enumerates the questions and says that among them the bifurcation of the Interior Ministry will be considered, as was agreed at Čierna nad Tisou.][40]

Brezhnev: And how is this question to be resolved? Will it be as we decided? I want to remind you, as you no doubt remember, that when this question was put to you, you turned to Černík. Černík said to you that the question had already been decided and that a candidate for the second post had already been designated, and within five days they would transmit orders about this to Smrkovský.[41] You then turned to Smrkovský, and he said that as soon as Černík issued this document, your council would resolve the matter within five days.

Dubček: Yes, he said that back in Čierna, but now the situation has fundamentally changed. We now have a process of federalization under way. There will be a federation of Slovakia with the Czech lands. And this question simply cannot be decided now by a central order for the country as a whole until Slovakia and the Czech Republic separately have adopted the corresponding decisions. For that reason, we at today's presidium meeting are able to resolve this question only as an instruction to the government and minister to prepare the requisite ideas for the final resolution of this matter somewhat later.

Brezhnev: How much later?

Dubček: In the month of October, toward the end of October.

---

[37] This summary comment was inserted by the transcriber.

[38] Since the Soviet leader and a number of top advisers were on vacation in the Crimea at this time, it would have been impossible for the "entire Politburo" to have been meeting or "exchanging views," unless some of the members were participating by phone (either during the session or by being consulted afterwards). A more likely scenario is that a core of senior members of the Politburo—Brezhnev, Podgorny, Kosygin, and perhaps one or two others—were meeting in the Crimea on behalf of the "entire Politburo." They probably received authority to do so at the session of the full CPSU Politburo on August 6th.

[39] Here again the transcriber inserts a third-person comment to summarize Dubček's response.

[40] This again is a summary of Dubček's response.

[41] Soviet officials expected that the "candidate for the second post"—that is, the new head of Czechoslovakia's State Security forces, which were to be separated from the rest of the Interior Ministry—would be Viliam Šalgovič, a notorious collaborator with the KGB.

Brezhnev: Well, what can I say to you about this, Sasha, except that it seems to be yet another manifestation of deceit. This is just one more sign that you're deceiving us, and I can't regard it as anything other than that, let me say to you in all honesty. If you're not even able to resolve this matter now, then it seems to me that your presidium in general has lost all its power.

Dubček: I don't see any deceit in this. We're trying to carry out the obligations we undertook. But we're carrying them out as best we can in a fundamentally changing situation.

Brezhnev: But surely you understand that this arrangement, this way of fulfilling the obligations undertaken at Čierna nad Tisou, will create a completely new situation which we, too, hadn't reckoned with, and that this obviously will compel us to reevaluate the whole situation and resort to new, independent measures.

Dubček: Cde. Brezhnev, you should resort to all the measures that your CC Politburo believes are appropriate.

Brezhnev: But if that's how you're going to answer me, I must say to you, Sasha, that this is a flippant statement.

Dubček: I'm not able to answer in any other way. We're working very hard to carry out the agreement. But in these conditions over the last week to ten days we haven't yet fully coped with it. We're not able to do more than what we've been doing. This is a large matter to deal with, and we're not able to complete all our work in just 10–15 days. How could it all be done in such a short time? I'm not able to take responsibility upon myself for doing everything in just five to seven days; this is a complex process, which has encompassed the whole party, the whole country, and the whole nation. And the party must keep control of this process, bringing the nation along with it in the construction of socialism. We see this as our duty and our obligation, but it's impossible to do this in as short a time as you are suggesting, Cde. Brezhnev. I tell you that if you don't believe me, if you believe we are deceiving you, then you should take the measures that your Politburo believes are necessary.

Brezhnev: Sasha, I understand that you're nervous, I understand that this situation is very complex for you. But don't you see that I'm talking with you as a friend, and that I wish only the best for you? If you recall the conversation you and I had one-on-one, as well as the conversation during our four-on-four sessions, and when you proposed your measures for restoring order in the mass media, it was we, not you, who pointed out that this would not be an easy task and that it would take time to bring the mass media back under control because the rightists had planted their agents everywhere, literally everywhere. In all the outlets of the mass media and information organs the rightists are firmly implanted, and the whole arrangement is being masterminded by Pelikán, Císař, Kriegel, and other scoundrels. But you at that time, in Čierna nad Tisou, said you could handle this work and that you didn't need any sort of help from us. We firmly agreed then that after Bratislava we would put an end to all polemics. I can understand that you're having difficulty, but the one thing I don't understand is why you've done nothing to overcome these difficulties. For example, let's turn back to the personnel questions. Again one can say that during the Čierna talks you also, without any pressure from us and completely of your own free will, said to us that you would be resolving all these questions literally as soon as possible.

Dubček: I can't just resolve these matters myself. It's not so simple, Cde. Brezhnev, to resolve such matters.

Brezhnev: Yet, how simple it was back in Čierna nad Tisou to have a conversation, are you now really implying that those were just irresponsible conversations at the level of the two highest organs of the leadership of the party? If it's clear that some question or other is difficult to resolve, then we shouldn't have had completely irresponsible discussions about it. That's how I understand

350

this matter. It's impossible to overstate, Sasha, how irritated I am by what you're doing now. You and I spoke about very important and very far-reaching matters, which will decide the fate not only of the Communist Party of Czechoslovakia, but also of the whole socialist camp. I'm not demanding anything new, and I haven't raised a single new issue for you. I only want to get from you a firm indication of when you're thinking of fulfilling the obligations on which we agreed at the meeting in Čierna nad Tisou. You have to understand that this isn't the way things are done—to have two fraternal parties meet and adopt a decision, and then just 10 days later have one side change its tune.

Dubček: We aren't changing our tune, it's just that the situation is complex and it requires a prolonged amount of time to carry out the agreement that was adopted.

Brezhnev: Well, fine, Sasha, then permit me to ask you openly and directly one additional question. Do you personally support the notion of fulfilling the obligations which you undertook at Čierna nad Tisou, or not?

Dubček: There will be a plenum, Leonid Ilyich, the plenum will decide everything.

Brezhnev: When will the plenum be?

Dubček: This question, I believe, will be resolved by us today in the presidium meeting. I think we'll convene a plenum before the end of the month. But I can't give you a precise date because if I don't get it right and the presidium schedules the plenum at a time different from the one I tell you, you'll again accuse me of having given you an insincere answer. This is difficult for me, Cde. Brezhnev, I still have a party congress ahead and I am completely unprepared for this congress.

Brezhnev: That's an entirely different matter. But by the way, since you've raised it, let me convey to you my personal view on this matter. I have participated in many congresses, and I've already conducted one congress independently as the first secretary of our party.[42] I personally can't imagine how it is possible to prepare a congress in such a short time. After all, the congress resolves weighty questions in the life of the party, and you must seriously prepare for such things, without any slip-ups. I'm surprised that you would even think a congress could be prepared in such a short time. But this, as they say, is your own affair.[43] I've digressed from our conversation.

Dubček: Yes. That's right, but since we have to deal with the situation as it exists, we are working night and day to prepare for the congress. We have an Action Program, draft party statutes, and personnel questions. In general, I think, we will succeed in preparing for the congress.

Brezhnev: Let's return to the thrust of our conversation. I don't know whether you'll be able to let your comrades on the presidium know about our conversation and tell them about the anxiety I've expressed to you at the way the situation is unfolding.

Dubček: Absolutely, without delay, I will tell Cdes. Černík and Smrkovský about this.

Brezhnev: Yes, that's good, you should tell Černík and Smrkovský, but I think, Sasha, that the other comrades are also full-fledged members of the presidium, and that you're obliged to say something to them about my phone call. I must tell you, Sasha, that they are very fond of you and can help you a great deal. I can assure you that these are your real friends both in their

---

[42] The congress to which Brezhnev refers here was the 23rd CPSU Congress in 1966. His formal title at that time had been changed to general secretary (the title used by Stalin) from first secretary (the title used by Khrushchev).

[43] Brezhnev uses the phrase here *"Eto vashe delo"* ("This is your own affair"), which has often been attributed to him in connection with the December 1967 unofficial visit to Prague (see Document No. 3).

past work—before the January plenum—and in carrying out the January plenum, and if you'd really like to know, I think they can help you more than Černík and Smrkovský can.

Dubček: Right now we already have a different agenda for the presidium meeting, but I'll try to find the opportunity to tell all the comrades about this conversation.

Brezhnev: Sasha, if I've understood you correctly, you're saying that at today's presidium meeting you won't be considering a single one of the questions we agreed on at Čierna nad Tisou.

Dubček: Only the question of the Interior Ministry.

Brezhnev: But as I understood you, you won't be deciding even this question the way we agreed—or at least not completely the way we agreed—in Čierna nad Tisou.

Dubček: [Very irritably repeats everything he said earlier about the difficulties attending the resolution of such matters.][44]

Brezhnev: Aleksandr Stepanovich, I regret that you're talking with me in such an irritable manner. On such momentous issues, emotions won't do anyone any good. What is needed here are common sense, reason, and will. Emotions here are of no help at all.

Dubček: I would be content to toss everything aside and go back to working at my old place. Why am I irritated? Because we're taking action here, we're working, we're doing everything we can to fulfill the agreement reached at Čierna nad Tisou, and yet the whole time you're accusing us. This is already the second conversation in which you've accused me of doing nothing, of deceiving you, and of not wanting to resolve the matters on which we agreed.

Brezhnev: Sasha, I'd like to believe you, but you must understand me. What troubles me most of all is that you haven't dismissed the three whom we agreed to dismiss, and this leaves a very big question. If you're sincerely convinced that you must release Císař, Kriegel, and Pelikán, and that this must be done, then I'm deeply convinced that a sincere effort on your part would allow you to do this very easily and simply.

Dubček: What reasons do you have for suggesting that this can be done quickly?

Brezhnev: We explained these things to you in Čierna nad Tisou. I'm not even referring here to the things that were not in the protocol—that is, the things we discussed in our one-on-one or four-on-four meetings. What I'm referring to are what was discussed in our plenary sessions, when we were all together. Go take a look at the stenographic report of my speech at the plenary session. You'll find there all our views. We told Kriegel directly that he is who he is.[45] We openly said this at the plenary session. What further basis can you possibly want, Sasha? Fine, you say that you're not able to resolve these questions in the presidium, and that it's necessary to convene a regular plenum. But from your answers, if you'll forgive me, I didn't understand whether even at the plenum you'll actually resolve these matters or not.

Dubček: At the regular plenum another CPCz CC first secretary will be chosen.

Brezhnev: Sasha, don't go to such extremes, this sort of talk is completely unnecessary. I don't know what would prompt you to speak with me this way; perhaps you feel uncomfortable about speaking with me more openly, or perhaps someone there is acting as a constraint on you. Well, then, let's agree that after the presidium meeting, Cde. Chervonenko will come to your office and you can tell him in greater detail when and how you are thinking about resolving the matters on which we agreed at the Čierna meeting.

[44] This summary has been inserted by the transcriber.
[45] Brezhnev is referring to the barrage of insults directed against Kriegel, including anti-Semitic slurs, that almost prompted the collapse of the talks.

Dubček: I can say nothing more. I already said everything there is to say, Cde. Brezhnev, and I can say nothing more to Cde. Chervonenko.

Brezhnev: Then let me ask you to tell me whether you'll be resolving these matters at the plenum or not.

Dubček: And who said that I won't?

Brezhnev: Again you're evading a direct response. You don't want to say whether you will or you won't.

Dubček: The last time I told you everything, and now I'm only able to repeat what I said earlier: that we're going to convene a plenum, that we must prepare for the plenum, and that we need time for this. If you believe that we're deceiving you, then take the measures you regard as appropriate. That's your affair.[46]

Brezhnev: Don't you see, Sasha, that we undoubtedly *will* be adopting the measures we believe are appropriate? You're absolutely correct in saying that this is our affair. But as far as this affair is not only ours but a matter of common concern, the measures would be easier for us to adopt if you and your comrades would more openly say that these are the measures you are expecting of us.

Dubček: We're able to resolve all these matters on our own, but if you believe it's necessary for you to adopt certain measures, then by all means go ahead.

Brezhnev: I'm not asking you why you didn't resolve any particular matter or another. I'm asking you something else, Sasha: namely, when you plan to resolve the things we agreed on.

Dubček: You're not asking me, you're rebuking me.

Brezhnev: I'm not rebuking you; I'm simply saying that in the wake of our meetings nothing has changed, and that we don't detect any sort of concrete actions aimed at fulfilling the agreement that exists between us. And insofar as that is the case, we are naturally alarmed. It seems to us that you're simply deceiving us and are completely unwilling to fulfill what we agreed on so firmly face to face, as well as during our four-on-four meetings. But if you're saying that at the regular plenum you'll resolve all the matters we agreed on at Čierna nad Tisou, then this of course will considerably alleviate our doubts. I'm not saying that our doubts will be eliminated altogether, but at least they'll be alleviated. After all, we're accustomed to believing you, and we see in you the leader of a fraternal party whom we can treat with great confidence.

Dubček: I'd just as soon go where it would be pleasant to work. I don't set great store by this post. Let whoever wants to occupy it, take it. Let whoever wants to be CPCz CC first secretary, take up the post. I can't work without enjoying support and in a situation of constant attacks.

Brezhnev: Sasha, I want to tell you openly that you yourself have created all the difficulties you're referring to. You saw how, before your very eyes, Císař and Kriegel installed their people in the press, radio, and television. These are people who have nothing in common with the Communist Party of Czechoslovakia. You yourself have created the personnel problem. You yourself have created all the problems you were mentioning. We didn't create these problems for you. It's precisely because of you that everything has gotten out of hand, and that you've lost power. And yet now you're bemoaning it. And I very much regret that you regard our conversation as an attack against you rather than a gesture of support. For it is precisely as a gesture of support that you should regard everything I've been talking about with you now. This hasn't been an attack against you.

---

[46] The phrase *"Eto vashe delo"* is used here again, this time by Dubček.

Dubček: Leonid Ilyich, I ask you to tell me how this can be.

Brezhnev: It's hard for me to give you any suggestions. But I want to tell you that if you continue to operate alone and if you continue to fluctuate between the leftists and rightists, you won't end up doing anything. Without the party *aktiv* you won't do anything. All around you are so many of your close comrades; they're good people and good communists. If you seek out the support of the party *aktiv* and rally them around you, there will no longer be any Císařs and Kriegels. In Čierna nad Tisou we were not inhibited about saying everything directly to Kriegel's face, without holding back. And yet you for some reason are still coddling him and sucking up to him.

You, Sasha, should take a close look around. I don't want to name names for you, but you know the people it would be worthwhile for you to rely on. By relying on them, you could resolve all your problems. I again say to you that by telling you this, by having this conversation, I am simply doing all I can to help you.

Right now we all are waiting: our party as well as the other fraternal parties from the Bratislava meeting and the documents of the Bratislava conference. I'm conveying all our doubts to you as frankly and openly and directly as I can. Let's just fulfill what we agreed on, and not an ounce more. As for your question of what will become of you, I can't give you an answer. If you want us to avoid a falling-out, let's just fulfill what we agreed on. Let's give an appropriate communist rebuff to the rightist forces. You'll have to strike a blow against them before the congress. It will have to be a blow from which they won't recover. Only in that case will the Communist Party of Czechoslovakia be able to show its best face at the congress.

Dubček: And you think that I don't want this?

Brezhnev: No, I don't think so. I believe you, Sasha. I believe that everything we wish for you is for the best, and that you will see what you will as your duty, while we for our part are ready to give you any help you need. But I ask you to understand that if you don't fulfill everything we agreed on—and I emphasize once again that these were things we agreed on; I'm not raising any new issues of any sort—then that will be an end to our trust in you. The whole point of our meeting in Čierna nad Tisou was to maintain the greatest trust in one another. All of our decisions were adopted in a spirit of enormous trust, and this is precisely what obliges us, in the most conscientious manner, to fulfill everything we agreed on. For a very long time you've been speaking in detail about the difficulties you've encountered while trying to carry out the decisions we reached and the agreement we arrived at. But I want to tell you that any question can always be made more complicated than it should be.

Dubček: We're not complicating anything; we're simply trying to deal with the situation that actually exists in our country.

Brezhnev: Why do you say this? Take this simple matter of dividing the Interior Ministry. Just as we agreed and as you yourselves said, this is a simple matter, one that you could resolve within the next five to ten days. And yet what has happened? You've done nothing.

Dubček: That's because the situation has changed. I told you that neither Černík nor I had foreseen that the situation would change. But our underlying view that such a step should be taken has not changed. We still firmly adhere to the view that this step should be taken. Only the situation has changed. But this means that the whole question must be approached differently. The outcome no longer depends on us alone.

Brezhnev: Sasha, let me ask you a question: What, if anything, *does* depend on your CC Presidium?

Dubček: Cde. Brezhnev, I once again ask you not to insist that I carry out this decision, considering that the situation has changed.

Brezhnev: Indeed I'm not insisting on it. I'm just saying that you on the CC Presidium are not in control of anything, and that it's a great pity we weren't aware of that during the meeting in Čierna nad Tisou. It now turns out that we were discussing things with an organ that is not in control of anything. It turns out that our conversation wasn't serious at all.

Dubček: The reasons for holding up the resolution of the matter are simply that Slovakia is now a federal territory while the ministry is a union-republic organ, and it's now necessary to follow a whole series of procedures if we are to settle this question once and for all.[47]

Brezhnev: I believe you, but you must also understand me. I'm not able to decide new matters behind the backs of the other members of my Politburo. I'm not able to give consent to any of your arguments. From what you've said it turns out that new circumstances have arisen for you, and so it's now totally unclear whether, or when at all, you'll be fulfilling our agreement about the division of the Interior Ministry. Doesn't it follow, then, that we have to reassess our whole agreement? You're aware that we agreed to these things at the very highest level. You and I spoke one on one. This is high level. We also spoke in four-on-four sessions. This was at the level of first secretaries, the level of chairmen of Councils of Ministers, and the level of chairmen of Supreme Soviets (or, as you have, a National Assembly). That is, our talks involved people who should be able to decide any matter. And it now turns out that these people can't decide anything. And now you're saying to me: "Take whatever measures the CPSU CC Politburo believes are necessary." Of course, one must obviously agree with you that we'll have to take whatever measures we believe are necessary. And by the way, I wanted to ask you something about the decisions we adopted during the four-on-four sessions. Did you convey the results to Cde. Bil'ak and the other comrades who are close to you?

Dubček: Yes, I informed Cde. Bil'ak about the things we decided during the four-on-four meetings.

Brezhnev: It's good that you did so, Sasha. These are your most dependable and closest friends. I would only urge you to rely on them. By relying on them, you can emerge triumphant. And you won't even need to wait for a plenum; with their help, you'll be able to resolve all these matters within the presidium.

Dubček: Please wait, nonetheless, Leonid Ilyich, until the plenum.

Brezhnev: Well, if this plenum is held soon, then of course I'll wait, and we all will wait.

Dubček: Leonid Ilyich, I well understand your benevolent intentions, and I only ask that you take into account the difficulties we are facing.

Brezhnev: I very clearly see your difficulties, Sasha, but you must put up a struggle against these difficulties. The struggle against them will be successful only on one condition, namely, that you yourself take direct charge of this struggle. You must surround yourself with reliable members of the party *aktiv,* and by depending on these comrades, you'll be able to overcome your difficulties.

Dubček: I'm running out of steam; it wasn't by chance that I told you that the new plenum would choose a new secretary. I'm thinking of giving up this work. Dear Leonid Ilyich, I ask that you forgive me for perhaps having spoken somewhat irritably today, I very much hope that you'll forgive me.

---

[47] Because the transcript here is somewhat garbled, this rendition of what Dubček says is somewhat cleaned up from the original.

Brezhnev: I understand, Sasha, it's your problems and your nerves. I want you to understand that in the context of what we agreed on at Čierna nad Tisou, you have to adopt measures and fulfill your obligations.

Dubček: Our desire is no less than yours, Cde. Brezhnev, to have these matters successfully resolved.

Brezhnev: Sasha, I take heart at your statement because the whole point of our conversation has been to help you fulfill these obligations. But you must also understand what it's like for us; for us, too, things aren't so easy. We reported back on that agreement to the plenum and to the Central Committee, and now we find it isn't being fulfilled. And so the party is asking us, as the leaders, why this is so. I want you to understand that good relations between our parties can be preserved only on the condition that there is mutual, honest fulfillment of the obligations by both sides. I think that you have no complaints about our party and our Politburo with regard to our fulfillment of the agreement achieved in Čierna nad Tisou.

Dubček: Leonid Ilyich, once again I affirm that we are *not* refusing to fulfill the agreement we reached in Čierna nad Tisou. The whole question is how much time we will be given to fulfill it, since there was no concrete timeframe specified in the agreement, and we still need more time to fulfill everything.

Brezhnev: You shouldn't pose the question that way, since on every issue a concrete timeframe was stipulated. If we said that this was all to be decided as soon as possible and before the congress, this establishes a well-defined deadline. That's not to imply it all had to be done in two to three days, but if we say "before the congress," then it's clear that everything should be resolved, say, in August.

Dubček: I promise you, Cde. Brezhnev, that I'll do everything necessary to fulfill our agreement.

Brezhnev: Good, we'll closely follow the course of events. I again earnestly request that you pass on my regards to all your working comrades and that you tell them about the alarm I've expressed to you. And now, Sasha, I would like to reach agreement with you on the desirability of continuing our conversations. If you don't want to meet Cde. Chervonenko, then let's agree that we'll continue our conversation after you're done with the CC Presidium meeting. I understand that it's awkward to have all your comrades sitting there while you've gone off to have a conversation with me.

Dubček: I agree. So let's definitely say that we'll speak again after the Presidium meeting.

DOCUMENT No. 82: The CPSU Politburo's Instructions to Ambassador Chervonenko for Meetings with Czechoslovak Leaders, August 13, 1968

Source: APRF, Prot. No. 38.

These Soviet Politburo instructions direct Ambassador Stepan Chervonenko to meet First Secretary Dubček again and reiterate the concerns expressed by Brezhnev in his telephone calls and by the CPSU leadership in its collective note to the CPCz Presidium. A second set of instructions calls for a meeting with President Svoboda, who, the Soviet leaders hoped, would influence "the course and outcome of events" in "the necessary direction." Chervonenko's conversations with Svoboda were designed to ensure that the ČSSR president would at least acquiesce in, and perhaps openly support, Soviet military intervention. The ambassador's instructions do not, however, include a discussion of military plans, suggesting that Soviet leaders remained uncertain about securing his active cooperation.

(See also Document No. 91.)

Proletarians of all countries, unite!

Communist Party of the Soviet Union. CENTRAL COMMITTEE

TOP SECRET

No. P94/101

To: Cdes. Brezhnev, Kirilenko, Andropov, Katushev, Ponomarev, Gromyko, and Rusakov.

Extract from protocol No. 94 of the session of the CPSU CC Politburo
on 13 August 1968

On Instructions to the Soviet Ambassador in Prague

To affirm the instructions to the Soviet ambassador in Prague (see attached).

CC SECRETARY

Regarding point 101 of Prot. No. 94

SECRET

URGENT

IMMEDIATE ATTENTION

PRAGUE
SOVIET AMBASSADOR

Urgently call on Cdes. Dubček and Černík and, referring to the instructions of the CPSU CC Politburo and USSR government, tell them the following:

We have already drawn the attention of the CPCz leadership to a number of serious facts attesting to the blatant violation by the Czechoslovak side of the agreement achieved in Čierna nad Tisou. Under this agreement, all the mass media—the press, radio, and television—were to be brought under the control of the CPCz CC and the government, and anti-socialist and anti-Soviet publications were to cease.

However, in recent days a number of press organs have featured new materials that cannot be regarded as anything other than anti-Soviet and anti-socialist. These materials distort the negotiations between our parties and the conference in Bratislava. An attempt is being made to provoke a deterioration of relations between the USSR and ČSSR and to evoke mistrust and hostility on the part of the Czechoslovak people toward the fraternal socialist countries.

The problem is not with some isolated excesses, but with an organized campaign. An especially unsavory role in this campaign is being played by *Literární listy*, *Mladá fronta*, *Reportér*, and *Práce*, which are relentlessly continuing to feature the publication of slanderous ravings against the Soviet Union and the other fraternal countries. These press organs have come to serve as the mouthpiece of the rightist, anti-socialist forces.

Issue No. 24 of *Literární listy* on 8 August published an article entitled "From Warsaw to Bratislava." Monstrous though this may seem, the article equates the policy of the fraternal socialist countries with the policy of Hitler. The press of the fraternal socialist countries is placed on a par with the Goebbels propaganda machine. The newspaper writes, in a style akin to its subject, that "the professional mode of thought of the propaganda machine, relying on its monopoly and distorting information through planned and deliberate misinformation, has not changed." The newspaper pins the label of "lackeys from the publicist world" on journalists of the socialist countries and shamelessly argues about "cohorts of authors who are prepared to attack everything and who, upon receiving instructions from their ideological chiefs, opened fire . . . against the Czechoslovak counterrevolutionaries."

This same anti-Soviet polemical spirit pervades the article "Friendship and Politics," published in the same issue of *Literární listy*. In the spirit of the bourgeois press, the article disseminates various insinuations and filthy rumors about the aims of the Soviet Union's policy. The newspaper states: "As far as Czechoslovakia is concerned, the Soviet leaders apparently are not overly confident about the capacity and desire of the people to maintain and develop socialism voluntarily and through democratic means, and the sole guarantee of inter-allied ties, in their view, comes from specific individuals."

The newspaper *Mladá fronta*, in its issue of 10 August, carries a slanderous assessment of the Bratislava Declaration and provocatively says: "Bratislava is not the end, but the beginning of discussions, possibly, and of polemics . . ."

The journal *Reportér*, in its most recent issue in August, has published an article entitled "Giving in to Illusions is a Luxury." It contains malicious slanders against the Soviet Union and the other socialist countries, and vilifies the socialist way of life. *Reportér* impudently asserts: "We are under the threat of bureaucracy, which slowly but surely has submerged and is continuing to submerge socialism on a global scale. To this end we can expect its fraternal solidarity as well as a spirit of mutual understanding or full unity of opinions on all questions under review. . . . We have brought forth the specter of the liquidation of absolute power wielded by the bureaucratic caste, which was created on an international scale by the Stalinist model of socialism."

At the same time, a boisterous campaign in defense of the remarks by General Prchlík against the Warsaw Pact continues to gather steam. We understand that the point of this campaign is not Prchlík himself, but the use of his name for greater and greater attacks against the Warsaw Pact. In this connection, we are bewildered by the statement in the newspaper *Mladá fronta* (if you can trust this newspaper) that Prchlík, as before, enjoys the full confidence of the CPCz CC Presidium.

Thus, there is every basis for regarding the emerging situation as a violation of the agreement achieved in Čierna nad Tisou. And this is the result not only of the active efforts of the rightist forces, but also the policy of "non-interference" by the leadership of the CPCz and the government in these processes. In effect this policy has ended up encouraging the actions of the anti-socialist elements. All of this we declare with full responsibility.

As you understand, we normally would feel obliged to react openly to such outbursts, to rebuff the provocative onslaught, and to declare that the Čierna nad Tisou agreement has been torn up by your side. However, we do not want events to develop this way and we hope that swift and forceful measures will be taken in connection with press organs like *Literární listy*, *Mladá fronta*, *Reportér*, and *Práce*, which indulge in anti-Sovietism.

We emphasize that the matter raised by you regarding the unfriendly expressions in organs of the Czechoslovak press is regarded in Moscow as extremely serious and urgent.

Regarding Point 101 of Prot. No. 94

SECRET
IMMEDIATE ATTENTION

PRAGUE
SOVIET AMBASSADOR

Visit the ČSSR president, Cde. Svoboda, and tell him that you have informed the CPSU CC Politburo about your conversation with him.

Let him know, in the name of Cde. L. I. Brezhnev, that the CPSU CC Politburo greatly values the understanding shown by Cde. President Svoboda towards our concern about the fulfillment of the agreement reached during the negotiations at Čierna nad Tisou, and about our evaluation of the danger posed by the rightist forces and their representatives in the CPCz leadership.

We view the president's intention to carry out active work among the ranks of the Czecho-slovak People's Army and among young people with great satisfaction, as well as his intention to make public statements supporting those working for the consolidation of friendship and unity between our countries and parties.

There is no doubt that at the present trying moment, Cde. Svoboda will have far-reaching influence, via his authority and direct participation, in determining whether the course and outcome of events move in the necessary direction, and in spurring the adoption and implemen-tation by the CPCz leadership and government of concrete measures aimed at fulfilling in practice the agreement achieved at our bilateral negotiations at Čierna nad Tisou and reaffirmed at the conference of fraternal parties in Bratislava.

Confirm by telegram.

DOCUMENT No. 83: János Kádár's Report on Soviet–Hungarian Talks at Yalta, August 12–15, 1968

Source: ÚSD, Sb. KV, Z/M 19.

János Kádár presented this report on his Yalta talks with Soviet leaders to a joint session of the HSWP Central Committee and the Hungarian Council of Ministers on August 23. The meeting took place between August 12 and August 15 with Brezhnev, Kosygin, and Podgorny.

This somber speech reflects none of the optimism of Kádár's report to the HSWP Central Committee Plenum a week earlier, and records his shift toward support for military intervention. At Yalta, the Hungarian leader affirms, he had been "able to justify the decisions we [in Hungary] adopted on military matters" and "to express things" during these "close and informal talks" that "could not have been said at formal international negotiations." Although there were "minor deviations" between some of his views and those of his Soviet counterparts, Kádár's remarks mark his evolution toward a hard-line position.

(See also Document No. 75.)

. . . [Pro forma introductory material has been deleted.]

I.

Cde. Kádár (accompanied by Cde. Károly Erdélyi) had talks at Yalta with Cdes. Brezhnev, Kosygin, and Podgorny. In an open, comradely exchange of views they had an in-depth discussion of numerous issues connected with the recent developments in Czechoslovakia. One reason for the discussion was that they wanted to assess the issues from all angles and draw the necessary conclusions. Cde. Kádár explained, in greater detail than he had at the talks involving representatives from several states, how the HSWP Central Committee and the Hungarian government saw the situation, what sorts of analyses they were carrying out, and what conclusions they had drawn from the situation as it had developed between December 1967 and the present. He did not want to repeat all this to the Central Committee since it was identical to what had been discussed and approved at its plenary sessions.

The aim of providing such detailed information in Yalta was to make the Soviet comrades fully aware of our position and motives. We also tried to get a thorough and detailed understanding of the position of the Soviet comrades.

We stressed that we agreed, and always did agree, on fundamental issues insofar as these were questions of principle for Czechoslovak society. We especially agreed that these questions should be settled in a socialist spirit and in the interest of socialism. The positions of our two countries with regard to objectives always were and will remain totally identical: We have always tried to act jointly with the CPSU leadership and the Soviet government to help settle the problems of Czechoslovak society in the interest of socialism.

However, when we assessed specific details, minor deviations in our positions were evident. When this occurred, our proposed solutions at times coincided, at other times diverged. We thought it proper to emphasize repeatedly that the Soviet Union lives and functions today, and will live and function tomorrow, and the day after tomorrow in unity with the HSWP and the other communist parties. From the point of view of the Hungarian people and from an internationalist point of view, we believe it is of cardinal importance to act at all times in complete accord with the Soviet Union. But it does occur that the Soviet comrades and our party have not always been assailed by the same types of factors, and not always to the same degree. We had the impression that the Soviet comrades were paying too little attention to the causes of the Czechoslovak crisis and to the errors and deformations that existed for many years. Only by remedying these shortcomings will it be possible to improve the situation. We emphasized this (perhaps a bit excessively) to make the Soviet comrades understand that no matter how difficult events may be and no matter what solutions prove necessary, the internal problems of Czechoslovak society—which are basically what everyone is concerned about here—can in the final analysis be remedied only by political means. A communist solution will be impossible if it does not clearly dissociate itself from the pre-January state of affairs and methods. In light of this, what matters is not a mere name (Novotný), but subjectivism and the other methods and mistakes that were the primary cause of the decline of the Czechoslovak party and of the crisis in that country.

Cde. Kádár is able to inform the Central Committee that the Soviet comrades now accept this extremely important and fundamental factor far more readily and will give it greater consideration.

We have always declared that political problems require political solutions. But it is also clear to us—and this is something we have always told our Czechoslovak comrades—that the use of administrative and coercive methods is occasionally necessary to safeguard and consolidate the social system. Furthermore, we have seen and recognized that military assistance may prove necessary on our part.[48] That is why our existing position, though stressing the need for maximum efforts to seek political solutions, includes statements such as: Let no one have any doubt that, if the need arises, we will be ready to offer even military aid. We have stressed that we will live up to this duty in any situation in accordance with the unconditional internationalist position of our party, government, socialist state, and working class.

Thus, at Yalta we were able to justify in detail the decisions we adopted on military matters, and we were able to express things that cannot not be said at formal international negotiations; such matters can be taken care of only in close and informal talks.

The talks with the Soviet comrades, which did not have a precise agenda, were extremely valuable for us in dealing with all matters. The Soviet comrades did not contradict our point of view on a single issue.

We also spoke about urgent matters connected with the internal Czechoslovak situation. The Soviet comrades expressed great and sincere concern as well as impatience when saying that the CPCz CC Presidium, and more particularly its top members, Dubček and Černík, had not yet taken the seemingly necessary steps in connection with the situation noted at the talks in Čierna nad Tisou and in Bratislava. What is more, events in Czechoslovakia were now worse than before the negotiations. Proof of this is a signature campaign in the streets demanding the dissolution of the People's Militia as well as the impertinent tone that reemerged in the Czechoslovak press only a few days after the Bratislava meeting. Even worse, at Čierna the Czechoslovak comrades made concrete commitments to stem the right-wing forces, yet they have drawn up no plan to this effect and have done nothing so far. Dubček himself admitted that they had placed someone at the head of the Interior Ministry (Pavel) who was totally unsuited for the job. Pavel had been a fighter in Spain, possibly a very good comrade, but is either unwilling or unable to take firm measures to protect Czechoslovak security.

During a visit by the Czechoslovak party and government delegation to our country, we said at our common talks that one cannot work without discipline and administrative measures. Every society, even under the most normal conditions, is forced to act against people who in any way violate the legal system.

At that time, the Dubčekites had already implied that they had found someone else (Šalgovič) to whom they intended to entrust the security portfolio.[49] Then they came up with the idea of bifurcating the Interior Ministry and creating a separate Ministry of Interior and Ministry for

[48] This assessment contrasts sharply with Kádár's August 7 report to the HSWP Central Committee that "the conflict [between Czechoslovakia and its allies] has ceased to exist and unity has been restored."

[49] See the annotation about Šalgovič in Document No. 77.

State Security. At Čierna they said this was a step their own presidium had already decided two months earlier. There was even a discussion there of why they had not gone ahead with it. Cde. Smrkovský replied that he would issue a directive if he were ordered to do so by Černík. Černík said that after returning home he would issue this instruction within an hour. The ministry was to be divided between 15 and 20 August at the latest. The presidium then discussed the matter on 13 August, and a report was presented by Pavel. The presidium took note of his report and voted to draft a proposal for the division of the ministry and its staff by 31 October. The proposal was to be drafted by Interior Minister Pavel.

There are many similar incidents in the current Czechoslovak situation, but this is a particularly telling example of how the leadership is functioning—or rather of its approach to dealing with problems.

The Soviet comrades have concluded that if the situation does not change after Čierna and Bratislava, if steps are not taken to reassert control over the mass media, and if no security measures are taken, nothing more can be expected from the current CPCz CC Presidium.

Cde. Kádár was asked to have one more talk with Dubček and point out that apart from the Soviet Union, the HSWP is the only party that can make some impression on them.

DOCUMENT No. 84: Reports on Warsaw Pact Military Communications Exercises and Marshal Grechko's Inspection Tours, August 9–16, 1968

Sources: Various Czechoslovak, Soviet, and Polish newspapers (noted after each dispatch).

The joint "Horizon" ("Gorizont") military communications exercises began on August 11, a day after the "Nemen" logistic maneuvers were completed. General Sergei Shtemenko, who only a week earlier (on 5 August) had been appointed chief of staff of the Warsaw Pact's Joint Command (replacing General Mikhail Kazakov) commanded the "Horizon" exercises, which included units from the Soviet Union, East Germany, and Poland. In addition, the Hungarian armed forces began bilateral maneuvers with the USSR's Southern Group of Forces on August 15—the first time since the crisis began that joint exercises with Soviet troops were conducted on Hungarian territory. The two sets of maneuvers, which continued until the very start of the invasion, enabled Shtemenko to establish and smooth out the complicated command, control, & communications (C^3) arrangements necessitated by Operation Danube's multinational invasion force.

As the news dispatches record, the "Horizon" and Soviet–Hungarian exercises were accompanied by a flurry of high-level military contacts between the Soviet Union and its allies. In the ten days before the invasion, Soviet Defense Minister Grechko traveled to each of the sites that would be crucial in coordinating the military operation: Minsk, the GDR, and Poland. After completing his inspection tours, Grechko returned to Moscow late on the 16th to take part in the decisive three-day meeting of the Soviet Politburo, where the final decision to invade was approved. The Politburo, at Grechko's suggestion, also decided to transfer all responsibilities from Marshal Yakubovskii and the Warsaw Pact's Joint Command directly to the Soviet High Command. Under the new arrangements, Army-General Ivan Pavlovskii, the commander-in-chief of Soviet Ground Forces, was designated the supreme commander of the whole invasion, accountable directly to the Politburo's representative on the scene, Kirill Mazurov.

"At the Concluding Stage"

. . . . It is already possible to say with confidence that the aims set for the extended large-scale logistic exercises were achieved. Many important problems that had arisen regarding the rear services of the Armed Forces in connection with changes in the nature, means, and forms of modern combat were studied and resolved in practice.

The exercises once again confirmed that the rear services of the Armed Forces are able to perform any tasks demanded by the communist party and the Soviet government.

Today the USSR Defense Minister, Marshal of the Soviet Union A. A. Grechko, arrived in the region where the exercises were conducted. The minister paid close heed to a briefing given by the commander of the exercises, Army-General S. S. Maryakhin. He also carefully studied the operational-tactical situation and circumstances of the forces, units, and logistical entities, and transmitted a series of instructions. . . .

Source: "Na zavershayushchem etape," *Krasnaya zvezda* (Moscow), 10 August 1968, p. 2.

* * *

"Meeting of Defense Ministers"

Berlin—The USSR Defense Minister, Marshal A. A. Grechko, who was visiting a formation of Soviet troops in the German Democratic Republic, met the GDR Defense Minister, Army-General Heinz Hoffmann on Wednesday. They exchanged views on general political matters and cooperation between the fraternal armies. They also exchanged experiences in combat training and political education and discussed the further improvement of cooperation among the leading organs of the troops in the continuing communications exercises.

In addition to Marshal Grechko, the talks were attended by the Commander-in-Chief of the Joint Armed Forces of the Warsaw Pact countries, Marshal of the USSR I. I. Yakubovskii.

Source: "Setkání ministrů obrany," *Mladá fronta*, 17 August 1968, p. 2.

* * *

"Exercises in Hungary"

Budapest—Over the next few days joint military maneuvers will be conducted in Hungary. Taking part will be certain communications staffs and units from the Hungarian People's Army and the Soviet forces temporarily stationed on Hungarian territory.

Source: "Cviceni v Maďarsku," *Mladá fronta*, 17 August 1968, p. 2.

* * *

"USSR Defense Minister Visits Soldiers from the Northern Group of Forces"

Northern Group of Forces, 16 August—Yesterday the USSR Minister of Defense, Marshal of the Soviet Union A. A. Grechko, arrived in the Northern Group of Forces. He was accompanied by the Commander-in-Chief of the Warsaw Pact Joint Armed Forces and First Deputy Defense Minister, Marshal of the Soviet Union I. I. Yakubovskii, and the Chief of the Main Political Directorate of the Soviet Army and Navy, Army-General A. A. Epishev.

They were met at the air base by the chief of staff of the Warsaw Pact Joint Armed Forces, Army-General S. M. Shtemenko, the commander of the Northern Group of Forces, Colonel-General I. N. Shkadov, the deputy chief of the Main Political Directorate of the Soviet army and Navy, Colonel-General N. A. Nachinkin, a member of the Military Council and Chief of the Northern Group of Forces Political Directorate, Colonel-General F. F. Kuznetsov, Air Marshal N. S. Skripko, and others.

The same day, the USSR Defense Minister, Marshal of the Soviet Union A. A. Grechko, and his entourage traveled around the units and formations of the group and monitored the combat and political preparations of the personnel. Marshal of the Soviet Union A. A. Grechko delivered a speech to the commanders and political workers.

Source: "Ministr oborony SSSR u voinov Severnoi gruppy voisk," *Krasnaya zvezda* (Moscow), 17 August 1968, p. 1.

* * *

"Meeting of Leaders of the Fraternal Armies"

On 16 August a meeting took place in southwestern Poland, in a cordial atmosphere of friendship and fraternity, between the USSR Minister of Defense, Marshal of the Soviet Union Andrei Grechko, and the acting minister of national defense and chief of the General Staff of the Polish Army, Div.-Gen. Boleslaw Chocha. Also present were the vice-minister of National Defense and chief of the Main Inspectorate of the Polish Army, Div.-Gen. Tadeusz Tuczapski, and the 1st deputy chief of the Main Political Directorate of the Polish Army, Brig.-Gen. Jan Czapla.

The meeting featured a mutual exchange of opinions on questions of cooperation between the fraternal armies and their joint efforts during the exercises of communications forces.

Taking part in the meeting from the Soviet side were the commander-in chief of the Warsaw Pact Joint Armed Forces and 1st Deputy Defense Minister, Marshal of the Soviet Union I. Yakubovskii, the chief of the Main Political Directorate of the Soviet army and Navy,

Army-Gen. A. Epishev, the chief of staff of the Warsaw Pact Joint Armed Forces, Army-Gen. S. Shtemenko, the representative to the Polish Army from the Staff of the Warsaw Pact Joint Armed Forces, Lt. Gen. A. Kozmin, the commander of the Northern Group of Forces, Col.-Gen. I. Shkadov, the deputy chief of the Main Political Directorate of the Soviet Army and Navy, Col.-Gen. N. Nachinkin, a member of the Military Council and chief of the Northern Group of Forces Political Directorate, Col.-Gen. F. Kuznetsov, and the chief of staff of the Northern Group of Forces, Lt. Gen. I. Kovalev.

Source: "Spotkanie kierownictw bratnich armii," *Trybuna Ludu* (Warsaw), 17 August 1968, p. 1.

DOCUMENT No. 85: Letter from Leonid Brezhnev to Alexander Dubček, and Dubček's Notes, Regarding the CPCz's Purported Failure to Carry Out Pledges Made at Čierna and Bratislava, August 16, 1968

Source: ÚSD, AÚV KSČ, F. 07/15, Zahr. kor. No. 822; Vondrová & Navrátil, vol. 2, pp. 187–189.

This is the last of the six personal letters Brezhnev wrote to Dubček during the 1968 crisis. A brief cover page to Ambassador Stepan Chervonenko, marked top secret, states: "Prague, Soviet ambassador. Visit Cde. Dubček and tell him that Cde. Brezhnev asked that the following be presented to him." When he received the letter, Dubček scribbled a series of notes on the front page and on an attached notecard.

Formal and reproachful in tone, Brezhnev's letter reiterates the complaints expressed during his phone calls on August 9, and 13. In closing, Brezhnev emphasized that he was hoping for a swift reply from Dubček as well as concrete measures to implement the Čierna and Bratislava accords.

Although Dubček took sharp issue with Brezhnev's charge that the situation had "deteriorated into counterrevolution," his handwritten notes on the letter indicate that the CPCz Presidium might eventually adopt certain of the measures demanded by the CPSU leadership. The notes support later assertions by Dubček that Soviet complaints about personnel, reformist groups and control of the media would have been addressed if the invasion had not occurred.

Esteemed Alexander Stepanovich,[50]

After the long telephone conversation with you on 13 August I am compelled once again to return to the subject we discussed.[51] I am doing this because of certain points in that conversation which I have no right or reason to ignore.

Above all, I wish to stress the seriousness and gravity of our talks with you concerning the results of the meetings between the CPSU CC Politburo and the CPCz CC Presidium when all members were present and also when just certain representatives from the CPSU CC Politburo and the CPCz CC Presidium got together. These results were of great significance for our parties, for our states, and for the entire socialist camp.

All of us, as representatives of the fraternal parties that met in Bratislava, attach enormous importance to these talks and to the decisions and commitments that were approved. It seems that, without question, the main thing now is to fulfill the programmatic clauses of the document adopted in Bratislava and also to take practical measures to fulfill the agreements reached in Čierna nad Tisou. The latter agreements include those adopted at the plenary session of the CPCz CC Presidium and the CPSU CC Politburo, as well as at the talks involving just four representatives per side from the CPSU CC Politburo and the CPCz CC Presidium.[52]

However, the course of events shows that the mass media have begun describing the results of the talks from right-wing positions and are continuing their anti-Soviet, anti-socialist attacks.

---

[50] This letter is undated, but the date of August 16 is cited in the collective letter that the CPSU Politburo sent to Dubček the following day, and in secret materials prepared for the plenum of the CPCz Central Committee in September 1969 (ÚSD, AÚV KSČ, F. 01, Sv. 210, A.j. 131), where Brezhnev's letter was reproduced on pages 85 to 87. The text of the letter was not made public until 14 May 1990, when it was published in *Rudé právo* ("Co psal Brežněv Dubčekovi: Hovoří dosud neuveřejněné dokumenty," pp. 1–2).

[51] See Document No. 81.

[52] The implication of this statement (and of a similar statement below) is that agreements were reached during the small, four-on-four negotiations at the end of the Čierna meeting that were not discussed in front of the full delegations. This seems plausible in light of Dubček's handwritten notes on the letter (see below) and his speech at the September 1969 plenum of the CPCz Central Committee.

A witch-hunt has begun against workers at the Auto-Praha factory.[53] I will not repeat all the facts I spoke you about on the phone. You must understand that the complexity of the situation in the CPCz and the organized attacks of right-wing, anti-socialist, and counterrevolutionary elements disturb us. For this very reason I decided to call you in the hope of receiving the proper replies. I want to be frank and say that as regards the measures taken by the CPCz toward the mass media, I have, in fact, received no reply. What specific measures are being taken by the CPCz CC Presidium on this matter?

During the talks in Čierna nad Tisou you told us about your decision to divide the bodies of the Ministry of Internal Affairs in order to strengthen the security of the country. At the time, Cde. Černík declared that a government decision on this matter was ready and would be turned over in the near future to Cde. Smrkovský in the National Assembly, and Cde. Smrkovský declared that by 25 August this bill would be passed.[54] During my phone conversation with you, I had the impression that the implementation of this decision was being postponed to an unspecified date.

On personnel matters:

In Čierna nad Tisou you told us firmly that you would release Cdes. Kriegel, Císař, and Pelikán from their posts.[55] During the telephone conversation, you for some reason seemed nervous when this point came up. It was difficult to understand what brought that on, and furthermore I did not understand what was being done in this regard.

Overall, I had the impression that the CPCz CC Presidium is not demonstrating the necessary initiative and determination in fulfilling the measures that we agreed upon. All these measures were meant to put up serious resistance to the rightist forces and the anti-socialist and counterrevolutionary elements, and to defend the CPCz and the gains of socialism in Czechoslovakia. Perhaps you were agitated by some sort of private matter, as sometimes happens in our lives.

At the end of our talk you apologized, but the questions that interest us were not explained satisfactorily. I do not wish to jump to conclusions about the reason for this delay, and therefore I decided to request you to send me an answer through Cde. Chervonenko.[56]

L. Brezhnev

* * *

[53] The reference here, as in Brezhnev's phone call to Dubček on 9 August (see Document No. 77), is to the 99 workers from the Czechoslovak automobile plant who had supposedly signed a petition that appeared in the Soviet press on July 30.

[54] For further details on this point, see János Kádár's remarks in Document No. 83.

[55] Toward the end of his life, Dubček heatedly denied, both in interviews and in his memoirs, that he had made any such commitment, regardless of what Brezhnev may have assumed. See, for example, Document No. 67. It should be emphasized, however, that at the September 1969 plenum of the CPCz Central Committee, Dubček did acknowledge in his speech that "we discussed the internal question of personnel" at the Čierna meeting and that "we presented a report at Čierna to our Soviet colleagues . . . regarding the personnel matters to which we intended to devote urgent attention during the pre-Congress CC plenum. . . . These matters were to be settled at the plenum, which was to be convened on 25 August." Dubček's additional handwritten comments on the notecard (see below) suggest Brezhnev may have been justified in assuming that Dubček had pledged to replace Kriegel, Pelikán, and Císař.

[56] Even though Brezhnev demands a reply, it is doubtful whether anything Dubček might have done or promised at this point could have forestalled the invasion. By the time Dubček received the letter and had a chance to peruse and act on it—August 17—the Soviet authorities had already arrived at a consensus in favor of intervention.

Dubček's Handwritten Notes on the Letter:[57]

1. Notes on the first page of the text:

I informed Cdes. Černík and Smrkovský and Cde. Svoboda. The whole spirit and content of the letter are out of keeping with the negotiations as far as "obligations" are concerned. These concerned only inf[ormation] about what the CC P[residium] is deciding on:

— the Soc[ial] Dem[ocrats],
— K-231—Černík's regulation,
— they were told that Císař must retain his post as ch[airman] of the ČNR,
— with regard to Pelikán: he's been in the party for many years, in an official post, etc.

Afterwards it was decided, by Dubček, Svoboda, Černík, and Smrkovský, that personnel ma[tters] will be decided at the next pl[enum] of the CPCz CC.[58]

I didn't raise this in the CC P[residium].

Indeed, as far as rad[io], tel[evision], and the major press organs are concerned, there was a definite turn for the better after Bratislava.

The situation improved polit[ically], and there's no basis saying it has deteriorated into counterrev[olution].

The CC [plenum] is being prepared as well as everything needed to safeg[uard] the congress.

The ČSSR has enough forces at its disposal—the army, sec[urity forces], and P[eople's] M[ilitia]—to intervene if necessary.

What's decisive for us is the posi[tive] relationship of the nation and the people toward the CPCz CC's poli[cies].

What seemed to be the case has in fact proven true: Čierna and then Bratislava were not sincere.

Dubček

2. Notes on the attached notecard:

It was decided (by Dubč[ek], Černík, Svoboda, and Smrkovský):

— to hold a pl[enum] of the CC and N[ational] A[ssembly][59] by the end of August,
— to deal with pers[onnel] changes involving the heads of the N[ational] F[ront] and television, and Císař's position at the ČNR,
— to prepare everything needed to pass the leg[al] measures—regarding the NF, the press organs, KAN, K-231—as was ind[icated] to them at Čierna.

I informed Cde. Brezhnev about this matter in the presence of Cde. Smrkovský when Cde. Brezhnev cited our failure to carry out the "agreement" reached at Čierna. With regard to

---

[57] Dubček's scribbled notes are nearly illegible in a few places and are written in a hybrid of Slovak and Czech that is not always easy to render into English, but they have been translated here as accurately and completely as possible. When Dubček used abbreviations, the full words have been written out for clarity's sake, with brackets around the portions Dubček omitted.

[58] According to Dubček's speech at the September 1969 plenum of the CPCz CC, all these matters would indeed have been resolved at the CC plenum that was scheduled for 29 August 1968, just after the Slovak CP Congress.

[59] The two-letter abbreviation Dubček uses here is NZ, which is in Slovak. The abbreviation in Czech would have been NS.

pers[onnel] mat[ters] Cdes. Kolder and Biľak were inf[ormed], and I told them why I didn't want to raise the issue in the CC P[residium] a long time beforehand, but just shortly before the CC plenum. I also spoke about this matter with other com[rades].

Measures were decided (by Dubč[ek], Smrkovský, and Černík)

— legally, in the CPCz CC P[residium] by the end of August,
— personnel, at the CC plenum and in the N[ational] A[ssembly].

DOCUMENT No. 86: Summary of Alexander Dubček's Meeting with János Kádár at Komárno, August 17, 1968

Source: ÚSD, AÚV KSČ, F. 02/1; Vondrová & Navrátil, vol. 2, pp. 216–219.

This memorandum of a conversation records a meeting between Dubček and Kádár on August 17—arranged that morning at Kádár's initiative. At the Yalta talks, Brezhnev had urged that the Hungarian leader intercede with Dubček one last time. The Komárno meeting, however, took place just after the Soviet Politburo had decided, on August 17, to give the final go-ahead for "Operation Danube" as the invasion was codenamed.

The meeting memorandum clarifies a longstanding discrepancy in the historical accounts of Kádár's motives—whether he sought to forestall an invasion by warning Dubček to take immediate action, or was simply engaging in a deceptive charade at Moscow's behest, as Dubček implied in his own memoir, Hope Dies Last. *Twice at the beginning of the conversation, Kádár indicates that he had spoken to Brezhnev, Kosygin, and Podgorny about his intention to meet Dubček, and had secured their approval. Those admissions would have been peculiar if Kádár had genuinely sought to mislead Dubček into thinking that the Hungarian leader was acting independently of the Soviet Union. Instead, by acknowledging from the outset the constraints imposed by his ties with the CPSU leadership, Kádár appears to be trying to signal to Dubček that the conversation could not be as free-ranging or explicit as either of them might have liked.*

Although Kádár made no reference to the pending likelihood of military aggression against Czechoslovakia, he is reported in Zdeněk Mlynář's account, Nachtfrost: Erfahrungen auf dem Weg vom realen zum menschlichen Sozialismus, *to have offered a final warning to Dubček as they parted in the train station: "Do you really not understand the sort of people you are dealing with?" Dubček, in his memoir, records Kádár's remark about the Soviet leaders as: "But you do know them, don't you?"—very similar, but not identical. These meeting notes do not contain this final exchange.*

The minutes were prepared by E. Újváry, a senior staffer at the CPCz CC's International Department.

. . . [Pro forma introductory material has been deleted.]

The Hungarian side was represented also by Cde. Erdélyi, a member of the HSWP Central Committee and deputy minister of foreign affairs.

The meeting, which took place in the building of the district committee of the Slovak CP at Komárno, was held at the request of Cde. Kádár.[60]

At the beginning of his remarks, Cde. Kádár said he wanted to have a personal meeting with Cde. Dubček with no protocol attached. The HSWP CC Politburo had agreed to his proposal. He said he was glad it had been possible to arrange the meeting. He mentioned the Bratislava meeting of the delegations from the six fraternal parties and noted that the brevity of the meeting as well as the heavy workload had not made it possible to discuss certain topical issues. That was why he had come up with the idea of having an additional meeting. Another factor that persuaded him of the need for such a meeting was, as he put it, some events that had occurred since the last bilateral meeting (at Komárno on Hungarian territory on 13 July 1968),[61] particularly the talks between the CPCz CC Presidium and the CPSU CC Politburo at Čierna nad Tisou and the Bratislava meeting of the six fraternal socialist countries. Cde. Kádár then informed Cde. Dubček that after the Bratislava meeting he had spoken several times to Cde. Brezhnev on the phone, who also thought a meeting between the first secretaries of the CPCz

---

[60] Kádár's own brief report on the meeting, presented to a joint session of the HSWP Central Committee and the Hungarian Council of Ministers, August 23, 1968, can be found in PTTI, 288, F. 4/94 oe. See also a one-paragraph description of the Kádár–Dubček meeting in Zdeněk Mlynář's *Nachtfrost: Erfahrungen auf dem Weg vom realen zum menschlichen Sozialismus* (Köln: Europäische Verlagsanstalt, 1978), p. 157, and Dubček's own account in his posthumously published memoir, *Hope Dies Last*, p. 173.

[61] See Kádár's statement in Document No. 52. See also Document No. 51.

and the HSWP would be useful. He added that on 12 August 1968, he had met Cdes. Brezhnev, Kosygin, and Podgorny in the Crimea.[62] This meeting had further convinced him of the need to meet Cde. Dubček. He had mentioned this to the Soviet comrades, who welcomed the idea and thought it a very good move.

After this brief introduction, Cde. Kádár said it would be good if they continued their discussion where they had left off at Komárom.

Cde. Dubček also said how pleased he was to have another meeting with Cde. Kádár and agreed to his proposal to have further talks.

Cde. Kádár said that since his meeting with Cdes. Dubček and Černík at Komárom, he had constantly thought about an idea which, he said, he had put forward in connection with the Moscow meeting of five fraternal parties.[63] That meeting, in his opinion, had created an unpleasant situation, and it was a mistake to have held it; but he added that this mistake was followed by another. He was referring here to the decision of the CPCz CC Presidium of 8 July 1968, dealing with the letters from the five fraternal parties of the socialist countries.

Cde. Dubček replied that this decision by the CPCz CC Presidium should not be seen as erroneous. The CPCz had expressed its position favoring meetings of the fraternal parties. As far as the Warsaw meeting of the five fraternal parties was concerned, Cde. Dubček said that the CPCz CC Presidium had not been informed that it would be held. They were first told about the meeting by the Czechoslovak News Agency.[64]

Cde. Kádár repeated that the decision of the CPCz CC Presidium on 8 July 1968 had created a new and difficult situation. He added that he did not at this point wish to elaborate on the causes of these mistakes, for what was important now were the bilateral talks held at Čierna nad Tisou and the Bratislava meeting of the six fraternal parties. The HSWP leadership viewed these meetings favorably and considered them to be of great importance. He remarked that the HSWP delegation had an easy time in Bratislava because it had welcomed both the bilateral negotiations at Čierna nad Tisou as well as the Bratislava meeting.

Cde. Dubček again averred that the CPCz CC Presidium's decision on 8 July 1968 could not be seen as an erroneous step. He said that the initial mistake had been the decision of the five fraternal parties to meet in Moscow, and the second mistake had been the convocation of the Warsaw meeting, again by the five fraternal parties.

Cde. Dubček went on to say that the leadership of his party had also informed the CPSU Politburo that it considered the Warsaw meeting of five fraternal parties to be a mistake, both in procedure and substance. In this context he added that the letter from the CPCz CC Presidium should have been discussed by the leadership of those fraternal parties to whom it had been sent before the Warsaw meeting as an expression of the CPCz's consistent respect for internationalist principles in relations among fraternal parties. But this was not done.

The Warsaw meeting, Cde. Dubček went on, adopted a document concerning one party. Apart from the fact that the meeting's evaluation of the situation differed from that of the party directly affected, the meeting was claimed to be in that party's interest. No one bothered to ask the party concerned whether this was really so. That is why, Dubček said, we considered this step to be a mistake not only vis-à-vis the CPCz but also vis-à-vis the whole international communist movement. Referring to the Bratislava meeting of the six fraternal parties and the document it adopted, Cde. Dubček said the document expressed a cause common to all the participants, for which we will all fight. That is why the CPCz is putting its entire weight behind this document. He said the content of the Bratislava document would be reflected in the proceedings and conclusions of the Extraordinary 14th CPCz Congress. The content of the document is reflected in several decisions and official statements made by the CPCz during the post-January period.

---

[62] See Document No. 83.

[63] For a transcript of this meeting, see Document No. 31.

[64] See Documents Nos. 51 and 62.

He said that after Čierna nad Tisou and Bratislava, the CPCz CC Presidium had taken a number of measures with regard to the clubs (K-231, KAN), the National Front (a law), the social democrats, and so forth, and that by the end of the month there would be a meeting of the CPCz Central Committee and of the National Assembly where legal, personnel, and other measures would be taken to implement the conclusions from Bratislava. Relevant measures are also planned in the CPCz CC Presidium.

Finally, Cde. Dubček again explained that the Bratislava document did not contradict the tasks and wishes of the CPCz. He emphasized that the document had created some basis for future unity, although it must be recognized that Czechoslovakia's internal political situation is more complicated than it was before the Warsaw meeting. The CPCz encountered these problems when carrying out tasks for the whole of society. Cde. Dubček also said he wondered whether some of the other participants interpreted the Bratislava meeting in the same way.

Cde. Kádár remarked that we ought to remember that these parties had not changed even after the Bratislava meeting, which did not mean, however, that we should not reinforce the platform jointly adopted in Bratislava.

DOCUMENT No. 87: General Semyon Zolotov's Account of the Final Military Preparations for the Invasion

Source: "Shli na pomoshch' druz'yam," *Voenno-istoricheskii zhurnal*, No. 4 (April 1994), pp. 17–19.

This excerpt from the memoirs of Lt. Gen. Semyon Mitrofanovich Zolotov, a top-ranking officer in the Main Political Directorate of the Soviet armed forces, covers the last two weeks of military preparations for "Operation Danube" and the first hours of the invasion.

Zolotov's account reveals how eager and impatient many of the Soviet commanders were as they readied their troops for the invasion. Most of the officers, as Zolotov recalls, were "genuinely alarmed" by what was going in Czechoslovakia, and wanted to resolve the crisis as soon as possible. This sense of urgency was shared by Soviet Defense Minister Marshal Andrei Grechko, who had long been warning of the dangers that would arise if events in Czechoslovakia were to continue unchecked. Zolotov claims that when Grechko conducted his inspection tours of Soviet military units in the second week of August before the Politburo had made its final decision, the defense minister informed the commanding officers that they should "expect to send their forces into Czechoslovakia in the very near future."

Zolotov also reports that Grechko expressed concerns about the prospect of NATO intervention on Czechoslovakia's behalf. When asked during one of his inspection visits what Soviet troops should do if they encountered violent resistance, Grechko responded that it was highly unlikely they would meet any resistance from the Czechoslovak army, but that the Soviet Union "could not exclude the possibility of an incursion from the west by NATO." Intelligence and diplomatic reports to the Kremlin demonstrated, however, that Western Europe and the United Stated did not intend to intervene to save the Prague Spring.

... It became known at around this time [in early August] that Army-General S. M. Shtemenko had been appointed the new chief of staff of the Joint Armed Forces of the Warsaw Pact member states.[65] He was highly respected in military circles for his outstanding organizational capabilities and for the vast experience he acquired during the Great Patriotic War and in the postwar period. In addition, the new appointment of Sergei Matveevich, who had headed the Operations Directorate of the General Staff during the Great Patriotic War and had thus been involved in planning all the most important wartime operations, made the possibility of conducting large-scale operations within the framework of the Warsaw Pact more likely.

Before long I received orders to return to the army command post. A good deal of work awaited me in acquainting myself with the new units and formations and with the way their combat and political preparations, troop service, and party-political work were organized. In accordance with the orders they had received, the troops remained in their field camps, concentrated in the Transcarpathian region. In addition to the standard formations of the army, there were already divisions from other regions redeployed here. Along with the commander, I ventured out to these formations and spoke to people. Although the officers did not refer directly to a possible thrust into Czechoslovakia, they understood very well why such a large buildup of troops was under way in the Transcarpathian region.[66] Many comrades expressed genuine alarm at the way events were developing in the ČSSR, and they were psychologically ready, it seemed, to take decisive action.

On 12 August the USSR Minister of Defense, Marshal of the Soviet Union A. A. Grechko, the chief of the Main Political Directorate of the Soviet Army and Navy, Army-General

---

[65] The announcement that Shtemenko would be replacing General Mikhail Kazakov as chief of staff of the Warsaw Pact came on 5 August.

[66] Although this segment, like the rest of Zolotov's memoirs, focuses primarily on the experiences of Soviet troops based in the Transcarpathian region, many of the events and impressions described here apply equally to other units involved in the invasion.

A. A. Epishev, and the commander-in-chief of the Ground Forces, Army-General I. G. Pavlovskii, visited our troops.[67] They stopped at the motorized rifle and tank regiments, and met personnel and staff.

On the following day, the leadership of the USSR Defense Ministry met the members of the Military Council and the command-political staff of the army in Uzhgorod. Marshal of the Soviet Union A. A. Grechko spoke about our problems and deficiencies and about our most pressing tasks. In particular, he pointed out the necessity of bringing all equipment up to a combat-ready state as soon as possible; of replenishing the stocks of combat material; of being ready to undertake a lengthy march across forested and mountainous terrain; of paying special attention to the training of the drivers and mechanics of tanks, armored personnel carriers, and infantry fighting vehicles and the drivers of other cars and trucks; and of ensuring a full complement and suitable replacements in all sections, crews, and detachments. The USSR minister of defense warned that in the very near future we could expect to send our forces to the ČSSR. I recall that one of the officers asked him a question: What should we do if we encounter armed resistance, should we use our weapons?

"Czechoslovakia is a friendly country. We are going to our brothers' homeland to help them defend socialism," A. A. Grechko staunchly declared. "On no account must we permit the spilling of blood of Slovaks and Czechs. I am certain that the CzPA will not put up resistance. However, we cannot exclude the possibility that NATO's forces will invade the ČSSR from the West. If that happens, we will have to act in accordance with the situation."

This meeting left an uneasy impression. It is possible that in August 1968 the world was again left teetering on the verge of a global war.

On Sunday, the 18th of August, we and our families went off to the mountain resort area at Yaremcha for a holiday. However, a policeman met us on the road and gave me a message saying that it was necessary to return immediately. Late that night I got back to Uzhgorod with my colleagues. There we found out that the situation in the ČSSR had deteriorated, and received orders to prepare the troops to move into that country.

It was necessary to ensure great vigilance and combat readiness and not to permit any frivolousness or lapses of discipline. To this end, the political department of the army was unstinting in its efforts to carry out intensive political education work.

On the eve of the introduction of the allied troops into the territory of the ČSSR, meetings and gatherings took place in the units and formations. The personnel were informed about a TASS statement, which said that party and state officials in the ČSSR had appealed to the Soviet Union and other allied states with a request that they provide urgent help, including the help of armed forces, to the fraternal Czechoslovak people. The statement said that this appeal had been prompted by the threat to the existing socialist order in Czechoslovakia and to the established constitutional state on the part of counterrevolutionary forces who had joined in a conspiracy with external forces hostile to socialism. The TASS statement was published in the Soviet press on 21 August 1968.

Soviet soldiers were informed that the introduction of allied troops into the territory of the ČSSR was prompted by the necessity of defending the fraternal Czechoslovak people against the intrigues of internal and external counterrevolution. No doubt, from today's standpoint the Czechoslovak events are regarded quite differently. But at that time, we perceived what was going on in the ČSSR in precisely the terms described in the TASS statement. My fellow officers and I saw the approaching operation as an unavoidable and appropriate response to the threat that had arisen. We believed that we were marching in to help our friends. . . .

At 1:00 A.M. on 21 August 1968 the units and formations of the army crossed the state border of the ČSSR. A huge procession of troops fitted out with modern equipment and weapons moved to the west. Until 3:00 A.M., the commander and I monitored the advance of tanks and vehicles,

---

[67] On the inspection tours by Grechko, Epishev, et al., see Document No. 84.

and then I moved ahead to the command post. There was no resistance at all from the Czechoslovak side. The front-line units marched forward intently. They crossed 250–300 kilometers within eight to ten hours. The motorized rifle division of Major-General G. P. Yashkin crossed 120 kilometers in four hours.

At first the march proceeded calmly. The local residents assumed that the large columns of our vehicles were moving to an ordinary exercise. Only when the radio and television of the ČSSR featured a broadcast about the violation of Czechoslovakia's sovereignty by allied troops did we sense that the nationalist sentiments of the Czechs and Slovaks had been affected. Crowds of agitated people now began meeting us on the roads. They were screaming and throwing things at us. Derogatory graffiti appeared on the streets and fences.

By the end of 21 August, the troops of the army had completed the tasks set out for them and had moved expeditiously into the territory of Slovakia and southern Moravia.

In a number of centers, Soviet troops took under their protection the most important facilities in local garrisons: staffs, command posts, lines of communication, air bases, combat vehicle depots, stocks of military equipment and weapons, ammunition, storage facilities for fuel and other materials, etc. We set up operative communications with the local authorities and the command of the CzPA. At the behest of Lt. Gen. Maiorov, the staff and field command of the army took up quarters in the city of Trenčín in the Central Slovak province, quartering in the same place as the staff of the CzPA's eastern military district. Despite the frictions and discord that arose at the outset, the commander of the eastern military district's troops, Lt. Gen. S. Kodaj, took the necessary measures to accommodate our troops and staffs on the territory of the district's military bases.[68] As stipulated in the directives of the ČSSR president and the minister of national defense, he ordered his troops not to oppose the Soviet soldiers and to help them in fulfilling their designated tasks. He was supported by the district's chief of staff, Major-General J. Pašek, and the head of the Political Directorate, Colonel J. Kovačík.

. . . On the first day of our march along the roads of the ČSSR, a tragedy occurred. En route between the cities of Prešov and Poprad, the path of a tank column was blocked by a group of women and children. As was later revealed, they had been planted there by extremists, who were hoping to provoke an incident involving a huge loss of human life. To avoid running over the people, the mechanic-driver of the vehicle at the head of the column swerved sharply to the side. The tank overturned from the sudden movement and, having fallen on its turret, caught on fire. Two soldiers serving in the tank received severe injuries, and one of them died as a result.

All told, our army lost 12 soldiers during the march into Czechoslovakia in August 1968, and 76 suffered wounds of varying intensity.

Seven combat vehicles were damaged, and more than 300 automobiles were damaged to one degree or another. These statistics were cited by Lt. Gen. A. M. Maiorov at a meeting on 23 August. At the same time he demanded that the soldiers exercise maximum restraint and that they avoid responding to provocations at all costs. Soviet soldiers did indeed abide by this code of behavior, as is evident from the fact that there was not a single instance in which the servicemen of the army used their weapons, despite the situations that arose in which the nerves of even combat-hardened veterans might have given way.

[68] Lt. Gen. Samuel Kodaj, who had previously been the head of the district's Main Political Directorate, was a notorious hardliner who collaborated with Soviet officials both before and during the invasion. With Kodaj in command of the CzPA's eastern military district, Soviet military planners knew that incoming troops would encounter no organized resistance.

DOCUMENT No. 88: The Soviet Politburo's Resolution on the Final Decision to Intervene in Czechoslovakia, August 17, 1968, with Attachments

Source: APRF, Prot. No. 38.

This resolution to invade and the accompanying documents were approved by the Soviet Politburo at the end of its lengthy three-day meeting on August 15, 16 and 17. The resolution codified the final decision to adopt "active measures in support of socialism in the ČSSR" and "provide help to the Communist Party and people of Czechoslovakia through military force."

The wording of the resolution indicates that the Soviet Politburo "unanimously" reached its conclusions about the situation in Czechoslovakia and "unanimously" decided to intervene with military force—suggesting that a firm consensus was achieved among Politburo members by August 17, without the need for a formal vote. The decision, as the document reflects, was assisted by the presentation of Soviet Defense Minister Marshal Andrei Grechko, who, the evidence suggests, presented the findings of his recent inspection tour of Soviet invasion units and sought the leadership's approval for a specific timetable and scale of the impending invasion.

The Politburo document also authorizes "travel for comrades to perform on-site work," a phrase that appears to apply to the mission in Prague undertaken by Kirill Mazurov. Under the code-name of "General Trofimov," Mazurov was responsible for overseeing the whole military-political undertaking and for keeping the Politburo closely informed of the operation's progress. Other officers designated by the Soviet High Command to exercise direct, on-site control of the invasion, including the commander-in-chief of Soviet Ground Forces, General Ivan Pavlovskii and his deputies, also traveled to Prague in strict secrecy.

The appended documents include a hasty invitation to the leaders of the Warsaw Five to come to Moscow for a final pre-invasion briefing on August 18; and a message to all members and candidate members of the Central Committee informing them of the decision to invade. In a procedurally unusual decision, no Central Committee plenum was held. Kremlin officials did, however, conduct a conclave of top party and state officials from the fifteen republics of the Soviet Union.

(See Documents Nos. 107, 112.)

Proletarians of all countries, unite!

Communist Party of the Soviet Union. CENTRAL COMMITTEE

TOP SECRET

No. P95/I

To: Cde. Brezhnev

Extract from Protocol No. 95 of the Session of the CPSU CC Politburo
on 17 August 1968

In regard to the situation in Czechoslovakia.

1. After comprehensively analyzing the situation and events in Czechoslovakia in recent days, and after reviewing the request from members of the CPCz CC Presidium and the ČSSR government to the USSR, Poland, Bulgaria, Hungary, and the GDR to offer them military assistance in the struggle against counterrevolutionary forces, the CPSU CC Politburo unani-

mously[69] believes that in recent days the course of events in Czechoslovakia has become as dangerous as possible. Rightist elements, relying on both overt and covert support from imperialist reaction, have carried out preparations for a counterrevolutionary coup and pose a threat to the socialist gains of Czechoslovak laborers and to the fate of the Czechoslovak Socialist Republic.

Bearing in mind that all political means of assistance from the CPSU and the other fraternal parties have already been exhausted in an effort to get the CPCz leadership to rebuff the rightist and anti-socialist forces, the CPSU CC Politburo believes the time has come to resort to active measures in defense of socialism in the ČSSR, and has unanimously decided to provide help and support to the Communist Party and people of Czechoslovakia with military force.

A proposal to the fraternal parties of the socialist countries—Bulgaria, Hungary, the GDR, and Poland—to convene in Moscow on 18 August for a meeting of party and state leaders to review the given matter would be desirable.

To affirm the draft instructions to the Soviet ambassadors in Warsaw, Budapest, Berlin, and Sofia (see attached).[70]

2. To affirm the text of the letter from the CPSU CC Politburo to the CPCz CC Presidium, as amended by the session of the CC Politburo (see attached).

To affirm the text of the instructions to the Soviet ambassador in the ČSSR on this matter (see attached).

3. To endorse the drafts of the following documents:

— An appeal to the citizens of the Czechoslovak Socialist Republic; and
— An appeal to the Czechoslovak People's Army.[71]

To introduce these documents for review at the forthcoming meeting of the leaders of the fraternal parties.

4. To endorse material for the text of the declaration (see attached).

To affirm the draft instructions on this matter to the Soviet ambassador in the ČSSR (see attached).

5. To instruct Cdes. Suslov, Ponomarev, Katushev, Gromyko, and Rusakov to prepare an information text for communist and workers' parties, taking account of the exchange of opinions at the CC Politburo session.

6. To instruct Cdes. Demichev, Katushev, Kapitonov, and Rusakov to prepare information for the members of the CPSU CC, the candidate members of the CPSU CC, the members of the CPSU Central Accounting Committee, and the CC first secretaries of the communist parties of the union republics, the regional party committees, and the oblast party committees.[72]

7. Special dossier.

8. To instruct Cdes. Kosygin, Suslov, Demichev, Ponomarev, Katushev, and Rusakov to prepare the draft of a document (Appeal of the ČSSR Government).

9. The information provided by Cde. A. A. Grechko is unanimously endorsed by the CPSU CC Politburo.

---

[69] The unanimity of the decision is conveyed by the word *edinodushno*, which is not quite as strong as another Russian word that is also usually translated as "unanimously," *edinoglasno*. Because the stenographic account of the Politburo meeting is not yet available, there is no way to tell precisely why the resolution used *edinodushno* (meaning united in spirit) instead of *edinoglasno* (unanimous by actual vote). It is possible that a few Politburo members initially expressed serious reservations about (or outright opposition to) the invasion, before agreeing to go along with the consensus.

[70] Of the attached documents appended to the resolution, two are not included here because they are featured below as separate records: the draft "letter of warning" from the CPSU CC Politburo to the CPCz CC Presidium (Document No. 89), and the draft appeal to the Czechoslovak army (see Document No. 95). The rest of the attachments are translated here in the order in which they appear in the resolution.

[71] See Document No. 95.

[72] For the text of this statement, see Document No. 94.

10. To instruct the CPSU CC Secretariat to prepare the travel arrangements for comrades to perform on-site work, taking account of the exchange of opinions at the CC Politburo session.

To invite to Moscow on 18 August the CC first secretaries of the union-republic communist parties, the chairmen of the union-republic Supreme Soviet Presidia, and the chairmen of the union-republic Councils of Ministers.

CC SECRETARY

Regarding point 1 of Prot. No. 95

TOP SECRET
IMMEDIATE ATTENTION

WARSAW
BUDAPEST
BERLIN
SOFIA

SOVIET AMBASSADOR

Promptly go in person to Cde. Gomułka (accordingly, Cdes. Kádár, Ulbricht, and Zhivkov) and transmit the following in accordance with the CC Politburo's instructions:

In connection with the unusually complicated situation that has emerged in Czechoslovakia and the need for urgent advice, the CPSU CC Politburo requests that you come to Moscow on Sunday, 18 August, at 10:00 A.M. Moscow time, acting at your own discretion.

L. Brezhnev

Regarding point 1 of Prot. No. 95

TOP SECRET
IMMEDIATE ATTENTION

PRAGUE
SOVIET AMBASSADOR

We are transmitting the text of a letter from the CPSU CC Politburo to the CPCz CC Presidium (sent by separate telegram).[73]

You must deliver it by Sunday morning.

Confirm by telegram.

[73] For the text of the draft letter, see Document No. 89.

Regarding point 1 of Prot. No. 95

PRAGUE
SOVIET AMBASSADOR

You are instructed to meet Cdes. Bil'ak and Indra and to pass on to them the text of the attached document, having indicated to them that the material in this document might be helpful to the friends in drafting an Appeal to the People.

Confirm by telegram.

DECLARATION
OF THE CPCz CC PRESIDIUM AND THE GOVERNMENT
OF THE CZECHOSLOVAK SOCIALIST REPUBLIC

Czechs and Slovaks,

Citizens of the Czechoslovak Socialist Republic!

Our motherland is going through a critical time. Socialism and the workers' regime are in danger. The counterrevolution is making a bid for power. It is trying to liquidate our socialist gains and turn the country back into the bourgeois path of development.

At this grave moment, the CPCz CC Presidium and the ČSSR government are appealing to you—the workers, peasants, representatives of the popular intelligentsia, soldiers and officers, and guards from the People's Militia—with a call to rise up in defense of the socialist gains that were achieved through the heroic struggle of Czechs and Slovaks against the Hitlerite tyranny and the selfless labor of our people during the years of socialist construction.

The Communist Party of Czechoslovakia, which at the January CPCz CC plenum came out in support of the perfection of forms of management of the national economy, the development of socialist democracy, and the rectifictaion of mistakes and shortcomings from the past, firmly declared its resolve, on the basis of Marxist–Leninist teachings and the successes achieved during the twenty years of popular rule, to continue a course aimed at building socialism in Czechoslovakia.

Unfortunately, events in the country have moved in a different direction. Forces that were always hostile to the cause of socialism in Czechoslovakia, the very forces that on the eve of World War II betrayed the Czechoslovak people to German Nazism, are now trying to commit new treachery. Their goal is to wrest the gains of popular rule away from the workers and to tear Czechoslovakia out of the commonwealth of socialist states and return it to its bourgeois past.

Organized, hostile forces led by certain centers, who are seeking to bring about a fundamental disruption of the existing social and state order by means of a "cold coup"[74] or, if needs be, by military force and resort to civil war, are active in the country. Hostile and unstable elements, having penetrated into the leadership of the party and government, have begun to yield one position after another, thus paving the way for the rise to power of the counterrevolution. In the capital, the cities, and the regions, a large number of legal and underground hostile groups have emerged, under the sway of non-proletarian classes and diehards from the exploiting classes.

The borders of the Czechoslovak state have been rendered vulnerable to penetration by foreign agents, spies, and subversives.

[74] Apparently, this was a takeoff of the phrase "Cold War" (as opposed to hot war)—that is, it was meant to indicate a normally violent event that was being accomplished without violence.

The anti-socialist, counterrevolutionary forces have directed their main blow against the Communist Party of Czechoslovakia, seeking to vilify it and undermine its leading role in society. They have inflicted a stream of slanders against honest communists and have done everything they can to disparage the achievements of the CPCz, the working class, and all those who have labored for the construction of socialism.

The lack of necessary and timely rebuffs to the intrigues of the enemies of socialism has caused events to reach the point where these forces have cast aside all restraint and pose a threat to the further existence of the very foundations of the socialist order. The rightist, revisionist elements, who have infiltrated the leadership of the party and state and who have heaped all sorts of promises on the people, have in fact shown themselves to be politically bankrupt. Their ascendance to power signaled an attack against the vital interests of the workers. They raised prices on a number of essential goods. Communists, laborers of the country, and all others to whom the cause of socialism is dear are decisively rejecting their position of accommodation with the counterrevolution.

Workers! Peasants! Popular intelligentsia! Soldiers of the People's Army, employees of the State Security organs, and warriors from the People's Militia! Young people and students! The duty of every citizen is to grasp the full extent of the danger and to safeguard the gains of socialism in Czechoslovakia.

The CPCz CC Presidium and government of the country are taking the initiative to unite all patriotic forces in the name of the socialist future of our motherland. The threat of a fratricidal struggle, which the reactionaries have prepared, has given us no choice but to appeal for help to the Soviet Union and other fraternal socialist countries. Our allies have responded to this request. They dispatched their troops to our country to offer us help during this arduous moment of travail.

The CPCz CC Presidium and the Revolutionary Government urge all citizens to offer assistance to the military units of our allies. After the threat from the counterrevolutionary forces is eliminated, the allied forces will be withdrawn from the territory of Czechoslovakia.

Today, at a time of daunting tribulations for the cause of socialism in the country—the cause to which Czechoslovak communists and all laborers gave and continue to give their energy, knowledge, and political experience—the newly formed CPCz CC Presidium and Revolutionary Government of the Czechoslovak Socialist Republic, having taken upon themselves full responsibility for supervising the affairs of the Czechoslovak state, have decided to issue this declaration on the internal and foreign policy of the country.

1. Internal Policy

The socialist order of the ČSSR is the unshakeable basis for the development of our state. The party and government will always regard the consolidation, development, and defense of the gains of socialism as their highest priority and most important duty.

In taking active steps to promote socialist construction, the party and government will strictly and consistently adhere to the principles of Marxism–Leninism and, above all, will strengthen the leading role of the working class and its communist vanguard. The leading and directing role of the communist party in the development of society is not the privilege but the duty of communists, and they will honorably fulfill it in the name of the present and the future of their people.

In creatively resolving the tasks of future socialist development, while taking full account of the specific national features and conditions in our country, the party and government will adopt measures to safeguard the dynamic development of socialist relations, the union of democracy with scientific leadership, the consolidation of the socialist way of life, the support of working-class and public discipline, and the exclusion of methods of subjectivism and willfulness in the leadership.

The party will consistently pursue a line aimed at bolstering the role of the National Front in the sociopolitical life of the country. The National Front is a tried form of cooperation among all the forces of our society who are committed to the cause of socialism.

The anti-socialist forces have made an effort to stir up nationalist passions, seeking to introduce and ignite discord between Czechs and Slovaks. The party and government will do everything to strengthen fraternal friendship of the Czech and Slovak peoples.

The party and government, as was indicated in the CPCz Action Program, will adopt all necessary measures to take advantage of all internal resources and opportunities that allow for the development of fraternal relations with the other socialist countries. In the process they will seek to achieve a higher rate of industrial production, increased productivity in our economy, and higher living standards for blue-collar and white-collar workers. Efforts will be carried out to perfect the supervision of the national economy, to improve planning, to develop the financial independence and initiative of state enterprise collectives, and to speed up the introduction of the achievements of modern science and technology in our productive base.

We are aware that current living standards still do not fully satisfy the growing demands of laborers. This applies both to the working class and to other segments of the population. The party and government decisively reject as incompatible with the fundamental interests of workers the suggestions by rightist forces to raise economic productivity at the expense of reduced living standards for the working class and other employees. These suggestions envisage market competition and mass dismissals of blue-collar and white-collar workers. Instead, the party and government will adopt measures to boost the real earnings of workers, to increase salaries and benefits from social funds, and to improve the pensions and medical care of workers on the basis of the development of social production. The government revokes the decision of _____ to raise prices on essential goods, regarding it as a measure directed against the interests of workers. Starting in _____, the government will set prices back to where they were before this decision was adopted.[75]

Constant attention will be given to problems of socialist agriculture and to increasing the welfare of the rural population.

One of the most important tasks for the party and government will be to consider how to achieve significant improvements in the country's housing stock. Great emphasis will be given to the urban planning of Prague and Bratislava.

The party and government will take all necessary measures to develop higher education, primary education, and elementary school education, as well as to develop science and culture in accord with progressive national traditions.

The state will display solicitude toward all segments of the intelligentsia, to people who perform intellectual labor, and to students and all young people, broadly encouraging them to take part in social and state affairs. The working intelligentsia, having proved its commitment to the cause of socialism, must occupy and will attain a worthy place in the life of the country and its political, social, and cultural activity.

The process of socialist democratization will unfold inexorably, aimed at attracting all segments of Czechoslovak society to take an active part in the building of socialism.

The party and government in their activity will broaden their reliance on mass organizations of laborers, seeking to encourage in every way possible the active participation of trade unions and youth organizations in state life and the process of socialist democratization.

The party and government will constantly pursue the rehabilitation of individuals who were condemned earlier without sufficient legal basis. The results of all cases of individuals that are reopened will be subject to public scrutiny.[76]

---

[75] These spaces for dates were left unfilled in the draft text.
[76] The phrase "public scrutiny" is used here to translate the word *glasnost'*, which was to become better known twenty years later.

All individuals who were the victims of slander or who suffered during the violation of laws will be given the opportunity to receive employment in accordance with the constitutionally guaranteed right to work.

All the so-called political clubs and societies, which recently emerged and became havens for enemies of socialism or fell under their direct supervision or hidden influence, are declared illegal.

The party and government will ensure that the press, radio, and television will be placed at the service of society and not exploited further by groups and individuals to the detriment of the Czechoslovak people, the cause of socialism, and the communist party, as well as to the detriment of the Soviet Union and the other fraternal socialist countries.

In view of the extraordinary circumstances that have emerged as a result of the anti-socialist acts of the counterrevolutionary forces, and bearing in mind that the question of convening a party congress was decided upon without necessary preparation, the CPCz CC has adopted a decision to defer the holding of the 14th Party Congress until a later date.

Steadfast devotion to Marxism–Leninism, the rearing of the popular masses in the spirit of socialism and proletarian internationalism, and an unflagging struggle against bourgeois ideology and against all anti-socialist forces—these are the guarantee of success in consolidating the positions of socialism and in thwarting the intrigues of imperialism.

2. Foreign Policy

The ČSSR is an indissoluble part of the socialist commonwealth of states. In the future it will continue to pay strict heed to the obligations that arise from this status in regard to foreign policy. The party and government declare their resolve to abide unwaveringly by the principles and clauses laid out in the declaration from the Bratislava Conference of Communist and Workers' Parties of Socialist Countries, as well as to strengthen the solidarity of the socialist states and their fraternal friendship, which were and remain a reliable basis for resolving socioeconomic and political tasks that lie before the socialist countries.

The fundamental basis of the country's entire foreign policy activity is friendship with the Union of Soviet Socialist Republics and with other socialist countries, as well as fidelity to the obligations undertaken by the ČSSR along with the other socialist states in the Warsaw Treaty and corresponding bilateral treaties based on the principles of equality, mutual respect, and internationalist solidarity. The party and government will be unswervingly guided by the interest of consolidating the sovereignty and independence of the ČSSR and expanding cooperation with the fraternal socialist countries.

Policy with respect to European security remains unchanged. The necessity of such a policy is dictated not only by the experience of the past and by the joint interests of the socialist states, but also by the fact that the main threat to European peace and to the security of the ČSSR still comes from West German militarism and revanchism, as is evident from the fact that the FRG still does not acknowledge that the Munich agreement was illegal from the very start. All of this increases the threat to the security and independence of Czechoslovakia.

Czechoslovakia will conduct a policy of peace and friendship among the peoples. It will take its place among the states that are forming a powerful anti-imperialist front, and will work alongside countries that are waging a struggle to respect the rights of peoples, to bring about the final elimination of colonialism, and to promote the Charter of the United Nations.

Czechoslovakia was and remains committed to a policy of stopping the arms race, a policy of disarmament, including nuclear disarmament, and a policy of doing away with this type of weapon and of achieving a complete ban on nuclear testing.

The ČSSR stood and will stand for a policy of peaceful coexistence between states of differing social systems and for the resolution of international disputes only by peaceful means.

In its foreign affairs, the ČSSR will strictly observe the international obligations it has undertaken in multilateral and bilateral treaties and agreements concluded with other states.

In the interests of developing the economy and boosting the people's welfare, the leadership of the country will devote great attention to the further development of economic and scientific-technical cooperation with the Soviet Union and other socialist countries both within the CMEA framework and on the basis of bilateral agreements.[77] Normal economic ties will be made with other states on the basis of the mutual benefit principle.

Dear countrymen!

The CPCz CC Presidium and government of Czechoslovakia urge you to display maximum responsibility and patriotism and to fulfill your duties honestly and calmly. We urge each of you at your workplace to gather closely around the communist party in putting an end to the counterrevolution and carrying out the internal and foreign policies proclaimed in this declaration.

To resolve all these tasks, the Czechoslovak people will rely on the fullest possible help and support of our tried and true friend, the Soviet Union, and of the other fraternal socialist countries. Every sincere patriot, every Czech and every Slovak, is well aware that the Soviet Union is the most reliable guarantor of the sovereignty, freedom, and independence of socialist Czechoslovakia.

All men and women of the Czechoslovak Socialist Republic!

The CPCz CC Presidium and the government triumphantly declare that they will apply all their strength and energy to protect the socialist gains of the working people, to raise the living standards of all laborers, to proceed with the further development of the democratic bases of society, and to enable our socialist motherland to flourish!

---

[77] The Council for Mutual Economic Assistance (CMEA) was the organization that handled trade and economic ties among the Soviet Union and its East European allies.

DOCUMENT No. 89: Draft "Letter of Warning" from the CPSU CC Politburo to the CPCz CC Presidium, August 17, 1968

Source: APRF, Prot. No. 38.

This draft of the CPSU Politburo's final "letter of warning" to the CPCz Presidium was approved by the Politburo on August 17 at the end of the three-day session that determined the invasion of Czechoslovakia. The draft was then promptly transmitted to the Soviet ambassador in Czechoslovakia Stepan Chervonenko, for delivery to the CPCz leadership. The instructions accompanying the draft stipulated that Chervonenko must hand over the document by the morning of the 18th, but delivery was held up until the evening of the 19th. (See headnote for Document No. 90.)

The Politburo's final "letter of warning" contained little other than the numerous previous critical communications from the Kremlin; it reiterated a litany of complaints and accusations that had been expressed before, either orally or in writing. Although the document stated that any delay by the CPCz in complying with Soviet wishes would be "extremely dangerous," it gave no direct or indirect indication of what the consequences would be, and therefore was not treated as an ultimate "warning" by Dubček.

(See Documents Nos. 82, 90, and 93.)

TO THE PRESIDIUM OF THE CENTRAL COMMITTEE
OF THE COMMUNIST PARTY OF CZECHOSLOVAKIA

Dear Comrades!

The development of events after our meetings in Čierna nad Tisou and Bratislava compels us to put a question to you: Has the mutual understanding that resulted from these meetings been upheld, and is the leadership of the CPCz truly ready to carry out the agreements that were reached?

In Čierna nad Tisou we told you frankly, in a comradely way, our fears for the fate of socialism in Czechoslovakia in connection with the growing threat of counterrevolution. Along with you we came to the conclusion that this question affects the vital interests of the entire socialist community. The CPCz CC Presidium acknowledged that conditions in the party and the country call for more active and decisive measures against those who are discrediting the CPCz, who are attacking the foundations of socialism, and who are attempting to undermine the fraternal friendship between Czechoslovakia and the Soviet Union and the other socialist countries. You assured us that the CPCz leadership would take the following concrete steps in the immediate future:

— assume control of the mass media;
— put a halt to the anti-socialist and anti-Soviet attacks in the press, on radio, and on television;
— put an end to the activities of various types of clubs, groups, and organizations supporting anti-socialist positions;
— carry out measures that would prohibit any activity by the Social Democratic Party; and
— carry out other relevant measures, including steps to strengthen the leading organs, with the aim of securing the leading role of the party and consolidating the positions of socialism in Czechoslovakia.

On the basis of the mutual understanding reached in Čierna nad Tisou in particular, we took joint measures to convene a meeting in Bratislava at which a joint statement was adopted. This statement evoked a positive response from the communist parties and peoples of the socialist countries.

As you will remember, we foresaw that when the anti-socialist elements in Czechoslovakia learned about this new conference and its results, they would try to use all means to compromise the decisions of these talks and to invigorate the struggle against our common cause and interests.

The CPSU and the other fraternal parties that took part in the Bratislava conference believed that you would embark on a struggle against such attacks. We told you that as far as our party was concerned, we were ready to provide unlimited help in this struggle.

We are compelled once again to remind you of this because a number of serious factors confirm that events are proceeding in a direction that scarcely corresponds to the idea of what we agreed upon, and that the CPCz CC Presidium is not adopting effective, concrete measures aimed at their practical application.

In phone conversations between Cde. A. Dubček and Cde. L. I. Brezhnev we mentioned our serious concern about the continuing offensive of the anti-socialist and counterrevolutionary forces whose main assault, in recent days, has been against the Marxist–Leninist principles of socialism and proletarian internationalism, against the healthy forces of Czechoslovakia, and against fraternal relations between Czechoslovakia and the Soviet Union and between Czechoslovakia and the other socialist countries.

In connection with this, at the behest of the CPSU CC Politburo the Soviet ambassador in Czechoslovakia Cde. S. V. Chervonenko spoke on two occasions to Cde. Dubček and Cde. Černík between 7 and 13 August.[78] Unfortunately, though, the situation has not changed for the better.

Therefore the CPSU CC Politburo, based on its concern for the development of events in the CPCz and in the ČSSR, has decided to appeal to the CPCz CC Presidium, which bears responsibility for implementing the agreement reached between us.

We wish to draw your attention to the fact that the press, radio, and television are interpreting the results of the meetings in Čierna nad Tisou and Bratislava as a victory for the CPCz over the CPSU and the other fraternal parties.[79] The Bratislava Declaration is being presented in a one-sided manner, often accompanied by a spirit of nationalism. We are not referring here to individual remarks, but to a general line.

Furthermore, the irresponsible assessments and conclusions that the press is publishing have been given *de facto* support by certain leading officials in the CPCz as indicated by their remarks.

Party and government officials who evaluate the results of the talks in Čierna nad Tisou and Bratislava objectively, from a Marxist–Leninist and internationalist position, are subject to vulgar attacks. They are being threatened, the public is being incited against them, and attempts are being made to depict them as "conservatives." The CPCz CC Presidium, however, prefers to remain silent about all this.

Political campaigns are still under way to subvert friendly relations between the ČSSR and the USSR, discredit the policy of the CPSU, and provoke hostility among the peoples of Czechoslovakia as well as distrust toward the fraternal parties and countries. In this inimical, unfavorable campaign against the Soviet Union and the other socialist countries, one cannot overlook the role played by the newspapers *Literární listy*, *Mladá fronta*, and *Práce*, and by the journal *Reportér*, which have long been transformed into the voice of right-wing, anti-socialist,

---

[78] In the final draft of the letter, the following sentence was added at this point: "Finally, on 16 August, Comrade L. I. Brezhnev personally appealed to Comrade A. Dubček in a letter in which, once again, he posed the questions that were considered in telephone conversations with Comrade A. Dubček on 9 and 13 August."

[79] In the final version of the letter, this wording was changed, at Chervonenko's suggestion, to "the results of the meetings in Čierna nad Tisou and Bratislava are being interpreted in the press, on the radio, and on television as a victory for the . . ." Chervonenko argued that it would be better to avoid implying that the whole press had been guilty of such acts.

and anti-Soviet forces.[80] These organs systematically vilify the Soviet Union, which brought freedom to the Czechoslovak people and which liberated them from fascist slavery.

Political attacks organized against the workers of the Auto-Praha factory—the signatories of the well-known letter published in *Pravda*, in which the workers voiced their fears, presented their assessment of events in the ČSSR, and expressed their friendly attitude to the Soviet people—all serve this objective.[81] In regard to this, we cannot refrain from mentioning that Cde. Císař, a secretary of the CPCz Central Committee, has played the role of an instigator in this harsh settling of scores. It is difficult to believe that such activities have a place in socialist Czechoslovakia.

Attacks are continuing against the Warsaw Pact. Insinuations are being made about the possibility of revising the Čierna nad Tisou and Bratislava decisions concerning relations with the allied, socialist countries. There is talk about the need to leave the Joint Armed Forces of the socialist community.

The press is mounting a hysterical campaign in support of General Prchlík, who, as is well known, openly attacked the Warsaw Pact.[82] The campaign in defense of Prchlík is being organized to put pressure on the CPCz Central Committee leadership and to demonstrate that the rightists control the personnel policy of the CPCz CC Presidium.

These and other facts confirm that right-wing, counterrevolutionary forces are being activated and are on the offensive.[83] Despite many statements by official representatives about the steadfast course of the ČSSR vis-à-vis friendship and alliance with the USSR, the mass media crudely slander the policies of the CPSU and the USSR. Rightists call mass meetings for no reason at which unscrupulous individuals speak out against the friendship between our peoples and parties. In Prague right-wing forces openly gather mobs of young rabble-rousers, who shout anti-communist slogans with impunity and throw stones at the building of the CPCz Central Committee. The rightists, using anti-communist slogans, are openly waging a campaign for the liquidation of the People's Militia.[84] The counterrevolutionary forces are busy collecting signatures in support of the liquidation of the communist party.[85]

Leninist principles of organization, which are universally accepted, are being violated in the CPCz along with its statutes. The Prague Municipal Committee is using its "non-stop conference" to exert pressure on the CPCz CC Presidium, and local party organs are using resolutions to alter the directives of the CPCz Central Committee.[86] This has occurred in such instances as the letter from Auto-Praha workers, and when "blacklists" of party officials were drawn up in order to

[80] At Chervonenko's suggestion, the newspaper *Student* was added to this list of publications in the final version of the letter.

[81] As in numerous earlier documents, this charge referred to the criticism directed against the 99 signatories of the letter that appeared in *Moscow Pravda* on July 30.

[82] This paragraph echoes the complaints in the Politburo's August 13 message (see Document No. 80). The repetition of such complaints at this point is peculiar, however, because on August 15 (two days after the previous message) the Czechoslovak Defense Ministry issued a statement officially disavowing Prchlík's comments. (See "Stanovisko Vojenské rady Ministra narodni obrany," *Rudé právo* [Prague], August 16, 1968, p. 2.) Newly declassified documents confirm that the ministry's statement was intended to accommodate Soviet demands. See, for example, "Stanovisko Vojenské rady MNO: Případ V. Prchlíka," August 13, 1968 (Top Secret), in VHA, F. Sekretariát MNO, 1968–1969, 129/AM.

[83] The allegations in this paragraph were repeated almost verbatim in a harsh editorial by I. Aleksandrov (a collective pseudonym for the CPSU Politburo), "Naglye vypady reaktsii," which appeared on p. 4 of *Moscow Pravda* the following day (August 18).

[84] The phrase "and are busy collecting signatures to support this demand" was added to this sentence in the final version of the letter. Evidence obtained by ČSSR Interior Minister Josef Pavel showed that these campaigns against the People's Militia were orchestrated by KGB and StB forces.

[85] At Chervonenko's suggestion, this sentence was deleted in the final version of the letter.

[86] The Prague Municipal Party Committee, headed by Bohumil Šimon, was one of the most ardently pro-reform organizations in the CPCz. Starting in early July, the committee established a "permanent session," which Soviet leaders construed as an attempt to forge an alternative power structure alongside the CPCz Central Committee and Presidium.

prevent them from being elected to the new Central Committee at the 14th Party Congress. In fact, the rightists are attempting to transform the Prague Municipal Committee into a second Central Committee and are seeking, in advance, to exert active influence on the results of the CPCz 14th Congress. The CPCz leadership is not offering any resistance to these actions.

Therefore, a situation has arisen in the country that is allowing anti-socialist forces to implement their plans and wage new attacks against the CPCz and the positions of socialism. Everything suggests that no decisive struggle has been organized so far against the anti-socialist forces. It is vital to strengthen socialism in Czechoslovakia.

We have the impression that there are forces in the CPCz CC Presidium who are inhibiting the development of this struggle and preventing the fulfillment of the agreements reached in Čierna nad Tisou and the declaration adopted in Bratislava.

The Politburo of the CPSU Central Committee wishes to stress, with all gravity, the urgency of fulfilling the commitments undertaken by you at this meeting and at the conference of fraternal parties without further delay. Any delay in this matter would be extremely dangerous.[87]

In sending this letter, the CPSU CC Politburo expresses its conviction that the CPCz CC Presidium will pay close attention to it, correctly understand our concern and anxiety, and adopt the necessary, urgent measures.[88]

The CPSU CC Politburo asks that all the members of the CPCz CC Presidium be informed immediately about the content of this letter.

17 August 1968

Politburo of the Central Committee of
the Communist Party of the Soviet Union

---

[87] This ambiguous statement is the closest the Soviet Politburo came in the letter to issuing a direct threat of military intervention.

[88] This exhortation raises doubts about Chervonenko's motives for seeking a delay in passing on the letter to Dubček. See Document No. 90 for further discussion.

DOCUMENT No. 90: Cable Traffic between the CPSU Politburo and Ambassador Stepan Chervonenko Amending the Text and Delivery Time of the "Letter of Warning," August 17–18, 1968

Source: APRF, Prot. No. 38.

This exchange of top-secret cables between the CPSU Politburo and the Soviet Ambassador in Czechoslovakia Stepan Chervonenko affected both the content and timing of delivery of the Politburo's final "letter of warning" to the CPCz Presidium. The small number of changes in the text of the document, including a full sentence added by the Politburo itself at the last minute, however, did not significantly alter the original draft. Of the three revisions proposed by Chervonenko, the most substantive is his recommendation that a sentence in the Politburo's draft—"The counterrevolutionary forces [in Czechoslovakia] are busy gathering signatures for the liquidation of the communist party"—be deleted because there is no evidence to substantiate it.

The change in the delivery time of the letter was far more important than the changes in content. Until these cables and a ciphered telegram stored at the Russian Foreign Ministry were declassified in the early 1990s, it was not known precisely when Chervonenko gave Dubček the letter. Even Dubček himself later cited two different dates—August 18 and late on the 19th—on which he received the letter. These cables and the document from the Foreign Ministry (which briefly recounts Chervonenko's final pre-invasion meeting with Dubček) confirm that Chervonenko was originally supposed to transmit the letter to Dubček on the morning of the 18th (see Document No. 88); but, with the Politburo's approval, he did not actually deliver it until the evening of the 19th, just 24 hours before the invasion began.

Chervonenko sought a delay on the grounds that "no one from the [CPCz] leadership would be in the CPCz CC building" on a Sunday—a specious argument since Chervonenko could easily have visited Dubček on Sunday morning either at home or at his office to pass on the letter. (That in fact is precisely what Chervonenko did the following evening.) The Soviet ambassador's chief motive in seeking the delay was simply (as he put it) to "avoid sparking off premature actions by the rightist forces." After consulting with Biľak and Indra, Chervonenko concluded that it would be best to allow as little time as possible for the CPCz leadership to consider the document. That way, there would be even less chance that Dubček would raise the matter at all in the Presidium until after the start of the invasion.

The document was very similar to the flurry of messages Dubček had been receiving from Soviet leaders over the previous two weeks; therefore he initially attached no special significance to the Politburo's latest admonitions. Even so, Dubček decided to bring the letter with him to the CPCz Presidium meeting on August 20, so that he and his colleagues could give the Soviet Politburo a collective response. During the meeting, when reports arrived that Soviet and East European troops had entered Czechoslovakia, he removed the document from his briefcase and read it to the other Presidium members.

Later, the leaders of the reinstated hard-line regime in Czechoslovakia, especially Gustáv Husák and Vasil Biľak, would accuse Dubček of having deliberately concealed the "letter of warning" from the other members of the CPCz Presidium on the night of August 20, allegedly because he feared the document would be used in a vote of no-confidence against him. This new documentation, however, clarifies that Dubček's "omission" was engineered by the Soviet Union itself. Although Dubček neglected to inform his colleagues about the letter until after word of the invasion came in, that was exactly the outcome that Soviet leaders—through Chervonenko's connivances—had sought.

(See also Documents Nos. 89 and 93.)

Proletarians of all countries, unite!

Communist Party of the Soviet Union. CENTRAL COMMITTEE

TOP SECRET

No. P95/2

To: Cdes. Brezhnev, Kirilenko, Suslov, Katushev, Gromyko, Kuznetsov, Rusakov

Extract from protocol No. 95 of the session of the CPSU CC Politburo
on 18 August 1968

On the Telegram to the Soviet Ambassador in the ČSSR.

To affirm the text of the telegram to the Soviet ambassador in the ČSSR (see attached).

CC SECRETARY

Regarding point 2 of Prot. No. 95

IMMEDIATE ATTENTION

PRAGUE
SOVIET AMBASSADOR

We agree with your suggestions for the text of the letter from the CPSU CC Politburo to the CPCz CC Presidium, and we agree that the time of delivery should be on Monday, 19 August.

In the text of the letter, to accommodate the request of our friends, a reference should be included to the personal appeal from Cde. L. I. Brezhnev to A. Dubček in his letter of 16 August, with the following changes:

In the existing text, after the sentence "In connection with this, at the instruction of the CPSU CC Politburo, the USSR ambassador to Czechoslovakia, Cde. S. V. Chervonenko, twice appealed to Cdes. A. Dubček and O. Černík between the 7th and 13th of August," add the following: "Finally, on 16 August, Cde. L. I. Brezhnev personally appealed to Cde. A. Dubček in a letter that once again laid out the matters raised by him during the telephone conversations with Cde. A. Dubček on 9 and 13 August," and then continue with the text as is.

MINISTRY OF FOREIGN AFFAIRS OF THE USSR
TOP SECRET

CIPHERED TELEGRAM[89]
FROM PRAGUE

IMMEDIATE ATTENTION

Because on Sunday, the 18th of August, there is no one from the leadership in the CPCz CC building, we believe it would be advisable to transmit the letter from the CPSU CC Politburo on Monday. Our Czechoslovak friends support this view, and they suggest that it would be more appropriate to transmit the letter in the usual manner, without attracting undue attention, in order to avoid sparking off premature actions by the rightist forces.

At the same time, Cdes. Biľak and Indra will be apprised of the contents of this letter independent of when exactly it is delivered to the CPCz CC Presidium. Simultaneously, we would ask that, before the official delivery of the letter, you examine and permit us to offer some amendments that, in our view, warrant attention.

The sentence "the counterrevolutionary forces are busy gathering signatures for the liquidation of the communist party" should be deleted from the text, since the embassy and the representatives of neighbors do not have such facts at their disposal. At the same time, at the end of the sentence "the rightists, under the banner of anti-communist slogans, are openly waging a campaign for the liquidation of the People's Militia," the following words should be added: "and are busy gathering signatures in support of this demand."

To the list of press organs that have been serving as the mouthpiece of rightists and others, the newspaper *Student* should be added.

In the sentence that says "the press, radio, and television are interpreting the results of the meetings in Čierna nad Tisou" and so forth, say the following instead: "the results of the meetings in Čierna nad Tisou and Bratislava are being interpreted in the press, radio, and television" and so forth. This change is necessary to avoid implying that the entire press is doing such things.

17. VIII. 68

Chervonenko

---

[89] In the copy of the telegram provided by the Russian government, several lines have been deleted from the beginning, and a few lines have been deleted at the very end. Because the text of the telegram is intact, one can infer that the deleted lines pertain to classification procedures.

DOCUMENT No. 91: Ambassador Stepan Chervonenko's Report on His Meeting with Czechoslovak President Ludvík Svoboda, August 17, 1968

Source: AVPRF, F. 059, Op. 58, P. 124, D. 574, Ll. 49–62.

This memorandum of a conversation recounts a secret meeting between Czechoslovak President Ludvík Svoboda and the Soviet ambassador in Czechoslovakia, Stepan Chervonenko, just a few hours after the Soviet Politburo had reached a final decision to go ahead with the invasion. Acting on orders from Moscow, the ambassador first provides a detailed explanation of the events that culminated in the Politburo's August 17 decision (without initially mentioning the decision itself). In direct language, Chervonenko informs Svoboda that the "use of extreme measures," including military force, "could not be excluded," although he offers no hint that the invasion is imminent. The document records the Czechoslovak president's dramatic warning: military intervention would be a "catastrophe" and would cause the Czechoslovak people to "lose all faith in the Soviet Union for many generations to come. . . . Don't you dare resort to military means to resolve the situation," Svoboda emotionally demands. At the end of his report Chervonenko nevertheless asserts that the Czechoslovak president would "stand with the CPSU" when "the most trying and critical moment came."

[Chervonenko began the conversation by describing the recent telephone conversation between Brezhnev and Dubček and by informing Svoboda about the CPSU Politburo's message of 13 August. He then referred to many of the CPCz's "obligations" that were still unfulfilled.]

Things will get even worse, I warned, unless a blow is struck against the rightist, anti-socialist, and anti-Soviet forces. . . . Dubček's and Černík's behavior after the Čierna and Bratislava meetings gives reason to believe that they are trying to deceive the CPSU CC Politburo and the leaders of the parties that met in Bratislava. This provides a basis for regarding the non-fulfillment of obligations that were undertaken at Čierna as a betrayal by the CPCz leadership of its fraternal relations with the CPSU and a betrayal of friendship with the USSR.

When this conclusion was drawn, Svoboda nearly shouted: "No! Dubček is not deceiving the CPSU! He is not deceiving the USSR! He's an honest man and a friend of the USSR; you must have faith in him! Have faith in us!"

. . . In response, I said that the question now is not about the personal side of things, but about the behavior of Dubček and Černík as political figures who are not free from concrete duties and responsibilities. On the contrary, they belong to the leadership of the party and state. Can the failure to uphold an agreement and fulfill obligations be regarded as normal in relations between parties and countries? I cited cases from the history of interstate relations, including relations between states with different social systems, when an open or secret agreement had been achieved and carried out in the name of a higher goal. There is simply no way to explain certain aspects of the behavior of Czechoslovak leaders, whose actions had caused the CPSU and other parties to trust them less and less. This may require the CPSU CC Politburo to respond to its party and world opinion by doing away with the secrecy surrounding the Čierna agreement and renouncing commitments that were valid only as long as the Czechoslovak leadership fulfilled its own commitments. I told the president directly that the CPSU CC Politburo will do what is required by the circumstances, but will never permit the socialist gains in fraternal Czechoslovakia to be damaged. As far as having trust in Dubček and Černík, this cannot somehow be divorced from their political behavior and their posture toward the USSR in deeds, not in words. I cited a number of arguments and factors regarding Dubček's behavior that evoke serious anxiety. It was evident that Svoboda began to lose his blind faith in Dubček; he was distressed and surprised, and at times, almost as in a cross-examination, he interjected comments to the effect of "How could this have happened?" "Why would Dubček behave this way?" and so forth.

One must bear in mind, of course, that Svoboda had been appointed to his post by Dubček. I noted that this appointment had been made through the direct initiative and support of the Soviet side, which Svoboda had not realized and which made a deep impression on him.

When the discussion turned to possible ways out of the crisis, the president sprang up and loudly exclaimed: "Don't you dare resort to military means to resolve the situation! That would be a catastrophe. If troops are brought here, Czechoslovakia will collapse and the republic will be lost. The Soviet Union, which the people of Czechoslovakia view as a symbol of freedom and a symbol of hope, will be seen in an entirely different light. Faith in the Russians as liberators will be lost for many generations. The national sentiments of Czechs and Slovaks are now very strained. Recall the history of our nation, the Hussite movement, Jan Hus, the age-old struggle of the Czechs and Slovaks for their independence.[90] Our people linked their freedom and independence with their own relentless struggle and with the great liberating mission of Russians and the Soviet Union. Don't put an end to that lofty sentiment among our people!"

Later, in a calmer tone, Svoboda began to say that "you should give us time and have patience." For my part, I did not yet disclose the intentions of the Soviet side and what methods we have in mind to lend decisive assistance to the healthy forces in Czechoslovakia. I noted that although this conversation did not imply that Soviet troops would be sent into Czechoslovakia the very next day, the circumstances were such that the CPCz leadership was merely shutting its eyes and adopting a compromising position. If a decisive struggle were not waged against the rightist and anti-socialist forces, the situation might deteriorate to the point where the use of extreme measures would be in order. I said directly that this could not be excluded.

I assured him that the Czechoslovak people look favorably upon the Soviet army. Despite the frenzied campaign that rightist and anti-socialist forces conducted against the continued presence of Soviet military formations in Czechoslovakia, there had not been a single instance of hostile behavior by the people against our soldiers and officers.

I also said that we should not confuse the people's true views with what had recently appeared in the Czechoslovak media, which are now under the control of rightist, anti-party, and counter-revolutionary forces. This is precisely the mistake that Dubček and other CPCz leaders made when they misconstrued the climate fostered by the media as a signal of the popular mood. That mistake frightened them off, and therefore they did not make any effort to rely on the people for support and to fight against a handful of anti-communists who, having seized key positions on the ideological front, were now brainwashing the public in an anti-socialist and anti-Soviet spirit.

Svoboda agreed, and said that if that were so and there was no alternative but to embark on a struggle not only using political and organizational means, then "you should give us a chance to adopt all measures, including the use of force, on our own. We can do it, have faith in us." I pointed out that the CPSU CC Politburo and the leaders of the other parties had long been urging Czechoslovak leaders to make a realistic assessment of the situation, to get to work in fighting against rightists and avowed enemies, to discard their illusions, and to stop acting in a utopian manner.

The president then requested that I talk to Dubček and Černík as candidly as I was talking to him. I responded that the CPSU CC Politburo and Leonid Brezhnev had spoken to Dubček many times. Likewise, Kádár and the leaders of other fraternal parties had spoken candidly to Dubček.[91] Many Czechoslovak comrades who champion the cause of socialism also spoke to him. I said that I myself had spoken to him many times on orders from Moscow, and I intended to speak to

---

[90] Jan Hus was a Czech religious reformer in the late 14th and early 15th centuries. He was burned at the stake in 1415. His martyrdom became a potent stimulus for the Hussite movement in Bohemia, which had both religious and nationalistic strands.

[91] That very day, in fact, Kádár was secretly meeting Dubček in Komárno in a last-ditch attempt to get the CPCz leader to change course. See Document No. 86.

him again on Monday.[92] Nonetheless, I was sorry to say that Dubček was either unwilling or unable, for reasons that were not quite clear, to embark on a struggle against the rightist and anti-socialist forces as they gained ever greater control of the situation. Such a lapse was bound to have a tragic outcome for the CPCz and the Czechoslovak people.

Svoboda said that he would talk to Dubček and Černík, and was confident that the situation could be reversed. But he also said that he now understood the complexity of the situation.

Svoboda said frankly that this conversation had placed a burden on him greater than any burden he had ever had to bear. He needed to think things over and to speak to Dubček and Černík.

I told the president that Czechoslovakia was truly passing through a historic phase. Its future as a socialist state would require wisdom, a clear-headed assessment of the situation, and a potent struggle against the openly raging counterrevolution.

I especially emphasized that I was frankly conveying to him the Soviet leadership's view that it was no longer possible to place any faith in the words and promises of Dubček and Černík. It was simply not right to do so. As regards the tactics of the struggle, Svoboda must also clearly see and understand that the Soviet leadership cannot in any way consent to having the resolution of the matter postponed until the 14th Party Congress. There was no reason to hope that the healthy forces could triumph at the congress without changes in the situation. Such an expectation would be dangerous and even reckless, and the current CPCz leadership would never be forgiven by communists and the nation as a whole.

Svoboda again began to lose his composure and said: "Do you want to get rid of Dubček, to replace him? Do you want to bring back Novotný or Novotný's supporters in place of Dubček and Černík?"

In response, I said explicitly to the president that he should not think this way about the intentions of the Soviet comrades, since the CPSU CC Politburo had many times declared its support for the new leadership's January course as well as its support for the new leaders themselves. Svoboda personally could not help but notice this. The Soviet leadership is coming to assist the Czechoslovak communists not by suggesting that they turn the clock back, but, on the contrary, by looking ahead into the future. Whether to leave Dubček in the post of first secretary or appoint someone else—that is a purely internal matter. The crux of the matter is that, at a time when developments in Czechoslovakia must be altered firmly and boldly, it would be far more difficult to do so after the congress.

Svoboda said that after the meeting in Čierna, the people of Czechoslovakia had breathed a sigh of relief. They still regard Dubček and the new leadership with great confidence. Dubček's authority has grown immeasurably. . . .

I reminded Svoboda how, at the Čierna meeting, Soviet leaders had emphasized that gaining prestige through nationalist propaganda in an anti-Soviet vein (by holding a so-called vote of confidence) would drive the new leadership of the CPCz and ČSSR to an impasse, and also inflict enormous damage on Soviet–Czechoslovak relations. I further noted that the outcome of the Čierna meeting was being portrayed as a triumph and a victory for Czechoslovakia's point of view over the views of the CPSU and the other four parties that signed the letter in Warsaw to the CPCz CC. Czechoslovak propaganda was making a fuss about it and bolstering the rightists, and this was clearly causing relations between the CPCz and the CPSU and other parties to deteriorate. Hence, it was necessary to relinquish spurious hopes of fostering so-called national pride through nationalist and anti-Soviet appeals. I asked Svoboda what options the CPSU CC Politburo could possibly have when, after placing its confidence in the CPCz leadership and stopping public polemics, it found that the violent anti-Soviet campaign in the Czechoslovak press had continued unabated after the Čierna meeting. After all, Soviet communists and the

---

[92] This indicates that Chervonenko had already put off the delivery of the CPSU Politburo's "letter of warning" until Monday, the 19th of August (rather than the 18th, as originally proposed), even though he had not yet received approval from Moscow to do so. No doubt, he was confident that his request would be approved.

Soviet people have just as much right as anyone else to expect to be treated respectfully. Evidently, the CPCz leadership has either naively or willfully discounted the possibility that its conciliatory stance vis-à-vis patently anti-Soviet and counterrevolutionary activities in Czecho-slovakia will irreparably damage the internationalist standing of the CPCz, which has been a source of pride up to now. That, I told Svoboda, is why the situation has to be viewed for what it really is.

When he again began to say that perhaps it might nonetheless be possible to change the situation in the ČSSR without resorting to decisive measures and struggle before the 14th Congress, I asked him a question: In this case could I inform the CPSU CC Politburo that he, Svoboda, will guarantee the victory of the healthy forces at the 14th Congress? If so, then he, Svoboda, will take upon himself full responsibility before the communists of Czechoslovakia, before the many hundreds of thousands who perished on the field of battle, including those whom he, Svoboda, fought alongside in the struggle for a free and socialist Czechoslovakia, and before the Soviet people and the world communist movement. This twist in the conversation forced Svoboda to regain his senses. He then began to say that he, unfortunately, can give no such guarantee, but that he will try to get Dubček and Černík to act and adopt meaningful steps that could change the situation before the congress. . . .

Judging from the conversation, the nature of Svoboda's view of the situation in the ČSSR and of the way to resolve it (to proceed without conflict before the congress) has been shaped by Dubček, Černík, and Smrkovský, in whom he maintained complete and unequivocal confidence up to now. . . .

Nevertheless, one can believe that at the most trying and critical moment, Svoboda will stand with the CPSU and the Soviet Union.

DOCUMENT No. 92: Leonid Brezhnev's Speech at a Meeting of the "Warsaw Five" in Moscow, August 18, 1968 (Excerpts)

Source: ÚSD, Sb. KV, Z/S 22; Vondrová & Navrátil, vol. 2, pp. 192–210.

One day after the Politburo decision to use military force, and two days prior to the invasion, Leonid Brezhnev delivered this keynote speech at a hastily convened meeting of the "Five" Warsaw Pact leaders in Moscow. The Soviet leader used this opportunity not only to spell out the rationale for the invasion, but to explain why the USSR had delayed up until this point. Even the "healthy forces" in the CPCz believed it made sense initially to try to enlist Dubček to their cause, Brezhnev states, according to the transcript: Only "after a long period, when they became convinced that Dubček had failed to support the healthy forces . . . and had actively joined the rightist forces," did they find it necessary to appeal for external military assistance. Brezhnev also points out that it would have been difficult for the "Five" to do anything earlier because the "healthy forces" had been slow in closing ranks. Not until very recently, he argues, had the pro-Moscow forces advanced beyond their earlier "vacillations" and "hodgepodge of plans."

During his speech Brezhnev reads a ciphered cable from the Soviet ambassador in Prague, Stepan Chervonenko, which arrived only a few hours before the meeting of the East European leaders. The cable, which recounted Chervonenko's latest meeting with Alois Indra and Oldřich Pavlovský at the Soviet embassy on August 17, indicates that the plan devised by the "healthy forces" to take power with Soviet military backing remained hazy and contingent. Indra and Pavlovský said they might "possibly" ask Černík to form a new government after the Soviet army entered Prague and would seek to have ČSSR Defense Minister Martin Dzúr remain in his post. Rather than work out a fall-back plan in case "Černík refuses" and "Dzúr wavers," the "healthy forces" hoped they could devise new arrangements on the spot, taking account of "the way things have progressed."

Although Chervonenko's cable reflects an optimism that the "healthy forces" would likely succeed—provided that they received adequate military backing from the Soviet Union—Brezhnev's speech conveyed a far more sober uncertainty of whether the "healthy forces" would "remain united to the end," much less whether they would be able to implement their proposals.

[Brezhnev begins with an overview of events after Čierna nad Tisou and Bratislava and previously voiced complaints about Czechoslovakia's failure to fulfill its "commitments."][93]

All of us had counted on serious changes in the actions of the CPCz CC Presidium and had expected that events would be turned around in a way that would reflect our joint declaration.

Unfortunately, we must affirm that this didn't happen. It is clear to all of us that the attacks of the Right not only haven't ceased, but in some respects have grown even stronger, that anti-socialist tendencies have not weakened, that attacks and slander against the Soviet Union and the other fraternal countries have not been curbed, and that attacks and slanderous denunciations against the healthy forces in the CPCz have also continued.

During this period there was the unprecedented incident of a witch-hunt against workers in the "Auto-Praha" factory; many of them have to have been thrown out of the trade unions and even fired because they signed the well-known letter published in our paper *Pravda*. It should be emphasized that the instigator of all this turned out to be Císař, the infamous anti-Leninist and anti-Marxist. He was the one who showed up at the factory at that particular moment.

---

[93] A transcript of the session first became publicly available in mid-1990 at the Modern Records Archive *(Archiwum Akt Nowych)* in Warsaw. The Russian government turned over a copy of its own 57-page transcript of the meeting to the Czechoslovak commission in 1992. The translation here was initially done from the Polish record of the meeting, but it has been adjusted in a few places to conform with the authoritative Russian text.

In Prague and in other cities these anti-socialist swine, to put it mildly, these elements organized by the Right, are collecting signatures on the streets and at enterprises calling for the disbandment of the People's Militia.[94] They also are holding demonstrations.

Not long ago they held a meeting at which there were all sorts of undignified ranting and shouting of slogans against the CPCz and leading individuals; stones were thrown at the Central Committee building; real acts of hooliganism are happening.

Nothing new has occurred from 3 August to this day in the decisions of the CPCz CC Presidium to indicate that even the most preliminary steps are being taken to implement what was agreed on and to carry out the document we adopted, along with you all, in Bratislava. No changes have taken place with regard to personnel even though during this time there was a session of the CPCz CC Presidium.[95]

Throughout this period we not only followed the course of events but considered it our duty, in one form or another which I will speak about later, to ask the CPCz leadership how they are fulfilling their commitments, what is being done, when the Central Committee plenum will meet, and when the personnel questions will be taken care of. . . .[96]

It should be said, based on our sources, that the healthy forces in the presidium, if they remain united to the end, number six full members as of today. This represents a majority compared to those who hold a right-wing or wavering position. The healthy forces have been waging a struggle the whole time, but the struggle inside the presidium is of a type that has not yet managed to succeed outside it. This whole struggle is taking place during formal sessions. No decisions are adopted. The right-wing forces keep silent. The sessions end, and neither the party nor the people have any inkling of what's going on. Everything is presented in such a way as to convey the impression of unity in the presidium, not a struggle. And on top of all this, as you know, the press, radio, and television, in conjunction with the hooligan elements, are carrying out their work on the street and among the masses.

At the same time, it should be said frankly that after monitoring the whole course of events, we can assure you that during this struggle a collective of healthy forces gradually coalesced. This collective gradually formed a monolithic body consisting of people ready to wage a decisive battle against the Right. At first their line was to carry on this struggle in conjunction with Cde. Dubček; but later, after a long period had passed, they became convinced that Dubček not only was wavering and had failed to support the healthy forces on which he could rely in the presidium, but also, in many instances, had done just the opposite in turning away from his comrades and—what is more—actively joining the rightist forces.

The healthy forces in the CPCz CC Presidium have begun to think it is necessary for them to conduct the struggle on their own.

As of late, their plans and ideas have given us the basis for thinking that as a result of this struggle their final plans have taken shape, plans that encompass their considered political views of the situation in the country and the measures to be carried out in practice, and also when these measures are to be implemented. Therefore, having received from them an official communication, we saw how this political crisis is developing, how there is a growing political demand to solve the question, and how the unity of the healthy forces in the CPCz CC Presidium is being consolidated in the process.[97] Having advanced beyond their well-known vacillations and earlier hodgepodge of plans, they have come closer and closer to agreement on a single plan of action, a single date, and a single assessment. Above all, they state that the right-wing forces do not

---

[94] The ČSSR interior minister, Josef Pavel, learned at the time that KGB and StB forces had orchestrated these campaigns calling for the dissolution of the People's Militia.

[95] Actually, by this time there had already been two sessions of the CPCz Presidium, on August 6 and 13.

[96] At this point, Brezhnev cited the steps the Soviet Union had taken to implement the Čierna commitments, as well as the letter from the CPSU Politburo to the CPCz Presidium of August 17, 1968.

[97] The "official communication" to which Brezhnev referred is the "letter of invitation" that was passed on to the Soviet leadership on August 3. See Document No. 72.

wish to engage in a real struggle and to separate themselves. Their line is to act very quietly and to bring the matter before the congress. They have accounts to settle at the congress when they achieve victory, and the healthy forces are taking that into consideration. We have official materials from which it is clear, for instance, that Husák is striving very hard to take power at the Slovak congress. There is every reason to believe what our friends say, namely, that the right-wing has done everything possible to compromise Biľak and will continue to do so until the congress. During the congress they will take all necessary measures to ensure that Biľak's position, which he had in mind to spell out to the congress—and he conducts himself coura-geously, along party lines—does not become known to the party and the people. Of course they will not allow it to become known, and will not allow him to be elected to the leading bodies. It is expected that a session of the CPCz CC Presidium will take place on the 20th. Therefore the healthy forces are reckoning that they must, in the coming days (that is, tomorrow or the day after), speak out decisively and demand the adoption of a number of decisions to fulfill what was agreed upon in Čierna, including the demand for personnel changes, and also fulfillment of the Bratislava Declaration.

According to all available information (and I shall soon read you one document), this is the last political battle-line to which we must turn our attention and treat with all due seriousness, for otherwise, it seems to us, we cannot give the most effective help to the healthy forces in the Central Committee of the Communist Party of Czechoslovakia and to the Czechoslovak people in defending their achievements.

I will read to you, comrades, a document that appears to be the concentrated expression of those plans to which the Czechoslovak comrades wish to call our attention and what they are asking of us.[98]

"Today I met Indra. He requested this meeting and came with Pavlovský.[99] Indra informed me that their group consists of the most reliable people and had just reviewed a plan of action for the CPCz CC Presidium session. If they receive a guarantee from us, then during the night of 20–21 August our troops should move into action. At midnight at the presidium session they will try to insist on a definitive split and adopt a resolution expressing political no-confidence in the right-wing and take upon themselves the *de facto* leadership of the party and government. A document will be prepared with an appeal to the people and fraternal parties to provide help to the healthy forces.[100] The Czechs will send us this document on Monday—that is, tomorrow. Along with those who signed the appeal that was transmitted to Cde. Brezhnev in Bratislava, it is already possible to affix the additional signatures of presidium members Barbírek and Rigo, and also government members Pavlovský, Hamouz, Štrougal, Hoffmann, Korčák, Laštovička, and Krejčí.[101] I'll tell you about this document later on. Because the document, in their view, should be published on the morning of 21 August, when our forces will already have entered Czechoslovakia, Indra guarantees that in the course of the night we'll receive no less than 50

[98] The author of these quoted passages was the Soviet ambassador in Prague, Stepan Chervonenko.

[99] Oldřich Pavlovský, like Indra, was a leading figure in the CPCz's pro-Moscow, anti-reformist faction. He had served as Czechoslovak ambassador in Moscow until the spring of 1968, when he was elevated to the government post of minister of internal trade. Chervonenko writes that Indra "requested this meeting," but it is worth noting that Chervonenko had intended to meet Indra and Biľak anyway in accordance with instructions he had received from the Soviet Politburo on August 17 (see Document No. 88).

[100] This document ended up being drafted in Moscow, and was published in leading Soviet newspapers on August 22. The purported signatories of the appeal were not named.

[101] The final name in this list is indecipherable in the Cyrillic typescript. It is likely to be Josef Krejčí, the minister of heavy industry (though it is worth noting that on August 21, Krejčí endorsed the government's resolution denouncing the invasion). The others in the list between Pavlovský and Krejčí are: František Hamouz, a deputy prime minister; Lubomír Štrougal, a deputy prime minister and chairman of the Economic Council; Karel Hoffmann, the chairman of the Central Board for Communications; Josef Korčák, the chairman of the Central Board for Energy; and Bohuslav Laštovička, who did not belong on this list because he did not hold ministerial rank (though he had been a member of the CPCz Presidium under Novotný).

signatures, including members of the Central Committee and the government. This will be in addition to those they have already obtained. Piller will be informed, but only at the very last minute, and they also hope to get his signature. He vacillates somewhat, though for now he is with them.

On 21–22 August a CC plenum will be convened, as will a session of the National Assembly, both of which, without question, will support their action and approve the appeal to the fraternal parties for military assistance. At the same time an appeal to the people by a large group of cultural figures will be published. That night, after the presidium meets, the printing house and offices of the paper *Rudé právo* will be seized and everything will be made ready for a special edition of the paper to appear. Through one of the most trustworthy activists of their group, radio and television will be shut down, as will all telephone and telegraph communications.[102] In the morning a speech by one of the representatives of their group will be broadcast on radio and television explaining the events. They wanted President Svoboda to speak, but will turn to him only when the troops are in control of the situation. Lists are being drawn up of the most trustworthy employees of the CPCz CC apparatus, as well as the secretaries of regional and district committees, to whom party leadership will be assured in the critical days. Some 20 to 30 radio and television commentators and newspaper journalists are being chosen to exercise control over the mass media. When it becomes clear to the presidium that the troops have entered, this group will possibly turn to Cde. Černík, counting on his conceit and cowardice, with an offer to head the government and act in concert with them. In the event that Cde. Černík refuses, they will declare that they are setting up a provisional revolutionary government headed by Cde. Pavlovský. The following individuals have been mentioned so far for the Council of Ministers:[103]

Dzúr will be asked to remain in his post and told to refrain from ordering his troops to resist the armies of the fraternal countries. . . .

If Dzúr wavers, the post of national defense minister will be given to one of his deputies. Then the question of members of the government will be decided as things progress, in the course of our actions.

An order will be issued through Cde. Šalgovič to seal off the western border. In the opinion of our friends, if we come to a favorable decision, the military operations should begin at midnight on 20–21 August, and by morning the basic strategic points should be taken, in particular, Prague, Brno, Bratislava, Košice, and other major cities.

For now they do not intend to resort to the People's Militia. It will be employed as soon as they are certain of the success of our operation.

Our friends believe that any postponement of the beginning of the operation to a later date, that is, until the period when the Slovak party congress is being held, is unnecessary since the congress will go on for four to five days and our entrance on the very eve of the 14th Party Congress will be used by Western propaganda to make a lot of commotion. Besides, they don't know whether they'll have another chance to carry out all the plans in the presidium they have just submitted to us.

Our friends ask for a final reply on Monday and once again urge that a letter be sent from the CPSU CC Politburo to the CPCz CC Presidium specifying the nature of the commitments adopted in Čierna nad Tisou.[104] They want us to transmit the letter not only to Dubček, but to the other presidium members as well. We have already done that. This will give them a reason to wage an open struggle with the rightist forces, including Dubček.

---

[102] The "trustworthy activist" responsible for shutting down the radio, television, and telephone system was Karel Hoffmann, who had served in 1967 and 1968 (until Novotný's ouster) as minister of culture and information. At the time of the invasion, he was chairman of the Central Board for Communications, which was an ideal vantage point from which to perform this task. As things turned out, however, Smrkovský was able to countermand Hoffmann's orders and ensure that the CPCz CC Presidium's condemnation of the invasion was broadcast over the Czechoslovak media.

[103] Unfortunately, the cable does not provide all the names.

[104] For a copy of this letter, see Document No. 89.

As was already indicated, Dubček concealed from the CC Presidium the fact that he had a telephone conversation with Cde. Brezhnev and received a letter from Cde. Brezhnev on 16 August, and also that he received an aide memoire in connection with the anti-Soviet campaign under way in the Czechoslovak press. Our friends ask that these documents be cited in the CPSU CC Politburo's letter so that they can force Dubček to admit to having received the items and force him to read them at the Presidium.[105]

In addition, Cde. Indra requested that today's *Pravda* publish an article which appeared in *Rudé právo* about hooligans. We saw to this, responded to their request, and published it in *Pravda*.[106]

In the meantime they ask for confirmation that we approve their request and will be ready to take concrete measures at the appointed hour."

So, comrades, I've finished reading the document to you. . . .

Yesterday, the day before yesterday, and three days ago the CPSU CC Politburo comprehensively examined and debated these questions. After a thoroughgoing analysis, we reached the conclusion that Dubček is not going to fulfill any of his commitments, that he has gone over completely to the side of the Right, and that in these circumstances a failure to support the healthy forces would cause the situation to become extremely difficult.

Having weighed all these circumstances, we unanimously[107]—the whole Politburo and the CC Secretariat—have decided to provide military assistance to the healthy forces and to agree to their plan of action, since we believe they are correct in arguing that there is and will be no more suitable time than now to do so. Of course, we understand that today or tomorrow the anticipated step will not be easy for us, but we see nothing else that would be any easier. We could only expect to find ourselves in an even more difficult situation. Therefore we came to this decision.

We were deeply convinced that the appeal of the healthy forces—this group of honest communists, including members of the CPCz Central Committee and members of the CPCz Presidium—would find ardent internationalist and fraternal support from all the other participants in the Bratislava conference. That's the first thing. And therefore we considered it our solemn duty to consult with you. And because so little time was left, we couldn't afford to delay and requested yesterday that you come today.[108]

I think you will excuse us and will understand that we had no other choice in handling things.

That, in effect, is the essence of the issue and the decision of our Politburo about which we have informed you. . . .

[105] All these documents were indeed cited in the CPSU Politburo's "letter of warning." See Document No. 89, as well as Documents Nos. 80, 82, and 85.

[106] The reference here is to the article on August 18 by I. Aleksandrov (a pseudonym for official Politburo statements), entitled "Naglye vypady reaktsii," p. 4. The article denounced the "outrageous hijinks of certain groups in Prague over the last few days," which "are endangering [Czechoslovak] society itself." As examples of these "hijinks," Aleksandrov cited the "slander campaign by reactionary elements against the People's Militia," the "frenzied campaign of persecution against the 99 workers from the Auto-Praha factory whose letter was published in *Moscow Pravda* on 30 July," and other "fierce new efforts by right-wing, reactionary forces, with encouragement from imperialist reaction abroad, to undermine the foundations of socialism [in Czechoslovakia], discredit the leading role of the working class and its party, and tear Czechoslovakia out of the socialist commonwealth."

[107] Brezhnev attributed the decision to the "entire Politburo" (a phrase that presumably included candidates as well as full members) and Secretariat, even though matters of this sort ordinarily would have been determined by a vote of just the *full* members of the Politburo. The candidate Politburo members and the junior members of the Secretariat (i.e., those who were not also full Politburo members) would have been permitted to take part in the debate, but would not have been eligible to vote. Brezhnev's effort to link all the members of the Politburo and Secretariat with the decision—and thus spread responsibility for the invasion as widely as possible—may simply indicate that no *formal* vote was taken because the debate had produced a clear but informal consensus by the end. The word Brezhnev used for "unanimously" *(edinodushno)* conveys the sense of "united in spirit" and does not necessarily imply that anyone actually voted. (By contrast, if he had used the word *edinoglasno*, which also translates into English as "unanimously," it *would* imply that every member of the two bodies formally voted in favor.)

[108] See the invitation in Document No. 88.

DOCUMENT No. 93: Cable from Ambassador Stepan Chervonenko to the Kremlin on His Meeting with Alexander Dubček and Oldřich Černík, August 19, 1968

Source: AVPRF, F. 059, Op. 58, P. 124, D. 574, Ll. 124–127.

Soviet Ambassador to Czechoslovakia Stepan Chervonenko transmitted this cable to Moscow on August 19, shortly after meeting Alexander Dubček for the last time before the invasion. Chervonenko requested the meeting primarily in order to hand over the CPSU Politburo's final "letter of warning." The letter originally was supposed to have been delivered to the CPCz leadership on the morning of the 18th but Chervonenko obtained the Politburo's approval to wait until the evening of the 19th so that Dubček would pay less attention to its significance and there would be less risk of "sparking off premature actions by the rightist forces." The ambassador's account of the meeting suggests that both Dubček and Černík regarded the letter as nothing more than the latest in a long series of Soviet protests and complaints.

(See also Documents Nos. 88, 90.)

. . . Dubček said that no obligations of any sort had been undertaken at Čierna, and that there was an exchange of views there, during which certain plans and intentions had been laid out, including personnel matters, which should have remained known only to those who had spoken in private with one another. Now the CPSU CC Politburo is asking him to inform the members of the CPCz CC Presidium about the letter that Cde. Brezhnev sent confidentially to him, Dubček, on 16 August. This means that it will be regarded by party activists and by the people as interference in internal affairs.

. . . I responded that he, as a political leader, should not present the matter as "interference," since what is at issue is whether there will or will not be a struggle against the rightist danger as the main danger, that is, whether they will or will not fulfill the decisions of the May plenum of the CPCz CC, the agreement at Čierna, and the declaration signed at Bratislava. A struggle against the rightist danger requires concrete measures to be adopted against the purveyors and inspirers of the rightist course in the CPCz, and above all the rightist course in the CPCz leadership. . . . I reminded him that he and others had several times linked Kriegel, Císař, and others with a second center and with the rightists. Consequently, the personnel side of things is an important part of the political line, since a political struggle against the rightists must be clear-cut and take a concrete form.

Dubček did not specify what sort of concrete steps and measures would be implemented in the struggle against rightist and anti-socialist forces. He said that they [in Moscow] do not trust him, and that no specific timeframe was set in Čierna for resolving any particular questions. At times he flared up and sputtered comments to the effect that "you want to restore Novotný or Novotný's methods."

Dubček said that in Moscow they do not understand that it is impossible to resolve problems that have been accumulating over a long period in just a week's time, and so forth.

I did not bother to argue any further because Dubček obviously had not made a realistic and concrete analysis of the situation in the ČSSR and did not reveal his plans and intentions. Černík was present, but he barely took part in the conversation. He was gloomy and only occasionally interjected remarks in a cold tone. Dubček said that on 20 August the letter would be considered by the CPCz CC Presidium and that an answer would be given later on.

DOCUMENT No. 94: Message from the CPSU CC Politburo to Members of the CPSU CC and Other Top Party Officials Regarding the Decision to Intervene in Czechoslovakia, August 19, 1968

Source: ÚSD, Sb. KV, Z/S 9; Vondrová & Navrátil, vol. 2, pp. 210–211.

The Soviet Politburo transmitted this communiqué to all leading officials in the CPSU's Central Committee apparatus and to the heads of republic, regional, and provincial party branches two days before the invasion. The document contains a vehement justification of the decision to "provide fraternal military assistance to the healthy forces in the CPCz," including a pledge that "the troops from our five countries will not interfere in the domestic affairs of fraternal Czechoslovakia." Senior party workers are instructed to use the same sorts of arguments when conducting "explanatory and mass political work among all segments of the public" after August 21. The need for a stepped-up campaign of "mass political work" is indicative of the unease that many Soviet leaders felt about the corrosive impact the invasion might have on the "cohesion of the party and the people" and on the "moral and political unity of Soviet society."

The number of officials who received the announcement was unusually large—a total of 643, including 350 from the CPSU Central Committee, 64 from the Central Auditing Commission, 75 from the union republic CC Secretariats, and 154 from the provincial and territorial party committees. No evidence has emerged that any of the recipients objected to the message, publicly or privately.

The message underscores the top-down character of Soviet decision-making. Although the Politburo was nominally accountable to the Central Committee, it was the Politburo that made all key decisions during the crisis and then informed other party organs.

TO: MEMBERS AND CANDIDATE MEMBERS OF THE CENTRAL COMMITTEE OF THE CPSU

TO: MEMBERS OF THE CENTRAL AUDITING COMMISSION OF THE CPSU

TO: SECRETARIES OF THE CENTRAL COMMITTEES OF COMMUNIST PARTIES OF THE UNION REPUBLICS

TO: FIRST SECRETARIES OF PROVINCIAL (AND TERRITORIAL) PARTY COMMITTEES[109]

The CPSU CC Politburo has systematically informed party activists about the situation in Czechoslovakia and about the emergence there of counterrevolutionary events that have endangered the socialist achievements of the Czechoslovak working people and the fate of the Czechoslovak Socialist Republic.

The CPSU CC Politburo, basing itself on the decisions of the April and July plenary sessions of the Central Committee, has used all possible political measures to influence the development of events in the ČSSR and to assist the healthy forces of the CPCz to sustain socialism and to prevent Czechoslovakia from moving into the imperialist camp.

In recent days events have assumed a most ominous character. The country was on the threshold of a counterrevolutionary coup.[110] By relying on the overt and covert support of reactionary imperialist forces and by exploiting the levers they had seized to run society and the mass media, right-wing forces have attempted to force the party and government of Czechoslovakia to follow a pro-Western policy and return Czechoslovakia to a bourgeois republic. They did not receive the support of a majority in the CPCz CC Presidium, the National Assembly, or the government. Instead, a majority who wish to defend the cause of socialism and the cause of the working class, the peasantry, and the working intelligentsia, have appealed to the Union of Soviet Socialist Republics, the Polish People's Republic, the People's Republic of Bulgaria, the

---

[109] Provinces *(oblasti)* and territories *(kraia)* were administrative divisions in the USSR. Smaller divisions of this sort included autonomous regions *(avtonomnye okrugi)*, cities *(goroda)*, and urban districts *(raiony)*.

[110] An apparent reference to the forthcoming 14th Party Congress.

Hungarian People's Republic, and the German Democratic Republic with a request to give them military assistance in the struggle against counterrevolution.

The CPSU CC Politburo, having considered this appeal, has concluded that the moment has arrived to undertake active measures in defense of socialism in the ČSSR.

Our assessment and conclusions are shared unanimously and supported by the leadership of the fraternal parties and socialist countries: the People's Republic of Bulgaria, the Hungarian People's Republic, the German Democratic Republic, and the Polish People's Republic.

Guided by feelings of internationalist duty and fraternal solidarity, the governments of the five countries have ordered their military units to take all necessary measures on 21 August to help the Czechoslovak working people in their struggle against reactionary forces and to protect Czechoslovakia's security against the intrigues of imperialism.

We have undertaken this decisive step on the basis of a deep and unwavering conviction that it will fully meet the desires and interests of the working people, the peasants, the people's intelligentsia, and all our Czechoslovak brothers.

The troops of our countries will not interfere in the internal affairs of fraternal Czechoslovakia. They will be withdrawn from its territory as soon as the danger to the independence and security of Czechoslovakia and to the socialist future of the Czechoslovak people is eliminated.

Our enemies should be fully aware that no one can or will ever be allowed to disrupt the inviolability of the borders of the allied socialist countries, and that no one will ever be permitted to break a single link in the community of socialist states.

Give serious attention to explanatory and mass political work among all segments of the public in order to promote the further cohesion of the party and people and to strengthen the moral and political unity of Soviet society.

The CPSU CC Politburo

DOCUMENT No. 95: Ciphered Telegram from Andrei Gromyko to Soviet Embassies in Eastern Europe Transmitting the Joint Text of an Appeal to the Czechoslovak People's Army, August 19, 1968

Source: AVPRF, F. 059, Op. 58, P. 127, D. 586, Ll. 33–35.

Soviet Foreign Minister Andrei Gromyko sent this telegram and its brief cover memorandum to the Soviet embassies in the four loyal East European countries on the day before troops were due to begin moving into Czechoslovakia. The cover memorandum directs the Soviet ambassadors in Poland, Hungary, East Germany and Bulgaria to present the leader of the respective country with the text of an "Appeal to the Czechoslovak People's Army," issued in the name of the commander of the joint interventionary forces, Army-General Ivan Pavlovskii. The text of the "joint" appeal claims that the intervention is being conducted at the invitation of "the leaders of the Communist Party and Government of Czechoslovakia;" it calls on Czechoslovak soldiers to support "the joint efforts to defend the cause of socialism in Czechoslovakia," and exhorts them "not to give in to provocateurs, who would try to sow confusion and discord in the ranks of the defenders of socialism." First Secretaries Todor Zhivkov, János Kádár, Walter Ulbricht and Władysław Gomułka all approved the brief appeal. It was released as planned two days later.

TOP SECRET
MAKING COPIES IS FORBIDDEN

EYES ONLY
SPECIAL CLASSIFICATION

19.08.68.

OUTGOING CIPHERED TELEGRAM

Destination: Sofia, Budapest, Berlin, Warsaw

Addressee: The Soviet Ambassador

Pay a call on Cde. Zhivkov (Kádár, Ulbricht, Gomułka) and, as agreed at the meeting in Moscow on 18 August, transmit to him personally the text of an Appeal to the Czechoslovak People's Army issued in the name of the Commander of Forces of the Bulgarian People's Republic, Hungarian People's Republic, GDR, Polish People's Republic, and USSR.
(The text of the Appeal is being transmitted to you in a separate telegram.)
Send a return telegram when you have carried out this task.

A. G.

TOP SECRET
MAKING COPIES IS FORBIDDEN

EYES ONLY
SPECIAL CLASSIFICATION

19.08.68.

OUTGOING CIPHERED TELEGRAM

Destination: Sofia, Budapest, Berlin, Warsaw

Addressee: The Soviet Ambassador

"To our fellow soldiers, officers, and generals of the Czechoslovak People's Army! Dear comrades-in-arms!

Faithful as it is to the cause of socialism and the vital interests of our peoples, and confronted by the overwhelming actions of counterrevolutionary forces, the leaders of the Communist Party and the Government of Czechoslovakia have summoned us for help.

Responding to this request, we have come to your country in order to provide fraternal assistance and, by our joint efforts, to defend the cause of socialism in Czechoslovakia.

Our fraternal countries are fulfilling their obligation as prescribed in the Bratislava Declaration of Communist and Workers' Parties of Socialist Countries. As is stated in the declaration, the defense of the socialist gains of every nation is the common international duty of all socialist countries.

The gains of socialism in Czechoslovakia are under threat. By using deceitful phrases, the enemies of socialism are trying to seize power from the working people and to destroy its avant-garde, the communist party, as well as to snatch Czechoslovakia out of the socialist common-wealth and transform it into a bourgeois state. These actions are creating a threat to the other countries in the socialist commonwealth as well, and also a threat to peace and security in Europe.

Dear friends! Not a single honest soldier can remain indifferent when such a threat is hanging over the socialist motherland. We cannot put off a minute longer dealing a rebuff to the counterrevolution.

We cannot permit the gains of the Czechs and Slovaks that were achieved during the years of popular rule to be crushed by the enemy.

We cannot permit the vital interests of the socialist community and the cause of peace and security in Europe to remain under threat.

Dear comrades and fellow soldiers!

Be vigilant! Do not give in to provocateurs, who would try to sow confusion and discord in the ranks of the defenders of socialism!

In accordance with the instructions of the governments, our forces will be swiftly withdrawn from the ČSSR as soon as the threat to the gains of socialism in Czechoslovakia has been eliminated.

The commander of forces of the socialist countries summons you to take part in joint efforts to defend the revolutionary legal order and safeguard Czechoslovak borders against any efforts by international imperialism and its agents to infringe on the sovereignty and independence of Czechoslovakia.

We are with you, brothers. Our common cause is invincible!

The Commander of Forces of the

People's Republic of Bulgaria,
Hungarian People's Republic,
German Democratic Republic,
Polish People's Republic, and
Union of Soviet Socialist Republics"

A. G.

DOCUMENT No. 96: Cable to Ambassador Stepan Chervonenko from Moscow with a Message for President Svoboda, August 19, 1968, and Chervonenko's Response, August 21, 1968

Source: APRF, Prot. No. 38; and ÚSD, Arch. Komise, Z/S—MID, Nos. 37, 39; Vondrová & Navrátil, vol. 2, pp. 211–212.

Moscow's efforts to ensure that Soviet and East European troops entering Czechoslovakia on August 20/21 would encounter no armed resistance are reflected in these cables. The first cable, sent via the "Hot Line" on 19 August by the CPSU Politburo, directs the Soviet ambassador in Prague, S. V. Chervonenko, to transmit a collective "Appeal" to President Svoboda on behalf of the "Five." The "Appeal" informs Svoboda that the Soviet Union and its allies have decided to "provide armed assistance" to "a majority of the members of the CPCz CC Presidium" who seek to "resist counterrevolution and defend the gains of socialism in Czechoslovakia," and pledges that the incoming troops will behave as "faithful friends of the Czechoslovak people" and will be withdrawn "whenever the president and government of the ČSSR deem this to be necessary." The message then politely but firmly urges Svoboda to "call on the army and people of Czechoslovakia not to resist the troops of the fraternal countries and instead to welcome them as friends," adding that this would be the only way to "avoid unnecessary incidents and victims."

Ambassador Chervonenko delivered the message to Svoboda shortly before midnight on August 20, when "Operation Danube" was already under way. The Soviet ambassador brought with him a draft appeal that Svoboda could issue to the Czechoslovak army and people, but the Politburo had instructed Chervonenko to be tactful when offering such assistance and to raise the matter only if Svoboda "responded favorably to the request of the fraternal parties." Chervonenko found it unnecessary to present Svoboda with the draft, however. Although the ČSSR president was disconcerted when he learned of the invasion, he immediately agreed to do whatever he could to prevent bloodshed, an objective that remained paramount during the entire post-invasion period. Svoboda soon ordered the army not to take up arms and delivered a brief public message calling on all ČSSR citizens to remain calm and avoid violence. The message was broadcast several times over Czechoslovak radio starting at 8:15 A.M. (along with numerous other appeals for calm) and was published in the second edition of Práce *on August 21.*

Ambassador Chervonenko's return cable to Moscow on August 21 reports Svoboda's position as positively as possible: Svoboda "doesn't welcome the intervention of the troops," Chervonenko writes, but pledges "never to cut his ties with the USSR."

Proletarians of all countries, unite!

Communist Party of the Soviet Union. CENTRAL COMMITTEE

STRICTLY SECRET

No. P96/IV

To: Cdes. Brezhnev and Gromyko

Extract from protocol No. 96 of the session of the CPSU CC Politburo
on 19 August 1968

On Instructions to the Soviet Ambassador in Prague

To affirm the draft instructions to the Soviet ambassador in Prague and the text of the attached material (see attached).

Regarding Point IV of Prot. No. 96

TOP SECRET
IMMEDIATE ATTENTION

PRAGUE
SOVIET AMBASSADOR

1. Visit President L. Svoboda and convey to him, orally, the content of the following Appeal from the Central Committees of the fraternal parties and the governments of the Soviet Union, Poland, Hungary, the GDR, and Bulgaria:

"Dear Ludvík Ivanovič!

The Central Committees of the fraternal parties and the governments of the Soviet Union, the Polish People's Republic, the Hungarian People's Republic, the German Democratic Republic, and the Bulgarian People's Republic received a request from a majority of the members of the CPCz CC Presidium and from many members of the ČSSR government to provide armed assistance to the Czechoslovak people to help them resist counterrevolution and defend the gains of socialism in Czechoslovakia.

All the matters that we worked out together and approved in Čierna nad Tisou and in Bratislava have not been resolved. This shortcoming is being exploited by counterrevolutionary forces to step up their struggle. Cdes. Dubček, Kriegel, Smrkovský, and Císař and several others are conducting themselves dishonestly and insincerely and, in fact, are supporting the activities of the reactionary forces.

You were informed by the Soviet ambassador about our most recent appeals to Cde. Dubček.[111]

Aware of the immediate threats to the existence of the socialist system in your country and the lack of necessary resistance against the overwhelming counterrevolution, and guided by the principles of socialist and fraternal solidarity and also by the relevant treaty commitments mutually agreed upon by our countries, we gave our consent to provide such aid. In accordance with this, the military units of our five countries will enter the territory of Czechoslovakia at midnight tonight. They will come to your country as faithful friends of the Czechoslovak people. They will not interfere in the internal affairs of your country. The military units of the five fraternal countries will leave the territory of Czechoslovakia whenever the president and government of the ČSSR deem this to be necessary.

The central committees of the parties and governments of our countries request that you, Comrade president, appeal to the army and people of Czechoslovakia not to resist the troops of the fraternal countries and instead to welcome them as friends. This would make it possible to avoid unnecessary incidents and victims, and would also help defuse provocations on the part of socialism's enemies.

We are deeply convinced that you, Comrade president, with your great experience as a military and government official, and as one who took a direct role in the liberation of Czechoslovakia from the German fascist yoke and in the creation of a socialist state, will understand the true aims of our actions. These actions are dictated by our concern for the interests of the Czechoslovak people, for the cause of socialism, and for our common interest in protecting the socialist states from the intrigues of imperialism and West German revanchism.

[111] See Document No. 91.

We are certain that you, as a reliable friend of the Soviet Union and of the other socialist countries, will not reject our request so that together we can stand up for the sacred cause of socialism, for the independence and sovereignty of Czechoslovakia, and for the security of the countries of the socialist commonwealth."

2. If the president responds favorably to the request of the fraternal parties, then, using the necessary tact, you can hand over to him as a draft the attached text of his Appeal to the army and the people.

For your eyes only:

We are transmitting to you the Appeal of the Central Committees of the fraternal parties and the Governments of the Soviet Union, Poland, Hungary, the GDR, and Bulgaria, which you should convey orally to President Ludvík Svoboda. You should do this, in our view, at 11:00 P.M. on 20 August, that is, one hour before the start of the operation.

You should recommend that he promptly get in touch about this with Cde. Dubček or with someone else from the leadership. We wanted to gauge your opinion on this point, and it is also essential to consult with Cdes. Indra and Biľak, because it is possible that they have a different view about what should be done. Try to get back to us about this.

Confirm by telegram.

8-yav
ks

ATTACHMENT

Czechs and Slovaks, citizens of the Czechoslovak Socialist Republic!

Our motherland is passing through an arduous moment of travail. The forces of counterrevolution by exploiting the irresponsible conduct of several officials who have recently been serving here in top posts, have placed the fate of our socialist state under threat and have brought our people to the brink of a fratricidal struggle.

The great freedoms and opportunities that socialism offers for the creative activity of the masses and for their effective participation in the life of our society were exploited by the reactionaries and used against the very foundations of the socialist order and our established constitutional state. The people, who were formerly united and strengthened by this, have become disunited as a result of the activities of hostile forces. Czechs have been set against Slovaks, workers and peasants have been set against intellectual laborers.

Foreign and internal reactionaries have been trying by political and psychological means to destroy our nation, vilifying its glorious achievements on the path to socialist construction and depriving it of faith in the future. They schemed to stop socialism and restore to the country a bourgeois order by means of a "cold coup" or even by civil war.

The enemies of our people intended to disrupt the bases of our national independence and security, which the Czechs and Slovaks paid for at such a high price during the struggle against German nazism and militarism. They wanted to tear our motherland from the fraternal family of socialist states and sever our friendly relations with the Soviet Union.

At the request of many leading officials, who have bravely come out in support of socialist gains, the fraternal socialist countries have come to our aid as our true friends.

The allied forces will return home as soon as the task of rebuffing the counterrevolution is completed and as soon as the government of the ČSSR believes that their further presence is no longer necessary.

My duty as the head of state, who is obliged to stand in defense of the constitution, sovereignty, and independence of the Czechoslovak Socialist Republic, compels me to appeal to you to join together in the name of the highest interests of the motherland.

I ask you, dear countrymen, to greet the soldiers and officers of the allied armies—the soldiers of the Soviet army, Poland, Bulgaria, Hungary, and the German Democratic Republic—as your friends. They came to us in the spirit of socialist solidarity. They came not to interfere in our internal affairs, but to permit us to fulfill the program for the perfection and development of socialism, as designed by the CPCz and endorsed by the people. This program will subsequently be brought to fruition.

I appeal to the soldiers and officers of the Czechoslovak People's Army to stand together with the fraternal armies in defense of the cause of socialism.

Soldiers, warriors from the People's Militia, all citizens of the Republic, I implore you to display the traits befitting our nation: calm, bravery, and loyalty to our socialist ideals and fraternal friendship with the Soviet Union and other socialist countries!

The unity of our people, and our unity with the fraternal socialist countries, provide the guarantee of a bright future for Czechoslovakia.

Glory to labor, glory to socialism!

Truth will win out!

8-afks

---

* * *

CHERVONENKO'S RESPONSE

21 August 1968.
"Hot Line"

Svoboda said he doesn't welcome the intervention of the troops, but if this is how we've decided to handle matters, he won't act against the allied states. He will do everything to ensure there is no resistance so that no blood will be shed. When I told him that Moscow and the other fraternal countries had expressed the hope that Cde. Svoboda will remain in his post and carry out his mission in the name of his homeland and fraternal friendship with the USSR and the other socialist countries, he replied that when he accepted the post of president he knew he would never cut his ties with the USSR.

When he learned that he was being summoned to the presidium he expressed the hope that he would not succumb to provocations and would remain firmly in the position he occupies.[112] The president promised that in this trying hour he would not deviate from what he has said.

Cde. Klusák was present at the talk.[113]

21. VIII. 68

Chervonenko

---

[112] As word of the invasion was coming in, Dubček called Svoboda and requested that he come over to the Presidium for urgent consultations. It was probably Svoboda's daughter, Zoe, who actually spoke to Dubček because Svoboda himself was meeting Chervonenko at the time, who was relaying the above cable from Moscow to the president.

[113] Milan Klusák, a Czechoslovak diplomat, was Svoboda's son-in-law.

The first units of the 20th Soviet Armoured Army in Liberec (the district town in Northern Bohemia)

The assault of Soviet tanks on one of the houses on Liberec's main square. There were two Liberec's citizens perished under the ruins

"The international help"

Invasion Soviet units in the district town Teplice, North-Western Bohemia

The construction of the barricade near the Czechoslovak Broadcast building,
August 21, A.M.

Dubček and Smrkovský surrounded by the inhabitants of Čierna nad Tisou during
the Czechoslovak–Soviet negotiations in the end of July 1968

Ať žijí
soudruzi
SVOBODA
DUBČEK
SMRKOVSKÝ
ČERNÍK
KRIEGEL

BYLI JSME
S VÁMI

JSME
S VÁMI

Long live comrades Svoboda, Dubček, Smrkovský, Černík, Kriegel.
"We were with you, we are with you"

Soviet tank in front of the Old Town Hall, with the well known astronomical clock

Prague street after the battle for the Radio (17 people killed, 5 wounded)

The typical scene from Aúgust's Prague: a group of young people with the flag stained by blood

Prague's houses in August "costume": the anti-occupation slogans and warning appeals regarding the activities of the state security collaborating with the occupants

DOCUMENT No. 97: Emergency Cable from the CPSU Politburo to Soviet Ambassadors around the World, August 19–20, 1968

Source: AVPRF, F. 059, Op. 58, P. 124, D. 548, Ll. 93–94.

This highly classified cable was transmitted by the CPSU Politburo to Soviet ambassadors in all major countries on the night of August 19, and the early morning hours of August 20. The cable directs Soviet ambassadors to strictly adhere to the official line when justifying the invasion. Ambassadors are also instructed to respond to "demonstrations and picketing of an unfriendly nature that might take place" outside the embassies and other Soviet buildings by meeting the demonstrators and explaining, as "patiently and tactfully" as possible, why the invasion had occurred. The final sentence of the cable appears to reflect concerns that embassy personnel might begin questioning the wisdom of the invasion if they were unduly swayed by "propagandistic, anti-Soviet campaigns" or by "attacks and provocations of various sorts launched by reactionary bourgeois circles." Almost no embassy employees or other Soviet officials opposed the invasion in private (much less in public), and the very few who did were swiftly dismissed.

SOVIET AMBASSADOR (EYES ONLY)[114]

We are letting you know in strict secrecy that within the next day or two there might be a joint effort by the five socialist countries—the Soviet Union, Poland, Hungary, the GDR, and Bulgaria—to provide assistance to the Czechoslovak people in dealing a blow to the counter-revolution and defending the gains of socialism. This help is being extended at the request of the Czechoslovak side.

You must bear in mind that there may be attacks and provocations of various sorts launched by reactionary bourgeois circles in the countries where you are stationed against the embassy (representation and consulate) and other Soviet institutions. These circles may also seek to engage in a propagandistic, anti-Soviet campaign.

It stands to reason that the embassy and other of our institutions must take all necessary precautionary measures. First of all, you must explain to all our citizens the purpose and significance of our action, relying on the appropriate materials you have at your disposal as well as whatever documents may be published.

Second, in discussions with foreign state and social officials, you must explain our policy toward fraternal Czechoslovakia, especially emphasizing that the aid to the Czechoslovak people is being undertaken at the request of the Czechoslovak side.

The whole job of explaining these matters must be conducted actively, with full awareness that our actions are just, and that they respond both to the interests of Czechoslovakia and other socialist countries and to the common interests of peace in Europe and the entire world.

In the event that demonstrations or picketing of an unfriendly nature take place outside the embassy building or other Soviet institutions, assess the situation and, if the participants in the demonstrations express the desire to speak to employees of the embassy (or of another institution), you do not have to avoid such discussions. You must patiently and tactfully offer them the necessary explanations.

All our employees and the members of their families must behave stolidly and must strictly observe party and professional discipline.

---

[114] The existence of this cable was confirmed in mid-1992, when a copy was released from the archives of the Russian Foreign Ministry.

DOCUMENT No. 98: Invasion Warning from Czechoslovak Ambassador to Hungary Jozef Púčik, August 20, 1968

Source: ÚSD, Sb. KV, K—Archiv MZV, Received Dispatches, No. 7723/1968.

The existence of this very brief though important document was first disclosed in 1972 by Ladislav Bittman, a former high-ranking State Security (StB) officer, in his book The Deception Game: Czechoslovak Intelligence in Soviet Political Warfare. *The document itself was released from the ČSSR Foreign Ministry archives in 1990.*

The cable reveals that a top-ranking Hungarian civilian or military official—only a few knew in advance of the exact schedule—tipped off the Czechoslovak Embassy in Budapest about the forthcoming invasion several hours before Dubček and his aides had any inkling of what was going on.

Ambassador Jozef Púčik's cable regarding this information arrived in Prague on the evening of the 20th. According to Bittman, the message was relayed to Dubček and Černík in the Central Committee building by 8:30 P.M. However, because the source was anonymous and no attempt at confirmation had been feasible, Dubček put the cable aside. Not until two hours later, when additional ominous reports of troop movements began flowing in, did Černík seek to verify the information. By then, however, it was too late to do anything.

(See Documents Nos. 100, 101.)

———————

Today, 20 August, at 5:00 P.M. an anonymous caller telephoned the ČTK correspondent in Budapest and told him in an agitated voice that the occupation of the ČSSR would commence at midnight tonight. He asked that the military attaché at the embassy be informed immediately.

Púčik 159

DOCUMENT No. 99: Report by Defense Minister Dzúr, June 9, 1970, Regarding His Activities on the Night of August 20–21, 1968 (Excerpts)

Source: ÚSD, AÚV KSČ, File for G. Husák.

General Martin Dzúr prepared this report for the CPCz Control and Auditing Commission in June of 1970. The section reproduced, "The Period from the Night of 20/21 August 1968 Through until the End of 1968," explains how Dzúr first discovered that foreign military units were crossing into Czechoslovakia and what measures he took to forestall a violent clash between those units and the Czechoslovak People's Army (CzPA). He cites the full text of a top-secret directive he issued to the CzPA "in encrypted form on 20 August at midnight," ordering all soldiers to remain in their barracks and desist from "the use of weapons under any circumstances."

(See Document No. 106.)

. . . On 20 August 1968, I was working at the National Defense Ministry as on any other normal working day. I received documents, had a pre-congress discussion with journalists, and so forth.

Late in the afternoon I got a telephone call from General Kodaj.[115] He asked me whether I knew what was being discussed at the CPCz CC Presidium. When I told him I didn't know, he suggested that I contact Cde. Biľak. I phoned Cde. Biľak at the CPCz Central Committee but didn't find him there. I told this to General Kodaj, who suggested that I call Cde. Hruškovič at the Slovak CP Central Committee. He referred me to Cde. Šalgovič. I phoned Cde. Šalgovič, who promised to call on me that evening in my home. But this didn't happen. I didn't know that the situation was so serious; I assumed there would be changes in the CPCz CC Presidium.

In the evening Cde. Ľudovít Bortel came to see me; we concluded that evidently something was going on in the CPCz CC Presidium.[116] We agreed that he would try to find out at the CPCz Central Committee what was happening. I lent him a car, and he left for the CPCz Central Committee, where he allegedly spoke to the first secretary. But when he returned, he told me that he had found nothing out.

At around 10 P.M. on 20 August 1968, Cde. Černík called me at home from the Central Committee. He asked me whether I knew what was happening on the borders. I replied that nothing special was going on. He replied that he wasn't interested in the border with Federal Germany and Austria but in the other borders. I told him I would have to ask Minister Pavel because I was responsible only for the western borders. Cde. Černík said he had been unable to contact Pavel and asked me to try to contact him and then let Cde. Černík know at the CPCz CC Presidium.

At that point the possibility of an intervention by the allied troops occurred to me for the first time. (Later I discovered that A. Dubček and Černík had already been informed from Hungary and Poland, but didn't see fit to let me know about it.)[117]

---

[115] Lt. Gen. Samuel Kodaj had recently been appointed commander of the CzPA's Eastern Military District, which corresponded exactly with the territory of Slovakia.

[116] Ľudovit Bortel was the ČSSR deputy minister of internal trade (primarily responsible for tourism), the general secretary of the Government Foreign Travel Committee, and a member of the Presidium of the Czechoslovak–Soviet Friendship Association. His responsibilities were very different from those of Dzúr, but the two men and Dubček had known each other in Slovakia when they were in earlier stages of their careers.

[117] Dzúr is referring here to the unconfirmed reports streaming into the ČSSR Foreign Ministry on the evening of August 20 (see Document No. 98). These cables, which were quickly passed on to the CPCz leadership, heightened the tense atmosphere at the CPCz Presidium meeting; but similar rumors had turned up before and had proven unfounded, so it comes as little surprise that Dubček and Černík did not immediately appreciate the full urgency of the warnings. Certainly there is no evidence that they were trying to conceal anything from Dzúr.

I was unable to contact anyone at the Interior Ministry. At about 10:20 P.M. I got a hold of Cde. Šalgovič. We agreed that he would come to see me in my home. I waited for him outside my house, and he arrived at about 10:30 P.M., but his reply was evasive and unsatisfactory.[118] Under the circumstances, I decided to act on my own because I realized that the situation was serious. I phoned the apartment of General Yamshchikov (the Soviet representative of the Joint Command) and requested a meeting.[119] He agreed and said he was prepared to meet me anywhere and at any time. I suggested we meet in his apartment and he agreed. I requested Cde. Šalgovič to drive me there because I didn't have my own car with me. At the same time I requested that the highest-ranking members of the Military Council of the Ministry of Defense be convened at the General Staff headquarters at 11 P.M.

I arrived at the home of General Yamshchikov at about 10:45 P.M. He informed me of the situation. Without the slightest hesitation, I took the decision given in my order, which I'll cite later. After this decision I was given more details. On the telephone I spoke to Cde. Chervonenko and Cdes. Brezhnev and Grechko, who provided additional information. They highly praised my decision, saying that the Soviet and Czechoslovak peoples and the CPSU and CPCz Central Committees would never forget this; they warned me that I would be placed in a difficult position, but asked me to hold out. Cde. Chervonenko told me he would inform the president and the CPCz CC Presidium.

At about 11:30 P.M. I reached the General Staff. The chief of the General Staff started to inform me of the situation. I interrupted him and told him of my decision, which was endorsed by the members of the Military Council who were present.

My decision was transmitted in encrypted form on 20 August at midnight to the commanders of the Western Military Region, the Central Military Region, the Eastern Military Region, the transport corps, the Antonín Zápotocký Military Academy, the Klement Gottwald Military Political Academy, the different training centers, and the other military formations of the Ministry of Defense. Here is the text:

"In connection with the entry of Soviet troops onto our territory I HEREBY ISSUE THE FOLLOWING ORDERS:

— all troops are to remain in their barracks;
— the corps units are to be summoned to their workplaces and are not to leave their peacetime garrisons;
— under no circumstances are weapons to be used; and
— Soviet troops who have entered our territory are to be given maximum all-round assistance.[120]

I also issue this specific order to the commanders of the Western Military Region and the Central Military Region:

Implement a heightened state of alert for the 20th, 19th, 2nd, and 15th motorized infantry divisions without having them leave their barracks.

[118] The "evasive and unsatisfactory" response that Dzúr got from Šalgovič is further evidence that Dzúr had not been privy to the plans beforehand. Šalgovič had long been actively supporting the efforts of the CPCz "healthy forces" and collaborating with Soviet officials, and he clearly was aware of what was transpiring. Even at this late stage, however, he did not want to tip off Dzúr.

[119] General Andrei Yamshchikov had previously been the deputy commander of the USSR's Northern Group of Forces in Poland, and he later served in a number of senior posts in Soviet military districts.

[120] This is the one point on which Dzúr's order diverged from the CPCz Presidium's statement that night condemning the invasion (see Document No. 100). The Presidium urged citizens to refrain from violence, but did not call on them to offer "assistance" of any sort to the Soviet troops.

Report on the fulfillment of this order to the Chief of the General Staff by 2 A.M. on 21 August 1968.

Minister of National Defense

Col.-General *Martin Dzúr*

20 August, midnight"

After that all my decisions were discussed with the Joint Command, and the more serious ones with Cde. Grechko personally.

DOCUMENT No. 100: Statement by the CPCz CC Presidium Condemning the Warsaw Pact Invasion, August 21, 1968

Source: ÚSD, Archiv UV KSČ, F. 02/1; published in *Práce*, second edition, August 21, 1968, p. 1.

Shortly after word arrived in Prague that tens of thousands of foreign troops were entering Czechoslovakia, the CPCz CC Presidium voted 7 to 4 to adopt a statement calling "on all citizens. . .to remain calm" and condemning the invasion as a violation of "all principles governing relations between socialist states." At Dubček's direction, Čestmír Císař and Zdeněk Mlynář prepared a draft of the statement on the spot; it was put to a vote with a few modest changes.

Contrary to Soviet expectations, the vote demonstrated that the "healthy forces" on the CPCz Presidium did not have a majority in support of the invasion. Vasil Biľak, Drahomír Kolder, Oldřich Švestka, and Emil Rigo voted against the resolution. But two members of the CPCz Presidium who the pro-Moscow faction had assumed would back the invasion, Jan Piller and František Barbírek, voted to condemn it. Both Piller and Barbírek would have supported a no-confidence motion against Dubček if one had been offered, but they were unwilling to go on record as condoning the military occupation of their country. The presidium's adoption of the statement marked the first in a series of crucial events that undermined the plot devised by the "healthy forces."

The text was conveyed to the central radio station for immediate broadcast and to Rudé právo for publication in the August 21 edition. The radio transmission was briefly interrupted when one of the pro-Moscow collaborators, the chairman of the Central Board for Communications, Karel Hoffmann, sought to replace it with the broadcast of a statement favoring the invasion. Publication of the resolution in Rudé právo also was temporarily disrupted when the editor-in-chief, Švestka, ordered the staff to publish a pro-invasion announcement instead. However, employees from the radio station and newspaper alerted Josef Smrkovský and he promptly intervened by phone from the Central Committee building and countermanded Hoffmann's and Švestka's orders, invoking his own authority as chairman of the National Assembly. The radio employees then promptly resumed transmission of the presidium's statement. At Rudé právo, where employees had halted publication of the newspaper's first edition for August 21 after Švestka had given his orders, a special second edition was issued that prominently featured the Presidium's resolution.

The Presidium's declaration inspired other leading party and state organs in Czechoslovakia, including the Council of Ministers, the National Assembly, the 14th Party Congress, dozens of regional and municipal party committees, trade union collectives, and numerous organizations affiliated with the ČSSR Academy of Sciences, to convene over the next two days and issue statements of their own condemning the invasion. Amidst the surge of non-violent civilian resistance in Czechoslovakia and the successful convocation of the 14th Party Congress, plans to set up a "Revolutionary Workers' and Peasants' Government" quickly came unstuck, and the "healthy forces" were unable to follow through with any of their promises.

To All the People of the Czechoslovak Socialist Republic

On Tuesday, 20 August 1968, at approximately 11 P.M., the armies of the USSR, Poland, the German Democratic Republic, the Hungarian People's Republic, and the Bulgarian People's Republic crossed the state borders of the ČSSR. This occurred without the knowledge of the president of the Republic, the chairman of the National Assembly, the prime minister, and the CPCz CC first secretary, and without the knowledge of these organs as a whole.

The border crossing occurred while the CPCz CC Presidium was meeting to make preparations for the 14th CPCz Congress. The CPCz CC Presidium calls on all citizens of the republic to remain calm and to refrain from putting up any resistance against the advancing troops, since it would now be impossible to defend our state borders.[121]

Accordingly, units of the Czechoslovak army and the People's Militia have received no orders to defend the republic. The CPCz CC Presidium believes the border crossing not only contravenes all principles governing relations between socialist states, but also violates the fundamental provisions of international law.[122]

All leading officials of the state, the CPCz, and the National Front are remaining in the posts to which they were elected as representatives of the people and of the members of their organizations, in accordance with the laws and other valid regulations in the Czechoslovak Socialist Republic.

The constitutional representatives have convened an immediate session of the National Assembly and the Government of the Republic. The Presidium of the CPCz Central Committee is convening a CPCz CC plenum to discuss the situation that has arisen.[123]

The CPCz CC Presidium

---

[121] The clause at the end of this sentence ("since it would now be impossible to defend our state borders") was included in Císař's and Mlynář's initial draft of the statement, but it was supposed to have been deleted in the final version. Dubček and his colleagues were concerned that any direct reference to armed resistance, even a negative one, might provoke an untoward reaction among the public. For some reason, however, the clause was reinserted during radio broadcasts after 4:30 A.M., and it also appeared in the text published in *Práce* and *Rudé právo* on August 21 [and then reprinted in *Sedm pražských dnů, 21.–27. srpen 1968: Dokumentace* (Prague: CSAV, September 1968), p. 6. The book is available in an abridged English translation as Robert Littell, ed., *The Czech Black Book* (New York: Praeger, 1969)]. Subsequently, all published versions omitted the clause. Confusion may have arisen when Hoffmann and Švestka tried to prevent the broadcast and publication of the statement; following Smrkovský's intervention, the broadcasters and journalists went back to the draft of the statement, unaware that the clause should have been excised.

[122] This sentence proved to be the most controversial part of the statement and, for a brief while, was the subject of heated debate. Even a few of the leading reformers initially were concerned that the charge of a "violation of the fundamental provisions of international law" might be too strong. In the end, however, all seven of those who supported the resolution were willing to go along with the phrase.

[123] The Presidium proclamation on the invasion set off a series of other resolutions and anti-invasion activities (see *Sedm pražských dnů*).

DOCUMENT No. 101: Report by a Czechoslovak State Security (StB) Official on the Arrest of Dubček and Other Members of the CPCz CC Presidium, August 21, 1968

Source: ÚSD, Sb. KV, A, from the documents left by L. Hofman, chairman of the Defense and Security Committee of the National Assembly in 1968.

Dubček and several other presidium officials were arrested in the early morning on August 21 by Soviet authorities at the first secretary's office in the CPCz Central Committee Headquarters. At about 4 A.M., a convoy of Soviet tanks and armored vehicles, headed by a Volga limousine from the Soviet embassy, arrived at the CPCz CC building, and Soviet special-operations forces (also from Taman) sealed off the premises and severed all phone links with the outside world. By 5:00 A.M. Soviet troops armed with machineguns had entered Dubček's office and detained Dubček, Smrkovský, Kriegel, Josef Špaček, Bohumil Šimon, Zdeněk Mlynář, Štefan Sádovský, Václav Slavík, and several other officials and aides. After hours of being kept under "room arrest," KGB officials removed Dubček, Smrkovský, Kriegel, and Špaček to another office. In the early afternoon they, along with Bohumil Šimon, were transported in armored vehicles to Ruzyně airport where they were joined by Prime Minister Černík (who had been arrested at 3 A.M. in the main government building by Soviet airborne commandos). From there the six were flown out of Czechoslovakia to Poland and eventually to a KGB barracks near Uzhgorod in the Carpathian Mountains, which effectively became their temporary prison.

This arrest report, compiled by a StB official for the Defense and Security Committee of the National Assembly, provides a first-hand account by Soviet and Czech security forces on the capture of the Czechoslovak leadership. Over and above a detailed description of the initial hours of the occupation, the StB agent's observations reveal tension between Soviet army and KGB officers about the assignment to arrest Dubček and his advisers. The report records that the colonel in charge of the army units demanded to know "why are they sending us there" after his army units had "come all the way from Dresden." The document also reveals that a special unit of Soviet KGB forces was given specific responsibility for tracking down Čestmír Císař. Císař was eventually arrested but escaped as Soviet troops were transferring him to the StB's Bartolomějská Street prison on the morning of the 21st.

---

21 August 1968

. . . Between 8:00 and 8:30 A.M. a group of six people were selected on orders from Lt. Col. Ripl.[124] Those orders were conveyed by Jaroslav Coufal.[125] The six included Mráček, Beran, and Šimon from the 5th Section of the 2nd Department of the StB Supreme Staff, and Kokta, Jelínek, and Škapa from the 7th Section.[126] The group was given the task of protecting the Soviet adviser at the counterintelligence unit, Mukhin, and another plainclothes Soviet security officer, who left for the Soviet embassy in separate cars. Their departure for the Soviet embassy was mentioned at the time, but the actual departure occurred only after a wait of about two hours. At the embassy a tank was already in place, along with a communications vehicle, the GDR ambassador's car, and several Bronevik-type armored vehicles. Soon afterwards, motorized formations were mobilized in a wide radius around the embassy.

Mukhin arrived at about 11:00 A.M. and divided out the duties: One StB official was to head the military convoy to the Central Board for Communications, another StB official was to go to the radio building, and other officials were assigned to the building of the CPCz Central Committee. The members of this last group, however, were ordered to stop first at the regional

---

[124] Lt. Col. Josef Rypl (whose surname is misspelled in this report as Ripl) was a top StB official in charge of the agency's main 2nd Department.

[125] Coufal was a secretary to Rypl and the chief of the 2nd Department's 10th Section.

[126] Five of these six names also are provided in *Sedm pražských dnů*, p. 69. But instead of Škapa, *Sedm pražských dnů* lists an agent named Burian, who, along with Jelínek, escorted a convoy to the Central Board for Communications.

StB administration to see Molnár.[127] The convoy heading for the CPCz Central Committee was accompanied by Major Marcel Šimon, an officer of the StB. It consisted of about 10 tanks, a communications vehicle, and a Volga car carrying a plainclothes Soviet security officer, a small, dark-haired man who was fairly young and moved briskly.[128] The military formation was under the command of a Soviet officer wearing a colonel's uniform. All three were seated in the Volga. From the conversation between the officer in uniform and the KGB official it appeared that the colonel was somewhat unhappy and kept asking "what are we going to do there", "why are they sending us there", "we've come all the way from Dresden," and so forth. The plainclothesman told the colonel that they had arrived the previous day as tourists and were afraid they might be discovered since the number plates of their cars were jotted down at the ČSSR border. He also said that immediately after arriving in the ČSSR their group had been given the task of tracking down Císař; they had looked for him but did not find him. They had even gone to his home.

At the CPCz Central Committee there were already 10 StB officials from the Prague regional police administration. They said they had been called that morning and dispatched to the Central Committee by Molnár to act as bodyguards for some members of the CPCz Central Committee. At around 9:00 A.M. the Soviet commander of the building asked these officials which of them would like to call Cdes. Dubček, Smrkovský, Kriegel, and Špaček out of the conference room. They were to be summoned on behalf of the StB and handed over to Soviet officers. This is precisely what happened. Several StB officials called out the above-named comrades and, on orders from a Soviet officer, took them to the office of the absent Čestmír Císař.[129] StB officials and a Soviet officer took turns standing guard over them.[130]

[127] Lt. Col. Bohumil Molnár was the chief of the main regional administration of the StB.

[128] The identity of this Soviet KGB officer is uncertain, but it may have been a high-ranking officer named Boris Nalivaiko (see August and Rees, *Red Star Over Prague*, p. 138). According to *Sedm pražských dnů*, there were 19, not 10, Soviet tanks in the convoy.

[129] The StB agents who carried out the arrests were named Dubský, Peroutka, and Hoffman. When one of them informed the four CPCz leaders that they were being taken into the custody of a "revolutionary government led by Cde. Indra" and would be judged by a "revolutionary tribunal," Smrkovský protested and tried to challenge the legitimacy of the arrests. Dubček, however, sensed that resistance at this point would be fruitless, and he quickly interrupted Smrkovský, saying simply: "Forget it, Josef!" The four CPCz officials were then taken to the vacant office of Čestmír Císař, where they were detained under armed guard for several more hours along with Bohumil Šimon, who was brought in about half an hour after the others.

[130] For other eyewitness reports and documents on these events see: The Institute of History of the Czechoslovak Academy of Sciences' collection in *Sedm pražských dnů, 21.–27. srpen 1968: Dokumentace* (Prague: CSAV, September 1968), esp. pp. 64–70; the eyewitness accounts presented by delegates to the Vysočany Congress, which became widely available when a partial transcript of the proceedings (based on tape recordings) and related documents in Jiří Pelikán, ed., *Panzer überrollen den Parteitag* (Vienna: Europa-Verlag, 1969). (A Czech edition was issued by the same publisher in 1970 under the title *Tanky proti sjezdu: Protokol a dokumenty XIV. sjezdu KSČ.*) Further information about the arrests was subsequently provided in a lengthy interview with Josef Smrkovský, "Nedokončený rozhovor: Mluví Josef Smrkovský," *Listy: Časopis československé socialistické opozice* (Rome), Vol. 4, No. 2 (March 1975), pp. 16–18; in a memoir by Zdeněk Mlynář, *Nachtfrost: Erfahrungen auf dem Weg vom realen zum menschlichen Sozialismus* (Köln: Europäische Verlagsanstalt, 1978), pp. 181–187; and in memoirs by several former Czechoslovak State Security officers, especially a volume by František August and David Rees, *Red Star Over Prague* (London: Sherwood Press, 1984), pp. 134–142.

DOCUMENT No. 102: The Arrest of the CPCz CC Presidium Members, as Recalled by Josef Smrkovský's Personal Secretary H. Maxa

Source: ÚSD, Sb. KV, A—D. Bárta and V. Holá, eds., "Sbírka dokumentů a svědectví z let 1968–69," pp. 60 et seq.

When the reformist members of the CPCz leadership spent several hours waiting in Dubček's large office suite after the Czechoslovak Presidium had adjourned at around 2:15 A.M. on August 21, 1968, numerous other people also were present, including three of Smrkovský's top aides. His secretary, H. Maxa, stayed in the suite the whole night and thus witnessed what happened when Soviet troops and Czechoslovak StB agents finally entered and arrested the top officials. While questioned many years later, Maxa recalled what he saw at around 9:00 on the morning of August 21, when Dubček, Smrkovský, Kriegel, and Špaček were summoned from the room and detained for another few hours in Císař's vacant office.

Maxa's testimony is largely consonant with other first-hand accounts of this scene, except for his intriguing comments about what the StB agents said when they arrested the four CPCz leaders.

At about half past eight a group arrived, though there was already quite a commotion all around. The group was led by a Soviet colonel, followed by two plainclothesmen, who appeared to be some of our people. They were wearing tweed jackets and open-neck shirts, and they came into the room and started looking for Cde. Dubček. I was standing some two meters from the door, and a young soldier with a machinegun stood on the other side. He was policing the area, and the moment the others saw Dubček, they immediately went up to him and said: "Cde. Dubček, you are to come with us straight away." And Dubček asked him: "Who are you, what do you want?" They replied: "The revolutionary committee." And Dubček again asked: "What and who are you?" And they again replied: "The revolutionary security committee." There was again confusion in the room. One of the two was fairly young; the older one was perhaps 1.7 m or 1.75 m tall. He had graying hair and was stocky, whereas the younger one was taller and thin. Then the colonel came in behind the two security agents and shook hands with everyone. He went up to Dubček and wanted to shake hands with him, too, but Dubček did not even speak to him, so he simply grabbed hold of Dubček's hand. He then went up to Smrkovský, who was standing opposite him with clenched fists, and the colonel tried twice to shake hands with him, but Smrkovský refused.

At that point they indicated who was to go with them: Dubček, Smrkovský, Špaček, and Kriegel. . . .

Question: It was also said that these plainclothesmen, when they came to make the arrests, uttered just one sentence: that they were arresting Dubček, Smrkovský, and Kriegel in the name of the revolutionary workers' and peasants' government headed by Cde. Indra. . . .

Answer: No, that's not where it happened. Later on I heard and saw and read reports about the testimony of a comrade from State Security who had concluded a bit too much from what preceded their entry into Cde. Dubček's office. He said that in the outer office there were two groups of six people each from our security officials, and that they had been chosen to arrest Dubček and the others. And that is where some official of the NKVD taught them the formula of arresting people: "In the name of the revolutionary workers' and peasants' government headed by Cde. Indra we hereby arrest you." . . . [131]

---

[131] NKVD was the old acronym (People's Commissariat of Internal Affairs) of what was known from 1953 to 1991 as the KGB.

But when they actually went inside, and only two of them and the Soviet official were present, they said what I just told you. I am absolutely certain of this, I was quite near them. Later on it was revealed that because they were so excited—those two who came in to take away the group of leading officials—that they forgot to recite the formula.

At that moment Dubček, Smrkovský, Kriegel, and Špaček were in Dubček's office and they were all taken away.

DOCUMENT No. 103: Alexander Dubček's Recollections of the Invasion and Its Immediate Aftermath

Source: "Alexander Dubček vzpomíná: Původní rozhovor pro *Občanský deník* o pozadí srpnových událostí roku 1968," *Občanský deník* (Prague), Part 3, August 17, 1990, p. 3.

Alexander Dubček's lengthy interview with Občanský deník *in 1990 before his death covers the events on the night of the invasion and the first two days immediately thereafter. Dubček recalls how "stunned" he was at news of the invasion, and the initial decisions he made "to prevent a military confrontation." He describes the way he and his colleagues were rounded up and spirited away by a team of Soviet KGB and Czechoslovak State Security officers and his growing comprehension after arriving in Poland that "this was not just a 100 percent liquidation measure." He notes that some of the others, especially Černík, were severely beaten and mistreated by the Soviet officers, and remembers screaming—in Russian—at his captors in Poland who were manhandling Černík to "let go of him immediately." The interview also includes valuable information on Dubček's emotional reactions to his Soviet counterparts in Moscow, but also to President Svoboda who had been brought to the Kremlin for negotiations. "Psychologically, everything affected me very badly," Dubček recalls.*

(See Document No. 67 for the first two parts of the Občanský deník *interview, and Document No. 120 for the final part.)*

PART 3

Občanský deník: We are interested in your personal testimony on the way the situation unfolded after Černík returned from the phone and informed you that Soviet troops had entered our country.

Dubček: When Černík came and officially announced that troops had crossed the borders, everybody reacted differently. I was stunned and I got up from my chair and started to walk gloomily around the room. I was taken aback by such treachery. I did not expect it. It might sound naive nowadays, but at the time I thought that maybe someone would call, that it might be possible to call Brezhnev, or that something else would happen. One thing was clear to me: we could not resign, we on the presidium had to do something. Gradually the view prevailed that we should adopt a position on the matter. The result was the famous declaration by the presidium in which we denounced the entry of troops as an illegal act, and so forth. I believed it essential to have the declaration published as soon as possible.

At the time I realized that another step was also extremely important: to decide whether or not to resist the military intervention. My position—which was espoused not only by me, but by those who thought in the same view—has often been judged in a negative light since. Yet even today, knowing all I know now, I would definitely act again the way I acted at that time, and would do everything I could to prevent a military confrontation. At the time I believed this was the right decision, and I still believe that today. To have done otherwise would have resulted in enormous and senseless bloodshed, and I am certain that the Soviet authorities did expect there to be fairly widescale armed resistance. Under the circumstances, we could have either given our consent to such action, or resistance could have taken place spontaneously. But my better judgment told me not to act the way the enemy was expecting us to act. That's why I told Černík and Svoboda: "Do not put up military resistance; let the invasion proceed without any sort of armed resistance."

Občanský deník: Did you consult the president or Dzúr about the possibility of defending the country, or was this your decision alone?

Dubček: We did not talk about it beforehand, nor was there any special meeting. We agreed unanimously and spontaneously about the matter, without any meetings. When I spoke about it to Černík and Svoboda, they did not present any alternative views. We did not even seriously consider an alternative; we simply agreed unanimously that there should be no military resistance.

Let's go back to that night. I kept turning to the phone the whole time, hoping that it would ring and someone would let me know what was going on. Nothing of the sort happened, and that reinforced my view that the intervention was far-reaching and that they would not negotiate with us. I no longer expected that any political official would contact us and instead waited for a military representative who would tell us something officially. But nothing of the sort transpired.

When troops finally entered the building and came into my office—there were seven soldiers in all, along with one officer—this was only the first wave. They were trying more or less to find out what was in my office. One went over to the window and another to the door, and in the meantime either the phone rang or I picked it up to make a call, I don't now remember which. One of the soldiers who had a machinegun ready pointed it at me, took the phone away, and pulled out the wires. At that stage nothing more happened.

Later on a major or lieutenant-colonel from the KGB arrived along with additional Soviet army officers and, I think, also an interpreter whom I had met somewhere before—he interpreted in Czech. This group also included some officials from our own State Security organs. The State Security agents officially, in the name of the revolutionary tribunal and the revolutionary government, announced that I was being arrested.[132] I could have resisted and put up a fight, but I didn't see any sense in that. I'd already lived through a war, so I told myself, so I should go voluntarily. At that time they took me to the adjoining office (which belonged to Císař), and later on others were brought there as well: Smrkovský, Kriegel, etc.

In the morning the KGB official ordered me to follow him. We went down the stairs, and they took me out onto the courtyard where there were tanks and armored combat vehicles. It was still morning, I am certain of that, although I didn't manage to look at my watch. When they took me into a tank, I asked whom they were giving me as a partner. Later they brought Kriegel. They drove us out of the courtyard, and I surmised they were taking us to the airport. At the airport we waited until the evening. Then I told my guards that after all those hours of waiting I had to be let outside into the fresh air. They demurred, went away somewhere, and then permitted me to go outside. Then they took me back inside, and I was there until that night. I said to myself that something must be going on and that they don't know what to do with me, because they had taken Kriegel away and I was left by myself. Then they took me aboard a plane, and I again had to wait a long while until it was dark—it was late at night. Then they took me out of that first plane and put me into another. The plane was a Tupolev, though precisely what kind it was I don't know. After a certain amount of flying time, they switched me onto another Tupolev; and in that plane we landed at an unfinished airport somewhere on Polish territory. Holes had been dug out there and a barracks had been built. When they took me to one of the barracks, I saw the same official—he was, I think, a KGB lieutenant-colonel—who had been present during my arrest. There I sensed that something was happening and that this was not just a 100 percent liquidation measure; instead, it was some kind of program.

At the barracks I met and spoke to Černík, and he described to me how he'd been arrested. He said that he had fought his captors and they'd had a difficult time regaining control over him. They then loaded us onto a train, and we were taken still further. This time they transported us to somewhere around Uzhgorod. Černík, Šimon, and I were there. At Uzhgorod station, some

---

[132] At this point, according to Jozef Smrkovský's personal secretary, H. Maxa, Dubček asked "Who are you, what do you want?" and the StB agents replied, "The revolutionary committee." KGB officers had coached the arresting agents to say "In the name of the revolutionary workers' and peasants' government headed by Comrade Indra we hereby arrest you," and some memoirs record them making this statement. But Maxa who was detained in the same room recalls that in the nervous tension of the moment, the agents forgot what they were supposed to say. See Document No. 102.

brawny and athletic young men weighing about 100 kilograms apiece were waiting for us, and they ordered us to get into their car. So I climbed in, and all of a sudden I could hear Černík screaming. They couldn't force him into the car. I scrambled out of the car and began yelling at them in Russian: "Do you know that you're dealing with the head of a government? Let go of him immediately!" When I was shouting at them in Russian, they stopped in surprise. And they let him go. They were all civilians. I don't know whether they were even aware that this was the head of a sovereign state. That's the reason I screamed at them, so that they would know.

They drove us to a house on the mountainside; I don't know how long it took us to get there. At least an hour. Based on what I know now, they drove the others there as well. I met up with Černík and Šimon, but I still didn't know what had happened to Kriegel, Smrkovský, and Špaček.

The next day they told me to come with them to the telephone. They put dark glasses on me and then took me to the elevator, which we took upstairs, where the OBKOM office was located. After a short while the phone rang, and it was Podgorny speaking. He talked to me very cordially, and then said that we needed to negotiate. I said to him: "Where?" He replied: "How about Moscow?" And I said into the telephone: "Well, fine, but in what capacity will I be brought there? As a prisoner? You see, I demand to know where the others who were arrested with me are. I am unwilling to discuss anything until we're all together."

Občanský deník: We need to determine precisely what time that conversation with Podgorny took place because the tone of it indicates that sometime before it the Soviet policy line must have started to change.

Dubček: This might have been sometime in the morning hours. At eleven o'clock the following day, 23 August. I lost sense of the time, but it was definitely sometime in the morning.

After we arrived at the Kremlin, they took me away separately to have a discussion. Brezhnev, Kosygin, Podgorny, and most likely Suslov were there, I don't recall precisely.[133] That talk was very brief. They said it would be necessary to hold negotiations with the members of the presidium, but I still didn't know where they were. I now know that earlier, while I was still in Uzhgorod, they had already had something like a preliminary meeting with the segment of the leadership that had been led to Moscow by Svoboda. There the Soviet authorities laid down for them their own ideas in a clear effort, as they were accustomed to doing, to plan something with one group first so that they could create a split between us. At that time they were mainly trying to decide what to do with us. Before I again sat down at a table with Brezhnev, once more they tried to gauge what my position would be. It was obvious that I was very upset, and I told them that I couldn't undertake any sort of negotiations with them because I didn't know what the situation was like back home. Under these circumstances, I didn't want to sit down and negotiate with them.

After I finished this brief discussion and made it clear that I would not be willing to take part in any joint negotiations, I went to another room. There I saw some of the members of the presidium, including Svoboda and others. When I saw Svoboda I reacted quite emotionally and impulsively. I don't know, but I think I dashed over to him. It was a real schoolboys' greeting. But when I look at him, I felt peculiar. I sensed in his face a certain stiffness. He had always been restrained on the outside, but we'd had a deep mutual respect and friendship. His reaction was strange. I'm not saying that he was not glad to see me, but he was having a tough time. I expected something different from him. He was terse the whole time, as though he were doing something he didn't really want to do. I never asked him about it because I forgot and because there were other, larger problems to contend with. But I did want to ask him about it at some point. However, I never got a chance to.

What else should I mention about the Moscow part.

---

[133] The fourth CPSU Politburo member who took part was Gennadii Voronov, not Mikhail Suslov. Otherwise, Dubček's recollection of the meeting and events surrounding it is accurate. See also Document No. 116.

Psychologically, everything affected me very badly. When it was decided that some kind of joint document would be prepared, I said: "They've done something which I'll never be able to reconcile myself to for the rest of my life. And under these circumstances I cannot and do not want to serve any longer as first secretary." I called Černík and asked him to accept my resignation. I told them that if I were to remain among them, they wouldn't succeed in achieving anything because I was in such a disoriented state of mind and I would most likely start fighting with them. I didn't take part in the negotiations until the very last day.

DOCUMENT No. 104: Oldřich Černík's Recollections of the Crisis (Excerpts)

Source: "Kak eto bylo: Byvshii Predsedatel' pravitel'stva ChSSR o sobytiyakh avgusta 1968 goda," *Izvestiya* (Moscow), December 5, 1989, p. 5; and "Bumerang 'prazhskoi vesny'," *Izvestiya* (Moscow), August 21, 1990, p. 7.

Oldřich Černík, Czechoslovak prime minister during the Prague Spring, provided two lengthy retrospectives on the crisis: the first appeared in Izvestiya *in late 1989 shortly after the communist regime in Czechoslovakia collapsed, and the second appeared in* Izvestiya *on the 22nd anniversary of the invasion in 1990. The first article, in which Černík offers a "different" perspective than those of Soviet officials interviewed earlier in* Izvestiya, *conveys the prime minister's broad view of events leading up to the invasion. His 1990 interview includes two anecdotes about Soviet General Secretary Leonid Brezhnev: the irritation that Brezhnev expressed at the slogan "socialism with a human face"; and how Brezhnev attempted to turn the reformers against one another by promising to secure new posts for them if they would heed his wishes. "He never doubted for a moment that it was his 'paternal' right to replace foreign prime ministers and designate the leaders of other countries' parties," Černík concludes about the Soviet leader.*

Černík's Recollections in 1989

. . . My view of the situation in the ČSSR in 1968 and the entry of troops from the five Warsaw Pact countries onto our territory is different from that expressed by K. T. Mazurov.[134] At that time I was a member of the CPCz CC Presidium and chairman of the ČSSR Government, and K. T. Mazurov was a member of the CPSU CC Politburo. . . .

The process of post-January development in our country lasted only eight months. There was not a single instance during that time when the authorities had to resort to coercive methods or apply pressure against anti-socialist forces. The reason for this was simply that there were no mass protest actions or anti-socialist demonstrations in the ČSSR during that period, none at all. Yet even so, this process was interrupted and terminated by military intervention from outside. Why?

The development of events in Czechoslovakia was not, and could not be, at that time an isolated, internal matter for Czechoslovak communists and the Czechoslovak people. This process also affected the interests of the fraternal communist and workers' parties of the countries in the socialist camp. The ideological legacy of the period of administrative-bureaucratic rule, an oppressive legacy of Stalinism, still prevailed in all the socialist countries in Eastern Europe. This was a defining element and was the basic principle for realizing the practical policies of the individual communist parties and of the whole socialist commonwealth. The theoretical line swamped the practical construction of socialism; principles that were far removed from reality stifled new and innovative decisions; and every attempt to fashion a new program—one that was responsive to the life's realities and would ease social tensions—was consistently thwarted by the concept of the leading role of the party. Every such attempt or even a mere search for independent solutions became suspect and was construed as an attempt at revising the principles of Marxism–Leninism.

In the military-political sense, that is, from the standpoint of the defense and security of the socialist countries, the special significance of Czechoslovakia—a country located in the very heart of Europe and at the same time forming an outer boundary of the socialist world—was emphasized. Czechoslovakia both before and after the Second World War was an industrially

---

[134] Černík is referring to the interview published in *Izvestiya* on August 19, 1989, which is translated as Document No. 107.

developed country; it was among the top ten developed countries in the world. The protracted influence of the administrative-bureaucratic methods of rule made it impossible to use new dynamic forces and exacerbated the extent of the party leadership's lag behind the development of society and the demands of the time. It is well known that, starting in 1956, the CPCz several times tried unsuccessfully to change the principles and methods of economic management. Every attempt to carry out economic reform ended in failure. A real danger arose of serious political conflicts between the CPCz and the workers of our country.

The key question examined at the last three plenary sessions of the CPCz CC in 1967 and 1968 was the notion of how to conceive of and implement in practice the leading role of the party. And when, after a wide-ranging discussion at the CPCz CC plenum, it became clear that the party must be given new leadership, L. I. Brezhnev arrived in Prague in December 1967 at the invitation of A. Novotný. After discussions with some of the members of the CPCz CC Presidium and before his departure from Prague, he uttered the words that capture all the complexity of the situation in which the CPCz and Czechoslovak nation found themselves in 1968: "That's your affair," said L. I. Brezhnev.[135] Yet only several months later he asserted that the methods of neo-Stalinism were absolutely identical for all countries in the community and bound them equally strongly. These two episodes marked precisely the beginning and end of the Czechoslovak reform movement 21 years ago.

. . .

In the opinion of the CPSU and the other parties, the CPCz and the Czechoslovak state at the time were headed by right-wing opportunist forces who through their policy of socialist reforms were seriously undermining the leading role of the CPCz and thus were fostering conditions conducive to the activity of anti-socialist forces. In the interests of defending the socialist gains of the ČSSR and preserving the development of socialism in the five other countries, on whom the course of events in Czechoslovakia had exerted a negative influence, it was necessary to ensure that before the 14th CPCz Congress (which was scheduled for September 1968) this leadership would be driven from power and that their program of reform for the CPCz and the Czechoslovak people would also be discarded.

I am convinced that the decision to resort to military force to resolve the Czechoslovak problem, that is, to liquidate the CPCz's reform policy, was made by certain political structures even before the meeting of officials from the six countries was held in Bratislava. . . .

Černík's Recollections in 1990

Interviewer: Millions of participants in the "Velvet Revolution" demonstrated on the streets of Czechoslovak cities and villages in November of last year not only to express their desire for change, but also to express their determination not to have their fate bound to a totalitarian system and to the CPCz any longer. Back during the "Prague Spring," by contrast, popular masses supported the CPCz. How do you account for this difference?

Černík: The "Prague Spring" was the widest possible movement of popular masses against the Stalinist—and later neo-Stalinist—conception of power in the so-called People's Democracies of Eastern Europe. The reformist wing of the CPCz led this historic movement. The people and the party in this case were genuinely united. For that reason, the CPCz enjoyed nearly universal support. This was a unique historical moment in the last four decades. The CPCz had never been accorded support on that scale before, and has not known anything of the sort since then, especially in recent years. The military intervention by the five Warsaw Pact countries liquidated the attempt by the Czechs and Slovaks to reform socialism. You're very familiar with

---

[135] This is the Russian phrase *"Eto vashe delo"* that Brezhnev reportedly used when he was asked by Novotný to intercede on behalf of the old CPCz leadership. Whether he actually said these words is unknown; see Document No. 3.

the expression "socialism with a human face." That expression greatly displeased Brezhnev. In one of the Kremlin corridors he kept asking Alexander Dubček. "What's with this human face? What kind of faces do you think we in Moscow have?" Dubček sought to mollify him by answering that this, you know, is just some catchy phrase that the people like.

. . .

Interviewer: What personally do you remember about the behavior of Soviet leaders when they "reasoned with" Czechoslovak officials in 1968?

Černík: Here's an example of what seems to be a personal trait. Twice Brezhnev himself nearly intervened on my behalf. The first time he threatened me: "Look, you either behave yourself or you'll lose your post as prime minister!" The next time, by contrast, he promised to do a favor for me: "Listen, don't you want to become first secretary of the CPCz?" It's amazing that both his threats and his affection were kneaded in a single dough: He never doubted for a moment that it was his "paternal" right to replace foreign prime ministers and designate the leaders of other countries' parties. . . .

DOCUMENT No. 105: János Kádár's Recollections of Events Preceding and Following the Invasion

Source: "Yanosh Kádár o 'prazhskoi vesne'," *Kommunist* (Moscow), No. 7, May 1990, pp. 101–103.

In a lengthy interview after the fall of the Soviet Union, former Hungarian leader János Kádár discussed events from early May to late August 1968, when the pressure for military intervention grew and the invasion finally took place. Kádár dates the first time Leonid Brezhnev directly raised the possibility of military intervention at the multilateral conference in Moscow on May 8th. Except for the Hungarian delegation, Kádár recalls, the East European officials at the meeting seemed quite willing, and even eager, to go along with that option. Even after the CPSU CC Politburo made its final decision in mid-August, Kádár claims, he still believed that political options were worth pursuing. He acknowledges, however, that "they were no longer listening to us by that point." General Secretary Brezhnev tried to purchase Hungary's support with "a petty bargain," according to Kádár's account: "János, contribute just one military unit, and you'll receive whatever you need." Yet, Kádár is evasive when the interviewer tries to ascertain why Hungary ultimately decided to support and participate in the invasion, answering that "the Czechoslovak comrades did not permit us to take steps to head off a catastrophe and they did not take those steps themselves either."

Kádár: In early May, Kosygin phoned and asked us to come to a meeting in Moscow. As it turned out, they wanted to discuss the results of the meeting that had just been held with the Czechoslovaks.[136] But there were no representatives from the CPCz at the Moscow meeting.

Brezhnev informed the leaders of the Soviet, Polish, East German, Bulgarian, and Hungarian parties about the meeting he'd had with Dubček, Smrkovský, and Biľak. The meeting was totally unsatisfactory. The leaders of the CPSU were disturbed that Czechoslovakia's borders had been opened. They also were concerned that the opposition forces in Czechoslovakia had become more and more aggressive and that anti-Soviet sentiments were being expressed. In the end we all agreed that troop maneuvers by the Warsaw Pact countries might have a beneficial effect both inside the country and beyond its borders.

During the negotiations Brezhnev raised the question of resorting to decisive measures if positive changes in Czechoslovakia did not materialize.

Interviewer: How did all of you react to this?

Kádár: Some approved the idea. But we said there was no need for rash action. In Dresden we raised our voices, but in this case we didn't have the right to do that.

Interviewer: The others were in agreement with you?

Kádár: No.

Interviewer: This was followed by Dubček's official visit to Budapest and by the extension of the Hungarian–Czechoslovak treaty. This appeared to be a political demonstration.

Kádár: We didn't think of it that way. These things had all been planned long before, so they had to take place. Of course, to the outside observer it might have seemed that it was just a demonstration. But in the middle of June, Warsaw Pact troop maneuvers took place in Czechoslovakia. We weren't sure that this step was necessary. We believed that the Czechoslovaks needed assistance, and that without them we wouldn't be able to do anything.

---

[136] This is a reference to the bilateral Soviet–Czechoslovak meeting held in Moscow on May 4, 1968. The larger Moscow conference was held on May 8, without the participation of either Czechoslovakia or Romania. See Documents Nos. 28 and 31.

Interviewer: What happened next?

Kádár: It seems that after this the leadership of the CPSU dispatched a letter to the CPCz. The Soviet party expressed its view that the situation in Czechoslovakia had deteriorated still further. Especially since the publication of the "Two Thousand Words" manifesto. From then on, events accelerated. We suggested in a letter that we repeat the Dresden meeting. The letter expressed solidarity with the CPCz and with the leadership of the party. The meeting took place in Warsaw, but the Czechoslovak comrades did not attend. Their absence from the meeting caused even greater tension. During the meeting in Komárno that preceded the Warsaw meeting, we tried to convince them to come to Warsaw.[137] But they didn't take any notice. We told them that they had put the Hungarian party into a difficult position and that concerns had already been emerging about the whole movement. If our paths were to diverge, with whom and where would they go? Dubček and Černík kept crying and constantly repeating that they could now see that all doors were closed to them.

Interviewer: How did the Warsaw meeting go?

Kádár: It didn't bring much happiness. Some of the other participants regarded us, the Hungarians, as scabs or strikebreakers because on the eve of the meeting we had met Dubček. Nevertheless, we informed the others about our talks in Komárno and suggested that we act in a way that would receive support in Czechoslovakia, in our own countries, and in the whole communist movement. By that point, however, these arguments went unheeded. The number of advocates of military intervention increased.

Interviewer: What were the arguments that could have been used against this option?

Kádár: The Hungarian experience of 1956. In connection with this we reminded the others of the historical responsibility of the CPSU. The Soviet comrades promised that they would phone Dubček from Moscow to arrange a new bilateral meeting. Next came the Čierna nad Tisou talks and a new multilateral meeting in Bratislava at the beginning of August. At Bratislava it seemed that everything would finally return to normal. The communiqué that everyone signed was good. But the jubilation was premature.

Interviewer: At the meeting in Bratislava agreement was achieved. Why did the jubilation turn out to be premature?

Kádár: Because soon after the Bratislava meeting a telephone call came through from Moscow. They asked us to come for bilateral negotiations and suggested that the meeting be held in Yalta. At the instruction of the party leadership, I went there with Cde. Károly Erdélyi. There we met Leonid Brezhnev, Aleksei Kosygin, and Nikolai Podgorny.

Interviewer: Why did they ask you to come to Yalta? What was the purpose of the bilateral negotiations?

Kádár: I think they wanted to meet us separately and discuss the situation in Czechoslovakia because they saw that we had developed good relations with the Czechoslovak leadership. Our ties with the CPCz leadership were direct and comradely, and the Soviet leadership hoped we could have some influence on them. The focus of the Yalta negotiations was on how to normalize the situation in Czechoslovakia and settle contentious issues by political means.[138] With these

---

[137] The bilateral Czechoslovak–Hungarian meeting in Komárno took place on July 13 at Dubček's and Černík's request. See Kádár's top-secret report on the meeting, "Cde. Kádár's and Cde. Fock's Meeting with Cde. Dubček and Cde. Černík" (PTTI, 288, F. 5/462 oe), which he presented to the HSWP Politburo on July 15, 1968.

[138] Here Kádár seems to overstate the Soviet leadership's willingness by this point to continue searching for a political solution; see Document No. 83.

aims in mind, we again arranged a meeting with Dubček and his colleagues in Komárno on 17 August. But the meeting did not lead to the results we had hoped for.

Interviewer: What happened after that?

Kádár: Right after the meeting in Komárno—possibly even the very next day—officials from the five fraternal parties gathered in Moscow.[139] In the name of the CPSU leadership, Brezhnev informed the participants of the Czechoslovak events and conveyed to them how the Soviet party leadership viewed the situation. In his assessment he expressed sharp condemnation of the CPCz CC Presidium and of Dubček personally, and he pronounced his view that the opportunities for a political resolution of the matter had disappeared and that, under the circumstances, military intervention was the only way to save the socialist order in Czechoslovakia. Only by means of military intervention would it be possible to head off a still greater danger.

Interviewer: Did everyone agree with his assessment?

Kádár: Not quite everyone. At least we, for our part, believed that it was still necessary to try to avoid armed intervention and that we should resort to it only if no other options remained and there was no other way out. But, as subsequent events showed, they were no longer listening to us by that point.

Interviewer: According to some reports, you came out against the plan for armed intervention.

Kádár: I don't know whether this is important or not, but in any event we agreed to it only when it became clear that there was no alternative.

Interviewer: What was the decisive argument in support of Hungary's participation?

Kádár: I don't remember that there was any single decisive argument. But if there was one, then apparently it would be that the Czechoslovak comrades did not permit us to take steps that would head off a catastrophe, and they did not take those steps themselves either. In Moscow it became obvious that we were being left isolated with the reforms we had only just begun.[140] The majority of the socialist countries were against us.

Interviewer: Is it true that Leonid Brezhnev personally demanded that you go along with the opinion of the majority?

Kádár: I don't remember whether he did so or not. But I recall that at a certain moment of the discussion he in fact requested that we not come out against the joint measures. He said something to this effect: "János, contribute just one military unit, and you'll receive whatever you need."

Interviewer: This, then, was the decisive argument?

Kádár: It's ridiculous to suggest that we would have made such a petty bargain at the expense of our Czechoslovak neighbors. After having done so much to try to salvage the situation, we could not be bought off so easily!

Interviewer: Not only in Hungary but in other global circles the view spread that you did not support the military action and that you expressed this opposition by not attending the Congress of the Polish United Workers' Party three months later.

---

[139] The meeting of the five Warsaw Pact leaders took place in Moscow on August 18, the day after the Komárno meeting. See Document No. 92.

[140] This is a reference to the "New Economic Mechanism" (NEM) which Hungary adopted in 1968. The NEM comprised a series of economic reforms that seemed bold at the time. Although these reforms were disrupted by the 1968 invasion, and again in the early 1970s by domestic retrenchment in Hungary, they survived and provided a relatively good starting point for Hungary's much more drastic reforms after the collapse of communism.

Kádár: What can I say? You see, whatever happened is over, and there's no turning back. Not everyone knew that our efforts were unsuccessful, and that it was not only me, but the entire party leadership, who sincerely regretted this.

Interviewer: Instead of sending you, the HSWP sent Béla Biszku as its representative to the PUWP Congress.[141]

Kádár: The Politburo took that decision.

Interviewer: It's clear that the interference in Czechoslovakia's affairs did not evoke general support. And today many people are questioning whether the decision that was taken was correct.

Kádár: In any event, the Yugoslav and Romanian governments were among the first to condemn the action. Many fraternal West European parties didn't support it either, and those who did come out in support of it ended up having a very hard time.

Interviewer: As far as we know, there was one further meeting in Moscow at which the events were analyzed and additional steps were considered.

Kádár: Yes, as far as I remember, Jenő Fock and Zoltán Komócsin went with me to Moscow at the end of August. We were there for four days and met the Soviet party leaders. At that time, if I'm not mistaken, they consulted with Gustáv Husák, Alois Indra, and Vasil Biľak about ways to rectify the situation. They told us about this. In their opinion, Gustáv Husák was the most appropriate official to cope with the situation that had emerged; they gave a very positive assessment of him.

Interviewer: And what was your opinion of him?

Kádár: We naturally supported any reasonable decision that would facilitate consolidation, but we said to Brezhnev. "Husák is our neighbor; we know that he is a decent person, but why are we being asked to speak on his behalf? Let the people of Czechoslovakia do that."

Interviewer: In your opinion, how much connection was there between the situation in Czechoslovakia and the slowdown of the reform process in Hungary?

Kádár: In international processes there are always influences of various sorts. It would be impossible to deny that these events had a negative influence on our country as well, and on the reformist initiatives that other socialist contries had undertaken.

Interviewer: What would you do today if you once again had to make this sort of decision?

Kádár: The question is badly formulated; the decision was made back then, and you can't compare today's situation with the situation twenty years ago. Relations between our parties and countries have completely changed. And the decision was not made by me alone. On the other hand, it's good that we can take into account that history always corrects mistakes. What we were unable to do back then for well-known reasons is now being implemented not only in our country but in other socialist countries, above all in the Soviet Union.

---

[141] Béla Biszku was a member of the HSWP CC Politburo and HSWP CC Secretariat from 1962 to 1978.

DOCUMENT No. 106: The Invasion in Retrospect: The Recollections of General Ivan Pavlovskii

Source: "Eto bylo v Prage," *Izvestiya* (Moscow), August 19, 1989, p. 5.

In August 1989, as a Soviet reevaluation of the Prague Spring crisis began, Izvestiya *conducted interviews with two key players in the invasion. One was with Soviet Army-General Ivan Pavlovskii, commander-in-chief of Soviet Ground Forces and deputy minister of defense in August 1968, and supreme field commander of the invasion. The initial plan for the invasion, General Pavlovskii confirms, called for Warsaw Pact Commander-in-Chief Marshal Ivan Yakubovskii to direct operations. Pavlovskii does not explain why control was transferred directly to the Soviet High Command, but other sources, including Pavlovskii's deputy, General Ivan Ershov, have suggested that the change occurred because the Soviet Defense Minister Marshal Andrei Grechko disliked Yakubovskii and persuaded the other members of the Soviet Politburo that orders might not be followed strictly enough within the pact's untested structures. General Pavlovksii acknowledges that he depended heavily on Yakubovskii to determine how the invasion should be carried out, and he also describes how closely Grechko and General Kirill Mazurov supervised the operation on behalf of the Politburo. Soviet military officers in the field had surprisingly little discretion of their own, even on relatively minor issues.*

(See also Documents Nos. 99, 104 and 107.)

Interviewer: Ivan Grigorievich, I suppose it was tough for you to accept the command of an operation that was so unusual for a general, one that was conducted on the territory of a fraternal country. . . .

Pavlovskii: I was appointed commander on 16 or 17 August, some three to four days before the start of the operation. Initially, it was suggested that Marshal Yakubovskii be placed in charge of the allied forces. He organized all the practical preparations. But suddenly Defense Minister Grechko summoned me: "You've been designated the commander of the units that will be entering Czechoslovakia."

I flew to Legnica (in Poland), and went to the headquarters of the Northern Group of Forces. There I met Yakubovskii. He showed me on the map which divisions would be used and what directions they'd be coming from. The operation was scheduled to begin on 21 August at 1:00 A.M. Grechko warned: "Orders will be sent to you from Moscow, and your task is to ensure that they're carried out."

At the designated hour the troops set off. I got another phone call from Grechko: "I just spoke to Dzúr [the ČSSR minister of national defense] and warned him that if, God forbid, the Czechs open fire on our troops, this will have dire consequences. I asked him to order Czechoslovak units not to move out anywhere and not to open fire, so that they won't come into confrontation with our forces."

Roughly an hour after the troops set out, Grechko phoned me yet again: "How's it going?" I reported to him that such-and-such divisions were in such-and-such a place. I also reported that in certain areas people had gone out onto the roads to block the convoys, but that our troops were managing to get around these obstacles. . . . He warned me not to leave the command post without his permission. And suddenly I got another call: "Why are you still there? Fly immediately to Prague!".

. . . We flew to Prague and circled two or three times above the airport; we couldn't see anyone and we couldn't hear any voices, nor could we see any airplanes. We landed. . . . Lt. Gen. Yamshchikov met me at the airport, and I went with him to the General Staff headquarters to see Dzúr.[142] We immediately got him to agree that there would be no fighting at all between our soldiers and that no one should think we had arrived with some sort of mission to occupy Czechoslovakia. We just brought our troops in, that's all. Anything beyond that would be left to political leaders to decide.

We settled down in the General Staff building and slept on the chairs and the floor. They gave me a room where I could sit with my telephones and radio operators. All orders were transmitted to me by Mazurov.

At the Soviet embassy they recommended that I meet the ČSSR president, Ludvík Svoboda. I took with me a Hungarian general, a Soviet general, and a German general. . . . I said: "Comrade president, you know that troops from the Warsaw Pact member states have entered Czechoslovakia. I've come here to report on this matter. And because you're an army-general and I'm an army-general—we're both soldiers—you'll understand that the situation has forced us into taking this step." He responded: "I understand . . ."

The president spoke in Russian. He had once lived in the Soviet Union and had been the commander of a Czechoslovak battalion, which he converted into a brigade and then into a corps. In May 1945 he brought his corps into Prague. I asked whether there were any hard feelings toward our troops. He answered: "Not especially." Then during the night there was gunfire involving tracer bullets, and that wasn't good. I myself did not witness such gunfire. But perhaps someone did it as a hooliganistic prank or in order to frighten someone. I gathered my commanders and ordered that they put a stop to any sort of nightime gunfire.

Kosygin flew to Prague in order to sign a treaty. A former member of the CPCz CC Presidium, Smrkovský, appealed to him: "Do you know that your troops have slaughtered all our game? They go hunting for pheasants and deer." Kosygin looked at me. I said: "That's not so. I can't say with absolute assurance that someone didn't kill a bird. After all, the troops are deployed in the forests and nearby. But it just isn't true that we've been organizing hunts. We've now begun to conclude agreements with local authorities on the delivery of vegetables and fruit, and the rest we supply ourselves."

Interviewer: How many of our tanks were in Czechoslovakia?

Pavlovskii: About five hundred . . . And to be frank about it, I wouldn't say that the population was particularly glad to see us. Even though it was our army that liberated Prague and we took part alongside Czechoslovak troops in combat operations against the Hitlerite forces, every Czech had a right to bear a grudge toward us. Why had we come there? We were dropping leaflets from an airplane that explained we had come with peaceful intentions. But you yourself understand that if I come as an uninvited guest to your house and begin giving you orders, you're not going to like it very much.

Interviewer: Over the last two decades has your assessment of the events of August 1968 changed at all?

Pavlovskii: You know, this reminds me of a play I saw in Malyi Theater about Ivan the Terrible. One of the monks came to him and began to complain that the tsar treated his enemies too harshly. The tsar got up from the throne and said: "Sit down here in my place and rule the country, and I'll see how you behave." In our country it's now accepted that everything should be criticized. But it wasn't all so simple! What if you consider this question in light of the military-political situation that actually existed? You'll have to forgive me, but I'm a man of principle. My views have not changed.

[142] Lt. Gen. Andrei Yamshchikov was the "resident representative" in Czechoslovakia (a position always reserved for a Soviet officer) from the Warsaw Pact Joint Command.

DOCUMENT No. 107: The Invasion in Retrospect: The Recollections of Kirill Mazurov

Source: "Eto bylo v Prage," *Izvestiya* (Moscow), August 19, 1989, p. 5.

In 1989, the Soviet newspaper Izvestiya *published an interview with Kirill Trofimovich Mazurov, who in 1968 was a full member of the CPSU CC Politburo and first deputy chairman of the Soviet Council of Ministers. He was intimately involved in all the top-level deliberations leading up to the invasion, and served as the Politburo's representative in Prague on the night that the troops moved in. Under the pseudonym of "General Trofimov," he oversaw all the military and political aspects of the invasion, issuing orders on behalf of the full Politburo.*

In this interview, Mazurov discusses some of the factors that motivated the invasion, including internal developments in Czechoslovakia, prospective changes in Czechoslovak foreign policy, tensions in Soviet–Czechoslovak relations, and pressure from hard-line East European leaders, especially Walter Ulbricht and Władysław Gomułka. Mazurov recounts the missions he performed once he got to Prague, stressing that he had been urged to "do everything [he] could to prevent a civil war" in Czechoslovakia. Mazurov returned to Moscow a week after the invasion, conceding that "there was still a long way to go before everything was over."

(For Mazurov's initial on-site reports and activities, see Document No. 112.)

Interviewer: Kirill Trofimovich, what particular aspects of the international situation leading up to August 1968 compelled the highest political leadership headed by Brezhnev to venture to send troops into a fraternal country?

Mazurov: This is difficult to understand today if we look at the past without trying to immerse ourselves in the circumstances of a different historical era. What has come to be called the "Cold War" was in full swing at that time. Relations were strained between the FRG and the GDR, and the construction of the Berlin Wall had provoked genuine hysteria in the West. The Cuban Missile Crisis had inflamed political passions. We had placed our hopes in a meeting with the U.S. president, but the meeting was thwarted by Powers' subversive flight.[143] We learned of plans that certain circles were hatching to provoke a nuclear attack against the Soviet Union. We could have retaliated and we were able to frighten them, but did we really have the quantity of weapons at our disposal that they did?

In their efforts to break up the socialist commonwealth, Western countries set their sights on Czechoslovakia. Situated in the center of Europe, a country with rich economic and cultural traditions, Czechoslovakia ranked among the ten most developed states. The opportunity was there to seize for those who wanted to exacerbate tension. The population had become dissatisfied with the adoption of the Soviet model of development. The mechanical copying of our procedures upset the balance of their economy. Likewise, discussions about the victims of repression in the 1940s and 1950s, which were tied to Stalinism, in one way or another affected us. The opponents of the new system attributed all the deformations to their cooperation with our country. The opposition openly expressed anti-Soviet and anti-socialist slogans.

The Soviet leadership was alarmed when it detected how fast the activities of right-wing forces were growing in Czechoslovakia. The CPCz CC lost control of the mass media. We pointed this out over and over to the Czechoslovak leaders at that time. In this difficult international situation we had only one desire, namely, to be united, to prevent war, and to ensure that everyone came

---

[143] This refers to the flight in May 1960 by Gary Francis Powers in a U-2 reconnaissance plane, which was shot down by a Soviet surface-to-air missile. The ensuing controversy resulted in the cancellation of a planned U.S.–Soviet summit in Geneva.

433

out unharmed. It came as a complete surprise to us when the ČSSR minister of foreign affairs dropped an obvious hint that Czechsolvakia would leave the Warsaw Pact.[144] By that time the border was opening between the ČSSR, on the one hand, and Germany and Austria, on the other. Hordes of Sudeten Germans began to penetrate the country. When Kosygin was on vacation in Karlovy Vary and saw how they were carrying on there, he cut short his vacation and returned to Moscow. He, as an eyewitness, confirmed the danger of what was going on.

After the ČSSR leadership refused to come to Warsaw for discussions with the leaders of the fraternal countries, we managed to arrange a meeting between the CPSU CC Politburo and the CPCz CC Presidium at Čierna nad Tisou. The meeting was painful. We sat opposite each other for several hours in some school building. Every time we raised an issue, they repeated that there was nothing for us to worry about. We parted on cold terms. On the return trip to Moscow no one could sleep; we were all thinking: what is to be done?

We compiled a note for the fraternal parties outlining the results of the meeting. They were constantly phoning us and offering suggestions. Ulbricht and Gomułka insisted on the harshest steps. Despite certain nuances, their general position was the same: we must intervene. It was difficult for us to imagine that a bourgeois parliamentary republic could take shape along our borders, one flooded with West Germans and behind them, Americans. This was totally incompatible with the interests of the Warsaw Pact. In the last week before the troops were sent in, the members of the Politburo barely slept or even went home: We were getting reports that a counterrevolutionary coup was expected in Czechoslovakia. The Baltic and Belorussian military districts were put on the highest state of combat alert. On the night of 20/21 August we once again gathered at a meeting. Brezhnev said: "We are going to send in the troops. . ."

A general sigh of relief was heard; finally, it had become clear what needed to be done. Brezhnev added: "It will be necessary to send one of us to Prague. The soldiers there might need some guidance. . . Let's send Mazurov."

Obviously, Brezhnev based his decision on the fact that I was a Second World War veteran and was on good terms with the military. But for me this development was completely unexpected. I went home, woke up my wife, and told her that I had to leave on an urgent trip to Kirgizia. At three o'clock in the morning the plane took off for Prague.

We circled above Prague airport for a long time, waiting for Soviet and Bulgarian commandos to free up the landing strip.

As I rode through Prague in the early morning hours—it was around five o'clock—tanks were already deployed in the city and the air was thick with their exhaust fumes. I myself was once a member of a tank crew and I had the sensation of wartime. I then remembered the parting words of the other Polituro members: "Do everything you can to prevent a civil war there."

Interviewer: I have heard from our comrades who were in Prague in those days that complete power was concentrated in the hands of General Trofimov. . .

Mazurov: That was my new name. In the uniform of a colonel (my military rank) and under the name of "General Trofimov," I issued orders to both military and civilian officials. Accompanied by my adjutant, I traveled around Prague in a jeep and rode out to the metal-works at Kladno and to the agricultural regions. Several times a day I spoke with Brezhnev and Kosygin, and received advice from them. The main task was to protect our soldiers from gunfire. You know, I was astonished by the restraint of the troops, by how they managed to keep calm even when the rabble-rousing young people on the streets insulted them and threw things at them. . .

.

---

[144] This remark prompted Jiří Hájek, the Czechoslovak foreign minister during the Prague Spring, to write a letter to *Izvestiya* denying that he dropped any such "obvious hint" in 1968. See "Rezonans: 'Eto bylo v Prage'," *Izvestiya* (Moscow), 15 September 1989, p. 6.

During the seven days I spent in Prague, I was able to sleep only an hour-and-a-half a day. At night there was gunfire in the city, enterprises had been shut down, stores were closed, and people were left without food. We designated the commander of the 20th division to be the commandant of Prague. "Do as you wish," I told him, "Drag the store managers out of their apartments if you have to; but see to it that the stores begin working again and that trading resumes, so that people won't starve."

On 27 August I returned to Moscow. Brezhnev was in a state of euphoria: "Thank God, everything is over. . . ." What he meant was that we'd succeeded in forestalling a military clash. But I knew there was still a long way to go before everything was actually over. And when I came home I said to my wife: "The main thing is not that I've returned, but that I've returned without having buried a single Czech. . . ."

You wish to ask me whether I would agree to conduct the same sort of operation today? No! Under no circumstances! But in the concrete situation of August 1968 I acted according to my convictions, and if the situation were repeated today I would conduct myself in the same way.

PART SIX

THE AFTERMATH

INTRODUCTION

The drama of August combined the military success of the invasion with its utter political failure. Although foreign troops overran Czechoslovakia in less than 24 hours, military force could not defeat the reform movement. The country's legitimate political representatives, led by Dubček were sitting in Moscow; yet, the Fifth Column of "solicitors" seemed to evaporate—at least temporarily—from political life. In Prague, the traitors swore that they had not betrayed the country leaving the Soviets with no political foundation, or even facade, on which to impose their will.

Initially, the reformers—Czechs and Slovaks alike—concluded that at least some of the fundamental elements of reform could be preserved. They believed that the champions of the reform movement themselves could be saved, and that after "normalization," it would be possible to make a gradual return to the Action Program, at least in its broadest outline. (On the other side of the barricade, Polish leader Władysław Gomułka continued to warn that counterrevolution was possible, even in the presence of the Soviet army.) For these reasons, the reformists in the end were willing to sign the Moscow Protocol.

The Soviet Goals

Forcibly detained in Moscow, Dubček had little bargaining power. The slight possibility that the Czechoslovak reformists could salvage a small part the Prague Spring depended, of course, on a dual *sine qua non*: the unity of the reform leaders and the unity of the Czechoslovak people in their confidence in, and support for, the reform leadership. On his return from Moscow, Josef Smrkovský, in a radio speech, made an analogy to a Czech fable about the three rods of the Moravian Prince Svatopluk (Document No. 123). As the prince demonstrated to his sons, individually the rods could be snapped. But, as long as the rods were held together, nobody could break them.

At the outset, the four principal Czechoslovak representatives—Dubček, Svoboda, Černík and Smrkovský—maintained similar positions, even under the direct duress of the Soviet authorities. Even Gustáv Husák, who had recently replaced Vasil Biľak as first secretary of the Slovak Communist Party (against Dubček's will), openly expressed his adherence to the reformers' approach on August 28: "So that is how the question stands," Husák intoned at the Extraordinary 14th Congress of the Slovak Party, "either to back Dubček and the others resolutely, or to express in them a vote of no confidence. There is no third way . . . I stand fully behind Dubček's concept. I was there when it was conceived, I will give it my full backing—either I will back him, or I will leave" (Document No. 122). At that moment there could have been no doubt about the unity and support of Czechoslovak society.

Apart from these domestic pillars of support, the position of the Western industrial powers was critical. Dubček and his associates were aware that the chances of preserving even limited reforms were predicated on the willingness of the West—notwithstanding their restraint in the face of the invasion—to now react to the use of Soviet force in Central Europe with commensurately forceful measures and apply significant political pressure on the Soviet leadership.[1] The Czechoslovak leadership hoped that external pressure on Moscow might help create maneuvering room for a limited, possibly "Kádár-style" Czechoslovak reform. However, this optimistic view, predominant as it was in the ranks of the CPCz, was not shared by other members of the reform movement. There was a widespread belief that the intervention had virtually eliminated the prospect of any democratic reform and that the Prague Spring was over, especially among communist intellectuals.

The Soviets and their allies had their own interpretation of the Moscow Protocol and their own ultimate objectives. On September 27, 1968, they met in Moscow to assess the aftermath of the invasion. Given the political fiasco in Prague, the members of the Five agreed that certain twists and turns of events were inevitable. They were more patient. "We see that the process under way in Czechoslovakia is of a long-term character," Brezhnev stated in his opening address. "We must work out a general position and follow it through right to the end" (Document No. 129).

The stenographic account of the meeting of the Warsaw Five on September 27 in Moscow clearly indicates that their political and strategic objectives went far beyond simply reinstating restrictions on the media, for example, or on political activity outside the framework of the National Front—as they had said to the Czechoslovaks at every earlier negotiation. What mattered most, as Brezhnev put it, was the "the political line pursued by the Czechoslovak leadership"—the fact that in spite of the Moscow Protocol, Dubček was still trying to salvage the remnants of the so-called post-January policy of reform. The representatives of the Five united in their determination to force Dubček and his associates to follow a course toward "normalization" of the communist party role, and Soviet-style system. "On this question it's essential that we break the resistance of Dubček," Brezhnev stated at the end of the meeting. "That is where the root of all evil lies" (Document No. 129).

Out of the September 27 meeting came a strategy intended to discredit Dubček before the Czechoslovak public and to undermine his widespread social support. The plans of Brezhnev, Gomułka, Ulbricht, Zhivkov, as well as Kádár amounted to a step-by-step elimination of the individual proponents of reform. Apart from harshly critical demands for immediate personnel changes—Smrkovský, Špaček, Mlynář, Šimon and Císař were mentioned in this connection—the Five leveled nothing but withering criticism at Dubček and Černík. At the same time, they showered praise on those who, according to the Soviet view, were acting in a "principled manner."

The Troop Deployment Issue

At the September 27 meeting, it also became clear that the main instrument for bringing about these changes would be maintaining an occupation force on Czechoslovak territory. An agreement on the deployment of troops, according to Brezhnev, was "one of the most important tasks" facing the Warsaw Pact. The effect, of course, would be to exert a form of permanent pressure on Prague. The Moscow meeting endorsed a Soviet proposal to provide a new contractual basis for this continuing deployment—demonstrating that Moscow and its allies had no intention of being tied to the Moscow Protocol which stated that the deployment was "temporary." Brezhnev made it amply clear that the Soviets had no wish either to negotiate or to be committed to any deadline restricting the presence of Soviet troops in Czechoslovakia.

These demands were submitted to a Czechoslovak delegation composed of Dubček, Černík and Husák, when they arrived in Moscow for negotiations with the Soviets on October 3–4, 1968 (Document No. 131). By making the journey, in a conciliatory and even humble manner, the

[1] The minutes of a National Security Council meeting on August 20 (by which time the invasion had already begun—Czechoslovakia was six hours ahead of Washington) show that the U.S. leadership was not, in fact, prepared to undertake measures (Document No. 109). As Vice President Hubert Humphrey noted, "We need to show caution. The Czechs touched the heart of the communist revolution. All you can do is snort and talk."

Czechoslovak side attempted to show good will in carrying out the fundamental provisions of the Moscow Protocol. True, Dubček did try to act as an equal party to a contract; for example, he proposed that both sides take steps to reduce persisting tensions created by the presence of allied troops on Czechoslovak soil. But his position was brutally rejected by the Soviet side. The future of the Soviet occupation force was non-negotiable.

The Czechoslovak position drew on the language of the Moscow Protocol, which spoke of the temporary stationing of troops and their complete departure after the conditions outlined in the protocol were fulfilled. The Soviets demanded that the new agreement be concluded and labeled any mention of the ultimate departure of the troops categorically unacceptable. "The troops remain without any fixed time limit," Prime Minister Kosygin told the Czechoslovak officials (Document No. 131). The text of a bilateral treaty on the "Temporary Presence of Soviet Forces on Czechoslovak Territory" was speedily drawn up and signed in Prague on October 16 by Černík and Kosygin (Document No. 133). At Soviet insistence, the Czechoslovak Parliament discussed the agreement two days later. In the morning, three parliamentary committees took up the matter, and in the afternoon a plenary session did the same. After a brief debate, in which only five deputies spoke, the National Assembly passed the accord. Of the 242 deputies present, 221 voted in favor, four (F. Kriegel, G. Sekaninová-Čakrtová, B. Fuková and F. Vodsloň) voted against, and ten abstained. From the number of deputies in attendance, it is clear that nearly one-fifth of the 300-strong Parliament did not take part in the voting, evidently as a sign of protest. Nevertheless, on that same day, October 18, the "agreement" was ratified by President Svoboda.

The agreement, in effect, codified the Soviet occupation of Czechoslovakia. As such, it definitively blocked the future of reform, even of a limited sort. As far as the Soviets were concerned, the accord carried an international legal status, which extricated them from diplomatic criticism and healed the wound inflicted on their superpower prestige after Czechoslovak citizens and government rejected the invasion and exposed the mendacity of its original justification.

During this critical period, Czechoslovakia's Western European neighbors proved unsympathetic and unsupportive of its plight. One European official belittled the Soviet intervention in the ČSSR as "a minor traffic accident" on the road of international relations. Nor did the United States offer any support for the reform movement, or put pressure on Moscow. The Johnson administration did not feel that the Prague Spring warranted placing its efforts to revive the SALT negotiations with the Soviets in jeopardy. In any event, the CIA reported on October 11 that Dubček's coalition was fragmenting under Soviet pressure. "Soviet psychological warfare has been partially successful as the unity of the Czech leadership has now weakened," according to an intelligence cable; and "resignation and pessimism" were spreading throughout the country (Document No. 132).

Czechoslovak society was placed behind an increasingly stiff information barrier; the population was aware only in broad outline about the negotiations between their representatives and the Soviets. Out of enforced ignorance, many citizens did not understand the struggle for democratic social changes would be lost. Indeed, some sectors of the population experienced continuing political progress. First of all, there were hundreds of thousands of workers on the scene who were mobilized. Second, the previous political structures, based on the hierarchical role of the communist party, were being replaced by new, spontaneously established horizontal relationships between individuals and social groups. Thus, the activities of organizations such as trade unions, student groups and cultural and artistic collectives combined with and reinforced each other—giving civil society a sense of dynamism despite the shadow of occupation..

But this development occurred as the Soviets were mounting another line of attack against the wounded reform movement. In early December, the Kremlin summoned Czechoslovak officials for a new set of talks, held in Kiev. The minutes of the Kiev meeting reveal Brezhnev, in a heavy-handed style, berating the Czechoslovak side for allowing certain officials, including Kriegel ("clearly anti-Soviet and a right-winger") and Smrkovský (a person who "violates party discipline"), to continue to speak out publicly on behalf of the CPCz. "This bespeaks great deficiencies in the activity of the CPCz CC Presidium and its Executive Committee," Brezhnev warned Dubček. "From our observations, matters are still far from satisfactory on the question of ensuring the leading role of the Communist Party of Czechoslovakia" (Document No. 136).

Replacing Smrkovský

The Soviets' demands at Kiev were no longer general or ideological in nature; rather Brezhnev and his aides made highly specific directives, particularly regarding personnel matters. In a lengthy monologue, Brezhnev declared the need "above all" for "unity", beginning with "highest party organs" and extending "down to the lowest branches." "For our part," he continued, "we never asked you to use repression. But the party reserves the right to name its cadres." Noting that "the principles of cadre policy have been seriously violated in your country," he pointedly remarked that "if in the Executive Committee itself there are those who violate party discipline, it is necessary to act decisively against them." It immediately became clear who the Soviet leader had in mind. "We don't hide our consternation about the way Smrkovský acts, and yet no one has been firm enough to call him to task" (Document No. 136).

This less-than-subtle demand that in the interests of "normalization" Smrkovský should be removed had a deeper significance. The forced resignation of this radical figure, which would expose Dubček's left flank, represented to the Soviets a fundamental prerequisite for the replacement of Dubček himself.

In Kiev, the Czechoslovak delegation could do nothing to prevent this gross interference with its sovereign right to appoint its own officials. With the exception of Dubček, who in the final stage of the negotiations tried to dilute Moscow's personnel demands by declaring them consultative in nature, the rest of the delegation offered little resistance.

By the time of the Kiev talks, others such as Svoboda and Husák had already defected to the Soviet camp, portending the eventual termination of Dubček's leadership. Svoboda had, in fact, already insisted on the replacement of the first secretary during the Moscow negotiations immediately following the Soviet invasion. Yet, at that time, Dubček continued to try to maneuver while professing to fulfill the Moscow Protocol faithfully; he hoped, among other things, to prepare the forthcoming November session of the Central Committee in a way that would allow at least the main body of reforms to be saved. "The November Resolution" which came out of that session did in fact include certain reform elements that were salvageable, in part because Czechoslovak society remained politically active in support of those measures.

November, however, marked one of the final crossroads of Czechoslovakia's poignant experience with reform. The political faction represented by Husák (and behind him the Slovak members of the Central Committee) seized control of the Central Committee along with the Czech conservatives. The latter were supported, in increasing numbers, by the party bureaucracy who in turn were urged on by ultra-left-wing groups of veteran communists and rising careerists. At that moment, Husák decided to comply with the most delicate conclusion of the Kiev meeting—the removal of Smrkovský. Husák himself had not chosen the timing for this; in Kiev, Brezhnev had pointed up the need to find suitable people to serve in the new federal bodies, primarily the Federal Assembly, and thus prevent the resurgence of the right wing. However, Husák did undertake a considerable political risk when, in the name of fulfilling the Kiev accords, he shrewdly exploited the legitimate demand of the Slovak people that one of the three top state functions (president, premier or parliament chairman) be filled by a Slovak. He used this demand as a justification to replace Smrkovský as chairman of the assembly.

To garner support for this move, Husák obtained the agreement of the Slovak Central Committee and then of the Slovak National Council. On the Czech political scene, the Slovak demand, with all that implied about the difficult question of a Czech-Slovak federation, became the source of the most profound political crisis of the post-August period. The struggle over

Smrkovský—next to Dubček he was the most popular personality in the reform movement—symbolized the struggle for democracy, civil liberty, independent development, and the restoration of full Czechoslovak sovereignty. At one point, a number of worker's unions threatened a general strike in support of Smrkovský. But the political leadership, including Smrkovský, were asking civil society to remain calm. (Smrkovský remarked to his close friends that, after all, he could not pit himself against the Slovaks.) The leaders assured their constituents that Smrkovský would continue to hold a high party or state office.

The Denouement of Dubček

The Kiev meeting was the last between top-level Czechoslovak and Soviet delegations during this decisive stage of "normalization." By the end of 1968, the Soviets were evidently convinced that they had done everything necessary to ensure that their military victory would be crowned by total political triumph.

The vehicle Moscow selected to impose "normalization therapy" on the country was the Czechoslovak People's Army. In so doing, the Soviets exploited the dual subordination of the Czechoslovak armed forces: to the Czechoslovak constitutional bodies on the one hand, and to the Joint Command of the Combined Armed Forces of the Warsaw Pact (i.e. the general staff of the Soviet army), on the other. At Kiev, the Soviets alluded to their plans. Brezhnev harshly criticized the situation in the army, especially among the commanders in the political branch. He then demanded that energetic measures be taken against the right-wing forces in the army, and its main institution—the Military Political Academy. A variety of steps were subsequently taken, including carrying out purges of so-called right-wing elements from among army commanders (10,000 members of the officer corps were eliminated in the course of normalization), and introducing a regime of severe discipline within the Czechoslovak armed forces. These measures succeeded in intimidating the army's remaining members and proved to be an effective method of both pacifying the military and creating the conditions for the army to become an obedient tool of state power—especially at home.

The army's readiness to fulfill its repressive functions was put to the test in the spring of 1969. The catalyst was unexpected and accidental, and certainly unique in history. From March 21–28, the World Ice Hockey Championship took place in Sweden. Twice, the Czechoslovak team defeated the Soviets. In Czechoslovakia, the public treated the victories not only as a sporting triumph but as a source of tremendous political satisfaction in the wake of the humiliations that had begun in August 1968. Literally within minutes of the final whistle ending the second game, some 150,000 citizens gathered in the center of Prague, and throngs crowded the streets of Brno, Plzeň, Olomouc, Bratislava, and Košice. In several other locations, demonstrations took place just outside the facilities of the Soviet occupation troops. In Prague, the office of Aeroflot, the Soviet airline, was demolished.

However this particular incident, as well as many others, were clearly staged by agents of the Czechoslovak State Security who were identified by members of the uniformed security units that had been called to the location in response. The spontaneous outburst of discontent and opposition to the diminished reforms, as well as to the continuing presence of Soviet troops, and to the ensuing acts of provocation by security agents escalated tensions and threatened to erupt into open conflict.

Although the Czechoslovak authorities restored order, the Kremlin's reaction to these events, which went down in the history books as the "ice-hockey crisis," was immediate and exceptionally harsh. The Soviet Politburo met in emergency session on March 30, characterizing the events as an open attack by Czechoslovak counterrevolutionary forces and severely criticizing the passivity of the Dubček leadership. The following day, Soviet Defense Minister Andrei Grechko arrived in Czechoslovakia unannounced. In a meeting with selected members of the Military

Council of the Minister of National Defense Grechko issued an ultimatum, threatening to use force, and specifically raising the prospect of a renewed occupation of the entire country if the situation was not brought under control. He assigned the Czechoslovak army commanders the task of putting direct pressure on the highest bodies of the communist party and the state to ensure that Soviet goals would be fulfilled.

Finally, Moscow had a pretext to remove Dubček from his post of first secretary. The so-called healthy core of the communist party joined the army in this effort. Svoboda and Husák were involved to no small degree in what became an internal, party coup. The army, meanwhile, went on combat alert beginning on March 30, and remained on standby until April 17, the day Dubček was actually removed. Armored car units, at the ready on the access roads to Prague, not only provided protection but plainly served as a tool for this power change.

The End of the Prague Spring

The appointment of Gustáv Husák, once an avid supporter of reform, to the top party post marked the real beginning of normalization, and the end of all the essential principles of the post-January 1968 policy. The new leadership restored the concept of rule by bureaucratic directive, so essential to the *de facto* dictatorship of the communist party; even the slightest traces of political pluralism were eradicated. The economy was returned to the principles of central planning. Censorship was restored, as was repression against basic civil and human rights. The authorities again placed cultural and artistic life in a strait-jacket. And the Czechoslovak government once more displayed its militaristic character.

On the first anniversary of the Soviet invasion, Czechoslovak society was treated to the violence of the old order. Spontaneous demonstrations broke out in protest of the conditions imposed by Moscow on the country and its political, economic, social and cultural system. Once again, the streets of Prague, Bratislava, Košice and other Czech and Slovak towns were filled, this time by crowds protesting not only the occupation but their own lack of political representation and empowerment. Units of the security services and the People's Militia together with more than 20,000 hand-picked Czechoslovak army troops brutally attacked their own people. The authorities sent tanks and armored cars against the demonstrators. Police and People's Militia forces not only used water cannon and truncheons but even opened fire against the unarmed crowds. In the streets of Prague and Brno alone, five people were left dead on the pavement. Dozens of others were seriously wounded.

The bloodshed marked the first heavy toll for "normalization" paid by Czechoslovak society. The following decades of communist bondage exacted an even heavier price. This was the final denouement to the "Prague Spring," followed by twenty years of winter that would last until the November revolution of 1989, when the sun suddenly rose again over Czechoslovakia.

DOCUMENT No. 108: Directive from the Commanders of the Southern Group of Soviet Forces Regarding Efforts to Disarm the Czechoslovak People's Army, August 1968

Source: Sb. KV, N—VHA.

General Konstantin Provalov, the commander of the USSR's Southern Group of Forces, and General Fyodor Marushchak, the chief of staff of the Southern Group of Forces, issued this directive shortly before the invasion. (The date of the order is not known but it was probably transmitted on August 20.) The directive called for a major redeployment of the 8th Motorized Rifle Division to be completed by 3:00 A.M. on the 26th, following preliminary reconnaissance and other detailed military preparations.

Provalov and Marushchak ordered that their units should "be prepared to suppress" any resistance by the CzPA and, if necessary, to "engage in rapid operations to crush" the Czechoslovak troops. The directive also ordered that those troops were to be disarmed of their "weaponry and combat equipment" even if they put up no resistance and remained in their barracks, and that "command posts, telephone exchanges, armories and warehouses" be occupied. The systematic disarming operations were suspended on August 26.

(See also Document No. 112.)

TO: The Commander of the 8th Motorized Rifle Division (1)

The 8th Motorized Rifle Division (the 6th, 14th, 33rd, and 63rd motorized rifle regiments, 31st armored regiment, and 22nd artillery regiment) must be prepared to suppress possible acts by the Czechoslovak People's Army and, if necessary, to engage in rapid operations to crush them. . . .

2. The following facilities of the Czechoslovak People's Army are to be occupied and disarmed by the following units:

— the Officers' Communications School at the Nové Mesto nad Váhom garrison by the forces of the 14th motorized rifle regiment;
— the 22nd anti-tank artillery regiment at Topolčany by the forces of the 63rd motorized rifle regiment;
— the 64th tank regiment at Levica by the 31st tank regiment minus one battalion;
— the 6th engineers' regiment and construction regiment at Sered, and the 6th independent radar regiment at Trnava by the forces of the 33rd motorized rifle regiment;
— the Central Repair Workshop at Hlohovec by the forces of the 22nd artillery regiment; and
— patrol formations at Nové Zámky by forces of the 6th motorized rifle regiment.

3. When occupying and disarming units and schools of the Czechoslovak People's Army in the division's sphere of responsibility, the division must take over all command posts, the telephone exchange, the armory, and all warehouses.

4. Commanders of divisions and regiments are required to exercise close surveillance over arms depots, warehouses, base facilities, and other major installations of the Czechoslovak People's Army.

They are required to perform covert reconnaissance round-the-clock to be able to detect any activities and to take other measures in deploying their units as well as security measures for preparing against an assault on their garrisons.

You are required to detect in good time any distribution of materials and arms by units, and from armories and warehouses, to the population and troops in order to act immediately to prevent such action.

Study the deployment of units and the deployment of heavy weaponry and combat hardware for the area you are occupying. Study the daily routine of the men in the garrison and in other installations, suitable access roads facilitating the covert advance of our own units, and the element of surprise in their movements.

Ensure a superiority of forces and material in disarming the forces of the Czechoslovak People's Army by rapid and resourceful maneuvers in all major directions.

Organize cooperation of units with lower echelon units in disarming formations and occupying installations to exclude the possibility of clashes between your own units.

If the need arises, even plan operations during the night.

5. The border of the area of the 8th motorized division is situated at Velký Krtíš, Prievidza, Nové Mesto nad Váhom, Piešťany, the Trnava airport, Sereď, Nové Zámky, and Štúrovo.

Patrols should be located at the 63rd motorized rifle regiment in the direction of Prievidza.

6. The 31st armored division of the 38th army will carry out similar duties from the north in the following regions: Olomouc, Žilina, Martin. . .[2]

From the northwest the 30th motorized division of the 38th army will operate in the following areas: Liptovský Mikuláš, Ružomberok, Banská Bystrica, Zvolen. . . .

Northward from your location the 112th Bulgarian motorized rifle regiment will operate in the area around Brezno and Banská Bystrica . . .

In the west, the Soviet 254th motorized division will operate in its originally defined area, it will occupy and disarm the main forces of the 3rd motorized division and other units and schools of the Czechoslovak People's Army. The division's area of duty is Bratislava.

7. The regrouping of the division is to be completed at 3 A.M., 26 August.

8. A state of readiness is to be reported by 5 A.M., 26 August 1968. . . .

Col.-General Provalov

Commander of the Southern
Group of Forces

Lt.-General Marushchak

Chief of Staff of the
Southern Group of Forces

---

[2] There are other names listed, but they are garbled.

DOCUMENT No. 109: Minutes of the U.S. National Security Council Meeting on the Soviet Invasion of Czechoslovakia, August 20, 1968

Source: National Security Council Box No. 3, Tom Johnson's Notes of Meetings, August 20, 1968, Lyndon Baines Johnson Library.

This document records an emergency meeting on August 20, 1968, of the U.S. National Security Council, called by President Lyndon Johnson. The discussion reflects the surprise, dismay, and caution of U.S. officials in the immediate aftermath of the invasion.

None of the officials appears to have anticipated a Soviet invasion. Most of the president's senior advisers voice opposition to any forceful response for fear of damaging relations with the Soviet Union or of provoking a Soviet retaliatory blockade against West Berlin. Vice President Hubert Humphrey represents the majority opinion when he declares that in this "delicate" situation "we need to show caution" and should do little more for the time being than "snort and talk." That view appears to be shared by President Johnson himself. The only time the possibility of a U.S. military response is addressed is when the chairman of the Joint Chiefs of Staff, General Earle Wheeler, flatly rules out any such options: "There is no military action we can take."

The NSC meeting notes were taken by White House Aide Tom Johnson.

SECRET

NOTES ON EMERGENCY MEETING OF THE
NATIONAL SECURITY COUNCIL

AUGUST 20, 1968

THOSE ATTENDING THE MEETING WERE:[3]

The President
Secretary Rusk
General Wheeler
CIA Director Helms
The Vice President
Ambassador Ball
Walt Rostow
Leonard Marks
George Christian
Tom Johnson

Secretary Rusk: This surprises me.

Secretary Clifford: It does me too.

General Wheeler: Ambassador Bohlen was uneasy about this.[4]

---

[3] In order, these were: President Lyndon Johnson; the Secretary of State Dean Rusk; the Chairman of the Joint Chiefs of Staff General Earle Wheeler; the CIA Director Richard Helms; Vice President Hubert Humphrey; the U.S. Ambassador to the United Nations (and former Under Secretary of State) George Ball; the Assistant to the President for National Security Walt Rostow; the Director of the U.S. Information Agency Leonard Marks; the Presidential Press Secretary George Christian; and a Top Personal Aide to the President Tom Johnson. Another participant in the meeting, who for some reason was not listed here, was the Secretary of Defense Clark Clifford.

[4] Charles Bohlen, the deputy under secretary of state for political affairs, had previously served as U.S. ambassador to the Soviet Union.

CIA Director Helms: This was what their big meeting was about today.

Walt Rostow: The evidence is: (1) Withdrew Soviet's planes to Poland. (2) Brought them back. [One line excised.] (4) Maneuvers.

CIA Director Helms: On 14 August exercise started.[5]

General Wheeler: Poland, Hungary, Bulgaria and USSR Troops have moved in:
   23 aircraft into Poland
   50 aircraft into border area
   50 aircraft entered Czechoslovakia

Walt Rostow: Aircraft: 50 in Czechoslovakia
   18 in S. W. Poland
   44 in central Poland
Prague domestic radio tells people not to resist.

The President: I asked you to come here because of the alarm of the last few hours. Ambassador Dobrynin called me late today with a very "urgent" message. He read from a long-hand note.[6] (INSERT A)
   I told him we would give it our attention. He said they were invading Czechoslovakia because the Czechs had asked them to come in.
   I notified the secretary of state and called this NSC meeting to analyze these actions and try to determine what our national interest is.
   It is one country invading another communist country. It is aggression. There is danger in aggression anywhere.
   We need to give immediate thought to the timing of the meeting with Soviets. The agenda is more full now than before. We must discuss all problems before us. Is October agreeable or should we meet earlier.
   There are serious questions: (1) Can we talk now after this. (2) Does our presence look as though we condone this movement.
   It demonstrates the difficulty the platform committee has in working out strategy at the Hilton Hotel. What do we do?

Secretary Rusk: First, I am surprised by the timing of this action. I am disappointed, particularly in light of their favorable messages on (1) nuclear explosion, (2) strategic missile talks (3) your meeting. This shows they hold the USA in contempt.

Walt Rostow: Read FBIS 07 Bulletin (INSERT B)

Secretary Rusk: We do not know yet if the Czechs will raise a voice. There is not a great deal we can do if they don't. We could support the Czechs in the United Nations and through USIA. If we do they can put pressure on the West, particularly Berlin. Khrushchev called Berlin the testicles of the West and when he wanted to create pressure he squeezed there.

Secretary Rusk: Draft reply to Dobrynin read.
   We have a public problem as well. We must decide what moral force and political force we should bring to bear. The big question is what the Czech reaction will be. I would not move ahead in next day or so.

---

[5] Presumably, this refers to the "Horizon" exercises, which actually began on 11 August.

[6] The Soviet Ambassador to the United States Anatolii Dobrynin, contacted President Johnson with a "very urgent" message a few hours before the president convened the NSC. The message turned out to be a cable from Moscow explaining that Soviet troops were entering Czechoslovakia "at the invitation of the Czechoslovak government" to remedy a "gravely deteriorating situation." The cable claimed that this action would "in no way affect U.S. state interests" and expressed hope that the move would not cause "a worsening of Soviet–American relations."

The President: We should talk to Dobrynin tonight.

Secretary Rusk: In order to let the press know I'll call him in to give him our views, it will be good to position ourselves publicly.

Walt Rostow: There are two points in Rusk's statement.

The President: I am amazed that Dobrynin told me it was at the request of the Czech government and the Czech government was never told.

We must talk to him about the other announcement.

The President: We reviewed information given by Ambassador Dobrynin.

The President instructed Rusk to ask Dobrynin in to discuss this matter. The Secretary could say:

(a) Astonished at this news.
(b) Not opportune time to make announcement tomorrow.

Tell allies we are dismayed and outline what should be anticipated.

Secretary Clifford: They had the first meeting. It seemed to go well. They had a meeting of the Warsaw Pact countries.[7]
I am not clear as to the reason why the Soviets took this action.

The President: We have been fearful that they have lost so much face that they had to return. They could not stand to move in until all the other ducks were lined in a row.

CIA Director Helms: It is not what has happened but what has not happened. They wanted to see if the Czechs would clamp down on the press. They did not.

The President: Wasn't this hard to swallow?

CIA Director Helms: Yes. Military exercises were designed to see how the troops could move in.

The President: Should the Secretary talk to Dobrynin tonight?

CIA Director Helms: Yes.

Secretary Clifford: Czechoslovakia is just one piece on the chessboard. This march will have an effect on Poland, Bulgaria, Rumania and Hungary. We must visualize what effect this will have on other countries.

Secretary Clifford: I agree we have to speak to Dobrynin. We have to delay this announcement.

The President: This seems strange in light of (a) peaceful uses of atomic energy and (b) the scheduled Geneva meeting. (c) The scheduled Geneva announcement. Then this bombshell.

Secretary Clifford: It may be that Supreme Soviet rumblings caused this.[8]

Ambassador Ball: They have been concerned about the internal structure of the Warsaw Pact and about not destroying the relationship with the United States.
This occurred just before the Democratic convention, just as the Hungarian invasion occurred before election.

---

[7] These appear to be references to the Čierna and Bratislava meetings.
[8] Clifford is likely confusing the Supreme Soviet with the CPSU Politburo or the CPSU Central Committee. The Supreme Soviet was a figurehead parliament that met only one or two days a year.

We can't be idle in the United Nations about this.

General Wheeler: There is no military action we can take. We do not have the forces to do it.

This approach is cynical to the Nth degree. They have had CPX exercise and troops on the border. I think this message is an insult to the United States.

They say keep your hands off.

Dean (Secretary Rusk) should say the future course of US–USSR relations depends on how this is handled.

The President: A. Do we send for him? B. Do we say no announcement? C. Do we say we are utterly dismayed by it. D. Cannot reconcile his statement with other statements we've received.

Secretary Rusk: Czechoslovakia is the 3rd arms supplier to Vietnam.

General Wheeler: That is because they were told to.

Secretary Clifford: Let's get to the heart of this matter. They may be sincerely conciliatory. Suppose there is no combat. Suppose there is a pullout. They had a lot of troops in there two weeks ago.

The President: I sympathize with General Wheeler's views. We do not have to say what we feel. 1. Call in Dobrynin. 2. Tell him we won't make announcement. 3. Tell him we asked Council to meet.

The Vice President: We need to show caution. The Czechs have touched the heart of the communist revolution. All you can do is snort and talk.

Your plan is right. We are in a more delicate situation than at the time of Hungary because of the developing relations with the USSR.

Ambassador Ball: What do we do effectively. What do we do publicly. We have a bad family problem. We may look like a paper tiger.

* * *

11:10 A.M.
President's Office

THOSE PRESENT:

The President
Secretary Rusk
Walt Rostow
George Christian
Tom Johnson

Draft statement read.

Secretary Rusk: I told the Soviet ambassador last night we could not reconcile statements.

George Christian: I prefer the tougher statement.

Secretary Rusk: The Czech mission at the UN.

The President: Ambassador Ball has been instructed to join with other nations in the United Nations and vigorously express our protest of this unwarranted action. And to insist upon the Charter rights.

DOCUMENT No. 110: Cable from Czechoslovak Ambassador to Washington Karel Duda, to Prague, August 21, 1968

Source: ÚSD, Sb. KV, K—Archiv MZV, Dispatches Received, No. 7765/1968; Vondrová & Navrátil, vol. 2, pp. 228–229.

Ambassador Karel Duda sent this cable to Prague on August 21, 1968. In it, he recounts a briefing from John Leddy, the assistant secretary of state for European affairs, who had been present when Secretary of State Dean Rusk met Dobrynin after the August 20 NSC meeting. Leddy communicated Rusk's muted challenge to the initial Soviet cable to Washington which described the invasion as a response to a "request of the ČSSR Government."

On 21 August at 2.30 A.M. I was summoned to Leddy's office. . . . Leddy first showed me the text of a cable the Soviet government sent to Johnson. It stated that the Government of the USSR deems it necessary to inform Johnson personally about the gravely deteriorating situation in the ČSSR, which was the result of a conspiracy against the social order in our country by "domestic and foreign forces." In response to a request by the Czechoslovak government for all military aid, the government of the USSR has ordered its military units to enter Czechoslovak territory. They will be withdrawn the moment the situation permits. The dispatch concludes that the move by the USSR in no way affects U.S. state interests, and expresses the hope that there will not be a worsening of U.S.–USSR relations, adding that "the government of the USSR continues to attach great importance to the development of those relations."

After receiving this information, Johnson convened the National Security Council and at 11:30 P.M. Rusk summoned Dobrynin to the State Department. The Americans at the meeting included Leddy and Ball. Rusk told them that a communiqué would have to be issued on developments in the ČSSR merely saying that after Dobrynin's talk with Johnson the National Security Council had met to assess the situation in the ČSSR; it instructed Rusk to have a meeting with Dobrynin. Rusk said off the record that the United States was concerned about the USSR's actions in the ČSSR and was particularly perplexed by the following points in the Soviet statement:

1) He did not understand the passage concerning "the request of the ČSSR Government," since, according to Prague Radio, the troops entered without the knowledge of the president, the prime minister, the CPCz CC 1st secretary, and the National Assembly.

2) It was not clear what was meant by the words "external forces" directed against the social order in the ČSSR. The US Administration "has no information to substantiate the allegation that non-socialist countries are involved in or are planning aggression against the ČSSR."

3) Under the circumstances, the State Department decided to postpone the talks about the currency and gold that were planned for today.

Duda 37

DOCUMENT No. 111: Occupation Order from the Soviet Commander in Trenčín, August 21, 1968

Source: ÚSD, Sb. KV, A—Gift from I. Šimovček of the Slovak branch of the Commission.

Colonel Nikolai Shmatko, commander of the local Soviet military garrison, formulated this occupation decree. The order was carefully translated into Slovak, and posted at conspicuous sites all over the western Slovak town of Trenčín within hours of the invasion.

Shmatko's decree ordered severe restrictions on movement, public gatherings, and freedom of expression. Failure to adhere to the directive, which included a demand to turn in all typewriters, would be regarded as "anti-socialist subversion," presumably punishable by death. Similarly harsh decrees were issued in numerous other areas in Slovakia and in several areas of the Czech Lands, reflecting Soviet knowledge of the degree of widespread opposition to the occupation.

ORDER

No. 1 FROM THE GARRISON COMMANDER

Trenčín, 21 August 1968[9]

Counterrevolutionary forces in Czechoslovakia, with the active support of special services in the USA and the FRG, have been disrupting order in the state.

Exploiting the current situation in the state, NATO armies are threatening to occupy the ČSSR, overthrow the people's regime, and create a regime to their own liking.

Out of loyalty to internationalist principles and to the Warsaw Pact, the Soviet Union and the other socialist countries—the Bulgarian People's Republic, the Hungarian People's Republic, the German Democratic Republic, and the Polish People's Republic—have dispatched their armies to help the Czechoslovak people and their institutions of people's power suppress the forces of counterrevolution and save their country from the threat looming over them.

To ensure strict order and an organized situation in the interest of the working people of the town, I issue the following directives:

1. As of 21 August 1968, I forbid anyone to leave their homes and go onto the streets between 8 P.M. and 5 A.M. Central European Time. Every citizen must unconditionally observe the regulations of conduct, issued by the Soviet military commander of the garrison.

2. Any attempts to disobey or resist the terms of this order will be punished immediately under military law.

3. Soviet military forces are to guard all important military offices, radio and television stations, teleprinter installations, and institutions of the press.

4. All citizens of the town are forbidden to carry firearms or any weapons that can be used for stabbing. Those who possess such arms must hand them over to the garrison administrator no later than noon.

5. Any movements of troops of the Czechoslovak People's Army from garrison to garrison are to be carried out only at the orders of the Soviet army command.

---

[9] Trenčín and the surrounding area were a stronghold of popular support for the Prague Spring, because of Dubček's ties to the region. Dubček was born in nearby Uhrovec and lived in Trenčín intermittently beginning in 1938, when his family returned from a prolonged stay in Soviet Kirghiziya. His political career began in Trenčín in June 1949, when he went to work for the district party apparatus. In the early 1950s Dubček served as the Trenčín district party secretary, his first major post. In that capacity he got to know an up-and-coming army officer, Martin Dzúr, who was stationed in Trenčín as deputy commander for logistics of the local military district. During the reform movement in 1968, Dzúr was appointed ČSSR minister of national defense.

6. All public and political organizations are ordered to report to the garrison administration by midnight. If this order is disobeyed in the town of Trenčín, I will regard such an act as illegal, and all citizens responsible will be regarded as elements hostile to the socialist system.

7. Meetings, demonstrations, gatherings, and other mass events are to be arranged only with the consent of the regime's legal institutions, local bodies of the Slovak CP, and representatives of the Soviet army command.

Patrols and representatives of the army command must have the unrestricted right to visit public institutions in order to establish and maintain order.

8. The dissemination of reports in the press, on radio, and on television broadcasts may be carried out only with permission from the Soviet army command and with the consent of local party and state bodies.

All typewriters, duplicating machines, copiers, and manual reproduction equipment are to be handed over to the administrator of the Soviet army command.

Violations of this directive will be regarded as subversive activity against the socialist forces.

9. The only personal identity document recognized is the identity card issued by the ČSSR authorities.

The inviolability of every ČSSR citizen is guaranteed upon presentation of the identity card.

10. For the duration of this order, departure beyond the confines of the town and the arrival of foreigners into the town may take place only with the permission of the Soviet army's military command.

All foreigners must register with the garrison administration no more than 2 hours after their arrival in the town.

Those who illegally conceal foreigners are liable to sanctions under military law.

Any attempt by a citizen to violate these orders and the provisions of conduct will be deemed an act against the law, against the national institutions of power and the Soviet military command, and against the Czechoslovak people and their socialist achievements.

Anyone who violates these orders will be subject to the most effective and expedient measures and sanctions under the circumstances.

SOVIET ARMY GARRISON COMMANDER

Lt.-Col. Shmatko

DOCUMENT No. 112: Initial On-Site Report by Kirill Mazurov to the CPSU CC Politburo, August 21, 1968

Source: AVPRF, F. 059, Op. 58, P. 124, D. 574, Ll. 184–186.

CPSU Politburo member Kirill Mazurov, the Soviet official designated to oversee the entire military-political effort in Czechoslavakia, filed this report fourteen hours after Warsaw Pact troops crossed into Czechoslovakia. Mazurov's report candidly describes the unfurling of the Soviet strategy to quickly establish a pro-Moscow regime made up of "healthy forces" in the CPCz.

(See also Document No. 99.)

. . . Our friends had gone somewhat haywire, but they really began to lose their nerve when the Soviet units were a bit late in arriving. As a result, time was lost and they failed to prevent the radio and television from operating. Also, an issue of *Rudé právo* was published with anti-Soviet reports, since Švestka was held under house arrest by the rightists until the editorial office was captured by Soviet troops. And even the commander in Prague himself is still, at 1:00 P.M. local time, unable to use the radio to issue his orders.

The rightists tried to stage disturbances, in some cases with the use of weapons, and they barricaded all approaches to the radio station, television center, and other establishments. The radio had to be seized by force, and as a result much of the equipment was destroyed. The soldiers are not using weapons, but thuggish elements have been throwing explosives and grenades at tanks, trying to provoke our soldiers. Crude, anti-Soviet broadcasts are being transmitted on radio and television from various stations throughout the day.

Dubček, Kriegel, and Smrkovský are being detained in the CPCz CC building, and Černík is in the government building. A search is under way for Pavel.

Our friends have gone to pieces, and are not showing the initiative and firmness of purpose that they should have displayed immediately. We are doing everything possible to shore them up, but they have not yet recovered from the shock. The only thing they have been able to accomplish so far is to broadcast their Appeal to the People twice. They have made no real progress in forming a new government or a new CPCz CC leadership. Clearly, in the situation that has emerged, it will be impossible to convene a CC plenum or a session of the National Assembly.

The situation demands prompt steps and clear-cut, concrete measures to calm the public and establish order in the city. We are insisting to our friends that they form a new government without further delay, and that they begin appealing to the people and reasserting control over the mass media.

DOCUMENT No. 113: Moscow CPSU Committee's Assessment of Local Citizens' Initial Reactions to the Invasion, August 21–22, 1968 (Excerpts)

Source: TsKhSD, F. 5, Op. 60, D. 1, Ll. 105–110 and 111–116.

These two reports are the first of many compiled under the auspices of Viktor Grishin, who served as both the Moscow party secretary and a candidate member of the CPSU Politburo. They were prompted by directives from the CPSU Politburo to lower-level party organizations throughout the Soviet Union to "conduct mass political-education campaigns" to ensure that ordinary citizens in the USSR would "understand the true essence of recent events in Czechoslovakia," and report back on the results.

Grishin's reports confirm that the reaction of Soviet citizens to the invasion was less supportive than the authorities publicly claimed. He notes a substantial number of "unsavory and at times even hostile views" from Soviets as well as from Czechoslovaks who happened to be in Moscow on the 21st. Grishin maintained that "opposition to the sending of troops onto ČSSR territory" was confined "primarily to members of the intelligentsia," but a close analysis of his reports (as well as other newly available evidence) suggests that this sentiment was expressed publicly and during private conversations.

(See also Document No. 96.)

SECRET[10]

To the CPSU CC

23372

INFORMATION
on the Reactions of Workers in the City of Moscow
to the Situation in Czechoslovakia

On 21 August, the Moscow municipal party organization launched its efforts to explain the TASS Statement to workers. At factories, plants, foundaries, and other workplaces a large number of party activists held discussions in accordance with materials published in the newspaper *Pravda* and featured in radio and television broadcasts.

. . .

During the discussions held with workers and during the collective readings in the factory divisions and at production sectors, Muscovites expressed many patriotic views, noting the cohesion of the Soviet peoples, as well as the effort to strengthen the ranks of the party and shore up the unity of the CPSU and the nation and the unity of the fraternal commonwealth of peoples of socialist countries. Alarm and worry also were expressed at what had just occurred in Czechoslovakia.

Along with this, in certain academic research institutes there were statements made against the measures taken by the Soviet government and the governments of the fraternal countries.

Thus, at a research institute for automated equipment, a senior research fellow and candidate of technical sciences, Andronov, who is not a party member, said that he does not understand who in Czechoslovakia, and on whose behalf, requested help from the Soviet Union and the other socialist countries, and he proposed a vote on a resolution at an assembly of researchers at the institute asking for clarification of the situation.

His speech was condemned by participants in the assembly.

---

[10] A routing slip attached to the memorandum reads "For the Information of the CPSU CC Secretaries." All the secretaries except Boris Ponomarev promptly saw the report. Ponomarev's absence is noted in handwriting on the back of the routing slip.

Certain individuals expressed unsavory and at times even hostile views in private discussions.

Thus, a producer at the Central Television Studio, Torstensen, who is not a party member, said: "Our actions do not square well with our statements about not interfering in the internal affairs of Czechoslovakia."

An instructor at the 1st Moscow State Pedagogical Institute of Foreign Languages, Korolkov, believes that "our government had no sound reasons for sending troops to the territory of Czechoslovakia."

An employee at the Gorky film studio, Kazaryants, declared: "The Soviet government is acting unjustifiably. You can't build a government authority on the bayonets of our army. I'm against the use of force."

Very similar views were expressed in conversations by an engineer at the Gipron farm, Petrov, by a nurse at Hospital No. 16, Sidorova, and by a welder at the electrovacuum glass research institute, Afanasev. (None are party members.)

The party committees and bureau are working individually with people who expressed incorrect views.

Information has come into the Moscow CPSU committee about the reaction to the TASS Statement among citizens of the ČSSR who are now in Moscow.

On 21 August three groups of Czechoslovak tourists came to the television factory, the "Paris Commune" plant, and Bread Factory No. 15. They arrived at the enterprises in a dispirited mood and behaved with reserve and caution. After the tour of the facilities and meetings with workers and managers at the factories, who received them warmly and with friendship, the behavior of the tourists changed. The tour of the factories and plant ended with toasts to the health of Czechoslovak–Soviet friendship, with songs, and with a performance by a Czechoslovak artistic ensemble.

Having learned about the entry of allied troops into their country's territory, a group of tourists from the ČSSR staying in the "Tourist" hotel emphatically expressed their dismay and tried to organize a demonstration. They marched out into the street shouting slogans of "We protest!" After discussions were held between activists from the Dzerzhinsky CPSU district committee and the leaders of the group, the tourists apologized for their behavior.

Having listened to the TASS Declaration, specialists from the firm "Tesla," who are temporarily working at the Moscow television scientific-research institute, declared: "This is a repetition of the Hungarian events. Your *Pravda* is a lie.[11] Your press, like the Chinese press, can only spread filth. Your press depicts all the events in a false light. Soviet troops are not helping Czechoslovakia, but occupying it. Your whole view is that whoever has more tanks must be right."

The Czechoslovak specialists Vlček, Přibáň, and Sokol, who were part of a technical exchange at the research institute, said: "We are stunned by the TASS Declaration. Why was this done? Why were Polish and German troops also brought in? Did they also come to us as liberators?!"

These Czechoslovak specialists are taking measures to arrange their immediate departure to the ČSSR.

There were no extraordinary incidents in the city during the past night. The night shifts worked as normal at the industrial enterprises. The workday began in a sound way. The city passenger transportation system, the railway stations, and the airports are all functioning without interruption. There is not a run on goods in the stores.

The municipal party organization is continuing to explain the TASS Statement to workers. ...

SECRETARY OF THE MOSCOW MUNICIPAL COMMITTEE OF THE CPSU

[signed] *V. Grishin*

21 August 1968
N. 259

---

[11] In both Russian and Czech, this would be a play on the word "pravda", meaning "truth."

454

To the CC CPSU

23448

INFORMATION

on the Organizational and Political Work of the Moscow
Municipal Party Organization to Explain to Workers
the TASS Message of 22 August 1968 and the Materials
Published in the Newspaper *Pravda*

At enterprises, factories, and institutions in Moscow, work is still under way to explain the situation in Czechoslovakia. . . .

Unanimous support for the joint actions and measures undertaken by the allied socialist countries was expressed at all workers' assemblies held today in Moscow.

However, certain individuals, primarily members of the intelligentsia, have shown that they fail to understand the situation in Czechoslovakia and have expressed their opposition to the sending of troops onto ČSSR territory. Thus, a senior employee at the Central Children's Library and member of the group of literary specialists for the "Soviet Writer" publishing house, Glotser, who is not a member of the party, declared: "They've lost their minds! This is fascism! There will have to be a war, since the Americans will not simply give on the ČSSR. Russia was once the gendarme of Europe, and it remains so to the present day."

The head of a laboratory at the Central Institute for Aircraft Engine-Building, Lebedev, who is a member of the CPSU, believes that "the sending of troops into Czechoslovakia attests to our demise on the ideological front."

An engineer at the Institute of Physical Chemistry of the USSR Academy of Sciences, Samoilov, who is not a party member, voted against the resolution of the assembly supporting the TASS Statement. In explaining his vote, he said that every country should have the right to resolve its own internal affairs.

In connection with this, the municipal party committee is directing its organizational and political work in such a way that it will be conducted not only in collectives but also individually with those who do not understand the significance of the measures to lend urgent help to Czechoslovakia through the use of armed force.

Workers in the district party committees, as well as party activists and members of collectives where these people work, are commenting on the TASS Statement and the TASS Message, are resolutely condemning their out-of-touch views, and are clearly affirming how ordinary workers, engineering-technical workers, and employees of other enterprises and institutions should view these items.

. . . .

Czechoslovak tourists, who were taking part in the MIREK Congress, were informed about the TASS Statement in the morning. The group was deeply upset by this news, especially the women. They were basically worried about their families and their children, and they expressed surprise at such a turn of events. Several participants in the congress were called out to visit the Czechoslovak embassy in Moscow. When they returned, they told the rest of the delegates that neither the president nor the prime minister nor the CPCz CC first secretary nor the chairman of the National Assembly had made a request for assistance. . . .

SECRETARY OF THE MOSCOW MUNICIPAL COMMITTEE OF THE CPSU

[signed] *V. Grishin*

22 August 1968
No. 260

---

[12] This report, too, has a routing slip attached for all the CPSU CC secretaries. All except Ponomarev signed it.

DOCUMENT No. 114: *Pravda* Editorial Justifying the Invasion, August 22, 1968 (Excerpts)

Source: "Zashchita sotsializma—vysshii internatsional'nyi dolg," *Pravda* (Moscow), August 22, 1968, p. 1.

The Kremlin used this unusually lengthy editorial in Pravda *to provide their initial rationale for the invasion. The editorial begins with an explanation of why the Soviet Union and its allies chose to fulfill the "request for military assistance" made by unnamed "party and state leaders" in Czechoslovakia, and then assails, in eight sections, the Prague Spring. It proclaims the "defense of socialism" in individual Warsaw Pact countries as "the most sacred internationalist duty for all socialist countries," especially for the Soviet Union.*

The language of the editorial reiterates, and in some cases repeats verbatim, arguments earlier set forth in the Warsaw letter, in the letters sent by the Soviet Politburo to the CPCz Presidium, and in Brezhnev's speeches at bilateral and multilateral meetings as well as at plenary sessions of the CPSU Central Committee. The editorial, however, marks the first time that the Soviet authorities publicly attacked Dubček by name, accusing him of heading a group of "right-wing opportunists" on the CPCz Presidium who had committed "perfidious and traitorous acts."

The article was published simultaneously in the form of a pamphlet for mass distribution in Czechoslovakia by the Soviet news agency Novosti.

The Defense of Socialism Is the Loftiest Internationalist Duty

Party and state leaders of the Czechoslovak Socialist Republic have asked the Soviet Union and other allied countries to give the fraternal Czechoslovak people urgent assistance, including assistance through military force.

The request was motivated by the existence of counterrevolutionary forces acting in collusion with external forces hostile to socialism. These forces combined, have created a threat to the existing socialist system in Czechoslovakia and to the statehood of Czechoslovakia as determined by the Constitution.

The need to adopt a historic decision in connection with the request to the Soviet Union and other fraternal socialist countries for help has been fully justified in the appeal by a group of members of the CPCz Central Committee, the ČSSR government, and the ČSSR National Assembly, which is published in today's *Pravda*.[13] This need was brought about by the danger of a fratricidal struggle that was being prepared by reactionary forces in the ČSSR.

. . . The governments of the USSR and of other allied countries have decided to comply with the above-mentioned request and to lend all necessary aid to the fraternal Czechoslovak people. The fraternal socialist countries are thus fulfilling their joint internationalist duty. . . .

The fraternal friendship and military alliance between the Soviet Union and Czechoslovakia were codified in the Treaty on Friendship, Mutual Assistance, and Postwar Cooperation, which was first signed in 1943 and then renewed in 1963. In accordance with this treaty, our states, our parties, and our peoples are obliged to come to each other's assistance whenever a threat emerges to the security of our borders and to the cause of socialism. . . .

. . .

. . . As time passed . . . an atmosphere of disarray, vacillation, and instability was beginning to take shape in the CPCz itself and reactionary, anti-socialist elements, backed by international imperialism, were beginning to rear their heads. . . .

. . .

[13] This "appeal" was published alongside the article on page 1 of *Moscow Pravda*, but the purported signatories were never identified either at the time or afterwards.

At the Dresden conference, the Czechoslovak comrades did not deny that certain negative phenomena were emerging in the country and that the radio, television, and press had eluded the party's control and were in fact under the control of anti-socialist elements. Nor did they deny that rightist forces were consolidating their positions. Even so, Czechoslovak officials asserted that overall the party was still in control of the situation and that there was no reason for alarm.

The Soviet officials at the conference and all the delegations of the other fraternal parties indicated as candidly as possible that they viewed the situation differently. They argued that a real danger existed in the emerging situation. Based on what was going on, they concluded that there was evidence of developments that could result in a counterrevolutionary coup. . . . The whole subsequent course of events substantiated the conclusions drawn by the fraternal parties and failed to vindicate the optimism expressed by CPCz leaders. . . .

Unfortunately, the hopes of the healthy forces in the party and the country, as well as the hopes of all the friends of the Czechoslovak people, were unwarranted. The decisions of the May plenum were not carried out.[14] . . . The incidence of anti-Soviet outbursts increased. The wave of the anti-socialist forces' attack intensified further in late June, when the counterrevolutionary forces published the "Two Thousand Words" statement in the press, which included an open summons to struggle against the CPCz and against the constitutional order. . . .

The CPSU CC has always emphasized that decisions can be successfully adopted only through the realization of the party's leading role and the retention of full party control over events. In this regard, we repeatedly noted that the slackening of party leadership was creating conditions conducive to stepping up the activity of right-wing forces and even of overtly counterrevolutionary forces, whose main task was to discredit the Czechoslovak Communist Party and dislodge it from power, to tear the ČSSR out of the socialist commonwealth, and ultimately to transform the whole socialist system in Czechoslovakia.

The CPSU Central Committee contended, and still contends, that the fate of the socialist gains of the Czechoslovak people, and the fate of Czechoslovakia as a socialist state linked by alliance obligations to our country and the other fraternal countries, are not merely the internal affair of the CPCz. They are the common affair of the entire commonwealth of socialist countries and the whole communist movement. That is why the CPSU Central Committee believes it has an internationalist duty to take every possible step to promote the consolidation of the CPCz, the preservation and strengthening of socialism in the ČSSR, and the defense of Czechoslovakia against the intrigues of imperialism. . . .

. . .

Unfortunately, some leaders of the CPCz Central Committee failed to draw the necessary conclusions from the fact that the country was being engulfed by a fierce anti-communist campaign directed by counterrevolutionary forces and overtly inspired by imperialist propaganda. Far from acting decisively to rebuff these attempts to destroy the party, they have continued to act in a way that is transforming the CPCz into an amorphous, impotent organization that is little more than a discussion club. . . .

. . . In addition to a grave weakening in organizational and political work, an equally grave threat to the cause of socialism in Czechoslovakia has come from the CPCz's relinquishment of control over the mass means of ideological influence to right-wing, anti-socialist forces. Many newspapers as well as the radio and television in Czechoslovakia were effectively controlled by certain groups whose objectives were manifestly anti-socialist. . . .

The vilification of the communist party, especially its activities over the last 20 years, the attacks against cadres, the transfer of control over the mass media to elements hostile to the party, and the violation of the principle of democratic centralism—all these phenomena undermined

---

[14] For information on the CPCz Central Committee's May plenum, see Document No. 37.

the morale of the large majority of communists, caused them to lose hope and confidence, gave rise to confusion in party organs, consolidated the influence of right-wing forces, and spurred increased activity on the part of counterrevolutionary forces.

. . .

Under the Soviet–Czechoslovak bilateral treaty, our countries have committed themselves to joint efforts and close cooperation in protecting their security and the security of other states of the socialist commonwealth. These obligations, together with the obligations of the other socialist states under bilateral treaties and the Warsaw Treaty, constitute a strong foundation that reliably protects the security of each of the members of the pact. . . .

It is impossible to tolerate a breach in this pact. Such a development would be inimical to the vital interests of all the member states of the Warsaw Pact, including the vital interests of the USSR. . . .

. . . . Recent developments show that anti-Soviet propaganda and anti-Soviet phenomena have been sharply increasing in Czechoslovakia. . . .

There is no question that the instigators of this malevolent anti-Soviet campaign will fail in their attempts to deny that Czechoslovakia can preserve its independence and sovereignty only as a socialist country and a member of the socialist commonwealth.

By attempting to undermine the ČSSR's relations with the USSR and the other socialist countries, the reactionary forces have been seeking to compel the Czechoslovak people to return to slavery under the imperialist yoke. . . .

. . .

As a result of the actions of right-wing, anti-socialist, and counterrevolutionary forces, a serious threat arose in Czechoslovakia that a counterrevolutionary coup would take place and the gains of socialism would be forfeited. . . .

. . . Far from being spontaneous, the counterrevolutionary, anti-socialist phenomena that occurred in Czechoslovakia were highly organized. The moments of action, the directions and targets of the attacks by anti-socialist forces, and the sequence and coordination of the actions were all carefully planned, linking together the right-wing revisionists in the CPCz, the anti-socialist and overtly counterrevolutionary forces inside the country, and their external supporters.

. . .

The line-up of forces in the CPCz CC Presidium became apparent during the Čierna nad Tisou meeting. A minority of the members of the presidium, headed by A. Dubček, espoused overtly right-wing opportunist positions, while the majority adhered to a principled line and recognized the necessity of undertaking a resolute struggle against the reactionary and anti-socialist forces and against collusion with the reactionaries.

However, right-wing revisionist elements in the CPCz leadership and the ČSSR government prevented the Čierna nad Tisou and Bratislava agreements from being carried out to defend the gains of socialism in Czechoslovakia, combat anti-socialist forces, and thwart the intrigues of imperialism. . .

. . . Everything that Czechoslovak workers have created over the last twenty years, and all the gains of socialism in Czechoslovakia, are endangered. A threat exists not only to the path of socialist democracy pursued by the Czechoslovak people since January, but also to the very foundations of socialism and to the republic itself.

A situation has emerged that is absolutely unacceptable to the socialist countries. In these circumstances, it was essential to act—and to act purposefully and decisively—before it was too late. That is precisely why the Soviet Union and the other socialist states have decided to meet the request made by ČSSR party and state officials to provide urgent assistance, including military assistance, to the fraternal Czechoslovak people. . . .

The defense of socialism in Czechoslovakia is not just an internal affair for that country's people alone; it is a collective problem of how to defend the positions of world socialism. . . . In providing fraternal internationalist assistance to our CPCz comrades and the entire Czechoslovak people, we are fulfilling our internationalist duty to them and to the entire international communist, workers', and national liberation movement. This duty, for us, is the loftiest of all.

DOCUMENT No. 115: Discussions Involving Certain Members of the CPCz CC Presidium and Secretariat, at the Soviet Embassy in Prague and the ČSSR President's Office, August 22, 1968 (Excerpts)

Source: ÚSD, AÚV KSČ, File for Gustáv Husák.

These meeting notes record efforts on August 22 to establish a "Provisional Revolutionary Workers' and Peasants' Government" in Czechoslovakia. Following the failure of the "healthy forces" in the CPCz to gain majority support on the CPCz CC Presidium for a quisling government while the invasion was underway, Soviet Ambassador Chervonenko convened a 5 P.M. meeting of thirteen Czechoslovak officials—who had not been arrested—at the Soviet embassy to hear their demands and urge them to implement the original Soviet plan for a transfer of power.

The thirteen officials who took part included: Vasil Biľak, Drahomír Kolder, František Barbírek, Emil Rigo, Jan Piller, and Oldřich Švestka, who were full members of the CPCz Presidium; Jozef Lenárt, who was a candidate member; Miloš Jakeš, who was the head of the CPCz Central Control and Auditing Commission; and Alois Indra, Štefan Sádovský, and Zdeněk Mlynář, who were members of the CPCz CC Secretariat. The other two participants in the meeting—Minister of Internal Trade Oldřich Pavlovský, and Deputy Interior Minister Viliam Šalgovič—were not members of the party leadership, but they were invited to attend because they had been working so closely with the "healthy forces." (The only members of the leadership not present were a candidate member of the CPCz Presidium, Antonín Kapek, and four members of the CPCz Secretariat—Čestmír Císař, Evžen Erban, Oldřich Voleník, and Václav Slavík apparently because of illness or, in Císař's case, because he was in hiding.)

The key demand of the thirteen officials was that Ambassador Chervonenko permit them to contact Brezhnev and seek the release of Dubček and the other Czechoslovak leaders who had been detained. Chervonenko kept the group waiting for several hours; when he finally appeared, he listened briefly and then left the room. He reemerged a half hour later and informed the delegation that it would be impossible to contact Moscow. Chervonenko advised the group to defer any proposals for obtaining the release of their arrested colleagues, and he urged them to try once again to form a "Revolutionary Workers' and Peasants' Government." Chervonenko then departed, and a formal meeting of the thirteen Czechoslovak officials began at the embassy, as recorded in these notes.

The notes reveal that the participants were uneasy about the situation they confronted. Alois Indra, whose unreservedly pro-Moscow orientation was well known both to his colleagues and to the public, acknowledges that "the stigma of treason [odium zradce] will be left on everyone who takes over." By the end of the meeting, none of the participants had yet agreed to be named the new CPCz first secretary; the person they had chosen to head the new government, President Svoboda, flatly rejected the idea when he was informed of it.

The second meeting recorded in these notes took place at Svoboda's office in the presidential Castle at around 11:00 P.M. Shortly before this meeting, Chervonenko conferred with Svoboda and urged him to take over as the leader of a "Provisional Revolutionary Government." The president refused, just as he had earlier declined to approve the formation of a "Revolutionary Workers' and Peasants' Government" headed by Indra, on the grounds that "ninety-five percent of the population are behind Dubček and Černík," and "if they are not released a great deal of blood will be shed." Svoboda declares that he would instead lead a small delegation to Moscow the next day to seek the release of all CPCz officials who had been arrested.

(See also Documents Nos. 96, 100, 118, 129.)

. . .

Cde. Biľak says it is necessary to agree on an alternative in case the negotiations with Cdes. Dubček and Černík are unsuccessful. He recommends the immediate formation of a provisional revolutionary government consisting of 11–15 people under the leadership of Cde. Indra. He also recommends Cde. Sádovský as vice premier, and Cdes. Jakeš, Štrougal, Korčák, Pavlovský, and Sucharda as ministers.

Cde. Pavlovský recommends that the least discredited figures be in the government. That is why he suggests Cde. Piller should head the government instead of Cde. Indra.[15]

Cde. Biľak says it is essential to activate and keep a hold on the party down there, in district committees.

Cde. Sádovský wholeheartedly agrees with the idea of a provisional revolutionary government, but asks to be able to work in Bratislava.

Cde. Jakeš recommends that they approach all current ministers, ask them to join the revolutionary government, and negotiate with them. For the Interior Ministry he suggests Cde. Neubert or Olejník, instead of himself. He agrees about the others. He suggests they draw up a wider list to facilitate the selection of ministers.

Cde. Kolder agrees because there is no other way out. He recommends they meet the remaining government so that the remaining part of the CC Presidium and the members of the Secretariat should not disperse, and asks that a regime be established. In Slovakia, Cde. Hruškovič would be at the head of the party and Cde. Piller should be put in charge of the Central Bohemian and Prague regions.[16] They should send only a delegation to the congress to convey the position, because if all of them go, it would confer legitimacy on the congress; they should insist on the postponement of the congress.[17] They must normalize the situation to ensure there will be no bloodshed.

Cde. Lenárt supports the formation of a revolutionary government as well as Cde. Kolder's suggestion that they should not all go to the congress. Only Cdes. Piller, Sádovský, and Mlynář should go, as long as the situation remains as described by Cde. Piller.

Cde. Mlynář agrees with the formation of a revolutionary government and, moreover, recommends they declare a state of emergency in the country, saying, for example, that the National Assembly, etc. are no longer valid and the purpose of the revolutionary government is to resolve pressing matters. As far as the congress is concerned, it is unrealistic to go without a full session of the Central Committee Presidium.[18] The new Central Committee will be declared counterrevolutionary and this will be followed by the arrest of the people who have organized it. He himself will do nothing against the party and will support it. He is convinced that this tragic moment need never have happened.

Cde. Sádovský: Has anyone checked to see whether Cde. Svoboda would appoint such a government?

Cde. Barbírek says consideration should be given to the composition and agrees with the size. They should win over a maximum number of members of the current government.

---

[15] Piller's name is misspelled (as Piler) here and everywhere else it appears in these notes; the mistake has been corrected throughout.

[16] Miloslav Hruškovič was the minister of technology; he was also a full member of the Slovak CP CC Presidium and a Slovak CP CC Secretary.

[17] According to Mlynář's memoirs, Piller was the first to suggest that a delegation consisting of himself, Mlynář, and Sádovský be dispatched to the Vysočany Congress. Mlynář speculates that this proposal may have stemmed from the hardliners' desire to get rid of him so that the "Revolutionary Government" could be set up forthwith.

[18] By suggesting that the full presidium must go to the Vysočany Congress, Mlynář may have been seeking either to avoid being sent off himself in a small delegation or to generate support for the release of the arrested leaders, or both.

Cde. Indra: The maximum number of current members of the government should be recruited, including Vlček and Kučera.[19] Agreement must be reached on the prime minister. The proposed candidates are Cdes. Piller, Indra, and Štrougal.

Cde. Piller: Cde. Indra is definitely the most suitable. But at the present moment, it will also mean hurting him. That is why I ask you to consider whether Cde. Štrougal should not be head of the government, and to press him and push him. Only the most necessary changes should be made in the government so that it will be flexible. I recommend that Cde. Biľak be entrusted with running the work at the Central Committee; he has all that is needed for this and, what is more, he is a Slovak.

Cde. Kolder recommends that Cde. Lenárt or Cde. Klusák be made foreign minister.[20]

Cde. Biľak: Leadership of the party should be entrusted to Cde. Lenárt, or else he should be made prime minister.

Cde. Lenárt: This would mean going back to the time before January.[21]

Cde. Indra: Different options are inevitable. The stigma of treason will be left on everyone who takes over.[22] We must consider the Soviet comrades. I would suggest Cde. Šalgovič or Cde. Jakeš for the Interior Ministry and Cde. Dzúr for the Ministry of National Defense, and as far as the Ministry of Culture is concerned, here we'll have to find someone other than Galuška or solve it as a group.[23]

Cde. Sádovský says we must establish the revolutionary government tonight; he suggests we talk to Štrougal straight away and if this isn't feasible, he proposes that Cde. Lenárt head the revolutionary government.

Cde. Mlynář: Cde. Svoboda must dissolve the National Assembly immediately. The government would be headed by the president and his deputies—Cde. Štrougal and Cde. Lenárt. Cde. Piller should be put in charge of the Central Committee.

Cde. Sádovský: If the president could be at the head of the government, then I would agree; otherwise I suggest that Cde. Lenárt head the revolutionary government.

Cde. Lenárt: We shouldn't make too many changes in the government. Under the Constitution, Cde. Svoboda can be in charge of the government and make only the most essential changes in the government. For the Central Committee he proposes Cde. Biľak and Cde. Piller; and here, too, not many changes should be made.

Cde. Piller in summing up, says the preferred alternative is for Cde. Svoboda, as the president, to head the revolutionary government and Cde. Štrougal would be executive vice premier. If this alternative is impossible, Cde. Lenárt should head the government. Cde. Biľak would then be entrusted to run the Central Committee. But if Cde. Svoboda does head the revolutionary government, Cde. Lenárt should be entrusted with running the Central Committee. Since neither

[19] Vladislav Vlček was the minister of health; Bohuslav Kučera, the chairman of the Socialist Party of Czechoslovakia, was the minister of justice.

[20] Milan Klusák, a Czechoslovak diplomat who headed the ČSSR mission to the United Nations in New York City, was President Svoboda's son-in-law. In 1968, he was an adviser to Svoboda and chairman of the socialist party.

[21] Presumably, Lenárt is referring to the fact that he served for a while as prime minister under Novotný.

[22] Articles in the Czechoslovak press on 21 and 22 August had been denouncing Indra, Biľak, and others by name as "traitors" and "collaborators," comparing them to officials in 1938–1939 who abetted the Nazi occupation and were later subject to "retribution" and "eternal contempt."

[23] Miroslav Galuška was the minister of culture and information at the time of the invasion.

Cde. Biľak nor Cde. Lenárt is willing to be in charge of the Secretariat of the Central Committee, Cde. Piller suggests not arguing about the first secretary; the comrades could take turns at being in charge. . . .[24]

. . .

* * *

Talks with Cde. Chervonenko with the participation of Cdes. Svoboda, Biľak, Piller, Kolder, Hamouz, and Machačová[25]

Cde. Biľak[26] informed the assembled officials about earlier talks and indicated that neither the 1st alternative nor the 2nd alternative had been accepted on the activities of the government without the return of Cdes. Dubček and Černík.[27] He also informed them about the proposal to send a delegation, headed by Cde. president Svoboda, to the negotiations in Moscow.

Cde. Hamouz said he had been authorized by the government to declare that the only solution that could help the situation in the country was a categorical request to allow Cdes. Černík, Dubček, and Smrkovský as well as the National Front—in other words, the legal institutions—to function. This is the only instruction we have received from the government.

Cde. Svoboda: Ninety-five percent of the population are behind Dubček and Černík. If they are not released a great deal of blood will be shed. If they return to their posts, Cde. Dubček will step down from his post the very first day, as will Černík.[28] Then let the government judge what mistakes he has made, assess everything, and solve it. If we proceed in this tactical way, the people will accept it and will consider it correct, and it will be done without bloodshed. Otherwise, 15 million people will curse the president and all members of the government and the CPCz CC Presidium as well as you, the ambassador.

I ask that measures be adopted so that I can meet the comrades in the CPSU CC Politburo. We will lose two days, but the government can start working today. If you release these comrades for a few days, Dubček will leave on his own accord. I urgently plead with you to do this.

Cde. Machačová: The whole government, aside from the comrades whose whereabouts we don't even know, was at the Vysočany congress. A new Central Committee is in session there and is electing a new CC Presidium.[29] Over there, they're all unanimously demanding the

[24] The meeting was leaked to the "unofficial" Czech media almost immediately, because Mlynář secretly phoned a radio journalist from the embassy. Broadcasts reported that "Indra and his cohorts" had gone to the Soviet embassy on August 22 to "present their quisling government."

[25] In his memoirs, Mlynář said that he and the others who took part in the previous meeting attended this meeting as well. The notetaker listed only Biľak, Piller, and Kolder, plus three newcomers: President Svoboda, František Hamouz, a deputy prime minister, and Božena Machačová, the minister of the consumer goods industry, who was serving as acting prime minister in Černík's absence. The reasons for this discrepancy are unclear.

[26] According to Mlynář's memoir, Piller was "designated to present the content of our negotiations at the Soviet embassy" because "Biľak and Indra did not feel up to it." It is unclear, therefore, why the notes from the meeting attribute these remarks to Biľak instead of to Piller.

[27] The two alternatives in question here are the ones that were proposed at the end of the previous meeting. The first alternative was for Svoboda to head the government and Lenárt to head the CPCz Central Committee; the second alternative (in case Svoboda rejected the first) was for Lenárt to head the government and Biľak to head the Central Committee.

[28] This was the crucial element in Svoboda's proposal. Although Dubček and Černík would be restored to power, they would have to resign as soon as they came back. Svoboda had not consulted either Dubček or Černík about this idea.

[29] At around 10:00 that evening (an hour or so before this meeting started), the new CPCz Central Committee convened to select a new presidium. Almost all the 28 members of the new body were ardent supporters of reform (even Gustáv Husák was perceived as such at the time). Dubček was chosen unanimously to remain as first secretary.

immediate release of those comrades and they're also demanding the immediate withdrawal of the troops. If funerals are to take place now, an immense effort will have to be made to keep control over the situation.

Cde. Svoboda says one must also look at the situation in light of the congress. If Cde. Dubček is released, he will declare the congress illegal; otherwise you will have to dissolve the congress yourself and this will be a great tragedy.[30] Cde. Černík was also pleased when I let him know what you said, that he will remain prime minister.

Cde. Chervonenko thanks them for the invitation and for explaining how they are approaching the situation. But it is necessary to consider one other thing. What guarantees can you give, as president, that a stop will be put to everything that has been done and is still being done? We already spoke about this, that there are matters which are your internal affairs. He explains the position of the CPSU toward post-January developments. The situation demands immediate solutions. Communists must realize that submission to right-wingers is impossible. On this there can be no compromise. The question of the armies and their withdrawal will be solved only once there are absolute guarantees.

---

[30] Svoboda's proposal is based on the assumption that Dubček would be willing to take certain measures—in this case, declaring the 14th Party Congress to be invalid—that would undo a key part of the Prague Spring. As it turned out, of course, Dubček did reluctantly agree to go along with Article 2 of the Moscow Protocol declaring the congress invalid (see Document No. 119).

DOCUMENT No. 116: Stenographic Account of Alexander Dubček's Talks with Leonid Brezhnev and Other Members of the CPSU CC Politburo, August 23, 1968 (Excerpts)

Source: ÚSD, Sb. KV, Z/S 10; Vondrová & Navrátil, vol. 2, pp. 234–250.

This stenographic transcript records Alexander Dubček's meeting in Moscow on August 23, only two days after he was detained by Soviet forces and placed in KGB custody. The meeting with the four Soviet leaders—Brezhnev, Kosygin, Podgorny, and Voronov—lasted over three hours during which they attempted to coerce Dubček to cooperate in publicly justifying the invasion, reversing the Prague Spring, and "normalizing" the situation. The transcript demonstrates Dubček's refusal to capitulate. Although the CPCz leader acknowledges that he is "in a very difficult emotional state," he explains, firmly and cogently, why the invasion is "a grave mistake" that will have "tragic consequences."

Soviet leaders decided to bring Dubček to Moscow for talks after the collapse of their initial effort to set up a hard-line regime in Prague on August 21. Dubček came against his will; Soviet leaders had failed to meet his precondition that he first be reunited with his other detained colleagues. Unbeknownst to Dubček, Černík was separately transported to Moscow and brought to the meeting as it was ending. Brezhnev also concealed from Dubček the fact that President Svoboda had arrived in Moscow earlier that day in an effort to gain Dubček's release.

STENOGRAPHIC RECORD OF THE NEGOTIATIONS

Cdes. Brezhnev L. I., Kosygin A. N., Podgorny N. V., Voronov G. I. with Cdes. Dubček and Černík[31]

Brezhnev: How is Cde. Černík feeling?[32]

Dubček: Bad, like everyone else.

Podgorny: Is it his health that's bad or his mood?

Dubček: It's the situation that's difficult.

Brezhnev: Let's agree not to rehash the past and to have a calm discussion, beginning with the situation that has now been created in order to find a solution that would be of benefit to the Communist Party of Czechoslovakia, so that it can act normally and independently in accord with the principles contained in the Bratislava Declaration. Let it act independently. We did not wish and do not intend to intervene in the future. Let the government base its actions on the principles of the January and May plenary sessions of the CPCz Central Committee. We spoke about that in our documents and are ready to reaffirm it. Of course, we can't say that you and the others are in a happy mood right now. But the question is not one of your mood. We have to conduct negotiations in a prudent and sober way in looking for solutions. It can be said simply that your failure to fulfill your commitments prompted the five countries to take extreme but unavoidable measures. The course of events since then has entirely confirmed that behind your back (in no way do we wish to imply that you were standing at the head of it) right-wing forces (we modestly

---

[31] Only Dubček was actually present during most of this meeting. Černík arrived near the end and spoke very briefly; excerpts from that part of the meeting are not provided here. The 52-page stenographic transcript of Dubček's initial meeting in Moscow, which was turned over by the Russian government to the Czechoslovak commission in mid-1992, contains some small gaps and is not quite complete.

[32] Presumably, this question was raised because Černík had been severely beaten after his arrest. See Dubček's recollections in Document No. 120. No doubt, the statement refers to Dubček's most recent encounter with Černík on the previous day, while the two were still in the KGB's custody. Some accounts (including Černík's own recollections) later suggested that Dubček and Černík had met in Moscow on 23 August just before Dubček's meeting in the Kremlin, but the transcript of the meeting tends to undercut that version of events.

call them anti-socialist) were preparing both the congress and all other steps.[33] Now even underground cells and ammunition caches have been uncovered. All this has now come to light. We don't wish to claim that you, personally, are to blame.[34] You might not have known about any of this; the right-wing forces organized all this on quite a broad scale.

We would like to find a more acceptable solution that could expedite the process of stabilization in the country, normalize the work of the party without the influence of the Right, and normalize the work of the government so that it, too, is free of rightist influence. . . .

We haven't occupied Czechoslovakia, we don't intend to keep it under "occupation," and we want it to be free to carry on the socialist cooperation we talked about in Bratislava. It is on this basis that we wanted to have a discussion with you and find a businesslike solution. If necessary, it can be done along with Cde. Černík. If we are silent, we will not improve the situation nor free the Czech, Slovak, and Russian peoples from tension. And with every passing day the Right will incite chauvinistic moods against all the socialist countries, particularly against the Soviet Union. In such conditions, of course, the troops cannot be removed; in general this doesn't help us. So, on these grounds, on this basis, we wanted to have a discussion about what we think is the best way to proceed from here. We are ready to listen. We are not dictating anything. Let's try together to find some sort of variant. . . .

Dubček: You've just said something by way of an introduction. I, too, would like to say a few words, Cde. Brezhnev, although I find myself in a very difficult emotional state. I haven't been home for three days.[35] I'd also like to say that it is indeed correct and necessary to look ahead again. That's true, certain realities now exist.

Podgorny: It is precisely for that reason that we wanted to talk, to look ahead.

Dubček: At present certain realities have been created. But, Cde. Brezhnev, I already sensed in Chop that it was necessary to look ahead.[36]

After Bratislava, conditions in Czechoslovakia and in the communist party were at first, and in all respects, favorable, even including the question of preparations for the congress and matters concerning the objectives of propaganda work: preparations for the congress and personnel issues. All this is included in the resolutions of the CPCz CC Presidium. Of course, I did not know how everything would end. I believed that you, too, would be interested mainly in the broad picture. But this in fact did not happen. I will not speak about the past, because on that score we made our opinion clear at Čierna and then in the joint document approved in Bratislava. The Bratislava Declaration is a document of the CPCz CC Presidium and our entire party and state. It received great support and was a significant document because it removed the question of the Warsaw meeting, which had become an internal, dynamic, and negative issue in inner-party and anti-state activities. Party and state activities were oriented in a favorable direction. I even said that it represented some sort of way out, based on the general interests written into it, since our CC Presidium always—both in January and after January, and in state documents—upheld the fundamental positions it proclaimed. And even now, it has in no way

---

[33] Brezhnev's asides here (and his subsequent disclaimers during this meeting) were disingenuous, to say the least. Contrary to Brezhnev's assertion that "we in no way wish to imply that you [i.e., Dubček] were standing at the head of the right-wing forces," this is precisely what was alleged in the long editorial in Moscow *Pravda* on 22 August ("Zashchita sotsializma—vysshii internatsional'nyi dolg"). Brezhnev obviously was hoping to mollify Dubček with these comments so that the CPCz leader would agree to cooperate in the "normalization."

[34] Here and elsewhere Brezhnev used the familiar form "ty" of the second-person pronoun when addressing Dubček. Dubček, by contrast, used only the formal "vy" when addressing Brezhnev.

[35] Dubček had been brought straight to the Kremlin by the KGB when he arrived in Moscow, without being permitted to rest or wash up; and the questioning began almost immediately.

[36] The stenographic account is in error here, either because Dubček misspoke or because the stenographer misheard him. Chop, like Čierna nad Tisou, is a major railroad crossing point at the juncture of the Slovak, Hungarian, and Ukrainian borders; it is on the Ukrainian side, whereas Čierna is in Slovakia (and Záhony is the crossing point on the Hungarian side of the border). Dubček must have been referring to Čierna nad Tisou, not to Chop.

deviated from its official policy, in either party or state work, from the general interests approved in Bratislava and proclaimed by us.

We welcomed them and along with you we worked on them because it serves our interests and our viewpoints, and because these issues were committed to paper as the basic points that the CPCz's policy had carried out previously. Therefore, I and my comrades cannot understand why, in such a short period—and I wish to stress this happened before the CC plenum of the party and before the congress—these military measures were undertaken by the five states. I said "before" the plenum of the party's CC because we could not have acted otherwise. Only on Tuesday did we approve the thesis on the federation, and the plenum had to be called at some point to clear up some matters in connection with the preparations for the congress. We drew your attention to this. The situation in the country and the party had improved. These extreme steps, these extreme measures were taken without warning the CPCz CC Presidium, or me, personally, or the president, the prime minister, or the chairman of the National Assembly. In my opinion, this has squarely confronted not only our two parties, but the whole international communist movement as well, with the most complicated problem it has ever faced.

It's hard for me, while I'm in such a difficult emotional state, to offer any immediate opinions about what should be done to take account of the situation that has been created. At this point, Cdes. Brezhnev, Kosygin, Podgorny, and Voronov, I don't know what the situation is like at home. On the first day the Soviet army arrived, I and the other comrades were isolated and were brought here without knowing anything. So I can't say what the response was to this act, what the opinion of the Czech and Slovak peoples was, or how it reflected on inner-party life and on an international scale. All of these things are very important for us to know if we are to take the right measures to solve this complicated matter. For now, I can only speculate about what has gone on. During the initial period, the presidium members with me in the secretariat were taken to the CC of the party under the control of the Soviet security organs.[37] Through the window I could see several hundred people who had gathered at the building, and through the glass we could hear them shouting: "We want to see Svoboda!", "We want to see the president!", "We want Dubček!" I heard several slogans. After that there was gunfire. That was the last scene I witnessed. From that moment on I knew nothing, and now I cannot imagine what is happening in the country and in the party.

Let me say, Cde. Brezhnev, something very important: namely, that I believe this act was prepared for neither through the government nor through the party and state authorities, and therefore it will be met inside the party with much misunderstanding, and I fear that this puts the party, the communists, against this act. I can only speculate about this, of course. . . . I would like the communists to understand the whole reality of the situation created by this, but I fear they will not understand, just as I do not understand. I believe such an armed attack was premature especially because the domestic armed forces and the other organs of power were not used. . . .

I cannot know how the working class reacted to such a deed. I think, comrades, the working class of Czechoslovakia reacted to it very negatively. Hence, it is necessary, realistically, without any illusions, to look truth in the face. It is necessary to face the real situation.

As a communist who bears great responsibility for future events, I am certain that not only in Czechoslovakia and in Europe, but in all communist movements this act will cause us to suffer the greatest defeat, and will bring about a collapse and a huge breach in the ranks of communist parties in foreign countries, in the capitalist states.

So, questions and situations, in my opinion, are complicated, although it was not until today that I got to read a newspaper for the first time. However, I can say, and let others think what they want about me, that I worked in the party for thirty years, our whole family did, we gave everything to the cause of the party and the cause of socialism. Come what may. I expect the worst to happen to me and I have reconciled myself to that. . . .

[37] See Documents Nos. 101, 102, and 103 above.

I believe that the conditions in the party and in the country are the kind I always feared when I informed you that all means of political struggle were not exhausted to rectify shortcomings and impediments and to overcome the attacks of various right-wing elements in diverse organizations. Although the situation today is difficult and complicated, I am still certain that this was a force with which we could have fully coped politically, in the literal sense of the word, insofar as the CPCz CC Presidium (perhaps it will sound immodest coming from my lips) enjoyed such enormous support within the party and among our people, on a scale that the party lacked until now, and perhaps since 1948. All the extant factors were working so that these circles could in no instance have assumed control of illegal preparations for the congress or of an illegal political struggle. After the May plenum, they were beating a headlong retreat. An urgent situation has emerged now. It is necessary for us to consider it together. But I would be acting improperly if I didn't tell you the truth, comrades. I think that what happened—the use of troops—was the greatest political mistake and one that will have tragic consequences. . . .

. . . .

DOCUMENT No. 117: Minutes of Soviet–Czechoslovak Talks in the Kremlin, August 23 and 26, 1968 (Excerpts)

Source: ÚSD, AÚV KSČ, F. 07/15; Vondrová & Navrátil, vol. 2, pp. 250–254, 265–271.

These minutes record two Soviet–Czechoslovak meetings held in Moscow shortly after the invasion. The first of the meetings, on August 23, was with ČSSR President Ludvík Svoboda, who led a party and state delegation to Moscow to request the release of the Czechoslovak officials. Brezhnev and his colleagues first held a brief private meeting with Svoboda, during which they continued to urge him— unsuccessfully—to approve the establishment of a "provisional revolutionary government." The meeting then expanded to include the whole Czechoslovak delegation, made up of ČSSR Defense Minister Martin Dzúr, ČSSR Justice Minister Bohuslav Kučera (who was a member of the socialist party, not the CPCz), ČSSR Deputy Prime Minister Gustáv Husák, Czechoslovak Ambassador in Moscow Vladimír Koucký, and hard-line members of the CPCz Presidium and CPCz Secretariat who had been working behind-the-scenes since July to bring about an invasion.

The second meeting, which began in the late afternoon of August 26, and lasted into the evening, included Dubček, Smrkovský, Černík, Špaček, and Šimon, as well as Zdeněk Mlynář and Miloš Jakeš. (The only member of the CPCz Presidium who did not take part in this meeting was František Kriegel who declined, out of principle, to take part in any formal negotiations with the Soviet Politburo and asked to be returned to his detention site outside the Kremlin.)

At this meeting, Dubček, who had not attended any meetings since August 23, offers a lengthy rebuttal to the Soviet arguments to reverse the Prague Spring. The CPCz leader insists that the invasion is a "grave mistake" which has "inflicted great damage" on the CPCz, posed a "threat of a split" within the party, and "created objective conditions" in Czechoslovakia "for the growth of anti-Soviet sentiment." These effects were unlikely to dissipate anytime soon, he states, especially while foreign troops were so conspicuously deployed on Czechoslovak territory. Dubček's comments prompt a scathing response from Brezhnev, who warns that Czechoslovakia would remain a part of the socialist commonwealth and that Moscow would never tolerate actions that "would negate our sacrifices in the Second World War." Further talks are "pointless," Brezhnev angrily interjects when Dubček tries to respond. Then the whole Soviet delegation, led by Brezhnev, demonstratively walks out in protest.

The talks resumed in the evening. At the outset, Brezhnev and Kosygin attempt to forestall any new exchanges, arguing that further questions of the legitimacy of the invasion would be a "big setback for all that we've done" and would "risk civil war." The two sides spend the rest of the evening going over a protocol drafted by the Soviets, article by article, finishing just before midnight. The Moscow Protocol, as it came to be known, established the ground rules for Czechoslavakia's "normalization" under Soviet occupation.

Minutes of the talks on 23 August in the Kremlin

For the ČSSR: Cdes. Svoboda, Biľak, Dzúr, Husák, Indra, Kučera, Piller, and Koucký.

For the USSR: Cdes. Brezhnev, Kosygin, Podgorny, Voronov, Kirilenko, Polyanskii, Suslov, Shelepin, Grechko, Gromyko, Katushev, Ponomarev.

The talks were opened by *Cde. Brezhnev.*

He emphasized his willingness to find a solution acceptable to all sides. We support the decisions of the January, April, and May plenary sessions. We never intended to replace anyone in the leadership. At Čierna nad Tisou we intended to find a political solution.

But we saw what was happening. Anti-socialist forces were attacking not only the USSR but were engaged in the ideological manipulation of the people so that the very cause of socialism was endangered. . . .

The reaction in the ČSSR to Bratislava was such that the propaganda organs began to depict it as a victory of the CPCz and so forth. Not even *Rudé právo* was able to find its bearings. I then spoke to Dubček, and Kosygin spoke to Černík. I last spoke to Dubček when the CC Presidium was meeting.[38] I asked him when the plenum was going to be held and when the measures on which we agreed would be taken, etc.[39] Dubček was very nervous. He said: "What do you want me to do, we have made no commitments." True, there were no signatures but a word of honor. . . .

Cde. Svoboda suggested that Cdes. Černík, Dubček, and Smrkovský should be returned home.[40] This would "defuse" the situation somewhat. We will do this provided that guarantees are given that Dubček and Černík will fulfill the pledges made at Čierna nad Tisou and that the so-called congress is declared illegal. If they insist on its legality, this will be impossible. The congress was not lawful. There's the old Central Committee, and the old CC Presidium. Some minor changes will have to be made. Two or three people will have to go. For example, the anti-Leninist Císař, let him be chairman of the Czech National Council, but he cannot be in the leadership of the party.

There must be guarantees that only a congress, properly elected, will deal with the question of the new organs.

This will not be easy. There will be attacks, but let Dubček deal with the matter.

One cannot expect the troops to leave just like that. If the underground radio continues to incite resistance, they obviously will not leave and there may even be a war.

Annulment of the illegal congress: That's the crux of the matter.

Postpone the Extraordinary 14th Congress.

If you fulfill the Čierna nad Tisou agreement, the troops will leave and you can continue along the path of the January plenum. . . .

. . .

Brezhnev's speech was followed by *Kosygin*.

A most serious situation has been created by the activities of the Czechoslovak leadership. Cde. Dubček holds great responsibility; he led the party and state.[41] That is why he, too, must take this responsibility upon himself.

We did not send our troops to bring back Novotný and his associates, contrary to what the underground radio station alleges. This is merely a provocation.

We said we agreed with the January, April, and May plenary sessions, but not with the way the situation developed after the May plenum. Developments went against friendship with the USSR and against socialism.

The USSR was unable to tolerate having Czechoslovakia set out on the road to capitalism. Our analysis was correct. Had the troops not arrived, the socialist forces would have been driven out either gradually or by the congress.

I cannot agree to accept that congress or the new presidium, not to mention the hostile propaganda against the USSR.

We must find a solution. But we're not the only ones who must look for a way out; that's your task as well. It's also the responsibility of Dubček. We must find a solution; otherwise there will be civil war in the ČSSR. You alone will bear the responsibility for that, especially Cde. Dubček.

---

[38] This refers to Brezhnev's phone conversation with Dubček on 13 August (see Document No. 81).

[39] Brezhnev was pressing Dubček to hold a CC plenum because that, according to Dubček, was the only forum at which personnel changes could be considered.

[40] In fact, by this point Brezhnev and his colleagues had already decided to bring Dubček and Černík to Moscow for negotiations, having given up hope that the CPCz hardliners would be able to form a "revolutionary workers' and peasants' government."

[41] Formally, this was not the case. Dubček led only the party, not the state. Svoboda, as president, was the formal head of state and Černík, as prime minister, was the head of government.

What has been proposed by Cde. Svoboda can essentially be accepted as the basis for an agreement.

There are two alternatives: war or an agreement. . . .

. . .

Cde. Biľak: The right-wingers were very well prepared and they had it all well thought out. But now the question is: what next? The responsibility rests with us. The congress was illegal. However, the Congress of the Slovak CP has been set to begin on 26 August. I asked for a postponement.[42] I think it will be impossible to hold the congress. The question is, who will declare the CPCz Congress illegal. It will have to be Dubček. . . .

. . .

* * *

Minutes of talks in the Kremlin on 26 August (4 P.M. local time)

For the ČSSR: Cdes. Svoboda, Dubček, Černík, Smrkovský, Husák, Biľak, Barbírek, Piller, Špaček, Švestka, Rigo, Šimon, Mlynář, Jakeš, Dzúr, Kučera, Koucký.

For the USSR: Cdes. Brezhnev, Podgorny, Kosygin, Voronov, Kirilenko, Polyanskii, Suslov, Shelepin, Shelest, Katushev, Ponomarev, Semyonov, Gromyko, Grechko.

At the outset, the text of a draft protocol was distributed. A discussion began on what procedure to adopt. The Soviet side suggested that they approve the draft page by page. *Cde. Černík* asked for the floor:[43]

We all feel the historical responsibility of this meeting. Our country has fallen into a situation for which there is no parallel in the postwar period. We, the Czechoslovak communists, feel an immense responsibility to our people.

We have to remember that some members of the presidium were informed about the talks only yesterday, after their arrival from Prague.[44]

We consider the situation in our country to be critical. There is still a danger of extensive bloodshed and an organizational split within the party. Putting the state institutions out of action has weakened the general running of society. We know that the events have had far-reaching international repercussions.

In our talks with you, the CC Presidium wants to look for an honest way of normalizing conditions and a future path for the advance of socialism. Under no circumstances do we want to rehash the causes of the situation and go back over this. The party leadership is aware of its responsibility for the way things now develop.

In a sincere attempt to promote the creative forces of the nation we embarked on a great mission after January. Every day we were striving to bolster socialism, and we wanted to consolidate the position of our country among the socialist states. We feel responsible for the inconsistent implementation of our tasks and for mistakes and shortcomings in our work. I would ask the CPSU CC Politburo to accept these words not as a hollow phrase but as an expression of profound awareness of the current situation.

---

[42] On 24 August, Slovak party officials spoke by phone with Dubček and Biľak, both of whom requested that the Slovak CP Congress be postponed until they had returned to the country from Moscow.

[43] Here, as on other occasions, Černík spoke in Czech. Dubček, by contrast, was able to speak in Russian; and his remarks below were delivered in Russian (though they have been translated here into English from a Czech transcript).

[44] Černík is referring here to CPCz officials who had not been arrested or been in Svoboda's original delegation; these would include Švestka, Rigo, Barbírek, Jakeš, and Mlynář.

Based on the May CC session, we stressed that in essence the process had assumed a clearly socialist character, but that there was still a threat both from the left and from the right.

The CC Presidium wishes to tell you that the occupation of the ČSSR by the armies of friendly countries took place without its knowledge, it never asked for this, and the Czechoslovak army, the People's Militia, and the security organs were not put on a state of alert beforehand.

We want to solve the difficult situation together with you. . . .

The CC Presidium has asked me to inform you that the press of the fraternal parties has described Cde. Dubček as the head of the right-wing forces in the party, and says that after Bratislava, he had moved further to the right. The presidium rejects such an assessment of Cde. Dubček's activities. . . .

. . .

Cde. Dubček: I saw your document—I am referring to your draft Protocol—and there is also our own draft.[45] I would therefore ask that both documents be part of the minutes of these deliberations. I would also ask that certain adjustments be made in the adopted document so that there should be no incorrect formulations in places. What we want, above all, is that no names be mentioned in the document we are going to adopt here, so that it should not be possible to interpret matters as a repetition of the 1950s.

We now have reports about the situation in our country. I want to point out that it is even worse than we had thought, both in the party and in the country as a whole. In the party, this is so because there is the threat of a split.

All that has happened since 20 August, when the allied armies arrived, has created an entirely new situation for us, which is all the more complex insofar as all activities of party and state organs have been impossible.

After the May plenum and especially after Bratislava, there was a great surge of activity in our party, mainly in connection with preparations for the congress. Neither the CC Presidium nor the entire party understands why the troops entered. I am saying this only to make you understand that concrete steps and the tactics of future moves must be determined only after a thorough examination of the situation at home. The entry of the troops has aroused the disagreement of the people, the party organs, and the working class.

You, too, must see the situation in our country and in our party realistically. All this has a devastating effect on the life of the people. It was a heavy blow to both the ideas and feelings of our people. We openly declare that we regard your move to be a serious mistake, which will inflict great damage on our party and the international communist movement. It is a fact—and I am saying this because we must now think of how to get out of this situation, which has the support neither of the people nor of the party—that this move jeopardizes our friendship and creates objective conditions for the growth of anti-Soviet sentiment. It cannot be expected that these effects will be eliminated in the near future. That job will be a long and arduous one, and that's why the CC Presidium is in a very difficult situation. . . .

. . .

---

[45] Soviet leaders had summarily rejected the Czechoslovak draft during a preliminary meeting the previous day. Even so, Czechoslovak officials were reasonably successful in obtaining improvements and modifications in the Soviet draft. Among the changes made in the Protocol were the excision of a clause referring to a "counterrevolution" in Czechoslovakia, which had been used to justify the invasion; the deletion of any reference to the Warsaw Letter; and the insertion of a clause supporting the CPCz CC's May plenum, which was an indirect way of endorsing the CPCz Action Program. Nevertheless, the Czechoslovak authorities had to make numerous concessions of their own, especially on personnel issues and on the status of the Extraordinary 14th CPCz Congress in Vysočany, which was ruled invalid by the Protocol. Moreover, they failed to gain any forthright commitment from the Soviet Union, either in Point 5 of the Protocol or elsewhere, to set a timetable for the withdrawal of Soviet troops from Czechoslovakia.

Brezhnev: I'm turning first to all our comrades, because I was ill yesterday and was unable to attend the meeting of our Politburo. However, I have been fully informed of its results and fully endorse them. We have already had preliminary talks, where a great deal has been clarified. But everything that Cde. Černík and Cde. Dubček have been saying today is a big setback for all that we've done. And if what you're saying here is also what you intend to say back home, things will get even worse. . . .[46]

Cde. Kosygin: The speeches by Cdes. Dubček and Černík have raised new considerations. We wanted you to understand why we sent the armies to your country and we understand your situation. We already thought we understood one another. But you've turned matters around here once again. The entry of the troops is, in fact, a historical event, if only because it will save socialism in the ČSSR. Cde. Dubček says we can expect anything, even provocations against the troops. He wants to make us responsible for everything, even for the split in the party. So what can we expect? I have a bad impression. In your speeches you are holding us responsible for everything, but you don't say how you yourselves intend to act in this situation. You've said nothing concrete here. We thought you had plenty of time here to consult each other and agree on what concrete steps we and you will take. You've been here two days, but once again you haven't come up with a program of what to do. . . .

After the experience we had with Čierna, we today are going to give you the agreement in writing and assume that this will be the program your party and government will follow. But now Cde. Dubček, as he says, sees no prospects. If that's the way you're going to talk back home, you're heading for civil war. The situation in your country is at present somewhat better than before the entry of the troops, and you'll be able to solve your problems together with our army. But to do this, you in the presidium must be united. . . .

. . .

---

[46] Brezhnev made this statement when the negotiations resumed following a Soviet walkout from the meeting in protest at Dubček's remarks. During the interruption, the CPSU Politburo had met and decided to finish up the talks as soon as possible.

DOCUMENT No. 118: Minutes of the First Post-Invasion Meeting of the "Warsaw Five" in Moscow, August 24, 1968

Source: ÚSD, Sb. KV, Z/M 21.

This stenographic summary of the first post-invasion meeting of the "Warsaw Five" records the positions of the Eastern European nations which participated in "Operation Danube." The summary is based on notes taken by an assistant to Hungarian leader János Kádár.

The document captures the hard-line position taken by the Polish, Bulgarian and East German leaders, all of whom explicitly called for the "imposition of a military dictatorship in Czechoslovakia" as Zhivkov suggested. Brezhnev and Kosygin argue that a viable political solution necessitated the return of Dubček and his high aides to Prague. Their position is forcefully opposed by Gomułka, Ulbricht and Zhivkov, who denounce any "compromise" with "the counterrevolution." Notwithstanding these consultations, the Soviets stay with their decision to involve Dubček in a less drastic political solution to the crisis.

The first meeting took place on 24 August between 10 A.M. and 11:50 A.M. Moscow time. The Soviet side was represented by Cdes. Brezhnev, Kosygin, and Podgorny; the Bulgarian side by Zhivkov and Velchev; the Hungarian side by János Kádár, Jenő Fock, and Zoltán Komócsin; the GDR side by Ulbricht, Stoph, and Honecker; and the Polish side by Gomułka, Cyrankiewicz, and Kliszko.

Cde. Brezhnev started by saying there was no need to explain why the meeting of officials from the five fraternal parties had become necessary; he added a short brief on the Czechoslovak situation and on the Soviet–Czechoslovak talks.

Our troops have accomplished their tasks in Czechoslovakia. The action started two hours early. They occupied the whole of Czechoslovakia, essentially without casualties, but political work has still not begun. By contrast, the counterrevolutionary and right-wing forces were exceedingly well prepared, and several illegal radio transmitters were operating on the territory of the state. A day after the occupation they were able to convene an extraordinary party congress, which they organized without the participation of members of the presidium. Everything indicates that the rightists are solidly organized. Secret weapons caches have been discovered.

Our expectations that the right-wing forces would be scared off after the entry of the troops proved unfounded. They have continued their activities. To make matters worse, the healthy forces did not succeed in launching their own activities and, in a certain sense, have acted in a cowardly manner. The rightists have the ideological centers (television, radio, and part of the press) firmly in their grip and will not surrender them. . . .

On the night of the 22nd, President Svoboda asked to come to Moscow at the head of a delegation. After thinking the matter over, the Soviet leadership agreed. Svoboda said a solution must be found that would be acceptable under current circumstances. A situation must be created that would enable the allied troops to leave Czechoslovakia and be seen off with flowers. The Czechoslovak delegation consisted of Svoboda, Biľak, Piller, Indra, Husák, Dzúr, and Kučera. Svoboda asked to be received officially, with the full honors normally accorded to a president.

Cde. Brezhnev said that they had held two meetings with the delegation so far. On the first occasion, he had a special meeting with Svoboda. Brezhnev asked that party matters be discussed with the delegation. Svoboda requested that the legal representatives of the Czechoslovak government be allowed to return to Czechoslovakia, and he said he wanted to meet them. To that end, he wanted to return to Prague that very evening.

The Soviet leaders declared they were ready to do whatever was required to normalize the situation. *But they needed to have Czechoslovak leaders who would carry out the agreements reached at Čierna nad Tisou and Bratislava.* Svoboda understood this. . . .

The Soviet leaders met Dubček and Černík twice. They explained the Soviet position that the old presidium and Central Committee must act in the spirit of the accords of *Čierna nad Tisou and Bratislava*. The Czechoslovak comrades must understand that *if they fail to do this there will be bloodshed in Czechoslovakia. In such a situation the allied troops cannot retreat even a single step.* Černík declared that he did not recognize the legality of the extraordinary congress which had met. The main question is to find someone on whom he can rely, and then he will fight until the end. If he does not succeed in carrying out the plan, he will resign. Dubček was more stubborn. He said he was expressing his own view, even though he respected Černík's opinion. He had to meet the full presidium, he said, because he needed to be informed about the situation back home, and only then would he be capable of dealing with the merit of the question. . . .

As regards the establishment of a new government, they spoke about *several options, including the establishment of a revolutionary government headed by president Svoboda.* Svoboda did not agree to this. *The second option would give the post of prime minister to Husák, and Černík would be secretary of the Central Committee.* Biľak and Svoboda maintained that such a solution was impossible. The third option would have Dubček remain first secretary and Černík remain prime minister. After a session of the Central Committee another solution could be found.

Cde. Podgorny said that president Svoboda was sincerely trying to find the best solution. *He criticized the Czechoslovak leaders who were now in Moscow, and pointed to the threat of civil war, after which Dubček suffered a heart attack.* According to the doctors, his condition was in no way serious, but he needed rest.

In a private discussion with the Soviet leaders, Svoboda said he did not trust Dubček and would do his utmost to have him dismissed from office after normalization.[47] But he suspected that for now if he were to return home without Dubček, it would be Dubček, not he, who would be proclaimed a hero.

Cde. Kosygin referred to Biľak, who had said that back home they would tell the Czechoslovak people, in a critical and self-critical spirit, about all the factors that had led to a counterrevolutionary threat in the state. Biľak and Svoboda believe that unless the Central Committee meeting takes place in a proper and orderly manner, it will turn against us. The Soviet side agreed with this and declared that in such an event the only solution would be the imposition of direct military rule.

Cde. Kosygin said that now the situation was different from before. We are now in a position of strength—he pointed to the presence of our troops in Czechoslovakia—and we will have an agreement. At Čierna we had an agreement but no strength to back it up.

Cde. Zhivkov said that the second option was the most significant, namely, the imposition of a military dictatorship in Czechoslovakia. . . .

Cde. Brezhnev repeatedly said that Dubček and Černík had to be included in the negotiations because otherwise *there would be no one to talk to.* Once an acceptable agreement was concluded, they, too, would be permitted to return to Prague. Before that, however, all members of the presidium would be invited to Moscow so that an agreement would be drafted in the presence of the full presidium and would be signed by all of them. No doubt, the first to return home would be Svoboda; and the rest of the presidium, led by Dubček, would return afterwards. Cde. Brezhnev emphasized that *counterrevolution had openly reared its head and that they must avoid giving the impression that the Soviet side would be ready to yield.* He said we would not retreat even an inch. At the same time, the complexity of the situation must be taken into account. Cde. Brezhnev asked the delegations of the four fraternal parties to remain in Moscow for 2–3 days

---

[47] Unfortunately, notes from the private meeting between Svoboda and the CPSU leadership on August 23 have not yet been released, so it is impossible to establish precisely what Svoboda said there about Dubček (as opposed to what Brezhnev *thought* he said). Still, based on other statements Svoboda had made about Dubček at the time, there is no inherent reason to challenge what Brezhnev said.

because in the current situation their help is essential. The situation may change from hour to hour, and that is why, while negotiations are under way with the Czechs, the delegations of the four socialist countries should consult with each other and adopt a unified position. . . .

Cde. Gomułka, too, proposed that Svoboda return home. He is to be followed by Dubček and Černík. *An armed struggle is probably inevitable.* There will be either a struggle or capitulation. *Our troops must be ordered to combat the counterrevolution.* After returning home, Svoboda must declare that negotiations can be successful only if there is calm. It is also possible, and we must reckon with this, that once the Czechoslovak leaders return home, they will say: "Let's go! Let's carry on the struggle." *If Svoboda, Dubček, and Černík fail to mobilize everyone for the cause of peace, we must issue orders to our troops.* We should acknowledge that in Czechoslovakia there is no communist party today, there are simply individual communists. The right-wing leadership is acting in collusion with the counterrevolution. In effect, Czechoslovakia has already left the Warsaw Pact, as the rightists and counterrevolutionaries demand neutrality for the country. The people are waiting passively to see what will happen, and the communists are incapable of taking a stand. The situation in Hungary was better than in Czechoslovakia today. Let us ask ourselves the question: What is going to happen? *If we fail to act with resolve, the next blow may be against the GDR. If so, we will be wiser from our experience, knowing that counterrevolution can be organized even in the presence of Soviet troops.* The situation is worse than we thought, Cde. Gomułka said. . . .

Cde. Ulbricht, too, stressed that we had not explained the real situation to the Czechoslovak people, nor had we explained the nature of the accords reached at Čierna and Bratislava. Dubček, Černík, and Smrkovský were claiming that there had been no accords and therefore were concealing them from the people. The gravity of the situation must be explained to the Czechoslovak working class, which must be asked to thwart the counterrevolution. And the healthy forces within the party must be activated. Dubček deceived us at Čierna and Bratislava. It would not be appropriate to establish a simple National Unity Government because it would lack the character of class struggle. *What is needed is a Workers' and Peasants' National Unity Government.*

Cde. Zhivkov underscored the complexity of the Czechoslovak situation. *He maintained that a confrontation with the counterrevolutionaries was inevitable.* The Czechoslovak leaders and *Svoboda must understand that civil war was brewing in the country. A Revolutionary Workers' and Peasants' Government must be established with Černík but without Dubček.* Our troops are being well received by the population. At this point, Cde. Brezhnev warned that the situation was different now. In Cde. Zhivkov's opinion, normalization of the situation must commence with the establishment of a workers' and peasants' government. The party can be resurrected later. . . .

In conclusion Cde. Brezhnev warned that we must expect the outbreak of civil war but we will never capitulate.

DOCUMENT No. 119: The Moscow Protocol, August 26, 1968

Source: ÚSD, Sb. KV, K—Archiv MZV, Gs "T"; Vondrová & Navrátil, vol. 2, pp. 271–275.

The Moscow Protocol established the political rules for rolling back the Prague Spring and "normalizing" post-invasion Czechoslavakia. The 11-page original Russian document, translated here, was signed in Moscow after three days of negotiations between Soviet authorities and Czechoslovak leaders, including Dubček and Černík. During the negotiating sessions, Soviet leaders had made clear that if the Czechoslovak delegation refused to sign a finished document, the Warsaw "Five" would establish a full-fledged military dictatorship in Czechoslovakia.

The document was based on a Soviet draft protocol presented to the Czechoslovaks on August 24. Soviet officials rejected efforts by Dubček's aides to substitute their own draft for negotiation. Nevertheless, the Czechoslovak negotiators did obtain some concessions. The final document no longer characterized events before the invasion as "counterrevolutionary," omitted any mention of the Warsaw Letter, and did not call for a return to the situation before January 1968. Nevertheless, the Protocol forced Dubček and his colleagues to concede to a virtual checklist of Soviet demands: nullify the 14th Congress in Vysočany, give much greater emphasis to central economic planning, ban political groups like KAN and K-231, prohibit the reemergence of the Social Democratic Party, reimpose censorship across the board, dismiss numerous reformist officials (understood to include Kriegel, Císař, Jiří Pelikán, Ota Šik, and Jiří Hájek, among others), refrain from dismissing or carrying out any reprisals against officials who had sided with the "healthy forces," subordinate Czechoslovak foreign policy completely to Soviet preferences, and retract the ČSSR's request for the UN Security Council to consider the situation in Czechoslovakia. Finally, the protocol offered no timetable for the withdrawal of Soviet and allied troops from Czechoslovakia; instead, it merely specified that withdrawals would "occur in stages" once "the threat to the gains of socialism in Czechoslovakia and the threat to the security of the countries of the socialist commonwealth have been eliminated."

PROTOCOL

on Negotiations between Delegations from
the Union of Soviet Socialist Republics
and the Czechoslovak Socialist Republic

On 23–26 August 1968, negotiations took place in Moscow between a delegation from the Union of Soviet Socialist Republics and a delegation from the Czechoslovak Socialist Republic. . . .

1. During the talks, the two sides considered questions linked with the defense of socialist gains of the Czechoslovak people in the circumstances that have arisen in the ČSSR. They also considered the highest priority measures dictated by this situation and by the presence of troops from the five socialist countries on the territory of Czechoslovakia.

During the talks, both sides abided by the generally recognized standards of relations between fraternal parties and countries, and by principles embodied in the final documents of the talks in Čierna nad Tisou and the conference in Bratislava. They reaffirmed their loyalty to the pledge by the socialist countries to support, strengthen, and defend the gains of socialism and to wage an irreconcilable struggle against counterrevolutionary forces, a struggle that is the common international duty of all socialist countries. They expressed the firm conviction that under present circumstances the main thing is to carry out what was formulated at the Bratislava conference regarding provisions and principles, along with the points agreed upon in Čierna nad Tisou. It is also imperative to consistently realize the measures which stem from the agreements reached there.

2. The CC Pesidium of the Communist Party of Czechoslovakia declared that the so-called 14th CPCz Congress—which was convened on 22 August without the approval of the CPCz

Central Committee, in violation of the statutes of the CPCz, in the absence of presidium and CC Secretariat members, in the absence of the delegates of communists from Slovakia, in the absence of most of the communist delegates from the Czechoslovak People's Army, and in the absence of communists from many other party branches—as well as the resolutions it adopted, are invalid. All relevant measures on this matter will be taken by the CC Presidium upon its return to Czechoslovakia.

The delegation declared that the Extraordinary 14th Congress of the Communist Party of Czechoslovakia will be convened after conditions in the party and the country have been normalized.

3. The CPCz delegation reported that in the course of the next six to ten days a joint plenary session will be held of the CPCz Central Committee and the Central Control and Auditing Commission.[48]

The plenum will consider questions of normalizing the situation in the country, topical issues of party and state life, questions about how to improve the work of party and state bodies, and problems of the economy and the standard of living of the people. The plenum also will consider strengthening all links in the supervision of the party and country and of removing from their posts those persons whose activities were not in keeping with the interests of ensuring the leading role of the working class and the communist party, or in keeping with the decisions of the January and May plenary sessions of the CPCz CC (1968), or in keeping with attempts to strengthen the position of socialism in the country and the further development of relations between the ČSSR and the fraternal countries of the socialist commonwealth.

4. The leaders of the CPCz declared it was necessary to carry out a number of immediate measures intended to reinforce the regime of the working masses and the positions of socialism.

In connection with this they especially emphasized the significance of such important measures as control of the mass media so that they are wholly at the service of socialism; the prohibition of anti-socialist and anti-Soviet expressions in the press, on radio, and on television; a ban on activities by various groups and organizations advocating anti-socialist positions; and a ban on activities by the anti-Marxist Social Democratic Party. With this goal in mind, steps will be taken in the coming days to bring about effective action.

Party and state bodies will regulate the situation in the press, radio, and television with the help of new laws and measures. Given the extraordinary nature of the situation, it is essential to approve special, temporary measures to bring order to these sectors so that the government will have effective powers at its disposal to act against the anti-socialist forces in the country. Moreover, if the need arises, the government can use these measures to combat the malevolence of certain persons or groups. The necessary measures regarding personnel will be undertaken to ensure the proper functioning of the press, radio, and television.

As at Čierna nad Tisou, the leadership of the CPSU expressed full solidarity with these measures, being convinced that they are in keeping with the basic interests of the entire socialist commonwealth and its security and unity.

5. Both delegations considered questions linked with the presence of troops from the five socialist countries on the territory of the ČSSR, and agreed that these troops and other bodies of allied countries will not interfere in the internal affairs of the ČSSR. When the threat to the gains of socialism in Czechoslovakia and the threat to the security of the countries of the socialist commonwealth have been eliminated, the allied troops will be withdrawn in stages from the ČSSR's territory.

Questions about the withdrawal and redeployment of troops from cities and villages will be considered by the High Command of the allied troops and the Command of the CzPA as soon as the organs of state power are able to maintain order.

---

[48] The CC plenum was convened on August 31. Before the invasion there had been plans to hold a CC plenum on August 29.

Allied troops will be deployed in barracks, training grounds, and other military zones. Deployment will be carried out after mutual agreement is reached between representatives of the allied and Czechoslovak armies.

The question of ensuring the security of borders with the FRG will also be examined. The number of troops and their structure and deployment are to be decided in cooperation with representatives of the Czechoslovak army.

To meet the material-technical, medical, and other needs for the temporary deployment of Soviet troops on ČSSR territory, an agreement will be drawn up and approved by the governments of the ČSSR and the USSR. All outstanding problems will be decided at the level of the ministers of national defense and foreign affairs. Controversial questions of principle will be decided by the governments of both states.

An agreement will be concluded between the allied states and Czechoslovakia regarding conditions for the deployment and full withdrawal of allied troops.

6. The Czechoslovak leaders stated that the armed forces of Czechoslovakia were given the necessary orders to prevent incidents and conflicts with troops of the allied countries or any other acts that might violate law and order.[49] The military command of the ČSSR was also given instructions to keep in contact with the commanders of the allied troops.

The CPCz CC Presidium and the government of the ČSSR will take immediate measures to prevent the press, radio, and television from carrying items that might cause conflicts and tension between the population and the allied troops stationed on the territory of Czechoslovakia.

7. The leaders of the CPCz declared that they will not permit officials and employees of the party to be dismissed from their posts—or, even more, to have any sort of repressive measures directed against them—simply because those individuals favored strengthening the position of socialism in the country against the anti-communist forces, or because of their friendly attitude toward the Soviet Union.

8. Agreement was reached that talks will be held in the immediate future on a broad range of economic questions in order to expand and deepen economic, scientific, and technical cooperation between the Soviet Union and the Czechoslovak Socialist Republic, bearing in mind, in particular, the need for the further development of the socialist economy of Czechoslovakia and support for the above-mentioned plans of the CPCz to improve the national economy of the country.

9. There is full consensus that the development of international conditions and the subversive acts of imperialism, directed against peace and the security of nations and against the cause of socialism, calls for the genuine strengthening and improvement of the effectiveness of the defensive Warsaw Pact in the future, as well as of other all-round and bilateral bodies and forms of cooperation among the socialist states.

10. The leaders of the CPSU and the leaders of the CPCz confirmed their determination to closely coordinate their actions on the international scene with the intention of promoting the cohesion of the socialist community and upholding the cause of peace and international security.

As in the past, the Soviet Union and Czechoslovakia will systematically pursue a policy on European affairs that is in keeping with the common interests of the socialist countries and the specific interests of each of them, as well as the interests of European security. They will decisively resist the militarist, revanchist, and neo-Nazi forces that are seeking to overturn the results of the Second World War and to challenge the inviolability of existing borders in Europe.

The parties to this agreement declare that they will scrupulously fulfill all commitments they have undertaken in multilateral and bilateral agreements concluded between the socialist states.

In close unity with the other countries of the socialist community, they will continue the struggle in the future against the subversive actions of imperialism and in support of national and international liberation movements.

---

[49] For evidence of how frequently these incidents were arising, see Document No. 127.

11. With regard to the UN Security Council's consideration of the so-called "Matter of the Situation in Czechoslovakia," the leaders of the CPCz and the government of the ČSSR declare that the Czechoslovak side did not request this issue to be brought before the Security Council.

The leaders of the CPCz stated that the government of the ČSSR had directed that its Czechoslovak representative in New York should categorically reject any examination of the situation in Czechoslovakia in the Security Council or in any other UN body and should categorically demand that this item be taken off the agenda.

12. The CPCz CC Presidium and the government of Czechoslovakia declared that they will evaluate the actions of members of the government outside the ČSSR concerning its domestic and foreign policy in the name of the ČSSR government, especially from the viewpoint of whether these actions are in keeping with the line of the CPCz and the government of the Czechoslovak Socialist Republic. The appropriate conclusions will be drawn from these assessments. In connection with this, the CPCz CC Presidium also believes it necessary to carry out several additional personnel changes in party and government bodies and organizations in order to secure consolidation in the party and the country as soon as possible.

These questions will be examined thoroughly after returning home. Furthermore, the actions of the Interior Ministry will also be examined and, on the basis of this, conclusions will be drawn about how to strengthen its leadership.

13. Agreement was reached to exchange party–government delegations as soon as possible to explore questions in greater depth pertaining to relations between their countries, as well as current international problems. Agreement also was reached that relevant decisions will be taken.

14. In the interest of both parties and to bolster friendship between the USSR and the ČSSR, the delegations agreed that the contacts between the leadership of the CPSU and the CPCz in the period after 20 August, and in particular the content of the current negotiations, should be regarded as strictly confidential.[50]

15. The leadership of the CPSU and the CPCz in the name of their parties and governments declare that the efforts of the CPSU, the CPCz, and the governments of the Soviet Union and the Czechoslovak Socialist Republic will be directed toward an improvement of the traditional and time-honored friendship between the peoples of both countries, bolstering their fraternal and permanent friendship.

By agreement of the two sides, both parties will sign the Russian-language text.

---

[50] Initially, the protocol was treated as a secret document, and no mention of it was made in the joint communiqué released after the Moscow negotiations. In the speeches that Dubček, Svoboda, Černík, and Smrkovský delivered when they returned from Moscow, they carefully refrained from making any direct reference to the protocol. Although a number of Western correspondents promptly learned of the existence and general content of the protocol, Soviet and Czechoslovak officials denied all reports about the matter. At a closed CPCz Central Committee plenum on August 31, Smrkovský revealed the terms of the document to the participants, but in public he still made no mention of the protocol. On September 8, *The New York Times* published a version, based on the Soviet *draft*, not on the final protocol. On September 9, Smrkovský publicly mentioned the protocol for the first time, though he did not specify its contents. A few days later, Dubček also referred explicitly to the protocol during a televised speech (which was published in *Rudé právo* on September 15), and he briefly alluded to some of the provisions. The document itself, however, was not actually published in Czechoslovakia until more than twenty years later.

DOCUMENT No. 120: Alexander Dubček's Recollections of the Moscow Negotiations and the Moscow Protocol

Source: "Alexander Dubček vzpomíná: Původní rozhovor pro Občanský deník o pozadí srpnových událostí roku 1968," *Občanský deník* (Prague), Part 4, August 24, 1990, p. 3.

This is the last of four excerpts from the lengthy interview with Alexander Dubček. In it, he recounts the negotiations in Moscow between Czechoslovak and Soviet leaders during the last week of August, and the evolution of his decision to join his colleagues in signing the Moscow protocol rather than resign his post as first secretary.

(For the rest of the Dubček interview see Document No. 67 [first two parts], and Document No. 103.)

PART 4

Občanský deník: At your first meeting with Brezhnev, according to certain accounts, prime minister Černík also took part.

Dubček: That's possibly and most likely true. I can't remember all of it. I just know that when I arrived there the first time, I didn't know what was going on back in Czechoslovakia and so I refused to negotiate. I remember that I learned about the support the people were giving us, about the international reaction, and about related matters only from other members of our delegation who arrived later on.

Občanský deník: At the time when you were still refusing to negotiate, our delegation was coming under pressure from the Soviet side to brand the results of the 14th Congress invalid. The resistance of our delegation began to crumble as a result of G. Husák, who said in Moscow that Slovakia could not accept the results of the 14th Congress because Slovak delegates had not been represented there. He threatened that it might lead to a split of the party between its Czech and Slovak components.

Dubček: What you are saying is correct. G. Husák also expressed these sentiments after he returned. In Moscow he felt he somehow had to exclude himself from the collective in order to demonstrate to the Soviets that he regarded their demands to be the key issue. In this way he had already shown in Moscow that he was willing to comply with their wishes.

The story regarding the congress did not end there. I felt, and other members of the delegation supported my view, that we had a certain responsibility to preserve at least part of the validity of the 14th Congress. I had tried to come up with a plan about what to do when we returned home already in Moscow. We needed to take steps that would substantially bolster the reformist wing of the Central Committee. But how? It occurred to me that for the sake of maintaining the unity of the party—at least that is how I presented it to Brezhnev—we could coopt a certain number of people from the Vysočany Congress into the old CC. In that way the old CC, which had proven loyal at a critical moment when the Warsaw Letter was under consideration, could be strengthened in the way we needed it to be.

At the first session of the CC immediately after our return on 31 August, we coopted a "certain number" of 87 people from the Vysočany Congress. But what then happened? During the session, which was taking place in the Castle in Prague, someone came over to me and said that I had a phone call waiting in the president's office.[51] It was Brezhnev asking what in the world we were

---

[51] The Castle, near the bank of the Vltava River across from the Old Town in Prague, was (and still is) the site of the presidential offices.

doing there at the CC by bringing in additional people through supposedly undemocratic methods. This was at a time when such a step was still only being discussed at the regional commissions. It had not even been approved when someone was already reacting to it from over there.

I explained to him that it was a political compromise, something that I had informed him earlier. Brezhnev said: "Da, vy govorili, no ne govorili skoľko." And I responded, "No vy tozhe ne govorili skoľko."[52]

We proceeded with the cooptation, but Brezhnev was very upset.

Občanský deník: It is a well-known fact that even during the final official meeting at the Kremlin on 26 August you refused to sign the protocol that had been prepared. In the end, however, you did sign the final version of the Moscow protocol. How did that occur?

Dubček: The other members of the delegation did not accept my resignation. The meetings were led on our side by Černík, and he was always asking me whether I would be willing to join them. No, I said, I wasn't willing to do so—and the important thing is how I conducted myself and why.

I had to decide these things in a difficult and complicated situation, when there was a danger lingering over our country that the resentment of the people toward the intervention might lead to a civil war. I could have acted in a way that would have promoted their defiance and resentment, which would inevitably have led to a confrontation, or, on the contrary, I could do everything possible to prevent such a confrontation. The second alternative was what I chose. And in the end I subordinated all other steps to that alternative.

I saw the people with whom I was personally connected—Svoboda, Smrkovský, Černík, Špaček, and others—collectively arriving at some sort of joint conclusion. I don't know whether I was under the sway of some kind of discipline, or whether it was the feeling that one must not abandon the others in a difficult and complicated situation and that one cannot and should not act only in accord with what one thinks is right. I also realized what might happen after we returned home if my signature did not appear alongside the signatures of Svoboda, Smrkovský, Černík and others, and if I did not return to my post. Then even these people could not have withstood popular scrutiny, and something would have happened that none of us wanted. I didn't feel justified in risking a confrontation between a morally courageous but unarmed populace, on the one hand, and the military machinery of a superpower, on the other.

Občanský deník: At that time did you have any concrete ideas about what would have happened if you had refused to sign? As far as we know, at the meeting with the part of the delegation that was headed by Svoboda, the Soviet side made a number of threats to the effect that there would be "either an agreement or a civil war." In subsequent meetings, were similar threats made?

Dubček: Not against me. But irrespective of what they said and did, I was convinced that from the very first night the Soviet army was just itching for a confrontation, and that I must do what I could to prevent that from occurring. If there had been a violent confrontation, they would have portrayed it all as a counterrevolution.

As concerns me personally, let me say this. Since the night of 20–21 August, when we voted on the famous declaration of the presidium, I had had no illusions about what I could expect. I had decided there already. It is not easy, but it is not as difficult when you are deciding only for yourself. And by the time they put me into the tank, I was already at peace with myself. I took account of the possibility that I might not come back at all. My eyes no longer shed tears at the thought.

---

[52] Dubček cites this exchange in Russian. The English translation would be: "Yes, you mentioned it, but you didn't say how many," "But you also didn't say how many."

And why did I sign the protocol? Why did I not hold out until the end as Kriegel did? If I had been in his place, I would have acted identically. But in my place I simply couldn't do that. I was accountable for far more than he was. I couldn't have abandoned the others.

My defiance, and my refusal to take part in the meetings and acquiesce in the diktat originally laid down by the Soviets, did bear fruits. It was not only my own countrymen who were interested in getting me to take part in the meetings, the Soviets were perhaps even more interested. When the option of using military intervention to underwrite the formation of a workers' and peasants' government didn't work out, they tried to find other options by way of the protocol.

They were particularly interested in ensuring that the protocol included these three things:

— we must acknowledge that the military intervention was justified and, therefore, that a counterrevolution had existed;

— we must acknowledge that the presidium and the CC plenum took an improper stance toward the Warsaw Letter; and

— we must discreetly abandon the Action Program.

We were not in a position to defend everything we had accomplished or to avoid making concessions. But on these three points we did prove successful and that was thanks to my refusal to go along.

Občanský deník: How did the process of actually signing the protocol take place?

Dubček: When Smrkovský and Černík were trying to persuade me to take part in the concluding ceremony, I didn't know whether I would have sufficient strength to do it. There still wasn't anything said in the protocol about our future political line, which we would be expected to adhere to after returning home. I finally realized that I could not exclude myself from the collective. But I warned that there was no guarantee I could make it through. As a result, they gave me some sort of sedative.

Well, I entered the meeting room. On the opposite side I saw the black eyebrows, the faces . . . I had to hold onto a table. Everything started to well up inside me. I ordered myself: "Hang on, hang on!" But in the end I couldn't stand it. I openly told them my view of what they had done and said I thought they had irreparably destroyed everything through their aggressive actions.

Obviously they couldn't put up with that, especially at an official meeting like this. The entire Soviet delegation led by Brezhnev demonstratively left the room, and the meeting broke up. I couldn't sense how long the interruption lasted, and I didn't know they were off somewhere debating what to do with me now that they couldn't count on me to guarantee the dictated agreements.

When the meeting resumed, the whole atmosphere was such that the Soviets backed down on the question of the Action Program. The protocol made no direct mention of it, but it did refer to the line of the January and May plenary sessions of the CC—and the May plenum had embraced about 99 percent of the Action Program. That was very important for me. There was still hope that the reformist forces who did not lose their positions might—on the basis of the political line of the January and May plenary sessions—be able to salvage at least part of the process of renewal and democratization. Our retreat after this did not appear so catastrophic. The outlook for us did not appear so hopeless, and that was a precondition for us to achieve unity after returning home. In that light, I came to believe that it would be possible to devise a political line that would overcome this difficult era. As it turned out, of course, it merely led to the rise of Husák and normalization.

Nowadays one might object that I was incorrect in my assessment of the situation. Perhaps I was. But how would history have judged us if we had decided not to sign and risked the outbreak of a civil war and the inception of a collaborationist revolutionary workers' and peasants' government, while failing to take advantage of the only opportunity we were offered? I signed.

DOCUMENT No. 121: Testimony by the Chief of the CzPA General Staff and the Head of the CzPA's Main Political Directorate at a Meeting of the Presidium of the National Assembly, August 26, 1968 (Excerpts)

Source: ÚSD, Sb. KV, O—Archiv NS, File for Meetings of National Assembly Presidium.

This document is a transcript of remarks made to the Czechoslovak parliament by two of the highest-ranking officers in the Czechoslovak People's Army—the chief of the CzPA General Staff, General Karel Rusov, and the head of the CzPA's Main Political Directorate, General František Bedřich—explaining what the army had done during and after the invasion on August 20. Both stressed that the army had acted in strict conformity with orders transmitted by the ČSSR president and by all other political leaders in Czechoslovakia. They acknowledged that their decisions had "created a good deal of tension within the army," but they emphasized that the invading troops had been prepared, if necessary, to annihilate the entire CzPA and dismember Czechoslovakia itself.

The transcript also records Bedřich's warning that Soviet commanders were trying to exploit the situation to achieve their long-standing aim of a permanent Soviet troop presence on Czechoslovak territory. This was the motive, according to Bedřich, for Soviet assertions that the poor morale among Czechoslovak troops "proved that [the CzPA] is incapable of defending [Czechoslovak] borders." Although Bedřich said "we are doing everything possible . . . to demonstrate that the [continued] presence of foreign troops in our country is unnecessary," he acknowledged it would be difficult to prevent the Soviet Union from establishing a Central Group of Soviet Forces on Czechoslovak territory.

. . .

General Rusov: . . . First of all I would like to assure you that from the very first moment of the occupation of our republic, the army command has fulfilled to the letter all orders issued by the country's commander-in-chief, President Svoboda. After consultations with Cdes. Černík and Dubček and the president, the army decided not to allow bloodshed in our country. Although these were difficult times, the army obeyed and there was not a single clash with the occupation troops in our republic. The result was that we were able to avoid the awful tragedy that would have occurred had we decided to put up any resistance. Had we done so, the result would have been the annihilation of the entire republic, the routing of the army, the elimination of our sovereignty, and a terrible bloodbath. They had all been prepared for this, especially the troops not directly controlled from the Soviet Union, who sought to disarm our soldiers immediately.[53] This step was prevented, and the army is functioning, its commanders are at their posts, and it is deployed with border guards on the state borders in advance positions of several divisions, while the rest of the troops are in their barracks or wherever they were caught by the situation. Although we are restricted in our actions—we are unable to train, patrol our air space, or be in a state of combat readiness—we will nonetheless fulfill our duties.

To give you an idea of what it would have meant if we had resisted—as certain madmen urged—I would like to point out that a huge force of our neighbors and the Soviet Union occupied our republic in just a matter of days.

Today some 27 full combat divisions with several army and front command staffs are deployed on our country's territory. Of these, there are twelve armored divisions, thirteen motorized infantry divisions, and two paratrooper divisions. In addition, there are 550 combat aircraft and 250 transport planes, or a total of 800 aircraft. We estimate that there are more than 6,300 tanks, some 2,000 artillery guns, and a strong air force with all types of equipment, including missiles. Most of the troops on the territory of the republic are from the Soviet Union, but there are also units from the GDR in western Bohemia and at some airfields in the ČSSR. Troops from Bulgaria

---

[53] Rusov is referring here, in particular, to Bulgarian, Hungarian, and East German troops.

are in southern Moravia and in southern Bohemia, Polish troops are in northeast Bohemia and in northern Moravia, and Hungarian units are in southern and central Slovakia. In Slovakia there are also Bulgarian soldiers with certain Soviet divisions.

Before the departure of the delegation to Moscow, we issued orders that came from the president of the republic and the minister of national defense—and yesterday from myself on behalf of the minister—to ensure calm, order, and a high degree of organization, and to prevent armed or unarmed troops from taking part in demonstrations or public gatherings. We were aware that if troops were to participate in such events anywhere, force would be used to liquidate them and disband the army.

Since the very first moment of the invasion the Ministry of National Defense and the General Staff headquarters have been occupied by a Soviet infantry and paratrooper battalion. The Ministry of National Defense was occupied by Soviet troops yesterday, without our consent. Despite this, our own organs are working and are commanding and controlling our troops. We are working among the people, we are visiting divisions and formations, and we are taking organizational measures to ensure that there is no lapse in normal functions.

Major-General Bedřich:[54] The situation in the army with regard to morale, as well as politically, does not differ from that of the entire nation. This explains why it is especially difficult to order officers and the rank-and-file to avoid confrontations that could lead to acts of violence and unnecessary bloodshed. Our soldiers find it hard to understand that we are particularly anxious to keep the army together even if the price of doing so is that it will be accused by the nation of failing to defend our country, and not for the first time either.

We want the National Assembly to understand that the forces who came to this country are so powerful that we would have been utterly incapable of defending ourselves against them. What is more, a fratricidal struggle would have benefited neither us nor the entire international workers' movement, even though the Soviet Union has violated all the commitments it undertook toward us as allies.

This situation is creating a good deal of tension within the army. It is not easy to deal with the situation, especially as the soldiers have nothing to do to keep them occupied. We are not allowed to train, we cannot operate our technical installations, and we are not permitted to leave our barracks. Because small groups have been leaving nonetheless and the population has been enticing them to join demonstrations, we are being accused of violating the position we originally adopted, and we are being warned that sanctions will have to be taken against us.

The first orders and the initial actions of the forces that came here made it clear that they expected a clash with us and planned to disarm our army completely. As soon as Hungarian, German, and Bulgarian units crossed the border, they began disarming all units they encountered. By 11:30 P.M. the Military Council had decided what we should do, and then General Yamshchikov and his staff arrived. He was informed of the decision by the Ministry of National Defense, and that is why the troops that occupied the General Staff building and the ministry were redirected by these generals toward other institutions such as the National Assembly, the government, and the Central Committee of the party. This put them in a situation in which they had no one to fight. The disarming operation was completely one-sided, and we insisted that since we were not fighting they had no right to disarm our units. But the process continued all the same. New orders were passed on very slowly, and certain Soviet, Hungarian, and Bulgarian units did not want to obey the Joint Command in any event. Finally we succeeded in preventing the rest of our units from being disarmed, but even then they were not allowed to use their hardware. For example, units at Mlada had their technical equipment removed, which is equivalent to being disarmed insofar as they now have only machine guns and firearms. This

---

[54] Bedřich was known as a notorious hardliner whose appointment as head of the Main Political Directorate (MPD) in late July 1968 reflected Soviet pressure to end the brief period of liberalization in the CzPA.

course is bound to continue as we are under the impression that the Joint Command is anxious to complete the disarming. It appears that attempts are being made to prove that our army is not capable of defending our borders, and to create a situation in which the allies would be forced to retain their armies on our territory. We are doing everything possible to maintain the integrity of the army in order to demonstrate that the presence of foreign troops is not essential. We are determined to achieve this objective, no matter what price we have to pay. We believe that this is more important for the army than anything else.

Deputy Rapos: Does our General Staff have any information regarding the morale and political situation in the occupation armies?

Maj.-General Bedřich: We know that their people are not satisfied. But yesterday morning I spoke to the deputy chief of the Main Political Directorate of the Soviet army, Nachinkin[55]—he is the commander of the troops on that front—who said: "It must be clear to the Czechoslovak army and the Czechoslovak people that we will defend socialism here even if an earthquake erupts. There is no force in the world that will drive us away from here. We will fulfill our mission. This is something you must understand unconditionally. No anti-Soviet campaign of incitement will stop us. If necessary, we will even resort to drastic measures."

---

[55] A reference to Col.-General Nikolai Aleksandrovich Nachinkin, who was one of the chief planners of the invasion.

DOCUMENT No. 122: Speech by Gustáv Husák at the Extraordinary 14th Congress of the Slovak Communist Party, August 28, 1968 (Excerpts)

Source: ÚSD, AÚV KSČ, F. UV KSS, CC plenary sessions; also published in *Pravda* (Bratislava), August 29, 1968, p. 1.

Gustáv Husák gave this speech at the Extraordinary 14th Congress of the Communist Party of Slovakia, held in Bratislava. His endorsement of the "great and bright period" of the Prague Spring reflected his reputation as a strong reformer. Over the next several weeks, however, Husák shifted his position. Following his selection as first secretary of the CPCz, Husák presided over the "normalization" of Czechoslovakia, implementing the Soviet program of dismantling the reform movement.

. . .

. . . Questions are today being asked whether or not we are betraying or will be betraying the road on which we set out in January, or whether we are not in some way going back to the 1950s, to certain cults and reprisals, or whether or not we are preparing to take a step backwards in the development of our party and our people. All that has happened in our country since January is, in a broader sense, a revolt against all the deformations and mistakes and against everything that met with a lack of understanding and even with opposition in the minds of the people. The aim was to renew the ideas of socialism, communism, and Marxism, to decide whether these ideas should be implemented, to create a freer situation for the life of our people, and to win broad sections of our people over to these ideas. During those eight months we were looking for ways of realizing these ideas. Those eight months were a great and bright period in the development of our party and our peoples. . . .

We want to retain and deepen all the positive aspects that we enjoyed during those months since the January plenum and the other sessions of the CPCz Central Committee. As for our Action Program, we want to deepen it and start to work on it once again in our society. . . .

We have been criticized that now and again we have not been capable of maintaining control of events, and that we permit the party, communism, Marxism, our allies, and other such things to be vilified. We understood events in our own way and had our own explanations. We said: we are preparing the congress, we will form new organs, and we will create the political prerequisites for a struggle against the real anti-socialist forces. Unfortunately, on these matters we reached no understanding. In the phase of discussions at Čierna and Bratislava, and even before and after that, we did not find a common language. The armies of the five socialist states have entered our territory. It must be said that the governing organs of our party and our state did not request this entry, they did not invite these troops to our territory. There has been a tragic misunderstanding, or a tragic lack of understanding. . . .

Through no fault of our own we have been placed in a situation where the territory of the Czechoslovak state has been occupied by the armies of five friendly states. . . .

This congress is now faced with a fundamental decision: either to accept the concept of Cdes. Dubček, President Svoboda, and Černík—and I fully agree with Dubček and the other leading comrades, that the only way out of the present situation is to advance toward the normalization of our lives on the basis of the accord that has been concluded, or to reject this concept, that is the only alternative.

There is no third alternative! If anyone has a better proposal, or if anyone can think of another concept, let them come forward! All party members, even the entire leadership, have been racking their brains. So that is how the question stands: either to back Dubček and the others resolutely, or to express in them a vote of no confidence. There is no third way. Any leading politician who does not have the full support of the decisive core of the party and public is incapable of carrying out his duties. In that case he must leave, in that case he cannot carry on. At that point one has to look for another team who are ready to set out on a different path. These are harsh words, but it is no more than a question of confidence, even for me, personally. I stand fully behind Dubček's concept. I was there when it was conceived, I will give it my full backing—either I will back him, or I will leave. . . .

DOCUMENT No. 123: Josef Smrkovský's Address to the People after His Return from Moscow, August 29, 1968 (Excerpts)

Source: *Sedm praľských dnů*, pp. 401 ff.

This transcription of Josef Smrkovský's address was broadcast to the nation over Czechoslovak radio on August 29. His detailed and somber speech conveys the harshness of the Moscow agreements and the severity of the constraints imposed by the "cruel reality of the Warsaw Pact's military occupation of our country." Although he makes no mention of the Moscow protocol, he does explicitly cite many of the steps the Czechoslovak leadership would have to take to comply with the protocol. In his address, Smrkovský also explains why he and his colleagues have decided to agree to a "compromise" with Soviet authorities.

. . . Our negotiations in Moscow were of an unusual nature. You know that we did not go there all together at the same time, and you are also aware of the circumstances under which each of us went there and negotiated there. I think I need not elaborate on this any further; for me as for Comrade Dubček and the others this is still a subject that is too difficult and painful.

Under the circumstances, as everyone will agree, deciding what to do was highly problematic. The occupation of the country by the Warsaw Pact armies was a cruel reality. Our contacts with home were limited; at first we had little, indeed almost no, information, and suddenly we had to rely more on our faith in the firm position of our people than on any knowledge of the facts of the situation. On the other hand, the position of our partners was conveyed to us very accurately. We even detected certain political difficulties that the military intervention was creating. We knew that the world was sympathetic toward us, but we also knew that the great powers prefer compromise solutions over everything else.

Under these circumstances we were faced by a dilemma to which there was no way out.

We could have rejected any compromise and forced events to the point where the foreign troops would remain on our territory permanently, with all the implications this would have for the sovereignty of our state, for political rights, for the economy, and possibly for greater human sacrifices, which such a deepening of the conflict would have clearly entailed. I want to point out that we even considered rejecting any accommodating solution, that sometimes it is better to face bayonets head-on in the interest of the honor and character of one's nation.

Nevertheless, we believed that such an extreme moment had not yet been reached, and that despite everything that had happened, there remained a second alternative which we, as politicians responsible for the future of the state, could not forsake. That is why we eventually tried to find another solution via an acceptable compromise. But even as we did so we were aware of the consequences, above all the moral and historical consequences that such a solution could have...[56]

---

[56] Smrkovský went on to explain several of the onerous steps the CPCz and the ČSSR government would have to take in the coming days and weeks. On August 27, several hours after returning from Moscow, he had addressed the National Assembly. This speech was followed by presentations by Dubček to the CPCz Central Committee and by Černík to the ČSSR Government. President Svoboda also addressed the country in a speech carried over the radio just after 2:00 P.M. on the 29th, and Dubček read out a longer statement via the radio a few hours later, speaking with great emotion and strain and often pausing for a minute or longer. In addition, the four leaders issued a joint statement on the 27th appealing for public calm and pleading with Czechoslovak citizens to avoid steps that might precipitate a "national catastrophe." The following day, Černík delivered a speech over the radio, and on the 29th Smrkovský did the same. All these speeches and statements can be found in a book compiled by the Institute of History of the Czechoslovak Academy of Sciences, *Sedm pražských dnů: 21.–27. srpen 1968: Dokumentace* (Prague: ČSAV, September 1968), pp. 380–407.

DOCUMENT No. 124: Situation Report by the U.S. State Department, August 29, 1968

Source: National Security File, Country File, Czechoslovakia, Czech Crisis 8/68, State Situation Reports, Box 182, Lyndon Baines Johnson Library.

This situation report was compiled by the Czech Task Force, a round-the-clock crisis monitoring unit established in the State Department in late July. The information was gleaned through intelligence channels or from the U.S. embassies in Prague, Moscow, and other Warsaw Pact capitals, as well as from newswire dispatches, broadcast monitoring services, and other open sources.

SECRET
DEPARTMENT OF STATE CZECH TASK FORCE

Situation Report 1200 Hours EDT, August 29, 1968

1. *Czechoslovak Leaders Encounter Mixed Reaction to Moscow Accords:* Press reports from Czechoslovakia today indicate that the Prague leadership is moving ahead with a slow modification of its liberal reforms. Opposition to the Moscow accords is still voiced from some quarters, but resistance appears to be subsiding in Prague as increasing numbers of people accept implementation of the accords as inevitable. According to the West German news agency DPA, *Literární listy*, the organ of the Czechoslovak writers and an outspokenly liberal journal, carried an article today calling on the Czechs to reject any compromise, insisting on "all the freedoms we have achieved" and the immediate withdrawal of foreign troops whom it was "our duty to hate."

A more moderate line was taken by the head of the Czech trade union council Karel Poláček in a speech broadcast this morning. Poláček urged all union members to support Svoboda, Dubček, and other leaders and to achieve "normalization" in order to permit the earliest possible departure of foreign troops. Tanyug reports members of the old and new Czechoslovak Central Committees—the pre-invasion CC and that "elected" by the extraordinary party congress on August 22—will meet on August 29 or 30, apparently to resolve the question of the validity of the decisions made by the extraordinary congress.

2. *Dubček Appears in Bandages:* Embassy Prague, citing an American medical scientist residing in Prague, reports that Dubček appeared at a meeting on August 28 heavily bandaged around the head and upper body, "presumably from mistreatment by Soviets." Reuters reported that Dubček had an "ominous-looking adhesive plaster" on his forehead on August 28, which he attributed to a bathtub fall.[57]

3. *Romania Backing Czech Emphasis on Troop Withdrawals, Avoiding Polemics:* The Statement of the Romanian Communist Party Executive Committee today underscored the party's "particular attention" to the August 23–26 Soviet–Czechoslovak talks in Moscow, reiterated its "unanimous anxiety and disapproval" of the "penetration" into Czechoslovakia, recalled Romania's insistence from the outset that the only way to "a reasonable solution" lay through negotiations, "appreciated" the return of the Czechoslovak leaders to Prague, and considered it of "utmost importance to carry into effect the complete withdrawal in the shortest

---

[57] Dubček's injury was, in fact, due to a fall, not to Soviet abuse, as Smrkovský revealed several years later in a posthumously published interview: ". . . As for all those rumors that spread about the scar Dubček had on his forehead, well, it happened in the bathroom. He fainted and fell over, and as he was falling he hit his forehead on the edge of the washbasin. And so he had a bandage, and our own doctors from the military hospital, whom Svoboda brought with him, took care of Dubček." See "Nedokončený rozhovor: Mluví Josef Smrkovský," *Listy: Časopis československé socialistické opozice* (Rome), Vol. 4, No. 2 (March 1975), p. 22.

time" of the occupation troops. This line is consistent with the Romanians' position on the invasion from the beginning, though the term "penetration," in lieu of their earlier-used "intervantion" and "occupation," represent a slight toning down of Bucharest's criticism of "the five." The Romanian press continues to avoid polemical exchanges with the powers that invaded Czechoslovakia—exchanges which today included a *Tribuna Ludu* attack in Warsaw on Romania's "impermissible" attitude on the crisis. Romanian ambassador Bogdan today indicated he thought the overall Czechoslovak crisis "was beginning to subside."

SECRET

DOCUMENT No. 125: Summary Notes of the 590th Meeting of the National Security Council, September 4, 1968 (Excerpts)

Source: Johnson Library, National Security File, NSC Meetings File, vol. 5. (Appears in *Foreign Relations of the United States, 1964–1968: Eastern Europe*, vol. XVII, [Washington, D.C.: U.S. Government Printing Office, 1996], pp. 272–278.)

Two weeks after the invasion, President Johnson and his top aides were still sorting out the facts—trying to decide what had motivated the Soviets, how broad the implications of the intervention would be, and how the U.S. should respond. During this NSC discussion, Ambassador Llewellyn ("Tommy") Thompson noted several reasons why Moscow may have decided to act, centering around a perceived threat to the leadership's "power position in the USSR." A major concern for the U.S. and its allies following the invasion was whether the Soviets would move against Romania, Berlin or possibly Yugoslavia. In fact, evidence had already begun to point in the opposite direction. Nonetheless, heightened fears about further Kremlin aggression would lead the members of NATO, which was due to disband the following year (20 years after its inception), to extend the treaty beyond its scheduled termination date—one of the most serious consequences of the action for the Soviets. Otherwise, U.S. and allied policies did not change appreciably as a result of the invasion. Although President Johnson privately scoffed at Moscow's attempts to cast its role in a moral light, the realities of superpower politics—particularly arms control—ultimately muffled Western reaction to the crisis, much as they had after the Hungarian revolution in 1956.

Washington, September 4, 1968, 5–7:25 P.M.

U.S., Europe and the Czechoslovakian Crisis

The President: The purpose of the meeting is to assess the impact of the Czechoslovakian crisis, to discuss how we can use the crisis to strengthen Western European defense and NATO, and to talk about our relations with the Russians and Eastern Europeans.

Secretary Rusk will summarize the issues and possible ways of dealing with them. Secretary Clifford will talk about the defense of Western Europe and the new disposition of Soviet troops in Central Europe.

Director Helms and Secretary Rusk will give us their views on the German reaction to the crisis. The press has already printed that the State Department was recommending additional reassurances to the Germans even before Secretary Rusk had made any recommendation to the president.

Secretary Fowler will speak on the financial problems.

If we speak out about a threatening situation and the situation does develop, we are accused of over-reacting. If we don't speak out and a serious situation does develop, then we are accused of not having done what we should have done. This is what happened following an indirect mention of the Romanian situation in the speech of last Friday.[58]

More meetings of the NSC should be held in the next few weeks so that all of the members may be fully informed on current foreign problems.

All political candidates' requests for briefings are to be granted. Mr. Temple[59] and Mr. Rostow are to clear Administration responses to requests for positions on foreign problems coming from candidates, advisors, task forces, etc.

Secretary Rusk: The gravity of the current situation cannot be overstated in view of the very high costs the Soviet government was willing to pay for intervening in Czechoslovakia.

The situation in Czechoslovakia has been developing since 1967. Dubček gained power over conservative communist party members in January, 1968. Press censorship was lifted and other

---

[58] August 30.
[59] Larry E. Temple, special counsel to the president.

reforms were initiated. Dissension between Czechoslovakia and the Soviet Union rose rapidly. The summer maneuvers of the Warsaw Pact were used to build up military pressure against the Dubček government in the hope that the liberals would slow down the reform campaign.

The day of the Soviet invasion, the president met Ambassador Dobrynin at 8:15 P.M. and then the NSC later that evening. Decisions were reached at the NSC meeting to take the Czech case to the United Nations immediately, and on a response to the oral message Dobrynin delivered earlier.

The response to Dobrynin's message emphasized two points:

a. Jefferson's quotation about governments based on the consent of the governed, and
b. denial that there was any U.S. or NATO attempt to intervene in Czechoslovakia as alleged by Moscow.

Dobrynin had said that U.S. state interests were not affected by the Soviet action. In response he was told that U.S. interests are involved in Berlin where we are committed to prevent the city being overrun by the Russians.

Although the Soviet military effort went smoothly, the Russians badly miscalculated the political reaction in Czechoslovakia. All Czechs opposed the movement of Soviet troops into their country. Their performance and discipline were superb. The Russians were unable to organize a puppet government to take over and legitimatize their invasion. Opposition outside Czechoslovakia to the Soviet move was world-wide and very strong.

The President: Asked to interrupt the meeting to deal with a proposed press release on the admission of Czech refugees to the United States. The statement was read. (Copy attached at Tab A.)

Secretary Rusk: The United States must grant refuge to those Czechs who want to leave their country or who are now outside, and do not wish to return. The number is not large. We have to open our doors because if we do not, the refugees might return to Czechoslovakia and oppose the existing government. This would not be in our interest.

Ambassador Thompson: We should not encourage Czechoslovakian refugees to come to the United States but only welcome them. If we appear to be urging them to come to the United States, the Soviet Union could use this policy to argue that we are, in fact, intervening in Czechoslovakian affairs.

Secretary Fowler: Are the borders of Czechoslovakia now open? Are we by this statement inviting another Berlin Wall?

The President: We can accept those who desire to come to the United States but not encourage them to come.

Director Marks: The draft statement would be read by the refugees as encouragement to come to the United States.

Ambassador Thompson: We should say no more than that the longstanding U.S. policy of offering asylum to political refugees remains unchanged. We should not appear to be accepting the entire burden because we want the Europeans to accept some of the refugees.

Secretary Fowler: The statement should say no more than that our asylum policy is unchanged.

Ambassador Cleveland: We should try for a uniform allied policy toward refugees.

Mr. Leddy: The humanitarian aspect is overriding. Let all refugees come who so wish. The refugees cannot resist in Czechoslovakia. The Soviets would like to have liberals, intellectuals, etc. leave Czechoslovakia.

The Vice President: Agreed with Secretary Rusk. We have to say something. We should reiterate our long-standing policy. Inevitably, many people will compare what we do for Czech refugees with what we did for Hungarian refugees.

Secretary Clifford: What did we do following the Hungarian crisis?

(Several recalled that thousands of Hungarian refugees came to the United States. Private organizations raised substantial sums to make possible the resettlement of Hungarians in the U.S.)

Director Helms: The statement as read was acceptable.

The President: Read a revised statement, commenting that he thought the State Department coordinated such statements. He suggested that the draft be further worked on taking into account all views expressed, and sent back for approval.

Secretary Rusk: Last week there were disturbing indicators and press reports that the Russians might invade Romania, states other than Czechoslovakia, possibly even Yugoslavia.

Read the evidence we had Friday, August 30. (Copy attached at Tab B.)

Ambassador Dobrynin Friday evening asked for an appointment for Saturday morning without mentioning the nature of his business. It was possible that his Saturday call would be to inform us of a Soviet move into Romania.

The President in his Friday speech referred to the rumors and issued a warning against another invasion.

Dobrynin was asked to call Friday night to deliver his message rather than wait until the next day; the message dealt with the Czechoslovak situation. During this call, Dobrynin was asked about reports that the Russians were going to invade Romania. He was told that such a move would have incalculable consequences. Dobrynin said he was without instructions but, as he had said previously, he personally doubted the Russians would move into Romania.

Saturday evening Dobrynin dropped by to say that Moscow had informed him that reports of an invasion of Romania were without foundation. This was interpreted to be reassurance that there would be no intervention in Romania. When asked, Dobrynin said his comments applied to Berlin as well, although he went on to mention many Berlin developments which the Soviets consider unsatisfactory.

Intelligence available Saturday evening indicated that the Russians were not going to move into Romania. The answer from the Soviet Union to our question about Romania came promptly after the President's Friday speech in San Antonio. Moscow had decided to hold down further troop movements for the present. However, no one can be sure that the Soviets won't hit Berlin and Romania in the days ahead.

General Wheeler: 19 Soviet divisions could move into Romania with two or three days notice. This force could quickly overwhelm any Romanian opposition. There would be little intelligence warning. The movement of Soviet planes, however, we would be able to detect.

Secretary Rusk: The Romanians have not been whipping up false scares. We have been careful, in talking to the Russians, to make clear that our sources of intelligence are not Romanian. We informed the Romanians of what we had done. The Romanian foreign minister has been in New York. Ambassador Ball will report on his conversation with him.[60]

It is important that everyone know we have never had any understanding with the Soviet Union about respective spheres of influence as de Gaulle alleges. The current difficulty arises out of Soviet violation of the Yalta Agreement, not out of that agreement itself which called for free elections in Eastern Europe.

There is a great difference between the Warsaw Pact and NATO with respect to internal affairs of members. NATO is operative only in the event of international aggression and grants no rights to a member to intervene in the affairs of another.

The Soviet Union is actively trying to put across the idea that its invasion of Czechoslovakia should not affect its bilateral relations with us.

We have a difficult problem of handling the American people as well as others throughout the world who would not approve if we act as if nothing had happened. We have cancelled

---

[60] Ball met Mănescu on August 30 and September 2, according to documents referred to in the *Foreign Relations of the United States* volume cited in the source note above. Ball found the Romanian foreign minister "basically relaxed though not unconcerned" about Soviet intentions toward Romania; Mănescu did remark that he hoped Washington would make clear to Moscow the costs of an invasion.

numerous activities of a good-will nature such as a visit of the Minnesota band to the USSR and a second inaugural flight to the U.S. of a Soviet civilian airliner.

On the other hand, Soviet action against Czechoslovakia has not eliminated many major world problems involving the USSR and the U.S. such as the Middle East, strategic missile control, and Vietnam.

We must not mislead the Soviet Union, the American people, or our allies.

The Soviet Union is trying to carry on business as usual with us. For example, they have told us they have ratified the Astronaut Treaty.

Western Europe reacted with shock following the Soviet invasion but it has not broken off trade relations with the USSR. Many European states have cancelled good-will projects.

NATO must consider the new Soviet deployments in Eastern Europe. There is a real need to reassure the Alliance.

The President: The members of the Council should know that when the Russians invaded Czechoslovakia, they took measures to insure that they would not be blocked. No further mention of this activity should be made but it is brought up for the benefit of those who are optimistic about Russian willingness to improve relations and reach agreements. (This apparently was a reference to the Soviet missile alert on the day of the invasion.)

Secretary Rusk: The effect of the Soviet action on the policy of detente has been serious. NATO members must consult with each other and be seen consulting. High level NATO meetings will be necessary. As to the future of NATO, it may be necessary to now extend the life of the treaty beyond 1969. The problem is what can we do to reassure NATO members that the treaty which does not require Senate approval and does not commit the new president will not disappear in 1969.

The President: We must not forget that a large number of senators not long ago favored a substantial immediate reduction in the level of U.S. forces deployed in Europe. Some wanted to reduce this number to 50,000.

Secretary Rusk: The country will now have to debate again the amount of its resources which it is willing to commit to keeping peace in the world. There is some isolationism in the United States. As NATO was warned at its last meeting held in Iceland, Soviet leaders' fears as they face a changing world create a dangerous attitude in Moscow.

Ambassador Thompson: The Soviet leaders decided to intervene in Czechoslovakia because they felt their power position in the USSR was threatened.

1. The Czech system was going democratic. For example, press censorship was abolished.

2. The other Warsaw Pact powers, especially East Germany and Poland, were worried as to the effect in their countries of the Czech liberal reforms.

3. The Czechs were printing, for the first time, suppressed accounts of the horrors of the Stalin regime. The Kremlin leaders were acutely embarrassed.

4. The Czechs were requesting financial backing from the USSR which came to a very large sum.

5. The Soviets concluded Dubček couldn't retain control of the Czech reform elements and that the result would cause serious difficulties for other European communist states and even within the Soviet Union itself.

We do not know what triggered the Soviet action.

1. East German Chairman Ulbricht reported to the Soviets following his August visit to Prague. He may have expressed his deep concern over developments in Czechoslovakia and their harmful effect in East Germany.

2. Brezhnev may have realized that the majority of the Kremlin leaders was shifting and therefore changed his position to that of supporting an invasion.

3. Soviet military leader's may have pressured the Politburo on grounds of the security of the USSR.

495

4. The Kremlin may have decided that Dubček either could not or would not carry out agreements reached earlier.

We do not know of any secret agreement reached in Moscow with Dubček. Nor do we know whether Dubček can carry out the terms of the agreement reached with the Russians.

It is very clear that the Russians totally misjudged the reaction of the Czech people to the invasion of their country by Warsaw Pact troops.

The Soviets are unlikely to invade Romania. There is no current threat to the communist system in Romania. The situation is quite different from the threat to Soviet and communist power which arose in Czechoslovakia.

. . .

DOCUMENT No. 126: Recommendations from the CPSU CC Propaganda Department on Efforts to Establish Political Control in Czechoslovakia, September 6, 1968 (Excerpts)

Source: "TsK KPSS," Memorandum No. 24996 (Top Secret), September 6, 1968, in TsKhSD, F. 5, Op. 60, D. 19, Ll. 200–206.

This memorandum, written by the deputy head of the CPSU CC Propaganda Department, Aleksandr Yakovlev, and the deputy head of Soviet television and radio, Enver Mamedov, recommends that Soviet propaganda efforts in Czechoslovakia be substantially upgraded and expanded. Their report is based on the findings of a Propaganda Department working group sent by the CPSU Politburo to Czechoslovakia during the last ten days of August.

The recommendations cover enhanced radio propaganda, expanded distribution of Soviet print materials, and KGB black propaganda in foreign newspapers on alleged connections between a "counterrevolutionary underground" in Czechoslovakia and Western intelligence services. The final group of proposals in the memorandum include additional political education programs directed at Soviet occupation troops and a number of measures to bolster the authority of ČSSR President Ludvík Svoboda, and provoke a split within the CPCz leadership.

"TsK KPSS," Memorandum No. 24996 (Top Secret), September 6, 1968[61]

. . .

There is a need to set up a broadcast center in either Poland or the GDR. Naturally, one can't exclude the possibility that the activity of this radio station could evoke strong protests from the CPCz and the ČSSR government. However, as anti-socialist propaganda in the press and radio in the ČSSR is still raging in full force both directly and covertly, and anti-Soviet propaganda continues in both Czech and Slovak on Western radio stations without any attempt at resistance made by the Czechoslovak propaganda organs, the activity of a radio station of the sort we have in mind (where we do not bear formal responsibility for what it broadcasts) is not only justified, but essential.

. . .

The KGB of the USSR Council of Ministers will be preparing and publishing a series of articles in the foreign press about the ties of the anti-socialist underground in Czechoslovakia with foreign radio broadcasters, above all with the intelligence organs of the USA and FRG.

. . .

The most important thing now is to strengthen and further consolidate the authority of L. Svoboda in order to encourage the incipient trend toward a deep schism in the leadership of the CPCz. In such circumstances, everything addressed to Svoboda and all meetings with him by our representatives in the ČSSR must be undertaken only with the approval of the Center. . . .

Visits and contacts by leading Soviet officials will be aimed at influencing the political situation and broadening the range of communications, thereby depriving a small group of Czechoslovak officials, above all Dubček, of a monopoly on the right to inform the leading party and state cadres in the ČSSR about our position on the concrete problems of Soviet–Czechoslovak relations that have arisen at any given stage.[62]

---

[61] A routing slip indicates that the document is for "the information of the CPSU CC Secretaries," and a handwritten annotation adds the names K.V. Rusakov, head of the CPSU CC Department for Ties with Communist and Workers' Parties for Socialist Countries, and N.I. Savinkin, head of the CPSU CC Administrative Organs Department, which supervised the military and internal security forces.

[62] For Yakovlev's follow-up report to the CPSU Secretariat on the impact of propaganda efforts see "Spravka o realizatsii predlozhenii po sovershenstvovaniyu informatsionno-ideologicheskoi raboty v svyazi s sobytiyami v Chekhoslovakii," 2 January 1969, in TsKhSD, F. 5, Op. 60, D. 19, Ll. 207–209.

DOCUMENT No. 127: CPCz Central Committee Notes on Problems Stemming from the Presence of Warsaw Pact Forces in Czechoslovakia, September 1968

Source: Cable No. 620 (SECRET), October 4, 1968, in TsKhSD, F. 5, O. 60, D. 311, Ll. 78–86.

This document contains notes prepared for the CPCz CC Presidium by the Information Department of the CPCz CC in late September 1968. The notes describe the clumsy attempts by Soviet troops to overcome the peaceful resistance they encountered from Czechs and Slovaks; they also chronicle a large number of accidents, fights, and other serious incidents involving the Warsaw Pact forces.

The Soviet embassy in Prague obtained these notes from "reliable sources," according to the Soviet ambassador in Czechoslovakia, S. V. Chervonenko. Chervonenko then transmitted the notes to CPSU CC Secretary Konstantin Katushev and Soviet Defense Minister Andrei Grechko.

ON ISSUES CONNECTED WITH THE PRESENCE OF WARSAW PACT FORCES ON THE TERRITORY OF CZECHOSLOVAKIA

Prepared on the basis of materials and communications received at the KSČ CC Department for Information, Planning, and Administration, along with some concrete first-hand observations regarding the presence of Warsaw Pact forces on the territory of our republic.

Opinions of Military Servicemen, Especially Soviet Servicemen

Representatives of the foreign troops bring up the following "arguments" to justify their presence on the territory of the ČSSR:

— The troops arrived in our country at the last minute. If they had arrived just two days later, we would have been occupied by the Germans. This has been confirmed by Soviet counterintelligence.

— Czechoslovak radio was able to continue broadcasting even after the liberation because it had linked up with Austrian and West German radio.

— Czechoslovakia's western borders were open. Troops from the five countries arrived to defend us, since the Czechoslovak army is worthless and is totally lacking in discipline.

— Dubček remains a revisionist, but now he will be forced to obey.

— Minister Pavel was hopeless. How was he permitted to occupy such a high post?

— In the ČSSR they are continuing to shoot at soldiers from the five countries. However, it would seem that the five have suffered no casualties.

— In Czechoslovakia there are over 2 million counterrevolutionaries.

— Some servicemen from the 5 countries acknowledge that there was no counterrevolution in our country, but say it could have developed into that.

— In the city of Tábor measures were taken to check the water, since the representatives of the troops of the five countries expressed concern that the water had been poisoned.

— Representatives of the troops of the five in the region of Chomutov say that enterprises there are stocked with weapons and that during negotiations with these entities, the representatives demand guarantees that these weapons will not be used against Soviet forces. Other demands of this sort have been going on for a whole month regarding the weapons belonging to the People's Militia.

Soviet representatives at the negotiations held in the KSČ raikom in the city of Vyskov, assert that according to official information from our citizens 120 soldiers were killed. This "fact" they adduce as evidence of the existence of counterrevolution.

— The majority of soldiers from the five countries are surprised that they are being called occupiers.

— The unity of our people is being presented as a matter playing into the hands of the counterrevolution.

— The servicemen of the forces of the five in conversations cite unsubstantiated instances and reports providing details and numbers of soldiers who have been shot in Czechos.

— There were cases of insults directed against A. Novotný.

— Representatives of the Soviet troops assert that our army and the state security are trailing our citizens so as to prevent them from conversing with the troops from the five countries (in western Bohemian oblast).

Information About Contacts with Troops from the Five Countries

During recent negotiations in the city of Chomutov, Lt.-Colonel Bakushkin declared that he does not trust the first secretary, Comrade Snigon, because the raikom of the KSČ does not make sufficient efforts to carry out the decisions of the higher organs and to arrange friendly contacts.

— In the city of Kroměříž negotiations with the city national committee did not lead to a common agreement. Neither side managed to convince the other about the reasons for the situation. Two other meetings with a group of young people have not been finished as yet and will be continued. The course of the meetings has been polite. However, opinions are still far removed.

— During an exchange of opinions in the city of Ostrava, the Soviet commander criticized the content of factory newspapers. The first secretary, Cde. Haj, after meeting with General Jashkin, summoned the general factory committees to carry out a review and ensure that the factory newspapers observe their agreements.

Colonel Komarov demanded that they not exclude Soviet films from the downtown cinema.

In the city of Olomouc a meeting took place with the teaching staff of the Palacký University. The Soviet commanders were interested in the start of the school year and the opinion of the university employees about the presence of the allied forces in Czechoslovakia.

On 16 September in the city of Olomouc a meeting took place with some directors and chairmen of the general factory committees of large enterprises. The opinions of the two sides were at odds. Our people spoke against the holding of discussions at enterprises, while the Soviet representatives, on the contrary, supported the practice.

In the Karviná and Frýdek-Místek provinces the Soviet commanders demanded the removal of statues of T. G. Masaryk. The local leaders declined to do so. The supreme command in the city of Ostrava took this refusal into account. The commander of the city of Vyškov directed a letter of ultimatum to the local leaders: If the statue of T. G. Masaryk is left standing, the troops will reenter the city and take other sanctions.

Citizens of gypsy origin show a definite eagerness to establish contacts with troops in Slovakia.

In some farm cooperatives in the province of Rimavská Sobota, parties were arranged in honor of the foreign troops on the day they arrived.

Attempts to establish contact with young people in Slovakia have not proven successful. Soviet soldiers dropped in, for example, to see students at the pharmaceutical faculty who are working in the state farm in Dechtjar, but the students dispersed.

Separate Instances of Contact

On 13 September the head of a forestry cooperative declared to the regional department of the public security organs that the forestry workers are refusing to come to work because they are afraid of being shot by Soviet soldiers. Earlier in the day in the forest, where these employees work, several shots were fired from a machine gun.

V. Kučera from Týn nad Vltavou told the provincial department of the public security organs that he and the members of his family are stopped every day by guards of the Soviet army and only after a prolonged detention are allowed to continue on.

On 15 September in Dolní Lhota, in the province of Jindřichův Hradec, eight Soviet soldiers were drinking at the local beer hall. Late in the evening during a debate near the beer hall, a student named Vladimir Motl was wounded in the leg by a shot from a pistol. Apparently, one of the soldiers had been playing with the pistol, but the soldiers fled the scene.

In the village of Dubá na Teplicku some residents invited soldiers into their apartments and provided them with alcoholic drinks. After this the Soviet soldiers, being drunk, engaged in a variety of disturbances (they shot at employees of the state security, for example). No one was wounded.

On 14 September at a hospital in Teplice a Soviet soldier named Anates Sankaevich (b. in 1947) was brought in with a wound in the side of his head. He died within five minutes, according to the doctor. He had been brought there by four soldiers and an interpreter, who asserted that the soldier had been shot while on duty by one of our citizens, who then fled. The commander of the formation in which this soldier served said, upon arriving at the hospital, that it had been an unfortunate accident and that they would handle the matter from then on.

In the Prague-9 district, an agreement was reached on the staging of training flights. Despite this agreement, on 12 September an incident occurred because the commander of the formations protecting the air training grounds had not been informed of the agreement. Fortunately, a tragedy did not occur and after further clarification the training flights took place.

Soviet soldiers are exchanging canned goods for money or wine in some provinces of the southern Moravian region.

In the western Bohemian region in August there occurred 15 traffic accidents caused by Soviet troops; extensive damage was inflicted on the property and health of our citizens.

On 13 and 14 September in the city of Ostrava the editorial board of the newspaper *Nová svoboda* was operating. The secretary of the KSČ city committee, Cde. Haj, and the editor of the newspaper *Nová svoboda*, Cde. Kubíček, were temporarily imprisoned.

On 15 September in the region between Františkova myslivna and Jelení chata in the town of Jeseník, a Soviet helicopter had an accident. The investigation into the accident was conducted only by Soviet organs, without cooperation with us.

On 10 September at 2:00 in the afternoon in the provincial village of Nový Dům (in the mid-Bohemian region) a dead Bulgarian soldier was found. It was confirmed that he had been shot and was brought to this place.[63] The incident is being investigated by our security organs and the commander of the foreign forces.

On 17 September the city committee of the Czechoslovak Youth Union in the city of Trenčín defied the Moscow agreements by organizing a campaign to collect signatures demanding the pull-out of Soviet troops. The text of the petition was laid out on one side of the placard and on the other the residents of the city signed their names. The Soviet patrols told the Soviet commander of the garrison in Trenčín about this matter, and he gave an order to deploy armored personnel carriers in all the streets leading to Peace Square. There occurred an incident and fist fights on both sides. Soviet soldiers used their rifle butts, and in the process, the chairman of the Czechoslovak Youth Union was wounded. The soldiers forced people into the armored personnel carriers and carted them off to the garrison to conduct interrogations. After the interrogations and judicial processing, all those who had been detained were released, thanks to intervention

---

[63] According to newly declassified reports, the shooting of this Bulgarian soldier was the only death attributable to deliberate action by a Czechoslovak citizen. Around 20 other Soviet/Warsaw Pact soldiers died during the operation, but their deaths were caused either by traffic accidents or by "so-called extraordinary events that accompany every large-scale troop movement." See "Oběti srpna žalují: Z důvěrné zprávy pro pět nejvyšších představitelů Československého podzimu 1968," *Občanský deník* (Prague), 31 July 1990, p. 3.

by the CPS raikom. This incident was handled directly by the Soviet garrison commander because he regarded it as a manifestation of counterrevolution and in the future intends to use more serious measures to apply pressure.

The commander of a railroad dispatch center in the city of Bohumín was visited by the city commandant, Lt.-Colonel I. V. Poratimov, who said he had learned about the arrival of new railroad troops in this center. Although Cde. Poratimov acknowledged he has no sort of directive, he regards the arrival of the fresh troops as a provocation and will give an order to reoccupy the barracks. The commander of the railroad center answered that this happened at the behest of the Ministry of National Defense. However, the lt.-colonel did not accept this and said that he only obeys orders from his own commander in Ostrava.

On 17 September in the province of Irklesy (Libava) [as given in text] in the first half of the day crossfire took place between Soviet soldiers, who reported that formations of the 92nd road-building battalion, which is deployed in this province, opened fire. The soldiers of this formation, along with the instructor Topič and the master Hošek, were arrested. After it was confirmed that they had no weapons, the soldiers were freed, but the instructor Topič and the master Hošek were interned.

In the city of Jestřebí a Soviet soldier was wounded in the shoulder. Negotiations and an investigation were conducted by our army and the Soviet army. The results of the investigation are not yet known.

DOCUMENT No. 128: Unofficial Enunciation of the "Brezhnev Doctrine," September 26, 1968 (Excerpts)

Source: S. Kovalev, "Suverenitet i internatsional'nye obyazannosti sotsialisticheskikh stran," *Pravda*, September 26, 1968, p. 4.

This lengthy commentary, which appeared in Pravda *five weeks after the invasion, constitutes the most elaborate articulation of the "Brezhnev Doctrine." The doctrine laid out the strict "rules of the game" for the socialist commonwealth; it linked the fate of each socialist country with the fate of all others, stipulated that every socialist country must abide by the norms of Marxism–Leninism (as interpreted in Moscow), and rejected "abstract sovereignty" in favor of the "laws of class struggle."*

"Sovereignty and the International Obligations of Socialist Countries"

. . . It is impossible to overlook the allegations being made in certain quarters that the action of the five socialist countries violates the Marxist–Leninist principle of sovereignty and the right of nations to self-determination.

Such claims are untenable insofar as they are based on an abstract, non-class approach . . .

. . .

. . . Without question, the peoples of the socialist countries and the communist parties have and must have freedom to determine their country's path of development. Any decision they make, however, must not be harmful either to socialism in their own country or to the fundamental interests of other socialist countries . . . Whoever forgets this in giving exclusive emphasis to the autonomy and independence of communist parties is guilty of a one-sided approach and of shirking their internationalist duties.

. . .

. . . V. I. Lenin wrote that a person living in a society cannot be free of that society, and it is equally true that a socialist state in a system of other states that make up the socialist commonwealth cannot be free of the common interests of that commonwealth.

The sovereignty of individual socialist countries cannot be set against the interests of world socialism and the world revolutionary movement. . . .

. . .

. . . Each communist party is free to apply the principles of Marxism–Leninism and socialism in its own country, but it is not free to deviate from these principles if it is to remain a genuine communist party. . . .

It must be emphasized that even if a socialist country tries to adopt a position "outside the blocs," it in fact retains its national independence only because of the power of the socialist commonwealth—and above all its chief force, the Soviet Union—and the strength of its armed forces. The weakening of any of the links in the world system of socialism directly affects all the socialist countries, and they cannot look indifferently upon this. . . . If Czechoslovakia were to be separated from the socialist commonwealth, that not only would contravene Czechoslovakia's own vital interests, but would also be of great detriment to the other socialist countries. . . . To fulfill their internationalist duties to the fraternal nations of Czechoslovakia and to defend their own socialist gains, the Soviet Union and the other socialist states were forced to act and did act in decisive opposition to the anti-socialist forces in Czechoslovakia. . . .

. . .

Those who "disapprove" of the actions of the five socialist countries ignore the crucial fact that it is precisely these countries who are protecting the interests of international socialism and the international revolutionary movement. . . .

Needless to say, communists in the fraternal countries could not have stood idly by in the name of abstract sovereignty while [Czechoslovakia] was under the threat of anti-socialist degeneration.

The action of the five socialist countries in Czechoslovakia corresponds with the vital interests of the Czechoslovak people themselves. . . . By encroaching on the foundations of socialism in Czechoslovakia, counterrevolutionary elements were undermining the basis of the country's independence and sovereignty. . . .

. . .

The assistance provided to workers in the ČSSR by the other socialist countries, which thwarted the export of counterrevolution from outside, was in fact a struggle to uphold the sovereignty of the ČSSR against forces that wanted to deprive it of this sovereignty. . . .

. . .

Those who claim that the actions of the allied socialist countries in Czechoslovakia were "illegal" forget that in a class-based society there is no such thing as non-class law and there never will be. Laws and legal norms are always subordinate to the laws of class struggle and the laws of social development. . . . The class approach to this issue can never be discarded under the pretext of legal considerations. . . .

Without question, the actions taken in Czechoslovakia by the five socialist countries, which were aimed at safeguarding the vital interests of the socialist commonwealth and especially at defending the independence and sovereignty of Czechoslovakia as a socialist state, will win ever greater support among all those who genuinely treasure the interests of the revolutionary movement, the peace and security of nations, democracy, and socialism.[64]

[64] Brezhnev himself reaffirmed the doctrine three months after the invasion in a speech before the 5th Congress of the Polish Communist Party. While acknowledging that the intervention had been "an extraordinary step, dictated by necessity," he insisted that "when internal and external forces hostile to socialism are threatening to turn a socialist country back to capitalism, this becomes the common problem and concern of all socialist countries." He warned that East European policies would have to conform with the "common natural laws of socialist development, deviation from which could lead to deviation from socialism as such." The Brezhnev Doctrine thus indicated that internal developments alone, even if unaccompanied by external realignments, might be sufficient to provoke a Soviet invasion, and that if the internal policies of a communist party were to "cause damage to socialism in its own country or to the fundamental interests of the other socialist countries," the Soviet Union would have not only a right but a "sacred duty" to intervene on behalf of the "socialist commonwealth." These basic principles of Soviet–East European relations remained in place until Mikhail Gorbachev abandoned them in 1989.

DOCUMENT No. 129: Stenographic Account of the Meeting of the "Warsaw Five" in Moscow, September 27, 1968 (Excerpts)

Source: ÚSD, Sb. KV, Z/S 13.

This transcript of a meeting of the "Warsaw Five" in Moscow, originally 66 pages in length and taken from tape recordings and participants' notes, records the Soviet Union's efforts to overcome the difficulties that emerged as a result of Dubček's alleged failure to abide by the Moscow protocol.

The meeting, which took place a day after the Politburo reviewed the Czechoslovak situation, focused on forcing Dubček to carry out the requisite changes of personnel in all major areas of Czechoslovak life: the party, the government, the mass media, the higher educational system, the security forces, and the army. Soviet leaders also wanted to prevent the CPCz first secretary from trying to salvage anything more of the pre-August reforms and, above all, to head off any attempt he might make to relax the censorship mandated by Article 4 of the protocol. The instrument for achieving these political goals, as decided both at the CPSU Politburo session and at the meeting of the Five, was the permanent Soviet troop presence in Czechoslovakia based on a formal treaty. The meeting transcript records Kosygin pointing out that making Dubček sign a status-of-forces treaty would discredit the CPCz leader in the eyes of all the "rightist forces" who had supported the Prague Spring. Over the longer term, the troops would be a convenient medium through which the Soviet Union could exert political pressure, precluding any renewed attempts at reform. For this purpose Brezhnev believed that around five divisions and command staffs would suffice because "if any real danger emerges, the number of troops can always be increased again."

The Russian government turned over a copy of this document to the Czechoslovak commission in the spring of 1992.

L. I. Brezhnev welcomes the leaders of the parties and governments of the fraternal countries and notes that events in Czechoslovakia have made it imperative that they meet, exchange information, calmly assess the situation, and reach agreement on what joint actions should be taken.

We will try to keep you informed of what we know and set forth our position and the measures to be taken in the immediate future. We expect that the process under way in Czechoslovakia is of a long-term character. We must work out a general position and follow it through right to the end. . . .

Moving on now to a brief report, which should provide a starting point for our negotiations, it is necessary to mention the following items, above all.

The month that has passed since the entry of our troops has fully confirmed both the need for our joint action and its timeliness. We have information about a whole series of facts attesting to the actions of the counterrevolutionary, anti-socialist underground in Czechoslovakia. The activity of the rightist forces, the revisionist wing in the CPCz, represents a great danger.

The main result of what we did is that we have blocked the road to counterrevolution in Czechoslovakia.

Furthermore, a strong blow was delivered to the right-wing forces in the CPCz itself; the prerequisites have been created for the gradual consolidation and activation of the healthy forces in the communist party.

On the whole, the groundwork has been laid for a renewal of the situation in both the party and the country. From a military-political standpoint, the entry of our troops demonstrated not only the capabilities of our countries in putting up a joint defense of the gains of socialism, but also our common resolve to use these capabilities when necessary. The military side of things provided ample confirmation of the high state of mobilized readiness of our armed forces and their efficiency in solving complicated tasks collectively.

It proved that the state interests and security of the Warsaw Pact countries are in fact guaranteed by the united might of our armies. . . .

The reaction of such socialist countries as Yugoslavia and Romania caused complications, as we all know; certain differences in assessing our actions also came up among a number of communist parties in capitalist countries.

We believe it would be appropriate to consider these questions at our meeting, bearing in mind the need to work out a line that would make it possible to make up for lost time relatively quickly and achieve the further cohesion and consolidation of the forces of our socialist commonwealth. All of us, obviously, are working strenuously in this direction and it would be useful to exchange opinions.

No doubt, you know the content of Cde. Husák's speeches. Of all the published pronouncements of Czechoslovak leaders these are the most principled and direct ones so far. They allow communists and the public to think and pay attention to the serious shortcomings and mistakes of the January line of the CPCz.

The impression we have gained as a result of a considerable number of meetings and talks between our comrades and individuals in the CPCz and the Czechoslovak government, especially with persons who still hold influential positions, tells us that many of these people are beginning to understand the necessity to make genuine corrections in the political line. They are beginning to understand that one cannot continue to play a double game, that it is necessary to fulfill one's commitments honestly, and to abide by the agreements reached. We are receiving more and more reports from key individuals in the CPCz and ČSSR government to the effect that Cde. Dubček is carrying out an incorrect policy, and that he, personally, is largely responsible for the situation that made it necessary for allied troops to enter.

Without exaggerating the significance of all these facts, we nevertheless must face up to them and take them into consideration.

Of the things that can be said to be positive developments, we might mention the major issue of the conclusion of a treaty providing for the deployment of units of our troops on Czechoslovak territory. When Černík came to Moscow on a visit, we brought this question up with him. We made it very clear that in this connection a certain portion of the troops who entered Czechoslovakia will remain there for an extended period, and we must now consider concluding a treaty on this question, as mentioned in the Moscow Protocol. We said that these talks should be held along government lines. As a preliminary step, we agreed to recommend that the defense ministers, Cdes. Grechko and Dzúr, prepare the draft of such an agreement. Before Cde. Grechko met Cde. Dzúr, we sent the draft to the capitals of the fraternal socialist countries so that we could secure agreement, in talks with your defense ministers, about the basic directions of our actions on this matter.

But even taking this all into account, comrades, we must not forget the main thing: the general political situation in the country, that is, the line being pursued by the CPCz leadership and its Central Committee in directing the work of the party itself and of the other party bodies—the regional, the district, and so on. In a word, we are talking about the political line pursued by the Czechoslovak leadership. Unfortunately, it is precisely in this regard that we cannot say things are going well. The problems begin with the fact that immediately after the Moscow talks ended, the Czechoslovak leaders convened a CC plenum.

Our view is that this plenum, from beginning to end, was not held in a spirit of the accords reached; rather, it was a violation of the Moscow Protocol. I am referring here primarily to personnel matters. You know, comrades, what changes were carried out there. A number of comrades who are known for their internationalist positions, for their friendly attitude toward the USSR and the other fraternal socialist countries were released from leading posts.[65] At the

---

[65] Article 7 of the protocol forbade any reprisals against officials who supported the "healthy forces" and the Soviet Union. The CPCz CC plenum on August 31 agreed to remove such prominent hardliners as Emil Rigo, Oldřich Švestka, Drahomír Kolder, and Antonín Kapek from the CPCz Presidium. All but Rigo had signed the "letter of invitation" to Brezhnev in early August 1968 requesting "fraternal military assistance" (see Document No. 72). Of the five signatories of the letter (including Alois Indra), only Vasil Biľak retained his post on the Presidium.

same time, through cooption, people who are clearly of right-wing persuasion, were named to the Central Committee and its presidium.[66] . . .

Yesterday we considered all these questions in our Politburo. We have come to the conclusion that our position should contain elements of self-restraint and patience in regard to a number of questions on the situation in Czechoslovakia, that is where patience is possible and appropriate. Beyond this, our position was, is, and will be one of principle on all basic questions. We will demand clear arrangements from the CPCz Central Committee and from Dubček for the whole party and all its branches with respect to the fulfillment of the Moscow Protocol and the Bratislava Declaration.

Our position also is one of principle on the question of personnel policy. We might note that at the last CPCz CC plenum the agreed principles concerning CPCz personnel were violated.

We also believe it is incorrect that Czechoslovak propaganda makes such a clamor about two personalities—Dubček and Smrkovský. It is not accidental that the rightist forces are doing such a thing.

We are clearly aware that key positions in the leadership of the CPCz Central Committee are occupied by such people as Cdes. Dubček, Špaček, Šimon, and Mlynář.[67] These individuals not only failed to act as consistent supporters of socialism and friendship with the USSR, but, on the contrary, are known for displaying unfriendly sentiments toward us. It is very difficult to expect such people to genuinely carry out a policy in the spirit of the Bratislava Declaration and the Moscow Protocol.

At the moment we believe one of the most important tasks is to prepare and conclude an agreement on the deployment of forces. Such an agreement should state that in conformity with the agreement reached in Moscow, and with various elements of the internal and international situation, our governments will conclude an agreement on the deployment of forces on the territory of Czechoslovakia. It also should state that the Czechoslovak side has various technical possibilities for their deployment, and so on. Afterwards, once the agreement is signed, it will be necessary for the Presidium of our Supreme Soviet and the National Assembly of Czechoslovakia to ratify it. We must link Cde. Dubček with a treaty on the retention of troops there. This, of course, will have a certain positive influence on the entire political situation in Czechoslovakia. And only after this, after such an agreement is concluded, can we proceed with the gradual withdrawal of a significant portion of our forces. Until such time, no forces at all will be withdrawn.[68]

Obviously, we all agree that to maintain such a large number of troops as there are at present in Czechoslovakia in winter conditions is virtually impossible. The Czechs simply cannot provide the necessary amount of housing for them. Even in principle we do not have to have so many troops there. If, for example, there are five divisions, an army command, a corps command, and liaison officers for all our allied countries, that in itself will be enough. After all, if any real danger emerges, the number of troops can always be increased again. The important thing is that our troops must remain in Czechoslovakia on a completely different legal basis.

[Participants in the meeting are given the draft text of an agreement between the governments of the ČSSR and the USSR on the question of troop deployments. A recess is declared.]

---

[66] Some eighty new members from the Central Committee elected by the Vysočany Congress were brought into the old Central Committee after the Vysočany Congress was ruled invalid. The same was true of the Central Control and Auditing Commission. Most of the new members were strongly pro-reform. As for the presidium, the new full members included Bohumil Šimon (previously a candidate), Zdeněk Mlynář, and Václav Slavík, all of whom were regarded as close associates of Dubček.

[67] Brezhnev's disparaging comments here about Mlynář are important evidence that the allegations of "high treason" against Mlynář in February 1992 may be unjustified. See Document No. 115 above.

[68] Brezhnev's position here is inconsistent with Article 5 of the Moscow Protocol (Document No. 119), which called for phased withdrawals after the situation had calmed down. It set no prerequisite for the conclusion of a treaty.

L. I. Brezhnev: Comrades, you've had a chance to familiarize yourselves with the text of the draft agreement. We prepared this draft as a working document, as a starting point for talks. Even if there are changes, the important thing is that approximately five divisions of our troops will remain in Czechoslovakia, and that four fully-equipped air bases, which can be used by our combat aircraft, will remain in our hands.

How should we proceed from here? Who wants to say something? Please speak your minds on all fundamental questions.

W. Gomułka: Where will the troops be deployed? On the western borders of Czechoslovakia?

L. I. Brezhnev: No, we think they should be stationed near the main cities of the country—Prague, Bratislava, and others. That also is the view of our military High Command. Czechoslovakia has 220,000–230,000 square meters of army housing space for personnel and about 150,000 square meters of storage space.

A. N. Kosygin: All this will cost a lot. We're paying for lodging, electricity, and water.

L. I. Brezhnev: Just to withdraw the military hardware we will need about 500 military trains.

A. N. Kosygin: The most important thing is to conclude a formal agreement and make sure it is signed by Cdes. Dubček and Černík. This is important for the outside world and for it to be perceived in Czechoslovakia itself. If they sign such an agreement, the rightist forces will rise up against them, and it would have many positive factors from a foreign policy standpoint.[69] After such an agreement is signed neither the United Nations nor anyone else will be able to make trouble for us.

W. Gomułka (translation): We believe the question is correct: We must conclude an agreement that will enable the troops to remain in Czechoslovakia. That's the most important thing. Concluding such an agreement will, in a certain sense, overcome any and all speculation. Up to now, Czechoslovak society, or at least a part of it, is convinced that . . .[70]

J. Kádár: Now, as far as personalities are concerned, I would like you to understand me properly. Since the Moscow talks, Cde. Husák and Cde. Svoboda have played the most positive role. Of the party officials, Cde. Husák, if you like, is the most decisive. We were acquainted with him in the past. In recent days we have spoken a great deal to Czechoslovak communists—the honest people—and these comrades, on the basis of their experience, say that Cde. Husák nowadays espouses a good position. But as far as the future is concerned, they're apprehensive. Cde. Husák is known as a person with very strong nationalist inclinations. Of course, people can change, but God only knows whether he is acting out of conviction now or whether he is acting only for tactical reasons. Therefore the most important thing is to insist on a defined policy and not to judge whether this or that person is the right one. . . .

W. Ulbricht (translation): We agree with the assessment of events presented here. All the comrades who spoke here stressed that the entry of allied troops into Czechoslovakia was timely and necessary, that the result of it was to block the path to counterrevolution, and that the right-wing in Czechoslovakia was dealt a blow. On the other hand, we must state that the consolidation of the communist forces in Czechoslovakia has not yet come about.

We agree with Cde. Brezhnev that the military tasks were solved very well by the High Command and the Command of Joint Allied Forces. This evoked a great international response, particularly from the West. They had to admit that the military action in Czechoslovakia indicates

---

[69] Kosygin's linkage of the troop deployments with the internal political situation in Czechoslovakia, as well as many of the other comments by different speakers below, belies later Soviet claims that the quest to deploy forces permanently in Czechoslovakia was based on military considerations.

[70] The transcript omits the rest of Gomułka's sentence.

a weakening of NATO's position and a barrier to Bonn's new *Ostpolitik*.[71] This is especially important with a view to the GDR's position which, as a result, has improved.

The statement of Soviet Ambassador Tsarapkin to Kissinger, that the Soviet Union will not permit a link in the system of socialist states to be broken anywhere or at any time, provoked a great response around the world.[72]

We believe the right-wing, counterrevolutionary forces in Czechoslovakia have been blocked. On the basis of the Moscow protocol we are now in a position to sign an agreement with Czechoslovakia on the deployment of allied troops there and their partial withdrawal. This makes our political course easier. We are now at a new stage, a stage when the center of attention will be directed to political activities. Signing an agreement on the deployment of troops can be used for political work.

We can say that in the past we failed to carry out the necessary political steps with the help of the *internal forces* in Czechoslovakia. We failed to do this in response to the publication of the "Two Thousand Words" Manifesto. We failed to do this when we sent in our troops on 21 August.

We sent in the troops on the basis of our correct political conception, but the internal forces did not come forward with their own, a Czechoslovak concept which would have directly addressed the interests of the Czechoslovak people and would have been targeted against the adventurist platforms of the Czechoslovak leadership.[73] There was no such concept. That is precisely where our weakness lies, a weakness that continues to the present day. The blame for this lies with the Czechoslovak friends inside the country, but to a certain degree the blame is ours as well—it is our weakness, the weakness of our "Five." I believe this matter should be at the forefront of our attention.

A treaty on the force deployments will be an incentive to raising political questions. . . .

As far as the draft treaty on force deployments is concerned, we agree with it. We, however, think it would be necessary to leave six divisions in Czechoslovakia and not five, as you thought.

Comrades, the CPSU CC Politburo and the Council of Ministers of the Soviet Union present this draft in the name of our five parties. In the end, this assumes that our meeting today will become officially known to the public. Perhaps we should publish a communiqué saying that the meeting took place but without disclosing the content of our negotiations. Clearly, we can't do without a communiqué of some sort. . . .

L. I. Brezhnev: . . . With regard to the presentations made at today's meeting, we would say that all the delegations of the fraternal parties added to our information and our assessment of the situation in Czechoslovakia. We see no differences in points of view on the situation in Czechoslovakia. We agree with all the remarks made by the comrades since our assessments coincide with and supplement one another. . . .

We are not occupiers, we came to Czechoslovakia as friends, as people worried about the fate of socialism in that country. Our soldiers are exposed to rain and wind, they eat at field kitchens, they sleep on the ground and on tanks. The troops are showing true magnanimity toward the people, helping them reap the harvest and putting economic life back on track. What other army can we say would behave this way?

Of course, nationalist passions have now surfaced in Czechoslovakia. The imperialists are using this and are creating a fuss about our joint action. It would be unnatural if they *didn't* attempt to use the situation to their own advantage. But let them make a fuss, the main thing has

---

[71] Ulbricht's comments here, like those of Brezhnev and Kosygin above, illustrate how much the leaders of the "Warsaw Five" were seeking to use the invasion to pursue their own political goals. Ulbricht was a vehement opponent of any compromise with the FRG and thus was hoping the invasion would put an end once and for all to the West German government's efforts to establish contacts with the Eastern bloc.

[72] Semyon Tsarapkin was the long-time Soviet ambassador at the Geneva Conference on Disarmament and the United Nations.

[73] Ulbricht's comments are a further reflection of how disappointed the leaders of the "Warsaw Five" were that the "healthy forces" proved unable to follow up on their promises.

been done—the path to counterrevolution in Czechoslovakia has been blocked and was dealt a serious blow. We all see eye-to-eye on this.

However, we must also draw another conclusion (which all the comrades here mentioned), that the situation in Czechoslovakia remains complicated not only in the leadership of the communist party, but also in the Central Committee, the regional committees, and the local branches. All that counterrevolutionary propaganda, all that furious anti-Sovietism, which kept on cropping up during the last ten months, inevitably left its mark. And added to this was the work of the illegal radio stations during August, the reaction of the people to the entry of the troops, and so on. Therefore we do not exclude the possibility, as the other comrades said, that there might still be all kinds of setbacks ahead, perhaps even sharper setbacks than we can imagine today.

If we are to speak of concrete measures, it seems to us we cannot allow the Czech congress to take place.[74] How to do this isn't a simple matter. We've begun to work in the following way. We explained our position to Husák, Černík, and Svoboda. In a telephone conversation, Cde. Svoboda advised us to put pressure on the Czechoslovak delegation when it comes to Moscow. If you, comrades, have a chance to use your influence, this clearly, would also be very helpful. After all, you have contacts there. It seems to us that if all of us together put pressure on the Czechoslovak leadership concerning this matter, they will agree not to hold a congress of the Czech Communist Party. Of course, one cannot guarantee such a decision, but based on recent conversations we get the impression that the Czechoslovak leadership might, for instance, convene a plenum instead of a congress with the participation of the secretaries of the Czech regional committees, or proceed along the lines of state measures (for example, resolving this matter by convening the Czech National Council).

Any attempt to hold a founding congress of the Czech Communist Party under the present circumstances would be undesirable. Dubček's talk about political guarantees is worth nothing, since not one of his assurances during this whole period, beginning in December of last year, was carried out. . . .

Along with this we should also consider several points that pose some danger. In the first place, the academic year in higher education institutions begins on 1 October. Students will return to their academic pursuits, and provocateurs might use this opportunity to encourage mass demonstrations of students, which might lead to clashes with our soldiers. The second is that some of the officers of the Czechoslovak army might fall under the influence of the right-wing, taking into account the situation in the country.

We must bear in mind these two dangers and be vigilant.

The two factors I've just mentioned might be significantly offset by the conclusion of a treaty on the deployment of a portion of troops in Czechoslovakia and the gradual withdrawal of the rest. This document would provide the legal basis for our troop presence in Czechoslovakia, and at the same time it will encourage the healthy forces who will be convinced that some of the troops will remain. This agreement also would have a favorable impact in the international arena, undercutting the fiery, hostile propaganda.

However, comrades, bear in mind that for now this document, the one we've been informing you about, is only a draft. Coming to an agreement with the Czechoslovaks on such a treaty will not be easy; we still don't know whether they will accept it in such a form.

We've already begun to work with the Czechs and to this end we used our talks with Černík who came to Moscow. We told him: Cde. Černík, you know that the troops will not leave, so think about how to arrange, in a formal way, for part of the troops to remain in Czechoslovakia.

---

[74] Before the invasion, the CPCz leadership had planned to create a federal structure for the communist party (with separate Czech and Slovak parties alongside a central CPCz) as well as for the state. The federalization of the state went ahead, but the Soviet authorities prevented Dubček from following through on the planned federalization of the communist party. Brezhnev is referring here to those soon-to-be aborted plans.

He was interested in how many we had in mind. In the preliminary arrangement, 10 to 12 percent of the present number was mentioned. We agreed to recommend that the ministers of defense hold talks in Uzhgorod. The ministers and our military specialists met for a working session, prepared materials, and returned home to report on their work to their respective leaderships. I phoned Dubček last week and was interested to know whether he had looked at the material on the deployment of troops. Dubček replied that he had not yet had the time, but intended to do so together with Černík. Several days later Dzúr began hinting to us that it would be difficult to reach agreement now on any long-term deployment of troops, and that most likely it would be possible to come to agreement just on the winter period. One can sense that they want to delay it.

Not long ago, Cde. Pavlovskii came to Moscow; he's the commander of our forces in Czechoslovakia, and he knows the situation very well. He spoke about both the negative and the positive features of the current situation and reported on his talks with Černík. As it turns out, president Svoboda expressed support for the deployment of Soviet troops in Czechoslovakia, but Minister of Defense Dzúr still takes an evasive position. Dzúr says that for the present there is no need for an agreement on deployments, but he approves the idea of stationing our troops in winter. These sorts of signals enable us to see that the talks will be difficult. True, preparations are now under way in Czechoslovakia to station the troops remaining there: Living areas are being readied, barracks are being repaired, etc. This is not a simple matter because stationing our officers there would require the Czechoslovaks to move out 7,000 of their own officers. This is the reason for certain views among Czechoslovak military personnel. So, on this question we undoubtedly will run into difficulties. . . .

W. Gomułka: In my view, the question of whether to publish a communiqué about our meeting today depends on whether there will be a conference of the "Six" or not. If we all agree to take part together in the negotiations with the Czechs on Thursday, then it isn't necessary to publish any message.[75] If we don't take part in the talks with the Czechs, then it would be expedient to publish a communiqué. And we might tell the Czechs directly: "We wanted to consult with one another because we all have our troops on your territory."

I think it would be advisable for all of us to take part in the negotiations with the CPCz. However, I doubt that the Czechs will accept the draft we will present. They'll say they can't solve such a serious question here, in Moscow, that it's necessary to consult back home, etc. If we send the draft to them before the meeting in Moscow, they'll bring their own counterproposal and they'll try to propose that instead of keeping our troops there permanently, the troops should stay only for the winter.

L. I. Brezhnev: Frankly, I also have strong doubts that the Czechs are ready to accept such a draft, although the barracks are all ready.

W. Gomułka: Obviously, they hope to provide the barracks for a stay only over the winter.

A. N. Kosygin: For tactical reasons it would not be advisable to send the draft to Prague. It is one thing to send the draft of a treaty there by post; they will get together and begin to review it. It would be another thing if we present the draft to them at the negotiations.

W. Gomułka: Perhaps we should send the draft treaty to Cde. Svoboda.

N. V. Podgorny: If they come with the officials they said they would, they can say that they're not authorized to sign such a treaty.

W. Gomułka: Insofar as this treaty is between states, those who sign it have to be properly authorized.

---

[75] Gomułka is referring to the meeting scheduled for October 3–4 in Moscow. See Document No. 131.

A. N. Kosygin: It is not necessary to sign the treaty immediately. At first it is necessary to speak to them and get their consent, and then to prepare the treaty for signing.

W. Gomułka: Does this mean that at the meeting on Thursday the treaty won't be signed?

A. N. Kosygin: You see, Cde. Gomułka, we'll try to gain their consent in principle to sign such an agreement.

W. Gomułka: I thought you intended to have this treaty signed immediately. Either way, it would be necessary to send the draft beforehand.

A. N. Kosygin: If Smrkovský receives such a draft, he'll speak to the National Assembly and he'll try to incite public opinion against the treaty.

W. Gomułka: One might tell them that the draft is secret.

A. N. Kosygin: That's unrealistic. Even if we were to do so, Smrkovský would give the secret away.

W. Gomułka: There's nothing terrible about that. After all, the Moscow protocol states that such a treaty should be concluded.[76]

A. N. Kosygin: If we had sent this protocol to Czechoslovakia in advance and then told the Czechs to come and consider it with us, I suspect there never would have been any such protocol.

W. Gomułka: We must devise a position and have options in reserve. What if the Czechs propose only a temporary deployment of the troops, allowing them to stay only over the winter?
I am for having representatives from the five parties take part in the talks with the Czechs. All of us have troops in Czechoslovakia. Let them hear our assessment of the situation.

W. Ulbricht: If the Soviet comrades conduct the talks on their own, they'll have an easier time. We should authorize them to speak in the name of all our parties.

T. Zhivkov: That's how it was, in fact, at past negotiations.

L. I. Brezhnev: The talks obviously won't be easy. They'll interpret the Moscow protocol in their own way. It'll be important to make them realize that some of the troops will remain in Czechoslovakia. They, of course, will say "the people will not understand" and "there's no need to conclude a treaty now," and then they'll stir up a frenzy around this question. So, let's have no illusions about their position.
From our point of view, it would be better if all of us took part in the negotiations with the Czechs. We're following a joint policy; all of us took part in the entry of troops; and all of us acted in a single front on the political level. What really disturbs me in this regard is that the Czechs didn't mention even once the possibility of a joint meeting. Today, during a conversation with Cde. Svoboda, I said that maybe all of us should get together and meet the fraternal parties. And he replied: "You should speak to the comrades about that." That means he doesn't want to take the matter upon himself, he doesn't want to express his opinion. Obviously, he'll tell Dubček and Černík about this idea. We'll await their reaction tomorrow. I don't exclude the possibility that they'll reply they want to consult only with us at this stage.

J. Kádár: In that case it will be necessary to issue a statement about our meeting today. . . .

A. N. Kosygin: I think it's better not to issue a communiqué to the press about our meeting today.

VOICE: It's not necessary.

---

[76] See Article 5 of Document No. 119.

A. N. Kosygin: In the first place, publication will provoke agitation in the world. Someone will write one thing, and others something else. They will maintain that we delayed our meeting with the Czechs in order to hold a conference of the Five. Would this be advantageous for us in the present circumstances? I think it would be disadvantageous because it would create obvious complications for the Czechs, and it would then be more difficult for us to exert pressure on them. At home they might say to the Czechoslovak leaders: They didn't invite you to this meeting, they don't trust you, they won't even give you the time of day. If that's the case we should be doing things not to start an argument with the Czechs but to find a solution that would be acceptable both to us and to them.

Based on your confidence in us, when they come to Moscow we can say to them that the questions we are asking them were agreed to by you. We will also say that the draft of the treaty on troop deployment received the approval of the Polish, Hungarian, German, and Bulgarian comrades.

L. I. Brezhnev: I think we don't have to hide from the Czechs the fact that we met today. We'll tell them directly that we got together, that we exchanged opinions on questions concerning the political situation, and that we shared observations. And, perhaps, it would be worth asking them by phone how they regard the possibility of a collective meeting. If they say that they want to only meet Soviet officials, it would be possible to go for that. But it would still be worthwhile suggesting a meeting of the Six. Particularly because I mentioned it today to Svoboda. He, no doubt, will tell this to Černík, Dubček, or Husák.

W. Gomułka: Taking account of all that's been said, I withdraw my suggestion.

L. I. Brezhnev: Are we all agreed then, comrades?

[All express agreement.]

W. Gomułka: But I still would propose that you ask the question about having a discussion with the Czechoslovak comrades.

N. V. Podgorny, L. I. Brezhnev: We haven't rejected this proposal, we will raise these questions.

W. Gomułka: It might be done by publishing editorial articles in newspapers. We can have our articles published in their papers, and they will have theirs published in our press.

L. I. Brezhnev: Císař made a speech in connection with the Marx jubilee, in which he essentially spoke out against Leninism and Lenin.[77] We replied to him in a theoretical article. And after that the Czechs began to say that we caused difficulties for them, that it was unnecessary to do it in such a way, and so on.

W. Gomułka: That was earlier, when circumstances were different. Now, for instance, we might aggressively set forth how we understand the concept of "normalization." That must be done insofar as the Czechs seem to have an incorrect understanding of what normalization should mean.

L. I. Brezhnev: On this question it's essential that we break the resistance of Dubček, Smrkovský, and the others. That is where the root of all evil lies. Resistance comes from them. We have only spoken about it and now, in forthcoming negotiations, we will raise this question pointedly. We'll ask Dubček what line he wishes to follow and what he wants to achieve. . . .

---

[77] Brezhnev is referring to the speech Císař delivered in connection with the 150th anniversary of Karl Marx's birth. See "Marxův myšlenkový odkaz je záštitou, oporou a inspirací: Večer k 150. výroči narození Karla Marxe," *Rudé právo* (Prague), May 7, 1968, pp. 1, 3; for further details see Document No. 30 above. An article by Fyodor Konstantinov, which bitterly attacked Císař's speech, appeared in Moscow *Pravda* on June 14, 1968; and Císař promptly responded to Konstantinov in a lengthy article, "V čem je síla živého marxismu-leninismu: Odpověd' akademiku F. Konstantinovovi," *Rudé právo* (Prague), 22 June 1968, p. 3.

DOCUMENT No. 130: KGB Report on the "Counterrevolutionary Underground" in Czechoslovakia, October 13, 1968 (Excerpts)

Source: TsKhSD, F. 4, Op. 21, D. 32, Ll. 99–157.

This 59-page document, compiled by the First Main Directorate of the KGB under the supervision of Aleksei Sakharovskii, provides a response to requests for information from the East German and Polish authorities. It is signed by KGB chief Yuri Andropov.

The first sections of the report address alleged activities of the "counterrevolutionary underground" before the invasion, although it fails to present any evidence that the reform process was subverted or manipulated by a small group of conspirators. The sections of the report focusing on the post-invasion situation highlight the extent of non-violent resistance to the invasion, and the hostile reception that Warsaw pact troops encountered everywhere they went, contradicting earlier KGB predictions that the invasion would be welcomed by the Czechoslovak public. The KGB authors blame the widespread opposition on the manipulations of the "right-revisionist and extremist elements in the CPCz leadership."

(See also Documents Nos. 20, 28, and 131.)

COMMITTEE FOR STATE SECURITY OF SPECIAL DOSSIER

THE COUNCIL OF MINISTERS OF THE USSR

13 October 1968

TOP SECRET

TO THE CPSU CC

In connection with the request by the German and Polish friends to transmit information to them about Czechoslovakia, the Committee for State Security believes it would be advisable to send the attached report about the activity of the counterrevolutionary underground in the ČSSR, which was prepared on the basis of intelligence materials, to the leadership of the GDR and PPR state security organs.

We request approval.

Attachment: 59 pages

CHAIRMAN OF THE COMMITTEE FOR STATE SECURITY

(signed) *Andropov*[78]

---

[78] The report was approved in mid-October 1968 by the KGB chairman, Yuri Andropov, who then sent it to the CPSU CC Secretariat for final approval. The text was edited for style and brevity by Mikhail Suslov, a senior member of both the CPSU CC Politburo and the CPSU CC Secretariat, whose handwritten changes were still present on the copy of the document stored in the former CPSU CC archives. When Suslov was done with his editing, he wrote "Approved" on the cover memorandum and signed it along with Konstantin Katushev and Boris Ponomarev. Next to their signatures is a subsequent comment that reads: "Comments incorporated. Andropov." On the back of the cover memorandum is an archival notation indicating that the revised document was transmitted to the East German and Polish state security organs, at Suslov's instruction, on 28 October 1968.

ON THE ACTIVITY OF THE COUNTERREVOLUTIONARY UNDERGROUND IN CZECHOSLOVAKIA

I. The Activity of Anti-Socialist Forces before the Entry of Allied Troops into the ČSSR[79]

Over a prolonged period the counterrevolutionary and revisionist forces in Czechoslovakia, relying on support from international imperialism, systematically and intently prepared to restore capitalism in the ČSSR and to tear it out of the socialist commonwealth. After the January plenum of the CPCz CC, which announced a course of "democratization" in the country's political life, the anti-socialist forces, having taken control of the mass media and exploiting the lack of unity in the CPCz leadership and the descent of a majority of the CPCz CC Presidium into right-revisionist positions, embarked on an open attack against the socialist order in the ČSSR and the leading role of the CPCz, and against honest communists in the party and state apparatus.

The counterrevolutionary forces regarded as one of their paramount tasks the demoralization of the army, the State Security organs, and the People's Militia, with the aim of eventually taking over these bodies.

A particular danger to the cause of socialism in Czechoslovakia is posed by the renewed activity of the Czechoslovak Social-Democratic Party (CzSDP), which has an elaborate program and enjoys support from West European socialist parties and the Socialist International. The CzSDP, according to its leaders, must become the main force of opposition to the CPCz. Despite the official ban on its activity, the CzSDP in a short time has created more than 200 primary organizations and cells.

The role of a "strike force" of the counterrevolutionary elements is performed by "Club-231," which numbers more than 40 thousand people who were repressed after 1948 for anti-state activity (some of whom were rehabilitated). The leaders of the club maintain links with reactionary emigrés and Western intelligence services, and receive financial assistance from them. One of the aims of the club is to bring about the complete collapse of the CPCz and the liquidation of the State Security organs and the People's Militia. At one of the meetings, the general secretary of the club, the former fascist Brodský, called for a violent confrontation with the communists.

At the session in June of the presidium of the local branch of "Club-231" in Bratislava, one of the leaders, VYNDRA, stated: "Our ranks must be more numerous than the ranks of the Communist Party of Slovakia so that when the time comes, we can destroy the communist party and liquidate socialism." Another activist in the club said: "The West knows about us, and it is waiting for concrete actions on our part and will support us. We need not be afraid now that victory is near."

In case "Club-231" was banned, the leaders devised a special "mobilization plan," which provided for the members to join non-communist parties and rise to leading posts in them so that they can continue their subversive work.

The "Club of Committed Non-Party Members" (KAN) is one of the largest anti-socialist organizations, consisting of reactionary members of the creative and scientific-technical intelligentsia. It has affiliates all over the country, at many large enterprises, and in several formations of the army. Many leading officials of KAN have links with the international Zionist organization "Joint." At the initiative of the spiritual leader of the club, the reactionary philosopher Sviták (who fled to the West after the allied forces entered the ČSSR), a provocative campaign was launched "to uncover all the circumstances" of the suicide of Jan Masaryk.

On the 3rd of May in the Old Town Square of Prague, a meeting organized by the leadership of KAN took place, with more than 1,000 people in attendance. The members of the leadership

---

[79] At times in the document, headings and sub-headings are not entirely consistent, and some of the brief identifications of individuals are misleading or erroneous. Where necessary, discrepancies have been pointed out in annotations, rather than in the text itself.

who took part in the meeting put forth demands to remove clauses about the leading role of the CPCz from the ČSSR Constitution and to liquidate the State Security organs. In their speeches, they asserted that the CPCz for some 20 years had "completely compromised itself," and that it was time to organize a "firm counterweight to the communists" in the form of KAN or the Czechoslovak Socialist Party. . . .

The reactionaries have succeeded in establishing broad links with cultural and scientific figures in Czechoslovakia, fostering a hostile mood among them, and receiving information from them about individual segments of the social, cultural, economic, and political life of the ČSSR.

At the 4th Congress of Czechoslovak Writers in June 1967, the reactionary core of the Writers' Union (Kohout, Liehm, Vaculík, Havel, Kundera) were able to force through a resolution in which a political platform opposed to the CPCz was laid out.[80] The platform asserted that the policy of the CPCz in the sphere of literature and art "retards the development of creativity," and it demanded an end to censorship and a policy of "absolute freedom of creativity."

The group of writers who subscribe to reactionary positions called for the readmission into the Writers' Union of someone who long ago was a professor at Charles University, Václav Černý, whom the reactionaries consider their "spiritual godfather" (as a member of the Syndicate of Czech Writers after 1945, Černý expressed anti-Marxist views and sought to propound the thesis that "literature and art have nothing in common with politics").

Černý established and still supports close ties with reactionary emigré circles of Czechoslovak writers, and also with officials in Western embassies in Prague. . . .

Long before the January plenum of the CPCz CC, Černý, along with the deputy chairman of the Writers' Union, Jan Procházka, put together an underground anti-party group. Taking part in the activities of this group were the writers Kohout, Vaculík, Liehm, Havel, and Kundera, and also the former chief of the General Staff of the Czechoslovak People's Army, Krejčí, a researcher in the Academy of Sciences, Konůpek, the editor of the newspaper *Svobodné slovo*, J. Černý, and others.[81]

The leaders of the underground group set out to discredit the CPCz in the eyes of the Czechoslovak nation, to undermine the foundations of socialism in the ČSSR, and to turn the country gradually onto the path of capitalist development.

The Černý–Procházka group worked out a phased plan to liquidate the CPCz. In the first phase, the aim of the group was to do everything possible to promote the "process of liberalization" and the criticism of the old leadership of the CPCz. Černý and Procházka declared that it was necessary to give the communists the opportunity to "wash dirty party linen" before the Czechoslovak public and thus to undermine the CPCz's authority and strength in the country.

In the second phase, when, according to the leaders of the group, the CPCz will lose its leading role and its ability to control the future development of events in the country, the group must take charge of the opposition forces in the ČSSR.

According to reliable data, this group is being orchestrated by reactionary Czechoslovak emigrés in Paris, who are connected with Western intelligence services. At the forefront of this center is an American agent, the editor of the emigré journal *Svědectví*, Pavel Tigrid (who in 1967 was convicted *in absentia* on charges of anti-Czechoslovak activity).[82]

Tigrid is constantly in touch with Czechoslovak scholars, journalists, and writers who come to Paris. With the help of Černý, Procházka, and other members of the underground group, he has succeeded in creating a wide and influential base for different sorts of anti-socialist and right-wing opportunist elements in Czechoslovakia. Tigrid has set the following tasks for his supporters: to create a force in Czechoslovakia that would drive forward the process of "democratization," to sow disarray in the organs of people's power (including the army, the State

[80] On this matter, see Document No. 1.
[81] See the KGB's earlier reports on these same matters in Document No. 20.
[82] On Tigrid, see the notes in Document No. 1.

Security organs, and the Workers' Militia), and to discredit and disorient the CPCz, with the aim of gradually removing it from its position as the leading force in Czechoslovak society. . . .

. . . The activity of the reactionary forces in Czechoslovakia facilitated the rise and operation of a "second center" in the CPCz CC alongside the CPCz CC Presidium. In the name of the party, this center organized the work of the mass media and took over a number of important posts in the party apparatus, the Interior Ministry, the Foreign Ministry, and other ministries and agencies in the ČSSR. The "second center" maintained contacts with different reactionary organizations and clubs, and coordinated their activities.

The chief of staff of the "second center" was Kriegel. Along with him, the leadership of the center included Šik, Císař, Mlynář[83] (Müller), Slavík, Pavel, Kolář, Šimon, Goldstücker, and Pelikán.

Actions are coordinated between the "second center" and the Černý–Procházka group; their plans essentially coincide and are both aimed at breaking up the workers' movement in Czechoslovakia, doing away with the political power of the CPCz by means of "restoring" the parties and organizations that joined the National Front, and reinstating bourgeois democracy in the ČSSR.

Kriegel, Goldstücker, and Šik have exposed themselves as active purveyors of Zionist influence in the ČSSR. They have established ties with foreign Zionist centers, in particular with Wiesenthal, an official from the organization "Joint" in Vienna.[84]

The leaders of the "second center" regularly meet to work out practical measures aimed at securing key positions for their supporters in the political, economic, and cultural life of the ČSSR. Kriegel was responsible for the general leadership and coordination of the activities of rightist elements in the CPCz; Císař and Goldstücker were instructed to organize the work of the mass media and the activity of youth organizations and of the creative and scientific intelligentsia; Mlynář was responsible for working out political conceptions of the "Czechoslovak model of socialism"; and Šik was assigned responsibility for economic policy questions. Slavík and Pelikán maintained contacts with non-communist parties in the country. Control over the activity of the "Club of Committed Non-Party Members," "Club-231," and other anti-socialist organizations was exercised through Mlynář and Pavel. "Club-231" was used as a "second center" for the transmission to the West of information about the situation in the ČSSR, especially information intended for the "Radio Free Europe" station in Munich.

Supporters of Kriegel planned to elevate Císař to the top post in the CPCz CC, and Šik to the post of prime minister.

According to the plan devised by the "second center," control over the Interior Ministry organs was the most important step in achieving its aims. After Pavel became head of the Interior Ministry, he heeded the instructions of the "second center" and immediately began purging the State Security organs of "people who had compromised themselves" and gave his approval to a campaign of "public exposure." At his insistence, Deputy Interior Ministers Záruba and Demjan were removed from their posts, as were the heads of directorates Spelina, Kosnar, Beran, Kovan, and Bokr, and a host of other senior officials who had supported an improvement of the situation in the Interior Ministry.[85] The "second center" planned gradually to dismiss all the appointed officials from the Interior Ministry and replace them with protégés of the "clubs" and other counterrevolutionary organizations.

---

[83] Mlynář is prominently cited in the report as one of the leaders of the "counterrevolutionary underground" both before and after the invasion. The KGB's treatment of him in this report raises questions about the charges of "high treason" leveled against Mlynář in 1992 for allegedly collaborating with the Soviet forces.

[84] A reference to Simon Wiesenthal, a survivor of Auschwitz who later gained renown for his efforts in tracking down escaped Nazi war criminals.

[85] Colonel Jan Záruba was the first deputy minister, and Colonel Štefan Demjan was one of five deputy ministers. The others mentioned here were department chiefs.

The "second center" also was carrying out a "purge" in the army so that it could use the army in its plans to seize power in the country.

The group of Kriegel, Císař, and Šik sought to disarm the People's Militia under the pretext that the country supposedly had only a trivial number of anti-socialist forces, and that therefore there was no need for armed detachments of workers. Simultaneously, Kriegel gave instructions to his people to set up special committees that would "control things" at enterprises and other institutions.

. . . In the press, on radio, and on television during this period a campaign was vigorously promoted to compromise the healthy forces in the CPCz as "closet conservatives" and to drive them from their posts. As a result of this campaign, more than 300 senior party officials were dismissed from their posts, and they still have no other permanent work. The instigators of this campaign, according to available information, were Šik and Císař.

. . . During the Šumava command-staff exercises and after the Warsaw Meeting, the leaders of the "second center" directed their main efforts at inciting a nationalist psychosis in the country against the presence of Soviet troops on the territory of Czechoslovakia. The press and other organs of the mass media were all used to whip up anti-Soviet fervor in the population under the pretext of the defense of the "sovereignty" and "independence" of the ČSSR. At the time of the meeting in Čierna, Císař and others promoted a campaign to collect signatures for the "Appeal of the Citizens to the CPCz CC Presidium."[86]

. . . Honest communists noted that, from January on, the reactionary forces launched direct attacks against the most important state institutions, the procuracy, the courts, the State Security organs, the Ministry of Justice, the Ministry of National Defense, and the CPCz CC apparatus in order to send them into disarray.

No measures at all were taken by the CPCz leadership to put an end to the subversive activity of the counterrevolutionary forces.

II. The Activity of the Counterrevolutionaries after the Entry of Allied Troops

The events that transpired after the entry of allied forces into the ČSSR dramatically affirmed that the counterrevolutionary underground in Czechoslovakia presents a serious threat to the nation's socialist gains and to everything that has been achieved during 20 years of popular rule. The counterrevolutionaries were consistently and intently preparing to overthrow socialism in Czechoslovakia not only by "peaceful means," but also through the use of armed force.

By the time allied troops entered the ČSSR, the counterrevolutionary underground had almost completely demoralized the staff of the Interior Ministry and, with the help of its protégé Pavel, had replaced all the leading personnel in the ministry and switched the staff of the most important units of the State Security organs to fulfill the aims of the counterrevolution. As early as July, the new leadership of the Interior Ministry had worked out a special operational plan for the reactionary forces in the event of an "emergency situation," so that they could protect and uphold conditions needed to continue activities aimed at restoring capitalism in the country.

At the end of August, during one of the conversations that Šik had in Belgrade, he said that "the occupation of Czechoslovakia will be prolonged and difficult for both the ČSSR and the USSR. It will strengthen the anti-Soviet mood among the Czechoslovak people and inflict damage on the Soviet Union." The "resistance movement," as he called it, can count on support from such officials as Císař and Pavel.

THE ACTIVITY OF THE COUNTERREVOLUTIONARY FORCES IN THE PARTY ORGANS

The Prague City Committee of the party, which assumed the role of an underground CC of the CPCz, became the counterrevolutionary core of the party organs. On the day that forces were

[86] See Document No. 63.

sent in, the Prague City Committee, whose top posts were long ago taken over by right-revisionist and extremist elements (Šimon, Litera, Lis, Šilhán, et al.), established itself as the underground leader of the counterrevolution and supervised the efforts of provincial and regional party committees, some of which had been operating partly or completely illegally from the first moment that allied troops marched in.

Through the Prague City Committee and an operational staff created within the Interior Ministry, the leadership set up a network consisting of underground radio stations, the press, television, armed counterrevolutionary groups, and supplies of weapons, ammunition, and equipment.

The Prague City Committee of the CPCz played an important role in the organization of protests against the five socialist countries. The leaders of the Prague City Committee were the initiators of the idea of convening the "14th CPCz Congress."

The Prague City Committee also played the main role in organizing hostile activities on the radio. . . .

By controlling the mass media, the Prague City Committee, with the help of an illegal radio network that it set up, fomented anti-Soviet hysteria in the ČSSR and confused the majority of the population, causing them to oppose the USSR. . . .

THE USE OF MASS MEDIA OUTLETS BY COUNTERREVOLUTIONARY ELEMENTS

At the moment that allied troops entered the ČSSR, all the mass media outlets—the radio, television, and press—were used by the counterrevolutionary elements against the socialist countries and their troops who moved into Czechoslovakia. Both overt and covert outlets of the mass media, which had been prepared beforehand, were brought into operation. Long before the allied troops entered, the counterrevolutionary forces had created a broad network of underground radio stations and transmitters, including state and army transmitters, as stipulated in a mobilization plan, plus amateur radio operators. Foreign radio stations—from Austria, the FRG, England, the USA, and other countries—came to the assistance of the counterrevolutionaries. Emergency television broadcasting channels were made available, and underground printing presses were geared up.

After the troops of the socialist countries entered the territory of the ČSSR on 21 August, a large quantity of active radio transmitters were in place on Czechoslovak territory. Provocative, anti-Soviet broadcasts, which clearly had been prepared in advance and been designated for special groups organizing counterrevolutionary work, were disseminated by these transmitters.

By the second half of 21 August the number of radio transmitters had begun to increase rapidly, and by 22 August transmitters were operating almost everywhere on the territory of the ČSSR.

By 28 August the location of some 35 powerful, illegal radio stations had been established.

The majority of the underground radio stations were stationary and were operating out of administrative buildings or on the grounds of a number of establishments, institutions, and organizations. Some of the radio stations were mobile. . . .

Three illegal Czechoslovak radio transmitters, which called for the population to resist the allied troops and engaged in broad counterrevolutionary propaganda, appealed to the authorities of Austria and the FRG to lend them technical assistance, that is, the opportunity to carry out broadcasts with the help of Austrian and West German radio stations and from the territory of these countries.

In connection with the events in Czechoslovakia, the radio broadcasting stations of the USA, the FRG, and England have sharply increased the volume of their Czech-language transmissions. . . .

The main organizer of all the preparations and activity of the underground radio network in the ČSSR was Hejzlar, who served as the *de facto* leader of the CPCz CC Ideological Department from 26 August on. Hejzlar set up a network of correspondents. At enterprises, establishments, and organizations, he arranged for anti-Soviet resolutions and protests to be adopted. Hejzlar continues to be in contact with Císař. . . .

Despite the official introduction of censorship, newspapers and magazines in the ČSSR are continuing to publish articles and materials with an anti-Soviet and anti-socialist slant. In thinly veiled form, the press materials justify the counterrevolutionary propaganda that was being purveyed by illegal radio stations and newspapers right after the entry of allied troops.

. . . The right-wing underground is actively distributing counterrevolutionary leaflets. . . . It has been established that many of the leaflets circulating in the ČSSR are being prepared in capitalist countries. . . . . [87]

ON THE EFFORTS BY THE COUNTERREVOLUTIONARIES
TO INCITE NATIONALISM AMONG THE POPULATION

After the entry of allied troops, the anti-socialist forces and counterrevolutionary elements launched an active campaign to condemn the "occupiers" of the ČSSR and to incite nationalism and hostility against the allied troops. This campaign was carried out with the endorsement, and later under the direction of, the central state and party organs in the ČSSR.

On 22–23 August, illegally published newspapers—*Práce, Večerni Praha, Svoboda, Česko-slovenský sport, Svět v obrazech,* and also a special edition of *Rudé právo*—were distributed. In these newspapers, and also in a large number of hastily published leaflets, demands were voiced for the withdrawal of allied troops from the country.

On 28 August the newspaper *Literární listy* published an appeal by Procházka, in which he called the Soviet Union a "gendarme" and described the foreign policy of the USSR as "Cossack diplomacy."

On 31 August, at a meeting of employees at the ČSSR embassy in Bern, Foreign Minister Hájek called for "active resistance and an increasing wave of protests against the occupation of Czechoslovakia."

At the beginning of September the rightists launched a provocative campaign demanding compensation for the economic damage caused by the entry of allied troops. In leaflets and illegally published newspapers they asserted that the total damage came to some 4 billion crowns, and the daily damage caused by the "occupation" in Prague alone came to 65 million crowns.

On 1 September the reactionary elements began a campaign to gather signatures calling for a "nationwide referendum" to demand the immediate withdrawal of the "occupying troops," the implementation of the CPCz Action Program, the release of state and party officials of the ČSSR, and compensation for damage from the "occupation."

The illegal radio station "Praha" not only conducted a hostile propaganda campaign, but was also an organizing center responsible for coordinating the activity of rightist forces against the presence of allied troops in the ČSSR.

On 5 September in the Prague cinema "Blaník," a tendentious documentary film was shown about the entry of the allied troops into the ČSSR. The film showed funeral marches commemorating Czechoslovak citizens "who perished during the entry of allied troops." The narrated part of the film was filled with malicious anti-Soviet propaganda characterizing the Soviet troops as "occupiers."

In book stores in Košice, anti-Soviet brochures entitled "Documents on the Occupation of the ČSSR" were on sale. The newspaper *Práce* featured an article about the placing of commemorative plaques honoring the "citizens who tragically perished," and it supported calls by individual reactionary regional committees to build "more worthy monuments in honor of those who perished."

---

[87] A lengthy section entitled "Facts About Provocations and Armed Attacks Against Allied Troops" has been omitted here because it is similar to events covered in Document No. 127.

The Czechoslovak trade representative in Bonn received a directive on 23 August from the ČSSR minister of foreign trade, which instructed all the ČSSR trade representatives abroad to come out actively against the entry of allied troops into the ČSSR.

The CPCz party committee and the trade union committee of the Plzeň factory "Škoda" opposed the contacts established by Soviet officers with the party organization and with workers of the factory. The plenum of the regional CPCz committee in Jihlava adopted a resolution supporting the immediate withdrawal of allied troops. At a plenum of the regional party committee in Kroměříž, a member of the CPCz CC Presidium and chairman of the National Committee of the Southern Moravian province, Neubert, called for "occupiers to be driven out of the country."[88]

Many legal press organs have called in veiled form for Czechoslovak citizens, especially young people, to put up all possible resistance against the Soviet troops. . . .

The CPCz Western Czech provincial committee gave instructions to its regional organizations not to meet Soviet servicemen or to have any contact with them, and the chairman of the collective farm cooperatives recommended not accepting any help from Soviet troops in gathering the harvest. Special representatives of this provincial committee warn the population that it should not establish contacts with servicemen of the USSR. . . .

THE PERSECUTION OF PEOPLE WHO WERE AMICABLY DISPOSED
TOWARD THE USSR OR WHO COOPERATED WITH SOVIET OFFICIALS

The counterrevolutionary forces unleashed terror against people who were committed to the cause of socialism and friendship with the Soviet Union.

On behalf of the CPCz CC, the underground radio issued many calls for anyone who established contacts with the Soviet troops to be regarded as an enemy of the people and to be subject to attack.

The underground radio station "Free Prague" broadcast the license plates of automobiles used by Soviet commanders, with instructions to destroy them and all those inside.

Following these broadcasts, the counterrevolutionaries have been terrorizing anyone who speaks out against them. . . .

A group of three workers at the ČKD factory, who signed a letter published in *Pravda*, appealed to the commander of a battalion of Soviet forces with a request to defend them, since they were threatened with reprisals.

At a meeting of press and television employees on 4 September, a member of the CPCz CC Presidium, Mlynář, said: "We must closely watch the 'time-servers,' who want to lick the boots of the occupiers."

Secret groups consisting of pro-rightist employees are actively operating in the 2nd Directorate of the ČSSR Interior Ministry. They are carrying out work against Soviet officials and Czechoslovak State Security agents who maintain contact with Soviet agents. . . .

At a session of the CPCz CC Presidium on 30 August, the CC Secretary Špaček and the presidium member Mlynář demanded that Biľak, Kolder, and Švestka be removed from the presidium because, as they put it, "only Soviet tanks, not the Czechoslovak people" stand behind the three. Beforehand, Dubček personally tried to persuade them to leave the presidium "voluntarily." According to certain data, surveillance of Kolder and Kapek was arranged to try to gather "compromising information" on them.

On 9 September the CPCz CC Presidium member Šimon, appearing at a meeting of the party *aktiv* at one of the Prague factories, spoke out against contacts between Czechoslovak citizens and Soviet servicemen. Šimon declared that once the Soviet troops have left the ČSSR, there will be an investigation of those who cooperated with the "occupiers."

[88] This refers to Karel Neubert, who, in addition to chairing the National Committee of the Southern Moravian Province, was a member of the CPCz Central Committee in 1968. He was elected to the presidium by the 14th Party Congress.

The counterrevolutionary elements are carrying out raids on the apartments of individuals who have been cooperating with Soviet officials, and they are threatening them and their families with physical reprisals. There was, for example, an attack carried out against the apartment of the Deputy Interior Minister Šalgovič.

On 28 August the secretary of the CPCz's Prague-8 regional committee, Suchý, told a group of old communists, who had refused to issue a protest against the "occupiers," that they were in danger of suffering reprisals from "patriots." On 30 August inscriptions were painted on the sides of the houses of these communists urging reprisals against them.

ON THE TIES BETWEEN THE COUNTERREVOLUTIONARIES IN THE ČSSR AND WESTERN SUBVERSIVE CENTERS

The Western powers are giving direct assistance to the counterrevolutionary elements in the ČSSR in their struggle against the healthy forces in Czechoslovakia and against the allied troops who entered their territory. Available information confirms that the West German government believes it is necessary to set up covert armed "resistance" groups consisting of students, workers, and servicemen. Such groups have already been created in a number of cities around the country, and they include soldiers and officers from the garrisons in České Budějovice and the Třeboň and Krumlov garrisons. The centers of such groups are in the environs of Prague and in the western part of the ČSSR in Kladno, Nimburg, and Mladá Boleslav. Resistance groups have been set up at factories in Plzeň and Strakonice. The FRG, judging from available data, has ties with certain "resistance" groups, provides them with help, and believes that other groups of this sort must be created.

Individual West European countries help the counterrevolutionary elements in the ČSSR with weapons and means of propaganda. Thus, for example, on the eve of the introduction of allied forces into the ČSSR, according to certain information, 500 Austrian policemen in civilian clothes arrived, bringing weapons into the country. Weaponry from Austria also has been brought into the ČSSR on ambulances. . . .

Austrian military intelligence has stepped up the activity of its agents in the ČSSR, especially those in the officer corps of the Czechoslovak army. The agents were given the task of creating underground organizations and carrying out terrorist acts against anyone who "opposes the process of liberalization." . . .

Western powers are giving material assistance to individuals who have come out in support of the counterrevolutionary forces or who have provided them with information about the events in the ČSSR. The U.S. embassy in Rome offered material help to some Czechoslovak diplomats. The leader of the Vienna branch of the Federation of Free Trade Unions, Matal, is meeting citizens of the ČSSR every day and offering financial help to those who will agree to gather information for him about the situation in the ČSSR. Packages and containers regularly flow in from the FRG to the West German representative in Prague without having to undergo any sort of customs inspection.[89]

Some of the counterrevolutionaries, in particular Šik, have broached the idea of creating a Czechoslovak government-in-exile. At the beginning of September, two right-wing representatives traveled to Austria to establish contacts with Šik. These representatives were instructed to inform Šik that he should not act prematurely in forming such a government, since this would compromise the current government in the ČSSR. At the time of his visit to Austria, Hájek expressed the view that it would not be advisable to hurriedly form a government-in-exile. In

---

[89] A two-sentence paragraph at this point in the KGB's original draft was crossed out by Suslov: "A member of the CPCz CC Presidium, Erban, traveled to England to hold negotiations with the leadership of the Labour Party. In connection with this, Hájek sent instructions to the ČSSR Embassy in London to provide Erban all possible assistance in conducting these negotiations."

his words, the socialist countries themselves would come to appreciate the "political disadvantage of maintaining the occupation." In connection with this, he noted the possibility of strengthening the "resistance movement" in the ČSSR, including the use of sabotage and methods of partisan warfare.

Evidence shows that Hájek, while in Switzerland, held consultations with a number of Czechoslovak diplomatic representatives in West European countries about the matter of convening an international conference of officials from communist and workers' parties to discuss the situation in the ČSSR. Hájek, in particular, instructed the Czechoslovak ambassador in Paris to find out the French Communist Party's view of this idea and to enlist its support.

A group of Czechoslovak journalists, who have recently left the ČSSR, created a secret organization with the help of Western intelligence centers to work against the Moscow Agreements. An important role in the group's activities toward this end is being played by the above-mentioned Tigrid. . . .

ON THE ACTIVITIES OF THE COUNTERREVOLUTIONARY FORCES IN THE ARMY

After the introduction of allied troops onto the territory of the country, the Czechoslovak People's Army (CzPA) as a whole preserved its neutrality. There was not a single instance recorded of a clash between Czechoslovak army units and the allied formations. However, the course of events showed that the rightist and counterrevolutionary forces conducted active work aimed at demoralizing the formations of the CzPA both during the presence of the allied troops in the ČSSR and long before their arrival.

The ideological basis of the counterrevolution in the army was the "Memorandum on Czechoslovak Military Doctrine" prepared by a group of military historians at the Gottwald Academy in accordance with the CPCz Action Program. The Memorandum contained a provision about the necessity of "theoretically" considering a version of defense for Czechoslovakia outside the framework of the Warsaw Pact, and also in the system of the other treaty obligations of the ČSSR.

Events confirmed that after the entry of the allied troops, the counterrevolutionary forces in the army began to rely on the political organs, where the rightist forces had succeeded in establishing their hold, thanks to the party organizations directly controlled by them.

After the introduction of allied troops into Czechoslovakia, many instances of anti-Soviet statements and hostile activity were recorded among the party workers and command staff of the army. The heads of the political departments of a number of units of the CzPA carried out anti-Soviet propaganda among the enlisted men. Some of them, upon coming into contact with Soviet officials, said that they were merely carrying out orders and were opposed to this sort of thing. The political officer of one of the aviation regiments of the CzPA said that the Czechoslovak army had "betrayed its nation" by not having offered resistance against the "occupiers," and that it must redeem itself by putting up an active struggle against the Soviet army. He issued instructions to prepare soldiers for partisan warfare. Like-minded officers arrived systematically from Prague to help him work out concrete subversive actions.

On 28 August the head of the political department of one of the CzPA brigades called on the soldiers in his brigade to struggle against the Soviet army, threatening to imprison or shoot anyone who refused to take part in this struggle. The party committees, political departments, and commanders of individual CzPA divisions spoke out against the Moscow negotiations and the Soviet–Czechoslovak communiqué.

In one of these CzPA military formations, deployed in Havlíčkův Brod, a sign was put up saying: "There will be no friendship with the occupiers for time eternal." An officers' meeting in the formation adopted a resolution to give back to the USSR a banner of Bohdan Khmelnitskii, which had been presented by a fraternal Soviet formation. On orders from the commander of one of the military units in Jihlava, several soldiers were interned in the guardhouse on 29 August after they spoke at a political gathering about their meetings with Soviet servicemen. . . .

On 29 August the commander of a Czechoslovak tank regiment deployed in Milovice appeared before his regiment and demonstratively tore a Soviet medal from his chest and threw it into the garbage.

In a number of units and formations of the CzPA in which the counterrevolutionary elements have obtained important military posts, they are ignoring orders and directives from the CzPA Commander-in-Chief and the Minister of National Defense Dzúr regarding the fulfillment of the Moscow Agreement.

The rightist elements in the CzPA, headed by Mencl, Prchlík, and Bižík, sent a group of 3–4 officers on 23 August to the heavy machine-building factory and shipbuilding factory in Prague to establish contacts with the staffs of the People's Militia in these enterprises with the aim of organizing demonstrations calling for the return of President Svoboda from Moscow. They recommended that workers come to the demonstration with weapons and that they use them if Soviet soldiers tried to break up the demonstration.[90]

The activity of the counterrevolutionaries in the army is not limited to anti-socialist and anti-Soviet propaganda. There is a great deal of evidence about attempts to create underground groups and detachments for a possible struggle against the allied forces, and there is also evidence of the direct participation by servicemen and command personnel in counterrevolutionary activities, including their use of army equipment for this purpose.

On 22 August at the Košice Higher Aviation School there was a meeting of officers, which approved a demand to begin an active struggle against the Soviet troops. One of those who spoke said that for this purpose he has caches of weapons, which he will distribute upon receiving a signal about the start of the "uprising." At the end of the meeting, all those present were warned, under the threat of death, not to divulge anything about the resolution adopted at the meeting. That very same day, an appeal from the personnel at the Košice Higher Aviation School to the "Commander of the Occupying Forces in the ČSSR," with a demand for the immediate withdrawal of troops, was circulated among the local population of Košice. The appeal claimed that responsibility for all consequences is borne by the "aggressors." The commanders of the school refused to grant lines of communication for the troops of the Carpathian Military District.

To carry out anti-Soviet broadcasts, the counterrevolutionary forces are actively using radio stations in the civil defense system and other means of communication reserved for military emergencies. To this end, a special device, which was prepared beforehand, is being used to thwart efforts to locate illegal radio stations. The military radio stations of the Ministry of National Defense and the General Staff are directly cooperating with the illegal radio stations to maintain the precise coordination of the activity of these stations.

According to information received here, around the 26th of August all the radar equipment of the Czechoslovak army was temporarily put out of commission so that it could not be used by the allied troops. All of the army's radio broadcasting facilities were temporarily shut down and were equipped with special codes in case efforts were made to reactivate them. Of the 35 radio stations belonging to the ČSSR Ministry of National Defense, which had been transferred by General Prchlík to the disposal of the counterrevolutionaries, 10 were dismantled and transported to the West.

In a number of cases, the counterrevolutionaries received military property to use for their own ends. In an illegal radio center that was uncovered in the populated area of Most, a military radio facility was being used. Regiments were using radio equipment deployed in the populated area of Klecany to bolster the output of low-power transmitters in their illegal radio stations.

It has been established that military communications equipment from some formations of the CzPA has been used by the counterrevolutionaries in operating the "Free Radio" station and in

---

[90] Two paragraphs at this point in the original draft—about the alleged efforts by CzPA officers to avoid any friendly contacts with Soviet troops, for fear of being deemed collaborators—were crossed out by Suslov because, according to a brief handwritten note, they merely repeated a section on page 45 of the draft.

maintaining contacts between Bratislava, and Brno. In the city of Svitavy, hostile radio broadcasts were carried out by tank radio stations of the Czechoslovak army.

On 30 August in the region of Gottwaldov, Soviet specialists discovered and destroyed an underground radio station in one of the watch towers. The towers were being guarded by Czechoslovak servicemen.

Personnel and equipment in formations were also used to publish and distribute anti-Soviet leaflets. . . . On 2 September in the city of Čáslav, leaflets were distributed from a military vehicle belonging to a tank regiment of the Czechoslovak army. These leaflets affirmed that the army "is prepared to struggle against the occupiers," although under current circumstances it is not well-situated to begin this struggle.

The measures recently adopted by the CzPA High Command have not yet resulted in any fundamental changes in the mood of the personnel of the Czechoslovak armed forces.

ON THE SUBVERSIVE ACTIVITY OF COUNTERREVOLUTIONARY ELEMENTS IN THE ČSSR INTERIOR MINISTRY AFTER THE ENTRY OF ALLIED TROOPS

The nature of the activities pursued by counterrevolutionary forces in the ČSSR Interior Ministry attests that Pavel and his supporters had been making the utmost preparations to respond if allied troops were sent to the territory of the ČSSR. Under the direct supervision of Pavel, a special operative plan was worked out to provide for the reorganization of Interior Ministry organs both at the center and on the periphery, to create a network of agents, detachments, and groups at key points, and to provide extra protection for the directors of radio and television as well as literary and artistic figures who had actively supported anti-Soviet positions.

Among the measures provided for in the plan was the maintenance of uninterrupted broadcasts by Czechoslovak radio and an end to the jamming of broadcasts by foreign radio stations, as well as the use of radio equipment, television, and the press for the aims of the counterrevolution.

Certain formations of the Interior Ministry were enlisted to take action against the allied troops. After fleeing underground, Pavel exercised general supervision over these formations via a system of communications officers and by telephone.

Pavel's staff organized the work of a number of illegal radio stations and provided help to the counterrevolutionaries in carrying out subversive work against the allied troops. At Pavel's direct order, street signs were taken down and the numbers on houses were removed. At the instruction of Pavel's staff, the mobilization system and means of civil defense were used against the allied troops.

Available data show that after the allied troops were sent in, CPCz provincial and regional committees and leading organs of State Security and of the police went underground in a number of places, having changed and concealed their new locations and having established secret caches of weapons. . . .

To ensure the uninterrupted activity of the counterrevolution after the allied troops were sent in, the rightists in the party and the operational leadership of the Interior Ministry not only put a complete freeze on the work of certain directorates and departments of the ministry, but also did all they could to remove representatives of the healthy forces from key posts in the State Security organs and to demoralize all those who, to one degree or another, disagreed with the line espoused by Pavel.

Pavel, while still in hiding, issued orders to remove a number of senior officials in the ČSSR Interior Ministry and tried to oversee the activity of all the ministry's organs.

On 31 August in Prague it was announced that Pavel had been removed from his post as ČSSR interior minister and that Jan Pelnář, a former chairman of the National Committee in the Western Czech province, had been appointed to this post.

The situation in the State Security organs of the ČSSR remains complicated. The supporters of Pavel have been left in a legally questionable situation, and some of them are trying to flee abroad. Roughly 50 percent of the operational staff of the directorate are pleased to see Pavel dismissed and are feeling more assured. However, the rightists at the head of the party committee in the Interior Ministry are consolidating their forces and are openly steering the operational staff in an anti-Soviet direction.

A grave situation has also emerged in the People's Militia organs. Eight months of uncontrolled operations by right-revisionist and anti-socialist elements in the organs of the mass media, and the sweeping replacements in the party leadership, have taken a negative toll on the moral spirit and combat readiness of the People's Militia. In a number of places, members of the People's Militia have gone over to support the counterrevolutionary forces and have left radio stations and weapons at their disposal.

The rightist forces are trying to cause the breakup of the People's Militia and to stir up a nationalist psychosis and anti-Soviet sentiments among its members. To this end they are acting through local party organs (regional and provincial committees) that are obedient to them. At a number of enterprises, the secretaries of party committees, who were sponsored in their rise by rightist forces, are trying to seize control of the People's Militia for themselves.[91]

* * *

The anti-socialist elements in Czechoslovakia have recently switched over to even more secretive methods of subversive activity. Without openly opposing the Moscow Agreement, they are stepping up underground activity to disrupt the fulfillment of the obligations flowing from the agreement and to organize "psychological terror" against the healthy forces in the party.

The mass propaganda organs, despite the replacement of certain individuals in the leadership, remain under the control of the rightists, who, as always, are steering public opinion in an anti-Soviet direction.[92]

In items featured in the press, on radio, and on television, the idea that the current "abnormal" situation in the country has been produced by the arrival of allied troops, who supposedly have disrupted the activity of the organs of authority and the work of enterprises, and have caused great damage to the ČSSR economy has been put forward.

The activity of underground radio stations has not ceased. Broadcasts continue to feature attacks against the USSR and the allied armies. Illegal publications are being circulated, as before. On the walls of buildings and in the shopwindows of stores in numerous cities (Košice, Prešov, Bánska Bystrica), lists of "collaborators" are being posted, along with demands for reprisals.

However, despite all the complexity and the contradictory nature of the situation, a process of internal political stabilization has recently gotten under way in Czechoslovakia. Thanks to the consistent Marxist–Leninist position of the leadership of the five socialist countries, public opinion in the ČSSR is becoming more diverse. An increasing number of Czechs and Slovaks are beginning to understand that the entry of allied troops was necessitated by the demands of the struggle against anti-socialist and counterrevolutionary forces and is aimed at helping the Czechoslovak people to normalize the situation in their country. . . .

CHIEF OF THE FIRST MAIN DIRECTORATE
COMMITTEE FOR STATE SECURITY
OF THE USSR COUNCIL OF MINISTERS

A. Sakharovskii

[91] Another paragraph at this point in the original draft—which claimed that no improvements were yet apparent in the state security organs and the People's Militia, despite the ouster of Pavel—was crossed out by Suslov.

[92] A sentence at this point in the draft, reading "The anti-socialist forces are actively exploiting the presence of allied troops in the ČSSR to inflame a nationalist psychosis among the population," was crossed out by Suslov.

DOCUMENT No. 131: Stenographic Account of Soviet–Czechoslovak Negotiations in Moscow, October 3–4, 1968 (Excerpts)

Source: ÚSD, Sb. KV, Z/S 14.

This transcript records the first session in a series of Soviet negotiations with Czechoslovak leaders in early October on a bilateral treaty providing for the "temporary" deployment of Soviet forces on Czechoslovak territory. The Soviets, represented by Brezhnev, Kosygin and Podgorny, wanted a quick agreement to ensure that their troops—now living in unsanitary conditions in Czechoslovakia—would have better quarters and a legal basis for adequate Czechoslovak government support before the winter set in.

The transcript reflects the resignation of Czechoslovak leaders to accept the indefinite presence of some 80,000 Soviet combat troops on their territory, although both Černík and Dubček still hoped they could ensure that such a military occupation would indeed be "temporary." In particular, they made a determined effort to persuade the Soviet delegates to insert a clause in the treaty providing for a bilateral review of the presence of the Soviet forces in the spring of 1969. The Soviet leaders rebuffed such requests. Brezhnev is recorded as declaring: "The crux of the matter is not an agreement on troop withdrawals, but an agreement on the presence of a certain contingent of our forces . . . without any fixed time limit."

A copy of this transcript was turned over to the Czechoslovak commission by the Russian government in the spring of 1992.

(See also Documents Nos. 121, 123.)

Taking part in the negotiations were:

for the Soviet side—Cdes. L. I. Brezhnev, A. N. Kosygin, N. V. Podgorny, K. F. Katushev, and K. V. Rusakov;

for the Czechoslovak side—Cdes. A. Dubček, O. Černík, G. Husák, and J. Šedivý.[93]

L. I. Brezhnev: . . . Let's follow our agenda literally. Let's ask Cdes. Kosygin and Černík to conclude the treaty on troop deployments in the interests of our countries and peoples.[94] We must formulate it in the most desirable way, perhaps by saying that it is essential for the security and defense of the borders. Perhaps by putting it in the same form that was used when corresponding treaties were concluded with Poland and Hungary.

A. N. Kosygin: We have such treaties with the GDR, Poland, and Hungary.[95]

N. V. Podgorny: It would be possible to conclude an agreement with Czechoslovakia along the same lines.

L. I. Brezhnev: We have to find the most appropriate format. The crux of the matter is not an agreement on troop withdrawals, but an agreement on the presence of a certain contingent of forces. We assure you we'll keep our word by withdrawing our troops in stages as normalization progresses.

A. N. Kosygin: It seems to me that, as a practical matter, it could be done this way. We've worked on the draft of a treaty. It was worked out by the defense ministers of our two countries.

---

[93] Presumably, the J. Šedivý listed here was Josef Šedivý, who worked for the CPCz CC Secretariat and was deputy head of the CPCz CC International Department — not Jaroslav Šedivý, a prominent specialist and commentator on foreign affairs, who had been outspoken in his support for far-reaching reform.

[94] It was in fact Kosygin and Černík who signed the treaty on 16 October. See Document No. 133.

[95] The Soviet status-of-forces treaty with the GDR was quite different from the treaties with Poland and Hungary insofar as it allowed the commander-in-chief of the Group of Soviet Forces in Germany to move his troops outside their garrisons without consulting the East German authorities, and empowered him to take a variety of emergency measures at his own discretion.

This document specifies the number of troops that will remain after the withdrawals to ensure the safety of the whole socialist community. And, as Leonid Ilyich proposed, this should be done in the framework of the Warsaw Pact, based on approximately the same conditions as in Poland, Hungary, and the GDR. The areas of deployment will be arranged by the defense ministers. We don't have to arrange that now, we're only signing an agreement in principle. This will settle the matter. We'll sign an agreement, our troops will begin to withdraw from there in the requisite numbers, and the only remaining troops will be ones needed to protect our common security. Of course it might be that these troops would not be numerous enough to protect our security on their own, but the point is that if anyone should touch them, then a completely different situation will arise.[96]

L. I. Brezhnev: There is one more question: in the ČSSR right now there are allied troops from the five socialist countries. There are Poles, Hungarians, and Bulgarians. What troops should be left there? We wanted to discuss that with the allies and also to hear your opinion on this matter.

G. Husák: We thought that only your troops might remain.

L. I. Brezhnev: That must be considered. Perhaps we should call them "allied" troops and then write "Soviet" in brackets.

G. Husák: There are difficulties with the Hungarian troops, because we have a Hungarian population and various disputes are arising.[97]

L. I. Brezhnev: I think we can come to agreement on this problem and leave only our troops, but not to announce that yet. I assume that, in fact, that's how it will be.

O. Černík: Could we sign such an agreement by 15 October?

A. N. Kosygin: I think we could even sign it today if you're ready to, and if not, then we can do so in a week.

O. Černík: One question, Cde. Brezhnev. The proposal about the number of troops, which we gave you, was agreed upon between Cdes. Grechko and Dzúr. It contains the following idea: In the political and military relationship it is clear we are speaking about the presence of troops in Czechoslovakia for an unlimited duration. What is important for us is to bring into harmony the presence of the troops with the numbers of our army.

We had in mind that after we had finished working out programs for the most immediate tasks, including those relating to the Czechoslovak army, we would return to the question of the troop presence next spring. Is it not possible in this agreement to return to the question of the presence of allied troops on Czechoslovak territory next spring?

A. N. Kosygin: The troops remain without any fixed time limit. As concerns the length of their stay, that question will be made clearer next spring. Is that how we are to understand you?

O. Černík: Yes. And now to the temporary stay of these troops. In the spring, questions will be devised by the Czechoslovak army and will be coordinated within the framework of the Warsaw Pact.

[96] Kosygin's intended message appears to be twofold: First, Soviet forces based in Czechoslovakia will serve as a tripwire; that is, any attack against them will provoke retaliation by the whole Soviet army. Second and more important, the size of the Soviet troop contingent will be drastically increased if needed to intimidate—or crush—"right-wing" and "counterrevolutionary" elements in Czechoslovakia.

[97] Ample evidence of this can be found in the CPSU CC and CPCz CC archives. See, for example, "Otdel TsK KPSS tov. Rusakovu K. V.," Cable No. 802 (SECRET) from F. Titov, Soviet ambassador in Hungary, to K. V. Rusakov, September 4, 1968, in TsKhSD, F. 5, Op. 60, D. 339, Ll. 72–73.

N. V. Podgorny: I think this question is clear. It should be written as it is in the agreement with the Poles and Hungarians: temporary stay, without any fixed time limit.

A. N. Kosygin: Leonid Ilyich, I think it would be possible for me to work on this question with Cde. Černík. Then we'll consult in the Politburo and resolve it.

N. V. Podgorny: We'll return to this question when needed.

O. Černík: It must be stipulated that we'll reconsider it in the spring.

A. N. Kosygin: Is there really any need for us to mention the time limit? In the agreements with the Poles and Germans there's no time limit set. In the agreement with the Hungarians it says the troops are deployed temporarily. That could mean a year, two, or three. Such a formulation gives you and us the right to return to this question whenever needed. There's no need to mention the time limit.

O. Černík: I'm not saying we should decide in the spring what the time limit will be for the withdrawal of the troops and the length of their stay—a year, two, or three. However, in present-day conditions the Czechoslovak army faces very definite tasks on a European scale. These tasks were defined under conditions, starting in 1945, when there were no foreign troops on Czechoslovak territory. If you believe that foreign troops must remain on the territory of Czechoslovakia then we must establish for ourselves, from the military point of view, the role of the Czechoslovak army. You, Cde. Brezhnev, mentioned how to solve the question concerning the air force, and other types of troops.

We want to think through the military problems and consult with you on this matter next spring. We therefore want to return to the question about the deployment of troops, not to determine when they will withdraw, but from the standpoint of the Czechoslovak army and of military needs, and to study the situation that will have developed.

A. N. Kosygin: And what is to prevent us from returning to any question in the spring?

O. Černík: If there is agreement on your part that we'll return to it, by all means we'll do so.
. . .

A. Kosygin: Cde. Černík, we guarantee you that if you wish to consider questions on the situation of the troops in the spring, we'll consent to that. After all, you're speaking about the mutual assistance provided by troops to one another, and we still don't know how events will unfold in NATO.

O. Černík: We must exchange letters on this question.

A. N. Kosygin: Let's carefully consider this question and then agree to it. We'll consult with the CPSU CC Politburo, and you with the CPCz CC Presidium. For now, though, let's come to an agreement in principle that in the course of 7 to 10 days we'll devise a solution to this question. We were ready to do this today, but if you don't wish to sign an agreement at this time, then let Cdes. Grechko and Dzúr meet, for preliminary work, in Moscow or in Prague.

L. I. Brezhnev: We accept the suggestion of Cde. Dubček to keep 70,000 to 80,000 troops on the territory of Czechoslovakia.

A. N. Kosygin: That helps us solve the biggest problem.

A. Dubček: So long as you keep in mind that later on it will be necessary to clarify the exact deployment areas and number of troops in all regions and districts. Obviously, we won't need that quantity of troops. That's why Cde. Černík is saying that in the spring we'll have to reconsider this matter.

N. V. Podgorny: The number of troops is determined by a government-to-government agreement, and the deployment sites will be arranged by the defense ministers.

A. Dubček: Perhaps in six months it will turn out that there's no need to have 70,000. Then we could return to this question.

L. I. Brezhnev: We'll instruct Cde. Kosygin and Cde. Černík to conclude an agreement on the presence of a certain number of troops on Czechoslovak territory, and we'll withdraw the other troops in stages. . . . We will not include a provision about reconsideration of this question in the spring of 1969. If we include such a provision, it will merely incite passions the whole time, and anti-socialist elements will exploit it. No good will come of it.

A. N. Kosygin: It won't be included. We'll agree that the troops will remain temporarily, and that's all, as in the other countries. And the examination of separate military questions can be done at any time.

[A break in the proceedings was announced.]

After the break, the talks continued between a smaller group of officials, including Cdes. Brezhnev, Kosygin, Podgorny, Katushev, Dubček, Černík, and Husák. No minutes were taken.[98]

---

[98] This group may have been "smaller," but only slightly so, than the original group. Of the original participants, only Josef Šedivý and Konstantin Rusakov were not listed here.

DOCUMENT No. 132: CIA Intelligence Information Cable, "Comments on the Growth of Disunity within Czech Leadership and Other Aspects of the Current Status of the Soviet Occupation of Czechoslovakia," October 11, 1968

Source: Czechoslovakia—Czech Crisis 8/68, Box 182, National Security File, Country File, Lyndon Baines Johnson Library.

The CIA prepared this information report drawing on intelligence gathered between September 18 and October 4, 1968. The report focuses on the "resignation and pessimism" spreading in Czechoslovakia, as well as the status of Soviet troops.

The first section of the intelligence memorandum reviews the mounting problems Dubček had encountered since his return from Moscow. Within the CPCz, CIA analysts reported, splits were emerging, in part because of Gustáv Husák's steady shift toward a pro-Moscow position. Disunity in the leadership was compounded by the marked rise in public discontent and disillusionment, as word of the Moscow protocol and other secret compromises and reversals filtered out. These trends, the CIA correctly predicted, eventually "may pave the way for the elevation by the Soviet Union of 'collaborators' to the top positions in the party and the government, and to the ultimate establishment of a new 'Soviet-friendly' government."

CIA intelligence also addressed the acute problems facing Soviet military personnel inside Czechoslovakia. These included decrepit barracks, unsanitary living conditions, and spreading disease with the "great danger that severe epidemics may strike."

CENTRAL INTELLIGENCE AGENCY
Intelligence Information Cable

STATE/INR DIA NMCC/MC (SECDEF JCS ARMY NAVY AIR) CIA/NMCC
NIC NSA SOO CNE CRS

[Handwritten:] EXO DO/I

[2 lines excised][99]

THIS IS AN INFORMATION REPORT. *NOT* FINALLY EVALUATED INTELLIGENCE.

[excised]   1117422   CITE [excised]

DIST 11 OCTOBER 1968

COUNTRY: CZECHOSLOVAKIA/USSR

DOI: 18 SEPTEMBER--4 OCTOBER 1968

SUBJECT: COMMENTS ON GROWTH OF DISUNITY WITHIN CZECH LEADERSHIP AND OTHER ASPECTS OF CURRENT STATUS OF SOVIET OCCUPATION OF CZECHOSLOVAKIA [excised]

PADA: [excised]

SOURCE: [block excised]

SUMMARY: [two lines excised]

---

[99] This document was declassified in 1991, with parts 6 and 7 deleted for national security considerations. Other sanitized sections appear to be classification codewords or names of sources.

The cautious optimism which prevailed after Dubček's first return from Moscow has now changed to a hard realistic resignation and pessimism. Soviet psychological warfare has been partially successful as the unity of the Czech leadership has now weakened. This drift towards disunity is accompanied by growing dissatisfaction and lack of sympathy by the Czech people for some of the Czech leaders and policies. [One or two words excised] this trend [Two or three words excised] might pave the way for the establishment of a new pro-Soviet government. [One line excised] Dubček and Smrkovský have considered stepping down from their positions.[100] The Czechs have not given the Soviets any support in their efforts to supply the occupation troops with the exception of sanitation supplies to prevent possible epidemics in the old Czech garrisons the Soviet troops are now moving into. Some sickness is already beginning to spread in the areas where the troops are quartered. *END SUMMARY.*

1. [Four lines excised] The cautious optimism which prevailed after Dubček's first return from Moscow, although not yet turned to depression, has changed to a hard, realistic resignation that the conditions which the Soviets have imposed on Czechoslovakia are harder than ever imagined. [One or two lines excised] the Soviet tactics of applying psychological pressures on the Czech leadership by continually postponing and obscuring any common understanding on "normalization" in order to sow disunity within the Czech leadership has already been partly successful. From prior to the Bratislava, Čierna talks until the middle of September there was complete unity among the Czechoslovakian leadership. This unity has now weakened and the leadership has dissimilar opinions and views on many various questions. The earlier unanimity in the presidium and government meetings has been replaced by meetings which are divisive and almost disorderly with arguments among leaders on all possible matters. This disagreement is accompanied by all possible types of rumors spread and circulated among the upper echelons of the party and government leadership. [One or two words excised] This drift towards disunity is accompanied by a growing dissatisfaction and lack of sympathy and understanding by the Czechoslovakian people for some of the Czech leaders and policies. [One or two words excised] This trend [Half-line excised] may pave the way for the elevation by the Soviet Union of "collaborators" to the top positions in the party and the government, and to the ultimate establishment of a new "Soviet-friendly" government. [One or two words excised] However, [One word excised] there is also a concerted effort by the Czechoslovakian leadership to preserve calm and to place in key positions men with good nerves who have status and prestige among the people and who are friendly to the progressive and liberal aspirations of the present leadership.

2. [One or two words excised] The last Moscow agreement was harder and much less favorable than had been hoped.

3. [One line excised] Dubček and Smrkovský have considered stepping down from their positions. First, they have contemplated that now that there is no possibility to execute the program which they have championed and which they believe is morally right and fully supported by the people, it might be better to leave as a protest against suppression of the program. Second, there is also the suspicion that Soviet tactics may aim at creating a situation in which the Czech people themselves become so tired of the compromising Dubček and Smrkovský that public pressures or even the Czech parliament will ultimately ask Dubček and Smrkovský to step down. In short, Dubček and Smrkovský have considered (and perhaps still do) that it might be preferable to leave at this early date than to postpone the decision until they are forced to leave as the result of Soviet tactics.

4. [Two lines excised] Much of the picture spread by the West regarding internal conditions in Czechoslovakia is false. [One or two words excised] Although Czech foreign policy is now stringently controlled by the Soviet Union, the internal economic reforms initiated by Dubček

[100] Headquarters Comment: This intention has been rumored but officially denied. [Footnote in original.]

continue, although markedly reduced. Also continuing but at a reduced pace, are many other cardinal internal policies of the Dubček regime. Although there is a certain degree of monitoring of the activities of the Czech national and local leaders by the Soviet Union and their incoming experts, it is only noticeable in non-concrete ways; local interference by the Soviet forces has not approached the exaggerated extent alleged by the western press. Tourism, also, functions almost normally. [One or two words excised] However, [one word excised] press freedom which was a reality in Czechoslovakia during the spring and summer, is now completely gone and a stringent censorship has replaced it.

5. [Two or three words excised] Although there is a growing bitterness among the people against the Soviet Union and its policies, there have been little or no provocations against the Soviet occupation forces. However, [One or two words excised] the Czechs have not given the Soviets any aid or support in their efforts to supply the occupation troops. They have not even sold bread to the occupying forces and even their water has to be transported from East Germany and Poland or must be obtained from natural sources. The troops, the number of which is being sharply reduced, are now moving into old Czech garrisons and camps. There is a great danger that severe epidemics may strike the Soviet occupying forces as the sanitary conditions of these old camps are extremely poor. Some sickness is already beginning to spread in the areas in which the troops are quartered because of the poor living conditions. The only supplies which the Czechs have given to the Soviet occupying forces has been chlorine and other sanitation supplies to prevent the spread of disease and epidemics. The Czechs have felt that because there is no agreement regarding aid to the occupation forces, the Soviets will have to supply and support their forces as best they can. Evidently the Soviets have taken this Czech position very hard.

6. [Four lines excised]

7. [Three lines excised]

DOCUMENT No. 133: Bilateral Treaty on the "Temporary Presence of Soviet Forces on Czechoslovak Territory," October 16, 1968

Source: "Dogovor mezhdu pravitel'stvom Soyuza Sovetskikh Sotsialisticheskikh Respublik i pravitel'stvom Chekhoslovatskoi Sotsialisticheskoi Respubliki ob usloviyakh vremennogo prebyvaniya Sovetskikh voisk na territorii Chekhoslovatskoi Sotsialisticheskoi Respubliki," *Pravda* (Moscow), October 19, 1968, p. 1.

This 15-article status-of-forces treaty, signed on October 16, 1968, codified a permanent Soviet military presence in Czechoslovakia. The Soviet–Czechoslovak treaty, like the USSR's earlier treaties with Poland (1956) and Hungary (1957), provided for unlimited duration (see Article 15), and contained no provision for the full withdrawal of the Soviet Union's new "Central Group of Forces." Nor did the treaty specify how many Soviet troops were to remain. Eventually, some five divisions, numbering 80,000 to 100,000 soldiers, stayed, and troops remained on Czechoslovak soil for another 23 years.

Other provisions of the treaty proved onerous for Czechoslovakia. The accord did not require the Soviet commander of the Central Group of Forces to obtain the consent of the host government before moving his troops outside their regular garrisons—providing Moscow with the discretion to order, or threaten to order, troops back into Prague at any time. The treaty also omitted any provision requiring compensation for physical damage caused by Soviet and allied troops during the invasion itself. This was one of the main concerns raised by opponents of the treaty when it came before the ČSSR National Assembly for ratification in October.

From Czechoslovakia's standpoint only three features of the treaty could be considered relatively positive. Article 1 ensured that the troops stationed in Czechoslovakia would be exclusively from the Soviet army, not from any of the East European armies which were to be pulled out "within the shortest possible time." Article 3 made the Soviet Union responsible for most of the costs of stationing the troops, apart from providing housing. And Article 9 gave the Czechoslovak authorities at least some ability to hold Soviet troops accountable for criminal acts.

TREATY

Between the Government of the Union of Soviet Socialist Republics and the Government of the Czechoslovak Socialist Republic on Conditions for the Temporary Presence of Soviet Troops on the Territory of the Czechoslovak Socialist Republic

Being determined to work for the strengthening of friendship and cooperation between the Union of Soviet Socialist Republics and the Czechoslovak Socialist Republic as well as between all countries of the socialist commonwealth, and being determined to work for the defense of the gains of socialism, in accordance with the Declaration of the Bratislava meeting of 3 August 1968;

Proceeding from the commitments adopted by the two sides under the terms of the Treaty on Friendship, Mutual Assistance, and Postwar Cooperation of 12 December 1943, as extended by the protocol of 27 November 1963;

and in accordance with the agreement reached at the Soviet–Czechoslovak negotiations in Moscow on 23–26 August and 3–4 October 1968,

the government of the Union of Soviet Socialist Republics and the government of the Czechoslovak Socialist Republic have decided to conclude this treaty and have agreed on the following:

ARTICLE 1: 1. The government of the Union of Soviet Socialist Republics, acting with the consent of the governments of the Bulgarian People's Republic, the Hungarian People's Republic, the German Democratic Republic, and the Polish People's Republic, and the government of the Czechoslovak Socialist Republic, have agreed that some of the Soviet troops now in the Czechoslovak Socialist Republic will temporarily remain on the territory of the Czechoslovak Socialist Republic with the aim of consolidating defenses against growing revanchist efforts by West German militarist forces.

The other troops of the Union of Soviet Socialist Republics as well as the troops of the Bulgarian People's Republic, the Hungarian People's Republic, the German Democratic Republic and the Polish People's Republic will be withdrawn from Czechoslovak territory in accordance with the documents of the Moscow negotiations of 23–26 August and 3–4 October 1968. The withdrawal of these troops will commence as soon as this treaty is put into force, and will take place in stages within the shortest possible time.

2. The number and locations of the permanent garrisons of Soviet troops remaining temporarily on the territory of the Czechoslovak Socialist Republic will be determined by an agreement between the governments of the Union of Soviet Socialist Republics and the Czechoslovak Socialist Republic.

The Soviet troops who are temporarily stationed on the territory of the Czechoslovak Socialist Republic will remain under Soviet military command.

ARTICLE 2: 1. The temporary deployment of Soviet troops on the territory of the Czechoslovak Socialist Republic does not violate the country's sovereignty. Soviet troops will not interfere in the internal affairs of the Czechoslovak Socialist Republic.[101]

2. Soviet troops and members of their families who are present on the territory of the Czechoslovak Socialist Republic will respect the legislation in force in the Czechoslovak Socialist Republic.

ARTICLE 3: 1. The Soviet side will be responsible for the expenses connected with the maintenance of Soviet troops on the territory of the Czechoslovak Socialist Republic.

2. For the duration of their temporary deployment in the Czechoslovak Socialist Republic, the government of the Czechoslovak Socialist Republic will offer Soviet troops and members of their families barracks and apartments in the barracks, service warehouses and other premises, airfields with permanent buildings and installations, facilities of the state communications network, transport facilities, electricity, and other services.

Military training areas, shooting ranges, and parade grounds will be used jointly with the Czechoslovak People's Army.

The method and conditions governing the use of the above-mentioned facilities as well as of communal, shopping, and other services will be laid out in an agreement between the contracting parties.

ARTICLE 4: Soviet military units, including troops and members of their families, will be permitted to travel to sites at which Soviet troops are deployed in the Czechoslovak Socialist Republic, and from the Czechoslovak Socialist Republic in direct trains and wagons belonging to the Soviet Union as well as by changing from the wagon of one country to the wagon of the other. They also will be permitted to travel in automobiles or by air.

Soviet troops and members of their families will be exempt from passport and visa checks on arrival, during their stay, and when leaving the Czechoslovak Socialist Republic.

Border crossing points and the procedures for crossing the Czechoslovak–Soviet border, as well as the checking method and the types and forms of pertinent documents, will be stipulated by agreement of the contracting parties.

---

[101] In April 1969, the Soviet Union threatened to reintroduce troops on a massive scale unless the Czechoslovak authorities agreed to replace Dubček with Gustáv Husák and make other far-reaching political changes. Despite this clause in the treaty, Soviet pressure demonstrated just how effective the "temporary" Soviet troop presence could be in "interfering in the ČSSR's internal affairs."

ARTICLE 5: The Czechoslovak side agrees that the following may cross the border of the Czechoslovak Socialist Republic without being subject to customs duty and exempt from border checks:

— Soviet troops and anyone serving with them who is traveling as part of the military formations, units, and commands,

— all military loads, including loads destined to secure the commercial and residence requirements of Soviet troops,

— Soviet troops traveling to the Czechoslovak Socialist Republic or from the Czechoslovak Socialist Republic either individually or together with members of their families and with their personal belongings on the basis of documents presented to the customs authorities, authorizing the crossing of the border of the Czechoslovak Socialist Republic.

Property brought by the Soviet side to the Czechoslovak Socialist Republic, military equipment, weapons, and combat installations may be exported to the Union of Soviet Socialist Republics without levying customs duty or other fees.

ARTICLE 6: 1. Commercial amenities and services for members of the Soviet troops and members of their families temporarily deployed on the territory of the ČSSR will be provided by Soviet commercial firms. . . .

ARTICLE 7: The government of the ČSSR will provide the government of the USSR with the quantities of Czechoslovak crowns needed to cover expenses connected with the temporary deployment of Soviet troops on ČSSR territory. . . .

ARTICLE 8: Procedures for payment for services mentioned in Article 3 and for the Czechoslovak crowns to be provided under Article 7 of this treaty will be arranged through a supplementary agreement between the two parties . . .

ARTICLE 9: Jurisdictional questions related to the temporary deployment of Soviet troops on ČSSR territory will be settled as follows: 1. In cases of crimes and misdemeanors committed by anyone serving with Soviet troops or by members of their families on ČSSR territory, Czechoslovak law will apply and the matter will be handled by the Czechoslovak courts, prosecutors' offices, and other Czechoslovak bodies empowered to prosecute criminal offenses. The military prosecutor's office and the military judicial organs of the ČSSR will investigate all criminal acts committed by Soviet servicemen.

2. The provisions of Point 1 of this article will not apply: (a) to crimes or misdemeanors committed by individuals serving with Soviet troops, or by members of their families, exclusively against the Soviet Union or against other individuals serving with Soviet troops or members of their families; and (b) to crimes or misdemeanors committed by individuals serving with Soviet troops in the performance of their duties in areas where the military units are deployed.[102] The exceptions specified in (a) and (b) come within the jurisdiction of Soviet courts, prosecutors' offices, and other legal bodies operating on the basis of Soviet law.

3. Those guilty of committing criminal offenses against Soviet troops temporarily deployed on the territory of the ČSSR or against individuals serving with those troops will bear the same responsibility they would if they had committed criminal offenses against the ČSSR armed forces or persons serving with them.

4. Authorized Soviet and Czechoslovak organs may request one another to exchange or accept jurisdiction in specific cases outlined in Points 1 and 2 of this article. Such requests will be looked upon favorably.

5. Authorized Soviet and Czechoslovak organs will provide legal and other kinds of assistance to one another in the prosecution of criminal offenses specified in Points 1, 2, and 3 of this article.

---

[102] This latter exemption provided a huge loophole if Soviet officials proved unwilling to cooperate.

ARTICLE 10: 1. The government of the USSR agrees to compensate the government of the ČSSR for any material damage done to the Czechoslovak state through actions or negligence on the part of Soviet military units or of anyone serving with them, as well as for damage that might be done by Soviet military units or anyone serving with them while performing their duties, to Czechoslovak citizens, to Czechoslovak institutions, or to citizens of third states. . . .

ARTICLE 11: 1. The government of the ČSSR agrees to compensate the government of the USSR for damage that might be done to property of Soviet military units temporarily deployed on Czechoslovak territory or to individuals serving with Soviet units if the damage results from actions or negligence of Czechoslovak state institutions. . . .

ARTICLE 12: Compensation for the damage specified in Articles 10 and 11 will be paid by the responsible parties no later than three months after a decision has been made by the Representatives for Matters Pertaining to the Temporary Deployment of Soviet Troops in the ČSSR or after a court decision has been reached. . . .

ARTICLE 13: To settle all matters connected with the temporary deployment of Soviet troops in the ČSSR as expediently as possible, the government of the USSR and the government of the ČSSR will designate Representatives for Matters Pertaining to the Temporary Deployment of Soviet Troops in the ČSSR.

ARTICLE 14: In this treaty the phrase "Soviet troops and those serving with them" refers to: (a) servicemen from the Soviet army; and (b) civilians with Soviet citizenship who are employed by Soviet military units temporarily based in Czechoslovakia. . . .

ARTICLE 15: This treaty will be put into force as soon as it is ratified by both sides and will remain in effect for the duration of the temporary deployment of Soviet forces on Czechoslovak territory.

The treaty may be altered with the consent of both parties.

DOCUMENT No. 134: The CPCz Leadership's Assessment of the Treaty on Soviet Troop Deployments, October 1968

Source: TsKhSD, F. 5, Op. 60, D. 19, Ll. 259–282.

This top-secret report was compiled by the Ideological Department of the CPCz Central Committee with assistance from relevant ČSSR government ministries shortly after the bilateral treaty on Soviet forces was signed and ratified.

The report provides the official Czechoslovak perspective on the political, legal, economic, and military aspects of the treaty. The authors claim that the treaty would "eliminate misunderstandings and restore trust in our relations" with the "Five" Warsaw Pact countries and "bring an end to a period in which our relations with the five socialist countries were very unclear, ill-defined, and seriously complicated as a result of the August events." While the report acknowledges that "the duration of the treaty was not definitively established," the writers optimistically insist that the "presence of the [Soviet] troops clearly [will be] only temporary." They also maintain that the Soviet troops in Czechoslovakia "are stationed here for our protection against foreign enemies" and "will not interfere in the internal affairs of the ČSSR." At the same time, however, the report notes that "the treaty establishes definite limits on the exercise of Czechoslovak state sovereignty" and that the Soviet "troops will have a certain influence [on Czechoslovakia's internal affairs] by the very fact of their presence."

The Central Committee intended this report only for internal use; but a copy quickly leaked to the Soviet embassy in Prague. The Soviet ambassador in Czechoslovakia, S. V. Chervonenko, then relayed the document "on a confidential basis" to senior officials in Moscow.

(See also Document No. 121.)

In Regard to the Czechoslovak–Soviet Treaty on the Conditions of the Temporary Presence of Soviet Troops on the Territory of the ČSSR

Contents:

I. Meaning and Contents of the Treaty

II. Juridical, Economic, and Military Aspects of the
   Presence of Soviet Troops

A publication of the CPCz CC Ideological Department
in cooperation with the Ministry of Foreign Affairs, the Ministry
of National Defense, and the Ministry of Finance

October 1968

35635

In Regard to the Czechoslovak–Soviet Treaty on the Conditions for the Temporary Presence of Soviet Troops on the Territory of the ČSSR

I. Meaning and Contents of the Treaty

The entry of troops from the five socialist countries onto the territory of the ČSSR in August of this year has created a new situation for us in terms of our internal development and our relations with these countries. One of the key problems of normalizing both spheres has been the question of the presence of the troops from these countries on our territory.

During the negotiations on the temporary presence of Soviet troops on our territory, the Czechoslovak party tried to accelerate the normalization of our internal life, and to find a means of enabling our partners to resolve the situation that arose in August of this year in a way that would eliminate the misunderstandings and restore trust in our mutual relations. The party took as its premises: first, that the matter at hand concerned troops from countries with which it is bound by common participation in a defense pact; second, that current developments in a divided world demand that we disallow a serious weakening of the forces of socialism and progress; and third, that the permanent foreign policy orientation of the ČSSR toward the development of cooperation among socialist states is of the utmost significance for our future.

The quest for a resolution to the emerging situation is common effort, above all in conjunction with the USSR. This was facilitated by the negotiations at the highest level which took place on 23–26 August and 3–4 October in Moscow, as well as the negotiations between the delegations from the Ministries of National Defense on 16–17 September in Mukachevo.[103] These negotiations were concluded on 8 October, and the treaty was signed on 16 October and ratified on 18 October of this year. The treaty brings to an end a stage in which our relations with the five socialist countries were very unclear, ill-defined, and all the more complicated as a result of the August events. The meaning, number, deployment, and juridical and economic aspects of the status of Soviet troops were precisely defined, and it was determined that the duration of their presence would depend on the general development of the situation in the country. Apart from the significance that the treaty has for the consolidation of life inside the country, one cannot overlook its foreign policy implications as well.

The final text of the treaty, which was worked out on the basis of points acceptable to both sides from the Czechoslovak and Soviet drafts, provides evidence that their positions are no longer far apart in regard to the best means of normalizing relations between the Czechoslovak Socialist Republic and the five socialist countries whose troops were sent onto the territory of the ČSSR. This is attested by the following:

— the action of the five was not further legitimated;

— the juridical basis for defining the nature of the presence of troops from the USSR on the territory of the ČSSR is a bilateral matter for the governments of the ČSSR and the USSR, just as it is for the other socialist countries in which Soviet troops are stationed;

— the treaty in question does not violate the sovereignty of the state, the rights of citizens, and the responsibility of the Czechoslovak constitutional organs except for obligations arising from the treaty;

— only Czechoslovak bodies and institutions, and no others, will be able to exercise jurisdiction over Czechoslovak citizens;

— on the question of the so-called commands, significant concessions were obtained from the Soviet side.[104] The commands will be eliminated in areas where no Soviet troops are deployed, and their role will be limited exclusively to the maintenance of communications between the Soviet troops and the Czechoslovak bodies or institutions for resolving questions that emerge, including, for example, the recovery of damages.

---

[103] See Documents Nos. 116, 117 and 131.

[104] The reference here is to the powerful Soviet *komendatury*, which had been established on August 21. (See, for example, Document No. 119.)

The treaty does not impose any conditions on the ČSSR with regard to the temporary presence of Soviet troops that are not comparable to conditions in treaties on the same matter between the USSR and Poland, Mongolia, and other countries.

The deployment of troops in the ČSSR is justified in the text of the treaty as serving the common interests of all socialist countries to preserve peace and security in Europe and in the whole world.

From the standpoint of international politics and the country's geographical position in Europe, the treaty on the temporary presence of Soviet troops in the ČSSR does not conflict with the efforts of the CPCz and the government to uphold the security of the republic and to do its part in upholding the security of the whole socialist commonwealth. The foundation of these efforts is the strengthening of across-the-board cooperation on the basis of Marxism–Leninism.

Therefore, the October treaty is acceptable to all sides as a means of resolving one of the most important aspects of the situation that emerged in August of this year as a result of the entry of the troops of the five socialist countries onto the territory of the ČSSR. In accordance with the treaty, the majority of foreign troops must be withdrawn from the ČSSR. With regard to the Soviet troops that will be temporarily deployed in our republic, the treaty precisely defines the purpose and conditions of their temporary presence here. Hence, the treaty will be an important means of normalizing both the internal life of the country and our relations with other socialist states. Our constitutional organs ratified the treaty in the firm belief that this is an important step both in the interests of the entire socialist commonwealth and in the interests of a bright future for the Czechoslovak Socialist Republic.

II. Juridical, Economic, and Military Aspects of the Temporary Presence of Soviet Troops on Our Territory

1. With Regard to Sovereignty in Accordance with the 2nd Point of the Treaty

In all instances the principle has been observed whereby, at any historical moment, the concept of state sovereignty is not and cannot be abstractly construed as an absolute and untrammeled right of a state to resolve its own internal affairs. The concept of sovereignty, which is defined under international law as the independence of a specific state and regime from any other sort of regime both in interstate relations and in internal affairs, is a concept that in practice cannot be realized in its absolute form. The limit on sovereignty is determined by the membership of a state in an international community of independent states, in which the sovereign rights of other states and the principles of international law must be respected.

In instances where a state assumes obligations in relation to other states—for example, through the signing of an interstate treaty—it further limits its sovereignty in that particular sphere of activity. Instead of the freedom of action that existed previously, the state is legally obliged to behave in a certain way. In the current stage of development of the world community, every state is encumbered by a multitude of international legal obligations that arise, on the one hand, from international law and, on the other hand, from the treaties that the given state has signed for its own purposes with other states.

The treaty between the government of the ČSSR and the government of the USSR on the conditions of the temporary presence of Soviet troops on the territory of the ČSSR is an agreed document in which the ČSSR extends certain powers to the USSR with the aim of temporarily stationing Soviet troops in selected areas.

The ČSSR extends to the USSR the following powers on Czechoslovak territory:

1. The deployment of Soviet troops at sites reserved for them and the withdrawal of these troops from Czechoslovakia.

2. Access to deployment sites for permanent garrisons, that is, the right of transit and overflight.

3. The use of military facilities and weaponry in sites for the deployment of garrisons, as agreed.

4. Exercises at military training sites.

5. The use of military hardware, as for example, at depots and other sites, etc.

6. The limit of judicial immunity for crimes and misdeeds committed by Soviet troops against one another or against the Soviet Union, and also for the performance of service obligations in deployment sites for permanent garrisons.

The treaty establishes definite limits on the exercise of Czechoslovak state sovereignty, but the extent of those limits is precisely defined by the treaty. Article 2 indirectly stipulates that apart from obligations which the ČSSR has assumed under the given treaty, there are not and cannot be any sort of other limits on the exercise of Czechoslovak state sovereignty connected with the temporary presence of Soviet troops on Czechoslovak territory.

Moreover, Article 2 specifically says that the troops and other people to whom it applies will not interfere in the internal affairs of the ČSSR and will be subject to the existing legal code in Czechoslovakia.

Similar formulations of this matter are included in the treaties that the government of the USSR concluded with the Polish government on 17 December 1956, with the Hungarian government on 25 May 1957, and with the GDR government on 12 March 1957 in regard to the temporary presence of Soviet troops on the territory of these states.[105]

2. On the Question of Jurisdiction (Article 9)

Article 9 stipulates matters of jurisdiction connected with the temporary presence of Soviet troops on the territory of the ČSSR. The basic principle of this article is that the Czechoslovak legal code is the only one in force on the territory of the ČSSR.

The provisions here are generally similar to provisions in the treaties concluded for the same purpose between the government of the USSR and the governments of Poland, Hungary, and the GDR.

In accordance with this article, Czechoslovak courts, procuracies, and other organs of the ČSSR—for example, the national committees and Public Security Organs—will operate on the basis of Czechoslovak laws in treating crimes and misdeeds committed on the territory of the ČSSR by Soviet troops. This also applies to the criminal responsibility of Soviet civilian workers stationed with the Soviet troops and to all family members accompanying the Soviet troops.

Two exceptions to this general principle of the subordination of Soviet troops to the Czechoslovak criminal code were stipulated: first, with respect to crimes or misdeeds committed by Soviet troops or members of their families against the Soviet Union or against other Soviet troops or members of their families; and second, with respect to crimes or misdeeds committed by Soviet troops in the fulfillment of their service obligations in deployment sites for permanent garrisons of military formations.

Such cases will be within the competence of Soviet organs, and will be treated under the Soviet criminal code. It is envisaged under the Treaty that in such cases, competent Czechoslovak or Soviet organs might turn to one another with a request for the transfer or assumption of jurisdiction. Such requests must be considered in good faith by both sides, so that the side which is making the request is obliged, on examination, to take full account of the basic interests of the other side in the exercise or transfer of jurisdiction in a particular instance. However, the nature of the particular case is what will determine the resolution of the matter.

The treaty emphasizes the legal accountability of Czechoslovak citizens for acts committed against Soviet troops or members of their families. The extent of accountability in these cases will be equivalent to the accountability for acts committed by our citizens against the Czecho-

---

[105] For texts of these earlier treaties, see Boris Meissner, ed., *Der Warschauer Pakt: Dokumentensammlung* (Köln: Verlag Wissenschaft und Politik, 1962).

slovak armed forces and soldiers. The crimes of our citizens will be treated in accordance with existing Czechoslovak laws and handled by Czechoslovak organs.

In cases when crimes and misdeeds are prosecuted, the appropriate Czechoslovak and Soviet organs will provide all possible help, including administrative power. Both parties to the treaty are working out a treaty about mutual legal assistance in cases connected with the temporary presence of Soviet troops on the territory of the ČSSR.

3. The Question of Empowerment (Article 13)

In accordance with this article, each party to the treaty will designate its own representative. The representative will be a special government organ with broad legal competence. The representatives will take up contentious matters and resolve all differences and disputes that might arise in connection with the temporary presence of Soviet troops on the territory of Czechoslovakia.

Besides this common specification of representatives, Article 10 and Article 11 provide for certain concrete tasks. In accordance with Article 10, the representatives must determine the amount of compensation for claims that might be filed by the Czechoslovak state, by Czecho-slovak citizens, or by institutions and citizens of a third country, or for claims arising from the negligence of Soviet troops or of persons affiliated with them. In accordance with Article 11, the representatives must determine the amount of compensation for damage inflicted on the property of Soviet troops by the actions or negligence of Czechoslovak state institutions. The amount of compensation for damage caused will be determined on the basis of claims filed by the party suffering the damage or by provisions of the Czechoslovak criminal code.

In both of the above-mentioned cases, the representatives will also resolve all disputes that might arise. In arriving at their decisions, they also will be obliged to adhere to the Czechoslovak criminal code.

In fulfilling their obligations, the representatives of both parties to the treaty will work, on the one hand, independently of one another and, on the other hand, through mutual help and consultation. In so doing, they will be fully subordinated to the governments of their respective states. To fulfill the obligations entrusted to them, the representatives must have an appropriate staff of qualified officials and specialists, including experts and advisers for the fulfillment of the tasks assigned to them.

If, during the consideration of particular problems and questions, the representatives are either unable to come to an agreed resolution of possible disputes or are unable to achieve a common point of view, such disputes or questions will be handled thereafter by diplomatic means, and the resolution will be left to the two governments that signed the Treaty.

4. Article 14—Interpretation of Concepts

Point 1 of Article 14 defines "Soviet troops" as consisting of soldiers of the Soviet army and civilians who are Soviet citizens performing certain functions in support of the Soviet troops. Point 2 of this article says that members of the families of these individuals include their wives, unmarried children, and other close relatives who are dependent on them.

All the above-mentioned individuals will be provided with appropriate documents. The documents will be supplied to them by the Soviet side, and the quality and means of regulating these documents by the appropriate Czechoslovak departments will be specified in supplemen-tary agreements between the two sides. In cases when doubts arise about the status of a particular individual, either as a soldier from the Soviet army or as a civilian performing services for Soviet troops, this question will be handled by the representatives that have been designated by both sides under Article 13 to resolve all contentious matters stemming from the temporary presence of Soviet troops on the territory of the ČSSR.

Point 3 of Article 14 defines the concept of "a site of permanent deployment" as a territory assigned to Soviet troops by the appropriate Czechoslovak organs, and also as a territory where these troops are temporarily deployed. Concretely, this covers barracks, exercise fields, test sites, and firing ranges.

The number and location of permanent contingents of Soviet troops temporarily located on the territory of Czechoslovakia are set out in a special agreement concluded between the two sides.

The sites of permanent deployment are subordinated to the principle of Czechoslovak state sovereignty, the observance of which comes within the competence of the appropriate organs of governmental authority on the territory in question—that is, the local national committees or the military districts that possess the same powers.

5. Article 15—Enforcement of the Treaty

Article 15 stipulates that the treaty comes into force after its ratification by both sides. According to the intra-governmental statutes in Czechoslovakia, the nature of the treaty required the National Assembly to give its consent before the treaty could be ratified by the president of the Republic.

The treaty was approved by the National Assembly on 18 October 1968. Of the 242 deputies in attendance, 228 voted in favor.[106] On that same day the treaty was ratified by the president of the republic, and an exchange of notes occurred via the Foreign Ministry whereby the ČSSR and USSR informed one another that the appropriate constitutional bodies of the two sides had approved and ratified the treaty. The treaty came into force on 18 October 1968.

The duration of the treaty was not definitively established. Article 15 only says that the treaty will remain in force "so long as Soviet troops are temporarily located on the territory of the ČSSR." International law provides for the annulment of such a treaty if both sides agree. The same applies to changes that might be made in the treaty.

The treaties that the government of the USSR concluded with the governments of Poland, Hungary, and the GDR on the temporary presence of Soviet troops do not set a specific duration either.

Regarding the review of this treaty, the National Assembly stipulated that the implementation of it will be reviewed at a suitable time, and also recommended that the government consider, in conjunction with the Soviet side, the following possible steps to clarify the effective duration of this treaty.[107]

In the text of the treaty itself, there is no provision for the possibility of holding negotiations about its extension, or about possible changes to be made at the initiative of one side or the other.

6. Economic Matters

The main problem of economic questions is the means of compensation for all the goods and services provided by the Czechoslovak side to units of the Soviet army that are temporarily deployed on the territory of the ČSSR. Both sides start from the basic premise that all damage connected with the temporary presence of the troops will be borne by the Soviet side, which will compensate Czechoslovakia for all damages (including payment for amortization of military facilities, etc.) in accordance with means to be specified beforehand. However, it would be necessary to review the approach of the Czechoslovak side to the magnitude of goods provided and also the magnitude of other types of services that are not directly tied to the military facilities and sites provided. It will also be necessary to review the types of services and the means of paying for them.

---

[106] Four deputies voted against the treaty, and ten abstained. Sixty deputies declined to show up for the vote.
[107] The steps are not further specified here.

After agreement was reached on a suitable means of resolving certain economic questions, Article 8 was approved, which says that the means of paying for services (for example, apartment rent, laundry, transportation, and so forth) specified in Art. 8 will be calculated in Czechoslovak crowns in accordance with Art. 7 and will be finally established in a supplementary agreement to be concluded within a month-and-a-half of the coming into force of the treaty. The recalculation of stipulated amounts of Czechoslovak crowns into convertible rubles will be based on the corresponding internal prices in the Czechoslovak Socialist Republic, and also on the basis of so-called contract prices in foreign trade averaged over a period of, say, 5 years, which have derived from prices on the world market.[108]

The Soviet side, in specifying its proposals, cited the concrete documents and practices already established to resolve similar problems with other socialist countries in which Soviet troops are temporarily stationed.

It is necessary to mention the following basic economic problems contained in the treaty between the government of the Union of Soviet Socialist Republics and the government of the Czechoslovak Socialist Republic establishing the conditions for the temporary presence of Soviet troops on the territory of the Czechoslovak Socialist Republic:

During the period of their temporary presence in Czechoslovakia, Soviet soldiers serving with the Soviet army and the members of their families will be furnished with barracks and living quarters on the territory of the barracks, service facilities, depots, and other facilities, airfields with stationary buildings, equipment, a state communications network, means of transport, electricity, etc. The payment for these facilities and tariffs, and the cost of providing services, must be provided by the Soviet army on the basis of accounting procedures existing in the ČSSR. However, it is recommended that the means and conditions of the use of facilities, including jointly operated ones, and of trade and other services be established by supplementary agreements.

For example, supplies of meat, vegetables, coal, electricity, and other goods to the Soviet Union will be carried out on the basis of contracts concluded between Soviet and Czechoslovak foreign trade organizations. These deliveries will be carried out on the basis of prices established by trade agreements between Czechoslovakia and the Soviet Union. These prices, in turn, are based on prices existing on the world market and on mutually beneficial arrangements. A list of goods will be defined, and they will be supplied in quantities that the Czechoslovak side is able and willing to provide. Goods that the ČSSR is not able to provide will be brought in directly from the USSR.

Soviet trade enterprises will supply goods and services for soliders of the Soviet army and members of their families. For these trade organizations, the Czechoslovak side will provide consumer goods in quantities to be decided in due course by the corresponding trade organizations of the USSR and ČSSR. The retail prices prevailing in the ČSSR will be used for these goods to calculate the extra trade charge (i.e., trade expenditures used by the Czechoslovak side will vary depending on the types of goods). The calculations for these deliveries will be done in Czechoslovak crowns. A provision for these deliveries will be in force, according to which the Czechoslovak side must carry out deliveries only if they correspond with the physical capabilities of the Czechoslovak economy.

It is recommended that in summing up the expenditures connected with the temporary presence of Soviet troops, the Soviet side will have an open account in Czechoslovak crowns. The volume of subsidies needed for this account will be determined by an agreement between the appropriate organs of the two sides.

In this connection it is necessary to mention that the Czechoslovak side officially informed the Soviet side that during the negotiations on the means of compensation for Czechoslovak

[108] The "convertible ruble" was an accounting unit (not a real currency) used for intra-CMEA trade. Despite its name, the convertible ruble was not convertible even within the Eastern bloc, much less outside it. From Czechoslovakia's perspective, it would be advantageous to have accounts settled in *koruny* (crowns).

deliveries—negotiations that must result in the conclusion of a special agreement within a month-and-a-half in accordance with Art. 8—the following provisions will be carried out:

Payment for all goods and services provided by the Czechoslovak side in connection with the temporary presence of Soviet troops on our territory will take place using a special means of accounting and compensation by supplies of Soviet goods at a level established by the protocol on the Exchange of Goods. The Czechoslovak side explained that it, in turn, hopes that these special economic relations will facilitate an expansion, and not a diminution, of the exchange of goods that would have occurred if the mutual supplies of goods and services had simply corresponded with traditional Czechoslovak export practices.

The question also remains open of where precisely the Czechoslovak crowns will come from that the Soviet side will need to pay for its debt. The Czechoslovak side officially announced that it will insist that this debt was specially established on the basis of Art. 7 during the negotiations. The Czechoslovak side argued this was so because of the difficulty of the situation on the internal market and the difficulties of balancing the incomes and expenditures of the population. The Soviet side announced that it could go along with such an approach, but that it wanted to review the Czechoslovak proposal before the start of bilateral negotiations.

During the negotiations, mutual consultation took place on the question of payments by the Soviet side until an agreement is reached to convert payments into payments in rubles in accordance with Art. 8 of the Treaty. They mutually agreed that after the signing of an agreement in accordance with Art. 8 of the Treaty, the balance will be swiftly compensated in accordance with the provisions of this new agreement.

7. Military Aspects

When discussing the tasks of the Soviet troops temporarily deployed on our territory and their influence on our economic and social life, it is necessary to begin with the provision of Art. 2, which stipulates that these troops will not interfere in the internal affairs of the ČSSR. From this it follows that they are stationed here for our *protection against foreign enemies* and thereby strengthen the defense of our country. The basis of our defense, however, remains the CzPA.

The established number of troops to be deployed also corresponds to this. If we bear in mind that they will be stationed in northern and northwestern Bohemia, in northern Moravia, and in central and southern Slovakia, we can see that their deployment is a veritable copy of the border between the socialist and capitalist states over a distance of 150–200 kilometers from these borders. This provides a second line of troops of the Warsaw Pact, which continues northward on the territory of the GDR, in several directions into Poland, and southward onto the territory of Hungary. It thus strengthens the common defense on this territory.

Thus, the troops will fill the gap on our territory that previously existed in this system, and will strengthen the operational routes on the territory of this country. In case an active defense is needed, they will bolster the striking power of the CzPA against a potential opponent.

With regard to deployment, the principle has been observed whereby Soviet troops will be presented, in return for payment, only barracks, depots, airfields, etc. In general, military training facilities will be used jointly with the CzPA.

Soviet air forces and air defense forces based on our territory strengthen our strategic air defense and increase the effectiveness of a retaliatory strike against violators of our airspace and against air attack. In so doing, naturally, they protect not only our country, but also the territory of other Warsaw Pact states.

The total number of Soviet troops, which comes to only about 1/3 of the size our own army, is appropriate for the main tasks just cited. This situation also shows that what is at issue is not any influence on the internal political development of the ČSSR, even though these troops will have a certain influence by the very fact of their presence.

However, the influence they will have is primarily non-political in nature—for example, the use of the transport and communications networks, of buildings, of means of communication, of training sites, and so forth, not to mention various types of communal services: the use of laundries, bakeries, and household utilities. All such services, of course, will be paid for in accordance with Article 3, Point 1 of the Treaty.

Although the majority of questions connected with the presence of troops will be decided by the military organs of the two sides, one cannot exclude the possibility that certain matters will also be considered by the appropriate national committees, which are receiving (or have partially received) necessary instructions by conventional means.

From the standpoint of the task set for the presence of Soviet troops on our territory, one must touch on the matter of relations with these troops. It is desirable that these relations be correct as one would expect of an alliance which provides for the equality of the two sides and respect for each other's interests. It is also necessary that they seek to resolve points of dispute in an amicable way, as provided for by the treaty.

As concerns the clearly temporary nature of the presence of the troops, it is essential to point out that this is necessitated by the current military-political situation in Europe and its development, which is unlikely to undergo any fundamental changes in the near future. It is also worth noting that the concept of the "temporary" deployment will depend in part on the capacity of the Czechoslovak People's Army to carry out its task of defending its territory with military force on a scale sufficient to overcome a potential adversary.

We thus come to the second part of the military aspects of the treaty, that is, *to the role, significance, and status of the Czechoslovak People's Army in the light of the new situation.*

The Czechoslovak Prime Minister Cde. Černík, in his speech before the National Assembly on 13 October 1968, said that "the Czechoslovak People's Army under present conditions remains a vital, indispensable component of the troops of the Warsaw Pact, and is prepared at any time to fulfill its internationalist obligations in defense of socialism. But now, its missions must be carried out in more complicated circumstances." This aptly defines the essence of the matter.

In the future, our army will continue to fulfill its basic task of coalition defense in the first strategic echelon of the Warsaw Pact against a possible ground and air attack from the West.[109]

The above-mentioned deployment of Soviet troops on our territory shows that the main task of the Czechoslovak People's Army is the direct defense of our western borders, that is, the 356-km border with the FRG, and the defense of our 578-km border with the neutral Austrian Republic. This task is well within the strength and capability of our army based on contemporary surveys of military prowess.

The task of defending the airspace of the ČSSR also arises, and this applies as well to the prevention of airborne incursions into the territory of the remaining socialist states. This mission exceeds the capabilities of the ČSSR and can be accomplished only within the framework of the unified system of air defense of the Warsaw Pact states.[110] This is evident from the enemy's capabilities in the airspace of Europe and from an analysis of the means of possible air attack. An important role in this regard also belongs to the air defense units of the Soviet troops on our territory.

The third important mission of the Czechoslovak People's Army is the defense of its territory against hostile landings and incursions stemming from various types of enemy operations on the

---

[109] Contrary to this statement, the CzPA was of little military use after 1968 because of the widespread demoralization caused by the invasion. The once-impressive Czechoslovak armed forces were no longer even assigned to first-echelon roles in Warsaw Pact strategy.

[110] On the Warsaw Pact's air defense system, see Mark Kramer, "Air Defense Forces," in George M. Mellinger, ed., *Soviet Armed Forces Review Annual*, Vol. 12: 1988–89 (Gulf Breeze, FL: Academic International Press, 1992), pp. 124–126; and Mark Kramer, "Air Defense Forces," in David R. Jones, ed. *Soviet Armed Forces Review Annual*, vol. 11: 1987–88 (Gulf Breeze, FL: Academic International Press, 1988), pp. 128–129.

whole territory of the state. It should be noted that the fulfillment of these missions is fully within the strength and capabilities of our army in conjunction with the other departments of state administration, although it is impossible to exclude the possibility that allied troops on our territory might assist in the fulfillment of these missions. Such assistance, of course, should be counted on only in emergency situations and would require action at the governmental level.

This means that the primary missions of the Czechoslovak People's Army remain essentially unchanged, even though they must now be accomplished under most complicated circumstances.

These circumstances arise above all from the limited quantity of living quarters as a result of the transfer of a number of barracks, facilities, and airfields to Soviet troops for their use.

The situation of living space in the Czechoslovak People's Army, even if extraordinary measures are taken, is not an easy one. Capital construction has lagged, and our public knows that the CzPA is still generally relying on the old barracks left over not only from the first republic, but also from the time of the Austro-Hungarian Empire. The CzPA was even forced to make do with certain fortresses and castles armed in the previous century.

If one takes account of the fact that the Soviet troops have been supplied with up to one-seventh of the total living quarters, it will be impossible to avoid certain measures that would help rectify the situation.

The latest period in the CzPA was marked by a redeployment of a significant number of garrisons and units. This redeployment was essentially carried out from 20 September until 15 October. The goal was to free up garrisons and other sites for Soviet troops on the basis of an agreement signed by the defense ministers of the two sides as well as on the basis of the negotiations in Moscow on 3–4 October. The redeployment took the form of a broad shift from Bohemia and Moravia to Slovakia, and the problems connected with it will be resolved in due course.

The results have been most noticeable in the apartment conditions and family situation of newly reenlisted personnel. Our public must understand that the army is the state institution that bears the heaviest burden of the newly emerging situation, and has the right to count on the public's assistance and understanding in the resolution of complex problems.

Morale under the new circumstances has inevitably declined a certain amount as a result of difficulties stemming from the redeployment, which will diminish over time.

In conclusion one can say that the CzPA, despite all the difficulties connected with the complex situation of recent weeks, is able to accomplish the missions assigned to it in accordance with the demands and interests of the state. Also, with the help of party and state organs, it can quickly achieve full combat readiness. Hence, it will facilitate the complete normalization of the situation in our state and remain one of the basic elements in the sovereignty of our state.

* * *

This material only explains the basic aspects of the entire Czechoslovak–Soviet treaty on the circumstances of the temporary deployment of Soviet troops on our territory. Certain financial and economic matters are not yet resolved. We will inform you about them later. Through internal party channels, we will also seek to respond to questions that arise among our public in connection with these questions.

DOCUMENT No. 135: The Soviet Politburo's Assessment of the Lessons of Operation "Danube" and the Tasks Ahead, November 16, 1968

Source: TsKhSD, F. 5 "OP," Op. 6, D. 776, Ll. 128–144.

At Brezhnev's instruction, this document was prepared three months after the invasion. It is considered an authoritative statement of the Soviet leadership's views on the invasion itself and the initial difficulties in accomplishing the Kremlin's goals in Czechoslovakia.

The assessment acknowledges that the political side of Operation "Danube" had been "extremely unsatisfactory." The authors attribute the surge of popular opposition to the invasion to "our failure to carry out propaganda"—underscoring the limits of Moscow's understanding of the widespread popularity of the Prague Spring. It does reflect, however, the Soviet leaders' awareness of the "difficult" and "protracted" process of reestablishing an orthodox pro-Soviet regime. Recommendations include "full-scale purges" in the CPCz leadership and in the ČSSR Interior Ministry and an effort to "topple Dubček and put an end to him as a viable political figure."

The report criticizes Soviet covert activities in Czechoslovakia in 1968, especially the KGB's failure to carry out more extensive penetration of the "counterrevolutionary underground." Policy recommendations at the end of the document include the suggestion that the Soviet Union "exploit the presence of [its] troops in Czechoslovakia" to "establish 10–12 powerful, clandestine intelligence centers at key points around the country." In addition, the authors criticize "the current [public relations] line of non-interference"—as stated in the Brezhnev doctrine among other statements by Soviet leaders—noting that "the dispatch of troops is the most extreme act of interference there can possibly be in the internal affairs of a state." In contrast to propaganda claims that "our troops will not interfere in the internal affairs of Czechoslovakia," the authors recommend "the most decisive interference in the affairs of Czechoslovakia and the exertion of pressure through all channels."

(See also Documents Nos. 109, 126, 128.)

SPECIAL DOSSIER

For oral presentation

STRICTLY SECRET
ONLY COPY

CPSU CC
3349
16 Nov. 1968

Must be returned to the
CPSU CC General Department

*Some Remarks Concerning Preparations for
the Military-Political Action of 21 August 1968*[111]

The decision by the CPSU Central Committee and the Soviet government to send allied forces into Czechoslovakia was wise, courageous, and timely. All recent events have shown that this step was the only way to prevent the restoration of capitalism in that country.

At the current stage of historical development, world reactionary forces are placing their main emphasis on the struggle against the socialist states, on the "peaceful" demolition of those states from inside. For this reason, the Soviet Armed Forces, in faithfully carrying out their interna-

---

[111] The actual authorship of this document remains unclear. Archival annotations indicate that the final recipient of the report was Brezhnev himself.

tionalist duty, were required to use force on three occasions to suppress counterrevolutions in fraternal socialist countries (in 1953 in the GDR, in 1956 in Hungary, and in 1968 in Czechoslovakia). It would be a profound mistake to suggest that after suffering a defeat in Czechoslovakia, imperialism has given up its insidious attempts to turn the course of events in the socialist countries to its advantage, using the same means that it employed in the GDR, Hungary, and Czechoslovakia. On the contrary, the intensification of the general crisis of capitalism means that such attempts will be made even more often, and they undoubtedly will be of an even more treacherous nature. Capitalism will not relinquish its positions without a struggle.

From this it follows that we must draw the necessary lessons for the future from the Czechoslovak events. What exactly are these lessons?

Propaganda Support of the Military-Political Action

With respect to propaganda, the preparations for sending allied troops into Czechoslovakia were extremely unsatisfactory. During the first week that our troops were present in the country, no active attempts were made to organize a broad counterpropaganda campaign against the fierce, skillful, and well-prepared propaganda of the anti-socialist forces. In principle, during the conduct of military-political actions like the one carried out on 21.8.1968, the work of the propaganda apparatus must drown out the roar of tank tracks. But during the August events, Soviet tanks moved forward amidst complete propaganda silence. A propaganda vacuum of sorts existed, thus providing maximum benefit to the counterrevolutionary forces.

It would have been appropriate to prepare, in a timely manner, many hundreds of thousands of leaflets in Czech, which would have explained to the population the nature of the measures undertaken. These leaflets should have been disseminated at the same time that our troops were advancing. However, this was not done. The first leaflet was not prepared until the fifth day that our troops were present in the country. Without question, it would have been advisable to have Soviet newspapers (*Pravda, Izvestiya, Sovetskaya Rossiya, Krasnaya zvezda*, and others) published in Czech at this time and widely disseminated around the country. It was necessary to take immediate control of the editorial boards of the major Czech newspapers and, from the very outset, to organize their publication under our direct supervision. However, this, too, was not done. All the editorial boards of the Czech newspapers went underground and remained a faithful weapon of the anti-socialist forces.

The same holds true about propaganda on radio. There was ample opportunity to organize the work of all the Czech radio stations, but the necessary personnel for this task had not been prepared. No programs were prepared for transmission over the radio. Only a single radio station, "Vltava," carried radio broadcasts in garbled Czech, and these were of very poor quality. Moreover, the station was successfully eclipsed by the more powerful Western radio stations. The television center was not used for propaganda purposes. It was completely paralyzed. At the same time, the rightist forces were able to organize television broadcasts through underground television transmitters. Radio broadcasting centers in all cities were in the hands of the rightists, and they used these for the widest dissemination of mass counterrevolutionary propaganda. Moreover, they encountered no difficulty at all in seizing the radio broadcasting centers. Thus, at the most critical moment of the situation, the rightist forces were the only ones fighting to win the hearts and minds of the Czechs, and they accomplished a great deal. It was precisely during the first week of our troop presence in Czechoslovakia that a frenzied process was underway to sway the consciousness of the Czechoslovak population. If, at the moment that our troops entered, we were able to count on the support and understanding of roughly 50–60 percent of the population, then by the end of the first week, as a result of our failure to carry out propaganda, this ratio had changed sharply to our disadvantage. Some 75–90 percent of the population, having been terrorized and demoralized by the counterrevolutionary propaganda, began to regard the entry of Soviet troops as an act of occupation. The lack of active propaganda work meant that the healthy forces began to behave diffidently and were reluctant to cooperate with us.[112]

The conduct of special military-political actions requires that, in addition to working out the military side of things, a more detailed plan be devised for propaganda measures, and that a strategy of propaganda support for military efforts be prepared, down to the smallest details. To this end, we must be sure to organize actions that could be broadly used for propaganda purposes. Nothing of this sort was provided for.

Diplomatic Support for the Operation. It was necessary to take measures to ensure that the question of the events in Czechoslovakia would not be brought before a session of the United Nations Security Council. This could only have occurred if the Minister of Foreign Affairs of Czechoslovakia Hájek had given the appropriate order to the Czechoslovak representative at the UN. Consequently, it was necessary to provide for the swift occupation of the Ministry of Foreign Affairs and to compel them to transmit the appropriate orders not only to the Czechoslovak representative at the UN, but to all the Czechoslovak embassies abroad. If the embassies abroad had properly informed their host governments about the events in Czechoslovakia from the very start, it would have been possible to forestall a significant number of anti-Soviet gestures and statements by bourgeois state officials in connection with the events in Czechoslovakia.

We should not have permitted Foreign Minister Hájek to be outside the country when our troops entered Czechoslovakia. There was ample opportunity to ensure that all members of the Czechoslovak government would be in Prague at that time. This would have deprived the counterrevolutionaries of the opportunity to form a government-in-exile.

Shortcomings in the Troops' Operations. In the military sphere, the operation to send our forces into Czechoslovakia was carried out flawlessly. The army displayed a high level of combat readiness and superb professional skill. However, it was hardly justified to "unleash a string of armored tanks" on the streets of Prague, Brno, Bratislava, and other cities. The streets and squares of these cities were clogged with tanks, armored personnel carriers, and artillery. This was detrimental in every respect: For one thing, it disrupted the normal rhythm of life; second, such a blatant demonstration of force had a negative effect on the patriotic sentiments of the citizenry (it's one thing when the population sees troops from morning to night, and quite another when they only hear them); and third, the idle equipment deployed on the streets proved vulnerable to subversive actions. If the situation had deteriorated into an open, armed confrontation, we would have suffered huge losses of equipment because of the way we had deployed our forces.[113] It follows that troops should be deployed at key points in the country, but not necessarily on the streets of cities.

Special Measures in Support of the Military-Political Action. Our special services carried out an enormous amount of work in Czechoslovakia, for which they deserve the highest credit. Without question, they succeeded in carrying out the tasks they were assigned. However, the following points should be noted.

The work in establishing appropriate operational positions in Czechoslovakia was begun late. This clearly limited our opportunities. The counterrevolutionaries decided as early as March to prepare for a transition to underground activity, but we did nothing to infiltrate this underground in a timely manner. As a result, we came up against an unusually well-organized network of underground resistance in the country; and if the situation had deteriorated into an armed struggle, our army and special organs would have found themselves in an extremely difficult plight. The timely organization of an underground on the scale of the entire state and at the very highest level of the party and state is an unprecedented event. This is a serious danger. We can overcome

[112] The second part of this statement is exaggerated. The "healthy forces" failed to establish a collaborationist government, but it was they who had promised too much, having assured their Soviet counterparts that the problem would be taken care of so long as allied troops were sent in.

[113] This in fact is precisely what happened with Soviet forces in Budapest in late October 1956. Without adequate infantry cover, Soviet tanks became inviting targets for Hungarian youths wielding grenades and Molotov cocktails.

it only if our special services carry out far-reaching internal penetration. Naturally this is easier to do when the underground is still being formed than when it has already begun its highly secret work. One must frankly say that during the Second World War not a single counterintelligence service in the world was able to paralyze the underground activity of the resistance movement. And that was at a time when the resistance movements in all countries were of an improvised nature. If the movements had been organized by state organs, then this would have been done as war was starting, and therefore would have been rushed. One certainly cannot overlook this.

The second important task for the special services was the implementation of a comprehensive program of disinformation vis-à-vis the adversary and the demoralization of enemy ranks. This task could be performed only by special means and only on the condition that these means were used boldly, on an exceptionally broad scale, and with a high level of professionalism. It was necessary to provoke a split in the ranks of the counterrevolutionaries, to cause them to mistrust one another, and to lead the foreign counterrevolutionaries along a false trail—all of which, in the end, would provide a sound basis for the adoption of the necessary political steps. Unfortunately, this task was not even placed on the agenda.

The third task that had to be carried out with the help of special means was, in all likelihood, the effort to bring about a polarization of forces among the deputies to the National Assembly and the members of the CC. One should not blithely assume that healthy forces will automatically gain the upper hand. No doubt, it was necessary to lend them assistance. And this was possible only by means of individual work with every person from the above-mentioned categories of officials, using the full arsenal of well-tried means.

The fourth task, whose implementation was necessary to stabilize the situation in Czechoslovakia, was the assertion of control over the organs of the Interior Ministry. Irrespective of any political settlement, it was necessary from the very start to interfere in the activity of this very important organ in the most decisive and most radical way possible, asserting control over all its posts. However, this, too, was not done. The Interior Ministry organs were under the control of one of the leaders of the right-wing forces, Pavel.

* * *

From the very start of the military-political action against Czechoslovakia, it was necessary to have a complex plan of propaganda measures, special measures, administrative measures, and other measures that, in aggregate with the establishment of military control, would have ensured the suppression of the counterrevolutionary opposition in the country. There was no such plan, and this, as one might expect, caused far-reaching complications.

The process of political normalization in Czechoslovakia has been dragged out. No doubt, the process will be a protracted one. For this reason, it is necessary now, as soon as possible, to work out an elaborate plan for the further stabilization of the situation in the country. This plan must be devised at the very highest state level.

In the most general sense, the point of departure for the plan must be the following basic propositions:

1. The normalization of the situation in Czechoslovakia requires us to recognize that the establishment of military control in and of itself cannot achieve the aims we set. Military control must be supplemented by political and administrative control. This means that there must be the most decisive interference in the affairs of Czechoslovakia and the exertion of pressure through all possible channels, including the presentation of uncompromising demands. The current line of non-interference is not only naive (considering that the dispatch of troops is the most extreme act of interference there can be in the internal affairs of a state), but is also counterproductive, since the rightist forces are exploiting this non-interference and our lack of resolve to strengthen their positions and demoralize the healthy forces.

2. The diffusion of counterrevolutionary influence among the masses in Czechoslovakia began when the rightist elements seized control of the mass media: the press, radio, television, and film industry. The reestablishment of socialism in Czechoslovakia will be possible only if all outlets of the mass media are brought under our firm and absolute control. The foremost task is to normalize the rightist forces without the mass media.[114] So long as the press, radio, and television—these powerful means of shaping public opinion—remain under the control of the rightists, it will be impossible to lay the basis for serious changes in the political leadership. At present the main issue on the agenda is the battle to win the hearts and minds of the Czechs. The ideological deformation of public opinion in Czechoslovakia is continuing. Without the assertion of control over the mass media, this process will be impossible to stop. Consequently, it will also be impossible to improve the situation, irrespective of how many of our troops are deployed there.

The rightists have preserved all their positions in the organs of the mass media. Moreover, they are strengthening these positions day by day. They control the newly-created Offices on Information and the Press.[115] Consequently, what will be at issue is formal control over the press, radio, television, and the film industry. There is no basis whatsoever for assuming that the press and radio will wage an active struggle against counterrevolution. That is out of the question. There is only one way to rectify the situation: by demanding that when the highest party and state leaders make appointments to the leading organs of the mass media, they choose people who are prepared to cooperate with us and who have actually proven their readiness to do so.

3. The second most important task is to establish genuine control over the organs of the Interior Ministry. The ousting of Pavel had barely any effect in weakening the positions of the rightists in the Ministry. This crucial state organ so far has remained a vital asset to the counterrevolution. Our aim will not be achieved if the organs of the Interior Ministry are simply neutralized. We must force them to consolidate the foundations of socialism and to wage a resolute struggle both against the intrigues of foreign intelligence services and against the internal counterrevolution. Without a far-reaching purge, it will be impossible to stabilize the situation in the country, but we must carry out this purge through the Czechs' own hands, that is, through the hands of the Interior Ministry organs. At present, these organs are not only preventing such tasks from being carried out, but are also actively opposing the Soviet state security organs and are still serving as an instrument of repression against the healthy forces.

A comprehensive purge must be carried out in the Interior Ministry organs, and this work must not be delayed.

4. V. I. Lenin often pointed out that policy depends on people. If we want to carry out a new policy, we must find new people. It is totally obvious that the former political and state leadership in Czechoslovakia is incapable of pursuing a new policy. They bear too great a burden for their past mistakes and delusions and for their direct betrayal of Marxism. The former leaders are hoping that as times improve, they will sabotage the Moscow Agreement in every way possible. If we are hoping to stabilize the situation in Czechoslovakia by relying on the former leadership, we will come to naught. Should that be the case, further complications are inevitable, and there is also the possibility of a major political and military crisis.

However, the replacement of the political and state leadership under present circumstances has been made possible through the existing party and state institutions, and through the National Assembly and the CPCz CC plenum. Consequently, we must pay the closest attention to these

[114] This is how the sentence appears in the document. Presumably, what is meant is that the rightist forces must be deprived of their control of the mass media.

[115] In accordance with the Moscow Protocol, one of the first actions by the Czechoslovak leadership upon returning to Prague was the reimposition of censorship and the establishment of new organs to oversee the press. A decree issued on 30 August 1968 provided for a state Committee for the Press and Information, plus Offices for the Press and Information in both Prague and Bratislava. These new bodies were responsible for preventing the publication of articles that were "at odds" with the vital interests of Czechoslovakia. Legislation passed by the National Assembly on 13 September formally codified the existence of the new agencies.

organs. We must rectify the crudest mistake that was committed previously, when we paid no attention at all to the members of the CC and the deputies of the National Assembly.

We must work out a wide-ranging plan of measures that would enable us to bring about the requisite polarization of forces in the National Assembly and in the CC. This will require concrete work with each deputy and each CC member. And we must use all available means: ideological appeals, the compromise of individuals, demoralization, economic levers, etc.

So long as the rightist forces maintain the monolithic unity of these important state and party organs, it will be difficult to speak of any sort of acceptable political solution.

The most important issue in the series of problems that must be resolved is the prestige of Dubček, Černík, Smrkovský, and other right-wing leaders. At the moment, their prestige is very high. It rose on the unsavory basis of nationalism and surged on a wave of so-called liberalization, which is to say, a wave of liberal demagoguery. But in any case, we must come to grips with it.

At present, the harshest criticism of Dubček within the country comes from the most right-wing circles. Extremist elements are voicing these criticisms. And we must frankly acknowledge that in the situation which has emerged, it is precisely this criticism from the Right that poses the most acute threat to Dubček's authority in the country. Consequently, we must offer support in every way we can for this critical trend. In this case the extremist elements are our fellow-travelers. Through the hands of the rightists, we must topple Dubček and put an end to him as a viable political figure.

5. The most important question at the current stage is the question of cadres. There can be no doubt at all that during the Czechoslovak crisis the healthy forces, having stood firmly behind Marxist positions, were decisively compromised by the rightist forces in the eyes of the nation. At present, they have no political authority. Moreover, they themselves also proved to be insufficiently consistent and steadfast in their Marxism. At the critical moment, they were not able to gain control of the situation. Consequently, from the standpoint of cadres, we must be oriented only toward new forces or, one might say, toward a third force, that is, toward people who only now will come onto the political stage and toward people who, though not well known, enjoy unquestioned authority in the business world or in the world of art and literature. We must prepare to move these people into the leadership. The first step in this direction, clearly, is to search for these people. The second step is to appoint them to senior posts. The question of the way in which these cadres must declare their political leanings will play an important role in moving them into the leadership. Do they criticize Dubček's positions from the left, or are they supporters of Dubček, or do they stand to the right of him?

In the situation now unfolding, the best thing would be if a settlement can be achieved under which the healthy forces, on whom we intend to rely in the first instance, will express loyalty to Dubček but will introduce new, constructive elements into the criticism of his policy. This political camouflage is absolutely necessary to enable the new cadres to shore up their positions. A frontal attack under present circumstances will not prove successful.

6. The political situation in Czechoslovakia at present is complicated enough, and measures must be taken to complicate it still further. To this end, it is necessary to devise a broad program of special measures of disinformation. We must strengthen popular distrust of the rightist leaders, undertake actions that will compromise them, and establish the widest possible contacts with these very same rightist elements so that the broad masses will have the opportunity to accuse the rightist leaders of collaborationism.

At present, the art of disinformation has attained an extremely high level. It is employed very intensively by our enemies and is achieving great results. It would be an unforgivable mistake if we, too, were not to make use of this technique. V. I. Lenin often pointed out that it would be criminal behavior on the part of a leader if, in a fight with the enemy, he were not to make use of all the means of struggle that his opponent is using. The counterrevolutionaries are widely using disinformation to undermine the positions of socialism in Czechoslovakia. They have sown the whirlwind, and now they must reap the storm.

7. At present, the healthy forces in Czechoslovakia do not have a center of gravity. Neither the party nor the government organs support them. Measures must be taken to ensure that such centers are created. The way to resolve this matter, apparently, is to replace the counterrevolutionary clubs around the whole country such as "Club-235" and the "Club of Non-Party Democrats"[116] with newly-created clubs for the revival of socialism and patriotic clubs with attractive programs, dynamic and sufficiently authoritative leaders, ample financial resources, and press organs.

At present, a split in the CPCz must be avoided, since any split will clearly impede efforts to stabilize the situation. Hence it would not be advisable to create any sort of social organizations that would set themselves against the party. A network of clubs would not in itself pose such a danger. Moreover, the network could have a salutary influence on public opinion and could assist the consolidation of leftist forces.

8. Efforts to ameliorate the situation in the Czechoslovak army will be an important part of attempts to stabilize things in Czechoslovakia. Thanks to the efforts of the rightists, the Czechoslovak army at present is in disarray. As an instrument of the Warsaw Pact, this army is not combat capable. There is a real threat that the Czechoslovak army might come over to the side of the rightists and be used by them under certain conditions to launch an armed attack against the Soviet army.

An improvement of the situation in the army will be possible only by means of a radical purge, which must begin as soon as possible in a categorical manner.

9. One of the most urgent special tasks is the need to penetrate the nationalist underground as widely as possible. At present, the extreme secrecy maintained by the underground forces has been weakened, and their vigilance has significantly eroded. We must take maximum advantage of this propitious opportunity. By establishing a firm presence in the underground, we will have the opportunity in the event of a crisis to paralyze it swiftly and painlessly.

10. It cannot be ruled out that the rightist forces are attempting to reduce the situation in the country to one of hunger and economic demoralization in order to lay the blame for this on the Soviet Union and strengthen their own positions. If the insult to patriotic sentiments is compounded by material deprivation, then a crisis is inevitable. The imperialists have a great interest in fomenting such a crisis, and there is no doubt that they will spend a good deal of effort trying to provoke it.

Given the possibility of such a development, we must adopt appropriate measures and, above all, we must draw the attention of the healthy elements to this danger.

11. We must exploit the presence of our troops in Czechoslovakia to strengthen our clandestine positions as much as possible.[117] It is insufficient to carry out special work solely through the legally established intelligence section in the embassy. We must establish 10–12 powerful, clandestine intelligence centers at key points around the country, and from these points we must carry out wide-ranging efforts to promote the activity of the healthy forces in exposing, disrupting, compromising, and apprehending the active figures in the counterrevolution.

12. The maximum expansion of official contacts along party, state, and other lines is on the agenda. These contacts must be expanded in a variety of ways. We must exploit personal ties

---

[116] The report misstates the names of both of these clubs. The first should be "K-231," and the second should be the "Club of Committed Non-Party Members" (or, more literally, "Club of Politically Active Non-Members of the Communist Party").

[117] The word "clandestine" has been used here to translate the Russian word "nelegal'nye," which usually means "illegal," but can also be used to mean "clandestine" or "covert." In the next sentence, the word "legal'nyi (usually meaning "legal") is used to describe the intelligence section in the embassy, contrasting it with the 10–12 "clandestine" centers that the authors of the report wanted to establish. The difference was that a legal agreement had been signed between the Soviet Union and Czechoslovakia providing for KGB representation in the embassy. Hence, the intelligence section in that case was "legally established," as opposed to "clandestine."

and personal influence to improve the situation. The expansion of contacts must not be of an arbitrary nature. It must be geared toward a concrete aim and be of a concrete nature.

13. At present, the counterrevolutionary forces are taking definite steps to enable a certain portion of their most compromised cadres to be spirited out to the West. We must oppose this in every way possible. We must intensify our operational work with regard to these cadres and our efforts to obtain materials that could be used to compromise the counterrevolution as a whole. As of now, unfortunately, we do not yet have at our disposal sufficiently convincing facts and materials that would enable us to undertake broad work in exposing the counterrevolutionary underground's ties with imperialism and its participation in the counterrevolutionary activity of foreign imperialist intelligence centers, though such participation is obvious. We must step up our efforts to obtain compromising materials.

14. A leading element of the rightist forces in Czechoslovakia is Zionism. No concrete work against the Zionists is being carried out in Czechoslovakia. There are no plans to undermine their positions, their ideology is not being exposed, and their subversive nature is not being laid bare. We must work out fully concrete plans to undermine the positions of Zionism in Czechoslovakia.

15. Without question, the course of events in Czechoslovakia would be positively affected by the appearance of some sort of document adopted by the communist parties of the five socialist countries that would: offer a profound political assessment of the processes that led to the crisis in Czechoslovakia; give a moral explanation of the events that took place; and lay out a broad program for the further stabilization of the situation in the country. It would be best if this document linked the crisis in Czechoslovakia with the intensification of the ideological struggle in the world, if it gave a pointed assessment of the deficiencies and mistakes that were made not only in the past, but also by the current Czechoslovak leadership, and if it exposed the Trotskyist, revisonist nature of their positions in the political system and economy. This document must contain an unambiguous statement that the socialist states are faithful to their internationalist duty and will use their armed forces and all other means to protect socialist gains in the future.

DOCUMENT No. 136: Minutes of the Soviet–Czechoslovak Negotiations in Kiev, 7–8 December 1968 (Excerpts)

Source: ÚSD, Sb. KV, Z/S 17.

This transcription of the Kiev meetings between Czechoslovak and Soviet authorities reflects Moscow's continuing pressure on Dubček to, as Brezhnev stated, "handle personnel matters"—purge the reformers from the leadership of the CPCz. Soviet leaders also emphasized the necessity of removing the "revisionist tendencies" within the Czechoslovak People's Army.

Brezhnev, Kosygin, and Podgorny led the Soviet delegation at these talks. They were accompanied by Pyotr Shelest, the Ukrainian party secretary, and Vladimir Shcherbitskii, the Ukrainian prime minister, both members of the CPSU Politburo (Shelest as a full member, and Shcherbitskii as a candidate). Shelest had attended earlier negotiations in Čierna and Bratislava. The Soviet delegation also included Konstantin Katushev, the CPSU secretary responsible for intra-bloc relations, and Vasilii Kuznetsov, the first deputy foreign minister who had effectively taken over from Chervonenko as ambassador to Czechoslovakia.

(See also Document No. 111.)

Minutes of the Soviet–Czechoslovak Negotiations in Kiev
7–8 December 1968

From the Soviet side: L. I. Brezhnev, A. N. Kosygin, N. V. Podgorny, P. E. Shelest, V. V. Shcherbitskii, K. F. Katushev, V. V. Kuznetsov.

From the Czechoslovak side: A. Dubček, L. Svoboda, O. Černík, G. Husák, L. Štrougal
. . .

L. I. Brezhnev: . . . We wish to express our thanks to you for agreeing to meet. The program for our meeting has not been fixed precisely, but we agreed with Cde. Dubček that we would listen to your reports on how the decisions of the November plenum are being implemented, how preparations are coming along for the December plenum, and, in particular, how you expect to handle personnel matters. . . .

A. Dubček: . . . In the two months that have passed since our last meeting in Moscow, the leadership of the CPCz has focused its efforts on reducing internal tension, isolating the right-wing forces, and strengthening the leading role of the party.[118] In doing so we used the conclusions we agreed upon together during our last meetings as our starting point.

To ensure fulfillment of the Moscow protocol means obtaining the support of the whole party and the majority of our society.

Of course, this is a long and complicated process when one considers the persistently negative mood that exists in Czechoslovakia. Our party rejects the views of those who believe that normalization of conditions can be achieved in one fell swoop—quickly, by using administrative measures. The adoption of such measures would cause further tension, which would entail resorting to extreme measures.[119] . . .

---

[118] In accordance with the Moscow Protocol, KAN and K-231 were effectively banned; censorship was reintroduced; the Social Democratic Party had been formally proscribed; measures to restrict public assembly had been enacted; several top reformers (Kriegel, Šik, Hájek, Pelikán, Pavel, and Hejzlar) had been dismissed or demoted; another reformer, Zdeněk Mlynář, had abruptly resigned at the November plenum of the CPCz Central Committee; and the status-of-forces treaty with the Soviet Union had taken effect.

[119] Dubček appears to be referring here to the imposition of martial law.

The concept of the right-wing forces is as follows: They want a repetition of what happened after the May plenum. On the one hand, they are trying in every way to downplay the importance of the November plenum resolution, and they speak out against it wherever possible. On the other hand, they raise political demands that are linked, formally, for instance, with our Action Program but that, in fact, confuse the essence of the political struggle now going on. They say they are "for the Action Program," but they make no mention of the fact that this program mentions friendship with the Soviet Union, loyalty to the Warsaw Pact, and participation in CMEA. Instead of mentioning these things, they emphasize aspects of the program which, under the new conditions, we are unable to carry out and don't want to resurrect, aspects that, as life has proven, were by no means sufficiently thought through. . . .

At present, a process of differentiation is going on. Only a month ago one could have spoken of the spontaneous support for the party leadership from the masses, but today it is a different story. Today they come forward with open criticism of the party leadership, against us. They accuse us of making political compromises, they maintain that either we "have betrayed the interests of the people" or that we "do not have the right to speak in the name of the people." These sorts of statements are not infrequent nowadays. Some non-party magazines are already criticizing Cde. Husák; tomorrow, perhaps, they will criticize Černík and Štrougal, and then Dubček, too. . . .

N. V. Podgorny: How were the decisions of the November plenum received in the Ministry of Defense?

O. Černík: They were, one might say, received with a certain amount of consternation in the Ministry of Defense and the General Staff. There are weak points there; for instance, the Military-Political Academy and in general the army's political apparatus.[120] This apparatus is unable to carry out the necessary work to ensure fulfillment of the plenum resolutions. Things are not so good in the intelligence agency section, either.[121] Štrougal might be able to say more about that; he was there not long ago. In a word, we still do not sense active support for the November resolution in the Ministry of Defense. . . .

L. I. Brezhnev: . . . Yet in your country people speaking in the name of the CC are explaining the plenum resolutions who should not have been entrusted to carry out this work. Take, for instance, Kriegel. This person is clearly anti-Soviet and a right-winger; he was against the Moscow protocol, he voted in Parliament against the status-of-forces treaty. Why is such a person to be found in the role of a CC spokesman explaining the November plenum? We simply can't understand that.

Or why should Smrkovský set the tone in a number of party branches in assessing the plenary session? He is a person who, as we know, often makes unexpected, unpremeditated, and irresponsible statements. He tries to play on nationalist feelings, and violates party discipline.

Naturally, you knew all that. Why is it that he nonetheless is permitted to address perhaps dozens of branches?

At one time we drew your attention to the conduct of the director of the CPCz CC Higher Party School, Hübl.[122] He is virulently anti-Soviet. It is hard to understand how he can occupy the post of Rector of the Party School, where there must be a crystal-clear communist. This Hübl

---

[120] The Klement Gottwald Military-Political Academy was the institution that produced a reformist "Memorandum" in the spring of 1968, with encouragement and guidance from General Prchlík. It was closed down in the spring of 1969, most of its faculty were dismissed, and its functions were transferred to the Zapotocký Academy in Bratislava.

[121] See Document No. 61.

[122] Milan Hübl had gained a reputation as one of the leading reformist intellectuals. He was elected to the CPCz CC Presidium by the Vysočany Congress, but was dropped from that body by the CPCz CC plenum on 31 August in the wake of the Moscow Protocol.

invited students to speak out against the Soviet Union, and he is in the front ranks of those sent by the CC as speakers to explain the plenum resolutions to party branches.

This bespeaks great deficiencies in the activity of the CPCz CC Presidium and its Executive Committee. For such matters one needs firm, reliable people. In mentioning this, we are thinking predominantly about your interests. Just remember, wherever Cdes. Dubček, Černík, Štrougal, Husák, Indra, and Biľak spoke and explained the plenum's resolutions, they received full support and approval. . . .

From our observations, matters are still far from satisfactory on the question of ensuring the leading role of the Communist Party of Czechoslovakia. For almost a year now the party has been persistently attacked. It has been forced the whole time to rebuff these attacks. It finds itself on the defensive when it should be in an offensive position and should occupy the leading role in society.

What is essential for this? Above all: unity. And this unity must begin with the highest party organs: from the Executive Committee, the CC Presidium, the Central Committee, and so on, down to the lowest branches.

Of course, it would be possible to write a resolution about unity, to adopt it, and not to go beyond that. But it is another thing to act in a united way, that is, to write a resolution and carry it out. For this there must be strict observance of party statutes and the implementation of measures outlined in the statutes to punish those who violate unity and discipline, including expulsion from the party. . . .

For our part we never asked you to use repression. But the party reserves the right to name its cadres. The party looks after these people, educates them, and shifts them around when necessary. That principle has been violated in your country. It is almost a year since we met in Dresden and talked, in particular, about Pelikán. But until now you have not found a proper person to head the television service. This is a sign of complacency, indecisiveness, and some sort of fear. The principles of cadre policy have been seriously violated in your country. Look, for example, now. In preparing to form a federal government you are acting on the principle: "At the head of each ministry and institution there should be one Czech and one Slovak." Can such a principle be considered basic in carrying out personnel policy? And it has even become clear that you consider it a success when you find one right-winger and one left-winger holding responsible positions in the party.

Cadre policy should be principled and strict and must entail respect for cadres. Without the leading role of the party there can be no solution to economic questions or to the question of the federal arrangement of the country. The federation; that's a complicated matter. We've been dealing with it for 50 years and we know what it means. New people take up jobs in new bodies, but first of all the party should unite them and mobilize them in the struggle to fulfill party decisions. You have the opportunities to undertake such work, especially after the creation of an Executive Committee of the CC Presidium.

The decisions of the Executive Committee must be binding for all. If in the Executive Committee itself there are those who violate party discipline, it is necessary to act decisively against them. We don't hide our consternation about the way Smrkovský acts, and yet no one has found enough strength to take him to task. . . .

At present you have created a very important body: the CPCz CC Bureau for the Czech Lands. It seems to us that it should be supported in every way. This body should play a very important role. It should be helped on cadre questions, helped in implementing the decisions it will adopt. Cde. Štrougal should be given all possible support so that the Bureau he heads becomes a body with genuine authority.

It stands to reason that this also concerns the Central Committee of the Slovak Communist Party. And the situation there looks like this: No sooner is Cde. Husák chosen for the leading post than some three months later he is being slandered. Certain people are not pleased by Husák.

And Štrougal, too, is coming under attack. One must know how to defend cadres; otherwise the party will not be stabilized.

A very important unit, comrades, is the army. We are your allies; together we are strengthening the defense of our states and defending their independence from our common enemy. For our part we always try to have the armies of our allies strong, well-armed, and firm on moral issues. Unfortunately, at the present time, the situation in the Czechoslovak army, clearly, is not good. Political work has weakened, discipline is lax, and, as a result, the combat ability of your armed forces is decreasing. That's the conclusion our military comrades have come to.[123] They had a chance to observe the situation first-hand. This can only make us anxious.

We can't say anything specific here about one or another cadre in your army. We don't intend to speak, for instance, about Cde. Dzúr or others. We have no personal objections to him, but one must analyze where the source of evil is, where the roots of the present unsatisfactory situation in the army lie.

N. V. Podgorny: And here, once again, the matter depends on the party's work.

L. I. Brezhnev: Yes, and that work is deficient in, above all, the army's political apparatus. Matters have reached a point where the chief hotbed of revisionist tendencies in the armed forces of your country is the Military-Political Academy. That is absolutely unforgivable! In our country, in both wartime and peacetime, the commissars and the political workers were always people devoted to the cause of the party and the spirit of the army. If the political workers have already become transformed into founts of reactionary thinking, what can it be like in the army itself? Can one rely on this army in the event of an extraordinary situation? . . .

One cannot permit such things in the army. In the army orders must be scrupulously observed and underpinned by sound educational work.

. . . The question of the situation in the army is extremely serious. There are many right-wing forces, especially in the political organs. This makes the army unreliable; you can't even put your trust right now in your own armed forces. What kind of trust can there be if a significant percentage of officers disapproves of the decisions of the November CC plenum and if they don't support the military alliance with us? This is dangerous; it puts us on our guard. And even more so because Czechoslovakia is one of the decisive and strategically most vital sections of our front. That's what our opponents believe. This is evident from the discussion at the last NATO Council session; Czechoslovakia is clearly regarded as a weak link in the socialist camp in view of the unreliability of its armed forces.[124] . . .

L. I. Brezhnev: How can one rely on an army in which the officers of the General Staff speak out against the decisions of the party's Central Committee?

A. Dubček: The General Staff didn't adopt any such resolution.

L. I. Brezhnev: Thank God it didn't, but that's not the point. The point is the mood of the officer corps.

L. Svoboda: That was in the Military Academy. There were actions in Brno.

A. N. Kosygin: There's no point in formal resolutions that do not reflect everything. The most dangerous enemies are masked. The essence of the matter is that you must have a politically healthy armed force, an army on which the party leadership and government can rely and the allies can depend.

---

[123] This was indeed the conclusion of numerous secret reports by top Soviet military and KGB officers; see, for example, Memorandum No. 8468 (TOP SECRET) from Army-General A. Epishev, chief of the Soviet army's Main Political Directorate, to K. F. Katushev, 23 October 1968, in TsKhSD, F. 5, Op. 60, D. 311, Ll. 141–148.

[124] For a detailed exposition of this point by a senior CPSU official, see Memorandum No. 23923 (TOP SECRET) from L. Tolokonnikov to K. V. Rusakov, 18 December 1968, in TsKhSD, F. 5, Op. 60, D. 311, Ll. 184–198.

L. Svoboda: After returning to Prague, I'll get in touch with your military comrades and ask them to inform me about all the negative things they're aware of in our army.

A. N. Kosygin: In short, you'll have to deal seriously with the situation in the army. . . .

L. I. Brezhnev: . . . I can't help but point out that in your National Assembly the tone is sometimes set by people who speak from an anti-party position. That's dangerous, especially now when you are making changes in the arrangement of the state, in connection with federalization. Are there any plans to make changes in the National Assembly?

A. Dubček: We'll have two chambers and a presidium of the National Assembly.[125]

L. I. Brezhnev: It's very important who serves at the head of the National Assembly. If it's a right-winger, you'll have a difficult time. The party should have its own people in the leadership of every important section of state work. . . .

We've exchanged views with you in a comradely way about the matters that trouble us. People often talk about "Moscow's influence." But what do we want? Our program is aimed at bolstering the position of socialism and strengthening our friendship with the Czechoslovak people and with the Communist Party of Czechoslovakia. In so doing we sometimes have to speak of unpleasant things. . . .

L. Štrougal: Much has been said about the situation in Bohemia. You mentioned events showing how complicated the situation is. There are many things that were said here with which one can agree. It's now essential to find a way out. In today's complicated situation it is imperative to define clearly what is the most important thing. We have to unite our forces. The Executive Committee must work out the party's tactics systematically.

The creation of an Executive Committee marks a big step forward. It's true that the Executive Committee is still not fully united, but we have all the potential to become united. It is also true that Cde. Smrkovský deviates a little from socialist rules.

The Executive Committee has only begun its work. Our main task, in my view, is to ensure control of the mass media. One cannot bolster the party without controlling the mass media. Several measures along these lines were considered even before the November plenum, particularly with regard to the press. Unfortunately, we were unable to follow them through in time. And after the plenum the journalists went on the offensive and limited our chances of implementing some of the resolutions. They began to attack the individuals we had wanted to appoint to responsible posts overseeing the mass media. As a result, these comrades refused to work in the positions for which they were recommended. . . .

The sphere where party action is essential is, of course, the cadre question. We cannot get along without personnel changes, although this produces conflicts. During changes of personnel there usually is a very unpleasant atmosphere, especially when the changes occur by administrative fiat or by party statutory measures. In such instances there are immediate outcries of "a return to the 1950s" and so on. The attacks of the right-wing are especially strong on cadre questions. The press, which is run by the right-wing, attacks comrades who defend the resolutions of the November plenum. The rightists claim that everyone who allegedly "took part in the deformations" is trying to incite mistrust in us. They demand the convocation of the CPCz and Czech party congresses, and they insist on having a new leadership that "enjoys the confidence of the people."

The CPCz CC has taken a clear and well-defined position with regard to comrades who are abroad. We can no longer be silent about Šik: He sends letters to factories in which he criticizes

---

[125] As of January 1, 1969, the National Assembly was renamed the Federal Assembly, reflecting the advent of the federal Czechoslovak state.

the resolutions of the November plenum. And yet he is a CC member, and his actions disorient the party. . . .

In conclusion, I wish once more to emphasize that our situation is serious. In fact, it is far more complicated than was said here. It demands concrete, focused, and comprehensive corrective steps on the part of our party. The Executive Committee of the CC Presidium must spearhead this work. The problems facing us will not be solved quickly, but we must not be on the defensive. The situation is dangerous. Perhaps I regard things too pessimistically. But I believe we are on the defensive and the right-wing is attacking us. They want to compel us to apply administrative measures on a broad scale. We must not allow this to happen. The main thing is to attack the right-wing politically, while giving only a secondary role to administrative measures. . . .

DOCUMENT No. 137: Vasil Biľak's Recollections of Preparations for the April 1969 CPCz CC Plenum, and the Removal of Alexander Dubček

Source: *Paměti Vasila Biľaka: Unikátní svědectvi ze zákulisí KSČ*, 2 vols. (Prague: Agentura Cesty, 1991), vol. 2, pp. 183–189.

In this excerpt from his memoirs, Biľak gives an interesting view into the process of the reorganization of the Czechoslovak power structure during the grim, early stages of "normalization". As part of the wholesale eradication of untrustworthy elements from the party, Biľak and his fellow hard-liners verified the political reliability of every member of the Central Committee. But the main task facing the country's pro-Moscow leaders in the spring of 1969 was to replace Dubček as CPCz CC first secretary. Initially, Oldřich Černík surfaced as the leading candidate, but when he was sent to Moscow for approval, he failed to provide the necessary guarantees that he would eliminate "right-wing opportunist members" from the party leadership and "pursue the policy of the Marxist–Leninist forces." In his place, Gustáv Husák got the nod. Despite some earlier signs that he had favored certain elements of reform, Husák would go on to complete the normalization process and rule the country until 1989.

Early in April it was clear that a political disentanglement was on the horizon in Czechoslovakia, that the political winter was coming to an end and that not only a symbolic but a genuine political spring had to follow. The situation had to be resolved one way or another. We were working with the members of the Central Committee actively and in a well thought out manner. We assessed every member of the CPCz CC against a political background and on the basis of their character. We needed to be certain and know what they were like. Whenever we did not know someone, and I am referring to those who were co-opted to the CPCz CC, we looked for someone who knew them and who was given the task of verifying their political qualities and character. There was a group like this in every region. We had to obtain a picture of each individual to be capable of foreseeing what would happen once things came to the crunch, to which side this or that member of the Central Committee would turn.

We realized that the preparations for the Central Committee session which was to be held in April [1969], as the CPCz CC Presidium had announced to the CPSU Central Committee, had to be well thought out down to the last detail. Even Černík and most other members of the presidium had begun to realize that Dubček must leave the post of first secretary of the CPCz CC. It became clear that the process of clarification had reached the phase that when the proposal for Dubček's dismissal as first secretary of the Central Committee was drawn up it would be adopted by a majority.

Comrades from Prague and messengers from various regions and districts met in my office at the CPCz CC for three or four weeks. Here we assessed the situation and determined further procedures. Among the most active were Comrades Drahomír Kolder, Karel Hoffmann, Alois Indra, Jozef Lenárt, Oldřich Švestka, Jan Fojtík, Václav David, Antonín Kapek, Josef Korčák, Vilém Nový, Miroslav Zavadil, Otakar Rytíř and others. It was a great help that Comrade Husák managed the situation correctly in Slovakia, which very much influenced the situation in the Czech Lands. Comrade Ján Janík, Ludovít Pezlár, Miloslav Boda, Ondrej Klokoč, Eugen Turzo and others worked with a great deal of initiative. Miloš Jakeš, chairman of the Central Control and Audit Commission of the CPCz, provided great support and assistance. In his position he was able to manage correctly and help with many questions.

Strong Marxist–Leninist groups were working in all regions behind the backs of many leading secretaries who hold right-wing positions. Links were established with regions, districts and major factories. This work meant that we had to obtain the necessary material resources. Many people were working in a dedicated manner, and voluntarily, but they were out of work and had to live on something. At a certain point I considered asking Černík for some money. Later I admitted this and Černík said, what a pity that I hadn't done so. He would have gladly given, say a million, and perhaps this would have helped him to retain his party card.

Gradually funds were obtained from other sources. Willingness to contribute was so great that proposals appeared to double the dues. Many comrades, especially in the Ostrava region, were prepared to donate part of their income for this purpose. That is how the idea came about to establish an illegal party leadership, a parallel Central Committee. I considered this proposal risky and kept postponing it. The danger, as far as I was concerned, was that there would be discussion rather on who was to be in the leadership, who had the greater merits, who was to be placed at the head of the party, and the main problem facing us would be omitted—i.e., to force Dubček to resign and create a party leadership that would support socialism.

Many comrades felt that the preparation of the Central Committee session was proceeding too slowly, that it didn't provide them with sufficient security and created a great deal of nervousness. [. . .]

Many urgent questions remained by the time of the CPCz CC session. The fact that Dubček had to be removed was clear but what was not clear was whom to elect first secretary of the CPCz CC. The mistake of January 1968 was not to be repeated. A fairly simple solution offered itself—to replace Dubček with Černík. He was one of the pillars who was not to be touched. Had he been we would have removed an important brick in the wall of right-wing counterrevolutionary forces so disorienting them but the question was whether this would have been a step forward. Would we turn events around in this way? Wouldn't we have to pay an excessively high price? Who would guarantee that Černík would behave as expected and that there wouldn't be a repetition of Dubček in a different form? Some proposed that we should try it, but the main thing was to remove Dubček.

We decided to risk it with Černík. I personally worked out seven options which would permit, or rather provide, guarantees that if Černík accepted any of the options we would make sure that the Marxist–Leninist forces understood his candidacy and approved it. The comrades who were working in various small groups in Prague agreed to try Černík as a temporary solution. The basis of each option was that Černík must give guarantees—not all verbally but in writing—to remove right-wing opportunist members from the party leadership and to pursue the policy of the Marxist–Leninist forces. But a promise from him was not enough for us. For this purpose we organized an invitation for Černík to go to Moscow.

This is what happened. Comrade Kosygin invited Černík as prime minister. He welcomed him at the airport, took him to the Kremlin where Comrade Brezhnev spoke to Černík the whole day. Unfortunately, Černík was too much in the grip of the atmosphere and emotions which he himself had tried to create. Although he wanted to be first secretary of the CPCz CC he was too scared to undertake any commitments. He did not believe that consolidation was possible in Czechoslovakia without certain people even if they were on the other side of the barricade. This was due to the fact that he did not trust the Marxist–Leninist forces. That was the problem with him. He did not even trust them when it was still possible that counterrevolution could be suppressed with our forces. He was incapable of admitting his share in the crisis which had arisen in Czechoslovakia. By hesitating he missed his last available chance.

When Moscow told us how the discussions were proceeding and their results, that Černík did not have the courage to help solve the situation, all the groups agreed that Comrade Husák should be proposed as first secretary of the CPCz CC. [. . .]

President Svoboda was very active in this respect. The Executive Committee met several times in the president's apartment without Smrkovský. Comrade Svoboda always briefed me in great detail about the meetings. We informed the Soviet leadership of our plan, of our preparations, of the removal of Dubček and of whom we were proposing to replace him in the post of first secretary of the CPCz CC. A very important, and for our side an exceptionally significant, meeting took place between Comrades Brezhnev and Husák at Mukačevo in April 1969. [. . .]

562

When the Executive Committee met the following morning in Comrade Svoboda's apartment and the need for the replacement of the first secretary of the CPCz CC was discussed, it was again proposed that Černík should replace Dubček as first secretary and Comrade Husák would be prime minister. They came back again and again to this question as the best solution. To achieve their aim they even deceived President Svoboda by claiming that the proposal was accepted by the Marxist–Leninists and even by Biľak.

The negotiations were adjourned. The president of the republic sent his son-in-law, Milan Klusák, to see me. Klusák was terrified, saying that the president of the republic would like to know why we had abandoned our original proposal for Comrade Husák. I was surprised no less than Comrade Svoboda. I again said that the only proposal that was acceptable and the only one to be submitted to the Central Committee was that after Dubček's removal Comrade Husák was to be elected first secretary of the CPCz CC.

During the break, due to the fact that Comrade Husák turned down the post of prime minister and said that under the circumstances he would remain first secretary in Slovakia, Comrade Štrougal came to see me. I gave Comrade Štrougal the same message I had sent to the president of the republic through Comrade Klusák. I repeated that this was the only solution and that any other would create a crisis. Comrade Svoboda informed Comrade Brezhnev about the situation that had arisen. Brezhnev phoned me to ask what had happened and why we were changing our proposals. This conversation took place in president Svoboda's office at Prague Castle. In the presence of president Svoboda I explained to Comrade Brezhnev that we were changing nothing, that it was the other side which had changed the proposal and that everything would be put right and that there would be only one single proposal as had been agreed. [. . .]

DOCUMENT No. 138: Talks between ČSSR Defense Minister Dzúr and Soviet Defense Minister Grechko, April 1, 1969

Source: AK, N—VHA, file MNO-SM.

While the Soviet-led invasion represented an easy military victory for Moscow, many of the documents in this collection show that the political battle for Czechoslovakia was far more problematic. In this vivid discussion, Soviet Marshal Andrei Grechko reacts furiously to the outbreak of widespread demonstrations following Czechoslovakia's victory over the Soviets at the world ice hockey championships on March 28. He accuses the Czechoslovak leadership of organizing the demonstrations, using the hockey match as a pretext. Amid charges that counterrevolution is on the advance, he comments, in the words of the Czechoslovak note-taker, that "the situation in our country is worse than on August 21, 1968."

Minutes of Talks between Representatives of the Czechoslovak People's Army Command and the Soviet Army

April 1, 1969 (10:00–12.30 P.M.)
in the building of the Ministry of National Defense

The ČSSR Minister of National Defense Col. General M. Dzúr received the USSR Defense Minister, Marshal of the USSR A.A. Grechko at his own request. In addition to Minister Grechko, the Soviet side was represented by:

— Col. Gen. Maiorov, commander of the Central group of forces in the ČSSR,
— Col. Gen. Povalin, head of the main operational administration and secretary of the State Defense Council,
— Maj. Gen. Zolotov, head of the political administration and member of the Military Council of the Central group of forces in the ČSSR.

In addition to the minister of national defense, the Czechoslovak side was represented by:

— Lt. Gen. V. Dvořák, state secretary of the ČSSR government at the Ministry of National Defense,
— Lt. Gen. K. Rusov, chief of the General Staff of the Czechoslovak People's Army,
— Lt. Gen. F. Bedřich, head of the main political administration of the Czechoslovak People's Army,
— Lt. Gen. A. Mucha, head of the main administration of land forces, deputy minister,
— Maj. Gen. J. Lux, head of the main rear, deputy minister,
— Col. Gen. M. Šmoldas, inspector general of the Czechoslovak People's Army, deputy minister.

Minister: stated at the outset of the talks that he had convened those members of the army command requested by Minister Grechko. The meeting is unexpected for us and it would have been more agreeable had it been possible to talk under different circumstances.

Grechko: stated that he, too, would have wished the situation had been better. He had come at the decision of the CPSU Central Committee and the USSR government to investigate the causes and consequences of anti-socialist outrages on March 28–29, 1969, directed against the Soviet army and the Soviet people. He would carry out the investigations with his own people.

It was a shameful thing and that is why he felt obliged to inform the minister of national defense and the command of the Czechoslovak People's Army on his opinion of the affronts directed against the Soviet army. A note from the Soviet government and the CPSU Central Committee would be handed over today in which they address the ČSSR government and the CPCz Central Committee, informing them of the inadmissibility of a repetition of similar outrages.

According to the reports they were receiving they knew what was being prepared. Yesterday (March 31, 1969) there was a meeting of commanders and political officers of the Central group of the armies where they convinced themselves how far counterrevolutionary groups had gone, insulting the peoples of the USSR and jeopardizing the friendship of our peoples and armies. They found out that these were not spontaneous actions, to do with ice hockey, but were well planned and organized demonstrations.

These are official talks and that is why he must lay down the facts concerning insults and acts of violence against the Soviet army. He would not even take the trouble to speak about Prague.

In Bratislava slogans appeared such as "occupiers", "fascists", "Brezhnev is a hooligan" and so on. Even members of the Czechoslovak People's Army took part in the demonstrations. We are talking about political demonstrations, organized political demonstrations by thousands of people with counterrevolutionary tendencies. If similar slogans directed against the ČSSR appeared in the USSR they would know how to cope with it immediately. In Bratislava Interior Ministry bodies did not intervene until three to four hours after the outbreak of the demonstration. The commander of the garrison had asked for help but nothing was done. However, Bratislava was the only city where the security bodies, General Pepich, finally intervened energetically.

At Ústí nad Labem the komandatura was surrounded, windows were shattered, a truck was burnt as were three motor-bikes, and soldiers took part as well.

At Turnov windows were also shattered and the barracks, housing Soviet troops, were besieged.

At Trutnov several thousand people wanted to force their way into the barracks.

In Olomouc several thousand demonstrators surrounded the staff of the corps and the military hospital. Columns of demonstrators were headed by soldiers, eight groups of soldiers, 50 persons each.

In Ostrava there were also thousands of people. Apart from slogans and insults there was even shooting. Machine-gun fire could be heard. After the end of the demonstration military vehicles were driving people around the town, praising other demonstrators. The commander of the security forces had given orders not to intervene.

At Jaroměř—a demonstration around the hospital, 30 windows shattered. Stones were thrown and even landed in the wards. A monument to the Soviet army was destroyed and wreaths were set on fire there.

At Havlíčkův Brod gangs gathered outside the komandatura.

At Pardubice mobs gathered near a Soviet tank where they set fire to a Soviet flag with a painted swastika.

The conduct of Czechoslovak soldiers in the presence of a delegation of the Transcarpathian Military Area with the Western military area was undignified. Soldiers were hurling Molotov cocktails and shouting obscenities. The question arises whether commanders are commanding their troops. If this happened in their country they would know how to deal with this even without the courts.

The problem has gone beyond all limits, a danger is looming. The leadership of the Ministry of National Defense has taken no measures to liquidate actions against Soviet troops and to protect the allied army. It would surely not have been difficult to bring out a regiment to protect at Olomouc even if it had arrived on the scene later. Once it [the Soviet army—editors] begins to defend itself many people will suffer.

Their patience has been exhausted. How much longer are they to stand for insults and violence? Nobody protects them, no one apologizes to them. Although they turned to the security forces, no one, except in Bratislava, took part in suppressing the disorders. How do you regard this? None of the leading personages was on the spot, but Smrkovský was. He said that now there was more at stake than just scores.

Minister: he said that this is not quite the way things went and measures had been taken.

Grechko: continued that they had their officers in plain clothes. They knew that this had all been done in an organized manner and here, everyone acts as though no one had seen anything. He expressed the indignation of Soviet troops, commanders, the army command and the government. He conveyed a protest to the minister of national defense at the insults hurled at the Soviet army which had shed its blood for the liberation of the ČSSR. He quoted from the note saying that in the event of a repetition of similar events the Soviet side would be compelled to take its own measures and feel free to choose what kind of measures to take, depending on what kind of measures the ČSSR would take.

He once again asks Comrade Dzúr to take steps if he honors the memory of Soviet soldiers, and protect the Soviet army against counterrevolutionary elements. We, too, have our pride, honor and dignity. He had ordered Soviet commanders not to shoot, to ask for help, to keep a cool head and use restraint.

They hear nothing but verbal assurances but it looks to them as though counterrevolutionary elements are gradually expanding the range of their activity and are becoming increasingly daring. No one explains anything but merely shudders. No proper political work is being done and no measures are taken to strengthen friendship. Soviet troops are not allowed to go near Czechoslovak ones; they do not need this kind of friendship.

He has given the commander of the Central group of forces orders which do not go beyond the provisions of the treaty:

1) to patrol from time to time with armored vehicles and tanks;

2) in the event of a threat, demonstrators are not to be permitted to come nearer than 500 meters to the barracks, and if lives are in danger firearms are to be used;

3) armored vehicles and tanks are to be sent to warehouses and bases where there are no troops and arms;

4) commanders of Soviet garrisons are to be instructed to inform the local state administration about this order;

5) if such events are repeated a curfew will be introduced, companies and tanks are to be deployed around existing komandaturas;

6) the possibility of increasing the number of Soviet troops by 10–15,000 to reach the number of 75,000 is being examined;

7) the Warsaw Pact states are being informed of the participation of certain members of the Czechoslovak People's Army in anti-Soviet demonstrations;

8) instructions have been issued for helicopters to patrol above areas where Soviet troops are deployed;

9) he has ordered the group of Soviet troops in the GDR, Poland and in Ukraine to prepare a plan to enter ČSSR territory and, in the event of a threat, to enter ČSSR territory without even prior warning to the Czechoslovak authorities.

He demands a strict investigation of and sanctions against soldiers who are guilty and material damage to be compensated. We leave the moral damage up to your conscience. He is bitter that he has to talk in this way since this then also reflects on the Soviet people. He asks to be received by the president, Comrades Dubček and Černík to express his protest and emphatically demands that measures be taken.

Dzúr: noted that the document he had prepared in many ways coincided with all that has been said. Several measures had been taken by the army. The only one who had asked for the assistance of troops was Pepich. We are specifying the situation in every respect. In Bratislava it had not been the soldiers but certain members of the Interior Ministry. Our inspection team left for Bratislava that same night. At Ústí nad Labem soldiers from the road battalion had been involved. A number had been summoned to the prosecutor.

He had and has thousands of troops ready, as well as a special plan. In agreement with the Interior Ministry he had taken measures and will take even more than had been requested. Every garrison commander has orders to help the security forces. In addition, there are special units. However, he himself cannot issue orders to the troops.

He was in contact with Comrades Dubček, Štrougal and Husák, but had been unable to contact the president and Comrade Černík. He had called on the commander of military counter-espionage and certain garrisons. On Saturday at 10 P.M. he was informed that everything was in order. All that needed to be done was done. He admits that certain factors were underestimated. He will summon the command, make his own evaluation and submit it to the party leadership, the government and the president.

Rusov: said that we felt miserable having to hear all this. Our information concerning the garrisons is more or less the same. We have a plan, the troops were prepared, all that was needed was for the political leadership to issue instructions. If soldiers did take part in the demonstrations, they were not from armored car or motorized divisions but from various rear supply units where there are soldiers with criminal records. We are investigating everything and shall take steps so the army will fulfill its duty. He informs the two ministers of the measures adopted.

Grechko: says the deputy commander of the group of forces had asked for assistance which was not given. Had he known that riots were being prepared throughout northern Bohemia he would have made a proposal to the government.

Dzúr: says that the Ministry of Interior, under pressure from us, has taken measures at Ústí. He explains that the deputy commander of the Central group of troops had telephoned between 12:30 A.M. and 1:00 A.M. when everything was essentially over. Everything had to be first clarified and specified through the Ministry of Interior. He himself is not authorized to bring the troops out without permission.

Grechko: This means that Dubček did not permit this.

Dzúr: argues that this was not the way he put it. Comrade Dubček ordered things to be clarified and specified. It was then that he called Comrades Štrougal, Husák, Pepich and others.

Maiorov: repeated the incident with the delegation of the Transcarpathian Military Area at lunch. When they were proposing a toast, explosives and Molotov cocktails were thrown outside and obscenities shouted. The commander of the Western military area and the commander of the 19th division were there. Of 36 garrisons 21 were in a state of disorder. He showed them on a map. A wireless engineering company was to have been deployed around Plzeň and Comrade Černík had spoken about this, but nothing is settled.

Rusov: specified that it was not near Plzeň but near Český Krumlov. We asked the government three times but received no answer.

Grechko: asked what our assessment was. He claimed that we were just looking on while the counterrevolution is running events. He again began to speak about counterrevolutionary slogans and banners and remarked that none of us had ever used the word counterrevolution. The allied troops had entered ČSSR territory to block the road to counterrevolution.

Dzúr: pointed out that he had said all he wanted to say.

Dvořák: noted that all that had happened and that is taking place cannot continue. The principles of friendship are being violated. The events on Saturday had been organized, and even if they had not, it's the results that matter. We have to apologize and take steps. He proposes that the Military Council thoroughly assess the situation, suggest measures and submit our evaluation and proposals to the leadership.

Dzúr: points out that this has been done. Agrees with Comrade Grechko that joint groups be set up to confront and verify facts with reports.

The question of guarding the western border is clear but as regards internal matters he is unable to state a decisive position. Then there is the political issue, the law on the press, censorship, the work of the judiciary, which also has its share.

He repeated how many and in which locations soldiers have been detailed to help the security forces. But he cannot send out a combat unit, for this he must receive instructions, consent. The commanders of the areas have the relevant orders.

Zolotov: division commander Novotný said he vouched for the senior officers but was unable to vouch for the younger ones.

Grechko: understands that Dzúr cannot send armed troops against the demonstrators. It was necessary to bar the road without arms.

He again came back to the insult of the Transcarpathian Military Area delegation. The commander does not command the regiment, the regiment has escaped subordination. In your country 40% of the soldiers say the main enemy is the USSR. And hundreds have taken part in anti-Soviet demonstrations. Relations with the USSR are getting worse. Counterrevolutionary forces are consolidating their positions. What are you doing in your political work? You call yourselves allies? Do you belong to the Warsaw Pact at all? We are defending socialism.

Both my hands were injured in battles for Czechoslovakia. I personally liberated many of the places where there were disturbances. You see this without any feelings. You are afraid to go to the troops and tell them the truth.

We warn you that we shall not tolerate a repetition of such acts. You said (that is, Comrade Dzúr), that you prevented clashes between Czechoslovak and Soviet troops. There was no need to say this. We shall make short shrift even of 100,000 counterrevolutionaries. We shall not let the ČSSR go. We shall withdraw neither this nor next year.

Nobody from the 21 garrisons came to apologize. This speaks for itself. You talk about this quite calmly. You should hear what our soldiers and commanders said. I am sorry but we shall not ask, we shall not ask your leadership, we shall not be afraid to adopt measures. You are afraid of a confrontation with counterrevolution.

There were signals of anti-Soviet slogans as far back as on March 21, yet this was no warning for you. You know the situation when ice hockey could turn into a political demonstration. You have no political vigilance.

Throughout the command of the Czechoslovak People's Army there is no good relationship with the Soviet army, otherwise measures would have been taken. What of it that the Military Council will meet, talk a while and then disband. Our people are waiting for someone to come and apologize.

At Mladá Boleslav, the commander asked three times until someone came and hit him with a stone. Things are verging on the terrible. Go to the soldiers and tell them the truth. Our soldiers are not permitted to mix with yours. I do not understand this and we cannot tolerate this. Measures must be taken, otherwise things will be really bad. One has to educate them, if not for friendship, then at least to show respect. Demonstrations are being prepared in your country and you are sitting still. I once again express the indignation of the Soviet command on the question of relations with the Soviet army. He not only asks but proposes that measures be taken.

Bedřich: agrees with the evaluation and understands the indignation. We have taken several measures but our results are not commensurate with our efforts. Czechoslovak–Soviet friendship is not being defended consistently. It is not easy to paralyze various influences on people's thinking. We must apologize for the events that have taken place and take steps towards strengthening lasting friendship.

Zolotov: is astonished how calmly the head of the main political administration is speaking. You often said that many political workers were an obstruction but you do nothing, you have them all at the main political administration. Those who want to work are angry that things are being dragged along and nothing is being done.

Maiorov: states that the treaty of October 16, 1968, is not being implemented, namely the passage which states that measures will be taken to strengthen relations. The Czechoslovak People's Army is not carrying out the president's decision on contacts. We are trying to fulfill it. The political leadership has laid down the line—the letter from the CPCz Central Committee to local branches speaking of the reinforcement of mutual relations. This applies to the army as well. An all-army assembly also underlined the demands to strengthen relations, but in practice nothing has changed. No political work is being done in carrying out the demand of the political leadership. If the army command did this the Soviet army would not be so isolated. There is still the Warsaw Pact. We made some good decisions there but what is needed is political education, friendship, love.

Grechko: none of this is felt, counterrevolution has gone onto an open offensive.

Dzúr: remarked that comrade Maiorov would be right if things were that simple in the state and among the people. There are many orders as well as speeches by leading representatives. We do not have the means to introduce love and friendship.

Maiorov: says he would dismiss a person if he were to find out that his men had harassed the allied army.

Dzúr: says he, too, will do this but only if the information is accurate.

Grechko: orders are given but how are they being fulfilled? We do not tell our people the kind of insults we hear. Or don't you think it necessary to summon your men, tell them, to come and see our men and talk to them?

Dzúr: is not too soft to do this. We, too, shall go there and explain.

Grechko: says it is essential to wage a real battle. He believes the situation in our country is worse than on August 21, 1968. If you don't take measures things will be in a bad way.

Dvořak: not only for us but for you as well.

Grechko: Smrkovský is always there when something against the USSR is taking place. He is surprised that we are so soft.

Dzúr: has spoken to the president and wants to brief him tomorrow at 10 A.M. The Bureau, the presidium is meeting and he is asking to be invited. He will inform them and state his opinion.

Grechko: asks Dzúr to inform them in the same way he informed the army command.

Dzúr: promises he will do this.

Grechko: asks Dzúr for an appointment for the whole delegation with the president, Comrades Dubček and Černík.

Dzúr: says he cannot promise that the president will see all of them. He stressed that we must make a profound analysis of all questions. It is not that simple. Your work is easier.

Grechko: we do not have people of the Smrkovský type. He (Grechko) would make use of this outrage by the counterrevolution and take a number of steps. He said he was glad shortcomings, the consequences of incorrect processes and so forth were being eliminated.

Dzúr: does not want to say a great deal. As regards the enemy from outside, the Czechoslovak People's Army will always be by the side of the Soviet army. The internal situation is something else. There are various linkages from which we shall learn lessons.

Grechko: again returns to the note, and remarks what it contains in this respect. Rejects the view that it was all unexpected. Go and explain and I, too, would like to go to our troops and explain certain matters.

The talks ended at 12.30 P.M.
April 1, 1969

PART SEVEN

DOCUMENTARY EPILOGUE

DOCUMENT No. 139: Vadim Medvedev's Account of the Legacy of the 1968 Crisis in the Age of *Perestroika*

Source: V. A. Medvedev, *Raspad: Kak on nazreval v "mirovoi sisteme sotsializma"* (Moscow: Mezhdunarodnye otnosheniya, 1994), pp. 137–154.

This excerpt from the memoirs of Vadim Medvedev, a top Soviet official during the Gorbachev period, focuses on Soviet–Czechoslovak relations in the late 1980s, including the legacy of the "Prague Spring." From 1986 to 1988 Medvedev was the CPSU CC secretary responsible for intra-bloc relations. From September 1988 on, he was both a full member of the CPSU CC Politburo and the CPSU CC secretary responsible for ideological affairs. In all these posts, he played a crucial part in relations with Czechoslovakia, including decisions on how to handle the "1968 Syndrome," as he called it. Having been the secretary of the CPSU's Leningrad branch (and a strong supporter of the invasion) in 1968, Medvedev knew from personal experience how different the calculations in the Soviet Union were in 1989.

Medvedev had a reputation as one of the most hard-line members of the Gorbachev-era Politburo, and some of that comes across in his memoir. He praises Gustáv Husák as an "honorable and open man," and writes that "Husák's willingness in April 1969 to assume leadership of the party and country was, in my view, the most courageous and responsible step possible." He also asserts that Husák's successor, Miloš Jakeš, "sincerely attempted to implement perestroika" in Czechoslovakia in 1988–1989 and "to engage everyone in the active work of perestroika." Despite these claims, Medvedev's account overall is solid and incisive, and is sharply critical of CPCz hard-liners like Vasil Biľak, Jan Fojtík, and Alois Indra. Moreover, Medvedev acknowledges that Jakeš "stopped half-way" in his efforts to adopt perestroika, and that "no decisive steps were taken to bring about national reconciliation and to do away with the 1968 syndrome."

The excerpts here are from a section entitled "The 1968 Syndrome." The section as a whole discusses the effect that Gorbachev's reforms had on Czechoslovakia—directly and indirectly—before, during, and after the "Velvet Revolution" of late 1989. Medvedev's account provides many new insights into this period and is especially valuable in conveying the shifting mood within the Soviet leadership as pressures for "new thinking" gained a life of their own. Medvedev rightly emphasizes the special problems posed by the legacy of the 1968 crisis. "For two decades," he writes, "the whole ruling elite [in Czechoslovakia] had been steeped in an ideology that totally rejected any model of society other than the one that was forcibly established in the country after 1968." Soviet efforts to reevaluate the 1968 crisis through the prism of "new thinking" were inherently constrained so long as CPCz leaders like Biľak, Indra, Husák, and Jakeš remained in power.

The extent of direct Soviet pressure on the Czechoslovak leadership during this crucial period is not entirely clear from Medvedev's account. On the one hand, Medvedev dismisses the notion that he or Gorbachev or any other Soviet official would have "delved into Czechoslovakia's internal affairs." Although CPCz hard-liners like Biľak and Indra strongly suspected that deals were being worked out "behind their backs" by Štrougal and Husák in connivance with Moscow, Medvedev denies that this was the case. On the other hand, Medvedev readily acknowledges that Gorbachev preferred certain CPCz officials (e.g., Štrougal) over others, and one can infer that the Soviet leader's preferences on this matter were conveyed, in one form or another, to the ruling elite in Prague. Moreover, the new Soviet position on the 1968 crisis, as Medvedev's account shows, could not help but affect the "internal affairs" of the CPCz leadership. Although Gorbachev himself refrained from any public condemnation of the 1968 invasion until after the "Velvet Revolution," the Soviet Politburo by 1988–89 was no longer willing to silence publicists and even some officials who wanted to reassess the whole crisis. That itself was a dramatic departure from the line of the Brezhnev period. Once individuals like Georgii Smirnov, the director of the CPSU Central Committee's Institute of Marxism–Leninism, began questioning the merits of the invasion, it became clear that a broader reevaluation was in the offing. The growing perception of impending dramatic changes in Soviet policy contributed to the demise of the Husák–Jakeš regime.

[By the mid-1980s] nearly 20 years had passed since the "Prague Spring" was crushed, and virtually nothing [in Czechoslovakia] had changed with regard to the development of democracy and *glasnost*. A strict ideological regime, a ban on pluralism of views, and a uniformity and sterility of the country's cultural life still prevailed.

Hundreds of thousands of people, who had been summarily expelled from the party and subjected to public ostracism, were, along with their whole families, still limited in their civil rights.

The party was still totally beyond any control by society, and as a result there were ever greater signs of decay, corruption, and malfeasance on the part of individual leaders. And all this in a country that had long been known for democratic and humanistic traditions and high European culture.

The beginning of *perestroika* in the Soviet Union generated a response throughout Czechoslovak society, spawning hopes that the situation in the country would change. The opposition was reanimated. Letters poured into the Central Committee. Demands grew for reform and for changes in the leadership.

And what did this leadership consist of? It had been kept almost intact since 1969, when it came to power after the suppression of a reform movement that was regarded at the time as counterrevolutionary and anti-socialist. The leadership was under the control of dogmatic conservative forces headed by a strongman, the "all-powerful" Vasil Biľak—"Vasilii Mikhailovich," as they called him in the Soviet Union. In essence, he held sway over the party, relying within the country on atavistic forces and openly exploiting for his own purposes his closeness to the Brezhnev leadership. . . .

. . . Soviet *perestroika* placed before the [CPCz] leadership an extremely difficult question: how to deal with it. The CPCz's unflinching loyalty and obedience to the CPSU ruled out the possibility of any sort of divergence from the new line of the Soviet leadership. In both the official documents of the CPCz CC and the speeches of its leaders, one could find no hint of disagreement with Soviet *perestroika*. The Czechoslovak leaders even began to compete with one another in their proclaimed enthusiasm for Soviet *perestroika*. They would accuse each other of not being sufficiently supportive of it. . . .

. . . From my meetings with the Czechoslovak friends, I reached the firm conclusion that their complete or partial aversion to *perestroika* was determined first and foremost by the 1968 syndrome, which dominated the country's leadership and defined the logic of its behavior. The problem was not only that someone was holding onto his sinecure, but that for two decades after the "Prague Spring" the whole ruling elite and party and state activists had been steeped in an ideology that totally rejected any model of society other than the one that was forcibly established in the country after 1968. . . .

. . . The dogmatic fundamentalist forces, with unyielding persistence, blocked any possibility of launching a renewal process. Without any sort of prompting on our part, our Czechoslovak colleagues began insisting to us that there was no need to rehabilitate the participants in the 1968 events because this matter had already been taken care of long ago. They noted that the measures adopted back then had been very lenient and had not infringed in any serious way on human rights and had not affected broad segments of society, etc. This line of a rhetorical embrace of *perestroika* continued even though democratic processes were in reality still frozen. . . .

When Czechoslovak leaders were in Moscow at the beginning of November 1987 to mark the 70th anniversary of the Soviet regime (Jakeš and Biľak accompanied Husák on the trip), a meeting took place between Gorbachev and Husák. As always, it was conducted in a very frank and comradely manner. Husák informed Gorbachev about the situation in Czechoslovakia and let him know that he was intensively contemplating the problem of changes in the country's leadership and was determined to find a considered solution. He referred positively to Jakeš and gave an upbeat evaluation of Štrougal's activities, and he said that he was preparing to reach a decision on himself. Husák informed Gorbachev that basic elements of *perestroika* in Czechoslovakia, and above all economic reforms, were due to be considered at a CC plenum in December, and that in connection with this there would be adjustments in the leadership.

Gorbachev did not delve into a consideration of possible adjustments in the leadership, having emphasized that this was a purely internal matter for Czechoslovakia. To this end he added that there was no one better than Husák himself to decide when the moment had arrived to resolve this question from the standpoint of the country's interests and his own personal interests. Gorbachev agreed to receive Štrougal in Moscow as soon as he wished.

While the Czechoslovak delegation was in Moscow, a highly unusual and important incident occurred. A statement by the director of the Institute of Marxism–Leninism, Smirnov, at a press conference—I don't recall in what connection it was held—cast doubt on the propriety of the actions taken by the allied governments in Czechoslovakia in 1968.[1] Even now I can't say for sure whether this was a coincidental or premeditated step. I can only note that such sentiments had begun spreading more and more widely in intellectual circles and among scholars. Of course, Smirnov was merely expressing his own viewpoint. But the point is that he was a CC member[2] and director of the CPSU CC Institute of Marxism–Leninism, and not long before had been an adviser to the general secretary. He hadn't received any sort of sanction, not to mention instructions, from the CPSU CC on this matter.

His statement caused great alarm on the part of the Czechoslovak delegation, especially Biľak. Having learned about it late in the evening, I found it necessary to make a special trip to the Lenin Hills, where the Czechoslovak delegation was staying. In a one-on-one conversation with Biľak I said to him that this was Smirnov's personal opinion, and I emphasized that we would not make even a single question that affected another friendly party and country without seeking the advice of that country's leadership. At the same time, we could not prohibit our scholars from reexamining historical problems.

He generally accepted this explanation, but nonetheless tried to shift the conversation into a review of the situation in the leadership, the need for changes, and so forth. This was not something I wanted to pursue, so I asked Biľak not to steer us into a consideration of such matters. These are your affairs, I said, and no one will decide them for you. With that, the conversation ended.

In mid-November, Štrougal arrived in Moscow. Ryzhkov held negotiations with him on economic matters, but the most important aspect of his visit was, of course, political. Štrougal met Gorbachev, who had a high regard for Štrougal's record as head of the government and his efforts to reform the economy. Along with this, the opinion was expressed that in moving to the plenum in December—the first plenum focusing on *perestroika*—one must be fully assured that the adopted resolutions will be serious and that the leadership can carry them out.

---

[1] The official in question is Georgii Lukich Smirnov, who was appointed director of the Institute in February 1987. He had long been one of the most influential theoreticians in the CPSU CC apparatus and was one of the early proponents of "new political thinking." Smirnov and two other prominent Soviet historians hosted a press conference on 4 November 1987 to discuss historical topics covered by Mikhail Gorbachev in his keynote 70th anniversary speech. When asked by a reporter whether it would soon be possible to reassess the 1968 crisis, Smirnov said there was "a need to reconsider the events of 1968 and the intervention" and "a need for a new assessment." He noted that the decision in August 1968 had been reached "with difficulty."

[2] Actually, Smirnov was only a candidate member of the CPSU Central Committee, not a full member.

Štrougal left for home feeling elated. He sensed that in Moscow they understand the situation and are not just blindly following the advice of certain diehard friends from the Czechoslovak leadership.

These discussions could not have been more timely. On 18 November, at the initiative of Biľak and his supporters on the CPCz CC Presidium, the question was raised of dividing the posts of president and first secretary of the Central Committee of the party. Apparently, Biľak and his supporters suspected that all matters had been arranged in Moscow behind their backs by Husák and Štrougal, and so they decided to act.

Indra directly asked Husák: Was the question of separating the posts raised during his visit in Moscow? Husák rightly gave a negative answer, emphasizing that in Moscow he had received full support for his efforts to carry out a line of *perestroika*. Biľak, for his part, "pressed" Štrougal: Didn't Štrougal indicate, when he was in Moscow, that there are opponents of *perestroika* in Prague, and didn't he cite specific names? Naturally, Štrougal, too, categorically denied these allegations. Biľak and his supporters referred, of course, to Smirnov's statement on the events of 1968. Everyone other than Štrougal and Kapek expressed a negative opinion of this statement. They authorized Biľak to seek reaffirmation of the previous assessments and the "Lessons of Crisis Development."

. . . . Overall Jakeš made some discernible efforts to embark on *perestroika*, but he stopped halfway when he proved incapable of traversing what for him was the main barrier. Hence, no decisive steps were taken to promote national reconciliation, eliminate the 1968 syndrome, and set forth a political course aimed at comprehensive and profound democratization and *glasnost*. Fundamental questions facing the public in Czechoslovakia were left unresolved. As a result, opposition sentiments grew rapidly and finally spilled over into the November "Velvet Revolution." . . .

I recall that on 17 November 1989—the same day that student demonstrations erupted on the streets of Prague, marking the beginning of the "Velvet Revolution"—I was meeting Jan Fojtík, my counterpart on ideological affairs, who happened to be in Moscow at the time. He privately briefed me on the student unrest, not yet suspecting where it all might soon lead.[3]

During the discussion, the question was raised about the reevaluation of the 1968 events. Fojtík tried to clarify whether we were preparing to make a reevaluation of 1968 in light of subsequent events and the new political thinking. He said that they, too, were coming under enormous pressure on this question. As a smart and, I would even say, crafty individual, he did not declare that this question was wholly off-limits for them. Moreover, he hinted that, in any case, the current Czechoslovak leadership no longer included people who had directly abetted the action of the allied states in August 1968 (by this time Biľak and Indra were no longer on the CPCz CC Presidium). "If you take some sort of steps in this direction," he said, "we, for our part, could respond."

I had to remind him of our position, which I had already expressed earlier—that neither on this issue nor on any other were we intending a unilateral resolution of matters that affected not only us, but our friends even more.[4] For us, since we had dissociated ourselves from the Brezhnevite course in the framework of new political thinking, a reevaluation did not pose any danger. On the contrary, it would be a logical step, but this would represent a direct statement

---

[3] For a detailed overview of the events in Czechoslovakia on 17 November 1989 that coincided with Fojtík's visit to Moscow, see the 3-part investigation "Ze závěrečné zprávy vyšetřovací komise Federálního shromáždění pro objasnění událostí 17. listopadu 1989," *Rudé právo* (Prague), part 1, 5 February 1992, pp. 7–10; part 2, 6 February 1992, pp. 7–10; and part 3, 7 February 1992, pp. 5–6.

[4] It is unclear how candid Medvedev is being here. Reliable sources, both at the time and afterwards, claimed that Georgii Smirnov informed Fojtík on 17 November that the Soviet leadership had prepared a statement condemning the invasion and would release it unilaterally unless the CPCz leadership acted promptly on the matter. Fojtík himself hinted at this in a public statement when he returned to Prague. In any case, the whole issue was swiftly overtaken by the "Velvet Revolution."

against the current Czechoslovak leadership, which continued to adhere to the positions of the "Lessons of Crisis Development." The initiative in reconsidering these positions, or at least in raising the question, must be up to the Czechoslovak comrades themselves.

The conversation was of a sufficiently pointed nature. But, naturally, Fojtík was unable to offer any sort of new position, since this matter had to be decided collectively at the highest level, with positive input from the leaders of all countries that had played a part in the events of 1968. Who could have foreseen that within less than a month, amid mass demonstrations, the CPCz CC and government would reconsider their earlier assessments of 1968 and condemn the action of the allied countries, and that the leaders of these countries would gather in Moscow and repudiate their earlier decision to send their troops to Czechoslovakia?

Right after our discussion, Fojtík returned to Prague, where events were assuming mass proportions and quickly spreading. The authorities had made a fatal decision to suppress the student demonstration by force. This action evoked a storm of outrage in society and soon led to a challenge to the existing regime, the removal of the party from power, and then to its collapse. Power passed into the hands of the opposition. . . .

DOCUMENT No. 140: Soviet and Warsaw Pact Apologies to Czechoslovakia, December 1989

Source: "Zayavlenie rukovoditelei Bolgarii, Vengrii, GDR, Pol'shi, i Sovetskogo Soyuza" and "Zayavlenie Sovetskogo Soyuza," both in *Pravda*, December 5, 1989, p. 2.

In early December 1989, just after communism had collapsed all over Eastern Europe (except in Romania, where a violent revolution was still to come), leaders of the Soviet Union and the four East European countries that took part in the 1968 invasion gathered in Moscow to issue a collective statement repudiating the "illegal interference" they had committed 21 years earlier against Czechoslovakia. That same day, the Soviet government issued a separate apology for its role in spearheading the invasion. These declarations marked the culmination of a reassessment of the 1968 invasion that had been under way in the Soviet Union—unofficially, for the most part—since the autumn of 1987.

By the time the two statements were issued, the East European countries that had contributed troops in 1968 had already conveyed apologies of their own to Czechoslovakia, starting with a resolution by the Polish parliament in mid-August 1989 that expressed "sorrow and regret" to the Czechs and Slovaks, declared the invasion to be a "violation of the inalienable right of every nation to self-determination," and explicitly "condemned the aggression of 1968, which set back the process of democratization in Czechoslovakia." Hungary issued a similar apology a few days later, and East Germany and Bulgaria both followed suit once the orthodox communist leaders in those countries had been overthrown. The individual East European statements were stronger than the declaration that the Soviet government later issued, but it was not until the Soviet Union had officially apologized that the Brezhnev Doctrine was fully renounced.

Statement by the Leaders of Bulgaria, Hungary, the GDR, Poland, and the Soviet Union:

The leaders of Bulgaria, Hungary, the GDR, Poland, and the Soviet Union, having gathered for a meeting in Moscow on 4 December of this year, declare that the introduction of forces into the ČSSR in 1968 amounted to interference in the internal affairs of a sovereign Czechoslovakia and must be condemned.

Having cut short the process of democratic renewal in the ČSSR, these unlawful actions had long-term negative consequences. History has confirmed how important it is, even in the most complex international situation, to use political means for the settlement of any problems and to adhere strictly to the principles of sovereignty, independence, and non-interference in internal affairs in relations between states, as required by the clauses of the Warsaw Treaty.

Statement by the Soviet Government:

Czechoslovak society is at a stage now where it is critically reevaluating the experience of its political and economic development. This process is natural and is something that many countries undertake in one form or another. Unfortunately, the necessity of constant socialist self-renewal and realistic assessments of continuing events were not always feasible. Especially in situations when such events assumed a contradictory shape and demanded bold responses to the needs of the time.

In 1968 the then-Soviet leadership sided with one of the parties in an internal dispute in Czechoslovakia that stemmed from festering problems. At the time, this unbalanced, deficient approach and this interference in the affairs of a friendly country were justified with respect to the tense confrontation between East and West.

We share the point of view of the CPCz CC Presidium and the ČSSR government that the entry of the armies of the five socialist countries into Czechoslovakia in 1968 was unjustified, and that the decision about it in light of all facts known now was mistaken.

MAIN ACTORS

Unless otherwise indicated,
titles and positions listed are those held in 1968

ALEKSANDROV-AGENTOV, ANDREI: chief foreign policy adviser to Leonid Brezhnev.

ANDROPOV, YURII: chairman, Soviet Committee on State Security (KGB), 1967–1982; candidate member, CPSU CC Politburo, 1967–1973; member, CPSU CC Politburo, 1973–1984; CPSU CC general secretary, 1982–1984.

BIĽAK, VASIL: member of the CPS CC Presidium and CPS CC secretary, 1963–1968; CPS CC first secretary, January to August 1968; member, CPCz CC Presidium, April 1968 until December 1988.

BREZHNEV, LEONID: CPSU CC general secretary, 1964–1982; chairman of Presidium of Supreme Soviet, 1977–1982.

CEAUŞESCU, NICOLAE: general secretary, Romanian Communist Party, 1965–1989; chairman of State Council RSR, 1967–1989.

ČERNÍK, OLDŘICH: ČSSR deputy prime minister and chairman, State Planning Commission, 1963–1968; ČSSR prime minister, 1968–1970; expelled from CPCz, 1971.

CHERVONENKO, STEPAN: Soviet ambassador in Prague, 1965–1973.

CÍSAŘ, ČESTMÍR: CPCz CC secretary, April to August 1968; chairman, Czech National Council, 1968–1969; expelled from CPCz, 1970.

DUBČEK, ALEXANDER: CPS CC first secretary, 1963–January 1968; member of CPCz CC, 1963–September 1969; CPCz CC first secretary, January 1968–April 1969; expelled from CPCz, June 1970.

DZÚR, MARTIN: ČSSR deputy minister of national defense, 1961–April 1968; minister of national defense, April 1968–1985.

GOMUŁKA, WŁADYSŁAW: first secretary, Polish United Workers' Party, October 1956–December 1970.

GRECHKO, ANDREI: marshal of the USSR; commander-in-chief, Warsaw Pact Joint Armed Forces, 1960–1967; Soviet minister of defense, 1967–1976; member, CPSU CC Politburo, 1973–1976.

GROMYKO, ANDREI: Soviet foreign minister, 1957–1985; member, CPSU CC Politburo, 1973–1989.

HÁJEK, JIŘÍ: ČSSR minister of education and culture, 1965–1968; ČSSR minister of foreign affairs, 1968; expelled from CPCz, 1970.

HUSÁK, GUSTÁV: ČSSR deputy prime minister, April–August 1968; CPS CC first secretary, August 1968–May 1969; member, CPCz CC Presidium, August 1968 to November 1989; CPCz CC first secretary, April 1969–December 1987; ČSSR president, May 1975–November 1989.

INDRA, ALOIS: ČSSR minister of transport 1963–April 1968; CPCz CC secretary, April 1968–December 1971; member, CPCz CC Presidium, 1971–1989; chairman, ČSSR Federal Assembly, 1971–1989.

JAKEŠ, MILOŠ: deputy minister of interior, 1966–April 1968; chairman, CPCz Central Control and Auditing Commission, April 1968–December 1977; secretary, CPCz CC, 1977–1987; member, CPCz CC Presidium, 1981–1989; first secretary, CPCz CC, December 1987–November 1989.

KÁDÁR, JÁNOS: first secretary, Hungarian Socialist Workers' Party, 1956–1989.

KAPEK, ANTONÍN: director of CKD Enterprise Prague; candidate member, CPCz CC Presidium, 1962–August 1968; member, CPCz CC Bureau for Party Work in the Czech Lands, September 1969–January 1970; leading secretary, CPCz Prague City Committee, December 1969–April 1988; full member, CPCz CC Presidium, January 1970–April 1988.

KATUSHEV, KONSTANTIN: CPSU CC secretary responsible for intra-bloc relations, 1968–1977; deputy prime minister, 1977–1980.

KOLDER, DRAHOMÍR: member, CPCz CC Presidium, 1962–1968; CPCz CC secretary, 1962–1968; removed from presidium on August 31, 1968; chairman, People's Control Committee, 1969–1972.

KOMÓCSIN, ZOLTÁN: HSWP CC secretary responsible for inter-party ties and foreign affairs.

KOSYGIN, ALEKSEI: member, CPSU CC Politburo, 1960–1980; chairman, USSR Council of Ministers, 1964–1980.

KRIEGEL, FRANTIŠEK: member, CPCz CC Presidium, April–August 1968; chairman, National Front Central Committee, April–August 1968; expelled from CPCz, May 1969; expelled from ČSSR National Assembly, October 1969.

KUZNETSOV, VASILI: Soviet first deputy minister of foreign affairs, 1955–1977; candidate member, CPSU CC Politburo, 1977–1986.

LENÁRT, JOZEF: ČSSR prime minister, 1963–April 1968; member, CPCz CC Presidium, 1962–1968; candidate member, CPCz CC Presidium 1968–1969; CPCz CC secretary, 1968–1970; CPS CC first secretary, 1970–1988; member, CPCz CC Presidium, 1970–1988.

LOMSKÝ, BOHUMÍR: ČSSR minister of national defense, 1956–April 1968.

MAZUROV, KIRILL: member, CPSU CC Politburo, 1965–1978; in August 1968 served under the code-name of "General Trofimov" as the Politburo's representative overseeing the political and military aspects of the invasion.

MLYNÁŘ, ZDENĚK: member, CPCz Central Committee, 1968–1969; member, CPCz CC Secretariat, April–November 1968; CPCz CC secretary, June–November 1968; member, CPCz CC Presidium, August–November 1968; removed from CPCz CC, September 1969; expelled from CPCz, 1970.

NOVOTNÝ, ANTONÍN: CPCz CC first secretary, March 1953–January 1968; ČSSR president, 1957–April 1968.

PAVEL, JOSEF: ČSSR minister of interior, April–August 1968; expelled from CPCz, 1970.

PAVLOVSKII, IVAN: army-general; commander-in-chief of Soviet ground forces; deputy Soviet defense minister; supreme commander of allied forces entering Czechoslovakia.

PELIKÁN, JIŘÍ: member, CPCz Central Committee; director, Czechoslovak Television Service; and chairman, Foreign Relations Committee of the ČSSR National Assembly

PILLER, JAN: member, CPCz CC Presidium; leading secretary, Central Bohemian CPCz Regional Committee, January 1968–1971.

PODGORNY, NIKOLAI: member, CPSU CC Politburo, 1960–1977; chairman, Presidium of Supreme Soviet, 1965–1977.

PONOMAREV, BORIS: CPSU CC secretary; head of CPSU CC International Department, 1961–1986; candidate member, CPSU CC Politburo, 1972–1986.

PRCHLÍK, VÁCLAV: army-general; chief, Main Political Directorate of the Czechoslovak People's Army, 1956–February 1968; head of CPCz CC State Administrative Department, February–July 1968; member of CPCz CC, 1958–1969

RIGO, EMIL: member, CPCz CC Presidium, January–August 1968; Deputy to Federal Assembly House of Nations, 1971–1986.

ŠALGOVIČ, VILIAM: chairman, CPS Central Control and Auditing Commission, 1962–1968 and 1970–1975; deputy minister of interior, June–August 1968; chairman, Slovak National Council, 1975–1988.

ŠEJNA, JAN: chief of party committee in Czechoslovak Ministry of Defense, 1963–1968; defected to the United States in February 1968.

Šɪк, Oтa: director of Economics Institute, Czechoslovak Academy of Sciences, 1962–1969; member, CPCz Central Committee, 1962–1969; ČSSR deputy prime minister, April–September 1968; expelled from CPCz, May 1969.

Smrkovský, Josef: member, CPCz CC Presidium, 1968–1969; minister of forest and water economy 1965–1968; chairman, National Assembly, 1968–1969; expelled from CPCz, 1970.

Špaček, Josef: leading secretary, South Moravian CPCz Committee in Brno, 1966–1969; member, CPCz CC Presidium, January 1968 to April 1969; CPCz CC secretary, August 1968–May 1969; expelled from CPCz, 1970.

Štrougal, Lubomír: CPCz CC secretary, 1965–1968; ČSSR deputy prime minister, April–December 1968; member, CPCz CC Presidium, November 1968–October 1988; ČSSR prime minister, January 1970–October 1988.

Suslov, Mikhail: member, CPSU CC Politburo, 1952–1953, 1955–1982; CPSU CC secretary responsible for ideological affairs.

Švestka, Oldřich: member, CPCz Presidium, removed on August 31, 1968.

Svoboda, Ludvík: minister of national defense, 1945–1950; deputy, ČSSR National Assembly, 1948–1968; ČSSR president, March 1968–May 1975; member, CPCz CC Presidium, August 1968–April 1976.

Tito, Josip Broz: general secretary/chairman, Yugoslav League of Communists, 1948–1980; president of Yugoslavia, 1953–1980; and supreme commander, Yugoslav armed forces, 1953–1980.

Ulbricht, Walter: first secretary, Socialist Unity Party (GDR), 1950–1971; chairman, GDR State Council, 1960–1983.

Yakubovskii, Ivan: marshal of the Soviet Union; commander-in-chief of the Warsaw Pact Joint Armed Forces; first deputy Soviet defense minister.

Zhivkov, Todor: first secretary, Bulgarian Communist Party, 1954–1989.

SELECTED ORGANIZATIONS

Club of Committed Non-Party Members (KAN) A loose association of citizens, mainly from the intelligentsia, who gradually formed a political "club" starting in April 1968. As the name of the club implied, all those who took part in KAN were not members of the CPCz. KAN functioned as a discussion group which subsequently could have become the nucleus of a new, non-communist political party. It was banned in September 1968 when the Ministry of Interior turned down the KAN statutes.

Communist Party of Czechoslovakia (CPC, or KSČ) A Marxist–Leninist political party that ruled Czechoslovakia from 1948 to 1989. The hierarchical structure of the party was based on "democratic centralism," a euphemism denoting strict conformity with central directives and rulings at all levels. The lowest organs of the party were the branches in workplaces and localities, directed by district committees that in turn were directed by CPCz regional committees. The highest organs were the Central Committee and the Presidium which it elected. The top official in the party was known as the "first secretary" from 1953 until 1971; in 1971 the title was changed to "general secretary." In principle, the supreme body of the CPCz was the Congress, which usually convened once every four years. The most recent congress before 1968 was the 13th, held from May 31 to June 4, 1966. In between congresses, decision-making rested with the Presidium, the Central Committee, and the district and regional party conferences. In 1968 two new party bodies were established. In response to the existence of the Communist Party of Slovakia and the demand to establish a separate Czech communist party (just as the Czechoslovak state was federalized in 1968), the CPCz CC plenum of November 1968 adopted a decree setting up a "Bureau" to run party work in the Czech Lands. Plans for the full-scale federalization of the party were abandoned at Soviet behest, however. The November 1968 CC plenum also decided to establish an Executive Committee of the CPCz CC Presidium as a body to run the party on a day-to-day basis. This organ was dissolved just five months later, however, by the CC plenum in April 1969.

Council for Mutual Economic Assistance (CMEA) An economic organization of communist states, established in Moscow in January 1949. Full members included all the Warsaw Pact countries as well as several communist states in the Third World.

Czech National Council (ČNR) Created in June 1968 in accordance with Constitutional Law No. 77/68 regarding preparations for the federalized restructuring of the ČSSR. The first elections to the ČNR took place on July 10, 1968. After the Czechoslovak federation was formally established, the ČNR became the legislative body of the Czech Socialist Republic.

K-231: An association of citizens who had formerly been imprisoned under Law No. 231/48 ("In Defense of the Republic"). K-231's main goals were to secure the rehabilitation of all political prisoners and to expedite the work of the Rehabilitation Commission. After a Law on Rehabilitations was passed on June 25, 1968, K-231 members actively contributed to the work of the Rehabilitation Commissions. The club was banned in September 1968 when the Ministry of Interior refused to approve its statutes.

National Assembly (NS) The highest legislative body in the ČSSR. In January 1969 it was renamed Federal Assembly in accordance with Constitutional Law No. 143/68. The legislature consisted of two chambers: the House of Peoples and the House of Nations. The National Assembly elected the president of the republic.

National Front (NF) An association of Czechoslovak political parties and mass organizations established in Moscow in March 1945 during talks involving Soviet and Czechoslovak communist officials. The CPCz controlled the activities of all nominally independent political parties and mass organizations through the NF. No political party or mass organization was permitted in Czechoslovakia unless it was represented in the National Front.

People's Militia (LM) Armed units of the CPCz established in February 1948 during the CPCz's bid to seize power. Subsequently, the LM's main purpose was to defend the communist regime and the "leading role" of the CPCz. The CPCz first secretary was the supreme commander of the LM. In 1968, when sentiment emerged in favor of a new role for the CPCz, many called for the disbandment of the People's Militia. Dubček sought to avoid this step by incorporating the People's Militia into the structure of the armed forces.

Slovak National Council (SNR) A parallel National Assembly for Slovakia, which was set up in 1944. The jurisdiction and powers of the SNR were constantly changed, especially in the 1960s. After the Czechoslovak federation was set up, the SNR became the legislative body of the Slovak Socialist Republic.

State Security (StB) Part of the National Security Corps. Its functions included intelligence and counterintelligence, and it was also a leading organ of internal repression.

Warsaw Treaty Organization (WTO) or *Warsaw Pact* A military-political group of communist states established in May 1955. The original members consisted of Albania, Bulgaria, Czechoslovakia, the German Democratic Republic, Hungary, Poland, Romania, and the Soviet Union. Albania ceased participating in the alliance in 1961 and formally withdrew from the pact after the 1968 invasion. The supreme political body of the pact was the Political Consultative Committee; the highest military organ was the Joint Command, which supervised the Joint Armed Forces of the participating countries. All the leading command posts in the WTO were staffed exclusively by Soviet officers. The commander-in-chief of the Pact in 1968 was Marshal Ivan Yakubovskii.

BIBLIOGRAPHY

Aczél, Tamás. "Budapest 1956—Prague 1968: Spokesmen of Revolution." *Problems of Communism* vol. 18, Nos. 4–5 (July–October 1969) 60–67.

Allison, Graham T. "Comment." *Studies in Comparative Communism* vol. XIII, No. 4 (Winter 1980) 329–330 [tk].

Ames, Kenneth. "Reform and Reaction," *Problems of Communism* vol. 17, No. 6 (November–December 1968) 38–50.

Andrew, Christopher and Oleg Gordievskii. *The KGB: The Inside Story of Its Foreign Operations from Lenin to Gorbachev*. New York: Harper-Collins, 1990.

August, František and David Rees. *Red Star Over Prague*. London: Sherwood Press, 1984.

Ball, George W. *The Past Has Another Pattern: Memoirs*. New York: W. W. Norton, 1982.

Benčík, Antonín. *Operace "Dunaj": Vojáci a Pražské jaro 1968*. Praha: ÚSD, 1994.

Bittman, Ladislav. *The Deception Game: Czechoslovak Intelligence in Soviet Political Warfare*. Syracuse: Syracuse University Research Corporation, 1972.

Bodensieck, Heinrich. *Urteilsbildung zum Zeitgeschehen: Der Fall ČSSR, 1968–69*. Stuttgart: Ernst Klett Verlag, 1970.

Bodner, Anne. *Die Ära Dubček: Untersuchungen zum Prager Reformkommunismus 1968/69*. Hamburg: Hoffman und Campe, 1971.

Bohlen, Charles E. *Witness to History, 1929–1969*. New York: W. W. Norton, 1973.

Brahm, Heinz. *Der Kreml und die ČSSR, 1968–1969*. Stuttgart: Verlag W. Kohlhammer, 1970.

Brandt, Willy. *People and Politics: The Years 1960–1975*. London: Collins, 1978.

Broue, Pierre, ed. *Ecrits à Prague sous la Censure. Aôut 1968–juin 1969*. Paris: EDI, 1973.

Brown, J. F. "Rumania Today: The Strategy of Defiance," *Problems of Communism* vol. 18, No. 2 (March–April 1969) 32–38.

Brus, Wlodzimierz, Peter Kende, and Zdeněk Mlynář. *"Normalization" Processes in Soviet–Dominated Central Europe*. Köln: Index, 1982.

Bukharkin, Igor. "Tsel' avgust 68-ogo goda..." *Pravda* (Moscow), 18 February 1991.

Burens, Peter-Claus. *Die DDR und der "Prager Frühling": Bedeutung und Auswirkungen der tschechoslowakischen Erneuerungsbewegung für die Innenpolitik der DDR im Jahre 1968*. West Berlin: Druckerei Humblot, 1981.

Československo roku 1968, 1. díl: Obrodný proces. Prague: Parta, 1993.

Československo roku 1968, 2. díl: Počátky normalizace. Prague: Parta, 1993.

Cigánek, František. Národní shromáždění, 21.–28. srpna, 1968. Brno: ÚSD, 1995.

Clifford, Clark M. with Richard C. Holbrooke. *Counsel to the President: A Memoir*. New York: Random House, 1991.

Craig, Richard B. and J. David Gillespie. "Yugoslav Reaction to the Czechoslovakia Liberation Movement and the Invasion of 1968." *Australian Journal of Politics and History* vol. 23, No. 2 (1977) 227–238.

Croan, Melvin. "Czechoslovakia, Ulbricht, and the German Problem." *Problems of Communism* vol. 18, No. 1 (January–February 1969) 1–7.

Crossman, Richard. *The Diaries of a Cabinet Minister* vol. 3. London: Hamish Hamilton, 1977.

Czerwinski, E. J. and Jaroslaw Piekalkiewicz, eds. *The Soviet Invasion of Czechoslovakia: Its Effects on Eastern Europe*. New York: Praeger, 1972.

Dahm, Helmut. *Der gescheiterte Ausbruch: Entideologisierung und ideologische Gegenreformation in Osteuropa, 1960–1980*. Baden-Baden: Nomos Verlagsgesellschaft, 1982.

Daix, Pierre. *J'ai cru un matin*. Paris: Laffont, 1976.

Daix, Pierre. *Prague au coeur*. Paris: Editions Juillard, 1968.

Dawisha, Karen. "Soviet Security and the Role of the Military: The 1968 Czechoslovak Crisis," *British Journal of Political Science* vol. 10, No. 1 (1980) 341–363.

Dawisha, Karen. "The 1968 Invasion of Czechoslovakia: Causes, Consequences, and Lessons for the Future," in Karen Dawisha and Philip Hanson, eds. *Soviet–East European Dilemmas: Coercion, Competition and Consent*. London: Heinemann, 1981, 9–25.

Dawisha, Karen. "The Limits of the Bureaucratic Politics Model: Observations on the Soviet Case." *Studies in Comparative Communism* vol. XIII, No. 4 (Winter 1980) 300–328 [tk].

Dawisha, Karen. "Rejoinder," *Studies in Comparative Communism* vol. XIII, No. 4 (Winter 1980) [tk].

Dawisha, Karen. *The Kremlin and the Prague Spring*. Berkeley: University of California Press, 1984.

de Gaulle, Charles. *Memoires d'Espoir — Le Renouveau*. Paris: Plon, 1970.

de Weydenthal, Jan B. "Polish Politics and the Czechoslovak Crisis in 1968," *Canadian Slavonic Papers* vol. 14, No. 1 (1972) 31–56.

Dean, Robert W. *Nationalism and Political Change in Eastern Europe: The Slovak Question and the Czechoslovak Reform Movement*, Monographs in World Affairs Series No. 10. Denver: University of Denver, 1973.

Devlin, Kevin. "The New Crisis in European Communism," *Problems of Communism* vol. 17, No. 6 (November–December 1968) 57–69.

Dubček, Alexander with András Sugár, *Dubček Speaks*, trans. by Kathy Szent-Györgyi. New York: I. B. Tauris & Co., 1990.

Dubček, Alexander. *Hope Dies Last: The Autobiography of Alexander Dubček*, trans. and ed. by Jiři Hochman. New York: Kodansha International, 1993.

Eidlin, Fred H. "'Capitulation,' 'Resistance,' and the Framework of 'Normalization': The August 1968 Invasion of Czechoslovakia and the Czechoslovak Response," *Journal of Peace Research* vol. 18, No. 4 (December 1981) 319–332.

Eidlin, Fred H. "Comment," *Studies in Comparative Communism* vol. XIII, No. 4 (Winter 1980) 332–342 [tk].

Eidlin, Fred H. "The Initial Political Failure of the Warsaw Pact Intervention in Czechoslovakia of 21 August 1968," *East Central Europe/L'Europe du Centre-Est* vol. 5, Pt. 2 (1978) 245–266.

Eidlin, Fred H. *The Logic of "Normalization": The Soviet Intervention in Czechoslovakia of 21 August 1968 and the Czechoslovak Response*. Boulder, Col.: East European Monographs, 1980.

Eidlin, Fred H. "Misperception, Ambivalence, and Indecision in Soviet Policy-Making: The Case of the 1968 Invasion of Czechoslovakia," *Conflict* vol. 5, No. 2 (1984) 89–117.

Erickson, John. "International and Strategic Implications of the Czechoslovak Reform Movement," in Vladimir V. Kusin, ed. *The Czechoslovak Reform Movement 1968: Proceedings of the Seminar Held at the University of Reading on 12–17 July 1971*. Santa Barbara, Calif.: ABC-Clio Press, 1973, 31–49.

Ermath, Fritz. *Internationalism, Security, and Legitimacy: The Challenge to Soviet Interests in East Europe, 1964–1968*, Memorandum RM–5909-PR. Santa Monica, Calif.: RAND Corporation, 1969.

Eugen, Löbl and Leopold Grünwald. *Die intellektuelle Revolution: Hintergründe und Auswirkungen des "Prager Frühlings"*. Düsseldorf: Econ Verlag, 1969.

584

Fejtő, François. "Moscow and Its Allies," *Problems of Communism*. vol. 17, No. 6 (November–December 1968) 29–38.

Floyd, David. "The Czechoslovak Crisis of 1968," in *Brasseys Annual: The Armed Forces Yearbook, 1969*. London: William Clowes and Sons, 1969, 70–81.

Frolík, Josef. *The Frolík Defection: The Memoirs of an Intelligence Agent*. London: Leo Cooper, 1975.

Garlicki, Andrzej and Andrzej Paczkowski, *Zaciskanie pętli: Tajne dokumenty dotyczące Czechoslowacji 1968 r.* Warszawa: Wydawn. Sejmowe, 1995.

Gellert, Andre. "The Diplomacy of the Czechoslovak Crisis: Why They Failed," *Studies for a New Central Europe* vol. 2, Nos. 3–4 (1968–1969) 43–53.

Golan, Galia. *Reform Rule in Czechoslovakia: The Dubček Era, 1968–1969*. New York: Cambridge University Press, 1973.

Golan, Galia. *The Czechoslovak Reform Movement: Communism in Crisis, 1962–1968*. New York: Cambridge University Press, 1971.

Groth, Alexander J. *Eastern Europe After Czechoslovakia*. New York: Foreign Policy Association, 1969.

Grünwald, Leopold, ed. *ČSSR im Umbruch*. Vienna: Europa-Archiv, 1968.

Gruša, Jiří and Tomáš Kosta. *Prager Frühling—Prager Herbst: Blicke zurück und nach vorn*. Köln: Bund-Verlag, 1988.

Gueyt, Remi. *La mutation tchécoslovaque: Analyse par un témoin. 1968–1969*. Paris: Editions ouvrières, 1969.

Haefs, Hanswilhelm, ed. *Die Ereignisse in der Tschechoslowakei, vom 27.6.1967 bis 18.10.1968: Ein dokumentarischer Bericht*. Bonn: Seigler & Co. K. G. Verlag für Zeitarchive, 1969.

Hájek, Jiří. *Dix Ans Après—Prague 1968–1978*, trans. by Claude Durand. Paris: Editions du Seuil, 1978.

Hájek, Jiří. *Intervence a odpor*. Praha: Logos, 1994.

Hamšík, Dušan. *Writers Against Rulers*. London: Hutchinson, 1973.

Hauner, Milan. "The Prague Spring—Twenty Years After," in Norman Stone and Eduard Strouhal, eds. *Czechoslovakia: Crossroads and Crises, 1918–88*. New York: St. Martin's Press, 1989, 207–230.

Heiman, Leo. "Soviet Invasion Weaknesses," *Military Review* vol. XLIX, No. 8 (August 1969) 38–45

Hejzlar, Zdeněk and Vladimir V. Kusin. *Czechoslovakia, 1968–1969: Chronology, Bibliography, Annotation*. New York: Garland, 1974.

Hejzlar, Zdeněk. *Reformkommunismus*. Köln: Europäische Verlagsanstalt, 1976.

Hodnett, Grey and Peter Potichnyj. *The Ukraine and the Czechoslovak Crisis*, Occasional Paper No. 6. Canberra: Australian National University Research School of Social Sciences, 1970.

Horský, Vladimír. *Prag 1968: Systemveränderung und Systemverteidigung*. Stuttgart: Ernst Klett Verlag, 1975.

Humphrey, Hubert H. *The Education of a Public Man: My Life and Politics*, ed. by Norman Sherman. Garden City, NY: Doubleday, 1976.

Institute of History of the Czechoslovak Academy of Sciences. *Sedm pražských dnů: 21.–27. srpen 1968*. Praha: ČSAV, September 1968.

"Interview with Jiří Pelikán: The Struggle for Socialism in Czechoslovakia," *New Left Review* vol. 71, No. 1 (January–February 1972) 3–36.

James, Robert Rhodes, ed. *The Czechoslovak Crisis 1968*. London: Weidenfeld and Nicolson, 1969.

Johnson, A. Ross, Robert W. Dean, and Alexander Alexiev. *East European Military Establishments: The Warsaw Pact Northern Tier*. New York: Crane Russak, 1982.

Johnson, Lyndon B. *The Vantage Point: Perspectives of the Presidency, 1963–1969*. New York: Holt, Rinehart and Winston, 1971.

Jones, Christopher D. "Autonomy & Intervention: The CPSU and the Struggle for the Czechoslovak Communist Party, 1968," *Orbis* vol. 19, No. 2 (Summer 1975) 591–625.

Josten, Josef. *Czechoslovakia, from 1968 to Charter 77: A Record of Passive Resistance*. Conflict Studies No. 86. London: Institute for the Study of Conflict, 1977.

Josten, Josef. *Unarmed Combat, as Practiced in Czechoslovakia Since August 1968*. New Delhi: D. K. Publishing House, 1973.

Juviler, Peter H. "Soviet Motivations for the Invasion, and Domestic Support," *Studies for a New Central Europe* vol. 2, No. 3 (1968–1969) 97–100.

Kadlec, Vladimír, ed. *Dubček — 1968: Selected Documents*. Köln: Index, 1987.

Kalvoda, Josef. *Czechoslovakia's Role in Soviet Strategy*. Lanham, MD: University Press of America, 1978.

Kaplan, Karel, ed. *Dans les archives du Comité Central: Trente ans de secrèts du Bloc sovietique*. Paris: A. Michel, 1978.

Király, Béla K. "Budapest, 1956–Prague, 1968: Parallels and Contrasts," *Problems of Communism* vol. 18, Nos. 4–5 (July–October 1969) 52–60.

Kirschbaum, Stanislav J. "National Self Assertion in Slovakia," in George W. Simmonds, ed. *Nationalism in the USSR & Eastern Europe in the Era of Brezhnev & Kosygin*. Detroit: University of Detroit Press, 1977, 380–400.

Kirschbaum, Stanislav J. "Kontinuität und politischer Wechsel in der 'Tschechoslowakei 1968'," *Bohemia-Jahrbuch* vol. 15 (1974) 279–291.

Klaiber, Wolfgang. *The Crisis in Czechoslovakia in 1968*. Arlington, Va.: Institute for Defense Analyses, 1970.

Klawitter, Karol. *Army of Revenge: Ulbricht's Occupation Forces in Czechoslovakia*. Köln: Markus-Verlag, 1968.

Klein, George. "The Role of Ethnic Politics in the Czechoslovak Crisis of 1968 and the Yugoslav Crisis of 1971," *Studies in Comparative Communism* vol. VIII, No. 4 (Winter 1975) 339–369.

Kohout, Pavel. *From the Diary of a Counterrevolutionary*. New York: McGraw-Hill, 1969.

Kosta, Jiři *et al. Prager Frühling und Reformpolitik heute: Hintergründe, Entwicklungen und Vergleiche der Reformen in Osteuropa*. München: Olzog, 1989.

Kosta, Jiři. "The Czechoslovak Economic Reform of the 1960s," in Stone, Norman and Eduard Strouhal, eds. *Czechoslovakia: Crossroads and Crises, 1918–88*. New York: St. Martin's Press, 1989, 231–252.

Kowalski, Lech. *Kryptonim "Dunaj": Udzial wojsk polskich w interwencji zbrojnej w Czechoslowacji w 1968 roku*. Warsaw: Ksiazka i Wiedza, 1992.

Kramer, Mark. "Inside the Warsaw Pact: New Sources on the 1968 Soviet Invasion of Czechoslovakia, Part I." Cold War International History Project *Bulletin*, No. 2 (Fall 1992) 1, 4 –13.

Kramer, Mark. "The Prague Spring and the Soviet Invasion of Czechoslovakia: New Interpretations, Part II." Cold War International History Project *Bulletin*, No. 3 (Fall 1993) 2–13, 54–55.

Kusin, Vladimir V. *From Dubček to Charter 77: A Study of "Normalization" in Czechoslovakia, 1968–1978*. Edinburgh: Q Press, 1978.

Kusin, Vladimir V. *Political Grouping in the Czechoslovak Reform Movement*. London: Macmillan, 1972.

Kusin, Vladimir V. *The Intellectual Origins of the Prague Spring*. New York: Cambridge University Press, 1971.

Kusin, Vladimir V., ed. *The Czechoslovak Reform Movement 1968: Proceedings of the Seminar Held at the University of Reading on 12–17 July 1971*. London: International Research Documents, 1973.

Leff, Carol Skalnik. *National Conflict in Czechoslovakia: The Making and Remaking of a State, 1918–1987*. Princeton, NJ: Princeton University Press, 1988.

Levy, Alan. *Rowboat to Prague*. New York: Grossman, 1972.

Liehm, Antonín J. *Socialisme à Visage Humain: Les Intellectuels de Prague au Centre de la Melee*. Paris: Albatros, 1977.

Liehm, Antonín J. *Trois Generations: Entretiens sur le Phénomène Culturel Tchécoslovaque*. Paris: Gallimard, 1970.

Littel, Robert, ed. *The Czech Black Book*. New York: Avon Books, 1969.

Lojin, Jaromír. *Hospodářské důsledky sovětské okupace Československá*. Praha: ÚSD, 1995.

Longuet, Robert Jean. *Im Herzen Europas: Prager "Frühling" oder Prager "Herbst"?* Luxembourg: Cooperative Ouvrière de Presse et d'Editions, 1979.

Lowenthal, Richard. "Sparrow in the Cage," *Problems of Communism* vol. 17, No. 6 (November–December 1968) 2–28.

Mackintosh, Malcolm. *The Evolution of the Warsaw Pact*. Adelphi Paper No. 58. London: International Institute for Strategic Studies, June 1969.

Mastný, Vojtěch, ed. *Czechoslovakia: Crisis in World Communism*. New York: Facts on File, 1972.

Mayer, Milton Sanford. *The Art of the Impossible: A Study of the Czech Resistance*. Santa Barbara, Calif.: Center for the Study of Democratic Institutions, 1969.

Meissner, Boris. *Die "Breschnew-Doktrin": Das Prinzip des "proletarisch-sozialistischen Internationalismus" und die Theorie von den "verschiedenen Wegen zum Sozialismus."* Köln: Verlag Wissenschaft und Politik, 1969.

Mezerik, A. G. *Invasion and Occupation of Czechoslovakia and the U.N.* New York: International Review Service, 1968.

Mlynář, Zdeněk, ed. *Der "Prager Frühling": Ein wissenschaftliches Symposion*. Köln: Bund-Verlag, 1983.

Mlynář, Zdeněk, ed. *Mráz přichází z Kremlu*. Praha: Mladá fronta, 1990.

Mlynář, Zdeněk, ed. *Nachtfrost: Erfahrungen auf dem Weg vom realen zum menschlichen Sozialismus*. Köln: Europäische Verlagsanstalt, 1978. Also available in English as *Nightfrost in Prague: The End of Humane Socialism*, trans. by Paul Wilson. New York: Karz Publishers, 1980.

Moravec, Jan. "Could the Prague Spring Have Been Saved? The Ultimatum at Čierna nad Tisou." *Orbis* vol. 35, No. 4 (Fall 1991) 587–595.

Moravus. pseud. "Shawcross's Dubček — A Different Dubček," *Survey* vol. 17, No. 4 (Autumn 1971) 203–216.

Müller, Adolf and Bedrich Utitz, *Deutschland und die Tschechoslowakei: Zwei Nachbarvölker auf dem Weg zur Verständigung*. Freudenstadt: Campus Forschung, 1972.

Müller, Adolf. *Die Tschechoslowakei auf der Suche nach Sicherheit*. Berlin: Berlin Verlag, 1977.

Navrátil, Jaromír. "Dzúrovo velení ČSLA a jeho nástupnická strategie." *Historie a vojenství* vol. XI, No. 6 (1991) 70–94; vol. XII, No. 1 (1992) 78–102.

Nitze, Paul H. *From Hiroshima to Glasnost: At the Center of Decision — A Memoir*. New York: Grove Weidenfeld, 1989.

Norden, Peter. *Prag, 21. August: Das Ende des Prager Frühlings*. München: W. Heyne, 1977.

Oxley, Andrew, Alex Pravda, and Andrew Ritchie, eds. *Czechoslovakia — The Party and the People*. London: Allen Lane, 1973.

Parrish, Michael. *The 1968 Czechoslovak Crisis: A Bibliography, 1968–1970*. Bibliography and Reference Series No. 12. Santa Barbara, Calif.: ABC-Clio Press, 1971.

Pataky, Ivan. "Zatiahnutie Mad'arska a Mad'arskej ľudovej armady do agresie proti Československu v roku 1968," *Historie a vojenství* No. 5 (September–October 1993) 54–69.

Pauer, Jan. *Der Einmarsch des Warschauer Paktes. Hintergründe–Planung–Durchführung*. Bremen: Edition Temmen, 1995.

Pelikán, Jiři, ed. *Ici Prague: L'Opposition interieure parle*. Paris: Editions du Seuil, 1973.

Pelikán, Jiři, ed. *The Czechoslovak Political Trials, 1950–1954: The Suppressed Report of the Dubček Government Commission of Inquiry, 1968*. London: MacDonald, 1971.

Pelikán, Jiři, ed. *The Secret Vysočany Congress: Proceedings and Documents of the Extraordinary Fourteenth Congress of the Communist Party of Czechoslovakia, 22 August 1968*. New York: St. Martin's Press, 1971.

Pelikán, Jiři. *Ein Frühling, der nie zu Ende geht: Erinnerungen eines Prager Kommunisten*. Frankfurt: S. Fischer, 1976.

Pecka, Jindřich. *Spontánní projevy Pražského jara, 1968–1969*. Brno: ÚSD, 1995.

Pecka, Jindřich, Josef Belda and Jiří Hoppe. *Občanská společnost (1967–1970)*. Brno: ÚSD, 1995.

Pichoya, Rudolf. "Czechoslovakia, 1968 go. Po dokumentam CK KPSS." *Novaia I noveishchaia istoriya*, No. 6 (1994) 3–20; No. 1 (1995) 34–38.

Pielkalkiewicz, Jaroslaw A. *Public Opinion Polling in Czechoslovakia, 1968–69: Results and Analysis of Surveys Conducted During the Dubček Era*. New York: Praeger, 1972.

Polk, James H. "Reflections on the Czechoslovakian Invasion, 1968," *Strategic Review* vol. 5, No. 2 (Winter 1977) 30–37.

Prague 1968: The Aftermath. Special Issue of *International Journal* vol. 33, No. 4 (1978) 663–874.

Pravda, Alex. *Reform and Change in the Czechoslovak System: January–August 1968*. Beverley Hills: Sage Publications, 1975.

Priess, Lutz. *Die SED und der "Prager Frühling" 1968: Politik gegen einen "Sozialismus mit menschlichem Antlitz"*. Berlin: Akademie Verlag, 1996.

Rainer, Laurent. *L'après de printemps de Prague*. Paris: Stock, 1976.

Rehm, Walter. "Neue Erkenntnisse über die Rolle der NVA bei der Besetzung der ČSSR im August 1968," *Deutschland Archiv* vol. 24, No. 2 (February 1991) 173–185.

Remington, Robin A. "Czechoslovakia and the Warsaw Pact," *East European Quarterly* vol. 3, No. 3 (September 1969) 315–336.

Remington, Robin Alison, ed. *Winter in Prague: Documents on Czechoslovak Communism in Crisis*. Cambridge, Mass.: The MIT Press, 1969.

Research Project on "The Experience of the Prague Spring 1968". Microform. London: Interpress, 1979 *et seq*.

Rice, Condoleezza. *The Soviet Union and the Czechoslovak Army, 1948–1983: Uncertain Allegiance*. Princeton, NJ: Princeton University Press, 1984.

Robinson, William F. "Czechoslovakia and Its Allies," *Studies in Comparative Communism* vol. 1, Nos. 1 and 2 (July–October 1968) 141–170.

Roll, F. and G. Rosenberger, eds. *ČSSR, 1962–1968: Dokumentation und Kritik*. München: Damnitz Verlag, 1968.

Rupnik, Jacques. *Histoire du Parti Communiste Tchécoslovaque*. Paris: Presses de la fondation nationale des sciences politiques, 1981.

Rusk, Dean. *As I Saw It*, ed. by Daniel S. Papp. New York: W. W. Norton, 1990.

Selucký, Radoslav. "The Dubček Era Revisited," *Problems of Communism* vol. 24, No. 1 (January–February 1975) 38–43.

Selucký, Radoslav. *Czechoslovakia: The Plan That Failed*. London: Nelson, 1970.

Shawcross, William. *Dubček*. London: Weidenfeld and Nicolson, 1970.

Šik, Ota. *Czechoslovakia, The Bureaucratic Economy*. White Plains, NY: International Arts and Sciences Press, 1972.

Sil'nitskaya, Larisa. "Recollections of Bratislava," *Radio Liberty Dispatch*, RL195/74, 2 July 1974

Šimečka, Milan. *The Restoration of Order: The Normalization of Czechoslovakia, 1969–1976*, trans. by A. G. Brain. London: Verso, 1984.

Simes, Dimitri K. "The Soviet Invasion of Czechoslovakia and the Limits of Kremlinology." *Studies in Comparative Communism* vol. VIII, Nos. 1 and 2 (Spring/Summer 1975) 174–180.

Simon, Jeffrey. *The Warsaw Pact: Problems of Command and Control.* Boulder, Col.: Westview Press, 1985.

Skilling, H. Gordon. *Czechoslovakia's Interrupted Revolution.* Princeton, NJ: Princeton University Press, 1976.

Sodaro, Michael J. "The Czech Crisis and Ulbricht's Grand Design: 1968," in *Moscow, Germany, and the West: From Khrushchev to Gorbachev.* Ithaca: Cornell University Press, 1990, 108–134.

Sontag, J. P. "Moscow and the Search for Unity," *Problems of Communism* vol. 18, No. 1 (January–February 1969) 44–50.

Spittmann, Ilse. "Die SED im Konflikt mit der UdSSR," *Deutschland Archiv* vol. 1, No. 6 (June 1968) 660–669.

Staar, Richard F., ed. *Yearbook of International Communist Affairs, 1969.* Stanford, Calif.: Hoover Institution Press, 1970.

Steiner, Eugen. *The Slovak Dilemma.* New York: Cambridge University Press, 1973.

Stepanek-Stemmer, Michael. *Die tschechoslowakische Armee: Militär-historische und paktpolitische Aspekte des 'Prager Frühlings' 1968.* Köln: Sonderveröffentlichung des Bundesinstituts für ostwissenschaftliche und internationale Studien, 1979.

Strmiska, Zdeněk. "The Prague Spring as a Social Movement," in Norman Stone and Eduard Strouhal, eds. *Czechoslovakia: Crossroads and Crises, 1918–88.* New York: St. Martin's Press, 1989, 253–267.

Švec, Milan. "The Prague Spring: 20 Years Later," *Foreign Affairs* vol. 66, No. 5 (Summer 1988) 981–1001.

Sviták, Ivan. *The Czechoslovak Experiment, 1968–1969.* New York: Columbia University Press, 1971.

Sviták, Ivan. *The Unbearable Burden of History — The Sovietization of Czechoslovakia.* vol. II: The Prague Spring Revisited. Prague: Academia, 1990.

Szulc, Tad. *Czechoslovakia Since World War II.* New York: Viking, 1971.

Szulc, Tad. *The Invasion of Czechoslovakia.* New York: Franklin Watts, 1974.

Tatu, Michel. "Intervention in Eastern Europe," in Stephen S. Kaplan *et al., Diplomacy of Power: Soviet Armed Forces as a Political Instrument.* Washington, D.C.: Brookings Institution, 1979, 205–264.

Tatu, Michel. *Power in the Kremlin: From Khrushchev to Kosygin.* New York: Viking, 1971.

Tatu, Michel. *L'herésie impossible: Chronique du drama Tchéchoslovaque.* Paris: B. Grasset, 1968.

Thomas, John R. *Soviet Foreign Policy and Conflict Within the Politburo and Military Leadership.* McLean, Va.: Research Analysis Corporation, 1971.

Tigrid, Pavel. *Le Printemps de Prague.* Paris: Editions du Seuil, 1968.

Tigrid, Pavel. *La Chute Irresistible d'Alexander Dubček.* Paris: Calmann-Levy, 1969.

Urban, George, ed. *Communist Reformation: Nationalism, Internationalism, and Change in the World Communist Movement.* New York: St. Martin's Press, 1979.

U.S. Congress. Senate. Committee on Government Operations. Subcommittee on National Security and International Operations. *Czechoslovakia and the Brezhnev Doctrine*, 91st Cong., 1st Sess., 1969.

Valenta, Jiři. "Czechoslovakia and Afghanistan: Comparative Comments." *Studies in Comparative Communism* vol. XIII, No. 4 (Winter 1980) 343–346 [tk].

Valenta, Jiři. "Eurocommunism and Czechoslovakia," in Vernon V. Aspaturian *et al.*, eds. *Eurocommunism Between East and West.* Bloomington: Indiana University Press, 1980, 157–180.

Valenta, Jiři. "Rejoinder." *Studies in Comparative Communism* vol. VIII, Nos. 1 and 2 (Spring/Summer 1975) 181–182.

Valenta, Jiři. "Soviet Decisionmaking and the Czechoslovak Crisis of 1968." *Studies in Comparative Communism* vol. VIII, Nos. 1 and 2 (Spring/Summer 1975) 147–173.

Valenta, Jiři. "The Last Chance." *Orbis* vol. 35, No. 4 (Fall 1991) 595–601.

Valenta, Jiři. "The Search for a Political Solution." *Orbis* vol. 35, No. 4 (Fall 1991) 581–587.

Valenta, Jiři. *The Soviet Intervention in Czechoslovakia, 1968: Anatomy of a Decision*, rev. ed. Baltimore: Johns Hopkins University Press, 1991.

Valenti, Jack. *A Very Human President*. New York: W. W. Norton, 1975.

Vida, István. "János Kádár and the Czechoslovak Crisis of 1968," *The Hungarian Quarterly* vol. 35, No. 2 (Summer 1994) 154–168.

Volkov, Vladimir. *Instinkt samosochranieniia: sovietskaia partokratiia I Prazhskaia vesna 1968 g.* Moscow: Rkp., 1994.

Vondrová, Jitka. "Dopisy L. Brežněva A. Dubčekovi." *Historie a vojenství*, rože. XL., č. 1 (1991) 141–166.

Vondrová, Jitka and Jaromír Navrátil. *Mezinárodní souvislosti československé krize, 1967–1970: Prosinec 1967—červenec 1968*. Brno: ÚSD, 1995.

Vondrová, Jitka and Jaromír Navrátil. *Mezinárodní souvislosti československé krize, 1967–1970: červenec — Srpen 1968*. Brno: ÚSD, 1996.

Vondrová, Jitka and Jaromír Navrátil. *Mezinárodní souvislosti československé krize, 1967–1970: Září 1968 — kveten 1970*. Brno: ÚSD, 1997.

Wechsberg, Joseph. *The Voices*. New York: Doubleday, 1969.

Weisskopf, Kurt. *The Agony of Czechoslovakia, 38/68*. London: Elek, 1968.

Weit, Erwin. *Ostblock intern: Dreizehn Jahre Dolmetscher für die polnische Partei- und Staatsführung*. Hamburg, 1970.

Weit, Erwin. *Eyewitness: The Autobiography of Gomulka's Interpreter*. London: Andre Deutsch, 1973.

Wenzke, Rudiger. *Die NVA und der Prager Frühling 1968: Die Rolle Ulbrichts und der DDR-Streitkräfte bei der Niederschlagung der tschechoslowakischen Reformbewegung*. Berlin: Chadwyck-Healey. Links, 1995.

Wenzke, Rudiger. *Prager Frühling — Prager Herbst: Zur Intervention der Warschauer-Pakt-Streitkräfte in der ČSSR 1968, Fakten und Zusammenhänge*. Berlin: Druckerei Humblot, 1990.

Wenzke, Rudiger. "Zur Beteiligung der NVA an der militärischen Operation von Warschauer-Pakt-Streitkräften gegen die ČSSR 1968: Einige Ergänzungen zu einem Beitrag von Walter Rehm," *Deutschland Archiv* vol. 24, No. 11 (November 1991) 1179–1186.

Western European Union. Committee on Defense Questions and Armaments. *Tchécoslovaquie, 1968*. Paris: WEU, 1968.

Whetten, Lawrence L. "Military Aspects of the Soviet Occupation of Czechoslovakia," *The World Today* vol. 25, No. 2 (February 1969) 60–68.

Williams, Kieran. *The Prague Spring and Its Aftermath: Czechoslovak Politics, 1968–1970*. New York: Cambridge University Press, 1997.

Wilson, Harold. *The Labour Government, 1964–1970*. London: Weidenfeld and Nicolson, 1971.

Windsor, Philip and Adam Roberts. *Czechoslovakia 1968: Reform, Repression, and Resistance*. London: Chatto and Windus, 1969.

Wolfe, James H. "West Germany and Czechoslovakia: The Struggle for Reconciliation," *Orbis* vol. 14, No. 1 (Spring 1970) 154–179.

Wolfe, Thomas W. *Soviet Power and Europe: 1945–1970*. Baltimore: Johns Hopkins University Press, 1970.

Zartman, I. William, ed. *Czechoslovakia: Intervention and Impact*. New York: New York University Press, 1970.

Zeman, Zbyněk A. B. *Prague Spring: A Report on Czechoslovakia, 1968*. Harmondsworth: Penguin, 1968.

INDEX OF NAMES

591

Stalin, Josip 1, 3, 4, 142, 155, 269, 495
Stepakov, V. 150
Stoph, Willi 474
Štrougal, Lubomír xxxviii, xxxix, 24, 38, 59, 397, 461, 462, 555–559, 563, 567, 571, 573, 574, 579
Suslov, Mikhail 166, 169, 216, 333, 377, 389, 422, 469, 471, 579
Švestka, Oldřich xxviii, xxxiv–xxxvi, 159, 280, 288, 313, 324, 325, 414, 452, 460, 471, 520, 561, 579
Sviták, Ivan 154, 514, 588
Svoboda, Ludvík xxviii, xxx, xxxiv–xxxix, 23, 85, 112, 117, 189, 204, 251, 311, 314, 321, 323, 348, 357, 359, 368, 391–394, 398, 405–408, 420–422, 432, 437, 439, 440, 442, 460–467, 469–471, 474–476, 482, 484, 487, 490, 497, 507, 509–512, 519, 523, 555, 558, 559, 562, 563, 579
Synek, Ivan 42

T

Temple, Larry 492
Thatcher, Margaret 1
Thompson, Llewellyn 492, 493, 495
Tigrid, Pavel 11, 96, 515, 522, 588
Tiso, Jozef 154
Tito, Josip Broz 87, 144, 147, 219, 257, 313, 318, 579
Todorov, Stanko 69, 317
Togliatti, Palmiro 78, 79
Trofimov, General xxxv, 433, 434
Trusov, N. 237
Tsarapkin, Semyon 508
Tuczapski, Tadeusz 364
Turzo, Eugen 561
Tutarinov, General 277

U

Udaľtsov, I.I. 61
Ulbricht, Walter xxvii, xxx, xxxiii, xxxviii, 4, 22, 32, 42, 58–61, 64, 69, 70,

73, 87, 96, 97, 102, 108, 124, 132, 136, 137, 139, 142, 167, 187, 188, 218, 219, 221, 230–233, 300, 309, 311, 312, 316, 322, 333, 341, 342, 345, 378, 403, 433, 434, 438, 474, 476, 495, 507, 511, 579

V

Vaculík, Ludvík xxvii, xxx, 8, 10–12, 91, 96, 177, 515
Velchev, Boris 474
Vlček, Vladislav 454, 462
Vokrouhlický, Zdeněk 252
Voleník, Oldřich 135, 460
Voronov, G.I. xxxvi, 465, 467, 469, 471
Výborný, O. 55, 145

W

Wiesenthal, Simon 516

Y

Yakovlev, Aleksander 497
Yakubovskii, Ivan xxviii, xxx, xxxii, xxxviii, 85, 86, 90, 112–114, 136, 161, 162, 183, 186, 187, 191–193, 199, 202–205, 239, 259, 260, 262, 263, 265, 294, 363–365, 431, 579, 581
Yamshchikov, Andrei 412, 431, 485
Yashkin, G.P. 375
Yeltsin, Boris 324
Yepishev, General xxxiii, 168

Z

Zagladin, Vadim 150
Záruba, Jan 516
Zavadil, Miroslav 561
Zhivkov, Todor xxvii, xxxviii, 87, 96, 97, 124, 132, 142, 188, 219, 221, 229–232, 309, 317, 378, 403, 438, 474–476, 511, 579
Zimyanin, M.V. 251
Zolotov, Semyon 202, 373, 564, 568, 569